PRESIDENTIAL PROFILES
THE NIXON-FORD YEARS

John Robert Greene

713825

✓ Facts On File
An imprint of Infobase Publishing

For Patty, T. J., Christopher, and Mary Rose

Presidential Profiles: The Nixon-Ford Years

Copyright © 2006 by John Robert Greene

Facts On File, Inc.
An imprint of Infobase Publishing
132 West 31st Street
New York NY 10001

Library of Congress Cataloging-in-Publication Data

Greene, John Robert.
  The Nixon-Ford years / John Robert Greene.
    p. cm. — (Presidential profiles)
  Includes bibliographical references and index.
  ISBN 0-8160-5280-8 (hc : alk paper)
  1. Politicians—United States—Biography. 2. United States—Politics and government—1969–1974. 3. United States—Politics and government—1974–1977. 4. Nixon, Richard M. (Richard Milhous), 1913–1994—Friends and associates. 5. Ford, Gerald R., 1913—Friends and associates, 6. United States—History—1969—Biography. I. Title. II. Presidential profiles (Facts on File, Inc.)
  E840.6.G745 2006
  973.924092'273—dc22 2005033993

Text design by Mary Susan Ryan-Flynn
Cover design by Nora Wertz
Maps by Sholto Ainslie

Printed in the United States of America

VB MSRF 10 9 8 7 6 5 4 3 2 1

This book is printed on acid-free paper.

CONTENTS

CONTRIBUTING EDITORS

Catherine A. Barnes
Columbia University

James Lewis Baughman
Columbia University

Jason Berger
City University of New York

Mel Bernstine
New York University

David Billington

Anthony F. Bruno
Boston College

Rachel Burd
City University of New York

Susan Burns
Catholic University

Gregory Bush
Columbia University

Carol Lea Clark
University of Houston

John D'Emilio
Columbia University

Trent Duffy
New York University

Andrew Eiler
University of Wisconsin

Donna Ellaby
New School for Social Research

Diane Elliot
University of Michigan

Carey V. Erickson
California Institute of the Arts

Amber Farr
Cazenovia College

Jefferson Flanders
Harvard College

Stephen Flanders
Brown College

Loren Goldner
University of California, Berkeley

Paula Goulden
Swarthmore College

John Robert Greene
Cazenovia College

PREFACE

❧

Since the initial publication of this work, in 1979, Nixon-Ford historiography has undergone a seismic shift. The epicenters of this shift are the primary source collections now available at the presidential repositories that deal most directly with these administrations. The Nixon collections have been more problematic in terms of their release to the public but are nevertheless strikingly rich in detail. Following two decades of legal wrangling, all material from the Nixon White House—including the Watergate-related material that since 1975 had been in the possession of the National Archives (College Park, Md.)—will be deposited at the Richard M. Nixon Presidential Library (Yorba Linda, Calif.). Since its opening in 1982, the Gerald R. Ford Library (Ann Arbor, Mich.) has made the papers of the Ford administration, as well as Ford's pre- and postpresidential career, available to scholars. The result of these additions to the historical record has been an increase in the scholarly studies on these presidencies, offering much fuller treatments than were available before the first publication of this volume. The newly expanded bibliography at the end of this volume only hints at the breadth of this literature.

Such a revision holds particular significance in light of the political history that was to follow. A list of principals who served in the Reagan, George H. W. Bush, and George W. Bush administrations reads like an alumni/ae list from the Nixon and Ford years. Indeed, both President Reagan and the elder President Bush cut their political teeth during these years, and several of the principals from the Nixon and Ford administrations served under Presidents Carter and Clinton as well. Clearly, the administrations of Nixon and Ford served as a primary training ground for politicians, government administrators, diplomats, and journalists—of both parties and all political ideologies—who would serve their country for the next three decades.

Thus the time was right to revisit the previous edition of this volume. This exercise was important not only to update for accuracy (a worthy task for any reference work) but also to integrate into the chronology, the entries, the documents, and the bibliography the full breadth of new scholarship and to extend the reach of the volume to the present day, to highlight the links between the Nixon-Ford years and the present political history of the nation. It is hoped that this revised edition will serve as a guide for scholars who wish to further plow the fertile fields of Nixon-Ford scholarship.

Grateful acknowledgment is due to those writers, contributors, and editors of the first edition of this book—it is upon their efforts that the present product is built. Thanks are also due to my colleagues at Cazenovia College, who make my writing endeavors a pleasure, particularly

President Mark Tierno and Dean of the Faculty Donald McCrimmon. Stanley Kozaczka and his staff at the Cazenovia College Library offered assistance without which this project would not have gone forward. Kaleb Wilson and Shannon Torgersen offered excellent research assistance, and Carol "Lolly" Kuntz provided invaluable support. I am grateful to Elisabeth Hayes and Elise Leipold for their clerical assistance. My usual thanks are reserved for my writing colleague, Shirley Anne Warshaw, at Gettysburg College. This is the second book I have completed with the help of Owen Lancer, an outstanding editor at Facts On File, who has guided my work to completion with grace and humor. And, as noted in the dedication, nothing is written from this desk without the support of my family.

INTRODUCTION

Public discontent with the Democratic administration of congressional wheeler-dealer Lyndon Johnson helped bring another Washington "old hand" into office—Republican Richard Nixon. From Lyndon Johnson through Richard Nixon to Gerald Ford, the public looked to experienced national politicians for leadership. Yet by the end of the Nixon-Ford years, the nation's bicentennial, the country was disillusioned and disappointed in the record of the recent presidency (regardless of party) and in a mood to experiment with men untainted by big government service. Richard Nixon came to office faced with problems of the war in Vietnam, inflation, and a crisis in public confidence, which was generally referred to as the "credibility gap." When the Republicans left office in 1976, only the Vietnam War was no longer an issue. Inflation and flagging public confidence not only remained, but had become even more acute.

Narrowly elected to office and representing the minority party of the nation, President Nixon soon embarked on a course to broaden his support base with "Middle America" (later christened the "silent majority") and to revitalize the Republican Party, which had been badly fragmented since the presidential candidacy of Barry Goldwater in 1964.

To help unify the party, the president named Representative Rogers C. B. Morton of Maryland as Republican National Committee chairman. Morton gave up a chance to be nominated as a senatorial candidate in 1970 to continue his work for the party. By the end of that year, Morton had put the Republicans in good financial shape, led them through the midterm elections with a creditable showing, and begun extensive preparations for the 1972 presidential campaign. The president not only praised Morton for uniting "the Party as no chairman in my memory has been able to do . . . in recent years," but also rewarded his faithful and effective service by appointing him secretary of the interior in January 1971.

In putting together his "official family," President Nixon chose a group of men much like himself—the sons of small-town America, self-made men and political middle-of-the-roaders. All the cabinet secretaries were white, male, middle-aged, business-minded Republicans. There were no token representatives of the Democratic Party or of either the Goldwater or the Rockefeller wings of the Republican Party. The composition of the cabinet raised considerable interest because of Nixon's announced intention of abandoning the JFK-LBJ operating style of powerful White House staffs and of returning to the Eisenhower style of "running the government through a strong cabinet."

The cabinet that President Nixon presented to a television audience of millions in mid-December 1968 was comprised of a few close friends, a couple of academics, and a number of practical politicians. He put friends in command of the strategic Departments of State (William P. Rogers), Justice (John Mitchell), and Health, Education, and Welfare (HEW) (Robert Finch). In addition to Rogers, he brought in another veteran of the Eisenhower administration—Maurice Stans—as commerce secretary. Both George Shultz as labor secretary and Clifford Hardin as agriculture secretary were academics with practical administrative experience. Most of the other cabinet members were elective officials. Politically astute Congressman Melvin Laird (R-Wis.) was named defense secretary, and three Republican governors joined the administration: George Romney of Michigan as secretary of housing and urban development (HUD), John Volpe of Massachusetts as secretary of transportation, and Walter Hickel of Alaska as secretary of the interior. The president repaid a campaign debt by naming David Kennedy as Treasury secretary in reward for his fundraising assistance. Finally, the appointment of conservative Alabama Republican Winton Blount as postmaster general appeared to be one of the administration's first moves in its southern strategy. At 43 Finch was the youngest cabinet member; most of the others were in their 50s or 60s. There were at least seven millionaires—Blount, Hickel, Kennedy, Rogers, Romney, Stans, and Volpe—but all had worked their way up from middle-class backgrounds.

Despite the fact that they seemed to fit the Nixon mold, few fared well in the administration. Postmaster General Blount presided over the transformation of the Post Office from a cabinet department to a government corporation and then left the administration

in 1971. Interior Secretary Hickel was fired in the autumn of 1970 after publicly complaining that he could not penetrate the "Berlin Wall," the layer of insulation that White House assistants John D. Ehrlichman and H. R. Haldeman had thrown up around the president. Midway through the term, Finch, Kennedy, and Hardin were eased out as their policy preferences and the president's began to diverge. Labor Secretary Schultz also left the cabinet in midterm to assume the directorship of the newly reorganized Office of Management and Budget (OMB). As part of this first major personnel shuffle of the administration, Undersecretary of State Elliot Richardson replaced Finch at HEW; Undersecretary of Labor James D. Hodgson was promoted to fill George Schultz's cabinet spot; Rogers C. B. Morton replaced Hickel at Interior; and former Texas governor and Democrat John Connally replaced David Kennedy at the Treasury Department.

Secretaries Romney, Volpe, and Laird lasted through the first term, but did not continue into the second. The president's oldest friend in the cabinet—William Rogers—held on to the title of secretary of state until the summer of 1973, even though National Security Affairs assistant Henry Kissinger had long since become the chief foreign policy adviser and negotiator. Finally, Maurice Stans and John Mitchell resigned from the cabinet to become respectively campaign fundraiser and manager for the reelection effort.

Despite Nixon's avowed intention of relying on a strong cabinet, it soon became evident that power and influence were gravitating toward the White House staff. The "Teutonic Trio" of Kissinger, H. R. Haldeman, and John D. Ehrlichman were soon envied for their access to and influence with the president. Also prominent among the staff were congressional strategist Bryce Harlow and domestic policy advisers such as the liberal Daniel Patrick Moynihan and the conservative Arthur Burns.

As the staff grew in prominence, it also grew in numbers. Clearly Nixon had learned during his years as Eisenhower's vice president that reliance on an extensive staff system helped conserve the president's time and energy. The buffering function of the staff was particularly important to Nixon because he had a low threshold for fatigue and was uneasy with most people. As a result of these factors, the president quickly acquired the largest staff in history—over 150 members, not counting secretaries and stenographers.

As a means of gaining support for the administration and enlarging the Republican Party's base, the White House evolved its southern strategy. The results of the 1968 election seemed to indicate that the Democratic hold on the "Solid South" was weakening and that the region held great potential for Republican gains. Therefore the administration undertook several actions designed to attract southern support. In 1969, in one of the first moves, Attorney General John Mitchell presented and won congressional support for a voting rights proposal that extended the provisions of the 1965 Voting Rights Act to the entire nation, rather than just targeting those states (primarily southern) that had a history of de jure discrimination against blacks.

Another major element of the southern strategy was the development of a more restrained policy regarding school desegregation enforcement, particularly through the use of busing. Beginning in the late summer of 1969, the administration, through HEW and the Justice Department, began to delay implementation of various desegregation orders. During 1970 the president made it clear that in his opinion, "education not integration" was the primary concern of the schools and that it was impossible to achieve "instant integration." He went on to state that his policy would be one of "cooperation, rather than coercion." In October 1970 the solicitor general, in oral argument

before the Supreme Court, pointed out that white students in the South might abandon public education if desegregation efforts were pressed too strongly, thus reinforcing Nixon's stated position opposing busing and favoring the "neighborhood school" concept.

While these moves won the applause of the southern conservatives, blacks and other minority groups and civil rights activists strongly disapproved. Indeed, the U.S. Commission on Civil Rights reported a "major breakdown" in federal efforts to fight discrimination, and a number of HEW officials and attorneys with the Civil Rights Division of the Justice Department resigned in protest of the administration's policies. Overall the White House position on civil rights issues from school desegregation and voting rights to housing and employment seemed to fit a policy proposed by one of the president's major domestic affairs advisers, Daniel Patrick Moynihan, which he described as one of "benign neglect."

Another tactic in the southern strategy was the use of the president's appointment power. As Nixon staffed his new administration, the *Baltimore Sun* estimated that a "higher number of Southerners had received patronage appointments . . . than ever before." However, Nixon's first two attempts to name southerners to the Supreme Court met bitter congressional opposition and eventual disapproval.

To replace Justice Abe Fortas, the president initially nominated South Carolina federal Circuit Court judge Clement F. Haynsworth. Criticized as a "racist" and a "laundered segregationist" and as "antilabor," Haynsworth faced questions at his Senate confirmation hearings about possible conflict-of-interest improprieties. On November 21, 1969, his nomination was rejected by the Senate. Two months later Judge G. Harold Carswell of the Fifth Circuit Court of Appeals in Florida was nominated, and he also encountered intense opposition. Like Haynsworth, Carswell was accused of being a racist and a segregationist, but to these criticisms were added objections that he was a mediocre jurist and thus not of the caliber befitting a member of the Supreme Court. When Carswell's nomination was also rejected, the president lashed out at the Senate, saying that "it [was] not possible to get confirmation for a judge on the Supreme Court of any man who believes in the strict construction of the Constitution . . . if he happens to come from the South. . . ." The president finally succeeded in filling the vacancy on the Court with the nomination of Circuit Court judge Harry A. Blackmun of Minnesota, who was unanimously confirmed in May 1970.

Far less controversial, but perhaps more important, was the nomination and confirmation of a new chief justice—Judge Warren E. Burger of the U.S. Circuit Court of Appeals for Washington, D.C. In contrast to the controversy surrounding the associate justice nominations, Burger easily won Senate confirmation to replace the retiring Earl Warren in 1969. By the end of his first term in office, the president had had the opportunity to appoint four men to the Court who he hoped would direct its constitutional philosophy toward a more conservative stance than that of the preceding Warren Court.

In 1971 President Nixon succeeded in naming a southerner, former American Bar Association president Lewis F. Powell Jr. to the Supreme Court. The same year he placed Assistant Attorney General William H. Rehnquist on the Court. Observers of the judicial process soon began to perceive a trend toward less "lenient" decisions in criminal matters, which was more in keeping with the Nixon administration's "law and order" campaign.

Along these lines the administration had submitted various crime control proposals to Congress in 1969, and in 1970 Nixon declared a "war on crime" and won legislative approval for four major crime bills—the Comprehen-

sive Drug Abuse Prevention and Control Act, the Omnibus Crime Control Act, the Organized Crime Control Act, and the District of Columbia Court Reorganization and Criminal Procedure Act (designed as a "model anticrime package" to redress Washington's reputation as the nation's "crime capital").

The war in Southeast Asia was a prominent issue throughout Nixon's first term of office. Committed to ending the conflict he had inherited from the Johnson administration, President Nixon initially encountered a lull on this front. During 1969 peace negotiations in Paris were stalemated. At home congressional criticism was restrained during the administration's "honeymoon period," and antiwar activity had decreased. But in the fall of 1969, issues of war and defense reemerged and were attended by heated debate, both congressional and public. Controversy over the funding and deployment of a Safeguard antiballistic missile (ABM) system culminated in a dramatic 50-50 Senate vote with a tie-breaking ballot cast by Vice President Spiro Agnew that allowed development of the ABM to continue. As the conflict in Vietnam dragged on, Senate criticism of the administration's war policies became more pronounced.

With students returning to school for the fall semester, campus protest increased. On October 15, 1969, the Vietnam Moratorium staged protests around the country and, a month later, brought 250,000 people to Washington for the largest demonstration in the capital's history. In an effort to extricate American forces from Vietnam and thereby quiet domestic dissent, President Nixon proposed a policy of "Vietnamization" of the war that involved a gradual shifting of military responsibility from U.S. combat troops to the South Vietnamese. The new policy, announced on November 3, 1969, marked the beginning of U.S. troop withdrawals from Vietnam. Vietnamization was an elaboration of an earlier foreign policy state-

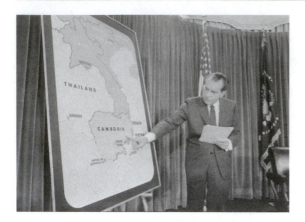

President Nixon points out the NVA sanctuaries along the Cambodian border in his speech to the American people announcing the Cambodian incursion, April 30, 1970. *(National Archives)*

ment by Nixon. In his "Asian Doctrine" of July the president had called for the maintenance of American commitments to Asian allies, but with a greater stress on self-help and economic development in the region and the avoidance of U.S. participation in future wars on the Asian mainland.

The president further developed this policy direction with the promulgation of the "Nixon Doctrine." Embodied in a 40,000-word "State of the World" message to Congress in February 1970, the Nixon Doctrine called for a change in U.S. relations with its allies, from one of American "predominance" to one of "partnership." Under this policy the United States would "participate in the defense and development of allies and friends but . . . cannot—and will not—conceive all the plans, design all the programs, execute all the decisions and undertake all the defense of the free nations of the world."

Despite the apparent intent to limit American military commitments around the world and withdraw from Vietnam, the president acted to broaden U.S. military involvement in Southeast Asia in 1970 by sending U.S.

forces into Laos and Cambodia. Initially the administration had cloaked its Laotian activities in a secrecy designed to help maintain that country's official neutrality. However, hearings by a Senate Foreign Relations subcommittee under Stuart Symington (D-Mo.) elicited an explanatory statement from the president in March 1970.

The revelation about the Laotian involvement generated apprehensions that the United States was still bogged down in the Southeast Asian war with no end in sight and thus set the stage for quick, strong reaction against the president's decision to send American troops into Cambodia to clean out Communist sanctuaries along the Vietnamese border. Nixon's action revived congressional concern about the extent of presidential warmaking and foreign-policy powers and set off an outburst of public antiwar sentiment. As a result the Senate engaged in a two-month debate over the Cooper-Church Amendment, which sought to restrain presidential authority to launch, expand, or sustain military activity in Cambodia without the concurrence of Congress. While the Senate on June 20 approved (58-37) the attachment of the Cooper-Church Amendment to a foreign military sales bill, opposition from conferees resulted in a six-month delay, and finally the amendment was dropped.

The Cooper-Church Amendment controversy was, however, only one example of renewed congressional concern about executive war powers. Senators George McGovern (D-S.D.), Mark Hatfield (R-Ore.), Alan Cranston (D-Calif.), Harold Hughes (D-Iowa), and Charles Goodell (R-N.Y.) proposed an end-the-war amendment that would have cut off funds for use in Vietnam after December 31, 1970, except for troop withdrawal purposes. In July the Senate passed a concurrent resolution repealing the 1964 Gulf of Tonkin Resolution, which many war critics considered a presidential carte blanche to wage the war in Vietnam.

(The House failed to pass a similar resolution.) The White House did not oppose the repeal of the Gulf of Tonkin Resolution, maintaining that the president had sufficient constitutional authority to continue the war. In effect the Senate resolution was merely a symbolic act, expressive of congressional dissatisfaction with a continuing, and apparently expanding, war.

The invasion of Cambodia also rekindled antiwar activity. Immediately following President Nixon's announcement of an American troop offensive into Cambodia, the Vietnam Moratorium Committee issued a call for a nationwide student strike. A strike at Kent State University in Ohio ended in the killing of four students by National Guardsmen. This tragedy galvanized the antiwar forces and helped produce a turnout of between 60,000 and 100,000 demonstrators in Washington on May 9. Although the president had labeled antiwar protesters "bums," he did greet the Washington group with a conciliatory pre-dawn appearance at the Lincoln Memorial. However, the effort proved fruitless. As public dissent tapered off, the scene of protest shifted again to Congress.

Despite public and congressional pressure for a quick end to U.S. involvement, the administration continued its policy of gradually removing American troops from Southeast Asia. Through 1971 the Paris peace talks remained stalled. Meanwhile, both houses of Congress finally approved a weakened version of the Mansfield Amendment, another measure calling for the withdrawal of U.S. troops from Indochina.

In keeping with the developing sentiment for a retrenchment of U.S. commitments around the world, and in response to the dissatisfaction over the course of the Vietnam War, the president moved toward fulfilling his campaign promise to replace the military draft with an all-volunteer force. Although the President's Commission on an All-Volunteer

Army reported that the draft could be abolished by mid-1971, Nixon set June 30, 1973, as the target date for the change. Meanwhile, draft quotas were reduced, and for a time the draft was suspended.

In its battle against antiwar dissent at home, the administration lost a 1971 Supreme Court decision to prevent the *New York Times* and other newspapers from publishing the *Pentagon Papers*, a Defense Department study of U.S. involvement and decision making in Southeast Asia, particularly in Vietnam. Although the information revealed in the *Papers* focused on policies followed under previous administrations, the Court's ruling rankled the president.

The administration's principal diplomatic concern at this time was the reopening of diplomatic contact with the People's Republic of China. In a sudden shift of foreign policy, the United States made a diplomatic approach to the Chinese, abandoning more than two decades of hostility between the two nations. During the summer of 1972 Nixon announced three major steps that radically altered America's position on China and shocked U.S. allies and adversaries. In June the United States ended its 21-year trade embargo of mainland China; a month later it was announced that Nixon would pay a state visit to Beijing in February 1972; and in August the State Department reported that it would back the admission of the People's Republic into the United Nations. These moves won the president accolades as a statesman working for world peace and boosted his popularity at home, but aroused uneasiness among America's allies, particularly Japan and the Nationalist Chinese government on Taiwan. The fears of the Nationalist Chinese and their conservative supporters in the United States were partially realized in October 1971. That month, while National Security Advisor Kissinger was in China preparing the agenda for Nixon's forthcoming trip, the United Nations voted to admit Communist China and to expel Taiwan, refusing to adopt the "two Chinas" policy proposed by the United States to retain Nationalist China while admitting the People's Republic.

The UN decision was greeted by angry suggestions that the United States retaliate by reducing its financial support of the organization to a more reasonable and appropriate sum. Such threats, however, were soon drowned out by the chorus of praise that accompanied the first visit of an American president to China, which was the highlight of the Nixon presidency. The Beijing trip ended with the issuance of the Shanghai Communiqué, which committed both the United States and China to "a peaceful settlement of the Taiwan question" and to a provision that neither nation "should seek hegemony in the Asia Pacific region and each is opposed to efforts by any other country or group of countries to establish such hegemony." Eventually diplomatic contact was reestablished between the United States and China. Opening the lines of communication marked American recognition of China's emergence as a central figure in world power politics.

A significant problem that confronted Nixon during his first term in office was the troubled state of the U.S. economy. In its initial efforts to curb inflationary growth without triggering recession, the administration followed a policy of "gradualism" that included the trimming of governmental expenditures, but determinedly eschewed wage and price controls. After more than a year of cautious restraint, anti-inflation strategy shifted in late 1970 toward efforts to spur economic recovery. By this time the president's handling of the economy was criticized not only by congressional Democrats and many private economists, but also by the public. Speculation arose that if Nixon did not take strong measures to improve the economic situation he might lose the presidential election of 1972.

In a major economic speech delivered on December 4, 1970, President Nixon announced changes in federal spending, monetary, and tax policies. Abandoning hopes of achieving a balanced budget, he announced the adoption of deficit spending to stimulate growth. He stressed that he had secured the agreement of Federal Reserve Board (FRB) chairman Arthur Burns, to "provide fully for the increasing monetary needs of the economy," thus easing the "tight money" situation created by previous FRB policies. He also tentatively entered the area of wage and price controls, warning that the government would take measures to offset oil price increases and would intervene in construction industry wage negotiations if salary demands and rising costs were not restrained.

Finally, after two and a half years of tenuous attempts to curb inflation and unemployment, the president took bold action in 1971, not only to improve the economic condition of the nation, but also to improve his standing with the public and therefore guarantee his prospects for reelection in 1972. On August 15, 1971, President Nixon froze wages and prices for 90 days; called for a variety of tax revisions to stimulate growth and investment; imposed a 10 percent surcharge on imports; cut the dollar loose from the traditional $35-an-ounce fixed price for gold; and established a Cost of Living Council to administer these policies.

Phase two of the stabilization program, announced on October 7, terminated the wage-price freeze and replaced it with a Pay Board and a Price Commission to regulate wage and price increases under specific guidelines. The president also asked for and received congressional approval of a tax cut proposal and a year's extension of his economic stabilization authority. The final step in this initiative was the devaluation of the dollar (December 18, 1971) as part of a general realignment of currency values among the major industrial nations. This move was designed to improve America's international trading position by eliminating the disadvantage created by an overvalued dollar against the undervalued currencies of other nations.

The initial overall effect of these efforts was generally favorable: the gross national product (GNP) increased, and wages rose faster than prices. But unemployment continued to be a problem, remaining well above the administration's goal of 4 percent. In September 1972 the unemployment rate stood at 5.5 percent, representing 4.8 million Americans out of work, or 2 million more than when President Nixon had assumed office. In addition to its economic implications the unemployment situation was a troublesome political problem, since the jobless might easily turn into a dissatisfied voting bloc in 1972.

The Nixon administration sought to address the unemployment problem within the context of its overall domestic policy orientation by trimming back "Great Society" programs started by the Johnson administration and by instituting a "New Federalism" approach. The major thrust of the New Federalism was to shift some power and program responsibility from the federal government to state and local governments. One of the first proposals in this strategy was a broad reform of the welfare system that would set minimum annual payments for welfare recipients (the Family Assistance Plan) and would link welfare to job-training programs administered by the states. Funding for these programs would come from a projected revenue-sharing system under which a portion of federal tax revenues would be returned to the state and local governments.

However, the administration's reform efforts, as well as other domestic initiatives in education, health, and labor, encountered substantial opposition in Congress. Although the House and Senate approved a 15 percent increase in basic Social Security payments in

1969, none of the administration's proposed reforms of the system were adopted. The Family Assistance Plan died in Congress during 1970. The two branches of government battled over health and education programs and revenue-sharing schemes, with the president vetoing various educational funding bills three years in a row and Congress voting to override his vetoes. Although the administration's manpower revenue-sharing program of 1971 was rejected, the seriousness of the unemployment situation elicited cooperation between the two branches on the passage of a $2.25 billion Democratic-sponsored program to create public service jobs at the state and local levels.

In his 1971 State of the Union message, President Nixon proposed "six great goals" to restructure government and to turn power "back to the people." These six goals were revenue sharing; executive department reorganization; initiatives to reduce pollution and preserve the environment; prosperity through a federal budget based on full-employment spending to stimulate the economy and efforts by labor and management to control wages and prices; major reform of the welfare system; and improvement of America's health care system.

The president's environmental proposals received favorable acceptance, because they coincided with a growing public concern about the environment, symbolized by the celebration of Earth Day in April 1970. During 1970 Congress approved administration bills to curb air and water pollution, as well as to establish the National Oceanic and Atmospheric Administration within the Commerce Department and an independent Environmental Protection Agency. Another presidential success was the establishment of a five-year revenue-sharing program, approved in 1972, to return $30 billion in federal revenues to state and local governments for spending as they saw fit.

One of the most politically controversial goals was reorganization of the executive departments, reducing them from 12 to eight, with most of the changes occurring in the domestic, constituency-oriented departments. State, Treasury, Defense, and Justice were to remain untouched, and Congress had already approved the conversion of the Post Office from a cabinet department into a quasi-public corporation in 1970. President Nixon proposed that the remaining seven departments be consolidated into four: Natural Resources (primarily Interior, with parts of Commerce and Agriculture); Human Resources (based on HEW, with parts of Agriculture and Labor); Economic Development (primarily Transportation, with parts of Labor, Commerce, and Agriculture); and Community Development (based on HUD, with parts of Agriculture). Congressional reaction to governmental reorganization of such scope was guarded, and beyond hearings in both houses, no action was taken.

Midway through the first term, Nixon and his advisers began to plan for the next presidential election. Dan Rather in *The Palace Guard* contended that immediately after the 1970 midterm elections Nixon became concerned about political threats from both the right and the left. On the left President Nixon feared Senator Edward Kennedy (D-Mass.) might rise above the potentially damaging Chappaquiddick incident to become a presidential contender. In addition, Senator Edmund Muskie (D-Me.) was becoming a potentially formidable contender and a spokesman for the Democrats. On the right George Wallace loomed as a potential third-party candidate who could seriously damage the Republicans' southern strategy and who might cut into the president's support from conservatives who favored lax desegregation efforts and strong law-and-order measures.

In the domestic area the Nixon administration had relatively little to show in the way of tangible accomplishments. Although the administration could point to "the most advanced environmental program in American history" and to a new revenue-sharing plan, inflation and unemployment remained serious problems. Relations with the Democratic-controlled Congress were strained and often antagonistic. During his first term Nixon vetoed 30 pieces of major authorizing or appropriating legislation and saw his veto challenged 11 times and overridden 14 times. In addition many of his legislative proposals were significantly modified, and his spending proposals were generally increased by Congress. On occasion, such as with Haynsworth and Carswell, the Senate had been not only unreceptive but hostile to the president's nominee. Clearly he had little hope of building himself a "monument" in domestic affairs, where the collaboration of Congress was so necessary. Thus his best opportunities for securing reelection, and a place in history, rested in the arena of foreign affairs, where the president had the ability to act without legislative approval and where he was confident of his abilities and those of his aides.

Early administration ventures in foreign affairs met with limited success. A serious policy blunder occurred during the December 1971 Indo-Pakistani War, when the United States decided to back Pakistan against India, which joined with East Pakistan in its struggle to gain independence. India beat Pakistan, and East Pakistan became the independent nation of Bangladesh. The Soviet Union, which had supported India in the conflict, claimed a victory over the United States. But the administration's failure soon faded in the shadow of the China rapprochement. The president's visit to Beijing in early 1972 was not only a diplomatic plum but also a most effective political maneuver. Major events of the trip were scheduled to coincide with prime-time television in the United States and to provide a statesmanlike contrast to the Democratic Party primary squabbles. The China trip constituted the launching of Nixon's reelection bid.

Soon after returning from China, Nixon flew to Moscow for a summit in May, becoming the first American president to set foot on Soviet soil since Franklin Roosevelt visited Yalta in 1945. During the Moscow summit Nixon and Soviet party secretary Leonid Brezhnev signed two agreements—one limiting each country to construction of two ABM missile sites and another freezing the deployment of new offensive strategic missiles on both sides. The ABM treaty was submitted to the Senate for ratification and was approved by an 88-2 vote in August. The executive agreement on offensive arms, while not requiring congressional action, was submitted to both houses. After weeks of debate and the adoption of several modifying amendments, the Senate and the House granted approval in September.

Yet the foundation for a strong record in foreign affairs had to encompass significant progress in ending the Vietnam War. Nixon had been elected in 1968 because of voter disenchantment and the Democratic administration's handling of the war and its failure to end U.S. participation in it. He had promised to bring the war to a close with an honorable peace, and after four years in office he would have to show major achievements toward that goal. The administration's Vietnamization policy was a step in that direction, as was the scheduled abolishment of the draft. But given the intensity of antiwar sentiment in the country, more substantial accomplishments were needed.

The Democratic presidential candidate, Senator George McGovern, made the war his major campaign issue. McGovern maintained that the Nixon administration had not gone far enough or fast enough in resolving the war. The attendant issue of the release of American prisoners of war (POWs) became a volatile and emotional topic in the campaign. Nixon considered his opponent the "most extreme of the antiwar candidates"—one who saw the war not as an issue but as a cause.

After three years of stalled peace talks, prospects of capitalizing on the Vietnam issue

appeared dim until shortly after the president's return from his trip to Moscow. Following some hopeful signs in the summer of 1972, a breakthrough in the peace talks seemed possible, perhaps because of Nixon's meetings with the leaders of both Communist China and the Soviet Union, or because of his decision to bomb prime military targets in the Hanoi area and to mine Haiphong Harbor. In mid-October, Kissinger reported that major progress had been made in the Paris peace talks. By the end of the month, the North Vietnamese broadcast the general provisions of a tentative agreement over Radio Hanoi, and Kissinger announced that "peace [was] at hand" and that "an agreement [was] within sight. . . ." McGovern called the announcement a "cynical effort" to win the election.

Although subsequent events showed that peace was not quite "at hand," it was within reach, and evidence of the diplomatic breakthrough was enough to give President Nixon another major foreign policy achievement on the eve of the election. It also seriously undercut the single-issue campaign of his opponent. McGovern had run as the peace candidate, and yet mere days before the election, Nixon seemed to be delivering a peace agreement. Not only was the administration apparently delivering on the Vietnam peace promise, but it had also recognized and played to the silent majority that was developing to the right of the Democratic Party. Author Theodore White maintained that starting in 1952 "the more liberal the Democratic candidate, the better Nixon did against him," until in 1972 his margin swelled to a landslide. The June break-in at the Democratic National Committee's headquarters in the Watergate office complex in Washington and the subsequent indictments of White House employees Howard Hunt and Gordon Liddy did not develop into a significant campaign issue, despite Democratic efforts to make it one.

Nixon waged a restrained campaign in which he minimized his own participation and left much of the public appearances to his

President Nixon and Vice President Agnew receive the acclamation of the 1972 Republican National Convention after their renomination, August 23, 1972. *(National Archives)*

family, Vice President Agnew, and select political supporters like John Connally, who organized "Democrats for Nixon." The election results provided Richard Nixon with his first overwhelming victory in the national political arena. In a landslide victory of near-record proportion, Nixon carried 49 states for a total of 521 Electoral College votes—the third largest vote in the nation's history. His 60.7 percent of the popular vote tally had been surpassed only twice before—by Franklin Roosevelt in 1936 and Lyndon Johnson in 1964. It also marked the defection of the Solid South from the Democratic Party—all the states of the old Confederacy plus all the border states had swung into the Republican column for the first time since the Reconstruction era. The Republican presidential mandate did not extend through the congressional or gubernatorial ranks of the party, however. While the GOP gained 12 seats in the House, it lost two seats in the Senate as well as one state house.

President Nixon began his second term of office riding a wave of popularity that was unprecedented in his political career. The economy seemed to prosper, and shortly before his second inauguration, the president announced phase three of his economic plan, which relaxed wage and price controls except in the food, health, and construction industries. Three days after his inauguration, the president announced a Vietnam peace agreement that included plans for the return of American POWs.

Following the election a major administration shake-up took place. Since Congress had displayed little interest in cooperating with his first-term proposals for governmental reorganization, the president now embarked on revamping the administration by executive fiat. According to his *Memoirs*, Nixon approached his second term with three major goals in mind—"to reform the budget and terminate wasteful and ineffective programs"; "to initiate a massive reorganization and reduction of the federal bureaucracy and White House staff"; and "to revitalize the Republican Party along New Majority lines."

Even before his second inauguration, Nixon began to construct the "administrative presidency" as a means of gathering in the reins of bureaucratic control. To avoid the typical "downhill" nature of second-term presidencies, Nixon felt he had "to change not only some of the players but also some of the plays. . . ." The keystone of his reorganization plan was the construction of a supercabinet of seven functional area coordinators. Presidential assistants Henry Kissinger and John D. Ehrlichman would preside over foreign affairs and U.S. intergovernmental affairs, respectively. In addition Roy Ash, former head of the president's Advisory Council on Executive Organization, was appointed director of OMB and presidential assistant for executive management.

Meanwhile, Treasury secretary Shultz was accorded concurrent status as assistant to the president for economic affairs, and agriculture secretary Earl Butz was given a similar White House title and responsibility for natural resources. In other cabinet changes George Romney was replaced at HUD by James Lynn, who was also named presidential assistant for community development. Elliot Richardson was moved from HEW to the Defense Department and replaced at HEW by former OMB director Caspar Weinberger, who was given overall responsibility for human resources. These attempts to centralize bureaucratic control also included the appointment of new secretaries of labor (Peter J. Brennan) and of transportation (Claude S. Brinegar). In all, the changes seemed to highlight men of known managerial ability and low public profiles. How successful the "administrative presidency" might have been as a tool for executive control became a moot point since such efforts were soon sidetracked and overwhelmed by the emerging Watergate scandal.

Events during 1973 seesawed between diplomatic drama and the tragic revelations of White House political abuses that eventually brought down the Nixon administration. Announcement of the Vietnam "peace with honor" agreement was soon followed by the creation of a Senate select committee to investigate Watergate. Confirmation hearings for a new FBI director, L. Patrick Gray III, revealed presidential counsel John Dean's involvement in the bureau's investigation of Watergate and led the trail of suspicion closer to the White House. In the midst of the hearings, the administration announced the opening of liaison offices between the United States and China to handle cultural and trade exchanges.

The Nixon administration received a staggering blow in April when two of the president's closest White House aides, H. R. Haldeman and John D. Ehrlichman, were forced to resign because of their apparent implication in the widening Watergate scandal. The following month two former members of the Nixon cabinet—John N. Mitchell and Maurice Stans—were indicted for illegal campaign finance activities during the 1972 elections. The president was also forced to agree to the appointment of an independent special prosecutor to handle the Watergate investigation to obtain confirmation of a new attorney general, Elliot Richardson, after Richard Kleindienst had resigned the post following controversy over the settlement of a Justice Department antitrust suit against International Telephone and Telegraph.

In June the White House scored another foreign policy success with the week-long visit of Soviet Communist Party leader Leonid I. Brezhnev to the United States. The meeting was hailed as symbolic of the new spirit of détente between the two nations, and several agreements were concluded. Although most of these agreements were rather minor in nature (regarding oceanographic, commercial, and cultural exchange matters), declarations of principles designed to accelerate the Strategic Arms Limitation Talks (SALT) and to avoid nuclear war were noteworthy.

However, on the domestic scene, both political and economic affairs continued to deteriorate. Inflation continued to soar, and the dollar weakened further on the international money market despite phase three of the president's economic efforts, which had included the imposition of a price ceiling on certain meats in response to a spring shoppers' boycott against record high prices. Acknowledging that neither voluntary wage and price guidelines nor the limited price control on meats had been effective, President Nixon, on June 13, reimposed a price freeze for 60 days. Meanwhile Congress, criticized for both inflation and the continuing war in Cambodia, took advantage of the president's preoccupation with Watergate to reassert itself and challenge the executive's war-making powers. On June 29 it passed the War Powers Act, which imposed an August 15 deadline for ending combat activities in Indochina and sought to impose limitations on the ability of presidents to exercise their war-making powers unilaterally and without consultation with and consent of Congress. Although the president vetoed the bill, Congress succeeded in overriding his veto.

For the rest of the summer of 1973, Watergate dominated the news. The surprise revelation of a White House taping system by a former White House assistant, Alexander P. Butterfield, to the Senate Watergate Committee touched off a nine-month political and legal battle for the release of these tapes. Throughout the summer the televised Watergate hearings brought the testimony of numerous former administration officials, such as Haldeman, Ehrlichman, Richard Helms, and L. Patrick Gray III, into the homes of millions of Americans.

There was also controversy over the nomination of National Security Advisor Henry Kissinger to succeed William Rogers as secretary of state. The nomination should have been welcomed by the Senate as an indication of better access to foreign policy-making information with Kissinger in a position of formal responsibility and of greater accountability to the Congress. Beclouding the confirmation hearings, however, was concern over Kissinger's role in authorizing the wiretapping of 17 government officials and newsmen from May 1969 to February 1971, in a search for the source of national security leaks. Despite this controversy Kissinger was confirmed and assumed the position of secretary of state late in September 1973.

Although untouched by the Watergate scandal, Vice President Spiro Agnew added another dimension to corruption within the administration. Under investigation for alleged conspiracy, extortion, and bribery, the vice president resigned on October 10 as part of a plea bargain that involved his pleading nolo contendere to a charge of income tax evasion. After accepting his sentence of three years

unsupervised probation and a $10,000 fine, Agnew made a farewell television address professing his innocence, denouncing witnesses as "self-confessed bribe brokers, extortionists, and conspirators," and attacking government prosecutors for "improperly and unconscionably" leaking grand jury proceedings to a press that published "scurrilous and inaccurate reports." He maintained that he had resigned because "the American people deserve to have a vice president who commands their unimpaired confidence and trust" and because he did not want to "subject the country to a further agonizing period of months without an unclouded successor for the presidency."

Two days later in a television ceremony, President Nixon announced his selection of a replacement for Agnew. Invoking for the first time the procedure in the Twenty-fifth Amendment for filling a vacancy in the vice presidency, Nixon announced his nomination of House minority leader Gerald R. Ford (R-Mich.). Ford's confirmation hearings moved quickly in both houses. Although he repeatedly stated that he did not seek "personal political aggrandizement" and did not intend to seek the presidency in 1976, his confirmation created considerable interest because of speculation that he would become president as a result of either the resignation or impeachment of President Nixon.

The drama surrounding the vice presidency was, however, only the beginning of administrative problems. On the same day that Gerald Ford's nomination as vice president was announced, the U.S. Circuit Court of Appeals for the District of Columbia upheld an earlier ruling by Judge John Sirica directing President Nixon to surrender Watergate-related tapes. The president, hoping to effect a compromise, offered to supply transcripts of the tapes verified by Senator John C. Stennis (D-Miss.) if special Watergate prosecutor Archibald Cox agreed not to subpoena additional tapes or documents.

Cox refused Nixon's compromise of tape transcripts, saying it would "defeat the fair administration of criminal justice." The president felt that Cox had "deliberately exceeded his authority" and that such a challenge to presidential authority would reflect badly on his prestige at a time of an imminent diplomatic showdown with the Soviets. Hence Nixon decided to fire the special prosecutor and directed Cox's immediate superior, Attorney General Richardson, to carry out his order. Richardson, feeling he had pledged himself to guarantee the independence of the special prosecutor, refused and tendered his resignation. Deputy Attorney General William Ruckelshaus also resigned rather than carry out the order. Finally the third-ranking official at the Justice Department, Solicitor General Robert H. Bork, now acting attorney general, fired Cox.

Public reaction to what became known as the "Saturday night massacre" was swift and intensely adverse. Characterized by White House chief of staff Alexander M. Haig as a "firestorm" of protest, the move precipitated the initiation of impeachment hearings and marked the beginning of the end of the Nixon presidency. Within two days of the firings, House Democratic leaders had tentatively agreed to have the House Judiciary Committee begin an inquiry into the grounds for impeaching the president. Realizing how badly he had underestimated public reaction to the dismissal of the special prosecutor, the president agreed to release the nine subpoenaed tapes and to allow the continuation of the special prosecutor's office under Texas trial lawyer Leon Jaworski, Cox's successor.

In the midst of the administration's domestic troubles, war had erupted in the Middle East between Egypt and Israel. In response to a U.S. announcement that it would supply Israel with military equipment, the Arab oil-producing nations imposed a ban on oil exports to the United States. On October 25 American military forces were put on a worldwide nuclear alert in reaction to the possibility of Soviet troop movement into the area. Within hours the situation was eased through Soviet agreement to a proposal for an international peace-keeping force without big power participation. Response to the alert varied widely. Senator Henry Jackson (D-Wash.) thought the incident had brought the world "right at the brink again." On the other hand there was considerable public skepticism that the crisis was real, and it was suggested that the alert was merely an administration tactic to divert attention from the Watergate scandals. Secretary of State Kissinger denied such speculation, calling it symptomatic of the "crisis of authority" the country was undergoing, and Nixon called it "the most difficult crisis we've had since the Cuban confrontation in 1962."

In the aftermath of the October 1973 Middle East war, Kissinger embarked on a round of "shuttle diplomacy" that brought the Egyptians and the Israelis to their first face-to-face diplomatic encounter in over two decades. The meeting led to an agreement for the exchange of prisoners of war and eventually to an Arab-Israeli peace conference in Geneva in late December 1973.

Dominating the first half of 1974 was the possibility that because of the Watergate scandal Nixon would become the first American president removed from office through impeachment. Probes into the affair had revealed additional campaign illegalities in which the administration was allegedly involved. In February the House Judiciary Committee began hearings into possible impeachment charges against the president. In March seven former Nixon aides, including Mitchell, Haldeman, and Ehrlichman, were indicted for conspiracy to cover up the Watergate burglary. In April the Internal Revenue Service (IRS) reported that Nixon owed over $450,000 in back taxes and interest for the period from 1969 through 1972.

Also during this month the House Judiciary Committee and the special prosecutor subpoe-

President Nixon delivers his farewell remarks to the White House staff in the East Room, with his family looking on, August 9, 1974. *(National Archives)*

naed tapes and documents relating to more than 60 presidential conversations. Nixon responded by releasing a 1,308-page edited transcript of these materials, but he declined to release the actual tapes and other documents, claiming these were protected by executive privilege. In the face of mounting congressional, legal, and public sentiment against him, the president continued to deny both knowledge of the Watergate burglary and participation in the subsequent cover-up.

On July 24 the Supreme Court, in response to a motion by the special prosecutor, handed down an 8-0 decision against the president's claim that executive privilege justified his withholding of the subpoenaed tapes. Nixon then announced, through his attorney James St. Clair, that he would turn over the tapes. Within a week the House Judiciary Committee approved three articles of impeachment charging Nixon with obstructing justice in the Watergate cover-up, misuse of presidential powers, and contempt of Congress for refusing to comply with congressional subpoenas. Bipartisan support within the committee for the articles strongly indicated that the House was likely to adopt at least one article of impeachment and thus send the president to trial in the Senate.

A week after the adoption of the articles of impeachment, Nixon provided the "smoking gun" in surrendering tapes of conversations on June 23, 1972, that clearly showed he had participated in the cover-up. With this evidence, remaining congressional support for the president collapsed. On August 8, in a televised speech, Richard M. Nixon tendered his resignation as president of the United States, effective at noon of the following day. He thus became the first president in American history to resign from office.

At 12:03 Vice President Gerald Ford was sworn in as the 38th president of the United States. He declared that the "long national nightmare" was now over, and the nation rallied behind him with a strong showing of popular and congressional support. Since he had been a generally well-liked congressman, it was hoped that under Ford interbranch relations would improve. The new president, in addressing a joint session of Congress, called for an "era of good feelings" between the executive and the legislature and expressed confidence that the Congress would be both his "working partner" and a "most constructive critic."

One of President Ford's earliest actions was to provide for the line of succession by nominating Nelson A. Rockefeller as vice president. Earlier in his career Rockefeller had twice turned down the job of vice president, calling it "standby equipment." Three times before, in 1960, 1964, and 1968, Rockefeller had made a run for the White House, and various political observers believed that he was going to make a fourth attempt in 1976. When the fall of Richard Nixon brought Gerald Ford to the White House and made him the de facto Republican front-runner for 1976, the former New York governor finally put aside his presidential ambitions and accepted the nomination as vice president.

The choice of this moderate veteran politician who had experience in both state and federal administration won widespread praise both from Republicans and Democrats as being complimentary to the conservative, congressionally experienced President Ford. Despite this initially favorable reaction to the nomination, the topic of Rockefeller's wealth generated considerable controversy during his confirmation hearings. During four months of grueling hearings, Congress questioned Rockefeller's habit of making loans and gifts to former members of his New York state administrations as well as the wisdom of placing the power of such wealth "only a heartbeat away" from the power of the presidency. Confirmation was finally secured, however, and Nelson Rockefeller was sworn in as vice president on December 19, 1974. Thus, for the first time in its history, the United States had both a president and a vice president selected under the provisions of the Twenty-fifth Amendment rather than by national election.

Less than three weeks after nominating his new vice president, Ford made a much more controversial decision. He granted former President Nixon a "full, free, and absolute pardon . . . for all offenses against the United States which he . . . has committed or may have committed" during his years as president. Seeking to put an end to the "bitter" and "divisive national debate" that had raged for over 18 months and to show the measure of mercy that his conscience dictated was "the right thing to do," Ford exercised his constitutional pardoning power and, in the process, ended his "honeymoon" period with the nation and the Congress. Ford was strongly criticized for circumventing the judicial process, and his credibility and popularity suffered. The House Judiciary Committee's Subcommittee on Criminal Justice convened hearings to investigate the reasons for the pardon, and in October Ford became the first sitting president to formally testify before a congressional committee. During that testimony Ford vigorously denied that he had made any secret arrangement with Nixon to grant a pardon in return for the former president's resignation.

The pardon had the effect of tainting Ford with the Watergate scandal. He was further criticized during 1974 for not moving quickly or decisively to replace the Nixon staff with choices of his own. Initial changes were slow and focused on the core members of the White House. Under a new chief of staff, Donald Rumsfeld, the mood in the White House began to relax from the tension and suspense that had permeated the Nixon administration. Cabinet changes trickled through Ford's first year in office as Attorney General William Saxbe was replaced by Edward H. Levi; Transportation Secretary Claude Brinegar by William Coleman; Commerce Secretary Frederick Dent by Rogers C. B. Morton, who was moved from Interior and replaced there by Stanley Hathaway; and HEW Secretary Caspar Weinberger by F. David Mathews. Since these changes were spread out over a year's time, their impact was fragmented. Thus, although President Ford made significant changes in the administration he had inherited, the public found it difficult to appreciate the extent of the turnover because of its piecemeal character.

Ford also inherited severe economic problems, which had been exacerbated by the sense of drift and the internal battling over economic policy that had occurred as President Nixon became more preoccupied with the Watergate affair. In October 1975 Ford unveiled his WIN ("Whip Inflation Now") program, which consisted of a 5 percent tax surcharge, voluntary efforts to hold down energy consumption, and a tight money policy accompanied by reduced federal spending. The WIN program was severely criticized in Congress as "misdirected and insufficient," and the program soon faded as the administration shifted attention, early in

Following Richard Nixon's resignation from the presidency as a result of Watergate, Vice President Gerald Ford is sworn in as president by Chief Justice Warren Burger. *(Ford Library)*

1975, from inflation to unemployment, which hovered above 7 percent.

Criticized for inadequacy in dealing with administrative and domestic problems, Ford found his public popularity declining steadily and his relations with Congress just as troubled (though less acerbic) as those of President Nixon. In reaction to the Watergate scandals, the public had sent a record number of Democrats to Congress in the 1974 midterm elections. The resultant number of liberal and reform-minded Democratic congressmen were dissatisfied and often at odds with the president. With inadequate congressional support, Ford's legislative strategy turned negative as he resorted to the frequent use of the veto and the veto threat. Although Congress frustrated many of the administration's economic, energy, and even foreign policy proposals, it was, however, unable to forge its own policy alternatives.

In contrast with its economic and political problems at home, the administration found the area of foreign affairs more rewarding. During the autumn of 1974 Ford traveled to Vladivostok to sign an arms limitation agreement with the Soviet Union. The following year he went to Europe three times and ended

1975 with a seven-day visit to China, Indonesia, and the Philippines. The European trips dealt with North Atlantic Treaty Organization (NATO) affairs, the formalization of territorial boundaries, and the Declaration of Rambouillet, which pledged Western nations and Japan to mutual economic cooperation.

The Ford administration presided over the final chapter of U.S. involvement in Southeast Asia. A series of military victories by the Communists in March and April brought down the South Vietnamese and Cambodian governments. With the final evacuation of Americans from the area in late April, Ford declared the war "finished as far as America is concerned." There was, however, another episode in the long American saga in Indochina. In response to the May seizure of an American merchant ship, the *Mayaguez*, by Cambodian Communists in the Gulf of Siam, the president ordered U.S. troops to recapture and free the ship and its crew. Despite questions as to whether Ford had fully complied with the congressional consultation provisions of the War Powers Act in sending in American troops, the *Mayaguez* incident prompted an overwhelming rally of congressional and public support for the president.

More troublesome issues emerged in the Middle East and Turkey. During Secretary of State Kissinger's efforts at shuttle diplomacy in the Middle East in the spring and summer of 1975, the administration announced a "total reassessment" of U.S. policy in the area. The announcement was viewed as an unsubtle form of pressure on Israel to agree to negotiating concessions that would facilitate the search for peace. The administration further fueled Israeli and Jewish-American opposition by trying to establish better relations with moderate Arab nations such as Jordan and Egypt. Despite these problems Kissinger finally succeeded in working out an agreement between Israel and Egypt that called for Israeli withdrawal from the Sinai mountain passes and oil fields in return for political concessions from Egypt.

Another major problem was the dispute between Turkey and Greece over Cyprus. Following Turkey's July 1974 invasion of Cyprus, congressional sentiment turned against Turkey, and, as a result, Congress sought to cut off U.S. military aid to that nation. Although Ford twice vetoed such efforts, Congress imposed an embargo on arms shipments to Turkey, which went into effect on February 5, 1975. The action did nothing to encourage a settlement of the Cyprus issue and worsened U.S.-Turkish relations. Turkey retaliated by taking over U.S. and NATO bases considered essential for Western intelligence gathering. Convinced that its hard-line policy was proving ineffective, Congress eased the embargo in October.

As 1975 ended, Ford reshuffled his national security team, appointed a new member of the Supreme Court, and began to assess his chances for nomination and reelection in 1976. As part of a sweeping personnel change in November, both Defense Secretary James R. Schlesinger and Central Intelligence Agency (CIA) Director William E. Colby were dismissed and replaced by Donald Rumsfeld and George Bush, respectively. Although the dismissal of Schlesinger was called a "Kissinger coup," Kissinger did not emerge from the shuffle unaffected. He lost his position as national security assistant, which was assumed by his assistant, Brent Scowcroft. Ford insisted that the changes were prompted by his desire to put together his "own team," but he also admitted that he had not been comfortable with Schlesinger.

Other personnel developments included the retirement of Supreme Court Justice William O. Douglas and the nomination of U.S. Circuit Court Judge John Paul Stevens as his replacement. Vice President Rockefeller withdrew from a potential Republican ticket headed by Ford in 1976. Rockefeller's withdrawal was interpreted as an effort by the president to strengthen his position with the conservatives of the party, who were opposed to Rockefeller and who were mounting a serious campaign for the nomination of their candidate, former California governor Ronald Reagan.

Ford's final year in office was preoccupied by the presidential nomination and election contests. Challenged on the right by Reagan's candidacy and pressured from the left by congressional Democrats, Ford found he had few of the usual advantages of an incumbent seeking reelection. The state of the economy, again a major issue of the campaign, was unstable and far from prosperous. Although the economic system seemed to be slowly recovering from the worst recession since the 1930s, the growth rate of the gross national product was low, and the unemployment rate remained above 7 percent.

In the aftermath of Watergate, the question of ethics and honesty in government became another major issue. Ford's strategy was to cultivate the idea that his administration had done much to heal the divisive wounds caused by White House scandals and a loss of the public's confidence in government. Yet the taint of

President Gerald Ford issues his controversial pardon of Richard Nixon for his role in Watergate. *(Ford Library)*

Watergate came back to haunt him because of his pardon of former President Nixon.

In the post-Watergate era, the American public wanted not only honest government but also strong leadership, after years of drift and disillusionment. President Ford's record of conflict with Congress, as well as his evident vulnerability within his own party, cast serious doubts about his ability to lead. Realizing that he was not an incumbent in the traditional sense and that he had never won a national elective constituency, Ford began campaigning in the fall of 1975 and made a good showing in the early primaries of 1976. His campaign organization, however, was weak and disrupted in late March by the resignation of his campaign manager, Howard H. (Bo) Callaway, who was accused of influence-peddling.

Because of these problems and a highly effective television campaign by Reagan, the tide began to turn against Ford with Reagan's success in the March North Carolina primary. Throughout the remaining primaries, Reagan and Ford ran neck and neck, with Ford emerging in June with only a slight delegate lead. As the Republican Convention convened in Kansas City in mid-August, the party was more evenly divided than it had been in over two decades. Ford threw all the status of the presidency into a last-minute push for the nomination, while Reagan overplayed his hand in an attempt to win wider appeal. Trying to woo liberal and middle-of-the-road Republicans to his banner (and to corner a large state delegation vote), Reagan announced his choice of a running mate just before the convention met. His selection of liberal Pennsylvania senator Richard Schweiker, however, backfired, alienating some of his conservative supporters and repelling, rather than attracting, some uncommitted delegates.

When the convention voted, Ford won on the first ballot with a thin margin of 1,187 to Reagan's 1,070. As a running mate Ford chose Kansas senator Robert Dole, an outspoken, aggressive political fighter. Furthermore, selection of the conservative Dole was designed to appeal to Reagan and his backers and thus promote party unity.

Meanwhile the Democratic side produced a multitude of candidates ranging from Alabama governor George Wallace to Arizona representative Morris Udall. Yet out of a field that included many well-known national and party figures, a dark-horse candidate, former Georgia governor Jimmy Carter, emerged as the front-runner. Carter's campaign did not so much emphasize issues as personal qualities like honesty, competence, and trustworthiness. Throughout the primaries Carter engineered and benefited from a process of elimination of the other contenders. Finally, as the indisputable leader in June, Carter won the Democratic nomination on the first ballot, amid the rallying of the various party segments behind him. After a long deliberative process, Carter selected Minnesota senator Walter Mondale, a protégé of Hubert Humphrey and the preference of labor and liberals, as his running mate.

The election campaign of 1976 presented an acutely undecided electorate with the prospect of a return to normalcy after the traumas of Vietnam and Watergate. While the issue of trust in government dominated the campaign, neither candidate seemed particularly able to generate or hold the public's confidence. Gerald Ford, the unelected incumbent, had been bloodied in the primaries and still carried the stigma of the Nixon pardon. Jimmy Carter, the "outsider," promised never to lie to the public and campaigned against the Washington establishment, yet he still appeared an unknown and untested leader. In such a climate of public uncertainty, both candidates needed to sharpen and improve their images. Hence both Ford and Carter saw advantages to engaging in the first televised debates between presidential candidates since those of Kennedy and Nixon in 1960.

After an initial lead in the popularity polls, Carter's rating dropped precipitously in late September. Contributing to this decline were an interview with Carter published in *Playboy* magazine and his poor showing in the first TV debate. The *Playboy* interview was Carter's most serious blunder, and his statements there came back to haunt him repeatedly during the campaign. He eventually apologized to Lady Bird Johnson for having said that Lyndon Johnson had lied, cheated, and distorted the truth. He never did quite live down the notoriety of his admission in *Playboy* to having "looked on a lot of women with lust" and to having "committed adultery in my heart many times." Carter, however, staged a comeback in the second and third debates. Particularly damaging to Ford was his assertion during the October 6 debate that "there is no Soviet domination of Eastern Europe," a statement he later recanted.

As the American voter went to the polls on November 2, 1976, the election contest was considered too close to call. When the votes were counted, Carter beat Ford narrowly by less than 2 million popular votes and by an Electoral College vote of 297 to 240.

The nation's bicentennial election contest produced a rural, southern Baptist ex-governor as the 39th president of the United States. For some Carter's election became a symbol for a South risen again and finally reintegrated into the Union. Carter began the country's third century with a call for "a new beginning, a new declaration . . . and a new spirit among us all" linked to the pursuit of "an old dream," that of "faith in our country—and in one another."

Carter's inauguration marked the end of the Nixon-Ford years. Those years had seen war, peace, and extensive diplomatic activity; nagging domestic problems, particularly those related to the economy; and scandal that had produced high political drama and tragedy. The eight Republican years, starting with Richard Nixon's election as president in 1968, had confronted the issues of peace, prosperity, and public confidence in government. When the Republican administration left office in 1976, the Vietnam War was ended, détente with the Soviet Union had been nurtured, and relations with Communist China had been reopened. Its record on the other two issues was, however, less commendable.

The economic situation was certainly no better, and probably worse, than eight years earlier. Inflation and unemployment seemed intractable problems, and over the years the American public had become less optimistic about the state of the economy and the prospects that better days were just around the corner. Public confidence had declined even further in the wake of the Watergate scandals and the resignation of both a president and a vice president disgraced in office. Thus after eight years only the issue of war had changed; the search for prosperity and for confidence in government and its officials continued.

Abernathy, Ralph D(avid)
(1926–1990) *president, Southern Christian Leadership Conference*

Born in Linden, Alabama, on March 11, 1926, the grandson of a slave, Ralph Abernathy was raised on his parents' 500-acre farm in Alabama. He was ordained a Baptist minister in 1948 and received his B.S. from Alabama College in 1950 and an M.A. in sociology from Atlanta University the following year. In 1951 Abernathy was appointed pastor of the First Baptist Church in Montgomery and became close friends with the Rev. Martin Luther King Jr., whom he accompanied in the early civil rights demonstrations. He and King, with several other black ministers, established the Southern Christian Leadership Conference (SCLC) in 1957 to end segregation and win full civil rights for southern blacks through nonviolent protest. (See *The Eisenhower Years* volume.)

During the 1960s Abernathy was King's closest friend and adviser. Their protest campaign in Selma, Alabama, attracted national attention and helped win enactment of the Voting Rights Act of 1965. During the late 1960s the SCLC leadership became interested in other economic and social issues affecting the poor, both black and white. After King was assassi-

nated in Memphis on April 4, 1968, Abernathy, who was with him at the time, became president of the SCLC and led the Poor People's Campaign in Washington. For several weeks in May and June, thousands of poor people camped out in "Resurrection City" in Potomac Park, attended sessions of Congress to present their demands, and demonstrated outside government buildings. (See *The Kennedy Years* and *The Johnson Years* volumes.)

Under Abernathy's leadership, the SCLC concentrated on broad social and economic issues other than civil rights. Still firmly committed to nonviolence, Abernathy was especially concerned with forging a coalition of all the disaffected groups rising to speak out. He regularly appeared at antiwar rallies, endorsed the grape pickers boycott sponsored by CESAR CHAVEZ and the United Farm Workers (UFW), and participated in a week-long UFW march through California in May 1969. The defense efforts of antiwar activists in the Chicago and Harrisburg conspiracy trials also received his support.

Targeting unemployment and poverty as the major civil rights issues, Abernathy took a leading role in the 1969 strike of hospital workers in Charleston, S.C. The strike began on March 20 after 12 union organizers were fired from their jobs. After a court injunction was issued against picketing, Abernathy led daily marches through the city, resulting in several hundred arrests. The strikers' demands for union recognition and a living wage were endorsed by major civil rights spokesmen, liberal senators and representatives, and union leaders. The demonstrations continued into June, when Abernathy was indicted on charges of inciting to riot after some protesters had damaged property. The strike was settled, however, on June 27 when the hospitals agreed to rehire all of the workers dismissed earlier and to recognize the union.

Abernathy, meanwhile, was organizing a second Poor People's Campaign, which began on May 12. Throughout the spring and summer, delegations of poor people from all races met with congressional officials, held small demonstrations in Washington, and lobbied intensively for social and economic welfare legislation. Their demands included jobs for all, a guaranteed annual income, a comprehensive health care program, quality education for all children, and a shift from defense expenditures to government spending on basic human needs.

In 1969 the SCLC sponsored an intensive voter registration drive in Greene County, Alabama, that resulted in the election of six blacks to local office and a black majority on the school board. It initiated demonstrations in Chicago during the summer of 1969 to protest the discriminatory hiring policies of the city's construction unions. In May 1970, after police in Augusta, Georgia, killed five young blacks during a protest march, Abernathy led 10,000 people on a 100-mile march to protest police violence against blacks. He supported the efforts of welfare recipients in Nevada to have arbitrary welfare cuts rescinded, and in April 1971 he was arrested in New York City during a demonstration against A&P hiring practices.

Abernathy found himself increasingly at odds with the NIXON administration. In Janu-

ary 1969 he and several other black leaders met with the president, who promised to do "more for the underprivileged and more for the Negro" than any other president. Four months later Abernathy met with Nixon again and later told the press that it was "the most disappointing and most fruitless of all the meetings we have had up to this time." He opposed the administration's proposed relaxation of school desegregation guidelines, the nominations of CLEMENT HAYNSWORTH and G. HARROLD CARSWELL to the Supreme Court, and the White House attempt to weaken the 1965 Voting Rights Act. By the summer of 1970 Abernathy was so disillusioned with Nixon's policies that he termed the administration "a repressive, antiblack, antipoor, antiyouth national government" under "fascist domination."

With other militant civil rights leaders and antiwar activists, Abernathy helped form the People's Coalition for Peace and Justice. In April and May 1971, the coalition sponsored a series of daily demonstrations against the war, poverty, and government repression. On April 29 Abernathy conducted a "teach-in" at HEW and led a mule train from the department's offices to the White House. The following day he read a "poor people's bill of particulars" against the Justice Department. The police began making mass arrests a few days later and held over 7,000 demonstrators in makeshift jails. The arrests and convictions were later overturned because of widespread violations of constitutional rights.

Despite Abernathy's energetic leadership, the SCLC was plagued by internal difficulties during the 1970s. In December 1971 its board of directors suspended the REVEREND JESSE JACKSON, head of the SCLC's Operation "Breadbasket," in a dispute over the use of funds. Jackson responded by resigning, announced the formation of his own organization, Operation PUSH (People United to Save Humanity), and took most of the SCLC's Chicago chapter with him. The following year the SCLC fired 21 workers at its national headquarters in Atlanta due to budget difficulties. Although in the late 1960s the SCLC had easily raised over $2 million a year, by 1973 income had fallen to approximately $500,000. On July 9, 1973, Abernathy announced his resignation as the organization's president. He blamed the SCLC's problems on middle-class blacks who "feel they have 'arrived' simply because they now occupy high positions, but will not support the SCLC financially." When the board of directors rejected his resignation, Abernathy agreed to stay on. By the mid-1970s, however, the SCLC was only a shadow of its former self and had ceased to play a leading role in the struggle for racial justice.

In 1977 Abernathy resigned from the presidency of the SCLC and ran unsuccessfully to fill the Georgia congressional seat vacated when President Carter appointed Representative ANDREW YOUNG as U.S. ambassador to the United Nations. Abernathy continued as pastor of an Atlanta church. He died on April 17, 1990, in Atlanta.

—JD

Abplanalp, Robert H.
(1923–2003) *businessman*

Born in Bronxville, New York, the son of Swiss immigrants, Abplanalp attended Villanova College for a short time before dropping out during World War II to open a machine shop in Yonkers, New York. There he perfected the aerosol valve and began manufacturing his invention at the Precision Valve Co. in 1949. The invention made Abplanalp a millionaire. By 1971 the company was grossing $50 million a year, and Abplanalp's personal fortune was estimated at $100 million.

Abplanalp contributed to RICHARD NIXON's 1960 presidential contest and was introduced to Nixon in 1963. Soon thereafter Nixon's New York law firm began representing Precision Valve Co. overseas. In 1966 Abplanalp bought the island of Grand Cay in the Bahamas and built a luxury compound. Nixon, by now a fast friend, paid frequent visits to the island, visits that became more frequent after Nixon became president.

The island was a refuge for the troubled president during the Watergate period. Often, Nixon and Abplanalp were in one another's company as Nixon prepared a new defense or recovered from new charges. In the worst days of Watergate, when impeachment loomed and Nixon withheld information even from his lawyers, a source close to Nixon said "the only people he will talk to candidly about Watergate are BEBE REBOZO and Bob Abplanalp." Rebozo was another millionaire who often joined Grand Cay fishing trips.

Abplanalp was also involved in Nixon's personal financing. Nixon's home in San Clemente, California, was purchased with the help of a $625,000 loan from Abplanalp, a financial arrangement that was revealed after a California newspaper charged that Nixon financed San Clemente with $1 million in unreported 1968 campaign funds.

In 1973 the General Services Administration reported that $10 million in new security arrangements ordered by Nixon and paid for by the government were detailed for Nixon's own homes in San Clemente and Key Biscayne, Florida, and at the Abplanalp complex at Grand Cay. The figures showed that $160,000 in communications equipment had been installed at Grand Cay, and a $16,000 bunk house for secret service agents was built for use during Nixon's visits.

Abplanalp was investigated by special Watergate prosecutor ARCHIBALD COX after a 1971 Justice Department decision to drop antitrust charges against Precision Valve Co. was revealed. Presidential critics said the charges were dropped because of Nixon's friendship with Abplanalp, but Cox found no evidence of price violations or presidential influence.

Abplanalp and Nixon remained friends following the president's resignation. He was a founding member and trustee of the Richard M. Nixon Library and Birthplace (Yorba Linda, California). Abplanalp died on August 30, 2003, in Bronxville, New York.

—BO

Abrams, Creighton W(illiam), Jr.
(1914–1974) *commander, U.S. Military Assistance Command, Vietnam; army chief of staff*

Born in Springfield, Massachusetts, on September 15, 1914, Creighton Abrams graduated from West Point in 1936 and during World War II distinguished himself as the commander of the 37th Tank Battalion. He served as chief of staff of several army corps in Korea in 1953 and 1954. While assigned to the Pentagon in the early 1960s, he was in charge of the federal troops who were placed on alert in the Deep South to prevent racial violence during desegregation. A general since 1956, Abrams was elevated to the rank of four-star general in 1964. He was deputy commander of the U.S. Military Assistance Command in South Vietnam in 1967 and 1968.

In June 1968 Abrams succeeded General WILLIAM WESTMORELAND as commander of the almost 500,000 American troops stationed in South Vietnam. Abrams's handling of the war was dictated in large measure by Johnson's decision in March 1968 to place a limit on U.S. military involvement in South Vietnam at its present level, to deescalate the fighting, and to renew efforts for a negotiated end to the conflict.

In May preliminary peace talks between the United States and North Vietnam began in Paris. The negotiations took a more sub-stantive form in January of the following year when, at Abrams' urging, the South Vietnamese entered the talks. He arranged for weapons aid and helped to overcome the Saigon government's reluctance to join negotiations that included the National Liberation Front. (See *The Johnson Years* volume.)

Abrams continued as the U.S. commander in Vietnam under President RICHARD NIXON. With the new administration came a change in war policy. No longer did the initiative for running the war come from the U.S. command in Saigon; it now came from the White House and HENRY KISSINGER. The Nixon administration had decided to "wind down" the war. While strengthening South Vietnamese forces in the difficult task of Vietnamization, a term to describe the goal of making South Vietnam capable of defending itself, Abrams was also charged with breaking contact with a still-able enemy and withdrawing U.S. forces. Troop withdrawals began in August 1969.

To carry out his new mission, Abrams modified Westmoreland's tactics. He deemphasized Westmoreland's search-and-destroy missions, designed to engage the enemy's large units in a war with no fronts. Abrams replaced ground forces with planes as troop reductions proceeded. He relied upon large deployments of artillery and precision B-52 strikes to defeat the enemy in medium- and large-scale engagements. Abrams gave subordinate commanders unusually wide latitude and increased night patrols and ambushes, favoring "spoiler" patrols of four or five men sent out to disrupt the enemy.

Abrams and other top military leaders resisted but went along with the Nixon administration's "orderly scheduled timetable" for the disengagement of U.S. forces from South Vietnam. The exact timetable was based on the pace of Vietnamization, progress at the Paris peace talks, and the extent of the Communist military threat.

In May 1970 President Nixon, in a move proposed since 1965 by a series of defense and foreign affairs advisers and strongly advocated by Abrams, ordered U.S. combat forces to attack North Vietnamese sanctuaries in Cambodia along the South Vietnamese border. The goal, which was accomplished, was to buy one year of grace from an enemy attack against South Vietnam to allow Vietnamization needed time. Domestic political reaction against the incursion prompted the administration to limit it to eight weeks. In pursuit of the same military results, the U.S. command furnished much of the logistical, air, and artillery support for the movement of South Vietnamese troops into Laos in February 1971.

Abrams was named army chief of staff in June 1972. His confirmation was delayed as the Senate Armed Services Committee looked into allegations by Lieutenant General John D. Lavelle that Abrams shared responsibility with him for unauthorized air strikes against North Vietnam in late 1971 and early 1972. Abrams denied the allegations before the committee. He said he did not know that Lavelle's raids were unauthorized, nor that false postaction reports had covered up the nature of the missions. The committee's investigation supported Abrams's claims, and his nomination was approved in October. Abrams appeared before the committee again in 1973 to answer charges that he had taken part in the cover-up of secret Cambodian bombing operations in 1969 and 1970. While acknowledging that he was fully informed of the secret B-52 raids, he denied responsibility for the falsification of reports, saying that special reporting procedures, authorized by the Joint Chiefs of Staff, had been used in the operation.

Abrams returned from Vietnam convinced that the army needed to reduce its "support tail." He abolished seven army headquarters around the world, reduced desk jobs in favor of more fighting strength, and worked to update the training of the reserve forces. As peace talks in Paris entered a new serious phase in October 1972, Abrams was ordered to South Vietnam to discover what additional arms would be needed by Saigon to make a cease-fire acceptable. Before the end of the month a massive airlift of planes, tanks, and ammunition began, based in part on Abrams's recommendations. After the Paris peace accords of 1973, Abrams, in his role as army chief, sought to stimulate subordinates to make the new volunteer army work.

Abrams supported the Nixon administration's pursuit of a policy of détente. However, the Strategic Arms Limitation Talks (SALT) I agreement between the United States and the Soviet Union, signed by Nixon in Moscow in 1972, caused some dissent among the Joint Chiefs. There were fears that the administration had given too much away. Abrams broke the silence of the military about détente in October 1973, during the Yom Kippur War in the Mideast, declaring, "the word 'détente' for some people evidently colors everything rose and turns their perceptions away from even obvious threats." He cautioned that it was necessary to keep the military's strength up to par. Abrams died in September 1974 at Walter Reed Medical Center (Washington, D.C.) of complications following lung cancer surgery.

—SF

Abzug, Bella (Stavisky)
(1920–1998) *member of the House of Representatives*

Born in New York City on July 24, 1920, Bella Stavisky, the daughter of a butcher, graduated from Hunter College in 1942. She then worked in a shipbuilding factory to help in the war effort. She met Maurice Abzug and married him in June 1944. After the war she returned to Columbia Law School and graduated in 1947. While at Columbia she was editor of the *Columbia Law Review.*

Abzug worked as a labor lawyer during the 1950s, representing fur workers, restaurant workers, auto workers, longshoremen, and civil rights workers. She was active in opposing Senator Joseph McCarthy's anticommunism and defended people accused of subversive activities, including several groups of New York schoolteachers.

Abzug won a reputation as a leader of liberal and radical causes during the 1960s. In 1961 after the failure of the nuclear test ban treaty, she and several other women founded the Women's Strike for Peace, which urged worldwide disarmament and an end to nuclear testing. In 1967 and 1968 she was active in the Democratic Party's "dump Johnson" politics, and in 1968 she was one of the founders of both the "Coalition for a Democratic Alternative," which supported the candidacy of Senator EUGENE MCCARTHY, and the Coalition for an Open Convention. After RICHARD M. NIXON was elected president in 1968, she joined with other Democrats to found the New Democratic Coalition.

In 1970 Bella Abzug won a House seat from New York City's 19th district, a polyglot district including the Lower East Side, Chinatown, Little Italy, Greenwich Village, and the Upper West Side. From her first moment in Washington, her unrestrained enthusiasm and flamboyance won her many enemies who felt that new representatives, and especially women, should be seen and not heard. In her first confrontation with her Democratic colleagues, she tried to have herself assigned to the House Armed Services Committee. Representative F. EDWARD HEBERT, (D-La.) the chairman of that committee, refused the request, and she was assigned to the Public Works Committee and the Government Operations Committee. On her first day in office after being sworn in, she introduced a bill calling for the withdrawal of troops from Vietnam by July 4, 1971. It was tabled within a week by the deft political maneuvering of conservative House members who were offended by her "brashness."

After the 1970 census returns verified that New York City had lost population and would therefore lose one of its four representatives, a struggle arose among New York politicians over which district would be gerrymandered. The state legislature led by a Republican majority decided that Abzug's district would be carved up. That left her with the option of challenging John Murray, a conservative from Staten Island; senior House member EDWARD KOCH from the Upper East Side; WILLIAM RYAN, a liberal candidate whose 20th district included 30 percent of Abzug's old district; or Charles Rangel, one of the few blacks in the House. She decided to challenge the ailing Ryan.

Abzug's decision split the district's liberal Democratic vote. Since both she and Ryan agreed on the issues and both had comparable liberal records, the contest came down to their personalities. In June Ryan won the primary. When Ryan died eight weeks before the November election, his supporters refused to concede to Abzug and ran Ryan's wife, Patricia, instead. In the general election Abzug won handily.

Bella Abzug made her impact felt on the House as an impassioned antiwar critic and as a feminist. She supported and spoke at many of the antiwar rallies both in Washington, D.C., and New York City. She and four other representatives were castigated by their more conservative House colleagues for "inciting to riot" a number of antiwar protesters whom they had invited to speak on the House steps during the May Day demonstrations of 1971. In April 1971 after the My Lai massacre had been exposed, she planned to head a war atrocities probe. Again in January 1972 after the bombings of Hanoi and the mining of Haiphong Harbor, she introduced a motion to censure President Nixon. On May 10 she offered an impeachment resolution based on Nixon's conduct of the war.

As a feminist Abzug supported the Equal Rights Amendment and spoke at and helped form the National Women's Political Caucus in July 1971. A month later she encouraged one of her staff members, Cynthia Edgar, to bring suit against the FBI, Attorney General JOHN MITCHELL, and FBI Director J. EDGAR HOOVER for sex discrimination. An FBI agent had told Edgar that women need not apply to the FBI for employment because they "do not command enough respect" and because they "could not handle combat situations."

During that same year she sponsored a $5 billion child care bill, eventually vetoed by President Nixon. In 1973 and 1974 she continued to champion such feminist causes as a women's credit rights bill, abortion rights, a national women's convention, equalization of pay between men and women, and welfare reform. Although her politics won her a 100 percent rating for both 1973 and 1974 from the liberal Americans for Democratic Action, they also earned her a place on President Nixon's "enemies list."

Close to the end of her term, Abzug decided, with four other Democrats, to seek the nomination for U.S. senator from New York. She lost the Democratic nomination to DANIEL PATRICK MOYNIHAN by less than 1 percent of the vote in a hard-fought and often rancorous battle. In 1977 she lost the Democratic primary for mayor of New York City to Koch. She ran unsuccessful congressional campaigns in 1978 and 1986. She spent her final years as an environmental advocate. Abzug died in New York City on March 31, 1998, of complications following heart surgery.

—SJT

Agnew, Spiro T(heodore)
(1918–1996) *vice president of the United States*

Born in Ocean City, Maryland, Agnew, whose father was a Greek immigrant, attended Johns Hopkins University and the Baltimore Law School before serving in the army during World War II. He received his law degree in 1947. Agnew became active in Maryland politics during the 1950s. He was appointed to the Baltimore County Zoning Board of Appeals in 1957 and was elected county executive in 1962, the first Republican to hold that post since 1895.

In 1966 Agnew ran for governor of Maryland. The strong segregationist views of his opponent, George Mahoney, led many normally Democratic blacks and liberals to cast their ballots for Agnew, who won the election handily. In his first year in office, Agnew secured passage of several liberal measures, including an open-housing law, a graduated income tax, and an expanded state-financed antipoverty program. However, he shifted direction abruptly in 1968 when he took a tough line against demonstrators, slashed state welfare spending, and won new police powers as head of the state militia. (See *The Johnson Years* volume.)

Agnew was an early supporter of the undeclared candidacy of New York governor NELSON ROCKEFELLER for the 1968 Republican presidential nomination. When Rockefeller firmly announced that he would not run, Agnew became a favorite-son candidate and eventually backed RICHARD NIXON, whose name he placed in nomination at the Republican National Convention. Nixon announced that Agnew was his choice for a running mate, and the convention accepted Nixon's wishes.

During the campaign, while Nixon sounded the statesmanlike themes of peace, prosperity, and a healing of the nation's wounds, Agnew spoke bluntly as a champion of "law and order." He attacked what he called "stylish forms of discontent," lashed into the "pie-in-the-sky" wastefulness of the Johnson administration's War on Poverty, and labeled Democratic candidate HUBERT HUMPHREY, "squishy soft on communism." In the November balloting he and Nixon won a narrow plurality of the total vote.

Once in office Agnew toned down his rhetoric and for a few months of the Nixon administration spoke in a conciliatory manner. At the National Governors Conference in February 1969, he successfully urged the rejection of a resolution sponsored by California governor RONALD REAGAN to have the Justice Department thoroughly investigate the sources of campus unrest. In April he voiced acceptance of nonviolent dissent as within "the limits of permissibility." Agnew told businessmen to increase their commitment to minority employment and business opportunities and promised the U.S. Conference of Mayors that Nixon's revenue-sharing plan would provide big cities with an "equitable and fair share" of federal funds. A strong supporter of the anti-ballistic missile (ABM), Agnew nonetheless cautioned the Republican Governors Conference against endorsing the ABM, saying that it should not become a divisive partisan issue.

Nevertheless, Agnew's comments were soon at odds with the policy statements of liberal administration officials. Shortly after the Apollo moon landing in July 1969, for example, Health, Education, and Welfare (HEW) secretary ROBERT FINCH and Housing and Urban Development (HUD) secretary GEORGE ROMNEY both urged a shift in spending from the space program to domestic needs. Agnew responded by declaring "we do not need a transfer of dollars from the space program to other programs. We need a transfer of its spirit—an infusion of American dedication to purpose and hard work." In September Agnew told the Southern Governors Conference that the Nixon administration opposed the use of busing to achieve school integration. Finch, a few days later, announced that HEW would use busing to bring school districts into compliance with desegregation guidelines.

By the autumn of 1969 Agnew's public comments had become outspokenly strident in their attacks on antiwar protestors, student radicals, and any group or individual who dissented vocally from the administration's policies. Over the next few years Agnew became a symbol of the tough law-and-order position of the Nixon presidency. He appealed to the millions of Americans who felt threatened by the social turbulence of the 1960s, playing upon their fears and confusion. With the repeated backing of the president, Agnew injected a level of vitriolic rhetoric seldom seen in American politics.

Administration concern over the impact of the antiwar demonstrations planned for the fall by the Vietnam Moratorium Committee provided the setting for Agnew's renewed attacks on dissenters. At a Republican fund-raiser in New Orleans shortly after the October 15 nationwide antiwar rallies, Agnew described the protesters as an "effete corps of impudent snobs who characterize themselves as intellectuals." Despite the overwhelmingly peaceful nature of these demonstrations, Agnew predicted that the November protests would be "wilder, more violent." Speaking against the dissenters at another fund-raiser on October 30, Agnew declared: "America cannot afford to divide over their demagoguery or to be deceived by their duplicity or let their license destroy liberty. We can, however, afford to separate them from our society—with not more regret than we should feel over discarding rotten apples from a barrel."

The following month, Agnew extended his attacks to the national television networks, accusing them of "a form of censorship" in their coverage of the administration's Vietnam policy and attacking the networks' executives as "a small and unelected elite." The response to Agnew's comments was immediate. FCC member Nicholas Johnson feared that "serious and permanent harm to independent journalism and free speech" might result, and the ACLU called Agnew's speech a "clear and chilling threat" of censorship. A few days later Agnew extended his criticism to the press, saying it had "grown fat and irresponsible" and singling out the *Washington Post* and the *New York Times* for their antiadministration stands. The vice president received considerable praise from President Nixon, who told the press on December 8 that Agnew had "rendered a public service" by his comments on the media.

Agnew's tough rhetoric stimulated an ongoing reaction. At the February 1970 hearings of the Senate Foreign Relations Committee on Nixon's Vietnamization policy, Senator HAROLD HUGHES, (D-Iowa) deplored the inhibiting effect that Agnew's comments were having on public debate. "First you pistol-whip the mass media," he said, "and then you commandeer it for political purposes." A report on student unrest issued by the American Council on Education in April 1970 concluded that "repressive and provocative pronouncements" by administration officials had an "inflammatory effect" on the campuses and warned against the "political exploitation of campus problems by some public figures." The United Automobile Workers and the Amalgamated Clothing Workers of America, at their spring 1970 conventions, attacked Agnew by name.

The vice president nonetheless persisted in his attacks on dissenters and his defense of administration policies in Vietnam. He defended the May 1970 invasion of Cambodia as "the finest hour in the Nixon presidency." After four students at Kent State University in Ohio were killed by the National Guard during a demonstration against the invasion, Agnew called the tragedy "predictable and avoidable" and blamed it on "the new politics of violence

and confrontation." Agnew's remarks provoked a reaction even within the administration. Interior secretary WALTER HICKEL wrote to the president asking him to bring an end to Agnew's attacks on the nation's youth; Robert Finch declared that the vice president's rhetoric "contributed to heating up the climate in which the Kent State students were killed."

No restraints, however, were placed on Agnew, who soon extended his barbs to Senate opponents of the war. He described as "reprehensible" the Cooper-Church Amendment to cut off funds for operations in Cambodia and accused Senators WILLIAM FULBRIGHT (D-Ark.), EDWARD M. KENNEDY (D-Mass.), and GEORGE MCGOVERN (D-S.D.) of having a "psychological addiction to an American defeat." Agnew called the McGovern-Hatfield Amendment "a blueprint for the first defeat in the history of the United States."

When the president's Commission on Campus Unrest issued a report that condemned "divisive and insulting rhetoric," Agnew turned his fire on Nixon's personal appointees and labeled the conclusions "more pablum for the permissivists." Meanwhile, he defended the assault on antiwar demonstrators by construction workers in New York City as "a wave in defense of the country."

Agnew became the chief administration spokesman in the 1970 congressional elections. In his first campaign speech, in San Diego on September 11, he said that the "great question" in the upcoming elections was "Will America be led by a president elected by a majority of the American people or will we be intimidated and blackmailed into following the path dictated by a disruptive radical and militant minority—the pampered prodigies of the radical liberals in the United States Senate?" The attack on "radical liberals" remained Agnew's central theme, and he campaigned heavily against liberal Democrats up for reelection.

He reserved special fire, however, for New York's Republican senator CHARLES GOODELL, who was an outspoken opponent of the war in Vietnam. Agnew's attack on a fellow Republican provoked a heated response in party circles. NELSON ROCKEFELLER, himself running for reelection, wrote to Nixon and asked him to "please let us handle our own political problems" in New York. "Outside intervention," he said, would be "prejudicial" to the state Republican ticket. Repudiating Agnew's position, 18 Republican senators, including minority leader HUGH SCOTT and minority whip ROBERT GRIFFIN, signed a public letter of endorsement for Goodell.

Agnew's attacks on Democratic candidates were so vitriolic that prominent Democrats purchased prime television time on the eve of the election to respond to his charges. Speaking for his party, Maine senator EDMUND MUSKIE asked voters to repudiate the "politics of fear." Pointing to the generally conservative legislative proposals of the administration, he told the working people of America that Nixon and Agnew "really believe that if they can make you afraid enough or angry enough . . . you can be tricked into voting against yourself."

For whatever reason, the election returns demonstrated that Agnew's rhetoric was not as effective as the administration had hoped. Although Goodell and Democratic senator ALBERT GORE of Tennessee, another Agnew target, were defeated, and the Republicans gained two Senate seats, the Democrats increased their margin in the House and won an additional 11 governorships. Perhaps in reaction there was a notable lack of inflammatory rhetoric on the vice president's part during the following year. In April 1971 Agnew actually praised the organizers of a massive antiwar demonstration in Washington, D.C., for "a very well-controlled rally."

Agnew served as an emissary of the Nixon administration to foreign governments during 1971. In June and July he made a month-long 10-nation tour of Asia, Africa, and Europe in which he reassured America's allies that the United States would not drift into isolationism. In October Agnew took another extended trip abroad.

In 1972 Nixon again chose Agnew as his running mate. While the president did little campaigning, Agnew became by far the most visible spokesman for the administration. Trying to cultivate a new image, he told the National Newspaper Association that "we all, whether government official or editor, might do well to forego harangue and cliché in favor of discussion based on reason." Agnew refrained from attacking most Democratic candidates and instead reserved his sharpest criticism for presidential aspirant Senator GEORGE MCGOVERN, whom he called "one of the greatest frauds ever to be considered as a presidential candidate by a major American party." When the ballots were counted in November, Nixon and Agnew had won an unprecedented landslide victory.

Nixon's second term had scarcely begun when it was overtaken by the deepening Watergate scandal. During the spring of 1973, as the Senate Watergate Committee conducted its nationally televised hearings on the affair, Agnew defended the president and attacked the investigation. In April he declared his "full confidence in the integrity of President Nixon." He called the press treatment of Watergate "a very short jump from McCarthyism," and said of the Senate hearing that they "can hardly hope to find the truth and can hardly fail to muddy the waters of justice beyond repair."

Agnew, however, was soon preoccupied with serious troubles of his own. On August 7 the *Wall Street Journal* reported that Agnew was the target of an investigation by U.S. Attorney George Beall in Maryland concerning allegations of kickbacks by contractors, architects, and engineers to officials of Baltimore County. The alleged violations of conspiracy, extortion and bribery, and tax statutes were supposed to have extended from the time Agnew was Baltimore County executive through his years in the vice presidency. In a news conference on August 8, Agnew vehemently denied the charges, labeling them "false, scurrilous, and malicious" and saying that he had "no expectation of being indicted." On August 21, in a nationally televised statement, Agnew denounced "leaks" to the press. "Some Justice Department officials have decided to indict me in the press whether or not the evidence supports their position," he said. Attorney General ELLIOT RICHARDSON, who was watching the investigation closely, hurriedly denied Agnew's charges but promised to investigate the source of the leaks.

News reports subsided early in September as the grand jury recessed, but on September 25 it was scheduled to begin hearing evidence against Agnew. The vice president, in an attempt to squelch rumors of his impending resignation and to block the investigation, contended that he could not be indicted while in office and asked the House of Representatives to begin its own inquiry under the impeachment provisions of the Constitution. When House Speaker CARL ALBERT rejected the request the next day, the grand jury began hearing evidence. Agnew's lawyers filed suit in federal district court on September 28 to stop the proceedings, but Judge Walter E. Hoffman allowed the grand jury to continue its hearings pending a decision. On October 3, in an unusual action, he authorized Agnew's attorneys to investigate the alleged news leaks with full subpoena power.

With the investigation continuing in the courts, Agnew renewed his appeals to the public. In a speech delivered in Los Angeles on September 29, he repeated the charges of deliberate news leaks designed to indict him

Spiro T. Agnew *(Library of Congress)*

in the press and promised that he would not resign even if indicted. Agnew's options, however, were rapidly dwindling as he became increasingly isolated. Meetings with the president on September 20 and 25 failed to get a strong, unequivocal statement of support, and rumors circulated that Nixon, buffeted by the Watergate revelations, asked Agnew to resign. On October 1, the White House confirmed that presidential counsel J. FRED BUZHARDT JR. was involved in plea-bargaining negotiations between Agnew's lawyers and the Justice Department.

On October 10, 1973, Agnew announced his resignation from office. Under the agreement reached with the Justice Department, Agnew was to resign office and plead nolo contendere (no contest) to a single charge of federal income tax evasion. In return the Justice Department would not proceed with indictments against Agnew on multiple charges of conspiracy, extortion, and bribery, although government lawyers did present the court with a 40-page document outlining alleged misconduct by Agnew. When Agnew appeared in court on October 10, Judge Hoffman informed him that the no-contest plea was the "full equivalent of a plea of guilty." Hoffman fined Agnew $10,000 and sentenced him to three years of unsupervised probation.

Agnew delivered a farewell address to the nation on October 15 in which he continued to protest his innocence and blame news leaks for his predicament. His decision to plead no contest, however, rather than simply resign and have his innocence judged in court, cast serious doubt on his claims. Coming in the midst of the Watergate revelations, moreover, Agnew's resignation deepened the shadow around the Nixon administration. By the time he left office, Agnew had lost virtually all credibility except among some diehard supporters.

In January 1974 a special three-judge panel in Maryland unanimously recommended Agnew's disbarment on the grounds that he was "unfit to continue as a member of the bar." In May the Maryland court of appeals carried out the recommendation, saying that "it is difficult to feel compassion for an attorney who is so morally obtuse that he consciously cheats for his own pecuniary gain that government he has sworn to serve."

After leaving public office Agnew became a lobbyist for Mideastern oil interests. He died on September 17, 1996, after being hospitalized for leukemia.

—JD

Albert, Carl B(ert)
(1908–2000) *member of the House of Representatives, Speaker of the House*

Born in McAlester, Oklahoma, on May 1, 1908, the son of a miner, Albert graduated

from the University of Oklahoma in 1931. A Rhodes scholar, he received two law degrees from Oxford University. Albert practiced law from 1934 to 1941 and served in the army during World War II. In 1946 he was elected to the U.S. House from Oklahoma's third congressional district, where he established a record as a liberal on social welfare legislation and a hawk on defense policy. Working under the tutelage of Speaker Sam Rayburn, he was elected Democratic whip in 1955 and rose to majority leader in 1962. (See *The Eisenhower Years*, *The Kennedy Years*, and *The Johnson Years* volumes.)

During the early Nixon years Albert maintained his moderate record, supporting the 18-year-old vote, the Equal Rights Amendment, the Philadelphia Plan, family assistance, tax reform, and consumer legislation. He supported strong controversial "no-knock" entry legislation. Despite ties to the petroleum industry, important in his district, he voted for a decrease in the oil depletion allowance from 27 percent to 20 percent, although he opposed efforts to reduce it further. In most other cases he backed the oil industry. Until 1973 Albert supported the administration's Vietnam war policy. That year, however, he backed a cutoff of funds for the bombing of Cambodia.

Albert succeeded JOHN MCCORMACK (D-Mass.) as Speaker in 1971. The selection was automatic and unchallenged, a reflection of the continuation of the tradition that the majority leader rose to Speaker upon the retirement of his predecessor. Albert's rise took place despite dissatisfaction with his leadership. Albert was generally viewed as a weak Speaker, unable to direct his party in opposition to the administration. The Speaker was a frequent critic of the Nixon administration, but he failed to develop Democratic alternatives to the president's programs.

Albert had risen through the House during a period when the Democratic Party was deeply divided between northern liberals and southern conservatives. His reputation as a conciliator and his penchant for compromise had been important in keeping the party together during the 1950s and 1960s. However, during the early 1970s when Albert was Speaker, the Democrats were overwhelmingly dominated by liberals. Rather than leading the party, marshaling its power in Congress, and galvanizing it into an effective legislative force, Albert preferred to work quietly behind the scenes, letting others take the headlines and guide the party. His natural reticence and desire for compromise was combined with an inability to use his staff or the media effectively. His power, therefore, was limited.

Nevertheless, he did occasionally wield power effectively. In 1973 Albert insisted that the members of the powerful Rules Committee be loyal to him. By appointing a few friendly members to the panel, he became the first Speaker in nearly four decades to have control over the House's legislative agenda. Albert also cooperated with the reformers in the House to shift the power base in the chamber away from the committees and to the majority party caucus and its steering and policy committee. This action resulted in the removal of three chairmen by the Democratic Caucus.

On two occasions Albert was second in line to become president because of vacancies in the vice presidency—once when SPIRO AGNEW resigned and again when GERALD FORD succeeded to the presidency. It was said of Albert that he was "running from the presidency" because he made every effort to avoid becoming president.

Albert encountered some personal criticism. At times he fell asleep while presiding over the House. It eventually became public that he had a drinking problem. In 1972 a car he was driving hit two cars, and some witnesses reported he had been drinking. However, no charges were brought against him.

At the time of his election as Speaker, Albert announced that he would retire at age 70 in 1978. (That was also the year in which he was eligible for maximum pension benefits.) However, because of growing opposition to his leadership, he decided not to seek reelection in 1976. He had served in Congress longer than any other Oklahoman. He died in McAlester, Oklahoma, on February 4, 2000.

—HML

Álvarez, Luis Echeverría
(1922–) *president of Mexico*

Luis Echeverría Álvarez rose through the ranks of Mexico's ruling Partido Revolucionario Institucional (PRI) as a reliable political appointee and obedient party loyalist. Though much of his political life and historical legacy were determined by his relationships with and service to controversial figures, Echeverría's own commitment to certain principles was unwavering. This commitment, however, was often eclipsed in the public mind and historical assessment by things beyond his control. Most significantly, the course and character of Echeverría's presidency, from 1970 to 1976, were dictated by events during the term of his predecessor, Gustavo Díaz Ordaz. Echeverría's complicity in the missteps of the Díaz Ordaz administration forced him into certain policies at home and abroad that were both understandable and untenable.

Echeverría began his rise through the ranks of the PRI in 1946 as private secretary to the president of the party, General Rodolfo Sanchez Taboada. After eight years in the general's employ, Echeverría moved to the Ministry of Education in the mid-1950s. When Gustavo Díaz Ordaz ascended to the presidency in 1964, Echeverría moved into the cabinet position that the president had previously held himself, minister of the interior.

From his post at the Ministry of the Interior, Echeverría was responsible for implementing the Díaz Ordaz administration's strict anticommunist policies, repression of the left, and crackdown on civil unrest. Such responsibilities brought Echeverría to the forefront of the controversy over the administration's heavy-handed dealings with the student protest movement of 1968, and in particular the October 2 massacre at La Plaza de las Tres Culturas in the Tlatelolco district of Mexico City. Echeverría was widely believed at the time to have been responsible for the repressive policies that culminated in the massacre. The administration's silence on the subject and Echeverría's own unwillingness to defend himself publicly led some to assume his complicity and others to admire his loyal service to the president. Regardless of his motivations, Echeverría's stoicism paid off in 1970, when he received Díaz Ordaz's endorsement for the presidency.

Like Díaz Ordaz, Echeverría ascended to the presidency through the Ministry of the Interior, and also like Díaz Ordaz, Echeverría faced a difficult campaign, one in which he had to distance himself from his boss and benefactor if he was going to win. In the election of 1970, Echeverría remade himself and his public image, abandoning the hard-line authoritarianism characteristic of the Díaz Ordaz administration in favor of old-style populism reminiscent of Lázaro Cárdenas in the 1930s. Echeverría pledged to move the country away from "stabilizing development" as an economic agenda and instead embrace state interventionism to promote economic prosperity and provide for a more just distribution of Mexico's resources.

Echeverría won the election in 1970 and immediately undertook the policies on which he had campaigned. The result was a Mexico less friendly to foreign investment, more hostile to U.S. interventionism, more nationalistic with its natural resources, and more supportive of the needs and agenda of organized labor.

None of these policies won the Echeverría administration many friends in Washington, and despite repeated diplomatic overtures, Mexico's relations with the United States became increasingly strained.

The situation worsened further in August 1971, when the Nixon administration imposed a 10 percent tax on all imports. Because Mexico sold 70 percent of its exports in the United States, this tariff dealt the nation's already fragile economy a severe blow. This compounded the problems already apparent from the failure of Echeverría's economic policies, and Mexico plunged into an economic decline that worsened throughout the 1970s and into the 1980s, when it culminated in a full-blown debt crisis and repeated currency devaluations. In the wake of the import tax, the Echeverría government decided that its efforts to maintain a "special" relationship with the United States were in vain, and Mexico embarked on a policy of economic diversification. In addition to asserting Mexico's economic autonomy, Echeverría also touted Mexico's diplomatic autonomy and took a more deliberately controversial stand on international issues. For example, in 1975 he became the first sitting Mexican president to visit Cuba. He also attempted to carve out for Mexico a leading role in the affairs of Latin America and the developing world.

Though Echeverría succeeded in creating a Mexico that was much more open and democratic than the one he inherited in 1970, economic problems and memories of the violence of 1968 dogged his administration and his postpresidential aspirations. Attempts to win a Nobel Peace Prize and be elected secretary-general of the United Nations, for example, both failed. Discredited at home and isolated abroad, Echeverría took a series of ambassadorships and left it to his successors to forge for Mexico a new and more beneficial relationship with the United States.

—JS

Anderson, Jack (Northman)
(1922–2005) *newspaper columnist*

Born on October 19, 1922, in Long Beach, California, the son of "straight-laced, honest, salt-of-the-earth Mormons," Anderson was brought up in Salt Lake City. While still a teenager, Anderson began his journalism career as a reporter for the *Deseret News.* By 1939 he was a staff reporter for the *Salt Lake Tribune.* He studied for a short time at the University of Utah and then served two years during the early 1940s as a Mormon missionary. At his request, Anderson began work as a war correspondent for the *Deseret News* in 1945. Two years later he moved to Washington, D.C., to begin work for Drew Pearson, who wrote the widely syndicated muckraking column "The Washington Merry-Go-Round." With Pearson he uncovered such important influence-peddling scandals as the "Five Percenters" in the 1940s, the Sherman Adams-Bernard Goldfine case in the 1950s, and the Thomas Dodd incident in the 1960s. In 1965 Anderson was finally granted an equal byline with Pearson. (See *The Johnson Years* volume.)

Anderson inherited the column after Pearson's death in 1969. His approach to the news was very different from that of Pearson. While the older man frequently reported personal gossip about public figures, Anderson attempted to uncover important problems in government.

During the Nixon administration, Anderson made headlines with several scoops revealing duplicity or wrongdoing in the White House. In 1972 the columnist published secret government documents revealing that despite the administration's public policy of neutrality, Nixon wanted to "tilt" U.S. support toward Pakistan in the war between that nation and India over Bangladesh. Although several critics opposed Anderson's publication of secret documents, his action was praised, and he received the Pulitzer Prize that year.

In February 1972 Anderson, using a memo reportedly written by International Telephone & Telegraph (ITT) lobbyist DITA BEARD, revealed that the Justice Department had settled a pending antitrust suit against ITT at a time when the giant conglomerate had pledged $400,000 to the 1972 Republican National Convention. He later revealed ITT attempts to stop the election of Marxist Salvador Allende in Chile.

During the Nixon administration, Anderson also uncovered evidence that the FBI had kept dossiers on persons opposed to administration policies and that the Central Intelligence Agency (CIA) had made attempts to assassinate foreign leaders, including Fidel Castro. In April 1973 Anderson began a series of columns that included a verbatim account of Watergate grand jury transcripts he had obtained during the jury's probe of the break-in. It was later revealed through White House sources that his access to these minutes was a factor in the president's decision to allow an open investigation of the case.

Other Anderson columns raised doubts about Senator EDWARD M. KENNEDY's (D-Mass.) account of events surrounding the accident at Chappaquiddick in which an aide drowned, revealed that Attorney General Robert F. Kennedy had known about FBI wiretapping of Martin Luther King Jr., and made public the CIA's large-scale spending in an unsuccessful attempt to raise a sunken Soviet submarine. Anderson was often criticized during this period for his methods, particularly his use of secret documents and his failure to check his sources adequately. In 1972 he publicly apologized to Senator THOMAS EAGLETON (D-Mo.), then the Democratic vice presidential candidate, for reporting false charges that the senator had been arrested for drunken driving. Anderson retired from journalism in July 2004, suffering from Parkinson's disease. He died of complications from Parkinson's on December 17, 2005, in Bethesda, Maryland.

—SBB

Anderson, John B.
(1922–   ) *member of the House of Representatives*

Born on February 15, 1922, Anderson, the son of Swedish-American parents who operated a small grocery store in Rockford, Illinois, graduated from the University of Illinois in 1942. After serving in the army during World War II, he received his law degree from the university in 1946. From 1952 to 1955 he served as an adviser to the U.S. High Commissioner for Germany while a member of the Foreign Service. Returning to Rockford, he was elected state's attorney for Winnebago County in 1956. He held the post until 1960, when he was elected to the House of Representatives from a predominantly agricultural and solidly Republican district in northwestern Illinois.

Anderson began his House career as a conservative Republican. He opposed funding what he called "warmed-over New Deal panaceas" like the antipoverty and Model Cities programs of the 1960s. Instead he favored greater involvement by the private sector in meeting social goals. He regularly opposed efforts to cut defense expenditures.

During the Nixon and Ford terms, Anderson generally supported the administration's legislative positions and regularly voted to sustain Nixon-Ford vetoes of spending legislation. At the same time, however, he began to shift away from his earlier conservatism on some issues. In 1971, for example, he supported the creation of an independent legal services corporation to aid the poor, a move the administration opposed. In 1973 he supported the successful effort to override Nixon's veto of the War Powers Resolution, which limited the president's authority to commit U.S. troops abroad. And even though he had been elected Republican Conference chairman in 1969, the third-highest Republican leadership post in the House, Anderson opposed his fellow Republicans almost as often as he supported them on party line votes, which pit a majority of Republicans against a majority of Democrats. Anderson's changing viewpoints angered many conservative Republicans in the House. In contrast to his 1969 victory of the conference chairmanship by a 122-65 vote, he was elected chairman in 1971 by only eight votes, when he faced conservative representative Samuel L. Devine (R-Ohio), who charged that Anderson's voting record was too liberal on domestic issues.

Anderson strongly supported "good government" reform efforts. In 1971 he and Representative MORRIS K. UDALL (D-Ariz.) headed the bipartisan campaign reform movement in the House. They cosponsored a four-part election reform package that called for tax credits on media expenditures by candidates and an agency to enforce campaign spending limits. The Federal Election Campaign Act of 1971, the first major federal election reform in 47 years, included many of the Anderson-Udall proposals.

Anderson and Udall advocated public financing for House and Senate races, as well as for presidential contests, when Congress was revising the 1971 law after the spending abuses of the 1972 campaigns had pointed out its many loopholes. Anderson and Udall favored public financing of elections as a way of limiting the increasing political influence of campaign contributions. Nixon and many in Congress opposed the concept, however, claiming that government financing undermined the democratic electoral process. The House refused to enact the Anderson-Udall proposal for public financing of House and Senate races, but it passed the Election Campaign Act Amendments of 1974, which provided for public financing of presidential primary and general election campaigns.

Anderson angered many Republicans when he called for a complete explanation of the unfolding Watergate scandal even before many Democrats had reacted. He quickly objected to the broad claims of executive privilege advanced by administration officials to restrict congressional inquiries into the Watergate affair. In May 1973 he cosponsored a resolution calling for the appointment of a special Watergate prosecutor as the only effective way to ensure an impartial and complete investigation of the scandal.

When the House Judiciary Committee formally opened its impeachment probe in early 1974, Anderson at first opposed the suggestion that Nixon resign so that impeachment could be avoided. He stated that the impeachment process was the only way to clear or convict the president and told Republicans that impeachment was "a Republican problem and we can't turn away from it." But he changed his position after reading the edited transcripts of taped White House conversations that were released to the Judiciary Committee in April 1974. Although Nixon always claimed he had not been aware of the cover-up until March 21, 1974, Anderson pointed out that the "transcripts made it quite clear he [Nixon] was deeply involved in Watergate on the 13th of March 1973." He then predicted the president would be impeached if he did not resign and called for Nixon's resignation so the nation could avoid the agony of impeachment.

Anderson's candor about Watergate did not damage him politically. He retained his conference chairmanship by a solid 85-52 margin after the 1974 elections swept many conservatives out of office. During the 1976 presidential primary campaign, he strongly supported Ford's candidacy over the more conservative RONALD REAGAN. During the Carter presidency, Anderson continued to advocate "good government" reforms, like reducing government regulation of business and televising House debates.

Anderson served in the House of Representatives until 1981. In 1980 he ran an unsuccessful independent candidacy for the presidency, being defeated by Republican RONALD REAGAN. Following his defeat, Anderson served on the faculty of several universities, including the University of Illinois, Brandeis University, Bryn Mawr College, and the University of Massachusetts. He is the president of the World Federalist Association and resides in Rockford, Illinois.

—AE

Arends, Leslie C(ornelius)
(1895–1985) *member of the House of Representatives*

Born on September 27, 1895, Arends left Oberlin College during World War I to enlist in the army. After the war he became a leading farmer and banker in his hometown of Melvin, Illinois, just outside of Chicago. In 1934 he was elected to the U.S. House of Representatives from the largely agricultural district that became a Chicago suburb. Arends emerged to be one of the House's leading conservative critics of the New Deal. In 1943 he became Republican minority whip and served in this position until 1974 except when his party controlled the House (1947–49, 1953–55), when he moved up to become majority leader.

Arends enthusiastically favored the defense and foreign policies of both the Democratic and Republican administrations in the postwar period. A fiscal conservative who deplored excessive spending, Arends opposed most liberal domestic legislation of the Democratic presidents. However, he backed the civil rights measures of the Johnson presidency. During the late 1960s Arends also supported President Johnson on the Vietnam War. (See *The Eisenhower Years*, *The Kennedy Years*, and *The Johnson Years* volumes.)

During the Nixon presidency Arends, in his position of whip, served as Minority

Leader GERALD FORD's (R-Mich.) chief legislative assistant. His most important function was to see that all House Republicans voted the party line on key legislation. Although Arends maintained a low profile as a leader, he made his presence felt through his knowledge of the party's House members and of House procedure. He kept tabs on the locations of all Republicans absent from the floor. Arends had legislative profiles of all his colleagues in the House to help determine how they would vote. Frequently Arends took informal polls of his peers before a key vote took place.

Aside from his position as minority whip, Arends was the ranking Republican on the Armed Services Committee. He worked with committee chairman F. EDWARD HEBERT (D-La.) to line up votes for the funds requested by the Pentagon. Throughout the Nixon presidency, in response to those who called for defense cuts, Arends raised the theme that the Russians should not be permitted to "bury us." Arends frequently expressed outrage at those in Washington who advocated the reallocation of defense money to social programs. He considered this a serious betrayal of the national defense.

In 1971 Arends voted against efforts to reduce the defense budget. Two years later he voted against an amendment introduced by Representative LES ASPIN (D-Wis.) to establish a defense ceiling of $20.5 billion. Arends avidly backed the Pentagon's desire to continue spending for new weapons systems. In 1971 he voted for the B-1 bomber, the F-14 fighter, and the antiballistic missile program.

Although a member of the congressional leadership, Arends was one of the leading defenders of the executive's right to conduct a foreign policy free from congressional interference. He voted to uphold Nixon's veto of the war powers bill designed to limit the president's authority to commit troops abroad. Arends opposed all attempts to end U.S. inter-

vention in the Vietnam War by withholding funds from the executive. A member of the top-secret committee overseeing the operations of the Central Intelligence Agency (CIA), Arends never questioned any CIA operation or the allocation of funds to the agency.

In domestic legislation Arends consistently voted conservative. He fought efforts to expand the federal contribution for increased local health services. During the 1973–74 recession Arends opposed measures to allocate funds for public works employment and to increase and expand unemployment insurance benefits in areas where the unemployed rate exceeded 6.5 percent. An opponent of proconsumer legislation, Arends resisted efforts to strengthen the powers of the Consumer Protection Agency.

With his seniority in Congress and his position in the House leadership, Arends kept up a close relationship with his constituency. Through his connections with the Pentagon, he obtained key defense contracts and an air force base for his district. In 1972 Arends faced a Republican challenger in the primary who campaigned on the issue of Arends's age. Arends easily defeated him but decided to retire in 1974. He died on July 17, 1985, in Naples, Florida.

—JB

Armstrong, Anne (Legendre)
(1927–   ) *counselor to the president; ambassador to Great Britain*

Born on December 27, 1927, the daughter of a well-to-do New Orleans coffee importer, Anne Legendre received her B.A. from Vassar College in 1949. The following year she married Tobin Armstrong, a wealthy Texas ranch owner. During the 1950s and 1960s she became active in Republican politics. From 1968 to 1973 Armstrong served as Republican national committeewoman from Texas. Acting on RICHARD NIXON's suggestion, the Republican National Committee made Armstrong its first female cochair in January 1971. She was put in charge of special programs. Armstrong worked to promote the party's "Open Door" policy to make the GOP and its leaders more accessible and prominent to the public. Working to recruit feminists into the party, she joined other Republican women in a successful effort to win a pledge from the GOP for an attempt to increase the number of women participating in the next party convention and to expand the antidiscrimination clause in the party's rules to include a prohibition on sexual bias. During the 1972 Republican Convention, Armstrong became the first woman to deliver a keynote speech for either party.

President Nixon named Armstrong counselor to the president on December 18, 1972. She was the first woman to assume the post. The appointment, coming at a time of growing bitterness toward the administration for its failure to assign women to positions of high authority, was labeled tokenism by many women's groups. As counselor, Armstrong was liaison between the White House and the GOP National Committee. In 1973 she described her function: "I have a rather generalist role, with diffuse responsibilities. That has advantage in that I don't have a special interest, or special department to take care of, as do other cabinet officers, and I can advise the president in a broader way." At the White House she served as chair of the Property Review Board, was a member of the Domestic Council, and became liaison with the cabinet committee on the Spanish-speaking, youth groups, and the Bicentennial Commission.

Armstrong supported the Equal Rights Amendment (ERA) and urged the use of more women in high-level positions. But she defended the administration's refusal to push the ERA in the states on the grounds that the federal government had no right to interfere in states' affairs. She was pleased that under

Nixon there was a threefold increase over past administrations in the number of women placed in top-level jobs.

Armstrong was a staunch supporter of Nixon during the White House Watergate controversy. She reported in May 1974: "I don't see an impeachment offense. . . . I think he has the guts to see it through in the proper way." But during the final days of the administration, she joined Senator BARRY GOLDWATER (R-Ariz.) in urging the president to resign.

Armstrong remained at the White House during the early months of the FORD administration. She was on the short list to be nominated as Ford's vice president in both 1974 and 1976. She resigned in November 1974 "because of unforeseen and pressing family responsibilities."

On January 28, 1976, the Senate announced its unanimous approval of Armstrong to fill the post of ambassador to Great Britain. In February she was sworn in as envoy to the Court of St. James's, becoming the 14th woman since World War II to hold an ambassadorship. Possessing the required wealth and sense of social graces necessary to maintain the position, Armstrong was welcomed in Great Britain. Before she resigned in March 1977, she was credited by the *Times* of London as "an assiduous ambassador . . . responding with womanly warmth to both our established habits and our changing ways."

From 1981 to 1990 Armstrong was chair of the president's Foreign Intelligence Advisory Board. In 1997 she was appointed a regent of Texas A&M University.

—SB

Armstrong, Neil (Alden)
(1930–   ) *astronaut*

Born in Wapakoneta, Ohio, Armstrong, a naval pilot during the Korean War, received a

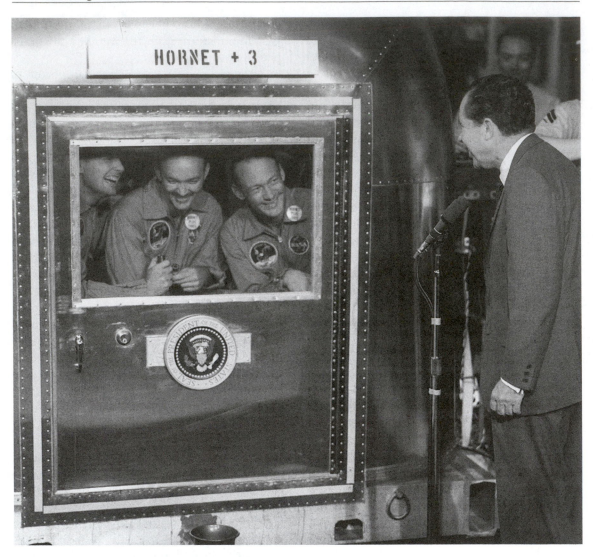

President Nixon visits the *Apollo 11* crew in quarantine, July 24, 1969. *(NASA)*

B.S. degree in aeronautical engineering from Purdue University in 1955 and an M.S. degree from the University of Southern California in 1970. In 1955 Armstrong became a civilian research pilot for the National Advisory Committee for Aeronautics, the predecessor of the National Aeronautics and Space Administration (NASA). Armstrong was selected in the second group of NASA astronauts in September 1962. In March 1966 Armstrong, as command pilot of the *Gemini 8* space mission with air force major David R. Scott, performed the first manual space docking in history.

In July 1969 Armstrong commanded the Moon flight with Colonel Edwin E. Aldrin Jr. and Lieutenant Colonel Michael Collins. While Collins maintained the command ship in lunar orbit, Armstrong and Aldrin descended to the Moon's surface in the landing module on July 20, 1969. Before a worldwide television audience estimated at more than 500 million people, Armstrong stepped on the Moon's surface and said, "That's one small step for man, one giant leap for mankind." Armstrong, joined by Aldrin, placed an American flag on the Moon, collected soil and rock samples, performed several scientific tests, and received the first Earth-to-Moon "phone call" from President NIXON. He left a plaque signed by the astronauts and President Nixon with the message "Here men from the planet earth first set foot on the moon. July 1969 A.D. We came in peace for all mankind."

Armstrong and the other two astronauts returned to worldwide acclaim. They received the Galabert International Aeronautics Prize for 1969 before they had even splashed down on Earth. Parades in major cities welcomed them as national heroes, and they received Medals of Freedom from President Nixon. They addressed a joint session of Congress and were received at the United Nations. Armstrong, Aldrin, and Collins went on a 38-day, 44,650-mile trip, which President Nixon called the most successful goodwill tour in history. The three were received by 20 heads of state and were decorated nine times.

The *Apollo 11* mission to the Moon added fuel to the controversy over the reordering of U.S. priorities. Numerous critics of the Johnson and Nixon administrations claimed that too much of the nation's money was being wasted on space and the military, particularly the war in Vietnam and reaching the Moon. By comparison, too little money was being spent to combat poverty, hunger, discrimination, disease, and other problems on Earth. There was also hostility over the relationship of the space program to the military-industrial complex, because the aerospace industry, which had produced most of the Apollo equipment, also produced military hardware. Critics speculated

that Apollo was really a quasi-military venture. Many scientists said that the space program received the largest share of the declining federal budget for nondefense research at the expense of other vital research.

The threat of Soviet competition in space, which had helped gain support for the U.S. space program in the beginning, faded as the Moon landing was achieved. At the time of Armstrong's mission to the Moon, the space program was being subjected to financial cuts and relegated to the status of a lesser national priority. The goal set by President Kennedy to land a man on the Moon before the end of the decade had been attained, and national attention turned elsewhere. The space program, however, continued, although with a reduced budget.

In 1970 Armstrong retired as an astronaut and became NASA deputy associate director, coordinating research and technology between government and private industry. The following year he resigned from NASA to become the first university professor of engineering at the University of Cincinnati. Yet Armstrong continued to serve NASA as a consultant.

From 1971 to 1979, he was professor of aerospace engineering at the University of Cincinnati. From 1982 to 1992 he was chairman of computing technologies for Aviation, Inc. He currently serves as chairman of the board of AIL Systems, Inc.

—CLC

Ash, Roy L(awrence)

(1918–   ) *chairman, President's Advisory Council on Executive Organization; director, Office of Management and Budget*

Roy Ash was born on October 2, 1918, in Los Angeles, California. Ash began his career at the Bank of America, where he worked from 1936 to 1942, and again from 1947 to 1949, attaining the rank of chief financial officer. Although he had never attended college, he earned an M.B.A. at Harvard in 1947. Ash worked at Hughes Aircraft from 1949 to 1953, when he left to participate in the founding of Litton Industries, Inc. Ash served as director and later as president of Litton from 1953 until 1972, and during his tenure the firm grew from a small defense contractor to a controversial holding company listed among the 50 largest corporations in the United States.

In April 1969 Ash became chairman of the President's Advisory Council on Executive Organization, known as the "Ash Commission." The first recommendations of the Ash Commission were sent to Congress in March 1970. The plans involved a reorganization of the White House, including the creation of a new Domestic Council and the supercession of the Bureau of the Budget by an Office of Management and Budget (OMB). The reforms, suggested in the commission's final report submitted in November 1970, were addressed to growing domestic discontent with government bureaucracy. In the government's view the reforms gave regional civil servants more power in funding and decision making and rendered the federal apparatus more responsive to local pressure groups. Ash's commission further recommended the elimination of the Office of Economic Opportunity (OEO) and the distribution of its functions among four new agencies. Ash proposed, among other things, to transfer the OEO's legal services to a congressionally chartered, nonprofit organization. This move would, in his view, insulate the services from politics and avoid the confusion engendered by OEO lawsuits against other government agencies.

Ash also proposed to transform the Departments of Labor, Agriculture, Commerce, Transportation, Housing and Urban Development, and Health, Education, and Welfare into four "super agencies," the Departments of Human Resources, Economic Affairs, Community Development, and Natural Resources.

In November 1972, shortly after his reelection, Nixon appointed Ash to head the Office of Management and Budget, which had replaced the Bureau of the Budget on Ash's recommendation. Shortly thereafter Ash was also appointed to a newly created Council on Economic Policy headed by Secretary of the Treasury GEORGE SHULTZ.

Ash's appointment, however, became the center of a confrontation between Congress and the White House. In early January 1973 the *Washington Post* alleged that Ash, while working for Hughes Aircraft, had falsified affidavits resulting in a $43 million overpayment on a defense contract. Admiral Hyman G. Rickover charged that Litton had "grossly exaggerated" the costs on a nuclear submarine. Two days after the *Post*'s charges, Nixon announced that he was moving ahead with all aspects of Ash's reorganization plan not requiring formal congressional approval, with the reduction of the White House staff from 4,000 to 2,000 a top priority.

In late January the conflict escalated when the Senate demanded formal review of appointees to the OMB directorship. Representative Les Aspin (D-Wis.) called for an investigation of Ash's sale of 85,000 shares of Litton stock in 1970 to determine if Ash had acted on "inside information." On February 5 Ash informed Congress that the Nixon administration was impounding $8.7 billion in federal appropriations from past legislation, citing the president's obligation to observe the legal limit on the national debt. Senator EDMUND MUSKIE (D-Me.) charged Ash with "a determined effort to butt back Congress's constitutional authority." On the same day the Senate legislated itself the right to review appointment to the OMB directorship, although Ash had been sworn in three days before. Nixon vetoed the measure, which the House overrode in May 1973. Nixon waited until March 1974 to sign the bill, which exempted the incumbent Ash.

In April 1974, as the Nixon administration was being paralyzed by the Watergate scandal, Ash had one of his last confrontations with Congress during his appearance there to promote alternative legislation to a pending bill establishing a Consumer Protection Agency (CPA). In the view of most supporters of the bill, the Nixon-backed alternative stripped the CPA of almost all effective power. On the day before Ash's testimony, consumer advocate RALPH NADER released a White House memo telling Ash to "signal hard veto from here on" unless the bill was "cleaned up," a move that gave more credence to congressional charges that the administration was "knuckling under to business lobbyists."

Despite his close association with the Nixon "inner circle," Ash survived Nixon's departure in August 1974. He helped to prepare GERALD FORD's September 1974 economic summit and was named to the Council on Wages and Prices, established to fight inflation. At the September 27–28 summit meetings, Ash was appointed to the Economic Policy Board.

After helping to ease the transition to a new administration, Ash announced his resignation in December 1974. He had participated in the Ford administration's policy turnabout from deflation to stimulation in November and December 1974, when the rapid collapse of U.S. production forced such a shift. Ash remarked that "the conditions of the economy are changing faster than we can change the budget." He left the OMB in February 1975 and returned to Litton Industries.

—LG

Ashbrook, John M(ilan)
(1928–1982) *member of the House of Representatives*

Born in Johnstown, Ohio, on September 21, 1928, John Ashbrook was the son of a newspaper publisher and conservative, anti-New Deal Democratic representative. After graduating from high school in 1946, he enlisted in the navy for a two-year tour of duty and then entered Harvard in 1948. Receiving a B.S. degree four years later, Ashbrook entered law school at Ohio State University. While in law school he took over the publishing of the family's weekly newspaper. Admitted to the bar in 1955, Ashbrook was elected as a Republican to the state legislature in 1956 and again in 1958. He was active in Republican Party organizations, becoming chairman of the Ohio League of Young Republicans in 1955 and chairman of the Young Republican National Federation in 1957. In 1960, in his first bid for national office, Ashbrook was elected to the House of Representatives.

A staunch conservative, Ashbrook quickly became a spokesman for the right-wing traditionalists of the Republican Party. Throughout the 1960s he consistently opposed the social welfare measures of the Kennedy and Johnson administrations, voting against federal aid to education, "war on poverty" funds, and other domestic spending programs. Although he opposed deficit spending and big government at home, Ashbrook nonetheless was a strong advocate of huge defense budgets.

One of the earliest supporters of BARRY GOLDWATER's presidential bid, he was a founder in 1963 of the Draft Goldwater organization. After Goldwater's defeat, Ashbrook helped found the American Conservative Union and served as its chairman from 1966 to 1971. In 1968 he surprised some right-wing Republicans when he came out in support of RICHARD NIXON's campaign for the Republican presidential nomination. (See *The Johnson Years* volume.)

During the Nixon years Ashbrook maintained his conservative voting record. He opposed giving enforcement powers to the Equal Employment Opportunity Commission and voted against extension of the Office of Economic Opportunity and against the federal minimum wage. Ashbrook was also one of the most outspoken foes of busing to achieve racial balance in schools and supported every antibusing measure in Congress. In 1974 he proposed an amendment to the Health, Education, and Welfare appropriations bill to prohibit the use of any federal funds for busing, even if ordered by the courts. Although it was accepted in the House, the Senate-House conference adopted a much weaker provision that allowed the funding of court-ordered busing.

Initially a supporter of President Nixon, Ashbrook became increasingly disenchanted with the administration's policies. A *Congressional Quarterly* study found that in 1972 Ashbrook voted against the president more than half the time. In December 1971 he accused Nixon of breaking 1968 campaign pledges and announced his candidacy for the Republican presidential nomination. Angered over continued deficit spending, the imposition of wage and price controls, and the administration's diplomatic initiatives toward Communist China, Ashbrook said that he intended his candidacy to halt the dangerous "leftward drift" of the Nixon administration. With the support of conservative writer William F. Buckley Jr., he entered the New Hampshire primary but received only 11 percent of the vote. Ashbrook fared badly in every primary he entered, never winning more than 10 percent of the vote. His effort had little impact upon the president, who easily won renomination at the Republican National Convention in August.

Ashbrook was critical of Nixon's handling of the Watergate affair. At a conference held by the American Conservative Union in January 1974, he cautioned against supporting the president out of personal or party loyalty. After reading the partial transcripts of the White House tapes released by the president in April 1974, Ashbrook announced that he no longer believed Nixon's version of his involvement. On July 30 he called for the president's impeachment.

Ashbrook opposed President FORD's selection of NELSON ROCKEFELLER as vice president, arguing that Rockefeller had "continually been rejected nationwide by the majority of the Republican Party." In 1975 he served on a committee sponsored by the American Conservative Union and Young Americans for Freedom to explore the possibility of a third party for the 1976 presidential elections. Abandoning that option, Ashbrook joined with other conservative Republicans in Congress in issuing a statement in June 1975 that called for an "open" convention in 1976. After RONALD REAGAN's entry into the Republican race, Ashbrook announced his support of Reagan, only to be disappointed by Reagan's choice of liberal senator RICHARD S. SCHWEIKER (R-Pa.) as his running mate. Ashbrook called the decision "the dumbest thing" he had ever heard and said that he had become a "former" Reagan supporter. Remaining aloof from the presidential campaign, Ashbrook was elected in 1976 to his ninth term in Congress.

In 1982, Ashbrook ran for the Republican nomination for the Senate from Ohio. In March he collapsed while campaigning and died a month later.

—JD

Ashley, Thomas L(udlow)
(1923–) *member of the House of Representatives*

Born in Toledo, Ohio, on January 11, 1923, into a rich, old Republican family, Ashley earned his B.A. at Yale in 1948 and his LL.B. at Ohio State in 1951. After working briefly for Radio Free Europe, Ashley ran for the U.S. House as a Democrat in 1954. He won by a narrow margin in Ohio's ninth district, a heavily industrial and ethnic area that includes most of Toledo. Reelected without difficulty through the 1960s, Ashley served on the Banking and Currency Committee and became a specialist in housing legislation. He promoted a national urban growth policy and was able to secure funds for the rebuilding of downtown Toledo.

During the Johnson years Ashley voted for all major Great Society legislation and maintained a solid liberal record. He did not, however, criticize Johnson's Vietnam policies. As a member of the banking and currency panel, Ashley helped to write the 1966 amendments to the Bank Merger Act of 1960 and win congressional approval of U.S. Export-Import Bank financing of a Fiat automobile plant in the Soviet Union. (See *The Johnson Years* volume.)

Ashley maintained a solidly liberal record during the Nixon administration, winning a 100 percent rating on selected issues from the Americans for Democratic Action in both 1968 and 1970. A member of the Banking Committee's Housing Subcommittee, he helped draft the Housing and Urban Development Act of 1970. He worked for passage of an amendment to fund urban renewal and aid new communities, spoke in favor of a national urban growth policy, and advocated the establishment of a three-member urban growth council in the executive branch. President Nixon opposed the council as an encroachment on executive prerogative. The provision was deleted from the final bill, but the act as passed did include a federal crime insurance program and an extensive Model Cities and metropolitan development program. Ashley's work on the bill was rewarded by the government's decision to build a new Model Cities town near Toledo.

During the early 1970s Ashley often teamed with Banking Committee Republican Garry Brown of Michigan to develop housing legislation acceptable to the administration. Ashley voted for the Housing Act of 1974, although he opposed the bill's special housing subsidy provisions for the elderly. The act, the first major piece of housing legislation since 1968, revised the nation's housing and urban aid programs. It provided block grants for development and established new programs of rental assistance for low- and middle-income families. The measure permitted communities to spend grants as they chose with only a few federal requirements for community development.

During 1975 and 1976 Ashley advocated new construction as the best way to stimulate the sagging housing industry and fought for the allocation of funds for new construction and public housing, a position opposed by the Ford administration. Ashley joined Republicans, however, in opposing a low-interest mortgage loan program for middle-income home buyers and was instrumental in developing the compromise emergency housing bill signed by President Ford in July 1975.

Ashley continued to win reelection through the 1970s, though his margin of victory dropped from 69 percent in 1972 to 53 percent in 1974, following his arrest for drunk driving in Toledo in 1973. He retired from the House in 1981 and is a consultant in Washington, D.C.

—DAE

B

Baker, Howard H(enry), Jr.
(1925–) *member of the Senate*

Born in Huntsville, Tennessee, on November 15, 1925, Howard Baker comes from a political family. His grandfather was a judge, and his father was a representative from the second Tennessee district from 1951 to 1964. He married the daughter of Senator EVERETT DIRKSEN (R-Ill.). Baker received his law degree from the University of Tennessee in 1949. He engaged in private law practice, banking, and business activities before running for the Senate in 1964 on what was essentially a conservative platform. He lost to a moderate Democrat. Adopting a more moderate political stance, he ran again in 1966 and defeated Democratic governor Frank G. Clement to become the first popularly elected Republican senator in the state's history.

In the Senate Baker compiled a relatively conservative record, voting to give state governors the power to veto federal grants in aid and supporting increased military spending. However, he backed major civil rights initiatives. (See *The Johnson Years* volume.)

Baker remained a conservative on matters pertaining to the courts and justice during the Nixon years. He voted for the nomination of conservatives CLEMENT F. HAYNSWORTH and G. HARR-OLD CARSWELL to the Supreme Court. He also voted for the District of Columbia crime bill's "no-knock" and preventive-detention clauses.

The senator continued supporting civil rights legislation. He backed extension of the Voting Rights Act in 1970 and 1972 and endorsed the nomination of Judge Ben Hooks to be the first black member of the Federal Communications Commission. He was, however, a strong opponent of forced busing to promote racial integration in the schools. He backed amendments to the Education Act of 1972 that limited the use of federal funds for busing.

He supported several environmental protection laws. He played an important role in the Senate Public Works Committee in the development of the clean air and water bills of 1970 and 1972 and the highway bill that permitted the trust fund to be used for mass-transit projects. But he voted in favor of the supersonic transport program and the construction of the Alaska pipeline. Baker was sponsor of every major revenue sharing measure to come before the Senate from 1967 until the successful enactment of the Revenue Sharing Act of 1972 in which the federal government distributed part of its revenues to state and local governments with few strings attached.

In foreign and national security policy, Baker generally sided with the Nixon and Ford administrations. He supported U.S. policy in Indochina until 1973, when he voted to force the United States to stop the bombing of Cambodia and Laos. He was a partisan of the president's prerogatives in foreign affairs and voted against the Cooper-Church Amendment of 1970, the McGovern-Hatfield Amendments of 1970 and 1971, and the Mansfield and Brooke Amendments of 1971 and 1972 to withdraw American troops from Indochina. He joined with most of his colleagues in 1973, however, in voting to override Nixon's veto of the war powers bill. He supported high military expenditures and voted in favor of the antiballistic missile system and the Trident submarine.

Baker rose to national prominence during the Watergate affair. He served as cochairman of the Senate Select Committee on Presidential Campaign Activities. More than any other committee member, Baker probed the motives of those involved in Watergate. Nixon had earlier been a supporter of Baker and had campaigned for him in 1966. Nixon staffers had expected Baker to be their friend on the committee. Baker, however, won praises from Democrats and Republicans for his impartiality and critical questions to Watergate witnesses. Baker served as a member of the Senate select committee investigating the Central Intelligence Agency. His attacks on a Republican president and the CIA drew criticism from some conservative Republicans.

Baker's name was mentioned as a possible vice president from the time it seemed that SPIRO AGNEW would step down. He supported GERALD FORD in 1976 and served as Ford's campaign manager in Tennessee. Baker was keynote speaker at the Republican National Convention in 1976.

Baker sought to become the Senate minority leader—a post once held by his father-in-law, Everett Dirksen. He lost in two attempts for the post, in 1969 and 1971. Seeking a new image and a more forceful opposition voice,

his party elected him to the post in January 1977. (See *The Carter Years* volume.)

Baker served in the U.S. Senate until 1985. From 1977 to 1981 he was that body's minority leader, and from 1981 to 1985 he served as majority leader. In 1980 he ran unsuccessfully for the presidency, losing the Republican nomination to RONALD REAGAN. He served on the president's Foreign Intelligence Board from 1985 to 1987, and again from 1988 to 1990. From 1987 to 1988 he served as Reagan's chief of staff. In 2001 President GEORGE H. W. BUSH nominated Baked as ambassador to Japan, a position he held to 2005. In March 2005 he joined Citigroup as a senior adviser. Baker was awarded the Presidential Medal of Freedom in 1984.

—HML and JRG

Baker, James A(ddison), III

(1930–   ) *undersecretary of commerce; national chairman, President Ford Committee*

Baker graduated from Princeton University in 1952 with a degree in the classics. He served two years in the U.S. Marine Corps and returned to earn his law degree from the University of Texas at Austin in 1957. That year, he joined Andrews and Kurth, a Houston law firm, where he worked until 1975. During that period he managed GEORGE H. W. BUSH's unsuccessful 1970 campaign for the U.S. Senate. One of Bush's oldest friends, Bush is godfather to one of Baker's daughters.

In 1975 Baker was named undersecretary of commerce in the Ford administration. In May 1976 he left that position to serve as a chairman for delegate operations in the Ford campaign against RONALD REAGAN for the Republican nomination for president. In August he was named national chairman of the President Ford Committee and managed Ford's unsuccessful fall campaign against JIMMY CARTER.

In 1978 Baker ran for attorney general of Texas and was defeated. From 1979 to 1980 he directed Bush's unsuccessful campaign to win the Republican presidential nomination. Ronald Reagan won the nomination, and Bush was chosen as his running mate. Baker was brought aboard the Reagan-Bush presidential campaign as a senior adviser. Baker served the entirety of the Reagan administration in several different capacities. He began as Reagan's chief of staff and was widely given credit for securing the passage of Reagan's 1981 tax reform bill. At the beginning of Reagan's second term, from 1985 to 1988, he served as secretary of the treasury; while there, he also chaired the president's Economic Policy Council. Baker resigned near the end of Reagan's second term to once again chair Bush's presidential campaign. Following Bush's election, Baker was the president-elect's first cabinet appointment, as he was nominated to be secretary of state. In August 1992, in an effort to jump-start Bush's faltering reelection effort, Baker was returned to the White House, where he was named chief of staff (replacing Sam Skinner) and counselor to the president (he was succeeded as secretary of state by Lawrence Eagleburger).

Following his service in the Bush administration, Baker returned to his position as senior partner of Baker and Botts, a law firm with offices in Houston and Washington. He received the Presidential Medal of Freedom in 1991, and in 2000 he served as chief legal adviser for the George W. Bush presidential campaign in Florida, where he oversaw the recount of the vote in that state.

—JRG

Barker, Bernard L.
(1917–   ) *convicted Watergate conspirator*

Born on March 17, 1917, in Havana, Cuba, Cuban-American Bernard Barker worked for Central Intelligence Agency (CIA) con-

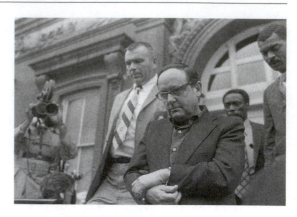

Bernard Barker is escorted from the courthouse after his arraignment for the Watergate burglary, June 22, 1972. *(Wally McNamee/Corbis)*

tact E. HOWARD HUNT during the CIA's early campaigns against Fidel Castro. Prior to the 1972 presidential election, Hunt and G. GORDON LIDDY put together a program of electronic surveillance, covert entry, and other "dirty tricks" for the Committee to Re-Elect the President (CREEP). Hunt sought Barker for various covert entry projects in connection with the program. In September 1971 Barker and two cohorts broke into the office of Dr. Louis Fielding, DANIEL ELLSBERG'S psychiatrist, in an effort to find information damaging to the antiwar activist. Ellsberg had been indicted on federal charges in connection with his release of the *Pentagon Papers*, a secret study compiled by the Rand Corporation documenting the history of U.S. involvement in Southeast Asia. They found no evidence, however.

In May 1972 Barker was one of several individuals who broke into the Democratic National Committee's (DNC) headquarters in the Watergate office building in Washington, D.C., to "plant" electronic "bugs" and photograph files. Because of an error in the placement of a phone tap, the team had to redo the job on June 17. During this second break-in, Barker and the other members of the entry team were discovered by a guard and arrested. Barker was carrying incriminating documents that led police investigators immediately to Hunt.

On September 15, 1972, Liddy, Hunt, Barker, and the other members of the entry team were indicted on charges in connection with the Watergate break-in. Barker pleaded not guilty and was released on bond.

The trial of the Watergate burglars started on January 10, 1973, with Judge JOHN SIRICA presiding. The following day Hunt pleaded guilty to all charges, and a week later Barker and the others followed suit. On March 23 Judge Sirica sentenced Barker and the other entry team members to a provisional maximum term of 40 years. He said he would not promise leniency but urged full cooperation with the federal grand jury and the Senate select committee investigating Watergate. During his testimony before the Senate select committee, Barker claimed that his motivation for committing the break-ins flowed from his belief that he was helping the anti-Castro movement. On November 9, 1973, Barker was sentenced to 18½ months to six years in prison. In July 1974 Judge Sirica reduced the sentence to time already served.

Barker and five other persons involved in the Fielding break-in were indicted for conspiring to deprive Dr. Fielding of his civil rights in March 1974. He and the others pleaded not guilty. In July Barker was convicted and given a maximum sentence of 10 years and a $10,000 fine. However, on July 22 the sentence was reduced to probation. On May 17, 1976, the court of appeals in the District of Columbia reversed Barker's conviction for his role in this incident. The court cited the failure of the trial judge to instruct the jury that Barker believed the break-in was legal because it had White House approval. Barker lives in Miami, Florida, where he oversees real estate businesses.

—RLN

Bayh, Birch E(vans), Jr.

(1928–) *member of the Senate*

Following graduation from Purdue University, Birch Bayh settled on a 340-acre farm outside his birthplace of Terre Haute in 1951. He entered politics in 1954, when he successfully ran as a Democrat for a seat in Indiana's house of representatives. While serving in the legislature, he studied law at night at Indiana University, which awarded him a degree in 1960. In 1962 Bayh won a seat in the U.S. Senate. As chairman of the Judiciary Committee's Subcommittee on Constitutional Amendments, Bayh gained national prominence when, in January 1965, he sponsored the Twenty-fifth Amendment, outlining the steps to be taken in case of a presidential disability and rearranging the order of succession in the event of the death of a president. (See *The Kennedy Years* and *The Johnson Years* volumes.)

During the NIXON and FORD administrations, Bayh, as chairman of the Constitutional Amendments Subcommittee, dealt with many of the major issues of the period. In 1970 Bayh's subcommittee held hearings and approved the Equal Rights Amendment and the Twenty-sixth Amendment, giving 18-year-olds the vote. Following the Supreme Court's 1973 decision striking down restrictive state abortion laws, Bayh's subcommittee received testimony on a constitutional amendment that would have permitted the states to ban abortions. With the vote deadlocked at 4-4, Bayh cast the deciding vote in 1975 that prevented the reporting of the amendment to the full committee and the Senate floor for consideration. Bayh introduced an "alternatives to abortion" package of legislation that would have provided a variety of social and medical services for young mothers and prohibited discrimination against unmarried mothers seeking health insurance benefits. Although Bayh personally opposed abortions, he pushed through the Senate a procedural vote that again barred a vote on the abortion amendment in 1976.

Bayh compiled a solid liberal record on domestic legislation. He was especially concerned with the passage of laws expanding day care centers and programs to help juvenile offenders. He backed legislation to control handguns. Bayh joined other liberals in the Senate to prevent the passage of legislation severely restricting the use of busing to facilitate integration. In 1969 and 1970 Bayh led the fight in the Senate that denied President Nixon's Supreme Court nominees CLEMENT HAYNSWORTH and G. HARROLD CARSWELL appointment to the high bench. It was Bayh and a number of staff members who publicized the conflict of interest charge that doomed the Haynsworth nomination. Bayh argued that Haynsworth's opposition to civil rights and the fact that so many of his decisions were overruled by an appeals court revealed he was not competent to sit on the nation's highest court. In foreign affairs Bayh supported the cutback of American troops in Europe and a reduction in defense spending for such projects as the Safeguard antiballistic missile system, the B-1 bomber, and the Trident submarine.

In 1971 Bayh tested the waters for the Democratic Party's presidential nomination. He toured the nation, concentrating on the states with future primaries, to raise money and make political contacts. He was usually well received because his staff did excellent advance work, and Bayh, who had always been a favorite of the AFL-CIO, received strong labor encouragement. Bayh ran on an anti-Nixon platform stressing his opposition to the Vietnam War and his support for domestic liberal legislation. The fight against the Carswell-Haynsworth nominations also became a central issue in the campaign. Bayh unexpectedly withdrew from the race in October 1971 because his wife had undergone "critical" sur-

gery for breast cancer, and he wanted to be at her side to help her recover.

In 1974 Bayh won a third term, with a narrow victory over Mayor Richard Lugar of Indianapolis. The economy was the dominant issue in the contest. Lugar accused Bayh of contributing to inflation by supporting excessive federal spending and refusing to go along with President Ford's budget cuts. Bayh's victory resulted primarily from an effective get-out-the-vote campaign by the state's unions.

In late October 1976 Birch Bayh became the ninth Democrat to declare his candidacy for the presidency. Running as a liberal, Bayh announced plans to be the front-runner of the left of center by the time of the April New York primary. He began his campaign with $150,000 supplemented by matching federal funds, but by the time of the New Hampshire primary, Bayh had run out of money. He and his staff had miscalculated the amount of donations they would receive. Bayh had planned large campaigns in Massachusetts and New York, where he had strong local support, but he did not have enough money. Following poor showings in New Hampshire and Massachusetts, Bayh withdrew from the race. (See *The Carter Years* volume.)

Bayh was defeated for reelection in 1980. He practices law in Washington, D.C.

—JB

Beame, Abraham D(avid)
(1906–2001) *mayor, New York, N.Y.*

The son of Polish-Jewish immigrants who had fled their native land to escape political persecution, Abraham Beame was born in London on March 19, 1906. His parents immigrated to the United States while Beame was still an infant, and he grew up on Manhattan's Lower East Side. Attending New York public schools and City College, he received an accounting degree in 1928 and founded a small accounting firm with a close friend. Beame moved to the middle-class Crown Heights section of Brooklyn in 1928 and became active in local Democratic Party politics. He attracted the attention of party leaders for his diligent work as an election district captain. In 1946 he was appointed assistant director of New York City's budget bureau, and in 1952 he became budget director, a position he held until 1961.

In 1961 Beame won election as city comptroller on an "antimachine" ticket headed by Mayor Robert F. Wagner. Encouraged by the respect he had won for his conservative approach to monetary matters, Beame unsuccessfully sought election as mayor in 1965. After his reelection to the post of comptroller in 1969, Beame became the focus for the "regular" Democrats opposed to Mayor JOHN LINDSAY. He entered the mayoral primary in 1973 and, after winning a plurality of the votes, defeated Herman Badillo (D-N.Y.) in the runoff. Presenting himself as an experienced administrator and budget expert, Beame won a landslide victory in November.

Beame took office at a time when cities across the nation were experiencing serious fiscal woes. The country's deepest recession in the postwar era had raised unemployment to near-depression levels and increased the demand for social services at a time when local revenues were in decline. Double-digit inflation, particularly the high cost of energy caused in part by the quadrupling of oil prices in 1973, placed a further drain on municipal budgets.

In May 1974 Beame presented an $11.1 billion "austerity" budget that eliminated low-priority programs and raised taxes. He opposed the FORD administration's effort to curb inflation by reducing federal expenditures, arguing that it would only worsen the plight of the nation's cities. He also lobbied hard for congressional approval of federal aid for mass transit.

Beame soon found himself in the midst of a fiscal crisis far worse than what other cities faced. By April 1975 New York City's publicly held debt totaled a staggering $14 billion. On April 2 Standard and Poor's Corp. suspended its "A" rating for New York City bonds. The city's cash-flow problems were so bad that state officials loaned the city $400 million. Beame promised a new austerity budget that included plans to fire 4,000 workers and to slash many city services. But he warned that even with these cuts the city still faced a $641 million deficit.

The crisis deepened in May when New York commercial banks refused to buy $280 million in city notes. Citing an immediate need for $1.5 billion by June 30 to meet the city's short-term debt obligations, Beame sought financial assistance from federal and state officials. He was rebuffed in Washington by President Ford, who instead urged the adoption of "sound budget policies" and the curtailing of "less-essential services and subsidies." Ford's response was echoed by Treasury secretary WILLIAM E. SIMON and Federal Reserve board chairman ARTHUR BURNS.

Although Republican leaders in the state senate initially rejected Beame's request, the threat of default was too serious to ignore. With the strong support of Governor HUGH CAREY, Beame won approval of a rescue plan. On June 10 the legislature created a new state agency, the Municipal Assistance Corp. (MAC), designed to alleviate the immediate cash-flow crisis and to supervise the city's long-range borrowing plans. "Big Mac," as it became known, was authorized to refinance New York's short-term debt of $3 billion, which was due for repayment in September, by floating long-term bonds guaranteed by the state. In return, MAC could limit the city's borrowing power and impose new, stringent budgetary procedures on the city. Although Beame was reluctant to relinquish control over the budget, New York's desperate financial situation left him with no alternative.

The state's rescue plan, however, was only the first in a long series of last-minute rescue operations designed to stave off bankruptcy. For months Beame presided over a city government periodically on the brink of insolvency and forced to make drastic cuts in essential services to survive. On June 30, 1975, Beame announced that 40,000 city workers, including firefighters, police, and sanitation workers, would be laid off. Sanitation workers struck, laid-off police conducted demonstrations, and firefighters called in "sick." The conflict eased on July 3 when Beame won agreement from state officials for a plan to increase the city's taxing authority to rehire some of the workers.

Meanwhile, MAC officials declared that Beame's austerity measures were insufficient. Accusing the agency of trying to "humiliate" him by becoming a "shadow government," he was nonetheless forced to comply with its demands. On July 31 Beame announced a wage freeze for all city workers, increases in mass transit and commuter rail fares, and a $375 million reduction in the city's capital budget. Despite these measures MAC failed to find buyers for its August bond issue, and the state again had to rescue the city. In a special session the state legislature passed a $2.3 billion aid bill, which also set stringent financial curbs on the city and gave control of city revenues to a newly created Emergency Financial Control Board. Beame angrily broke with Governor Carey over the measure, charging that it destroyed the city's independence as a self-governing municipality. Another crisis was narrowly averted in October, when the municipal teachers' union agreed to purchase $250 million in MAC bonds with pension fund money.

The inability of state and local efforts to permanently avert a financial collapse led to a concerted attempt aimed at securing federal assistance. In October the Congressional Budget Office released a study concluding that default by the city was a near certainty unless new aid was obtained. On October 12 Vice President NELSON ROCKEFELLER broke ranks with the administration and urged aid for New York City. Arthur Burns warned that if New York's "financial crisis is not resolved, it could injure the recovery process under way in our national economy." On October 29, however, President Ford delivered a strong speech in which he vowed to veto any bill providing federal loans for New York. Blaming the crisis on "fiscal mismanagement," he said that federally guaranteed loans would allow New York City officials to "escape responsibility for their past follies" and warned that only additional austerity measures would lead him to reconsider his stand.

Ford's tough position forced state and city officials to take further action. Beame announced more cutbacks in municipal employment and services, and in late November the state approved a new tax package to raise city revenues. Pressure began to mount for congressional action. The U.S. Conference of Mayors supported federal aid for New York, and the Bank of America warned that if New York defaulted, "the entire nation would suffer." The House and Senate Banking Committees both initiated hearings on loan legislation.

On November 26, the day after New York state approved its latest rescue operation, Ford ended his opposition to federal aid and asked Congress to approve legislation making up to $2.3 billion a year in direct federal loans available to New York City. Congress quickly complied, and on December 9 Ford signed the three-year loan package.

Although federal legislation virtually eliminated the danger of default or bankruptcy, the crisis had a continuing impact on New York City. The price of federal and state aid was the imposition of austerity budgets for the remainder of Beame's administration. The mayor was forced to curtail city services drastically, reducing police and fire protection to dangerously low levels. He also had to order the closing of schools, hospitals, libraries, and day care centers; cut back funds for the city's parks; and end free tuition at City University. The quality of life in the nation's largest city deteriorated badly.

Beame sought reelection in 1977. He was opposed by several candidates, including liberal Democratic representatives BELLA ABZUG, Herman Badillo, and EDWARD KOCH and New York's secretary of state Mario Cuomo. Beame was the target of all the candidates, and in the September primary, in which no one received the required 40 percent of the vote, he failed to make the runoff. He was succeeded as mayor by Representative Edward Koch.

Beame retired from politics but served as head of the advisory board of UMB Bank and Trust. After suffering a heart attack in July 2000, Beame remained hospitalized until his death on February 10, 2001.

—JD

Beard, Dita D(avis)
(1918–) *lobbyist*

Dita Beard's father was an army colonel. Beard held various odd jobs following high school. With the onset of World War II, she went to work for the Board of Economic Warfare before joining the Red Cross. During the late 1940s and early 1950s she was married and divorced twice.

After her second divorce Beard went to Washington, D.C., with her five children. With no child support payments from either of her former husbands, she was forced to find work as a secretary for the National Association of Broadcasters. She was actively involved in RICHARD NIXON's 1960 campaign for the presidency.

The following year, she began working for the International Telephone and Telegraph's (ITT) new Washington, D.C., office, initially as a secretary. But because of her extensive experience with D.C.'s social and political life, ITT president HAROLD GENEEN promoted her to lobbyist and general troubleshooter. Beard's professional relationship with Geneen remained close. Indeed, she occasionally aroused the ire of her superiors by going over their heads and reporting directly to the president. In 1966 *Fortune* magazine identified her as one of Washington's major lobbyists, noting her penchant for blunt language and actions and her keen knowledge of "what makes congressmen tick." She was particularly adept at establishing contacts with politicians by making various ITT services available to them free of charge.

During the Nixon administration her influence increased even further—as a lifelong Republican, she was on friendly terms with a number of the new faces at the White House, such as defense secretary MELVIN LAIRD.

In the first half of 1971, the Republican Party was searching for a city to host its 1972 national convention. President Nixon strongly favored San Diego because of its proximity to his home in San Clemente. Local leaders, however, were far from convinced that the business the convention would bring to the city was worth the great expense required. But the Republican Party continued to show an interest—White House staffers visited in June, long after the deadline for convention bids had passed without any action on San Diego's part.

ITT, whose subsidiary Sheraton Hotels had recently opened a new hotel in San Diego, was also interested in having the Republican convention there. In May ITT's annual general meeting was held in San Diego. Dita Beard, who had been in San Diego for the past few months, gave a dinner party in which White House aides, local politicians, and ITT officials discussed the convention question. Out of this informal gathering came a quiet ITT pledge of considerable support, in money and services, to defray the cost of the convention. In July the Republican National Committee, meeting in Denver, chose San Diego as the convention site.

Later that same month a government antitrust suit against ITT was settled out of court. The settlement, which permitted a merger between ITT and the Hartford Insurance Group, was largely along the lines ITT had desired. As word of ITT's support for the San Diego convention site circulated, suspicions of a "deal" between ITT and the Republican Party emerged in Washington. In December Democratic Party chairman LAWRENCE O'BRIEN wrote to RICHARD KLEINDIENST of the Justice Department, questioning the implications of the settlement. Rumors of a deal were emphatically denied.

But in February 1972 Washington columnist JACK ANDERSON obtained an ITT memorandum written by Dita Beard to William Merriam, head of ITT's Washington office, during the height of the San Diego convention negotiations in June 1971. Beard stated in the memo that ITT's promise of financial support for the convention had "gone a long way toward our negotiations on the mergers eventually coming out as Hal (Harold Geneen) wants them." The memo not only confirmed a connection between ITT's proposed contribution to the San Diego convention and the ITT–Hartford Insurance merger, but also indicated that President Nixon and Attorney General JOHN MITCHELL were aware of the arrangement.

Anderson passed the document to his associate Brit Hume, who contacted Dita Beard and arranged two meetings during which she reportedly confirmed the authenticity of the memorandum. Hume told Anderson that Beard took the credit for finalizing the ITT commitment with John Mitchell in May 1971 at a Kentucky Derby social gathering held by Republican governor LOUIS NUNN. Both Nunn and Mitchell denied the allegations when Hume confronted them with Beard's statements.

Nonetheless, the substance of Brit Hume's investigations appeared in the February 29 edition of Anderson's column. Two days later another column implicated Richard Klein-dienst in the ITT settlement, directly contradicting Kleindienst's December 1971 assurances to Lawrence O'Brien. The Senate was then considering the confirmation of Kleindienst to replace Attorney General Mitchell, who had stepped down to run President Nixon's re-election campaign. Kleindienst immediately requested a chance to appear before the Senate Judiciary Committee to refute the claims of Anderson and Hume.

When the hearings began on March 2, Dita Beard figured prominently in the testimony of such witnesses as Mitchell and Governor Nunn. Nunn portrayed Beard as unreliable, stating that she had been intoxicated at the Kentucky Derby social. Harold Geneen testified that his connection with Dita Beard was a distant one and denied any knowledge of the events described in the memo.

Meanwhile, Dita Beard had vanished from Washington, D.C., at about the time the hearings began. The FBI eventually located her in the coronary ward of a Denver hospital, where she had apparently gone after being taken out of Washington by G. GORDON LIDDY, who would play a key role in the Watergate scandal later that year. Her personal physician, Dr. Victor Liska, told the FBI that she was too ill to give evidence to the committee. Dr. Liska testified at the hearing that Beard had been suffering from a heart ailment for some time—implying that her physical and mental condition affected her competency at the time she wrote the memo. Liska's own credibility, however, was damaged when it was learned that the Justice Department was investigating him and his wife on charges of Medicare fraud.

It was not until March 17 that Beard made her first public response to the proceedings in Washington. In a sudden reversal she released a statement through her lawyer that referred to the memo as "a forgery, a fraud, and a hoax." Several members of the Judiciary Committee then flew to Denver to take testimony from Beard in her hospital room. Although she conceded that some of the less controversial passages did sound familiar, intensive questioning was prevented when Beard's attending physicians cleared the room, claiming she was showing symptoms of a relapse. In April two independent physicians associated with the hospital stated there was no evidence, except her own complaints of chest pains, that Beard suffered from any heart ailments. In any event there was no further testimony from Beard.

The balance of the hearings involved more conflicting testimony, various experts with differing opinions on the memo's authenticity, the introduction of yet another memo, which ITT claimed was the "real" Dita Beard memorandum—in short, a bewildering array of evidence that made a clear determination of the facts increasingly difficult. Ultimately the committee and the full Senate confirmed the nomination of Kleindienst as attorney general.

Dita Beard never returned to her old post in Washington. She was transferred by ITT to Denver and retired in June of 1975 to a farm near Shepardstown, West Virginia.

—MDQ

Bennett, Wallace F(oster)
(1898–1993) *member of the Senate*

Wallace Bennett was born on November 13, 1898, in Salt Lake City, Utah. A graduate of the University of Utah in 1919, Bennett began an apprenticeship in his father's paint-manufacturing and glass-distributing firm the following year. Under his father's tutelage he rose from office clerk to company president by 1938. In 1939 he founded the Bennett Motor Company,

a Ford dealership. In addition, during these years he was active civically and served on the boards of a number of western banks. Bennett's business acumen and leadership ability became widely recognized, and in 1950 he was urged to run for the Senate. After an energetic campaign he defeated the Democratic incumbent, Elbert D. Thomas, who had been a key figure in the New Deal. Bennett was subsequently reelected in 1956, 1962, and again in 1968. (See *The Truman Years*, *The Eisenhower Years*, *The Kennedy Years*, and *The Johnson Years* volumes.)

A steadfast fiscal conservative and ardent supporter of the free enterprise system, Bennett gained prominence as a leading monetary expert. The ranking Republican on the Senate Finance Committee, he stressed the necessity of building a more flexible international monetary system that would determine the value of the dollar based on supply and demand in world markets. Bennett regarded the U.S. gold reserve for domestic currency as an anachronism, since the gold standard had been abandoned in 1934. Based on Finance Committee recommendations, Nixon suspended convertibility between gold and the dollar in 1971 and instead permitted the international market to decide dollar value.

As a member of the Senate Banking, Housing, and Urban Affairs Committee, Bennett opposed the increasing number of bank acquisitions by industrial conglomerates and in 1969 introduced the Bank Holding Company Act. The bill broadened the existing definition of bank holding companies, thus reducing loopholes that enabled multibillion-dollar corporations or banks to acquire large and diverse financial and nonfinancial businesses. The bill was enacted into law in a modified form in 1970. Bennett played a key role in the shaping of revenue-sharing legislation that provided local and state governments with federal funds based on population, local tax revenues, and per-capita income. Thus, funds to impoverished areas would exceed funds to wealthy suburban communities. The State and Local Fiscal Assistance Act passed in 1972.

An opponent of antipoverty programs during the Johnson administration, Bennett advocated responsible legislation structured to effectively meet the needs of the poor and avoid excessive drain of revenue at the taxpayer's expense. In 1972 he introduced the Allied Service Act, which was designed to coordinate federally financed social service programs on a state and local level. The bill was rejected by Congress, however. He also cosponsored a bill that provided funds for bilingual job-training programs and the Minority Business Equity Investment Act, which established investment opportunities in minority businesses.

Bennett staunchly supported the antibusing legislation passed by the House in 1972 because it provided federal aid to disadvantaged students, retained the neighborhood school concept, and offered remedies to help achieve equal educational opportunities.

A vociferous foe of organized labor, Bennett supported a 1973 Senate resolution giving union employees the right to end a strike by secret ballot vote. He also backed legislation that increased presidential power to end strikes. In 1972 he opposed a bill to increase the minimum wage because he considered it inflationary in its recommendation for an immediate wage increase.

Throughout his final senatorial term Bennett provided unwavering support of Nixon administration policies. "Nixon," he stated, "has raised the level of our leadership to new and greater heights and made America the symbol of hope for peace among all nations in all the world."

Bennett decided against a fifth term in office and retired from the political arena at age 77. He died in Salt Lake City in 1993.

—DGE

Bentsen, Lloyd (Millard), Jr.
(1921–2006) *member of the Senate*

Born on February 11, 1921, Lloyd Bentsen grew up in the citrus country of the Rio Grande Valley, in southern Texas, where his father and uncle had a real estate business. Bentsen took his LL.B. degree at the University of Texas at Austin in 1942. He served in the U.S. Army Air Corps during World War II.

After discharge from the army in July 1945, Bentsen returned to McAllen, Texas, and entered private law practice. He was elected judge of Hidalgo County in 1946. In December 1948, the last day of the 80th Congress, he was sworn in as the youngest member of the U.S. House of Representatives after winning a special election. During his years in the House Bentsen generally supported the interests of Texas farmers and fruit growers. He was a militant anticommunist, favoring U.S. involvement in Indochina and opposing alleged communist domination of U.S. labor unions.

Bentsen decided not to run for reelection in 1954. Instead, he returned to Texas to become a businessman. With his father's multimillion-dollar financial help, he founded Lincoln Consolidated, a holding company that owned Lincoln Liberty Life Insurance Co. and controlled stocks worth hundreds of millions of dollars.

Bentsen challenged liberal senator Ralph Yarborough (D-Tex.) in the May 1970 Democratic senatorial primary. With the support of former governor JOHN B. CONNALLY and others of the conservative Democratic establishment in Texas, Bentsen waged a heavily funded, highly organized campaign. Associating Yarborough with the domestic disorders of the late 1960s, he managed to defeat the incumbent, who had the backing of a coalition of liberals, blue-collar workers, blacks, and Mexican Americans.

Bentsen and GEORGE H. W. BUSH, the Republican candidate for the Senate in 1970, differed little in their general positions. Both supported Nixon's Vietnam policies and measures to aid the oil industry while opposing social welfare programs. Bentsen was helped by a large voter turnout. Two proposed amendments to the state constitution allowing saloons throughout the state and giving tax breaks to undeveloped land turned out the conservative Democratic vote enabling Bentsen to win with 53 percent of the ballots. Bentsen classified himself as part of the loyal opposition to the president. He criticized the Nixon administration for its neglect of education, health, and the environment and for economic policies that resulted in inflation and high unemployment. Bentsen declared support for a limited form of national health insurance and supported allocation of federal funds to promote medical education, scientific research, rural area development, and improved day care programs.

The federal budget deficit was an issue of utmost importance to the senator. He demanded cuts in government spending and tax reform as an alternative to increased taxes. In keeping with his conservative fiscal stand, Bentsen voted against the Revenue Sharing Act of 1972. His reason was that he knew of no revenue to share, only federal deficits, and he believed that in the long run revenue sharing would not improve local government. Bentsen also supported welfare reform, although he opposed the guaranteed income plan proposed by the Nixon administration because he believed it lacked sufficient work incentives. In another effort to stop needless federal spending Bentsen proposed an unsuccessful amendment to cut increased expenditures on the Trident nuclear submarine.

Bentsen was concerned about the erosion of power from the Congress to the executive branch of the federal government. He objected to the tendency of U.S. presidents to enter into executive agreements rather than to make treaties, which must be ratified by a two-thirds

vote of the Senate. In 1972 Bentsen cosponsored a Senate resolution asking the executive branch to comply with the Constitution and submit such agreements to the Senate as treaties. When the administration did not comply, the Senate voted to deny the money needed to implement such agreements unless they were resubmitted as treaties. He also supported the War Powers Act of 1973, which limited the president's power to commit U.S. forces to combat without consent of Congress.

Bentsen supported measures that would allow Congress to make its own evaluation of social programs and budgets. He advocated one measure, a national goals and priorities bill, that would have created a three-man president's council of social advisers that would submit an annual report to the Congress evaluating social programs. The measure would also have created an office of national goals and priorities to advise Congress on social programs. Bentsen also worked for the adoption of the Congressional Budget and Impoundment Act of 1974. The act provided for the staff and information needed by Congress to make independent decisions on budget policies.

Bentsen continued his early career interest in the American farmer. The senator disapproved of the handling of the 1972 United States–Soviet Union grain trade. He stated that a few giant trading companies made immense profits while many farmers in early harvest areas actually lost money. He introduced legislation that would have authorized the secretary of agriculture to make special deficiency payments to wheat farmers. The measure was defeated.

In February 1975 Bentsen announced his candidacy for president in the 1976 election. He stated that the paramount issue of the election was economic recovery. He pledged to "restore the meaning of America's two great promises: opportunity at home and moral leadership." Bentsen's campaign raised a lot of money but little popular support. He was reelected to the Senate in 1976.

In 1988, Democratic presidential nominee Michael Dukakis chose Bentsen as his running mate. In one of the more memorable moments of the campaign, during the vice presidential debate against Republican Dan Quayle, Bentsen responded to Quayle's claim that he had more experience than did John F. Kennedy when he ran for president with this quip: "Senator, I served with Jack Kennedy. I knew Jack Kennedy. Jack Kennedy was a friend of mine. Senator, you are no Jack Kennedy." Bentsen resigned from the Senate in 1993 to serve as President Bill Clinton's secretary of the treasury, a position he resigned for health reasons in 1994. Bentsen suffered two strokes in 1998. He died on May 23, 2006, in Houston, Texas, at age 85.

—CLC and JRG

Ben-Veniste, Richard
(1943–) *Watergate assistant special prosecutor*

Upon completion of Columbia Law School, Ben-Veniste joined the Special Prosecutions Section of the U.S. Attorney's Office in New York City. After a year he was promoted to chief of the Official Corruption Section and was credited with the successful prosecution of a number of organized crime figures for income tax fraud and collusion with union officials in kickback schemes. In 1973 ARCHIBALD COX, special Watergate prosecutor, recruited Ben-Veniste for his staff. Assigned to the Watergate Task Force in mid-July, his responsibilities included investigating allegations of hush money, destruction of documents, and illegal wiretapping as well as charges that NIXON had advance knowledge of Watergate activities.

Ben-Veniste was the attorney who subpoenaed the White House tapes during July.

When Nixon refused to supply the tapes on the grounds of national security and executive privilege, Ben-Veniste helped prepare the prosecution's case, which was argued before Judge JOHN SIRICA. Sirica ruled in the prosecution's favor.

Ben-Veniste was involved in further legal battles for additional tapes and was one of the attorneys responsible for analyzing them once turned over to the Watergate prosecutor. His analysis helped develop the case for Nixon's complicity in the Watergate cover-up. Ben-Veniste later presented evidence of complicity by high administration officials to various grand juries investigating the affair, evidence that led to the indictment of several former members of the Nixon administration. He continued to probe the case until the special prosecutor's office was officially disbanded in the latter part of 1975, soon after Nixon's resignation.

Ben-Veniste is a partner in the Washington law firm of Mayer, Brown, Rowe, & Maw. From May 1995 to June 1996, he served as chief counsel of the Senate committee investigating the Whitewater scandal. From 2001 to 2004 he served as a commissioner on the National Commission on Terrorist Attacks on the United States.

—DJE

Bernstein, Carl
(1944–) *journalist, author*

Born on February 14, 1944, the son of labor and political activists, Carl Bernstein grew up in Silver Spring, Maryland, and attended the local public schools. At age 16 Bernstein worked as a copy boy for the *Washington Star* and at 19 was named to the *Star*'s reporting staff as a summer replacement. His bylined, human interest stories dominated the front page of the *Star*'s local news section. In 1965

Bernstein dropped out of the University of Maryland to work at the *Elizabeth (N.J.) Daily Journal*, where he covered the November 1965 New York City blackout and won several prizes in local press association competitions.

Landing a job on the metropolitan staff of the *Washington Post* in 1966, Bernstein covered the police department, city hall, and the Virginia state legislature. On his own initiative, Bernstein wrote discursive articles on Washington's ethnic neighborhoods, investigative pieces on slum landlords, and rock music reviews.

Although not initially assigned to cover the Watergate break-in, Bernstein produced a sidelight story on the five apprehended suspects, and later "polished" BOB WOODWARD's piece identifying JAMES W. MCCORD JR. as a salaried security adviser for the Committee to Re-Elect the President (CREEP). In July 1972 the *Post*'s editors named Bernstein to the Watergate team, where he combined his efforts with Woodward.

Woodward and Bernstein ("Woodstein") relied on two principal investigative techniques to solve the Watergate riddle. They attempted to trace the "money chain" all the way from the apprehended burglars to higher officials in CREEP, and they located employees in the White House and CREEP who might be persuaded to provide them with small pieces of the puzzle. "The thing is to work from the bottom up," Bernstein told journalist Leonard Downie.

In pursuit of his story, Bernstein on several occasions employed methods that he questioned in others, such as using clandestine sources to get telephone and credit card records of major figures in the case. Woodward and Bernstein were also criticized for their surreptitious attempt to contact members of the special Watergate grand jury hearing evidence in U.S. district court in Washington. But through persistent and imaginative questioning of disgruntled CREEP employees, arduous checking of records, and tiring legwork, Woodward and Bernstein followed the "money chain" of secret funds all the way up to former attorney general JOHN N. MITCHELL, the director of CREEP at the time of the break-in.

Woodward and Bernstein provoked angry denunciations from White House spokesmen for their October 10, 1972, scoop tying campaign "dirty tricks" and financial irregularities to the president's reelection team. The *Post* was accused of printing stories based on "thirdhand information" and the "shabbiest journalistic techniques." The attacks intensified after Woodward and Bernstein incorrectly reported on October 25, 1972, that CREEP treasurer HUGH W. SLOAN, JR. had named H. R. HALDEMAN in grand jury testimony as the head of a secret slush fund that financed the Watergate break-in and other illegal operations. To prevent further blunders, the *Post*'s editors tightened their control over the reporting team. In addition to requiring two cross-checks for every fact, the editors subjected the team to intensive cross-examinations.

For the first nine months, the *Post* had pursued the Watergate case virtually alone. Following McCord's letter to Judge JOHN J. SIRICA in March 1973, however, other news media joined the hunt. Sharpened by the competition, Woodward and Bernstein compiled an impressive record of scoops, including E. Howard Hunt's clandestine visit to International Telephone and Telegraph (ITT) lobbyist DITA BEARD and CREEP's manipulation of TV public opinion polls after the mining of Haiphong Harbor. From April 1973 until Nixon's resignation, the team concentrated on uncovering the president's involvement in Watergate.

Woodward and Bernstein's "story within the story" was told in *All the President's Men*. Written in the third person, the book traced the two reporters' steps from the break-in to the Senate Ervin Committee hearings in May

1973. Published in late spring 1974, *All the President's Men* was an immediate best seller.

Urged to continue the story begun in *All the President's Men*, Woodward and Bernstein next focused on Nixon's last 15 months in office, paying particular attention to the final two weeks. The result was *The Final Days*, published simultaneously with the release of the film version of *All the President's Men* in April 1976. Gossipy, titillating selections in *Newsweek* excerpts of the book provoked strong criticism from former Nixon associates, particularly from HENRY KISSINGER, who was outraged by their version of a drunken, tearful Nixon. The book shot to the top of the *New York Times* best-seller list within days of its publication, hovering around the top for more than six months. Bernstein returned to his desk at the *Post* in June 1976 after an extended leave of absence, during which he wrote a long article on McCarthy-era Washington for the *New Yorker*.

Bernstein resigned from the *Washington Post* in 1976. He worked as a senior correspondent for ABC News and contributed to *Time* magazine until 1981, when he returned to the *Washington Post* as assistant managing editor for investigations. He wrote *Loyalties: A Son's Memoir* (1989) about the experience of his parents with McCarthyism and coauthored *His Holiness: John Paul II and the History of Our Time* (1998). In May 2005 MARK FELT announced that he was the source known as "Deep Throat," a revelation that both Woodward and Bernstein corroborated the following day.

—JAN and JRG

Berrigan, Daniel
(1921–   ) *antiwar activist*

Born on May 9, 1921, in Virginia, Minnesota, Berrigan's father was a socialist and union organizer. Berrigan entered a Jesuit seminary near Poughkeepsie, New York, in 1939 and was ordained a Roman Catholic priest in 1952. He was attracted to social activism, being influenced by French worker-priests. He became a staunch critic of the Catholic Church's views on social consciousness and of American political and social institutions. He taught and lectured on college campuses and served as an editor of *Jesuit Missions*, a liberal publication. He was active in the civil rights movement and participated in Civil Rights teach-ins and sit-ins. In 1965 Berrigan founded Clergy Concerned about Vietnam (later Clergy and Laymen Con-

The Reverend Daniel J. Berrigan is taken into custody in Providence, Rhode Island, on charges of burning draft cards, August 11, 1970. *(Bettman/Corbis)*

cerned about Vietnam). He went to Hanoi in 1968 to help gain the release of three American prisoners of war. An ardent antiwar activist, he and his brother Philip (also a Catholic priest) became leading critics of the war and were once described as "the shock troops of the peace movement." In May 1968 the two brothers and seven others raided the Selective Service office in Catonsville, Maryland, outside of Baltimore, and destroyed the draft board's files. (See *The Johnson Years* volume.)

In October 1968 Daniel Berrigan was tried and sentenced to three years in prison for the Catonsville raid. He immediately went into hiding. Berrigan was captured in Rhode Island in August 1970 and served 18 months in a federal prison in Danbury, Connecticut. As a poet and writer, he dramatized the antiwar activities of himself and his associates in his play *The Trial of the Catonsville Nine.* He described his attempt to avoid imprisonment in his book *No Bars to Manhood.*

Berrigan was named by a federal grand jury in 1972 as an unindicted coconspirator in a case in which his brother Philip was charged with conspiracy to kidnap HENRY KISSINGER and to blow up the heating systems of federal buildings in Washington. The conspiracy charges against Philip and six other defendants in the case were eventually dropped by the government.

Berrigan continued his antiwar protests. He became the center of a storm of protest when in late 1973 he addressed a meeting of the Arab University Graduates Association in Washington, D.C. In that talk he blasted Israel as a "nightmare military-industrial complex . . . the creation of millionaires, generals, and entrepreneurs." He was sharply criticized for his anti-Israel views. Accusations were made that he was anti-Semitic, a charge he ardently denied. Some leading antiwar activists, such as Donald Harrington, Nat Hentoff, and Arthur Hertzberg, condemned Berrigan for his anti-Israel position.

With the ending of the war in Vietnam, Berrigan dropped out of the national spotlight. Only his Middle East views catapulted him to prominence again. He continued to teach, write, and lecture. He was arrested several times for protest activities after 1973. Berrigan turned his attention to the nuclear arms race and was arrested at a Pentagon protest in 1976.

In the 1980s Berrigan and his brother Philip began the "Plowshares Movement" to protest nuclear arms proliferation. On September 9, 1980, a group of protesters led by the Berrigans entered the General Electric Nuclear Missile Reentry Division in King of Prussia, Pennsylvania, defacing documents and attempting to destroy two nose cones. Arrested on April 10, 1990, the group was resentenced to and paroled to time served. Berrigan has continued to lead protests around the world against such issues as the 1991 Gulf War and the post-September 11 war on terror.

—HML and JRG

Black, Hugo L(a Fayette)

(1886–1971) *associate justice, U.S. Supreme Court*

Born on February 27, 1886, Black grew up in rural Clay County, Alabama, and received his law degree in 1906 from the University of Alabama Law School. He practiced in Birmingham and held several local offices there before his election to the U.S. Senate in 1926. Reelected in 1932, Black proved to be an ardent New Dealer. He became Franklin Roosevelt's first Supreme Court appointee in August 1937. On the bench Black supported federal and state economic and social welfare legislation and favored strong enforcement of national labor and antitrust laws.

More important, Justice Black developed a judicial philosophy that was to have a significant impact on American law. As he explained in a June 1947 dissent, Black believed that the Fourteenth Amendment had "incorporated," or made applicable to the states, all the guarantees of the first eight amendments to the Constitution. The justice also argued that the provisions in the Bill of Rights should be interpreted literally. As a result of that approach, he viewed the scope of most criminal rights very broadly. Black considered the First Amendment "the heart of our government" and was especially ardent in its defense. He believed its guarantees of free thought and expression were fundamental to all other liberties, and he insisted that the amendment prohibited all government interference with freedom of speech and of the press. (See *The Truman Years* and *The Eisenhower Years* volumes.)

Until the 1960s Black frequently voiced these positions in dissents in criminal rights, loyalty-security, and other First Amendment cases. When a liberal majority emerged on the Warren Court, however, many of Black's views finally prevailed. Few justices adopted his absolutist position on the First Amendment, but the Warren Court gave significantly greater protection to its guarantees in areas such as free press, libel, obscenity, and loyalty-security. Similarly, though a majority never accepted Black's "total incorporation" doctrine, the Court applied most of the Bill of Rights to the states on a case-by-case basis. The Court also took an expansive view of the criminal safeguards in those amendments and broadened the rights afforded defendants in federal and state courts. During the 1960s a majority also adopted Black's long-held views on legislative reapportionment and ordered congressional and state redistricting according to a one-man, one-vote standard.

Just when Black seemed vindicated and at the height of his influence, he began taking "conservative" positions that surprised many observers. He dissented, for example, when the majority invalidated a Connecticut anticontraceptive law in June 1965. The justice also voted in a series of cases beginning in 1964 to uphold the convictions of civil rights demonstrators. (See *The Kennedy Years* and *The Johnson Years* volumes.)

During his last years on the bench, Black continued in this vein. He dissented in February 1969 when the Court held that public school students had a right to nondisruptive political expression. He also objected to a June 1971 ruling in which the majority overturned the conviction of a demonstrator who had entered a courthouse wearing a jacket inscribed with a vulgarism condemning the draft.

Black protested when the Court in June 1969 limited the area that police could search without a warrant incident to a suspect's arrest. In March 1970 his opinion for the Court held that a disruptive defendant could be expelled from the courtroom and could even be bound and gagged, if necessary, to maintain order during a trial.

Justice Black also resisted efforts to expand the rights of debtors and of illegitimate children through the courts. He considered welfare a "gratuity," not an entitlement, and dissented from rulings in April 1969 and March 1970 that broadened the rights of welfare recipients. Black cast the deciding vote in a set of December 1970 cases in which the Court held that Congress could lower the voting age to 18 for federal elections but not for state and local elections. For a five-man majority in June 1971, the justice ruled that Jackson, Mississippi, officials had not violated the Constitution when they closed all public swimming pools rather than desegregate them.

Based on such decisions, some observers charged that Black was backsliding and "going conservative" in his old age. Others, including Black himself, said the justice had not changed and that his views were consistent with those expressed years before. Black had always maintained, for example, that government could regulate the time and place of speech, though never its content. Thus, he believed it could forbid political expression and demonstrations in schools or on other public or private property. In contrast to his broad approach to most criminal rights guarantees, the justice had repeatedly taken a narrow view of the Fourth Amendment's prohibition on unreasonable searches and seizures and had frequently voted against expanding the scope of this provision. Similarly, Black had long inveighed against policy making by judges. He had objected when the Court's conservative majority in the 1930s read its own economic notions into the Constitution, and he protested late in his life when he thought liberal justices, using the due process and equal protection clauses, were attempting to graft their personal social and political ideas onto the Constitution. Black's literalism, as some commentators pointed out, limited him to the express provisions of the Constitution and kept him from recognizing any new constitutional rights, such as a right to privacy. Other analysts remarked that Black's conservatism demonstrated simply that the judicial revolution he had started had passed him by. Many of Black's goals had essentially been achieved. When a younger generation sought to move beyond them, Black tried to confine constitutional change within the bounds he had originally set.

For all the talk of Black's alleged conservatism, the justice remained in the forefront in his defense of certain rights, even in his final years on the bench. In a March 1969 majority opinion, Black held that the *Miranda* ruling applied once a suspect was taken into custody, not just before questioning at a police station. He dissented in February 1971 when a new majority authorized the use of incriminating statements obtained in violation of *Miranda*, at trial to impeach a defendant's credibility on the witness stand. Black voted in June 1969 to make the provision against double jeop-

ardy applicable to the states and in June 1970 to extend the right to counsel to preliminary hearings. He objected in June 1971 when the majority ruled that juveniles had no right to trial by jury.

In February 1970 Justice Black's majority opinion extended the one-man, one-vote rule to state and local elections for specialized bodies such as school boards. In June 1969 he upheld a federal district court order requiring the Montgomery, Alabama, school board to desegregate faculty and staff according to a specific numerical ratio. In a majority opinion in a January 1970 case, the justice held that the Selective Services System lacked authority to reclassify a youth with a valid student deferment as punishment for turning in his draft card to protest the Vietnam War. Five months later Black's opinion of the Court ruled that a person was entitled to conscientious-objector status when he possessed deeply held moral or ethical beliefs against war, even if his beliefs were not religiously based.

Black adhered to his absolutist views on freedom of speech and of the press. In a May 1970 majority opinion, he overturned, as a violation of the First Amendment, a federal law making it a crime for an actor to wear a U.S. military uniform in a production critical of the armed forces. In three February 1971 suits he voted to invalidate state requirements that applicants for admission to the bar take a loyalty oath or disclose membership in subversive organizations. On June 30, 1971, Black joined the majority to deny the government's request for an injunction prohibiting newspaper publication of a classified study of U.S. involvement in Vietnam known as the *Pentagon Papers*. In a separate opinion the justice insisted that freedom of the press, like other First Amendment rights, was unassailable and that no judicial restraint on the press was permissible.

The opinion was Justice Black's last. On August 28, 1971, he entered the hospital, and on September 17, after 34 years on the Court, Black resigned because of ill health. Two days later he suffered a stroke. Within a week he was dead at age 85.

—CAB

Blackmun, Harry A(ndrew)
(1908–1999) *judge, U.S. Eighth Circuit Court of Appeals; associate justice, U.S. Supreme Court*

Born on November 12, 1908, in Nashville, Illinois, Blackmun grew up in St. Paul, Minnesota, and graduated from Harvard College, Phi Beta Kappa, in 1929. He received a degree from Harvard Law School in 1932 and then clerked for a year for a judge on the U.S. Eighth Circuit Court of Appeals. From 1934 to 1950 Blackmun practiced with a large Minneapolis law firm, where he specialized in taxation and estate planning and became a general partner in 1943. He also taught part time at several area law schools. In 1950 he began serving as resident counsel at the Mayo Clinic in Rochester, Minnesota.

A Republican, Blackmun was named a judge on the Eighth Circuit Court in 1959 by President Dwight D. Eisenhower. On the circuit bench he developed a reputation as a cautious and basically conservative judge who respected precedent and favored a policy of judicial restraint. An expert on taxation, Blackmun was a moderate on civil rights and civil liberties issues and a conservative on criminal rights. He was well regarded within his circuit and was considered a fair and scholarly jurist of complete integrity who wrote thorough and careful opinions.

On April 14, 1970, President RICHARD NIXON appointed Blackmun to the Supreme Court seat vacated by ABE FORTAS in May 1969. The Senate had rejected Nixon's two previous nominees for the post, CLEMENT HAYNSWORTH and G. HARROLD CARSWELL. However,

Blackmun's record withstood close scrutiny, and his nomination was well received. He was confirmed by the Senate, 94-0, on May 12, 1970. Blackmun was sworn in on June 9 by Chief Justice WARREN BURGER, with whom he had been friends since childhood.

As most observers had expected, Justice Blackmun was generally conservative in his interpretation of the Constitution and restrained in the use of judicial power, especially in criminal cases. He voted in favor of the prosecution in almost all Fourth Amendment cases. He also took a very narrow view of the Fifth Amendment's privilege against self-incrimination. In an opinion for the Court in June 1971, Blackmun ruled that juvenile defendants were not guaranteed the right to trial by jury. Two years later the justice held that a defendant's counsel did not have to be present during a pretrial display of photographs to witnesses for the purpose of identifying the accused. Although personally opposed to capital punishment, Blackmun voted in June 1972 and July 1976 to sustain state death penalty laws against the charge that they violated the constitutional ban on cruel and unusual punishment.

On racial issues Blackmun followed a moderate course. He spoke for the Court in February 1973 when it upset a suburban swim club's policy of excluding all blacks from membership, and he participated in decisions interpreting provisions of the 1964 Civil Rights Act favorably to blacks. However, the justice also joined in several rulings that limited the scope of remedies for school segregation and in a June 1971 decision allowing a city to close its public swimming pools rather than desegregate them.

Blackmun voted to overturn most laws discriminating against women and illegitimate children and to hold most forms of state aid to parochial schools unconstitutional. In other areas, however, he was wary of invalidating federal or state statutes. For a five-man majority in April 1971, he upheld a federal law revoking the citizenship of individuals born abroad of one American parent who failed to meet a U.S. residency requirement. Although he joined in a March 1972 decision upsetting a one-year state residency requirement for voting, Blackmun supported a 50-day state registration requirement in March 1973 and several laws establishing lengthy registration requirements for voting in party primaries. He backed most state welfare regulations and voted to sustain laws authorizing the seizure of goods or wages from an allegedly delinquent debtor without notice or hearing. In his first few years on the Court, Blackmun almost always voted in favor of the government in First Amendment cases. He dissented in June 1971 when the Court refused to grant an injunction against newspaper publication of the *Pentagon Papers,* and he joined in several June 1973 decisions giving the states greater leeway to suppress allegedly obscene materials.

In January 1973 Blackmun made a notable departure from his policy of judicial restraint and, for a seven-man majority, held laws prohibiting abortions during the first six months of pregnancy an unconstitutional violation of women's right to privacy in *Roe v. Wade.* During the 1974 and 1975 Court terms, commentators detected in Blackmun signs of greater self-confidence and independence. In March 1975, for example, he spoke for the majority to hold that officials in Chattanooga, Tennessee, had violated the First Amendment by denying the use of a municipal theater for a production of the controversial rock musical *Hair.* In June 1975 and May 1976, the justice overturned on First Amendment grounds Virginia laws prohibiting advertisements for abortion services and of drug prices. As the justice overseeing the Eighth Circuit, Blackmun acted independently in November 1975 to invalidate parts of a Nebraska judge's "gag" order restricting

media coverage of a mass murder case. In June 1976 he joined with the rest of the Court to overturn the remaining portions of the order. Blackmun once again spoke for the majority in July 1976 to upset state laws requiring women to get the consent of a spouse or parent before having an abortion. He protested a June 1977 ruling holding that states and municipalities were not constitutionally required to fund elective abortions for indigent women. In 1994, in a dissent written in *Collins v. Collins,* Blackmun announced that "from this day forward, I shall no longer tinker with the machinery of death." He retired later that year and died in 1999 following hip replacement surgery.

—CAB

Blatnik, John A(nton)
(1911–1991) *member of the House of Representatives*

John Blatnik was born in Forest Heights, Maryland, on August 17, 1911. A former high school chemistry teacher and Minnesota state senator from 1940 to 1946, John Blatnik was elected to the U.S. House in 1947 on the Democratic-Farmer-Labor ticket. His heavily industrial ore-mining district in northeastern Minnesota bordered on Lake Superior and included Duluth and the iron-rich Mesabi Range. Beginning with his vote against the Taft-Hartley Bill in 1947, Blatnik compiled a strongly prolabor, liberal record during the Truman and Eisenhower administrations. He voted for all of the civil rights legislation of the late 1950s and advocated a foreign policy based on economic aid and cultural exchange rather than on armament.

During the 1950s Blatnik became known as a conservationist and a crusader for clean water legislation. As chairman of the Public Works Committee's Rivers and Harbors Subcommittee, he sponsored the Federal Water

Pollution Control Act of 1956, steering it through the proindustry committee and a hostile Congress.

Blatnik maintained his liberal record on most issues during the 1960s. But he ceased to be a vigorous proponent of pollution control legislation. In 1968, when interior secretary Stewart Udall ordered an investigation of pollution in Lake Superior, a task force of five Interior agencies found the beginning of widespread pollution by mining wastes being dumped into the lake by the Reserve Mining Co. The task force recommended that Reserve Mining's permit to dump be revoked within three years. Blatnik, on close terms with officials of the company, which provided more than 3,000 jobs in his district, spoke out publicly against the report, saying that it had "no official status" and later denouncing it as "completely false." In 1968 Blatnik tried unsuccessfully to block a plank in the Minnesota Democratic-Farmer-Labor Party's platform declaring Lake Superior off-limits as a dumping ground for mining and industrial wastes. (See *The Eisenhower Years* and *The Clinton Years* volumes.)

At a water pollution enforcement conference in 1969 in Duluth, government scientists were unable to develop an indisputable case of interstate pollution against Reserve Mining. Findings as early as 1967 by the Duluth National Water Quality Laboratory, opened through Blatnik's efforts, had shown the ill effects of Reserve Mining's dumping, but the results of studies were suppressed by Washington headquarters and a Blatnik supporter, known to be sympathetic to the interests of Reserve Mining, appointed assistant director of the laboratory. By 1971 every Lake Superior polluter had been given a clean-up deadline except for Reserve Mining.

In 1971 Blatnik acceded to the chairmanship of the powerful Public Works Committee. While his leadership on pollution control matters within the strongly proindustry com-

mittee continued to be weak, he still retained something of his old reputation as an environmentalist. His committee helped write a new Water Pollution Control Act, which was passed in 1972 over President RICHARD NIXON's veto. When the president announced his plan to cut by more than half the congressional allocations for state waste treatment plants, Blatnik joined Senator EDMUND S. MUSKIE (D-Me.) in denouncing the president's move as indicative of his "halfhearted commitment to the cause of clean water."

Blatnik announced his retirement from Congress in February 1974. He went into private consulting and died in 1991.

—DAE

Blount, Winton M(alcolm)
(1921–2002) *U.S. postmaster general; chairman, Postal Board of Governors*

Born in Union Springs, Alabama, on February 1, 1921, Blount left the University of Alabama in his sophomore year to manage his father's asphalt plant. After serving in the army air force during World War II, he took over his father's failing sand and gravel business. With his brother's help Blount invested in war surplus equipment and built the Blount Brothers Corp. of Montgomery into one of the nation's largest general contractors, moving into the field of nuclear energy, missile bases, and space development projects. He served as director of the Central Georgia Railway Company and of the First National Bank of Montgomery and had numerous other business affiliations.

Blount was elected 41st president of the U.S. Chamber of Commerce in April 1968 after serving for several years as director and chairman of the manpower training panel. Responsible for studying and defining national economic problems, he warned against inflation, which he blamed in part on excessive wage increases, and declared that the most effective way to end urban rioting was to crack down on the "lawless hoodlums" who threatened the rights of businessmen and ghetto residents.

Originally a Democrat, Blount supported the presidential candidacy of Dwight D. Eisenhower and helped lead the southern campaign of RICHARD M. NIXON in his 1960 bid for the presidency. He joined the Republican Party in the early 1960s and by 1968 termed himself "conservative." Blount's position as president of the Chamber of Commerce prevented him from taking part in Nixon's successful 1968 campaign.

When President-elect Nixon designated him postmaster general in December 1968, Blount announced that he would sever all business connections in accepting the position. Acting upon the 1968 recommendations of the President's Commission on Postal Organization, Blount put forward a plan in early 1969 for converting the Post Office Department into a nonprofit, nonpolitical government-owned corporation. He also planned to end post office patronage by filling vacancies on a strict merit system.

In March 1970 an eight-day postal workers' strike for higher wages, the first in the history of the federal postal system, stopped mail in New York and other cities across the country. President Nixon declared a national emergency and ordered in federal reserve troops to help move the mail, while Blount ordered a mail stoppage to New York and obtained a federal court injunction to bar the illegal strike of federal workers. AFL-CIO president GEORGE MEANY condemned the use of troops but urged the strikers to return to work. The administration promised to enter negotiations with the postal unions once the strike ended. After meeting with the heads of seven postal unions, Blount pledged that President Nixon was committed to obtaining congressional approval of any agreement reached in negotiations. Within

a few weeks Congress passed a 6 percent pay raise for all postal and civil service employees and military personnel.

In July 1970 Congress approved the plan to make the U.S. postal system a semi-autonomous federal agency. The new system was to be financed by its own revenues and congressional appropriations, and governed by a board of nine presidential appointees, who in turn would appoint the postmaster and deputy postmaster general. A special five-member Postal Rate Commission would make recommendations on rates, classifications of mail, and services. Blount presided over the transition and agreed to stay on as chairman of the postal service governing board after the change occurred in July 1971. At a press conference in January 1971, Blount cited as his accomplishments the abolition of the patronage system for appointing the postmaster, the passage of antiobscenity laws to help curb the distribution of pornographic mail, and the recruitment of businessmen to improve postal services. Repeated postal rate increases and continued poor service, however, provoked much criticism of the system. Democratic Party national chairman Lawrence F. O'Brien charged that the post office was "bogged down in partisan politics, service cutbacks, and financial ineptitude," while Senator JENNINGS RANDOLPH (D-W.Va.) accused officials of bypassing the commission authorized by Congress to establish postal rates.

In a move he had apparently been planning for six months, Blount resigned as chairman of the postal service board in October 1971 to run against incumbent Democratic senator John J. Sparkman of Alabama. Political observers considered this a test of Nixon's "southern strategy" to gain congressional seats for the Republican Party by wooing the traditionally Democratic Deep South with conservative stances. Blount's campaign was managed by Allison, Treleaven, and Rietz, a Washington firm who had worked for Nixon in 1968, and the former postmaster received strong administration support. During the campaign, Blount emphasized his ties with the Nixon administration and focused his criticism on the Democratic presidential ticket headed by liberal senator GEORGE MCGOVERN of South Dakota. Sparkman, who wielded great power as chairman of the Senate Banking and Currency Committee, was as critical of Senator McGovern as his Republican opponent. With the support of banking interests and an endorsement by former Alabama governor GEORGE WALLACE, the 72-year-old Sparkman swept to an easy victory over Blount, providing a major setback for the Republican effort to win southern congressional seats.

After the election Blount returned to private business, as chairman of the board of Blount, Inc. He died in 2002.

—DAE

Boggs, (Thomas) Hale
(1914–1972) *member of the House of Representatives; majority leader*

Born in Long Beach, Mississippi, Boggs studied journalism and law at Tulane University, from which he graduated in 1937. In 1941 he won a seat in the U.S. House. After being defeated in 1943, he joined the navy. He returned to the House in 1947, where he was a protégé of Speaker Sam Rayburn. In 1962 he became majority whip under JOHN MCCORMACK (D-Mass.), Rayburn's successor. Boggs also was a ranking Democrat on the Ways and Means Committee. The Louisiana representative compiled a moderate record, liberal by southern standards. Although he voted against early civil rights measures, he supported the voting rights and open housing legislation of the late 1960s and helped direct Great Society legislation through the House in the Johnson years. (See *The Eisenhower Years*, *The Kennedy Years*, and *The Johnson Years* volumes.)

Boggs maintained his moderate stand during the NIXON years. He voted for the amendment lowering the voting age to 18, tax reform, and family assistance programs as well as the Philadelphia Plan, revenue sharing, and the "no knock" entry legislation. He opposed busing; environmental legislation; and, although backed by labor, efforts to aid migrant workers. Many of Boggs's votes were based on the specific needs of his district. As a representative of a large urban area, he introduced bills designed to provide tax incentives to builders for slum clearance and rehabilitation. Because New Orleans had several important defense and space industries, he backed large-scale spending by the Defense Department and the National Aeronautics and Space Administration. Although he voted against the Cooper-Church Amendment of 1970, Boggs eventually became a critic of the war.

Boggs played a major role in the passage of the measure extending the income surtax in 1969. Because of the illness of Chairman WILBUR MILLS (D-Ark.), Boggs pushed the bill through the Ways and Means Committee and the House. He met heavy opposition from liberals who attempted to prevent passage of the surtax unless the House took up general tax reform. Boggs, the floor leader for the measure, urged bipartisan support for the bill, which he argued was needed to limit inflation. He also promised that the House would consider tax reform. The surtax passed by five votes.

In 1971 Boggs waged a difficult campaign to win the post of majority leader. He was opposed by liberals MORRIS UDALL (D-Ariz.) and James O'Hara (D-Mich.), both of whom had the backing of labor, and by moderate B. F. Sisk (D-Calif.), who had the support of the California delegation as well as much of the South. His critics termed Boggs haughty and aloof, called his personal behavior erratic, and described his performance as whip as minimal.

However, as a House leader and member of the Ways and Means Committee, Boggs used his ability to deliver choice committee assignments to parlay votes, and he won the post in January.

In 1971 Boggs became embroiled in the growing controversy over the conduct of J. EDGAR HOOVER and the FBI. He delivered a speech on the House floor accusing the FBI of tapping telephones of members of Congress and calling for Hoover's resignation. His allegations were later proven correct following administration and congressional probes of the agency. Boggs himself came under criticism because he had permitted a wealthy builder to perform $40,000 worth of improvements on his Bethesda home at a fraction of the cost. In 1972 Boggs was killed in a plane crash in Alaska.

—HML

Bork, Robert H(eron)
(1927–   ) *solicitor general*

Born in Pittsburgh, Pennsylvania, on March 1, 1927, Robert Bork attended the University of Chicago Law School, where he graduated as managing editor of the law review in 1953. From 1955 to 1962 he practiced law with a Chicago firm. During the 1960s he taught at Yale Law School, where he was a leading expert in the field of antitrust law and the most conservative member of the law faculty. A believer in free market economics, Bork favored an aggressive antitrust policy by the government. He served the Johnson administration as a member of the presidential task force on antitrust in 1968.

Bork was a critic of the Warren Court, which he believed "represented a sharp challenge to the traditional relationship of the judiciary to the process of democratic government." He was a strong supporter of the presidential candidacy of RICHARD NIXON in 1968 and 1972 and considered Nixon an "intellectual politician." Bork assisted in drafting the Nixon administration's proposal for a moratorium on busing to achieve racial balance in public schools and defended the constitutionality of the proposals in testimony before Congress. He disagreed with the administration's antitrust policy, however, on the grounds that it was insufficiently activist in promoting competition.

In June 1973 Nixon appointed Bork solicitor general of the United States. As head of the small but prestigious solicitor general's office in the Justice Department, Bork controlled the flow of cases through the appellate system, deciding which cases the government would appeal and what line of argument its appeals would follow. Bork himself often argued the important cases before the U.S. Supreme Court. Bork's first major public act was the filing of a brief in Baltimore federal court on October 5 arguing that a sitting vice president could be indicted and tried on criminal charges. Vice President SPIRO T. AGNEW, under investigation for taking bribes, had tried to block a grand jury investigation with the argument that criminal proceedings could not be commenced against a sitting vice president until he had been impeached. Agnew resigned on October 10 and pleaded nolo contendere to income tax evasion.

Bork's most dramatic and controversial official act occurred a few weeks later as part of the "Saturday Night Massacre" of October 20. On that night President Nixon attempted to fire Watergate special prosecutor ARCHIBALD COX, who had refused to obey Nixon's command to drop his legal effort to secure certain White House tapes for the Watergate grand jury's investigation. After Attorney General ELLIOT RICHARDSON resigned rather than carry out Nixon's order to fire Cox, and Deputy Attorney General WILLIAM RUCKELSHAUS was fired for his refusal to discharge Cox, Bork, third in command in the Justice Department, became acting attorney general and dismissed Cox. "I believe a president has the right to discharge any member of the Executive branch," Bork said in defense of his act.

Two days later Bork placed HENRY PETERSEN, assistant attorney general in charge of the criminal division, in direct charge of the Watergate case. In response to an avalanche of public criticism over his removal of Cox, however, Nixon on October 26 announced that Bork would appoint a new special prosecutor. On November 1 Bork announced the appointment of Houston lawyer LEON JAWORSKI to the post. Bork said Jaworski would have the same charter as Cox, the "full cooperation" of the executive branch, and no restrictions placed on his freedom of action if he sought additional presidential documents. Nixon also appointed Senator WILLIAM SAXBE (R-Ohio) as attorney general; with Saxbe's confirmation, Bork returned to his position as solicitor general. He remained the government's chief advocate until early 1977, when he returned to Yale as Chancellor Kent professor of law.

From 1982 to 1988, Bork served as a circuit judge for the U.S. Court of Appeals from the District of Columbia Circuit. In 1987 he was nominated to the U.S. Supreme Court by President RONALD REAGAN. His confirmation hearings were the most contentious of the century. Liberal groups rose in heated opposition, most notably to his testimony that since there was no stated right to privacy in the Constitution, he would vote to overturn *Roe v. Wade*. The full Senate rejected Bork's nomination on October 23, 1987, by a 58-42 vote.

Following his defeat, Bork joined the American Enterprise Institute for Public Policy Research as a senior fellow and taught at the University of Richmond Law School. He is currently on the faculty of the Ave Maria School of Law in Ann Arbor, Michigan, and is a visiting fellow at the Hoover Institution.

—TO and JRG

Bradlee, Benjamin C(rowninshield)
(1921–   ) *journalist, author*

Benjamin Bradlee was born on August 26, 1921, in Boston, Massachusetts. Bradlee developed an early interest in politics and news reporting through his family, staunch Massachusetts Republicans, and at his prep school, St. Mark's in Southborough, Massachusetts, where Bradlee landed his first newspaper job, copy boy on the *Beverly (Mass.) Evening Times*. He entered Harvard College in 1939 and wrote for the *Harvard Crimson*. After graduation and a stint in the U.S. Navy, he helped launch the *New Hampshire Sunday News* in Manchester, N.H. He sold his interest in the paper in 1948 and became a police reporter for the *Washington Post*. In 1951 he left the *Post* to become a press aide at the U.S. embassy in Paris but returned to journalism in 1953 when he was hired by *Newsweek* as chief European correspondent.

In 1957 Bradlee was transferred to Washington, D.C., where he became a lasting friend of then senator John F. Kennedy. The relationship boosted Bradlee's career and *Newsweek*'s circulation. The *Post*, in the midst of reorganization under publisher KATHARINE GRAHAM, persuaded Bradlee to return as deputy managing editor.

He soon became the paper's managing editor and hired such political reporters as David Harwood and former *New York Times* newsman David Broder to enliven the sometimes colorless product. On September 30, 1968, Bradlee was named vice president and executive editor.

His plan to enhance the *Post*'s image and make it the nation's most respected paper suffered a sharp blow in 1971 when the *Times* became the first paper to publish the *Pentagon Papers*, a secret study of the Vietnam War. The *Post* obtained a copy of the classified Defense Department documents three days after the *Times*.

The paper's image improved after a police report about a break-in at the Democratic National Committee's Watergate headquarters set in motion a story that would topple the Nixon administration and bring a Pulitzer Prize to the *Post*. Bradlee pushed his senior editors to get complete details on the break-in from the beginning, despite the administration's characterization that the incident was just a "third-rate burglary." The *Post* ran 80 column inches about the burglary on June 18, 1972, the day after the break-in.

Bradlee was not dismayed when others, both on the *Post* and outside it, disagreed with his emphasis on the story. "Editors throughout the country really downplayed the story," Bradlee said, "as a vagary of the *Post*." He allowed two young reporters, BOB WOODWARD and CARL BERNSTEIN, to work full-time on the story and defended them inside the hierarchy of the paper as the complex details of their story linked the break-in to the president. In May 1973 the *Post* broke the details of the cover-up that followed the break-in and of White House involvement in several other scandals. The *Post* named top administration officials in connection with the illegal acts.

The White House retaliated by limiting *Post* contacts and denouncing both the paper and Bradlee. Senator ROBERT DOLE (R-Kan.), head of the Republican National Committee, called Bradlee a "Kennedy coat-holder," and White House press secretary RON ZEIGLER said the *Post* practiced "shabby journalism" based on "hearsay and innuendo." As the administration sank, however, *Post* stories held up, and the paper received the Pulitzer Prize for public service in 1973.

Bradlee retired as the *Post*'s managing editor in 1991. He now serves as that paper's vice president.

—BO

Brennan, Peter J(oseph)
(1918–1996) *secretary of Labor*

Brennan was born in a New York City tenement on May 24, 1918. Following his graduation from high school, he became a painter and jointed the Painters, Decorators, and Paperhangers of America. During this period he began attending the City College of New York on a part-time basis, receiving a degree in business administration in the early 1950s. Brennan saw action in the navy during World War II and then resumed his career in the painting trade. He rose gradually in the union movement, eventually becoming head of the Building and Construction Trades Council of Greater New York by the late 1950s.

Brennan came to national prominence as a result of a series of violent confrontations between student demonstrators and New York "hard hats" in May 1970. Following the Cambodian invasion, a series of antiwar demonstrations occurred protesting the fatal shootings at Kent State and Jackson State colleges. At a rally on Wall Street on May 8, 200 well-organized construction workers violently broke up the student protest, leaving 70 bloody victims, including three policemen; six workers were arrested. Brennan was credited with organizing the attack and a series of confrontations that occurred over the next five days. His efforts culminated on March 20, when approximately 100,000 construction, longshore, and office workers rallied at City Hall in support of President RICHARD NIXON's war policies. The demonstration was officially sponsored by Brennan's Building and Construction Trades Council. Brennan supported Nixon in the 1972 presidential election and rallied traditional Democratic labor support behind the Republican incumbent.

Three weeks after his overwhelming victory, on November 29, 1972, Nixon nominated Brennan to be secretary of labor to succeed

I. D. HODGSON. Not since Martin P. Durkin, former president of the plumbers' union, held the position under Eisenhower, had a trade unionist been secretary. The nomination received only lukewarm approval by GEORGE MEANY, president of the AFL-CIO. It was strongly criticized by civil rights leaders who felt that Brennan had obstructed integration of the building trades in New York. Nevertheless, Brennan was overwhelmingly confirmed by the Senate on January 31, 1973.

During the two years Brennan held his post, he became fully embroiled in the major issues affecting the Nixon administration. His stand on wage-price control policies and support of Nixon during the Watergate crisis alienated him from many leaders of organized labor.

Despite his initial opposition to the plan, Brennan supported the president's program to raise the minimum wage but set a lower rate for youths during 1973. He alienated labor further by recommending that the public employment program established by the Emergency Employment Act of 1971 be phased out as unemployment dropped. Yet in 1974 he introduced administration plans to find summer jobs for youths and presented a minimum wage bill that contained a compromise on the issue of substandard wages for youths.

On April 31, 1974, federal wage-price controls, which had been in effect since August 1971, were suspended, precipitating the greatest strike wave since World War II. Brennan urged workers not to strike and accept voluntary wage restraint in the face of mounting inflation.

Brennan favored collective bargaining and voluntary arbitration as a major tool in cutting down strike activity. He did, however, strongly oppose compulsory arbitration. While he supported workers' right to strike, he also endorsed the management-labor collaboration efforts of the president's Commission for Industrial Peace.

The Watergate crisis put Brennan in a difficult position. The AFL-CIO called repeatedly for Nixon's impeachment because he had created a "special and personal secret police" and in Meany's words used "tools of repression" to violate individual rights. Brennan sought to neutralize this criticism by insisting that "labor should not lead these attacks" against the president. He implored organized labor to stand by Nixon, insisting that the president "could make mistakes like anyone else" and that until Nixon was proven guilty "we have to work within the administration."

During the early months of the Ford presidency, Brennan helped formulate the administration's plans to create jobs as unemployment rose. He served on the newly created Council of Wage and Price Stability, formed to help consolidate administration anti-inflation policy. In September 1974 Brennan outlined administration plans to launch public service jobs if unemployment topped 5.5 percent. He announced that the government would double existing outlays of $500 million to create 100,000 jobs and increase the funding for job creation as unemployment rose. If unemployment rose to 7 percent a $4 billion program would be launched. He also urged workers to accept voluntary wage guidelines as their contribution to fighting inflation. Organized labor opposed these proposals as insufficient to deal with unemployment. They also insisted that they could not comply with the guidelines and keep pace with inflation. As a result of this pressure, Brennan began speeding up dispersal of funds to finance 85,000 public sector jobs and dispatch monies to communities hardest hit by unemployment.

Out of a September economic summit to deal with "stagflation," President GERALD R. FORD announced the creation of two special commissions with Brennan actively connected to both. The top-level Economic Policy Board was established to coordinate federal economic affairs. The second commission, the White

House Labor-Management Committee, was a bipartisan group of 16 labor-management representatives that sought to "help assure effective collective bargaining and promote sound wage and price policies."

Brennan resigned as secretary of labor in February 1975 and reassumed his position as president of the Building and Construction Trades Council. He retired in 1992 and died of lymphatic cancer in 1996.

—DR

Brennan, William J(oseph), Jr.
(1906–1997) *associate justice, U.S. Supreme Court*

Born on April 25, 1906, in Newark, New Jersey, Brennan graduated from the Wharton School of Finance in 1928 and from Harvard Law School in 1931. A labor law specialist who practiced in Newark, he served as a state court judge from 1949 until September 1956, when he was named to the U.S. Supreme Court.

From the start Justice Brennan voted with the Court's liberals. Although not an absolutist or literalist in his approach to the Constitution, Brennan was deeply committed to procedural fairness by the government, and he believed the protection of individual rights from government intrusion to be a primary function of the Court. He took an expansive view of most of the criminal safeguards in the Bill of Rights and favored extending those guarantees to the states. The Court's main spokesman in obscenity cases, Brennan wrote opinions that liberalized this area of the law. He also broadened freedom of the press in a series of rulings that put limits on libel judgments against the media. Justice Brennan was a key member of the Warren Court's activist and liberal majority and the author of some of its most significant opinions. (See *The Eisenhower Years*, *The Kennedy Years*, and *The Johnson Years* volumes.)

On the Burger Court, Brennan's role changed significantly. He became a frequent and vocal dissenter from the decisions of a new, more conservative Court majority. In most of the Court's terms after 1970, Brennan ranked second only to Justice WILLIAM O. DOUGLAS in the number of dissents he entered, and he was identified with Douglas and THURGOOD MARSHALL as part of a liberal trio that protested majority rulings on criminal rights, reapportionment, racial discrimination, and free expression. Because of the antilibertarian trend he perceived on the Supreme Court, Brennan urged litigants to turn to the state courts and state constitutional provisions to secure greater expansion and protection of individual rights.

In criminal cases Brennan opposed Court decisions sanctioning warrantless searches and arrests. He spoke out strongly against limitations on the exclusionary rule, which barred the use of illegally obtained evidence in court. He dissented from February 1971 and December 1975 decisions cutting back on the 1966 *Miranda* ruling. Brennan also protested a May 1972 judgment permitting nonunanimous jury verdicts in state courts, but he did join in June 1970 and June 1973 decisions authorizing juries of less than 12 members. In June 1970 Brennan's opinion for the Court extended the right to counsel to preliminary hearings, and he dissented from a June 1972 ruling limiting the right to counsel at police lineups to those conducted after a defendant's indictment or arraignment. A strong proponent of equal justice for rich and poor, Brennan's majority opinion in a March 1971 case overturned a Texas law limiting punishment for traffic violations to fines for those able to pay but allowing imprisonment of those who could not pay. In June 1972 and July 1976 cases, Brennan argued that the death penalty violated the Eighth Amendment's ban on cruel and unusual punishment because, under current moral standards, it did not comport with human dignity.

Justice Brennan took a broad view of the equal protection clause and voted to overturn laws discriminating against the poor and illegitimate children. In an April 1969 majority opinion, he overturned state residency requirements for welfare as a denial of equal protection and an unconstitutional restriction on the right to travel. Brennan urged a strict standard of review in cases alleging sex discrimination. He wrote the opinion of the Court in several cases in the 1970s invalidating distinctions between men and women in military dependency benefits, in Social Security law, and in state laws governing the sale of liquor. In racial discrimination cases, Brennan maintained an activist position. His opinion in a March 1976 case held that under the 1964 Civil Rights Act, an individual denied employment by a company because of race and then later hired by the company may be awarded seniority retroactive to the date of his or her initial job application.

Brennan insisted that the government use fair procedures in taking away from an individual any benefit or entitlement. In a March 1970 majority opinion, he ruled that welfare recipients were entitled to a hearing before their benefits could be cut off. He also voted to grant hearings to debtors before their wages or property was seized by creditors, to drivers before revocation of their licenses for involvement in an accident, to federal civil service and municipal employes before dismissal, and to public school students before a disciplinary suspension.

The justice supported the one-man, one-vote standard for legislative apportionment and, in an April 1969 majority opinion, ruled that no deviation from that standard, no matter how small, was acceptable in congressional districting without strong justification. He objected to February and June 1973 decisions that held that state legislative apportionment did not have to meet the same exacting degree of compliance.

In First Amendment cases Brennan continued to vote in favor of individual rights. In a plurality opinion in a June 1976 suit, he held patronage firings of public employes a violation of their rights of freedom of belief and association. The justice further expanded the protection of the press from libel judgments in a June 1971 ruling and objected in June 1974 and March 1976 when the majority narrowed this protection in cases involving private citizens rather than public figures or officials. Brennan also dissented from several June 1973 decisions in which the Court gave the states greater leeway to regulate allegedly obscene material. In a significant departure from his earlier position in such cases, Brennan said that the Court's attempts to establish a clear, workable definition of obscenity had failed. Rejecting his own past opinions, he urged the Court to abandon the effort and to overturn all obscenity laws for willing adult audiences. The only Roman Catholic on the bench, Brennan advocated strict separation of church and state and repeatedly voted against state aid to parochial schools.

After the ABE FORTAS affair in 1969, Brennan gave up virtually all off-the-bench activities. He became the senior justice on the Court following William O. Douglas's retirement in 1975. Brennan retired in 1990; only Douglas had written more opinions. From 1990 to 1994 Brennan taught at the Georgetown University Law Center. In July 1997 he died in a nursing home in Arlington, Virginia.

—CAB

Brezhnev, Leonid Ilich
(1906–1982) *general secretary of the Communist Party of the Soviet Union*

Born in the Ukraine, Brezhnev was a land surveyor in the 1920s. He joined the Communist

Party in 1931, studied at the Dniprodzerzhinsk Metallurgical Institute (graduating in 1935), and worked throughout the 1930s as both a director of a technical school and in a series of positions within the party. By 1939 he had risen to the post of secretary of the regional committee of Dnipropetrovsk. During World War II he rose in rank until he became a major general and the head of the political commissars on the Ukrainian front. After the war he advanced through the party ranks until he was a member of the party's central committee and a candidate for election to the Politburo. However, the death of Joseph Stalin in March 1953 slowed Brezhnev's progress; he was stripped of his positions on the central committee and became the deputy head of the political department of the Ministry of Defense. However, Nikita Khrushchev, who emerged from the post-Stalin party struggle as the Soviet premier, resurrected Brezhnev's career by making him second secretary of the Kazakhstan Communist Party, a position from where Brezhnev vigorously implemented Khrushchev's agricultural policies; by 1957 he had been reinstated to his posts on the central committee and had been elected to the Politburo; in 1960 he became chairman of the Presidium of the Supreme Soviet. In 1964 Brezhnev participated in the coup that overthrew Khrushchev from power; after a period of joint leadership with Premier Alexei Kosygin, Brezhnev, now the general secretary of the Communist Party of the Soviet Union, surfaced as the de facto leader of the Soviet state.

Brezhnev's forte was foreign and national security affairs; later observers, most notably Mikhail Gorbachev, would blame Brezhnev for ignoring the Soviet economy, thus bringing on the calamitous situation of the 1980s that led to the fall of the Soviet Union. An unabashed hard-liner, Brezhnev masterminded the buildup of the Soviet military until it was at rough parity with that of the United States. His enforcement

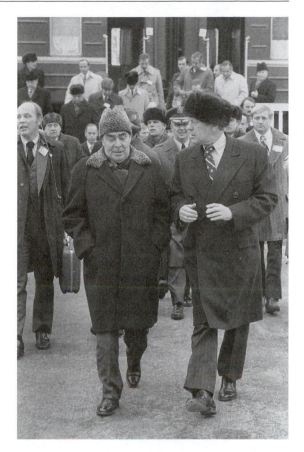

President Ford (right) and Soviet general secretary Leonid I. Brezhnev during the president's trip to Vladivostok, November 23, 1974 *(Ford Library)*

of the "Brezhnev Doctrine"—which contended that the Soviet Union had the duty to intervene militarily if one of its satellites was threatened from without—was used to justify the Soviet invasion of Czechoslovakia in 1968, thus ending that nation's attempt to moderate its socialist state—the "Prague Spring." Brezhnev also was well noted for his unilateral military assistance to satellite nations who were challenging the United States, most notably North Vietnam. Thus, it came as a considerable surprise when in 1971 Brezhnev agreed to open a discourse with President Nixon that might lead to an easing of tensions between their two nations. This move toward détente was consummated by Nixon's 1972 visit to the Soviet Union and the negotiation of a Strategic Arms Limitations Treaty (SALT I, signed in May 1972) with the United States. During the Ford administration, Brezhnev committed his nation, at least on paper, to respect worldwide human rights when it signed the Helsinki Accords (1975).

However, when a SALT II treaty was rejected by the U.S. Senate, Brezhnev retaliated by scuttling détente, invading Afghanistan (December 1979), and aiding in the suppression of the Polish Solidarity movement. Brezhnev died in 1982 at age 75.

—JRG

Brinegar, Claude S(tout)
(1926–) *secretary of transportation*

Claude Brinegar was born on December 16, 1926, in Rockport, California, and joined the air force in 1945 for a two-year tour. He graduated from Stanford in 1950 and received his Ph.D. there four years later. Brinegar was an economic consultant before joining the Union Oil Company of California in 1953. He worked at Union Oil for 20 years, rising to president of the gasoline division and member of the company's board of directors.

At the start of his second term in 1972, President NIXON nominated Brinegar to be the nation's third secretary of transportation, succeeding JOHN VOLPE. Brinegar was considered an unknown political quantity, but observers, citing his association with Union Oil, saw him as a conservative addition to the cabinet. The Highway Action Coalition, an antihighway lobby, said it was "outraged" at the nomination because of Union Oil's involvement in the oil spill off Santa Barbara in 1966. The lobby also pointed out that the oil company had contributed $30,000 in the early 1970s toward the defeat of propositions in California that would have allowed the

state's gasoline taxes to be used for mass transit. At his confirmation hearings, however, Brinegar pleaded unfamiliarity with the issues and declined to say whether federal highway funds should be used for mass transit or to comment on oil pollution. The Senate confirmed his nomination in January 1973.

During his tenure, Brinegar was deeply involved in the question of mass transit subsidies. In 1973 both houses of Congress passed different versions of a bill authorizing $800 million of the Highway Trust Fund to provide operating subsidies for deficit-ridden urban mass transit systems. Brinegar testified that he supported the use of Highway Trust Fund monies for capital expenditures, but he reiterated the administration's opposition to the federal underwriting of operating expenses, saying this would be the "easy way out" and merely encourage inefficiency and an "accelerating subsidy program." The House-Senate conference, fearing a presidential veto, postponed further action until the following year.

Congress began consideration of the same measure in 1974. Brinegar, though he now agreed to the principle of subsidized operating expenses, unexpectedly denounced the bill as "heavily weighted to a handful of big cities with large and expensive rail transit systems" and said he had urged the president to veto the measure. After a series of complex legislative maneuvers, the House Public Works Committee returned a bill that apportioned more funds to smaller cities wishing to expand their transit facilities, while sharply cutting funds to the larger cities, especially New York. The bill broadened the scope of the earlier proposal, extending it from two to six years as the administration had urged, but it authorized $20.4 billion, which Brinegar said was excessive. In the first major success of President FORD's policy of fighting inflation by curbing federal spending, Congress reduced the appropriation to $11.3 billion, and Ford signed the bill in November.

Faced in 1973 with the near-bankruptcy of several railroads, including Penn Central, serving the populous Northeast, Brinegar proposed a reorganization plan that depended on private financing. Declaring that the problem must "be solved within the broad framework of the private sector," Brinegar advocated a pruning of unprofitable lines and the establishment of a board, whose members would be named by the president, that would select the carriers to serve the remaining "essential" routes. Later in the year he modified his plan to include more public funding and participation in the new system. In the meantime the Federal Railroad Administration announced a $17 million loan to Penn Central.

In December Congress passed a version of the administration bill, reorganizing Penn Central and six other bankrupt railroads in the Northeast into one profitable system. A Federal National Railway Association would plan and finance the network and have the authority to raise $1 billion in federally backed bonds. Brinegar first opposed some provisions as too expensive, but faced with deteriorating trackage and a larger role projected for railroads because of the energy crisis, he reversed himself and endorsed the measure. Labor organizations objected to the proposed abandonment of more than 15,000 miles of track, and industry spokesmen said that the plan was a step toward nationalization. Brinegar replied that the remaining trackage could handle 96 percent of the traffic currently carried and that although the government might eventually have to take over the railroads, they should not "be permitted to slide into the morass of nationalization."

In other financially troubled areas of public transportation, Brinegar tried to follow a policy of government support short of direct subsidies or takeover. In September 1974 he announced the government's refusal to pay a monthly subsidy of $10.2 million to Pan American Airways, which had lost $174 million since 1968. Instead he outlined a strategy of belt-tightening, international fare hikes, and consolidation of competitive routes with other airlines. Later in 1974 Brinegar met with auto industry officials to work out a long-range program for increasing fuel efficiency. Although the plan was a voluntary one, Brinegar said it was no "sweetheart deal." Gasoline usage in 1974, he said, was 5 million barrels per day, a per-auto average of 14 miles per gallon (mpg). The administration's goal was 19.6 mpg for 1980 model cars, which he said could be accomplished by smaller automobiles and engines and simple design changes.

In December, as part of a gradual transition from a Nixon to a Ford cabinet, Brinegar resigned effective February 1975 and returned to Union Oil. He was replaced by WILLIAM T. COLEMAN, a Philadelphia transportation lawyer. Brinegar was elected senior vice president of Union Oil and served on the transition from the JIMMY CARTER to the RONALD REAGAN administration. After his retirement from Union Oil, Brinegar was elected to the board of directors of Conrail.

—FLM

Brooke, Edward W(illiam)
(1919–   ) *member of the Senate*

Born in Washington, D.C., on October 26, 1919, Brooke was the son of a prosperous Veterans Administration lawyer. He received a bachelor of science degree from Howard University in 1941, served in the army during World War II, and graduated from Boston University's law school with LL.B. and LL.M. degrees in 1948 and 1949, respectively. During the 1950s Brooke practiced law and made several unsuccessful attempts for state office.

Brooke was elected attorney general of Massachusetts in 1962 and reelected two years later with a plurality of almost 800,000 votes, the largest margin of victory of any Republican in the country that year. He was a speaker at the 1964 Republican National Convention in San Francisco but declined to endorse presidential candidate BARRY GOLDWATER.

In 1966 Brooke became the first black in history to be elected to the U.S. Senate by popular vote. His success in defeating liberal Endicott Peabody by more than 4,000 votes was widely attributed to a singular ability to defuse the issue of his race. As a senator Brooke was mildly critical of the Johnson administration's Vietnam policies. In January 1967, in a move that puzzled his critics and admirers alike, he stated after a visit to Indochina that suspension of the U.S. bombing in North Vietnam would not produce fruitful negotiations. It was widely thought at the time that Brooke had succumbed to the famous Johnson "treatment" of persuasion and pressure. (See *The Johnson Years* volume.)

Although Brooke had campaigned vigorously for the NIXON-AGNEW ticket in 1968, he soon found himself clashing with the administration on substantive issues. In 1969 he opposed the Supreme Court nomination of CLEMENT W. HAYNSWORTH and was considered a significant force in Haynsworth's ultimate rejection by the Senate in November of that year. He also opposed the nomination of G. HARROLD CARSWELL to the High Court in 1970. Carswell's "self-proclaimed conservatism," Brooke said, "cannot excuse the behavior and decisions which tend more to confirm than to contradict the thrust of his initial views on racial supremacy." Using a similar argument, Brooke unsuccessfully challenged WILLIAM H. REHNQUIST's appointment to the Court in 1971.

In January 1970 Brooke strongly criticized the Nixon administration's civil rights record. He stated that the administration had not acted vigorously enough on desegregation of public schools. He charged that the decision not to seek an extension of the 1965 Voting Rights Act represented a step backward for the cause of civil rights.

In March of the same year, Brooke declared that the White House had made a "cold, calculated political decision" to shun the needs of blacks in the United States in favor of pursuing a "southern strategy" of wooing southern whites to ensure reelection in 1972. Brooke further stated that he and other Republicans who had worked for Nixon's election in 1968 because of his promise to "bring us together" were now "deeply concerned about the administration's lack of commitment to equal opportunities." It was Brooke's belief that his clashes with the administration over its civil rights record and Supreme Court nominations had greatly damaged his effectiveness as a senator and resulted in cutbacks and impoundments of his housing legislation.

Throughout his career Brooke was particularly interested in housing legislation, which became the cornerstone of his work in the Senate. Brooke's most important achievements in housing were the proposals he offered to a 1969 housing bill. As passed in the 1970 Housing and Urban Development Act, the Brooke Amendment provided that tenants in federally assisted public housing would have to pay no more than 25 percent of their income for rent. The act also required the federal government to pay the difference between the 25 percent ceiling and the housing authorities' operating expenses and provided $75 million for the management of housing facilities to improve maintenance and services. Under an amendment introduced by Brooke to the 1972 Housing Act, low-income tenants of government-subsidized housing in Massachusetts received extended allowances to assist them in buying standard housing.

As a legislator, Brooke also showed a special interest in reforming the nation's system of justice. In 1971 alone he sponsored eight bills that included provisions for establishing training centers for prison officials, for accelerating court trials, for orienting prisons toward manpower and community correctional programs, and for rehabilitating juvenile delinquents.

In foreign policy matters Brooke voted a generally liberal line. He supported every antiwar amendment from 1970 until the end of the Vietnam War. In 1972 Brooke introduced an amendment calling for the withdrawal of U.S. troops from Indochina within four month's of the bill's passage pending release of U.S. prisoners of war. The Senate adopted the measure in August.

On April 22, 1973, Brooke spoke out for the first time on the Nixon administration's deepening Watergate crisis. He stated that Nixon could not escape the responsibility for Watergate "under any circumstances." On November 4 Brooke became the first Republican senator to publicly call for Nixon's resignation. "There is no question that President Nixon has lost his effectiveness as the leader of this country, primarily because he has lost the confidence of the people of the country, and I think . . . that he should step down, should tender his resignation." Brooke added that he did not know of anything that the president could do to reverse the situation.

On May 22, 1974, Brooke publicly questioned the wisdom of Nixon's planned summit meeting with Soviet leader LEONID BREZHNEV in June when "the question of impeachment could be coming to a head in the House of Representatives." Almost three months later, on August 8, Brooke and Republican representative John H. Buchanan Jr. of Alabama introduced companion resolutions expressing "a sense of Congress" that Nixon should not be prosecuted after he left office but that the measure would not be binding on the prosecu-

tion or the courts. Brooke explained the next day, however, that he would not press for passage of the resolution because of the lack of contrition and confession in Nixon's televised resignation announcement.

Brooke maintained cordial relations with President FORD, and was viewed as a possible running mate in 1976 until he removed his name from consideration. Brooke seconded Ford's nomination for president at the Republican National Convention in Kansas City on August 19, 1976. Brooke lost his reelection bid in 1978, in part as a result of his controversial divorce, which revealed possible perjury in statements over loan dispositions during the proceedings. The Senate Ethics Committee discussed the possibility of hearings into Brooke's financial affairs. But with this defeat the committee announced it would not institute a probe because the panel had lost its jurisdiction over Brooke. After his defeat Brooke chaired the National Low-Income Housing Coalition. Diagnosed with breast cancer in September 2002, Brooke lives in Florida.

—FHM

Brown, Edmund G(erald), Jr.
(1938–) *governor of California*

Born on April 7, 1938, in San Francisco, Edmund Jr., the only son of California governor "Pat" Brown, attended parochial schools and spent four years at a Jesuit seminary in California. He obtained his B.A. degree from Berkeley in 1961 and his law degree from Yale in 1964. After spending a year as a law clerk for the California supreme court, Brown took an extensive trip through Central and South America. Upon his return in 1966 he joined the Los Angeles law firm of Tuttle and Taylor.

During the late 1960s Brown became active in efforts to organize migrant workers and antiwar groups. In 1970 he won the election for secretary of state in California and was the only Democrat to survive a Republican sweep of state offices that year.

Over the years the position of secretary of state had become unimportant, but Brown used his powers in a series of bold, highly publicized reform campaigns that soon made his nickname, "Jerry," as well known among voters as his father's had been. He filed suit against three major oil companies—Standard Oil, Gulf, and Mobil—charging that they had made illegal contributions of up to $95,000 to politicians who opposed diverting gasoline tax revenues into rapid-transit development funds. He issued new, stricter regulations on the reporting of campaign funds by candidates for office in California. Angry legislators responded by cutting Brown's budget, but this only made him more popular with the voters.

In March 1972 Brown initiated a court action against the International Telephone and Telegraph Corp. ITT had become involved in a major scandal following reports by columnist JACK ANDERSON that the corporation had offered to contribute to the upcoming Republican Convention in San Diego in return for a favorable settlement of an antitrust suit. Brown's suit sought to prohibit ITT from sponsoring the convention and to return the funds already committed. Eventually the Republicans decided to hold their convention in Miami instead of San Diego.

In January 1974 Brown's office charged that a deed for President RICHARD M. NIXON's gift of his vice presidential papers to the National Archives had been falsely predated to avoid a federal law prohibiting tax deductions for such gifts. It was not the first confrontation between Brown and the president. He had already become one of the first politicians demanding the impeachment of Richard Nixon on the grounds that the president had lied to Congress about the conduct of the war in Southeast Asia.

In January 1974 Brown announced his candidacy for California's Democratic gubernatorial nomination. His platform called for restrictions on campaign spending and lobbying activities. Brown won the primary against such prominent opponents as San Francisco mayor Joseph Alioto and California state assembly speaker Robert Moretti. In the general election campaign against Republican state controller Houston Flournoy, Brown pledged to bring a "new spirit" to state government.

Brown's positions were a curious amalgam of liberal and conservative themes. He supported abortion rights for women and aid to California's farm workers and poor. But Brown also expressed doubts about increased government spending to solve social ills. He adopted a strict law-and-order stand, stating at one point that prisons were for punishment, not rehabilitation. In November Brown was elected by a narrow margin.

Brown swiftly set a new, austere image in his administration. He dispensed with elaborate inauguration ceremonies, turned down the customary chauffeured limousine, and refused to occupy the new governor's mansion. He canceled a raise for himself and cut the salary of his staff. Brown selected his staff not from the established party functionaries but from generally young, well-educated poverty lawyers and consumer advocates.

Brown established a liberal reputation as governor. In the spring of 1975 he personally oversaw the passage of a major bill of his administration, the farm labor relations measure. It set up the machinery for secret ballot elections of worker representatives who were to monitor the labor practices of growers. The bill also sanctioned consumer boycotts, one of the key strategies of the United Farm Workers. Later Brown signed a bill reducing to a misdemeanor the possession of an ounce or less of marijuana. In 1976 Brown signed into law a right-to-die bill permitting adult patients suffering from terminal illness or injury to make a "living will" that would authorize doctors to turn off life-sustaining equipment if it was evident that death was inevitable. In 1977 Brown vetoed a death penalty bill, but the veto was successfully overridden by the legislature.

Brown's theme of limited governmental powers and his image of thrift and austerity struck a responsive chord with voters. In December 1975 they gave him an approval rating of 84 percent. Critics, however, including some former members of his staff, claimed that behind his media image Brown was an indecisive leader who avoided grappling with the state's more complex problems. Yet as the 1976 presidential election year began, Brown was one of the most popular politicians in the country.

That year Brown entered several presidential primaries. In Maryland he called for "a new generation of leadership" and a foreign policy with a "moral base." He characterized the campaign of former Georgia governor JIMMY CARTER as "all just smiles." Carter accused Brown of "not really running for president," but merely acting as part of a "stop Carter" movement organized by the Democratic Party establishment. In May Brown defeated Carter in Maryland by a substantial margin. Later that month, in Nevada, he defeated the state's former governor and placed a strong third in Oregon, considered a good showing since Brown had conducted only a write-in campaign in that state. After Brown visited New Jersey, pledging a presidency that "would restore honesty to the White House and put a paycheck in every pocket," the state's uncommitted delegates threw their support to him and HUBERT HUMPHREY.

Victories in California and New Jersey in early June brought Brown's total delegate count to 225 after a campaign that cost $1 million. Carter had done poorly in the final series of primaries, but his early lead was so strong that his opponents withdrew one by one and announced their support for Carter's candidacy. Brown was one of the few holdouts. In a paid national TV address in June, Brown repeated his familiar themes but added that he would "enthusiastically support" Carter should the governor win the nomination. In July Brown finished third at the Democratic Convention. During the fall he campaigned across California with Carter, referring to the former governor as a "fine, dedicated human individual" and predicting Carter would be "a great president." Although Carter was victorious in the November election, California gave its electoral votes to his opponent, GERALD FORD.

In 1978 Brown ran for governor and was reelected. (See *The Carter Years* volume.) In 1980 he ran unsuccessfully for the Democratic presidential nomination. In 1982 he ran unsuccessfully for a seat in the U.S. Senate. In 1989 he became chairman of the California State Democratic Party, a position he held until 1991. In 1992 he ran unsuccessfully for the Democratic presidential nomination. In 1998 he was elected mayor of Oakland, California.

—MDQ

Bruce, David K(irkpatrick) E(ste)

(1898–1977)   *chief negotiator, Paris peace talks; chief liaison officer to the People's Republic of China; ambassador to the North Atlantic Treaty Organization*

Born on February 12, 1898, into one of Maryland's most prominent families, David K. E. Bruce enjoyed a comfortable childhood. He left Princeton University in 1917 during his sophomore year to enlist in the army. After completing his law studies at the University of Maryland, Bruce was admitted to that state's bar in 1921 and elected to the Maryland state legislature in 1924. During the 1930s Bruce became a "gentleman farmer" in Virginia and was elected to Virginia's house of delegates in 1939. Bruce helped in the formation of the Office of Strategic Services (OSS) during World War II and commanded the OSS in Europe from 1943 to 1945. Following the war Bruce became an important diplomat in Europe and was the only ambassador to hold three major posts: France from 1949 to 1952; West Germany from 1957 to 1959; and Great Britain from 1961 to 1969. (See *The Truman Years, The Eisenhower Years, The Kennedy Years,* and *The Johnson Years* volumes.)

In July 1970 President NIXON called Bruce out of retirement to replace HENRY CABOT LODGE JR. as chief negotiator at the Paris peace talks. At his first session with the Communists, on August 6, Bruce expressed confidence that an agreement could be reached provided that both sides negotiated with sincerity and quiet resolve. On September 17 the chief delegate of the National Liberation Front, Mme. Nguyen Thi Binh, made the first Communist initiative in 16 months. Although pressing for a reunified Vietnam, the Communists suggested a June 1971 deadline for American troop withdrawal rather than their oft-repeated demand for an immediate pullout. Once the United States accepted this deadline, Binh would agree to discuss the prisoner-of-war issue. The Communists also expressed a willingness to negotiate the fate of Saigon's government, provided Nguyen Van Thieu, Nguyen Cao Ky, and Premier Tran Thien Khiem were excluded. Bruce interpreted these proposals as "old wine in new bottles."

On October 8 Bruce submitted President Nixon's five-point peace plan to the Communist delegation in Paris. Describing the plan as an effort to deceive world opinion, the Communists rejected the proposals, which called for a cease-fire in place, expansion of the peace conference to include Laos and Cambodia, negotiation of a timetable for U.S. troop withdrawal, a political settlement to meet the needs

of all South Vietnamese, and an immediate release of all prisoners of war. Bruce continued as chief negotiator until July 31, 1971, when he resigned for health reasons. Throughout his stay in Paris, Bruce continually blamed the Communists for not negotiating in good faith and attacked their treatment of war prisoners. Bruce was replaced by William J. Porter.

During his historic 1972 visit to mainland China, Nixon found the Communist Red Chinese reluctant to establish liaison offices because of the Vietnam War. In February 1973, three weeks after a cease-fire was declared in Vietnam, Secretary of State HENRY KISSINGER was again in Beijing. Many observers found it no coincidence that Chou En-lai issued a communiqué stating that the time was now "ripe for accelerating normalization of relations."

On March 15, 1973, Nixon summoned Bruce to head the U.S. liaison office in Beijing. Bruce's staff of 20 included two notable China hands: Kissinger's adviser John Holdridge and the State Department's director of Asian Communist Affairs, Alfred Jenkins. Bruce remained in Beijing from May 1973 to September 1974, when President GERALD R. FORD replaced him with Republican Party national chairman GEORGE H. W. BUSH. While in China Bruce dealt mainly with cultural exchanges and trade matters. A major unresolved issue during this period was the recovery of $78 million in Chinese assets that were frozen in the United States and approximately $195 million in U.S. claims for private property confiscated by the Communists in 1949.

With a sense of duty that made virtually any call to public service obligatory, Bruce accepted President Ford's request in November 1974 to serve as ambassador to the North Atlantic Treaty Organization at its Brussels headquarters, where he remained until his retirement from the Foreign Service in January 1976. On February 10, 1976, President Ford presented Bruce with the nation's highest civilian honor, the Medal of Freedom, for his 50 years of distinguished diplomatic service. Bruce died of a heart attack on December 5, 1977, at age 79.

—TML

Buchanan, Patrick J(oseph), (Jr.)
(1938–   ) *special assistant to the president, consultant to the president*

Patrick Buchanan was born on November 2, 1938, in Washington, D.C. He graduated with a B.A. in English from Georgetown University in 1961 and received his M.S. in journalism from Columbia the following year. He then became an editorial writer with the *St. Louis Globe Democrat*. He was named the paper's assistant editorial editor in 1964. In 1966 Buchanan became an assistant to RICHARD M. NIXON in New York. At the time the former vice president, who was a partner in a Wall Street law firm, was campaigning for Republican victories in congressional and state elections in anticipation of a run for the presidency in 1968. In 1967 Buchanan accompanied the future candidate on a trip to Africa and the Middle East, one of four such foreign study tours Nixon made to prepare for the 1968 election. During the campaign Buchanan worked as a speechwriter.

Buchanan came to the White House with the new administration as a senior writer on the research and writing staff headed by James Keogh. Nixon would turn to Buchanan for his generally conservative analysis and hard-hitting style. He prepared the president's tough speech defending the military service from "unprecedented attack," which was delivered at the Air Force Academy in June 1969. In April 1970 he drafted Nixon's address explaining the U.S. military incursion into Cambodia.

A strong critic of the press, Buchanan wrote Vice President SPIRO AGNEW's blister-ing November 13, 1969, attack on the three major TV networks' news coverage in which he protested the kind of "instant analysis and querulous criticism" that had followed the president's speech to the nation on Vietnam 10 days earlier. Agnew questioned the validity of a "small band of network commentators and self-appointed analysts" inheriting an audience of 70 million Americans gathered to hear the president's address. Again during the 1970 campaign Buchanan was enlisted to assist the vice president in his carefully articulated criticism of press coverage of the administration.

Buchanan played an important conceptual role in the off-year elections. He helped to design a Republican campaign strategy aimed principally at disaffected Democrats, including blue-collar workers and working-class white ethnics. In 1971 Buchanan drew up a provocative memorandum warning that on such traditional Republican issues as balancing the budget and reducing the federal bureaucracy, President Nixon was not doing enough and risked being labeled a liberal. He urged the administration to concentrate on constructing "the new majority," which, in his 1973 book of the same name, he identified as an alliance of disparate political groups moving away from New Deal–type coalitions and toward the decentralization of power from the federal to the local level.

In 1973 Buchanan was named a consultant to the president. His time became increasingly devoted to Watergate. In April of that year he stated in a memorandum to Nixon that aides H. R. HALDEMAN and JOHN D. EHRLICHMAN should voluntarily leave if they could no longer maintain their effectiveness. He later pushed for their resignation. Buchanan was the first witness when the Senate Watergate Committee opened the second phase of its probe, in September 1973, focusing on alleged political sabotage during the 1972 presidential campaign. The committee majority set out to show that the policy groundwork for alleged campaign sabotage in 1972 had been firmly laid in early political strategy memorandums. The committee produced memos revealing Buchanan's urgings to Nixon supporters to knock out one Democratic contender—Senator EDMUND MUSKIE (D-Me.)—and to elevate another—Senator GEORGE MCGOVERN (D-S.D.)—considered a weaker challenge to the president.

Buchanan denied any illegal or unethical tactics. He told the committee that he had been willing to use "anything that was not immoral, unethical, illegal, or unprecedented in previous Democratic campaigns." He asserted that he had neither suggested nor participated in anything beyond acceptable political operations. He declared that Nixon had won his record landslide reelection not because of Watergate and dirty tricks but in spite of them.

The Supreme Court on July 24, 1974, ordered President Nixon to surrender the tapes of 64 conversations subpoenaed by the special prosecutor. A review of the tapes by White House lawyer J. FRED BUZHARDT JR. led several aides to believe that the transcripts of discussions between Nixon and Haldeman on June 23, 1972, were sufficiently damaging to cause the president to resign. Buchanan was among the aides who successfully argued that it would be better to release the transcripts first and then evaluate the reaction. He reasoned in that way there would be no doubt about whether the resignation was necessary.

After leaving the White House following Nixon's August 1974 resignation, Buchanan wrote a nationally syndicated newspaper column and was a charter member (along with liberal Tom Braden) of the CNN political talk show *Crossfire*. Buchanan returned to active politics in 1989, when he joined RONALD REAGAN's White House speechwriting team. However, Buchanan's persistent attempts to get Reagan to voice a hard conservative line led to tension within the White House, and Buchanan resigned in 1987.

In 1992 Buchanan ran against GEORGE H. W. BUSH for the Republican presidential nomination. In the New Hampshire primary, he finished a surprising second to Bush, garnering 34 percent of the vote. In February 1993 Buchanan founded the American Cause. Buchanan ran again, also unsuccessfully, for the presidency in 1995. Since 1995 Buchanan has been active as a newspaper columnist and media pundit.

—SF and JRG

Buchen, Philip W(illiam)
(1916–2001) *counsel to the president*

Born on February 27, 1916, in Sheboygan, Wisconsin, Philip Buchen received his A.B. from the University of Wisconsin in 1939 and remained at that university to earn his J.D. two years later. He was admitted to the Michigan bar soon after graduation. In November 1941 he opened a law office with fraternity brother GERALD R. FORD. As novices, their clients were primarily indigents whose cases had been referred by local courts. The partnership was short-lived, however; when Ford joined the navy in April 1942, Buchen joined one of Grand Rapids's leading law firms, Butterfield, Keeney, and Amberg. (Buchen had been crippled by polio as a child and was unable to serve in the armed forces during World War II.) He remained in private practice in Grand Rapids through 1974, entering political affairs only as part of the original "Ford for Congress" group in 1948. Buchen also assisted Ford politically in preparing for the proposed vice president's confirmation hearings in 1973.

In March 1974 Buchen came to Washington, D.C., as counsel for the Domestic Council's Committee on the Right of Privacy, a group chaired by Vice President Ford. Two months later Buchen began working with the head of the Office of Telecommunications, Clay Whitehead, for what Ford's old friend saw as the eventual move of the vice president to the presidency. Whitehead and Buchen initially worked without Ford's knowledge. But as the Watergate crisis deepened, they were forced to involve the vice president.

On July 24 the Supreme Court ruled that President Nixon must give potentially damaging tape recordings pertaining to the Watergate burglary to the special prosecutor. Following the release of tape transcripts detailing Nixon's intricate knowledge of and participation in the subversion of efforts to investigate the burglary, Buchen worked closely with Ford on the likely transition. It was Buchen who helped assemble Ford's White House staff and prepare his initial speech on the assumption of office.

Buchen was appointed presidential counsel shortly after Ford became president in August 1974. Immediately after assuming his new position, Buchen became immersed in legal proceedings involving the Watergate burglary investigation and upcoming trial. He and Ford ordered the retention of Nixon's tapes and documents pending the resolution of legal issues raised by the special prosecutor. Buchen at first denied the defendants access to their files; he later permitted them to see the documents but would not allow notes or copies to be made.

Buchen also helped work out an agreement with Nixon's attorney giving the former president ownership and control of material still stored in the White House. The pact was soon challenged by the Reporters' Committee for Freedom of the Press and the American Political Science Association, which sought to keep the papers available for public use. The suit argued that the material was "prepared on government time by government employees in the discharge of their public duties." The mate-

rial was ultimately put in the permanent custody of the General Services Administration.

On September 8, 1974, Ford granted "a full, free, and absolute pardon" to ex-president Nixon. Buchen acted as a liaison between the White House and the various other parties involved; he queried special prosecutor LEON JAWORSKI on the possible timing of a Nixon trial and asked a friend of Ford's to go to San Clemente and meet with Nixon's counsel. Buchen told the press that no demands had been made upon Nixon as a condition for the pardon, which he described as an "act of mercy." Although an admission of guilt was not requested of Nixon, Buchen said that the granting of a pardon "can imply guilt—there is no other reason for granting a pardon."

Buchen served as the president's counsel until Ford left office. He died in Washington, D.C., in 2001.

—RB

Buckley, James L(ane)
(1923–   ) *member of the Senate*

Born on March 9, 1923, in New York City, James Buckley attended Yale College and graduated in 1943. After serving in the navy during World War II, he studied at Yale Law School and completed his degree in 1949. He practiced law in New Haven, Connecticut. Buckley entered political life by managing the unsuccessful campaign of his brother, William F. Buckley Jr., when the latter sought the post of mayor of New York City in 1965.

In 1968 James Buckley ran unsuccessfully as a Conservative Party candidate for the U.S. Senate. He ran again in 1970 and succeeded in defeating CHARLES GOODELL, the Republican incumbent, and the Democratic candidate, Richard Ottinger. Buckley received only 38.7 percent of the vote, but that was enough to gain him the victory. He was aided in his campaign by RICHARD NIXON, whose support in the election had probably been decisive.

Buckley immediately became a leading conservative figure in the Senate. Both in domestic and foreign policy, he spoke for and voted for conservative programs. He was opposed in principle to government programs designed to strengthen the welfare state and to intervene in the management of a free-enterprise economy. He voted against government guarantees to the Lockheed Corp. He fought against federally financed and controlled day care centers. Buckley voted against a federal bail out of New York City and suggested that New York City would be better off if it went into bankruptcy. He cast his ballot against the minimum wage bill of 1974 and opposed increased Social Security benefits and vocational rehabilitation for the handicapped.

Buckley backed strong anticrime measures and drug abuse laws. He opposed the Equal Rights Amendment in 1972 and introduced a constitutional amendment to outlaw abortions except when the mother's life is in danger.

Buckley supported the Nixon and FORD administrations in their Indochina policy. He opposed the McGovern-Hatfield Amendment calling for the withdrawal of U.S. troops from Vietnam by the end of 1971. He also was an advocate of high defense spending. A staunch critic of communism, he advocated a hard-line American foreign policy to deal with the Soviet Union and its allies. He endorsed the preservation of the president's foreign policy prerogatives and voted against the war powers bill and other measures that would weaken the president in the conduct of foreign policy.

On a number of issues, Buckley gathered the support of some liberals. He joined with former senator EUGENE J. MCCARTHY to file a federal court lawsuit challenging the Federal Election Campaign Act Amendments of 1974. In that suit they contended that the federal financing provisions of the act violated con-

stitutional restrictions on federal taxing and spending power, prevented taxpayers from supporting candidates or parties, and discriminated against minor parties and independent candidates.

Buckley supported legislation, moreover, to protect student rights. The "Buckley Amendment" of 1976 gave parents and adult students the right to inspect school records and restricted the rights of institutions to pass on the content of students' files to outsiders.

Buckley became the first conservative to call for Nixon's resignation. He suggested that Nixon resign as "an extraordinary act of statesmanship and courage" because of the Watergate scandals. This statement undermined Nixon supporters who argued that the liberals wanted Nixon to resign.

In 1976 Buckley lost his reelection bid to DANIEL PATRICK MOYNIHAN. He was also defeated for election to the Senate from Connecticut in 1980. From 1981 to 1982 Buckley served as undersecretary for security, science, and technology in the State Department. From 1982 to 1985 he was the seventh president of Radio Free Europe/Radio Liberty. In 1982 he was appointed federal judge of the Washington, D.C., Circuit of the U.S. Court of Appeals, a position he held until 1996. He resides in Sharon, Connecticut.

—HML and JRG

Bunker, Ellsworth
(1894–1984) *ambassador to South Vietnam*

Born in Yonkers, New York, on May 11, 1894, Ellsworth Bunker was the son of a wealthy sugar manufacturer. After graduating from Yale in 1916, Bunker worked for his father's firm, the National Sugar Refining Company, until 1948. Three years later he left business to accept an appointment as ambassador to Argentina.

Through the 1950s and into the 1960s, Bunker handled his diplomatic duties skillfully and gained a reputation as a formidable mediator. He served as ambassador to Italy and to India under President Eisenhower and undertook two special assignments for President Kennedy, mediating armed confrontations in Indonesia and Yemen. Kennedy designated Bunker U.S. representative to the Organization of American States (OAS), and President Johnson approved the appointment, which became official in 1964. (See *The Truman Years, The Eisenhower Years,* and *The Kennedy Years* volumes.)

Bunker approved of OAS programs "designed to enhance the internal security capabilities of the military and police forces of Latin America," and supported U.S. intervention in situations involving threats to the security of the hemisphere. After armed U.S. intervention in the civil war–torn Dominican Republic in 1965, Bunker undertook a year-long assignment as head of a three-man OAS peace mission.

In 1967 President Johnson named Bunker to succeed Henry Cabot Lodge as ambassador to South Vietnam. The appointment was applauded by both "hawks" and "doves." Bunker became one of the strongest supporters of the war in the Johnson administration, severely damaging his reputation as a disinterested mediator. As the number one American in Vietnam, he gave final approval to all important military and political decisions and, according to *The New Republic,* was in large part responsible for the continued U.S. presence in Indochina during the Nixon era. Bunker took an optimistic view of U.S. involvement in the war, asserting that progress was being made even after the disastrous Tet offensive of January 1968. He favored border incursions into Laos and Cambodia and was a strong supporter of the repressive regime of South Vietnamese president Nguyen Van Thieu, whom he regarded as

"an extremely reasonable, open-minded man." (See *The Johnson Years* volume.)

In January 1969 Bunker agreed to stay in his Saigon post at the request of President-elect Richard M. Nixon. He continued to favor U.S. participation in the war and spoke publicly of the progress of the South Vietnamese against the Communists. Bunker supported the 1970 invasion of Cambodia by South Vietnamese and U.S. troops as part of the administration's policy of Vietnamization of the war. The destruction of North Vietnamese bases in that country, he stated, would give "more time to develop the South Vietnamese forces." Fearing political repercussions at home and in Vietnam if the government of Nguyen Van Thieu failed to win a democratic mandate from the Vietnamese people, Bunker worked to give the October 1971 presidential elections in South Vietnam the appearance of a free contest. He urged South Vietnamese vice president Nguyen Cao Ky and General Duong Van Minh to run against Thieu and reportedly offered to finance Minh's campaign. Both men withdrew from the elections, charging U.S. interference and a conspiracy by President Thieu to rig the elections. Thieu ran unopposed and was reelected.

Bunker resigned his Saigon post in March 1973, returning to Washington as ambassador-at-large. He worked closely with Secretary of State HENRY KISSINGER, accompanying Kissinger to Saudi Arabia in a futile effort to seek lower oil prices. In November 1973 Bunker took charge of the deadlocked Panama Canal treaty negotiations. He left in December to head the U.S. delegation to the Geneva Mideast Peace Conference.

Bunker continued his Panama negotiations through the FORD administration, maintaining steady progress at the bargaining table. By the time Sol Linowitz joined Bunker in Panama at the beginning of the JIMMY CARTER administration, most of the work had been done.

Bunker won Pentagon support for the treaty by separating the issues of canal operations and canal defense. On August 10, 1977, the negotiators announced that they had reached an "agreement in principle," and Bunker devoted himself to achieving Senate ratification of the pact. After accompanying President Carter to Panama in June 1978 for ceremonies accompanying the signing of the treaty, the 84-year-old diplomat announced his retirement to his Vermont farm. (See *The Carter Years* volume.) He died in Brattleboro, Vermont, in 1984.

—DAE

Burch, Dean

(1927–1991) *chairman, Federal Communications Commission; special counselor to the president*

Born on December 20, 1927, in Enid, Oklahoma, the son of a federal prison guard, Dean Burch worked his way through the University of Arizona law school, graduating in 1953. From 1955 to 1959 he was administrative assistant to conservative senator BARRY M. GOLDWATER (R-Ariz.) and then entered private law practice. In 1963 Burch left his practice to serve on Goldwater's presidential campaign staff. Following Goldwater's nomination for president at the 1964 Republican National Convention, the senator named Burch chairman of the Republican National Committee (RNC). Burch, who never served in a national campaign, knew little about the committee's operations, but Goldwater felt that his position as chairman would help keep the GOP national organization in conservative hands even if Goldwater lost the election.

As RNC chairman Burch was responsible for running Goldwater's campaign and made most of the major strategy decisions. Unprepared for his leadership role, however, he proved a poor campaign director and failed to efficiently organize the RNC. He antagonized

liberal-moderate Republicans by packing the RNC executive committee with conservative loyalists and brought in his own aides to run the national organization, shattering morale among permanent RNC employees. In the 1964 elections the Republican Party suffered its worst defeat since 1936. Under pressure from Richard M. Nixon and other influential moderate Republicans, Goldwater agreed to Burch's replacement by the nonideological Ray C. Bliss of Ohio. Burch returned to his Phoenix law practice and in 1968 directed Goldwater's successful campaign for reelection to the U.S. Senate. (See *The Johnson Years* volume.)

In September 1969 President NIXON appointed Burch chairman of the Federal Communications Commission (FCC). Before announcing Burch's appointment, the president had cleared it with broadcasting executives, who expected the new chairman, with his conservative ties, to uphold their interests. At first Burch supported the large broadcast companies, who were being threatened for the first time in 42 years by private groups seeking to wrest their licenses. However, Burch soon challenged the power of broadcast industry chiefs in the area of television news commentary. Instead of waiting the customary 30 days, he requested immediate transcripts of network commentaries on President Nixon's November 3 speech on Vietnam. Broadcast executives saw this move as a subtle threat of federal censorship of TV news presentations. On November 14, 1969, Burch again surprised industry chiefs when he endorsed Vice President SPIRO T. AGNEW's attack on the biases of TV news coverage. Democratic congressional leaders protested that Burch was trying to suppress criticism of the Nixon administration and to stifle open news coverage and analysis. Burch denied the charges of federal censorship, stating that he hoped news coverage would change as a result of public pressure and decisions within the industry. Burch's position was supported by liberal Democrats on the FCC, who feared the potential influence of network power and corporate control in biasing news reportage.

In October 1971 Burch and Nicholas Johnson, a liberal FCC member who often opposed Burch's views, appeared together before the Senate Subcommittee on Constitutional Rights to defend the FCC against broadcasters' charges that the commission had interfered with news programming. When Dr. Frank Stanton, president of the Columbia Broadcasting System (CBS), stated that there was "ample evidence" of attempts by government officials to intimidate the press, Burch cited cases in which the FCC had purposely avoided judging controversial news journalism, including the coverage of the 1968 Democratic National Convention and two CBS documentaries, "Hunger in America" and "The Selling of the Pentagon." Burch and Johnson saw the real threat of news censorship as coming from the networks and their attempts to maximize profits. Burch's criticism of the major networks was welcomed by opponents of the Pastore bill, legislation that would have made it even more difficult for small private groups to apply for broadcast licenses.

Burch left the FCC in the winter of 1974 to become presidential counselor for domestic affairs. Political observers saw the move as an attempt by the president, whose involvement in the Watergate scandal had deepened, to shore up his defenses against impeachment. Through the spring of 1974, while Nixon refused to turn over subpoenaed tapes and documents dealing with Watergate to Special Prosecutor LEON JAWORSKI, Burch urged Republicans to remain loyal to the president and to link their political futures to his. In April 1974 Burch assured the RNC that Nixon would soon turn over to the House Judiciary Committee a "massive body of evidence" that would establish the truth of the Watergate affair.

When in May the White House finally released edited transcripts of the Watergate tapes, Burch defended their tone and content to a public appalled by the revelation of the inner workings of the White House. In a letter to the *Chicago Tribune* Burch argued that the transcripts showed "life as it is" in "government, politics, industry, and business." He continued to denounce the deliberations of the House Judiciary Committee as a "black spot on jurisprudence," even as it became clear that both Democrats and Republicans believed Nixon guilty of impeachable offenses.

After Nixon's resignation in August 1974, Burch remained on the White House staff as President GERALD R. FORD's campaign coordinator for the 1974 elections. Although Burch left the president's staff in 1975, he filed the organizing papers for the President Ford Committee with the Federal Elections Commission in June 1976. His major role during the 1976 Ford presidential campaign consisted of his efforts to dissuade his former boss, Senator Goldwater, from supporting California governor RONALD REAGAN for the Republican presidential nomination. From 1975 Burch worked for the Washington law firm of Pierson, Ball and Dowd, which specialized in communications. In 1985 he was named chairman of the U.S. delegation to the World Administrative Radio Conference on Space of the International Telecommunication Union. He died in 1991.

—DAE

Burger, Warren E(arl)

(1907–1995) *judge, U.S. Court of Appeals for the District of Columbia; chief justice of the United States*

Warren Burger was born on September 17, 1907, in St. Paul, Minnesota. Burger worked his way through the St. Paul College of Law, graduating third in his class in 1931. A partner in a St. Paul law firm from 1935 to 1953, he maintained a varied general practice while teaching part time at his alma mater. Burger, a Republican, worked to elect Harold Stassen governor of Minnesota in 1938. He was floor manager for Stassen's unsuccessful presidential bids at the 1948 and 1952 Republican National conventions and shifted his support to Dwight D. Eisenhower at an important moment during the 1952 gathering. Burger was named assistant attorney general in charge of the Civil Division of the Justice Department in 1953. In June 1955 Eisenhower nominated him to a judgeship on the U.S. Court of Appeals for the District of Columbia. Burger was sworn into office in April 1956.

In his 13 years as a circuit judge, Burger developed a reputation as a conservative, particularly in criminal cases. In often articulate, quotable opinions, he opposed the reversal of convictions for what he considered legal technicalities and was a critic of the *Durham* rule, which broadened the definition of criminal insanity. Off the bench Burger challenged various aspects of the American criminal justice system, criticized the Warren Court's approach in criminal rights cases, and urged reform of the penal system. Active in the American Bar Association (ABA), he was a leader in efforts to improve the management and efficiency of the courts.

On May 21, 1969, President RICHARD NIXON nominated Burger as chief justice to replace the retiring Earl Warren. Nixon had made the Warren Court's criminal rights rulings a target during his 1968 campaign and had promised to appoint "strict constructionists" to the bench. He selected Burger for the Court largely because the judge's record demonstrated a philosophy of judicial conservatism, especially on criminal issues. Burger's appointment was confirmed by the Senate on June 9 by a 74-3 vote. He was sworn in on June 23, 1969, at the end of the Court term.

In criminal cases Chief Justice Burger usually took a conservative stance. He voted to uphold searches and arrests made without a warrant and vigorously attacked the exclusionary rule that prohibited the use of illegally seized evidence at trial. He took a narrow view of the Fifth Amendment's privilege against self-incrimination and joined in several decisions limiting the scope of the 1966 *Miranda* ruling. Although he voted to guarantee indigent defendants free counsel in certain misdemeanor cases, Burger opposed extending the right to counsel to preliminary hearings, preindictment lineups, and displays of photographs of a suspect to witnesses. He supported the use of six-member juries and nonunanimous jury verdicts and voted repeatedly to uphold the death penalty against constitutional challenge. In December 1971, however, Burger ruled that prosecutors must adhere to their part of plea bargaining agreements. He joined in several decisions banning the imposition of jail terms on convicts solely because they could not pay fines.

In July 1974 Burger spoke for the Court in the celebrated case of *U.S. v. Nixon*. He ordered the president to surrender the tapes and documents subpoenaed by special prosecutor LEON JAWORSKI for the pending Watergate cover-up trial of six former presidential aides. Nixon's claim of executive privilege, Burger ruled, had to yield in this case to the demonstrated need for evidence in a pending criminal trial. Conversations recorded on several of the tapes that Nixon surrendered in response to the Court's order led directly to his resignation from office on August 9, 1974.

In free speech cases the chief justice generally sustained government action against individual rights claims. For a five-man majority in June 1973, he reversed a 16-year Court trend lowering restrictions on pornography and set new guidelines for obscenity laws that gave the

President Nixon announces the nomination of Warren E. Burger to fill the post of chief justice of the U.S. Supreme Court, May 21, 1969. *(National Archives)*

states greater leeway to regulate pornographic materials. He dissented in June 1971 when the Court denied the government's request for an injunction to halt newspaper publication of the *Pentagon Papers*. Burger joined the majority a year later in holding that journalists had no First Amendment right to refuse to testify before grand juries about information obtained from confidential sources. However, he spoke for the Court in June 1974, to invalidate as an infringement on freedom of the press, a Florida law requiring newspapers to print replies from political candidates whom they criticized. He also overturned a judicial "gag" order restricting pretrial news coverage

of a Nebraska mass murder case in June 1976 as an unjustified prior restraint on the press.

Burger wrote several significant opinions on government and religion. In May 1972 he ruled that the application of a state law for compulsory secondary education to the Amish denied the sect their right to free exercise of religion. His May 1970 majority opinion held that tax exemptions for church property used solely for religious purposes did not violate the First Amendment's ban on government establishment of religion. However, Burger overturned several programs for direct state aid to parochial schools in June 1971, because they would result in excessive government entanglement with religion. In later cases he voted to sustain state aid programs in which the benefits went to the individual parents or children rather than directly to the religious schools.

In a widely publicized April 1971 case, Burger spoke for a unanimous Court to uphold court-ordered busing as one means of eliminating state-imposed school segregation. In July 1974, however, he overturned a plan to remedy segregation in Detroit's school system by merging it with suburban districts. For a five-man majority, Burger held such an interdistrict plan inappropriate when segregation had been established only in one district and there was no evidence showing that school district lines had been drawn in a discriminatory way. In other racial discrimination cases, Burger followed a moderately conservative course.

The chief justice applied the constitutional guarantee of equal protection of the laws to women for the first time in November 1971, when he invalidated an Idaho law favoring men over women in the administration of estates. In later sex discrimination suits and other equal protection cases, however, Burger again took moderate to conservative positions. He concurred in January 1973 when the Court upset state laws prohibiting abortions within the first six months of pregnancy as a denial of due process. However, he was otherwise wary of invalidating government action on due process grounds. Burger usually upheld the states' power to establish voting requirements. Nevertheless, for a unanimous Court in March 1974, he ruled that states requiring political candidates to pay a filing fee had to provide some alternative means of access to the ballot for individuals too poor to pay the charge. The chief justice joined in numerous rulings limiting the Court's jurisdiction to hear cases. He voted, for example, to set restrictive requirements for bringing federal class action suits, to tighten standing requirements, and to limit state prisoners' right of appeal in federal courts in certain instances.

As chief justice, Burger took a leading role in promoting administrative efficiency and reform in the courts. He publicized the problems of the courts through annual State of the Judiciary addresses given before the ABA, press interviews, and public speeches. He suggested a variety of administrative improvements and successfully urged establishment of state-federal judicial councils, a national center for state courts, and an institute to train court managers. Burger devoted special attention to what he considered an excessive workload in all of the federal courts. To remedy it, he urged Congress to remove certain cases from federal jurisdiction and to consider the impact of all new legislation on the courts before passage. He also favored studying the possibility of limiting the right of appeal and of having certain types of cases, such as family law problems or prisoner complaints, settled in some other forum than the courts. Burger appointed a seven-man committee in the fall of 1971 to study the Supreme Court's caseload. In a controversial December 1972 report, the committee recommended establishment of a new national appeals court to screen all the petitions for review of cases currently filed in the Supreme Court. Burger also promoted penal reform and proposed special training and certification for trial attorneys. Burger retired from the Court in 1986 and died of heart failure in 1995.

—CAB

Burns, Arthur F(rank)

(1904–1987) *counselor to the president; chairman, Board of Governors, Federal Reserve System*

Arthur Burns was born on April 27, 1904, in Austria and immigrated to the United States with his parents prior to World War I. After growing up in Bayonne, New Jersey, he attended Columbia University, where he took his B.A., his M.A. and finally, in 1934, his Ph.D. in economics. While still a graduate student, Burns began teaching at Rutgers University, and in 1930 he was hired as a research associate at the National Bureau of Economic Research (NBER), a private institute established for the study of business cycles. In 1941 Burns returned to Columbia as a visiting professor, becoming a full professor in 1944. The following year he was appointed director of research at the NBER and became NBER president in 1957.

Burns's early career was not limited to teaching and research. Through his association with the NBER, he had served as a consultant to various government agencies and departments. In 1953 President Eisenhower appointed Burns chairman of the Council of Economic Advisers (CEA). Burns, in his three-year tenure as chairman, was widely credited with bringing the council to the center of U.S. economic policy making.

Because of his early critique of Keynesian economics and other writings, Burns was generally viewed as a conservative but repeatedly proved to be, above all, a pragmatist who could shift policies as the situation demanded. Thus, to combat the recessions of the 1950s, he on occasion pressed for more extensive credit policies against the tight money bias of the Eisenhower administration. In the early 1970s, reversing a position he had taken in an influential 1965 article, Burns emerged as a leading spokesman for wage and price controls.

Burns's career first became interwoven with that of RICHARD NIXON when he correctly informed the vice president in 1960 that without adequate economic stimulus the Republicans would lose the upcoming presidential elections. After Nixon's defeat Burns served on the Advisory Committee on Labor-Management Policy under Kennedy and Johnson. When Nixon was elected to the White House in 1968, Burns became counselor to the president, with cabinet status. In January 1970 he succeeded WILLIAM MCCHESNEY MARTIN as chairman of the Federal Reserve Board.

Burns took over the Fed at an auspicious moment. The Nixon administration had come into office amid promises to combat inflation and to balance the federal budget, and under Martin the Federal Reserve had pursued what some observers felt was a draconian credit policy. Just before Burns took office, the nation's money supply had been held to an unprecedented five months of zero growth, prompting Nixon, at Burns's inauguration, to end his introductory remarks with the plea: "Dr. Burns, please give us more money!"

Burns was in fact preparing to ease monetary conditions. In his Senate confirmation hearings in December 1969, he had stated that he was in favor of a relaxation of current tight money "under normal conditions," although he had gone on to say that conditions at the time were by no means "normal."

Burns was under pressure from many quarters, including the White House. In appointing Burns Nixon had acclaimed the chairman's "independence" but added his hope that "independently he [Burns] will conclude that my views are the ones that should be followed." Burns admitted at a May 1970 convention of the American Bankers' Association (ABA) that the administration's exclusive reliance on monetary and fiscal policy to combat inflation could cause "a very serious business recession." In the same speech he voiced support for a "modest" incomes policy, though not for full-fledged wage and price controls. Two weeks later, at a White House dinner for top U.S. businessmen, Burns alluded to the widespread concern about U.S. corporate liquidity and promised action by the Fed to avert any liquidity crisis.

Events quickly put Burns to the test. In June 1970 congressional opposition to government-guaranteed loans for the Penn Central Railroad forced the company into bankruptcy, despite initial support by Burns and the administration for such loans. Over the weekend prior to the Penn Central's public declaration of bankruptcy, Burns mobilized the Federal Reserve System for the largest rescue operation in its history.

Burns correctly feared that the Penn Central's default on $80 million in commercial paper might produce a general panic in the financial markets, forcing numerous other corporations into default and bankruptcy. The Federal Reserve Bank notified all member banks that it was prepared to issue standby credits through its discount window to enable capital markets to function smoothly, and a panic was thereby averted. In July 1970, testifying before the Joint Economic Committee (JEC) of Congress, Burns proposed the creation of a new federal lending corporation to guarantee loans to creditworthy corporations cut off from normal borrowing channels.

In December 1970, with the U.S. economy in serious recession and inflation still at high levels, Burns proposed an 11-point anti-inflation plan. Among his proposals were more vigorous use of antitrust regulations, expanded federal training programs to produce more skilled workers in high-wage sectors of the economy, a liberalized depreciation allowance for corporations, a suspension of the Davis-Bacon Act requiring union wages to be paid on federal construction projects, and compulsory arbitration of public interest labor disputes. Burns also voiced his support for a wage-price review board, intensifying his campaign for controls that were still officially anathema to the Nixon administration.

Burns's relations with the administration entered a crisis in July 1971. In testimony before the JEC, Burns had stated that there had been "very little progress" in the fight against inflation. Widespread rumors began to circulate that Nixon was furious at Burns's remarks and exasperated by his repeated calls for wage-price controls. Other rumors, which were somewhat coolly denied by White House Press Secretary RONALD ZIEGLER, implied that Nixon was considering steps to double the size of the Federal Reserve Board with his own appointees. Two days after Ziegler's remarks, Treasury Secretary JOHN CONNALLY, countering Burns, stated that "very substantial" progress had been made against inflation. Finally, rumors appeared in the press asserting that Burns was hypocritically seeking a $200,000-per-year increase in his own salary.

These rumors were later traced to White House aide and future Watergate figure CHARLES COLSON. The *Wall Street Journal* editorialized that the White House wanted to embarrass Burns "either to diminish his impact on public opinion or to force him to resign and make room for a more docile central bank head." In early August Nixon himself was compelled to "set the record straight" about the rift, calling Burns "the most responsible and statesmanlike" Fed chairman in memory.

Behind this atmosphere of rumor and denial, however, a policy struggle of the gravest consequences was at stake. The U.S. economy remained stagnant, and the international crisis of the dollar had forced America's Common Market trading partners into a joint currency float in May 1971. According to Charles Coombs, who managed the foreign exchange desk for the Federal Reserve Bank of New York and was thus in charge of defending dollar parity, communication had virtually ceased between the administration and Connally's Treasury Department on one side and the Federal Reserve on the other.

In Coombs's view, Burns "alone of Washington officialdom . . . had recognized the danger inherent in the Treasury policy stance." On the weekend of August 14–15, 1971, Burns participated with Connally, Office of Management and Budget Director GEORGE SHULTZ, Nixon, and other leading administration figures in the "Camp David II" talks, where Burns's long-advocated domestic wage-price controls were adopted in the drafting of Nixon's "New Economic Policy (NEP)" announced on national television on the evening of August 15. Although victorious on wage-price controls, Burns fought and lost to Connally on the plan to end legal gold backing of the dollar in international settlements. Burns was aware that such a unilateral action by the United States would only fuel the criticisms that the Nixon administration, with Connally, was practicing a "malign neglect" policy in international monetary matters. Nevertheless, Connally carried the day.

With the end of Phase One and the 90-day wage-price freeze, more permanent control mechanisms were established for Phase Two. President Nixon appointed Burns to head a newly created Government Committee on Interest and Dividends, whose purpose was to keep bank and other interest rates and stock dividend increases at appropriate levels. His appointment drew fire from critics who either feared Burns's increased power to influence capital markets or who saw a possible conflict of interest between Burns's functions on the committee and his role as Fed chairman.

Nixon's NEP launched the U.S. economy on a two-year boom that was later criticized as hyperinflationary and politically motivated by the president's desire to be reelected in 1972. This criticism was necessarily rebounded to Burns, who permitted the domestic money supply to expand through 1972 at unprecedented rates. Burns later admitted that the 1972 monetary expansion had been too rapid.

Burns also played a key role in the international arrangements related to the NEP. In the intense international negotiations in the fall of 1971 over the establishment of new fixed parities for the world's currencies, Burns represented the United States at the International Monetary Fund (IMF) Group of 10 meeting in London in September. With Connally and

PAUL VOLCKER, undersecretary of the Treasury for Monetary Affairs, Burns negotiated the final articles of the Smithsonian Agreements, signed in Washington in December 1971, which were called the "most important monetary agreement in the history of the world."

Sixteen months later, the Smithsonian Agreements collapsed. Burns, more than most U.S. officials, had understood the fragility of the new accords and was more adamant than most that the United States should take some of the responsibility for maintaining the stability of the dollar, which in the 1971 crisis had devolved largely onto foreign central banks who sought to save their own currencies from unnecessary appreciation.

In May 1972, at an American Bankers' Association convention in Montreal, Burns elaborated a 10-point program for monetary stability that appeared to many to contain gestures of conciliation toward U.S. trading partners, particularly in its acceptance of a continued role for gold and its emphasis on a "symmetrical" division of responsibilities. Immediately after Burns's speech, Undersecretary Volcker took the floor and emphatically reminded the convention that Burns "was not speaking for the U.S. government." Thus, the Fed-Treasury rift on international questions continued into the second dollar crisis of 1973. In the interim, with Burns's support, the Federal Reserve Bank of New York continued to make limited interventions to bolster the dollar in foreign exchange markets.

The end of Phase Two controls in January 1973 initiated a new period of intense international pressure on the dollar from foreigners, who correctly anticipated a new wave of U.S. inflation. In early February Burns told the Senate Banking Committee that enforcement of Phase Three guidelines would be "very tough indeed" and called for presidential standby authority to reimpose wage-price controls. Nevertheless, intense selling of the dollar on foreign exchanges forced a new dollar devaluation by mid-March. In early March Burns attended a crisis session with President Nixon on the matter and several days later told the House Banking Committee that he wanted a prompt international solution to the crisis. Burns then flew to Paris for the international meetings that ended the Smithsonian Agreements, realigned currencies, and established a floating-rate system of international exchange.

The takeoff of inflation in early 1973 brought the Government Committee on Interest and Dividends into a showdown with the banking system. In February 1973 Burns had forced the major commercial banks to roll back an increase in the prime lending rate. In March, with increased pressure from inflation, Burns and the banks negotiated a "split" rate system of one rate for nationally known borrowers and another for small businesses dependent on local capital markets. In April Burns, acting in his capacity as Fed chairman, sent a letter to all Federal Reserve member banks urging them to "avoid a credit crunch" and to be cautious in their lending. A week later, however, he was forced to concede that his "jawboning" efforts had resulted in artificially low rates, and by the end of 1973, the prime commercial rate had risen from approximately 6.5 percent to 10 percent.

The problem of accelerating domestic inflation, compounded by the quadrupling of oil prices in the fall of 1973, confronted the Federal Reserve with the possibility of a new U.S. recession, of which many observers considered Burns to be a major architect. In April 1974 congressional testimony, Burns defended the Fed's application of the monetary brakes, which had begun to deeply depress the housing and mortgage markets. "To shape monetary policy with an eye to the fortunes of home building and to neglect the grave and very dangerous problem of inflation would be extremely unwise," said Burns. "We're having

a veritable explosion of business loans." In July 1974 Burns told the House Banking Committee that inflation was the result of "loose fiscal policies" and defended the slowing of monetary growth by the Fed. In August he urged the JEC to channel $4 billion into the creation of 800,000 public service jobs if unemployment passed the 6 percent mark.

By the fall of 1974 U.S. industrial production entered the worst downturn since the Depression years of 1929–33, and Burns increasingly devoted his public statements to detailed analyses of its causes. In October he told the JEC that the United States was in "a most unusual recession" with "no precedent in history." Burns pointed to the potentially illiquidity of the international banking system brought about by "petrodollar recycling," saying that such recycling was "piling debt upon debt, and more realistically, bad debt on top of good debt." Attempting to quiet fears in the wake of the bankruptcy of the Franklin National Bank, Burns revealed that the Fed had made some temporary loans to "a few other institutions" in order to allow financial markets to "function in an orderly manner."

Burns recognized that long-term trends were at work in the recession. He addressed an ABA convention in late October 1974, pointing to the long-term deterioration of U.S. bank liquidity and indicating that "the capital cushion which plays such a large role in maintaining confidence in banks has become thinner, particularly in some of our largest banking organizations." He went on to say that the federal regulatory system had "failed to keep pace" with these changes and called for a sweeping overhaul of the Federal Reserve, the Federal Deposit Insurance Corporation (FDIC), and the Comptroller of the Currency, whose overlap was "indeed a jurisdictional tangle that boggles the mind."

When economic recovery began in mid-1975, Burns attempted to keep the U.S. money supply expanding at a 5 percent to 7 percent rate, adequate to fuel a "modest" increase of production. Representative HENRY REUSS (D-Wis.) had used the collapse as an opportunity to introduce legislation forcing the Fed to expand the money supply at a 6 percent annual rate, a measure that Burns vehemently opposed as tying the hands of the central bank to a mechanical target. Reuss's measure was eventually turned into a sense of Congress resolution, but under congressional pressure, Burns made the unprecedented concession of revealing Federal Reserve Board monetary targets a year in advance on a quarterly basis.

In a September 1975 speech Burns proposed a series of sweeping "structural reforms" to eradicate the inflationary bias of the U.S. economy. He called on the U.S. government to act as the "employer of last resort" with public works programs, at the same time calling for a reduction of unemployment insurance payment periods from 65 to 13 weeks and a modest set of voluntary wage and price controls. He also urged policy makers to stretch out environmental and job safety goals because of their "dampening" effect on business.

Burns repeatedly had to weather criticism of the Federal Reserve, particularly from labor leaders and liberal congressional opponents of his monetary policies. In 1971, in opposition to Burns's advocacy of wage-price controls, AFL-CIO president GEORGE MEANY charged that "Chairman Burns . . . [and others] . . . have been engaged in the shocking and blatant use of a double standard while providing subsidies and aid for the banks and big business." As the United States entered the 1974–75 recession, Meany called for the ouster of Burns and other Nixon appointees.

Similarly, congressional advocates of tighter governmental control of the Fed and the banking system, such as Representative WRIGHT PATMAN (D-Tex.) and Representative Henry Reuss, repeatedly attempted to push

through legislation making the Fed more accountable to Congress. In 1971 when Congress was considering two bills that authorized the government to regulate interest rates, credit flows, and wages and prices and to permit the Fed to channel credit into desired sectors of the economy with variable reserve requirements, Burns opposed this increase of the Fed's powers, arguing that such legislation would put the central bank "in the political arena in a big way."

In May 1976 Burns vehemently opposed a watered down Reuss bill that made a Fed chairman's term roughly concurrent with a presidential term and introduced other measures to effectively "politicize" Fed policy. Burns also opposed attempts by Reuss and Patman to use the January 1976 leak of the comptroller of the currency's "problem list" of commercial banks to force greater disclosure practices.

Burns played an important role in the 1975 New York City fiscal crisis. With secretary of the Treasury WILLIAM SIMON and CEA chairman ALAN GREENSPAN, Burns emerged as an opponent of federally guaranteed loans to the city in the summer and fall of 1975. In May, like many critics, he stated that the city had lost its credibility and that default was inevitable. However, by November 1975 national and international opinion had begun to sense that a New York City default might do serious damage to U.S. capital markets and hence to the shaky world economic recovery. Thus, while telling the Senate Banking Committee in early November that a default would not set off a chain reaction, he began to express growing concern over its effects. On November 12 FELIX ROHATYN of the Municipal Assistance Corp., established to oversee the city's finances, announced that Burns had given "an A-minus" to New York state governor HUGH CAREY's rescue plan for the city. At the same time top U.S. officials, including Simon and Greenspan, were also beginning to favor some form of aid. Nevertheless, in a December 1975 meeting with Carey over the imminent bankruptcy of the state's Housing Finance Association, Burns denied Federal Reserve aid to the agency.

After the election of Jimmy Carter to the White House, Burns stayed on as Federal Reserve chairman. He clashed openly with Carter on several occasions over monetary policy, and when his term expired in January 1978, he was replaced by William Miller. Burns returned to the private sector and died in 1987.

—LG

Bush, George H(erbert) W(alker)

(1924–) *ambassador to the United Nations; chief, liaison office, People's Republic of China; director, Central Intelligence Agency*

Born on June 12, 1924 in Milton, Massachusetts, the son of Senator Prescott Bush (R-Conn.), George Bush attended the Phillips Academy and joined the U.S. Naval Reserve upon his graduation in 1941. After the war Bush majored in economics at Yale University, graduating in 1948. Bush declined a position with his father's banking firm in New York, and instead he became an oilfield supply salesman in Texas. In 1954 he founded the Zapata Off-Shore Co., a contract oil-drilling firm. This enterprise expanded rapidly and made Bush a millionaire in his own right.

Bush entered politics in 1964 with an unsuccessful run for a U.S. Senate seat. He won election in 1966 to the U.S. House from Houston's wealthy seventh congressional district. In his two terms in the House, Bush served on the Ways and Means Committee and earned a 77 percent rating from the conservative Americans for Constitutional Action. Although Bush favored state "right-to-work" laws and "freedom of choice" alternatives to school desegregation, he supported the John-

son administration's open-housing legislation in 1968 over intense opposition among his constituents. Bush also supported the 1969 voting rights amendment and the NIXON administration's 1970 Family Assistance Plan. Although Bush defended the interests of the oil companies, he favored stringent environmental legislation.

Bush was considered for the 1968 Republican vice presidential nomination on the strength of his southern constituency and reputation as a Nixon backer, but Nixon chose SPIRO AGNEW. Bush launched a second unsuccessful campaign for the Senate in 1970.

President Nixon appointed Bush U.S. ambassador to the United Nations in December 1970. Although initially regarded with skepticism as a politician, Bush earned the admiration of the other delegates in 1971 with his informal style and access to the White House. Bush advocated the Middle East peace proposals of Secretary of State WILLIAM ROGERS and called for stronger world action to control the illegal narcotics trade. In October 1971 he guided the Nixon administration's attempt to admit Communist China to the U.N. under a "two Chinas" proposal that would have continued Nationalist Chinese membership in the General Assembly. The United Nations rejected the American proposal, however, and expelled Taiwan. Bush defended the administration's "tilt" toward Pakistan in the Indo-Pakistani war of December 1971 but pledged U.S. relief aid to Bangladesh in May 1972. He also defended the administration's decision to blockade North Vietnam in May 1972.

Following the 1972 elections, Nixon appointed Bush chairman of the Republican National Committee. Bush sought to translate the Republican "new majority" of 1972 into greater Republican congressional power by broadening the party base to include workers and ethnic groups. The unfolding Watergate scandal soon absorbed most of Bush's attention, however, throwing the Republican Party on the defensive. Although maintaining that Nixon would survive the scandal, Bush resisted administration pressure to involve the Republican Party in the president's defense. The crisis nevertheless slashed financial contributions to the party by one-third and produced a series of bielection losses to the Democrats, who won a landslide victory in the congressional elections of 1974.

In September 1974 President FORD appointed Bush to head the U.S. Liaison Office in Beijing. Bush impressed the Chinese with his friendly informality by touring Beijing on a bicycle and by holding hamburger and hot-dog parties in the American compound. He helped to host President Ford's state visit to China in December 1975.

In November 1975 Ford appointed Bush to replace WILLIAM COLBY as director of the Central Intelligence Agency (CIA). Although at first suspected as a "political" director, Bush stayed out of the 1976 campaign. He helped the agency to improve its professionalism by making structural reforms and by promoting younger personnel. In response to previous disclosures of CIA misconduct, Bush carried out President Ford's executive order of February 1976 to reform the intelligence community. The order prohibited abuses, upgraded the interagency committee on covert operations to cabinet-level, tightened measures to prevent unauthorized disclosures, and enlarged the responsibilities of the CIA director for overall management of the intelligence community.

George Bush was again considered for the Republican vice presidential nomination in 1976, but President Ford chose Senator ROBERT DOLE (R-Kan.) instead. After leaving office in 1977, Bush served as chairman of the First National Bank of Houston. In 1980 Bush sought the Republican nomination for president. Though he lost the nomination, he became RONALD REAGAN's running mate

and served two terms as vice president, from 1980 to 1988. In 1988, upon the conclusion of Reagan's second term, Bush won the Republican nomination for president. On January 20, 1989, George Herbert Walker Bush was sworn in as the 41st president of the United States of America. In 1992, after weathering a tough challenge from PATRICK BUCHANAN (a conservative political columnist), Bush received the Republican nomination for the presidential race. However, in the fall election he was beaten by Arkansas governor Bill Clinton.

Currently, George H. W. Bush is a resident of Houston, Texas, and summers in Kennebunkport, Maine. He is on the board of visitors of M. D. Anderson Hospital, on the board of the Episcopal Church Foundation, and serves on the vestry of St. Ann's Episcopal Church in Maine. He is the grandfather of 14 children and father of the 43rd president, George W. Bush.

—GB and JH

Butz, Earl L(auer)
(1909–   ) *secretary of agriculture*

Born on July 3, 1909, Butz grew up on his family's 160-acre farm in Albion, Indiana. He attended Purdue University and received a doctorate in agricultural economics in 1937. Nine years later he became a full professor at Purdue. From 1954 to 1957 Butz served as assistant secretary of agriculture in the Eisenhower administration. He was dean of Purdue's school of agriculture during the late 1950s and early 1960s and a director of the Ralston Purina Company and several other agribusiness corporations.

In response to declining agricultural income and rising discontent among farmers, President NIXON in November 1971 announced the resignation of Secretary of Agriculture CLIFFORD HARDIN and the appointment of Butz to replace him. The nomination aroused strong opposition because of Butz's association with the conservative policies of the Eisenhower administration. For the first time the National Farmers Union opposed a presidential nominee for agriculture secretary. The Senate Agriculture Committee narrowly voted in favor of confirmation, 8-6, with two Republican farm state senators voting against Butz. On December 2 the Senate approved Butz's nomination 51-44.

Although he favored a return to free market forces and a minimum of federal support for agriculture, Butz released agricultural appropriations impounded by the Nixon administration. In December he announced the purchase of large amounts of corn, and other grains on the open market to bolster farm prices. He also increased the subsidies paid to farmers to retire land from production and raised environmental conservation payments. In a gesture to congressional liberals he announced in January 1972 a reversal of planned cutbacks of $200 million in the food stamp program.

Butz advocated improved income levels for the nation's farmers. In a February 1972 speaking tour of farm states, he opposed controls on farm prices and blamed middlemen for rising food costs. His statements, however, were at odds with the administration's wage and price controls and quickly provoked dissenting reactions. C. Jackson Grayson, head of the federal Price Commission, deplored Butz's comments, saying that if other federal officials thought only of their own constituents, "the efforts to achieve price stability would be wrecked."

Butz looked to foreign sales of U.S. grain and other agricultural products as a way of bolstering farm income. At the urging of the White House, which was concerned about the persistent balance of payments deficit, Butz visited the Soviet Union in April 1972. In July he announced a three-year agreement with the Russians for the purchase of a "minimum" $750 million of U.S. wheat, corn, and other grains on the open market. The Soviet Union would be eligible for long-term credits from the Department of Agriculture's Commodity Credit Corporation, and the domestic sellers would be eligible for government subsidies to bring the market price of the grain up to parity.

The Soviet grain deal, which was timed to coincide with the 1972 presidential campaign, quickly embroiled Butz in a storm of controversy that lasted two years. The sale also played a major part in wrecking the administration's efforts to achieve price stability.

On August 30 the Consumers Union asked the Justice Department to investigate possible conflict of interest by two Agriculture Department officials who were involved in the negotiations and then left the department to take jobs with major grain-exporting firms. A Senate Agriculture Committee staff memo reported evidence of a "coziness between the Department of Agriculture and private grain exporters" that led to windfall profits for the corporations. On September 8 Democratic presidential candidate Senator GEORGE MCGOVERN attacked the deal as "another example of the big business favoritism" of the Nixon administration and charged the big grain companies with acquiring huge stocks of grain, based on inside information, early in July when prices were low. A few days later Butz called McGovern's charges "a bald-faced lie."

Despite Butz's denial the public outcry was so great that the Justice Department and the General Accounting Office (GAO) began formal investigations. In July 1973 the GAO reported that the Department of Agriculture's mismanagement of the sale had resulted in $300 million in unnecessary subsidies paid to grain exporters and the escalation of food prices. That same month the Justice Department concluded no evidence of criminal fraud or conflict of interest existed. Nevertheless, the final report of an inquiry by the permanent investigations subcommittee of the Government Operations

Committee in the summer of 1974 severely criticized Butz for a "$300 million error in judgment." "At virtually every step," the report declared, "from the initial planning of the sales to the subsidy that helped support them, the grain sales were ineptly managed."

Although the grain sale eventually led to higher prices paid to farmers, it had a disastrous impact on domestic inflation, driving up the cost of feed grains for cattle producers and the retail price of food. The skyrocketing price of beef led consumer groups to declare in March 1973 a national meet boycott, but prices remained firm. Butz placed temporary export curbs on 41 commodities in July to prevent domestic shortages and ended all production controls to increase supplies. In June the administration, over Butz's opposition, froze food prices for a month and beef prices for three months. In response cattle producers refused to bring steers to market, leading to widespread meat shortages in many parts of the country. Consumer food prices rose 22 percent in 1973 and another 14 percent in 1974. In September 1974 Butz warned consumers that prices would rise another 8 to 10 percent before leveling off.

Butz announced in January 1973 that the administration would impound $1.2 billion in funds appropriated for agriculture, including monies for disaster loans and food stamps. In March, however, a federal district court in Minneapolis ordered the restoration of disaster aid and the following year issued a similar ruling on $278 million in food stamp funds.

Despite the furor surrounding the 1972 Soviet grain sale, in October 1974 Butz reported a $500 million sale to the Russians, but President GERALD FORD canceled the purchase because of its inflationary impact. A smaller export agreement was announced later.

In December 1974 cattle producers from South Dakota organized a "cross-country beef-in" to protest Butz's policies. Widespread evidence of corruption and bribe taking among grain inspectors licensed by the department of Agriculture was uncovered by the Department of Justice in May 1975. Grand juries in Houston and New Orleans handed down over 50 indictments. In August 1975 the General Accounting Office charged that faulty crop forecasting by the department had resulted in policy decisions that led to $1.67 billion in unnecessary federal expenditures.

Butz's tenure as agriculture secretary ended abruptly during the 1976 presidential campaign when former White House counsel John Dean related in a magazine article a slur against blacks made by an unidentified administration official. "I'll tell you why [the Republicans] can't attract coloreds. Because coloreds only want three things. You know what they want? . . . first, a tight pussy; second, loose shoes; and third, a warm place to shit. That's all." A few days later another magazine revealed Butz as the source of the comment.

Reaction to Butz's remark was swift and furious. On October 1 President Ford gave Butz a "severe reprimand" for making a "highly offensive remark." Ford was forced to accept Butz's resignation when no one came to his defense and the public outcry continued to mount. On October 4 Butz resigned, admitting merely to a "gross indiscretion" and "unfortunate choice of language." He later resumed his professorship at Purdue University. In May 1981 Butz pled guilty to charges of tax evasion. The next month he was sentenced to five years in prison; all but 30 days of the sentence was suspended.

—JD

Buzhardt, J. Fred, Jr.
(1924–1978) *counsel to the president*

Born on February 21, 1924, and raised in South Carolina, Buzhardt graduated from the U.S. Military Academy in 1946. He served in the air force until 1950 and received his law degree from the University of South Carolina in 1952. He practiced law until 1958, when he became administrative assistant to Senator STROM THURMOND (R-S.C.). He became chief aide to Secretary of Defense MELVIN LAIRD following the 1968 election.

In 1970 Buzhardt was appointed general counsel to the Defense Department. From 1971 to 1973 he represented the Department of the Army in the prosecution of two Rand Corp. consultants accused of leaking the classified *Pentagon Papers*, which detailed the U.S. entry into the Vietnam War. The consultants, DANIEL J. ELLSBERG and Anthony J. Russo, were charged with conspiracy to obtain classified government documents, theft, espionage, and receiving unauthorized government property. On May 11, 1973, after 89 days of trial, charges were dropped.

Following the *Pentagon Papers* trial Buzhardt became counsel to the president and was put in charge of the Watergate defense. For the next 16 months Buzhardt tried to coordinate the myriad of presidential legal battles, spending most of his time protecting presidential documents. He invoked "executive privilege" in numerous court appearances. His argument was based on a July 7, 1973, letter in which RICHARD NIXON informed the Senate Watergate Committee that he would cooperate fully with its investigation "except in those instances where I determine that meeting the Committee's demands would violate my constitutional responsibility to defend the office against encroachment by other branches."

Buzhardt first used the argument shortly after existence of the White House tapes was discovered and special prosecutor ARCHIBALD COX subpoenaed them. He lost in the court of appeals on October 12. The court ruled that criminal prosecution took precedence over executive privilege. Later that year Buzhardt informed the court that two of the subpoenaed

tapes were missing and that there was an 18-minute gap in another.

In October 1973 Buzhardt played the role of go-between in the resignation of Vice President SPIRO AGNEW. Buzhardt, representing the administration, met with Agnew's lawyers on October 5. Agnew, it was agreed, would be free to deny criminal charges submitted by the Justice Department and would be able to review the government's evidence against him. Following the review, Agnew entered a plea of no contest to one count of tax evasion and resigned on October 10.

On January 4, 1974, Buzhardt was removed as chief Watergate counsel but remained Nixon's chief legal adviser. When Nixon agreed to provide the House Judiciary Committee with edited transcripts of subpoenaed tapes, Buzhardt was put in charge of the project. He turned over 1,254 pages of text on April 30. In June Buzhardt was assigned to protect presidential papers against former aide JOHN D. EHRLICHMAN's attempt to use them in his own defense. Buzhardt suffered a heart attack June 13 but continued to advise the president. Following the July 24 Supreme Court decision ordering that all the subpoenaed tapes be turned over to the special prosecutor, Buzhardt urged the president to resign.

Buzhardt resigned as presidential counsel on August 15, 1974, a week after Nixon's departure. He returned to South Carolina and private legal practice. He died of a heart attack on December 16, 1978.

—BO

Byrd, Harry F(lood), Jr.
(1914–) *member of the Senate*

Born on December 20, 1914, Byrd was the son of Senator Harry F. Byrd (D-Va.), whose organization dominated Virginia politics from the late 1920s to the mid-1960s. Upon the elder

Byrd's retirement in 1965, his son, known as "Little Harry," assumed the vacant seat and was elected to the Senate one year later. One of the staunchest conservatives in the upper house, Byrd opposed civil rights measures and large government expenditures, especially for social welfare programs.

During the NIXON administration, Byrd maintained his conservative record, voting against establishment of a consumer protection agency, government aid for abortions, and busing and for farm subsidy legislation and Nixon's conservative nominations to the Supreme Court. In foreign and defense affairs, he voted against foreign aid and attempts to limit troop commitments abroad. In 1974 he received a 100 rating from the conservative Americans for Constitutional Action. Byrd remained a staunch supporter of American policy in Vietnam. In 1972 he sponsored an amendment to prohibit U.S. assistance to North Vietnam without prior congressional consent. The amendment banned expenditures of any funds from the Defense Department or other federal budgets for any kind of assistance, direct or indirect, to North Vietnam.

In the belief that he would have difficulty winning the 1970 Democratic primary in Virginia because of opposition to the Byrd machine, Byrd ran and was reelected as an independent. Nixon strategists hoped that if the Republicans gained control of the Senate, Byrd would be free to switch parties and lead an exodus of southern conservatives to the GOP. When the Democrats won, Byrd was able to maintain his seniority on the powerful Armed Services and Finance Committees by voting with the party when it organized the Senate.

In September 1971 Byrd spoke out in opposition to the UN embargo of the white supremacist government of Rhodesia, a measure that prohibited the importing of chrome needed by American defense industries. He presented an amendment to a defense procurement bill providing that the president could not regulate the amount of goods imported from any noncommunist country as long as the United States was importing the same material from a communist country. Since approximately 60 percent of America's chromium ore came from the Soviet Union, the measure required the United States to end the embargo. Byrd stated that the purpose of his proposal was "simply to end the dependence of the United States upon the Soviet Union for chrome ore." The measure passed and was implemented in January 1972. However, in December 1973 the Senate passed a bill that brought the U.S. back into compliance with UN sanctions.

In the 1976 general election, Byrd, running as an independent, defeated the Democratic candidate, retired ADM. E. R. ZUMWALT, by over 200,000 votes. Byrd did not stand for reelection in 1982 and lives in Winchester, Virginia.

—FHM

Byrd, Robert C(arlyle)
(1917–   ) *member of the Senate*

Born on November 20, 1917, in North Wilkesboro, North Carolina, the son of an itinerant West Virginia coal miner, Robert Byrd drifted with his family from one mining town to another. Raised in poverty, he worked his way through high school but could not afford to go to college; instead he became a butcher in his hometown. He eventually received a law degree from American University in 1963. In the early 1940s Byrd moved to Baltimore to be a welder in a shipyard. He then returned to West Virginia after the war to open a grocery store and teach a Bible class. A born-again Baptist with an intense evangelical fervor, Byrd became so popular that he was invited to broadcast his sermons. In 1946 he won a seat in the state legislature and six years later won a seat in the U.S. House. In 1959 Byrd moved over to the Senate, where he established a conservative record. During the Kennedy and Johnson years Byrd opposed efforts to end the cold war with the Soviet Union. He also voted against civil rights and welfare legislation but supported regional redevelopment, labor, and education measures.

In 1967 Byrd's colleagues elected him secretary of the Democratic Conference, a minor post with a great deal of potential. Byrd was responsible for the scheduling of debates, informing senators about votes on the Hill, polling his peers, pairing votes when necessary, stalling a roll call to accommodate a delayed senator, and keeping tabs for the majority leader of senators' birthdays and other celebrations. Because Senators RUSSELL LONG (D-La.) and EDWARD KENNEDY (D-Mass.), the two whips Byrd served until 1971, focused most of their attention on legislative issues, Byrd inherited their routine responsibilities as the majority leader's deputy. He was, in essence, MIKE MANSFIELD's (D-Mont.) de facto whip. Holding such power, Byrd ingratiated himself with most of his colleagues. Many owed him favors; others were simply impressed with him for mastering the intricacies of running the day-to-day operations of the Senate. Thus, in January 1971 Byrd challenged Edward Kennedy for the position of whip. Support for Byrd crossed ideological lines, and he defeated the Massachusetts senator.

During the early years of the NIXON administration, Byrd generally supported the president on most issues. He backed defense spending including funding for the Safeguard antiballistic system and development of the supersonic transport. Byrd supported the war in Vietnam and opposed many of the end-the-war amendments during the period. On domestic issues he voted for the confirmation of conservative nominees CLEMENT HAYNSWORTH and G. HARROLD CARSWELL to the Supreme Court. Nixon even considered appointing Byrd to the High Court, but the American Bar Association suggested that the West Virginian was not qualified. Byrd was a staunch law-and-order advocate and favored antiriot, preventive detention, and "no knock" entry legislation. Nevertheless, he voted with the liberals to preserve the major social service programs, such as Social Security, unemployment, housing, and education. In 1972 he supported the Equal Rights Amendment.

After becoming the whip, Byrd became more moderate and started to break frequently with the administration. As a member of the Judiciary Committee, Byrd expressed doubts in the spring of 1972 about appointing RICHARD KLEINDIENST attorney general. His staff joined with Senator Kennedy's in investigating the Kleindienst link to the ITT scandal. Byrd was one of 19 Democratic senators who voted against confirmation. He also led the opposition to the appointment of L. PATRICK GRAY as FBI director. He obtained secret material questioning Gray's controversial handling of an air hijacking attempt in which Gray had ordered agents to fire on the plane's tires.

Byrd also moderated his strident anticommunist posture. He called for a review of American relations with Cuba as a step toward possible normalization of relations. Byrd proposed that the United States withdraw from the Southeast Asia Treaty Organization, and after visiting China in the fall of 1975, he recommended that the U.S. normalize relations with the Beijing regime.

Byrd remained a conservative on civil rights, however. He vigorously opposed busing and in 1971 supported a constitutional amendment to permit the desegregation of schools based on a freedom-of-choice principle. Byrd also supported the Gurney Amendment aimed at restricting the courts' right to desegregate schools. In 1975 he secured passage of an amendment that would partially repeal the 1964 Civil Rights Act's prohibition of racial discrimination in federally funded projects.

In January 1977 Byrd succeeded Mansfield as majority leader. His only serious contender, HUBERT HUMPHREY (D-Minn.), who was seriously ill, withdrew when it became apparent that he could not win. During the early Carter presidency, Byrd supported the administration on most issues. He helped steer the Panama Canal treaties through the Senate. On a number of occasions, however, Byrd criticized the president for his failure to develop a coherent anti-inflation and energy policy.

Byrd served as Senate majority leader from 1977 to 1980 and from 1987 to 1988, and as Senate minority leader from 1981 to 1986. He has chaired the Appropriations Committees and has twice been elected president pro tempore of the Senate (1989–94; 2001–02).

Byrd has been a consistent critic of the policies of George H. W. Bush with respect to the war on terror. On March 19, 2003, when Bush announced the invasion of Iraq, Byrd bemoaned, "Today I weep for my country." Later that year, Byrd criticized the "cowed members of the Senate" who continued to support the president's policies.

Byrd has become the unofficial guardian of Senate rules and traditions and is often called upon to resolve disputes over parliamentary procedures. He is at present the longest-serving member of the U.S. Congress.

—JB and JRG

Callaway, Howard (Bo)
(1927–) *secretary of the army*

Born on April 2, 1927, into a prominent Georgia textile family, "Bo" Callaway received a B.S. degree from West Point in 1949. He was commissioned and served as a platoon leader in Korea for a year. As a civilian Callaway was active in various business, educational, and civic affairs before turning to politics in the early 1960s.

Abandoning the party of his family, Callaway became a registered Republican and a delegate and fundraiser for Senator BARRY GOLDWATER in 1964. That same year he was elected to represent Georgia's third congressional district, thus becoming the state's first Republican congressman since Reconstruction. Callaway spent his one term in Congress compiling a near-perfect conservative voting record; he staunchly opposed most Great Society programs, particularly bills pertaining to civil rights.

In 1966 Callaway ran for governor of Georgia. Although he won a narrow plurality of the popular vote in a three-way contest, he lost the governorship when the Democratic legislature decided the election in favor of Lester Maddox. During 1968 he was RICHARD NIXON's chief preconvention scout in the South

and then his southern campaign director. His comment during the campaign in Mississippi that "perhaps we can get Governor GEORGE C. WALLACE on our side, that's where he belongs," reportedly angered Nixon, who refused Callaway any significant appointment during his first administration. Callaway was relegated to a three-man Advisory Commission on Intergovernmental Relations to "foster better federal-state-local relations."

In mid-1973 Callaway was nominated secretary of the army. The major objection at his Senate confirmation hearing concerned his racial views. At a time when the army was experiencing racial tensions, it was suggested that Callaway would "lack credibility . . . in dealing with the service's race relations." Such objections, however, were offset by support for his nomination from Georgia representative and civil rights activist ANDREW YOUNG.

During his two-year tenure as secretary of the army, Callaway's major accomplishment was to "sell" the concept of an all-volunteer army and then preside over its implementation. He resigned from this post in June of 1975 to become President FORD's campaign manager. Reportedly Callaway was chosen because Ford needed an "enthusiastic advocate" with strong conservative credentials capable of countering "the Reagan threat from the right" and with "only limited ties to the 1972 Republican campaign."

Almost immediately Callaway became a controversial figure. His repeated public insistence that Vice President NELSON ROCKEFELLER was the president's biggest problem enraged Republican liberals and moderates. Callaway, however, was encouraged to voice such sentiments by Ford's chief of staff, DONALD RUMSFELD, who had his own eye on the vice presidential nomination.

Although he bore the title of campaign manager, much of the actual strategy was decided at the White House first by Rumsfeld and his deputy, RICHARD CHENEY, and later by Cheney and Jerry Jones, who headed a "scheduling committee." In addition to alienating the vice president, Callaway also encountered problems with the White House press staff over "communication lapses" and "resistance in the government to his repeated efforts to establish a program that would coordinate public appearances by 'appropriate' cabinet and administration officials to help sell Mr. Ford's candidacy to the voters."

Within the party organization Callaway was criticized for courting conservatives "instead of managing the overall campaign," lacking "experience in presidential politics," and having "no organizing ability." Republican director of organization Lee Nunn resigned in October of 1975, accusing Callaway of outright incompetence, while finance chairman DAVID PACKARD implied that fundraising was lagging because of Callaway's interference.

Despite such complaints President Ford retained Callaway and tried to "paper over his deficiencies" with the appointments of former Reagan political technician Stuart Spencer as Callaway's deputy and ROGERS C. B. MORTON as White House counselor and campaign adviser. The president finally became convinced that Callaway was a political liability after the disclosure that as secretary of the army he had

furthered his family's interests in a Colorado ski resort by "persuading" the U.S. Forest Service to drop environmental objections to the resort's expansion plans.

Callaway announced in March 1976 that he would "step aside until the air cleared." In January 1977 a Senate investigation subcommittee found Callaway guilty only of "poor judgment," while a Justice Department investigation cleared him of any conflict-of-interest charges.

In 1980 Callaway ran an unsuccessful campaign for the U.S. Senate from Colorado. From 1981 to 1987 he was chairman of the Colorado Republican Party. From 1987 to 1993 he served as chairman of GOPAC. He presently serves as chairman of Callaway Gardens in Pine Mountain, Georgia, and resides in Crested Butte, Colorado.

—MJW

Calley, William L(aws), Jr.
(1943–   ) *army officer*

Born on June 8, 1943, in Miami, Florida, Calley worked as a bellhop, dishwasher, and railroad switchman until 1966, when he enlisted in the army. He graduated from Officers Candidate School and was then ordered to Hawaii to join Company C, First Battalion, 20th Infantry, under the command of Captain Ernest L. Medina. Calley was given charge of the rifle company's first platoon.

Company C arrived in Vietnam in December 1967 and was assigned to the Americal Division in the northern I Corps zone as part of the new 11th Infantry Brigade. On March 16 it was part of a task force that swept through the South Vietnamese village district of Son My in an effort to destroy a suspected Vietcong stronghold in the hamlet of My Lai.

No Vietcong were encountered in either engagement. However, helicopter pilots who circled the area during the action reported massive civilian casualties. Both Colonel Oran K. Henderson, the new commander of the 11th Brigade, and Major General Samuel W. Foster, commanding officer of the American Division, looked into the reports and decided nothing unusual had occurred at Son My.

In April 1969 a Vietnam veteran, Ronald L. Ridenhour, reported alleged war crimes by U.S. soldiers at Son My in the operation a year before. In November the army appointed Lieutenant General William R. Peers to head a board of inquiry into the events of March 16 and to determine whether there had been a deliberate cover-up by the American Division command.

That same month Calley was charged with the premeditated murder of 102 civilians at My Lai. His court-martial, postponed several times, began a year later. In his defense Calley argued that he had been ordered by Medina at a briefing the day before the attack to destroy My Lai and kill every living being in the hamlet because "they were all enemy." Medina rebutted Calley's testimony.

On March 29 an army court-martial jury found Calley guilty of the premeditated murder of at least 22 South Vietnamese civilians. He was sentenced to life imprisonment at hard labor, dismissal from the army, and forfeiture of his pay and allowances, pending the outcome of an automatic review of the case by another command.

Eventually Calley believed that he was made a scapegoat for the army, taking the blame while his superiors escaped responsibility. Chief of Staff General WILLIAM C. WESTMORELAND later stated the army's position: "Judging from the events at My Lai, being an officer in the U.S. Army exceeded Lieutenant Calley's abilities. Had it not been for educational draft deferments, which prevented the army from drawing upon the intellectual segment of society for its junior officers, Calley probably never would have been an officer.

Denied that usual reservoir of talent, the army had to lower its standards."

Calley's conviction provoked an immediate and sharply divided outcry. JIMMY CARTER and GEORGE WALLACE were among the governors and other public officials who expressed indignation at the verdict. On April 1 President Nixon ordered Admiral THOMAS H. MOORER, chairman of the Joint Chiefs of Staff, to release Calley from the stockade and return him to his apartment on the base while his conviction was under review. Two days later Nixon announced that he would personally review Calley's case.

In August of the same year, Calley's sentence was reduced to 20 years. In 1973 both the Army Court of Review and the Court of Military Appeals upheld his conviction. Calley was released on bail in March 1974. In April Secretary of the Army HOWARD CALLAWAY reduced his sentence to 10 years. The following month the Pentagon announced that Nixon had reviewed the case and decided that no further action was "necessary or appropriate." Calley's conviction was overturned on technical grounds by a U.S. district court in September but was reinstated a year later by a circuit court of appeals. He was released on parole in November and given a dishonorable discharge. The Supreme Court refused to hear Calley's appeal in 1976.

The Peers Report, released in 1972, was critical of the entire command structure of the American Division. Calley was not the only individual charged in the incident. Several other officers and enlisted men were investigated and tried. However, Calley was the only one found guilty. Calley is now a jeweler in Columbus, Georgia.

—SF

Cannon, Howard W(alter)
(1912–2002) *member of the Senate*

Born on January 26, 1912, in St. George, Utah, Cannon worked on his father's ranch as a cowboy before entering Arizona State Teacher's College. He earned his B.E. in 1933 and an LL.B. in 1937 from the University of Arizona. Prior to entering military service in March 1941, Cannon worked as an attorney in Utah. He served with distinction as an air force pilot during World War II. After the war Cannon became a partner in a Las Vegas, Nevada, law firm until his election to the Senate in 1959. Supporting most of President Kennedy's programs in the early 1960s, Cannon became identified as a moderately liberal Democrat. After winning reelection in 1964 by 48 votes, Cannon's support of liberal programs dropped.

In the late 1960s and early 1970s Cannon supported legislation to preserve natural resources. A representative from a silver-producing state, he urged Congress to take steps to conserve the diminishing U.S. silver supply and provide for future needs through industry incentives and other inducements to encourage producers. In April 1969 he spoke out on behalf of the lead-zinc quota that he hoped to be the beginning of a natural minerals policy. According to Cannon the major issue of the 1970s was man's ability to reverse the environment's deterioration. He cosponsored the Water Quality Improvement Act of 1970 and introduced a bill to establish a world environment institute. In 1971 Cannon cosponsored the Federal Water Pollution Control Act Amendment, which established the federal government's commitment to clean up all navigable rivers by 1985. He also supported the 1971 Wild Mustang Protection Act empowering the federal government to protect, manage, and control an estimated 17,000 remaining mustangs. On the international scene, Cannon supported the president's "Vietnamization" policy. He voted for the Cooper-Church Amendment of 1970 to limit U.S. military involvement in Cambodia. In June 1971 he supported the Mansfield end-the-war amendment calling for withdrawal of all U.S.

forces from Indochina within nine months in return for the phased release of American war prisoners. He also backed the Senate's refusal to authorize continued foreign aid programs in October 1971. Cannon believed it was time to reassess foreign aid in light of the world's changing political, economic, and social conditions.

Cannon was chairman of the Senate Rules and Administration Committee in October 1973 when President NIXON nominated Representative GERALD R. FORD (R-Mich.) to succeed SPIRO T. AGNEW. Although Cannon criticized the Justice Department's restrictions on the committee's access to FBI files, he gained access to a wide range of documents. In this manner Cannon's committee was credited with rebuilding public confidence in government. The panel approved Ford's nomination in November. When President Nixon's Watergate-induced resignation made Ford president in August 1974, Cannon's committee conducted an inquiry into Ford's vice-presidential nominee, NELSON A. ROCKEFELLER. Cannon expressed concern over Rockefeller's gifts to associates over the years but in the end supported his confirmation.

Because of Watergate, Cannon maintained that campaign spending reform was still unexplored territory despite the 1971 Federal Elections Campaign Act, which he cosponsored. Subsequently, Cannon's Rules and Administration Committee hammered out a revised campaign spending bill, known as the 1974 Federal Election Campaign Act Amendments. The act imposed overall limitations on campaign expenditures and contributions and procedures for filing campaign expense reports and for public financing of presidential nominating conventions and presidential primary elections.

Throughout the remainder of Ford's administration, Cannon received attention for his inquiries into the airline industry. In 1974 he charged that the Civil Aeronautics Board

(CAB) had the power to deal with the problem of unfair foreign competition with American international air carriers, particularly over the North Atlantic. He criticized foreign governments for violating bilateral capacity agreements and the World Bank for subsidizing foreign-owned air carriers. In October 1976 he proposed that the CAB approve air carriers to service routes on which present carriers charged too much or offered poor service. This was designed to help Pan American World Airways compete in the domestic market for routes finding their way into overseas lines.

In 1982 Cannon was upset by Republican Chic Hecht. His bid for reelection was hurt by a difficult primary battle as well as by a trial in which members of the Teamsters Union were charged with trying to bribe him. In 2002 Cannon died of congestive heart failure at a Las Vegas hospice.

—TML

Carey, Hugh L(eo)

(1919–   ) *member of the House of Representatives; governor of New York*

Born on April 11, 1919, and raised in New York City, Hugh Carey earned a Bronze Star during World War II. Following his graduation from St. John's University Law School in 1951, he worked for his family's oil company. A political unknown in New York's 12th congressional district, Carey challenged Representative Francis E. Dorn in 1960. Carey, running on a liberal platform, narrowly defeated the incumbent in the Kennedy landslide of that year. During the Kennedy-Johnson years Carey emerged as a leading urban liberal in the House of Representatives. As a member of the Education and Labor Committee, he was a principal architect of bills providing federal aid to education and to the handicapped.

In 1969 Carey ran unsuccessfully for the Democratic nomination for New York City Council president. During the 1970s he continued his focus on social welfare legislation and aid to cities. He recommended that Congress shift more funds from RICHARD NIXON's revenue-sharing program to urban areas and in 1971 suggested that Congress double the revenue-sharing grants to the cities. In addition he lobbied for national health insurance and for the removal of the Social Security tax burden from the middle and working class. However, few of Carey's proposals became law.

Initially a supporter of U.S. involvement in Vietnam, by the 1970s Carey was an opponent of the war in Indochina. In 1971 he voted for the Fraser Amendment barring the assignment of draftees to Vietnam; the Mansfield Amendment calling for a pullout from Vietnam within nine months subject to a prisoner-of-war release; and the Boland Amendment cutting off funds for the war after June 1. Carey also supported attempts to cut defense spending and to limit the deployment of antiballistic missiles. Despite his liberal stance, Carey worked well with the established leaders in the House and opposed efforts to modify the seniority or committee systems.

In 1974 Carey campaigned for New York's Democratic gubernatorial nomination. Relatively unknown in upstate New York, he challenged the popular Howard Samuels, who had the support of party bosses and many liberals. Carey ran as a reformer against a coalition of liberals and the Democratic machine. In November he won a surprise victory. His success was due to determination; generous campaign donations, including a substantial contribution by his brother Edward, the sole owner of an oil company; and excellent media work by Dave Garth. In the November election Carey crushed the lackluster incumbent, Malcolm Wilson. Carey's victory margin exceeded that of Al Smith and Franklin D. Roosevelt, the two most popular Democratic governors of the state.

During his first two years in office, Carey was primarily concerned with the impending bankruptcy of New York City. In May 1975 New York City officials announced an immediate need for $1.5 billion by June 1975 to meet the city's short-term debt obligation. Carey, Mayor ABRAHAM BEAME, and other city officials sought assistance on many fronts but met rejections from President FORD, the New York state legislature, and the city's leading commercial banks. After meeting with the president on May 14, Carey announced that Ford's response showed a "level of arrogance and disregard for New York that rivals the worst days of Richard Nixon and his gang of cutthroats." However, he finally convinced the legislature to approve on June 10, one day before the bankruptcy date, a bill to create the Municipal Assistance Corp. (Big Mac). Its first task was to gradually refinance the city's current short-term indebtedness and then work with city hall to supervise budge cuts to bring spending in line over a three-year period.

During the summer Carey worked to prevent a possible default in October by persuading large municipal unions to invest in Municipal Assistance Corp. bonds and by lobbying for government loans. The city escaped default at the last hour when the New York City teachers' union agreed with the other municipal unions to invest its pension funds. Carey's pleas for federal aid met with little success. Ford continued to insist that federal aid would create a dangerous precedent. Only after Carey persuaded the legislature to pass a tax increase, for which he assumed full personal responsibility, did Ford relent. On November 26 he asked Congress to approve the legislation making up to $2.3 billion in direct federal loans available annually.

Carey's skill as a negotiator with the bankers, unions, upstate Republicans, and the administration, as well as his forceful presentation of the city's case through the media, earned him national praise for salvaging what appeared to be a hopeless situation. That same year Carey helped organize aid for the Urban Development Corp., the nation's largest builder of public housing.

Carey inherited a state that was also in financial trouble. During the Rockefeller and Wilson administrations, state spending had increased by $1 billion a year, and the area was losing its tax base. Carey therefore increased taxes and put curbs on spending increases. During the recession of 1975–76, he was forced to hold down spending on social services. He successfully reduced the number of state workers by 7 percent. Although he had championed free tuition in the City University system, Carey was forced to impose tuition on that institution, a step that angered city residents.

Conditions in the state improved in 1976, and the unemployment rate declined. Still, Carey kept a lid on spending and instituted a tax cut to stimulate business. Because he was occupied with the state's financial problems, Carey was unable to institute the sweeping program he wanted in criminal justice, corrections, and mental health. He was also unable to give guidance to his own administrators. Although he remained popular, his aloof, arrogant style and his distaste for state legislators alienated politicians in the state. He was unable to project a clear image to the public. Conservatives were outraged with him for opposing the restoration of the death penalty, although he did sponsor legislation instituting mandatory sentencing and punishments for juvenile offenders.

In the summer of 1978 Carey faced challengers in his own party for reelection. He won the primary by a narrow margin and waged an uphill fight against his Republican opponent, Perry Duryea, in the general election campaign. Helped by an effective media blitz that focused on his accomplishments, Carey defeated his rival with 53 percent of the vote. Carey returned to the practice of law in New York City, where he resides.

—JB

Carswell, G(eorge) Harrold
(1919–1992) *judge, Court of Appeals, Fifth Circuit*

Born on December 12, 1919, in Irwinton, Georgia, Harrold Carswell graduated from Duke University in 1941 and served in the navy during World War II. Following his graduation from Mercer University Law School in 1948, Carswell, raised in a family active in Georgia Democratic politics, ran unsuccessfully for the state legislature. He then moved to Florida and opened his own law practice. In 1969, after serving appointments as U.S. district attorney and district judge for northern Florida, Carswell was named judge of the U.S. Court of Appeals for the 5th Circuit (Georgia, Florida, Alabama, Mississippi, Texas, Louisiana).

In keeping with his stated objective to nominate a conservative southern jurist to fill the Supreme Court seat vacated by ABE FORTAS, RICHARD NIXON, on January 19, 1970, sent Harrold Carswell's name to the Senate for confirmation. Because the Senate had just emerged from a bitter fight resulting in the defeat of CLEMENT HAYNSWORTH to fill the Fortas seat, the appointment was expected to be approved with minimal opposition. But controversy developed immediately when the press publicized a Carswell statement made in 1948 supporting white supremacy and later attempts to circumvent integration of public facilities. These accusations and testimony of witnesses reviewing Carswell's hostile behavior toward civil rights lawyers and questionable rulings in voting rights and desegregation cases monopolized the hearings of the Senate Judiciary Committee, which finally voted their approval in February.

Confirmation still seemed assured despite the growing opposition of the legal community, which was reacting to the results of research on Carswell's judicial record: 60 percent of Carswell's published opinions had been reversed by higher courts; his decisions in all areas of law were characterized as mediocre, confused, and ignorant of precedent.

But after WILLIAM SAXBE (R-Ohio) released a letter from Richard Nixon that in effect claimed that the Senate was usurping the power of the president to appoint justices and evidence was produced to show that Carswell had lied during his confirmation hearings about his role in attempts to forestall desegregation at private facilities, the appointment was threatened. A number of senators became convinced that Carswell's nomination was an act of vengeance by Nixon for not confirming Haynsworth. Carswell was defeated on April 8 by a vote of 51-45. Nixon blamed the defeat on antisouthern prejudice.

Carswell did not return to the bench; he ran for and lost the Florida Republican senatorial primary in September 1970, returned to private law practice, and served as a bankruptcy referee to become eligible for a federal pension. In 1976 Carswell, semiretired, was hospitalized with a nervous condition after having been arrested on vice charges. He died in 1992.

—JMP

Carter, Jimmy
(1924–   ) *governor of Georgia*

Jimmy Carter was born on October 1, 1924. His father, James Earl Carter, was the most prominent citizen of Plains, Georgia, a small junction farm town. The elder Carter owned a farm supply store, was a peanut trader, and after the birth of his son acquired large tracts of farmland. Carter studied for a year at Georgia Southwest College and Georgia Institute of Technology before being admitted to the United States Naval Academy at Annapolis in 1943. Three years later he graduated 10th in his class. Following the death of his father in 1953, Carter left the navy to run his father's numerous business enterprises. In 1962 Carter won a seat in the state senate. He ran unsuccessfully for governor in 1966 but won four years later.

As governor, Carter took a strong stand on civil rights. He opened up more state political positions to blacks than any governor before him. A number of Carter's programs, especially in education, health, and prison reform, greatly helped the blacks of his state. For such endeavors Carter was applauded as the representative of the "New South," the new brand of southern politician who sought to unify the races rather than divide them.

Carter's administrative reforms impressed the nation. He reduced the number of state agencies from 65 to 22, increasing efficiency and saving the taxpayer money. However, a number of Carter's critics claimed these reforms were more cosmetic than real. But they did concede that he improved the quality of service by Georgia's civil servants. Carter also introduced a "sunshine law" that opened most government deliberations to the people. His "zero-based budgeting" program made all departments accountable for money spent. Carter expanded state programs to help the mentally ill. His prison reform activities received national praise. Conservationists were impressed with his interest in protecting Georgia's environment, especially the state's threatened swamps.

The publicity Carter enjoyed as governor catapulted him into national prominence as a southern alternative to conservatives GEORGE WALLACE and LESTER MADDOX. Efforts were made to win him the vice presidential nomination in 1972. In 1974 Carter served as the Democratic Party's national campaign committee chairman. He traveled throughout the nation speaking on behalf of many candidates and making himself valuable contacts. Carter served on the Trilateral Commission, an international think tank of leaders from the United States, Western Europe, and Japan who engaged in economic forecasting and planning. On December 12, 1974, Carter announced his candidacy for the Democratic nomination for the presidency. He proclaimed himself the southern liberal alternative to George Wallace who would restore honesty and integrity to government.

Throughout the spring of 1976 Carter ran on a platform promising to end inflation and high unemployment, expand aid to the cities and the poor, and implement a national health insurance program. Even with these programs Carter promised to attain a balanced budget. Calling the American tax program a national disgrace, he promised to plug the loopholes. He pledged to maintain a rigid control of the FBI and the Central Intelligence Agency. In foreign policy Carter endorsed the substance of the Nixon-Kissinger diplomacy but objected to the style as secretive, manipulative, and unilateral. The obscure, one-term southern governor astounded the nation by proceeding to defeat his rivals in most of the primaries. In July the Democratic convention gave him the nomination on the first ballot.

In the fall Carter's lead in the polls began to evaporate. In comparison to the exciting primary campaigns, Carter made a number of strategic errors, and his style appeared lackluster. He barely won the election with 51 percent of the vote.

Following his presidency, Carter became a professor at Emory University (Atlanta). He then founded the Carter Center, also in Atlanta. The first such center to be linked to a presidential library, the Carter Center focused on public policy issues, both international and domestic. Both Carter and his wife, Rosalyn, played an active role in developing the mission of the center and its work, particularly as it evolved into an agent of international conflict mediation. Since its inception, the Carter Center has sent 47 international election-monitoring delegations around the world. The work of the Carter Center has led observers to dub Carter the most influential former president since John Quincy Adams. In December 2002 Carter was awarded the Nobel Peace Prize. In March 2004 Carter publicly censured President George W. Bush for waging a needless war against Saddam Hussein's Iraq.

—JB and JRG

Case, Clifford P(helps)
(1904–1982) *member of the Senate*

Case was born on April 6, 1904, the son of a Dutch Reformed minister and the nephew of a future New Jersey supreme court chief justice, Clarence Case. He graduated from Rutgers and Columbia University Law School, joined a Wall Street law firm in 1928, and soon began winning local political office as a Republican. He served in the U.S. House of Representatives from 1945 to 1953 and after a brief stint as president of the Fund for the Republic, retained a seat in the Senate for 24 years.

Case was long viewed as one of the most liberal Republicans in the Senate. The senator's voting record on domestic issues reflected the interests of the most urbanized state in the Union, where a heavy concentration of labor union members existed, along with teeming ghettos and a chaotic transportation system. Case consistently earned ratings of between 80 percent and 100 percent from the liberal Americans for Democratic Action and ratings of from 0 percent to 18 percent from the conservative Americans for Constitutional Action. He also won the support of labor unions. He

was not considered personally magnetic or particularly activist in introducing legislation. Unusual to the Senate, he had no press secretary, although he retained a loyal and competent staff. He was often thought to be reclusive. His liberalism put him firmly in the political camp of Governors NELSON ROCKEFELLER and WILLIAM SCRANTON in the 1964 Republican presidential contest. He eventually withheld his endorsement of the convention's designated candidate, BARRY GOLDWATER. Four years later Case allowed his own pro-Rockefeller, favorite-son candidacy to continue long after the likelihood of RICHARD NIXON's nomination became evident.

The senator voted against three of President Nixon's choices for the Supreme Court— CLEMENT HAYNSWORTH, G. HARROLD CARSWELL, and WILLIAM REHNQUIST. He voted against the federal funding of the SST in 1971 and for various attempts to extend minimum wage provisions to include domestic household employees. In 1972 the New Jersey lawmaker voted for the mass transit bill that allocated $11.8 billion over six years and provided for federal funds to be available as operating subsidies for mass transit. During the FORD administration Case voted for the Consumer Protection Agency and against a prohibition on the use of food stamps for the families of those on strike in November 1974.

Perhaps the heart of Case's political philosophy and legislative interests can be appreciated by his belief that an educated public requires the maximum feasible public disclosure of the financial and political affairs of those involved in political decision making. Toward that end he introduced full disclosure bills in every session of the Senate from 1957. The legislation would have revealed the sources of income of public officials as well as their official written communications with other governmental functionaries. He proposed amendments to open up the appropriations of Radio Free Europe and Radio Liberty to public scrutiny rather than retaining them under needlessly secretive CIA auspices. In 1974 he also voted for 17 amendments to the Freedom of Information Act that made government-held information more accessible to the public. The president vetoed the measure, but the Senate overrode him.

The New Jersey legislator was appointed to the Foreign Relations Committee in 1965 and was the ranking Republican member in his last years in the Senate. His influence became important in the reassertion of congressional power during the two Republican administrations. In 1969 he voted against the antiballistic missile, then the following year voted for a narrowly defeated appropriations reduction for Pentagon public relations and for a $5.2 billion cut in a Defense Department appropriations bill. In February 1971 Case sponsored a bill, which eventually became law in 1972, requiring that the text of all international agreements accepted by the president be presented to both houses of Congress within 60 days for their approval.

Although becoming critical of the levels of American involvement in Vietnam during the Johnson administration, Case, along with many other members of Congress, held off on his criticism of the Nixon administration's policies for a number of months. His dissatisfaction mounted so that by June of 1970 he voted for the Cooper-Church Amendment that limited presidential authority to conduct ground operations in Cambodia. In January 1973, after the renewal of bombing of Hanoi and Haiphong, Case presented an amendment with Senator FRANK CHURCH (D-Idaho) that mandated a deadline to cut off all funds for U.S. military involvement in Indochina. It passed the Senate but was defeated in the House.

The war was still an important issue in 1975 when the Ford administration attempted to procure new aid for the American evacua-

tion of Vietnam. Case rejected such aid saying "there was an inevitability about what happened that no change in our policy or amount of money could have affected significantly." Case ran for reelection in 1978 at the age of 74 but was defeated in the primary by a narrow margin. The senator had relied on his standing in public opinion polls and with Republican county chairmen to win and had not campaigned extensively until the last two weeks before the election. The Republican nominee, Jeffrey Bell, was a national organizer for conservative Republicans who ran an effective, well-financed campaign that concentrated on taxpayers' frustrations and Case's vote in support of the Panama Canal Treaty. Case resumed his law practice and taught at Rutgers University until his death in 1992.

—GB

Celler, Emanuel
(1888–1981) *member of the House of Representatives; chairman, Judiciary Committee*

Born on May 6, 1888, in Brooklyn, New York, Emanuel Celler received his B.A. in 1910 and LL.B. in 1912 from Columbia University and then practiced law in New York. In 1922 he was elected for the first of 25 consecutive terms to represent Brooklyn's 10th district as a Democrat in a largely Jewish area of Flatbush. In the House, Celler compiled a liberal record. He was a lifetime advocate of liberalized immigration and naturalization laws and voted consistently for the social welfare legislation of Democratic administrations. During his quarter of a century tenure as chairman of the Judiciary Committee, Celler became an authority on antitrust, civil rights, and civil liberties legislation.

During the 1950s Celler amassed a prodigious legislative record in the field of antitrust. He coauthored the 1950 Celler-Kefauver

Antimerger Act and his Antitrust Subcommittee conducted extensive investigations into the monopolistic practices of American industry. Celler also opposed the creation and extension of the House Un-American Activities Committee and fought to temper the political hysteria of the McCarthy period.

Celler's most notable legislative efforts in the 1960s were in the field of civil rights. He sponsored or managed the passage of all the major civil rights acts, guided the Twenty-fourth Amendment (abolishing the poll tax) through the House, and managed the 1965 Voting Rights Act. In the area of civil liberties, Celler warned against and opposed the inclusion of court-supervised wiretapping and antiriot provisions in the legislation of the late 1960s.

Celler's last years in Congress were marked by repeated conflict with an administration attempting to win the loyalty of the South. In June 1969 he fought administration attempts to weaken enforcement provisions of the 1965 Voting Rights Act extension by applying its sanctions to the North as well as the South. Celler held hearings in an attempt to undermine the momentum behind the support of the proposed changes but was unsuccessful at that time. However, he managed the extension of the original bill the following year, after the Senate had succeeded in striking out the administration's proposed change.

In April 1970 Representative GERALD FORD (R-Mich.) reflected the administration's bitterness over the defeat of their nominee to the Supreme Court, conservative southerner G. HARROLD CARSWELL, by calling for an impeachment investigation of Justice WILLIAM O. DOUGLAS, whom Ford termed a "hippie-yippie type" revolutionary with ties to the "underworld." Celler fought the resolution, and after it passed he defeated impeachment by appointing himself to head the five-man investigating panel and dragging out the

process until December, when he released a report that cleared Douglas of all charges.

In February and March of 1972, southern Democrats introduced a constitutional amendment to prohibit the busing of school children to achieve racial integration. In an attempt to appease the southerners but head off a protracted emotional battle across the country, the NIXON administration proposed a busing moratorium and introduced statutory antibusing provisions. Celler, clearly opposed to this whole movement, successfully killed approval of the proposed constitutional amendment by conducting hearings but was less successful in defeating the administration's proposals, which he termed "an unconstitutional interference with the judicial power" in view of the 1971 Supreme Court decision that ruled that busing was a legal means to achieve racial integration.

Celler also found himself in conflict with some of the favorite issues of the left in the 1970s. He refused to consider abortion reform legislation and proposals of amnesty for Vietnam war resisters. Charging that the Equal Rights Amendment would invalidate laws that protected women and that "there is more difference between a male and female than between a horse chestnut and a chestnut horse," Celler held up the ERA for 20 years until a discharge petition forced its release in 1970.

Criticism was also leveled at the way Celler ran his committee, particularly his propensity to delay or refuse to hold hearings on proposals that he did not like. And although Celler's staff issued a report in 1971 that called for more effective antitrust laws and he conducted hearings on six major conglomerates, Celler was accused of neglecting antitrust issues. Intimations were also made that Celler was protecting corporate interests who were also clients of his New York law firm.

In 1972 Celler was up for reelection at the age of 84. When ELIZABETH HOLTZMAN, a young New York lawyer, announced her candidacy for Celler's seat, Celler remarked, "She doesn't exist, as far as I'm concerned." Celler did not campaign, did not have an office in his district, and chose to remain in Washington and rely on his past record and the Democratic machine for reelection.

In a campaign largely ignored by the press, Holtzman covered the district on foot, with leaflets and through a small army of volunteers. She attacked Celler's record in opposition to the ERA and his reluctant support for the Twenty-fifth Amendment, which gave 18-year-olds the right to vote, and charged Celler with accepting legal fees from defense contractors. But most importantly, she argued that Celler had neglected his constituency and taken it for granted. Celler received no help from the Brooklyn Democratic machine, which was preoccupied with the reelection of Representative JOHN ROONEY (D-N.Y.), and lost the primary by 609 votes. Although Celler remained the Liberal Party candidate, he conceded the November election to Holtzman after conducting an unsuccessful court suit to declare the primary void on grounds of fraud and voting irregularities. Celler returned to his law practice and died in Brooklyn in 1981.

—JMP

Chafee, John H(ubbard)

(1922–1999) *secretary of the navy, member of the Senate*

Chafee was born on October 22, 1922, into a family long active in Rhode Island politics. He graduated from Yale in 1947 after service with the Marines during World War II. Three years later Chafee earned a law degree from Harvard. After another tour with the Marines in Korea, he began a law practice in Providence in 1953.

A liberal Republican, Chafee won election to the Rhode Island house of representatives in 1956. He was reelected in 1958 and 1960 and house minority leader from 1958 to 1962. Chafee served as governor of Rhode Island from 1963 to 1968. He worked closely with a Democratic legislature to pass liberal legislation, including a state Medicare program, which earned recognition as "a state version of the Great Society." Chafee was defeated for reelection in 1968 largely due to advocacy of a state income tax. He supported George Romney for the 1968 Republican presidential nomination and backed Nelson Rockefeller after Romney's withdrawal. Following the nomination of RICHARD NIXON, Chafee sought unsuccessfully to block the vice presidential nomination of Spiro Agnew in the hope of gaining the nomination for himself.

In January 1969 President Nixon appointed Chafee secretary of the navy. The appointment was intended as a gesture of reconciliation toward the more liberal Republicans of the Northeast. Chafee's duties included carrying out Nixon's Vietnamization program and modernizing the U.S. fleet. He provoked a controversy in May 1969 by overruling a naval court of inquiry that had recommended courts-martial for officers of the U.S.S. *Pueblo*, an electronic intelligence-gathering ship captured by North Korean gunboats in January 1968. He also supported the service reforms of Chief of Naval Operations ELMO ZUMWALT.

Chafee resigned in May 1972 to challenge incumbent senator CLAIBORNE PELL (D-R.I.). He won the Republican nomination but lost the election in November. In 1976, however, he won the U.S. Senate seat vacated by retiring Democrat John Pastore. Chafee was reelected to the Senate four times and served until his death of a heart attack in 1999. He was posthumously awarded the Medal of Freedom in 2000.

—DB

Chapin, Dwight
(1940–   ) *Watergate figure*

Born on December 2, 1940, in Wichita, Kansas, in 1959 Dwight Chapin enrolled as a freshman at the University of Southern California (USC) in Los Angeles. He was active in student politics and belonged to a student group, the Trojans for Representative Government. The Trojans distributed false campaign literature, stuffed ballot boxes, and planted spies in the opposition camp. In 1962, a year before their graduation, Chapin and his friend GORDON STRACHAN were asked by a former Trojan and USC graduate, RON-ALD ZIEGLER, to join him and H. R. HALDEMAN in Richard Nixon's 1962 campaign for governor of California. Although Nixon lost, Haldeman was impressed with Chapin's style and initiative and offered him a job at J. Walter Thompson advertising agency after graduation in June 1963.

When RICHARD NIXON decided to run for the presidency in 1965, he asked Haldeman to be his chief of staff. Haldeman's protégés Ziegler and Chapin became respectively Nixon's press secretary and his personal aide. After the election Ziegler stayed on as Nixon's press secretary, and Chapin was named the president's appointments secretary. However, since all of Nixon's appointments were cleared through Haldeman, Chapin was as much Haldeman's aide as Nixon's.

Chapin, like the rest of the people Haldeman gathered about him, was an ambitious corporate functionary with little political experience. As a Haldeman aide his official duties included preparing the itinerary and seeing to the details of the president's domestic and foreign trips. As was the case with most of the White House staff, however, he had political duties, too. At the beginning of 1971, when Haldeman was forming the strategy for the reelection campaign, Chapin and Gordon Strachan were tapped to organize a "dirty tricks" unit to harass the Democrats in the 1972 primaries.

In the spring of 1971 Chapin and Strachan contacted DONALD SEGRETTI, another USC classmate, to have him organize a "non-CHARLES COLSON" dirty tricks operation in the field. In June 1971 they flew Segretti to Washington and formally offered him a job as a political prankster working for Richard M. Nixon's reelection. In August Segretti met with HERBERT KALMBACH, President Nixon's personal lawyer, and was offered a salary of $16,000 a year plus expenses.

Segretti assembled an "intelligence unit" of 28 people in 17 states who devoted themselves to wreaking chaos in the Democratic candidates' primary campaigns. Chapin told Segretti to concentrate on Senator EDMUND MUSKIE's campaign, since he was considered the president's most formidable rival. The dirty tricks campaign involved forging letters and distributing them under the candidates' letterheads, making dossiers on the candidates' personal lives, and seizing confidential campaign files. The tricksters leaked false statements, manufactured items for the press, and threw the candidates' campaign schedules into disarray by phoning ahead to cancel appearances and/or schedule appearances that the candidates could never make.

In October 1972 *Time* magazine and *Washington Post* reporters began to make the connections between the Watergate burglary, the Committee to Re-Elect the President (CREEP), and the Segretti operation. After Haldeman, JOHN EHRLICHMAN, and JOHN DEAN agreed that the cover-up had to be maintained to protect the president and "the presidency," they decided that Chapin would have to leave his White House job. In January 1973 Chapin resigned from the White House staff and accepted an executive position with United Airlines.

When called before the Watergate grand jury in April 1973, Chapin denied specifically encouraging Segretti to concentrate his activities on Senator Edmund Muskie. In March 1974 Chapin, with other former Nixon aides, was indicted on four counts of perjury stemming from his April 1973 testimony. On April 5, 1974, Dwight Chapin was convicted of two counts of perjury, and on May 15 he received a jail sentence of 10 to 30 months. In December 1975, after his appeals had been exhausted, his sentence was reduced to from 30 to 6 months at the federal prison in Lampoc, California. Upon completing his sentence, Chapin worked for W. Clement Stone Enterprises (Chicago) and published a magazine, *Success Unlimited.*

—SJT

Chavez, Cesar E(strada)
(1927–1993) *president, United Farm Workers Organizing Committee*

Cesar Chavez was born on March 31, 1927 in Yuma, Arizona. When Chavez was 10 years old, the foreclosure of his family's farm forced them to move on, to travel among labor camps in search of work. Although officially schooled through the seventh grade, he finally taught himself to read and write in his 20s and 30s. He served in the U.S. Navy in 1944–45.

In 1952 Chavez was recruited into Saul Alinsky's Community Service Organization (CSO), a Mexican-American self-help group. Chavez became general director of the CSO in 1958; he resigned four years later after the board of directors voted down his plan to organize farm workers. He then founded the National Farm Workers Association (NFWA) and over the next few years attempted to organize the migrant workers of southern and central California. In 1966 the NFWA merged with the Agricultural Workers Organizing Committee (AWOC), an AFL-CIO affiliate, to form the United Farm Workers Organizing Committee (UFWOC). The union's name was later shortened to the United Farm Workers of America (UFW).

From 1965 to 1970 Chavez and the union conducted a strike against the California grape growers. The long and bitter strike had elements of both a labor dispute and a crusade

for migrant workers. Chavez led his workers in long marches similar to those used by black civil rights groups. In 1966 he called for a national boycott of table grapes that lasted into the late 1970s. These tactics and Chavez's personality brought together a coalition of liberal supporters, including Robert F. Kennedy and WALTER REUTHER. The strike ended in 1970 when growers signed a three-year contract.

Jurisdictional disputes between the UFWOC and the International Brotherhood of Teamsters (IBT) often stymied Chavez's attempts to negotiate. The first pact marking the unions' territories was signed in July 1967; the Teamsters would represent workers in the commercial sheds, while the UFWOC would handle the field workers' affairs. Three years later, however, the IBT announced they had signed contracts for field workers with Salinas, California, fruit and vegetable growers. Another agreement was worked out between the unions in August 1970 that essentially followed the tenets of the earlier pacts. This "peace pact" lasted only two and a half years; late in 1972 the director of the Western Conference of Teamsters (WCT) announced his union's renegotiation of contracts with lettuce growers. As UFW contracts expired the following year, the WCT reported signed contracts or in-progress negotiations.

Chavez denounced the WCT agreements as "sweetheart contracts," favoring the growers rather than the workers, and pressed for secret ballot elections to allow the workers to choose their representation. Secret ballot elections did begin in September 1975, but only following passage of the California Agricultural Labor Relations Act (CALRA) earlier in the year. So many elections were contested that the newly formed state Agricultural Labor Relations Board (ALRB) ran out of funds in February 1976. Pressure from a grower-supported coalition of Republicans and rural Democrats in the state legislature stalled the governor's recommended supplemental appropriation for the board. The

ALRB received its annual budget in July 1976 and reopened the following November. A five-year territorial pact was signed between the WCT and the UFW in March 1977; under the agreement the Teamsters represented all workers covered under the National Labor Relations Act (which specifically excluded farm workers), and the UFW received jurisdiction over laborers covered under the CALRA.

Use of pesticides became a major bargaining point for Chavez in 1969. Early that year, in a letter to the growers' organization, he emphasized the discussion of "economic poisons . . . even if other labor relations problems have to wait." The UFWOC filed suit in Delano, demanding access to public records on pesticide use kept by the Kern County Agricultural Commission (KCAC). A Kern County superior court judge, while noting that "many commonly used pesticides . . . are highly toxic and can constitute a hazard to human health and welfare,"

refused the union permission to see the KCAC files. He claimed the union's primary purpose was "to keep alive controversy with the growers . . . and to force unionization." The union appealed the decision and filed several suits to end the use of DDT in California. This pressure, plus national publicity on the pesticide's harmful effects, resulted in a statewide ban of DDT effective January 1, 1970.

Chavez served as president of the 30,000-member UFW until his death in 1993. In 1994 he received the Presidential Medal of Freedom (posthumously) from President Bill Clinton.

—RB

Cheney, Richard B.
(1941–   ) *chief of staff*

Born in Lincoln, Nebraska, on January 30, 1941, Cheney attended Yale University and

President Ford meets with Richard Cheney. *(Ford Library)*

Casper College before taking his B.A. (1965) and M.A. (1966) from the University of Wyoming. Without obtaining a degree, Cheney did additional graduate-level work at the University of Wisconsin, and he was awarded a Congressional Fellowship for 1968–69. Immediately following his fellowship, Cheney became a special assistant to DONALD RUMSFELD, then the director of the Office of Economic Opportunity. Cheney moved up in the NIXON White House in 1971 when he became a White House staff assistant, then director of the Cost of Living Council, where he served until 1973.

Upon the resignation of Nixon in August 1974, Cheney served as a member of a short-lived transition team to the FORD White House, headed by Rumsfeld. When Rumsfeld became Ford's White House chief of staff in 1974, Cheney became his deputy; when Rumsfeld was chosen secretary of defense in November 1975, Cheney was promoted to Ford's chief of staff, a position he held to the end of the Ford administration in 1977.

In 1978 Cheney was elected to the House of Representatives as the at-large congressman from Wyoming. He served in that capacity until 1989. He served as chairman of the Republican Policy Committee, chairman of the House Republican Conference, and minority whip.

Cheney served as secretary of defense in the GEORGE H. W. BUSH administration from 1989 to 1993. Following that service, he became a senior fellow at the American Enterprise Institute. In 1995 he explored the idea of a run for the presidency but finally dismissed it (most reporters cited Cheney's health—to that point, he had had three heart attacks). Later that year Cheney was named chief executive officer of the Halliburton Company, a leader in energy service products. In 2001, after a challenge to the vote in Florida, Cheney was elected vice president of the United States on a ticket headed by George W. Bush. He was reelected in 2004.

—JRG

Chisholm, Shirley (Anita) (St. Hill)
(1924–2005)   *member of the House of Representatives*

Born November 30, 1924, as Shirley Anita St. Hill, the daughter of an unskilled laborer, she emigrated from the West Indies to Brooklyn when she was 11. She graduated cum laude from Brooklyn College in 1946. While she was in college, she became active in the Urban League and the NAACP. In 1952 she received her master's degree from Columbia in childhood education. In October 1948 she married Conrad Q. Chisholm.

From 1953 to 1959 Chisholm worked as the director of the Hamilton-Madison Child Care Center in New York, and from 1959 to 1964 she served as an educational consultant in New York City's Bureau of Child Welfare. She was also active in the Brooklyn branch of the NAACP, the Democratic Women's Workshop, the League of Women Voters, and the Bedford-Stuyvesant Political League. Chisholm served in the New York state assembly from 1964 to 1968, where she was recognized as a feminist and a black leader.

In 1968 Chisholm ran against JAMES FARMER, the founder of the Congress of Racial Equality, for a seat in the U.S. House. Since they both agreed on basic issues, Farmer unwisely chose to base his campaign on male chauvinism. He charged that the black community needed "a strong male image" and "a man's voice in Washington" to counteract sociologists' claims that blacks suffered from "matriarchal dominance." That November Chisholm defeated Farmer by a margin of two to one.

As the first black woman ever elected a U.S. representative, Chisholm quickly found herself at odds not only with the NIXON administration, but with her fellow Democrats and black male colleagues as well. Her initial encounter with the Democratic leadership came during her first month in the House, when she refused to sit on the Agriculture Committee after having requested the Education and Labor, the Post Office and Civil Service, or the Foreign Affairs committees. In a perhaps unprecedented reversal, Representative WILBUR MILLS (D-Ark.), chairman of the Ways and Means Committee, placed her on the Veterans Affairs Committee.

Chisholm's voting record from 1969 to 1973 established her as a liberal, antiwar feminist. In her first year in the House, she voted against such Nixon proposals as the antiballistic missile system and the SST, the "no knock" provision of the anti-crime bill, and jet fighter planes for Taiwan. She also opposed Nixon's nominations of CLEMENT F. HAYNSWORTH and G. HARROLD CARSWELL to the Supreme Court.

The same year Chisholm supported a full employment bill, appointment of a national commission on Afro-American history and culture, enlargement of the powers of the Department of Housing and Urban Development, establishment of a cabinet-level department of consumer affairs, and federal reimbursement (up to 90 percent) of state welfare programs. She cosponsored with her colleague and friend BELLA ABZUG (D-N.Y.) a comprehensive bill to establish day care facilities in most major cities at a cost of $5 billion. President Nixon, however, vetoed the day care bill. In 1970 she opposed Nixon's welfare bill, charging that it was totally inadequate and demeaning to the poverty-stricken applicant.

As an antiwar activist, Chisholm backed and spoke at several of the marches on Washington in the late 1960s and early 1970s. She voted for the Cooper-Church Amendment following the Cambodian invasion of 1970 and supported legislation for an all-volunteer army. A dedicated feminist, she spoke in favor of the Equal Rights Amendment, the right of all women to abortion, day care centers, and the equalization of pay between men and women. In July 1971 she joined with other national women political leaders to form the National Women's Political Caucus. On other social issues she consistently voted for equitable health, education, and welfare benefits for the poor, worked to establish a national SEEK program (a remedial education project for minority students), and continued to press for passage of full-employment legislation. In 1971 Chisholm and Ronald Dellums (D-Calif.) held a series of hearings to investigate racism in the army.

In December 1971 Chisholm announced that she would seek the Democratic nomination for president in 1972. She entered almost all of the primaries and went to the national convention in Miami Beach with 152 delegates. However, during the convention she withdrew and threw her support behind GEORGE MCGOVERN.

In 1973 Chisholm launched a legislative effort that for the first time united blacks, women, and labor behind an amendment to include domestics in the minimum-wage bill. Congress passed the bill in June 1973 and overrode Nixon's veto in March 1974.

In the mid-1970s Chisholm continued to oppose large defense budgets, to actively support federally funded abortions for welfare recipients, and to lobby for a department of consumer affairs. Amid criticism that she was not responding to the needs of her disadvantaged constituency, Chisholm won a difficult reelection in 1976.

Chisholm retired to Florida in 1982. In 1992 she was nominated as ambassador to Jamaica but withdrew due to poor health. She died in Ormond Beach in 2005.

—SJT and JMP

Church, Frank (Forrester)
(1924–1984) *member of the Senate*

Frank Church was born on July 25, 1924, in Boise, Idaho. After a bout with cancer, in which doctors only gave him six months to live, Church earned his law degree from Stanford University in 1950. Running as a Democrat in a traditionally Republican state, Church lost a number of elections for local offices. In 1956 he upset archconservative senator Herman Welker (R-Idaho) in a bitterly contested election. Church championed public ownership and development of power facilities and conservation against his rival, who was supported by the private utilities and lumber and mining interests. Throughout the Kennedy-Johnson years Church compiled one of the most liberal records in the Senate, voting for civil rights acts, War on Poverty programs, Medicare, and conservation legislation.

It was in foreign policy that Church broke with the Johnson administration. A member of the Foreign Relations Committee, Church became one of the Senate's most vocal critics of the Vietnam War. In 1965 Church called for direct negotiations with the Communists, free elections in South Vietnam, and American disengagement from the conflict. Yet Church continued to vote for appropriations bills for the war.

During the NIXON administration, Church, fearing an expansion of the war, began to campaign to get Congress to use its funding power to force the president to seek peace in Asia. In the spring of 1970, Church and Senator JOHN SHERMAN COOPER (R-Ky.) introduced an amendment to a foreign military sales bill barring funds for future military operations in Cambodia. Capitalizing on the outrage many in the nation expressed toward the escalation of the war into Cambodia, Church and his supporters got the amendment passed by the Foreign Relations Committee. After a seven-week filibuster, the Senate passed it in late June by a vote of 58 to 37. The House, however, rejected the measure. A watered-down version was passed in December as part of a defense appropriation bill. The rider prevented the introduction of ground troops into Laos or Thailand. The adoption of the Cooper-Church Amendment represented the first limitation ever voted on the president's power as commander-in-chief during a war situation.

In April 1972 Church, this time joined by Senator CLIFFORD CASE (R-N.J.), introduced an amendment to a State Department appropriations bill authorizing a cutoff of funds for all U.S. combat operations in Indochina after December 31 subject to an agreement for the release of American prisoners of war. The Foreign Relations Committee and the Democratic Party Caucus approved the Church-Case Amendment, but the Senate reduced its effectiveness by attaching a rider that made it effective only if an internationally supervised cease-fire was negotiated.

Church also questioned other administration defense and foreign policies. He called for a reduction of American troops in Western Europe. Church voted against the deployment of the antiballistic missile system, backed ending the construction of the C5A plane, and opposed arms aid to repressive regimes.

In January 1975 the Senate created a bipartisan, select committee to investigate alleged abuses by the Central Intelligence Agency, the Federal Bureau of Investigation, and other government intelligence and law enforcement agencies. Church was selected chairman. Over the next year and a half the Church Committee heard testimony from cabinet heads, top military officials, the leadership of the CIA and the FBI, retired intelligence operatives, and those Americans who felt victimized by the unconstitutional activities of both organizations. Among other things, the probe revealed CIA involvement in plots to assassinate world leaders and in the coup against Chile's Marxist president Salvador Allende. It also uncovered a series of covert operations by the FBI against organizations J. EDGAR HOOVER had considered radical.

In a November 1975 letter to Church, President FORD requested that the panel not make its assassination report public because it would "do grievous damage to our country" and be "exploited by foreign nations and groups hostile to the United States." Church responded that the committee's intention to make the report public had "long been clear." Moreover, he felt the national interest would be "better served by letting the American people know the true and complete story" behind the death plots. The committee's report charged the U.S. government had ordered the assassination of two foreign leaders—Fidel Castro and Patrice Lumumba—and had been involved in assassination plots against three other foreign officials—Raphael Trujillo, Ngo Dinh Diem, and Rene Schneider. Although four of the five leaders were assassinated, none of them died as the direct results of the plans initiated by U.S. officials.

In its April 26 report on the CIA, the Church Committee described the U.S. intelligence community as routinely engaged in covert operations that were often without merit and frequently initiated without adequate authorization. Two days later the committee charged the FBI had conducted investigations, often employing illegal or improper methods, not only against individuals and political groups on the right and left but also against religious groups, prominent politicians, advocates of nonviolence and racial harmony, and supporters of women's rights. The report astonished the American people by listing such FBI targets as Dr. Martin Luther King Jr., Adlai Stevenson, and Justice WILLIAM O. DOUGLAS. In its final recommendation, the Church Committee advocated greater oversight of the agencies by Congress and the White House to prevent future excesses.

Frank Church decided to enter the 1976 Democratic primaries, using his investigation as his major issue against the Ford administra-tion. Declaring his candidacy in March 1976, he hoped to rally liberals who had been disappointed with MORRIS UDALL (D-Ariz.) and fearful of JIMMY CARTER and Senator HENRY JACKSON (D-Wash.). For two months Church actively campaigned, running on his solid liberal record during the Nixon-Ford presidencies. Church supported conservation, opposed placing limits on busing, and voted to override the vetoes of Nixon and Ford of appropriations to cities and poverty programs. Although Church won the Nebraska, Idaho, and Oregon primaries, it appeared certain to him by June that Carter would obtain the nomination. Church, therefore, endorsed the former Georgia governor.

During the early Carter presidency, Frank Church became one of the president's closest foreign policy advisers. He worked with Carter for the ratification of the Panama Canal treaties. A staunch pro-Zionist, Church broke with the administration on its desire to sell arms to Israel's enemies to secure a military balance of power in the Middle East. In 1980 Church was defeated for reelection by Republican Steve Symms. He died of cancer in 1984.

—JB

Cleaver, (Leroy) Eldridge
(1935–1998) *Black Panther Party leader*

Born on August 31, 1935, in Wabbaseka, Arkansas, Cleaver grew up in the Watts section of Los Angeles, where his mother was a school janitor. He became involved in a series of legal offenses, including rape, that landed him in reformatories and jails for various periods of time until his self-imposed exile from the United States in 1968. While in prison he became attracted to the discipline and self-pride of the Black Muslims and became one of its ministers. He also began writing on radical subjects. Many of his magazine articles were included in his book *Soul on Ice*, published in

1968, which became one of the best-selling radical works in the United States in the late 1960s and early 1970s. In 1966 Cleaver was released from prison. He joined the Black Panther Party the following year and was the party's presidential candidate in 1968. In April 1968 Cleaver was involved in a gun battle with police. His parole was immediately revoked, and he was returned to jail. He was later released by a superior court judge, but the state appealed the ruling and in November 1968 higher courts ordered Cleaver back to jail. He refused to comply, went underground, and finally fled the country. He lived in Cuba until July 1969, when he moved to Algeria. He was in exile for six years, during which time he visited North Korea and several other countries.

Cleaver attempted to keep his identification with the revolutionary struggle within the United States during his exile. He wrote an article for the Black Panther Party newspaper in 1969 in which he asserted: "in order to transform the American social order, we have to destroy the present structure of power in the United States. . . . The only means possible is the violent overthrow of the machinery of the oppressive ruling class." That same year he also wrote, "I love the angels of destruction and disorder as opposed to the devils of conservation and law and order." In October 1970 he made a broadcast through Radio Hanoi to the U.S. forces in Vietnam in which he called on black soldiers to dissent from the policies of the armed forces.

In 1971 Cleaver was expelled from the Black Panther Party as a result of conflicts within the party's leadership over ideology and personality clashes with party chairman Huey P. Newton. The official reason given for the expulsion was that Cleaver still championed a violent position for the party, which was shifting toward a nonviolent approach to change. Cleaver's expulsion symbolized the decline in the fortunes of the party, which henceforth contained its activities to electoral contests and the social needs of the few communities in which it operated.

Relations grew uncomfortable between Cleaver and the Algerian government after hijackers associated with the Panthers arrived in the country in August 1972. Cleaver therefore moved to Paris. In the early 1970s he began to tire of exile. He wanted his children to know the United States. He also thought that after Nixon's resignation from the presidency in 1974, the political climate in the United States would be less repressive. Cleaver had, in his own words, undergone a religious conversion while he was in France and became a "born-again Christian."

On November 18, 1975, Cleaver ended his self-imposed exile by surrendering to the FBI at Kennedy Airport in New York. He spent the first nine months in the United States in prison before being released on $100,000 bail. Upon his return Cleaver altered his ideology almost completely. He expressed faith in "the limitless possibilities of the American dream." He asserted that "I'm having a love affair with the U.S. military" and apparently meant it. Cleaver praised HENRY KISSINGER's policy on South Africa, eschewed even the NAACP, and found Secretary of Agriculture EARL BUTZ's controversial remarks on blacks "sort of funny, nothing much to get excited about."

Cleaver published *Soul on Fire* in 1978, describing much of his more recent thoughts. The book was widely thought to be inferior to his earlier *Soul on Ice*. Aside from writing and lecturing, Cleaver began to travel on the evangelical circuit with the Reverend BILLY GRAHAM. Cleaver ran for the Republican nomination for the Senate from California in 1986. In 1992 he was convicted of cocaine possession and burglary. In 1994 he was nearly killed in a drug-related assault. He died in 1998.

—GWB

Cohen, William S.
(1940–   ) *member of the House of Representatives*

William Cohen, the son of a baker, graduated in 1962 from Bowdoin College. He earned his law degree from Boston University Law School in 1965 and became a partner in a Bangor law firm. He was active in the Maine Trial Bar Association and served as assistant editor in chief of the *Journal of the American Trial Bar Association* from 1965 to 1966. He was an instructor at Husson College in 1968 and at the University of Maine from 1968 to 1972. He was mayor of Bangor in 1971–72. In 1972 he ran for the U.S. House, conducting a 600-mile walking campaign through his congressional district. He won the seat that had been vacated when Democratic representative William D. Hathaway successfully challenged longtime Maine senator MARGARET CHASE SMITH (R-Me.) in the 1972 election. Cohen's victory was considered an upset.

In the House Cohen compiled a moderate record. He supported the NIXON and FORD administrations only slightly more than 50 percent of the time. He usually voted to override Nixon-Ford vetoes of spending and social welfare measures. Cohen frequently backed consumer and labor legislation. His support of administration defense policy was mixed. He opposed Nixon's program to develop the B-1 bomber and voted against increasing military assistance for South Vietnam and the continued funding of the Safeguard antiballistic missile system. He backed the administration's demands to maintain defense appropriations budget spending levels and opposed cutting military aid for South Korea.

Cohen gained national attention when he became one of the most outspoken Republicans favoring impeachment during the House Judiciary Committee's impeachment proceedings in 1974. Shortly before the panel held public hearings, Cohen said, "If we are to have

confidence in the concept of even-handed treatment under the laws, then we simply cannot condone" the kind of conduct the committee had discovered during its investigation. Five other Republicans were also thought to be leaning toward impeachment, while 10 Republicans were firmly opposed. It was not easy for a freshman Republican to support impeachment. At the time the strategy of the Republican House leadership was to brand impeachment as a purely partisan affair, supported mostly by the president's liberal political enemies. The party position was that Nixon, a Republican president, deserved the support of Republicans in Congress.

Cohen took a leading role in the impeachment debate during the committee's public hearings. He challenged Nixon's chief committee defender, Representative CHARLES E. WIGGINS (R-Calif.), by pointing out how Wiggins had quoted selectively from the tape transcripts when he was making out the case for the president. Cohen helped revise the proposed impeachment articles so they more closely reflected Republican views on impeachable conduct and on the evidence.

Cohen was one of six Republicans who joined all 21 Democrats to vote for the first two articles of impeachment adopted by the committee. The first article accused President Nixon of obstructing justice, and the second accused him of misusing federal agencies to violate the rights of citizens. The committee adopted a third article that Cohen opposed. The article accused Nixon of failing to comply with the committee's subpoenas. Cohen also opposed the two articles the committee rejected. The articles accused Nixon of waging an illegal war in Cambodia and of income tax evasion. Cohen never had to defend the difficult political choice he had made. After the White House was forced to release the contents of tapes that showed that Nixon had discussed using the CIA to halt the FBI's

Watergate probe, almost everyone in the House supported impeachment.

Cohen's leading role in the impeachment hearings established him as a strong statewide candidate in Maine. He briefly considered challenging Senator EDMUND MUSKIE (D-Me.) in 1976 but decided against it. Two years later Cohen won a Senate seat from incumbent senator William D. Hathaway (D-Me.), the man Cohen replaced as the second district's representative.

Cohen was elected to the U.S. Senate in 1978 and reelected to two succeeding terms. His service on the Armed Services Committee and the Senate Committee on Intelligence earned for him the reputation as one of the leading experts on security issues in the Republican Party. His role in the drafting of the Goldwater-Nichols Act of 1986, which restructured the nation's defense hierarchy, was notable. He was also an influential member of the 1986 Senate probe into the Iran-contra scandal. Cohen was one of only three Republicans who signed the majority report that held Reagan responsible for the affair.

Cohen declined to run for a fourth Senate term in 1996. In December of that year, claiming his desire to have a truly bipartisan cabinet, President Bill Clinton named Cohen his secretary of defense. Cohen served in that position until 2001. He is presently chairman of The Cohen Group, a business consulting service.

—GWB and JRG

Colby, William E(gan)
(1920–1996) *director of Central Intelligence*

Born on January 4, 1920, Colby, the son of a career army officer, graduated from Princeton in 1940. He served as a member of the Office of Strategic Services during World War II and received his law degree from Columbia in

1947. He then practiced law in New York City. Colby joined the Central Intelligence Agency (CIA) in 1950. Under cover of diplomatic title he served the agency in Sweden and Italy during the 1950s. Colby played a major role in CIA attempts to block the expansion of the Italian Communist Party.

Colby became CIA station chief and first secretary of the American embassy in South Vietnam in 1959. Three years later he was appointed head of the Far East division of the clandestine services, where he presided over the CIA's expanding programs throughout Southeast Asia. He played an important role in social development programs designed to win the allegiance of the South Vietnamese people as well as in Operation Phoenix, an effort to coordinate American and Vietnamese attacks on the Communist infrastructure.

The latter program proved extremely controversial. Critics charged that American officials condoned and participated in the torture of political prisoners and that during its first two and a half years over 20,000 suspected Communists had been killed. In 1970 and 1971 Colby was called before congressional committees to explain and justify the program. He pointed out that many of the dead had been killed in battle, but when asked to state categorically that there had been no assassinations under the program, he refused. His testimony failed to quiet criticism of the program, which was generally accounted a failure.

In June 1971 Colby resigned his post and returned to Washington because of the serious illness of his eldest daughter. He became executive director-comptroller of the CIA, its third ranking position, in 1972. He had no direct influence on policy, but because he had control of the budget, Colby could influence the development of various programs. He refined the agency's budgeting procedures to permit financing of unanticipated projects and presented budget requests to Congress.

CIA director William Colby before the House Intelligence Committee, August 1975 *(Library of Congress)*

Colby was aware of various high-level CIA programs including "Track I," the agency's efforts to prevent the election of Marxist Salvador Allende in Chile in 1970. He was also aware of Track II, the top-level program authorized by Nixon and revealed to no one outside the CIA, designed to prevent Allende from assuming office. The program failed. He also knew of the existence of Operation Chaos, an effort to investigate possible foreign links with domestic antiwar groups. In 1972, as a result of prompting by Colby, the focus of the operation was turned from the antiwar movement to antiterrorist activities. However, no effort was made to destroy the illegal information gathered.

Colby was deeply involved in the agency's reaction to Watergate, following identification of the burglars as former CIA agents. Director of Central Intelligence RICHARD HELMS spelled out the agency's fundamental strategy: distance the CIA from the event to every extent possible. He also asked Colby to coordinate the agency's efforts in the case. The CIA provided responses to what it considered legitimate demands from law enforcement agencies but would not volunteer information.

Shortly after JAMES SCHLESINGER was named director of Central Intelligence (DCI) in January 1973, Colby became deputy director for plans. (He later changed the title to deputy director of operations to clarify to the public what his functions were.) At this post he reformed the clandestine services, paring down its staff and reducing its influence. Colby also reorganized the division to limit the power of James Angleton, a cold warrior who opposed détente and had been active in supervising some of the illegal domestic operations. (After Colby became DCI in 1974, he succeeded in forcing Angleton's retirement.) Colby reoriented the service, moving it from traditional clandestine operations to the use of sophisticated technology to collect intelligence. He also placed greater stress on the area of economic intelligence.

Under Schlesinger's direction, Colby compiled a list of what were termed the agency's "family jewels," questionable or illegal operations. In addition to CIA actions in Chile and operations against the antiwar movement, they included the opening of domestic mail, attempts to assassinate or have assassinated such foreign leaders as Patrice Lumumba and Fidel Castro, experimentation with mind-control drugs on unknowing subjects, and exchanges with domestic agencies of information on possible subversives. The list was compiled in an effort to identify potentially dangerous issues and reform internal procedures.

President NIXON named Colby DCI in May 1973. He was confirmed in August. Colby attempted to continue the reforms he had initiated as deputy director of operations. In an effort to establish better communications and interchange between policy makers and analysts, he abolished the Office of National Estimates and replaced it with a group of 11 specialists in functional and geographical areas known as National Intelligence Officers. These individuals were responsible for intelligence collection and production in their designated fields and reported directly to Colby.

Soon after Colby's appointment, the agency became the focus of public and congressional attention as its illegal activities became public. Therefore, most of Colby's time was absorbed in responding to these developments. During 1974 and 1975 the agency was investigated by a presidential commission led by Vice President NELSON ROCKEFELLER, a Senate committee under the direction of Senator FRANK CHURCH (D-Idaho), and a House panel headed by Representative OTIS PIKE (D-N.Y.). It also became the target of a number of investigative reporters. Against the advice of such individuals as HENRY KISSINGER, Colby chose to cooperate with these panels, revealing information that he thought would not damage national security or endanger CIA agents. He did, however, unsuccessfully attempt to prevent an investigation of assassination plots on the grounds that the agency had assassinated no one and that the probe would only damage the reputation of the United States. He also failed to prevent revelation of the CIA's efforts to use the *Glomar Explorer*, a technically advanced ship built by HOWARD HUGHES's interests, to salvage a Soviet submarine.

During September 1975 Colby was threatened with contempt of Congress for refusal to give the Pike Committee classified documents unless permitted to delete passages he felt jeopardized national security. A settlement was reached under which disputes between the committee and Colby over deleted passages would be mediated by the president.

In testimony before the various committees, Colby reiterated his contention that the CIA's domestic misdeeds were few and that they had been stopped in 1973. He also repeated his statements that the CIA had assassinated no one and argued that certain aspects of the probes could damage national security. In September he revealed that the agency possessed a poison cache in direct opposition to a presidential order given by Richard Nixon to destroy it. This last revelation proved the catalyst for President FORD to demand Colby's resignation. The White House had been disturbed by the continuing probes and revelations, Colby's handling of the situation, and the impression given that the CIA was an unsavory world of cloak and dagger spies.

Colby announced his resignation in November. His departure was delayed until January 1976 to give his replacement, GEORGE H. W. BUSH, time to return from his diplomatic assignment in Beijing. After he left government service, Colby set up law practice in Washington, D.C. In 1982 the government began legal proceedings against Colby for disclosures made in his 1978 memoir *Honorable Men* (Colby agreed to pay a $10,000 fine in an out-of-court settlement). He died on April 27, 1996, following a canoeing accident at his Maryland home.

—ES

Coleman, William T(haddeus), Jr.
(1920–   ) *secretary of transportation*

Born on July 7, 1920, into a middle-class family with connections to many of America's most distinguished black leaders, William T.

Coleman was educated in the public schools of Philadelphia and at the University of Pennsylvania. Following service in the army air corps during World War II, Coleman received degrees from Harvard Law School, where he edited the *Law Review* and graduated first in his class. Admitted to the Pennsylvania bar in 1947, Coleman became a law clerk in 1948 for Supreme Court justice Felix Frankfurter. He was the first black ever to hold such a post. In 1952 Coleman joined the Philadelphia law firm of Dilworth, Paxson, Kalin, & Levy, becoming a senior partner in 1956.

Although specializing in corporate and antitrust litigation, Coleman acquired a reputation as an expert in transportation law. He represented Philadelphia, Cincinnati, and other cities in mass transit and labor matters, in time becoming special counsel and negotiator for both the Philadelphia Transportation Authority and the Southeast Pennsylvania Transportation Authority. Coleman's corporate directorships included, among others, Pan American World Airways and the Penn Mutual Life Insurance Corporation, as well as membership on the board of governors of the American Stock Exchange.

Deeply involved in civil rights law, Coleman coauthored the brief presented to the Supreme Court in the *Brown v. Board of Education* case, which led to the 1954 decision banning school segregation. In 1971 he was elected president of the NAACP's Legal Defense and Education Fund, of which he had been a member for years.

A long-standing member of the Republican Party, Coleman entered government during the Eisenhower administration, serving from 1959 to 1961 on the President's Commission on Employment Policy. In the 1960s and 1970s Coleman was a consultant to the U.S. Arms Control and Disarmament Agency, an assistant counsel to the Warren Commission, and a member of the U.S. delegation to the UN General Assembly. On January 14, 1975, Coleman accepted President FORD's offer to become secretary of transportation. Sworn into office March 7, 1975, Coleman succeeded CLAUDE S. BRINEGAR as head of the fourth-largest federal agency.

Coleman's priorities upon taking office were to settle transportation problems during a period of retrenchment in government spending. Several months of study produced *A Statement of National Transportation Policy*, which Coleman sent to Congress in September 1975. The 53-page document set forth measures that Coleman believed would lead to "a more safe, efficient, diverse, and competitive transportation system." In general Coleman recommended less governmental interference in the operation of railroads and airlines, an extensive reformation of federal regulations pertaining to rate structures, and a more equitable distribution of federal funds among the various branches of transportation policy. Although it contained few new ideas, the *Statement* marked the first serious effort by the federal government to formulate a comprehensive national transportation policy.

An architect of the Ford administration's efforts to change regulations in the transportation industry, Coleman recommended that financial aid be provided to airlines to help defray the cost of modifying old planes to meet new FAA noise standards. Under the Coleman proposal such aid would have been funded by diverting 2 percent of the 8 percent airline ticket tax. However, Coleman took a tough stance against certain other transportation subsidies, such as free use of waterways by barge operators. Similarly, Coleman approved a new $378 million federal budget allocation for Amtrak in 1976, higher than the $350 million of the previous year but considerably less than what Amtrak had requested.

Coleman's most controversial decision as secretary of transportation was his ruling on

February 4, 1976, to allow limited service by the British-French supersonic transport Concorde to New York and Washington on a 16-month basis. Although the decision stirred environmental opposition, President Ford announced that he would "stand by" Coleman's ruling. Excluding noise, Coleman said that he did not consider the environmental consequences of the decision "to be substantial." The Concorde decision was found to be legal and reasonable on May 19, 1976, by a three-judge panel of the U.S. Court of Appeals for the District of Columbia.

Despite demands for increased safety controls on automobiles, Coleman ruled on December 6, 1976, against requiring auto manufacturers to equip all new cars with air bags as a protective device against accidents. Instead of mandatory air bags, Coleman proposed a demonstration project, declaring his concern over the public's rejection of "unfamiliar and controversial technology." Coleman is the senior partner of O'Melveny and Myers law office. On September 29, 1995, President Clinton gave him the Presidential Medal of Freedom.

—JAN

Colson, Charles (Wendell)
(1931–   ) *special assistant to the president*

Charles Colson was born on October 16, 1931, and raised in a comfortable home in Boston, where his father worked for the Securities and Exchange Commission. When he was 18 he turned down a full scholarship to Harvard because he thought the school was too radical and because a shocked admissions officer told him that no one had ever done that before. Colson went to Brown University and graduated in 1953. He served in the Marines from 1953 to 1956. After his discharge he went to Georgetown Law School and graduated in 1959. The following year he became Senator Leverett

Saltonstall's (R-Mass.) campaign manager and then served as his administrative assistant on Capitol Hill. From 1961 to 1969 he enjoyed a prominent law practice in Washington and continued to be active in Republican politics, working for Senator BARRY GOLDWATER in 1964 and RICHARD NIXON in 1968.

In 1968 Colson joined the Republican presidential campaign as an "issues man," helping Nixon think through his position on various issues. In 1969 he was brought to the White House to work as a political strategist under H. R. HALDEMAN, the president's chief of staff. Colson worked out the Nixon strategy to court the potentially conservative, ethnic labor vote away from the Democrats on the issues of Vietnam, public school integration, and birth control. Colson's influence was seen in Nixon's pardon of Teamster president JAMES HOFFA and in his appointment of PETER J. BRENNAN of the New York Building Trades as secretary of labor.

Colson liked to describe himself as a "flag-waving, kick-'em-in-the-nuts, antipress, antiliberal Nixon fanatic." He was known at the White House for his insensitivity and ruthlessness and had once exclaimed to astonished reporters, "I would walk over my grandmother if necessary" to ensure Richard Nixon's reelection.

The year 1970 proved to be a turning point for both the Nixon White House and for Charles Colson. In May 1970, after the Cambodian invasion and the resulting student strikes culminating in the public outcry over the shooting of college students at Ohio's Kent State and Mississippi's Jackson State colleges, the Nixon administration found itself increasingly on the defensive. Its response, carried out by the White House staff under Haldeman, JOHN EHRLICHMAN, JOHN DEAN, and Colson, was a series of deceptive letter-writing campaigns designed to convince the public and government officials that the American people supported Nixon's policies.

Colson and JEB STUART MAGRUDER set up a White House letter-writing campaign to influence citizens and politicians about the correctness of the president's foreign policy. Colson's office used Republican National Committee lists of editors, governors, congressmen, and media representatives and sent them letters and telegrams that expressed concern about their positions on Nixon policies. The letters and telegrams appeared to come from private citizens but in fact came from the White House. Colson specialized in the establishment of dummy "citizens' committees" organized to give the impression to both people in influential positions and to voters that Nixon policies had a broad base of support. He also supported the so-called Huston Plan to create a domestic security group to spy on "disruptive elements" within society. Nixon approved the project, but J. EDGAR HOOVER vetoed it.

After the 1970 elections Colson moved to a key position with Haldeman and Ehrlichman as a special assistant to the president. For the next two years Colson was in daily contact with the president, speaking with him often as many as five or six times a day, and had a key role in creating the "Plumbers" unit, drawing up the "political enemies list," and establishing the security operation of the Committee to Re-Elect the President (CREEP).

The White House special investigations unit, or the Plumbers (as it was known in the White House), was established in June 1971 at Richard Nixon's directive that the White House "plug the leaks." The directive arose from the publication of the secret *Pentagon Papers*. John Ehrlichman and Colson served as supervisors of the unit, which was to identify people suspected of leaking information and harass, intimidate, and embarrass them publicly.

In 1971, in response to Nixon's growing fear and hostility to criticism from Democrats and liberals, Charles Colson had his staff draw up elaborate lists in categories like "political enemies" and "media enemies," with suggestions about which government agencies might appropriately deal with them.

In addition to the enemies project, Colson was involved in a myriad of other clandestine and illegal activities. These included having E. HOWARD HUNT forge a cable implicating the Kennedy administration in the 1964 assassination of President Diem of South Vietnam, which Colson then leaked to *Life* magazine. In the spring of 1972, during the International Telephone and Telegraph (ITT) scandal that erupted during the RICHARD KLEINDIENST confirmation hearings, Colson dispatched Hunt to discuss the case with DITA BEARD, who had written a memo suggesting that a "deal" had been worked out between the Nixon administration and ITT to end an antitrust suit against the company in return for funding the Republican National Convention planned for San Diego, near President Nixon's San Clemente, California, home. After Hunt had met with her, Dita Beard issued a statement claiming her memo was a fraud. Then in the summer of 1971, Colson suggested to John Caulfield, a member of the John Dean's staff, that he arrange for the firebombing of the liberal Washington-based Brookings Institute.

By winter 1972, when the Nixon administration started gearing up for the 1972 reelection effort, a pattern of widespread illegalities under the direction of H. R. Haldeman, John Ehrlichman, and Charles Colson had been well established. The Committee to Re-Elect the President, established as a Haldeman operation to circumvent the influence of JOHN MITCHELL, was staffed by the young men from the White House who had been involved in these questionable activities for two years or more.

Although Colson was not involved in the formation of G. GORDON LIDDY's "Gemstone" plan for electronic surveillance of LAWRENCE O'BRIEN, chairman of the Democratic National

Committee, he provided encouragement and support for the project. After the burglars were caught in June 1972, Colson supervised the destruction of the contents of E. Howard Hunt's White House safe, which included a psychological study of DANIEL ELLSBERG and the forged Diem cable. Colson promised Hunt clemency for his continued silence and urged that the White House continue its financial support of the defendants.

After Nixon's reelection in the fall of 1972, when people in the media and in Congress began to make connections among the Watergate burglary, the CREEP staff, and the White House staff, Colson announced that he was submitting his resignation. In early 1973 he left the White House and returned to his lucrative law practice, bringing to the firm a $100,000-a-year retainer from the Teamsters Union.

In spring 1973 JAMES MCCORD, one of the Watergate burglars, broke his silence and wrote a letter to Judge JOHN SIRICA, who had tried the Watergate case, charging that the defendants had been paid for their silence and that the deeds of wrongdoing extended far beyond those committed by the burglars or those traceable to CREEP.

In spite of his 11th-hour announcement that he had been "converted to Christ" and would dedicate himself to "working for the Lord," Colson was among seven top Nixon officials—including John N. Mitchell, H. R. Haldeman, and John Ehrlichman—indicted by the Watergate grand jury in March 1974 for conspiracy to "commit offenses against the United States," for obstruction of justice, for their political activities from 1969 to 1972, and for lying to investigative officials and agencies about those activities.

In lieu of facing a possible 15 years in prison and citing his recent Christian conversion, Colson promised to plead guilty and to be a cooperative witness in the other investigations and lawsuits provided the most serious charges against him were dropped. On June 3, 1974, he pled guilty to a charge of obstructing justice and was sentenced to one to three years in a minimum-security prison. In February 1975, after serving seven months of his sentence, Colson was released from jail. In 1976 he founded Prison Fellowship Royalties from Colson's 20 books are donated to that organization. In 1991 Colson began a daily radio show, *BreakPoint*, carried nationwide.

—SJT

Connally, John B(owden), Jr.

(1917–1993) *secretary of the treasury; special adviser to the president*

Born on February 27, 1917, the son of a tenant farmer, Connally attended the University of Texas at Austin, where he earned his law degree in 1941. His introduction to state and national politics, however, took place in 1938 when Lyndon B. Johnson, a freshman Democrat in Congress, invited him to Washington to serve as Johnson's aide. Connally joined the U.S. Naval Reserve in 1941 and worked in the office of the chief of naval operations and on the planning staff of General Dwight D. Eisenhower. Later, as a fighter plane director aboard the aircraft carrier USS *Essex* in the Pacific, he was awarded the Bronze Star. Connally returned to civilian life in 1946 and two years later managed Johnson's successful bid for the U.S. Senate. Connally worked as Johnson's administrative assistant in 1949. Thereafter he remained active in Texas Democratic Party politics and helped Johnson take over the party machine in 1956. In 1960 Connally managed Johnson's unsuccessful campaign for the Democratic Party's presidential nomination. Connally also worked as an attorney representing the oil interests of his state.

In early 1961 President John F. Kennedy appointed Connally secretary of the navy on the recommendation of Johnson and Secretary of Defense ROBERT S. MCNAMARA. Connally resigned his post in December 1961 to enter the Texas gubernatorial race, in which he defeated his Republican opponent the following year.

On November 22, 1963, Connally was riding in the presidential limousine in Dallas at the time of the assassination of John F. Kennedy and was himself seriously wounded. Connally's near-assassination made him a nationally known political figure and facilitated his reelection as governor of Texas in 1964 and 1966. Connally was generally a conservative, probusiness governor, stressing the need for economic growth and promoting expansion of the Texas educational system.

In 1968 Connally headed the Texas delegation to the Democratic Party Convention in Chicago, where HUBERT HUMPHREY was nominated for president. Although his own hopes for a place on the ticket were dashed, Connally played a key role in mobilizing the party apparatus behind Humphrey and pushing through a prowar plank in the face of liberal challenges inside the convention and massive rioting in the streets outside. Connally gave Humphrey only modest support in the subsequent election and in 1969 returned to his private legal practice in Texas.

In December 1970 President Nixon appointed Connally to succeed DAVID KENNEDY as secretary of the treasury. Connally's appointment was seen on all sides as a shrewd political move by Nixon. The incipient economic recession and Democratic gains in the off-year elections of November 1970 prompted Nixon to shake up his administration. Connally had attracted Nixon's attention while serving on the President's Advisory Commission on Executive Organization, headed by ROY ASH, which had been set up to streamline the executive branch. At a March 1970 cabinet meeting in which Ash had made a rather listless and unconvincing

presentation of the commission's recommendations, Connally had come to Ash's rescue with an impromptu summary of the advantages of the reorganization and had put at ease cabinet officials who feared their own jobs were being downgraded. On December 1, 1970, Nixon appointed Connally to the prestigious Foreign Intelligence Advisory Board, and days later, when David Kennedy offered to step down to facilitate a revamping of the administration, Nixon offered the Treasury post to Connally.

The reaction to the appointment of a Democrat to Nixon's cabinet was swift. Connally had not even consulted former president Lyndon B. Johnson, with whom he had discussed every previous move of his political career. Johnson was shocked at Connally's decision. One Washington commentator stated, "To my dirty mind, this appointment means only one thing: the start of 'Democrats for Nixon in 1972.'" Speculation that Nixon would replace SPIRO AGNEW with Connally as his running mate in 1972 began to circulate. A newspaper story concerning $225,000 in executor's fees that Connally had allegedly received from the estate of a former employer, Sid Richardson, while serving as governor of Texas created some friction at his Senate confirmation hearings, but Connally nonetheless assumed office in early February 1971.

Connally took over the Treasury while the United States was mired in recession. His appointment had been greeted with some skepticism by observers who questioned his ability to handle a post usually given to a banker. "I can add," Connally told a reporter who had asked him about his qualifications in economic matters. Connally imposed a grinding schedule on himself, reading widely to deepen his grasp of day-to-day Treasury operations and economics in general. In one of his first public actions, he attacked the Chase Manhattan Bank for boosting the prime interest rate at a time when credit for industry was already tight.

Connally's style was widely seen as a refreshing contrast to the rest of the Nixon administration. In September 1971 *New York Times* columnist James Reston described Connally as "the spunkiest character in Washington these days. . . . He is tossing away computerized Treasury speeches, and telling American business and American labor off the cuff to get off their duffs if they want more jobs, more profits and a larger share of the increasingly competitive world market."

Connally quickly emerged as the main spokesman in Congress for the administration's economic program. One of his first assignments was the promotion of the $250–$300 million White House bail-out plan for Lockheed Aircraft before a skeptical Congress. The issue had extensive international ramifications. The bankruptcy of Rolls-Royce, the British-owned maker of jet engines, was threatening to bankrupt Lockheed, which had spent millions designing its new L-1011 jet with Rolls-Royce engines. Connally's credibility in these matters was already strained by his statement that development of the supersonic transport (SST) by the United States would provide "$22 billion in the nation's foreign trade account over the next 20 years," a figure that caused even Council of Economic Advisers (CEA) chairman PAUL MCCRACKEN to criticize Connally for "numerical science fiction."

Senator JOSEPH MONTOYA (D-N.M.) argued that Connally, in advocating a loan for Lockheed, was effectively asking Congress to bail out a British firm. Connally replied that it would cost Lockheed $50 million to redesign the L-1011 to use different engines and emphasized how many jobs would be created by the firm's rescue. "The impact on the economy by the bankruptcy of Lockheed would be enormous, in my judgment," Connally told the Senate Finance Committee. Connally's personal sponsorship of the Lockheed loan drew the fire of economist JOHN KENNETH GALBRAITH, who

used the incident to assert that "the military-industrial complex is alive in Washington and doing well." Galbraith saw Connally as "a new boy in town and a Democrat in a Republican administration . . . needing to prove himself with the president." In contrast to Connally, Federal Reserve chairman ARTHUR BURNS and Deputy Secretary of Defense DAVID PACKARD were cool to the Lockheed bailout.

In addition to numerous appearances before congressional committees to promote the administration's domestic economic policies, Connally played a key role in U.S. foreign economic policy in 1971–72, a time of the worst monetary crisis since World War II.

In May 1971 Connally entered the arena that was to occupy his attention for the rest of his tenure at the Treasury. President Nixon sent him as the ranking representative to the International Banking Conference of the American Bankers' Association in Munich, where Connally spoke on the international monetary crisis that had just forced the European countries into a joint currency float earlier that month. In his speech Connally articulated the arch-nationalist tone that characterized his stance with Europe and Japan over the following year. Connally attributed the exchange crisis to a shift of economic power from the United States to Europe and Japan. He complained about restrictions on U.S. industrial and agricultural exports to foreign nations and underlined the failure of other countries to share the defense burdens of the West. The "unalterable position" of the United States concerning the dollar, as expounded by Connally, was: "We are not going to devalue. We are not going to change the price of gold."

The position of the U.S. dollar and the U.S. economy continued to deteriorate throughout the summer of 1971, however, and by early August it was obvious that drastic action was necessary. From August 13 to 15, Connally, Nixon, Office of Management and Budget director GEORGE SHULTZ, Federal Reserve Board chairman Burns, Council of Economic Advisers Chairman McCracken, and New York Federal Reserve Bank president PAUL VOLCKER conferred on the situation at Camp David, Maryland. Connally throughout the conference was an advocate of aggressive action, including the "closing of the gold window," or an end to the U.S. legal obligation to exchange its gold reserves for dollars held by foreign central banks.

When Burns, Connally's major opponent on the gold question, argued that such a move would severely tax the goodwill of the major U.S. trading partners, Connally replied, "We'll go broke getting their goodwill." Connally's views prevailed, and on the night of August 15, in a nationwide television broadcast, Nixon announced his "New Economic Policy" (NEP), which included a closing of the gold window, a 10 percent surcharge on foreign imports, and an 8 percent devaluation of the dollar.

Throughout the fall and winter of 1971, Connally was chief U.S. representative in all economic negotiations over the realignment of exchange rates. His first foreign appearance after his May 1971 speech in Munich was at the Group of Ten meeting of September 15–16 in London, which Connally chaired. He reiterated the administration's general policy, announcing the U.S. intention to promote a $13 billion swing in its balance-of-payments deficit over the next year, a figure whose dimension frightened the European representatives because they saw a shift for the worse in their own trade positions as a result. Connally also repeated his demands that U.S. trading partners reduce their tariff barriers to U.S. goods and share defense expenses more equally.

On September 26, at a second Group of Ten meeting, Connally said that appropriate currency revaluations by foreign countries would make it easier for the United States to drop the 10 percent import surcharge. At the annual meeting of the International Monetary Fund in Washington from September 27 to 30, Connally again defended the U.S. position and, in a closed session, attacked Latin American countries who encouraged U.S. investment and then expropriated U.S. companies. In October Connally said that the surcharge "is going to stay on for a while because it is frankly to our advantage to keep it on for a while." Shortly thereafter he went to Japan for top-level talks about a revaluation of the yen. He was widely referred to as "Typhoon Connally" in the Japanese press because of the hard bargaining position he took.

Connally's actions in the international economic sphere created serious tension in the high echelons of the Nixon administration. Both BURNS and HENRY KISSINGER, National Security Council Advisor, were appalled by Connally's apparent lack of concern for the sensibilities of America's allies. Representative HENRY REUSS (D-Wis.) had publicly called on Nixon to replace Connally with Arthur Burns as the top U.S. negotiator abroad. Kissinger, who had only a limited interest in economic matters, was equally worried about Connally's impact on U.S. foreign relations in general, a concern complicated by a certain rivalry growing out of Connally's intrusion into what Kissinger considered his domain.

Burns and Kissinger allied to convince Nixon of the dangers posed by Connally's behavior, and Burns urged Nixon to allow Dr. J. Zijlstra, president of the Bank of International Settlements, to draw up a currency realignment plan without Connally and to present the plan to the November 1971 meeting of the Group of Ten in Rome. Connally became incensed at Burns's intrusion into his activities and refused to have anything to do with Zijlstra's plan. At the time of his departure for Rome, Connally also refused to include any State Department officials in his delegation, a direct slap at Secretary of State WILLIAM ROGERS, who was a passive ally of Burns and

Kissinger in the struggle for Nixon's allegiance. Finally, on November 24, Burns and Connally met with Nixon to discuss the situation, and at that meeting, in one observer's comment, Connally "got the message."

At the December 1971 Smithsonian monetary meeting Connally, confronted by a uniformly hostile group of foreign finance ministers alienated by six months of his unilateral actions and pressure tactics, pulled perhaps the most dramatic coup of his period in office. Tensions were mounting in the negotiations after long hours during which Connally had coaxed the European and Japanese representatives for greater revaluations of their own currencies against the dollar, without the slightest hint that the United States would reverse its refusal to readjust the dollar against the price of gold. After a French negotiator had snapped at Connally, "If that is your position, we can all go home," French finance minister Giscard d'Estaing asked the secretary what the U.S. contribution to realignment would be. Connally answered laconically: "Well, we leave that up to you. What change in the gold price do you want, 8, 9, 10 percent?"

After the stunned Europeans and Japanese had digested this first hint that the United States would raise the gold price, a British representative remarked that Connally's negotiating tactics were "not economics, but jujitsu." After the conclusion of the Smithsonian conference, at which the United States obtained much greater revaluations, particularly from Japan, than anyone thought possible, British chancellor of the exchequer Anthony Barber remarked that "a lesser man, a man less tough than Connally, could not have done it."

Connally's relations with Congress showed more mixed results in the period of the New Economic Policy. In late November the Emergency Loan Guarantee Board (ELGB), established by Congress to oversee loans to Lockheed, approved further credits to the ailing corporation, a victory for Connally. Connally was briefly embarrassed by the discovery that he owned a large amount of stock in an insurance company destined to benefit significantly from tax legislation pending before Congress. Connally denied any personal knowledge of the bill, however, and the incident had no further consequences.

In spring 1972 the Lockheed affair again complicated Connally's relations with Congress. General Accounting Office (GAO) controller general Elmer B. Staats told a Senate subcommittee that Connally was obstructing the GAO's authority by refusing to provide documents and records of the aircraft company, making review of the loans impossible. Connally replied that "it was not the intent of Congress that the decisions of the ELGB be reviewed by the GAO," prompting Senator WILLIAM PROXMIRE (D-Wis.) to accuse Connally of defying the authority of Congress.

Connally's relations with labor suffered during his last months at the Treasury. He carried on a verbal battle with GEORGE MEANY over the need to limit wage demands, in reference to which Meany stated that Connally knew nothing about the problems of labor.

Even Connally's relations with U.S. business deteriorated. In January 1972 he addressed the U.S. Chamber of Commerce, defending the Nixon administration's new shift to anti-recessionary deficit spending and predicting a $35–$40 billion deficit for the current fiscal year after almost balanced budgets in the previous two years. He went on to chide U.S. businessmen for not taking advantage of the investment tax credit included in Nixon's NEP package: "You asked for it. You got it. What have you done with it? Nothing." A week later Connally went before a hostile House Ways and Means Committee to ask for a $50 billion increase in the federal debt ceiling.

During the months before he left the Treasury, Connally began to move toward open identification with the Republican Party, feeding new rumors that he would be Nixon's choice for vice president in the November 1972 elections, in preparation for a Connally run at the presidency in 1976. On April 30 Connally received Nixon at his Texas ranch, where he introduced the president to 200 members of the state's political and business elite in a show of his own regional power base. He also moved closer to the inner circle of Nixon's advisers, supporting Nixon in the decision to mine Haiphong Harbor on May 10. The announcement of Connally's resignation on May 16 took most observers by surprise, particularly in view of an imminent meeting of the Organization of Economic Cooperation and Development (OECD), where critical negotiations on international monetary questions were to take place. Indirectly acknowledging recognition of his problematic role during the previous year, Connally said, "Charging up that hill to do battle hasn't been as exciting the last nine months as it was during the first six." Nixon said that Connally had initially agreed to serve at the Treasury for only a year but had stayed on "because of the very, very sensitive monetary negotiations that were taking place."

Connally began campaigning for Nixon in the early summer of 1972 and on August 9 announced the founding of "Democrats for Nixon" in response to the Democratic Party's nomination of Senator GEORGE MCGOVERN. "[McGovern] . . . is so far out of the mainstream of American politics," said Connally, "he has no business being president of the United States." In September Nixon kicked off his campaign with a dinner on Connally's ranch, and the McGovern forces seized the occasion to announce that "John Connally and his oil billionaire friends" were lining up behind the president and his "special-interest administration." In October Connally made a 30-minute television plug for Nixon that, in the view of many observers, came close to red-baiting the Democratic candidate.

Immediately after the Nixon landslide, Connally met with the president at Camp David but denied he was seeking a cabinet post amid rumors he would be secretary of state. In his 1977 television interviews with David Frost, Nixon admitted that he had almost given that post to Connally, but, fully aware of National Security Council Advisor Henry Kissinger's intense rivalry with Connally and weary of the feud between Kissinger and outgoing secretary of state Rogers, Nixon gave the portfolio to Kissinger.

On May 1, 1973, Connally announced that he was switching to the Republican Party, and on May 10 the White House announced that Connally would serve as a special adviser to the president on domestic and foreign affairs. By early June, however, Connally was already thinking about resigning, and on June 20 he held a press conference at which he announced his departure: "Obviously, I'm not being fully utilized in an advisory capacity. I have no operational responsibilities. . . ."

By this point, however, Connally was already becoming associated with the political scandals of the Nixon administration, which ultimately destroyed his chances to run for president in 1976. As early as November 10, 1972, the Watergate special prosecutor had focused on Connally's alleged role in facilitating higher federal price supports for the dairy industry in exchange for contributions to Nixon's 1972 presidential campaign. In March 1973 a House subcommittee charged that Connally had been a key administration figure in delaying a Securities and Exchange Commission (SEC) probe of the International Telephone and Telegraph Corp. (ITT) and had interfered in government appeals of three antitrust cases against the corporation. In June 1973 former White House counsel JOHN DEAN testified that Connally had participated in top-level discussions on how to "turn off" the Watergate probes, suggesting ways to pressure WRIGHT PATMAN (D-Tex.) into canceling the hearings. In August the Senate Watergate committee made public a memo by White House staff member CHARLES COLSON, dated March 30, 1972, warning that the confirmation hearings for Attorney General-designate RICHARD G. KLEINDIENST, then in progress, might link Nixon and many top administration officials, including Connally, with the controversial out-of-court settlement of an antitrust suit against ITT. A week later *Business Week* alleged that Connally had personally halted U.S. aid to Ecuador pending settlement of that country's expropriation of an ITT subsidiary.

The controversy over milk price supports refused to die. On November 15 Connally testified before the Senate Watergate committee that he had always favored higher price supports for the dairy industry, but he refused to discuss the question of campaign contributions by the dairy lobby. On December 27 the Justice Department filed a civil antitrust suit against the Mid-American Dairymen, Inc., for political contributions made in exchange for a relaxation of government price controls on milk. In November 7 testimony that led to the suit, a dairy spokesman admitted he had personally discussed the issue with Connally in 1972 and that Connally had assured him "he would do all he could."

In January 1974 the White House was obliged to issue a 17-page paper explaining its 1971 increase in price supports for milk. The report indicated that Connally had called the administration's attention to the power of the milk lobby in March 1971 and had urged action to appease the dairymen. On May 31, 1974, the Senate Watergate committee issued its report on the dairy lobby question, concluding that there had indeed been a link between the government's decision on price supports and the millions of dollars in dairy association contributions to Nixon's 1972 presidential campaign. The committee's report also alleged that Connally had received a $10,000

bribe from the Associated Milk Producers, Inc. (AMPI).

On July 19 the House Judiciary Committee released a report on the March 1971 increase in milk price supports. Included in the report was a transcript of a White House meeting of Nixon, his aides, and Connally at which Connally had argued that there were excellent political reasons for the increase. At that meeting Connally urged swift action on price supports.

On July 28, 1974, the Watergate grand jury indicted Connally on five counts of accepting a bribe, conspiring to obstruct justice, and committing perjury in connection with his acceptance of $10,000 in two cash payments from dairy lobbyists in 1971. In the following week two former AMPI officials pleaded guilty to charges of bribing Connally, but on August 9 Connally entered a not-guilty plea at his own trial. In April 1975 Connally was acquitted on the charge of accepting a bribe after his defense attorney had successfully convinced the court that the guilty pleas of the AMPI officials were made solely for plea-bargaining purposes.

Within weeks of his acquittal, Connally plunged back into Republican Party politics. President GERALD FORD had deemed it acceptable to pay a private visit to Connally even before his acquittal. Yet in his May 1975 appearance on the TV program *Meet the Press*, Connally mildly criticized Ford while denying that he planned to run for any elective office in 1976. In April 1976 Ford in turn denied that Connally would be his new secretary of state if he were reelected. At election time Connally merely endorsed Ford's candidacy.

Connally resumed his legal practice and business activities and remained active in Republican Party politics throughout the late 1970s. In 1980 Connally ran for president, pledging to bring home the American hostages held in Iran by any means necessary, including nuclear weapons. After his 1980 defeat, he returned to his business interests and to running his cattle ranch. Connally died in 1993.

—LRG

Cooper, John S(herman)
(1901–1991) *member of the Senate*

John Cooper was born on August 23, 1901, in Somerset, Kentucky. Following graduation from Yale University and Harvard Law School, Cooper won election to the state legislature. He became a local judge in 1928 and a district judge in the 1930s. He held these positions in intervals throughout the 1940s and 1950s. Cooper also served as a consultant to Secretary of State Dean Acheson and sat on the American delegation to the United Nations during that period. He was ambassador to India and Nepal in the Eisenhower administration. Cooper won special elections to the U.S. Senate in 1946, 1952, and 1956, although he lost two regular elections during the period. He won his first full term in 1960.

During the Truman, Eisenhower, and Kennedy administrations, Cooper established himself as a liberal Republican with an interest in foreign affairs. In domestic concerns he was a defender of small business and agriculture. Cooper was a moderate on civil rights.

Cooper was one of the Senate's earliest critics of the Vietnam War. Starting in January 1966 he began to criticize the bombing of North Vietnam, and at the time of the Tet offensive in February 1968 he warned against an escalation of the conflict. In 1969 he introduced an amendment to a procurement bill barring the president from using funds for U.S. combat support in Laos and Thailand. The bill passed the Senate 86-0 in September. Cooper teamed with Senator FRANK CHURCH (D-Idaho) to introduce another amendment to an appropriations bill barring the president

from spending any funds without congressional approval after July 1 for American troops fighting in Cambodia, for support of advisers or troops from other countries aiding Cambodia, or for air combat operations. The measure barred the introduction of U.S. ground troops into Thailand and Laos and forbade the spending of funds for "free-world forces" used to provide military support for the Laotian or Cambodian governments. The stipulation did not restrict the use of funds for action to safeguard the withdrawal of U.S. troops. The Senate passed the measure, but the House deleted the Cooper-Church amendment from its bill. A modified version of the amendment restricting the powers of the president in the Vietnam War passed both houses of Congress in December. In 1971 Cooper charged that the administration violated this amendment by ferrying South Vietnamese troops into battle in Cambodia and providing air cover for them.

Cooper abstained in 1972 in the vote on the Church-Case Amendment that provided for a cutoff of funds for all U.S. combat operations in Indochina subject to an agreement for the release of American prisoners of war. Instead he supported the Nixon-sponsored bill that tied this proposal to an internationally supervised cease-fire. The senator explained his opposition to the original amendment was based on fear that it would undercut Nixon's bargaining position in the upcoming peace talks.

Cooper, a longtime opponent of the cold war, opposed the administration-sponsored Safeguard antiballistic missile (ABM) system. In 1969 he charged that this system would provoke an arms race. Cooper supported Senator MIKE MANSFIELD's (D-Mont.) call for a moratorium on both sides in weapons development projects. In seeking a compromise on this issue, Cooper and Senator PHILIP HART (D-Mich.) introduced an amendment to the ABM bill that would have provided funds for research but not the deployment of the system. The Senate defeated this measure by a vote of 51 to 49. In 1971 he backed an ABM system deployed at a low level just to give the U.S. bargaining strength at the SALT negotiations.

Cooper also voted against the administration on a number of domestic issues. In 1969 he opposed the nomination of conservative judge CLEMENT HAYNSWORTH to the Supreme Court, but the following year he backed the nomination of G. HARROLD CARSWELL to the high bench. Rather than support the administration's voluntary health plan program, Cooper joined the bipartisan Senate group that introduced a federally financed national health insurance plan in September 1970.

Cooper retired from the Senate at the end of his term in 1973. From 1974 to 1976 he served as ambassador to East Germany during the period that witnessed the opening of the Communist state to Western trade. He retired at the end of the Ford administration. He resumed his law practice in Washington, D.C., where he died in 1991.

—JB

Cox, Archibald
(1912–2004) *Watergate special prosecutor*

Born on May 17, 1912 in Plainfield, New Jersey, Archibald Cox attended St. Paul's, Harvard College, and Harvard Law School. After a year's service as clerk to Judge Learned Hand, he practiced law with the Boston firm of Ropes, Gray, Best, Coolidge, & Rugg. During World War II he worked in Washington, D.C., first for the National Defense Mediation Board, then in the office of the solicitor general of the Department of Justice, and from 1943 to 1945 in the Department of Labor as associate solicitor. After the war Cox returned to Harvard Law School, becoming in 1946 a

full professor, one of the youngest men in the school's history to attain that rank.

An expert in labor law, Cox was frequently called away from the university to arbitrate labor disputes or accept temporary government positions. During the Korean War he served as cochairman of the Construction Industry Stabilization Commission and as head of the Wage Stabilization Board. In the late 1950s Cox served as an adviser on labor legislation to Senator John F. Kennedy (D-Mass.). During the 1960 presidential campaign he was a member of Kennedy's brain trust, directing an academic team that researched and drafted speeches on major issues for the candidate. After his election Kennedy appointed Cox solicitor general, the third-highest official in the Justice Department and the government's chief advocate before the Supreme Court.

Cox served as solicitor general until 1965, when he returned to teaching at Harvard. He returned to the Supreme Court on occasion to argue cases as a private attorney, as in 1966 when he urged the Court to uphold the constitutionality of the 1965 Voting Rights Act. He also served as a special mediator in the 1967 New York City school strike and as chairman of a five-man commission investigating the violent disturbances at Columbia University in the spring of 1968. In 1969 Cox represented three welfare clients before the Supreme Court, challenging the constitutionality of the one-year residency requirement for welfare benefits in Connecticut, Pennsylvania, and the District of Columbia. The Supreme Court declared the residency requirement unconstitutional in a landmark decision on April 21.

In May 1973, under public and congressional pressure to appoint an independent special prosecutor to take command of the Watergate investigation, Attorney General-designate ELLIOT RICHARDSON, a former student of Cox, chose the Harvard professor for the post. Cox was given jurisdiction over the investigation of the Watergate burglary and coverup, as well as "all allegations involving the president, members of the White House staff, or presidential appointees," and endowed with the full range of prosecutorial powers, including the power to contest in court any refusal by the White House to produce subpoenaed evidence. On May 21 Richardson assured the Senate Judiciary Committee that Cox would have full independence and support and would be fired only for "extraordinary improprieties." *Newsweek* characterized the appointment of Cox as a "master stroke," which brought "an infusion of unshakable integrity to the administration's sometimes suspect handling of Watergate and related scandals."

Before long Cox chose a staff of about 30 lawyers, averaging about 30 years in age, mostly graduates of Ivy League law schools. He divided the special prosecutor's office into a series of task forces, each covering a major area of suspected criminality: the Watergate break-in and cover-up, the main case, the activities of the White House "Plumbers" unit, the "dirty tricks" of White House functionaries during the 1972 elections, the alleged special treatment of an antitrust suit against the International Telephone & Telegraph Co. (ITT) in return for campaign contributions, and assorted violations of campaign finance laws. Throughout the summer of 1973 the special prosecutor's office quietly went about its task of amassing evidence for presentation to the grand jury.

The startling revelation on July 16, 1973, that President Nixon had been tape-recording his White House conversations since 1971 set in motion the dramatic chain of events that led to Cox's firing three months later. On July 18 Cox wrote to the White House requesting eight tapes of conversations important to the Watergate probe. On July 26 Nixon announced that he would not surrender any tapes to the grand jury or the Senate Water-

gate Committee. Cox then requested that U.S. district court judge JOHN SIRICA issue a subpoena compelling production of the requested tapes.

White House lawyer CHARLES WRIGHT attempted to quash the subpoena by arguing that the president was not subject to the ordinary processes of law and that the doctrine of executive privilege was a barrier to the demand for any evidence from the conversations of the president. During his oral argument before Judge Sirica on August 22, Wright added the claim that some tapes contained sensitive "national security" information, the disclosure of which would harm the national interest. Cox contended that the president was subject to legal processes and that executive privilege did not cover possible evidence of criminal conduct. His brief stressed that the tapes were necessary for the grand jury to determine the criminal culpability of the president's aides, not the president himself. One week later Judge Sirica ordered Nixon to turn over the eight tapes to him for the judge's determination of whether they were covered by executive privilege.

On October 12 the U.S. court of appeals affirmed Sirica's decision that Nixon must turn over the tapes. Rather than seek Supreme Court review, Nixon offered Cox a "compromise" plan, whereby Nixon would provide the special prosecutor with "summaries" of the taped conversations rather than the tapes themselves. Nixon selected Senator JOHN STENNIS (D-Miss.) to listen to the tapes in question and verify the accuracy of the summaries. A final part of the compromise was that Cox would agree to make no further attempt to subpoena any more tapes or presidential papers.

On October 19 Cox rejected the Nixon proposal. The proposed summaries would violate the court order and destroy the evi-

Archibald Cox (center) is sworn in as special Watergate prosecutor by Judge Charles Eahy (left) on June 8, 1973. Looking on is Attorney General Elliot Richardson (right). *(Bettman/CORBIS)*

dentiary value of the tapes, for summaries of the tapes would be inadmissible as evidence at trial. The president's order to forgo any further attempts to obtain presidential tapes and other papers violated the pledge of independence given to Cox by the attorney general at his confirmation, Cox said. Acceptance of the president's directive, he said, would "defeat the fair administration of criminal justice. It would deprive prosecutors of admissible evidence in prosecuting wrongdoers who abuse high government office. . . . I cannot be party to such an arrangement."

On October 20 Nixon ordered the attorney general to discharge Cox. Richardson resigned rather than carry out the order, and Deputy Attorney General WIL-

LIAM RUCKELSHAUS was fired for his refusal to do so. Solicitor General ROBERT BORK, then appointed acting attorney general, finally discharged Cox. Nixon announced that he had abolished the special prosecutor's office and transferred the investigation back to the Justice Department. Cox issued a one-sentence statement: "Whether ours shall continue to be a government of laws and not of men is now for Congress and ultimately for the American people [to decide]."

The public response to what was dubbed the "Saturday Night Massacre" was a deluge of criticism of the president's act. Western Union in Washington was inundated with a record 220,000 telegrams of protest by October 24, while public figures called for

Nixon's resignation or impeachment. Nixon soon reversed his position on the tapes and on October 23 announced he would obey the subpoena to turn them over to Judge Sirica. On October 26 he announced that Bork would appoint a new special prosecutor. A week later Bork announced the appointment of Texas lawyer LEON JAWORSKI to fill the position.

Almost unnoticed amid the furor over the tapes and dismissal of Cox was Cox's first major accomplishment as special prosecutor: the plea of guilty on October 19 by former counsel to the president JOHN DEAN. As part of a bargain negotiated with Cox, Dean pleaded guilty to a single count of conspiring to cover up the truth about the Watergate break-in and agreed to be a prosecution witness in return for Cox's promise not to bring other charges, with the exception of perjury, against him. Two of Cox's assistant prosecutors wrote that Dean's guilty plea was a result of Cox's "personal determination that Dean be prosecuted no matter what. Dean became an *idée fixe* for Cox."

Cox's firing gave him heroic stature in the eyes of many, who saw him as the embodiment of integrity and dedication to constitutional principles, in addition to being a distinguished legal scholar. Returning to Harvard after his dismissal, he continued to play an occasionally prominent role in public affairs. In July 1976 Cox gave the nominating speech for Representative MORRIS UDALL (D-Ariz.) at the Democratic National Convention.

Cox went on to become the chairman of Common Cause. In October 1978 Cox appeared before the Supreme Court to defend the University of California's affirmative action program in the important *Bakke* case. He was made an honorary member of the Order of the Coif in 1991 and died at his home in Maine in 2004.

—TO

Cramer, William C(ato)
(1922–2003) *member of the House of Representatives*

Born on August 4, 1922, in Denver, Colorado, Cramer served in the navy during World War II and graduated Phi Beta Kappa from the University of North Carolina in 1946. He earned his law degree in two years at Harvard and returned to St. Petersburg to lead the successful revitalization of the long-dormant Pinellas County Republican Party. In 1950 he won election to the state House of Representatives and served as minority leader. Four years later the 32-year-old Cramer became the first Republican representative elected from Florida since 1875. He easily won reelection through the 1960s. His early success and statewide partisan labors made him, as journalist Neal Peirce observed, "virtually the founding father of the present-day Republican Party in Florida."

In the House Cramer almost always voted with the conservatives. He opposed President Johnson's Great Society programs and voted against civil rights legislation with the singular exception of the 1965 Voting Rights Act. After three consecutive summers of racial rioting, Cramer introduced in 1966 an amendment to the Civil Rights Act on open housing aimed at "those professional agitators" who travel interstate to incite riots. Cramer, who had not originally intended to support the open-housing law, voted for the final version passed in 1968 because it contained his anti-riot provision.

Cramer continued his opposition to civil rights during the NIXON administration. He had been outraged at the presence of Resurrection City, a civil rights protest set up near the Washington Monument during May and June of 1968. The next year, to forestall any similar incident that he said would be "potentially explosive and potentially disruptive" to the government, Cramer sponsored a bill banning any future encampment or overnight sit-in on federal property or in public parks and requiring protest leaders to post bond if officials considered it appropriate. The bill passed overwhelmingly in the House but died in the Senate.

Cramer clashed with environmentalists in the debate over the Water Quality Improvement Act of 1970. The issue was the extent of an oil company's responsibility in the event of an oil spill at sea. The Senate passed a version of "absolute liability," that is, exempting the company from paying cleanup costs only if the spill were the result of an act of God, war, or governmental negligence. The looser House version, strongly backed by Cramer, held the companies liable only in the event of willful negligence. Cramer held fast, and it seemed that in the House-Senate conference his version would prevail until a series of oil spills in California and the Gulf states swung the House over to the tougher doctrine of "absolute liability."

In 1969 Cramer joined the House Republican leadership when he was elected unopposed as conference vice chairman. At that time he all but dominated the party in his home state. A year later, at President Nixon's "personal" urging, Cramer entered the race for the U.S. Senate. In April of that year, less than two weeks after the Senate had refused to appoint him to the Supreme Court, Judge G. HARROLD CARSWELL resigned from the U.S. Court of Appeals for the 5th Circuit to run for the same seat. Although Carswell was backed by the state's top Republicans, Governor CLAUDE R. KIRK JR., and Senator EDWARD GURNEY, Cramer soundly defeated him in a primary that severely split the state's GOP.

In the general election Cramer ran a "law and order" campaign, inviting voters "to join the fight to stop cop killers, bombers, burners, and racial revolutionaries who would destroy America." Although Nixon visited Florida twice on his behalf, Cramer lost in November to Lawton Chiles, who ran a low-key campaign stressing the economy and large cutbacks at Cape Kennedy. Cramer then retired to private life. Cramer died in Florida in 2003.

—FLM

Curtis, Carl T(homas)
(1905–2000) *member of the Senate*

Carl T. Curtis was born on March 15, 1905, in Minden, Nebraska. After attending the University of Nebraska and teaching school for a short time, Curtis studied law and was admitted to the bar in 1930. He was elected to the House of Representatives in 1938, where he served for 16 years before moving to the Senate in 1955. During his career Curtis was widely viewed as one of the Senate's most conservative members on social, economic, and foreign policy issues. Coming from a state considered the most Republican in the Union, he frequently joined southern Democrats in thwarting spending programs for the disadvantaged. He was a strong supporter of President Johnson's Vietnam policies. (See *The Eisenhower Years, The Kennedy Years,* and *The Johnson Years* volumes.)

Curtis favored RICHARD NIXON in 1968 for the Republican presidential nomination and backed the new president's handling of the Vietnam War as well as his defense policy. He voted for most major military spending programs including the Safeguard antiballistic missile system. Curtis sought to avoid tying the hands of the president in the execution of foreign policy, opposing a 1973 appropriations bill that prohibited the use of funds for bombing Cambodia, as well as the Cooper-Church Amendment in 1970 restricting presidential authority to conduct military operations in Cambodia.

Curtis held no such reservations when it came to funding for domestic programs. He was one of the most powerful members of the Finance Committee because of his attendance record. (Many liberal Democrats on the committee were frequently absent.) He opposed deficit spending and supported legislation to put the federal government on a pay-as-you-go basis in the absence of war or a grave national emergency. Curtis voted against the 20-percent increase in Social Security payments proposed in 1972, despite the fact that Nebraska had a high proportion of elderly people. He went on record against Nixon's 1973 budget proposal because of its $25.5 billion deficit.

Curtis resigned his post on the Government Operations Committee in 1969 to accept a position on the Agriculture and Forestry Committee. In that capacity he favored the generous spending of federal funds aimed at raising farm income, although he objected to such programs as food stamps. He sought a limitation on meat imports as well as legislation to create a rural affairs council. He helped write the Rural Development Act of 1972 to assist rural communities in their search for new industries.

Curtis voted for the nominations of WIL-LIAM REHNQUIST, CLEMENT HAYNSWORTH, and G. HARROLD CARSWELL to the Supreme Court, cosponsored antiabortion legislation in 1973, and voted against extension of the Office of Economic Opportunity. Generally considered antilabor, Curtis sought to exempt businesses having 25 or fewer employees from provisions of the Occupational Safety and Health Act, which was designed to protect workers against hazardous job conditions.

During the Watergate controversy Curtis was a firm supporter of Nixon, and in July 1973 he led a delegation of 10 Republican senators who met with Nixon in a show of their support. After Nixon resigned, Curtis approved of his pardon by President FORD. He also endorsed the elevation of Nixon's rival NELSON ROCKEFELLER to the vice presidency.

Curtis voted for the resumption of aid to Turkey in 1975. The same year he opposed legislation allowing striking workers eligibility for food stamps and establishing a federal consumer protection agency. He lauded President Ford's decision to attack Cambodia to facilitate the release of the merchant ship *Mayaguez*. Curtis beat Senator JACOB JAVITS by a vote of 23 to 14 for the chairmanship of the Senate Republican Conference, a party policy-making body. At the Republican Convention in 1976, Curtis was a major proponent of the platform plank calling for morality in foreign policy—seen as a not-so-subtle jab at the leadership of HENRY KISSINGER.

Curtis chose not to run for reelection in 1978 and retired at the end of his term. He practiced law in Lincoln, Nebraska, until his death in 2000.

—GWB

Cushman, Robert E(verton), Jr.
(1914–1985) *deputy director, Central Intelligence Agency; commandant, U.S. Marine Corps*

Born on December 15, 1914, in St. Paul, Minnesota, Robert Cushman graduated from Annapolis in 1935 and was commissioned a second lieutenant in the marines. He saw action in World War II as a battalion commander. After the war Cushman spent 12 years in a succession of school, staff, and training positions. From 1949 to 1951 he was assigned to the Central Intelligence Agency (CIA). Cushman began a four-year association with RICHARD M. NIXON in February 1957, when he became Vice President Nixon's assistant for national security affairs. During those years Cushman, then a brigadier general, worked closely with CIA in addition to advising Nixon on security matters.

Cushman went to Vietnam in April 1967 to succeed Lewis W. Walt as commanding general of the 3rd Marine Amphibious Force. For the next two years he commanded 163,000 army and marine troops in the I Corps Area, in the northernmost provinces of South Vietnam. This was the largest battle command ever given to a marine officer. During his tour of duty Cushman strongly advocated tactical mobility instead of static siege warfare. He and the marine command believed that the major goal in Vietnam was the achievement of the pacification program and the primary task of the military was the protection of pacification areas.

In April 1969 President Nixon named Cushman deputy director of the CIA. The agency's director was RICHARD M. HELMS, a civilian and career CIA officer. The law provided that a civilian must hold the position of either director or deputy director, and the traditional practice was to divide the two posts between the civilian and the military. Cushman's major responsibility was to represent the CIA on the U.S. Intelligence Board, the National Security Council's central coordinating committee for the intelligence community. In 1971, following the reform of the CIA, Helms turned over many of the operating responsibilities to Cushman.

In December 1971 Nixon chose Cushman to replace the retiring general Leonard F. Chapman Jr. as commandant of the Marine Corps. When he took command, the armed services had suffered a decline in morale because of the Vietnam War, and defense spending cutbacks had made decisions about priorities all the more difficult. At the time the nation was heading toward volunteer military service, forcing each branch to do more to attract recruits. Cushman joined many marine leaders in advocating a return to the traditionally smaller, more elite corps. He identified one of his most serious tasks

as that of assuring fair treatment for blacks. Recent years had witnessed persistent racial problems between black and white military personnel. In July 1972 Cushman issued a sweeping order that banned segregation practices in the corps, even where segregation was voluntary.

In early May 1973 E. HOWARD HUNT JR. testified before a Washington grand jury investigating the Watergate break-in that the CIA had given him and G. GORDON LIDDY assistance in preparing for the September 1971 burglary of the office of DANIEL ELLSBERG's former psychiatrist, Lewis J. Fielding, in Los Angeles. The *New York Times* reported May 7 that Cushman, as deputy director of the CIA, provided Hunt and Liddy with false identification papers, disguises, a tape recorder, and a miniature camera. This aid, the *Times* said, came at the request of the president's domestic adviser JOHN D. EHRLICHMAN, who had been ordered by Nixon in 1971 to investigate a series of national security leaks.

On May 9 CIA director JAMES SCHLESINGER told a Senate subcommittee the agency had been unaware that Hunt and Liddy were preparing to break into Fielding's office. He noted that aid to Hunt and Liddy had been discontinued one week before the break-in occurred because Cushman was becoming "increasingly concerned" over Hunt's repeated requests for assistance. Two days later Cushman confirmed before a series of House and Senate panels that he had provided aid in July 1971 to Hunt at the request of Ehrlichman.

Later in the month Ehrlichman denied before a Senate subcommittee having called Cushman about Hunt. In response to the Ehrlichman denial, Cushman told a news conference that a search of records had turned up minutes of a daily CIA staff meeting for July 8, 1971. Cushman said he had mentioned at the meeting a conversation with Ehrlichman the day before about giving aid to Hunt. In August

Cushman produced for the Senate Watergate committee the transcript of a conversation he had had with Hunt in his CIA office on July 22. The conversation indicated that Ehrlichman had made the call to Cushman. In his testimony Cushman insisted that he did not know that Hunt intended to use the equipment to break into Fielding's office. He contended that he did not learn of the break-in until it was made public on April 27, 1973, during Ellsberg's trial for releasing the *Pentagon Papers* to the press. Cushman retired in May 1975 and died in 1985.

—SF

D

Daley, Richard J(oseph)
(1902–1976) *mayor of Chicago*

Born on May 15, 1902, in a blue-collar district of Chicago, Daley worked his way up the city's Democratic political machine. At age 21 he was a precinct captain for Chicago's Democrats. He rose to head the Cook County Democratic organization, the machine that dominated Chicago politics. In 1955 he was elected mayor of Chicago, a post he successfully won in six consecutive elections. He held jointly the positions of mayor of Chicago and head of the Cook County Democratic organization. He was responsible for encouraging a revitalization of downtown Chicago. Funds from local, state, and national government agencies and private sources poured into Chicago's development projects. At the time that other cities were experiencing immense decay, Chicago was undergoing a rebirth.

By 1968 Daley's power had begun to ebb; he was frequently labeled "the last of the bosses" by the media. In that year he reacted strongly to the riots that took place in Chicago in the aftermath of the assassination of Dr. Martin Luther King Jr. and gave his famous "shoot to kill" order to police in dealing with arsonists. Daley's role at the Democratic Party Convention in Chicago gave him further national attention. He was blamed by critics for creating the conditions that led to fighting between police and antiwar activists outside the convention hall. It was the television coverage given to this conflict that contributed to the defeat of HUBERT HUMPHREY, the party's presidential standard-bearer.

Although he had exercised an important role in national politics, the 1968 Democratic National Convention was the high mark of his national influence. In part because of the reaction against the manipulations of Daley during the 1968 convention, reforms were instituted in the Democratic Party nominating procedures requiring representation of minorities in state delegations. Daley refused to comply with the new rules for selecting delegates to the 1972 Democratic Convention. As a result his delegation was not seated. Instead a group led by William Singer, an independent Democrat, and the Reverend JESSE JACKSON, the black leader of Operation PUSH, unseated the Daley-dominated delegation. Daley could not get along with the Democratic presidential nominee GEORGE MCGOVERN and his liberal supporters, and the antagonism was mutual. Daley, however, supported McGovern in the election.

After the disastrous McGovern defeat of 1972, Daley was welcomed back into national

Democratic Party influence. He played a major role at the Democratic miniconvention in Kansas City in 1974. At the meeting the party adopted a charter that proscribed mandatory quotas for delegations to the 1980 national convention and limited the ability of groups to challenge delegations on the basis of delegation composition or primary results. In 1976 his support of JIMMY CARTER for the presidential nomination was slow in coming, although he actively endorsed him in the election. However, GERALD FORD carried Illinois in the contest against Carter.

From the time he rose to power as Cook County chairman in 1953, Daley always exercised an important role in state and local matters. His power even in these areas showed signs of deteriorating after 1968. In the Democratic primary of 1972, Dan Walker defeated the mayor's choice for gubernatorial candidate and went on to win the election. In that same year, moreover, Daley's choice for state's attorney also lost.

When the NIXON administration assumed power, it appointed James Thompson as U.S. attorney for the Chicago district. Many of Daley's closest lieutenants were indicted and convicted on federal and county charges of conspiracy and bribery. The news that Daley's youngest son may have been involved in receiving local government insurance contracts for his firm further weakened the reputation of the mayor. In 1976 Thompson defeated the Daley-backed gubernatorial candidate.

In 1974 Daley suffered a stroke and was out of any active involvement in politics for four months. It was believed that he would not run for reelection. He did, in fact, run again and despite the opposition of Chicago newspapers, was reelected handily. He died of a heart attack in December 1976 after serving 21 years as mayor of Chicago.

—HML

Dash, Samuel
(1925–2004) *chief counsel, Senate Watergate committee*

Born on February 27, 1925, in Camden, New Jersey, the son of immigrant Russian Jews, Dash graduated from Temple University in 1947 and Harvard Law School in 1950. Following a year as a teaching associate at Northwestern University, he served as a trial lawyer for the Justice Department. Dash was appointed district attorney of Philadelphia in 1955. The next year he went into private practice. In 1959 he published *The Eavesdroppers*, a study of electronic surveillance. In 1965 Dash joined the faculty of the Georgetown University Law Center.

In February 1973 Dash was chosen by Senator SAM ERVIN (D-N.C.) to serve as chief counsel of the Senate select committee established to investigate the Watergate incident. Dash was given considerable independence to select his own staff, eventually numbering over 40, and investigate the facts wherever they led. Dash, for the first time in a congressional investigation, used a computer to keep track of the massive amounts of information generated by the Watergate inquiry.

The first break in the investigation came at the end of March when Judge JOHN SIRICA disclosed the contents of a letter from JAMES MCCORD, one of the Watergate burglars. Dash met secretly with McCord, who informed him that JEB MAGRUDER, second in command of the president's reelection campaign, had perjured himself when testifying that he knew nothing about Watergate. In an effort to get other participants to come forward with information, Dash informed the press that McCord had identified more persons involved in the scandal.

In May Dash began meeting secretly with JOHN DEAN, former counsel to President NIXON, to determine if the committee should offer him immunity in return for testifying. In an unorthodox procedure Dash promised Dean he would tell no one, except Ervin, what was said in the interviews. This meant that the committee would have to follow Dash's recommendation concerning immunity without any other information. Dash recommended immunity. The committee approved it over the opposition of Senators HOWARD BAKER (R-Tenn.) and EDWARD GURNEY (R-Fla.). Baker and Gurney subsequently changed their votes to present a unified image to the public.

Working closely with Ervin, Dash began planning for public hearings to begin in May 1973. They hoped to educate as many people as possible on the threat that Watergate posed to the democratic process. Dash wanted television coverage. He proposed they start with little-known witnesses who could gradually provide the necessary background for the public to understand the testimony of the major witnesses.

The nationally televised hearings opened on May 17. Dash helped Ervin prepare his opening statement, which warned of the threat to democracy posed by the affair and stressed that the purpose of the hearings was broadly educational, not prosecutorial. Throughout the hearings Dash was well prepared on the complex facts of the case and usually began cross-examination of witnesses. He also supplied senators on the committee with questions ahead of time.

In the first week of June, ARCHIBALD COX, special Watergate prosecutor, requested a suspension of the Watergate committee's hearings, arguing that they jeopardized the pending criminal proceedings. Dash strongly opposed this move, asserting that the committee had a much broader responsibility than the courts, namely, to publicly expose all the facts and recommend remedial legislation. The committee voted to refuse Cox's request. A few days later Dash argued before Judge Sirica against

a motion by Cox to limit the hearings. Dash won. Sirica denied Cox's motion and granted Dean and Magruder immunity before the committee.

At the end of June, Dean began his testimony by reading a 245-page statement that Dash had helped him prepare. This statement linked President Nixon directly to a cover-up of Watergate. At the beginning of Dash's cross-examination, he forced Dean to admit that he had personally participated in the cover-up. (Later Dash wrote a letter to Judge Sirica recommending a lenient sentence for Dean because of his cooperation with the committee.)

In the first week of July, Dash secretly agreed to share the mountain of information collected by his staff with the House Judiciary Committee, which was considering an impeachment inquiry. In the middle of July, Dash's staff uncovered the existence of a taping system at the White House, a fact subsequently revealed in the public hearings. After Nixon rejected a request for certain tapes, the committee issued a subpoena. When Nixon refused to comply, the committee filed suit in federal district court to force the president to relinquish the tapes. In October Judge Sirica ruled against the suit on the grounds that the committee had failed to prove the amount in controversy exceeded $10,000, a requirement for a civil suit to be tried in federal court. Dash appealed the decision but lost. Even though the committee subpoenaed many more conversations, they never succeeded in obtaining a single presidential tape. (Eventually the special prosecutor, Cox, and the House Judiciary Committee did succeed.)

The first phase of the hearings ended on August 7, 1973, after 33 witnesses had been heard and 7,537 pages of testimony had been compiled. At the end of September the committee reopened hearings covering questionable campaign contributions and "dirty tricks" during the 1972 elections. Since

Dash's staff was still in the midst of these investigations, the evidence was fragmentary, and the procedures never captured the public's attention like the summer hearings. The second phase of hearings adjourned in late November. In February 1974 the committee voted to end public hearings on Watergate, yielding to the courts and the House impeachment inquiry.

Dash played an important role in writing the final report of the committee, which was made public in July 1974. The report summarized the factual evidence of wrongdoing and made over 40 recommendations for legal and institutional reform. Among the committee's major proposals were: an independent and permanent office of "public attorney" with powers similar to those of the Watergate special prosecutor; a federal elections commission with supervisory and enforcement powers; limits on cash campaign contributions by individuals; reforms in reporting procedures; restrictions on solicitation of campaign funds by presidential staff; and tightening of laws involving use of federal agencies to aid the election of candidates. A year later Dash testified before the Senate Government Operations Committee recommending Watergate reform legislation. In a book on Watergate published in 1976 Dash expressed strong disappointment that more had not been done to prevent future Watergates.

After his service on the committee Dash went back to his position as professor of law and director of the Institute of Criminal Law and Procedure at the Georgetown University Law Center. In 1994 Dash served as ethics adviser to Kenneth Starr, the independent counsel investigating the Whitewater scandal. In 1998 Dash resigned, charging that Starr was an "aggressive advocate" of impeaching Bill Clinton rather than an objective investigator. Dash died in 2004.

—TFS

Davis, Angela Y(vonne)
(1944–)   *political activist*

Born on January 26, 1944, the daughter of schoolteachers, Angela Davis grew up in a segregated neighborhood in Birmingham, Alabama. With her mother she took part in civil rights demonstrations during the mid-1950s. In 1959 she moved to New York City to attend a private high school on an American Friends Service Committee scholarship. Davis received her B.A. from Brandeis University in 1965. After two years of graduate study in West Germany she enrolled in 1967 in the philosophy department of the University of California at San Diego to study under the Marxist philosopher Herbert Marcuse. Within two years Davis, whose gifted intellect was widely acknowledged by her professors, had completed all of the requirements for a doctorate except her dissertation.

Throughout these years of study Davis was steadily becoming more radical politically. While in Paris, she was friendly with Algerian revolutionaries. Strongly influenced by Marcuse's criticism of industrial capitalist society, Davis became increasingly active in the militant black power movement in California. In June 1968 she joined the Communist Party.

Immediately after Davis was hired by the philosophy department of the University of California at Los Angeles in 1969, she became the focus of controversy. When a Los Angeles newspaper revealed that she was a member of the Communist Party, the California Board of Regents refused to approve her appointment despite the favorable recommendation of the faculty and the university chancellor. In October 1969 she was reinstated by court order, but the regents would not renew her contract at the end of the year, and this time the courts upheld their decision.

Davis, meanwhile, had thrown herself into the work of the Soledad Brothers Defense

Committee. The "Soledad brothers" were three black convicts, including prison activist George Jackson, who was accused of murdering a white prison guard. After receiving numerous threats to her life, Davis legally bought several guns. On August 7, 1970, Jackson's younger brother Jonathan entered the Marin County courthouse in San Rafael, California, where a black convict was on trial. With the guns purchased by Davis, he freed the defendant and seized five hostages, including the judge and district attorney. A shoot-out followed, and Jackson, the judge, and two inmates were killed.

Because the guns were owned by her, Davis was indicted on charges of murder, kidnapping, and conspiracy (under California law, an accessory to a capital crime is considered as equally guilty as the perpetrator). After going into hiding, she was placed on the FBI's 10-most-wanted list and became the object of a nationwide search. Arrested in a New York City motel on October 13, 1970, she was extradited to California.

Davis's trail quickly became an international cause célèbre, with demonstrations in her support occurring around the world. After several procedural delays the trial finally began in March 1972. The prosecutor charged that Davis's motive in supplying the fatal weapons was "a passion for George Jackson" that "knew no bounds," but Davis dismissed the argument as evidence of "male chauvinism." On June 4, 1972, the jury acquitted her on all counts.

Davis continued to be a controversial figure. Elected to the Central Committee of the Communist Party (the party's governing body) in 1972, she undertook a worldwide speaking tour during which she denounced the U.S. criminal justice system and called for socialism in the United States. In 1975 she taught at Claremont College in California and in 1976 at Stanford. In both cases angry alumni threatened to withdraw their financial support.

Davis was actively involved in support of Joanne Little, a North Carolina black woman accused of murdering a white prison guard, and of the "Wilmington 10," civil rights activists appealing their 1972 convictions on charges of arson and conspiracy. In 1974 she published *Angela Davis: An Autobiography.* The author of seven books, she continues to raise consciousness regarding the state of America's prisons and teaches at the University of California, Los Angeles.

—JD

Dean, John (Wesley), III
(1938–   ) *counsel to the president*

Born on October 14, 1938, John Dean lived with his family in Akron and in Evanston, Illinois, before they settled down in Greenville, Pennsylvania, where his father was president of the Jamestown Manufacturing and Machine Co. Dean attended Staunton Military Academy in Virginia, Colgate University, and Wooster College in Ohio, graduating from Wooster in 1961. He enrolled in American University's graduate school in government and married the daughter of Senator Thomas Hennings (D-Mo.) before he entered Georgetown Law School in 1962. After receiving his law degree in 1965, Dean became an associate with Welch and Morgan, a Washington law firm specializing in communications law. After six months Dean was fired for an outside business involvement that his employer considered a conflict of interest.

Following this mishap, Dean acquired a succession of political jobs and became known as a capable staff man. His first position was chief counsel to the Republican minority on the House Judiciary Committee. In mid-1967, under the sponsorship of Representative Richard Poff (R-Va.), Dean became associate director of the National Commission on the Reform of Federal Criminal Law. In the 1968 presidential campaign Dean helped write position papers on crime for candidate RICHARD NIXON's "law and order" campaign. Brought into the Justice Department by Deputy Attorney General RICHARD KLEINDIENST after Nixon's election, Dean worked closely with Attorney General JOHN MITCHELL in the administration's drug control and crime bills.

In July 1970 Dean moved to the White House with the title of counsel to the president, the post formerly held by JOHN EHRLICHMAN. Dean did not inherit Ehrlichman's power and prominence, however. He had little authority, rarely saw the president, and was originally confined to dealing with relatively trivial matters. Dean sought to expand his little "law firm," he recounted in his book *Blind Ambition*, by making his office's advice available to White House staff members on any subject they requested, from the technicalities of divorce and immigration laws and possible conflicts of interest by White House staffers to the propriety of suing or otherwise harassing certain magazines critical of the Nixon administration.

The counsel's office built up a reputation for intelligence investigations as well. "I became the White House collecting point for antiwar intelligence reports, and I funneled information directly to the president during emergencies," particularly during the May 1971 "Mayday" demonstrations when thousands of antiwar protestors descended on Washington and disrupted government functions. By 1972 Dean had won the confidence of Nixon assistants Ehrlichman and H. R. HALDEMAN and was regularly chosen to handle important and sensitive assignments, such as interviewing potential nominees to the Supreme Court. Dean also sought to discover evidence that a memo written by DITA BEARD, an International Telephone and Telegraph Co. lobbyist, was a forgery. The memo stated that

ITT had contributed $400,000 to the Republican Party in return for a favorable antitrust settlement. However, the FBI confirmed the authenticity of the document.

Soon after the break-in on June 17, 1972, by agents of the Committee to Reelect the President (CREEP) at the Watergate offices of the Democratic National Committee, Dean became engaged in the strenuous effort by the White House to conceal the responsibility of high CREEP officials for the planning of the crime. The White House strategy was to contain the criminal investigation at a low level—the high-level CREEP officials denied any involvement, while the seven men caught and ultimately convicted for the break-in did not reveal the source of their orders in the CREEP hierarchy.

Under the general direction of Haldeman and Ehrlichman, Dean orchestrated the day-to-day cover-up of responsibility for the Watergate break-in. As the White House liaison with the Justice Department investigators, he passed along information to CREEP officials and coordinated their denials and cover stories. He also supervised payments of "hush money" to the arrested burglars. "The cover-up blistered on," he wrote, "with me throwing water on it. Each day brought threats, dramas and more legal strategies. Clandestine conversations with [HERBERT] KALMBACH and [FRED] LARUE about hush money . . . Constant messages between [John] Mitchell and the White House. Crisis calls from [CHARLES] COLSON and [ROBERT] MARDIAN. Coaching sessions for the witnesses being interviewed by FBI agents or paraded before the grand jury." Dean wrote: "I was not the source of authority for the cover-up, yet I became the linchpin." In October Dean worked vigorously to block an investigation of the break-in by Representative WRIGHT PATMAN's (D-Tex.) Banking and Currency Committee. The effort succeeded, ending any chance of a congressional inquiry before the elections. By the time of Nixon's reelection in November Dean had managed to keep a lid on the Watergate investigation.

Dean was first propelled into the public spotlight in February 1973 during Senate confirmation hearings on the nomination of FBI acting director L. PATRICK GRAY. Gray revealed to the Judiciary Committee that he had passed FBI investigative reports to Dean and that Dean had sat in on FBI interviews with White House personnel. The committee asked Dean to appear and testify before it, but Nixon refused to allow his aide to appear in person, citing the doctrine of executive privilege on which Dean had been his chief adviser. The jockeying between the committee and the president over Dean's appearance ended with

Gray's withdrawal of his name from nomination on April 5.

In February and March Dean met frequently with Nixon. The two discussed, among other things, the cover-up and the criminal liabilities of White House and CREEP officials. Facing the probability of eventual prosecution for his own heavy involvement in the cover-up, Dean began meeting secretly with prosecutors in April, relating his knowledge of the cover-up to them, except for Nixon's involvement. During this period Dean in effect broke from his White House superiors. On April 19 the *Washington Post* published a letter from Dean in which he declared he would not become a "scapegoat" in the Watergate case. On April 30 Nixon announced that he had accepted the

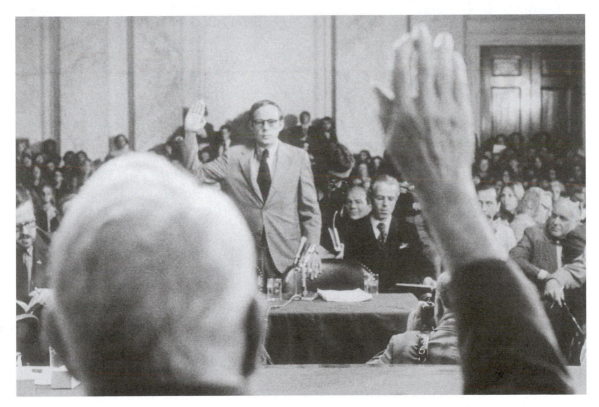

John W. Dean III is sworn in before the Senate Watergate committee. Senator Sam Ervin, chairman of the committee, administers the oath, June 25, 1973. *(Bettman/CORBIS)*

resignations of Haldeman, Ehrlichman, Dean, and Kleindienst. In contrast to his praise of Haldeman and Ehrlichman as "two of the finest public servants it has been my privilege to know," Nixon merely said of Dean that he had "requested and accepted" the resignation of his counsel.

On June 12 Judge JOHN SIRICA granted Dean "testimonial" immunity for his upcoming testimony before the Senate Watergate committee, meaning that no evidence derived from Dean's testimony could be used in prosecuting him. The prosecutors consistently rebuffed Dean's attempts to gain complete immunity from prosecution, however. At a subsequent appearance before the grand jury, Dean repeatedly invoked the Fifth Amendment to protect himself from self-incrimination.

Dean was the star witness of the Watergate committee, the first to accuse Nixon of involvement in the cover-up. From June 25 to 29 he testified before the committee and a national television audience in a dry monotone that belied the startling nature of his testimony. Dean commenced his testimony by reading a 245-page account detailing his own involvement in the cover-up conspiracy, the involvement of his colleagues, and his discussions with Nixon. He testified that on September 15, 1972, Nixon had congratulated him for containing the investigation of the break-in. In February and March, Dean related, he had discussed with Nixon the possibility of executive clemency for some of the conspirators and "hush money" payments to maintain the cover-up. Nixon told him the money was "no problem" on March 13. On March 21, Dean said, he told Nixon there was a "cancer growing on the presidency" and that he doubted whether continued perjury and payments could maintain the cover-up, but Nixon did not appear concerned.

Dean calmly refuted attacks on his credibility by the White House and hostile commit-

tee members. The White House charged Dean with being the "mastermind" of the cover-up, but Dean insisted that his main role was as a conduit between Haldeman and Ehrlichman and CREEP. Under questioning by Senator EDWARD GURNEY (R-Fla.), Dean admitted that he had used, and replaced, Republican funds from his safe to finance his honeymoon. Gurney's hostile questioning, however, was unable to shake Dean's account of Nixon's knowledge of the cover-up. Gurney called Dean a "shoddy turncoat," but Senator JOSEPH MONTOYA (D-N.M.) voiced the majority opinion that Dean was "a very credible witness."

Along with his testimony Dean submitted 47 documents to the committee. One, the Nixon "enemies list," created a minor sensation in the press. The enemies list contained names of individuals, largely liberal Democrats, deemed "enemies" of the Nixon administration for their political postures and activities. In an August 1971 memo Dean had suggested to his superior ways in which "we can use the available federal machinery to screw our political enemies." Techniques included denial of federal grants and contracts, litigation, prosecution, and harassment by the Internal Revenue Service, among others.

Through the rest of the summer former Nixon administration officials appeared before the committee and disputed Dean's version of events. On July 16 it was first revealed that Nixon had been taping his White House conversations. The tapes, played subsequently during the trial of the Watergate conspirators and the House impeachment hearings, ultimately confirmed Dean's account down to the smallest details.

On October 19 Dean pleaded guilty to a single count of conspiring to obstruct justice. The plea was part of a bargain with Special Prosecutor ARCHIBALD COX whereby Dean agreed to be a prosecution witness in return for Cox's promise not to bring further charges against him, except in the case of perjury. On August 2, 1974, Judge Sirica sentenced Dean to one to four years in prison. He began serving his sentence on September 3. On October 2 Dean was barred from practicing law by the District of Columbia Court of Appeals.

Most of Dean's prison sentence was spent either in preparing to testify at the Watergate conspirators' trial, testifying, or waiting to be called to the stand. Two of the prosecutors wrote that he was "the most conscientious witness anyone connected with Watergate had ever seen" and marveled at his retentive memory. In October 1974 Dean, the key witness, testified for eight days at the cover-up trial of Ehrlichman, Haldeman, John Mitchell, ROBERT MARDIAN, and Kenneth Parkinson. He told the same basic story he had related before the Watergate committee. The jury convicted all the defendants except Parkinson on January 1, 1975.

On January 8 Judge Sirica ordered Dean and two other Watergate figures, HERBERT KALMBACH and JEB STUART MAGRUDER, freed from prison, having reduced their sentences to time already served. No longer able to practice law, Dean embarked upon a career as a writer. In October 1976 he published *Blind Ambition*, a regretful account of his White House years that presented an unflattering picture of Dean and his associates and quickly became a best seller. The book also charged that GERALD FORD, the House minority leader, played a role in the Watergate cover-up. In the same month Dean once again shook up a Republican administration with a scandalous revelation. Covering the Republican National Convention for *Rolling Stone* magazine, Dean reported a conversation with a cabinet officer, soon revealed to be Secretary of Agriculture EARL BUTZ, in which Butz made jocular racial slurs against blacks. The story generated a storm of criticism against Butz, who resigned a few days later. Now a writer and speaker, Dean

has published books on Chief Justice WILLIAM REHNQUIST, a biography of Warren Harding, and a study of the presidency of George W. Bush. Dean also works as an investment banker and lives in Beverly Hills, California.

—TO

Dent, Frederick B(aily)
(1922–) *secretary of commerce*

Frederick Dent was born on August 17, 1922, in Cape May, New Jersey. Dent took his B.A. at Yale in 1943 and served the following three years in the navy. After completing his military service he took a job with a family firm, the Joshua A. Baily Co. of New York, and in 1947 went to work for Mayfair Mills, a textile company in South Carolina.

As the U.S. textile industry began to feel the increasing pressure of foreign imports, Dent became an industry spokesman and a critic of prevailing laissez-faire attitudes. In 1970, while serving as chairman of the Committee on International Trade of the American Textile Manufacturers' Institute, Dent attacked trade negotiations then under way among the United States, Japan, and other textile-producing nations, calling for an immediate termination of the talks and for legislation establishing an "effective, comprehensive, qualitative limitation on imports of all textile articles." A year later, when Japan agreed to voluntarily curtail textile exports to the United States, the textile trade association called the move "worse than no agreement at all," and Dent called on President NIXON and Congress "to disavow and disregard the proposal and continue working for a real solution."

Dent's appointment to the post of secretary of commerce in late 1972 represented a concession to domestic producers eager for tariff protection against foreign competition. After assuming office in January 1973, however,

Dent was plunged immediately into the growing raw material and agricultural shortages that surfaced in the hyperinflationary boom conditions of that year. In June 1973, with Secretary of Agriculture EARL BUTZ, Dent placed export controls on soybeans and cottonseed to prevent a domestic livestock feed shortage. In July Dent extended the controls to 41 other farm commodities. Several weeks later he was one of two cabinet-level officials to attend the annual conference of the Joint Japan–United States Committee on Foreign Affairs, at which the Japanese delegation attempted to assure Japan of a "stable supply" of key commodities.

Dent was also involved in the wider aspects of the administration's economic policy. In August 1973 President Nixon instituted the Phase 4 plan, which ended the price freeze then in effect and instituted a system of mandatory compliance with a regimen of price controls. Shortly afterward Dent told a conference of U.S. businessmen that Phase 4 would be a "phase-out" of controls and announced an imminent return to a free market economy. He accompanied Secretary of the Treasury GEORGE SHULTZ to Belgrade for trade talks in October 1973 and held further talks in Moscow and Sofia as part of the administration's overall détente effort. In March 1974 Dent became briefly embroiled in a legal battle with the General Accounting Office (GAO) when it questioned the legality of certain Export-Import Bank loans to Eastern European countries, leading to a suspension of the loans on March 11. Dent stated that the GAO's action was endangering jobs in the United States, and on March 22 the loans were declared legal. As the U.S. economy slid into recession in the fall of 1974, President Ford appointed Dent to the Council on Wage and Price Stability and later to the Economic Policy Board.

In February 1975 Dent was named a U.S. trade negotiator and one month later stepped down as secretary of commerce. Once again

he became immersed in the protectionist issue. In March 1976 President Ford threatened to impose three-year quotas on U.S. imports of specialty steels unless an "orderly market agreement" could be negotiated with the nation's trading partners. In announcing the move Dent, who had also been appointed a U.S. representative to the General Agreement on Trade and Tariffs in Geneva, expressed the hope that Ford's decision would not "kick off a trade war." A month later Dent announced the president's decision not to implement a similar restriction on nonrubber shoe imports. When in June 1976 Ford did approve import quotas on specialty steel imports, Dent was sent to negotiate an "orderly market agreement" with Japan after failing to win voluntary export restraint from Sweden and the European Economic Community (EEC) in the same areas. In 1976 Dent also served on a cabinet-level task force to review U.S. corporate payoffs in overseas operations.

When President Ford left office, Dent stepped down as U.S. trade negotiator and returned to private business. He was president of Mayfair Mills Corp. and a trustee of both Yale University and the Institute of Textile Technology (Charlottesville, Virginia).

—LG

Diggs, Charles C(ole), Jr.
(1922–1998) *member of the House of Representatives*

Born in Detroit, Diggs, the first black congressman from Michigan, was the son of a wealthy Detroit undertaker who also served for many years in the Michigan state senate. His father's popularity in the community boosted Diggs's own political career.

Diggs attended the University of Michigan and Fiske University before entering the army air force in World War II. After the war

Diggs received a degree in mortuary science from Wayne State University and studied at the Detroit College of Law. Diggs entered the family business, one of the state's largest black funeral establishments. He also worked as a disc jockey and news commentator on the family's weekly radio show. In 1950 Diggs won a seat in the state senate, and four years later he was elected to the U.S. House as a Democrat.

During the 1960s Diggs's success in winning reelection in the poor, black downtown Detroit district he represented depended less on his voting record, which reflected a high rate of absenteeism, than on services he offered his constituents. His office expedited the delivery of Social Security checks, speeded the processing of Small Business Administration loans, and performed numerous minor legal services for voters.

During the Nixon-Ford administrations, Diggs maintained that he was particularly concerned with legislation designed to protect and extend the rights of minorities. Yet his continued absenteeism limited his effectiveness. He became chairman of the Senate Foreign Relations Committee's African Subcommittee in 1969. As chairman he was an outspoken critic of U.S. policy toward southern Africa, which he felt supported the status quo of white racism and Portuguese colonialism. By 1971 Diggs began to push openly for changes in U.S. policy. After being denied a visa to visit Rhodesia, he denounced that government as the "new world's light-heavyweight champion of racism." He warned the Democratic Platform Committee in 1971 that "southern Africa holds the frightening, but real, potential for another Vietnam." He said that the United States must act to avoid a racial holocaust and that U.S. business involvement formed a "bulwark for the status quo for apartheid."

As part of his U.S.-African relations activities, Diggs was involved in a congressional effort to repeal the 1971 "Byrd Amendment,"

which allowed the United States to import chrome from Rhodesia despite UN mandatory sanctions for which the United States had voted.

In 1971 Diggs's subcommittee made an extensive inquiry into the conduct and nature of American business in South Africa. As a result of the probe, it proposed a resolution to "protect United States domestic and foreign policy interests by making fair employment practices in the South African enterprises of U.S. firms a criterion for eligibility for government contracts." This proposal was reintroduced in the 93rd and 94th Congresses but was never passed. In 1973, 1974, and 1975 Diggs introduced bills in Congress to prevent U.S. companies in South Africa from practicing racial discrimination with respect to wages, fringe benefits, hiring, and training and advancement opportunities.

As subcommittee chairman, Diggs liberally used his prerogatives to travel, making several trips to Africa and to Europe. After a trip to South Africa and the Portuguese colonies of Guinea-Bissau and Cape Verde in 1972, Diggs issued an "Action Manifesto," which he sent to Secretary of State HENRY KISSINGER, urging the United States to condemn the use of violence by Portugal and the South African government to remain in power. Among its 55 specific proposals the manifesto suggested ending Export-Import Bank loan guarantees to South Africa, terminating a U.S. sugar quota for South Africa, and a justifying agreement with Portugal over the leasing of a military base in the Azores.

In October 1974, at Diggs's insistence, the House International Relations Committee agreed to hold closed hearings on CIA activities in southern Africa and to include in the hearings investigation of U.S. policy toward the Portuguese colonies since the Portuguese military coup in the spring of 1974.

In a 1976 interview with *Africa* magazine Diggs commented that "the record of the Ford administration and its predecessor, the Nixon administration, in the field of African affairs has left much to be desired, to put it in a kindly context."

In October 1978 Diggs was convicted of mail fraud and falsification of congressional payroll data. He was sentenced the following month to a maximum of three years in prison. Nevertheless, in the November 1978 elections he was returned to the House for a 12th term. Diggs was censured by the House in 1978, and his committee and subcommittee chairs were taken from him. Diggs resigned from the House in June 1980 and served seven months of his prison term. Upon his release he opened a funeral home in Prince George's County, Maryland, and earned a degree in political science from Howard University. He died in Washington, D.C., in 1998 of a stroke.

—MLB

Dirksen, Everett McKinley
(1896–1969) *member of the Senate*

Born on January 4, 1896, the son of German immigrants, Dirksen grew up in the farming town of Pekin, Illinois. He entered the University of Minnesota in 1914 but left in 1917 to serve in the army. He was general manager of the Cook Dredging Co. from 1922 to 1925, when he joined his brothers in a bakery business.

Dirksen was Pekin commissioner of finance from 1927 to 1931. He was elected to the U.S. House in 1932 and served there until 1948. Although opposed to many New Deal domestic measures, Dirksen favored Social Security and minimum wage laws. He was an isolationist in the years prior to American entry into World War II but supported the Marshall Plan during the Truman administration. Dirksen supported the presidential candidacy of Senator Robert A. Taft and was a bitter-end supporter of Wisconsin senator Joseph McCarthy, opposing

that senator's censure in 1954. Elected to the U.S. Senate from Illinois in 1950, Dirksen rose to become minority whip in 1957 and minority leader in 1959.

The leading conservative in Congress after Senator Taft's death in 1953, Dirksen insisted upon government economy and devoted his energies to reducing President Eisenhower's budgets. During Eisenhower's second term he became more cooperative with the moderates in the Republican Party. Known as the "Wizard of Ooze" for his grandiose oratory, Dirksen gained new respectability as Republican leader and "political soothsayer" during the Democratic administrations of Kennedy and Johnson. In 1963 his support carried the nuclear test ban treaty through the Senate, and in 1964 he pushed through the epoch-making Civil Rights Act, reversing his previous opposition. He backed the Voting Rights Act of 1965 and the Housing Act of 1968. Despite his opposition to much Democratic social legislation, Dirksen remained a strong supporter of the presidents' foreign policies, including the Vietnam War.

Dirksen was seldom consulted by the president during RICHARD NIXON's first months in office, and his influence declined during his last months in the Senate. Manifesting an increasingly rigid attitude, he was confronted by "Young Turk" liberal Republicans who sought to displace him from leadership of the party. He was unanimously reelected minority leader in 1969 but suffered a personal defeat when his candidate for minority whip, conservative ROMAN L. HRUSKA, was defeated by liberal HUGH SCOTT.

Dirksen generally proved a devoted advocate of the president's domestic and foreign policies. As a member of the Senate Finance Committee, he supported Nixon's efforts to extend the income tax surcharge and after initial opposition backed his expensive Safeguard antiballistic missile project. He joined the

Nixon administration's clandestine campaign to force the resignation of Supreme Court Justice ABE FORTAS after *Life* magazine disclosed Fortas had accepted a $20,000 fee from the Wolfson Foundation. Dirksen suggested that the Senate Judiciary Committee, to which he belonged, inquire into the matter.

A steadfast supporter of Nixon's Vietnam policy, Dirksen favored a gradual deescalation of the war and praised the president's announcement in June 1969 that 25,000 U.S. troops would be withdrawn from Vietnam as "the first tangible, specific, immediate step to de-Americanize" the war. He opposed Senate passage of the Fulbright Resolution of June 25, 1969, which prohibited the president from sending troops or money to foreign countries without congressional approval. Serving as a Nixon spokesman, Dirksen announced the president's opposition to any resolution limiting the executive's war powers but indicated that Nixon preferred the Republican-sponsored Mundt Resolution, which gave the president independent authority in cases of "a direct and immediate threat to the national security." Following Nixon's trip to Romania and the Far East in August 1969, Dirksen, after meeting with the president, expressed confidence that American involvement in the Vietnam War was drawing to a close. Although he said the president had informed him that further U.S. troop withdrawals were imminent, White House press secretary RONALD ZIEGLER commented that this decision had not yet been made.

Dirksen was less accommodating to Nixon's civil rights policies, regarding them as too liberal. He attacked the Labor Department's decision that a federal program to guarantee jobs for blacks in the construction trades (the "Philadelphia Plan") was legal. On July 8, 1969, he told Nixon that the program violated the Civil Rights Act of 1964 by imposing employment quotas and urged him to postpone its implementation.

Entering Washington's Walter Reed Hospital on August 31 for treatment of a malignant lung tumor, Dirksen died of cardiac arrest on September 7, 1969. The Senate passed a resolution that his body lie in state in the Capitol rotunda, an honor that until then had been bestowed on only one other senator, Robert A. Taft, in the 20th century. Nixon delivered a 12-minute eulogy there on September 9. In 1972 one of the Senate office buildings was renamed to honor Dirksen.

—AES

Doar, John M(ichael)
(1921–) *special counsel, House Judiciary Committee*

Born in Minneapolis on December 3, 1921, John Doar grew up in New Richmond, Wisconsin, where his father had a successful law practice. He served in the air force and attended Princeton University and the University of California at Berkeley's law school. From 1950 to 1960 Doar worked in the family firm. He then joined the Justice Department's Civil Rights Division. Four years later he became assistant attorney general and chief of the division. Doar played a major role in the civil rights movement. In September 1962 Doar stood with James Meredith as he attempted to register as the first black student in the history of the University of Mississippi. He was the lead prosecutor in the trials revolving around the murder of civil rights worker Viola Liuzzo and the 1964 murders of three civil rights workers near Philadelphia, Mississippi.

In 1968 Doar left government and made his home in New York City. He was elected president of the New York Board of Education that October. A proponent of decentralization, Doar, a Republican, opposed the United Federation of Teachers' (UFT) demands for the same job security standards in the demonstration district as applied in the rest of the city. The episode somewhat tarnished Doar's reputation since, as some city officials complained, he dragged out the resulting teachers' strike through his intransigence and rigid belief in the morality of his own position. Doar's term as board president ended in 1969. In December 1973 Representative PETER RODINO (D-N.J.) asked him to join the House Judiciary Committee as special majority counsel.

The Judiciary Committee and Chairman Rodino were about to consider the evidence for the impeachment of President RICHARD NIXON on Watergate and other matters. It was Doar's responsibility to compile the evidence, working with his own staff and the special counsel to the committee's Republican minority, Albert Jenner. Seeking to avoid publicity and any show of partisanship, Doar carefully put together his case. He preferred to use documents and existing records rather than witnesses. Doar was almost universally considered fair, although some Democrats found him too cautious.

By February 1974 the committee's work was in full operation with broad subpoena powers from Congress. The two counsels told the committee that violation of criminal law need not be the basis for impeachment. Since the Constitution set no standards, they adopted a general standard from English history, which could include "constitutional wrongs that subvert the structure of government, or undermine the integrity of office and even the Constitution itself." The president's "entire course of conduct in office" as well as individual acts were to be considered. Although some Republicans on the committee believed that only criminality should constitute the basis for impeachment, Doar argued that to confine the case to criminal offenses "may well be to set a standard so restrictive as not to reach conduct that might adversely affect the system of government." For that reason Doar's staff examined not only the Watergate burglary and cover-up—which Nixon always insisted was the only issue at stake—but also the president's taxes and personal finances, "dirty tricks," domestic surveillance activities, the use of federal agencies for political purposes, the secret bombing of Cambodia, and the impounding of congressionally mandated funds.

Doar skillfully directed preparations for the committee's investigation. He successfully opposed a delay in the probe and got the Watergate grand jury's secret report despite the objections of the indicted men's lawyers. He would not allow the president's counsel, JAMES D. ST. CLAIR, to sit in on prehearing staff proceedings. Nonetheless, Doar restrained some committee Democrats who wanted to pressure the White House by an immediate subpoena of White House tapes. He preferred to patiently seek Nixon's compliance and use subpoenas only as a last resort. And in April Doar's firm stance softened enough to allow St. Clair to state his client's case at panel meetings, although cross-examination, which Doar deemed inappropriate to the panel's function (he compared it to that of a grand jury's), was forbidden.

On May 9 Doar began to present the committee with the evidence for impeachment, deliberately speaking in a boring monotone to underscore his nonpartisanship and emphasize the sheer weight of the facts. His performance lasted six weeks, covered 7,200 pages of evidence, and listed 650 findings of fact. In early July the first witnesses were heard. By mid-July the first committee members were visibly bored and exhausted by the whole process. The presentation of evidence had apparently not been so overwhelming as to move the majority of committee Republicans to favor impeachment. Therefore, although all the evidence had still not been presented, Rodino pressured Doar to present his 306-page summary of evidence with analysis, forcefulness, and even some passion.

On July 19 Doar, seconded by Jenner (who would be replaced as minority counsel two days later by a lawyer friendlier to the president's cause), urged a Senate trial of the president on one or more of five impeachment charges: obstruction of justice in the Watergate cover-up; abuse of presidential powers through the invasion of the privacy and civil rights of citizens and the manipulation of government agencies; contempt of Congress and the courts through his defiance of subpoenas for Watergate tapes; denigration of the office of the presidency through income tax evasion and the use of federal money for personal purposes; and the usurpation of Congress's power (as in the bombing of Cambodia). Doar admitted that based on the available evidence, it could not be precisely ascertained at what point the president knew about Watergate, but the "enormous crime" at issue was Nixon's "conduct of his office." The counsel asserted that he had "not the slightest bias against President Nixon . . . I would not do him the smallest, slightest injury. But I am not indifferent . . . to this matter of presidential abuse of power by whatever president." The evidence showed such a systematic "subversion of constitutional government" that "reasonable men acting reasonably would find the president guilty." Doar's speech was uncharacteristically passionate. Many Republicans criticized Doar, but when the committee voted at the end of July, a number of the GOP members joined the Democratic majority to approve three impeachment articles (on the obstruction of justice, the abuse of powers, and subpoena defiance). The House impeachment debate was then scheduled for August 18, but on August 9 Nixon resigned.

In 1975 Doar became a partner of the New York law firm of Donovan, Leisure, Newton, and Irvine. From 1987 to 1993 he would serve as a member of the Committee on Rules of Practice and Procedure of the Judicial Conference of the United States.

—JCH

Dole, Robert J(oseph)

(1923–   ) *member of the Senate; Republican vice presidential candidate*

Born on July 22, 1923, in Russell, Kansas, the son of a grain elevator manager, Dole attended the University of Kansas for two years before enlisting in the army during World War II. He rose in rank to captain and was seriously wounded while leading a combat platoon in Italy. Doctors thought that he would never walk again. Despite this prognosis, a combination of willpower and physical therapy enabled Dole to walk out of a Veterans Administration hospital, but his right arm remained immobile. Dole received his B.A. from the University of Kansas in 1949 and earned his law degree from the same university in 1952. While in law school he won a seat as a Republican in the Kansas house of representatives. Nine years later he was elected to the U.S. House. He focused his attention on the problems of his farm district, fought to preserve rural domination of the legislature, and supported legislation to aid the handicapped. A conservative on most issues, he backed civil rights measures and tax incentives for business to help rebuild cities. In 1968 Dole moved up to the Senate after carrying his state with 60.5 percent of the vote.

Robert Dole emerged in the early years of the Nixon presidency as the administration's leading defender. Often known to be arrogant, abrasive, and brash, he frequently launched sarcastic attacks on liberals. He once termed Ramsey Clark a left-leaning marshmallow. His biting sarcasm and insulting humor won him few friends on the opposite side of the aisle but did earn him the praise of his conservative colleagues and the White House. Dole took it upon himself to be the most persistent Republican defender of the Vietnam War, the antiballistic missile, and Nixon's conservative nominations to the Supreme Court. In gratitude for such

Vice President Nelson Rockefeller, vice presidential candidate Bob Dole, President Gerald Ford, and First Lady Betty Ford celebrate winning the nomination at the Republican National Convention, Kansas City, Missouri, August, 1976. *(Library of Congress)*

loyalty, the president appointed Dole chairman of the Republican National Committee in 1971. The selection angered a number of Senate moderates. Republican senator WILLIAM SAXBE of Ohio called Dole "a hatchet man" who was so arrogant he "couldn't sell beer on a troop ship." Throughout 1971 Dole toured the nation speaking for the party, defending the president's war policies, and collecting funds for the upcoming election campaign. He soon found to his dismay that the White House had shut him out of any decision-making role in the 1972 presidential campaign. Thus, Dole was able to prove ignorance when responding to any charge that he knew of the Watergate break-in. Following the president's reelection, Dole's relationship

with the White House staff was so strained that he resigned in January 1973. During the Watergate controversy Dole warned Nixon against hiding from the people but attacked the press for hounding the president.

In 1974 Dole ran for reelection in a race that emphasized the abortion issue. Dole opposed abortions and favored a constitutional amendment giving the states the right to restrict them. His opponent, Dr. William R. Roy, a Catholic physician who had performed abortions, supported abortions. Right to Life forces descended on Kansas to aid Dole in this test case. Leaflets such as one showing dead fetuses were widely circulated. Dole disclaimed any knowledge of this part of his supporters' campaign, but he refused to disassociate himself from the antiabortion forces. He carried the state in a close election by 13,000 votes.

Robert Dole had always been on good terms with Gerald Ford, although he had broken with the president over the Nixon pardon in 1974 and Ford's veto of a consumer protection agency bill. At the 1976 Republican Convention, Ford chose Dole to be his vice presidential running mate. Behind in the polls, the president hoped Dole's abrasive debating style would add color to the campaign. In addition, Dole was close to the conservative forces, and Ford hoped his choice would reunite the party. In the fall campaign Dole, more than Ford, went on the offensive in attacking JIMMY CARTER's and WALTER MONDALE's liberalism.

At Dole's historic Houston debate with his Democratic counterpart, the candidates exchanged verbal jabs on domestic issues. Dole accused the Democratic Party of bankrupting the nation, while Mondale tried to portray his adversary as a heartless conservative who showed no compassion for the poor, the unemployed, or the elderly. It is generally believed that Mondale won the debate. Following the defeat of the Republican ticket in November, Dole returned to the Senate. During the first years of the Carter administration he led the opposition to the Panama Canal treaties.

In 1980 Dole made his first run for the Republican nomination for president, being defeated by Ronald Reagan. In 1984 Dole was elected Senate majority leader, a position he kept for two years, until the Republicans lost control of the Senate in the 1986 off-year election; then Dole was elected to the post of Senate minority leader. In 1988 Dole ran again, this time losing the nomination to Vice President GEORGE H. W. BUSH. Following his defeat by Bush, Dole returned to his leadership role in the Senate. Dole continued his leadership service in the Senate until 1996, when he resigned to devote his full attention to his run for the presidency. That year he won the Republican nomination but was defeated by Bill Clinton in the fall election. Following his defeat Dole formed Bob Dole Enterprises, which monitors his business affairs. He has also been a member of the International Commission on Missing Persons and was influential in the planning of a World War II memorial, dedicated in Washington, D.C., in 2004.

—JB and JRG

Douglas, William O(rville)

(1898–1980) *associate justice, U.S. Supreme Court*

Douglas was born in Maine, Minnesota, on October 16, 1898. After an impoverished childhood in Yakima, Washington, Douglas worked his way through Columbia Law Shool, graduating second in his class in 1925. He became a leading corporate and financial law expert while teaching at Columbia and Yale law schools. As chairman of the Securities and Exchange Commission from 1937 to 1939, Douglas effected a reorganization and reform of the stock exchange. Named to the Supreme Court in March 1939, Douglas used his financial law background over the years to write significant court opinions in the fields of bankruptcy, antitrust, and patent law.

Justice Douglas became best known, however, as one of the foremost defenders of individual liberties in the Court's history. He gave a preferred position to the First Amendment and insisted that its guarantees of freedom of belief and expression could not be breached by government. He favored extension of the criminal safeguards in the Bill of Rights to the states and interpreted those rights, such as the right to counsel or the privilege against self-incrimination, very broadly. The justice also took an expansive view of the guarantee of equal protection. Underlying many of his views was a strong concern for protecting the individual from the power and intrusiveness of big government, especially if the individual was socially or economically disadvantaged and powerless. Any changes in Douglas's position while on the Court were all in the direction of giving greater scope to constitutional liberties.

Douglas shared many of his views with Justice HUGO BLACK, and during the 1960s the two men saw the Court adopt positions they had earlier espoused in dissent. In the late 1960s, however, Douglas surpassed even Black in his protection of individual freedoms, voting, for example, to protect the rights of antiwar and civil rights protesters, of debtors, of welfare recipients and illegitimate children, and of criminal defendants. Outspoken and personally nonconformist, Douglas became a symbol of the liberal judicial activism that characterized the Warren Court. Partly because of that position, he was the target of an impeachment attempt in 1970. On April 15, after the Senate had rejected two of President RICHARD NIXON's nominees for the Court, House minority leader GERALD R. FORD (R-Mich.) launched a move to impeach Douglas for alleged improprieties in his professional conduct. Ford challenged the justice's association with the Albert Parvin Foundation prior to 1969 and with the Center for the Study of Democratic Institutions. He criticized the views Douglas expressed in his book *Points of Rebellion*, the publication of excerpts from the book in an allegedly pornographic magazine, and Douglas's participation in several cases in which Ford detected a conflict of interest. A special House Judiciary Subcommittee began investigating the charges on April 21. In a report released December 15, the subcommittee cleared Douglas of all the allegations and declared there were no grounds for impeachment.

On the WARREN BURGER Court Douglas resumed the role he had played earlier in his judicial career of dissenter from the rulings of a more conservative majority. From the 1969 Court term on, he entered far more dissents than any other justice, and he staked out a position as the most liberal member of the high bench. Especially notable were Douglas's numerous dissents from Court decisions refusing to hear cases such as those challenging the legality of the Vietnam War. Douglas favored making the Court an accessible forum where the aggrieved could obtain a remedy for deprivations of their civil and constitutional rights. He urged the Court to take more cases, and he opposed rulings that limited the Court's jurisdiction to decide lawsuits.

Douglas also dissented from many Burger Court criminal decisions. He objected to all rulings that in any way limited the scope of the 1966 *Miranda* decision and to judgments sanctioning warrantless searches and electronic surveillance. In May 1971 and May 1972 dissents, he maintained his position that the Fifth Amendment's privilege against self-incrimination barred the government from compelling anyone to confess to a crime, even with an immunity guarantee. Douglas did join the majority in June 1970 to validate six-member juries in state courts, but he opposed a May 1972 decision allowing nonunanimous jury verdicts. He urged the Court to extend the right to a jury to all trials and to juvenile court proceedings. In a June 1972 opinion for the Court, Douglas held that an indigent defendant could not be jailed, even for a misdemeanor, unless given free counsel.

Justice Douglas continued to express his concern for those who were disadvantaged and different from the rest of society. A longtime critic of vagrancy laws he wrote the majority opinion in a February 1972 case overturning a municipal vagrancy ordinance because it was vague and subject to arbitrary enforcement. The justice voted to overturn the death penalty in June 1972, largely because under existing laws judges and juries could discriminate against the poor and minorities in imposing the death sentence. Douglas retained a predominantly activist stance in racial discrimination cases and opposed all forms of discrimination against illegitimate children, the poor, and women. In a June 1969 opinion he overturned state laws permitting garnishment of a debtor's wages prior to any hearing. In subsequent cases Douglas voted to guarantee hearings to welfare recipients before termination of their benefits, to parolees before revocation of their parole, and to public employees prior to dismissal. He also favored removing restrictions on the right to vote based on age, residency, or status.

In First Amendment cases Douglas adhered to his absolutist position. He opposed all loyalty oaths and obscenity laws in these years and favored giving constitutional protection to a wide variety of symbolic forms of expression such as wearing a black armband or putting a peace symbol on the flag to protest the Vietnam War. He believed freedom of the press was unassailable and voted against the government's request for an injunction to halt newspaper publication of the *Pentagon Papers* in June 1971. Douglas also opposed all state aid to parochial education as a violation of the First Amendment. He was the lone dissenter in May 1970 when the Court upheld tax exemptions for church property used solely for religious purposes.

A dedicated conservationist and naturalist, Douglas wrote several important environmental law opinions. In an April 1973 case he ruled that the states could establish stiffer penalties for maritime oil spills than the federal government. A year later Douglas sustained a municipal zoning ordinance that barred communal living groups. He believed the ordinance a legitimate land use law aimed at preserving a quiet, uncongested residential area. When the majority ruled in April 1972 that the Sierra Club did not have the necessary legal interest to challenge the building of a ski resort in

Sequoia National Forest, Douglas entered a widely discussed dissent that argued that inanimate objects such as trees and rivers should be accorded legal standing and be allowed to sue in their own name for their preservation.

Douglas was known to the public not only for his constitutional views but also for his many off-the-bench activities. A colorful and controversial figure, he disputed the notion that the Court was overworked and used his free time to travel, hike, mountain-climb, and write and lecture. A vigorous, energetic man when well into his 70s, Douglas suffered a stroke on December 31, 1974. He retired from the Court on November 12, 1975, when he found that the aftereffects of the stroke kept him from performing his share of the Court's work. He had served on the Court longer than had any other justice. Douglas died in Washington, D.C.'s, Walter Reed Hospital on January 29, 1980.

—CAB

Dunlop, John T(homas)

(1914–2003) *director, Cost of Living Council (CLC); chairman, CLC; secretary of labor*

Born in Placerville, California, Dunlop was raised in the Philippines, where his father was a missionary. He received his A.B. and Ph.D. from the University of California at Berkeley. He joined the Harvard faculty in 1938 and served at one time as dean of the Harvard Faculty of Arts and Sciences. During the postwar period he participated in numerous boards and committees in and out of government as a mediator, arbitrator, and adviser—mostly in the construction industry.

In 1971 Dunlop was named chairman of the NIXON administration's Construction Industry Stabilization Committee (CISC). As chairman of that panel, Dunlop fought many open and bitter battles with Nixon's Pay Board formed to monitor wages. The board had insisted that Dunlop adhere to its guidelines in judging construction industry contracts. Dunlop, however, demanded to have autonomy for his committee and, in fact, retained the authority he sought. It was generally believed that he brought some order to the collective bargaining process in the construction industry. He was acclaimed for deflating wage pressures in that industry.

Dunlop became head of the Cost of Living Council (COLC) in January 1973 and was, consequently, responsible for directing Nixon's price and wage controls. He encouraged the federal government to use its power as a major buyer and seller to help keep market prices down. He played a role in convincing Nixon to speed up the sale of government-owned metals and rubber. When the price of steel scrap surged upward, he encouraged the Maritime Administration to double its sales of scrap from obsolete ships. Dunlop presided over the easing, and then ending, of price and wage controls in Phases 3 and 4 of Nixon's economic policy. His role was limited, however, because he ruled over a dying program.

In March 1975 President GERALD FORD appointed Dunlop to be his secretary of labor. Dunlop came to his post with strong support from organized labor. He took the job with the assurance by Ford that he would be given a role in the formulation of economic policy. Although he served for only nine months in this cabinet post, he was a strong secretary. He staged a major shake-up in the Labor Department's Occupational Safety and Health Administration. He set up the department's first office for enforcing the new federal pension law. He began an investigation of the Teamsters Union Central States Pension Fund. He helped to steer legislation through Congress that would increase permanently the number of workers eligible for unemployment insurance. He successfully mediated the dispute between the AFL-CIO and the White House that eventually allowed a long-term Soviet-American grain agreement. He played a role in formulating Ford's tax cut in 1975.

Dunlop put much of his energy into bringing peace to the construction industry. His solution for an industry plagued by unemployment and high wages was composed of two elements he hoped would be enacted into law. First, a Construction Industry Collective Bargaining Committee composed of employer and employee representatives would get involved in local disputes to try to solve them without inflationary pressures emerging from local unions. Second, to get union support for the first part of his program, Dunlop included provisions that would have permitted a union to picket an entire construction site even if the union was only having a conflict with one of several contractors working at the site. President Ford had promised to sign the bill that contained this package. When Ford vetoed it, Dunlop felt that his usefulness as labor secretary had come to an end. He believed he would no longer have the confidence of organized labor. He resigned in January 1976.

After JIMMY CARTER was elected president, Dunlop's name emerged as a possible labor secretary in the new administration. Civil rights and women's groups objected. They were critical of the orders he had given as labor secretary under Ford for the new enforcement regulations governing the contract compliance program in which federal money could not be spent in those enterprises where workers faced discrimination on the job. Dunlop had objected to employment goals and timetables. Although the AFL-CIO had favored Dunlop for the post, he was not named by Carter. Dunlop died in Boston's Brigham and Women's Hospital on October 3, 2003.

—HML

E

Eagleton, Thomas (Francis)
(1929–) *member of the Senate*

Born on September 4, 1929, the son of a local St. Louis politician and prominent lawyer, Eagleton earned his B.A. from Amherst University in 1950. In 1953 he received his LL.B. from Harvard, graduating cum laude and as editor of the *Law Review*. Eagleton then returned to St. Louis to join his father's law firm and pursue a career in politics. In 1956, running as a Democrat, he became the youngest circuit court attorney in St. Louis history. In 1960 he was elected state attorney general. Besides introducing administrative reforms that facilitated the processing of cases, Eagleton earned a liberal reputation by opposing the death penalty, championing consumer protection, and endorsing Supreme Court decisions protecting the rights of the accused. In 1968 Eagleton entered the Democratic primary for a U.S. Senate seat. He defeated the incumbent, Edward V. Long (D-Mo.), and then narrowly won the election running on an antiwar, liberal platform in a conservative state.

Eagleton emerged as one of the leading liberal freshman in the Senate. He opposed the Vietnam War, voting for both the Cooper-Church and McGovern-Hatfield end-the-war amendments, and questioned excessive defense spending. He successfully led the fight to ban funds for the development of the MBT-70 tank, a weapon he deemed obsolete. In domestic legislation he lobbied for programs to assist the elderly, protect the consumer, encourage clean air and water, improve the nutrition of Americans, and plug tax loopholes. He also opposed the development of the SST.

At the 1972 Democratic National Convention, presidential nominee GEORGE MCGOVERN, impressed with Eagleton's record, offered him the vice presidential nomination. He did so after only a cursory check of the senator's background, which revealed that he had been hospitalized for "fatigue and exhaustion." McGovern and his staff thought that Eagleton, an urban Catholic, would strengthen the ticket in the ethnic neighborhoods suspicious of the antiwar movement. Eagleton gladly accepted the offer and delivered to the convention an impassioned acceptance speech calling for an end to the war and a renewal of liberalism.

Rumors immediately began to spread suggesting that Eagleton had been hospitalized for a nervous breakdown. McGovern was aware of this, and when discussing the issue with Eagleton, both had agreed it would not hurt the ticket. Perhaps, they thought, the matter might even help them because of Eagleton's underdog status. However, shortly after the convention two reporters for the Knight newspaper chain learned that Eagleton had been institutionalized on a number of occasions. Before they released the story to the press, they reported it to McGovern's campaign manager, FRANK MANKIEWICZ. To blunt the impact of this revelation, McGovern and Eagleton held a joint press conference at Sylvan Lodge, South Dakota. Eagleton announced that he had voluntarily checked himself into a hospital three times in the 1960s for nervous exhaustion. He admitted that he had undergone shock therapy and drug treatments and conceded that the breakdowns occurred after undertaking three grueling campaigns. McGovern announced that he was 1,000 percent behind Eagleton and was satisfied with the senator's explanation.

Soon after this press conference, JACK ANDERSON stated that Eagleton had been apprehended for drunken and reckless driving. Eagleton angrily denounced Anderson's charges. The columnist then retracted the story as completely false because his informant had proven to be unreliable. Nevertheless, Eagleton's credibility was severely challenged. The leading newspapers of the nation, including the *New York Times* and the *Washington Post*, called for him to step down or be ousted from the ticket. They questioned his ability to assume the vigorous duties of the presidency if necessary and criticized his dissembling to McGovern. Leading Democratic officials also began to pressure McGovern to remove Eagleton. They feared that by having him on the ticket, the party, already in trouble, would do even worse in the polls. Contributors to the party treasury declined. Yet McGovern persisted in publicly claiming that he would keep Eagleton on the ticket, and Eagleton continued to campaign, trying to exploit his underdog image.

After several days of uncertainty, however, McGovern leaked reports that he was going to drop Eagleton to the press. Eagleton picked up these signals and announced on July 31 that he would leave the ticket. He reiterated that he considered himself mentally fit and explained that he made this decision because he feared questions concerning his health would divert discussion from the issues in the campaign.

In analyzing the Eagleton affair, critics accused McGovern of showing little courage when he leaked those reports rather than confronting Eagleton and personally requesting his resignation. McGovern and his staff were also charged with failing to do a proper background check. Eagleton recalled McGovern asking him only, "Do you have any old skeletons rattling around your closet?" Eagleton said no; he believed that what McGovern was asking referred to something sordid. However, his critics wrote that Eagleton should have been honest with McGovern.

Eagleton returned to the Senate and remained one of the leading critics of the administration's Southeast Asia and defense policies. In 1973 Eagleton introduced an amendment to an appropriations bill barring funds for military operations in Cambodia and Laos. He further lobbied for a cutoff of military aid to Turkey after that nation's invasion of Cyprus. In 1973 the liberal Americans for Democratic Action gave Eagleton a 90 percent rating. As one of the Senate's most important liberals, Eagleton supported appropriating more funds for urban mass transit and nutritional programs. In February 1973 he was floor manager of the Older American Act, a bill designed to assist the elderly. Eagleton advocated tighter regulation by the federal government of the cosmetics industry, especially to protect the consumer from hazardous products. Only in the area of busing did Eagleton break from his liberal colleagues. He supported an effort in 1974 to restrict busing.

During the Carter presidency, Eagleton continued to be one of the leading liberals in Congress. He supported the president on the Panama Canal treaties and the SALT initiative. Eagleton continued to press for legislation to help the elderly. After retiring from the Senate in 1987, Eagleton returned to Missouri. He is a partner at the St. Louis law firm of Thompson Coburn, where he served as the chief negotiator in the successful effort to lure the St. Louis Rams football team from Los Angeles. He also serves as a professor of public affairs at Washington University (St. Louis).

—JB

Eastland, James O(liver)
(1904–1986) *member of the Senate*

A Mississippi native, Eastland practiced law, managed the family's 5,400-acre cotton farm, and served briefly in the state's house of representatives until 1941, when he was appointed temporarily to the U.S. Senate. Two years later Eastland was elected to the Senate. Although a Democrat, Eastland compiled one of the most conservative records in the Senate, opposing federal social welfare and civil rights legislation. In the early 1970s the conservative Americans for Constitutional Action gave him a cumulative rating of 73. Eastland strongly supported agricultural programs, particularly cotton interests important to his state. In 1956 he became chairman of the Judiciary Committee. He also served on the Agriculture and Forestry Committee, chairing the Immigration and Naturalization Subcommittee. In July 1972 Eastland was elected president pro tempore of the Senate.

Although Eastland shunned publicity and was little known outside of Congress, he was one of the most powerful men on Capitol Hill. Because of his seniority and committee positions, he was able to block the flow of much liberal legislation. As chairman of the Judiciary panel, Eastland had control over all civil rights, crime, and gun-control legislation, as well as judicial appointments. Eastland waged a continuing fight against all civil rights legislation and saw to it that no civil rights bill or

resolutions received a favorable report from the Judiciary Committee. A staunch anti-communist, he contended that communists had infiltrated civil rights organizations and were seeking to destroy communication and cooperation between persons of good faith of all races. As chairman of the Immigration and Naturalization Subcommittee, he attempted to check many State Department policies regarding foreign travel, passports, and admission of undesirable aliens. During his career Eastland introduced more than 30 bills aimed at increasing internal security, including one to control travel by "subversives" from the United States to other countries such as North Vietnam.

During the NIXON administration, Eastland voted against the majority of Democrats in the Senate more often than he voted with them. He backed the president's position three out of four times in 1970 and supported the conservative coalition 99 percent of the time. Eastland defended the civil rights record of President Nixon's controversial Supreme Court nominees, CLEMENT F. HAYNSWORTH JR., G. HARROLD CARSWELL, and WILLIAM H. REHNQUIST. He opposed federal aid to primary and secondary schools. The senator maintained that such aid was unconstitutional and that control of education belonged to state and local authorities. He warned that continued federal interference with education would result in "one conglomerate mass of people." In 1969 and 1970 Eastland spoke against busing plans to achieve racial balance in schools. He asserted that the plans were particularly aimed at the South and ignored racial discrimination in the North.

Despite the poverty of his home state, where the median income was the lowest in the nation, Eastland opposed federal programs for the poor. He voted against increasing appropriations for food stamps in 1970 and authorization of funds for antipoverty programs in 1971. The Mississippi lawmaker believed that persons trafficking in narcotics should be severely punished. He supported proposed legislation mandating life imprisonment without parole for sellers of hard drugs. In February 1973 Eastland introduced a bill calling for a reduction of sentences for those dealers who revealed to law enforcement officials their source of narcotics.

By virtue of his seniority on the Agriculture and Forestry Committee, he was appointed adviser to the Senate Appropriations Committee. He proved effective in restoring funds for research, Extension Service, and school lunch and milk programs. His record was unsurpassed in the protection of minimum cotton allotments for small farmers. In 1970 the senator, who owned a large plantation, opposed a measure limiting farm subsidies to a maximum of $55,000.

As chairman of the Senate Forestry and Soil Conservation Subcommittee, Eastland played a significant role in drafting legislation to salvage areas laid waste by silt, flood, or mismanagement. In 1975 Eastland offered a Senate resolution to provide all government aid possible for the protection of the U.S. coastal fishing industry against excessive foreign encroachment.

On the international scene, Eastland maintained that as a free nation, the entire U.S. population was responsible for foreign policy. As an ardent anticommunist, Eastland believed that every weapon needed for victory should be made available to U.S. troops in Vietnam and thus "rattle the teeth of the Reds" in Moscow and Beijing. On June 30, 1970, Eastland voted against the Cooper-Church Amendment to halt American military action in Cambodia. He also opposed the administration's economic sanctions against Rhodesia and described Nixon's 1970 decision to close the U.S. consulate in Salisbury, Rhodesia, as a "colossal folly." He charged that Americans ignored international law and followed the emotional dictates of African politics.

In 1971 Eastland endorsed congressional action permitting the importation of Rhodesian chrome ore into the United States, a break in the UN-mandated economic sanctions against the country. He observed that Communist China's admission to the United Nations demonstrated the futility of using foreign aid to buy votes. When he voted against the continuance of all foreign aid in October 1971, Eastland charged that such assistance had degenerated into a wasteful and inefficient program. He remained a staunch advocate of military aid to assist free nations vigorously resisting the spread of communism. Eastland opposed attempts to limit defense appropriations and supported construction of the Safeguard antiballistic missile system and the C-5A aircraft. He voted against the Nuclear Nonproliferation Treaty of 1969, the volunteer army in 1971, and the reduction of U.S. troop levels in Europe in 1971.

In May 1978 Eastland announced he would not seek reelection, thus ending a 35-year congressional career. He retired to his home in Doddsville, Mississippi, where he died in February 1986.

—TML

Ehrlichman, John D.
(1925–1999) *counsel to the president; assistant to the president for domestic affairs*

Born on March 20, 1925, John D. Ehrlichman's family originally emigrated from Austria to Seattle in the late 19th century and soon thereafter abandoned their Orthodox Jewish faith to become Christian Scientists. His father was a land developer. Ehrlichman grew up in Santa Monica, California, and attended the University of California at Los Angeles (UCLA). In 1943, after his freshman year at UCLA, he enlisted in the army air corps and flew 26 missions over Europe as a B-24 navigator.

After World War II he returned to UCLA on the GI Bill. Ehrlichman attended Stanford Law School, from which he received a law degree in 1951. Thereafter he joined a Los Angeles law firm for a short time before setting up his own law firm in Seattle. He built on his family's substantial connections in the real estate business community and established a prosperous specialization in zoning and land use law.

As a legal expert in land use, Ehrlichman had frequent dealings with state and local officials of both parties, and it thus behooved him to sustain a low level of partisan involvement. Even during his years on President NIXON's White House staff, Ehrlichman was virtually unknown to many of his state's leading Republicans. This was largely because Ehrlichman never had a strong ideological-partisan commitment; instead, his political commitment was to a single man—Richard M. Nixon.

Ehrlichman was drafted into Nixon's political career by his old college friend H. R. HALDEMAN, who had been a fervid Nixonite since the late 1940s. In 1959, when Haldeman became chief advance man for the 1960 Nixon presidential campaign, he called on his friend to help out. During the course of that campaign, Ehrlichman was captivated by the excitement and scale of national politics and also became a committed Nixonite. He returned after the 1960 defeat to help in Nixon's unsuccessful 1962 race for the California governorship. Convinced that his candidate's career was finished, Ehrlichman returned to Seattle and his law practice.

Republican intraparty strife during the mid-1960s revived Nixon's political fortunes. In an effort to win the presidential nomination, Nixon and his forces actively campaigned for Republican candidates across the country and in the process tested the political waters for a possible comeback. As part of this 1966 campaign effort, Ehrlichman assisted in training some advance men. Thereafter he (and Haldeman) helped direct some of Nixon's early comeback and primary campaign efforts, although he maintained an attitude of reserve and incomplete commitment until he was convinced that Nixon was on a winning course.

After signing on full time, Ehrlichman set up Nixon's headquarters for the 1968 Miami Beach Republican Convention and played a role in carrying out convention strategy. After Nixon secured the presidential nomination, he was appointed tour director and put in charge of the logistics of the campaign.

After his November victory the grateful Nixon offered Ehrlichman the position of counsel to the president. The president recognized in him qualities that he valued: "diligence, caution, an open mind, an absence of distracting personal flair, and above all, orderliness and efficiency." Ehrlichman accepted, feeling that this was exactly the kind of unpretentious and uncontroversial job he could handle and yet not get shunted off into the executive branch's bureaucratic maze.

His first two projects as counsel were the composition of a conflict-of-interest code for the new Nixon appointees and the management of the president's personal finances, which included the purchase of the Nixon homes at San Clemente and Key Biscayne. Gradually he emerged as something of the "White House fireman," dampening political fires and anticipating bureaucratic blazes. As presidential counsel, he assumed a prominent role in reconciling interagency disputes and in turning legislative ideas into specific proposals. Without firm policy opinions or an inclusive ideological frame of reference, Ehrlichman was well suited to the role of idea broker. Furthermore, as an unpresupposing character, he could interface with the president's more, flamboyant domestic advisers, the liberal DANIEL PATRICK MOYNIHAN and the conservative ARTHUR BURNS. Indeed, the president experimented with Ehrlichman as a domestic policy referee in mid-1969 when he returned from his European tour. Ehrlichman remembered that at that time the White House was "long on advocates and short on honest brokers" and that "the president himself was often left as the only honest broker . . . [which] was inefficient and wasteful of his time."

Clearly the president had neither the time, the personal disposition, nor the political interest to referee most domestic policy quarrels. But to delegate that task, he needed to find someone he knew and trusted and who was like-minded. On both counts Ehrlichman fitted the bill. He was regarded as a cautious, nonideological pragmatist who had the leanings of an "instinctive conservative." Furthermore, as one White House colleague observed, "He is a guy the president knows, trusts, and likes to work with," which was particularly important to a president like Nixon who did not "like to work closely with too many people."

In November 1969 the president institutionalized Ehrlichman's role as domestic policy coordinator by naming him assistant to the president for domestic affairs. The change in Ehrlichman's title (although not his duties) came as part of a series of staff changes designed to streamline the president's domestic policy-making machinery and strengthen his grip on the executive branch. The moves were touched off by the impending departure of one of the president's chief domestic policy advisers, Arthur Burns, to assume the chairmanship of the Federal Reserve Board. As part of the change, both presidential assistants Daniel Patrick Moynihan and BRYCE N. HARLOW were accorded cabinet rank and named counselors to the president. The post of assistant for domestic affairs was also created and bestowed on Ehrlichman.

Ehrlichman viewed his new assignment as "essentially operational"—"to serve as a strainer" or as an "honest broker between warring points of view" on domestic policy issues. He was expected to coordinate the develop-

ment of policy alternatives and specific programs. The White House announcement of his appointment stated that "advice and policy guidance will be channeled to the domestic affairs staff from the Urban Affairs Council, the Cabinet Committee on Economic Policy, the Environment Quality Council, and the counselors to the president, as well as the departments and agencies." Thus, all of the president's messages to Congress, speeches, administrative policy statements, and specific legislative proposals on domestic affairs had to be cleared through Ehrlichman's office.

Comparison was immediately made to the advisory-administrative setup under HENRY KISSINGER for foreign affairs. If the comparison was valid, then Ehrlichman was much more than a mere technician with minimal policy influence. And, in fact, a *Newsweek* story on the staff changes called Ehrlichman a "domestic czar" with powers roughly equivalent to those of Joseph Califano in the Johnson presidency.

Certainly the president hoped that from this new position Ehrlichman could bring an order and neatness to domestic policy formulation and execution that would be comparable to Kissinger's system for foreign affairs. Yet despite the apparent similarities between Ehrlichman in domestic affairs and Kissinger in foreign affairs, there were two important differences.

Foremost, Kissinger was a theoretician, an idea generator in his area, whereas Ehrlichman laid "no great claim to creativity in policy making" for domestic affairs. Instead Ehrlichman had to work with two other White House assistants of equal, if not superior, status who were to act as the substantive policy advisers in the domestic arena. It was Moynihan and Harlow who were given the responsibility to "anticipate events, think through the consequences of current trends, question conventional wisdom, address fundamentals, and stimulate long-range innovation." From this perspective Ehrlichman's task was "essentially managerial and judicial." He acted "like an editor, trimming, revising, expanding, or compelling a complete overhaul of the literary products" of the idea men. Thus, the combination of influential staff competition and a projected administrative function seemed to indicate that the new assistant for domestic affairs would be destined for a less significant role than the assistant for foreign affairs.

A second important difference between these two presidential assistants and their bailiwicks concerned presidential attitudes and interests. Foreign affairs were the focal point of the president's personal and political interests, and they were the topic of the creatively innovative policy impulses of his presidency. In contrast, domestic affairs were generally less interesting to President Nixon and more often the target of negative policy impulses to cut back, consolidate, or retrench. Thus, since Kissinger acted as majordomo and confidential adviser in the area of major presidential concern, his influence with the president and over policy formulation was quite evident. On the other hand, since Ehrlichman acted in less of a substantive capacity over an area of less intense presidential interest, the president may have been more inclined to delegate affairs to him. It is therefore difficult to pinpoint the character and extent of Ehrlichman's influence over domestic policy. Although comparable in a formal sense, Kissinger's influence was more in the character of a pilot, while Ehrlichman's was that of a steward.

To achieve his coordinating task, Ehrlichman established a pyramidal organizational structure to channel ideas. First he assembled six aides to perform two essential roles: to determine how well government bureaus were executing the president's instructions and to supervise interagency "project teams" that would conduct research, develop legislative programs, and "present policy options to the president." At a

secondary level he collected a "pool of technicians organized into groups to solve specific problems and run specific programs." Through this system Ehrlichman became a "traffic manager," directing ideas up to the president and passing down policy choices made by the president for implementation.

Criticism of Ehrlichman in this position generally followed two themes. On the one hand, comment focused on his inexperience. One White House aide said that Ehrlichman's relentlessly linear mind could not comprehend the untidiness of getting things accomplished in Washington. "He has not been around here long enough to understand that when Congress seems to make little sense to an orderly mind, that is frequently when Congress makes the most sense."

While admitting that he was not an expert, Ehrlichman saw certain advantages to his inexperience. He remarked: "My knowledge of the kind of things we're dealing in here is very limited and I'm the first to realize that. . . . Sometimes it helps to be uneducated, so you can ask stupid questions that need to be asked and get some hard answers—questions like, 'Do we have to do this at all?' and 'Why can't the states do this?'" This process may have been considered particularly useful to an administration convinced that many federal programs that were a legacy of the New Deal and Great Society eras needed pruning, weeding, and consolidating.

The other critical theme contended that instead of being a traffic manager, Ehrlichman (as well as other members of the White House staff) was acting more like a roadblock, cutting off direct access to the president and isolating him from political realities. As the character of the Nixon White House began to evolve, the Teutonic trio of Haldeman, Ehrlichman, and Kissinger were accused of building a "Berlin Wall" around the president. Ehrlichman, in particular, incurred the enmity of domestic cabinet officers since, in operational details, he had broad authority to place the key domestic departments directly under his control.

With few exceptions, domestic cabinet secretaries were forced to adjust to the idea that they had to deal with Ehrlichman before they could reach the president and, frequently, instead of the president. One cabinet member who felt particularly estranged was Interior Secretary WALTER HICKEL, whose frustration finally erupted into the public domain when his letter to the president protesting the handling of the Kent State demonstration strongly implied that the president was being isolated both from the public and from his administration. Hickel suggested in the letter that Nixon "consider meeting on an individual and con-

versational basis with members of . . . [the] cabinet."

Despite the complaints of an occasional Hickel or the grumblings about "Von" Ehrlichman's "Berlin Wall," Ehrlichman's importance was implicit and played down during President Nixon's first term, when he was portrayed as merely a middleman—a conduit between the president and his domestic administrators. Within weeks of Nixon's reelection in 1972, however, the extent of Ehrlichman's influence in domestic affairs became more evident.

In mid-December of 1972 Ehrlichman was relieved of his responsibilities for supervising the day-to-day activities of the Domestic Council. These operational duties were assumed by his former deputy, Kenneth B. Cole Jr., to free Ehrlichman "for additional

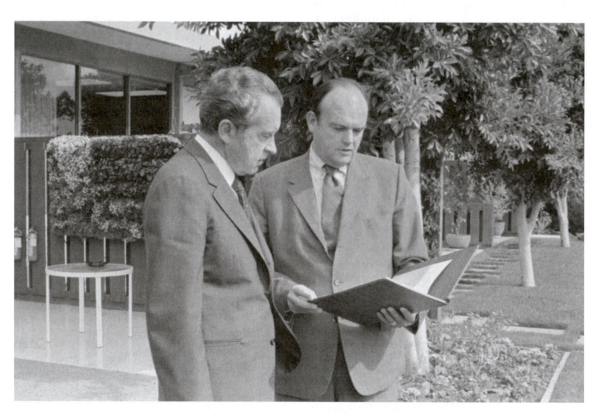

President Nixon with John Ehrlichman, February 12, 1973 *(National Archives)*

responsibilities beyond being the president's chief domestic adviser." Given the president's desire to avoid most domestic affairs, he was glad to merely indicate what he wanted in broad, vague terms and leave Ehrlichman to handle the specifics. This virtually made Ehrlichman a surrogate president for domestic affairs, and as his power grew and became more evident, he outgrew the rather unpretentious and unassuming style he had brought to Washington. Instead, he became arrogant in his power, regarding the cabinet and agency heads as irrelevant nuisances who wasted his and the president's time.

Once the administration had been reelected, Ehrlichman helped develop a bureaucratic reorganization plan that displayed his disdain for the cabinet, his suspicions of the permanent bureaucracy, and his newfound enjoyment and thirst for power. In all these things he was empathetic with the president's preferred style of dealing with a minimum of people and his view that something had to be done to bring a generally recalcitrant bureaucracy under presidential control.

Ehrlichman furthered the administration's earlier reorganizational study, the Ash Commission Report, by coordinating a task force effort with the Justice Department and the Office of Management and Budget to develop the "administrative presidency." His approach was to find effective ways of gathering the reins of bureaucratic control into the president's hands without having to go to the Democratically controlled and often uncooperative Congress to ask for new laws. An important part of his scheme was for the president to elevate four cabinet members to concurrent status as assistants to the president. This quartet was to be given coordinating responsibilities for the areas of economic affairs, human resources, natural resources, and community development. In addition, Ehrlichman was to assume direction of the Office of Intergovernmental Relations, thereby dealing with the mayors and governors of the nation. Meanwhile, Henry Kissinger would continue to preside over the foreign affairs sphere.

These six individuals would constitute a supercabinet and the core of the projected "administrative presidency." A second step in the process of gaining control of the bureaucratic behemoth was the installation of loyal, White House–experienced personnel in each agency and bureau to establish an informal network of "old boys" who could help the president and his supercabinet.

Yet in attempting to grasp control of the bureaucratic machinery for domestic affairs, Ehrlichman projected the president's negative disposition toward this policy area. As Dan Rather in *The Palace Guard* observed, Ehrlichman and Haldeman "had a clear understanding of what the Nixon White House was *against* [but] they were never quite certain what it should be for. As a result, domestic policy under Ehrlichman's reign was essentially negative, both in tone and substance."

Another problem with Ehrlichman's supervision of domestic policy was his style of dealing with Congress. Not only was he inexperienced in the ways of Capitol Hill but he also chose to cloak his deficiencies with an arrogance of power—both his own and the president's. He used to like to say that "the president is the government." He dealt with Congress as if it were the enemy, and his favorite tactic was the veto. His approach finally resulted in a series of stalemates and setbacks that caused the defeat of the president's policies for welfare reform, national health insurance, and the SST. Indeed, the administration's second-term record on domestic issues was conspicuously lackluster and in contrast to the modest achievements of the preceding term (such as revenue sharing and environmental legislation). It seemed that as his self-assurance and influence with the president grew, his concern to get along with others, such as administration members and congressmen, lessened.

Ultimately the most damaging exhibition of Ehrlichman's arrogance in power, his inexperience in public affairs, and his loyalty to the president was his involvement in establishing the White House "Plumbers" unit. The unit was initially created to deal with the *Pentagon Papers* leaks and eventually perpetrated the break-in at Democratic national headquarters in the Watergate office building and the burglary of DANIEL ELLSBERG's former psychiatrist's office. Although Ehrlichman claimed that he did not order the Watergate break-in, he admitted learning of it soon after the fact, at which time his response was to instruct the "Plumbers," such as EGIL KROGH, E. HOWARD HUNT, and GORDON LIDDY, that he "did not agree with this method of investigation" and that they should not repeat such tactics.

Thereafter, as subsequent investigations revealed the scandal, Ehrlichman's prominent role in the cover-up effort was exposed, and he came under considerable public criticism. Within four months of Nixon's second inauguration, Ehrlichman and other major administration figures were seriously implicated in a number of possibly illegal and unethical political activities, ranging from the actual Watergate break-in through secret "hush money" payments and the Ellsberg burglary to obstruction of justice. Two days after the Hunt and Liddy connection to the Ellsberg break-in had been uncovered, it became clear that the scandalous trail led straight into the White House and directly to John Ehrlichman. Thus, the president regretfully announced his acceptance of the resignations of Ehrlichman and Haldeman, as well as that of Attorney General RICHARD KLEINDIENST.

In his letter of resignation, Ehrlichman wrote: "For the past two weeks it has become increasingly evident that, regardless of the actual facts, I have been a target of pub-

lic attack. The nature of my position . . . has always demanded that my conduct be both apparently and actually beyond reproach. I have always felt that the appearance of honesty and integrity is every bit as important to such a position as the fact of one's honesty and integrity." He went on to complain that given his circumstances he was forced "to conclude that [his] present usefulness . . . and ability to discharge [his] duties [had] been impaired by these attacks, perhaps beyond repair."

From one perspective Ehrlichman's resignation appeared as the ultimate proof of his loyalty. To deflect some of the controversy directed at the White House and to help keep the Nixon presidency afloat, Ehrlichman and Haldeman had resigned. From the president's perspective it was a bitter loss of "two of [his] closest friends and most trusted assistants" and "two of the finest public servants it [had] been [his] privilege to know."

In a deposition made public on June 7, Ehrlichman placed much of the blame for Watergate on JOHN DEAN, former counsel to the president, and on JEB STUART MAGRUDER, former deputy director of the Committee to Re-Elect the President. He also implicated former attorney general JOHN MITCHELL, in contradiction to H. R. Haldeman's statement issued the same day.

Six weeks later, in late July 1973, Ehrlichman testified before the Senate Watergate committee. Unlike most other witnesses, Ehrlichman, according to the *New York Times*, came across as "a tough, unapologetic Nixon stalwart who obviously felt that a good offense was the best defense." He vigorously denied John Dean's contention that a Watergate cover-up had preoccupied the White House between June 17 and September 15, 1972. He stated that during the latter part of 1972, the president had been busy with domestic policy issues and that only "about one-half of 1 percent [of his time] was spent on politics and campaigning." He also disputed Dean's testimony concerning the possibility of executive clemency for the Watergate defendants.

In further testimony, Ehrlichman defended the Ellsberg break-in as a valid exercise of the president's constitutional powers to protect the welfare of the nation by preventing the betrayal of national security secrets. This line of constitutional interpretation brought Ehrlichman into heated argument with the Senate committee chairman, Senator SAM ERVIN (D-N.C.), who insisted that the break-in violated the Fourth Amendment. Later Ehrlichman also clashed with the majority counsel, SAMUEL DASH, "over definitional matters," such as whether he had administered the Plumbers in a "literal sense" or an "actual sense." Ehrlichman's exchanges with Dash elicited the most obvious public display of partisan differences on the committee when Senator HOWARD BAKER (R-Tenn.) and the minority counsel accused Dash of improper questioning and of interpreting the witness's answers.

The resignations of Ehrlichman and Haldeman from the White House staff late in April 1973 indicated that the administration's efforts to ride out the Watergate storm by "stonewalling" it were not proving very successful. Shortly thereafter the revelation of a White House taping system and the halting release of taped conversations between the president and various aides increased public indignation and helped propel the impeachment inquiry.

The depth and seriousness of the Watergate scandal was further highlighted by the March 1974 indictment of Ehrlichman, Haldeman, and John Mitchell for conspiracy and obstruction of justice with regard to the Watergate break-in and cover-up. In addition, Ehrlichman was charged with lying to both the grand jury and the FBI. He was also indicted in the Plumbers case for conspiracy and perjury to both a grand jury and the FBI.

The Plumbers trial opened in Washington on June 28, with the prosecution contending that the burglary of Dr. Lewis Fielding's office was "a willful, arrogant act of men who took the law into their own hands and felt above the law." While Ehrlichman maintained that he had agreed to a "covert operation, not a break-in or illegal operation," the prosecution argued that he was clearly "implicated in knowledge of and approval of the break-in."

Considering the importance of the defendants and the political ramifications of the hearing, the trial was speedily concluded. On July 12 the jury found Ehrlichman guilty of three counts of perjury and one of conspiracy. In sentencing him to serve at least 20 months in prison, Judge GERHARD GESELL told Ehrlichman that he must bear "major responsibility for this shameful episode in the history of our country." The conviction of the Plumbers, in combination with the progress of the House impeachment hearings and the Supreme Court's ruling against the president on the tapes, demonstrated both the precarious and culpable position of the president and his men. President Nixon resigned 10 days later and, on September 8, 1974, was pardoned by President Ford for all federal crimes that he "committed or may have committed or taken part in" during his time in office. Thus, by the time Ehrlichman and other former administration officials came to trial in October for the Watergate cover-up, the president was free and clear of any legal sanctions.

At the trial, which opened on October 14, 1974, the defendants pursued a go-it-alone strategy, and Ehrlichman openly broke with his former colleagues and with the president. Ehrlichman's counsel contended that "Richard Nixon deceived, misled, lied to, and used John Ehrlichman to cover up his own knowledge and his own activities. . . . In simple terms John Ehrlichman has been had by his boss, who was the president of the United States."

The climax of the trial occurred on December 10, Ehrlichman's second day on the witness stand. According to his version of the Watergate affair, he had been deceived by the president and unaware of the extent of the cover-up until late March 1973. In recounting the circumstances of his resignation as the president's chief domestic adviser, the composure of the usually assured Ehrlichman cracked, and he momentarily broke into tears.

On New Year's Day 1975 the jury turned in a verdict of guilty against the three former top political aides of President Nixon. Ehrlichman was convicted of conspiracy, of obstruction of justice, and of making false declarations to a grand jury. In addition to these convictions, he was subsequently disbarred.

Of the nearly 30 former Nixon aides who pleaded guilty to or were convicted of Watergate-related crimes, Ehrlichman was one of the most visibly changed by the experience. He left his wife, moved from Seattle to Santa Fe, and abandoned his clean-cut image for a bearded and more relaxed demeanor. In addition to his novel based on his White House years, *The Company*, Ehrlichman undertook some low-profile activities in civic projects in Santa Fe, where he felt "his knowledge of government" would be helpful. In 1982 he published *Witness to Power*, his memoir of his years working for Nixon. He also worked as a talk-show host and for a quality control firm. Ehrlichman died in 1999 of complications from diabetes.

—MW

Ellsberg, Daniel
(1931–   ) *economist, political scientist*

Born on April 7, 1931, Daniel Ellsberg grew up in Chicago and Detroit, where he attended an exclusive prep school on a scholarship. He received a B.A. in economics from Harvard in 1952 and studied in England for a year. In 1954 he enlisted in the Marines. Returning to Harvard after two years in the service, he wrote as his dissertation an analysis of strategic military planning. In 1959 Ellsberg joined the Rand Corp., a West Coast "think tank," where he researched game theory and the risks involved in nuclear warfare. He was a consultant to governmental officials during the early 1960s and joined the staff of John T. McNaughton, an assistant secretary of defense, in 1964. Touring Vietnam in 1965, Ellsberg was decidedly "hawkish" on the war and lobbied on behalf of the Johnson administration's policy of escalation.

After returning to the Rand Corp., Ellsberg participated in the research for a massive history of U.S. involvement in Southeast Asia commissioned by Secretary of Defense ROBERT S. MCNAMARA in 1967. Ellsberg's work convinced him that the war was unjust, the result of several presidents' unwillingness to bear responsibility for the loss of South Vietnam to the Communists. After reading the entire study, he decided that from the start, it had been an "American war" in which the United States was guilty of "foreign aggression." Believing that he could be most useful by "working within the system," Ellsberg sent numerous memos and position papers to government officials in which he urged immediate withdrawal from Vietnam, wrote magazine articles urging an end to the war, and spoke at antiwar rallies.

By the autumn of 1969 Ellsberg was prepared to take drastic action to stop the war. Using his top secret clearance to obtain a copy of the Pentagon study, he rented a copying machine and reproduced the study with the aid of a Rand colleague, Anthony J. Russo Jr. He sent a copy to Senator J. WILLIAM FULBRIGHT (D-Ark.), who declined to use it, and approached other prominent opponents of the war, who likewise were unwilling to take action. Finally Ellsberg approached Neil Sheehan, a *New York Times* reporter, who in March 1971 accepted the documents on behalf of the *Times*. On June 13 the *Times* began publishing excerpts of the study. When the government obtained an injunction against the paper, the *Washington Post*, the *Boston Globe*, and other newspapers continued to print excerpts. On June 30 the Supreme Court ruled in favor of the *Times*'s right to publish the documents.

Ellsberg, meanwhile, had gone into hiding. Indicted by a Los Angeles grand jury on charges of theft of government property and violation of the Espionage Act, he surrendered to federal marshals in Boston on June 28. Ellsberg readily admitted that he was the source of the *Pentagon Papers*, as they were called, but denied he had broken any laws. In December 1971 12 additional charges of theft, violation of the Espionage Act, and conspiracy were lodged against Ellsberg. Anthony Russo also was named in the indictment.

After several unexpected procedural delays, Judge Matthew Byrne Jr. declared a mistrial on December 8, 1972. A new jury was selected, and the trial began on January 18, 1973. The defense based its case on the argument that no laws had been broken, claiming that Ellsberg's clearance allowed him access to the study and that nothing in the documents endangered national security. The defense called as witnesses several prominent former government officials, including MCGEORGE BUNDY, ARTHUR M. SCHLESINGER JR., and JOHN KENNETH GALBRAITH, who testified that the top secret classification assigned to the Pentagon study was routinely used and indiscriminately applied to documents regardless of their contents.

In late April and early May, before the case went to the jury, Judge Byrne made a series of shocking revelations. On April 27 he released a Justice Department memo that G. GORDON LIDDY and E. HOWARD HUNT, convicted Watergate conspirators, had burglarized the office of Ellsberg's former psychiatrist, Lewis J. Field-

ing, in September 1971 to find evidence that would embarrass and discredit Ellsberg. A few days later it was revealed that JOHN EHRLICHMAN, Nixon's domestic affairs adviser, had ordered the investigation of Ellsberg that led to the break-in. Byrne also announced that Ehrlichman had recently offered him the post of FBI director. Finally on May 9 came the disclosure that the FBI had wiretapped the home of Morton Halperin, head of the *Pentagon Papers* study and a close friend of Ellsberg, and had made tapes of Halperin's conversations with Ellsberg. When Byrne ordered the prosecution to turn over transcripts of the conversations, the government announced that it had lost all the relevant records.

Incensed at the government's action, Byrne declared a mistrial on May 11, 1973, and dismissed all the charges against Ellsberg and Russo. He accused the government of "gross misconduct" that disgraced the judicial system. In September 1973 indictments were handed down against Ehrlichman, Liddy, and several others for the burglary of Fielding's office, and in July 1974 all were found guilty.

Ellsberg remained active in the antiwar movement, writing extensively and speaking at rallies and on college campuses across the country. After the Communist victory in South Vietnam in 1975, he turned his attention to other causes, becoming especially active in the growing movement against nuclear weapons and in favor of disarmament. In October 1976 Ellsberg was arrested with 40 others at a demonstration in front of the Pentagon. In March 1978 he organized and led a protest march on the nuclear weapons plant at Rocky Flats, Nevada. Continuing his antiwar activism, Ellsberg spoke out against the 2003 invasion of Iraq and testified in 2004 at the conscientious-objector hearing of Camilo Mejia. In 2002 he published *Secrets: A Memoir of Vietnam and the Pentagon Papers*.

—JD

Ervin, Sam(uel) J(ames), Jr.

(1896–1985) *member of the Senate; chairman, Government Operations Committee; chairman, Senate Select Committee on Presidential Campaign Activities*

Sam Ervin, a descendant of Scotch-Irish Calvinists, was born on September 27, 1896, one of 10 children of parents living in Morganton, North Carolina, a community in the foothills of the Blue Ridge Mountains. He received his B.A. from the University of North Carolina in 1917 and his LL.B. from Harvard University Law School in 1922. Ervin then returned to Morganton to practice law intermittently for the next three decades. He served three terms in the state assembly in the 1920s and 1930s. From 1935 to 1937 he was a judge in the Burke County criminal court and later served in the North Carolina supreme court from 1948 to 1954. When in the early summer of 1954 U.S. senator Clyde Hoey died, Governor William B. Umstead named Ervin to fill his seat. He won election in November 1954 and was handily reelected to three full terms as a Democratic senator. Although he had no formal power base in the state, his folksy political style and dramatic use of the Bible and the works of Shakespeare appealed to his constituents.

During the 1950s and 1960s Ervin's strict constructionist view of the Constitution was the basis for his opposition to many important administration policies. He opposed numerous civil rights bills that he found to be invasions of states' rights. He opposed aid-to-education bills and voted against such programs as Medicare, Model Cities, aid to mass transit, child care, and Project Head Start. He did, however, build a record supporting environmental legislation and attempted on numerous occasions to strengthen the civil liberties of various types of citizens, such as Native Americans, mental patients, and federal employees.

During the NIXON administration, Ervin continued his policy of fully supporting the president and the military in the prosecution of the Vietnam War, and he voted against legislation such as the Cooper-Church Amendment to limit presidential authority to conduct military operations in Cambodia. Ervin attempted to keep the levels of military spending at what he considered to be adequate levels. But in August 1969 he voted for the amendment to the defense appropriations bill to delete funds for research and development of the Safeguard antiballistic missile system.

On domestic issues Ervin continued his conservative voting pattern except on matters of personal liberty that he saw to be transgressed by the power of government. His father, the senator once said, had instilled in him the idea that "the greatest threat to our liberties comes from government, not from others." Government, Ervin believed, has "an insatiable thirst for power and is never satisfied." He opposed the Equal Rights Amendment when it came to a vote in March 1972, and in proposing nine changes to the amendment aimed at narrowing the impact of its coverage, he warned that adoption of the measure unchanged would destroy the social fabric of America. Women would be crucified "upon the cross of dubious equality and specious uniformity." All of his amendments were rejected by substantial margins.

Reflecting both his political constituency and his constitutional beliefs, Ervin voted against the use of federal funds for the busing of school children to achieve racial balance. Never a strong labor advocate, he opposed the Nixon administration's Philadelphia Plan giving the federal government power to force the hiring of minority workers on federally financed construction projects. He supported the nomination of fellow southerner G. HARROLD CARSWELL to the Supreme Court in April 1970. The nomination was a controversial one because of allegations that Carswell was a racist and had a poor record as a lower court judge. A firm believer in free enterprise, Ervin voted against legislation appropriating an additional $289 million for the development of the SST. However, he opposed any limitation on the amount of farm subsidies paid by the government.

Aside from serving on the Armed Services Committee, Ervin spent his last three years in Congress presiding over the Government Operations Committee and was chairman of three subcommittees of the Judiciary Committee. These positions gave him considerable power that he used with great effectiveness. In 1971 he effectively challenged Nixon's impoundment of funds allocated by Congress for federal programs. In hearings called to investigate the right of the president to spend money only where he desired, the senator said that "what concerns me is the use of impounding practice to void or nullify congressional intent." Ervin surprised many observers by obtaining a list of the impounded funds from the Office of Management and Budget and then publishing it in the *Congressional Record* to give a clearer and broader appreciation of the differing priorities of the president and Congress.

Ervin fervently opposed the concept of preventive detention under which certain types of individuals charged with "violent" or "dangerous" crimes or with threatening a witness or juror could be held for 60 days without being brought to trial. The senator admonished that "such flagrant violation of due process smacks of a police state." In 1970 he said of the model District of Columbia Court Reform and Criminal Procedure Act (the D.C. Crime Bill) sponsored by the Nixon administration that "this . . . is as full of unconstitutional, unjust and unwise provisions as a mangy hound dog is full of fleas . . . a garbage pail of some of the most repressive, nearsighted, intolerant, unfair, and

vindictive legislation that the Senate has ever been presented . . . an affront to constitutional principles and to the intelligence of the American people. . . ."

Alarmed at the increase in surveillance of civilians by government and private industry, the senator held hearings in 1969 addressing the problems of government coercion of citizens into supplying personal information for statistical data banks. Two years later he presided over hearings that addressed an allegation by CBS newsman DANIEL SCHORR that an investigation into his activities by the FBI was an attempt to quiet his criticism of Nixon administration policies. The administration denied the charges by responding that Schorr was actually being considered for a position in the government and the FBI was merely engaged in a background clearance check. The issue died down, but suspicions of improper intimidation remained.

In 1970 Ervin's Constitutional Rights Subcommittee looked into revelations first published in *Washington Monthly Magazine* that the army had conducted "surveillance" on 800 Illinois citizens, including many considered to be liberal politicians. The public cleansing that followed was supposed to limit collection practices, but it possessed, Ervin said, "qualifications, exceptions, and ambiguities which permit surveillance even within the confines of an otherwise restrictive policy."

Ervin was catapulted into national prominence early in 1973 after he had been chosen to head the seven-member committee to investigate the Watergate affair. The panel was formally labeled the Senate Select Committee on Presidential Campaign Activities. The main reason that he was chosen to lead the investigation was the fact that his advanced age precluded any potential charges of his grandstanding because of presidential ambitions. But Ervin's reputation for honesty and his skill as an interpreter of the Constitution also were in his favor. The probe by the Watergate committee was soon to parallel the investigation of the special prosecutor, ARCHIBALD COX, but the panel had the unofficial, broader mission of educating the public about the nature of the crimes committed. After choosing SAMUEL DASH, professor of law at Georgetown University Law Center, as chief counsel, the members settled on a strategy of calling witnesses before televised hearings on an ascending scale of political importance. The committee sought to create a detailed basis of understanding before the major witnesses close to the president were called to testify.

Some of the earlier testimony involved numerous revelations of illegal espionage directed from the White House. JEB STUART MAGRUDER, the first major witness and former deputy director of the Nixon reelection campaign, not only admitted his own role in various illegal actions but also implicated nearly every important person around the president. He was soon followed by former White House counsel JOHN DEAN, who not only corroborated much of Magruder's testimony but also said that Nixon himself had known of the cover-up activities as early as September 27, 1972. Ervin was probably best remembered for his questioning of MAURICE STANS, the former secretary of commerce and finance director of the Nixon campaign committee. After Ervin berated Stans for not following ethical guidelines on campaign contributions, which Ervin implied should have been superior to the minimum requirements of the criminal law, the single Nixon loyalist on the committee, Senator EDWARD GURNEY (R-Fla.), objected to the North Carolinian's harassing manner. In reply Ervin, ever the actor with a mask of innocence and a skilled sense of rhetoric, responded: "I am an old country lawyer and I don't know the finer ways to examine the witness. I just have to do it my way."

One minor witness, White House aide Alexander Butterfield, testified in July that a secret taping system had recorded most presidential conversations in the White House. Ervin and the committee soon agreed to subpoena five tapes of conversations between the president and Dean. Ervin then told television viewers that the country was more interested in finding out the facts about Watergate than in "abstruse arguments about the separation of powers or executive privilege." And he concluded: "I think that Watergate is the greatest tragedy this country has ever suffered. I used to think the Civil War was the greatest tragedy, but I do remember some redeeming features in the Civil War in that there was some spirit of sacrifice and heroism displayed on both sides. I see no redeeming features in Watergate." In the fall of 1973 controversy over the tapes continued. Ervin at one time agreed to a compromise whereby Mississippi senator JOHN STENNIS would authenticate White House summaries of the tapes, but Special Watergate Prosecutor Cox refused, thereby causing his own dismissal in what became known as the "Saturday night massacre" in which Attorney General ELLIOT RICHARDSON and Deputy Attorney General WILLIAM RUCKLESHAUS were forced to resign rather than fire Cox.

Although the committee unearthed widespread abuses of campaign activities, it faded from existence in early 1974 as the main attention shifted to the newly appointed special prosecutor, LEON JAWORSKI, and the House Judiciary Committee, where formal impeachment hearings were to begin.

In the final committee report submitted in July 1974, the question was raised whether there had been a genuinely fair election in 1972. Ervin, in a separate section setting forth his own views, wrote that the first objective of the "various illegal and unethical activities" studied by the committee was to "destroy insofar as the presidential election of 1972 was concerned the integrity of the process by which the president of the United States is nominated and elected."

Among the proposals of the Ervin committee was the establishment of a public attorney to be appointed by the judiciary and confirmed by the Senate. Further curbs on intelligence-gathering activities in the White House and a ban on the examination of tax returns by anyone in the executive office were among the many other recommendations submitted.

Ervin declined to run for reelection in 1974 and retired to his home in Morganton. He died in 1985 of respiratory failure.

—GWB

Farmer, James L(eonard)

(1920–1999) *assistant secretary of health, education, and welfare; civil rights leader*

James L. Farmer was born on January 12, 1920, in Marshall, Texas. The son of the first black man in Texas to hold a Ph.D. degree, Farmer graduated from Wiley College in 1938 and received a bachelor of divinity degree from Howard University in 1941. Refusing ordination because the Methodist Church in the South was then segregated, he turned his energies toward social activism. From 1941 to 1945 Farmer was race relations secretary for the Fellowship of Reconciliation, a pacifist organization. Later in the 1940s and 1950s he worked as a labor organizer for a number of trade unions, served as a program director for the NAACP, and was a commentator on a United Automobile Workers radio program in Detroit. Farmer also wrote and lectured extensively on race relations.

In 1942 Farmer, with some students at the University of Chicago, founded CORE, the Congress of Racial Equality. An interracial group pledged to the eradication of racial discrimination, it applied Gandhian techniques of nonviolence to the struggle for racial equality. CORE staged its first successful sit-in at a Chicago restaurant in 1943 and thereafter

grew slowly until the 1960s. From 1961 to 1966 Farmer was the organization's national director. He led its efforts to achieve desegregation of public facilities, to register black voters in the South, and to end discrimination in employment and housing in the North. On March 1, 1966, Farmer resigned from CORE's directorship, expecting to receive an Office of Economic Opportunity grant to establish a nationwide program to improve literacy and job skills among unemployed blacks. The proposal was never approved, however, and in September 1966 Farmer joined the faculty of Lincoln University as a professor of social welfare.

Farmer surprised many of his friends in the civil rights movement when he joined Black Independents and Democrats for Rockefeller in July 1968. When RICHARD NIXON received the Republican nomination, Farmer denounced his civil rights record as "apathetic at best and negative at worst." Shortly before his inauguration, however, Nixon met with several black leaders and promised to do "more for the underprivileged and more for the Negro than any president has ever done." He offered Farmer the position of assistant secretary of health, education, and welfare (HEW), with special responsibility for relations with black youths. Farmer accepted the offer and was confirmed by the Senate in March 1969. Of all the blacks appointed to office by Nixon, Farmer was by far the most prominent.

It quickly became apparent, however, that the Nixon administration's policies were antagonistic to the goals of the civil rights movement. In January 1969 HEW secretary ROBERT FINCH announced that he was extending the deadline for southern school districts to comply with desegregation guidelines. In June the administration presented a substitute proposal for extension of the 1965 Voting Rights Act that would have seriously weakened the legislation. The nominations of CLEMENT HAYNSWORTH and G. HARROLD CARSWELL, both of whom had poor civil rights records, to the Supreme Court was a further blow to Farmer and others who had placed faith in the new administration.

In late February 1970 a memo by White House adviser DANIEL PATRICK MOYNIHAN, in which he urged a policy of "benign neglect" toward blacks, was leaked to the press. Several days later Farmer and 36 other black officials in the administration conferred with Nixon on civil rights. They reported that they were feeling heavy pressure from the black community and that only stronger presidential action on behalf of civil rights would relieve it. Farmer asked Nixon in particular "to clarify his posture" on school desegregation, one of the more volatile issues.

Farmer resigned from HEW on December 7, 1970. At the time he declined to criticize Nixon and cited personal reasons for his resignation. Farmer said that the "ponderous bureaucracy" prevented him from achieving gains "sufficient, or fast enough, to satisfy my appetite for progress." In January 1973, however, Farmer acknowledged that he had had "great difficulty" remaining in the administration because the president isolated himself from blacks and instead relied on white aides for advice on racial matters.

After resigning from government office, Farmer pursued his idea of a training program for blacks. Still unable to obtain funding for a community organizing project, he announced in July 1973 the formation of the Public Policy Training Institute in conjunction with Howard University. The purpose, he said, was to study the impact of government policy on blacks and to bring teachers from black colleges to Washington to gain understanding of how public policy is set.

In February 1976 Farmer quit his membership in CORE after its director, Roy Innis, announced that CORE was recruiting black mercenaries to assist anti-Communist forces fighting in the Angolan civil war. In 1985 he published his memoir, *Lay Bare the Heart.* Eventually hospitalized for diabetes, Farmer would lose both legs and his sight before his death in 1999.

—JD

Felt, William Mark, Sr.
(1913–   ) *deputy associate director, Federal Bureau of Investigation*

Felt was born in Twin Falls, Idaho, and received a B.A. from the University of Idaho in 1935. While serving as a staff member for U.S. senator James P. Pope (D-Idaho) and David Worth Clark (D-Idaho), Felt attended George Washington University School of Law, from where he earned his J.D. in 1940. After a short stint at the Federal Trade Commission, Felt joined the FBI in January 1942. Between 1942 and 1962 he served at several field offices around the country, returning to Washington in 1962 as assistant to the bureau's assistant director in charge of the Training Division. In 1964 he became assistant director of the bureau, and in 1971 he was promoted to deputy associate director. Upon the death of FBI director J. Edgar Hoover on May 2, 1972, President

W. Mark Felt *(Corbis)*

"I'm the guy they used to call Deep Throat." "Deep Throat" was an aphorism given to a key government source for *Washington Post* reporters BOB WOODWARD and CARL BERNSTEIN, who reported on the early stages of the Watergate investigation. The day after the *Vanity Fair* story appeared, Woodward and Bernstein acknowledged that Felt had, indeed, been "Deep Throat." Woodward had met Felt in 1969, when Woodward was an aide to Admiral THOMAS MOORER, and when Woodward became a reporter for the *Post*, Felt had served as a source for several Woodward stories, including his reporting on the attempted assassination of GEORGE WALLACE in 1972. From his position at the FBI, Felt had kept Woodward and Bernstein's Watergate reporting on line, confirming their leads but always remaining in deep background as an anonymous source (an agreement had been reached between Woodward and Felt that "Deep Throat's" identity would not be revealed until after his death, but members of Felt's family had pressed for the 2005 article in an attempt to gain for their father a measure of public acknowledgment for his efforts). Felt lives in Santa Rosa, California.

—JRG

Richard Nixon appointed L. PATRICK GRAY as the acting head of the FBI, bypassing Felt, who chose to stay with the bureau. As associate director, Gray saw all field reports and communications traffic regarding the bureau's investigation into the Watergate affair. In 1980 Gray and several others were prosecuted by the JIMMY CARTER administration for planning and executing several break-ins into the homes and offices of suspected radicals in the 1960s and 1970s (known as "black bag jobs"). Felt was convicted and assessed a fine, but he was later pardoned by President RONALD REAGAN in 1981.

On May 31, 2005, *Vanity Fair* magazine published an interview with Felt, claiming that

Finch, Robert H(utchinson)
(1925–1995) *secretary of health, education, and welfare*

Robert Finch was born on October 9, 1925, in Tempe, Arizona. The son of an Arizona state legislator, Finch was a Republican Party activist beginning with his organization of 13 Young Republican clubs while a student at Occidental College in Los Angeles. After graduating in 1947 Finch went to Washington as administrative aide to California representative Norris Paulson. Working in the House, he met freshman congressman RICHARD NIXON and began a long political and personal relationship. After graduating from the University of Southern California Law School in 1951, Finch made two unsuccessful bids for the U.S. House and became a local party chairman. He returned to Washington in 1958 as administrative assistant to Vice President Nixon.

During the 1960s Finch concentrated on building a strong Republican Party in California. He managed Nixon's unsuccessful presidential campaign in 1960 but disapproved of and kept aloof from Nixon's 1962 race against Edmund Brown for governor of California. After managing George Murphy's upset victory over Pierre Salinger in the 1964 Senate race, Finch ran for lieutenant governor of California and won the 1966 election with more votes than the newly elected governor, RONALD REAGAN. As lieutenant governor Finch mediated between conservative Reagan and the liberal legislature, managing to mold a bipartisan coalition behind measures to aid minorities and urban areas.

When Richard Nixon campaigned again in 1968 for the presidency, Finch was his close adviser. After Nixon won the Republican nomination, he turned down an offer to run for the vice presidency so that Nixon would not be criticized for "nepotism." After the national election President-elect Nixon offered him the job of attorney general, but Finch wanted to be secretary of health, education, and welfare (HEW), with its 250 programs and $50 billion budget. He believed that was where the tremendous social questions facing America could be addressed.

Although Finch was widely regarded as Nixon's closest political adviser in 1969, the two were poles apart in political strategy and administrative goals. Finch had remarked that 1968 would be the last election won by "the unblack, the unpoor, and the unyoung." Nixon, however, was constructing a permanent political coalition aimed at adding conservative white southerners to the Republican Party. In

discharging his responsibility to enforce Title VI of the Civil Rights Act, the legal authority for school desegregation, Finch vowed, "We're going to be hard. We're going to stick to the guidelines." But the president's strategy was to appease influential southern senators by pushing back guideline compliance dates for eliminating de jure segregation from fall 1969 to fall 1970.

In response to pressure from Senators STROM THURMOND (D-S.C.) and Charles Jonas (D-N.C.) to postpone a scheduled January 29, 1969, cutoff of funds to school districts in their states that failed to submit desegregation plans, Nixon prevailed on Finch to allow a 60-day delay. This new deadline was subsequently pushed back at Nixon's request to the fall of 1969. Finch, who had staffed HEW's civil rights and education offices with liberal activist reformers, was caught in the middle. The result was indecision and finally compromise.

By summer 1969 demands from southern senators for relief from the fall deadline became intense. On July 3 Finch and Attorney General JOHN MITCHELL issued a joint statement retaining the fall deadline but noting "there may be sound reasons for some limited delay."

By August the period of compromise was over. Senator JOHN STENNIS (D-Miss.) told Nixon that he would abandon leadership of the fight for the antiballistic missile unless the federal government dropped its court advocacy of immediate school desegregation in Mississippi. Finch was forced to send a letter to fifth circuit court judge John Brown expressing disapproval of plans written by his own staff, and Attorney General Mitchell sent Justice Department lawyers into court opposing HEW plans for 33 other school districts.

Finch's staff was now openly defiant. Leon Panetta, head of the civil rights division, vigorously protested the administration's policy on desegregation in court. Nixon aides forced Panetta's resignation. In May 1970, after Nixon's Cambodia invasion, the HEW staff demanded a meeting with Finch on the issue. Finch scheduled a May 19 meeting but was hospitalized one hour before it was to take place. HEW employees booed Finch's statement supporting the president's Cambodia policy.

By June 1970 Nixon was convinced that Finch was incapable of leading HEW. Finch had begun efforts to reorganize the department and had extended consumer and environmental services. He had banned cyclamates, set a deadline on the use of DDT, implemented reorganization plans and family-planning services, and helped develop the administration's Family Assistance Plan. However, the press, once favorable to him, began to show its disappointment.

On June 6 Nixon announced that Finch would leave HEW to become White House counsel to the president. But it was apparent that Finch was kept on the periphery of the Nixon circle, and in December 1972 Finch resigned to resume his political career in California. In September 1974 President FORD appointed Finch to a nine-member clemency board to consider the cases of convicted Vietnam deserters and draft evaders.

In June 1976 Finch lost the Republican senatorial nomination in California to S. I. Hayakawa. Finch retired from politics and taught at the University of Southern California until his death in 1995.

—JMP

Findley, Paul
(1921–) *member of the House of Representatives*

Paul Findley was born on June 23, 1921, in Jacksonville, Illinois. Findley graduated from Illinois College and after World War II founded a county weekly, the *Pike Press*, in Pittsfield, Illinois. In 1960 he was elected as a Repub-

lican to the House of Representatives from Illinois's largely rural 20th district. First known as a tough conservative, Findley consistently called for a balanced budget and received high ratings from the conservative Americans for Constitutional Action. He opposed the Kennedy administration's domestic programs and fought many of President Lyndon B. Johnson's Great Society measures, including the antipoverty, Medicare, and federal aid to education bills. Throughout the early and middle 1960s, Findley led the fight against extension of food to communist bloc nations and opposed trade with these countries except on a direct cash basis.

During the NIXON administration Findley moved toward more moderate stands on some issues. He voted for urban renewal, child care facilities, and benefits for families of black lung victims. A member of the House Agriculture Committee for most of his congressional career, Findley persistently criticized U.S. farm policy, opposing the conservative southern cotton growers whose representatives dominated both the House and Senate Agriculture Committees. In his book *The Federal Farm Fable*, published shortly before the 1968 election, Findley attacked price supports, acreage allotments, marketing quotas, and farm subsidies. Beginning in 1969 Findley, with Representative Silvio O. Conte (R-Mass.), led the House floor fight to limit cash subsidies to farmers, an effort that finally resulted in the 1973 passage of a $20,000-per-farmer subsidy limitation. Findley was unsuccessful, however, in tightening the loopholes in the law by which rich farmers subdivided their lands to collect more subsidy payments.

A member of the House Foreign Affairs Committee from 1966 on, Findley was a passionate advocate of the "Atlantic Union" concept, arguing that world peace and order depended on a strong union between European democracies and the United States. He consistently opposed cuts in the number of American troops stationed in Europe and advocated giving U.S. allies in NATO a larger decision-making role, particularly with regard to the use of nuclear weapons.

Seeking to maintain free international trade, Findley testified in 1970 before the Ways and Means Committee against the imposition of import quotas on textiles and shoes. During the late 1960s he softened his views on trade with communist bloc nations, sponsoring bills to facilitate trade with Romania and the USSR. Prior to President Nixon's trip to China in 1972, Findley advocated reopening relations with Communist China in hopes of developing trade markets there.

Findley's views on the war in Southeast Asia vascillated. Prior to 1967 he supported the conflict, but by the fall of that year he questioned the legality of U.S. involvement. Nevertheless, he voted for war appropriations and opposed attempts to set rigid timetables for U.S. withdrawal. In 1970 he proposed a substitute to the Reid Amendment that would have barred the use of funds from the military appropriations bill from financing American troops in Laos, Cambodia, or Thailand. Findley's amendment, endorsed by Nixon, would have prohibited funding for troops in those areas except where the president found the lives of U.S. troops in danger and quickly informed Congress. The proposal was tentatively approved but rejected in the final vote.

Findley remained a conservative in budget matters, voting against environmental proposals. However, he supported the Equal Rights Amendment (1971) guaranteeing constitutional rights to women and busing as a means of achieving school integration. He approved the Nixon administration's wage and price controls but opposed government controls on food prices. In 1973 Findley tried to initiate impeachment proceedings against Vice President SPIRO T. AGNEW following revelations of corruption in office and in August 1974 moved to censure President Nixon for his role in the Watergate scandal.

Findley lost his reelection bid in 1982. The next year he was appointed to the Board of International Food and Agricultural Development, a post he held to 1994. Findley founded the Council for the National Interest and is currently its chair. He travels the lecture circuit, arguing that the terrorist attacks of September 11, 2001, were caused by American support for Israel. He is the author of several books, including *They Dare to Speak Out: People and Institutions Confront Israel's Lobby* (1978) and *Silent No More: Confronting America's False Images of Islam* (2001).

—DAE and JRG

Fitzsimmons, Frank E(dward)
(1908–1981) *president, International Brotherhood of Teamsters*

Born on April 7, 1908, in Jeanette, Pennsylvania, Fitzsimmons, the son of a brewery worker, left school at age 17. He worked as a truck driver in Detroit, where he befriended JIMMY HOFFA. During the Depression Fitzsimmons helped Hoffa organize Local 299 of the International Brotherhood of Teamsters. In 1937 he became the local's business manager and three years later its vice president. In contrast to Hoffa's flamboyant style, Fitzsimmons, acting the role of his loyal lieutenant, quietly rose in rank behind the controversial Hoffa. He was particularly known for his organizing ability and his blind devotion to the Teamster leader. In 1961 Fitzsimmons became the International's vice president.

After Hoffa was convicted of jury tampering and misuse of union funds, he designated Fitzsimmons his successor. In 1966 the union elected Fitzsimmons general vice president, a post created to fill any vacancy in the presidency. When Hoffa went to prison in March 1967, Fitzsimmons took over his functions. He assumed power in the midst of confusion. The union was negotiating a contract with the trucking industry, and talks had been stalled as a result of Hoffa's departure. The new leader immediately negotiated a favorable contract that many observed surpassed what Hoffa had previously obtained.

Fitzsimmons's style of leadership differed from that of Hoffa. Lacking Hoffa's personal power, he restored autonomy to the regional and local heads to negotiate and authorize strikes. Complaints against trucking firms and union officials were handled at the local or regional levels rather than at the national level. This change was favorably received by a number of union heads who had chafed under Hoffa's domination. Investigations by the press later revealed that Fitzsimmons relinquished daily control of the union to Murray Miller, the secretary-treasurer, while major union policy was made by William Presser, who had long-standing ties to the underworld and had been convicted of misuse of union funds. Before Hoffa went to jail, Fitzsimmons had promised to do anything he could to free his friend, and he later authorized the "Spring Jimmy" campaign. Yet Hoffa soon questioned Fitzsimmons's sincerity as he saw the union leader controlling his organization rather than taking orders from the jailed leader. In his autobiography, Hoffa considered the naming of Fitzsimmons as acting president one of the worst mistakes of his life. (See *The Johnson Years* volume.)

The issue of Hoffa's pardon became closely tied to the NIXON White House during the 1970s. When Nixon took office, the pardon was stalled as a result of efforts by White House aide CHARLES COLSON, a friend of Fitzsimmons. Colson observed that it would be beneficial for the new president to work with Fitzsimmons rather than Hoffa, since it appeared that Hoffa had lost his grip on the union. Colson argued that the pardon should be delayed until after the Teamsters' 1971 summer convention so that Fitzsimmons could be elected president in his own right.

Fitzsimmons persuaded Hoffa to officially resign in June 1971, a move that Fitzsimmons argued would strengthen Hoffa's appeal for parole. Once out of jail, Fitzsimmons suggested, Hoffa could easily win reelection as the union's president. Desperate to get out of jail, Hoffa resigned. He later found that the parole board rejected his appeal. The union's executive council designated Fitzsimmons acting president, and the convention elected him to that office. Hoffa's supporters later charged that Fitzsimmons, through his White House connections, was keeping Hoffa in jail and had tricked him into resigning to gain control of the union. Hoffa was eventually paroled in December 1971 with the stipulation that he could not participate in union business for nine years. His allies maintained that Fitzsimmons had arranged the provision with Colson. Fitzsimmons was the only prominent labor leader to support Nixon and in 1971 was appointed to Nixon's Wage-Price Control Board. He backed the president's economic policies and supported Nixon during Watergate. Fitzsimmons was a frequent golfing partner of Nixon, and he later developed a close personal relationship with President FORD.

Fitzsimmons's administration was marred by charges of corruption and mismanagement, particularly on the local and regional level. Leading newspapers and journalists charged that he was keeping company with organized crime figures. His decentralized administration of the union enabled such Teamsters as William Presser and Tony Provenzano to continue shaking down truckers. Teamster pension funds were still invested in questionable activities in Las Vegas, and the pension fund system contained so many loopholes that many members found themselves without old age coverage.

Attempts to investigate the giant union often met with opposition from government officials. The *Los Angeles Times* claimed in 1973 that the Justice Department dropped charges in a fraud case against Fitzsimmons's son because of White House intervention. In the same year the *New York Times* reported "two ranking officials of the Justice Department" had halted court-approved wiretaps "that had begun to penetrate Teamster connections with the Mafia." In 1975 investigators from the Labor Department, Federal Bureau of Investigation, and Internal Revenue Service probed the Teamsters' financial dealings and connections with the underworld. Fitzsimmons himself was criticized for his relationship with suspected mobsters and his trusteeship of the union pension fund.

Within the union a grassroots movement, the Professional Drivers Counsel (PROD), encountered apathy and violence in its attempts to clean up the Teamsters. It maintained that the union's power amounted to "a national scandal." The PROD leaders asserted that Teamster officials were overpaid, that there had been innumerable thefts and kickbacks from the pension fund, and that members' support for the union was based on fear of bodily harm. PROD pressed for democracy in the union, pension reform, and the purging of gangsters. At the 1976 convention a number of PROD members were beaten up. During the meeting Fitzsimmons told the rank and file, including a small PROD contingent, "For those who would say it's time to reform this organization . . . I should say to them go to hell." The union delegates voted a dues increase to help finance a 25 percent pay raise for officials. Fitzsimmons also pushed through authorization for an unlimited number of patronage jobs, with payments set by himself. He was given a standing ovation when he denounced government "witch hunts" against the Teamsters.

During the late 1960s and early 1970s, the Teamsters engaged in a bitter struggle with the United Farm Workers Union led by CESAR CHAVEZ over representation of California migrant farm workers. The use of strong-arm tactics and sweetheart contracts reflected poorly on the union, and the Teamsters failed in many of their organizing drives.

Jimmy Hoffa mysteriously disappeared in July 1975 and was probably murdered by individuals opposed to his return to office. Fitzsimmons was not connected with the incident, and he easily won election in 1976. He died of lung cancer in 1981.

—JB

Flanigan, Peter M(agnus)

(1923–) *White House political and economic adviser*

The son of the chairman of Manufacturers Trust Co. (later Manufacturers Hanover), Peter M. Flanigan was born on June 21, 1923, and raised in New York City. Following service in the navy during World War II, Flanigan graduated from Princeton in 1947. In the same year he joined the investment banking firm of Dillon, Read, & Co. By the time he left Dillon, Read in 1969 to work in the NIXON White House, Flanigan had become a senior partner and vice president of the firm.

Flanigan's association with Nixon dated from 1960, when he headed "Citizens for Nixon" in New York. After Nixon moved to New York in 1963, Flanigan introduced him to potential campaign contributors and helped him plan strategy for the 1966 congressional elections. In 1968 Flanigan served as Nixon's deputy campaign manager. A year later he joined the White House staff as a political and economic adviser, serving as a consultant on high-level appointments, a trade negotiator, and general liaison with the business community.

As the president's chief talent scout, Flanigan brought in more than 300 senior officers to the Nixon team. Flanigan's White House responsibilities included the arrangement of foreign embassy appointments, one of the choicest of patronage plums. Flanigan's manipulative abilities acquired him a reputation as Nixon's "Mr. Fixit," responsible for shifts in presidential policy favorable to big business.

In 1970 Flanigan was accused of using improper influence to gain a Treasury Department waiver permitting an oil tanker to engage in coastal shipping trade. The tanker was owned by officials of Dillon, Read, & Co. Flanigan also held a share in the vessel and disposed of it only five days before the waiver was granted. The following year Flanigan directed a White House task force aimed at overturning an earlier government decision to eliminate quotas on oil imports. Anticipating repercussions from oil-rich Republican contributors who were angered by the earlier decision, Nixon had ordered a new study of oil import quotas, which recommended retention of tariffs.

In 1972 Flanigan helped to arrange a favorable decision for the International Telephone and Telegraph Corp. (ITT) in an antitrust suit brought by the Justice Department. The department had earlier ruled ITT's acquisition of the Hartford Fire Insurance Co. illegal. Flanigan arranged for Richard J. Ramsden, a former White House aide, to prepare a study of the case. The Ramsden report stressed the "unfavorable" economic consequences that would result should ITT be forced to divest its recent acquisition. Despite the fact that Ramsden was at that time employed by Dillon, Read, which held $200,000 in ITT stock, and that his report was based on a brief authored by ITT's own attorneys, the Justice Department reversed itself and abandoned pursuit of the case.

HERBERT KALMBACH, Nixon's former personal attorney, testified at the House Judiciary Committee's impeachment inquiry in 1974 that Flanigan brokered ambassadorships in return for massive contributions to the 1972 Nixon presidential campaign. Flanigan acknowledged telling Kalmbach that a potential ambassadorial nominee, Dr. Ruth B. Farkas, was "a good prospect for solicitation." According to Kalmbach Flanigan had advised him to contact Dr. Farkas since she was interested "in giving $250,000 for Costa Rica." Dr. Farkas, Kalmbach said, thought Costa Rica not worth that much, but by contributing $300,000, she was eventually named ambassador to Luxembourg.

Flanigan resigned from the Nixon administration in July 1974. Several months later President Ford named him ambassador to Spain. The Flanigan nomination soon ran into opposition. At a Senate Foreign Relations Committee hearing on October 2, 1974, Senator THOMAS F. EAGLETON (D-Mo.) denounced the nomination as "a disgrace to the United States." The White House announced the withdrawal of the Flanigan nomination November 16, 1974, after Flanigan requested that it not be resubmitted because of the "current political climate." In January 1975 Flanigan returned to Dillon, Read, as a managing director and executive officer. He continues as an investment banker.

—JAN

Fonda, Jane
(1937–) *actress, political activist*

Born on December 21, 1937, Jane Fonda attended Vassar College, studied art in Paris, and then enrolled at the Art Students League in New York. During the 1950s and 1960s she starred in a number of movies, including *Tall Story* (1960), *A Walk on the Wild Side* (1962), *Period of Adjustment* (1962), *Sunday in New York* (1963), and *La Ronde* (1964). By the early 1970s she had established herself as one of the nation's leading motion picture actresses.

During the late 1960s and early 1970s Fonda became known for her outspoken opposition to the Vietnam War and her support of the feminist movement. Fonda joined other members of the film community to form Entertainment Industry for Peace and Justice. The group's major production, "Free the Army," was well received by civilian and military audiences during its international tour and was honored with an Obie award after its New York performance. Fonda's political activities won her a degree of notoriety with the American public and even inspired the Maryland general assembly to entertain a bill declaring her persona non grata in the state. In 1972 she traveled to Vietnam, where she broadcast on Hanoi Radio in addition to directing a film, *Viet Nam Journey*, relating her experience of the war.

In 1973 Fonda married antiwar activist TOM HAYDEN. As the war wound down, Fonda moved out of the public spotlight. But in 1977 she resumed her full-time movie career. A year later Fonda starred in *Coming Home*, the story of a Vietnam veteran whose war injury had left him a paraplegic, and in 1978 she played a leading role in *The China Syndrome*, a movie about the possibility of an accident at a nuclear power plant. After the nuclear accident at Three Mile Island in Pennsylvania, Fonda emerged as a spokeswoman of antinuclear power forces. In the 1980s Fonda produced a number of highly successful fitness tapes. In 2005 she published a memoir, *My Life So Far*.

—PM

Fong, Hiram L(eong)
(1907–2004) *member of the Senate*

Born on October 1, 1907, Hiram Fong, the son of indentured plantation workers, worked his way through the University of Hawaii and Harvard Law School. Fong stood out among a generation of upwardly mobile Chinese Americans who challenged the Caucasian plantation owners' economic leadership on the islands. He worked as a deputy city attorney in Honolulu and later founded the city's first multiracial law office. So successful was the firm that Fong was able to invest in a variety of businesses. His assets totaled several million dollars by 1960. Fong was elected as a Republican to the Hawaiian territorial legislature in 1938 and served as Speaker of that body from 1948 to 1954. During that time he developed a working relationship with the powerful International Longshoremen's and Warehousemen's Union (ILWU). When he ran for U.S. senator in Hawaii's first general election as a state in July 1959, Fong was the only Republican candidate backed by the normally Democratic ILWU.

Fong won the Senate race and designation as senior senator from Hawaii with a special term that expired in 1964. Characterized as a Republican moderate, he tended to take more liberal stands on domestic issues than on foreign policy. After winning reelection by a comfortable margin in 1964, Fong proved a leading supporter of civil rights legislation. He backed the 1965 Voting Rights Act and wrote a key amendment to include poll watchers in the bill. As a member of the Judiciary Committee's Immigration and Naturalization Subcommittee, Fong worked to eliminate the traditional immigration restrictions against Asians. Also during the Johnson administration, Fong pressed for gun control legislation and was one of the few Republicans to support the president's proposal for an Administration on Aging. In 1968 he joined six other members of the Judiciary Committee in voting against Johnson's nomination of Supreme Court justice ABE FORTAS for chief justice.

Fong became highly partisan and more conservative during the NIXON years. He consistently voted for large defense appropriations and used his seat on the Judiciary's

Refugees and Escapees Subcommittee to defend the Nixon administration's Vietnam policy. He also served as ranking Republican on the Appropriations Committee's Foreign Operations Subcommittee, where he argued for the continuation of military aid programs. On the floor Fong voted against any curtailment of funds for Vietnam and against any cutbacks in the Defense Department budget. He voted for the Safeguard antiballistic missile system (ABM) and the supersonic transport (SST). Fong received a 100 percent rating for 1969–70 from the American Security Council.

Although Fong's unstinting support of Nixon's Vietnam policy hurt his popularity in Hawaii and weakened his relationship with the ILWU, the strength of his personal organization carried him to a narrow reelection victory in 1970. During the 92nd Congress, as ranking Republican member of the Constitutional Amendments Subcommittee, Fong supported the Equal Rights Amendment. On other domestic issues, including welfare and tax bills, his voting record was mixed. In 1972 he voted against any federal action to foster busing as a means of integrating schools and in 1973 opposed voter registration by mail. Fong supported President Nixon's veto of the U.S. Information Agency bill on the grounds that its access-to-information clause was an unconstitutional encroachment on executive prerogatives.

In January 1971 Fong's office was rocked by a major scandal involving his longtime administrative assistant Robert Carson. Fong courageously stood by his aide, who was indicted and subsequently convicted in New York federal court for allegedly trying to bribe Deputy Attorney General RICHARD KLEINDIENST with $100,000 in campaign funds. Though Fong emerged blameless from the scandal, he announced his retirement in 1976, at the end of his third term. He was succeeded by Spark

M. Matsunaga, formerly a Democratic representative from Hawaii. Fong served as the chairman of Finance Enterprises Ltd. until his 2004 death from kidney failure.

—DAE

Ford, Gerald R(udolph)

(1913–   ) *member of the House of Representatives; president of the United States*

Gerald R. Ford was born on July 14, 1913, in Omaha, Nebraska. Raised in Grand Rapids, Michigan, Ford attended the University of Michigan, where he was a college all-star football player, and Yale Law School, where he earned his law degree in 1941. After serving in the navy during World War II, he practiced law in Grand Rapids. In 1948, at the urging of Arthur H. Vandenberg, Ford successfully challenged an isolationist incumbent U.S. representative in the Republican primary. Ford then easily defeated his Democratic opponent and, in 12 subsequent elections, always captured over 60 percent of the vote. During the 1950s he aligned himself with the Eisenhower internationalist wing of the Republican Party and became a staunch proponent of large defense budgets and military alliances to prevent communist expansion. Fiercely partisan, Ford compiled a conservative voting record in domestic affairs.

During the 1960s Ford emerged as a leader of House Republicans, who elected him chairman of the House Republican Conference in 1963 and minority leader in 1965. He opposed most of the social welfare legislation of the Kennedy and Johnson administrations and consistently voted to reduce appropriations for such programs as model cities, the War on Poverty, and aid to education. Although he was on record as a supporter of civil rights, Ford generally played an obstructionist role until the final vote, when he supported enactment

The Ford family in the Oval Office prior to the swearing in of Gerald R. Ford as president, August 9, 1974 (left to right) Jack, Steve, Betty, Gerald, Susan, Gayle, and Mike *(Ford Library)*

of civil rights protection. Ford served on the Warren Commission to investigate the assassination of President John F. Kennedy and in 1965 helped write *Portrait of the Assassin,* which defended the commission's conclusion that Lee Harvey Oswald had acted alone. He frequently spoke out against President Johnson's conduct of the Vietnam War, arguing that the United States was not prosecuting the war aggressively enough.

During RICHARD NIXON's first term in office, Ford proved himself a staunch administration loyalist and maintained his conservative voting record. In 1970 the liberal Americans for Democratic Action gave him only a 17 percent rating. Ford supported Nixon's decision in March 1969 to seek appropriations for deployment of the Safeguard antiballistic missile system (ABM) and accused its opponents of proposing unilateral disarmament "in the face of a serious threat from the Soviet Union." Ford led a low-key campaign in the House to continue funding of the controversial supersonic transport plane (SST). In May 1971 he engineered a reversal of a previous House vote to cut off funds, but the Senate ultimately killed the measure. In January 1972 Ford signed a petition to discharge an antibusing constitutional amendment from the House Judiciary Committee.

The rejection by the Senate of Nixon's conservative Supreme Court nominees CLEMENT HAYNSWORTH in November 1969 and G. HARROLD CARSWELL in April 1970 led Ford to call for an inquiry into the possible impeachment of liberal Supreme Court justice WILLIAM O. DOUGLAS. In a speech on the House floor on April 15, 1970, Ford demanded the removal of Douglas from the Court. He accused the associate justice of having ties to the underworld and of publishing an article in the "hard-core pornography" magazine *Evergreen Review* that advocated "hippie-yippie-style revolution." Ford cosponsored a resolution to have the House investigate whether grounds existed for impeachment. When a subcommittee of the House Judiciary Committee released in December 1970 a report that outlined a "mountain of evidence" against impeachment, Ford labeled the investigation a "whitewash."

Ford consistently supported Nixon's Vietnam policy. In September 1969 he denounced the proposals of antiwar activists for immediate troop withdrawal as "tantamount to surrender." He voted against all efforts to curb military spending in Southeast Asia and to place a time limit on American troop involvement in the war. In 1971 he voted to extend the draft and in 1973 voted against the War Powers Act. In the spring of 1972 he defended the intensified bombing of North Vietnam as "the right course." In May, when Nixon announced the mining of North Vietnamese harbors, Ford praised the president as "generous in his bid for peace but firm in his determination that we will not surrender."

On October 12, 1973, two days after the resignation of Vice President SPIRO T. AGNEW, President Nixon named Gerald Ford to replace Agnew. The choice was widely viewed as an effort to win congressional support for the administration in light of the growing Watergate scandal. The initial reaction in Congress was overwhelmingly favorable since Ford, though extremely partisan, was also well liked and admired for his extreme honesty and candor. The following day Ford promised a complete disclosure of his personal finances and also barred a 1976 campaign for the presidency.

Although favorably disposed to him, Congress conducted a thoroughgoing investigation of Ford's record. In the Senate Rules Committee, which opened hearings on November 1, Ford was repeatedly questioned about such matters as executive privilege, the separation of powers, impoundment of funds, the independence of a new special Watergate prosecutor, and whether the president had a right to withhold information concerning criminal activity in the executive branch. Ford walked a tightrope in his answers. He denied that a president had "unlimited authority" in the areas of executive privilege, said that documents concerning "serious allegations" of criminal behavior should be made available, and said that even though he was convinced of the president's innocence, an impeachment inquiry would "clear the air." When asked if in the event of Nixon's resignation he would try to halt an investigation into the president's affairs, Ford replied "I don't think the public would stand for it."

On November 20 the Rules Committee unanimously approved Ford's confirmation, and on November 27 the full Senate voted 92 to 3 in his favor. Although some opposition to Ford emerged in the House Judiciary Committee, largely on the basis of his conservative voting record and whether he had the leadership qualities required of a president, the House on December 6 voted 387 to 35 to confirm Ford. Later that day he was sworn in as the nation's 40th vice president.

As vice president, Ford traveled widely around the country, trying to bolster the sagging fortunes of the Republican Party, which was being buffeted by the Watergate scandal. Ford unequivocally defended Nixon. The day after he was confirmed, the vice president declared that there was "no evidence that would justify impeachment." In January he characterized the president's opponents as "a few extreme partisans" and reiterated his conviction that Nixon had "no prior knowledge of the Watergate break-in" nor "any part in the cover-up." Ford did urge the president, however, to release the White House tapes to lay to rest doubts about his innocence. Even after Nixon released in April 1,200 pages of transcripts that were damaging to his case and led to the defection of much of his Republican support, Ford remained loyal. As late as July he said that "the preponderance of the evidence favors the president" and that Nixon was the victim of "Democratic partisan politics."

On August 9, 1974, Nixon resigned from the presidency after admitting that he had ordered a halt to the FBI probe of the Watergate break-in, and Gerald Ford was sworn in as the nation's 38th president. In addressing the country he said, "Our long national nightmare is over. Our Constitution works. Our great republic is a government of laws and not of men." He pledged an administration of "openness and candor" and moved quickly to meet with cabinet members, congressional leaders, national security officials, and economic policy advisers. Ford took office with a great reservoir of goodwill. The public rallied to support him, and leaders of both parties predicted an extended "honeymoon" with Congress.

Ford risked much of his popularity when, on September 8, he granted Nixon a full pardon for all federal crimes he may have committed while in office. The decision provoked an uproar, since the previous month Ford's press secretary, JERALD TERHORST, had reiterated the president's statement that the public would not stand for a pardon. TerHorst immediately resigned in protest. A Harris poll in October indicated that 67 percent of the public opposed the pardon, and Ford's approval ratings plummeted. In October he testified before a House Judiciary subcommittee that was investigating the pardon that "no deal" had been made. The following month the subcommittee voted to drop the inquiry.

Ford balanced his pardon of Nixon by announcing on September 16 a program of limited amnesty for Vietnam era draft evaders and military deserters. Although he had adamantly opposed any such efforts while in Congress, as president he said he had a responsibility to "bind up the nation's wounds." His proclamation offered clemency to those who swore an oath of allegiance to the United States and agreed to perform 24 months of alternate service work. For men already convicted, Ford set up a clemency board to review cases and recommend pardons. The clemency program received the support of Congress but was condemned by veterans groups as going too far and by antiwar groups as inadequate. When the program expired on March 31, 1975, only about one out of six who were eligible had signed up, and the American Civil Liberties Union concluded that the effort was a "fraud."

The most pressing problem that Ford faced on taking office was the state of the economy. The removal of price controls in 1973 and the quadrupling of oil prices by the Organization of Petroleum Exporting Countries (OPEC) that fall led to rapidly escalating prices. The Wholesale Price Index rose almost 18 percent in the 12 months ending in August 1974. In a nationally televised address to Congress on August 12, Ford called inflation "our domestic public enemy No. 1" and told the legislators that "my first priority is to work with you to bring inflation under control." At Ford's request Congress quickly passed legislation establishing a Council on Wage and Price Stability to monitor wage and price increases without, however, any enforcement powers. The president also announced plans for a White House economic summit conference in late September that would make specific recommendations for fighting inflation.

On October 8 Ford presented his anti-inflation program to Congress. Offering fiscal and monetary restraint as the main cure, he pledged to keep the federal budget for 1975 under $300 billion. Ford's program avoided mandatory controls and instead relied on appeals for "self-discipline" and "voluntary restraint," urging Americans to "drive less, heat less" as a way of cutting the consumption of high-priced fuel and heating oil. He set as a goal a reduction in oil imports of 1 million barrels a day without specific proposals to accomplish it. He asked Congress to enact a 5 percent surtax on incomes of middle and upper income families and on corporate profits, to liberalize investment tax credits, to create a board to develop a coherent energy policy, and to extend the length of unemployment benefits. In line with his emphasis on voluntary efforts to curb inflation, Ford announced on October 15 a "great citizens mobilization" under the slogan WIN (Whip Inflation Now). Among other things he suggested that Americans plant WIN gardens to reduce the cost of food.

Ford's initial response to the nation's economic woes provoked widespread criticism, especially from organized labor and congressional Democrats. AFL-CIO president GEORGE MEANY disputed the targeting of inflation as a priority. "We are in a recession," Meany declared and argued that job creation and economic stimuli were most needed. Speaker of the House CARL ALBERT decried the "old-time religion" of fiscal and monetary restraint. Liberal Democrats almost unanimously opposed Ford's suggested tax increases and deplored the absence of programs to create new jobs. Rebelling at the president's insistence on balancing the budget, Congress in October overrode a veto of a railroad workers pension bill and in December enacted a substantial increase in veterans' educational benefits over another Ford veto.

By the end of 1974 the evidence of recession was unmistakable. Unemployment rose from 5.3 percent in July to 7.2 percent in December.

Auto sales fell 23 percent below 1973 levels, real gross national product declined 2.2 percent for the year, the purchasing power of workers in manufacturing dropped, and productivity declined for the first time since 1947. In addition, inflation continued at a galloping pace, with wholesale prices for the year up 20.9 percent and consumer prices 12.2 percent higher than a year earlier. Economic analysts agreed that the nation was in the worst recession since the 1930s and coined a new term, "stagflation," to describe the unprecedented concurrence of rising prices with declining production.

Although the depth of the recession forced a drastic shift in Ford's economic policies, the combination of inflation and recession stymied efforts to devise a coherent approach to economic recovery. Ford's difficulties were evident in his 1975 State of the Union address to Congress. In it he proposed a $16 billion dollar tax cut, mostly in the form of a rebate to taxpayers, to stimulate the economy. He also abandoned his goal of a balanced budget and instead predicted a deficit of from $30 billion to $50 billion for 1975 and 1976. His proposed budget for fiscal 1974 was a record $349.4 billion, but it contained no new social welfare or job-producing legislation, and Ford promised to veto any new spending bills. To counter the nation's dependence on high-priced foreign oil, Ford said he would invoke his emergency powers as president to raise the tariff on imported oil, increasing its price to discourage consumption. He also urged Congress to deregulate the price of new natural gas to encourage domestic exploration and asked for authorization to lease the government's petroleum reserves to commercial development.

The effort to enact his economic program led to a serious deterioration in Ford's relations with Congress. Upset at the inflationary effect of his energy proposals, Congress passed legislation in March to suspend his powers to raise import fees but was unable to override a presidential veto. Controversy over Ford's energy plans continued throughout the year. In July he presented a proposal for the phased decontrol of domestic oil prices in an effort to both cut consumption and encourage exploration of domestic oil. Instead, Congress passed a bill that month to roll back the price of domestic oil in an effort to limit the inflationary impact of fuel consumption. Ford's veto of the bill led to a stalemate with Congress that continued until December, when compromise legislation was enacted. The final version of the energy bill provided for an immediate rollback in domestic crude oil prices while also phasing out all controls over a 40-month period. As part of the compromise Ford agreed to remove the tariff on imported oil.

There were also substantial differences between Ford and Congress over tax and spending proposals. In March Congress enacted a $22.8 billion tax cut, which Ford signed even though it was significantly larger than his original request. He did, however, successfully veto in May a $5.3 billion appropriation for public works employment and a $1.2 billion emergency housing bill the following month. But by the summer unemployment had reached 9.2 percent, the highest post–World War II level, and congressional Democrats and liberal Republicans joined forces to override presidential vetoes of a number of domestic spending programs. Over Ford's opposition Congress approved a $2 billion health care bill in July, a $7.9 billion education bill in September, and an expanded school lunch program in October.

The recession, meanwhile, was having a particularly adverse effect on state and municipal governments. High unemployment led to a sharp decline in tax revenues, and many state and local governments, having reached the limits of their borrowing power, were forced to cut back on social welfare programs at a time when they were most needed. New York City, on the verge of default throughout the spring and summer of 1975, pleaded with federal officials to support federally guaranteed loans to save the city. Ford, strongly backed by Treasury secretary WILLIAM SIMON, adamantly opposed such guarantees and as late as October 29 promised to veto any legislation to "bail out" New York. As evidence accumulated, however, that a default might jeopardize the banking system and the nation's economic recovery, the president was forced to relent. On November 26 he asked Congress for legislation to provide up to $2.3 billion annually in loans to New York and the following month signed the bill into law.

By the end of 1975 statistics indicated that the economy, though slowly recovering from the depths of the recession, was still very weak. Unemployment in December measured 8.3 percent of the labor force, and consumer prices rose 9.1 percent for the year. In his January 1976 economic report to Congress Ford declared that the "underlying fact about our economy is that it is steadily growing healthier." The persistence of high rates of unemployment and inflation, however, made the recovery shaky, and it was evident that the state of the economy would weigh heavily in the 1976 election campaigns.

While coping with the problems of the economy, Ford also found himself presiding over a somewhat new era in American foreign policy. Although he had entered politics as a cold war advocate, as president he pursued a policy of détente with the Soviet Union and sought to defuse tensions in the Middle East. The legacy of Vietnam, moreover, affected his conduct of foreign affairs. Congress was unwilling to let the president have a free hand in the making of foreign policy, and public pressure against further entanglements abroad forced a generally low profile for the United States.

Ford voiced strong support for HENRY KISSINGER and kept him on as both secretary of state and head of the National Security Council. Kissinger was viewed as the chief architect of East-West détente, and in October 1974 he visited the Soviet Union in pursuit of a new arms limitation agreement. Upon Kissinger's return Ford announced that he would travel to the Soviet port city of Vladivostok in November to meet Soviet leader Leonid Brezhnev. There the two heads of state announced an agreement to limit the numbers of all strategic offensive nuclear weaponry, including the controversial MIRV delivery system. In contrast to the 1972 Strategic Arms Limitation Agreement (SALT), the new pact set the principle of equivalency in offensive weaponry for the two nations. Ford also revealed that SALT II talks would resume in Geneva in January and described the pursuit of a further agreement as in "the best interest" of the United States. Little further progress was made, however, and a year later, in November 1975, Ford was forced to concede that the "timetable doesn't look encouraging" for a new SALT pact in the near future.

Ford also encouraged Kissinger's efforts at "shuttle diplomacy" to achieve a peace settlement in the Middle East. In March 1975, after Kissinger failed to win agreement for a second Egyptian-Israeli troop withdrawal from the Sinai, Ford angrily announced that his administration was totally reassessing Middle East policy and pointedly said that if Israel "had been a bit more flexible" the chances for peace would have been better. In June Ford held separate meetings with Egyptian president Anwar Sadat and Israeli premier Yitzhak Rabin, which led to a revival of Kissinger's peace-making efforts in August. On September 4 Ford was able to announce that a new Sinai pact had been reached that called for a further Israeli troop withdrawal from the Sinai and the stationing of U.S. civilians there to monitor the pact. The agreement received widespread approval.

In other areas of foreign policy, Ford found his freedom to maneuver hampered by increasing congressional assertiveness. Revelations by the press of massive illegal intelligence operations by the Central Intelligence Agency (CIA) led Ford, in January 1975, to appoint a commission headed by Vice President NELSON ROCKEFELLER to investigate the charges. The report, issued in June, acknowledged violations of law but disputed claims that the violations were serious or widespread. Both the Senate and the House, disturbed by reports that the CIA had plotted assassinations of foreign leaders, conducted their own investigations that caused Ford to warn against "sweeping attacks" on foreign intelligence operations. In September 1975 he refused to grant the House Select Committee on Intelligence access to classified material until it yielded any right to make the information public, a concession the House granted. Concern about CIA activities, however, remained widespread, and in December 1975 Congress, over the strong objections of Ford and Kissinger, voted to cut off funds for covert CIA operations in the Angolan civil war. Ford called the decision "a deep tragedy" but was powerless to do anything about it.

Congressional wariness about military involvement abroad also was apparent in its response to the final stages of the Vietnam War. Concerned about the upsurge in fighting there, Ford asked Congress in January 1975 for an additional $522 million in military aid for South Vietnam and Cambodia. As the Communist offensive in both countries intensified and it became obvious that victory was imminent, Ford pleaded for action, but Congress remained adamant and merely approved funds for an emergency evacuation of American personnel from South Vietnam. After the capture of the capitals of Pnom Penh and Saigon in April, Ford blamed Congress for the collapse but admitted that the end of hostilities "closes a chapter in the American experience."

Shortly thereafter, on May 12, 1975, Cambodian forces seized an American merchant vessel, the *Mayaguez*, and its American crew in the Gulf of Siam. Ford called the action "an act of piracy" and two days later ordered a dramatic rescue operation involving air, sea, and ground forces. Although the action was successful and received praise from leaders of both parties, some analysts saw it as an excessive display of force intended to symbolize the willingness of the United States to take firm action in world affairs.

In September 1975 Ford was the target of two separate assassination attempts. On September 5 in Sacramento, a member of the Charles Manson cult, Lynette Fromme, standing a few feet away from Ford as he shook hands in a crowd, pointed a gun at the president. The revolver failed to fire, and Fromme was quickly subdued by Secret Service personnel. On September 22 in San Francisco, Sara Jane Moore, an FBI informant, fired at the president. The gunshot was deflected by the quick action of an onlooker, and Ford escaped injury.

On July 8, 1975, Ford formally announced his candidacy for the 1976 Republican presidential nomination. Ironically, Ford faced opposition from the conservative wing of the party with which he had been most closely identified while in Congress. His choice of Nelson Rockefeller as vice president, the huge budget deficits of his administration, and the Vladivostok arms limitation agreement all contributed to conservative disenchantment. Ford tried to mollify the opposition by appointing a conservative southerner, HOWARD CALLAWAY, as his campaign manager and intensifying his attacks on a free-spending Congress. In November, moreover, Rockefeller withdrew himself from consideration for the 1976 vice presidential spot. Nonetheless, California's conservative ex-governor RONALD REAGAN announced his candidacy on November 20, and a December Gallup poll showed Ford trailing Reagan.

Early primary victories by Ford in New Hampshire, Florida (where Reagan had predicted a two-to-one victory for himself), and Illinois buoyed the president's campaign, and attention shifted to the May 1 Texas primary. Reagan focused on the issues of détente and defense, charging that under Ford the United States had fallen behind the Soviet Union in military strength. Ford accused Reagan of raising "false alarms" and said that the ex-governor was so "simplistic" that as president he would make "irresponsible and fundamentally harmful policy decisions." Ford nonetheless lost by a huge margin, suffering the worst defeat ever sustained by an incumbent. A string of losses in Indiana, Georgia, Alabama, and Nebraska added to Ford's worries, but he bounced back with victories in Michigan and Maryland on May 18. In late June Ford picked up the important endorsement of conservative senator BARRY GOLDWATER (R-Ariz.), but when the delegate selection process was completed in July neither Ford nor Reagan had enough to clinch the nomination. The decision rested with the uncommitted delegates. Ford was slightly ahead, however, and the fact that he was the incumbent gave him the edge. On August 19 the Republican National Convention nominated Ford on the first ballot. To mollify conservatives he chose Senator ROBERT DOLE (R-Kan.) as his running mate.

Having defeated the conservative opposition in his own party, Ford had to confront the opposition of liberals and moderates in the general election. The slowness of the economic recovery and Ford's numerous vetoes of spending programs to create jobs and expand social welfare measures meant that organized labor and racial minorities were solidly arrayed against him. His opponent, former Georgia governor JIMMY CARTER, capitalized on the nation's disenchantment with Washington politicians of the Vietnam and Watergate era. Avoiding as much as possible specific solutions

President Ford meets with his National Security Council to discuss the *Mayaguez* situation, May 13, 1975. *(Ford Library)*

to problems, Carter promised to bring a new morality and a new approach to the nation's affairs. The election results were close. Ford won 27 states, including most of the Midwest and all of the West except Hawaii, while Carter captured the South and most of the heavily populated industrial Northeast. Carter received 51 percent of the popular vote to Ford's 49 percent, and 297 electoral votes in contrast to 241 for Ford.

Following his defeat in 1976, Ford moved to Rancho Mirage, California, where he was immediately tapped to join several influential boards of directors. In 1980 he considered a second run against Jimmy Carter but decided against making the campaign. However, at the Republican Convention that August, pre-sumptive party nominee Ronald Reagan, after entering into negotiations with former Nixon and Ford secretary of state Henry Kissinger, surprised most analysts by offering Ford the second place on the Republican ticket. Ford surprised even more observers by seriously entertaining the offer. Ford, however, jumped the gun by discussing the offer during a live interview with CBS newsman Walter Cronkite, and an angry Reagan withdrew the offer. This effectively ended Ford's political life. Retiring to his homes in California and Vail, Colorado, Ford maintained an active speaking schedule until declining health (hip and knee replacements) forced him in 2003 to begin to refuse most invitations to speak.

—JD and JRG

Fortas, Abe
(1910–1982) *associate justice, U.S. Supreme Court*

Abe Fortas was born on June 19, 1910, in Memphis, Tennessee. After receiving a B.A. from Southwestern College in Memphis in 1930, Fortas attended Yale Law School, where he graduated first in his class in 1933. He taught at Yale from 1933 to 1937 while also working part time for several New Deal agencies. After 1937 Fortas held posts in the Securities and Exchange Commission and the Interior Department, serving as undersecretary of the interior from 1942 to 1946. In the latter year he began a private practice with several other New Dealers. Arnold, Fortas, & Porter was soon a flourishing and prestigious Washington firm with a roster of corporate clients including Coca-Cola, Lever Brothers, Philip Morris, and Pan American World Airways. Fortas himself became known as a skilled corporate counselor and appellate advocate, but he and his firm also developed a reputation for their civil liberties work. They defended various individuals charged with being security risks during the McCarthy era and took several loyalty cases to the Supreme Court. Serving as Court-appointed counsel, Fortas won a landmark ruling from the Supreme Court in 1963 in which the justices unanimously held that the states must supply counsel to indigent defendants accused of serious, noncapital crimes.

In 1948 Fortas secured a Supreme Court order that enabled Lyndon Johnson to get his name on the general election ballot in Texas. Johnson went on to win a U.S. Senate seat that November. The incident launched a long and close friendship between the two men, with Fortas becoming one of Johnson's most trusted advisers. During Johnson's presidency Fortas acted as an unofficial counselor on appointments and legislation and on issues ranging from racial controversies to the Vietnam War.

He turned down several offers of appointment to public positions but at Johnson's insistence finally agreed to accept a Supreme Court nomination on July 28, 1965.

On the bench Fortas immediately aligned himself with the Warren Court's liberal justices. He voted with the majority in the June 1966 *Miranda* decision and wrote the opinion of the Court in a May 1967 case extending most of the criminal safeguards in the Bill of Rights to children in juvenile court proceedings. Justice Fortas voted repeatedly to sustain civil rights claims and to invalidate state loyalty oaths, but he took a more moderate position in free press and obscenity cases.

On June 26, 1968, Johnson nominated Fortas as chief justice to succeed Earl Warren, who planned to retire. A coalition of Republicans and conservative Democrats managed to block Senate confirmation of the appointment, and it was withdrawn early in October. Foes of the nomination objected to Fortas's liberalism, to his advisory relationship with Johnson, which had continued even after he joined the bench, and to having a "lame duck" president select the new chief justice. In addition, it had been disclosed in September that Fortas had received $15,000 for teaching a summer school course in 1968 and that the money had been raised by one of his former law partners from five prominent businessmen, one of whom had a son involved in a federal criminal case.

Despite the defeat of his nomination as chief justice, there was every expectation as the 1968 Court term opened that Fortas would have a long, productive, and influential career as an associate justice. He seemed at ease on the bench and had won respect for his intelligence and legal craftsmanship and for opinions that were thorough and scholarly yet also crisp and colorful in style. During the term Fortas wrote several significant opinions for the Court that advanced the libertarian views he espoused. In November 1968 the justice held that Arkansas's "monkey law," which forbade the teaching of the Darwinian theory of evolution in public schools, violated the First Amendment's ban on establishment of religion. A week later Fortas ruled that a court order restraining the National States Rights Party from holding a public rally for 10 days was an unconstitutional violation of free speech because the injunction had been granted at a hearing without prior notice to party representatives. For a seven-man majority in February 1969, Fortas declared that the First Amendment guaranteed public school students the right to peaceful, nondisruptive political expression such as the wearing of black armbands to protest the Vietnam War.

In another February 1969 case involving "jailhouse lawyers," Fortas's majority opinion held that the states could not bar a prisoner from giving legal aid to illiterate or poorly educated fellow inmates when no other provision was made for those inmates to receive legal assistance in appealing their convictions. In an April 1969 opinion Fortas ruled that a lineup identification of a suspect could not be used as evidence at trial when the lineup was arranged so that the defendant stood out as the likely criminal.

Off the bench Justice Fortas and his wife, a leading Washington tax attorney, enjoyed a life of comfort and culture. Their Georgetown home contained antique furniture, contemporary works of art, and Chinese scrolls and paintings. They drove a Rolls-Royce and had a summer house in Connecticut. An accomplished amateur violinist, Fortas played in a string quartet at least once a week.

Fortas's judicial career ended suddenly in May 1969, when he resigned from the Court in the wake of disclosures of questionable financial associations. On May 4 *Life* magazine reported that in January 1966 Fortas had accepted $20,000 from the family foundation of industrialist Louis E. Wolfson. He had returned the money in December 1966 after Wolfson was twice indicted on federal stock charges. Since then, Wolfson had been convicted and imprisoned for selling unregistered securities. On the same day Fortas issued a statement declaring that he had "not accepted any fee or emolument" from Wolfson or his foundation but then conceded that the foundation had tendered him a fee in 1966 for research and writing services. Fortas said he had returned the fee when he concluded that he could not undertake the assignment. He insisted that he had not intervened in any way in Wolfson's case.

Nonetheless, some members of Congress began calling for Fortas's resignation, and there was talk of impeachment. The pressure increased when *Newsweek* magazine revealed on May 11 that Attorney General JOHN MITCHELL had visited Chief Justice Warren on May 7, reportedly to tell him that the Justice Department had "far more serious" information about Fortas than had already been disclosed. Fortas submitted his resignation May 14 and made it public the next day along with a letter to Earl Warren explaining his action. In the letter Fortas stated that late in 1965 he had made an agreement with the Wolfson Foundation that gave him $20,000 a year for life in exchange for services to the foundation. He had received the first fee in January 1966 but had canceled the agreement that June because his Court duties were taking more time than anticipated. Fortas had returned the money in December 1966 following Wolfson's indictment. The justice declared he was resigning for the good of the Court and flatly denied any wrongdoing on his part. On May 20, 1969, the American Bar Association's Committee on Professional Ethics concluded that Fortas's association with Wolfson was "clearly contrary" to the Canons of Judicial Ethics. The Justice Department, which had been conducting its own inquiry, decided that Fortas had done nothing criminal and closed its file on the case.

The first justice ever to leave the Court under the pressure of public criticism, Fortas made no further public statement about the Wolfson episode and returned quietly to private life. He spent some time writing a book that he later decided not to publish, and he gradually undertook some legal work. By the spring of 1970 Fortas had joined a small new law firm in Washington, where he practiced law until his death in 1982.

—CAB

Friedman, Milton
(1912–) *economist*

Born on July 31, 1912, the son of immigrant merchants, Milton Friedman grew up in Rahway, New Jersey, and graduated from Rutgers University in 1932. He did graduate work in economics at the University of Chicago, a citadel of classic economic theory. In 1935 he joined the National Resources Committee, a federal agency, as a statistician, leaving in 1937 to do a study of independent professional practice for the National Bureau of Economic Research. Friedman taught economics, and from 1941 to 1943 he was the principal tax research economist at the Treasury Department. After obtaining his Ph.D. from Columbia University in 1946, he joined the faculty at the University of Chicago, where he spent the next three decades.

By the 1960s Friedman had become the foremost academic apostle of free market economics and an iconoclastic critic of the Keynesian theories prevalent among government economists. In *Capitalism and Freedom* (1962) he made a vigorous laissez-faire case against virtually all government interference with the private market. He favored the elimination of most federal agencies as well as tariffs and farm price supports, arguing that the best guarantee of prosperity and consumer welfare was an unfettered price system. Friedman believed that Social Security should be abolished and called for the abandonment of minimum wage legislation on the grounds that such a wage floor increased unemployment. He advocated turning over public schools and public transportation to the private sector.

Within the academic community Friedman won prominence with his persistent and provocative advocacy of the quantity theory of money, or "monetarism," as it became known. According to this theory, the dominant factor in the economy is the amount of money in circulation, not, as the Keynesians held, the fiscal policy of the federal government. In *The Monetary History of The United States*, Friedman correlated contractions in the money supply with the occurrence of recessions and depressions. His chief policy prescription was to strip the Federal Reserve of its discretionary control of the money supply and mandate that the supply be increased at the steady rate of 4 percent each year.

An active supporter of the unsuccessful presidential candidacy of Senator BARRY GOLDWATER (R-Ariz.) in 1964, Friedman reached the peak of his influence with the election of RICHARD NIXON in 1968. Although he was not an official member of the Republican administration, Friedman saw his ideas reflected in several of the new administration's policies and personnel. Nixon's first chairman of the Council of Economic Advisers, PAUL MCCRACKEN, described himself as "Friedmanesque." The administration's basic economic policy of cutting government spending and taxes to halt the inflation and stimulate investment followed the outlines of Friedman's thought. By late 1969, however, the Federal Reserve allowed a slow and steady expansion of the money supply.

The creation of an all-volunteer army and the publication by the Federal Reserve of regular reports on the money supply were other Friedman proposals implemented during the

Nixon years. The administration tried to enact Friedman's substitute for welfare, the negative income tax, as part of its Family Assistance Plan, but Congress rejected the measure. The administration did not attempt to implement many of Friedman's favorite libertarian schemes, such as his proposal to replace public schools with a system of government-awarded tuition vouchers that would enable parents to send children to the school of their choice.

After the Nixon administration's wage-price freeze of August 1971, Friedman regularly excoriated the controls. To Friedman the controls were not only economically unsound but "deeply and inherently immoral." "By substituting the rule of men for the rule of law and for voluntary cooperation in the marketplace," he wrote, "the controls threaten the very foundations of a free society." Friedman was also a frequent critic of the Food and Drug Administration (FDA), whose extended procedures for approving experimental drugs were, according to Friedman, costly, inefficient, and self-defeating. Friedman wrote in *Newsweek* in January 1973 that the FDA's regulatory procedures "condemn innocent people to death." Friedman's confidence in the market led him to dispel fears of an energy crisis and continually escalating oil prices after the Organization of Petroleum Exporting Countries dramatically hiked oil prices in October 1973. Friedman predicted in June 1974 that the oil cartel would break up and prices would return to pre-October 1973 levels.

At the same time Friedman stimulated a lively debate with his suggestion, unusual for a conservative, that the United States adopt a system of automatic wage-price increases to keep pace with inflation. He cited Brazil's successful use of the mechanism, known as "indexing," in reducing its inflation without inhibiting economic growth. He maintained that indexing would give greater protection to the poor and those on fixed incomes from the inflationary spiral. Some critics charged that the Brazilian technique spawned black markets, while others criticized Friedman's idea as a surrender to inflation that would weaken the political resolve to try more orthodox techniques, such as reduced government spending.

In March 1975 Friedman visited Chile and recommended an economic "shock treatment" to combat inflation. In line with his advice, the military dictatorship instituted a rigorous economic austerity program, which included sharp government spending cuts, tax increases, and regular devaluations of the currency. Friedman, who acknowledged that the program would be hardest on the poorest section of Chile's population, was severely criticized in America for associating with the repressive regime.

In October 1976 the Swedish Royal Academy of Sciences named Friedman winner of the 1976 Nobel Prize in Economics for his achievements in the fields of consumption analysis, monetary history and theory, and his demonstration of the complexity of stabilization policy. The selection was controversial, with several former Nobel Prize winners publicly protesting the award to Friedman because of his association with the Chilean regime and 2,000 leftists demonstrating outside the Stockholm ceremony. Since 1977 Friedman has been with the Hoover Institution of Stanford University.

—TO

Fulbright, J(ames) William
(1905–1995) *member of the Senate; chairman, Foreign Relations Committee*

Born on April 9, 1905, the son of a wealthy businessman and banker, Fulbright was raised in Fayetteville, Arkansas, where his family moved in 1906. After graduating from the University of Arkansas in 1925, he studied at

Oxford University on a Rhodes scholarship. He returned to the United States and studied law at George Washington University. Admitted to the bar in 1934, Fulbright became an attorney for the Justice Department, then taught law at the University of Arkansas and served as president of the university from 1939 to 1941. As a Democrat he was elected to the House of Representatives in 1942 and two years later won a seat in the Senate.

In the Senate Fulbright generally supported liberal legislation in the areas of health, education, and welfare, but, reflecting the sentiments of the white majority in his state, he consistently opposed civil rights legislation. Throughout his career in Congress, Fulbright was concerned primarily with foreign affairs. In 1943 he introduced the "Fulbright Resolution," approved by the House, which favored the creation of an international organization to maintain world peace. Three years later he introduced the bill that set up the educational exchange program that bears his name. Becoming chairman of the Senate Foreign Relations Committee in 1959, he used his position to conduct highly publicized hearings to educate the American public on foreign affairs. Fulbright first voiced doubts about U.S. policy in Vietnam during the spring of 1965. He conducted televised hearings on the war in February 1966 and questioned the wisdom of continued escalation of the conflict. By the end of the decade he had become the symbol of congressional opposition to the Vietnam War and was credited with making criticism of the war respectable in Congress.

During the NIXON years Fulbright continued his criticism of U.S. foreign policy. His first major clash with the new administration came in March 1969 after Nixon requested congressional approval of funds for the Safeguard antiballistic missile system. In hearings conducted by the Foreign Relations Committee, Fulbright accused Secretary of Defense MELVIN LAIRD of using "the technique of fear"

to justify deployment of the ABM. Charging that Safeguard had little military value and was "purely a political gimmick," he deplored the decision to go ahead with its deployment before completing arms limitation talks with the Soviet Union. In June 1969 Fulbright signed a statement with other members of Congress urging a moratorium on the deployment of the Safeguard system. In August he voted in favor of the Cooper-Hart Amendment to a defense procurement bill to bar funds for the ABM. The amendment was defeated, however, and in November Congress finally approved the appropriation.

In 1970 Fulbright published *The Pentagon Propaganda Machine*, an expanded version of speeches he delivered in the Senate in December 1969. In it he accused the Defense Department of waging "a coordinated high-pressure propaganda and public relations campaign" to win approval of the ABM. The Pentagon was guilty of "subterfuge," he said, in its efforts to manipulate public opinion. Fulbright also warned that the "monster bureaucracy" at the Pentagon had become an active participant in making foreign policy, at the expense of both the State Department and Congress, and that militarism was "slowly undermining democratic procedure and values."

Fulbright led efforts to restore the constitutional balance between Congress and the executive in foreign affairs. In February 1969 he introduced a "national commitments" resolution that reasserted a congressional voice in decisions pledging the United States to the defense of foreign nations. The resolution, as approved by the Senate in June, stipulated that the use of troops abroad "results only from affirmative action by the legislative and executive branches" of the government. As a sense of the Senate resolution, however, it did not have binding power on the president, and later in the year Fulbright pushed for more forceful measures.

In December 1969 Congress voted to prohibit the commitment of U.S. ground troops to Laos and Thailand. The action came after Fulbright won acknowledgement from the administration of a secret "contingency plan" with Thailand and after reports surfaced of U.S. involvement in the Laotian civil war. Throughout 1969 and 1970 the Senate Foreign Relations Committee conducted an inquiry on U.S. military activities overseas. Highly critical of the extensive use of executive agreements in foreign affairs rather than treaties that required Senate approval, its final report, issued in December 1970, charged that "creeping commitments" threatened to trap the nation into global military responsibilities. In 1972 Fulbright supported legislation requiring the secretary of state to submit to Congress the text of any international agreement made by the executive branch.

After Nixon took office in 1969, Fulbright initially muted his criticism of the Vietnam War. He praised the eight-point peace plan that Nixon offered in May and applauded the president's announced intention gradually to withdraw all U.S. troops. By the autumn, however, Fulbright had resumed his criticism of the war. In October 1969, after nationwide protests against the war captured the attention of the public, he deplored Nixon's call for a moratorium on dissent and instead urged a "moratorium on killing." The next month Fulbright declared that Nixon had taken "fully as his own the Johnson war" by acting on the assumption that the war was a fight against an international communist conspiracy.

In a major speech in St. Louis in December, he attacked "Vietnamization" as another form of waging "a continuing war of stalemate and attrition" and warned that "every day this war goes on the sickness of American society worsens." In February and March 1970 Fulbright held extensive public hearings on the effectiveness of Nixon's Vietnamization policy. He expressed skepticism that the prospects for peace had improved, and a report by his committee's staff cast serious doubt on the chances of Vietnamization succeeding.

Fulbright attacked the president's decision to invade Cambodia and in June 1970 supported the Cooper-Church Amendment to cut off funds for combat operations in Cambodia. In 1971, after the United States provided support for a South Vietnamese invasion of Laos, Fulbright announced that he would hold "end the war" hearings to propose legislation to curb the president's war-making powers. He supported legislation aimed at that purpose that Senator JACOB JAVITS (R-N.Y.) introduced. As finally passed by Congress, the 1973 War Powers Act limited to 60 days the president's ability to commit U.S. troops to combat abroad without congressional approval.

Fulbright presented his most extreme attack on American foreign policy in his 1972 book *The Crippled Giant*. Surveying U.S. policy abroad since World War II, he charged that the nation's policymakers seemed "driven by a sense of imperial destiny." The exercise of power had become an end in itself, he charged, "purposeless and undisciplined" in its use. "History did not prepare the American people for the kind of role we are now playing in the world," he said. Fulbright warned that the unbridled resort to force in foreign affairs would cripple the United States, leaving a "moral wasteland." Already it was destroying the constitutional balance of power between Congress and the president, and unless it was stopped, the "ultimate casualty" would be democracy itself.

After HENRY KISSINGER became secretary of state in 1973, Fulbright's criticism of the Nixon administration's foreign policy lessened. Fulbright respected Kissinger's abilities and approved of his willingness to abandon cold war myths in the conduct of foreign affairs. He supported Kissinger's pursuit of détente with the Soviet Union and approved of the friendly initiatives toward mainland China. Kissinger's reassertion of a strong role for the Department of State in making foreign policy and his obvious preference for negotiation and diplomatic initiatives over the use of force was more in line with Fulbright's own thinking. The senator also praised Kissinger's even-handed approach to a Middle East peace settlement.

Fulbright's preoccupation with foreign affairs put him increasingly out of touch with the voters of his state. In 1974, in his bid for a sixth term in the Senate, he lost the Democratic primary to Governor Dale Bumpers. When Fulbright retired from the Senate he had amassed the longest tenure as chairman of the Foreign Relations Committee of any previous senator. He joined the Washington law firm of Hogan and Hartson, where he served until his death in 1995. In 1993 President Clinton awarded Fulbright the Presidential Medal of Freedom.

—JD

G

Gardner, John W(illiam)
(1912–2002) *chairman, National Urban Coalition; chairman, Common Cause*

John W. Gardner was born on October 8, 1912, in Los Angeles, California. Gardner earned his doctorate in psychology at Berkeley in 1938 and taught at Connecticut College for Women and Mount Holyoke. He began work at the Carnegie Corp. in 1946 and became its president in 1955. He served as secretary of health, education, and welfare under Lyndon Johnson from 1965 to 1968. Gardner left the administration in March 1968, contending that he could deal more effectively with solving urban problems from a position outside of government. To that end, he became chairman of the National Urban Coalition, a private association organized in 1967.

In the fall of 1970, Gardner formed Common Cause, an organization that soon became one of the most effective public interest groups. According to Gardner, the agenda of Common Cause was "how to get responsive government, government that you can hold to account, government to which the citizen has access."

Under Gardner's leadership Common Cause became active in many areas of public policy and government structure. It sought, among other goals, to depoliticize the Jus-

tice Department, end illegal covert police and intelligence activities, terminate the war in Vietnam, give high priority to solving problems of poverty, reform legislative machinery, halt construction of the B-1 bomber and supersonic transport, and establish a federal consumer protection agency.

Common Cause achieved much notoriety because of its early criticism of the NIXON administration. The organization filed the lawsuit that forced Nixon to disclose the contributors to his 1972 presidential campaign. In the aftermath of Watergate, Common Cause moved with considerable success to institute election reforms dealing with limits on campaign spending and public financing of presidential elections. It played a role in weakening the seniority system in the House and in deposing the chairmen of some congressional committees.

At the height of its influence in 1973, Common Cause had 320,000 members, most articulate and well educated. Its membership declined to 250,000 by 1977, however. By 1975 it had a staff of 80 Washington employees and 14 lobbyists.

Gardner was not without his critics. His name was included on Nixon's "enemies list." Representative WAYNE HAYS of Ohio referred to Common Cause as "common curse." Gardner stepped down as chairman in 1977 and was succeeded by Nan Waterman, a civic activist from Muscatine, Iowa. In 1978 he became the chair of the Commission on White House Fellowships. Following that service he returned to California, where he served as a trustee and professor at Stanford University until his death in 2002.

—HML

Garment, Leonard
(1924–) *special assistant to the president; acting legal counsel to the president*

Leonard Garment was born on May 11, 1924, in New York City. Originally a jazz saxophonist who played with such icons as Billie Holiday and Woody Herman, Garment received his law degree from Brooklyn Law School in 1949 and then joined the prestigious law firm of Mudge, Rose, Guthrie, and Alexander. A specialist in litigation, Garment befriended RICHARD NIXON when the former vice president joined the law firm in 1963. Frequently Nixon visited Garment's Brooklyn Heights home. Garment introduced Nixon to his New York friends; many of them were liberals and many were active in the arts. When Nixon decided to pursue the Republican nomination for the presidency, Garment, a liberal Democrat, joined his campaign staff. Garment headed the media division throughout the primary run and the fall campaign. Following election day Garment participated in the selection of the cabinet. Nixon asked Garment to join the administration as a White House adviser on minority problems.

On July 12, 1969, Nixon appointed Garment director of the National Goals Research Staff. Garment also dealt with a number of civil rights problems the administration confronted. Following a July 1970 NAACP attack on the administration for being antiblack, Gar-

ment wrote the White House response, which declared that "the president and the administration are committed to achieving equal opportunity for every American, and are determined to maintain their efforts to reach that goal." Garment further persuaded Nixon not to veto the Voting Rights Act of 1970, which promised to continue to protect the newly enrolled 1 million black voters in the South and added 18-year-olds to the voting rolls. Garment argued that Nixon could not afford to alienate the young and the minorities.

As the Watergate crisis grew more ominous, Nixon consulted Garment for advice. At Garment's urging the president fired H. R. HALDEMAN and JOHN EHRLICHMAN, his top advisers, who were implicated in the cover-up. Nixon asked Garment to replace JOHN DEAN, who also was fired, as the acting counsel for the president for Watergate matters. Garment's first responsibility was to assist speechwriter RAYMOND PRICE in composing a statement announcing the ousters. Garment then joined with the other White House lawyer, J. FRED BUZHARDT, to answer reporters' questions concerning the shakeup in the White House staff and Watergate.

At this press conference Garment quickly discovered that there were many gaps in the White House case. He thus requested access to presidential tapes and documents on the case so he could prepare a better defense for the president. Nixon refused to permit him to look at the material. Throughout the remainder of 1973 Garment found it difficult to function as the president's lawyer because he could not examine the material in question. He further feared that he might be implicated in obstructing justice as long as the president denied the special Watergate prosecutor access to the material.

On November 3, 1973, Garment and Buzhardt flew to Key Biscayne to confront their client on this issue. They outlined to

ALEXANDER HAIG, Nixon's chief aide, the legal problems the president faced, and they argued they could not defend him as long as he denied them the right to see the evidence. Both found Nixon's position so hopeless that they requested permission to see him to persuade him to resign. After seeing Nixon, Haig reported that the president would neither resign nor see them. Garment then quietly resigned his counsel position but remained on the White House staff.

President FORD appointed Garment U.S. representative to the United Nations Human Rights Commission in 1975. In a number of stormy sessions, Garment defended the Israeli treatment of the Arabs in the occupied territories. He also fought against passage of the "Zionism as racism" resolution. In 1977 Garment returned to practice full-time law in New York. In 1977 he published *Crazy Rythym*, a memoir; in 2000 he published *In Search of Deep Throat*, which named John Sears as the executive department informer during Watergate.

—JB

Geneen, Harold S(ydney)
(1910–1997) *chief executive officer, International Telephone and Telegraph Corporation*

Born on January 22, 1910, in England, Geneen spent much of his youth in a Connecticut boarding school, leaving at age 16 to become a page at the New York Stock Exchange. After acquiring a degree in accounting in 1934, he rose quickly through a succession of companies, including Bell & Howell and Jones & Laughlin Steel Corp., before winning his reputation of master manager as vice president of Raytheon Manufacturing, which he joined in 1956. Dividing the large electronics firm into 12 semiautonomous units, Geneen applied a system of strict financial control and constant monitoring of each division by top management.

Geneen brought the same management principles to International Telephone and Telegraph (ITT) when he assumed the presidency of the communications carrier in 1959. Through an aggressive program of mergers, acquisitions, and diversification, both in the United States and overseas, he succeeded in boosting ITT's sales to $8.5 billion annually by the early 1970s.

During the 1970s Geneen and ITT became embroiled in several scandals implicating high NIXON administration officials in possible conflict of interest and influence peddling. In 1970 the conglomerate purchased the Hartford Fire Insurance Co. as a consistent source of fresh revenue. The Department of Justice immediately filed an antitrust suit. The suit was about to be appealed to the Supreme Court when it was settled in 1971 by an out-of-court agreement that permitted ITT to keep the insurance company. However, the company was forced to divest itself of other holdings, including Avis Rent-a-Car and the Canteen Corp.

In February 1972 columnist JACK ANDERSON released a confidential memorandum allegedly written by ITT lobbyist DITA BEARD linking the antitrust settlement with an ITT pledge of $400,000 for the 1972 Republican National Convention, which was tentatively scheduled to be held in San Diego, where ITT owned hotel property. On March 17 Beard denied writing the Anderson memo and called it a "forgery" and a "hoax," but the Senate Judiciary Committee launched an immediate investigation into Anderson's charges. Geneen testified before the committee on March 29 and stated that the firm's contribution to the Republican Convention was conditional on establishment of convention headquarters for President Nixon at ITT's hotel in San Diego.

On March 20, 1972, Anderson charged that ITT had attempted to influence U.S. policy in Chile, a country where the conglomerate had six affiliates with over 7,000 employees. Anderson said his material revealed ITT efforts and "fervent hopes for a military coup" in Chile in 1970 to prevent the election of Marxist Salvador Allende as president.

In March 1973 a Senate Foreign Relations Committee special Subcommittee on Multinational Corporations began a two-year investigation of the influence of those firms on the U.S. economy and conduct of foreign policy. Testifying before the committee on March 21, John A. McCone, former director of the Central Intelligence Agency (CIA) and a director of ITT, stated that he had met with HENRY KISSINGER and CIA director RICHARD HELMS in mid-1970 to offer the U.S. government $1 million in financial aid on behalf of ITT. The money was to be used to block the runoff election of Allende as president. The funds had been authorized by Geneen, and according to McCone they were to be channeled to people who "support the principles and programs the U.S. stands for against the programs of the Allende Marxists." He denied charges that the money was intended for "surreptitious" purposes or would be used to create "economic chaos." Instead he maintained it was to be used to support conservative politicians and for housing and agricultural projects.

The plan was rejected, but Helms put Geneen into contact with William Broe, director of clandestine operations in Latin America for the CIA. Earlier testimony by ITT vice president William Merriam had revealed that Geneen had arranged to establish a working relationship between the corporation and the CIA to prevent Allende's election and failing that to bring about the "economic collapse" of Chile. When the results of the presidential election were still in doubt, Broe and ITT worked together to put economic pressure on the nation. On April 2 Geneen, testifying before the panel, admitted offering the government money. He justified the gesture as an "emotional reaction" of fear that the U.S. government would do nothing to prevent the Allende election. He reiterated McCone's testimony that the money was to be used for social projects.

The investigations by several government agencies into ITT's antitrust settlements with the Justice Department continued in 1973. The House Interstate and Foreign Commerce Committee's special Subcommittee on Investigations made public March 19 a confidential document prepared by the Securities and Exchange Commission (SEC) that revealed the extent and success of ITT's attempt to pressure the administration in the 1971 Hartford Fire Insurance Co. settlement. The document implicated seven present and former administration officials, including Vice President SPIRO AGNEW, presidential assistant JOHN D. EHRLICHMAN, and former attorney general JOHN MITCHELL.

On July 19, 1974, two volumes of evidence on the administration's handling of antitrust cases against ITT were released by the House Judiciary Committee. While no evidence appeared to substantiate allegations that President Nixon had personally ordered the Justice Department to drop its appeal before the Supreme Court of the Hartford antitrust case in 1971, the documents did reveal numerous meetings in the 1969–71 period between high administration officials and ITT executives. The executives waged an intense lobbying campaign to have the antitrust charges dropped. Although the case was filed for appeal with the High Court, the settlement was reached before arguments could be heard. Geneen retired as chief executive officer of ITT in 1977 and died in 1997.

—FHM

Gesell, Gerhard A(lden)
(1910–1993) *U.S. district court judge*

Gerhard A. Gesell was born on June 16, 1910, in Los Angeles, California. Gesell earned his law degree from Yale in 1935 and became counsel for the Securities and Exchange Commission.

He left the commission in 1941 and practiced law until 1967, when he was appointed judge in the U.S. district court for the District of Columbia by President Lyndon Johnson.

He established a reputation as a liberal with a pair of controversial rulings. The first came in November 1969, when Gesell ruled that a law that severely restricted abortions was unconstitutional. In another decision Gesell upheld charges of mismanagement and conspiracy against the United Mine Workers' pension fund and the union-owned National Bank of Washington. An out-of-court settlement, approved by Gesell, resulted in the payment of $53 million to 17,000 retired miners and miners' widows during the first year of a reorganized fund.

This liberal reputation was enhanced in June 1971, when Gesell refused a request from the Justice Department to block the printing of the *Pentagon Papers*, classified documents describing the U.S. entry into the Vietnam War that had been leaked initially to the *New York Times*. Gesell held that to prevent publication would constitute prior restraint and violate the First Amendment. Later in the year the *Pentagon Papers* issue again came before Gesell's court when two congressmen asked the judge to compel the government to release the entire 47-volume set of documents. This time, however, Gesell refused the request, noting that the bulk of the papers had already been released and saying "the government must have some degree of privacy."

In 1973 Watergate-related cases began to appear before Gesell. The cases would take up much of his time for the next year. The first Watergate case came before the judge when DONALD H. SEGRETTI entered a guilty plea to three misdemeanor charges involving "dirty tricks" during the 1972 Florida Democratic primary. Gesell sentenced Segretti to six months in jail and three years of probation. In November 1973 Gesell ruled that the firing of special Watergate prosecutor ARCHIBALD COX by President NIXON was illegal, holding that Justice Department regulations establishing the position had the force of law. The regulations stipulated the prosecutor could not be removed except "for extraordinary improprieties," a condition the judge said did not exist in the firing of Cox. A plaintiff in the suit, Representative BELLA ABZUG of New York, said Gesell's ruling established obstruction of justice by the president and could be used as grounds for impeachment.

All of Gesell's rulings did not go against the president, however. When the Senate Watergate committee subpoenaed five White House tapes in February 1974, the judge dismissed the suit, saying publicity surrounding release of the tapes could be harmful to criminal prosecutions.

Gesell heard the first case brought by the new special Watergate prosecutor, LEON JAWORSKI, in April 1974. DWIGHT L. CHAPIN, appointments secretary to the president, was convicted on two counts of perjury after covering up for Segretti. Gesell's sentencing, as it had been with Segretti, was light, giving Chapin 10 to 30 months in jail.

Gesell's most important case related to Watergate was as trial judge in the prosecution of six members of the White House Special Investigations Unit dubbed the "Plumbers." The six were charged with planning and executing a break-in at the office of DANIEL ELLSBERG's psychiatrist with the intention of finding damaging evidence against Ellsberg, the man who leaked the *Pentagon Papers*. Charged were EGIL KROGH, aide to presidential adviser JOHN D. EHRLICHMAN and head of the unit; CHARLES COLSON, special counsel to the president; Ehrlichman, White House liaison to the unit; and G. GORDON LIDDY, BERNARD L. BARKER, and Eugenio Martinez, the convicted Watergate burglars who carried out the break-in. Krogh pleaded guilty well before the trial and was separated from the case after agreeing to cooperate with the Watergate prosecutors.

In pretrial hearings the defense indicated it would use national security as justification for the break-in, but Gesell immediately quashed the argument, saying that the Fourth Amendment's protection of privacy was more fundamental in the case than any national security consideration. The White House then refused to produce documents subpoenaed by Ehrlichman and Colson, drawing the wrath of the judge. He told presidential counsel JAMES D. ST. CLAIR, "It is not up to the president which documents to produce." Gesell added that by withholding evidence "the president must know he is acting deliberately [in] aborting this trial," and raised the possibility that Nixon could be held in contempt of court. This eventuality was avoided when Gesell agreed to a White House plan whereby the judge privately examined the presidential documents to determine relevancy to the trial.

On the eve of the trial, Colson entered a guilty plea, leaving four defendants to face the court. After a week of testimony Gesell told the jury that "an individual cannot escape criminality because he sincerely, but incorrectly, believes his acts are justified in the name of patriotism." All of the defendants were found guilty of violating the civil rights of Lewis B. Fielding, Ellsberg's psychiatrist, and Ehrlichman was found guilty of three additional counts of making false statements. Ehrlichman received a stiff sentence of 20 months to five years, Liddy was given one to three years, and Barker and Martinez were placed on probation. Colson had previously been sentenced to one to three years and fined $5,000, and Krogh had been given a six-month sentence. Gesell remained on the bench until 1993, when he died of liver cancer.

—BO

Glenn, John H(erschel), Jr.

(1921–   ) *member of the Senate*

Born on July 18, 1921, the only son of a railroad conductor and proprietor of a heating and plumbing business, Glenn enlisted in the marines when the United States entered World War II. He remained on active duty through the Korean War and flew 90 missions in Korea. He earned the nickname "MiG-mad Marine" after he shot down three Communist MiGs over the Yalu River in the closing days of that war. After the war Glenn became a navy test pilot, and in 1957 he set a speed record in the first nonstop transcontinental supersonic flight. Two years later he was made a lieutenant colonel in the marines. Glenn was among the seven men who were chosen from 110 military test pilots to become the first American astronauts. On February 20, 1962, Glenn became the first American to orbit the Earth, circling the globe three times in under five hours.

Glenn resigned from the space program in January 1964 and announced his Democratic candidacy for the U.S. Senate seat from Ohio, challenging incumbent senator Stephen M. Young. But he was forced to withdraw from the race on March 30 after a severe injury suffered in a bathroom fall. In the fall of 1964 Glenn was named vice president of corporate planning for Royal Crown Cola Co.'s domestic operations. He also bought an interest in several Holiday Inn franchises across the country. Glenn hosted a series of television programs based on historical explorations called Great Explorations, which were aired on NBC in January 1968.

In the 1968 presidential primaries, Glenn strongly supported Robert Kennedy's campaign. Following the New York senator's assassination, Glenn was appointed chairman of the newly formed Emergency Committee for Gun Control, a coalition of groups formed to lobby for tough firearms control.

John Glenn *(Library of Congress)*

After Young announced his decision not to seek reelection in 1970, Glenn declared his candidacy for the Senate seat. He ran his primary campaign on a platform favoring wage and price controls, busing, and the withdrawal of U.S. troops from South Vietnam and Cambodia. Glenn lost the primary election to a Cleveland lawyer, Howard Metzenbaum, by over 13,000 votes. Metzenbaum outspent Glenn five to one during the campaign. Metzenbaum lost the general election to ROBERT A. TAFT JR. Stunned by his defeat, Glenn spent the next few years building a political base in his home state.

Glenn ran again for the Democratic senatorial nomination in 1974 against Metzenbaum, who had the support of Ohio governor JOHN GILLIGAN. A bitter campaign followed over the issue of Metzenbaum's use of tax shelters and an IRS suit against the millionaire for back taxes owed in 1969. Glenn suggested that Metzenbaum had used legal tax shelters to avoid paying taxes in 1969. He claimed that no one should use such shelters to avoid paying taxes, even if they were legal. During the campaign Glenn called for the return of integrity in government. He went on to beat Metzenbaum in the May primary by more than 94,000 votes. Glenn scored this victory despite the fact that he lacked the support of the state Democratic organization and the local labor leaders. He swept the general election in November with a landslide 64.6 percent of the vote, beating Ralph Perk, the Republican mayor of Cleveland, by 1 million votes.

In the Senate Glenn compiled a moderate record. On economic issues he recommended an end to deficit spending, strict enforcement of antitrust laws, and reform of the national tax system. He proposed a "countercyclical" aid program for providing federal funds to U.S. cities to enable them to maintain essential services without raising taxes during times of recession. He approved of the creation of a consumer protection agency. Always a strong advocate of education, Glenn criticized the inequity of funding education solely through property taxes. The Ohio senator also supported the right of teachers and other public employees to organize and bargain collectively. Glenn was a strong supporter of national health insurance legislation, and he favored increasing federal grants for basic medical research and the expanded use of paramedical personnel.

Glenn was a major spokesman for campaign and congressional reform. He especially favored public financing of political campaigns. Rather than advocating a system of full or nearly complete federal financing of campaigns out of tax revenues, he supported a program that would give incentives to the small donor. He proposed the creation of a statewide campaign finance office in each state and advocated shortening the length of campaigns. A proponent of congressional reform, he criticized what he termed "the disproportionate influence lobbyists wield over members of Congress." Glenn scorned the seniority system and spoke of opening up the deliberations of Congress to the public.

Glenn was an outspoken critic of the FORD administration's Project Independence, which was designed to make the United States self-sufficient in energy by 1980. He spoke out against the cost of the program and claimed that it would involve shifts of income from consumers to owners of energy-related assets. Glenn played a major role in helping formulate the Democratic response to the president's energy program. As a member of the Interior and Insular Affairs Committee, he criticized the Republican gasoline tax plan, claiming it would take money from the hands of consumers and increase the profits of energy producers, possibly by as much as $1 trillion, without guaranteeing that imports of foreign petroleum would decrease.

Glenn instead proposed a vague program of import quotas, admitting that despite intensive study of the question he did not possess a comprehensive plan. During congressional debate of the issue in the spring of 1975, his thought matured. He recommended increased production of natural gas and increased use of interstate pipelines to distribute fuel and proposed enforcing ceiling prices on "new" domestic oil developed after 1972 at the same level as that existing for foreign oil imports as of January 31, 1975. In April 1975 the Senate passed a bill cosponsored by Glenn that extended price controls on domestic oil until March 1, 1976, after which a federal-state energy consumption reduction plan was to be implemented. The bill gave the president emergency powers to ration gasoline, prohibit

oil imports, and allocate oil supplies subject to congressional veto within a 10-day period. Glenn's major contribution to the bill was the price ceiling on "new" oil produced after 1972, which had previously been uncontrolled. The bill's aim was to cut U.S. energy consumption by 4 percent annually through fuel conservation rules and guidelines drawn up by the Federal Energy Administration with the approval of Congress and administered by the states. The president signed the Energy Policy and Conservation Act in December.

Glenn delivered the keynote address to the Democratic National Convention in 1976. Before the meeting he was considered one of the top candidates for the vice presidential nomination. However, Glenn's uninspiring address and relative inexperience led the presidential nominee, JIMMY CARTER, to select Senator WALTER MONDALE (D-Minn.) as his running mate. During the first two years of the Carter administration, Glenn supported the Panama Canal treaties. In 1978 Glenn was the chief author of the Nonproliferation Act and from 1978 to 1995 served as the chairman of the Committee on Governmental Affairs. In 1998 Glenn flew as a payload specialist on the space shuttle *Discovery*. After retiring from the Senate in 1999, Glenn served on several national commissions.

—GMS

Goldberg, Arthur J(oseph)
(1908–1990) *political leader*

Born on August 8, 1908, the son of Russian Jewish immigrants, Goldberg was raised on Chicago's West Side. After working his way through college and law school, he established a private practice and occasionally served as counsel for trade unions in Chicago. Appointed general counsel in 1948 for both the United Steelworkers of America and the Congress of

Industrial Organizations, he played a major role in the merger of the CIO with the American Federation of Labor in 1955 and thereafter served as its special counsel.

Picked as secretary of labor by President Kennedy at the start of his administration, Goldberg adopted a "public interest" activist posture, frequently intervening in labor disputes to achieve a settlement. Elevated by Kennedy to the Supreme Court in October 1962, Goldberg took advanced positions on civil liberties issues. In a 1963 opinion he first raised questions about the constitutionality of the death penalty and the following year wrote the majority opinion in the landmark *Escobedo v. Illinois* case, which protected the rights of suspects under police custody. In July 1965 Goldberg stepped down from the Court to become ambassador to the United Nations. Although told by President Johnson that he would play a major part in shaping foreign policy and in ending the Vietnam War, Goldberg in fact was excluded from high-echelon decision-making meetings regarding the war and found his efforts to start negotiations only weakly supported. He did, however, play an important role in the March 1968 reassessment of American policy, arguing strongly for a complete halt to the bombing. Resigning from his post in April 1968, Goldberg took an active part in Hubert Humphrey's presidential campaign.

During the first years of the NIXON administration, Goldberg remained active in public affairs, generally taking a critical stance toward the president's foreign and domestic policies. He urged the president to push for ratification of the nuclear nonproliferation treaty and came out in favor of recognition of Communist China. In April 1969 Goldberg formed a national citizens' committee to marshal opposition to Nixon's proposal to continue funding development and deployment of an antiballistic missile system. Remaining a strong propo-

nent of civil rights and civil liberties, he joined with NAACP executive director ROY WILKINS in December 1969 in forming a citizens' panel to conduct a "searching inquiry" into police clashes with the Black Panther Party. In March 1970 Goldberg denounced as unconstitutional the contempt convictions of the Chicago Seven and their lawyers, and later that year he attacked Nixon's preventive detention bill for the District of Columbia as an infringement of the rights of the accused.

Goldberg became more outspoken in his criticism of the Vietnam War during Nixon's tenure in the White House. At an October 1969 moratorium rally in the nation's capital he called for a "straightforward" statement from Nixon that he accepted the principle of "a prompt withdrawal of all American forces" from Southeast Asia. The following month, when Vice President SPIRO AGNEW assailed the major television networks for their coverage of antiwar protests, Goldberg deplored his comments as "inflammatory." In 1970 he played a key role in organizing lawyers around the country to lobby against the war.

Despite earlier disclaimers, Goldberg announced his candidacy on March 19, 1970, for the Democratic nomination in the New York state gubernatorial race. Receiving the official endorsement of state party leaders, Goldberg faced a challenge in the primary from industrialist Howard J. Samuels but defeated Samuels by a narrow margin. His opponent was three-term governor NELSON ROCKEFELLER, and Goldberg took the position that the New York race was "nothing less than a referendum on the Nixon-Agnew administration." He campaigned on a standard liberal platform, urging a continuation and expansion of existing social welfare programs to solve urban problems, and spoke out strongly against Rockefeller's increasingly tough law-and-order stance. Although he received the endorsement of New York City mayor JOHN LINDSAY, who praised Goldberg for resisting the "ominous political trend to the right," Goldberg's lackluster campaign style failed to arouse the voters. Rockefeller, moreover, won the support of normally Democratic white ethnic voters who were angered by Goldberg's opposition to the war and who were reacting against the rising tide of urban disorders and student protests. Outspending Goldberg by over $800,000, Rockefeller defeated him by more than 500,000 votes in the November election.

After his electoral defeat, Goldberg returned to the practice of law and continued to speak out occasionally on public issues. In 1974, during the Senate confirmation hearings on Rockefeller's nomination to the vice presidency, it was revealed that the millionaire politician had financed a derogatory biography of Goldberg during their gubernatorial race. In 1977 President JIMMY CARTER chose Goldberg to be U.S. ambassador to the Belgrade Conference on Human Rights. Carter awarded Goldberg the Presidential Medal of Freedom in 1978. Goldberg died of a heart attack in 1990.

—JD

Goldwater, Barry M(orse)
(1909–1998) *member of the Senate*

Barry M. Goldwater was born on January 1, 1909, in Phoenix, Arizona. Goldwater left the University of Arizona after one year to join the family department store, Goldwater, Inc., and he became the firm's president in 1937. He served as a noncombat flyer with the Army Transport Command in the Far East during World War II. Goldwater became active in Republican politics and helped build the party in Arizona during the 1950s, when the state was almost completely dominated by the Democrats. He was elected to the Phoenix city council in 1949. Goldwater won election to

the U.S. Senate in 1952, where he established a conservative record. During the 1950s and 1960s he became the party's most effective fundraiser and spokesman of its conservative wing. Goldwater captured the 1964 Republican presidential nomination, beating the disorganized opposition to his candidacy. He ran on a conservative platform that alienated many of the moderates in the party. In November he lost the election to Lyndon B. Johnson in a landslide. Goldwater, who gave up his Senate seat to run for president, surrendered his party leadership position after the election and spoke out only occasionally on political issues. In 1968 he was reelected to the Senate.

As a conservative who wanted to stop federal programs, Goldwater staunchly supported the NIXON-FORD administrations' efforts to limit federal spending for social welfare measures. He opposed allowing striking workers to get food stamps; establishing federal standards for a uniform national no-fault auto insurance system; using federal funds for abortions; and creating a federal consumer protection agency. As a staunch anticommunist he consistently supported defense spending and voted for every major controversial weapons system advocated by the administration. These included the Safeguard antiballistic missile system, the Trident submarine, and the B-1 bomber.

Goldwater was one of the Senate's strongest advocates of America's Vietnam involvement. In 1972, for example, he attacked critics of the renewed bombing offensive against North Vietnam begun by Nixon after the Communists had started an offensive in the South. When raids against the port of Haiphong raised fears about Soviet involvement if Russian ships were hit, Goldwater said the raids were better than the "dilly-dally" bombing of supply lines that had gone on before.

Goldwater opposed all congressional efforts to legislate an end to the war. These included the 1970 Cooper-Church Amendment to limit the president's authority to conduct military operations in Cambodia and the 1973 amendment by Senator THOMAS F. EAGLETON (D-Mo.) to halt American combat operations in Laos and Cambodia. At the same time, Goldwater supported the Nixon administration's attempts to end the war through negotiations. When a peace treaty was concluded in 1973, Goldwater warned the Saigon government not to be an obstacle to the peace agreement the United States had signed. Goldwater was one of the strongest congressional supporters of the Saigon government. He continued to support military aid for South Vietnam after the peace treaty was signed. When the Senate Armed Services Committee debated the Ford administration's request for additional military aid in April 1975, two weeks before the Communists captured Saigon, Goldwater favored sending at least an additional $101 million. The committee rejected both this proposal and a $70 million proposal, which Goldwater opposed as inadequate.

While an advocate of a strong defense posture, Goldwater was one of the leading congressional opponents of the military draft. In 1970 he was one of 12 senators who introduced legislation to implement the recommendations of a presidential commission that studied the creation of an all-volunteer force. The commission, headed by former secretary of defense Thomas S. Gates, called for ending the draft when the draft law expired on June 30, 1971. As requested by the Nixon administration, Congress extended the draft until 1973, when an all-volunteer force was established.

In 1974 Goldwater played a key role in forcing Nixon's resignation after the release of transcripts of White House conversations that showed that Nixon had discussed using the Central Intelligence Agency (CIA) to head off the FBI's Watergate probe. Goldwater had consistently defended Nixon as the Watergate scandal unfolded during 1973 and 1974. At the

same time, however, he condemned the scandals and urged the president to reveal the full story. In April 1973 he warned that Watergate was hurting the Republican Party. In May 1973 he cosponsored a Senate resolution calling on Nixon to appoint a Watergate special prosecutor. But he initially opposed suggestions made by Republicans that Nixon resign. In March 1974, when Senator JAMES L. BUCKLEY (R-N.Y.) urged resignation, Goldwater opposed it. He defended Nixon, saying resignation would involve questions of fair play and precedent "whereby any man in the White House who was unacceptable to certain politicians and segments of the media might be forced to resign." But he also said, "If any evidence of criminal acts on the part of the president is proven, I shall change my position and support the Buckley proposal."

The August release of the incriminating tapes furnished the proof Goldwater demanded, and he ended his opposition to resignation. On August 7 Goldwater, Senate minority leader HUGH SCOTT (R-Pa.), and House minority leader JOHN J. RHODES (R-Ariz.) met with Nixon to discuss the political situation in Congress. The meeting occurred the day after the Senate Republican Policy Committee had reached a consensus that the president should be told of his erosion of support in the Senate. Goldwater and Scott told the president that he had less than 15 supporters left in the Senate, far fewer than the number he needed to avoid conviction. After the meeting Goldwater said the group had not made any suggestions to the president about what he should do. But when Goldwater, who had been opposing resignation, agreed that the situation looked "damn gloomy," other words were unnecessary. Nixon announced his resignation the next day.

After Ford became president, Goldwater supported NELSON A. ROCKEFELLER's nomination as vice president. He also noted, however, that

Rockefeller would not be acceptable to "rank and file" Republicans in 1976 and pointed out that Rockefeller was not the one to put the party back together again. Goldwater, however, was one of seven who eventually voted against the nomination in the Senate after congressional hearings disclosed Rockefeller's financial dealings with political figures. Goldwater did not object to Rockefeller's millions but questioned "whether or not he's used these millions of dollars to buy power. I think that's wrong."

In 1976 Goldwater backed Ford for the Republican presidential nomination, declining to support the conservative RONALD REAGAN. Goldwater strongly opposed the Carter administration's efforts to normalize relations with mainland China, which also ended U.S. diplomatic relations with the Nationalist government on Taiwan. During the Reagan years Goldwater developed libertarian views that put him in opposition to much of administration policy. Goldwater retired in 1987 and died in 1998 of complications of Alzheimer's disease.

—AE

Goodell, Charles E(llsworth), (Jr.)
(1926–1987) *member of the Senate*

Born on March 16, 1926, the son of a Jamestown, New York, physician, Goodell served in the naval reserve during World War II. He received his B.A. degree from Williams College in 1948 and his law degree from Yale three years later. Goodell remained at Yale to receive his master's degree in political science in 1952. Following a short stay at Jamestown, where he practiced law, Goodell moved to Washington to serve from 1954 to 1955 as a congressional liaison assistant with the U.S. Department of Justice. He returned to his home in 1955 to become a partner in a local Jamestown law firm.

Active in local Republican politics, Goodell won election to the U.S. House in 1959. During the Kennedy and Johnson years he compiled a record as a moderate Republican. He was a leader of the "Young Turks" who replaced the conservative party leadership with moderates headed by GERALD FORD.

In September 1968 governor NELSON ROCKEFELLER appointed Goodell to complete the Senate term of the late Robert F. Kennedy (D-N.Y.). Goodell's short, stormy term in the Senate from 1968 to 1970 became controversial as New Yorkers observed their senator trying to emulate Kennedy's brand of politics. Conservative critics of Goodell defended his political move to the left by pointing out that he had supported liberal legislation in the past.

Charles Goodell thus became for Nixon one of the least reliable Republican senators the president could count on in key votes. Goodell opposed the G. HARROLD CARSWELL and CLEMENT HAYNSWORTH Supreme Court nominations, voted against the antiballistic missile system, and became the leading and most visible Republican critic of the Vietnam War. In late September 1969 Goodell introduced one of the Senate's earliest end-the-war resolutions, calling on the president to withdraw all troops from Vietnam by December 1970. He then began an extensive tour of colleges, criticizing the administration's war policy. Goodell opposed the American invasion of Cambodia in 1970 and spoke at numerous rallies against the action. He enthusiastically voted for the Cooper-Church Amendment aimed at ending the war.

Goodell's antiwar activities incensed the powerful conservative faction of New York's Republican Party. A "dump Goodell" movement was organized to bar him from obtaining the party's senatorial nomination in 1970, but Governor Rockefeller's powerful control of the organization prevented Goodell from being denied a chance to run for a full term.

Disgruntled Republicans thus flocked to support the state's Conservative Party candidate, JAMES BUCKLEY, who pledged to vote with the Republicans if elected to the Senate. Goodell, who made no such pledge, thus found himself in a three-way race. The Democrats nominated Representative Richard Ottinger (D-N.Y.), who questioned Goodell's commitment to liberalism by citing his often conservative votes in the House.

Vice President SPIRO AGNEW also campaigned against Goodell. In a speech in San Diego on September 11, Agnew said, in reference to Goodell, "In my view, this fall, any candidate of any party who voices radical sentiments or who courts and enjoys the support of radical elements ought to be voted out of office by the American people." On September 30, in South Dakota, Agnew called Goodell a "radical liberal" who "has left his party." The following day, in Salt Lake City, Agnew stated that Goodell "has strayed beyond the point of no return." Goodell defended himself by accusing Agnew of using "inflammatory and divisive rhetoric." "What is involved," said Goodell, "is the right of people to differ with official policies, and to do so with power and effectiveness." Goodell charged that the vice president's "rhetoric suggests that people who question the administration's views are somehow dangerous and irresponsible, have no place in public life, and should be discredited in the public eye."

In response to Agnew's attempt to purge the party of one of its leading liberals, moderate and even some conservative Republican senators came to Goodell's defense. In New York liberals feared the Goodell candidacy would siphon from Ottinger enough votes to guarantee a Buckley victory. They failed in their attempt to persuade Goodell to withdraw from the race. The liberals' fears proved correct as Buckley garnered 39 percent of the vote to Ottinger's 37 percent. Goodell's 24 percent, a large percentage of it liberal, would have easily gone to Ottinger. Following this defeat Goodell resumed his private law practice in Washington, D.C., where he died in 1987. Goodell also chaired the Presidential Clemency Board for President Ford from 1975 to 1977.

—JB

Goodpaster, Andrew J(ackson)
(1915–2005) *supreme commander, allied forces (NATO), Europe*

Andrew Goodpaster was born on February 15, 1915, in Granite City, Illinois. Goodpaster graduated second in his class from West Point in 1939. During World War II he saw combat in North Africa and Europe. Detailed to Princeton University after the war for graduate study in engineering and international relations, Goodpaster took an M.S.E. in 1948 and a Ph.D. in political science in 1950. From 1950 to 1954 Goodpaster served with the newly formed North Atlantic Treaty Organization (NATO). In Paris Goodpaster worked to organize the alliance's military arm and develop political aims.

Goodpaster served as White House staff secretary from 1954 to 1961. During the Johnson administration General Goodpaster held a series of high-level positions at the Pentagon and was often consulted by the president. He was a member of the U.S. delegation to the Paris peace negotiations from May to July 1968, when he became deputy to general CREIGHTON W. ABRAMS, commander of the U.S. forces in Vietnam. Goodpaster was made a full general at the time.

At the request of President-elect RICHARD NIXON, Johnson called Goodpaster to Washington in December 1968. He remained there throughout the presidential transition period, serving as chief military adviser to Nixon. At a time when the new administration was formulating its policy on Vietnam, Goodpaster reportedly informed Nixon that a continued display of patience and determination was necessary for America to bring about an acceptable end to its role in the conflict. Reflecting the thinking of top military leaders, he counseled against the United States settling for anything less than the maintenance of South Vietnam. Goodpaster argued that a disadvantageous outcome in that country would precipitate political troubles in particular in other Asian countries, but also in other parts of the world that were of interest to the United States.

In March 1969 Goodpaster became supreme allied commander of NATO forces in Europe. He arrived in Europe at a time of growing concern over NATO. The renewed interest resulted primarily from the Soviet invasion of Czechoslovakia in 1968. During the mid-1960s the support of European governments for the alliance had declined. American attention meanwhile had been focused on Vietnam. There was also the feeling in European capitals that they had not been consulted by previous administrations. Because of the failure of some European governments to contribute their quotas, Goodpaster found the forces he had helped Eisenhower organize 20 years earlier suffering from chronic troop shortages. This led to fears that NATO would be forced to rely on nuclear weapons. Goodpaster let it be known that he believed in a policy of flexible response that was not dependent on nuclear weapons alone.

Goodpaster worked to improve the communication between Washington and its European allies. In October, three months after taking command, he told an annual meeting of the North Atlantic Assembly, composed of parliamentarians from the 15 NATO countries, that the alliance "must pay the more modest costs for peace" to avoid the larger costs of war. He listed steps necessary for maintaining NATO's ability to deter a Soviet attack in Europe and the Mediterranean area. These included increasing and improving troop and war stock levels and the expansion of reinforcement capabilities.

As supreme allied commander, Goodpaster warned repeatedly against NATO troop reductions, particularly by the United States. Goodpaster asserted that the Soviet Union's armed forces constituted a concentration of military power beyond anything the world had previously seen. Congressional efforts to cut forces were rejected during the period.

The military lessons and experiences of the 1973 Arab-Israeli War brought on a reevaluation of NATO's forces and their tactics and strategy. Goodpaster began the modernization of NATO forces that resulted from the West's study of Soviet weapons systems in action during the Yom Kippur War. Improved tactical nuclear artillery weapons, electronic warfare, night fighting capability, and antitank warfare received specific attention.

By 1974 the United States was developing miniature nuclear warheads to replace the larger warheads spread across Europe. Nevertheless, Goodpaster maintained that as the United States and the USSR reached nuclear parity, a strong conventional capability was as important a deterrent as a nuclear capability.

President FORD named General ALEXANDER M. HAIG to succeed Goodpaster at NATO in October 1974. Goodpaster retired from the army and became a senior fellow in security and strategic studies at the Woodrow Wilson International Center for Scholars. In retirement he was a founder of the Committee on the Present Danger. The committee was organized to publicize the belief that the Soviet Union's military threat was underestimated and that the United States needed to maintain a strong defense. In 1977 President JIMMY CARTER called Goodpaster out of retirement to become commandant of West Point, where he served until 1981. Until his death from cancer in 2005, Goodpaster was a senior fellow at the Eisenhower Institute.

—SF

Gore, Albert A(rnold)
(1907–1998) *member of the Senate*

Born on December 26, 1907, Gore, the son of a Tennessee dirt farmer, earned his law degree from the Nashville YMCA Night School, where he studied while serving as a county school superintendent. A Democrat and staunch New Deal supporter, Gore was elected to the House in 1938. He won a seat in the Senate in 1952. In the Senate Gore matched the liberalism of his fellow Tennessean Senator Estes Kefauver. He was a leading supporter of tax reform and backed the bulk of President Johnson's Great Society legislation. He had a mixed record on civil rights.

Gore generally opposed the NIXON administration's legislative programs. He was one of the few senators from the South who opposed the Supreme Court nominations of conservative judges CLEMENT F. HAYNSWORTH in 1969 and G. HARROLD CARSWELL in 1970. In 1970 he voted against the administration's controversial anticrime bill that authorized "no-knock" search warrants.

Gore continued his battle for tax reform into the Nixon administration. He consistently waged battles in the Senate Finance Committee and on the Senate floor to close tax loopholes that benefited corporations and wealthy individuals and led the fight to decrease the oil depletion allowance. Gore pushed the effort to raise the personal income tax exemption when the Senate Finance Committee was considering the House-passed Tax Reform Act of 1969. Describing the $600 personal exemption as the unfairest part of the entire tax law, Gore wanted to increase it to $1,250, a move that was opposed as prohibitively expensive even by fellow tax reformers such as senator EDWARD M. KENNEDY (D-Mass.). When the Finance Committee defeated Gore's proposal to raise the exemption to $725, he took the issue to the Senate floor and led the fight to raise the

exemption to $800, a proposal that would have cut individual taxes by about $2.2 billion per year. He won despite President Nixon's threat to veto the bill if it included the $800 exemption. As enacted, the law raised the personal exemption to $750 over a three-year period.

Gore was one of the leading Senate opponents of the Safeguard antiballistic missile system, which the White House proposed as an alternative to the more extensive system advocated by the Johnson administration. His Disarmament Subcommittee of the Foreign Relations Committee held numerous hearings on the issue during 1969 and 1970. At the hearings Gore routed the administration's claims that the system was needed to protect U.S. deterrent forces from a first-strike attack by the Soviet Union. He pointed out that the proposal to build two missile sites would protect only about 10 percent of the total U.S. deterrent forces. He asserted that the Safeguard deployment would "endanger our security" and "make an arms limitation agreement more difficult, if not impossible, to attain." Gore's subcommittee produced a mass of academic and scientific testimony opposing the deployment of the ABM system on technical and practical grounds. Congress, however, agreed to build the system in 1969, but six years later voted to dismantle it after having spent $6 billion on the project.

Gore, an early and consistent critic of the Johnson administration's Vietnam policy, was also an outspoken opponent of the Nixon administration's Vietnamization program. When Nixon announced the initial withdrawal of 25,000 American troops as part of the Vietnamization program, Gore objected to the "piecemeal withdrawal" as a plan for "prolonging the war." In February 1970 he warned about increasing U.S. involvement in Laos and accused the administration of misleading the American people about the situation. He said the White House was refusing to release congressional testimony on U.S. involvement in

Laos because it would reveal that the activities violated the 1962 Geneva Accords on Laos. He consistently supported efforts to legislate an end to the war.

Gore became the administration's number one target during the 1970 election campaign. His criticism of Nixon's Vietnam policy and his votes against the two southern Supreme Court nominees had undermined his political popularity at home. President Nixon persuaded Representative William E. Brock III (R-Tenn.), a four-term House member, to challenge Gore's bid for reelection. President Nixon and Vice President SPIRO T. AGNEW both campaigned against Gore in Tennessee and strongly attacked his stand on the Supreme Court nominations and his liberalism. Brock attempted to exploit racial prejudices in a well-financed media campaign that attacked Gore for being a traitor to the South, for supporting school busing, and for opposing prayer amendments to the U.S. Constitution. Gore fought back by attacking Brock's votes against Medicare and the Appalachia poverty program and by pointing to his own efforts to win tax reforms and increased Social Security benefits. Gore's campaign fell short, however, and he lost the Senate race by 42,000 votes.

After his defeat Gore left public life. He became a law instructor at Vanderbilt University from 1970 to 1972 and was named chairman of the board of the Island Creek Coal Co., the nation's third-largest coal producer. He lived in Carthage, Tennessee, until his death in 1998.

—AE

Graham, Billy (William Franklin)
(1918–   ) *evangelist*

A descendant of pre-Revolutionary Scottish pioneers, Graham was born on November 7, 1918, and raised on his family's prosperous dairy farm near Charlotte. He experienced a religious conversion at age 16 and made his "decision for Christ." After attending Florida Bible Institute and fundamentalist Wheaton College, Graham became active as a preacher on the so-called sawdust trail. A sensationally successful crusade in Los Angeles in 1949 brought him notice in the press, especially in the Hearst papers, and Graham rapidly rose to preeminence as an evangelist.

Over the next 20 years Graham conducted crusades throughout the world, addressing more than 60 million people. Through the careful use of radio, television, and film and through magazines and syndicated newspaper columns, he became perhaps the most widely known evangelist in the world. With his fundamentalist fervor and charismatic style, Graham preached a message of repentance and faith in Christ. Often named in polls as one of the most admired men in America, Graham found himself invited to the White House by every president from Truman through Johnson. Although he claimed to avoid mixing politics and religion, Graham's rousing sermons frequently contained a strong measure of patriotic zeal.

Graham had an especially close relationship with President NIXON. In January 1969 he gave the first of a series of White House religious services, and at Nixon's second inauguration in 1973 Graham was invited to deliver a short prayer. During Nixon's first term in office, as protests and demonstrations against the administration's Vietnam war policy rose in size and frequency, the two men often appeared in public together, and Graham had Nixon address the friendly and enthusiastically patriotic audiences that gathered to hear the evangelist.

In May 1970 Graham invited the president to a rally of 88,000 in Knoxville, and in October of the following year Nixon addressed a well-attended tribute to Graham in Charlotte. At a Fourth of July 1970 Honor America Day

Rally in Washington, D.C., organized by the president's supporters, Graham gave the keynote address. Telling the participants that there was "too much discouragement, despair, and negativism in the nation," he said that Americans "deserve to wave the flag a bit."

Graham remained loyal to Nixon through much of the revelations surrounding Watergate, and as late as December 1973 he publicly expressed his "confidence in the president's integrity." After reading the transcripts of White House tapes in May 1974, however, Graham called it "a profoundly disturbing and disappointing experience." When Nixon finally resigned from office, Graham urged Americans to pray for him.

In 1975 the Billy Graham Evangelical Association, with a yearly income in excess of $28 million, lost its status as a charitable gift fund in the state of Minnesota for failure to submit financial reports. Two years later the *Charlotte Observer* reported that the association had amassed a $23 million secret fund under another corporate name. Graham quickly issued a six-page defense in *Christianity Today* in which he denied any wrongdoing and said that the fund had "some of America's most reputable businessmen in control."

—JD

Graham, Katharine (Meyer)
(1917–2001) *president, Washington Post Company; publisher, the* Washington Post*; chairman of the board, Washington Post Company*

Born on July 16, 1917, Katharine Meyer was the daughter of an investment banker and philanthropist. In 1935, two years after her father, Eugene, purchased the *Washington Post*, Katharine Meyer graduated from the Madeira School in Greenway, Virginia, where she worked on the student newspaper. After graduation from the University of Chicago

in 1938 she worked as a reporter for the *San Francisco News*.

In 1939 her father asked her to join the *Washington Post*. She became part of the editorial staff of the *Post*, and from 1939 to 1945 she worked in the circulation and editorial departments of the Sunday edition. In June 1940 she married Philip L. Graham, a brilliant Harvard Law School graduate and a law clerk for Felix Frankfurter. In 1946 Graham became publisher of the *Post*. Two years later Eugene Meyer sold all the voting stock of the company to the Grahams for a dollar. Like many women of her generation, Katharine Graham spent the 1950s raising children and entertaining friends in her stylish Georgetown home. In 1963 the Grahams' domestic tranquillity was shattered when Philip Graham killed himself.

In September 1963 Katharine Graham assumed her husband's position as president of the *Washington Post*. In 1961 Philip Graham had purchased *Newsweek* and held a 50 percent interest in the *Los Angeles Times* with a news service wire. The Post Company also held several radio and television stations in Washington, Miami, Jacksonville, Cincinnati, and Hartford. Newspeople considered Katharine Graham's most important decision to be her hiring of BENJAMIN C. BRADLEE, the Washington bureau chief for *Newsweek*, as the managing editor for the *Post*. Under Bradlee's direction the *Washington Post* soon became one of the best daily papers in the country.

Virtually from the beginning the liberal *Washington Post* was critical of the NIXON administration. For instance, a 1968 editorial compared the nomination of SPIRO AGNEW as Republican vice president with Roman emperor Caligula's appointment of his horse as proconsul. The editorial fueled Agnew's attack on the news media in general and on the *Washington Post* in particular as being part of the "liberal establishment" out to get the

Nixon administration. In 1971 the *Washington Post* with the *New York Times* was sued by the Nixon administration for publishing the *Pentagon Papers*, a study of U.S. military involvement in Vietnam during the Johnson years. In June 1971 the Supreme Court upheld the newspapers' right to publish the study.

In October 1972 two young *Washington Post* reporters, CARL BERNSTEIN and ROBERT WOODWARD, broke the story of the DONALD SEGRETTI "dirty tricks" operation during the 1972 presidential campaign. When the Nixon White House not only denied the story but also attacked the reporters and the *Post*, Katharine Graham stood behind her staff. Although both Richard Nixon and JOHN MITCHELL threatened the paper with antitrust suits if it persisted in its Watergate coverage, Katharine Graham supported the probe and insisted only that the reporters verify their information and print the truth.

In February 1973 Graham, Bernstein, and Woodward from the *Post* and reporters from the *Washington Star News*, the *New York Times*, and *Time* magazine were issued subpoenas in a civil suit brought by the Committee for the Reelection of the President (CREEP) and were ordered to surrender "all notes, tapes, and story drafts in their possession regarding Watergate." They refused to comply, and Katharine Graham declared that she would go to jail as the paper's representative before she allowed the freedom of the press to be threatened in that way. The judge agreed with the press's position and disallowed CREEP's subpoenas of Graham and her staff. Although she conceded the important role the press and the *Post* played initially in raising public awareness about the deeds of the Nixon White House and of CREEP, Graham insisted that "in the long run it was minor compared to that of the courts, the grand juries, the Judiciary Committee, and the American people."

Graham announced her plans to retire as publisher of the *Post* in January 1979. In 1998 she won a Pulitzer Prize for her memoir *Personal History*. She died in July 2001 after falling on a sidewalk while attending a conference in Idaho.

—SJT

Grasso, Ella T(ambussi)
(1919–1981)   *governor of Connecticut*

The daughter of Italian immigrants, Ella Tambussi was born on May 10, 1919, and raised in the small town of Windsor Locks, Connecticut, where her father was a baker. Encouraged by her mother to pursue her education, she attended Mount Holyoke College, receiving her B.A. with honors in 1940 and an M.A. in economics in 1942. She worked for the War Manpower Commission during World War II and became a member of the League of Women Voters, which aroused an interest in politics. Joining the Democratic Party, Grasso, who married a school principal in 1942, became the protégé of the powerful state party chairman, John Bailey. She worked hard for the party machine and in 1952 was elected to the state assembly, where she served two terms and became assistant assembly leader. Elected secretary of state in 1958, she retained that position for 12 years and turned her office into a "people's lobby" where ordinary citizens could air their complaints.

On the national level Grasso was a member of the Democratic Party's platform committee in 1960 and cochaired the resolutions committee at the party's national conventions in 1964 and 1968. At the latter convention she played a major role in the composition of a minority report that opposed continued U.S. involvement in Vietnam. Grasso was one of the delegates who walked out of the convention as a protest against the provocative tactics of the Chicago police toward antiwar demonstrators. In 1970 Grasso ran for the U.S. House in the district represented by Republican Thomas Meskill, who was running for governor, and won a narrow victory. In 1972 she was reelected by a substantial margin.

Assigned to the Education and Labor Committee, Grasso supported most social welfare legislation and was a strong advocate of increased federal spending to reduce unemployment. She was among the most active proponents of the Emergency Employment Act of 1971 and also supported a 1971 emergency aid to education bill, an increase in the minimum wage to $2 an hour, and extension of coverage under the law to an additional 6 million workers. Though she supported congressional efforts to limit the president's war-making powers, Grasso displeased antiwar activists by her support of military appropriations bills, a position attributed to Connecticut's heavy dependence on defense industries. A practicing Catholic, Grasso received a poor rating from the feminist Women's Lobby because of her unequivocal opposition to abortion and her failure to support child-care legislation.

A 1973 poll by the *Hartford Times* indicated that Grasso was by far the most popular choice among voters to succeed Thomas Meskill as governor. In January 1974 she announced her candidacy, and in July the state nominating convention chose her by acclamation. Running against a House colleague, Robert H. Steele, Grasso won the election handily, thereby becoming the first woman in the nation's history to win a governorship in her own right. She was also the first person of Italian descent to be elected governor of Connecticut.

Grasso's first two years in office were difficult ones as Connecticut was particularly hard hit by the nationwide recession. Unemployment in the state was over 10 percent, and in April 1975 Connecticut was forced to borrow $106 million from the federal government to pay unemployment benefits, having exhausted its own fund the previous month. With a projected deficit of $90 million, the state also saw its credit ratings downgraded by Standard and Poor's Corp.

In February Grasso presented the state legislature with an austerity budget that called for higher taxes, a wage freeze for state employees, a lengthening of the workweek for government employees to 40 hours, and the transfer of veterans' pension funds to the general budget. Her proposals aroused widespread opposition, and state civil unions threatened to strike if the measures were enacted. Although the legislature raised the sales tax to 7 percent, making it the highest in the nation, they balked at the other measures. Grasso convened a special session of the legislature in the autumn, but when she failed again to win approval of her austerity measures, she announced the layoffs of several hundred state employees. The following year, with economic conditions still poor, she won a compromise extension of the workweek to 37½ hours.

Taking office in the post-Watergate era, Grasso attempted to make government more responsive to the people. She bypassed normal patronage routes in making appointments to office. In 1975 she won passage of a state Freedom of Information Act. The law ensured public access to government meetings and to the records of state agencies. Grasso also held public hearings throughout the state on her budget proposals and opened her office for a number of hours each week to hear the complaints of ordinary citizens.

Longtime state party chairman John Bailey's death in April 1975 created disarray among Connecticut Democrats. In 1976 Grasso attempted to oust Bailey's successor, assembly majority leader William A. O'Neill. Her failure to do so, coupled with the unpopularity of her two austerity budgets, raised speculation that she might not win renomination to a second term. Further opposition to Grasso came from feminist leaders in the state who were dismayed by her failure to appoint more women to state office and by her strong stand against public funding of abortions. When the U.S. Supreme Court ruled on June 20, 1977, that states were not constitutionally required to pay for abortions for poor women, Grasso immediately ordered a halt to state funding.

In January 1978 Lieutenant Governor Robert Killian announced that he would challenge Grasso for the gubernatorial nomination. Improved economic conditions, however, had decreased dissatisfaction with Grasso. The governor won reelection in November. In December 1980 Grasso resigned due to ovarian cancer; she died five weeks later.

—JD

Gravel, Mike
(1930–) *member of the Senate*

Born on May 13, 1930, the son of French-Canadian immigrants, Gravel was a counterintelligence officer with the army in Europe from 1951 to 1954. After graduating from Columbia University in 1956 with a B.A. in economics, he moved to Alaska and went into real estate. Gravel won election to the Alaska house of representatives in 1962 and became Speaker of the house in 1965. Three years later he defeated incumbent senator Ernest Gruening in the Democratic primary and went on to win the election.

In the Senate Gravel generally aligned with liberal Democrats, supporting most social welfare legislation and opposing President NIXON's impounding of funds for domestic programs. Occasionally he broke ranks to back the president: in 1969 he voted to confirm CLEMENT HAYNSWORTH to the Supreme Court and two years later supported continued funding of the controversial SST.

Largely inconspicuous during his first two years in the Senate, Gravel suddenly received national attention in spring 1971 when he placed portions of the *Pentagon Papers*, a top secret Defense Department study of U.S. involvement in Southeast Asia, into the Senate record. On June 28 a federal grand jury had indicted DANIEL ELLSBERG, a former Defense Department aide, on charges of stealing the *Pentagon Papers*. The next day Gravel responded by calling reporters to a late-night session of his Subcommittee on Public Buildings and Grounds, where he read aloud from a copy of the *Pentagon Papers* for three hours. Senate minority leader HUGH SCOTT of Pennsylvania threatened to have Gravel censured, but majority leader MIKE MANSFIELD of Montana blocked any such attempt. In a major Court decision on congressional immunity, the Supreme Court on June 29, 1972, ruled 5-4 that although Gravel and his aides could not be subpoenaed or indicted for reading the documents to the press, immunity did not extend to the circumstances surrounding their acquisition. No action was taken against Gravel.

Gravel took an increasingly active role in the Senate's opposition to the war in Vietnam. During the summer of 1971 he led a three-month filibuster against extension of the draft. One of four senators to vote against the military appropriations bill of 1971, Gravel consistently supported attempts to cut off funding for the war. In May 1972, after President Nixon announced the mining of North Vietnam's major harbors and a resumption of bombing, Gravel read portions of another classified government report on Vietnam into the *Congressional Record*.

Concerned about the economic development of his underpopulated state, Gravel was a strong proponent of the Alaska oil pipeline. He helped win passage in 1971 of the Alaska Native Claims Settlement Act, which provided the state's native population with 40 million acres of land and almost $1 billion in compensation.

However, the act prohibited the state or native Alaskans from claiming lands selected by the secretary of the interior for a pipeline corridor. In 1973 Congress passed a $3.5 billion appropriation to build the pipeline. The measure included an amendment introduced by Gravel barring further court challenges to the pipeline by its opponents, thus assuring construction of the pipeline.

Gravel also was a vocal critic of nuclear power. He supported passage in 1974 of the Energy Research and Development Act, which abolished the Atomic Energy Commission and created in its place the Nuclear Regulatory Commission. In 1975 he tried unsuccessfully to win passage of a bill to increase the liability of nuclear power companies in damage suits filed by private citizens. After failing to win a seat on the Joint Atomic Energy Committee, he charged in 1976 that Senate leaders had denied his request because of his opposition to the nuclear power industry.

Gravel served one more term as senator and was defeated for renomination in 1980. Residing in Arlington, Virginia, he continues to be active in public affairs.

—JD

Gray, L(ouis) Patrick

(1916–2005) *acting director, Federal Bureau of Investigation*

Born on July 18, 1916, the son of a railroad inspector, L. Patrick Gray grew up in Houston, where he studied at Rice University and trained with the naval reserve. After four years at Rice, he won an appointment to the Naval Academy at Annapolis, Maryland, graduating in 1940 with a B.S. and a commission as ensign. After serving aboard a submarine in the Pacific during World War II, Gray was chosen in 1946 to attend George Washington University Law School in Washington, D.C.,

as a navy postgraduate student. Receiving his J.D. with honors in 1949, Gray advanced to the rank of captain during the 1950s.

In the Korean War Gray commanded three submarine combat patrols and after the war was stationed at the School of Naval Justice, Newport, Rhode Island. In 1958 he was named military assistant to the chairman of the Joint Chiefs of Staff and special assistant to the secretary of defense for legal and legislative affairs. In these posts Gray served principally as a liaison between the Pentagon and Congress and had frequent dealings with the staff of Vice President RICHARD NIXON.

When Nixon began organizing his 1960 presidential campaign, Gray left the navy to become an aide to ROBERT FINCH, head of Nixon's vice-presidential staff and chairman of his campaign. After Nixon's defeat by John F. Kennedy in 1960, Gray joined a New London, Connecticut, law firm and established a small-business investment company. Throughout the 1960s he maintained his political contacts with Nixon, serving as a fund raiser for the Republican Party. Early in 1968 he met with Nixon to pledge his support in the race for the presidential nomination. During the campaign Gray prepared a position paper elaborating Nixon's views on the small-business investment field.

After his victory in November 1968, Nixon recruited Gray as executive assistant to Robert Finch, who was designated secretary of health, education, and welfare (HEW). Gray quickly became known as "a very strong loyalist to the president and the administration and the party." In a speech given to HEW's political appointees soon after joining the department, Gray stressed that all appointees owed their jobs to the Nixon administration and must be willing to subjugate "personal goals to a deep personal commitment to serve our president, our secretary, and our nation." Though not highly visible in his HEW work, Gray played a key role in the department's internal organization and earned the president's gratitude for his service. A death in his family led Gray to leave HEW and return to his law practice in January 1970, but he continued to serve the Nixon administration as a cabinet-level consultant on school busing and desegregation.

In December 1970 Gray was persuaded to return to Washington as assistant attorney general for the Justice Department's Civil Division. In this post he was responsible for handling antiwar demonstrations on federal property. In April 1971 he obtained a federal court restraining order to keep the Vietnam Veterans against the War from camping on Capitol Hill. When the White House decided against forcibly evicting the veterans, many of whom were paraplegics, Gray was left the embarrassing task of asking the court to withdraw its order. Gray was also given the responsibility of enforcing the wage and price controls specified in Nixon's Economic Stabilization Act.

In February 1972, when Nixon nominated RICHARD G. KLEINDIENST to replace JOHN N. MITCHELL as attorney general, Gray was nominated for the post of deputy attorney general. Both men were still awaiting confirmation, pending the Senate's investigation of Kleindienst's handling of an antitrust case against International Telephone and Telegraph, when FBI director J. EDGAR HOOVER died on May 2, 1972. It was rumored that Nixon's appointment of Gray as acting FBI director on the following day had been planned far in advance. Nixon promised to evaluate Gray's performance after several months before deciding whether to nominate him for the permanent position, which required confirmation by the Senate.

When Gray took over as head of the FBI, he faced the problem of winning the loyalty and respect of an organization that had idolized Hoover, the bureau's tough, idiosyncratic chief, for almost 50 years. Some of Gray's immediate reforms, such as his relaxation of dress and

weight codes for agents and his inclusion of agents' wives in bureau activities, were welcomed by the FBI field offices. Many of these changes, however, including Gray's policy of hiring women as special agents, drew criticism from Hoover loyalists at bureau headquarters. These top officials, often at odds with the agents in the field offices, resented the elevation of an outsider to the bureau's top post and feared that Gray's background might lead him to politicize the traditionally independent FBI. Gray's selection of non-FBI people as his top staff advisers fueled the resentment of veteran bureau officials, many of whom resigned soon after Gray's appointment. Unfamiliar with the daily operations of the FBI, Gray relied heavily on his deputy director, W. MARK FELT, to deal with the vast amount of paperwork that crossed his desk. Instead of concentrating on learning FBI routines, Gray spent much of his time visiting the bureau's 59 field offices and fulfilling speaking engagements in what many saw as a "campaign" for the bureau's permanent directorship.

In February 1973 Nixon announced Gray as his choice for permanent FBI director. During 10 days of confirmation hearings before the Senate Judiciary Committee, the senators attacked such controversial areas of FBI policy as the handling of fingerprints and arrest records, the bureau's efforts against organized crime, its secret files on government officials, and the gathering of domestic intelligence on U.S. citizens who had never been charged with a crime.

Most damaging to Gray, however, was the review of the FBI's Watergate investigation. The committee exploded when it learned that during the initial investigation of the break-in at Democratic headquarters, Gray had regularly provided JOHN DEAN, the president's special counsel, with copies of "raw" unevaluated investigative materials, including summaries of the telephone conversations that were originally intercepted with

L. Patrick Gray III is escorted to the witness stand to continue his testimony before the Senate Judiciary Committee on his nomination to be FBI director, March 22, 1973. *(Bettmann/CORBIS)*

the electronic devices illegally installed at Democratic headquarters in the Watergate complex. In addition, Gray had allowed attorneys at the Committee to Re-Elect the President (CREEP) to sit in on FBI interviews of CREEP employees and had agreed to the White House demand that John Dean monitor the FBI's interviews of 14 White House aides.

Defending his actions, Gray stated that "you've got to operate on a basic presumption of regularity," pointing out that Dean was, after all, counsel to the president. Yet Gray was unable to explain why his dealings with Dean had been carried out in secrecy, to the extent that Gray had insisted Dean personally pick up packets of Watergate materials instead of having them delivered by Justice Depart-

ment courier. When Gray offered during his confirmation hearings to provide the Judiciary Committee with the same "raw" Watergate materials he had given to Dean, he incurred the wrath of the White House as well. After Gray testified on March 22 that John Dean had probably lied to FBI agents about the activities of HOWARD HUNT, a former White House aide who had helped engineer the Watergate break-in, the Judiciary Committee met secretly to dispose of Gray's nomination by indefinitely postponing action on it. In early April Gray wrote to President Nixon asking that his name be withdrawn.

Following his disastrous confirmation hearings, Gray told Senator Lowell Weicker (R-Conn.) that John Dean and presidential aide JOHN EHRLICHMAN had, in June 1972, given Gray two envelopes from Howard Hunt's files, suggesting that they were "political dynamite" that "should not see the light of day." Gray told Weicker that he had burned the files, which were later revealed to have contained State Department cables doctored by Hunt to demonstrate that John F. Kennedy had ordered the assassination of South Vietnamese president Ngo Dinh Diem during the early stages of U.S. involvement in the Vietnam War. The documents were to have been used in the event that senator EDWARD KENNEDY (D-Mass.) challenged Nixon in the 1972 presidential election.

The story, which was leaked to the press by Weiker, made banner headlines on April 27, 1973. Gray immediately resigned as acting director of the FBI and returned to his private law practice in Connecticut. Later Gray revealed to the Senate Watergate committee that he had warned President Nixon of the Watergate cover-up effort on July 6, 1972, about three weeks after the break-in.

In 1978 Gray was indicted for having approved illegal "black bag" break-ins during his tenure as FBI director. The charges were dropped in 1980, and President RONALD REAGAN pardoned him the following year. In 2005 Gray's deputy at the FBI, W. MARK FELT, confessed to being "Deep Throat"—the executive department source who provided *Washington Post* reporters BOB WOODWARD and CARL BERNSTEIN with information on their investigation of the Watergate scandal. On July 6, 2005, Gray died of complications from pancreatic cancer.

—DAE and JRG

Greenspan, Alan

(1926–   ) *chairman, Council of Economic Advisers*

Greenspan was born on March 6, 1926, and raised in New York City. The son of a stockbro-

ker, he took his B.S. in economics from New York University (NYU) in 1948 and acquired his M.A. in 1950. In the same year he began a doctoral program at Columbia under ARTHUR BURNS but gradually lost interest in academic economics. While still a student at NYU, Greenspan had already worked as an economist for the Conference Board, a private business research organization, and in 1953, with business counselor William Townsend, Greenspan founded the consulting firm Townsend-Greenspan & Co. He also began teaching economics at NYU.

Beginning in 1952 Greenspan was influenced by Ayn Rand and her controversial philosophy of laissez-faire capitalism. Rand, he explained later, showed him "why capitalism is not only efficient and practical, but also moral." In the 1960s Greenspan published articles in Rand's magazine *The Objectivist* and in one of them characterized the modern welfare state as "nothing more than a mechanism by which governments confiscate the wealth of the productive members of a society." Greenspan's association with Rand later provoked Arthur M. Okun, former member of the Council of Economic Advisers (CEA) under Lyndon Johnson, to remark that "when Greenspan came to Washington . . . I had an image of him as the worst, flaming right-wing bastard in the world."

In 1967 Greenspan was recruited from his consulting firm to work on RICHARD NIXON's 1968 presidential campaign. Greenspan had deeply mixed feelings about involving himself in national politics and at the 1968 Republican Convention told a reporter: "I'm disturbed. Every single decision is governed by politics, and the narrowest kind of politics." After Nixon's election Greenspan declined any full-time post with this administration but served as Nixon's personal representative to the Bureau of the Budget during the transition period and also was appointed chairman of the Task Force on Foreign Trade Policy.

In 1969 Greenspan returned to his consulting firm in New York City but remained a part-time adviser to the administration, serving on the Task Force on Economic Growth, the Commission on an All-Volunteer Armed Force, and the Commission on Financial Structure and Regulation. Greenspan kept his distance from the official economic spokesmen of Nixon's administration, correctly predicting in his newsletter, despite government optimism to the contrary, that the recession of 1969–70 would continue well into 1971. After the events of August 1971, when Nixon introduced his "New Economic Policy" and effectively became, in his own words, a "Keynesian," Greenspan was quite critical of the turn and called for the "old-time religion" of conservative fiscal and monetary policies, which he would later advocate as chairman of the CEA. Despite his criticisms of Nixon's economics, Greenspan agreed to work on the president's 1972 campaign, repeatedly attacking Democratic nominee senator GEORGE MCGOVERN for "fiscal irresponsibility." In early 1974 Nixon offered Greenspan the chairmanship of the CEA, which Greenspan declined.

After the administration's six-month search had failed to turn up another economist for the CEA post, Federal Reserve Board chairman ARTHUR BURNS, Greenspan's college professor, persuaded Greenspan to reconsider, citing the dire situation of the United States and world economies as they entered the deep recession of 1974–75. Greenspan's nomination was pending in the Senate at the time of Nixon's resignation in August 1974, and despite some initial reluctance by the Senate to accept a Nixon appointee, Greenspan became CEA chairman on September 1, 1974.

Greenspan was initially the symbol of a commitment to classic economic conservatism by the new FORD administration. But at the time he assumed office, the tight money policies and fiscal restraint designed by Burns

and Treasury Secretary WILLIAM SIMON were rapidly being made obsolete by the accelerating fall in production, giving Greenspan an opening for a more flexible economic policy. This flexibility became apparent in Greenspan's endorsement in 1975, over the objections of Burns and Simon, of Ford's proposed $23 billion tax cut to inject consumer spending power into the economy.

Greenspan was not a classic conservative. In a September 1974 meeting with AFL-CIO leaders, he produced charts and graphs showing conclusively that inflation was seriously outstripping wage gains and effectively refuting the traditional conservative claim that inflation was the product of a "wage-price spiral." Not all of his public appearances were so successful, however, and a few weeks later Greenspan committed a major public relations blunder. Speaking before hearings on the economy held by Health, Education, and Welfare (HEW) officials and attended by many poverty organization representatives, Greenspan said: "Everyone is hurt by inflation. If you really want to examine percentagewise who was hurt most in their income, it was Wall Street brokers." Jeers and catcalls drowned out the remainder of Greenspan's remarks, and the ensuing outcry, which seized on the incident to portray the Ford administration as strictly a government of big business, compelled Greenspan to state one week later. "Obviously, the poor are suffering more."

Greenspan's stature as an administration spokesman was based on his ability to call the turns of the economy with considerable accuracy. Greenspan had predicted a "mild" recession for 1974 before accepting the CEA chairmanship, and though he consistently underestimated the rise of the unemployment rate, he correctly predicted that the recession would "bottom out" by mid-1975. In January 1975, when U.S. production was falling at the fastest rate since 1931, Greenspan told the Joint

Economic Committee (JEC) of Congress that the economic outlook for the year was "neither pleasant nor reassuring," warning that "a sharp contraction of production and employment still has several months to run" with the economy continuing to decline "into the summer." With unemployment figures approaching 9 percent, Greenspan said that the "recession has come upon us much more suddenly than we generally anticipated" and agreed that strong action by the government was necessary to "dissipate the extraordinary sense of uncertainty and gloom that businessmen and housewives have about the economy."

Nevertheless, in early May 1975 Greenspan told the JEC that "the economy may wobble on the bottom for a while, but the worst does appear to be behind us." Production had in fact bottomed two months earlier. In June 1975 Greenspan stated definitively in a television interview that the recession was over, warning against any "overexpansion of the money supply" and echoing Treasury Secretary Simon's concern about the danger of federal borrowing "crowding out" the private sector in capital markets.

Greenspan's ability to foresee with accuracy the turns of the economy made him invaluable to the Ford administration. One White House official stated in the spring of 1975 that "Greenspan has a unique personal relationship with Ford . . . Alan spends time alone with the President on economic policy, and on economic policy Alan is a heavyweight." By July 1975 Greenspan was able to tell the JEC that the business recovery was "ahead of schedule."

Greenspan, with Simon, was most closely associated with a general shift in economic philosophy that became apparent in the final year of the Ford administration. Although Greenspan's backing of the 1975 tax cut had appeared to many as a surprising policy from a conservative, Greenspan and Simon felt that the real prob-

lems of the U.S. economy would not be solved until a serious revamping of U.S. industry was made possible by an investment boom in capital goods. To bring about such a boom, they felt a fundamental shift in tax incentives was necessary to encourage corporations to make large-scale investments. In the 1976 debate over extending the tax cut, Greenspan said he preferred a tax cut to a deficit increase but looked to more fundamental changes for a long-term solution. Ford's defeat in the 1976 election, however, ended any more serious reform of corporate depreciation allowances and similar measures.

After the 1975 turnaround in production, Greenspan saw his major task as preventing a rekindling of inflation. In 1974 he had already stated that "if inflation continues, our system will not hold together in its present form," and called for a reduction in government borrowing, tightening of the money supply, and a federal surplus as means of combating inflation. In 1975–76, despite record peacetime federal deficits to finance the Ford "reflation" program, Greenspan warned Congress against "excessive" deficits or tax cuts. He also expressed concern about costly labor settlements. When the International Brotherhood of Teamsters, after a brief strike in April 1976, won a large wage increase in excess of administration recommendations, Greenspan stated that the Teamster settlement, while "not inflationary," was "somewhat higher than I would have liked to see."

In the late summer of 1976, the recovery of the U.S. economy reached a plateau that lasted several months, leading many observers to prematurely announce the end of the 1975–76 recovery. Greenspan correctly argued that the economy had merely entered a "pause" and that "the basic recovery is solidly in place with no evidence of underlying deterioration." The economy stayed flat into the fall of 1976, however, and was an important factor in the electoral defeat of Gerald Ford.

With the election of JIMMY CARTER in 1976, Greenspan returned to New York City to his consulting firm of Townsend-Greenspan. Following the 1981 election, President RONALD REAGAN then named Greenspan to serve as chairman of the National Commission on Social Security Reform (1981–83). During the Reagan administration Greenspan was also appointed to the president's Economic Policy Advisory Board (1981–87) and the president's Foreign Intelligence Advisory Board (1983–85).

When PAUL VOLCKER, the chairman of the Federal Reserve Board, unexpectedly announced his retirement in June 1987, President Reagan nominated Greenspan to the Board of Governors of the Federal Reserve Board. Greenspan accepted the nomination and was confirmed by the Senate on August 11, 1987. In 1988 Reagan named Greenspan chairman. In 2005 Greenspan announced that he would step down from his post at the Federal Reserve effective January 2006.

—LSG and SAW

Griffin, Robert P.
(1923–   ) *member of the Senate*

Robert P. Griffin was born on November 6, 1923, in Detroit, Michigan. Following his graduation from Central Michigan College of Education in 1947, Robert Griffin obtained his law degree from the University of Michigan in 1950. He practiced law in Traverse City until 1956, when he won a seat in the House of Representatives. Griffin earned national distinction during Eisenhower's second term for his cosponsorship of the Landrum-Griffin Act in 1959 and his lobbying efforts to increase federal assistance to education. (See *The Eisenhower Years* volume.) As a representative during the Kennedy and early Johnson years, Griffin compiled a moderate record supporting civil rights, federal aid to education, and Medicare.

In 1963 Griffin and a number of other young Republicans, called the "Young Turks," staged a revolt against the party hierarchy by voting for representative GERALD R. FORD (R-Mich.) for chairman of the House Republican Conference Committee instead of representative Charles Hoeven (R-Iowa). Two years later they unseated minority leader Charles A. Halleck (R-Ind.) in favor of Ford.

Griffin was appointed to the Senate in May 1966 following the death of Patrick McNamara. He won election to that Senate seat in November. Griffin achieved national prominence in 1968 when he led Republican opposition to President Johnson's nomination of ABE FORTAS as chief justice of the Supreme Court.

In October 1969 the Senate Republicans elected Griffin their minority whip. Griffin thus became one of the leading congressional spokesmen for the White House. He consistently backed RICHARD NIXON's Vietnam War policies, especially during the turbulent period of the spring of 1970 as demonstrations mounted against the war. Griffin opposed the Cooper-Church Amendment prohibiting the president from sending combat troops into Cambodia without the consent of Congress. On the Senate floor he stated that he knew the amendment sponsors did not intend "to aid the enemy," "but it does aid the enemy when we tie the hands of the commander in chief."

Griffin backed Nixon's vetoes of bills to increase funds for education, health, and manpower training programs because he felt they were inflationary. He also opposed increasing food stamp allotments and voted against most proconsumer legislation. In 1972 the conservative Americans for Constitutional Action gave Griffin a rating of 74 and in 1973 of 88. Nevertheless, Griffin supported liberal legislation in several areas of interest to him. In 1972 he called for the elimination of monthly premiums that Medicare recipients had to pay for supplementary coverage. Griffin also introduced a bill to revamp the nation's health coverage system by requiring all employers to contribute to a privately run health care insurance program for their workers. Those not covered by the program and ineligible for Medicare would be included under a government-paid program. Griffin cosponsored a 1970 constitutional amendment calling for direct election of the president and vice president by popular vote. Griffin also supported the Equal Rights Amendment in 1972 and backed the stiff Federal Election Campaign Act of 1971.

In 1971 a federal court ordered Detroit and its suburban school systems to integrate through busing. In response Griffin introduced a constitutional amendment to abolish forced busing. On February 25, 1972, the Senate adopted Griffin's amendment by a vote of 43-40, but five days later, in another vote, the same measure was rejected, 48-47. Griffin was successful in persuading the White House to sponsor the repeal of the 8 percent automobile excise tax to stimulate his state's automaking industry.

Griffin opposed the administration on a number of issues. He voted against the nomination of CLEMENT HAYNSWORTH to the Supreme Court because of "legitimate and substantial doubt" about Haynsworth's "sensitivity to high ethical standards demanded by the bench." Griffin opposed the allocation of funds to develop the supersonic transport because of the "unresolved questions about the SST's impact upon the environment." The Michigan senator backed his liberal friend senator CHARLES GOODELL (R-N.Y.) against the White House attempt, led by Vice President SPIRO AGNEW, to purge Goodell from the Republican Party.

During the early period of the Watergate controversy, Griffin gave the president the benefit of the doubt concerning his statement on the innocence of the White House in the cover-up. He sat in on a number of strat-

egy sessions to discuss Nixon's best possible response to public pressure for an explanation of the president's relationship with the break-in. But Griffin soon grew disenchanted with how Nixon was handling the whole affair. In the spring of 1974 he joined with other Republican congressional leaders in privately urging the president to release all material related to the case. By failing to do so, the leaders warned, Nixon would be setting himself up for impeachment.

On August 3 Griffin notified the president that if he defied a Senate demand for the tapes in the expected impeachment trial, he would vote for conviction. Two days later Griffin appeared before television cameras to call for Nixon's resignation. "I think we've arrived at a point where both the national interest and his own interest will best be served by resigning," Griffin said. "It's not just his enemies who feel that way. Many of his friends, and I count myself one of them, believe now that this would be the most appropriate course."

Griffin supported the economic and foreign policies of his friend President Ford. He endorsed Ford in his drive for the presidency and campaigned for him in the fall. During the first two years of the JIMMY CARTER presidency, Griffin emerged as one of the leading Republicans challenging the new president on his foreign and economic policy programs. He was defeated for reelection in 1978, served as a justice of the Michigan supreme court from 1987 to 1994, and lives in Traverse City, Michigan.

—JB

Griffiths, Martha W(right)
(1912–2003) *member of the House of Representatives*

Born on January 29, 1912, the daughter of a letter carrier, Griffiths received her B.A. from the University of Missouri in 1934 and her

LL.B. from the University of Michigan in 1940. Admitted to the Michigan bar in 1941, she worked in the legal department of an auto insurance company and during World War II was a contract negotiator for army ordnance in Detroit. In 1946 she opened a law office, which later became a partnership with husband Hicks G. Griffiths and former classmate G. Mennen Williams, who was governor of Michigan.

Griffiths served as a state representative from 1948 to 1952, fighting for unemployment compensation. In 1952 Griffiths ran unsuccessfully for the U.S. House. She won the seat two years later. Griffiths's interest in human rights and welfare surfaced early in her House career. She sponsored bills to increase the pay of post office workers, to promote library service in rural areas, and to provide food stamps for the poor and housing for the elderly.

In 1963 the House Democratic Caucus elected Griffiths to the powerful Ways and Means Committee, seats on which are reserved for representatives whose electoral strength in their own districts allows them to take independent stands. By 1970 she emerged as the fifth-ranking member of the committee, helping to write tax and welfare legislation and to decide on all other House Democratic committee assignments. In the 91st Congress she steered the Women's Rights Amendment to passage, only to see it die in the Senate. A longtime advocate of free trade, Griffiths voted against an amendment to President RICHARD NIXON's 1973 trade reform proposals that would have set mandatory quotas on imports that had taken over 15 percent or more of the U.S. market. Also in 1973 Griffiths supported the Older Americans Act, though she opposed the proliferation of welfare programs and felt such benefits should be administered by the Social Security system.

A member of the Joint Economic Committee, Griffiths ordered a survey of poverty benefits programs by the General Account-

ing Office. In response to the report issued May 27, 1973, which found that substantial inequities prevailed in the distribution of welfare funds, Griffiths denounced the inadequacy of the federal welfare effort, pointing to work disincentives built into the program.

During the 93rd Congress Griffiths voted with the bipartisan majority on 56 percent of all floor votes, supporting President Nixon on 40 percent and President GERALD FORD on 31 percent of the bills on which each had declared positions in 1974. Griffiths was one of three Ways and Means Committee Democrats to be named in 1974 to the new House Budget Committee. Also in that year she sponsored the Health Security Act, the most comprehensive national health insurance plan of its kind presented to the Ways and Means Committee. No action was taken the same year on Griffiths' plan, which called for health benefits for all Americans, without deductibles or copayments, to be financed by general federal revenues and new payroll taxes. Griffiths announced her retirement in 1974 at the end of her 10th consecutive term. She was succeeded by Democrat William M. Brodhead.

She served as lieutenant governor of Michigan from 1982 to 1991, and was inducted into the National Women's Hall of Fame in 1993. Griffiths died in 2003 at her home in Armada, Michigan.

—DAE

Gurney, Edward J(ohn)
(1914–1996) *member of the Senate*

Edward Gurney was born on January 12, 1914, in Portland, Maine. Gurney received his B.S. in 1935 from Colby College and his LL.B. from Harvard in 1938. He served in the army in World War II. In 1948 Gurney established a law practice in Winter Park, Florida. His political career began four years later, when he became Winter Park's city commissioner, remaining in the position for six years. In 1961 he was elected mayor of Winter Park. The following year he won a seat in the U.S. House, where as a Republican he established a conservative record.

Gurney ran for the Senate in 1968, forging the same conservative Democratic-Republican coalition on a statewide level that had worked so effectively within his congressional district. On the campaign trail he denounced the riots in the black sections of Newark and Detroit and endorsed "bombing the hell" out of Vietnam. His conservative stands, plus the active support of such prominent senators as JOHN TOWER of Texas and EVERETT DIRKSEN of Illinois, resulted in a stunning victory in November in which Gurney received the largest number of votes in Florida history.

In the Senate Gurney was a strong RICHARD NIXON supporter. He backed Nixon's nomination of conservative appeals court judge CLEMENT HAYNSWORTH to the Supreme Court and sponsored the nomination of G. HARROLD CARSWELL, both of which met defeat. Gurney was a consistent supporter of antibusing proposals. Because his state contained a large number of elderly, he worked for the expansion of government programs for the aged.

Gurney was a particularly vocal advocate of Nixon's handling of the war in Indochina, including the president's decision to send American troops into Cambodia to attack Communist strongholds along the border in the spring of 1970. In the wake of the Cambodian incursion and the killing of four students at Kent State University during an antiwar protest, demonstrations and strikes were triggered in colleges across the country. In June, during debate in the Senate on funds for the Office of Education, Gurney offered an amendment that would have withheld such funds from any institution of higher learning that closed

or suspended classes to allow participation in nonacademic political affairs, except for elections. The amendment was rejected. That same month Gurney voted against the Cooper-Church Amendment, which set a specific cutoff date for military appropriations for use in Cambodia.

By 1973 the scandal resulting from a break-in at the Democratic Party's headquarters in Washington's Watergate complex had become a major political crisis. In February the Senate created a seven-member select committee to probe the break-in and the general question of political espionage in the 1972 presidential elections. Gurney was one of the three Republican senators chosen for the committee.

The hearings began in May. Throughout the probe Gurney supported Nixon. He warned that an elaborate investigation could jeopardize the conduct of the presidency.

Gurney carefully cross-examined JOHN DEAN, who in late June testified that Nixon knew of the cover-up. The senator focused on September 15, 1972, the date that indictments were handed down in the Watergate case. Those indicted were only minor figures in Nixon's reelection campaign organization. Dean testified that on that day, the president had commended him on "doing a good job"—which Dean asserted was further indication of Nixon's awareness of the cover-up operation. Gurney countered this claim, saying to Dean, "your whole thesis on saying that the president of the United States knew about Watergate on September 15, 1972, is purely an impression. There isn't a single shred of evidence." In July Senator Lowell Weicker (R-Conn.) suggested that Nixon himself testify in rebuttal. Gurney labeled Dean a "shoddy turncoat" and said that it would be "demeaning" to respond to his charges. The following month he again urged a swift conclusion to the hearings.

But by October Gurney was facing political problems of his own. That month he acknowledged reports that he was under investigation by the Justice Department on charges of maintaining a secret "boosters' fund" of more than $300,000 in contributions from Florida builders. One of these builders had accused Gurney aide Larry E. Williams of demanding a $5,000 contribution in exchange for federal approval of two government funded housing projects. Gurney denied any knowledge of the incident.

The *Miami Herald* reported in December that Williams gave sworn testimony to federal investigators in which he said that Gurney knew of $50,000 delivered to his office in Washington in July 1972, which was not reported as required by new federal election laws. In April 1974 Gurney was indicted by a Leon County grand jury in Tallahassee for violating state campaign laws. Gurney called the move a "political Pearl Harbor" engineered by Democrats seeking his seat. The indictment was dismissed in May.

Two months later a federal grand jury indicted him on seven counts of bribery, conspiracy, and perjury, accusing him of using his influence in the Department of Housing and Urban Development in exchange for campaign funds. At the urging of Florida Republicans, he withdrew from his reelection campaign. That same month the final report of the Senate Watergate committee was issued. In his own personal statement in the report, Gurney said, "In my opinion, the evidence gathered by the committee does not indicate that the president had knowledge of the cover-up." He attacked "careless handling of cash contributions, which should be barred from future elections," and strongly differed with the report's endorsement of a permanent special prosecutor in Washington. Gurney was acquitted of all charges against him in 1975 and 1976.

In September 1978 he won the Republican primary contest in his attempt to win back the seat that had launched his career in Washington, but he lost the general election. Gurney retired to his home in Winter Park, Florida, where he died in 1996.

—MDQ

Haig, Alexander M.

(1924–   ) *assistant to the president; supreme allied commander, North Atlantic Treaty Organization*

Born on December 2, 1924, the son of a Philadelphia lawyer, Haig worked his way through high school to finance his college education. After studying at the University of Notre Dame for two years, he was admitted to the United States Military Academy at West Point in 1944. Despite his unimpressive class rank of 214th out of 310, Haig advanced rapidly after his graduation in 1947. From 1953 to 1955, while he was tactical officer at the U.S. Military Academy, he studied business administration at Columbia University. Later he took a two-year course of study at Georgetown University in international relations, which culminated in an M.A. degree awarded in 1961. Among these extensive and diverse courses of study, Haig served in Japan, Korea, and Vietnam and performed in various staff capacities at the Pentagon. During the early 1960s, he was a staff officer in the Department of the Army, where he attracted the attention of Joseph Califano, who was then general counsel of the army. Califano later recommended Haig to the secretary of the army, Cyrus Vance, who took him on as his military assistant. When Vance became deputy defense secretary late in 1964, Haig remained with him as his deputy special assistant. In the mid-1960s Haig saw action in Vietnam as commander of the 1st Battalion of the 26th Infantry. Upon his return to the States in June 1967, he was appointed regimental commander of the 3rd Regiment of the Corps of Cadets at West Point. A month later he was promoted to the rank of colonel, and in June 1968 he became deputy commandant of cadets.

During the transition between the Johnson and NIXON administrations late in 1968, LBJ's domestic adviser, Joseph Califano, recommended Haig to the incoming national security assistant, HENRY KISSINGER, calling Haig "one of the new breed of sophisticated army officers." Kissinger, who was looking for a military man with field service rather than a defense intellectual, made Haig his military assistant at the National Security Council (NSC).

Haig cemented his relationship with Kissinger by being a discreetly inconspicuous and competent staff man who solidly supported his superior on controversial policies like the mining of Haigphong Harbor and the bombing of Hanoi during the final phase of the Vietnam War. Haig's staff responsibilities evolved and expanded as Kissinger's prominence as a top presidential adviser became evident.

Haig reorganized the NSC staff to improve the flow of ideas and information, screened all intelligence information to prepare a daily summary for the president, served as liaison between the Pentagon and the State Department, and took charge of NSC meetings when Kissinger was absent. He quickly gained a reputation for "meticulous staff work" and was regarded by Kissinger as a virtually "indispensable deputy." This status was recognized by his promotion to the position of deputy assistant to the president in June 1970.

Haig was often used as a "diplomatic troubleshooter," particularly in Southeast Asia. As early as 1970 he began a series of visits to Vietnam to provide the president with a firsthand, on-the-spot assessment of the situation there.

Then, as negotiations for a peace settlement began to gain momentum during the summer of 1972, Haig became the major diplomatic courier between President Nixon and South Vietnamese president Nguyen Thieu. Between October 1972 and January 1973 Haig made over a dozen trips to South Vietnam, acting in both a fact-finding capacity and in a persuasive effort to keep President Thieu from sabotaging the Paris peace talks. He was particularly effective in explaining President Nixon's "difficult domestic situation" with a presidential election looming on the horizon and with the conduct of the war as a major campaign issue.

Although Haig in Saigon and Kissinger in Paris worked diligently toward negotiating a diplomatic breakthrough before the 1972 presidential election, both Haig and the president "felt that the North Vietnamese would be more likely to make concessions after the election," when Nixon would have more freedom of action as a result of his expected landslide victory.

Since a settlement was not worked out before the election, Haig continued his shuttle diplomacy during the winter of 1972. Fully aware of the president's belief that the prospect of the new and more dovish incoming Senate made a speedy settlement of the Vietnam conflict imperative, Haig took a tough line with President Thieu. Yet because Thieu also respected Haig's views as "a soldier and as someone completely familiar with Communist treachery," Haig finally succeeded in securing South Vietnamese acquiescence to the January 27, 1973, cease-fire accord.

In the midst of this diplomatic troubleshooting, Haig also found time to serve as the president's advance man for the Nixon trip to China in February 1972. He made all final arrangements for the president's arrival and touring in China, personally checking out each stop on the president's itinerary as well as providing for press coverage and a television relay system.

In these various diplomatic missions, as well as in his administrative work at the NSC, Haig had established himself as second only to Kissinger as the president's most trusted diplomatic troubleshooter. Both in recognition of his exemplary service and in deference to his desire to return to his military career, the president promoted Haig from a two-star major general to a four-star general in September 1972 and designated him army vice chief of staff.

Although the president regretted Haig's departure from the White House staff, the president acted in response to the urgings of his secretaries of defense and of the army to promote upwardly mobile young officers to bring new, young blood into the armed forces command structure. To promote Haig, the president bypassed the routine recommendation process of the Pentagon and passed over more than 240 top-ranking officers with greater seniority. Haig's assumption of the position of vice chief of staff in January 1973 took him out of the White House just as the president was beginning his second term in office. Shortly thereafter, evidence of White House involvement in the Watergate affair began to develop.

By mid-1973, as politically damaging and explosive revelations about the Watergate cover-up forced the resignations of two of the president's closest top aides—H. R. HALDEMAN and JOHN EHRLICHMAN—Haig was brought back to the White House, initially on a temporary basis, to help restore some semblance of order to the staff. Haig's appointment as assistant to the president, replacing Haldeman, was the first step in a complete reevaluation of the operations of the White House.

In appointing a military man to replace a scandal-tainted civilian chief of staff, the president was following the tactic he had seen President Eisenhower use in 1958 when he replaced a discredited Sherman Adams with General Wilton P. Persons. Observers of Eisenhower's maneuver concluded that the appointment had been designed to bolster public confidence in White House operations. Nixon hoped to accomplish the same end with the appointment of a man whose service with both Republican and Democratic administrations had won him a reputation as a tough, hardworking, effective, and dependable administrator.

Haig's temporary appointment soon became permanent as President Nixon came to rely on him heavily as the Watergate crisis worsened. The president had known that asking Haig to stay at the White House (and subsequently resign from the army) would probably torpedo his bright prospects of becoming army chief of staff and perhaps

President Gerald Ford meets with his chief of staff, Alexander Haig. *(Ford Library)*

even chairman of the Joint Chiefs of Staff. Haig also was aware of the sacrifice he was making and the problems he would face in undertaking the job as presidential chief of staff. While he could joke that he was a "historical phenomenon—the first active-duty general who had to retire from military service to enter combat," a more serious evaluation of his position was that duty left him "no alternative but to come" and that having "commanded units in combat in which the ultimate sacrifice was demanded . . . [he was] conditioned to a degree."

Unlike his predecessor, Haig functioned in a relatively relaxed, open manner. Cabinet officials no longer had to work through the chief of staff to report to the president. Not under attack himself, Haig even managed to reintroduce a sense of humor and pleasantness to staff operations that had been lacking under the besieged and dour Haldeman. LEONARD GARMENT, another presidential assistant, commented that Haig "never lost his composure . . . but dealt with the problems of the wounded with both compassion and detachment." Despite being a military man accustomed to a clear chain of command, Haig was apparently less authoritarian than his predecessor. As one Nixon aide observed, "Haldeman issued orders. You work with Haig as an equal."

Even though President Nixon had not intended Haig to become preoccupied with the Watergate saga, he turned to Haig for advice on the matter almost as soon as he joined the White House staff. In June 1973, when JOHN DEAN told a Senate investigating committee that the president had discussed "hush money" for the Watergate burglars, Nixon contemplated resigning. President Nixon recalled that when he asked Haig's opinion, he got a "robust no" and was urged "to listen to the tapes of the Dean meetings and to construct an unassailable defense based on them."

A month later, when the existence of a White House taping system was revealed to the Ervin committee, Haig was again consulted. At that time the general counseled against destroying the tapes, arguing that such action "would create an indelible impression of guilt."

The more intensive the political fire on the White House became, the more Haig rallied to the president's aid and support. He took his responsibilities as chief of staff seriously and restructured staff operations to prevent any possible recurrence of the kind of mistakes that he felt had spawned the Watergate affair. In addition to these duties, he became a primary counselor to the president on his political troubles. To handle the double load, Haig put in 12- to 14-hour days, seven days a week. Despite his importance to the president, Haig never achieved the intimacy that Haldeman had had with Nixon. Instead he maintained an air of military formality, which he believed was both to his own and to the president's preference.

Soon after joining the staff, Haig saw the need for the president to begin marshaling a legal team, and he was responsible for getting FRED BUZHARDT, a Pentagon lawyer, appointed special counsel for Watergate affairs. He was also confronted with the need for extensive bureaucratic restaffing. While he moved quickly to fill the most necessary positions and to reenlist men like JOHN CONNALLY, MELVIN LAIRD, and BRYCE HARLOW, more confusion and frustration followed, since almost no one knew where he fit into the new hierarchy or the measure of either his access or his authority.

Within a few weeks of assuming command of the staff, Haig became aware of yet another calamity brewing—the investigation of Vice President SPIRO AGNEW on charges of conspiracy, extortion, bribery, and tax fraud. Throughout the summer Haig monitored developments until Attorney General ELLIOT RICHARDSON and special counsel Fred Buzhardt agreed that there was a solid and serious case against the vice president. Worried at the prospect that possible impeachment hearings against the vice president would merge with and fuel the Watergate issue, Haig and Buzhardt launched a campaign with Richardson and Agnew to negotiate a plea rather than provoke a constitutional crisis with an indictment and subsequent trial or impeachment proceedings. Much later Haig remarked that "arranging that cop-out was one of the greatest feats of bureaucratic skill in the history of the art."

As the Watergate investigation proceeded through the appointment of ARCHIBALD COX as special prosecutor and more and more White House tapes were subpoenaed, Haig handled negotiations between the Oval Office and Attorney General Richardson over the course of Cox's investigation and tried to work out a compromise over the tapes. When relations with special prosecutor Cox broke down completely during the October 1973 Arab-Israeli War, Haig tried to persuade the attorney general not to resign in protest, or at least to delay any action until the Mideast crisis was resolved.

Though he was unsuccessful in this effort to prevent, or at least limit, the "Saturday Night Massacre," Haig immediately set about finding a new special prosecutor. After consulting with the then acting attorney general, ROBERT BORK, Haig recommended LEON JAWORSKI and within days secured the president's approval of this appointment.

Soon after the Supreme Court decision requiring Nixon to release the White House tapes in July 1974, Haig heard the infamous "smoking gun" tape of June 23, 1972. He knew that the president was doomed and set out to salvage the presidency from a state of complete collapse. Whether Haig presided over the demise of the Nixon presidency or he orchestrated the president's resignation is a matter

of contention and is likely to remain so, since Haig has chosen to maintain a loyally discreet silence about events that were agonizing for his commander in chief.

Throughout the first seven days of August 1974, Haig kept the government functioning as a virtually "acting president." He prepared the groundwork for the imminent transfer of power, and for a short time the new President FORD retained General Haig as his White House chief of staff.

During the six weeks that Haig continued as Ford's chief of staff, the president issued the Nixon pardon, and some speculation held Haig responsible for convincing Ford to grant it. Haig, however, while admitting he favored the pardon, maintained that he was not even consulted on the matter.

Despite his evident competence, Haig could not long survive the fall of Richard Nixon. He was "the most visible symbol of the continued presence of Nixon men in the White House," and until he left the White House the administration's character would remain a Nixon legacy. Indeed, to many of the new Ford men, Haig had become "a symbol of Ford's inability to get rid of the Nixon taint."

Unlike many other Nixon staff members, when Haig left the corridors of power in late September 1974, he did so with his honor and dignity intact. President Ford recalled the general to active duty and awarded him the two most prestigious foreign military positions available for an American officer—supreme allied commander, Europe, and commander in chief, American forces, Europe.

Once again military critics grumbled that Haig lacked sufficient command experience to head a multiservice, international force. Yet precedent and the nature of the job seemed to indicate otherwise. In an era of evolving détente and of defensive reevaluation, General Haig's primary task at NATO was seen as one of convincing the United States' "allies to remain equipped and trained to fight even as the United States itself [was] beginning to debate the importance of its own military commitment in Europe." This required the talents of a soldier-statesman well versed in diplomacy, politics, and public relations—skills Haig had honed to a fine point during his White House years.

Although there was some congressional concern over the appointment, Haig successfully weathered these reactions and assumed command of the NATO forces in December 1974. His only comment on the politically controversial overtones of his appointment was a request "to be judged on . . . performance, and not [on] how [he] got here." General Haig continued in command of NATO until 1979. In 1981 RONALD REAGAN chose Haig as his first secretary of state, a post from which Haig resigned in 1982. In 1988 Haig ran unsuccessfully for the Republican nomination for the presidency. In 1984 he published a memoir, *Caveat*.

—MJW

Haldeman, H(arry) R(obbins)
(1926–1993) *assistant to the president*

Born on October 27, 1926, a third-generation Californian with midwestern roots, Haldeman came from a comfortable, business-minded, conservative family. His paternal grandfather, Harry Marston Haldeman, had been an early anticommunist and helped found the Better America Foundation after World War I to combat the purported Bolshevik threat.

His father was a shrewd businessman whose sixth sense about market trends had enabled the family to successfully weather the Depression and prosper. H. R. Haldeman inherited his grandfather's ardent anticommunism and his father's business sense.

Although of near-genius intelligence, Haldeman did not originally do well in public school and was ultimately sent to a strict private school, where he acquired "a zest for regimen and rigid command structure." Just young enough to miss service during World War II, he did take part in the navy's wartime V-1 training program during his first two years of college, first at Redlands University and then at the University of Southern California. He finished his college career at the University of California at Los Angeles (UCLA), graduating with a B.S. degree in business administration in 1948.

During his years at UCLA, Haldeman met and became friends with another future White House assistant, JOHN EHRLICHMAN. In the late 1940s Haldeman became a RICHARD NIXON enthusiast, avidly following and applauding the House Un-American Activities Committee investigation of Alger Hiss and Whittaker Chambers.

During the years that Nixon served in the House and the Senate, Haldeman remained a political spectator while he actively built a career in advertising. Initially a market researcher with Foote, Cone, and Belding, he soon joined the advertising firm of J. Walter Thompson Co. From 1949 to 1959 he was an account executive with the firm in New York, Los Angeles, and San Francisco and handled or supervised accounts like those of Disneyland, Seven-Up, Aerowax, and Black Flag insecticide. In 1959 he was named vice president and manager of the Los Angeles office.

Meanwhile, Haldeman began to act on his admiration for Richard Nixon. Although he volunteered to work for Nixon's first vice presidential campaign, in 1952, it was not until the 1956 campaign that he was taken on as one of the vice president's advance men. In that role Haldeman put his advertising and managerial skills to good use in Nixon's service.

He combined "crisp organization, precise attention to detail, and a strong sense of image" with a "fervid personal commitment to the candidate." His work in 1956 and in the subsequent congressional campaign of 1958 impressed key Nixon advisers like ROBERT FINCH and HERB KLEIN. When Finch became manager for Nixon's presidential campaign in 1960, he convinced Haldeman to take a leave of absence from the Thompson Co. to become chief advance man for the presidential campaign. Although his candidate was narrowly defeated by John Kennedy in 1960, Haldeman learned a great deal from the mistakes of that campaign and would later take care to avoid repeating them when he managed the 1968 campaign.

During the 1960 campaign Richard Nixon was only superficially acquainted with Haldeman. In the months following the electoral defeat, however, Haldeman became a Nixon intimate by volunteering to stay and help Nixon research and write the book that became *Six Crises*. In that effort Haldeman was "a combination sounding board and cheerleader." He was a self-effacing and reassuring listener during these months, convincing Nixon of his loyalty and, in turn, winning his trust.

Haldeman tried to dissuade Nixon from running for governor of California in 1962, but when Nixon persisted he remained faithful and managed the unsuccessful campaign. In retrospect, Haldeman's part in that campaign was noteworthy for an incident similar to the kind of "dirty tricks" that came to light years later in the Watergate scandal. With Nixon's approval Haldeman organized a mailing campaign against the Democratic opponent, incumbent governor Edmund "Pat" Brown. The letter, from a bogus Committee for the Preservation of the Democratic Party, was designed to discredit Brown within his own party. When the ruse was discovered to be a violation of California's election law, the Democrats took the matter to court and won a ruling against the Republicans. But by that time the election had already ended in Nixon's defeat.

H. R. Haldeman *(National Archives)*

During the 1960s, when Nixon was largely out of public affairs, Haldeman advanced in the advertising world, excelling at promotional strategy and staff-building. Hugh Sutherland, a boyhood friend who worked for Haldeman at J. Walter Thompson Co., observed that he "had a gift for recognizing whether or not [a product] would sell, and if so, exactly what advertising and publicity techniques would be most effective." Haldeman was also adept at recruiting and molding individuals into an efficient, enthusiastic staff. Indeed, a number of his protégés from the advertising agency—men like RONALD ZIEGLER, DWIGHT CHAPIN, Larry Higby, Kenneth Cole, and Bruce Kehrli—later moved with Haldeman to Washington and the Nixon White House, where they were nicknamed "the beaver patrol" because of their eagerness.

Haldeman tentatively reenlisted in political activity as Nixon began to nurture hopes of a political comeback in the wake of the crippling intraparty struggle between BARRY GOLDWATER and NELSON ROCKEFELLER and the subsequent Republican rout in the 1964 presidential election. Although he declined to help train some new advance men to help Nixon's midterm campaign efforts in 1966, he did suggest a substitute—his college friend John D. Ehrlichman.

During 1967 and early 1968 Haldeman cautiously monitored Nixon's chances and aided Operation Comeback on a part-time basis, helping to set general strategy and directing Nixon's travels and promotional affairs for the primary contests. Dan Rather in *The Palace Guard* speculated that Haldeman and Ehrlichman refrained from making a definite and full commitment to Nixon's 1968 presidential campaign effort until June 1968, when they felt that Nixon was assured of the Republican nomination and that his Democratic opponent would not be another Kennedy (as in 1960).

Named campaign manager, Haldeman worked out a campaign for the "new" Nixon designed to rectify what he considered to be the tactical errors of the 1960 race. Knowing that Nixon tired easily and had a tendency to push too hard on the campaign trail, Haldeman plotted a restrained and highly controlled campaign designed to keep the candidate rested, relaxed, and as remote as possible from both the press and from unstructured and potentially unfriendly audiences. He pursued this strategy by strictly controlling access to Nixon and by personally acting as liaison between the protected candidate and the official campaign apparatus. The remote and controlled campaign that the Republicans implemented in 1968 and that advertising executive Haldeman had designed to sell the new Nixon was tailored not only to the political situation of the moment but also to the candidate's likes, dislikes, strengths, and weaknesses. It also prefigured Haldeman's operating style at the White House.

Within five weeks of the election, Haldeman emerged as the administration's first éminence grise under the title of assistant to the president. In this capacity he was the president's gatekeeper and image overseer. This was essentially the same role he had performed during the campaign—that of "human link between the president and the machinery."

It was his job to arrange the president's schedule, screen his calls, and decide who saw him and what memos, reports, or papers crossed the president's desk. His most evident predecessor (although he denied the similarity) was Eisenhower's chief of staff, Sherman Adams, who had held the same title of assistant to the president.

Although the parallel to Sherman Adams was clear, there were important differences. Adams restricted himself primarily to coordination and administration, leaving command over public relations to press secretary James Hagerty. Within Nixon's White House, Haldeman, as chief of staff, was responsible for all administrative matters, including the press. To facilitate this control, he took pains to assure that the man appointed press secretary, Ron Ziegler, was one of his protégés. Whereas Adams had quickly become primus inter pares on the Eisenhower White House staff, Haldeman emerged as as one of the Nixon staff triumvirate. Although he was given an even broader administrative coordinating role than Adams, Haldeman had to share prominence with two other equally influential staff members who had substantive concerns: John Ehrlichman for domestic affairs and HENRY KISSINGER for national security-foreign affairs. These were the three men who saw the president most frequently.

Haldeman characterized his role as that of a "coordinator rather than an innovator, a technician rather than a policy man." He considered it his main mission to marshal "the use of the president's time, to make him as effective as he can be . . . [and to be] . . . the one to get done the things he wants done."

The role of coordinator was, however, not so simplistic. Although some felt that Haldeman always did what the president wanted done without argument, even when it was not in the best interest of the president, he saw himself as something of a "devil's advocate" who was responsible for presenting contrary views to the president before he made decisions. An associate said that on occasion Haldeman would even delay implementating what he considered an unwise presidential decision to give the president time to reflect on it. A short time later Haldeman would return to the president and ask if he really wanted the decision carried out. The fact that the president sometimes changed his mind seemed to support Haldeman's belief that he could serve Nixon so well because he thought like the president.

Observers suggested that Haldeman exercised such broad administrative control with little effective internal opposition because he eschewed a policy-making role. According to one White House staff member, although everything was channeled through Haldeman and Ehrlichman, "Haldeman [was] not at all interested in policy, and Ehrlichman [was]. This explains how they manage to get along." Haldeman himself maintained that "we have Moynihan and Kissinger and Burns and an entire executive apparatus to make policy" and that his job was "to make sure that the people who do make policy get a hearing with the president."

As presidential assistant, Haldeman was on virtual 24-hour call. HERB KLEIN, Nixon's communications director, observed that Haldeman was "the only Nixon man who [had] no schedule of his own," tailoring his time

exclusively to the president's. In his book *The Ends of Power*, Haldeman recounted that he kept "himself totally at the president's beck and call." He accompanied the president on all trips, including holiday and weekend vacations, usually pursuing his photographic hobby of taking home movies of the president and of big state events. Rarely more than a few feet away from the president during working hours, Haldeman was "in Nixon's office so often . . . he [was] usually trying to get out at the same time everyone else [was] trying to get in."

Accused of isolating the president, Haldeman's access and intimacy with Nixon and his gruff style irritated many with less access. Indeed, the prominence of individuals with a Germanic background—Haldeman, Ehrlichman, and Kissinger—was quickly parodied by their antagonists and by the press. The three became known as "the Berlin Wall" around the president. Kissinger called his two compatriots "the Praetorian Guard," and Haldeman was sometimes likened to the "Iron Chancellor."

Haldeman pursued his tasks as chief of White House operations and administration with loyalty, self-righteousness, and an "intellectual preoccupation with the techniques of modern management." Haldeman's fundamental loyalty was to a well-ordered American society, and he viewed Richard Nixon as essential to that vision. Haldeman's wife commented after the 1968 election victory, "Thank goodness Nixon won, because now Bob will have something to devote his life to." This unswerving loyalty to a man, rather than to a set of principles represented in a political party or in a process of government, helped cultivate a White House environment that tolerated and condoned Watergate-related activities. In *The Ends of Power* Haldeman recognized that in being a perfectionist taskmaster, he put too much pressure on men under him and indoctrinated them with the view that "the job must be done" and that results, not alibis, were expected of them.

Haldeman's loyalty without personal political ambitions, his ideological compatibility with the president, and his rigid staff control gave him an almost unprecedented concentration of power. Although Haldeman seldom made his views on policy issues known, Deputy Press Secretary Ken Clawson said that "there is no policy that Haldeman is responsible for, yet there is no policy that he doesn't have a hand in somehow."

Added to this unswerving personal loyalty to the president was a desire to protect him not only from "the unending flow of public officials who just had to see the president" but also from his own "dark side," which was petty, vindictive, insecure, awkward, and rigidly disciplined. In terms of personal style, Haldeman was ideally suited to be Richard Nixon's doorkeeper. Puritanically moral, Haldeman was incorruptible about money and neither smoked nor drank and frowned on those who did. It was thus with a certain amount of smug glee that Haldeman and other White House strategists looked forward to the reelection campaign of 1972, when their virtuous incumbent would face a weak Democratic contender like HUBERT HUMPHREY or EDMUND MUSKIE instead of TED KENNEDY, who had been morally discredited by the Chappaquiddick incident.

Throughout the campaign of 1972, Haldeman continued to be President Nixon's primary image molder, even though this brought him into bitter dispute with Nixon's campaign manager, JOHN MITCHELL. In this vein Haldeman orchestrated the presidential trip to Beijing in February 1972 as the kickoff of the reelection campaign. It was the high point of the Nixon presidency, showing him at his most self-assured and presenting a dramatic, statesmanlike contrast to the squabbling Democratic contenders, who were fighting their way through the New Hampshire snows to the primaries.

Nixon thrived on Haldeman's hero worship and was impressed by his efficient management. Both men had a passion for neatness, precision, and attention to detail that complemented their day-to-day working relationship. In addition, the president valued Haldeman as his hatchet man. For Richard Nixon, who had always abhorred unpleasant face-to-face confrontations, a "no-man" was essential, and Haldeman was just the man for the job. Haldeman liked to say that "every president needs an SOB" and that he was Nixon's. He accepted this role as a necessary part of keeping the president free from avoidable tensions and demands.

Ironically, Haldeman was in some ways responsible for the downfall of the Nixon presidency. The fundamental criticism of his White House style centered on the intense concentration of power in the hands of a few presidential assistants and the indoctrination of much of the staff to follow orders, not discuss them. This resulted in an isolation and inflexibility in the White House and a consequent inability to realistically assess public and political sentiment to administration policies and actions. Such a system of staff operations provided fertile soil for overzealous, unscrupulous attitudes that produced the Watergate break-in and cover-up.

Haldeman was also instrumental in setting up the White House taping system that in the end proved to be Nixon's undoing. In 1970 Haldeman had convinced the president to install an elaborate taping system to provide an unparalleled historical record of his presidency. If the tapes had not existed, or if their existence had not been revealed by one of Haldeman's protégés, Alexander Butterfield, the Nixon presidency might have survived the Watergate inquiry and been saved the painful trip down the road to impeachment.

As the unorthodox and illegal means Nixon and his assistants had taken to assure the president's reelection in 1972 slowly came to light in the Senate hearings, Haldeman and other high-ranking White House officials became deeply implicated. As public scrutiny intensified, efforts to cope with or cover up the scandal preoccupied the time and attention of many presidential assistants and led to a near paralysis of the administration. In a desperate attempt to keep his administration afloat, the president announced the resignations of Haldeman and Ehrlichman on April 30, 1973, calling it "one of the most difficult decisions of my presidency" to accept the resignations of "two of the finest public servants it has been my privilege to know." The president went on to state that the resignations were not to be taken as an implication of any personal wrongdoing on their parts, but rather that their ability to function had been impaired by rumors, accusations, and charges generated by the Watergate investigations.

In resigning, Haldeman said he had "hoped and expected to have had an earlier opportunity to clear up various allegations and innuendos that have been raised," but it had become "virtually impossible . . . to carry on . . . regular responsibilities in the White House." He noted that he intended "to cooperate fully" with the investigation and would consult with his attorneys and with the Senate select committee investigating the case.

In July 1973 Haldeman's appearance before the Senate Watergate Committee caused a new flurry over the presidential claim of executive privilege regarding tapes that both the Senate committee and the special prosecutor wanted. Haldeman testified that he had been allowed to listen to and take notes of a tape recording of the September 15, 1972, conversation among himself, John Dean, and the president to prepare his testimony. Subsequently, Watergate special prosecutor Archibald Cox used this incidence of access of nonprivileged individuals to White House material as an argument against the president's assertion that the tapes could not be subpoenaed because they fell under the protection of executive privilege.

In this testimony Haldeman said that the Watergate scandal had not come to presidential attention until March 1973. In two days of restrained, courteous testimony, Haldeman continued to defend the president and, in his concluding statement, spoke of the "high standards Nixon set for the White House staff and of his deep regret and sorrow that in a few instances there was a failure to live up to them."

The resignations of Haldeman and Ehrlichman from the White House staff late in April 1973 marked a turning point in the Watergate investigations and seemed to indicate that administration efforts to "stonewall" were not proving effective. The revelation of a White House taping system and Haldeman's testimony concerning such tapes during the summer of 1973 added further fuel to the public fires of indignation. This eventually culminated in the "Saturday night massacre," firings of the special prosecutor and the attorney general and his deputy in October. This action in turn precipitated the opening of impeachment hearings against the president. Later the March 1974 indictments of Haldeman, Ehrlichman, and John Mitchell for conspiracy and obstruction of justice hastened the demise of the Nixon presidency.

Haldeman was charged, among other things, with conspiring to impede the Watergate investigation through the improper use of government agencies, the covert raising and distribution of payoff funds, and the concealment or destruction of records and documents. He was also charged with three counts of perjury relating to his testimony before the Senate Watergate committee. Although Haldeman did not actually come to trial and sentencing until after President Nixon resigned, his indictment, with other influential former members of the White House staff, led to the establishment of presidential involvement in the Watergate cover-up.

On January 1, 1975, H. R. Haldeman was convicted in a U.S. district court in Washington, D.C., of one count of conspiracy, one count of obstruction of justice, and three counts of perjury before the Senate investigating committee with regard to his own (and the president's) knowledge of the payment of "hush money" and other cover-up activities. He was originally sentenced to from two and a half to eight years, but this was later reduced to from one to four years. Eventually he was paroled after serving six months in the federal minimum-security facility at Lompoc, California.

Although Haldeman never became as critical of President Nixon or his conduct of the Watergate affairs as did his former colleague and friend John Ehrlichman, he was reportedly spurred by Nixon's television interviews with David Frost to publicly discuss his part and the president's flaws because he felt that the former president was trying "to offload the guilt for Watergate on him and Ehrlichman."

The criticisms found in his book *The Ends of Power* were restrained and appeared to be the remarks of a man who had been disappointed by his lifelong hero but who was still loyal. Ultimately, Haldeman seemed to have reached the conclusion, so typical of the Nixon circle, that the true indictment of the Nixon administration concerning the Watergate affair was that it failed. Haldeman admits that "morally and legally it was the wrong thing to do—so it should have failed." But he goes on to say that "tactically, too many people knew too much" and that "there were many mistakes . . . [that] can be summed up in that we totally failed to get out ahead of the curves at any point." Haldeman worked as a real estate developer in Southern California until his 1993 death of abdominal cancer.

—MW

Hanks, Nancy
(1927–1983) *chairwoman, National Council on the Arts, National Endowment for the Arts*

Born on December 31, 1927, Hanks grew up in Miami, where her father was a corporate lawyer and the president of the Miami Water Power Co. After graduating magna cum laude from Duke University in 1949, she began a career in Washington in 1951 as a receptionist in the Office of Defense Mobilization. The following year she became a secretary for the President's Advisory Committee on Government Operations, where she became acquainted with the committee's chairman, NELSON A. ROCKEFELLER. Rockefeller retained Hanks as his assistant following his appointment as undersecretary of health, education, and welfare in 1953 and his assignment to President Eisenhower's Special Projects Office two years later.

In 1956 Hanks came to New York to be executive secretary of the Special Studies Project of the Rockefeller Brothers Fund. Over the ensuing years she coordinated the fund's research into foreign policy, defense, and financial and educational issues. In 1963 she directed a study of the performing arts in America. Published two years later under the title *The Performing Arts: Problems and Prospects*, it was hailed as the first major report of its kind. Urging the creation of state and community arts councils across the nation, *The Performing Arts* anticipated many of the policies Hanks would pursue during her years with the National Endowment for the Arts, which was created by the Johnson administration in September of the same year.

Hanks subsequently became a board member of the private, nonprofit Associated Council of the Arts (ACA), an organization promoting and assisting arts councils around the country. In June 1968 Hanks was elected ACA president. The following year President NIXON appointed her chair of the National Endowment for the Arts (NEA) and of its advisory body, the National Council for the Arts. The appointment was a highly popular move. The Senate swiftly confirmed her nomination, and she was sworn into office in October 1969.

The NEA's budget was $9 million when Hanks became chairwoman. The conditions described in the 1965 Rockefeller Brothers Fund report—increasing costs in the arts coupled with decreasing sources of private revenue—had become even more critical. Hence, in preparing the 1970–71 budget of the NEA, Hanks sought a major increase in funding to $20 million—more than double that granted her predecessor in his last year. When Congress seemed destined to cut most of her requests, Hanks and her assistant personally spoke to over 150 senators and representatives. Approximately 100 of them changed their previously negative votes, and most of the budget was passed.

Hanks's considerable success with Congress was due not only to her personal skills as a lobbyist but also to her philosophy of a nationwide, "grassroots" approach to arts funding. During the NEA's years under Roger Stevens, the emphasis was on "rescuing" established arts institutions such as the American Ballet Theatre and the American National Theatre and Academy from financial peril. Hanks sought a wider dispersion of the arts. In her first month in office she announced a series of grants to various performing arts groups in theater, dance, and music that would enable them to tour small communities. In subsequent years funds spent on touring dance companies and the creation of local dance troupes helped foster a major revival of interest in dance, much of it outside the New York area and other traditional arts centers.

This trend was furthered under the NEA's Expansion Arts Program, which encouraged the development of local artists and arts programs outside of the large institutions. A prominent example was the Michigan Artrain, a traveling museum jointly financed by the NEA and the Michigan Arts Council containing exhibits on the history of the visual arts, artworks by contemporary artists, and a workshop where artists could be seen at work.

Thus, while Congress criticized the NEA's sister organization, the National Endowment for the Humanities, for "elitism," there was widespread approval on Capitol Hill for Hanks's populist approach to the arts. Some critics, however, argued that the funds should be disbursed on the basis of who could use them most effectively, rather than the politically expedient standard of geographic distribution. Uniform, top-quality art could not be expected from every part of the country, it was argued, and funding practices that did not take this into account threatened to weaken the standards of excellence American art should seek to attain.

Another program that attracted some controversy in the artistic community was the NEA's Artists in the Schools program, described as a "national, state-based program which places professional artists in elementary and secondary schools to work and demonstrate their artistic disciplines." The program began in 1969 on a budget of $145,000 that soon grew into the millions. While many educators were enthusiastic about the program, others complained that it was superficial and too transient to have any real effect on students. In 1973 Stanford University education professor Elliot W. Eisner urged the NEA to undertake an evaluation of the program's effectiveness. When the NEA finally commissioned such a study in 1974, the contract went to a foundation that was itself partially funded by the NEA. The resultant report was so one-sided in its praise for the program that Eisner referred to it as a "public relations document, rather than a professional evaluation of a publicly funded program."

Under Hanks the NEA budget almost doubled every year. While this represented the greatest commitment ever made by the U.S. government to the arts, it also resulted in a growing bureaucracy that frustrated many artists. The procedure for grant application became more complex, to the extent that some feared it would inhibit requests for small amounts of assistance.

Nonetheless, when Hanks announced her resignation from the National Endowment for the Arts and the National Council on the Arts at the conclusion of her second term, the consensus of opinion was that she had played a major role in the growth of the arts in the United States. "Eight years are enough," was her comment at the official White House announcement in August 1977, though there was little doubt that had President JIMMY CARTER chosen to reappoint Hanks, she would have accepted.

In responding to her resignation the president wrote, "Under your thoughtful and creative stewardship, the Endowment has . . . firmly established in the country's consciousness the importance of broad-based public and private support for the arts." Hanks died of cancer in 1983.

—MDQ

Hardin, Clifford M(orris)
(1915–   ) *secretary of agriculture*

Born on October 9, 1915, Hardin, the son of a Quaker farmer, was raised on his father's 200-acre grain and livestock farm in Indiana. He received a B.A. from Purdue in 1937, an M.A. from the university in 1939, and his Ph.D. in agricultural economics in 1941. From 1941 to 1944 he was on the University of Wisconsin faculty. In 1944 he moved to Michigan State College (later University), where he held several research and administrative posts. He was

the dean of the College of Agriculture when he left Michigan in 1954 to become the chancellor of the University of Nebraska. Under Hardin's leadership the university's enrollment jumped from 7,200 to 30,000 students.

A leading international developmental economist, Hardin was always interested in the problem of world hunger and agricultural development in the less-developed countries. He was a U.S. delegate to the International Conference on Agricultural Economics in 1947; he organized agricultural training programs and educational development projects in South America, Asia, and sub-Saharan Africa; and he introduced the background papers presented at the World Food Conference in New York in 1968, papers he later edited and published as *Overcoming World Hunger* (1969).

RICHARD NIXON appointed Hardin secretary of agriculture in 1969. When Hardin assumed office, federal farm policy was governed by the Food and Agriculture Act of 1965. Under this law the government tried to regulate production by establishing acreage allotments that specified how much land a farmer could use to grow various crops. Farmers who accepted the allotment controls could get government price support loans for their crops. Farmers could either repay these loans if the market price for the crops exceeded the price support level for the loan, or they could default on the loan and turn their crop over to the government if market prices were below the price support level. The government also made direct subsidy payments to farmers who voluntarily used less than their allotted acreage. The law was scheduled to expire in 1969, but Nixon urged Republicans to support a one-year extension to give his administration a chance to develop a new farm policy.

Hardin worked to change this policy. He favored a land retirement program as the key element of a new farm policy. He also wanted to relax the strict federal controls over agricultural production. Hardin believed that the problems of the small, marginal farmer had to be separated from those common to the large, commercial farmer. Government subsidy payments were inadequate for marginal farmers and merely encouraged them to remain on the farm in poverty. Hardin felt the government should encourage the marginal farmers to move off the farm by paying them to retire their land. At the same time Hardin believed that the commercial farmers needed a more market-oriented policy that gave them additional flexibility in deciding what to produce and that relied more heavily on market prices to set price support levels.

The administration program Hardin presented to the House Agriculture Committee in September 1969 retained the old acreage allotment formulas, direct subsidy payments, and price support loan programs but implemented them in a new way. Hardin proposed a "set aside" programs under which farmers would agree to set aside, or leave unplanted, a portion of their acreage allotments for feed grains, wheat, and cotton. Farmers who did so could then grow whatever crops they wanted on the remaining land and be eligible for price support loans on all the crops they produced. The price support levels would, however, be set at world market prices rather than at some fixed price. Farmers who agreed to set aside additional land could get direct subsidy payments in lieu of what they would have produced.

Farm groups opposed Hardin's proposals and submitted their own plans to Congress. A coalition of 24 farm groups wanted to extend the 1965 law permanently. But they also wanted to raise the price support levels. The American Farm Bureau Federation, which represented the larger commercial farmers, wanted to return to a free market in agriculture by phasing out acreage controls, marketing quotas, and direct subsidy payments to wheat, feed grain, and cotton growers. The Farm Bureau also wanted

to reduce agricultural production to maintain free market prices by requiring the secretary of agriculture to retire 10 million acres from farm production during each year from 1971 through 1975. Urban legislators, on the other hand, wanted to set a ceiling on the amount of subsidy payments farmers could get. Hardin proposed a $110,000-per-crop ceiling, but urban legislators wanted a $20,000 ceiling.

The Agriculture Act of 1970, which Congress enacted in November after 16 months of hearings and negotiations, was a compromise between Hardin's proposals and those made by the other groups. Congress enacted the set-aside proposal and eliminated strict commodity-by-commodity production controls by allowing farmers to plant whatever they wanted after they had set aside the required acreage. Congress also gave the administration some flexibility in setting prices for the price support loan program but protected farmers by establishing minimum price support levels for such loans. Finally, Congress established a ceiling of $55,000 per crop on subsidy payments, which was later reduced to $20,000.

Hardin had to increase farm subsidies for corn and wheat growers less than a year after the new law went into effect. In 1971 farmers produced a record 5.4 million bushels of corn. The set-aside targets Hardin announced in October 1971 increased the set-aside for feed grain lands for the 1972 crop from 18.2 million acres to 38 million acres. He also increased subsidy payments for leaving land out of production, which raised the cost of the program by over $300 million.

Hardin's food stamp policies were strongly criticized in Congress, which failed to enact the administration's food stamp reform proposals that Nixon announced in May 1969. The reforms would have limited the maximum amount paid by food stamp recipients. Hardin, however, implemented some of the reforms by revising departmental rules so that families did not have to spend more than 25 percent of their income for food stamps. Hardin's proposal to give free food stamps to families earning less than $30 per month was attacked by liberals, who called the program inadequate, and by conservatives, who said that deadbeats who can but will not work should be prevented from getting free food stamps. But Congress enacted the program in 1970. Responding to congressional pressures, the administration raised its funding requests for the food stamp program for fiscal 1970 and 1971. However, when congressional liberals wanted to increase fiscal 1970 spending even more, Hardin thwarted their efforts by telling Congress that the administration could not reasonably spend more than the amount it had requested.

Hardin was sued by conservation groups in early 1970 for imposing only a partial ban on the use of DDT in November 1969. Hardin defended his action by claiming that since scientific evidence had so far failed to show DDT was an "imminent hazard to human health," he would not completely ban the use of the pesticide while his department was still studying the question. The DDT suit and other environmental issues were, however, taken out of Hardin's hands when the Environmental Protection Agency was created by a presidential executive reorganization in 1970. Hardin opposed the creation of the new agency but was overruled by President Nixon, who insisted that a central agency was the best solution for dealing with environmental issues that cut across several jurisdictions.

Hardin vigorously advocated the administration's $1.1 billion special revenue-sharing proposal for rural community development, which Nixon announced in 1971. Hardin testified that the program was needed to promote balanced growth between urban and rural areas. He pointed out that half the counties in the United States had lost population during the 1960s and that most of these counties were in rural areas. He said that the revenue-sharing proposal would consolidate federal funding and grant programs for rural areas and equitably allocate funds to the states. Congress refused to enact the proposal and adopted instead the Rural Development Act of 1972, when Hardin was no longer in office.

Hardin's action to raise milk price supports in 1971 became a major political issue the following year when Ralph Nader and three consumer groups sued the Department of Agriculture to rescind the increase. Hardin had refused to increase the price support level on March 12, 1972, claiming the hike was unjustified. But he reversed himself 13 days later and raised the price support level for milk. The Nader suit charged that the increase had been granted "illegally" in return for "promises and expectations of campaign contributions for" Nixon's reelection drive. According to the suit, Hardin's reversal occurred after milk producers had contributed $10,000 to various Republican fund-raising committees on March 22 and 16 dairy industry spokesmen had met with Hardin and the president on March 23. The suit also claimed that milk producers had donated $322,500 to GOP campaign committees by the end of 1971. The suit alleged that Hardin had received no new evidence or information bearing on the issue since his earlier denial of the price support increase.

Hardin was no longer in office when the suit came to trial. He resigned on November 11, 1971. Reports of Hardin's departure had already circulated in Washington a year before he resigned. Hardin could not establish effective relations with Congress and was the sixth member of Nixon's original cabinet to leave office. He became a vice president of the Ralston-Purina company in St. Louis, Missouri.

—AE

Harlan, John Marshall

(1899–1971) *associate justice, U.S. Supreme Court*

Born on May 20, 1899, into a family distinguished in the law, Harlan graduated from Princeton in 1920 and then studied law while a Rhodes scholar at Oxford for three years. He received a degree from New York Law School in 1924 and joined a large Wall Street firm, where he became a partner in 1931. Although he held a number of public service positions, Harlan devoted himself mainly to private practice until 1954. He specialized in corporate and antitrust cases and became a leader of the New York bar. A Republican, he was named a judge on the U.S. Second Circuit Court of Appeals in January 1954. He was appointed to the U.S. Supreme Court 10 months later. Grandson of a Supreme Court justice, Harlan took his seat on March 28, 1955.

On the bench Harlan was soon aligned with Justice Felix Frankfurter in philosophy as well as votes. Like Frankfurter, Harlan believed that judges should approach issues in a dispassionate, reasoned fashion and that the Court should exercise restraint. He placed great value on adherence to precedent and thought the Court should limit its role, leaving other branches of government free to work out solutions to the nation's problems. Harlan was deeply committed to the maintenance of federalism. He believed Court interference should be minimal in areas where state power was preeminent. He resisted, for example, the effort to extend all of the Bill of Rights to the states and argued that the Fourteenth Amendment's due process clause only required state criminal procedures to be "fundamentally fair." Harlan also respected the doctrine of separation of powers and was wary of invalidating federal legislative or executive action. Although he could be rigorous in his application of the Bill of Rights to the federal government, the justice believed individual rights had to be balanced against government interests in each case. He also thought the Court should not deal with political questions such as reapportionment and vigorously protested the Court's establishment and extension of the one-man, one-vote standard. Harlan insisted that reform was a legislative and not a judicial function and criticized many of the major trends of the activist and liberal Warren Court.

Justice Harlan was no inflexible conservative, however. His judicial views on matters such as due process allowed for considerable discretion and made it hard to predict his stance in particular cases. He voted in June 1963, for example, to overturn a 21-year-old precedent and require the states to supply counsel to indigent defendants accused of a felony. He also joined in a June 1965 ruling overturning a state anticontraceptive law, which he considered an invasion of the right to marital privacy. Harlan concurred in May 1967 when the Court extended certain constitutional safeguards such as the right to counsel to juvenile court proceedings.

Because of personnel changes, Justice Harlan found himself more often at the center of the Court during his final years on the bench. He remained, though, as thoughtful and dispassionate and as independent and difficult to predict as before. On criminal rights questions, for example, Harlan dissented in June 1969 when a majority applied the provision against double jeopardy to the states. Nevertheless, he concurred when the Court extended the right to counsel to preliminary hearings in June 1970 because recent Court rulings supported such a decision, a ruling he had personally disagreed with. The justice joined in March 1970 and June 1971 rulings guaranteeing juvenile defendants the right to have their guilt proven "beyond a reasonable doubt" but not the right to trial by jury. In two June 1971 cases Harlan's opinion for the Court held that the states did not deny due process by giving juries in capital cases complete discretion in deciding whether to impose the death penalty or by allowing such juries to determine both a defendant's guilt and his punishment in one proceeding.

Since he demanded high procedural standards in federal criminal cases, Harlan voted in January 1969 and June 1971 to overturn federal convictions where he thought there had not been sufficient cause for a search warrant to be issued. He also dissented from an April 1971 judgment upholding "third-party bugging" in which a federal informer used an electronic device, without a warrant, to transmit a conversation between himself and another person. In June 1970 the justice concurred when the Court upheld the use of six-member juries in state trials. However, he objected when the majority at the same time overruled a long-standing precedent requiring 12 members for federal juries.

Harlan maintained his opposition to the one-man, one-vote standard in reapportionment cases decided in 1969 and 1970. He believed that the states had the power to set reasonable voting requirements. Harlan therefore dissented in June 1969 and June 1970 when the Court invalidated state laws limiting voting for school board members and on bond issues to those considered to have the most immediate stake in the results. In December 1970 Harlan took the position that Congress could neither lower the voting age to 18 for state or federal elections nor limit state residency requirements for presidential elections to 30 days.

Justice Harlan generally supported state welfare regulations. Nevertheless, he did join the majority in March 1970 to hold that due process guaranteed welfare recipients the right to a hearing before their benefits could be terminated. He also opposed the Court's increasing use of the equal protection clause against economic rather than racial discrimination. However, his majority opinion in a March

1971 decision ruled that the states could not deny poor persons a divorce solely because they could not pay the court costs. In civil rights cases Harlan backed school desegregation orders in June and October 1969 decisions. Yet he dissented in December 1969 when the majority used an 1866 civil rights law to rule that a black family could not be excluded from membership in a community recreation club when a club share was included in their lease of a house in the neighborhood.

In April 1969 Harlan spoke for a five-man majority to reverse a conviction for making derogatory statements about the American flag a violation of the First Amendment. His majority opinion in a June 1971 case also overturned the conviction of a demonstrator who had entered a courthouse wearing a jacket inscribed with a vulgarism condemning the draft. In June 1971, when a majority refused the government's request for an injunction to halt newspaper publication of a classified study of U.S. involvement in Indochina, Harlan strongly objected to the haste with which the cases were handled. He maintained that the Court should have allowed more time for consideration of the serious issues involved. On the merits, the justice dissented from the majority in the *Pentagon Papers* case because he thought that the Constitution gave control of foreign affairs to the executive branch and that the scope of judicial review of foreign policy matters was severely limited. Justice Harlan retired from the Court on September 23, 1971, and died three months later of cancer.

—CAB

Harlow, Bryce N(athaniel)

(1916–1987) *assistant to the president; counselor to the president*

Bryce N. Harlow was born on August 11, 1916, in Oklahoma City. Harlow received his B.A.

from the University of Oklahoma in 1936 and his M.A. from the same institution in 1942. In the interim he had worked as an assistant librarian for the House of Representatives. He rose to the rank of lieutenant colonel in the army during World War II. He worked on the staff of the Armed Services Committee from 1947 to 1951. President Eisenhower appointed Harlow to the White House staff in 1953. He served throughout both terms as an assistant to the president. From 1961 to 1968 Harlow was the director of governmental relations for the Procter & Gamble Manufacturing Corp. in Washington.

When President-elect RICHARD NIXON began to name key administration aides in November 1968, his first appointee was Harlow, designated to be an assistant to the president for legislative and congressional affairs. A year later the White House announced that Harlow had been raised to counselor with cabinet rank responsible for national affairs and relieved of operational duties. Harlow reported directly to the president. The change was coordinated with the expected departure of domestic adviser ARTHUR BURNS, whom Nixon had nominated to the Federal Reserve Board.

Harlow worked to generate support for the administration's domestic legislative program—federal revenue sharing, welfare reform, alterations in manpower training programs—which was bottled up in Congress. In an action typical of his responsibilities as counselor, he wrote Republican congressmen in January 1970 seeking support for Nixon's position of federal budget restraint during congressional debate of an appropriations bill the president had threatened to veto because of what he considered inflationary increases over his funding requests. Despite such lobbying, the bill and many other such measures passed the heavily Democratic Congress.

That same month it was announced that Harlow would work with a cabinet-level task force established by Nixon to counsel southern school districts on implementation of court-ordered desegregation plans. After the U.S. military incursion into Cambodia in the spring, Harlow attempted to modify the language of many of the resolutions introduced in Congress seeking to limit U.S. involvement in that country. In June he accompanied a high-level delegation sent at the president's behest to inspect the war theater in Southeast Asia.

In December Harlow resigned from the administration and resumed his career with Procter & Gamble. In the spring of 1973, during the growing Watergate crisis, he informally advised Nixon that White House aides JOHN DEAN, H. R. HALDEMAN, and JOHN D. EHRLICHMAN would have to leave "if they have undertaken actions which will not float in the public domain." For Harlow there was "too much at stake to hang on for personal reasons." In the subsequent reorganization after their resignations, Harlow took a leave of absence from Procter & Gamble to return at Nixon's request to the White House.

Harlow, again as counselor to the president, immediately found himself involved in such controversial Watergate issues as the audits of Nixon's finances and the release of the White House tapes to the courts. Along with other close and longtime Nixon aides, he attempted to rally the president's cause. After the dismissal of Watergate special prosecutor ARCHIBALD COX, he relayed the suggestions of Republican members of Congress to Nixon that he appoint a new special prosecutor. When the House Judiciary Committee began its proceedings early in 1974, Harlow urged that the panel adopt tighter rules to govern its hearings. At issue were committee leaks and the fact that the procedure's format did little to distinguish accusation from evidence.

Harlow again resigned from the White House in April. He returned to Procter & Gamble as a vice president. The following year he helped plan President FORD's 1976 campaign. He received the Medal of Freedom in 1981. Harlow died on February 17, 1987, in Harpers Ferry, West Virginia.

—SF

Harrington, Michael J(oseph)
(1936–1989) *member of the House of Representatives*

Born on September 2, 1936, Harrington was exposed to politics at an early age, when his father was elected mayor of Salem, Massachusetts. Educated at Harvard, Harrington received a law degree in 1961 and subsequently did graduate work in public administration. His interest in Latin America, dating to his years at Harvard, became the focus of his concerns in the House of Representatives. Harrington had already begun his political career by the time he graduated from law school. He served on the Salem city council from 1960 to 1963 and as state representative from 1964 to 1969. In 1969 Harrington entered the House of Representatives as a Democrat after winning a special election to fill the vacancy created by the death of William H. Bates. During the campaign Harrington opposed U.S. involvement in Vietnam and heavy military spending, especially on the antiballistic missile system (ABM). His victory was thus regarded as a vote of no confidence for the NIXON administration's foreign and defense policies.

Harrington maintained a vigorous anti-administration stance during the Nixon and FORD years, receiving a rating of 100 from the liberal Americans for Democratic Action (ADA) in 1973. He was appointed to the House Foreign Affairs Committee in 1973 after serving four years as one of the few doves on the Armed Services Committee.

As a member of the Foreign Affairs Committee's Subcommittee on Inter-American Affairs, Harrington was an outspoken critic of the Central Intelligence Agency (CIA). He

became aware that U.S. policies of economic "deprivation" had contributed to the downfall of Chile's Marxist Allende regime in 1973. At Harrington's urging the Subcommittee on Intelligence of the Armed Services Committee called CIA director WILLIAM COLBY to testify about his agency's operations; Colby revealed in a closed session that the CIA spent $8 million to eliminate Allende and that this was a "laboratory experiment" in overthrowing governments.

After reviewing the transcript of Colby's secret testimony, Harrington disclosed portions of it to "unauthorized" persons in an attempt to convince the House and Senate international relations committees to investigate CIA operations. In the process Colby's revelations were leaked to the press. The resulting public outcry spurred presidential and congressional investigations of intelligence activities. In the meantime, Harrington sued the CIA in federal court to enjoin its covert operations.

Harrington, after working to establish a congressional watchdog panel for intelligence activities, became a member of the newly created House Select Committee on Intelligence. However, his criticism of committee chairman Lucien Nedzi, backed by other committee Democrats, impaired the committee's effectiveness. Neither Harrington nor Nedzi was reappointed when House Speaker CARL ALBERT reconstituted the committee.

Shortly after the original leak of Colby's testimony in September 1974, the Armed Services Committee reprimanded Harrington for disregarding House secrecy rules. During the controversy between Harrington and Nedzi in June 1975, the issue was revived: the Armed Services Committee denied Harrington access to its classified files and this time brought charges before the House Ethics Committee. The committee later dismissed the complaint against Harrington on the grounds that Colby's testimony was taken under conditions that violated House rules.

Harrington continued to criticize the CIA's covert operations, especially in Chile, although he admitted the need for covert intelligence-gathering. During the Ethics Committee's later investigation of leaks by CBS News reporter DANIEL SCHORR, Harrington maintained that the priorities of the House were wrong if attention could be diverted from illegal intelligence activities to congressional ability to keep secrets.

Harrington was reelected in 1976. He did not run in 1978, preferring to return to his law practice. He wrote a memoir, *The Long-Distance Runner: An Autobiography*, published in 1988; he died the following year.

—PG

Harris, Fred R(oy)
(1930–   ) *member of the Senate*

Fred R. Harris was born on November 13, 1930, in Walters, Oklahoma. Following the completion of college and law school at the University of Oklahoma, Harris entered the Oklahoma state senate at age 33. Within three years he headed the Democratic Party Caucus and was a leader of the civil rights movement. In 1964 Harris won a seat in the U.S. Senate. He was a loyal Johnson supporter, voting for the Great Society legislation and civil rights measures and defending the war in Vietnam. He backed the oil depletion allowances that favored the oil interests of his state. Married to a Comanche Native American, Harris was the most militant advocate of Indian rights in the Senate. In the 1968 campaign Harris worked for HUBERT HUMPHREY.

Following RICHARD NIXON's victory Harris moved farther to the left. His membership on the President's Advisory Commission on Civil Disorders under Johnson had persuaded him that a major effort must be undertaken to eliminate poverty in the nation. Harris angrily

observed that the Vietnam War had been diverting needed funds for domestic programs and moved into the antiwar camp. In 1970 he voted for the Cooper-Church Amendment. That same year he introduced his own welfare reform bill as an alternative to the administration's plan. Harris proposed a national guaranteed minimum income of $3,600 a year for a family of four. The Harris program would also allow a family of four to retain additional earnings to raise its yearly income to $6,000 without losing the guaranteed payments. He maintained that the president's proposal of a $1,600 national minimum would plunge more people into poverty. The Senate rejected Harris's plan.

Harris was particularly concerned with Native American affairs. He lobbied for more land to be given to the Native Americans in Alaska. In 1970 he sponsored a bill to grant the Taos Pueblo Native Americans title to 48,000 acres of New Mexico land, which included the tribe's sacred Blue Lake. Enjoying bipartisan support, his bill passed both houses and was signed by the president.

In early 1969 Harris became chairman of the Democratic National Committee. Aside from his role as the leading partisan critic of the Republican administration, Harris began the implementation of the reforms in the party that opened up greater opportunities for minorities, young people, and women to participate in the 1972 Democratic National Convention. He resigned as chairman in 1970. Two years later he decided not to seek reelection because of his fear that his liberal stands had doomed his chances. Instead, Harris waged a short-lived run for the 1972 Democratic presidential nomination. Four years later Harris ran again. Campaigning from a trailer, he toured the nation promising to break up the major corporations, end tax loopholes, and restore morality to American diplomacy. The neopopulist enjoyed strong grassroots support from many veterans of the 1972 McGovern campaign. Although he had found receptive audiences while campaigning, Harris's recognition in the polls remained low, and his proposals made him a weak contender. In the early 1976 primaries he did poorly, losing even his own state's party caucus to JIMMY CARTER. Harris withdrew from the race in April for lack of funds but promised his supporters to remain active in the party to move it farther to the left. Harris took a position as professor of political science at the University of New Mexico; he currently resides in Corrales, New Mexico.

—JB

Harris, Patricia R(oberts)
(1924–1985) *chairwoman, Democratic National Convention Credentials Committee*

Patricia Harris was born on May 31, 1924, in Mattoon, Illinois. Harris, the daughter of a railroad waiter, graduated from Howard University in 1945 and held a variety of jobs before deciding to attend George Washington University Law School. After her graduation in 1960, Harris worked as an attorney in the Criminal Division of the Justice Department and then taught law at Howard University until President Johnson appointed her ambassador to Luxembourg in May 1965, becoming the first black woman to hold that position. Harris returned to Howard University in 1967 to resume her teaching career and served as alternate delegate to the United Nations in 1966 and 1967.

In December 1969 the National Commission on the Causes and Prevention of Violence issued a report that in part condemned civil disobedience and nonviolent protest action. Harris, a member of the commission and a participant in early civil rights sit-ins while a student at Howard, issued a dissenting report that argued that if persons were willing to accept the penalty, civil disobedience "can

represent the highest loyalty and respect for a democratic society."

Harris had confronted such action herself as dean of Howard University Law School in February 1969 when students occupied the law building. She obtained a court injunction, and the students left the building, but Harris resigned after charging that President Nabrit had undermined her authority by negotiating with the students behind her back.

Long active in the Democratic Party, Harris had been a member of the Democratic National Committee, seconded the nomination of Lyndon Johnson at the 1964 national convention, and was appointed to a number of commissions by Presidents Kennedy and Johnson. In October 1971 the Democratic national committee met and elected Harris temporary chairwoman of the Credentials Committee for the 1971 national convention.

That post was considered a measure of the party's progress toward fulfillment of reform proposals made in the wake of the 1968 Democratic Convention disruptions. Harris was backed by national chairman LAWRENCE O'BRIEN, labor and party regulars including Max Kempleman, a Humphrey supporter, and copartner in Harris's law firm. Reform elements including blacks and presidential hopefuls GEORGE MCGOVERN, FRED HARRIS, EUGENE MCCARTHY, and EDMUND MUSKIE supported Senator HAROLD HUGHES (D-Iowa), who was nominated by SHIRLEY CHISHOLM.

When the Credentials Committee met in late June and early July 1972, Harris was elected permanent chairwoman. She faced over 80 challenges to state delegations, two of which threatened to expose party infighting on the convention floor. The committee voted to invalidate California's winner-take-all primary, a setback for McGovern, who had won the primary, and to oust the Illinois delegation led by Mayor RICHARD DALEY in favor of a more representative delegation, a move by McGovern forces angry at the California decision. Harris's performance was assessed as strict and fair, but the struggle between party regulars and reformers was fought out at the national convention.

From 1970 to 1971 Harris was a partner in a Washington, D.C., law firm and was elected to the boards of directors of the National Bank of Washington, Scott Paper Co., and IBM. From 1973 to 1976 she was member-at-large of the Democratic National Committee. On January 20, 1977, the Senate confirmed President JIMMY CARTER's nomination of Harris as secretary of the Department of Housing and Urban Development. In 1980 she became a professor at the George Washington National Law Center. Harris died on March 23, 1985, of breast cancer.

—JMP

Hart, Gary (Warren)

(1937–) *director, Senator George McGovern's campaign for president; member of the Senate*

Born Gary Hartpence (he changed his name in 1961) on November 28, 1937, Hart received his B.A. degree in 1958 at Bethany Nazarene College and also attended Yale Divinity School. He earned a law degree from Yale in 1964 and moved to Washington, D.C., where he served as an appellate attorney in the Department of Justice and as a special assistant to Secretary of the Interior Stewart L. Udall. In the late 1960s Hart taught law in Colorado and was a consultant for the National Water Commission and the Public Land Review Commission. He also entered private law practice in Denver.

Hart volunteered his services to Senator Robert F. Kennedy when Kennedy declared his candidacy for president in March 1968. He continued working for Democratic Party candidates following Robert Kennedy's assassination. Hart organized the Colorado hear-

ings of the Reform Commission, also called the Commission on Party Structure and Delegate Selection. He was one of the earliest of Senator GEORGE MCGOVERN's supporters for the presidency and became his first full-time staff member in March 1970. He agreed to manage McGovern's national campaign in August 1970.

In organizing McGovern's national campaign, Hart promoted a policy of decentralization. Instead of giving the national staff full authority in campaign decisions, Hart delegated responsibility to volunteers on the local level. This method increased communication between national headquarters and local offices as well as encouraged a sense of increased involvement for all the volunteers. McGovern's people worked at the grassroots level, canvassing neighborhoods and talking to voters.

McGovern announced his presidential candidacy in January 1971. Some political contributions arrived at this point, but lack of money was a continuing problem. Hart created the "McGovern for President Club," in which members contributed $10 per month and in return received current news on McGovern's campaign. It proved to be an effective strategy. Hart felt that the willingness of ordinary citizens to invest in the political process was "a revolutionary event in American politics."

McGovern captured the leadership of the liberal wing of the Democratic Party and secured the nomination for the presidency on the first ballot at the Democratic National Convention in July 1971. Hart organized the McGovern campaign by concentrating on the states that HUBERT HUMPHREY had either won or narrowly lost in his campaign for president in 1968. Hart urged his field organizers to reevaluate these states and to move in with media campaigns and public appearances when the time was right.

Although he originally felt it would be easier for McGovern to beat President RICHARD NIXON than for the senator to get the Democratic presidential nomination, Hart eventually concluded that the campaign was doomed after McGovern's first vice presidential choice, THOMAS EAGLETON (D-Mo.), withdrew following revelations that he had been hospitalized for psychiatric problems. But neither Hart nor McGovern anticipated the dramatic defeat in November. Nixon was reelected by a plurality of nearly 18 million votes and carried 49 of the 50 states.

Hart returned to Denver, resumed his law practice, and began work on a book recording his personal history of McGovern's campaign. In *Right from the Start* he concluded that McGovern and his advisers did not offer workable solutions to America's problems or clearly identify the national issues. Hart also felt that liberalism in the United States had become extremely removed from the problems of the working class. He proposed reestablishing effective communication with the people to develop a new generation of national leaders.

Hart won a U.S. Senate seat from Colorado in 1974. As senator he worked for national health insurance, the restoration of run-down residential buildings in inner-city areas, and the protection of Colorado's natural beauty.

Hart was reelected to a second term in the Senate in 1980. In 1984 he embarked on the first of several campaigns for the presidency. After defeating former vice president WALTER MONDALE in that year's New Hampshire primary, Hart and Mondale traded primary victories throughout the spring. However, Mondale's famous "Where's the beef?" quip (mimicking a famous fast-food restaurant advertising slogan of the day) to respond to Hart's "new ideas" served to dull Hart's momentum and was instrumental in Mondale's winning the crucial New York and Pennsylvania primaries; after those defeats Hart withdrew from the race.

In 1987 Hart declined to run for a third Senate term, concentrating instead on a presidential run the following year. However, the campaign, which began with Hart as the clear front-runner, was derailed by the revelation that he had had an extramarital affair with Donna Rice, a 29-year-old model (a blunder that was compounded by Hart's arrogant challenge to the press to "follow me around" to see if he really was having an affair). When the *Miami Herald* published compromising photos of Hart and Rice on a sailboat called *Monkey Business,* Hart was forced to withdraw from the race on May 8, 1987. Hart reentered the race in December 1987, but his poor showing in the February 1988 New Hampshire primary led to his final withdrawal.

Hart returned to the practice of law. He cochaired the Hart-Rudman Commission, formed by President Bill Clinton to investigate homeland security. He now lives in Kittredge, Colorado.

—CE and JRG

Hart, Philip A(loysius)
(1912–1976) *member of the Senate*

Philip A. Hart was born on December 10, 1912, in Bryn Mawr, Pennsylvania. Following graduation in 1937 from the University of Michigan Law School, Hart established a law practice in Detroit. He served in the army during World War II and then returned home to resume his practice. Governor G. Mennen Williams, a former law school classmate of Hart, appointed his friend Michigan's corporation and securities commissioner in 1949. He made Hart his legal adviser in 1953. Hart was elected lieutenant governor of Michigan in 1954 and served two terms. In 1958 he won a seat as a Democrat in the U.S. Senate with strong labor support. In subsequent campaigns Hart also was aided by the wealth of his wife, an auto parts heiress. Hart immediately joined the liberal coalition in the Senate. An open, frank man known as the conscience of the Senate, Hart built a reputation as a quietly effective legislative technician with a special interest in civil rights, consumer protection, and antitrust matters.

During the NIXON administration Hart earned consistently high marks from the liberal Americans for Democratic Action. In 1969 and again in 1974 the organization gave him a 100 rating. Hart voted for federal campaign subsidies, busing, and government aid for abortions while opposing "no-knock" entry legislation. In defense and foreign affairs he opposed the deployment of the Safeguard antiballistic missile system and supported the ban on importing chrome from Rhodesia and cuts in military spending. He was an early critic of the Vietnam War and voted for attempts to limit presidential authority to conduct the war and efforts to end the conflict.

Hart's liberal voting record often proved unpopular at home. His battle for stiff air pollution and safety devices on cars angered Detroit and the auto unions. In 1972 he introduced a bill to restrict the ownership of hand guns that alienated Michigan's rural voters. Hart's most controversial stand was his support of school busing at a time when Detroit and its suburbs were embroiled in a dispute over the issue.

As chairman of the Judiciary Committee's Subcommittee on Antitrust and Monopoly, Hart frequently challenged the power of the nation's insurance companies. In August 1972 he introduced legislation to establish a national no-fault insurance program. The Senate recommitted it, thus killing the bill. Hart then chaired hearings in the spring of 1973 to expose the questionable selling practices of life insurance companies. Hart proposed a truth-in-insurance bill, but the Senate failed to act on this also.

Hart's subcommittee also held hearings throughout the Johnson and Nixon years on the power of the largest corporations to stifle competition. Hart found that existing antitrust and

antimonopoly laws were rarely enforced and that big business engaged in practices presumably outlawed. To rectify this situation he introduced the 1972 industrial reorganization bill aimed at breaking up monopolies in seven major industries—automobiles, chemicals and drugs, steel, electronics, energy, electrical machinery, and nonferrous metals. Hart's bill stipulated that corporations would be liable to divestiture if the businesses earned over 15 percent of their profits after taxes, if four or fewer companies accounted for 50 percent of sales in a given industry, or if there was a lack of price competition. To enforce these stiff requirements Hart proposed a commission to prosecute the conglomerates in a special federal court. The law would have specifically affected such corporations as IBM, Xerox, Procter & Gamble, Ford, Chrysler, and General Motors, all with corporate headquarters in Hart's home state. Responding to charges that he was antibusiness, Hart answered that on the contrary he was probusiness because he desired to return fair competition to the economy. Hart's bill was defeated, but his exposé contributed to the Justice Department's decision to sue for the breakup of IBM.

Through 1976 Hart battled cancer. He died in December of that year. Before his death the Senate, in an unprecedented move, named its new office building after him.

—JB

Hartke, R(upert) Vance
(1991–2003) *member of the Senate*

Born on May 31, 1919, the son of a small-town Indiana postmaster, Hartke received his law degree from Indiana University in 1948. He practiced law in Evansville, where he was also active in local Democratic Party politics. In 1955 the city elected him mayor; four years later, he became the state's first Democratic senator in 20 years. Earning high rankings by the liberal

Americans for Democratic Action, Hartke supported the Great Society legislation of Lyndon Johnson. He was the principal author of the Higher Education Act of 1965 and the Adult Education Act of 1967, both of which made college education readily available to those who could not afford it. Originally a supporter of the Vietnam War, Hartke became one of the leading Senate doves after a visit to Asia in 1965.

As chairman of the Surface Transportation Subcommittee and a member of the Aviation Subcommittee, both under the Commerce Committee, Hartke was particularly concerned with improving safety features in the nation's transportation system. He led efforts for legislation to authorize the Department of Transportation to set national uniform safety standards for airlines, highways, and railroads as well as natural-gas pipelines. Hartke had lost a sister in a car crash and had been impressed with critics' charges that American automobiles were inherently unsafe. Beginning in 1966 Hartke unsuccessfully pressed for a mandatory prison term for those in the automobile industry who willfully violated auto safety in their designs. Hartke also was a leading critic of the Federal Aviation Administration, which he accused of failing to enforce safety precautions.

Hartke played a major role in the passage of the Rail Passenger Service Act of 1970. The measure provided for the establishment of the National Rail Passenger Corp. known as Amtrak, a quasi-public corporation providing passenger service between major cities throughout the nation. It was hoped that Amtrak would relieve the railroads of the financial burden of operating commuter routes that frequently ran deficits. Hartke's Hazardous Materials Transportation Act, signed by Ford in 1975, restricted the shipments of radioactive and hazardous materials on passenger aircraft. To ensure a uniform system of track maintenance, Hartke introduced in 1970 the Railroad Safety Act, which was subsequently passed. Two years later his more ambitious Inter-

state Railway Act provided for the rehabilitation of main-line tracks and roadbeds through a program of federal grants and loans.

In 1973 Hartke became chairman of the Veterans Affairs Committee. He obtained in 1974 cost-of-living increases for G.I. education benefits. Hartke also sponsored similar increases in pensions given to wartime veterans and their survivors for service-connected disability and death.

Hartke was a major supporter of organized labor, which was a major power in Indiana politics. Hartke coauthored with Representative James A. Bourke (D-Mass.) the AFL-CIO–sponsored foreign trade and investment bill, which sought to safeguard American jobs and industry through a protectionist tariff system and a discriminatory tax levied on multinational American corporations flooding the domestic market with cheap imports. This bill, as well as the one he introduced in 1971 to curb imports of steel, was defeated.

In foreign affairs Hartke opposed the Vietnam War policies of the NIXON administration, voting, for example, for the Cooper-Church and McGovern-Hatfield amendments. Because of Hartke's opposition to the war, the administration made him a priority target for defeat in his 1970 campaign. The Republican Party poured money into the state to aid his rival, and Vice President SPIRO AGNEW toured the state speaking for the Republican challenger. Hartke won the election in one of the closest senatorial elections in recent memory. His opponent, Representative Richard L. Roudebush, challenged the results, but the Supreme Court in 1972 declared Hartke the winner.

In January 1972 Hartke announced his candidacy for the Democratic nomination for the presidency. Running as a liberal with little funds and no press coverage, Hartke did poorly in both the Florida and New Hampshire primaries. He withdrew in April in favor of HUBERT HUMPHREY. In 1976 Hartke lost in his bid for a third term to the popular Indianapolis mayor Richard Lugar. Hartke established a law firm in Falls Church, Virginia, where he lived until his death in 2003.

—JB

Hatfield, Mark O(dum)
(1922–   ) *member of the Senate*

Mark O. Hatfield was born on July 22, 1922, in Dallas, Oregon. After earning his master's degree in political science from Stanford University in 1948, Hatfield taught political science at Willamette University. In addition to his academic responsibilities, the Republican Hatfield concurrently served in both houses of the Oregon legislature. In 1957 Oregon voters elected him secretary of state; two years later he became his state's youngest governor. In 1966 he won a seat in the Senate on an antiwar platform.

During the NIXON administration Hatfield was one of the major doves in the Senate. In June 1970 he suggested that the Nixon-Agnew team might have to be replaced because it failed to deliver on its promise to end the war. In May 1970, when Nixon ordered American troops into Cambodia, Hatfield cosponsored with Senator GEORGE MCGOVERN (D-S.D.) an amendment to the arms appropriations bill providing for the termination of funds for the Vietnam War after December 31, 1971. The Hatfield-McGovern Amendment became the rallying cry for the antiwar movement among activists, who collected petitions, held demonstrations, and lobbied in Congress for its passage. The Senate defeated the amendment twice, once in 1970 and again in 1971. Hatfield also lobbied for the replacement of the draft with a voluntary army. His bill, first introduced in 1967 and on a number of occasions thereafter, never passed, but the administration eventually ended the draft on its own initiative.

Hatfield was particularly concerned with a number of major constitutional reforms. He joined the group in the Senate that had been urging the abolition of the Electoral College. Hatfield further proposed special elections for the vice president and other cabinet officials to create a "plural executive" and forestall the trend toward one-man rule. Hatfield also sponsored a constitutional amendment that sought to restrict senators to two six-year terms and representatives to 12 years. Following a mandatory sabbatical of two years, those congressmen whose terms had expired would be permitted to seek office again. Hatfield argued that this plan would restore democracy to the Congress by undermining the seniority system.

Hatfield's record during the Nixon-Ford years also revealed concern for both the conservation of natural resources and the sanctity of what he believed to be human life. Hatfield lobbied for legislation to preserve the forests and asked for the decentralization of national control over forest areas, especially in his home state. In 1973 Hatfield cosponsored a constitutional amendment barring abortions except to save the life of the mother. Although he opposed abortions, he was in the forefront of those who desired a stronger federal commitment to encourage family planning.

During the JIMMY CARTER administration Hatfield's interest in foreign policy and in domestic liberal legislation made him a reliable Republican vote for the new president in these areas. Retiring from the Senate in 1997, Hatfield became an adjunct professor at Portland State University, George Fox University, and Willamette University.

—JB

Hawkins, Augustus F(reeman)
(1907–   ) *member of the House of Representatives*

Born on August 31, 1907, in Shreveport, Louisiana, Hawkins moved to Los Angeles with his family when he was 10. He attended the

University of California at Los Angeles and received a B.A. in economics in 1931. After working as a volunteer in Upton Sinclair's End Poverty in California campaign, Hawkins was elected to the state assembly in 1934. He served there for 28 years.

In 1962 Hawkins won election to the House of Representatives. A black Democratic representative from a predominantly black district in Los Angeles, Hawkins consistently supported President Johnson's Great Society programs. After the 1965 Watts riots, which occurred in his district, Hawkins was able to win large amounts of federal aid for his constituents. He was an early critic of the Vietnam War on the grounds that it diverted badly needed funds from antipoverty programs.

Hawkins continued his opposition to the war during the NIXON years. In 1970 he was a member of a House fact-finding mission to Vietnam. Although the majority of the group issued a report on July 6 that was optimistic about the success of U.S. military policies, Hawkins and another member of the group, Representative William R. Anderson (D-Tenn.), issued a report highly critical of conditions and treatment of civilian political prisoners. Hawkins described the "tiger cages" on Con Son Island as "the worst" prison he had ever seen. The revelations led to congressional hearings on the matter and a great deal of unfavorable publicity for the South Vietnamese government.

Hawkins quickly became a vocal congressional opponent of President Nixon, whose domestic policies and appointments appeared to threaten the gains made by the civil rights movement during the 1960s. Nixon's nomination of CLEMENT HAYNSWORTH and G. HARROLD CARSWELL to the Supreme Court, the extension by the Department of Health, Education, and Welfare of school desegregation deadlines in the South, and administration proposals to weaken the Equal Employment Opportuni-

ties Commission (EEOC) and to dismantle the Office of Economic Opportunities (OEO) angered Hawkins and other black members of Congress. In February 1970 they sought a meeting with Nixon but after several months were informed that it could not be fit into the president's schedule.

During the summer Hawkins released to the press a letter he had addressed to the president that said that the administration's policies were "destined to destroy all possibilities of unity and brotherhood" between blacks and whites. With other black representatives he announced the formation in October 1970 of a "shadow cabinet" on civil rights, and the following year, at the start of the 92nd Congress, he helped organize the Congressional Black Caucus, of which he was chosen vice chairman. Finally granted a meeting with the president on March 25, 1971, the caucus members presented Nixon with 60 legislative goals, including a guaranteed annual income for all Americans, federal funds for minority businesses, the nationalization of welfare, and expansion of the federal government's low-income housing program. The caucus later denounced Nixon's response as disappointing and inadequate.

Hawkins, meanwhile, was working on proposals to strengthen the enforcement powers of the EEOC. In 1969 he introduced legislation to give the commission the power to issue cease-and-desist orders in cases of job bias, but no action was taken. In 1971 he introduced a similar bill with the cosponsorship of Representative Ogden Reid (R-N.Y.). Although approved by the Education and Labor Committee in June, it was defeated on the House floor in September. In its place was adopted a weaker administration measure that limited the EEOC to bringing suit in federal court. The weakened bill was finally cleared by Congress in March 1972 and became law.

Hawkins also opposed efforts to dismantle the OEO. In March 1971 Nixon asked for a simple two-year extension of the OEO pending the development of a reorganization plan that would transfer many of its programs to other agencies. Hawkins denounced the proposal as a disguised attempt at "dismantling the OEO and stripping it of all its programs" so that there would no longer be an "advocate for the poor" among federal agencies. In 1973 Nixon attempted to scuttle the OEO without congressional approval but was blocked by court order. The following year Hawkins sponsored the legislation that replaced the OEO with a new independent Community Services Administration to handle federal programs for the poor. Aided by a recession and rising unemployment rates that highlighted the need for aid to the poor, the bill was approved by Congress in December 1974 and signed into law the following month by President FORD despite his reservations.

On June 20, 1974, Hawkins proposed a full-employment bill in the House. Introduced in the Senate by HUBERT HUMPHREY in October, the Humphrey-Hawkins bill quickly became a priority legislative item of liberals, blacks, and organized labor. The measure called for a national unemployment rate of 3 percent to be achieved within 18 months of enactment for those 16 years of age and older, with the federal government as an employer of last resort. Throughout 1975 and early 1976 Hawkins and Humphrey held hearings around the country to mobilize support for the legislation.

On March 12, 1976, a revised version was introduced extending to four years the timetable for reaching full employment. The House Education and Labor Committee approved the measure in May, and the bill had the endorsement of Democratic presidential hopeful JIMMY CARTER. The Republican Party criticized the bill in its platform as a "quick-fix solution" to unemployment, and Ford attacked the measure as an "election-year boondoggle."

In response to these criticisms and in an effort to broaden support for the bill, Hawkins agreed to a compromise version approved by the committee in September. The revised bill strengthened the anti-inflation sections, provided for a goal of 3 percent unemployment for workers over 20 years of age, and made clear that last-resort government jobs would be low paying. Despite these compromises no action was taken on the bill by either the full House or the Senate in 1976.

In 1977 President Carter expressed further reservations about the full-employment bill. In November he and Hawkins worked out a compromise that raised the unemployment target to 4 percent, restricted federal action to fiscal and monetary policies, and established no new jobs programs or spending programs to create jobs for the unemployed. Furthermore, the measure would not guarantee government jobs for the hard-core unemployed. On October 27, 1978, President Carter signed a significantly weakened version of the original Humphrey-Hawkins bill based on this compromise.

Hawkins served in the House until 1991, when he retired. He currently resides in Los Angeles.

—JD

Hayden, Thomas E(mmett)
(1940–) *radical, antiwar leader*

Born on December 12, 1940, Hayden, raised in a conservative suburb of Detroit, was the only child of a Chrysler Corp. accountant. After graduating from the University of Michigan in 1961, he worked full-time with the Student Nonviolent Coordinating Committee in the South. Returning to Ann Arbor, he helped form a campus chapter of the newly organized Students for a Democratic Society (SDS). He wrote the initial draft of SDS's "Port Huron Statement," which became the manifesto of the New Left, and served as president of SDS in 1962 and 1963.

With the escalation of U.S. involvement in Vietnam in 1965, Hayden increasingly focused his attention on the growing antiwar movement. In December 1965 he traveled to North Vietnam with other antiwar activists. In September 1967 he attended a conference in Czechoslovakia with North Vietnamese leaders. A second trip to North Vietnam later that year led to the release of three American prisoners of war as a gesture of good faith by the Vietnamese Communists. Hayden participated in the student occupation of Columbia University in April 1968, and as project director of the National Mobilization Committee to End the War in Vietnam, he organized the antiwar demonstrations outside the Democratic National Convention in Chicago in August. During the bloody clashes between demonstrators and police, which the National Commission on the Causes and Prevention of Violence later described as a "police riot," Hayden told the crowds, "It may be that the era of organized, peaceful, and orderly demonstrations is coming to an end."

On March 20, 1969, Hayden, along with seven other leaders of the antiwar movement, was indicated on charges of crossing state lines with intent to riot and conspiring to incite a riot. The indictments were the first ones issued under the antiriot provisions of the 1968 Civil Rights Act. The trial, which opened on September 24, 1969, was widely publicized as a test of the limits of dissent and became a cause célèbre of radicals. The courtroom was the scene of numerous confrontations between the defendants, their lawyers, and Judge JULIUS HOFFMAN. When the trial ended in February 1970, Hoffman imposed heavy contempt-of-court sentences on the defendants and their lawyers, including a 14-month sentence on Hayden. The jury acquitted all of the defendants of the conspiracy charge but found Hayden and four others guilty of crossing state lines with intent to riot.

After the verdict was announced, protests erupted in numerous cities. In November 1972 an appeals court overturned the convictions, charging Judge Hoffman with improper rulings and conduct, and the Justice Department decided not to seek a retrial. In December 1973 Hayden's contempt conviction also was overturned.

Hayden continued to be active in the antiwar movement. In May 1971 he was arrested at a demonstration in Berkeley commemorating the second anniversary of "People's Park," when a student was killed by state troopers. Hayden spoke and wrote extensively about the war and about the intensifying government repression directed at antiwar radicals and other dissenters. In 1970 he published *Trial* and in 1972 *The Love of Possession Is a Disease with Them*. In January 1973 Hayden married antiwar activist and actress JANE FONDA, and together they directed the efforts of the newly organized Indochina Peace Campaign toward ending U.S. clandestine involvement in Vietnam and all U.S. aid to the Thieu regime in South Vietnam. As the Saigon government approached its final collapse in April 1975, Hayden declared, "Indochina has not fallen—it has risen."

With the end of the Vietnam conflict and the decline of the mass protest movements of the 1960s and early 1970s, Hayden turned toward electoral politics. Declaring that "the radicalism of the '60s is fast becoming the common sense of the '70s," he announced on June 2, 1975, his candidacy for the U.S. Senate seat held by John V. Tunney of California. In response to charges that he had abandoned his radicalism. Hayden answered that he had "redefined" it. Campaigning against the power of big business and big government, Hayden sought the support of minorities, blue-collar workers, the poor, and young middle-class voters from the student movement of the 1960s. Although pollsters and professional politicians initially dismissed his candidacy, Hayden waged a vigorous campaign and won almost 40 percent of the vote—over 1,000,000 votes—in the June 1976 primary.

After the primary Hayden transformed his campaign organization into the California Campaign for Economic Democracy, a grassroots coalition opposed to the concentrated wealth and power of big corporations. He was also active in the National Conference on Alternative State and Local Policies, a loose coalition of activists and progressive public officials, many of whom were leaders of the protest movements of the 1960s. Hayden's career in California politics accelerated in 1982, when he was elected to the state assembly. He served in that body until 1992, when he was elected to the state senate, where he served until 2000. In 1997 he ran unsuccessfully for mayor of Los Angeles. In 2003 he published a memoir, *Rebel: A Personal History of the 1960s.*

—JD

Haynsworth, Clement F(urman), Jr.
(1912–1989) *chief judge, Court of Appeals, Fourth Circuit*

Clement F. Haynsworth Jr. was born on October 30, 1912, in Greenville, South Carolina. In 1933 Haynsworth graduated from Furman University, a school founded by his great-great-grandfather. After receiving his LL.B. from Harvard Law School in 1936, Haynsworth began a 20-year career (interrupted only by his service in World War II as a navy ensign) in a law firm founded by his great-grandfather. In 1957 Haynsworth was appointed judge of the U.S. Court of Appeals for the Fourth Circuit (Maryland, West Virginia, Virginia, North Carolina, and South Carolina), and in 1964 he became chief judge.

In August 1969 RICHARD NIXON nominated Haynsworth to fill the Supreme Court seat of ABE FORTAS, who had resigned in May following charges of financial improprieties. In nominating Haynsworth, a southerner, a Democrat, an Episcopalian, and a conservative jurist, Nixon broke the tradition of reserving the seat for a Jewish justice. He selected a nominee consistent with his "southern strategy": to capture the political loyalty of the white southerners whose historic affiliation with the Democratic Party was believed to have been weakened by the party's support of the civil rights movement. Nixon selected a nominee acceptable to influential southern senators STROM THURMOND (D-S.C.), JAMES EASTLAND (D-Miss.), and JOHN MCLELLAN (R-Ark.), men who sought a halt to enforcement of guidelines for implementation of school desegregation plans and reversal of recent Supreme Court opinions in support of immediate desegregation.

The nomination provoked an angry response from civil rights organizations who argued that four of Haynsworth's opinions supported racial segregation in schools. Organized labor also denounced some of Haynsworth's decisions. Decisive opposition developed during Judiciary Committee hearings in September over Haynsworth's judicial ethics when it was revealed that the judge had purchased stock in a corporation after he had decided but before he had announced the ruling in a suit involving that company.

Many Republicans who could not in good faith support a candidate whose ethics were as questionable as those of Abe Fortas announced their opposition, and ROBERT GRIFFIN (R-Mich.) led the floor fight against his nomination. On November 21 Haynsworth was rejected by a vote of 55 to 45; 40 percent of Senate Republicans had voted nay.

Richard Nixon blamed Haynsworth's defeat on "antisouthern, anticonservative, antistrict constructionist" prejudice and persuaded Haynsworth to remain at his post. In 1972 Haynsworth sided with a majority in overturning a district court order to bus students between predominately black Richmond and predominately white suburbs to achieve school desegregation. Haynsworth assumed senior status on the Fourth Circuit in 1981. He served on that court until his death in 1989.

—JMP

Hays, Wayne L(evere)

(1911–1989) *member of the House of Representatives; chairman, House Administration Committee*

Wayne Hays was born on May 13, 1911, in the area of southeastern Ohio marked by an abundance of coal and poverty. He graduated from Ohio State University in 1933 and entered Duke University to study law. But financial conditions eventually forced him to find employment as a schoolteacher in Flushing, Ohio.

In 1939 Hays was elected mayor of Flushing, a position he held for three terms. In 1941 he also began a term as state senator. Shortly after the attack on Pearl Harbor by the Japanese in December 1941, Hays volunteered for army duty. Nine months later, however, he received a medical discharge. In 1948, after two years as a county commissioner, he won a seat in the U.S. House.

Hays attracted little attention during his early years in the House, usually siding with the Democratic majority on roll call votes. Domestically he generally supported the social policies of Truman's Fair Deal. On foreign policy matters he pursued a hawkish course that would remain a consistent theme of his entire political career. He was a strong believer in massive military aid to the North Atlantic Treaty Organization (NATO) and approved of actions taken against the Communist Party in the United States. Hays was a vocal critic of political "witch-hunting" during the 1950s.

The vitriolic and abrasive style Hays employed against his opponents, directly contrary to the Capitol Hill tradition of at least outward courtesy, was to become a widely recognized trademark of the Ohio representative.

Hays supported such civil rights legislation as the Civil Rights Act of 1964 and the Voting Rights Act of 1965. However, during the NIXON years he opposed such specific remedies as busing to achieve school integration and the "Philadelphia Plan," which provided for specific minority-hiring targets at federal construction sites.

Hays was a staunch advocate of the Indochina War. Beginning in 1966 he backed all Pentagon requests for funds to fight the war, as well as the transfer of funds from other defense programs to finance the Vietnam effort. He frequently delivered scathing attacks on the war's opponents from the House floor. In October 1969, during the nationwide antiwar moratorium, he referred to a group of dovish congressional representatives as "self-appointed emissaries from Hanoi." In December of that same year he cosponsored a resolution supporting the president's conduct of the war. In July 1970 he opposed the Cooper-Church Amendment to limit U.S. involvement in Cambodia.

Hays competed against four other Democratic congressmen for the position of House majority leader in 1970. He came in second to last—even he conceded that the vote reflected the animosity existing between him and many of his colleagues. In January 1971 Hays became chairman of the House Administration Committee. Under previous chairmen the Administration Committee had been little more than a housekeeping body for the lower chamber of Congress. But Hays was able to use its various powers to reap major influence in the House. Aside from managing such pedestrian yet essential aspects of the House bureaucracy as office and stationery expenses, travel allotments, and the like, the committee determined the budget for all other committees with the exception of Appropriations.

Hays's power was further enhanced in July 1971 when the House granted his panel the authority to determine the benefits and allowances of representatives. This move was popular in the House because it prevented controversial increases in benefits from reaching the House floor, where debate would perhaps attract adverse publicity. Coupled with his chairmanship of the Democratic Congressional Campaign Committee, Hay's control of the House Administration Committee made him one of the most powerful members of Congress.

One of the first issues Hays faced as the new chairman was campaign reform. There had been no major revision of the laws in this area since the Corrupt Practices Act of 1925. There was a particular need for legislation concerning the financing of election campaigns. In June 1971 Hays introduced to the Administration Committee a resolution setting a limit on campaign spending and placing responsibility for complete disclosure of funds on the candidates themselves. The legislation was modeled after Ohio campaign laws. Proponents of campaign finance reform urged swift action on the resolution, but Hays stated he would not be pressured. The bill was finally reported out of committee in October 1971, but by this time the House had agreed to the Senate version of the same legislation, and the Hays bill was dropped. Hays insisted that the vote be delayed until after the Christmas recess, and thus it was not until January 1972 that the Federal Election Campaign Act was passed. This had the effect of delaying the date that the bill became effective.

The new law required that all campaign contributions in excess of $100 be reported and the contributor be fully identified. The House clerk, the secretary of the Senate, and the comptroller general were to receive copies of the reports. Hays became involved in a bitter dispute with House Clerk Pat Jennings when Jennings appeared before the Administration Committee to request additional staff and funding to help implement the law. After a closed committee hearing, which reportedly included threats and name-calling, Hays granted Jennings half the staff requested.

The fall of 1974 saw fresh debate on campaign financing as the House considered a new federal elections bill. Hays opposed the much-discussed concept of public financing of elections, particularly congressional races. In August he stated that the plan was "a scheme to break down the two-party system." Hays also opposed the establishment of an enforcement commission to monitor compliance with the election laws.

In 1973 the House attempted to curtail foreign travel "junkets" at taxpayers' expense by requiring that members list their traveling expenses in the *Congressional Record*. Hays, however, was able to render the resolution ineffective by adding an amendment that merely called for such expenses to be "available for public inspection." Hays had long possessed a reputation among congressman as one of the most frequent users of the traveling privileges extended to representatives. Citing his responsibilities as head of the U.S. delegations to NATO and chairman of a House Foreign Affairs subcommittee, Hays traveled so extensively that Senator Stephen Young of Ohio referred to Hays as the "Marco Polo of the Ohio delegation." During a debate in October 1974 on reform of House committees, Hays opposed an amendment to prevent congressmen who were defeated in elections or retiring from using government funds to travel during the last weeks of their terms.

During the summer of 1973, Hays expressed increasing anger at the mounting Watergate scandal. In January 1974 he would become one of the first major congressional figures to call on Richard Nixon to resign from the presidency.

The 1974 elections were held almost immediately after the resignation of President Nixon and the virtual conclusion of the Watergate scandals. The result was a dramatic increase in freshman congressmen the following January, many of whom had campaigned on promises of bringing reform to Washington. When the Democratic Caucus met in January 1975, the new representatives were instrumental in removing such veteran committee chairmen as Representative WRIGHT PATMAN of the House Banking Committee and Representative F. EDWARD HEBERT of the House Armed Services Committee from their influential positions. Many observers predicted Hays would be next. But Hays was once again able to use his political clout as head of the Administration Committee to curry favor with congressmen. He was also able to gain the support of Representative PHILLIP BURTON, newly elected chairman of the Democratic Caucus, who owed his position in part to Hays's backing. Thus, Hays retained his chairmanship. Subsequently, however, he seemed to make a determined effort to soften his well-known abrasive personality when dealing with colleagues.

In 1976 Hays divorced his wife of many years, from whom he had been separated since 1970, to marry Patricia Peak, head of his Ohio office. But his professional and personal life was suddenly shattered in May when Elizabeth Ray, a secretary on a Hays subcommittee, told the *Washington Post* that Hays kept her on the payroll simply in exchange for her services as a mistress. Initially Hays denied the charges, only to stand before the House later and admit them. Initially he gave up the chairmanship of the Administration Committee, but in the face of continued pressure, Hays resigned from Congress in August,

bringing to an abrupt end an 18-year congressional career.

Returning to his farm in Ohio with Patricia Peak, Hays avoided the limelight for two years. In 1978, however, he won a seat in the Ohio senate. He served in the senate only one year before returning to his retirement; he died in 1989.

—MDQ

Hebert, F(elix) Edward

(1901–1979) *member of the House of Representatives; chairman, House Armed Services Committee*

Edward Hebert was born on October 12, 1901, in New Orleans, Louisiana. A newspaperman from 1919 to 1940, Hebert helped expose corruption in the administration of Louisiana governor Richard W. Leche in 1939. Capitalizing on his fame, Hebert successfully ran for the U.S. House in 1940 and in subsequent elections faced little opposition. Hebert, a member of the southern Democratic bloc, opposed liberal domestic programs and supported the 1948 presidential campaign of Senator STROM THURMOND (D-S.C.), who ran on the States' Rights Democratic ticket. As chairman of the House Armed Services Special Investigations Subcommittee, Hebert led an investigation of Defense Department procurement procedures during the 1950s. During the 1960s he opposed the Kennedy and the Johnson administrations' attempts to impose stronger civilian control over the Pentagon. Hebert was a strong supporter of the war in Vietnam.

With the death of MEDEL RIVERS (D-S.C.), Hebert rose to the chairmanship of the Armed Services Committee in January 1971, proclaiming that "my goal is the same as his . . . that the United States have an uncontestable military defense and overwhelming offensive power." As chairman he was considered to be less dictatorial than Rivers, but his control stayed firm into 1973.

Hebert remained a staunch supporter of the Vietnam War, backing the president's requests for defense funds, voting against the December 31, 1971, deadline for mandatory withdrawal of troops, and favoring the resumption of the bombing of North Vietnam in January 1973. In 1972 he forced the armed services to stop sending military personnel to study at universities that had banned ROTC. It was a move aimed against the schools of the Northeast, which he said was "where most of the draft-dodgers come from." He opposed the president's plans for an all-volunteer army as impractical.

Hebert's control of military spending began to erode in 1973. In July Pentagon critics and fiscal conservatives joined forces to pass an amendment to Hebert's defense procurement budget that restricted funds for weapons research and acquisition during fiscal 1974 to the same levels as 1973. The passage of the amendment, which left the Pentagon with $1.5 billion less than it had requested, marked the first time a recommendation for defense spending by the Armed Services Committee had been reversed by the House. The passage of a similar bill the following year and a rejection by the House in April 1974 of an administration request for increased military aid to South Vietnam marked further defeats for Hebert. In 1975 the Armed Services Committee rejected President FORD's request for emergency military aid to the falling government of South Vietnam despite Hebert's efforts.

In January 1975 opponents of the seniority system, given further impetus by newly elected Democrats who regarded the Louisiana Democrat as too amenable to Pentagon pressure, succeeded in stripping Hebert of his chairmanship.

In 1976 Hebert retired after serving 36 years in the House. He died in 1979.

—FLM

Helms, Jesse A(lexander)
(1921–   ) *member of the Senate*

Born on October 18, 1921, Jesse Helms was educated at Wingate Junior College and Wake Forest College. During World War II Helms served four years in the navy. Following the war he became city editor of the *Raleigh Times* and director of news and programs for the Tobacco Radio Network and WRAL Radio in Raleigh. In the early 1950s Helms was an administrative assistant to Senator Willis Smith and Alton Lennon in Washington. From 1953 until 1960 Helms was executive director of the North Carolina Bankers Association. Elected to the Raleigh city council in 1957, Helms was reelected in 1959 and served as chairman of the Law and Finance Committee. As a television commentator for WRAL-TV in Raleigh and the Tobacco Radio Network Helms criticized President NIXON for "appeasing Red China" when Nixon visited Beijing.

In 1972 Helms ran for the U.S. Senate. Helms handily defeated his Democratic opponent, Representative Nick Galifianakis, in what had been forecast as a close race. Helms won by more than 12,000 votes, with 56 percent of the vote. Not only did Helms carry the Piedmont and western part of North Carolina, where Republicans have historically been a factor, but he also carried the traditionally Democratic eastern countries by a 53 percent to 47 percent margin. Helms was assisted in the election with a campaign stint by President Nixon.

In his first term of office Helms was one of the most conservative members of the Senate. The conservative Americans for Constitutional Action gave Helms a 100 rating in both 1973 and 1974 and again in 1976. He voted against busing, the licensing of handguns, and efforts to give the president discretionary power to deal with the energy crisis. He also opposed the establishment of a consumer protection agency and federal campaign subsidies. A fiscal conservative, he proposed a balanced budget in 1975. In foreign affairs Helms voted against reducing troop commitments abroad, foreign aid, and the ban on importing Rhodesian chrome.

A strong supporter of the Vietnam War, in May 1973 Helms introduced an amendment with Senator ROBERT DOLE (R-Kan.) to weaken a bill that called for the cutoff of all funds for combat activities in Cambodia and Laos. The amendment, which failed, would have delayed the fund cutoff if President Nixon determined that North Vietnam had failed to account for U.S. soldiers listed as missing in action. Helms was one of only two senators to vote against allocating over $300 million in aid to Vietnamese refugees. As an alternative he proposed funding the refugee program with private voluntary contributions and attached a check of $1,000 to his amendment. He proposed that each member of Congress do the same. However, the Senate rejected the proposal by a vote of 75 to 5.

Helms led the fight on Capitol Hill against legalized abortions. In March 1974 he proposed a constitutional amendment aimed at rescinding the 1973 Supreme Court decision upholding a woman's right to have an abortion. The amendment set out to guarantee, without exception, the right to life at the instant of conception. Two years later he proposed another constitutional amendment that would have outlawed abortions even for those women who were raped or for those whose lives were endangered by pregnancy. The Senate tabled the measure.

In February 1975 Helms called for the drafting of a conservative platform at the second annual Conservative Political Action Conference. He also headed a group of conservative Republicans, the Committee on Conservative Alternatives, which established a panel to research state election laws in preparation for a possible third party presidential

bid in 1976. That June he was one of a group of conservative Republicans who called for an "open convention" in 1976.

In the 1976 presidential campaign Helms threw his support initially behind the candidacy of former California governor RONALD REAGAN. The senator was nominated for the vice presidency, but he withdrew his name after using the opportunity to address the convention and call for the upholding of conservative principles.

During the JIMMY CARTER administration Helms was one of the Senate's fiercest opponents of the Panama Canal treaties. During the 1980s and 1990s Helms led the charge for conservative causes in the Senate. He chaired the Foreign Relations Committee from 1995 to 2001. He currently lives in Raleigh, North Carolina, where he was active with the Jesse Helms Center.

—GMS

Helms, Richard M(cGarrah)
(1913–2002) *director of Central Intelligence; ambassador to Iran*

Richard M. Helms was born on March 30, 1913, in St. Davids, Pennsylvania. After receiving his secondary education in Europe, Helms graduated from Williams College. He then worked as a news correspondent for U.P.I. Following a short stint in the navy in 1942, he was transferred to the Office of Strategic Services (OSS), the nation's wartime intelligence-gathering agency. Following the war Helms remained in the OSS and then helped organize the Central Intelligence Agency (CIA) in 1947. He moved up in the agency to become one of its leading operatives and administrators. From 1965 to 1966 Helms served as its deputy director. He became director of Central Intelligence (DCI) in June 1966.

During Helms's tenure the agency was involved in numerous domestic activities that were illegal under the agency's charter, which forbade CIA operations in the United States except to protect intelligence sources. These efforts included mail-opening operations, projects to obtain background information on campus radicals, and probes of possible foreign links with domestic antiwar groups.

The CIA also was involved in a number of projects designed to ensure the establishment and preservation of friendly foreign governments. The most dramatic of these operations was the effort to strengthen the moderate Chilean government of Eduardo Frei and prevent the election of Marxist Salvador Allende as president. During the late 1960s the agency gave monetary support to political and intellectual groups, established leftist splinter parties to draw support away from Allende, and continued propaganda and liaison activities with Chile's internal security and intelligence services to meet any threat posed by leftists.

The effort failed, and in 1970 Allende won election. At the request of President NIXON Helms then began a top-secret program to block Allende's assumption of office. Allende had to be voted into office by the Chilean Congress, since he had obtained only a plurality in the general election. The CIA was to see that he did not get the vote and, if necessary, was to turn to the Chilean military for help. Funds were allocated to bribe Chilean congressmen, but this tactic proved unworkable. The agency then investigated the possibility of kidnapping the head of the army, General Rene Schneider, the most prominent military supporter of Allende. It was thought that if he were to be removed from power, the army might act against the Marxist. The CIA canceled its plans because it found the organization it had contacted to carry out the kidnapping ineffective. But the group still abducted Schneider, who was killed resisting. The agency's efforts were terminated, and Allende was installed in office. The CIA continued efforts to undermine him during the early 1970s and directly subsidized

the strikes by Chilean middle-class groups in 1972 and 1973. The strikes helped precipitate the military coup that toppled Allende in September 1973. Allende was killed during the coup.

Helms became involved in domestic politics during the Watergate controversy. Following identification of the Watergate burglars as former CIA agents, he ascertained that they had no current connection with the agency and developed the CIA's fundamental strategy during the investigations of the incident that followed. Helms handed down a directive to distance the CIA from the event to every extent possible. The agency provided responses to what it considered legitimate demands from law enforcement groups but would not volunteer information. Several days after the break-in, Helms and Deputy Director VERNON WALTERS were called to the White House. There JOHN EHRLICHMAN ordered Walters to inform the FBI that a probe of the matter would endanger CIA operations in Latin America. Walters complied, but when FBI director L. PATRICK GRAY asked for a written statement to the effect that CIA interests were at stake before he called off the probe, Walters, at Helms's instruction, informed him that no operations were in jeopardy. As a result of Helms's actions, the CIA was kept on the periphery of the Watergate scandal.

At the end of 1972 Helms was replaced as DCI, ostensibly because of his failure to institute needed reforms in the agency. However, former CIA operative Victor Marchetti reported that another factor in his dismissal was his connections with liberal congressmen on President Nixon's "enemies list." His refusal to cooperate during the Watergate controversy also may have been a factor. Helms was appointed ambassador to Iran in January 1973. His confirmation hearings were stormy. He was asked about CIA activities in Chile and replied that the agency had not attempted to overthrow the government there or to pass money to Allende's opponents. He was confirmed in February.

Helms was frequently called back from his post to defend his activities as DCI during the congressional and presidential probes of the CIA from 1973 to 1976. In contrast to Director WILLIAM COLBY, Helms publicly denied the existence of covert domestic projects. He asserted that the charges remained unsupported and had been "undermined by contrary evidence in the press itself." But he admitted that in collaboration with the FBI, the CIA did discover in the late 1950s and 1960s that the upsurge in radicalism was "inspired by, coordinated with, or funded by anti-American subversion mechanisms abroad."

In January 1975 the Senate Armed Services Subcommittee on Intelligence asked Helms to reconcile his previous testimony denying CIA involvement in Chile with revelations of agency actions published in the *New York Times* and the findings of the Senate Foreign Relations Committee. Helms replied that there was "no doubt" in 1970 that former president Nixon wanted the Allende government overthrown. He admitted that the administration had requested a "very secret probe . . . just to see if there were any forces to oppose Allende's advent as president . . . and no further effort was made along these lines." In recognizing that he might have perjured himself, Helms said that he should have stated "off the record" during the confirmation hearings that the CIA was involved in Chile. But, he added, he felt that he did not have to provide the Foreign Relations Committee with such information. He claimed that he was only obliged to discuss such a sensitive activity with the CIA Oversight Subcommittee. Critics of Helms demanded he be indicted for perjury, and the Justice Department commenced an investigation.

In the fall of 1977 the Justice Department completed its probe and planned to request a perjury indictment from the grand jury. Helms's attorney, Edward Bennett Williams, informed the department and the White House that if a trial were held he would have to subpoena secret documents. In addition, Helms was prepared to provide names of other Americans who had been in intelligence who had misled Congress. Through the process of plea bargaining, sanctioned by President JIMMY CARTER and Attorney General Griffin Bell, Helms's trial was averted. Helms pleaded guilty to two misdemeanor counts for failing to answer senatorial questions "fully, completely, and accurately." He was fined $2,000 and received a two-year suspended sentence. Liberals condemned the deal, while Helms's defenders pointed out that all Helms was doing was trying to protect the nation. He asserted that he should never have even been indicted.

Following his retirement as ambassador in 1977, Helms opened a consulting firm in Washington, D.C. In 1983 RONALD REAGAN awarded Helms the National Security Medal. Helms died of unknown causes in 2002.

—JB

Hickel, Walter J(oseph)
(1919–   ) *secretary of the interior*

After spending his early life in Kansas, Walter Hickel moved to Alaska in 1940, where he made a fortune with his own construction business. He later became active in Republican politics and was a supporter of RICHARD NIXON for the 1964 Republican presidential nomination. He was elected governor of the state in 1966. During his one term he gave top priority to the economic development of the state, particularly opening up the Arctic for mining and drilling. He often received criticism from conservationists for his neglect of environmental issues. He was one of the first governors to support Nixon for president in 1969.

Hickel's appointment as interior secretary sparked immediate controversy. Known for his conservative beliefs and strong antienvironmental opinions ("A tree looking at another tree really doesn't do anything."), his confirmation was delayed in January 1969 because of extended questioning by the Senate Interior and Insular Affairs Committee. During the hearings such organizations as the Sierra Club, American Indians United, and Eskimos of the North Slope opposed his confirmation. These groups believed that Hickel was too closely allied with oil interests. Nevertheless, the Senate committee approved Hickel's nomination by a 14-3 vote on January 20.

Hickel's most important environmental decision came shortly after he took office as a result of the Santa Barbara, California, oil leak that occurred on January 31, 1969. A total of 235,000 gallons of crude oil spilled into the Santa Barbara channel, destroying marine life and wildlife and washing oil onto 30 miles of Southern California beaches. Controversy over the accident intensified when the president of Union Oil Co., which owned the well responsible for the disaster, was widely misquoted as saying, "I am amazed at the publicity for the loss of a few birds."

On February 5 Hickel ordered all drilling and pumping stopped in the channel. Twelve days later he announced regulations making all oil firms drilling on federal leases on the continental shelf responsible for cleaning up any pollution that resulted from offshore operations, whether or not the pollution resulted from company negligence.

On February 27 Hickel reversed his decision and permitted Union Oil to reactivate several wells in the channel. He stated that the authorization was a safety measure to stem seepage from the ocean floor. A presidential task force, commissioned February 11 to study the spill, recommended a resumption of drilling "to prevent forever" future blowouts,

because the 11-member panel had concluded that pumping the field dry was the only way to guarantee leaks would not reoccur. On June 2 Hickel authorized unlimited drilling in the channel.

During his tenure Hickel became increasingly concerned with conservation. In June 1970 he banned the use of 16 pesticides on 534 million acres of public land controlled by the Interior Department. The department prohibited the use of DDT, aldrin, mercury compounds, and other pesticides.

In May 1970 Hickel clashed with Nixon over environmental policy. Angered because the administration was unwilling to make Earth Day—April 22—a national holiday, and possibly influenced by the environmental concerns of his six sons, Hickel accused the administration of failing the nation's youth. He reserved special criticism for Vice President SPIRO AGNEW, accusing him of making "a continued attack on the young."

In a letter outlining his views, Hickel also appealed to the president to meet "on an individual and conversational basis" with members of the cabinet. In his 15 months in office, Hickel had seen the president privately on only two occasions. The letter was quickly leaked to the press. After the letter was made public, Hickel was immediately cut off from several White House functions, and White House staff members began to speak of him with contempt. Thereafter a government reorganization plan was implemented that removed all major antipollution programs from the Interior Department.

Despite considerable pressure from the administration, Hickel refused to resign. On November 23, during a private meeting with the president, Hickel was fired as secretary of the interior.

In 1972 Hickel seconded Nixon's nomination at the Republican National Convention in Miami Beach. But the next year his name appeared on the administration's "political enemies" list. In August 1974 he lost the Alaska Republican gubernatorial nomination to conservationist Jay S. Hammond. He returned to running his construction business in Anchorage, where he later built and operated an inn.

In 1990 Hickel was reelected governor of Alaska on the Independence Party ticket. He served until 1994. Hickel has founded the Institute of the North at Alaska Pacific University, works as a real estate developer, and is chairman of Hickel Investment Company.

—FHM

Hills, Carla A(nderson)

(1934–   ) *secretary of housing and urban development*

Born on January 3, 1934, Carla Anderson grew up in a wealthy Los Angeles family and graduated from Stanford University in 1955. Resisting her father's wish that she enter the family's building supplies business, she fulfilled her childhood ambition to become a lawyer by obtaining her LL.B. from Yale in 1958. Hills worked as an assistant attorney in the Los Angeles civil division of the Justice Department for three years before joining her husband, Roderick Hills, in private practice, where she specialized in antitrust law. In 1974 Hills was appointed assistant attorney general in charge of the civil division.

Betty Ford, advocate of placing more women in top government positions, claimed part of the credit for President FORD's nomination in February 1975 of Carla Hills to succeed Fred T. Lynn as secretary of housing and urban development (HUD). Some members of the housing industry and Senator WILLIAM PROXMIRE (D-Wis.), chairman of the Senate Banking, Housing, and Urban Affairs Committee, protested that this was no position for

someone lacking knowledge of the severely depressed housing industry. They also pointed out that Hills had had no experience in dealing with an extensive bureaucracy. Nevertheless, the Senate confirmed Hills in March by a vote of 85 to 5.

Carla Hills brought to HUD a philosophy shared by the Ford administration: fiscal conservatism and restrained government intervention in the economy. Hills demonstrated how that philosophy translated into housing policy in two programs legislated during the NIXON administration.

Section 8 of the 1974 Housing and Community Development Act appropriated monies for rental subsidies to landlords to place low and moderate income level families in existing, rehabilitated, or new housing. Hills made implementation of section 8, which had not begun, her first priority. But her emphasis was upon existing and rehabilitated housing, and the policy became to "recycle," not to subsidize new public housing. As Hills explained, HUD was "no longer emphasizing clearance and removal but . . . preservation and restoration." After demanding realistic projections and temporary deadlines, Hills was able to report the initial processing of 92,000 rental units.

Section 235 of the housing law provided interest subsidies to enable low- and moderate-income families to become homeowners, but the program had been abandoned by Nixon and ignored by Ford until October 1975, when a General Accounting Office lawsuit pressured Ford into releasing $264.1 million of the funds. Hills reshaped the program to address the moderate-income groups by increasing the minimum down payment required and decreasing the interest subsidy, thus limiting the risk and the fiscal generosity of the program. Hills felt that "home ownership for the poor [was] unrealistic," and that "When the plumbing backs up, when the heating acts up . . . these people do not have the wherewithal to deal with those problems."

Hills's administration of these two programs became the focal point of congressional activity in the spring 1976 housing authorization and HUD appropriation bills. Democrats fought for a revival of old public housing programs by earmarking funds for that purpose and extension of section 235. Hills objected to the revival of public housing as wasteful and expensive and protested that the earmarking of funds would destroy flexibility in HUD administration. She recommended that Ford veto the measure. The bills, which passed and Ford signed, did earmark funds for new construction of housing and extend section 235. But they reduced somewhat the amount of funding for new construction that Democrats had proposed, continued to place major emphasis on section 8 rental subsidies as Hills desired, and did not change the operation of the various programs in HUD that Hills administered.

Although Hills's leadership at HUD was essentially supportive of the Ford administration's philosophy, she did publicly oppose Ford's recalcitrant position on aid for financially crippled New York City and backed the 1975 congressional loan guarantees because bankruptcy would have retarded the housing investment market.

Hills was criticized for underutilization of appropriations and for using the department to further Ford's 1976 election campaign. But she had earned a reputation as a professional, exacting, thorough administrator.

After JIMMY CARTER's 1976 presidential victory, Hills was elected to the board of directors of IBM. She also continued to practice law until 1989, when GEORGE H. W. BUSH appointed Hills his U.S. trade representative, with cabinet-level rank. Hills served as USTR until 1993. She is now chair and CEO of Hills and Company international consultants.

—JMP

Hodgson, J(ames) D(ay)
(1915–   ) *secretary of labor*

Born on December 3, 1915, James Day Hodgson was the product of a small Minnesota lumber town. He graduated from the University of Minnesota and a few years later moved to California. In 1941 he started working for Lockheed Aircraft Corp. as a personnel clerk. For the next 28 years, except for three years during World War II when he was a navy officer, Hodgson remained at Lockheed. He rose to the position of vice president for industrial relations, responsible for corporate policy regarding Lockheed's 100,000 employees. As a labor negotiator he gained the unions' respect for being "a straight-shooting management man." Hodgson was instrumental in organizing one of the first corporate efforts to hire and train the hard-core unemployed.

Hodgson accepted RICHARD NIXON's offer to become undersecretary of labor in February 1969, even though the position meant a drop in salary and a change in party allegiance from Democrat to Republican. When Secretary of Labor GEORGE SHULTZ was elevated to the newly created White House post of director of the Office of Management and Budget in June 1970, Hodgson was moved up to labor secretary. He was only the second businessman to serve in that post.

Hodgson's belief in encouraging employment of the disadvantaged carried over into his tenure in public office. As undersecretary he was a prime supporter of the Philadelphia Plan, a quota system that required contractors working on federal projects in Philadelphia, and later Washington, D.C., to hire a fixed number of minorities. In July 1970, one month after his nomination, Hodgson warned the construction industry to open up more jobs for blacks or the government would enforce federal hiring quotas. The following January he proposed quota rules that would require unions to adopt "affirmative action plans." His policy would be that "decisions on work and employment will increasingly be influenced by social and human needs rather than just private purpose." In spite of strong union opposition, by that summer the Labor Department had imposed quota plans on Chicago, San Francisco, Seattle, and Atlanta. Within one year 55 other cities had voluntarily adopted "hometown" plans geared to their minority populations.

Nixon's stance on this program altered drastically when he was faced with an election year. In a Labor Day speech in 1972, he opposed job quotas for minority groups, calling them "a dangerous detour away from the traditional value of measuring a person on the basis of ability." Hodgson dealt with Nixon's withdrawal of support by defining the Philadelphia Plan not as a quota system but as a system of "goals and timetables" to which a "good-faith effort" must be directed. Herbert Hill, an NAACP labor director, accused Hodgson of sending a memo that implied abandonment of the Philadelphia Plan and similar programs and charged that the reason was "in large part, part of a political payoff to the AFL-CIO for its neutrality in the presidential election."

Besides the problem of persuading the construction unions to accept more minority membership, Hodgson also attacked their inflationary wage settlements. In January 1971 the secretary noted that while the Labor Department deplored the excessive increases, it still observed a "hands-off policy." He personally felt these settlements contributed to the high 11 percent unemployment rate in construction. Hodgson observed that during the first nine months of 1970, construction wage increases had averaged 15.7 percent, in contrast to only 8 percent in manufacturing. In March 1971 Nixon signed an executive order setting up a primarily industry-regulated system of "constraints" to stabilize wages and prices that Hodgson had worked out with industry rep-

resentatives. The objective of the wage-price plan was to keep the industry increases to about 6 percent. Administration officials denied that the plan represented controls. Hodgson said that he did not regard the presidential order as a policy switch but a signal that any industry that permits its wages and prices to range "far out in front" of others is "in danger of getting itself singled out by the government." At the end of 1971 Hodgson remarked that "the level of wage increases has been brought down markedly, employment is up, and the industry is generally healthier than it was before this plan was put in operation."

Construction industry strikes were rife prior to the wage-price stabilization, but they were not the only labor disturbances. There were also long strikes in the coal industry and on the docks on both the East and West coasts. Hodgson, though a firm supporter of collective bargaining, believed that strikes in the transportation industry created emergency situations. To deal with this situation, in the beginning of 1971 the administration proposed the emergency public interest protection bill, which revised procedures for settling transportation disputes. In all forms of transportation—railroads, trucking, airlines, longshore, and maritime industries—the president would be empowered to end strikes. His power would include the most drastic and final step: an imposed solution. The bill became stalled in Congress, however. The following year, after a long lobbying blitz, the White House removed the bill from the legislative priority list two days before the Teamsters Union was to vote on a presidential endorsement. After the Teamsters endorsed Nixon for reelection, Hodgson admitted at a press conference that the removal of the legislation was politically motivated.

Throughout Hodgson's term in office the economy and unemployment were front-page news. The longest sustained boom in U.S. history ended in late 1969, and 1970 was a year of economic recession and high unemployment. When Hodgson took office, the unemployment rate was 5 percent and climbing. By September of 1970 it had hit 5.5 percent, and in 1971 the figure hovered around the 6 percent mark. The figures were so depressing that in May 1971 the Labor Department stopped holding press briefings on the unemployment figures and the consumer price index. With an increase in economic activity, the figure dropped back to 5.5 percent in October 1972.

Because of the jobless millions, unemployment benefits were extended, and programs were developed to increase jobs in both the public and private sectors. In August 1971 the public service jobs bill was enacted. Hodgson was given the authority to spend $1 billion to create 120,000 jobs in state, county, and city government. The life of the subsidized work, however, was limited to two years. Nixon had vetoed a similar bill the year before because it did not have this provision. Job preference was given to veterans.

With the returning Vietnam veterans entering the labor market (more than 3 million returned to civilian life between 1969 and 1971), the problems of the jobless were intensified. In June 1971 Nixon announced a high-priority job placement program for the Vietnam veteran. At that time about 10.8 percent of veterans were unemployed compared to 8.4 percent of nonveterans in the same age bracket. Hodgson headed the drive, which was coordinated with private industry efforts. By May of the following year Hodgson noted that almost one-fourth of the new jobs created in the United States in 1971 had gone to veterans, though their jobless rate was still high, at 8.6 percent.

In June 1971 Hodgson announced a $20 million manpower program for migrant farm laborers. The program was immediately denounced by several migrant groups because it was to be administered by the Farm Labor Service (FLS). Critics charged that the FLS had served the growers by guaranteeing them a cheap supply of labor and that it was guilty of discrimination. Although the name of the agency was changed to the Rural Manpower Service (RMS), after a 10-month study the Labor Department found many of the charges to be true. Widespread evidence pointed to discrimination against blacks, Chicanos, and women and the RMS's cooperation in the exploitation of migrant workers. Hodgson admitted that past reforms had been ineffectual but promised new efforts. Farm worker and civil rights groups were unimpressed with the proposed reforms and filed suit in October 1972 to prevent Hodgson from giving the manpower money to the RMS. The Labor Department indicated that "implementation of the reforms has begun but everything can't be done overnight."

For much of Hodgson's time in office he was concerned with Nixon's economic policy. First, there was the 90-day wage-price freeze imposed in August 1971, followed by a system of wage-price controls instituted in mid-November 1971. In both Phase One and Phase Two, Hodgson was involved as a participant as a member of the Cost of Living Council and as a defender of these policies before organized labor. At the outset labor unions came out strongly critical of the freeze, complaining that profits were not frozen but workers' earnings were. Hodgson accused GEORGE MEANY, president of the AFL-CIO, of being negative and "out of step" with his union members. Asked about his personal confrontation with Hodgson, Meany commented: "I don't pay much attention to the secretary of labor. After all, when you have a problem with the landlord, you don't discuss it with the janitor."

In August 1971 Hodgson made a surprise visit to AFL-CIO headquarters in Washington and pledged to Meany that organized labor would be consulted on any controls retained after the 90-day freeze. Labor was not mollified, and at the AFL-CIO Executive Council meeting in February 1972 the members attacked Nixon's economic programs. For the first time in the union's 17-year history, the secretary of labor was not invited to speak at the meeting. Nevertheless, with adroit handling Nixon gained labor's neutrality in the upcoming November election.

Following Nixon's reelection Hodgson resigned, ostensibly because he wanted to return to private life. However, he appeared to have become a casualty of the president's continuing effort to dissolve labor's alliance with the Democratic Party. His replacement was a construction union president, PETER BRENNAN. In February 1973 Hodgson rejoined Lockheed as vice president for corporate relations. In June 1974 he was named ambassador to Japan and served until 1977. In 2000 he published *Doing Business with the New Japan*.

—MW

Hoffa, James R(iddle)
(1913–1975) *president, International Brotherhood of Teamsters, Chauffeurs, Warehousemen, and Helpers of America*

James R. Hoffa was born on February 14, 1913, in Brazil, Indiana. Because of his father's death, Hoffa had to quit school to support his family. After moving to Detroit, he became involved in the activities of the Teamsters union, heading Local 299 at age 18. During the 1940s Hoffa gained control of the entire midwestern branch of the organization as leader of the Central States Drivers Council. To achieve such power Hoffa had no reservations about using strong-arm tactics to win contracts or destroy rivals. He made alliances with Chicago's Capone mob and Detroit's Purple Gang to protect his activities and in exchange employed hoodlums as business agents and secretly channeled union dues to finance illegal activities. Businessmen who had connections with organized crime or who solicited its help received preferential treatment from Hoffa in contract negotiations. The terms of such "sweetheart contracts" enriched Hoffa's leaders and the mobsters. In 1952 Hoffa became a Teamsters vice president. Five years later he succeeded Dave Beck, who was indicted for tax fraud, as president of the corrupt International Brotherhood of Teamsters (IBT).

From 1957 to 1961 Senator JOHN MCCLELLAN's (D-Ark.) Permanent Investigations Subcommittee heard testimony detailing Hoffa's links with organized crime and the embezzlement and misuse of union dues and pension funds. When Robert F. Kennedy, who had served as chief counsel to the subcommittee, became attorney general in 1961, he organized a "Get Hoffa" task force in the Justice Department to put the union leader behind bars. Meanwhile, Hoffa attempted to portray himself as a reformed labor statesman and issued a ban on sweetheart contracts. In 1963 he was charged with jury tampering in Nashville. Concurrently he was indicted in Chicago for pension fraud. Found guilty of both charges, Hoffa was sentenced to 13 years in prison. He began serving his term in 1967. Hoffa left the day-to-day operation of the union to his loyal national vice president, FRANK FITZSIMMONS, but he did not resign the IBT presidency formally until June 1971. Running the union from his prison cell, Hoffa coordinated contract negotiations and had the final say about the investment of pension funds.

After RICHARD NIXON won the presidency, White House aide JOHN EHRLICHMAN began to press for a pardon for Hoffa. Reports circulated that the Teamsters had secretly donated $100,000 to the Nixon campaign to secure Hoffa's release from prison. Hoffa was still popular with the union, and the administration believed a pardon would improve Nixon's position with labor, which for the most part had been distrustful of him.

But the pardon did not come immediately. Presidential assistant CHARLES COLSON, a close friend of Fitzsimmons, prevailed on Nixon to keep Hoffa in jail until after the union elections in 1971 so he could not challenge Fitzsimmons for the presidency. Colson succeeded in blocking the Hoffa pardon until Fitzsimmons won election in July. To protect Fitzsimmons from a future Hoffa challenge, Nixon issued a Christmas pardon that barred Hoffa from engaging in union activity for nine years.

Nixon's action ingratiated his standing with the union rank and file, who still revered Hoffa and were unaware of how Colson and their leader intrigued to keep him in jail. Fitzsimmons was indebted to Nixon for keeping Hoffa in jail long enough to consolidate his control of the union. A frequent golfing partner of the president, Fitzsimmons had, among union leaders, the closest relationship with the president. Teamster donations aided Nixon in his 1972 reelection campaign. For his role in the Hoffa affair Colson became the union's general counsel in 1973.

In addition to the ban on his participation in union affairs, Hoffa was placed under constant surveillance. Ostensibly he toured the nation lecturing on prison reform, but he secretly discussed Teamster activities with those disturbed by Fitzsimmons's conduct. He learned that Fitzsimmons had approved huge loans from the pension fund to gangsters, a practice Hoffa began to discourage in the 1960s. Hoffa also was angered by Fitzsimmons's refusal to continue his ban on sweetheart contracts, which had enriched the organizations of crime figures Anthony Provenzano and Anthony Giacalone, former Hoffa associates with whom Fitzsimmons had developed close relationships.

In July 1975 Hoffa left his Detroit home to meet Giacalone and Provenzano. He was not heard from again and presumably was executed by mobsters. Provenzano and Giacalone denied knowledge of the meeting or the reasons for Hoffa's disappearance. In 1983 he was declared legally dead. Hoffa's body was never found.

—JB

Hoffman, Julius J(ennings)
(1895–1983) *U.S. district judge*

Born on July, 7, 1895, Julius Hoffman was the son of German Jewish immigrants. Raised on Chicago's North Side, he attended Northwestern University and received his B.A. in 1912 and a law degree in 1915. He was admitted to the Illinois bar in 1915 and began a highly successful practice as a corporate lawyer. A substantial contributor to the Republican Party, Hoffman served as a superior court judge in Cook County from 1947 to 1953. Appointed to the U.S. District Court for Northern Illinois in 1953, he presided over many widely publicized trials of Chicago mobsters during the 1950s and early 1960s.

Hoffman received national attention in 1969 and 1970 as presiding judge in the famous Chicago conspiracy trial. On March 20, 1969, eight radicals and antiwar activists, including TOM HAYDEN, BOBBY SEALE, and David Dellinger, were indicted on charges of conspiracy and of crossing state lines with intent to riot in connection with demonstrations at the 1968 Democratic National Convention in Chicago. The indictments were the first under the antiriot provisions of the 1968 Civil Rights Act, and the trial was seen as a test of the limits of dissent. The trial began on September 24, 1969, and throughout the proceedings the courtroom was the scene of heated confrontations between Judge Hoffman and the defendants and their lawyers.

The trial opened with procedural battles between Hoffman and defense lawyers William Kunstler and Leonard Weinglass. Hoffman denied several pretrial motions presented by the defense and then ordered the arrest of four absent defense lawyers on charges of contempt. The lawyers, who were hired only to work on pretrial preparations, had written to Hoffman to ask that they be excused, a standard judicial procedure. Hoffman's contempt sentence was condemned by many lawyers, and on September 29 over 150 attorneys picketed the court building. That same day a U.S. court of appeals overruled Hoffman and allowed the defense lawyers to be excused in writing.

During the first weeks of the trial, controversy centered around defendant Bobby Seale, national chairman of the Black Panther Party. Seale's lawyer, Charles Garry, had been unable to appear in court for the trial's opening since he was recuperating from surgery in a California hospital. Hoffman refused Seale's request for a delay and instead ordered William Kunstler, attorney for the other defendants, to represent Seale. Kunstler did so under protest, but Seale adamantly demanded to conduct his own defense. When Hoffman denied Seale's request, the defendant accused Hoffman of being a "racist" and a "fascist." After numerous outbursts, Hoffman had Seale gagged and shackled in the courtroom on October 29 over the protests of Kunstler and the other defendants. On November 5 Hoffman declared a mistrial for Seale, severed his case from the others, and set April 23, 1970, as the date for a new trial. He also convicted Seale of 16 counts of contempt of court, sentenced him to four years in prison, and denied bail pending appeal, calling Seale "a dangerous man."

Courtroom confrontations continued after the removal of Seale. Kunstler tried to demonstrate that the defendants were being tried for their political beliefs, that the police had engaged in deliberate provocation and had initiated the violence in Chicago, and that actions to oppose the Vietnam War were within the constitutional rights of the defendants. His attempts to prove his case by calling respected political figures as defense witnesses were stymied, however, by Hoffman's rulings. On January 28 Hoffman denied the defense request to call former attorney general RAMSEY CLARK as a witness. On February 2 Hoffman similarly prevented civil rights leader RALPH ABERNATHY from testifying for the defendants. The decision provoked a sharp interchange with Kunstler, who told Hoffman that "these men are going to jail by virtue of a legal lynching and Your Honor is wholly responsible."

Minutes after the jury retired to deliberate on February 14, Hoffman handed down heavy contempt-of-court sentences against all of the defendants. The following day he convicted attorneys Weinglass and Kunstler of contempt, sentenced Kunstler to four years in prison, and accused him of a deliberate effort to "continuously disrupt the administration of justice and sabotage the functioning of the federal judicial system." When the jury returned a guilty verdict against five of the defendants on charges of intent to riot (all of the defendants were acquitted of conspiracy charges, and two of them, John Froines and Lee Weiner, were acquitted of the riot charge), Hoffman handed down the maximum five-year sentence and refused to release the defendants and their lawyers on bail.

Hoffman's behavior and rulings during the trial received heavy criticism. The board of directors of the American Civil Liberties Union called his contempt sentences "extraordinary and unconstitutional," and former Supreme Court justice ARTHUR GOLDBERG released a similar statement. On March 31, 134 Wall Street lawyers petitioned the U.S. Judicial Conference "to investigate and consider the censure and condemnation" of Hoffman for his courtroom actions. The contempt sentences also provoked demonstrations of student radicals in cities across the country.

Over the succeeding months and years, most of Hoffman's judicial decisions in the conspiracy trial were overturned. On February 28, 1970, a U.S. court of appeals released all of the convicted defendants and their lawyers on bail pending appeal. In May 1972 an appeals court ordered a retrial on the contempt-of-court sentences, and in November the riot convictions were overturned due to improper rulings and conduct by Hoffman. In its decision the appeals court rebuked Hoffman in unusually emphatic terms for his "deprecatory and often antagonistic attitude toward the defense." In January 1973 the Justice Department announced that it would not seek a retrial on the riot charges.

Meanwhile, District Judge Edward T. Gignoux was placed in charge of the contempt trial of the defendants and their lawyers. In November 1972 he dropped the charges against Seale and reduced the other sentences to 177 days. The following year he handed down his final decision in the case. Acquitting Froines, Weiner, Weinglass, and Hayden of contempt, he nonetheless found defendants Dellinger, Abbie Hoffman, Jerry Rubin, and Kunstler guilty but declined to impose any sentence, citing the improper behavior of Judge Hoffman as his reason.

In 1982 the executive committee of the U.S. District Court ordered that Hoffman no longer be assigned cases. He died in 1983.

—JD

Holtzman, Elizabeth

(1941–) *member of the House of Representatives*

Born on August 11, 1941, Elizabeth Holtzman, the daughter of a lawyer and a professor, graduated from Radcliffe in 1962 and Harvard Law School in 1965. In 1970, after two years in a New York state law firm and an appointment as mayoral assistant in the JOHN LINDSAY administration, Holtzman was elected Democratic state committeewoman from Flatbush. In 1972 Holtzman ran against veteran representative EMANUEL CELLER (D-N.Y.), powerful chairman of the House Judiciary Committee, who had represented the 16th congressional district for 50 years. Campaigning with less than $50,000 against Celler's support of the Vietnam War, his anti-ERA vote, and his insensitivity to the needs of his constituency, she won the primary and the general election.

In the House Holtzman established a solidly liberal record. She received a 100 rating from the liberal Americans for Democratic Action and the AFL-CIO's Committee on Political Education. Holtzman's legislative aspirations were clear: stop the war in Southeast Asia, reduce the defense budget, and reestablish the solution of domestic social problems as the nation's first priority. In foreign affairs and defense matters she supported the cutoff of arms aid to Turkey and opposed the development of the antiballistic missile and the B-1 bomber. In domestic issues she supported busing, government aid for abortion, and the Equal Rights Amendment. She backed conservation and consumer protection legislation. Coming from an area dependent on mass transit, Holtzman voted for subsidies for public transit systems.

During her first term Holtzman played a significant role in formulating the rules of evidence for federal courts. After President NIXON ordered the bombing of Cambodia in early 1973, a number of bills were introduced to prohibit bombing after August 15, 1973. In addition, Congress began creating legislation to define the president's power to conduct war. The result was the War Powers Act, passed over Nixon's veto in November 1973. Holtzman refused to vote for these bills because they gave congressional sanction to the bombing of

Cambodia until August 15, and in stipulating what the president could do, they conferred war-making power on the president.

Instead, on April 18, 1973, Holtzman filed suit in U.S. district court in New York to enjoin the Cambodia bombings on the grounds that they had not been authorized by Congress and were therefore unconstitutional. On July 25 a federal court ordered a halt to the bombings within 48 hours and then allowed a stay of the order until the government could obtain a hearing on appeal. The decision was overturned on appeal. Convinced that a definitive ruling on the need for congressional authorization of war was vitally important, especially for an era in which a president could initiate a nuclear war, Holtzman pressed an appeal to the Supreme Court. On August 13 Chief Justice WARREN BURGER denied the request for a hearing. Holtzman voted in November to override the Nixon veto of the War Powers Act. In December she successfully fought for an amendment to the National Energy Emergency Act that prohibited the export of petroleum products for military purposes in Southeast Asia.

During the nationally televised House Judiciary debates in July 1974 on the impeachment of President Nixon, Holtzman earned a reputation for her well-reasoned, competent argument in support of a broad definition of impeachment. Holtzman voted for all five of the articles of impeachment and specifically supported an article that charged the president with illegally and secretly invading Cambodia in 1970. The committee defeated the article.

When President FORD appeared before the Criminal Justice Subcommittee in October 1974 to submit to questions on the pardon of President Nixon, Holtzman, incensed at the subcommittee's intent to conduct a mild, pro forma hearing, objected to the five-minute time limit on questions and hurled a series of politically explosive questions at Ford. "Why

was no crime cited, no guilt confessed? Why was the action done in haste and secrecy without consultation with the attorney general or the special prosecutor?"

In 1975 Holtzman won an assignment to the Budget Committee, where she fought unsuccessfully for the passage of a budget that stated national priorities. Holtzman continued her opposition to large defense appropriations and her defense of women's rights.

In 1980 Holtzman was narrowly defeated in her bid for the U.S. Senate from New York. In 1981 she was elected Kings County District Attorney. In 1989 she was elected New York City comptroller. In 1992 she lost the Democratic primary for the U.S. Senate, and in 1993 she was defeated for reelection as comptroller. She now practices law in New York City.

—JMP and JRG

Hoover, J(ohn) Edgar

(1895–1972) *director, Federal Bureau of Investigation*

J. Edgar Hoover was born on January 1, 1895, in Washington, D.C. Hoover supported himself through George Washington University Law School by working days as an indexer for the Library of Congress. After obtaining his law degree, he began his lifelong association with the Justice Department as a clerk in 1916. He assisted Attorney General A. Mitchell Palmer in the roundup of Communists during the Red Scare of 1919–20. As a result of his performance, he was appointed assistant director of the department's Bureau of Investigation (the name was changed in 1935 to the Federal Bureau of Investigation). In 1924 Attorney General Harlan Fiske Stone appointed Hoover, known for his integrity and dedication, to take over the scandal-ridden, politicized bureau. During Hoover's long tenure as head of the bureau, he oversaw the vast expansion of the FBI's power.

In the 1930s and 1940s the bureau was given authority to investigate all major interstate crimes and monitor those on the right and on the left suspected of subversive activities. The bureau also kept President Franklin Roosevelt informed on the activities of his political enemies. The security needs of World War II further enhanced Hoover's power. His agents tracked down Nazi and Japanese spies, used the security pretext to spy on the activities of unions and civil rights organizations whose conduct Hoover and the administration deemed detrimental to national unity, and kept a close surveillance on American Communists. The director promised that all these pursuits would be terminated when the national emergency had ended. America's entry into the cold war, however, justified the retention of Hoover's power.

In the postwar period Hoover was particularly concerned about Communist infiltration of the American left, and during the McCarthy era he played a major role in the government's loyalty programs and investigations. In the Eisenhower years the FBI continued to investigate the loyalty of civil servants, with expanded authority to conduct wiretaps. Hoover, by that point the self-proclaimed expert on American communism, continued his campaign to urge Americans to ferret out subversives from the nation's life. Using Communists as a catch-all for all dissenters, Hoover questioned the patriotism of such movements as those lobbying for free speech, civil rights, disarmament, academic freedom, and increased trade and cultural contacts with the communist world. During the 1950s Hoover's agents made a number of spectacular spy arrests and continued the policy of observing the activities of administration opponents.

In the 1960s the bureau carried out a series of operations of questionable constitutionality against civil rights organizations and radical groups that Hoover considered subversive. COINTELPRO, as the operation was known, had originally begun in 1956 against the Communist Party of the United States. But in the 1960s it was expanded to include the Southern Christian Leadership Conference and the Congress of Racial Equality. It also carried out operations against the Socialist Workers Party, white hate groups such as the Ku Klux Klan, and black power groups such as the Black Panthers. COINTELPRO operations included sending anonymous or fictitious materials to groups to create internal dissension; leaking of informant-based or nonpublic information to friendly media sources; using informants to disrupt group activities; informing employers, credit bureaus, and creditors of members' activities; informing or contacting businesses and persons with whom members had economic dealings of the members' activities; attempting to use religious and civic leaders and organizations in disruptive activities; and informing family or others of radical or supposed immoral activities. Probably the most controversial activity was inciting radicals to commit illegal acts. The FBI also conducted illegal wiretaps, including the bugging of members of Congress.

Beginning in 1971, revelations of these questionable activities embarrassed Hoover and the bureau. Antiwar activists raided the Media, Pennsylvania, FBI office and stole confidential documents damaging to the bureau. These were published in a number of leading newspapers, including the *New York Times* and the *Washington Post*. Liberal senators and representatives also began waging a campaign against the bureau by publicizing the extraconstitutional activities of the FBI. Individuals and organizations believing they had been harassed by Hoover released anti-FBI material obtained through the Freedom of Information Act of 1966. Investigative reporting by newspapers and radio and TV networks contributed to a demand for a thorough appraisal of the bureau and the conduct of its leader.

In response to the growing leaks, Hoover ended COINTELPRO in 1971. During his last years in office he flatly denied any wrong-doing. President NIXON, Vice President SPIRO AGNEW, and Attorney General JOHN MITCHELL backed Hoover's claims that the accusations were a cheap ploy by Democrats and liberals to embarrass the administration and undermine the FBI chief. Hoover tried to distract critics of the bureau by announcing in 1972 the existence of a plot hatched by the Reverend Philip Berrigan and other militant antiwar Catholics to kidnap HENRY KISSINGER and blow up buildings in Washington.

Although Hoover was not adverse to the extraconstitutional activities of the bureau, he did resist the attempts by the Nixon administration to centralize all countersubversive operations in the White House. In July 1970 Tom Charles Huston, coordinator of security affairs for the White House, sent a memorandum to H. R. HALDEMAN suggesting the creation of a "working group consisting of the top domestic intelligence officials" of the FBI, CIA, Defense Intelligence Agency, National Security Agency, and the three military services. Huston recommended an increase in "electronic surveillance and penetrations" of both "individuals and groups in the United States who pose a major threat to the internal security"; the removal of all restrictions on legal mail covers; the lifting of restrictions against surreptitious entry or burglary to obtain vitally needed material; and an expansion of the monitoring of "violence-prone and student-related groups." Hoover objected to the plan, not for constitutional reasons, but because he felt it threatened his authority. He persuaded Mitchell and Halde-man to force Huston to withdraw the recommendation.

Amid all the turmoil surrounding his years as director, especially the growing demand that he retire or be ousted, Hoover died on May 2, 1972. President Nixon and the rest of the administration joined leading American conservatives in eulogizing Hoover as a patriot.

Yet just before his death Hoover's popularity slipped in the public opinion polls. A Harris poll reported that the American people were evenly split concerning Hoover's performance in office. Even members of the administration had seriously contemplated forcing Hoover to retire following the 1972 election.

In 1975 and 1976 the FRANK CHURCH committee held hearings on intelligence activities not only of the FBI but also the CIA and other information-gathering groups. From its hearings as well as earlier accusations made against the bureau, the nation learned of the extensive illegal operations conducted during Hoover's years in office.

—JB

Hruska, Roman L(ee)
(1904–1999) *member of the Senate*

Born on August 16, 1904, in a rural Nebraska Czech community, Hruska earned his law degree from Omaha's Creighton University College of Law in 1929. He engaged in private practice until he entered the House as a Republican in 1953. The following year he won a special election to the Senate. Throughout the Eisenhower, Kennedy, and Johnson years Hruska compiled one of the most conservative records in the upper house. He enjoyed near-perfect ratings from the conservative Americans for Constitutional Action. Hruska opposed urban aid, Medicare, federal aid to housing, and gun control legislation. He voted for the major civil rights legislation but opposed busing. Sitting on the Judiciary Committee, Hruska cast votes against anti-trust legislation and improved regulation of business. Hruska's strict laissez-faire beliefs did not influence his consistent support for legislation beneficial to his state's farming and cattle interests. An avowed anti-Communist who began his political career as an admirer of Senator Joseph R. McCarthy (R-Wis.), Hruska opposed any attempt to relax cold war tensions and backed the Johnson Vietnam War policies.

During the NIXON-FORD years Hruska was the ranking Republican member of the Judiciary Committee. In this capacity he had great power in determining the nation's legal legislation. Campaigning for Hruska in 1970, Richard Nixon called him "Mr. Law Enforcement." The Nebraska senator helped shape the Omnibus Crime Control and Safe Street Act of 1968 and two years later the Omnibus Crime Control Act of 1970. Both laws increased federal anticrime assistance. Hruska introduced a number of amendments to the second act that made it illegal to invest money derived from criminal activities. This, Hruska hoped, would strengthen the federal prosecution of organized crime. Hruska's opposition to gun control legislation gratified the National Rifle Association. Speaking for the sportsmen whom Hruska believed gun control would penalize, he led the campaign that successfully prevented meaningful regulation. In his committee Hruska also opposed attempts to provide federal aid for legal help to the poor.

Hruska gained national attention in 1970 during the congressional battle for confirmation of President Nixon's conservative nominees to the Supreme Court. During the Johnson years Hruska had voted for the president's liberal appointments; therefore he expected liberals to do the same with Nixon's conservative choices. The opposition to CLEMENT HAYNSWORTH incensed Hruska. He was G. HARROLD CARSWELL's principal defender. Hruska found him to be "well qualified and well suited for the post . . . learned in the law . . . experienced . . . a man of integrity." To the press Hruska responded to the charges that Carswell was mediocre by saying, "Even if he were mediocre, there are a lot of mediocre judges and people and lawyers, and they are

entitled to a little representation, aren't they? We can't have all Brandeises, Frankfurters, and Cardozos."

Hruska also waged a campaign against consumer legislation. His threat to filibuster a 1970 bill that would permit consumers to join in class action suits against defective goods killed the measure. He unsuccessfully led the forces in 1971 to delete money from an appropriations bill for the Federal Trade Commission to enable it to study methods to improve consumer grievance procedures. Hruska thought the bill would enhance the power of bureaucrats in Washington.

In foreign and defense matters Hruska backed the Nixon-Ford policies. He remained an enthusiastic supporter of the Vietnam War. Hruska voted for all the defense spending proposals, including the ABM. In 1970, running in one of the most Republican states in the nation, Hruska barely won reelection. He decided to retire in 1976. He died in April 1999 of complications following a broken hip suffered in a fall.

—JB

Hughes, Harold E(verett)
(1922–1996) *member of the Senate*

Born on February 10, 1922, and raised in rural poverty, Harold Hughes attended the University of Iowa for a short time before being called into the army in late 1942. Following his discharge in 1945 Hughes returned to his home state to become a truck driver. For the next seven years Hughes struggled with alcoholism, and through his involvement with the Methodist Church and Alcoholics Anonymous he was able to overcome the habit. Hughes then made a lifelong commitment to serve his church. For a while he even contemplated entering the ministry. In the mid-1950s Hughes worked as a trucking association executive. He became involved in state politics and was elected governor in 1962. During his four years in office Hughes was responsible for modernizing the state's services in such areas as prisons and hospitals and creating a civil rights commission. He won a seat in the Senate in 1968.

Hughes entered the Senate as a Democrat with two overriding interests: ending the Vietnam War and dealing with the problem of alcohol and drug abuse. His first major speech was in opposition to the war. He became one of the nation's most popular antiwar politicians. Hughes voted for the major resolutions to end the war such as the Cooper-Church, McGovern-Hatfield, and Mansfield amendments. Hughes also was a leading critic of the administration's defense policies. Sitting on the Armed Services Committee, Hughes cast numerous negative votes against new weapons systems. In 1969 he was one of the leaders against the deployment of the ABM missile system. His amendment to totally scrap the project, far more ambitious than the Cooper-Hart resolution, failed by a large measure.

As chairman of the Armed Services Subcommittee on Drug Abuse in the Armed Forces, Hughes worked for a more humane federal policy for alcoholics and drug addicts. His committee conducted hearings throughout the nation to gather material for new legislation. The Senate unanimously passed the Comprehensive Alcohol Abuse and Alcoholism Prevention, Treatment, and Rehabilitation Act of 1970, which provided funds for treatment and educational opportunities for alcoholics. Although President Nixon signed the bill, he impounded funds for its implementation. Hughes then lobbied to successfully force the president to release the money. On a personal level Hughes helped a number of his congressional colleagues to combat drinking problems. Hughes also was concerned with the drug problem. He favored the expansion of methadone programs and the decriminalization of the possession of marijuana.

Coming from a farm-belt section, Hughes was particularly concerned with the impact of Secretary of Agriculture EARL BUTZ's policies on the small farmer. He opposed Butz's nomination, calling it "a blow to farmers not only because of Mr. Butz's devotion to agribusiness, but because of his obsession with agribusiness." In the Senate Hughes continued to press for relief for the small farmer.

In his first two years in the Senate, Hughes compiled a 97 percent rating from the liberal Americans for Democratic Action. His record and his prominence as an antiwar politician made him a dark-horse candidate for the Democratic presidential nomination in 1972. Hughes toured the nation following the congressional election of 1970. In the style of a Methodist preacher, he called for the restoration of morality in American politics and blasted the administration for continuing to wage a war that divided the people. The Iowa senator, only on the national political scene for two years, promised to unify the American people through a liberal program at home and peace abroad. Although he obtained support from the antiwar movement, especially among students, Hughes found the rank and file Democrats unresponsive to his unannounced candidacy. Part of this apathy was due to Hughes's refusal to court the party professionals. He withdrew from the race in the summer of 1971. Six months later he endorsed EDMUND MUSKIE (D-Me.) for the nomination.

Hughes decided to retire in 1975 to devote the rest of his public career to serve his church. On a number of occasions he returned to the nation's capital to hold prayer breakfasts with his colleagues. He served as the chairman of the Harold Hughes Centers for Alcoholism and Drug Treatment until his death in 1996.

—JB

Hughes, Howard R(obard)
(1905–1976) *industrialist*

Howard Hughes was born on December 24, 1905, in Houston, Texas. At age 18 Hughes inherited his father's oil well drilling equipment company, which provided the young man with an income of close to $2 million annually. Hughes turned his attention to filmmaking and the aircraft and airline industries. In 1935 he founded the Hughes Aircraft Co., which later held a number of profitable wartime contracts, and that same year purchased Trans World Airlines (TWA), the first international air carrier. In the 1950s the onetime playboy millionaire became known as the "spook of capitalism." Hughes shunned publicity and secluded himself in a number of secret retreats in the United States, the Caribbean, and Europe. His behavior became even more eccentric in the following decade. The once tall, handsome Texan resorted to eating strange diets, taking drugs, and avoiding contacts with all humans outside of his bodyguards for fear they were carrying germs.

In the late 1960s Hughes was forced to sell his controlling interest in TWA when other investors won a case charging that he had used the company to finance other investments. Hughes then invested in Las Vegas hotels, purchasing the Desert Inn, the Sands, and the Frontier hotels and attempting to purchase the Dunes Hotel. He also began investing in Nevada mineral land. In addition, he purchased Air West, a regional airline that served Canada, the West, and Mexico.

Hughes's name figured prominently in the Watergate controversy. In 1969 and 1970 a Hughes aide gave Nixon's friend CHARLES "BEBE" REBOZO two cash donations of $50,000 each, presumably to be used to support the Republican congressional campaigns and aid Nixon's reelection bid. At the time Hughes was negotiating with the Justice Department for an anti-trust ruling that would permit him to buy the Dunes. The department gave a favorable ruling, but the deal fell through for financial reasons. Fearing disclosure of the donation, Nixon's friend placed the money in a safe deposit box. It was returned in 1973. During the Watergate controversy some investigators speculated that the money had been used to help pay for Nixon's San Clemente estate. However, no charges were brought in the case.

J. Anthony Lukas of the *New York Times*, in his book *Nightmare: The Underside of the Nixon Years*, claimed the Watergate burglars had broken into the Democratic National Committee's office to find out what the party knew of the Hughes-Rebozo transaction. LAWRENCE O'BRIEN, chairman of the Democratic National Committee, had been Hughes's chief Washington representative from 1968 to 1970. Lukas speculated that O'Brien might have had in his safe damaging documents concerning the link between the donation and permission to purchase the Dunes. This was a claim that was corroborated by several of the Watergate principals in recent years.

In 1974 the government indicted Hughes for a major stock swindle in the purchase of Air West. At the time the industrialist was living in the Bahamas, and he could not be extradited on the charge. There were charges made during the period that Hughes had used his connection with the White House to prevent extradition. In 1972 Hughes, who shunned publicity, was continually in the news when Clifford Irving announced he had written an authorized biography of the reclusive billionaire. The book was later discovered to be a hoax. In the last years of his life, Hughes lived in seclusion in the Caribbean and Mexico. He died in 1976 aboard a plane en route to Houston for emergency medical treatment. Following his death a complicated legal battle centered on the question of who would inherit his estate.

—JB

Humphrey, Hubert H(oratio)
(1911–1978) *member of the Senate*

Born on May 27, 1911, the son of a South Dakota druggist, Hubert Humphrey was profoundly influenced by his father's reverence for William Jennings Bryan and Woodrow Wilson. He was a star debater and class valedictorian in high school, but he had to leave the University of Minnesota early in the Depression to work in his father's drugstore. He became a registered pharmacist and managed the store while his father participated actively in South Dakota Democratic Party politics. Humphrey returned to the University of Minnesota in 1937, earning his B.A. in 1939 and M.A. in political science from Louisiana State University a year later. His master's thesis, titled "The Political Philosophy of the New Deal," was a glowing tribute to Franklin D. Roosevelt's response to the Depression.

Humphrey taught in college and worked for the War Production Administration before plunging into Minnesota politics. He played a key role in the 1944 merger of the Farmer-Labor and Democratic parties and won election as mayor of Minneapolis the next year. As mayor he waged an antivice war, created the first municipal fair employment practices commission in the United States, expanded the city's housing program, and took an active part in settling strikes. Reelected in 1947, Humphrey helped to organize the liberal, anti-Communist Americans for Democratic Action (ADA) and fought a successful battle to purge the Communist faction from the Democratic-Farmer-Labor (DFL) Party. He gained national attention at the 1948 Democratic National Convention with a stirring oration in favor of a strong civil rights plank, one of the most memorable convention speeches of modern times. In November Minnesota voters elected Humphrey to the Senate over the conservative Republican incumbent.

Humphrey quickly moved into the vanguard of the Senate's liberal minority, promoting a wide variety of social welfare, civil rights, tax reform, and prolabor legislation. The first bill he introduced was a proposal to established medical care for the aged financed through the Social Security system, which was finally enacted as Medicare in 1965. In his early career Humphrey's aggressive debating style and effusive liberalism alienated powerful Senate conservatives, and their hostility reduced his effectiveness.

Gradually he eased his way into the Senate "establishment," toning down his fervid ideological approach and working closely with the Democratic leader, Senator Lyndon Johnson, who used Humphrey as his liaison with liberals and intellectuals. Humphrey, moreover, combined his advocacy of social reform with unwavering anticommunism. He introduced the Communist Control Act of 1954, which outlawed the Communist Party. In foreign affairs Humphrey leavened his anticommunism with Wilsonian idealism. He became a leading advocate of disarmament and the distribution of surplus food to needy nations. By the late 1950s Humphrey was the most outspoken congressional champion of the welfare state, the premier symbol of postwar American liberalism.

Humphrey's first run for the presidency began in January 1959 and ended in May 1960 with his defeat in the West Virginia primary by Senator John F. Kennedy (D-Mass.). Humphrey reached the peak of his legislative influence during the Kennedy administration. As assistant majority leader, or majority whip, he became the administration's most ardent ally in the Senate, working tirelessly to win passage of Kennedy programs. In the process he helped to enact several measures, such as the Peace Corps and the nuclear test ban treaty, that he himself had long promoted. Humphrey was the floor manager of the landmark Civil Rights

Act of 1964, the culmination of his career-long advocacy of the cause of equal rights.

Elected vice president in 1964, Humphrey defended the Johnson administration's domestic and foreign policies with his characteristic ebullience. His zealous support for Johnson's Vietnam policy cost him the support of many antiwar Democrats in his 1968 presidential campaign. Despite a dramatic surge in the last month of his troubled campaign, Humphrey lost the election to Republican RICHARD NIXON by a narrow margin.

After his defeat Humphrey taught at the University of Minnesota and Macalester College. He also traveled widely on speaking engagements, wrote a $200-a-week syndicated newspaper column, and became a consultant and member of the board of directors for Encyclopaedia Britannica, Inc., at a salary of $75,000 a year. He publicly expressed his approval of Nixon's Vietnam policy. With Senator EUGENE MCCARTHY's (D-Minn.) announcement that he would not seek reelection, an avenue opened for Humphrey's return to political office. He easily won the nomination in September 1970 and in November defeated his Republican opponent, Representative Clark MacGregor (R-Minn.), with 59 percent of the vote, his largest percentage victory in a Senate race.

On his return to the Senate Humphrey requested but was denied assignment to the Appropriations Committee. He was assigned to the Government Operations, Agriculture, and Joint Economic committees instead. Lacking seniority and the institutional power he had once enjoyed, the junior senator from Minnesota experienced frustration in pushing his usual host of legislative initiatives. In May 1971 he proposed a national domestic development bank to provide a new source of capital funds for state and local governments. His proposal received little attention, as did his bill to establish an environmental trust fund to enable communities to set up their own envi-

ronmental action plans. Humphrey's call for national health insurance was eclipsed by Senator EDWARD KENNEDY's (D-Mass.) conspicuous activity in the area. He worked vigorously for passage of a new fair labor standards law in 1972 and 1973 that would have expanded coverage to another 8.4 million workers and combated age and sex discrimination in employment, but President Nixon vetoed the measure in 1973. In 1974 a compromise version raising the minimum wage and covering 7 million more workers became law.

Humphrey's backing in March 1971 of a successful Senate move to cut off further funding for the proposed $1.3 billion SST signaled a shift to the left from his centrist course. Organized labor had strongly supported the plan. At the same time he endorsed a resolution of the Democratic Policy Council condemning Nixon's Vietnam policy and calling for withdrawal of all American forces by the end of 1971. This was a critical turning point for Humphrey. A day later, in his first major speech since returning to Congress, he criticized the administration's slow movement on arms control negotiations with the Soviet Union and urged the United States to accept a Soviet offer to limit deployment of the antiballistic missile.

In January 1972 Humphrey again became a candidate for the Democratic presidential nomination. Out of a crowded field of contenders, Humphrey's candidacy survived until the climactic California primary in June, his last chance of catching the front-runner, Senator GEORGE MCGOVERN (D-S.D.). Humphrey's vigorous campaigning and sharp criticisms of McGovern's proposals for a guaranteed annual income and sweeping cuts in the defense budget reduced the South Dakotan's lead, but McGovern's margin of victory was still substantial, effectively ending Humphrey's candidacy. As he had done after his primary defeat in 1960, Humphrey campaigned hard for the Democratic ticket.

In his last years in the Senate Humphrey became that body's foremost proponent of national planning. In 1973 he proposed a balanced national growth and development bill that would have created an executive office and a congressional committee to oversee policy and prepare long-range programs dealing with economic growth, population, environmental protection, housing, welfare, and other areas of national concern. The ambitious plan made little headway in Congress, however.

As sponsor of the Humphrey-Hawkins full-employment bill, Humphrey spearheaded the movement to force the federal government to create a massive number of jobs for the unemployed. First introduced in 1976, the bill committed the federal government to being the employer of last resort for the unemployed who could not otherwise find jobs. The measure was the focal point for labor and liberal agitation to combat unemployment and for Humphrey, the most prominent embodiment of governmental activism in America. Stymied during Humphrey's lifetime, the bill passed in diluted, largely symbolic form 10 months after his death in 1978. The bill declared that it was a national goal to reduce the unemployment rate to 4 percent by 1983, as well as cut the inflation rate to 3 percent by that year and reduce the federal share of the economy to the lowest possible level "consistent with national needs and priorities."

During the Watergate scandal it emerged that Humphrey had received some illegal contributions from dairy producers. Humphrey acknowledged the contributions but said he had not known they were from corporate funds and thus illegal. Jack Chestnut, Humphrey's campaign manager in 1970 and 1972, was sentenced in 1975 to four months in prison and fined $5,000 for accepting illegal campaign contributions.

In 1976 Humphrey almost made another bid for the Democratic presidential nomination but finally decided not to enter the primaries. At the July convention he nominated a protégé, Senator WALTER MONDALE (D-Minn.), for vice president. Reelected to the Senate in November, Humphrey made his final effort for a higher office, that of Senate majority leader. Although he held the affection and respect of his colleagues, Humphrey was unable to match the support conscientiously gathered by his foe, Senator ROBERT BYRD (D-W.Va.), and withdrew before the vote in January 1977. As a consolation, Senate Democrats created a special post for Humphrey, that of deputy president pro tem of the Senate, which carried a $7,500 salary increase.

In October 1976 Humphrey underwent surgery for bladder cancer. In August 1977 doctors found terminal cancer in his pelvis. In the ensuing months Humphrey performed his public duties while his physical condition deteriorated. He died on January 13, 1978. President JIMMY CARTER eulogized him as the "most beloved of all Americans."

—TO

Hunt, E(verette) Howard, Jr.

(1918–   ) *convicted Watergate conspirator*

E. Howard Hunt Jr. was born on October 19, 1918, in Hamburg, New York. Hunt's father was a lawyer with business interests in New York and Florida. A 1940 graduate of Brown University, Hunt entered the naval reserve and was commissioned at Annapolis in 1941. After an injury while on duty in the North Atlantic, he was given a medical discharge. Hunt wrote a novel, *East of Farewell*, based on his wartime experiences and continued to write some 50 adventure and espionage books in the following three decades.

Hunt became a writer for the news series "The March of Time," then transferred to *Life* magazine as a South Pacific war correspondent. In 1944 he volunteered for the Office of Strategic Services and worked with partisan groups until the end of the war. After several postwar writing jobs, Hunt joined Marshall Plan ambassador Averell Harriman in Paris as a press aide. While there Hunt met his wife-to-be, Dorothy de Goutiere, and was recruited into the Central Intelligence Agency (CIA).

As a CIA agent Hunt served in Europe, the Far East, and Latin America and was a major figure behind the overthrow of the Marxist government of Guatemala in 1954. In 1961, under the cover name Eduardo, Hunt was the CIA contact in Miami for anti-Castro Cubans involved in the abortive Bay of Pigs invasion of Communist Cuba.

After 21 years in the CIA, Hunt retired from the agency in May 1970 and began working for a Washington-based public relations firm, Mullen & Co. In July 1971, recruited by fellow Brown alumnus CHARLES COLSON, Hunt went to work for the NIXON White House as a part-time consultant. With presidential assistant G. GORDON LIDDY, Hunt was involved in a number of covert activities for the administration, some of them aimed at damaging the reputations of possible Democratic presidential candidates in 1972. Hunt unsuccessfully tried to uncover damaging evidence of Senator EDWARD M. KENNEDY's culpability in the 1969 drowning death of a female campaign worker on Martha's Vineyard. At Colson's urging Hunt also tried to fabricate State Department cables linking President John F. Kennedy to the assassination of South Vietnamese president Ngo Dinh Diem in 1963. (Hunt later stated that several cables possibly damaging to the Kennedy administration were already missing from the files.) Hunt unsuccessfully attempted to pass off the doctored cables as authentic to a *Life* magazine reporter.

During the summer of 1971, the Nixon administration began looking for ways to dis-

Convicted Watergate conspirator E. Howard Hunt testifies before a new round of hearings by the Senate Watergate committee, September 24, 1973. *(Bettmann/CORBIS)*

credit former Defense Department analyst DANIEL ELLSBERG, who had been indicted for leaking the *Pentagon Papers*, classified documents that detailed the U.S. buildup in Vietnam. Hunt became one of a team of officials known as the "Plumbers," assigned by the White House to investigate such leaks to the news media. Liddy and Hunt developed a plan to break into the office of Ellsberg's psychiatrist, Dr. Lewis Fielding, to photograph his files on Ellsberg. Nixon aides hoped to leak damaging information about Ellsberg from the files, and they feared that the Ellsberg defense might enter an insanity plea when the case went to trial. At one point, at Hunt's suggestion, a CIA psychiatric profile of Ellsberg was obtained, the first one the agency had ever prepared on a U.S. citizen. Hunt and other White House aides believed that Ellsberg was possibly a Soviet agent. Hunt later wrote of his suspicions, "If Daniel Ellsberg viewed the legitimate government of the United States as 'criminal,' then we perceived him as treasonist and alien." After obtaining clearance from EGIL KROGH JR. and presidential adviser JOHN EHRLICHMAN, Hunt and Liddy put the break-in plan into operation. In the early morning hours of

September 4, 1971, they directed three Cuban Americans, BERNARD BARKER, Eugenio Rolando Martinez, and Felipe De Diego, in a covert entry of Fielding's office. But the three found no records on Ellsberg. When JOHN W. DEAN revealed the illegal break-in in 1973, charges against Ellsberg and a codefendant in the *Pentagon Papers* trial were dismissed.

In March 1972 Hunt flew to Denver to interview International Telephone and Telegraph Co. (ITT) lobbyist DITA BEARD, who was recuperating from a heart ailment. Beard had allegedly written a memo establishing a connection between the settlement of a Justice Department antitrust suit then pending against ITT and ITT's contribution to the 1972 GOP presidential campaign. During the interview Hunt used a disguise and a false name. After his visit Beard denied writing the memo, and ITT presented evidence disputing the memo's veracity. Hunt later claimed that after the Beard episode, he stopped accepting money for his White House consultant work.

During the spring and summer of 1972 Hunt and Liddy drew up plans for a massive political espionage campaign to be directed against President Nixon's Democratic rivals. Hunt named the plan "Gemstone." Approved by former attorney general JOHN MITCHELL, who left that post to head the Committee to Re-Elect the President, the Gemstone plan involved electronic surveillance, "dirty tricks," and the introduction of paid informers onto the campaign staffs of Democratic candidates. In the belief that Senator GEORGE S. MCGOVERN (D-S.D.) was receiving funds from Cuban president Fidel Castro, Hunt and Liddy arranged an entry into the Democratic National Committee's (DNC) Washington headquarters in the Watergate office building.

On May 27, with Hunt and Liddy stationed nearby, a team led by former CIA agent JAMES MCCORD and recruited by Hunt entered the DNC offices, planted electronic surveillance devices, and photographed files. But because of a mistake in planting the bugs, the team had to repeat the entry on June 17. This time a security guard discovered them and called the police, who arrested McCord, Barker, Martinez, FRANK STURGIS, and Virgilio R. Gonzalez. Hunt's name was found in the address books of two of the men arrested. He deposited some of the break-in equipment in his White House safe and fled Washington, traveling to California on the advice of Liddy.

After his departure Dean broke into Hunt's White House safe and removed the documents there. Then, with Ehrlichman present, Dean turned the materials over to acting FBI director L. PATRICK GRAY for destruction, telling Gray that they were "political dynamite." Gray had the files burned on July 3, an action that eventually led to his resignation. Among the documents destroyed were the faked cables linking the Kennedy administration to the Diem assassination and papers dealing with the Gemstone operation, the Plumbers unit, and other covert projects. Hunt later claimed that the destruction of the documents robbed him of evidence he needed for his defense. He argued that his constitutional rights were thereby violated, and like Ellsberg, the charges against him should have been dropped. The FBI began a nationwide search for Hunt on July 1 but called it off six days later when Hunt, still in hiding, said through his lawyer that he would meet with federal authorities. Shortly afterward he was fired from his job at Mullen & Co.

On September 11 he was named in a civil suit initiated by the Democratic Party against the Watergate entry team and GOP officials for conspiracy to commit political espionage. The $6.4 million suit was settled out of court in February 1974 for $775,000. On September 15 the five-member burglary team, along with Hunt and Liddy, were indicted on several criminal charges in connection with the Watergate break-in. After pleading not guilty, as did the other six, Hunt was released on a $10,000 bond.

After the indictments, money for the defendants was covertly funneled through Hunt's wife, Dorothy. Hunt felt the amounts were insufficient for legal costs and family support, and after Nixon's reelection in November, he felt the White House was unresponsive to his complaints. On December 8, 1972, Dorothy Hunt took $10,000 in cash and boarded a flight to Chicago, but her plane crashed before landing near Midway Airport, killing her. Hunt claimed the money was earmarked for investment in a motel management company owned by friends in the Midwest. After his wife's death, Hunt's attitude underwent a marked change. Believing that he could not stand the stress of a trial and convinced that the government was concealing evidence that showed him acting in good faith, Hunt decided to plead guilty, "in the hope that leniency would be accorded me."

U.S. district court judge JOHN J. SIRICA refused to allow Hunt to plead guilty to three charges, as had been agreed to by chief prosecutor Earl J. Silbert. Therefore, Hunt, on January 11, 1973, pleaded guilty to all six charges against him. After being freed on $100,000 bail, Hunt told reporters that he believed all of his activities were "in the best interests of my country." Sirica sentenced Hunt on March 23 to a provisional maximum prison term of 35 years and gave the other defendants similarly long sentences. Sirica recommended that they cooperate with the federal grand jury and the Senate select committee investigating the Watergate case.

Hunt later denied that he had been paid hush money by the White House to plead guilty and remain silent on the administration's involvement with the Gemstone and Watergate operations. He also denied claims by Dean that he had demanded large sums of money and a guarantee of executive clemency in exchange

for his silence. He claimed any requests he had made were "routine" actions to provide security for his family and to pay overdue legal fees. His portrayal as a blackmailer, Hunt contended, was a White House strategy to make him a scapegoat for the Watergate affair. Hunt disclosed that he gave $156,000 of the funds to his attorney William O. Bittman, who withdrew from the case under government pressure in August 1973.

Hunt appeared before the Watergate grand jury for three days of testimony in March 1973. The second session was interrupted to grant Hunt immunity from further prosecution so he could answer questions. According to testimony released in May 1973 at the *Pentagon Papers* trial. Hunt had revealed his attempt to fabricate cables linking the Kennedy administration to the Diem coup d'état.

In September 1973 Hunt filed a petition for dismissal of the charges against him, contending that he thought he had been acting lawfully, "pursuant to the president's power to protect national security." Hunt also claimed misconduct by government officials in his case and asked to have his guilty plea withdrawn.

Also in September, Hunt went before the Senate Watergate committee. On September 24 he told the panel that he considered his actions to be "a duty to my country." He said that after a career as a spy, "following orders without question," he never thought to question the legality or propriety of the Watergate entries. While he said he regretted his role, he maintained that the break-ins were "unwise" but "lawful." He also related his personal plight in the aftermath of Watergate, noting that he had been attacked and robbed and had suffered a stroke in his six months in prison "isolated from my four motherless children." He claimed he had been "crushed by the failure of my government to protect me and my family, as in the past it has always done for its clandestine agents."

On September 25 he reiterated his belief that the Watergate entries were sanctioned by high government officials for legitimate national security purposes. He also denied having sought executive clemency and repeated his denials of having accepted hush money. He suggested that the Watergate conspirators were "trapped" by a double agent and named the possible informer as former FBI agent Alfred C. Baldwin III, who acted as lookout during the break-in. Hunt's attempt to link Baldwin to the Democrats was sharply disputed by Senator Lowell P. Weicker Jr. (R-Conn.). Weicker identified one of Baldwin's relatives as Raymond Baldwin, a former Republican senator and governor.

On November 9 Sirica sentenced Hunt to from 30 months to eight years in prison and fined him $10,000, making him eligible for parole in the fall of 1975. Hunt was freed December 28 without bail by the U.S. court of appeals in the District of Columbia pending the appeal of his case.

On February 25, 1975, the U.S. court of appeals unanimously rejected Hunt's petition, and he was returned to prison April 25. Although Sirica reduced the sentences of the four Cuban Americans involved on July 11, 1975, he refused to take similar action in Hunt's case. Hunt was paroled on February 23, 1977, after paying his $10,000 fine a week earlier. He had served 32 months of the sentence.

In November 1978 Hunt called a news conference in Miami to deny that he was in Dallas on the day of President John F. Kennedy's assassination in 1963 or that he was involved in any way with Kennedy's death. Hunt said he had made those denials before a subcommittee of the House Select Committee on Assassinations. Hunt had been plagued by reports linking him to the Kennedy assassination, including reports that he and Frank Sturgis were the "tramps" arrested near the scene of the killing. The House Assassinations Committee had rejected that theory and claimed a photograph taken at the time was not of Hunt and Sturgis. In 1981 Hunt won $650,000 in a libel suit against the Liberty Lobby, which had published an article accusing him of complicity in the Kennedy assassination. Hunt declared bankruptcy in 1995. He lives in Miami, Florida, where he is a spy novelist.

—JF

I

Inouye, Daniel K(en)
(1924–) *member of the Senate*

Daniel Inouye was born on September 7, 1924, in Honolulu, Hawaii. After serving with the all-Nisei 442nd Infantry in World War II, Inouye returned to Hawaii, graduated from the University of Hawaii in 1950, and received his law degree from George Washington University Law School in 1952. In 1953 he set up private practice and was appointed assistant public prosecutor for Honolulu. After serving two terms in Hawaii's territorial house of representatives and one term in the territorial senate, Inouye won election in 1959 as the first representative from the new state of Hawaii. In Congress Inouye, acutely aware of the discrimination against his fellow Japanese Americans, supported attempts to pass civil rights legislation. In 1960 Inouye backed Lyndon Johnson's candidacy for the Democratic presidential nomination and at Johnson's request gave the seconding speech at the Democratic National Convention.

In 1962 Inouye was elected to the Senate, where he became a strong supporter of the Kennedy and Johnson administrations' policies, especially those concerning civil rights and social welfare. He also served on the Democratic Policy Committee, became vice chairman of the Democratic Senatorial Campaign Committee, and was chosen assistant majority whip in 1966. In 1968 Inouye was reelected with 83 percent of the vote.

Inouye became opposed to the Vietnam War in the NIXON years, voting for the Cooper-Church Amendment to cut off funding for military operations in Cambodia. He cosponsored with 58 other senators the War Powers Act of 1973, which limited presidential authority to commit American forces and military aid to combat situations without congressional approval.

Inouye's major legislative initiatives during the Nixon years were promoting and protecting Hawaii's maritime and tourist industries. As chairman of the Commerce Committee's Subcommittee on Foreign Trade and Tourism, Inouye encouraged aggressive federal promotion of American commercial interests in foreign countries, supported water pollution control and land use policy legislation, and successfully sponsored in 1971 the Public Interest Protection Act, which gave Hawaii's governor the power to rent naval ships to move goods when dock strikes exceeded 30 days.

Inouye gained national prominence in the spring and summer of 1973 when he sat on the Select Committee on Presidential Campaign Activities, the "Watergate committee." Inouye's conduct in questioning key administration aides and officials was widely regarded as fair and competent, and Inouye evoked great outpourings of sympathy after BOB HALDEMAN and JOHN EHRLICHMAN's lawyer, John J. Wilson, referred to Inouye before TV cameras and reporters as "that little Jap." On October 22, 1973, Inouye became one of the first members of Congress to publicly call for Nixon's resignation from the presidency. He supported and worked for the 1973 campaign reform bill and the 1974 Federal Election Campaign Amendments, the first such legislation that resulted from the Nixon administration scandals.

Throughout the Nixon years Inouye was consistent in his advocacy of generous appropriations for social welfare programs and civil rights legislation. He voted for the Equal Rights Amendment in 1972 and supported busing to achieve integration. He opposed the administration's strict anticrime legislation. Reflecting the importance of organized labor in Hawaii, he promoted labor legislation and received high ratings from the AFL-CIO's Committee on Political Action.

In 1976 Inouye was assigned to the newly created Select Committee on Intelligence formed after investigations of the Nixon administration revealed extensive illegal and suspect activities of U.S. intelligence agencies in domestic and foreign affairs. In 1977 Inouye became chairman of that committee, a post he relinquished in 1979. Inouye continues to serve in the Senate.

—JMP

J

Jackson, Henry M(artin)

(1912–1983) *member of the Senate; chairman, Interior and Insular Affairs Committee*

Henry Jackson was born on May 31, 1912, in Everett, Washington. After two years in private legal practice, "Scoop" Jackson won his first elective office in 1935. Five years later as a Democrat he was elected to the House of Representatives, where he compiled a generally liberal voting record. He advanced to the Senate in 1952. As a member of the Armed Services Committee, he evolved into a prototype "cold war liberal," advocating large defense expenditures to counter growing Soviet military power. He forged close ties with organized labor.

Jackson's influence in defense matters declined under a Democratic administration. He was skeptical about Kennedy's efforts to control the arms race and even opposed the 1961 bill creating the Arms Control and Disarmament Agency. He refused to vote for the 1963 nuclear test ban treaty until his "safeguards" were added to the treaty terms. His adherence made ratification possible.

The senator was a staunch supporter of the Johnson administration's Vietnam policy, although he tended to favor the Pentagon's military solutions over the Defense Department's. He also compiled a notable record in sponsoring conservationist legislation. In December 1968 President-elect RICHARD NIXON approached Jackson with an offer to head the Defense Department. Jackson declined, apparently wishing to leave open more options for his political future.

Jackson, as chairman of the Interior and Insular Affairs Committee, deftly managed passage of the National Environmental Policy Act of 1969. A landmark piece of legislation, the bill established a national policy for the environment, authorized studies on natural resources, and set up a three-member Council on Environmental Quality in the executive branch. All federal agencies were required to determine the environmental impact, if any, of all policies and proposals. Jackson had qualified administration endorsement of the bill, in part because he was one of the few Senate Democrats who supported White House Vietnam and defense policy. Especially gratifying to Nixon was Jackson's support of the ABM in 1969. Not surprisingly, throughout 1969–70 Jackson fought for the administration's decision to develop the Supersonic Transport (SST), whose prime contractor was the Boeing Co., located in Washington. The SST was defeated in March 1971.

Jackson's liberalism in the domestic social welfare area remained untainted. One example was his sponsorship of the Youth Conservation Corps, which cleared Congress in August 1970. He voted against Nixon's controversial Supreme Court nominees CLEMENT HAYNSWORTH and G. HARROLD CARSWELL. Particularly unexpected was his support of the Cooper-Church Amendment in June 1970.

Jackson's modus vivendi with the White House bore some substantial benefits. Since 1968 antiwar Democrats had succeeded in taking over a number of local Washington Democratic organizations. Up for reelection in 1970, Jackson had to face a peace opponent in the primary and was embarrassed at the state convention by the adoption of the peace group's platform. Yet, with ample financial backing—much of it provided by Republicans—and relying on a record of service to his constituents, he won the primary, taking 84 percent of the vote. He received the same figure in the November election. The vote-getting feat was made easier because of pressure put on Washington Republicans by Nixon and other GOP leaders to choose a weak opponent for Jackson.

In November 1971 Jackson announced his candidacy for the 1972 presidential election. Theoretically, his primary chances looked promising. With most of the candidates taking antiwar positions, he could win most right-wing and many centrist Democratic votes, assuming that Alabama governor GEORGE WALLACE did not enter the race. He appealed to diverse constituencies, including minorities, labor, large segments of industry, and the military. Since 1948 he had been an unswerving supporter of Israel. Unlike most other Democratic candidates, Jackson did not believe that the war would be a viable campaign issue, since he trusted that the president was gradually ending U.S. involvement in Indochina. Rather, he thought the president most vulnerable on the issue of the economy. He advocated full employment measures and government action to prime the economy.

But there were weaknesses in Jackson as a candidate. His passion for expansion and growth was beginning to appear outdated in a decade in which the "less is more" philosophy was gaining currency. Many conservationists, in view of his SST position and support for the Alaskan oil pipeline, did not find his environmental record as perfect as had been thought. Although AFL-CIO president GEORGE MEANY liked him, some younger labor leaders preferred other candidates. Jackson's principal shortcomings, however, were probably his lack of national recognition and his mediocre speaking voice.

Jackson fared far worse in the primaries than expected. Wallace's entry into the February 1972 Florida primary crushed the senator's hopes of capturing the "law and order" vote and pushed him into proposing an antibusing amendment that led to the further alienation of liberal voters. He came in third behind Wallace and Senator HUBERT HUMPHREY (D-Minn.), with 13 percent of the vote. In May he announced his withdrawal from future primaries following dismal showings in such industrial states as Ohio and Pennsylvania, but he indicated that he still hoped to win the presidential nomination. At the Democratic National Convention in July Jackson placed second to Senator GEORGE MCGOVERN (D-S.D.), getting most of organized labor's support after Humphrey withdrew from the race. He grudgingly agreed to support McGovern, whom he had attacked violently during the primaries. But immediately after the November election he and Humphrey backed the formation of a group designed to win back control of the Democratic Party for its more conservative elements.

During the 1970s Jackson was one of Congress's most powerful figures. He increasingly used his power to attack the Nixon administration's policy of détente and détente's chief architect, Secretary of State HENRY KISSINGER.

He criticized the May 1972 Strategic Arms Limitation Talks (SALT) accords on defensive nuclear weapons with the Soviets by arguing that the "agreements are likely to lead to an accelerated technological arms race with greater uncertainties, profound instabilities, and considerable costs." At the same time, he claimed that they gave strategic advantages to the Soviets. Jackson's price for ratification of the treaty was an amendment that contained hard-line instructions for SALT negotiators. It requested that any future permanent treaty on offensive nuclear arms "not limit the United States to levels of intercontinental strategic forces inferior to" those of the Soviet Union. Any treaty was to be based on "the principle of equality."

Jackson's suspicions of the Soviets and his concern for Soviet Jews were made clear again in October when he and 75 Senate cosponsors introduced an amendment to the East-West Trade Relations Act aimed at denying the USSR most-favored nation status as long as it barred emigration or imposed "more than a nominal tax . . . on any citizen as a consequence of emigration." The Soviet leadership responded strongly to the action, calling it unjustified interference in internal matters. Both the Soviets and the administration were embarrassed, but in June 1974 Kissinger reportedly got a pledge from the Soviets to allow the emigration of 45,000 Jews a year. Jackson found the figure inadequate. Kissinger later carried more Soviet assurances to Jackson, and in December 1974 the comprehensive trade bill with the Jackson amendment was passed by Congress. The USSR canceled the treaty the next month because of the emigration clause. Jackson claimed that Kissinger and President FORD were seeking to blame Congress, and him specifically, for their failure.

In the midst of the Watergate investigations in February 1973 the Government Operations Committee's Permanent Subcommittee on Investigations, which he chaired, initiated research on the circumstances surrounding the sale of grain to the USSR in the summer of 1972. Jackson charged the Department of Agriculture with mismanagement that led to excessive profits for the grain exporters and bargain prices for the Soviets at the expense of farmers and consumers. In the subcommittee's final report of August 1974 Jackson said that the "great grain robbery" resulted in depleted U.S. grain reserves, higher food prices, and a crisis in the livestock industry. His pressure led to a temporary halt of grain shipments in October. The subcommittee also investigated the energy crisis beginning in January 1974. The sponsor of an emergency energy bill, Jackson suggested that the oil companies were manipulating the petroleum shortages to their own advantage. His bill, which proposed a 30 percent rollback on domestically produced oil, was vetoed by Nixon in March.

In February 1975 Jackson announced his intention to seek the presidency again, pledging to help "the little people—little business, the elderly, the young." The polls showed him to be the front-runner, and in the Massachusetts primary of March 1976 he won his first contest outside of Washington, getting 23 percent of the vote. His platform included opposition to busing and détente and support for disarmament and national health insurance. As in the past, he enjoyed the support of organized labor. Yet, by the time he won the April New York primary (he won 38 percent of the vote but had predicted a landslide), JIMMY CARTER, a former governor of Georgia, was gaining momentum and leading in the race for delegates. Following his loss in Pennsylvania Jackson decided to end active candidacy, since without a win in Pennsylvania his candidacy was no longer "viable." In June he endorsed Carter and turned his attention to winning reelection to the Senate. He received 85 percent of the September Democratic primary vote against two opponents and was reelected in November in another landslide. Jackson died in 1983. He posthumously received the Presidential Medal of Freedom in 1984.

—JCH

Jackson, Jesse
(1941–   ) *national director, Operation Breadbasket*

Born in Greenville, South Carolina, Jackson attended the University of Illinois from 1959 to 1960 on a football scholarship. He then transferred to North Carolina A&T State University at Greensboro, where he took his B.A. in sociology in 1964 and, as a senior, began to become active in the civil rights movement in the South. He then enrolled at Chicago Theological Seminary and was ordained a Baptist minister in 1968. But he delayed his full-time studies to work full time in the movement (he would receive a Master of Divinity degree from Chicago Theological Seminary in 2000). In 1965 Jackson joined the Southern Christian Leadership Conference (SCLC), where he worked closely with the Reverend Martin Luther King Jr. In 1966 Jackson founded the Chicago branch of Operation Breadbasket—the economic wing of the SCLC. While some controversy still exists as to whether Jackson was the last man to talk to King alive, he was with King in Memphis, Tennessee, at the time of his April 4, 1968, assassination.

In 1971 Jackson was suspended from the SCLC when its leaders claimed he was using that organization as a platform for his own ambitions. Later that year Jackson founded Operation PUSH (People United to Save Humanity) in Chicago, and in 1984 he founded the National Rainbow Coalition in Washington, D.C., an organization wedded to reform within the Democratic Party. The two organizations merged in 1996 to form the Rainbow/PUSH Coalition.

Jackson's first campaign for the Democratic nomination for the presidency, in 1984, was credited with registering more than a million new voters. However, he lost that campaign; one mistake of many was his reference to New York City as "Hymietown." In 1988 another million were registered as Jackson once again sought the presidency. After scoring several impressive early victories, Jackson lost ground to Michael Dukakis, the eventual nominee. Nevertheless, Jackson did not withdraw from the race until the convention.

Following the 1988 election Jackson redirected his political energies toward the District of Columbia. In 1989 he floated some trial balloons in advance of a possible run for mayor of Washington but later decided against the race. In 1991 Jackson became one of two "shadow senators" for the District of Columbia—in effect, a lobbyist for statehood. In 1992 he supported Bill Clinton for the presidency. From 1992 to 2000 he hosted *Both Sides with Jesse Jackson* on CNN. In 1999 he helped get the release of three American military prisoners in Yugoslavia. In 2000 Clinton awarded Jackson the Presidential Medal of Freedom.

—JRG

Javits, Jacob K(oppel)
(1904–1986) *member of the Senate*

Born on May 18, 1904, the son of Jewish immigrants, Jacob Javits was raised on the Lower East Side of New York City. Working his way through law school at New York University, he received his law degree in 1926 and was admitted to the bar in the following year. With his older brother he established a law firm that specialized in bankruptcy and corporate reorganization. A supporter of Mayor Fiorello La Guardia, Javits joined the Republican Party in the 1930s. After serving in the army during World War II, he won election to the House of Representatives from the Upper West Side of New York City in 1946 and served there until 1954. In the House Javits broke ranks with the Republicans on most issues and established a reputation as a liberal. He ran for attorney general of New York in 1954 and was the only Republican elected that year to statewide office. In 1956 he defeated New York City mayor Robert F. Wagner Jr. in a race for the U.S. Senate. Javits's liberalism, combined with his Jewish religious affiliation, made him one of the most successful candidates in New York state history, and he easily won reelection to the Senate in 1962, 1968, and 1974. During the 1960s Javits supported most of the social welfare proposals of the Kennedy and Johnson administrations and was an outspoken advocate of civil rights legislation. Blocked from influence in the Republican Party because of his liberal voting record, Javits tried to make up for his lack of power in the party by serving on many committees and informing himself on a wide range of issues.

During the NIXON and FORD administrations, Javits sponsored legislation in several areas. An early advocate of consumer protection, he introduced in 1970 with Senator ABRAHAM RIBICOFF (D-Conn.) a bill to establish an independent consumer protection agency. Filibusters killed the bill on the Senate floor in 1972 and again in 1974. Finally passed by both houses of Congress in 1975, the bill died in conference because of a threatened veto by President Ford. Javits also was a prime mover behind legislation to regulate private pension plans. As a member of the Senate Labor and Public Welfare Committee, Javits first introduced such legislation in 1970. With Senator HARRISON WILLIAMS (D-N.J.) he conducted a two-year study of private pension plans and held hearings throughout the country to gather data on abuses. Their study showed that most

workers seldom received benefits and recommended legislation to regulate funding of pension plans and to guarantee to workers at least a part of their pensions even when they changed jobs. In 1974 Congress finally passed a bill establishing minimum federal standards of investing and financing for private pension plans.

Javits also supported attempts to establish a national health insurance program and to provide federal subsidies for mass transit. In 1972 he led the fight for passage of a law that gave the Equal Employment Opportunities Commission the power to take cases of job discrimination to court. In 1973 he supported extension of unemployment compensation benefits, and in 1974 he helped win passage of the first increase in the federal minimum wage since 1967. A strong advocate of civil rights, Javits opposed attempts to slow the pace of school desegregation and to place restrictions on the use of busing to achieve integration.

During the Nixon years Javits became increasingly critical of the war in Vietnam. In May 1969 he called Nixon's Vietnam policy "sterile" and asked the president to set a timetable for the withdrawal of U.S. troops. In 1970 he voted for the Cooper-Church Amendment to cut off funds for combat operations in Cambodia and in 1971 supported the McGovern-Hatfield end-the-war amendment. As a member of the Senate Foreign Relations Committee, Javits voted for a 1972 proposal to cut off funds for all combat operations in Southeast Asia by the end of 1972.

Concerned about the apparent erosion of congressional authority in the area of foreign policy, Javits introduced legislation in 1970 to limit the war-making powers of the president. Finally passed by both houses of Congress on November 7, 1973, over President Nixon's veto, the War Powers Act limited to 60 days the president's ability to send U.S. troops into combat without receiving congressional approval. It marked the first time in the nation's history that Congress had undertaken to define the powers of the president as commander in chief. In 1973 Javits wrote *Who Makes War: The President versus Congress*, in which he outlined the rationale for the War Powers Act.

Javits also took an interest in other areas of foreign policy. Visiting Cuba in 1974, he called for an end to the trade embargo against Cuba, an easing of restrictions on travel to the island, and a resumption of diplomatic relations with the Castro regime. In December 1975 Javits led the successful effort in the Senate to bar the use of defense appropriations in the civil war in Angola. A vocal proponent of American aid to Israel, Javits condemned the 1975 UN resolution that called Zionism a form of racism.

Javits found himself at odds with the JIMMY CARTER administration over U.S. policy toward the Middle East. Javits was sharply critical of the State Department's call in 1977 for Israeli withdrawal from all occupied Arab lands and for Israeli agreement to the establishment of a Palestinian state as a condition for peace. In 1978 he led the unsuccessful fight against Carter's package arms deal for the Middle East. Defeated for reelection in 1980, Javits returned to his law practice. He died of complications of amytrophic lateral sclerosis ("Lou Gehrig's disease") in 1986.

—JD

Jaworski, Leon
(1905–1982) *Watergate special prosecutor*

The son of immigrant parents, Jaworski was born on September 19, 1905, in Waco, Texas, where his father was an evangelical minister. He graduated from Baylor University and Baylor Law School and in 1925 became the youngest person ever admitted to the Texas bar. Six years later he joined the Houston firm of Fulbright, Crooker, Freeman, & Bates and soon became a partner in the firm. During the 1930s he gained a reputation as a skillful courtroom strategist and tactician. After serving as a colonel in the army during World War II, Jaworski headed the war crimes trial section of the judge advocate general's office. Following the war he returned to his law partnership and gradually assumed a prominent place among the state's leading businessmen, bankers, and politicians. During the 1960s he took a hardline stance against lawlessness, and as president of the American Bar Association in 1971–72, Jaworski expressed his dismay over "errant lawyers" and the diminishing respect for the law.

In early November 1973 Jaworski succeeded ARCHIBALD COX as the Watergate special prosecutor. President NIXON had fired Cox when he refused to accept summaries of taped White House conversations subpoenaed as possible evidence in the cover-up of the burglary at the Democratic Party's Washington headquarters in the Watergate complex on June 17, 1972. Jaworski agreed to take the job only after receiving strong assurances from White House staff members that he would have complete independence and could not be discharged by the president without the consensus of the leaders of both parties in the House and Senate and on the House and Senate Judiciary committees. The new prosecutor also was guaranteed the right to take the president to court.

Jaworski was sworn in on November 5 amid considerable skepticism in Congress and the press about the viability of another White House–appointed prosecutor. No less skeptical were the members of the special prosecutor's staff, who were badly shaken by the firing of Cox. Shortly after Jaworski took over, however, the prosecutor's office obtained from district court judge JOHN J. SIRICA relevant portions of seven of the nine tapes Cox had subpoenaed months before. The White House reported that two tapes were missing and a third tape contained an 18 1/2-minute gap.

Of the material provided, the tape from March 21, 1973, was the most damaging to the president's contention that he was innocent of any involvement in the Watergate cover-up. In a conversation with White House counsel JOHN DEAN and chief of staff H. R. HALDEMAN, Nixon not only approved but also urged the payment of a large amount of cash to secure the continued silence of E. HOWARD HUNT, a convicted participant in the Watergate burglary. In another March 21 conversation the president coached Haldeman on how to testify untruthfully without committing perjury. From these revelations Jaworski proceeded to build a case against Nixon, and in late December he advised the president's new chief of staff, ALEXANDER M. HAIG, to get the "finest criminal lawyer you can find" to study the tapes.

Jaworski requested additional tapes and documents that he believed relevant to the Watergate cover-up case and the 1971 break-in at the office of psychiatrist Lewis Fielding, whose patient DANIEL ELLSBERG was accused of leaking the *Pentagon Papers* to the press. The break-in had been traced to a White House investigative unit known as the "Plumbers," established to plug such leaks. By the end of January, however, Jaworski was told he had all the material he needed and that no more tapes would be forthcoming from the White House. Nevertheless, a month later the special prosecutor's office asked for indictments in both the Watergate and Fielding cases based on evidence already supplied by the president and information provided by the Senate Watergate Committee and former members of the administration and the Committee to Re-Elect the President (CREEP). Among those who at this point had pleaded guilty and cooperated with the prosecutor in the investigations were John Dean, former Plumbers chief EGIL KROGH, and ex-CREEP deputies JEB

STUART MAGRUDER, HERBERT KALMBACH, and FREDERICK LARUE.

On March 1 a grand jury in Washington, D.C., indicted seven former White House and CREEP officials for conspiracy to obstruct justice, to defraud the United States, and to make false statements and declarations in covering up the Watergate burglary. The accused were top presidential aides H. R. Haldeman, JOHN D. EHRLICHMAN and CHARLES W. COLSON; ex-attorney general JOHN N. MITCHELL; former assistant attorney general and CREEP officer ROBERT C. MARDIAN; CREEP counsel Kenneth W. Parkinson; and White House assistant GORDON STRACHAN. Each of the seven pleaded not guilty to all charges.

Despite evidence of President Nixon's complicity in the conspiracy, the grand jury did not indict him because of doubts, raised by Jaworski, that the Supreme Court would allow the indictment of a sitting president for obstruction of justice. However, Nixon was named an unindicted coconspirator so that his taped statements could be used later as evidence in the trial of his former associates. At the same time the jury gave Judge Sirica, who had assigned himself to the case, a sealed report detailing all the information compiled by the special prosecutor on the president's involvement in the cover-up. After judicial review the report was transmitted, on the grand jury's recommendation, to the House Judiciary Committee, which was considering whether to impeach the president.

In a separate action on March 7, a grand jury charged Ehrlichman, Colson, and four of the alleged principals in the Fielding break-in with conspiracy to violate civil rights. The four included G. GORDON LIDDY, a member of the Plumbers and CREEP, and BERNARD BARKER and Eugenio Martinez, all of whom had been convicted a year earlier in the Watergate burglary trial. Again the accused pleaded not guilty to the conspiracy.

Leon Jaworski, testifying before Congress for the first time since being sworn in as special Watergate prosecutor, November 8, 1973 *(Bettmann/CORBIS)*

In mid-April Jaworski obtained a subpoena from Judge Sirica for 64 presidential conversations, after the White House had repeatedly ignored his requests for additional material to be used in the cover-up trial, scheduled for the fall. The president's lawyer, JAMES D. ST. CLAIR, sought to have the subpoena quashed on the grounds that the tapes were covered by executive privilege and the dispute between the special prosecutor and the president was an "intrabranch affair," not justiciable by the courts. Sirica denied the motion, and St. Clair petitioned the court of appeals for Washington, D.C. To avoid an extended delay of the trial, Jaworski took the matter directly to the Supreme Court, which agreed to bypass the appellate court and hear the case under the "imperative public importance" rule, invoked only twice since the end of World War II.

On July 24, 1974, the Supreme Court ordered President Nixon to turn over the subpoenaed conversations, ruling that the claim of executive privilege in this case "must yield to the demonstrated, specific need for evidence in a pending criminal trial." The decision also affirmed the right of the special prosecutor to take the president to court over the tapes.

Shortly after the decision Nixon released transcripts of three conversations held on June 23, 1972, in which he had instructed H. R. Haldeman to use the Central Intelligence Agency to halt the FBI's investigation of the Watergate burglary. The transcripts showed that the president actively participated in the cover-up just six days after the burglary. With this disclosure Nixon's remaining support collapsed, and he resigned on August 9.

Jaworski was deciding whether to prosecute the former president for obstruction of justice in the cover-up when President FORD pardoned his predecessor on September 8 for all possible federal crimes committed while in office. Although he was not consulted on the move, Jaworski maintained that Ford had a constitutional right to issue the pardon. He also believed that Nixon could not have received a fair trial because of the vast publicity surrounding the Watergate affair.

Jaworski resigned as special prosecutor to return to his law practice on October 25, 1974, shortly after the opening of the cover-up trial. By that time the prosecutor's staff had obtained convictions of Ehrlichman, Colson, Liddy, and two other defendants in the Fielding break-in. It had successfully prosecuted DWIGHT L. CHAPIN, President Nixon's appointments secretary, for perjury in connection with a political espionage campaign directed against the Democrats and secured guilty pleas from eight individuals and corporations charged with making illegal campaign contributions. On January 1, 1975, Ehrlichman, Haldeman, Mitchell, and Mardian were found guilty of covering up the Watergate burglary. In 1977 Jaworski served as special council to the U.S. House of Representatives Committee on Standards of Official Conduct as it investigated the "Koreagate" scandal. He died of a heart attack at his Texas ranch in December 1982.

—JR

Jordan, Barbara C(harline)

(1936–1996) *member of the House of Representatives*

Born on February 21, 1936, Jordan, the daughter of a Texas Baptist minister, graduated from Texas Southern University in 1956 and Boston University Law School in 1959. Back home in Houston, Jordan set up a private law practice and became active in the local Democratic Party organization. After campaigning for John F. Kennedy in 1960 and losing two bids for a seat in the state house of representatives, Jordan, in 1966, became the first black woman ever elected state senator in Texas. She was an effective legislator; 50 percent of her bills, including one that created a state Fair Employment Practices Commission and another establishing the state's first minimum wage law, were enacted. Jordan was elected president pro tempore of the state senate in March 1972. She won a seat in the U.S. House that fall. She represented Houston's 18th district, which is 44 percent black and 19 percent Hispanic.

In the House she maintained a liberal record. During her freshman year she cosponsored a bill with MARTHA GRIFFITHS (D-Mich.) to extend Social Security coverage to housewives, actively supported the inclusion of domestics in the minimum wage bill, backed free legal aid to the poor, and advocated increased appropriations for cities. In November 1973 she voted against the confirmation of GERALD FORD as vice president because of his weak civil rights record. That vote, combined with her outspoken opposition to increased military expenditures and support for the attempts of Congress to halt the bombing of Cambodia, earned for Jordan a 100 percent rating in 1973 from the liberal Americans for Democratic Action.

In 1975 she successfully fought for the inclusion of bilingual ballots for "language minorities" in the Voting Rights Act and in 1976 engineered the adoption of mandatory civil rights procedures by the Law Enforcement Assistance Administration and the Office of Revenue Sharing. Jordan was consistent in her views on military expenditures and foreign policy. She voted for reductions in the defense budget, opposed appropriations for the B-1 bomber, and voted against arms sales to Turkey and Chile.

In 1975 and 1976 liberals criticized Jordan for her close ties to what was known as the "Texas Club" (together, WRIGHT PATMAN, GEORGE MAHON, W. R. POAGE, Olin Teague, and Jack Brooks chaired one-third of the House standing committees) and for her vote in favor of the deregulation of natural gas in February 1976. To Jordan, that was practical politics. She was willing to work with her powerful conservative colleagues and support some of their proposals if she thought she could win their support for her proposals in return.

As a member of the Judiciary Committee, Jordan gained national attention during the committee's 1974 hearings into the impeachment of President NIXON. Her powerful oratory and brilliant delivery set the mood of serious deliberation, "My faith in the Constitution is whole," she said, "it is complete, it is total, and I am not going to sit here and be an idle spectator to [its] diminution." Jordan presented a case for a broad interpretation of the grounds of impeachment and argued that the charges before the committee were a worthy test of the Constitution's value. She voted for all five articles of impeachment; three were passed.

In 1976 Jordan delivered the keynote address at the Democratic National Convention. She thrilled the meeting with a ringing call for "a national community" where everyone is equal. "We cannot improve on the system of government handed down to us by the founders of the Republic," she said, "but we can find new ways to implement that system and realize our destiny." Her own role that night, she asserted, showed "that the American dream need not forever be deferred." Jordan was the first black and the first woman ever to be the party's keynoter.

After the overwhelming response to Jordan's speech, rumors spread about her chances for the vice presidential nomination. But the only position Jordan would accept from JIMMY CARTER was attorney general, an offer that never came. In November 1977 Jordan keynoted the National Conference of Women in Houston.

In 1973 she had begun to suffer from multiple sclerosis. In 1977 she declined to seek another term in Congress. She became a professor at the University of Texas, and in 1992 she was once again the keynote speaker at the Democratic National Convention. She was awarded the Presidential Medal of Freedom in 1994 and died of pneumonia in 1996.

—JMP and JRG

K

Kalmbach, Herbert W(arren)
(1921–   ) *attorney*

Born in Port Huron, Michigan, Kalmbach graduated from the University of Southern California in 1949 after serving in the navy during World War II. In 1951 he received a law degree from the same institution and the following year was admitted to the bar in California. In 1952 he became vice president of the Los Angeles Security Title Insurance Co., a position he held until 1957, when he entered law practice. Kalmbach first became involved in the political career of RICHARD NIXON when he quit his job to work on the 1960 presidential campaign. After Nixon's defeat he returned to the business world and the practice of law.

In 1968 Kalmbach was one of the chief fund-raisers for Nixon's presidential campaign. A great deal of money came to Kalmbach through the Lincoln Club, an exclusive group of wealthy businessmen in Newport Beach, California, who were staunch supporters of Nixon. Kalmbach reportedly raised more than $6 million. Nixon expressed his gratitude by offering the lawyer the post of undersecretary of commerce in the new administration, which Kalmbach turned down. Kalmbach's practice soon expanded greatly as he became known as the "president's lawyer." In addition to local clients, his firm began to attract large corporations such as United Airlines, the Marriott Corp., and the Music Corp. of America.

Soon after Nixon was installed in the White House, CHARLES COLSON, special counsel to the president, formulated an "enemies list." This list contained the names of left-wing people and organizations, leading Democrats, media people, and countless others who were considered to be either hostile or threatening to the president. To keep an eye on these people, presidential aide JOHN EHRLICHMAN organized an investigative force, which originally consisted of two former members of the New York City Police Department's Bureau of Special Services, John Caulfield and ANTHONY ULASEWICZ. The funds for the investigations came out of a secret trust that had been established in Kalmbach's name. The money in the trust was a surplus from the 1968 campaign, and in early 1969 it amounted to $1,668,000. Kalmbach dispersed the moneys in banks in New York, Washington, and later in California, keeping ready cash in safe-deposit boxes and the rest of the money in checking accounts. Not only did Kalmbach disburse funds for the investigations but also paid Ulasewicz's salary. During the Watergate investigation Kalmbach testified that he used the funds at the direction of H. R. HALDEMAN for others acting on his behalf.

The White House soon established another secret fund that was made possible in large part by Kalmbach's fund-raising abilities. This fund was used to aid favored candidates in the 1970 congressional campaign. Kalmbach alone raised $2.8 million out of a total of $3.9 million. From the basement of a townhouse in Washington, funds were distributed to candidates in at least 19 states. The "townhouse project" was illegal because the participants were acting as a political committee, and a committee could not support candidates in two or more states without having a treasurer who filed public reports with Congress.

In late 1970 Kalmbach began raising funds for the 1972 presidential campaign. He was able to elicit contributions from major corporations and organizations, such as the Associated Milk Producers, Inc. (AMPI), that were dependent on favorable government regulations. The AMPI had given money to Kalmbach in 1969, part of which he put into his secret fund and part into the townhouse project. A $2 million pledge was obtained from the AMPI for the 1972 campaign. Eighteen other corporations, including American Airlines, Gulf Oil, and Goodyear Tire and Rubber, contributed a total of $754,540. Political contributions out of corporate funds were prohibited during this time. Kalmbach was also able to secure large contributions from those who were interested in government posts, usually ambassadorships. Even though the administration was not always forthcoming after a contribution had been made, the tactic remained a successful one.

In February 1972 Kalmbach's role as fundraiser was made official when he received the title of associate chairman of the Finance Committee to Re-Elect the President. He held this post until April, when a new law requiring more stringent reporting of contributions went into effect. Kalmbach closed out his secret trust fund and transferred $915,037 to HUGH W. SLOAN JR., treasurer of the Finance Committee.

In addition to raising large amounts of money for the 1972 campaign, the White House also developed a policy of harassing the Democratic Party and its candidates. As the incumbent, Nixon had a decisive edge over his Democratic opponent, but his paranoia and that of his aides led to the sabotage and spying that caused the downfall of his second administration. Two White House aides, DWIGHT CHAPIN and GORDON STRACHAN, with the approval of Haldeman, recruited a lawyer, DONALD SEGRETTI, to harass the Democrats and to foster hostility within the party. In August 1971 Segretti met with Kalmbach, who offered him a salary of $16,000 per year plus expenses. Over the next eight months he received $45,336; $22,000 was for expenses and $9,000 of that went to various agents he hired.

During the summer of 1972, Kalmbach worked secretly to raise funds for the Watergate defendants. He delivered the cash to Anthony Ulasewicz, who in turn distributed it to the defendants and their families. For three months Kalmbach worked with Ulasewicz, using code names and secret drops for the hush money, until he realized what he was doing was illegal and decided that he could not take part in it any longer.

During the Watergate investigation of 1973, Kalmbach's illegal dealings came to light. In February 1974 he pleaded guilty to raising secret contributions for congressional campaigns and to promising an ambassador a better diplomatic post in return for a campaign contribution. He was sentenced to a jail term of six to 18 months and ordered to pay a $10,000 fine for violating a federal disclosure law governing campaign funds. Kalmbach was also directed to serve a concurrent six-month prison term for promising the ambassadorial appointment. Kalmbach was freed from prison in January 1975. He is currently a counsel for Baker and Hostetler LLP.

—NK

Kastenmeier, Robert

(1924–   ) *member of the House of Representatives*

Robert Kastenmeier was born on January 24, 1924, in Beaver Dam, Wisconsin. Kastenmeier, whose father was a farmer, served in the army during World War II. He received his law degree from the University of Wisconsin in 1952 and went into private practice. Kastenmeier won election as a Democrat to the U.S. House in 1958. His district, which centered around the University of Wisconsin at Madison, with its 30,000 students, was well matched to Kastenmeier's strong liberal convictions.

Kastenmeier was an opponent of the Vietnam War, and he generally opposed the NIXON-FORD administration legislative programs. He backed the positions of labor, consumers, and conservation groups; he consistently voted to override Ford-Nixon vetoes of welfare and social programs; and he strongly opposed the military draft, favoring instead a volunteer army. He often opposed administration requests for increased military spending, foreign military aid, and the development of controversial weapons programs such as the B-1 bomber.

Kastenmeier's opposition to the Vietnam War continued into the 1970s. He remained a consistent opponent of the Nixon-Ford Vietnam policy. In 1969 he joined 55 other House members to vote against a resolution condemning President Nixon's efforts to achieve "peace with justice" in Vietnam. In 1972 he supported an amendment calling for an end to American involvement in Vietnam after American prisoners of war were released and those missing in action were accounted for. On May 1, 1975, the day Saigon was secured by Communist forces, he voted against a Ford administration request for supplemental military aid to South Vietnam.

Kastenmeier served continuously on the House Judiciary and the House Internal and Insular Affairs committees. In 1969 he became the chairman of the Judiciary's Subcommittee Three, which was renamed the Subcommittee on Courts, Civil Liberties, and the Administration of Justice when the Judiciary Committee was reorganized in 1973. During his chairmanship the subcommittee concentrated on prison reform, copyright law revision, and civil liberties issues. Under his leadership it became an unusually close-knit group that often cosponsored legislation and reported bills unanimously. His panel was the first judiciary subcommittee to hold open mark-up sessions where members debated and voted on the actual wording of bills.

In 1971 Kastenmeier's subcommittee handled the repeal of the Emergency Detention Act, which had allowed the president to order the detention of persons who might engage in espionage or sabotage activities during a national emergency declared by the president. Calling the repeal one of the biggest victories of his career, Kastenmeier said "that it showed you couldn't have concentration camps in America." The Nixon administration supported repeal, but it was opposed by the House Internal Security Committee (formerly the House Committee on Un-American Activities). The repeal was a rare defeat for that committee.

In 1975 Kastenmeier publicly exposed the scope of two government operations that threatened civil liberties. On March 21 he released secret testimony given by the chief postal inspector to his subcommittee about the CIA's mail-snooping operations from the 1950s to the 1970s. On October 22 he released FBI documents including a list of persons to be detained in national emergencies.

Kastenmeier's commitment to prison reform led to the enactment in 1976 of a law to reform parole procedures that his subcommittee had worked on for five years. The law reorganized the U.S. Parole Board and established procedures requiring that parole decisions be reached openly using fair and reasonable processes that granted prisoners some rights.

One of Kastenmeier's major legislative achievements was the enactment of a copyright revision law in 1976, the first major revision of the 1909 copyright law. The effort to revise the law started in 1955 when Congress authorized the Copyright Office to study comprehensive revision. Among other changes the 1976 law extended the copyright duration to 50 years beyond the death of the author and provided for a "fair use" doctrine, which had been sporadically developed by the courts. The doctrine allowed limited free use of copyrighted materials.

Kastenmeier played an important but low-key role during the House Judiciary Committee's 1974 impeachment proceedings. He was a member of the committee's Impeachment Advisory Group, and his vote could be counted on for impeachment before most people had expressed a position on the issue. Kastenmeier firmly insisted that each article of impeachment be debated and voted on separately. Some members supporting impeachment wanted to delay the vote on all the articles until they had all been debated. Kastenmeier's firm position ensured that the committee followed a procedure that required the members to show the public how each of them interpreted the evidence pertaining to each impeachment article and how they voted on the article following its debate.

In 1977, as chairman of the Subcommittee on Courts, Civil Liberties, and the Administration of Justice, he led an investigation of access to federal courts. He was named as one of the House managers appointed to conduct the 1986 impeachment proceedings against Harry E. Claiborne (Nevada). Kastenmeier was defeated for reelection in 1990 and currently resides in Wisconsin.

—AE

Kelley, Clarence M(arion)

(1911–1997) *chief of police, Kansas City, Mo.; director, Federal Bureau of Investigation*

Born on October 24, 1911, Clarence Kelley grew up in Kansas City. Missouri. He received his B.A. from the University of Kansas in 1936 and his LL.B. from the University of Kansas City Law School in 1940. Shortly after graduating, Kelley joined the FBI as a special agent. During his 21 years in the agency, Kelley served in 10 cities, handling criminal cases and administrative operations rather than security investigations. During the late 1950s he was promoted to special agent in charge of the Birmingham, Alabama, field office and in 1960 headed the Memphis, Tennessee, office. When Kelley reached the optional retirement age of 50, he was recommended by, among others, Attorney General Robert F. Kennedy and various FBI officials to the Kansas City Board of Police Commissioners, who were searching for a new police chief. Kelley returned to Kansas City to take the job in 1961.

In a reorganization of the demoralized department, Kelley fired many men who had been involved in corruption scandals under his predecessor. He then began a series of innovations that made the Kansas City Police Department a national law enforcement model. In 1968 he introduced the first around-the-clock helicopter patrols in any major U.S. city and created the Automated Law Enforcement Response Team (ALERT), a system of computerized police records that eventually covered 10,000 square miles as smaller towns in the Kansas City area hooked into the system. At first the names of "mentals," activists, and militants were fed into the computer with the names of convicted criminals, but pressure from civil rights groups and the local American Civil Liberties Union forced the police to purge their files.

Kelley also vetoed the practice of gathering information on student demonstrators and reprimanded officials of a suburban town for passing ALERT information about newcomers to landlords and employers. Another Kelley innovation was the "metro squad," a mini-FBI that could be called in for homicides and other major crimes. He experimented with a more open department, initiating regular discussions between patrolmen and officers as an alternative to the quasi-military precinct organization; increased police pay; and offered educational incentives. Modern equipment and the addition of 400 men to the force helped reduce Kansas City's crime rate by 24 percent between 1969 and 1972.

The major controversy during Kelley's tenure as Kansas City police chief centered on his handling of racial problems. By 1968 Kansas City's population was over 20 percent black, but its police force was 95 percent white. The police were distrusted in the black community, and racist attitudes in Kansas City hardened in reaction to the civil rights movement. Essentially a conservative, Kelley made little attempt to ease the situation.

On April 9, 1968, the day of the funeral of Dr. Martin Luther King Jr., a group of schoolchildren marched to city hall demanding that the schools be closed in King's honor. They were dispersed with tear gas and billy clubs by police in full riot gear. Kelley requested National Guardsmen from the governor and adopted a hard-line policy, refusing to join the mayor in apologizing for the use of tear gas at city hall. During the ensuing riots six unarmed black men were shot. In retrospect Kelley admitted that some officers might have acted unwisely, but he took no disciplinary action.

When on June 7, 1973, President RICHARD NIXON designated Kelley permanent director of the FBI, political commentators expected Kelley's Senate confirmation hearings to center on the issue of racism. However, the controversy over Kelley's handling of the 1968 riots had subsided, and members of the Senate Judiciary Committee were more concerned with establishing Kelley's freedom from involvement in the Watergate scandal and his willingness to cooperate with Congress. Traditionally the FBI had operated as an independent investigative agency with very little supervision from Congress or the executive branch.

The death in 1972 of J. EDGAR HOOVER, FBI director for nearly 50 years, and the resignation of Acting Director L. PATRICK GRAY in April 1973, after his admission of burning documents connected with Watergate, left the bureau in a state of growing crisis. Abuses during the Hoover period, including infringements of civil liberties involved in the FBI's "domestic security" investigations, were beginning to surface. The Senate wanted assurance that the new FBI director would stop these questionable practices and be willing to submit to congressional supervision.

During his confirmation hearings Kelley stated, "I have never bowed to political pressure," and informed the committee that he would report to Congress regularly and cooperate in a strong congressional oversight relationship. After hearings that lasted only three days, Kelley was enthusiastically endorsed by the Senate Judiciary Committee and confirmed by the Senate. President Nixon flew to Kansas City to swear Kelley in on July 9, 1973.

As FBI director, Kelley disappointed those who had hoped for immediate sweeping reforms of bureau policies. While Kelley faced external pressure from the Justice Department and Congress to reform and modernize bureau practices, he also had to deal with considerable pressure from within the FBI hierarchy to remain true to the methods of former chief J. Edgar Hoover. Many observers saw Kelley's choice of veteran agent and Hoover loyalist Nicholas P. Callahan as his associate director and of other Hoover supporters for key positions as an indication that he had capitulated to the traditionalist.

When Kelley appeared before the House Subcommittee on Civil Rights and Constitutional Rights, which was investigating the FBI's counterintelligence programs (COINTELPROs), he was accompanied by at least six bureau officials. Denying pressure from within the FBI, Kelley nevertheless refused to condemn COINTELPRO activities that had taken place under Hoover during the political upheavals of the 1960s. These activities included attempts to have persons lose their jobs, their apartments, and their credit ratings because of their political affiliations. Kelley issued orders in December 1973 forbidding FBI personnel to engage in investigative activities that would abridge the civil liberties of U.S. citizens. However, he defended the COINTELPRO activities of the 1960s, stating that Hoover thought them necessary at the time to deal with "revolutionary elements" and that FBI agents should not be prosecuted for their participation in these activities.

While some saw Kelley as a Hoover loyalist, others felt that he was shrewdly gaining the trust of the slow-moving bureau hierarchy to gradually introduce reforms. Kelley brought in independent advisers to help him run the bureau and convened a series of regional management symposia for assistant directors, inspectors, and special agents in charge of field offices. By 1976 he had redirected more FBI resources toward the prosecution of white-collar and organized crime and had cut the "internal security" investigations, which had formed a large part of bureau activity during the 1960s, by 98 percent. Kelley removed the categories of "extremists" and "internal security" from the domestic intelligence division and, under new Justice Department guidelines, restricted political investigations to those who had already broken the law.

Despite Kelley's reforms, when the newly formed Senate Select Committee on Intelligence held its first FBI oversight hearings in September 1976, the bureau faced the worst internal crisis in its history. The committee unearthed new evidence of illegal activity, internal corruption, and abuse of power. Kelley himself was almost fired by President GERALD FORD when it was discovered that he had accepted gifts of furniture and appliances from his subordinates and that carpenters from the bureau's Exhibit Division had done some work in his apartment. Although Kelley's integrity was later vindicated, it became clear that such favors had been common under Hoover and that FBI officials had accepted kickbacks on electronic equipment. The committee also gathered substantial evidence of illegal wiretappings and the "systematic theft" of government property by FBI agents, abuses that dated back to the 1930s when the FBI was first authorized to gather information about the political beliefs of U.S. citizens.

In January 1977 President JIMMY CARTER and Attorney General Griffin Bell decided that the FBI needed a new director, someone free of any connection with FBI scandals. Both Carter and Bell praised Kelley's leadership and reforms but felt he was moving too slowly in his attempts to change FBI policy. The president appointed Kelley to a special eight-man selection committee to search for his successor.

Kelley announced his intention to retire in June 1977, but when his designated successor, federal judge Frank Johnson, had to decline the directorship due to health problems, Kelley agreed to remain in his position through February 1978. On February 15, after more than four years of service, Kelley retired as director and was replaced by federal judge William H. Webster. Kelley moved back to Kansas City, where he created Clarence M. Kelley and Associates, specializing in white-collar crime investigations.

—DAE

Kennedy, David M(atthew)
(1905–1996) *secretary of the treasury*

David Kennedy was born on July 21, 1905, in Randolph, Utah. Kennedy obtained his bachelor's degree from Weber College in 1928. He began a 16-year period at the Federal Reserve Bank in 1930 but continued his education at George Washington University, earning an M.A. in 1935 and an LL.B. in 1937. He completed his formal schooling with a degree from Rutgers University's Graduate School of Banking in 1939. In 1946 Kennedy was appointed vice president of the Continental Illinois National Bank and Trust Co. of Chicago. By the time he left Continental Illinois in 1969 he had risen to be chairman of the board. Under his leadership Continental Illinois had become active in promoting business and economic opportunities for Chicago's black population. Kennedy was a special assistant to the secretary of the treasury in 1953–54.

Kennedy was part of the team that in December 1969 planned the economic policy that the NIXON administration pursued for the first two years of its existence and that it began to abandon as Kennedy left office. The policy essentially involved a series of deflationary measures, above all manifest in a tightening of interest rates and a slowing of monetary growth, as well as a commitment to balancing the federal budget. In his confirmation hearings Kennedy fully endorsed these goals.

His nomination encountered some resistance when Senator ALBERT GORE (D-Tenn.) accused Kennedy of conflict of interest as a stockholder of Continental Illinois, but Kennedy agreed to place his stock in trusteeship. He had also created a minor stir in December 1968 by implying that a rise in the official price of gold—for over a decade anathema to Treasury officials concerned with the prestige of the dollar—might be considered to help stabilize the U.S. currency. This remark triggered a speculative surge in the European gold markets. However, in one of his first statements after assuming office, Kennedy reaffirmed his commitment to the long-standing Treasury policy. The market price of gold in Europe immediately took a sharp fall.

Kennedy added his voice to the administration's attempts to educate the American people to tight money after eight years of Keynesian policies. In February 1969 he called for "fiscal restraint" but also warned against a too-rapid reflation with its untoward consequences for employment. He warned against a repetition of the abrupt shift in Federal Reserve policy when the Fed had reverted to easy money even before its 1965–66 tight-money policies had borne fruit. He foresaw even larger federal surpluses for fiscal 1970 than the $3.5 billion estimated by the administration and opposed proponents of the abolition of the 7 percent investment tax write-off.

Kennedy came under fire from antibanking members of Congress such as WRIGHT PATMAN (D-Tex.) on several occasions. When Kennedy testified on a proposed bill that restricted bank-owned holding companies to banking activities alone, warning that without such restraint "within a few years . . . we would find ourselves in a structure dominated by some 50 to 75 centers of economic and financial power," Patman brushed aside the criticism and argued that the legislation was not tough enough. In July 1969, after a further prime-rate interest rise by commercial banks, Patman, a longtime advocate of low interest rates, criticized Kennedy for having failed to prevent it.

In late 1969 and early 1970, as the U.S. economy began to slow down in response to the administration's measures, Kennedy continued to serve as a spokesman for these policies. He warned against possible wage-price controls if Congress failed to extend President Johnson's surtax and told the Joint Economic

Committee that a 4 percent rate of unemployment was "acceptable" to the administration. Shortly thereafter he reaffirmed the need to wait for a recession before undertaking any expansionary policies. He complained that the American public did not understand the need for fiscal restraint.

By the time of the November 1970 congressional elections, the Nixon administration's tight-money policies had begun to show their effects: unemployment had risen from 4 percent to 6 percent, the stock market had fallen over 300 points, and production was falling. The Democratic Party thus made what were considered excessive gains for an off-year election. White House press secretary RONALD ZIEGLER did not deny that a cabinet shakeup was in the offing. Thus, in mid-December Nixon informed Congress that former Texas governor JOHN CONNALLY, a Democrat, would succeed Kennedy at the Treasury, thereby giving economic policy a "bipartisan" quality. Although it was stated that the "soft-spoken" Kennedy—a description that was underlined to some observers by the style of his successor—had agreed to serve only two years upon assuming office, Treasury officials confirmed rumors that Kennedy had offered to resign as a "scapegoat" after the disappointing election results. Kennedy was thus appointed ambassador-at-large with cabinet status and left the Treasury in early 1971.

As ambassador-at-large, Kennedy was primarily involved in negotiating and signing trade agreements with major importers to U.S. markets. A growing chorus of protectionist sentiment was one major response to the recession. Thus, in 1971, because of the Nixon administration's opposition to overt protectionist measures, Kennedy signed a series of "voluntary restraint" agreements with Italy, Japan, and Taiwan affecting shoe and textile shipments to the United States.

In December 1971 Kennedy was given additional duties as ambassador to the North Atlantic Treaty Organization. One year later he was replaced at that post by DONALD RUMSFELD, and in early 1973 he retired to private life in Illinois. He died in 1996.

—LG

Kennedy, Edward M(oore)
(1932–   ) *member of the Senate*

Edward M. Kennedy was born on February 22, 1932, in Brookline, Massachusetts. Kennedy, brother of President John F. Kennedy and Senator Robert F. Kennedy (D-N.Y.), entered Harvard University in 1950. After he was suspended from the university in the spring of 1951 for cheating on an examination, he served a two-year hitch in the army. Readmitted to Harvard, he graduated in 1956 but was denied admission to the university's Law School. He earned his law degree from the University of Virginia in 1959. Kennedy worked in his brother's 1960 presidential campaign and won election to the U.S. Senate in 1962.

In the upper house Kennedy established a liberal record, supporting a wide variety of social welfare legislation as well as efforts to end the cold war with the Soviet Union. He gradually established a reputation as an effective legislator.

During the NIXON-FORD years Kennedy generally opposed the administration. He regularly voted to override the Nixon-Ford vetoes of spending legislation for social and welfare measures, usually voted to cut defense spending and weapons development programs, and often spoke out against the administration on foreign policy issues. Kennedy was a strong advocate of consumer legislation, federal election reform, and gun control. In 1975 Kennedy, a Catholic, led the Senate floor opposition that prevented antiabortion forces from attaching an antiabortion amendment to the fiscal 1976 appropriations for health services. Kennedy, who was the floor manager for the health services bill, also tried to compromise with the Ford administration on the funding issue by accepting the lower funding voted by the House. Ford still vetoed the bill, but Congress overrode the veto.

As a Democratic spokesman on foreign policy issues, Kennedy urged the normalization of relations with Communist China and introduced legislation to end the U.S. embargo on trade with Cuba established during his brother's presidency. He supported efforts toward international disarmament. Kennedy was an outspoken opponent of the Vietnam War and supported the congressional efforts to legislate an end to American involvement.

In 1969 Kennedy was considered the front-runner for the 1972 Democratic presidential nomination until the July 18 auto accident on Chappaquiddick Island in which a young woman drowned. Kennedy left the scene of the accident and failed to report it for 10 hours. He eventually pleaded guilty to a charge of leaving the scene of an accident and was given a two-month suspended sentence, the minimum under Massachusetts law. On July 25 he made a televised speech to Massachusetts voters in which he gave his account of the accident and appealed to voters to help him decide whether he should remain in the Senate. Polls showed that more than 80 percent of the voters wanted him to stay in office, and he resumed his Senate duties. On July 30 he announced that he would not run for president, that he would run for reelection to the Senate in 1970, and that he would serve out his full term if reelected.

Kennedy became known as "Mr. Health" during the 1970s when he provided strong leadership for national health insurance. He became the chairman of the Labor and Public Welfare Committee's Subcommittee on Health in 1971. Kennedy was one of the 100 members of the Committee on National Health Insurance

established by United Automobile Workers president WALTER P. REUTHER. The committee recommended a national health insurance bill that Kennedy sponsored with 14 other senators in 1970. The comprehensive health insurance proposal, then estimated to cost $40 billion, encouraged group medical services and preventive medicine. It would have established national standards for hospitals and doctors; supplemented health manpower training programs for medical professionals; and developed national health policies. The federal government would have administered the proposed program, which would have covered most personal health care services. It would have been financed partly from payroll taxes and partly from general federal tax revenues. The bill failed that year and in subsequent years.

Kennedy sponsored the Developmental Disabilities Services and Facilities Construction Amendments of 1970, which extended and broadened programs begun under the Mental Retardation Facilities Construction Act of 1963. The new program covered both mental and developmental disabilities, such as epilepsy. Also in 1970 Kennedy favored a three-year extension of the Hill-Burton hospital construction program. Nixon vetoed the bill, but the veto was overridden. Kennedy sponsored the 1973 law that provided federal funding for health maintenance organizations and the 1974 act to create a network of local health systems agencies.

During the JIMMY CARTER administration Kennedy became an important critic of the president's economic and energy programs. Chappaquiddick and its accompanying publicity led Kennedy to defer a presidential bid until 1980, when he mounted a challenge to then incumbent JIMMY CARTER. Kennedy lost the nomination to Carter, largely because of Chappaquiddick and questions about his character. Following that defeat Kennedy concentrated on securing his legislative legacy. He has chaired the Committee on the Judiciary, the Committee on Labor and Human Resources, and the Committee on Health, Education, Labor, and Pensions. His support was of significance in the passage of the No Child Left Behind Act of 2001. At present he has been reelected seven times and is the second most senior member of the Senate.

—AE

Kissinger, Henry A(lfred)
(1923–   ) *special assistant to the president for national security affairs; secretary of state*

Heinz Alfred Kissinger was born on May 29, 1923, into an Orthodox Jewish family. The family fled Nazi Germany in 1938, going first to England and then to New York City, where Kissinger studied accounting at City College and worked in a shaving brush factory. He was drafted in 1943 and worked in army intelligence. After serving as a district administrator with the military government of occupied Germany from 1945 to 1946, Kissinger enrolled at Harvard. He received a B.A. summa cum laude in 1950 and Ph.D. in 1954. His dissertation, later published as a book, concerned European diplomacy during the post-Napoleonic period. The work sought to show how the archconservative Prince Metternich brought order, stability, and an era of peace to Europe through maintenance of a balance of power in which each country had a vested interest. Kissinger admired Metternich's skillful use of personal and secret negotiations unhampered by the demands of bureaucracy and public opinion and of his occasional threat of force to preserve order. Kissinger's study reflected his own pessimism and fear of instability and served as the basis for his approach to international power politics.

In 1954 Kissinger became study director of a Council on Foreign Relations project seeking to explore alternatives to the massive-retaliation policy of the Eisenhower administration. The project report, published in 1957, accepted Eisenhower's view that the Soviet Union was an expansionist power seeking to undermine the stability of the West but proposed a strategy based on the limited use of nuclear weapons as an alternative to massive retaliation.

In 1956 NELSON A. ROCKEFELLER appointed Kissinger a director of a Rockefeller Brothers Fund special project formed to study the nation's major domestic and foreign problems. The project's final foreign affairs report, published as *The Necessity for Choice: Prospects for American Foreign Policy* (1961), warned against optimism over prospects for a Soviet-American détente and stressed the need for a strategy centered on tactical nuclear weapons. It called for an expanded nationwide civil defense system and for a major increase in defense spending to meet the expected Soviet challenge.

Kissinger returned to Harvard as a lecturer in the government department in 1957 and eventually became a professor in 1962. From 1959 to 1969 he was director of Harvard's Defense Studies Program. Kissinger also served as a consultant to the Arms Control and Disarmament Agency from 1961 to 1967 and to the State Department from 1965 to 1969. Between 1961 and 1962 he was an adviser to the National Security Council. During the late 1960s he visited South Vietnam as a State Department consultant. On the basis of personal interviews with many nongovernment Vietnamese, Kissinger concluded that an American victory was impossible but that it was also unacceptable to withdraw from Vietnam in a manner that would cause the United States to lose its "honor" and credibility in the eyes of its allies. Nonetheless, he published an article that justified U.S. policy as necessary to stem communist expansion.

Kissinger wrote speeches for Rockefeller's bid for the 1968 Republican presidential nomination. He also produced a peace plan that incorporated elements of the plan he would pursue as Nixon's foreign-policy adviser, including a proposal for the gradual withdrawal of U.S. troops and their replacement by South Vietnamese. In addition, the plan recommended the withdrawal of troops on both sides, the imposition of an international peacekeeping force, internationally supervised free elections, and negotiations for the reunification of Vietnam.

Rockefeller's failure to win the nomination upset Kissinger, who considered RICHARD NIXON a demagogue without purpose or a sense of history and a man who did not "have the right to rule." Nixon, however, had been impressed by Kissinger's work and, through his aides, induced the professor to act as a foreign-policy consultant for the Republican campaign. In late November 1968 Kissinger was offered the post of head of the National Security Council (NSC) and the position of special assistant for national security affairs.

Politically the offer was a clever move aimed at hurting Nixon's old rival Rockefeller: Rockefeller was not offered a post in the new administration, and at the same time one of his closest advisers was taken from him. Moreover, the appointment added an intellectual to the White House staff and won Nixon some rare praise from liberal and academic critics.

Kissinger quickly altered his opinion of Nixon. He discovered that he and Nixon agreed on their approach to foreign policy and shared a contempt for the bureaucracy and a pessimism about the limits of American power. They both believed that there was need for more flexibility, more thorough planning, and a better-defined philosophy in the conduct of foreign affairs. Nixon realized that the American public was tired of the cold war rivalry with the USSR and particularly of the Vietnam War. Both men wanted to maintain an active international role for the United States and subtly resist what they viewed as the new isolationist tendencies of Congress and the public.

The new president claimed expertise in foreign affairs and wanted to make policy himself, not delegate the task to the traditional departments, State and Defense, as it had been under Lyndon Johnson. Both men agreed that Johnson had been hampered in foreign affairs because he had delegated authority and only heard what his advisers thought he wanted to hear. The new president wanted Kissinger to coordinate the thinking and recommendations of the various departments and then present him with a reasonable array of alternatives for a given foreign policy issue. Nixon aimed to rationalize and centralize the foreign policy bureaucracy and to make Kissinger the channel through which recommendations from below were passed, criticized, and refined. From the beginning Kissinger's position was clearly superior to those of the secretaries of defense and state. Subsequently his skill at political infighting, his capacity for hard work, and the president's growing dependence on him amplified that superiority. He quickly recruited an NSC staff, appropriating some of the most highly regarded Pentagon and State Department personnel.

The contrast between Kissinger's mode of operation and that followed during Johnson's period was evident in one of his first tasks, preparation of an options memorandum on the progress of the Vietnam War. Identical questions were directed to second-echelon staffers of various departments. Thus, many officials evaluated areas outside their field of expertise. In contrast, Johnson's information about military matters always came from top people in the Pentagon. One result of the Kissinger report, called the National Security Study Memoranda (NSSM), was a wider range of opinions and therefore greater accuracy and honesty. But a further result—and one Kissinger did not foresee—was the virtual ineffectiveness of cabinet departments in determining policy. The NSC, in fact, supervised studies on a wide range of policy issues, working through an Interdepartmental Group (IG) composed of assistant secretaries or their deputies from State, Defense, Commerce, Treasury, and other relevant departments. The IG never made recommendations. It produced "area" options for NSC consideration. Kissinger himself chaired the committees that reviewed the defense budget, intelligence policy, and clandestine intelligence operations, as well as the Washington Special Action Group (WSAG), the top-level crisis group, and the Verification Panel, which oversaw monitoring of the nuclear arms agreements with the Soviet Union. Thus, whatever went to the president had to pass through Kissinger. Unwittingly, the Nixon White House became as isolated as Johnson's.

The Soviet Union was the centerpiece of Kissinger's foreign policy. In his view success in any other area of foreign policy was in some way dependent on the administration's relations with the Soviets. While he no longer thought of the communist world as an aggressive monolith, he still believed that the USSR was a capricious power not yet reconciled to the international status quo. It was Kissinger's aim to get the Soviet Union to act as a responsible nation-state convinced that working with the United States to maintain an international balance of power was in its best interest. To accomplish this he developed the concept of "linkage." If the Soviets wanted American trade and technology, Kissinger argued, then they had to make concessions. Most importantly, the Soviets would have to put pressure on the North Vietnamese to negotiate an end to the Indochina conflict.

Nuclear weapons constituted another crucial issue dividing the two powers. Aside from the realization that nuclear war between the superpowers was unthinkable, Kissinger knew that neither the United States nor the

Soviet Union could tolerate the costs of an accelerated arms race. He also believed that it was in the mutual interest to defuse tensions in central Europe and in other trouble spots. In addition, the United States should share some of its heavy defense burden with its allies. This was essential not only in economic terms but also because Kissinger felt that American foreign policy since World War II had been too paternalistic. Without retreating into isolationism, the United States no longer needed to confront international crises single-handedly, although in practice Kissinger himself acted unilaterally. Nixon was in agreement on the necessity for détente with the USSR and restraint on unilateral U.S. action in local conflicts.

Nixon and Kissinger, because of their emphasis on linkage, were less disposed to rush into the Strategic Arms Limitation Talks (SALT) than were many of their advisers, such as Secretary of State WILLIAM ROGERS. Nixon responded to early Soviet calls for SALT by saying that talks would be feasible "in a way and at a time that will promote, if possible, progress on outstanding political problems at the same time—for example, on the problem of the Middle East and other outstanding problems in which the United States and the USSR, acting together, can save the cause of peace." Meanwhile, he supported the development of the Safeguard antiballistic missile and the MIRV (multiple independently targeted reentry vehicle) to strengthen America's bargaining position when talks began. The Russians took this expression of linkage to be a form of blackmail or extortion. Government bureaucrats and members of Congress, despite Kissinger's explanation of the concept, feared that it would endanger SALT's future and viewed support of weapons development as lack of interest in arms control.

Kissinger ignored early calls for wide-ranging discussions with the Soviets to give his staff time to prepare a study on the relative military strength of the two superpowers. One part of the study provided the basis for the president's approval of the nuclear nonproliferation treaty negotiated by the Johnson administration. It was sent to the Senate in February 1969. The other part of the study put into question Nixon's campaign pledge to ensure "clear-cut military superiority" over the Soviet Union. Superiority was impossible in the decade ahead, especially in view of the Soviets' enormous defense budgets. Nixon accepted the findings and publicly substituted Kissinger's "sufficiency" for "superiority," asserting that the administration would guarantee "sufficient military power to defend our interests and to maintain . . . commitments." The Helsinki SALT discussions did not begin until November 1969. Although the Soviets had not yet offered to satisfy U.S. demands in the Middle East and Vietnam, Kissinger hoped that progress in the negotiations would encourage greater Soviet accommodation.

Vietnam was the most pressing foreign—and domestic—problem inherited from the Johnson administration. It also proved harder to resolve than Kissinger expected, because he underestimated the tenacity of Hanoi and the National Liberation Front (NLF). At the 1969 Paris peace talks the North Vietnamese rejected Kissinger's "two track" formula, which projected a military settlement between Washington and Hanoi and a political settlement between Saigon and the NLF. Kissinger, as his former aide Roger Morris pointed out, was unable to understand the North Vietnamese position that the conflict was a civil war. It was for this reason that he insisted—until May 1972—on mutual withdrawal of troops, a proposition that Hanoi considered unreasonable and unacceptable.

Both Kissinger and Nixon recognized that a military victory was impossible in Vietnam. But they refused to consider a U.S. withdrawal, which they thought would be an ignominious act unworthy of a great power and a signal to enemies and allies that the United States could not be trusted to keep its commitments. Instead, in June 1969 they proposed a policy of Vietnamization, gradually giving the South Vietnamese Army the responsibility for conducting the war. But Kissinger had little faith in Saigon's military capacity, and he ultimately placed his hopes in a combination of personal diplomacy and periodic "savage, punishing" military escalations. He initiated his personal diplomacy in secret Paris meetings in August 1969, and between February and April of the following year he met with Le Duc Tho, a member of Hanoi's Politburo. Little was accomplished, and even less was achieved in the official talks, which only served as a cover for the secret conferences. Meanwhile, the administration pressured the North Vietnamese militarily. In March 1969 secret B-52 raids began over Cambodia, in spite of Washington's official recognition of that nation's neutrality, in an effort to keep enemy troops from moving across the border.

Kissinger's early efforts at diplomacy engendered criticism from several quarters, and despite his efforts to end U.S. involvement in Vietnam, the antiwar movement remained active. As an academic in whom some intellectuals had put their hopes for a speedy settlement, Kissinger was especially subject to severe criticism from the left. His penchant for secrecy and tendency to show sympathy for the views of whatever groups or individuals to whom he was speaking earned him a reputation for duplicity. Members of Congress resented Kissinger's refusal to appear before their committees under the cloak of "executive privilege." (As a personal adviser to Nixon, he was not required to testify.) Kissinger's standing fell even further when he supported Nixon's decision to invade Cambodia in May 1970. With one exception his principal aides, who had tolerated his demanding regimen and abusive treatment because of their faith in him and in spite of their aversion to Nixon, quit. Academic colleagues advised Kissinger to resign; others asked him to "stop that madman."

That liberal critics came to view Kissinger as equally villainous as Nixon reflected a growing public awareness that Kissinger was, as some said, "the second most powerful man" in the country and that he, not Rogers, shaped U.S. foreign policy. Kissinger was deemed so important that the Harrisburg Six, a group of pacifists, were indicted in January 1971 for allegedly conspiring to kidnap him and put him on trial for war crimes. Kissinger sought to maintain contact with his critics and even spoke with members of the Harrisburg group, one of whom said, "The scary part of it is he really is a nice man."

Yet Kissinger was popular with the general public. With the exception of Nixon, he was the only member of the administration to make the 10 "most admired" persons list, which was compiled annually on the basis of a national poll. The admiration was due in part to the largely uncritical attitude of the national media, which was impressed by his intellectual credentials, charmed by his combination of arrogance and self-deprecating wit, and aware of the marketability of his romantic secret shuttle diplomacy. Kissinger, unlike Nixon and his media-hating staff, cultivated the press. A divorced bachelor, Kissinger was photographed in the company of elegant women and was depicted as a cocktail party "swinger" who still found the time to unveil frequent diplomatic marvels. In November 1972 he ascribed his popularity to the "fact that I have acted alone. . . . The Americans love the cowboy . . . who comes into town all alone on his horse. . . ." It was not until after Watergate that the nonradical press would evaluate him somewhat more critically.

One of the least disputed triumphs of the Nixon-Kissinger era was the establishment of ties with the People's Republic of China. It was a case in which the initiative was clearly Nixon's. Both Kissinger and the president had long held the cold war view of an irresponsible, fanatical China bent on world conquest. Kissinger, whose international bias was clearly European, admittedly knew almost nothing about China and was slower to change his views than Nixon. Yet he appreciated that an approach to China could exploit strained Sino-Soviet relations and be used as leverage in dealings with the Soviet Union, which was obsessed with a fear of the Chinese. Besides, it was consistent with Kissinger's philosophy to give powerful nations a stake in maintaining the international balance of power. Throughout 1969 Nixon put out diplomatic "feelers" to the Chinese via the French, Romanians, and Pakistanis. Kissinger applauded the president's diplomatic challenges to the Soviets—and to the cautious State Department as well—such as his August 1969 visit to Romania, which was on bad terms with the Soviets and close to the Chinese. More substantive moves (e.g., easing restrictions on American travel to China and ending U.S. naval patrols in the Taiwan Strait) came at the same time border clashes broke out between the Russians and the Chinese. The first direct contacts with the Chinese were made in December 1969 in Warsaw, over the objections of both Soviet specialists in the State Department and hardliners in the Chinese government. In October 1970 the White House publicly suggested that it was ready to adopt a two-China formula in the United Nations. After Chairman Mao Zedong (Mao Tse-tung) and Premier ZHOU ENLAI (Chou En-lai) were convinced that the South Vietnamese invasion of Laos in February 1971 was not the prelude to a U.S. invasion of China, they invited an American envoy to Beijing, suggesting either Rogers or Kissinger. Nixon chose Kissinger.

With the exception of a group of Ping-Pong players, Kissinger was the first American to officially enter China since 1949. During a July 1971 Asian tour he flew secretly to Beijing via Pakistan. The meetings with Zhou were marked by cordiality and apparently genuine personal rapport. The initial climate of good-will that Kissinger fostered was considered to be his most important contribution to the successful approach to China. At the talks he also conceded that the Americans would now consider Taiwan a part of China, allowing its political future to be settled between the two Chinese governments. Kissinger also laid plans for Nixon's February 1972 visit.

Nixon's surprising announcement of the China visit won wide national support, with the exception of some extreme conservatives, and helped his popularity ratings. As Kissinger expected and even hoped, the Soviets were upset. But American allies, especially the Japanese and the Nationalist Chinese, resented not being consulted on the move. Nixon and Kissinger, however, enjoyed the theatricality of the trip and the impression it gave of diplomatic initiative and daring. The administration proceeded to cut back its troop strength in Taiwan and supported the quest of the People' Republic for seats in the UN General Assembly and on the Security Council, although it publicly claimed it would oppose any effort to oust Taiwan from the international organization.

The Chinese breakthrough was combined with the adoption of a firmer policy toward the Soviet Union. Kissinger and the president had been battling with Rogers and the State Department over linkage and Nixon's hard-line approach to the Russians. In the autumn of 1970 Kissinger, over State's objections, orchestrated the threatening U.S.-Israeli military moves that appeared to stop Moscow's client Syria from toppling the pro-Western regime of Jordan's King Hussein. During the same period Kissinger, employing "tough" language, warned the Soviets not to construct a nuclear submarine base in Cuba, since it was a violation of the post-1962 missile crisis understanding between the United States and the USSR. According to CIA reports, the Soviets stopped construction of the base. The Soviets, besieged by problems with China and Warsaw Pact nations, finally agreed in May 1971 to link limitation of offensive and defensive weapons in any SALT accord. Two months after Kissinger's visit to Beijing, the Americans and Russians began preparations for a May 1972 Moscow summit. In April 1972 Kissinger made a secret trip to Moscow to lay plans for the May summit and to get the Soviets to pressure the North Vietnamese to become more flexible in the Paris peace talks. The summit, so important to Kissinger's grand designs, produced a large number of cultural, scientific, environmental, and trade agreements and eventually the first SALT treaty, which set a limit on certain defensive weapons. SALT gave a crucial boost to Nixon's reelection chances. Larger trade arrangements, including the grain sale to the Soviets, were negotiated by Kissinger in September. In addition, a few weeks after the summit Soviet president Nikolai Podgorny flew to Hanoi to recommend more flexible negotiations with the United States, since Moscow felt that Nixon was actually ending American involvement and the fall of Saigon was inevitable anyway.

Kissinger's strategy did not always produce the desired results. His famous "tilt" toward Pakistan in the December 1971 India-Pakistan War, conditioned by his and Nixon's emotional dislike of the Indians and their gratitude to Pakistan for its help in making contact with Beijing, had disastrous results. The United States was put in the position of supporting a military dictatorship against the world's largest democracy and opposing Bangladesh's struggle for independence. India won; Pakistan lost Bangladesh, formerly East Pakistan; and the Soviets, who supported the Indians, claimed a victory over the Americans and Chinese (who also supported Pakistan). Biographers Marvin and Bernard Kalb reported that the policy failure led Kissinger to briefly consider resignation. Records of secret meetings about the war were leaked to JACK ANDERSON, who published parts of them in his column, proving a great embarrassment to Kissinger. He reportedly suspected that White House aides JOHN EHRLICHMAN and H. R. HALDEMAN, who were jealous of his influence with the president, were responsible for the leaks.

During 1972 Kissinger focused his attention on ending the Vietnam War, which he regarded as a nuisance that kept him from more important business and which jeopardized Nixon's chances for reelection. In the months preceding the 1972 presidential election, he circled the globe in an effort to end the U.S. involvement in Vietnam. Nixon's critics, including his Democratic opponent for the presidency, Senator GEORGE MCGOVERN (D-S.D.), suggested that the president was "manipulating" public opinion and raising expectations by keeping Kissinger in the spotlight. Kissinger even appeared in a Republican campaign film in which he praised Nixon for making possible through SALT a "generation of peace." He also attended GOP contributors' dinners in a "nonpartisan" capacity. He met frequently—in highly publicized secret meetings—with Le Duc Tho and before the election stated "peace is at hand," which many interpreted as an obvious ploy to improve the president's reelection chances. In October Kissinger completed a peace settlement with the North Vietnamese. However, he was unable to get the North Vietnamese to accept changes that the South Vietnamese insisted on before agreeing to the proposal. In December Nixon, with Kissinger's approval, resumed B-52 raids on the North to pressure Hanoi into resuming negotiations.

A peace agreement was signed in January 1973. It followed the one Kissinger had negotiated in October. The terms included a cease-fire; the complete withdrawal of U.S. troops and the dismantling of U.S. bases within 60 days; and a prisoner-of-war (POW) exchange. The cease-fire allowed North Vietnamese troops to remain "in place," that is, they were left in control of those areas in the South that they actually occupied. Foreign troops were to leave Laos and Cambodia, and troop and supply movements through these countries were banned, but no deadline was set. The DMZ would be the provisional dividing line between North and South until reunification could be achieved peacefully. An international commission would deal with the release of POWs, elections, etc., and President Thieu would remain in office pending elections. The peace, as Kissinger had hoped, provided a "decent interval" between U.S. withdrawal and Communist victory. After the Americans left Indochina, however, an increasingly contentious Congress obstructed Kissinger's plans for further involvement there. In March and April 1973 Kissinger pleaded unsuccessfully for the continued bombing of Cambodia to force Hanoi to abide by the Paris accords and bring about a cease-fire. His support of an aid program for Hanoi struck congressional conservatives as an admission that the United States owed reparations to the enemy. In June Kissinger concluded a round of talks with Le Duc Tho about observance of the terms of the January agreement. The resulting communiqué did not provide for an end to the Cambodian and Laotian conflicts. The poor results of the talks, some analysts suggested, only reflected the condition of an administration weakened by the Watergate scandal.

One of Kissinger's greatest triumphs was his handling of the delicate situation in the Middle East, an area that occupied much of his time during Nixon's final months in the White House and during the FORD administration. In Nixon's first administration the area had been left largely to the State Department because, as analysts noted, State needed something to do and it was thought that Kissinger's Jewish ancestry might prejudice the Arabs against him. However, during the mid-1970s Kissinger handled Middle Eastern diplomacy on a personal level. His ethnic background eventually became an asset because it proved difficult to accuse him of anti-Semitism when he showed sympathy for Arab interests.

In October 1973 Egyptian president Anwar Sadat precipitated the Yom Kippur War with Israel to force the return of Egyptian land lost to the Israelis six years before. For years the United States had been staunchly pro-Israel. Kissinger, though not possessed of strong emotional ties to that nation, saw Israel as a U.S. ally and the Arab states, with the exception of the conservative monarchies, as Soviet clients. He blamed the Soviets for supplying offensive arms to the Arabs and encouraging the attack on Israel. Their actions, he felt, were inconsistent with détente. Yet because of Defense Department hesitation, the United States only slowly matched the Soviet effort in supplying military aid to its ally. Secretary of Defense JAMES SCHLESINGER," a frequent critic of Kissinger's policies, hesitated to give Israel massive support because such aid might precipitate an oil embargo threatened by the Arabs. However, Nixon finally overrode Schlesinger. In view of his Watergate problems, the president realized that failure to aid Israel would result in an overwhelmingly negative public and congressional reaction and what he saw as weakness in the face of a Soviet challenge. In response to the U.S. aid to Israel, the Arab nations instituted a total ban on oil exports to supporters of Israel.

American aid made possible a spectacular Israeli counteroffensive, and the Soviet Union consequently called for a cease-fire. Kissinger went to Moscow with authorization from Nixon to sign anything in his name. The secretary of state and Brezhnev worked out a cease-fire providing for direct Egyptian-Israeli talks. The cease-fire was precarious, however, and a few days after meeting with Brezhnev, Kissinger called for a worldwide nuclear alert of U.S forces in response to what he claimed were Soviet military moves to intervene in the conflict on the side of the Arabs. Kissinger's action, some skeptics believed, was a dangerously reckless tactic to divert domestic attention from the president's role in Watergate. Military and political analysts at least thought that the Russians' behavior, though belligerent, did not warrant preparations for nuclear war.

Soviet unwillingness to pursue an active role in achieving a Middle East settlement worked in Kissinger's favor. He was able to personally direct the negotiations. His shuttle diplomacy, rather than multilateral discussions in Geneva, provided the basis for a series of agreements leading to the Egyptian-Israeli peace treaty of 1979. U.S. influence in the Middle East and Kissinger's prestige benefited from the new situation.

The embargo dictated a more evenhanded U.S. policy in the Middle East. It was Kissinger's aim, then, to keep Israel from winning complete victory. Israeli victory would make the oil embargo permanent and peace impossible, since the Arab states, especially Egypt, would never resign themselves to the loss of their territory. Without the return of Arab lands, there could be no peace, and without peace, it was likely that the oil producers would refuse to sell to the United States.

Kissinger's diplomatic offensive in the Middle East began in November 1973 and lasted through 1976. He developed an apparently warm and intimate relationship with Sadat, who had shown signs of desiring better relations with the United States since 1972, when he expelled Soviet advisers from Egypt. Kissinger arranged two Sinai disengagements, in January 1974 and September 1975, which gave Egypt back its land and some measure of pride and offered Israel a measure of security it had been unable to attain in four wars. He also produced a disengagement on the Golan Heights between Israel and Syria in May 1974, although relations between the two nations remained hostile. The Mideast oil embargo was ended, and relations with Saudi Arabia were restored. Such triumphs were as much responsible for Kissinger's international "Super K" reputation as the opening of relations with China. However, in some places his achievements were viewed more critically. Jewish-American opinion, already angered that détente ignored the plight of Soviet Jews, attacked Kissinger's sympathy for the Arab position. Israeli public opinion, too, reflected the view that Kissinger had forced the Israeli government into disadvantageous settlements as the price of continued U.S. support. Moreover, some analysts noted that Kissinger had been unable to moderate sufficiently the position of the more militant Arab states, particularly Syria. Most importantly, his diplomacy ignored the question of the stateless Palestinians, who were, in fact, the key to any permanent Middle East peace.

The Middle East oil embargo gave rise to further friction in the relations between the United States and its traditional allies, Western Europe and Japan. Ironically, it was Kissinger's reputedly less-idealistic "European" style of diplomacy that contributed to the deterioration of the alliance with Europe, which had already been adversely affected by disagreements over trade, monetary, and military policies. Kissinger had once criticized American policy makers for their failure to consult with the allies on world issues and to consider those countries in terms of their national interests. Yet in his diplomatic initiatives with the Soviets and the Chinese, Kissinger usually failed to advise the governments of Western Europe

and Japan beforehand. The behavior was partly due to Kissinger's stress on secrecy, but it also arose out of the assumption that the United States was a great power with global interests. Europe, in contrast, was considered a regional power. Conscious of the neglect, Kissinger in April 1973 announced the "Year of Europe," proposing a new Atlantic Charter that would include the Japanese and require a cooperative comprehensive policy on energy, military, monetary, and commercial issues. The proposal was spurned more than once. British prime minister Edward Heath and French president Georges Pompidou made it clear in May that they wanted issues considered separately. European Economic Community (EEC) spokespersons warned the United States that Europe would act as a "distinct unity" in world affairs.

The Arab oil embargo prompted Kissinger to propose in December 1973 a cooperative effort by the industrialized nations to develop long-term energy planning. The proposal conflicted with a French call for an Arab-EEC summit. Kissinger continued arguing in favor of oil-consuming nations' solidarity in the face of high prices imposed by the Organization of Petroleum Exporting Countries (OPEC). He noted, however, that the burden of high prices weighed most heavily on underdeveloped nations. Kissinger recommended vigilance to ensure that "petrodollars" invested in the industrial economies did not threaten the sovereignty and security of the individual nations. Another proposal suggested that oil-consuming nations establish a $25 billion lending facility to provide funds for nations unable to meet balance-of-payments obligations.

European unwillingness to cooperate with the United States exasperated Kissinger, who in March 1974 declared that the Europeans constituted the nation's biggest foreign policy problem. The statement irritated the Europeans, who believed that it was in their self-interest to cultivate closer ties with the Arab world. Kissinger, in their view, was taking an excessively hard line against the Arabs. Particularly unwise, they thought, were statements by Kissinger and other members of both the Nixon and Ford administrations, suggesting that the Americans might be forced to occupy Arab oil fields in case the Arabs became unreasonable in their policy on petroleum exports. In addition, the Europeans shared with the Arabs concern over the Americans' inability or unwillingness to fortify the dollar. Kissinger was never able to mend relations strained during the oil crisis, and Europe remained a source of tension throughout his tenure.

Despite his triumphs and reputation, Kissinger, like most members of the Nixon administration, was touched by Watergate and related issues. In May 1973 it was revealed that he had approved wiretaps of officials and newsmen in efforts to stem policy leaks. Kissinger admitted that he had authorized the taps, but he claimed that the idea had been suggested and put into operation by FBI director J. EDGAR HOOVER and ATTORNEY GENERAL JOHN MITCHELL. They assured him, he alleged, that the taps were legal. Besides, Kissinger argued, it was essential to stop the leaks to the press, which were damaging national security. Also harmful to Kissinger's image was information made available in 1973 and 1974 about his role in the secret bombing of Cambodia and efforts by the CIA and International Telephone and Telegraph to overthrow the democratically elected Marxist government of Salvador Allende in Chile. It appeared that Kissinger was as likely to resort to covert means to achieve his goals as were the political advisers who surrounded Nixon.

Watergate had a significant effect on Kissinger's conduct of foreign affairs. When he went to Moscow in late 1973, he found the Soviets uninterested in reaching any substantive agreements on arms control issues. They were evidently unwilling to deal with a lame-duck administration that might not be able to carry out its part of any bargain. Kissinger warned the American public that obsession with Watergate could damage the nation's international role and destroy the unique opportunity then available to ensure world peace. He privately urged the president to cut off all ties with Haldeman and Ehrlichman and to provide all the White House tapes requested by the Senate Watergate committee and the special Watergate prosecutor. Kissinger reportedly considered resigning during the crisis but soon decided that the best solution to a political nuisance—his view of Watergate—that was obstructing foreign policy was the resignation of the president.

Nixon made Kissinger secretary of state in May 1973. Aside from a supposed desire to humiliate Rogers, Kissinger wanted the post to guarantee that he alone would control the direction of foreign affairs at a time when Nixon was, in his opinion, so desperate that he was liable to act irrationally. Moreover, Kissinger hoped to strengthen his strategic position within the administration against his newest White House rivals, White House chief of staff ALEXANDER HAIG and Secretary of the Treasury JOHN CONNALLY. The president also hoped that naming Kissinger secretary of state would help lift his faltering position. Kissinger was Nixon's most prestigious aide, and his diplomatic triumphs had given luster to the administration. The new appointment was designed to give the White House a measure of legitimacy. Without Kissinger, observers hypothesized, Nixon had no chance of survival.

In reaction to Watergate, the new secretary of state promised that secrecy would no longer be as necessary in his work as it had been in the past. Secret diplomacy, he explained, had been essential to implement "some revolutionary changes," but the foundations had now been laid. The conduct of foreign policy

Secretary of State Henry Kissinger (left) confers with Vice President Rockefeller (center) and President Ford. *(Ford Library)*

in the future, he predicted, would be less secretive and less dramatic. Kissinger's reputation received another boost in October 1973 when he won the Nobel Peace Prize for his Vietnam negotiations, although the choice was not universally applauded.

Nixon, trying desperately to avoid confronting the question of his role in the Watergate cover-up, sought to take refuge in the less compromising realm of foreign policy to emphasize his indispensability. He specifically tried to take advantage of the enormous public acclaim Kissinger was winning through his Middle East shuttle diplomacy. In the spring of 1974, soon after Kissinger had worked out agreements between the Israelis and their Arab neighbors, Nixon toured the Middle East. The president traveled abroad as often as possible, even irritating foreign leaders by his desire to publicize the significance of routine conferences, which they thought unnecessary in the first place. The June 1974 summit meeting with Brezhnev produced nothing.

Kissinger resented Nixon's attempts to share the spotlight with him. He also feared that the president's frenetic travels could have undesirable effects on the work he had already done. Moreover, Kissinger felt that unless Nixon resigned, he, too, would be dragged irretrievably into Watergate.

In a June press conference in Salzburg the secretary of state complained about "innuendos" that he had participated in illegal wiretapping. Speaking so emotionally that some critics called it a "tantrum," Kissinger said that he did not think it "possible to conduct the foreign policy of the United States under these circumstances when the character and credibility of the secretary of state is at issue. And if it is not cleared up, I will resign." He requested that the Senate Foreign Relations Committee investigate charges against him. (In August the committee cleared him of charges that he had perjured himself in testimony about his role in the wiretaps.) Although highly sensitive to criticism, Kissinger in this case appeared to be demanding that Nixon take responsibility for all illegalities and resign.

In Nixon's last days, however, Kissinger, whose relationship with the president had always been solely professional, sought to soothe his superior's vanity by assuring him that history would look favorably on Nixon's achievements, particularly in the area of foreign affairs. In a conversation between Nixon and Kissinger related in *The Final Days*, the secretary of state reportedly knelt down in prayer beside the weeping president. Nixon resigned in August 1974. His successor, Gerald Ford, asked Kissinger to remain.

Kissinger's last three years in government lacked the drama of the first five. Relations with China progressed slowly, in part because of internal political struggles in that country. The two nations agreed, however, to the establishment of liaison offices in Washington and Beijing. Détente with the Soviets slowed, too, and SALT II negotiations were not completed while he was in office. However, the Ford-Brezhnev Vladivostok summit of November 1974 produced a tentative agreement on ceilings for strategic delivery vehicles and MIRV missiles. An effort to provide the Soviets with most-favored-nation status in a trade treaty met with fierce congressional opposition. The legislators, led by Senator HENRY JACKSON (D-Wash.) and supported by the American Jewish lobby, wanted any U.S. trade concessions tied to a Soviet agreement to liberalize their emigration restrictions on Soviet Jews. The furor embarrassed both Kissinger and the Soviets and led to Soviet cancellation of the treaty in January 1975. Conservatives began to regularly accuse Kissinger of "selling out" to the Russians, and some extremists even referred to him as the "Jewish Communist." Liberals continued to attack what they considered his hard-line attitude, and there was a wider consensus that believed that Kissinger was unconcerned about human rights and moral issues.

In 1975 the site of East-West confrontation shifted from Indochina and the Middle East to Africa. Both the State Department and the NSC had been unprepared for "destabilization" in Africa. They had not foreseen the Portuguese withdrawal from its African colonies nor the development of black liberation movements in areas controlled by whites. A 1971 NSC memorandum concluded that black insurgents were not "realistic or supportable" alternatives to white regimes. However, the appearance of Cuban troops in the Angolan civil war in 1975 prompted Kissinger to employ threatening language against the Soviets and to reevaluate U.S. African policy.

In September 1975 Kissinger made a strong statement against apartheid and indicated American displeasure with South Africa's policy in Namibia, expressing support for Namibia's complete independence. He sought to identify the United States with the aspirations of black Africa. He realized that past American policy, exemplified by unstinting support for the Portuguese in Angola and backing of the Biafrans' attempted secession from Nigeria, showed an inability to perceive the direction of the flow of power on the continent. A tour of black Africa in early 1976 gave evidence of the shift in U.S. sympathies. In a speech in Nairobi in May, Kissinger proposed a multibillion-dollar raw-materials development program intended to benefit African nations. He also called for a $7.5 billion international drought-relief program for the sub-Sahara. Most importantly, Kissinger decided that the United States could no longer support the white supremacist regime in Rhodesia. He even promised aid to any southern African nation that joined the campaign against Rhodesia. Together with the British, Kissinger put pressure on Rhodesian prime minister Ian Smith to agree to the end of white rule and preparations for a coalition government that would include moderate black leaders. To force Smith to accept the plan, he sought to persuade South Africa to stop supplying Rhodesia. The interim government plan for Rhodesia was accepted by Smith in November 1976.

It was not clear to political observers whether Kissinger under President Gerald Ford determined foreign policy as completely as he had in Nixon's last year in office. Ford depended on Kissinger, but he also saw the secretary of state as more of a liability than Nixon ever had. In Ford's two years in office, there were repeated rumors that Kissinger would be replaced; the rumors were usually followed by denials from Ford and, in some cases, by a diplomatic coup that temporarily silenced Kissinger's critics. Nonetheless, in May 1976 Kissinger told a reporter that he expected to resign in 1977, even if Ford was elected to a full term. Kissinger's sins, in the opinion of his critics, were many. Even his biggest successes were interpreted as failures. Although the left remained hostile to Kissinger, particularly for his role in the overthrow of Salvador Allende's Marxist government in Chile, it was criticism from the Republican Party's radical right wing that most worried Ford.

Ironically, Kissinger, who had called the nuclear alert in 1973 and had advocated massive bombing of North Vietnam, was considered "soft" on communism in the eyes of the right. Proponents of a big defense budget argued that SALT had given the Soviets an advantage over the United States and that Kissinger was fully conscious of what he had done. Secretary of Defense James Schlesinger claimed that Kissinger made too many concessions and was reluctant to accuse the Soviets of violating previous agreements. Schlesinger argued that the Vladivostok accord had set too high a limit on the number of MIRVs, thus failing to reduce the threat presented by Moscow's huge new missiles. The Kissinger-Schlesinger enmity led to the ouster of Schlesinger in November

1975. To give the appearance that Kissinger's authority was also being reduced, Ford replaced Kissinger as head of the NSC. However, his successor in the NSC was known to be an adherent of Kissinger's policies and likely to carry out the recommendations of the former chief.

Congress also provided a forum for criticism of Kissinger's foreign policy. Senator Jackson, a supporter of both Israel and the defense establishment, led the attack on détente and the new Middle East policy. Supporters of Israel were especially angered by the United States's condemnation in the United Nation of Israel's settlements on the West Bank of the Jordan River and its occupation of East Jerusalem. Just as the American Jewish community influenced congressional opinion, the nation's considerable Greek community stirred a sharp reaction against Kissinger's "tilt" toward Turkey on the Cyprus issue. In May 1975 Congress banned military aid to Turkey, justifying its action on the grounds that the law prevented the use of U.S. weapons for purposes other than defense (the Turks had used American weapons in the invasion of Cyprus).

Kissinger's handling of foreign policy became a major issue during the 1976 presidential campaign. RONALD REAGAN, running against Ford in the Republican primary, argued that the Helsinki accords had recognized the status quo in Eastern Europe and thus abandoned the "captive" nations of the Warsaw Pact to perpetual Soviet domination. Reagan even attacked Kissinger's position on Rhodesia for favoring "revolutionaries" at the expense of legitimate governments. In March 1976 Reagan, relying on information provided by Admiral ELMO ZUMWALT, claimed that Kissinger had once compared the United States to Athens and the USSR to Sparta. According to Reagan, Kissinger had said that the job of "secretary of state is to negotiate the most acceptable second-best available." Reagan insisted that the United States could never be second best and that it should never abandon its ideals. Reagan was able to tap a strong chauvinist sentiment in the Republican Party that could not be reconciled to Kissinger's pragmatic approach to diplomacy. The Reagan wing of the party still objected to relations with China and condemned Kissinger's efforts begun in 1973 to work out an agreement giving Panama control over the Panama Canal. The Democratic candidate, JIMMY CARTER, hit on the idealism-morality issue when he charged that Kissinger's foreign policy was based on "the assumption that the world is a jungle of competing national antagonisms where military muscle and economic muscle are the only things that work."

Following the end of the Ford administration, Kissinger formed Kissinger and Associates, an international consulting firm. In 1980 he was instrumental in negotiating the ultimately failed attempt to have Reagan ask Ford to join him on the Republican ticket as his running mate. In addition to his original firm, Kissinger also formed Kissinger McLarty Associates, with Mack McLarty, former chief of staff to President Bill Clinton. In 2002 President George W. Bush named Kissinger chairman of a commission to investigate the September 11, 2001, terrorist attacks. However, claims by congressional Democrats of conflict of interest forced Kissinger to resign from the commission in December 2002. Kissinger has been awarded the Presidential Medal of Freedom (1977) and the Medal of Liberty (1986).

—JCH

Klein, Herbert G(eorge)
(1918–) *director of communications for the executive branch*

Herbert G. Klein was born on April 1, 1918, in Los Angeles, California. Klein received a degree in journalism from the University of Southern California and began his career as a reporter for the *Post-Advocate* in Alhambra, California. After service in the navy during World War II, he returned to the *Post-Advocate*. In 1948 Representative RICHARD NIXON, a friend of Klein's, asked him to be press agent for Nixon's reelection campaign. Klein accepted, thus beginning a political relationship that lasted for a quarter of a century. He served as a publicist during Nixon's successful Senate race in 1950 and his 1952 vice presidential campaign. In the 1956 general election Klein was assistant press secretary to Nixon. He became editor of the *San Diego Union* in 1959. During the unsuccessful 1960 presidential contest and the 1962 California gubernatorial race, Klein acted as Nixon's press secretary. But his influence with the candidate declined as a result of losses in these elections.

Although Klein was again press secretary for Nixon in his 1968 presidential bid, he was significantly eclipsed by campaign chief of staff H. R. HALDEMAN and Haldeman's associates. Within weeks of Nixon's election victory, the president-elect announced that Klein would serve in the new post of director of communications for the executive branch. His responsibilities were described as including the formulation of information from all departments in the executive branch, not merely the White House.

California representative John E. Moss, a Democrat who headed the House Committee on Freedom of Information, asserted the new office amounted to an "information czar" with "awesome powers." Yet because Klein did not have daily access to the president, his influence remained largely peripheral.

Klein was a major spokesman of the Nixon administration. He helped write SPIRO AGNEW's 1969 address in which the vice president accused television news organizations of reflecting the biases of a small, northeastern liberal elite. The Agnew speech represented the opening salvo in a public confrontation between the administration and the news media. Shortly after the speech Klein said that Agnew's charges represented the widely held view in the White House that "all of the news media needs to reexamine itself, in the format it has and in its approach to problems of news, to meet the current issues of the day."

Klein was a vigorous supporter of the Vietnam War and defended the Cambodian invasion of 1970. He also was a strong opponent of antiwar demonstrators, who he maintained expressed the minority public opinion.

During the 1972 presidential campaign Klein was one of several administration officials appearing as a surrogate for Nixon. He stumped the country as the president's stand-in during the early months of the race. It was part of a campaign strategy of having Nixon "act presidential" rather than directly confront Democratic opponent Senator GEORGE MCGOVERN (D-S.D.), whose candidacy was having trouble after the party's national convention.

In September Klein accused McGovern of using Senator EDWARD M. KENNEDY (D-Mass.) as a "crutch" in his campaign appearances. McGovern responded angrily, "Is he [Klein] campaigning for the presidency? Instead of sending Mr. Klein up here, the president ought to come himself."

RALPH NADER also objected to the surrogate strategy for different reasons. In November he named Klein in a suit to recover government funds paid to White House aides for campaigning on behalf of Nixon. Nader said taxpayers should deplore "any attempts to have the federal government unlawfully finance a candidate for office."

Nixon won by a landslide in November. It was Klein's last campaign. In June of the following year Klein announced his resignation, saying he would have left earlier except that he did not wish to create the impression that his departure was a result of the growing Watergate scandal.

Klein joined the Metromedia communications conglomerate as a vice president. In May 1974 he returned briefly to the White House to help coordinate the release of the transcripts of the White House tapes to the House Judiciary Committee. In 1980 he became editor in chief of Copley newspapers, a job from which he retired in 2003. At present he is a fellow at the American Enterprise Institute.

—MDQ

Kleindienst, Richard G(ordon)
(1923–2000) *attorney general*

Born on August 5, 1923, Richard Kleindienst, the son of a railroad brakeman who later became a minor government officer, was raised in a small town in Arizona. He entered the University of Arizona in 1941 but was called to active duty in the army in 1943. After his discharge in 1946 from Italy he finished his last two years of college at Harvard University on the G.I. bill. He received his law degree from Harvard in 1950 and returned to Arizona to practice law.

During the 1950s and 1960 he was active in Republican politics and served on the Republican National Committee from 1961 to 1963. In 1964 he was instrumental in winning the presidential nomination for BARRY GOLDWATER and became the senator's national director for field operations.

In 1964 he ran unsuccessfully for governor of Arizona. Kleindienst served as the general counsel of the Republican National Committee in 1968 and was RICHARD M. NIXON's director of field operations. He became deputy attorney general in 1969. As deputy attorney general, Kleindienst was in charge of the supervision and direction of the Justice Department, formulating department policies, and was the department's liaison officer with Congress and other government agencies. During his tenure Kleindienst ordered the mass arrest of 7,000 protestors during the 1971 May Day antiwar demonstrations, accepted wiretapping for organized criminals and in national security cases, and supported the enforcement of preventive detention legislation. He directed "Operation Intercept," which called for strict controls and stiff penalties for people caught smuggling marijuana across the Mexican border into the United States. Kleindienst was a foe of busing to achieve racial integration in city school systems, but he favored the preferential employment of minorities in government service.

In February 1972 JOHN MITCHELL resigned as attorney general to become campaign director for the Committee to Re-elect the President (CREEP). Richard M. Nixon nominated Richard Kleindienst to take Mitchell's place. During the last weeks of February, before the Kleindienst nomination reached the floor of the Senate, JACK ANDERSON, a Washington columnist, broke the story that the antitrust division of the Justice Department had been influenced by Kleindienst and the White House to settle out of court a $7 billion antitrust suit against International Telephone and Telegraph (ITT). In exchange the company was to underwrite the expenses for the upcoming Republican Convention, to be held in San Diego. The ITT deal was spelled out in a memo from DITA BEARD, a company lobbyist, to ITT's Washington vice president, William Merriam. It was later learned that Kleindienst had spoken with FELIX ROHATYN, an ITT director, at least five times just before the suit was settled. The Watergate tapes also revealed that he had discussed the suit with President Nixon, who lambasted him for not making an easy settlement with ITT.

During his confirmation hearings, Kleindienst denied that ITT had received preferential treatment by the Justice Department, that he had had meetings with Rohatyn to

discuss the antitrust suit, or that he had been pressured by the White House to settle out of court. Kleindienst was confirmed.

Although Kleindienst subordinates ROBERT C. MARDIAN, PATRICK GRAY, and HENRY PETERSEN were involved in various aspects of the Watergate cover-up, no evidence was ever produced that Kleindienst knew about the break-in plans or participated in the cover-up. In fact, when G. GORDON LIDDY approached him to see if he would use his influence to have the burglars released, he told Liddy that they would get no special treatment.

In April 1973 when Kleindienst found out that John Mitchell, H. R. HALDEMAN, and JOHN EHRLICHMAN were deeply involved in the Watergate burglary and cover-up, he decided to resign. Although Kleindienst was cleared of any wrongdoing in the Watergate affair, the Watergate tapes revealed that he had committed perjury in his Senate testimony in the ITT case. LEON JAWORSKI, special prosecutor for Watergate, let him plead guilty to a lesser charge of refusing to testify. In June 1975 Kleindienst was sentenced to one month in jail and given a suspended sentence. Although the Arizona bar voted to censure him, they did not vote to disbar him. Kleindienst returned to his law practice in Arizona, where he died of lung cancer in 2003.

—SJT

Kleppe, Thomas S(avig)

(1919–) *member of the House of Representatives; director, Small Business Administration; secretary of the interior*

Born on July 1, 1919, and raised in rural North Dakota, Thomas S. Kleppe left Valley City (N.D.) State College after one year for a succession of bookkeeping jobs in several North Dakota banks. Following army service during World War II, Kleppe became the bookkeeper for Gold Seal Co., a Bismarck firm that manufactured and marketed cleaning wax, bath soap, and laundry detergent. Kleppe became the firm's president in 1958. By 1964, when he left Gold Seal to join Dain, Kalmar, & Quail, a Minneapolis-based investment bank, Kleppe had amassed a fortune of $3.5 million.

Kleppe entered politics in 1950, serving a four-year term as mayor of Bismarck. In 1964 he ran unsuccessfully for a U.S. Senate seat. Two years later Kleppe was elected to the U.S. House of Representatives from North Dakota's second congressional district. As a Republican in the House he established a conservative record, consistently supporting the conservative coalition of Republicans and southern Democrats. But he opposed the expansion of the Vietnam War into Cambodia and supported the Senate's Cooper-Church Amendment.

Encouraged by RICHARD NIXON and Republican Party officials, Kleppe made a bid for a Senate seat in 1970. Despite strong backing from the Nixon administration, he lost to the incumbent, Quentin Burdick, by a large margin. Shortly afterward, Nixon offered Kleppe a job as head of the Small Business Administration (SBA). Kleppe was confirmed by the Senate in February 1971.

Kleppe's record for integrity was brought into question when a scandal was uncovered during a 1973 investigation of SBA operations by the House Banking Committee's Subcommittee on Small Business. It was disclosed that Thomas F. Regan, the SBA's Richmond, Virginia, director, had approved loans of up to $11.7 million to companies with which his brother-in-law was associated. Although advised to fire Regan in 1971, Kleppe had refused to take action. Previously, House Banking Committee chairman WRIGHT PATMAN had accused Kleppe of failing to discharge his responsibilities. Minority representatives complained that the SBA was not doing enough to help minority businesses and that the agency was a conservative and unresponsive bureaucracy.

Separate investigations by the House Banking subcommittee and the FBI revealed that White House pressure had been used to obtain SBA approval of loans for political purposes. In August 1975 a Civil Service Commission report confirmed the subcommittee's findings, concluding that under Kleppe's administration "political interests were allowed to influence appointments in a style approximating a patronage system." Although Kleppe was not charged in the report, a longtime observer of the SBA commented that management of the agency "had always been bad, but it's been worse under Kleppe."

In September 1975 President FORD nominated Kleppe to succeed Stanley K. Hathaway as secretary of the interior. Despite criticism from environmental and conservation groups who charged him as "not qualified" for the Interior post, Kleppe was confirmed unanimously by the Senate on October 17, 1975.

As head of the Interior Department, Kleppe promoted a policy of "cautious development of natural resources," yet his administration was again marked by controversy. In February 1976 Kleppe authorized the sale of offshore oil and gas leases in previously unexplored areas despite repeated requests for an indefinite postponement by the Environmental Protection Agency. In keeping with its "accelerated program" for energy independence, the Ford administration had held a sale in December 1975 of oil leases off Southern California. Kleppe's approval of the sale came amid persistent criticism of the oil lease program, particularly in regard to the lack of coordination between federal and state policies and the lack of distinction between exploration and production.

In August 1976 Kleppe's last-minute requests for changes in the Jackson-Murphy oil lease bill nearly raised havoc on Capitol Hill. The sponsors of the legislation had worked out a series of compromises between the House and Senate versions that would revise the competitive bid system for oil leases and provide for greater state control over drilling decisions. Kleppe's proposed amendments (favored by the oil industry) would have, according to the *Washington Post*, "gutted every major provision of the bill." The amendments were not adopted.

Among Kleppe's other proposals for coping with the growing energy crisis was the leasing of federal lands for coal mining on a competitive basis, beginning in 1977. However, in September 1977 U.S. district court judge John H. Pratt ruled against that policy, stating that he considered the government's required environmental impact statement deficient. The judge was especially critical of the role granted private industry in determining leasing sites on publicly owned land.

Following Ford's defeat in the 1976 election, Kleppe joined the faculty of the University of Wyoming. He is now retired and living in Bethesda, Maryland.

—JAN

Knauer, Virginia H(arrington) (Wright)

(1915–   ) *special assistant to the president for consumer affairs*

Virginia Knauer was born on March 28, 1915, in Philadelphia, Pennsylvania. Knauer studied art at the University of Pennsylvania, where she received her B.F.A. in 1937. After graduation she spent one year doing postgraduate work at the Royal Academy of Fine Arts in Italy. During the 1940s Knauer focused on her family and artistic pursuits; the latter included portrait painting and collecting antiques. Her political activities began in 1952 when she joined the Citizens for Eisenhower and Nixon. In 1956 she founded the Northeast Council for Republican Women and served as its president for eight years; she subsequently held high

offices in the Philadelphia County Republican Committee and the Philadephia Congress of Republican Councils. In 1959 Knauer became the first Republican woman ever elected to the Philadelphia city council. She served two terms before losing her third bid, in 1967.

After leaving the city council, Knauer was appointed to head the Bureau of Consumer Protection of the state's justice department. During the year she held this position, Knauer helped speed up complaint processing and pushed for two state laws strengthening her bureau: one giving the bureau permanent status and the other expanding its powers to subpoena witnesses and seek injunctions against fraud. Both bills were enacted in December 1968.

In April 1969 Knauer was appointed special presidential assistant for consumer affairs. She also assumed the chair of the President's Committee on Consumer Interest and the post of executive secretary of the Consumer Advisory Council; the former body was a government agency designed to coordinate federal activities on consumer issues, and the latter sought to bring private citizens together to represent consumer views to the president.

Knauer took over an office with very little effective power. As a presidential assistant she lacked permanent legislative authority as well as enforcement and investigative powers. The government's efforts for consumers were divided among over 400 agencies, none of which Knauer had the authority to coordinate or control. Her most effective function was processing complaints to other agencies.

During Knauer's tenure reformers and consumer advocates made several efforts to establish an independent consumer protection agency with effective powers. Knauer's reaction to these proposals reflected the Nixon administration's changing policies on consumer affairs. In 1969 she opposed a bill establishing an independent nonregulatory agency with broad powers to represent consumer interests before federal agencies and in courts. Instead she backed an administration bill, sponsored by Senator JACOB JAVITS (R-N.Y.), establishing a White House Office of Consumer Affairs and a consumer protection division in the Justice Department. The White House office would have the "central responsibility for coordinating all federal activities in the consumer protection field," but major jurisdiction would be delegated to existing agencies. Knauer said this would "utilize existing programs without creating another cumbersome bureaucratic structure." Both measures failed.

Over the next few years the debate changed from whether a consumer protection agency (CPA) should be established to what powers it should have. In 1974 Knauer supported a House compromise bill that dropped consumer advocates' demands that a CPA be allowed to intervene in state and local agency and court proceedings. The bill was defeated, however, when its Senate companion proposal was filibustered to death. The following year Knauer offered President FORD's alternative suggesting a series of consumer representative plans: 17 executive departments and agencies would appoint one person each to handle complaints and comments and represent consumer interests in the agencies' activities. The heads of five consumer groups issued a joint statement calling the proposal "toothless rhetoric." The Ford alternative failed.

Knauer supported a variety of consumer legislation, but her efforts were criticized by more liberal reformers who wanted stringent laws to protect the consumer. She backed efforts to protect the public against inaccurate consumer information, set federal standards for warranties, and passed more stringent food inspection measures. In 1969 she demanded a comprehensive system of safety standards. A moderate, Knauer opposed measures giving consumers full legal recognition as a class.

Knauer left government service at the end of President Ford's term. The following year she set up Virginia Knauer and Associates, a private consumer consultant agency. Knauer served as President RONALD REAGAN's chief consumer adviser (within the office of Public Liaison) from 1981 to 1983.

—RB

Koch, Edward I(rving)
(1924–) *member of the House of Representatives*

Koch was born on December 12, 1924, to Polish-Jewish immigrant parents. He served in the army during World War II and received his law degree from New York University in 1948. For the next 20 years he was a practicing attorney in New York City, helping to found a Wall Street firm in 1963 with himself as a senior partner. He became active in Democratic politics during the 1950s and in 1966 won election to the city council. In 1968 Koch ran for a seat in the U.S. House on a platform stressing opposition to the Vietnam War and supporting the presidential candidacy of Senator EUGENE MCCARTHY (D-Minn.). He won the three-way Democratic primary and the general election for what was known as the "silk stocking" or the "perfumed stockade" district that ran north in Manhattan from Greenwich Village to Spanish Harlem. It was a predominantly white-collar area, with the fourth-highest median income of any district in the nation.

During the NIXON-FORD years Koch was both an ardent reformer in domestic affairs and a virulent critic of military spending and the Vietnam War. His rating from the liberal Americans for Democratic Action was frequently placed at 100. On numerous occasions he sought cuts in military spending and voted against the antiballistic missile system, the B-1 bomber, and federal funding for the SST. Koch also voted against the Lockheed loan guarantees. He worked hard for passage of the

Cooper-Church Amendment, which sought to limit presidential authority to conduct military operations in Cambodia. He voted against appropriations legislation for support of bombing in Cambodia in 1973.

A steadfast supporter of Israel, Koch promoted aid to that country and legislation that would permit Jews to immigrate to the United States from the Soviet Union. In December 1975 Koch voted against legislation that gave approval to U.S. participation in the African Development Fund as a response to the UN vote equating Zionism with racism. Others had argued against amendments that imposed such a general foreign policy position on such a specific piece of valuable legislation, but Koch asserted that "for these people [the Development Fund supporters] there is never a right time nor the right place."

On domestic issues Koch voted in favor of school busing, government aid for abortions, various subsidy proposals for public transit systems, increased appropriations for public broadcasting, and establishment of a consumer protection agency. In a congressional district in which 56 percent of the population were unmarried adults, Koch, a bachelor, sought several times to end discriminatory legislation against single persons, especially regulations involving the Internal Revenue Service.

Although identified as an outspoken liberal, Koch demonstrated an ability to be independent from ideological stereotyping as well as earning the respect of conservatives in certain areas. In concert with Representative Barry Goldwater Jr. (R-Ariz.), Koch shared sponsorship of the bill that became the landmark Federal Privacy Act of 1974, which sought to prevent invasions of privacy by the federal government. In addition, the act established the Private Protection Study Commission, to which both Koch and Goldwater belonged. The commission investigated the problems of protecting individuals from intrusive investigation by nongovernmen-

tal sources such as banks, credit card issuers, and insurance companies and made numerous recommendations in its 1977 report.

Koch was instrumental in getting federal loan guarantees for the city of New York in 1975, recognizing early that "the executive branch is not going to take any lead in this area." Koch ran for mayor of New York in 1973 on a platform that dismayed many liberals, since it stressed the importance of combating street crime. He had trouble raising funds and dropped out by March 1973 because of the myriad of other candidates in the race and his own inability to gain the support of the influential New Democratic Coalition.

Koch again declared his candidacy for mayor in November 1976, a time when New York was still bickering over the severity of the financial crisis facing the city. He was not widely known outside of his own district, where his popularity was preserved by peripatetic service to his constituents and frequent personal appearances. In his second mayoral bid he again stressed crime control issues and endorsed capital punishment. He also became incumbent mayor ABRAHAM BEAME's most outspoken critic. What was probably the most influential determinant in his 1977 campaign, however, was his use of consultant David Garth, a man who had crafted numerous winning political campaigns by skillful use of the media. Garth's commercials for Koch stressed the crime issue and the competence of the candidate in contrast to the clubhouse politics of Beame and the charisma of former mayor JOHN LINDSAY. Koch's November general election victory was an impressive 50 percent share of the vote over three challengers.

Koch assumed the office of mayor in January 1978. Although immediately involved in seemingly endless squabbles over the city's financial condition, he was able to achieve a renewal of federal loan guarantees for New York.

In 1982 he ran unsuccessfully for governor of New York, losing to Mario Cuomo in the Democratic primary. In 1989 he lost his bid for a fourth term as mayor, losing in the Democratic primary to David Dinkins. Koch then practiced law and opened a second career as a television personality and commentator (serving for a brief period as the judge on the syndicated show *The People's Court*). He continues to be a public advocate for Jewish causes and for the state of Israel.

—GB

Krogh, Egil (Bud), Jr.
(1939–) *White House aide*

Born in Chicago, Illinois, on August 3, 1939, Krogh graduated from Principia College in 1961 and then went on to secure a law degree from the University of Washington. He then joined a firm in Seattle, where he was an associate of JOHN EHRLICHMAN. When Ehrlichman went to Washington in 1969 to assume the post of Nixon's chief domestic council, Krogh became his assistant.

According to members of the press, White House staffers considered Krogh a man of "unusual piety" and jokingly referred to him as "Evil Krogh" because of his presumed incapacity for wrongdoing. As a White House staff official and Ehrlichman assistant, Krogh was responsible for overseeing a number of ongoing projects designed to curtail the flow of narcotics into the United States. Krogh maintained up-to-the-minute progress reports and served as a liaison for Ehrlichman when other pressing matters prevented his attendance. His ability to adhere to administrative priorities and his staunch loyalty to White House policy served to endear him to the president, who appointed Krogh cochairman of the Special Investigations Unit in 1971.

Because of a series of government leaks that culminated in the publication of the *Pentagon Papers* by the *New York Times* in 1971, Nixon established the unit to uncover the sources of confidential information. Because of its overriding concern with leaks the unit was soon referred to as the "Plumbers."

With the disclosure by former Defense Department employee DANIEL ELLSBERG that he was responsible for the leak, Nixon ordered the Plumbers to uncover all available information concerning Ellsberg's motives and associates, since the FBI was handling the matter lethargically. Krogh and David Young, in need of additional staff, recruited veteran intelligence officer E. HOWARD HUNT and former Treasury Department official G. GORDON LIDDY.

Since the authenticity of the *Pentagon Papers* was never in doubt, the unit focused their attention on discrediting Ellsberg to undermine any possible national sympathetic response to his criminal action. When it was discovered that Ellsberg had previously undergone psychiatric care, the unit became determined to expose any potentially embarrassing information. However, Ellsberg's psychiatrist cited doctor-patient confidentiality and refused to discuss Ellsberg.

According to testimony subsequently provided by JOHN DEAN in August 1971, the Plumbers then decided to burglarize the offices of the psychiatrist. Hunt, relying on his former Central Intelligence Agency connections, recruited a team of Miami-based Cubans for the operation, and together with Liddy they headed to the West Coast to carry out their clandestine mission. Krogh had informed Ehrlichman that the burglary was the only means to secure the necessary information to mount a smear campaign against Ellsberg, and Ehrlichman endorsed the operation provided it was carried out in such a fashion as to be "untraceable" to the White House. After the operation was completed, both Liddy and Hunt returned to Washington, where they became involved in intelligence activities for the Committee to Re-elect the President (CREEP). Krogh and Young were then assigned to uncover the source of JACK ANDERSON's column that documented White House support for Pakistan in the India-Pakistan War. They were unsuccessful, and the Plumbers' unit disbanded after the Anderson probe.

Still a member of the White House domestic counsel staff, Krogh continued to function as assistant to Ehrlichman, and with Nixon's reelection in 1972 he was given a post as undersecretary of the Department of Transportation. The appointment took effect in February 1973.

As momentum began to build regarding White House connections to the Watergate burglary, an investigation of the break-in of Ellsberg's psychiatrist's office also pointed to possible White House complicity. Together with Young, Liddy, and Ehrlichman, Krogh went on trial for the burglary in 1974. They cited "national security" as adequate defense. The jury was unimpressed, and Krogh, faced with an inevitable conviction for his role, entered a plea of guilty in February 1974. Krogh received a six-month prison sentence; he was released in June 1974. From 1975 to 1980 Krogh taught ethics at Golden State University. He now practices law in Seattle.

—DGE

L

Laird, Melvin R(obert)
(1922–) *secretary of defense*

Born in Omaha, Nebraska, Melvin Laird received his B.A. from Carlton College in 1942. After military service in World War II, Laird, a Republican, was elected to the Wisconsin state senate, where he served from 1946 to 1952. In that year he was elected to the U.S. House, where he remained until RICHARD NIXON made him his first secretary of defense in 1969. As a representative, Laird emerged as a prominent figure in the Republican Party. He served on the House Appropriations Committee and was a member of the Republican Coordinating Committee, vice chairman of the Platform Committee of the 1960 Republican Convention, and chairman of the same committee at the 1964 convention. During his years in Congress he also served as chairman of the national defense project of the American Enterprise Institute, a conservative "think tank" in Washington, D.C. He supported NELSON A. ROCKEFELLER for the 1968 Republican nomination, but his backing of the Nixon presidential candidacy, combined with his background in Congress and his knowledge of defense matters, prompted the new administration to appoint him secretary of defense.

Laird took office at a time when the fortunes of the U.S. armed forces were at a historical low, with antimilitarist sentiment widespread in the United States as the country attempted to disentangle itself from the Indochina War. A major focal point of the changing attitude toward the military was the defense budget, which liberal sentiment in Congress and at large wished to reduce substantially. Such a reduction was also implied in the "Vietnamization" of the war carried out during Laird's tenure. In March 1969 the Nixon administration announced a $2.5 billion cut in defense spending for fiscal 1970, the first such cut since the beginning of the Vietnam War. Testifying before Congress in April 1969, Laird placed these cuts in the context of the administration's overall anti-inflation policy, asserting that the United States was in an "extremely difficult and dangerous economic and fiscal situation" that made defense reductions imperative. Later that month Laird ordered the closing of 36 U.S. military installations at home and abroad and in August 1969 announced a further $3.6 billion reduction, bringing military spending to $74.9 billion for the following year, to be achieved by a withdrawal of personnel from Southeast Asia and the deactivation of 100 navy ships. Laird stated that these cuts would not mean "an inevitable weakening of our worldwide military position," but that further cuts would be "counterproductive."

These trends continued as the United States slipped into economic recession in 1970–71; Laird in January 1970 announced that 1,250,000 defense-related jobs were going to be phased out as a result. In this context Laird, with other administration officials, proposed a 1-million-man reduction in total armed forces strength. These trends were reversed in 1971, however, when Laird asked Congress for an $80 billion defense budget, and again the following year, when he called for a massive $6.3 billion increase, so large that even prodefense congressmen such as Senator JOHN STENNIS (D-Miss.) questioned its wisdom. Many observers interpreted the 1971–72 turnabout as a move to stimulate the stagnant U.S. economy through arms production.

Laird was deeply involved in the extended controversy over the Sentinel antiballistic missile (ABM) system, which the Nixon administration inherited from the Johnson era and which became the focus of a major confrontation with liberal antimilitary sentiment in Congress. During early 1969 the administration repeatedly underlined its desire to achieve "sufficiency," not superiority, relative to Soviet military capacity. In initial hearings on the ABM issue, Laird told Congress that the Soviet Union spent 3.7 times as much on similar systems as did the United States and in 1970 again warned against a major Soviet arms buildup to justify expenditures that many congressmen felt unwise and unnecessary.

A question closely tied to that of the ABM was the Nixon administration's effort to reach a strategic arms limitation agreement with the Soviet Union. Laird told Congress in April 1969 that he did not feel that the Soviet Union would "be so foolish" as to make a first-strike attack against the United States but warned of Soviet superiority in several years if the arms buildup under way continued. At the beginning of the following year, he again cited the Soviet arms buildup and defended the ABM as a necessity if

no arms limitation agreement could be reached. Laird told Congress in March 1971 that the United States was adopting a new defense posture, which he described as a "prudent middle course between two policy extremes—world policeman or a new isolationism." After the United States and the Soviet Union arrived at a treaty limiting their respective arsenals of antiballistic missiles in early 1972, Laird insisted that Congress approve the treaty only if it was willing to grant the administration its requests for new weaponry.

The new world strategic conception inaugurated under Laird placed greater emphasis on regional military alliances and on enlisting U.S. allies in combat commitments. Laird was concerned about conveying this shift to the European member states of the North Atlantic Treaty Organization (NATO). In May 1969 he flew to Canada to urge the Canadian government not to reduce its NATO troop commitments. A year later he stated his aim of achieving greater sharing of costs by member countries, relieving the United States of untenable economic burdens. He toured U.S. bases in Spain in June and endorsed that country's entry into NATO. At the same time he assured America's allies that all treaties would be honored and that no U.S. troops would be withdrawn precipitously from Europe. In December 1972, at the annual NATO ministers' conference in Brussels, Laird hailed the decisions of West Germany and Great Britain to increase their defense budgets.

Two major domestic issues tied to defense during Laird's tenure at the Pentagon were chemical-biological warfare (CBW) and the military draft. In July 1969 a group of congressmen called for a halt to CBW tests pending studies of their effects. A month later, when the Senate voted curbs on the use of CBW, Laird supported the move but warned of the Soviet Union's high CBW capacity and the need for the United States to "keep up."

Laird supported a reform of the draft in September 1969 while President Nixon announced decreased induction calls for the month ahead. Laird said the reduction was the result of lower manpower needs for the war in Vietnam and a desire to lessen inequities in the 1967 draft law. In 1971 military manning requirements fell to new lows, and in January of the following year the draft was suspended for several months. Laird nonetheless opposed amnesty for draft dodgers.

Much of Laird's efforts at Defense were consumed by the Indochina War. In March 1969 he toured Vietnam, emphasizing the administration's desire to "Vietnamize" the war as quickly as possible by replacing American combatants with Vietnamese troops. In the spring of 1970, Laird again toured Vietnam, denying any U.S. buildup in Laos. It was rumored in May that Laird opposed the U.S. invasion of Cambodia, but publicly he fully backed the administration's policy. The U.S. invasion of Laos in February 1971 discredited Laird's earlier denial of a buildup in that area, but Laird insisted that the invasion had the sole aim of shortening the war and protecting American lives. He also stated that there would be a prompt, scheduled withdrawal. In January 1972 Laird announced a 70,000-man withdrawal from Vietnam. Four months later he firmly endorsed the U.S. blockade and mining of Haiphong Harbor. He attacked Senator GEORGE McGOVERN's (D-S.D.) prisoner-of-war exchange plan put forward that summer in the latter's campaign for the presidency. In October 1972 Laird conceded that the May bombings of North Vietnam had in fact hit the French embassy in Hanoi, a charge earlier denied by the Pentagon.

Laird also had to confront the crisis in morale of the U.S. armed forces. In response to widespread drug use in the military in May 1969 he announced new tests to identify drug addiction in U.S. troops. When the Nixon administration formed an international drug panel in September to stop the worldwide drug traffic, Laird was a prominent member. In February 1970 Laird also acknowledged widespread racism in the U.S. military, stating that "the armed forces have a racial problem because the country has a racial problem." When the Pentagon released a report that November showing systematic racial discrimination within the armed services, Laird said that equality in the military was the "essence of an ordered, free society."

Laird participated in top-level defense discussions on crises in other parts of the world. During the 1970 crisis in which the troops of King Hussein and Israeli forces both attacked the Palestinian guerrillas operating in Jordan, Laird made public statements assuring Israel of U.S. support and promised to replace any equipment lost in combat by Israeli forces. In December he met with Israeli defense minister Moshe Dayan to discuss the results of the military campaigns against the Palestinians.

In November 1972 Laird announced his resignation at the end of Nixon's first term, and ELLIOT RICHARDSON was appointed to replace him. Laird made his final report to Congress in January 1973 but returned to the White House five months later as a domestic adviser to President Nixon in the Watergate affair. After the resignation of Vice President SPIRO AGNEW in October, Laird was discussed as a possible successor and played a role in the eventual selection of GERALD FORD for that post. Two months later Laird resigned from his post, calling for an "early impeachment vote" to bring the issue to a head in Congress and to end the growing paralysis of government that Watergate had brought about.

After this final departure from the Nixon administration, Laird became a senior counselor for the Readers' Digest Association and assumed several corporate directorships of such companies as Metropolitan Life Insurance and Phillips Petroleum. In May 1975 he met with a group of top-level Republican political experts to prepare the groundwork for Gerald Ford's 1976 electoral strategy. In 1985 he was awarded the Harry S. Truman award for distinguished service in defense. He currently resides in Washington, D.C.

—LRG

LaRue, Frederick C(heney)
(1928—2004) *Watergate figure*

Born in Athens, Texas, Frederick C. LaRue came from a family scarred by scandal and tragedy. His father, Ike Parsons LaRue, was sent to jail for banking violations. Following his release he struck oil in Mississippi. That oil strike made the family rich and led to Frederick LaRue's prominence in Mississippi as a political financier. In 1957 LaRue sold the field, reportedly for $30 million. That same year Frederick LaRue shot and killed his father in a hunting accident in Canada.

In the early 1960s LaRue became active in Mississippi Republican politics and served on the Republican National Committee from Mississippi. In 1964 he was a big contributor to the BARRY GOLDWATER presidential bid and four years later was an early donor to the RICHARD NIXON campaign. When Richard Nixon assumed the presidency in 1969, he took LaRue with him to the White House. Described as a "skilled behind-the-scenes operator," LaRue, with no title, no salary, and no listing in the White House directory, became one of the most trusted members of the Nixon administration.

In January 1972, when JOHN N. MITCHELL resigned as attorney general and became campaign director for the Committee to Re-Elect the President (CREEP), LaRue moved from the White House to the "Mitchell group" at CREEP, which included ROBERT C. MARDIAN

and Henry S. Fleming. LaRue was present at the March 30, 1972, meeting in which JEB STUART MAGRUDER presented G. GORDON LIDDY's "Gemstone Plan" for the Watergate burglary to John Mitchell for final confirmation.

After the break-in LaRue and Mardian were in charge of the CREEP cover-up. They supervised the shredding of documents and the destruction of financial records and helped to prepare key CREEP officials for their interviews with the various law enforcement agencies. LaRue also was a principal conduit for "hush money" payments from White House fund-raisers to the Watergate burglars and their attorneys.

By June 28, 1972, it was clear that if the Watergate defendants were not supported, they would tell all they knew about the Watergate break-in and the other White House and CREEP "national security" operations. From September 1972 to March 1973, when JAMES MCCORD broke his silence, LaRue raised funds and distributed the money to the burglars' lawyers. One reporter estimated that the total amount of money paid to the defendants and their lawyers came to $429,500.

On July 30, 1973, at the trial stemming from his indictment by the Watergate grand jury, Frederick LaRue pleaded guilty to one count of conspiracy to obstruct justice. He was sentenced to six months in prison. After serving his sentence, he returned to private life in Mississippi. He worked there in his family's real estate and oil businesses until his death in 2004.

—SJT

Levi, Edward
(1911–2000) *attorney general*

Born in Chicago the son of a scholarly family and descended from a long line of rabbis, Edward Levi was educated at the University of Chicago. He was awarded a Ph.D. degree in

1932 and a J.D. in 1935 by the University of Chicago and served as editor of the law review. He was a Sterling fellow at Yale University, where he earned a Doctor of Juristic Science degree in 1938.

Appointed to the Chicago law faculty in 1939, he took a leave of absence the following year to work in Washington at the Justice Department under Thurman Arnold. Levi first served as special assistant to the attorney general and later became first assistant in the department's war division. In 1944 he was named first assistant of the antitrust division, where he handled many suits against oil companies.

After leaving the Justice Department in 1945, Levi pursued an academic career at the University of Chicago while occasionally returning to government councils. Considered "one of the two most brilliant scholars in the antitrust field in his generation," Levi was chief counsel to the House Judiciary Committee's Antitrust Subcommittee in 1950. From 1966 to 1967 he was a member of the White House Panel on Education and acted as a consultant to the Department of Health, Education, and Welfare and the Office of Education.

Levi shunned party labels and did not even maintain the minimal party identification of registering for purposes of primary voting. His legal philosophies stressed the strict interpretation of the Constitution and balance among the different branches of government. In addition, he seemed to subscribe to traditionally Republican views supporting less government intervention and strengthening states' rights.

At the University of Chicago Levi earned a reputation as an "acerbic and articulate legal scholar" and "a hard-nose administrator." As a law professor he both dazzled and terrorized his students and had little tolerance for either dullness or misguided crusades. As dean, a post he assumed in 1950, Levi presided over an extensive revision of the curriculum, empha-

sizing an interdisciplinary approach joining the study of law with a knowledge of economics, sociology, and political theory. His goal was to train lawyers who could pursue justice, advise on policy matters, and be "capable of cutting through the clichés of [their] own time." When Levi was named university provost in 1962, one of his major concerns was faculty recruitment, and by the end of his term he had been instrumental in substantially upgrading the intellectual caliber of the faculty. In 1968 Levi became president of the university.

In December 1974 President GERALD FORD nominated Levi to be attorney general. He was confirmed the following month. He inherited the post at a time when public confidence in the Justice Department was low and staff morale was badly shaken by the Watergate scandal and the personal involvement of Attorneys General JOHN MITCHELL and RICHARD KLEINDIENST. Five attorneys general in as many years had left the department directionless and badly tainted for breaking, rather than upholding, the law. Lacking partisan passions and of proven legal and administrative ability, Levi seemed well suited for depoliticizing and remotivating the department. As a man of "unquestioned integrity and strength" whom Republican Senator CHARLES PERCY commended as "beholden to no one," Levi's appointment was another step toward dispelling the NIXON administration's legacy of cronyism, duplicity, and frequently unprincipled pragmatism.

His appointment also was significant as the first cabinet-level change of the Ford presidency. Nominated in December of 1974 to replace the controversial WILLIAM SAXBE, Levi's appointment was heralded as a sign of changes that would finally mark the evolution of a distinctive Ford administration, rather than a Nixon holdover. Hailed by the American Bar Association as a "brilliant nomination," it seemed to demonstrate that the Ford administration could attract an individual of high quality to its councils and would steer its own course.

During his tenure as attorney general Levi had to deal with the thorny issue of establishing guidelines for the FBI. He chose the rather controversial method of a study commission, a decidedly unorthodox move by FBI standards. The committee was headed by a woman, Mary Lawton, who was from the Justice Department rather than the bureau. It also included, over FBI objections, a number of outside consultants, such as former acting FBI director WILLIAM RUCKELSHAUS and some academics. In March 1976 the committee issued a first set of guidelines covering domestic security investigations, White House personnel security and investigation, and reporting on civil disorders and demonstrations involving a federal interest. In April 1976 the attorney general formed a three-member unit to monitor the use and effectiveness of the guidelines and to suggest possible changes and refinements to them.

In other areas the department vigorously prosecuted antitrust cases, instituting a record number of criminal and civil suits, which reflected Levi's view that "antitrust enforcement can promote competition without increasing government regulation." Along the same lines Levi argued that the Justice Department "should take from the CAB [Civil Aeronautics Board] its authority to sanction airline agreements and mergers that otherwise would be subject to antitrust prosecution." Although Levi was not successful in persuading the president to endorse such a move, the administration did sponsor legislation that gave the Justice Department increased rights to review and intervene in CAB decisions.

In the area of civil rights, Levi was responsible for the decision not to ask the Supreme Court to reconsider a 1971 ruling that authorized busing as a means of achieving school desegregation. As a result the administration switched to a legislative tactic, and the attorney general helped draft a bill proposing that busing be limited to cases of demonstrated de facto segregation resulting from state action and that busing orders be restricted to a three-year period followed by court review of their effectiveness.

Levi served until the end of the Ford administration and then returned to the University of Chicago as Glen A. Lloyd distinguished service professor. He also was the Herman Pfleger visiting scholar at Stanford University Law School from 1977 to 1978. In 1986 he was elected president of the American Academy of Arts and Sciences and served as a trustee of both the University of Chicago and the MacArthur Foundation. He died in 2000 of complications due to Alzheimer's disease.

—MW

Liddy, G(eorge) Gordon B(attle)
(1930–   ) *Watergate figure*

The son of a prominent patent attorney, Liddy spent his youth in a quiet New Jersey suburb. Following graduation from Fordham University in 1952, he joined the army because, as a friend maintained, "he felt we had to stop the Communists in Korea." After his discharge he entered Fordham Law School and received his degree in 1957. He then became an agent with the FBI. In 1962 he relocated to upstate New York, and after four years in private practice he became assistant district attorney in Dutchess County. In 1968 he ran unsuccessfully for the Republican nomination for a seat in the U.S. House. He campaigned on a "law and order" platform.

In 1969 Liddy became special assistant to Assistant Secretary of the Treasury Eugene T. Rossides. His first assignment was in the Bureau of Narcotics and Firearms Control as a member of Operation Intercept, a program designed to undermine drug trafficking at the Mexican border. Although Operation Intercept had little if

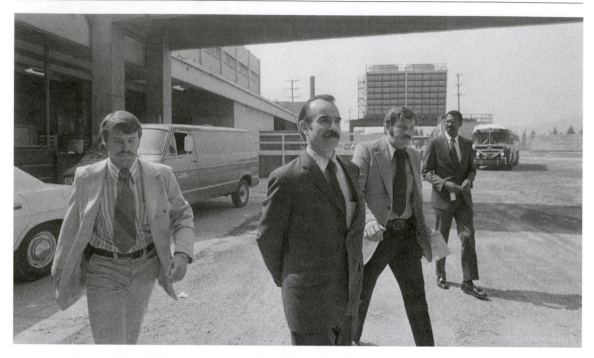

A handcuffed G. Gordon Liddy (second from the left) is escorted to the Los Angeles County jail to await arraignment on charges of conspiracy and burglary, September 19, 1973. *(Bettmann/CORBIS)*

any impact on drug trafficking, Liddy's forcefulness as a speaker and his unrelenting enthusiasm for the job impressed EGIL KROGH, the White House staff coordinator for the project.

Krogh considered Liddy an invaluable asset to the White House, and in July 1971 Liddy joined E. HOWARD HUNT as a member of Nixon's Special Investigations Unit. The ad hoc agency, headed by Krogh and David R. Young Jr., had been established only months earlier to provide a thorough investigation of DANIEL ELLSBERG and the publication of the *Pentagon Papers* and also to uncover the source of government leaks. Consequently it became known as the "Plumbers" unit. Because of Nixon's instructions to give the Ellsberg case priority, Liddy together with Hunt began an intensive examination of Ellsberg's associates and his motives in an attempt to unearth a possible conspiracy. After a review of FBI files it was discovered that Ellsberg had undergone psychiatric care, but his physician refused to provide information, citing patient-doctor confidentiality.

Motivated by a campaign to discredit Ellsberg and uncover the full extent of the conspiracy, Liddy and Hunt, with the approval of Krogh and presidential counsel JOHN D. EHRLICHMAN, plotted a break-in of Ellsberg's psychiatrist's office. With the assistance of three expatriot Cubans, the Plumbers implemented their burglary plan but were unsuccessful in their attempted acquisition of damaging evidence. Ehrlichman, fearful of possible exposure of the bungled burglary, purportedly insisted that future Plumbers' work pursue a conventional means of investigation only. With the exception of a brief investigation of JACK ANDERSON due to his disclosures of White House involvement in the India-Pakistan War, by the end of 1971 the

Plumbers were out of business. In November 1971 Krogh recommended Liddy for a position with the Committee to Re-Elect the President (CREEP).

With a complex new campaign finance law in effect, Liddy was responsible for coordinating CREEP's expenditures in addition to meeting the requisite filing requirements of all 23 states where Nixon entered the primaries. Liddy, with the help of Hunt, also formulated a "broad-gauged intelligence plan" to secure Nixon's reelection. In January 1972 he prepared a detailed draft of his scheme that bore the code name "Gemstone" and presented it to JOHN MITCHELL, head of CREEP; JEB STUART MAGRUDER; and JOHN DEAN, counsel to the president. Liddy's "$1 million bottled-in-bond espionage plan" included the abduction of radical leaders to halt planned demonstrations at the Republican National Convention, break-ins at Democratic headquarters, wiretapping and surveillance of Democratic candidates, and the use of call girls to compromise Democratic politicians. According to later testimony, everyone present was "stunned and appalled" by the plan. Liddy later informed security coordinator JAMES MCCORD that the plan was presently unaffordable, and the project had to be reorganized.

In subsequent meetings Liddy presented a scaled-down version that restricted the project to wiretapping of the Democratic National Committee headquarters only. A reduced budget was submitted and later approved. Within months Liddy, Hunt, and McCord and a four-man back-up team, plotted the break-in of the party's headquarters at the Watergate complex.

In May 1972 the group succeeded in planting wiretaps, but the equipment began to malfunction in June, and a return visit was necessitated. Because of a night watchman's suspicion, McCord and the four-man back-up team were arrested on the premises.

As the Watergate episode began to unfold, Liddy was subpoenaed before a grand jury in August 1972. He was later indicted, tried, and convicted for his role in the burglary. In November 1973 Liddy was sentenced to 6 to 20 years. Stubborn to the end, he refused to testify either on his own behalf or against his colleagues and superiors. President JIMMY CARTER commuted his sentence, and he was released from prison in September 1977. In 1982 Liddy published his memoir, *Will*. After touring on the lecture circuit, Liddy became host of *The G. Gordon Liddy Show*, syndicated on talk radio.

—DGE

Lindsay, John V(liet)
(1921–2000) *mayor, New York, N.Y.*

Born on November 24, 1921, the son of an investment banker, Lindsay was educated in fashionable private schools and at Yale University, which awarded him a law degree in 1948. Active in the Young Republicans as an Eisenhower stalwart, he worked as executive assistant to Attorney General Herbert Brownell from 1953 to 1956. In 1958 Lindsay was elected to the House of Representatives from Manhattan's East Side "silk stocking" district, a bastion of the GOP's eastern establishment and one of the few Republican districts in New York City. He became one of the most liberal Republicans in Congress, sponsoring civil rights legislation and opposing anti-Communist-inspired attacks on civil liberties.

In November 1965 Lindsay upset New York's Democratic political machine by winning the mayoralty election on the Republican and Liberal lines. Once in office he frequently found himself embroiled in difficult negotiations with the city's traditionally Democratic public service unions. Strikes were frequent. Despite winning handsome contracts from the city, many white union members, as well as other working- and middle-class whites, came to dislike Mayor Lindsay with growing intensity. Ironically, one reason was the dramatic increase in the city budget, which required higher taxes and transit fares. Another was the mayor's close relationship with the black and Hispanic communities. His support of school decentralization against the demands of the United Federation of Teachers (UFT) led to the 1968 teacher strikes, increased—at least temporarily—black-white polarization, and eroded his popularity among traditionally liberal Jews (a large percentage of the UFT membership was Jewish). Meanwhile, Lindsay's relationship with New York governor NELSON ROCKEFELLER, one of the major financial backers of the 1965 campaign, deteriorated, as Rockefeller occasionally exercised gubernatorial prerogatives to the detriment of the mayor and New York City.

In 1969 Lindsay faced an uphill battle for a second term. He had to win if he hoped to fulfill early predictions that he would someday be a presidential candidate. In New York he was still popular among the nonwhite minorities and some liberals and, as the charming host of "Fun City," among chic Manhattanites. One of the most appealing and photogenic national political figures—he was almost invariably described as "handsome" or "tall, tanned, and mediagenic"—he was, as one local politician said, "the most popular mayor in the country outside of New York." Some found him arrogant and self-righteous. Scandal beset Lindsay, too, when a key aide was jailed for bribery. The mayor therefore began his unofficial campaign early, appearing as often as possible in the news and visiting white communities in the boroughs. He repeatedly admitted making mistakes, but New Yorkers were reminded by his supporters that his was the "second toughest job in America." He deemphasized his glamorous "Fun City" image and sympathy for minorities. Instead, he stressed his admin-

istration's achievements in the areas of budget, employment, rapid transit, housing, education, and the war on crime. He noted that his government had made city parks more available to the public. He took tough public stands on civil disorder.

Lindsay was defeated in the June Republican primary by John Marchi, a conservative state legislator from Staten Island. Jarred by the first electoral defeat of his career, Lindsay nonetheless benefited from the loss. Having won the Liberal Party endorsement, he was free of the constraints imposed by the Republican label. Although Rockefeller refused to back him, New York's two liberal Republican senators, JACOB JAVITS and CHARLES GOODELL, offered their support. The mayor himself rejected "rigid party loyalty" and decided to "support candidates on the basis of their performance and record on behalf of New York City." He was also the only liberal in the field for November, since Democratic voters chose a "law and order" candidate, Mario Procaccino, in their primary. The mayor continued to emphasize his "solid" accomplishments and made a concerted effort to win the crucial Jewish vote, but he was careful not to compromise his liberalism beyond the point of credibility. He used Vietnam as a campaign issue, arguing that the war diverted money and attention from urban and other domestic problems. In November Lindsay won reelection with 41 percent of the vote, running on the Liberal and a special Independent line.

Political analysts speculated whether Lindsay would switch party allegiance. But Lindsay moved slowly, declaring his intention to remain Republican and refusing to discuss future political ambitions. Meanwhile, polls showed Lindsay to be an attractive figure nationally, particularly among the young, the college-educated, and women.

During the NIXON administration the mayor was spokesperson for the nation's cities. In March 1970 he helped unite the big cities through the U.S. Conference of Mayors to lobby for "congressional and state actions to meet city needs." The mayors would concentrate on five areas of pending congressional legislation: revenue sharing; welfare reform; federal mass transit aid; urban renewal and Model Cities; and crime control. For the next few years a task force of 17 mayors, Lindsay's creation, visited each other to publicize urban problems and keep the demand for revenue sharing alive. In December 1970 Lindsay drew a standing ovation at the National League of Cities convention by calling for a $10 billion revenue sharing program in 1971. As chairman of the Conference of Mayor's Legislative Action Committee, he led the cities' attack on Nixon's 1971 budget. He developed the concept of the "national city," which would bypass state government and deal directly with Washington.

Lindsay grew increasingly critical of Nixon administration policies. Speaking in April 1970, he assailed administration efforts to quash dissent as "the most significant threat to freedom from our own government in a generation." The following month he lauded the young men who refused to serve in Vietnam as he traded attacks with Vice President SPIRO AGNEW. Lindsay and Agnew chose opposite sides again in the fall, when Lindsay backed Senator Goodell's bid for reelection, while Agnew indirectly endorsed Conservative candidate JAMES L. BUCKLEY. More surprising was Lindsay's public support for Democrat ARTHUR J. GOLDBERG in the gubernatorial contest against Governor Rockefeller. This decision marked the final break with Rockefeller.

Lindsay faced recurrent municipal crises. In May 1970 construction workers, abetted by police inaction, attacked antiwar demonstrators in Manhattan. In the following month ghetto riots, punctuated by arson, erupted. In August and September inmates of four city prisons revolted and took over the jails. The prison affair generally enhanced Lindsay's stature, since the mayor appeared to act with firmness but without an excessive use of force. Some liberal critics, however, blamed Lindsay for the riots, charging that his administration, while spending enormous amounts on the police, had done little to improve the backlogged court system, prison overcrowding, and inmate medical and rehabilitation programs. More clearly damaging to Lindsay were the Knapp Commission hearings on police corruption held in late 1971. Evidence presented to the commission indicated that in 1967 the mayor had been informed of police officers' complaints about widespread corruption in their department but had chosen to ignore their reports.

In August 1971 Lindsay announced his switch to the Democratic Party. In part because of the mixed reaction from national and state Democratic leaders, he did not immediately announce his presidential candidacy. Nonetheless, he said that he was "firmly committed to take an active part in 1972 to bring about new national leadership." He scorned the Nixon administration for "indifference" to urban problems, drug addiction, inflation, and gun control. He noted the failure to end the Indochina War, but "the most troubling development" was "the government's retreat from the Bill of Rights," citing telephone tapping, military spying on citizens, mass arrests of protesters, and "minimum enforcement" of minority rights. After a period spent making contact with Democrats across the nation and assessing his modest performance in the Gallup and Harris polls, the mayor declared his presidential candidacy in December.

Lindsay pictured himself as an "outsider" competing with primary opponents who were "good and honorable men" but trapped in "a capital closed to the ordinary citizen, but open to bankrupt corporate giants, foreign dictators, and to those wealthy enough to buy privileged protection with campaign cash." Aided by friendly New York labor leaders, he made a strong effort to appeal to the blue-collar vote. Yet, unlike his primary opponents, he had no established constituency within the Democratic Party. Even a January 1972 convention of liberal New York State Democrats voted to back Senator GEORGE MCGOVERN (D-S.D.), giving Lindsay only 1.4 percent of the votes. His primary runs were disastrous. He won only 7 percent in the Florida primary in March and came in sixth with 7 percent in the April Wisconsin primary. He then announced his withdrawal from the race.

Lindsay campaigned actively for McGovern in the fall, heading the Mayors for McGovern Committee. He decided not to seek reelection in 1973. He took up law practice again in New York. In 1980 he was defeated for the Democratic nomination for the U.S. Senate by ELIZABETH HOLTZMAN. His final years saw two of his law firms go out of business and found Lindsay in a series of health-related problems. He died at a retirement community on Hilton Head, South Carolina, weakened by Parkinson's disease.

—JCH

Lodge, Henry Cabot
(1902–1985) *chief negotiator, Paris peace talks; special envoy to the Vatican*

Lodge was born on July 5, 1902, into a distinguished New England family that traced its ancestry to the Massachusetts Bay Colony and later included several cabinet members and congressmen. He was raised by his grandfather Senator Henry Cabot Lodge Sr., noted for his opposition to U.S. participation in the League of Nations in 1919. Subsequent to his graduation from Harvard in 1924, Lodge pursued a journalism career until his election

to the Massachusetts house of representatives in 1933. In 1936 he was elected to the U.S. Senate. Lodge served two duty tours during World War II.

Reelected to the Senate in 1946, Lodge identified with the eastern wing of the Republican Party supporting bipartisan foreign policy to contain communist expansion and federal programs to deal with selected economic and social problems. During 1951–52 Lodge worked for the election of Dwight D. Eisenhower as president. In so doing, Lodge ignored his own political career, losing his senatorial reelection bid to Representative John F. Kennedy. Lodge served as ambassador to the United Nations until 1960, at which time he became the Republican Party's vice presidential nominee. Lodge served as ambassador to South Vietnam twice, from August 1963 until August 1964 and from July 1965 until April 1967. From April 1968 until January 1969, Lodge served as ambassador to West Germany.

In January 1969 President RICHARD NIXON appointed Lodge chief negotiator to the Paris Peace Conference, replacing veteran diplomat W. Averell Harriman. Lodge's credentials marked him as an ardent anticommunist, meaning that the North Vietnamese could anticipate few concessions from the new administration. New York attorney Lawrence Walsh and ambassador to Indonesia Marshall Green were named Lodge's assistants. The American proposals called for complete withdrawal of all outside forces within one year, a cease-fire under international supervision, and free elections under international supervision. The North Vietnamese rejected consideration of these proposals and demanded the immediate and total withdrawal of all Americans from South Vietnam. Frustrated by Hanoi's "take it or leave it" attitude, Lodge asked to be relieved in October 1969. Nixon's failure to immediately replace Lodge upon his resignation on December 8, 1969, indicated that the administration was momentarily downgrading the peace negotiations.

In July 1970 Lodge became President Nixon's special envoy to the Vatican, a position accepted without pay and not requiring residence in Rome. The post held significance because the Vatican was a center of worldwide information and provided an opportunity for possible peace negotiations with North Vietnam and inquiries concerning the fate of American prisoners of war there. Also in July 1970 Lodge was named chairman of a special presidential commission to study U.S. policy toward Communist China. After hearing testimony from 200 witnesses in six U.S. cities, the commission recommended in April 1971 that the United States seek Communist China's admission to the United Nations without the expulsion of Nationalist China.

During the 1970s Lodge maintained his home in Beverly, Massachussets, primarily tending to personal business. He attended the 1976 Republican National Convention but did not play a significant role. He died at his home in 1985.

—TML

Long, Russell B(illiu)

(1918–2003) *member of the Senate; chairman, Finance Committee*

Born on November 3, 1918, Russell Long, son of the populist Louisiana governor and U.S. senator Huey Long, obtained his law degree in 1942. He served in the navy during World War II and then entered politics by working on his uncle Earl K. Long's successful 1947 gubernatorial campaign. The following year he won a seat as a Democrat in the U.S. Senate. Long assumed the chairmanship of the powerful Finance Committee in 1966. As chairman, Long became the Senate's most influential voice on federal economic and tax policy.

Long combined the "poor boy populist" image of his father with his own energetic and determined advocacy of policies favored by Louisiana's major industries—oil, natural gas, sulfur, sugar, and shipbuilding. He fought for oil depletion allowances for the oil and natural gas industry, the deregulation of natural gas prices, and price supports for the sugar industry. He opposed breaking up the large, integrated oil companies. But he also said that it would "probably be right to break up big fortunes" and that it would be beneficial to spin off Chevrolet and Buick from General Motors. He opposed what he called "give-away" programs like the Communications Satellite Corp. (COMSAT) and government patent policies that grant patents on research results obtained under federally financed research projects. And he wanted to tighten up tax breaks given to foundations and those given for charitable contributions.

During the NIXON-FORD administrations he worked for limited pension reform and for a national health insurance to cover catastrophic illness. In foreign affairs he supported the Vietnam War and opposed the 1970 Cooper-Church Amendment to limit the president's authority to conduct military operations in Cambodia and the 1971 Mansfield Amendment calling for American withdrawal from Vietnam within nine months of the release of U.S. prisoners. But when President Ford requested additional military aid for Vietnam during the final Communist offensive in 1975, Long opposed it.

Long played a major role in the formation of the Tax Reform Act of 1969. He guided through his committee the bill extending the income tax surcharge and revised the House-passed tax reform measure so it was more in line with the administration's more limited reform proposals. The panel diluted reform measures that cut off tax loopholes and reduced individual tax relief measures. It entirely deleted reforms dealing with foreign income, especially from oil, and increased the oil depletion allowance to 23 percent after the House had cut it to 20 percent. The Senate, however, added several major floor amendments before passing the bill. These included a 15 percent increase in Social Security benefits and increases in the income tax exemptions for tax payers and their dependents. Long supported an unsuccessful Republican move to return the amended bill to his Finance Committee. Nixon at first threatened to veto the reform bill but eventually signed it, and the Tax Reform Act of 1969 became the most comprehensive tax reform law in the nation's history. The same year Long successfully led the opposition that defeated the Nixon administration's Family Assistance Plan (FAP). The FAP was expected to check what were described as family welfare costs by increasing the incentive to work. The plan had two features: one aided the unemployed poor; the other aided the working poor who would be eligible for assistance payments until their annual income reached $3,920.

The House adopted the basic features of the administration's proposals in April 1970, but the plan immediately ran into the combined opposition of liberal Democrats and conservative Republicans on Long's Finance Committee. The liberals and welfare groups opposed the plan because the benefit levels were too low; the conservatives opposed it on principle because they saw it as the beginning of a guaranteed annual income system whose costs would increase substantially over the years. After three days of hearings in April, Long sent the measure back to the White House for redrafting. At July hearings Long denounced the Family Assistance Plan as "a massive and costly experiment which proposes adding 14 million Americans to the welfare rolls." Instead, he proposed increasing the federal minimum wage as a way to raise living standards for the working poor and to cut fed-

eral welfare costs. The administration rejected this idea. Welfare reform was effectively killed in the 91st Congress when Long's Committee rejected the FAP by an 8-6 vote in November 1970.

The following year Long was a major force behind attempts to include the family welfare features of the FAP in an omnibus Social Security bill. After his second defeat on the family welfare reform plan, Nixon announced in February 1973 that his administration would not resubmit it to Congress.

During 1972 Long helped shape the Nixon-proposed federal revenue-sharing program Congress enacted in 1972. The administration had first proposed the program in 1969. The revised 1971 proposal called for a $5 billion general revenue-sharing program and an $11 billion special sharing program that reorganized and regrouped existing grant programs. But Congress failed to move on special revenue sharing.

Long's Finance Committee substantially revised the House-passed version of the program. They rewrote the aid distribution formula to increase the amounts made available to smaller, rural states at the expense of the more populous ones. Senators from urban states strongly opposed the aid formula. Long admitted that his bill gave less money to more populous states than did the House version. But he also claimed that his bill gave more money to the cities and poorer areas because it distributed less money to the well-to-do suburbs. The Senate accepted the Long formula.

Tax reform, national health insurance, welfare reform, and energy policy were high on the JIMMY CARTER administration's agenda when it took office in 1977. They all had to confront Russell Long and his Finance Committee. Retiring in 1987, Long practiced law in Washington, D.C., and Baton Rouge, Louisiana, until his death in 2003.

—AE

Love, John A(rthur)

(1916–2002) *governor of Colorado; director, Office of Energy Policy*

John A. Love was born on November 29, 1916, in Gibson City, Illinois. Love attended the University of Denver, receiving his bachelor's degree in 1938 and his law degree in 1941. After serving in the armed forces in World War II, he practiced law in Colorado Springs. As a political novice, he entered the Colorado gubernatorial race in 1962 and won. He held that office until 1973 and, consequently, served longer than any other Colorado governor. He was regarded as a political moderate.

He resigned as governor to become President NIXON's director of a newly created Energy Policy Office. From the winter of 1972 until Love's appointment in July 1973, Nixon had already gone through four top energy advisers—General George Lincoln, PETER FLANIGAN, JOHN EHRLICHMAN, and GEORGE SHULTZ. When Love was appointed, the president seemed to give the energy problem new attention.

From the outset Love ran into trouble. He took the spotlight in the public criticism of summertime gasoline shortages and forecast of a possible heating oil and propane gas shortage. His lack of experience in energy matters combined with other factors to make his job difficult. When Nixon appointed Love, he gave him only eight persons to work in the energy office. In addition, Love found himself sidestepped on energy matters, meeting challenges from officials in the Treasury and Interior departments.

Love was regarded by the administration as indecisive and ineffectual. Dissatisfaction became widespread in the summer of 1973 when Love resisted mandatory allocations of heating oil supplies, a policy the Nixon administration finally adopted after months of indecision. Love, too, changed his mind on allocations when criticism came from governors, oil distributors, and Congress.

When the Yom Kippur War broke out in the Middle East in October, the administration became increasingly convinced that Love was not the person to take charge of the energy crisis. Nixon decided to create a Federal Energy Administration. Reports circulated in Washington in December that WILLIAM E. SIMON, then deputy secretary of the treasury, would be the head of the new energy agency. It was reported, moreover, that Love would remain in the administration as assistant to the president but would no longer be coordinating energy policy for President Nixon. On December 3 Love resigned, causing the White House to upset its plans to announce the setting up of the Federal Energy Administration. Love apparently believed that the Energy Policy Office would be absorbed in the new energy agency and that his job would lack influence. Nixon's continuing legal problems over Watergate contributed to Love's demise. "To be honest," Love was quoted as saying after his resignation, "it's been difficult to try to do anything meaningful and even to get the attention of the president."

In 1976 Love supported the nomination of GERALD FORD on the Republican ticket. Love succeeded in blocking the at-large sweep of Colorado delegates to the Republican convention that the RONALD REAGAN camp had predicted. Reagan received the support of 15 of the 16 at-large convention delegates; the lone opponent was Love, who sided with Ford. Love became the CEO of Ideal Basic Industries and taught history at the University of Northern Colorado. He died in 2002.

—HML

Lowenstein, Allard K(enneth)

(1929–1980) *member of the House of Representatives*

Born on January 16, 1929, the son of a prominent physician and restaurateur, Allard

Lowenstein grew up in the suburbs of New York City. He studied at the University of North Carolina and Yale Law School, where he received his law degree in 1954. As president of the National Student Association during the early 1950s, Lowenstein coordinated a nationwide student-volunteer effort to aid the presidential campaign of Democrat Adlai Stevenson. Later, as an educational consultant to the American Association for the United Nations, he toured South-West Africa, an international territory under the jurisdiction of the Republic of South Africa. As a result of his trip, he published in 1962 *Brutal Mandate*, an impassioned indictment of South Africa's racial policies in the territory.

In 1960 he managed the successful congressional campaign of reform Democrat WIL-LIAM FITTS RYAN of New York. Lowenstein taught political science at Stanford University and North Carolina State University. Active in the civil rights movement, he donated his legal services to jailed civil rights workers, helped organize voter registration drives in Mississippi, and was an adviser to the Southern Christian Leadership Conference.

Lowenstein, an early critic of the Vietnam War, became the chief organizer of the "dump Johnson" movement in 1967–68. He used his strong ties to the student movement to bring antiwar Democrats and campus activists together. Convinced that only a change in leadership would end the war, he canvassed antiwar senators to find a candidate willing to challenge President Johnson in the primaries. When Minnesota senator EUGENE MCCARTHY agreed to run, Lowenstein mobilized large numbers of student volunteers to work for the senator in the New Hampshire primary. McCarthy's impressive showing led Johnson to announce on March 31, 1968, that he would not seek reelection.

At the Democratic Convention in Chicago in August, Lowenstein worked for a strong peace plank. He also opposed Vice President HUBERT HUMPHREY's nomination but later supported Humphrey in the campaign. While putting a peace coalition together for the convention, Lowenstein also ran for a seat in the House of Representatives from New York's Nassau County. Campaigning as a peace candidate and with the aid of large numbers of student volunteers, Lowenstein narrowly defeated his Republican opponent in November 1968.

In Congress Lowenstein compiled a consistently liberal voting record. He opposed the NIXON administration's District of Columbia anticrime bill, a proposal to cut off financial aid to student demonstrators, and most military appropriation bills. He voted for tax reform, for reform of the Selective Service System, and for liberalization of the food stamp program. In 1970 the Americans for Democratic Action gave him a 100 percent rating.

Lowenstein's primary concern while in Congress remained the Vietnam War. With Representatives PAUL MCCLOSKEY (R-Calif.), Donald Riegle (R-Mich.), and Donald Fraser (D-Minn.), he tried to coordinate the efforts of antiwar representatives to enact peace legislation, especially proposals to cut off funds for combat operations in Southeast Asia. But the antiwar forces in the House were much weaker than those in the Senate, and the efforts of Lowenstein and others were frequently stymied. MENDEL RIVERS (D-S.C.), the powerful chairman of the House Rules Committee, was a strong supporter of the war, and he generally imposed severe time limits on House debates over war-related issues.

In April 1970, when the Rules Committee restricted debate on a military procurement bill, Lowenstein attacked the lack of democratic procedures and accused the House leadership of contributing to "widespread erosion of faith" in democracy among the nation's youth. His remarks had little effect, however. Later that year the House Rules Committee allowed only one hour to debate the controversial Cooper-Church Amendment.

Lowenstein continued to be active in the antiwar movement outside of Congress. On October 6, 1969, he released a statement with eight other members of Congress that urged all Americans to support the student-led nationwide protests planned for October 15. He also endorsed the November march to Washington to protest the war. Throughout 1969 and 1970 Lowenstein spoke on college campuses and at antiwar rallies around the country.

Although he was defeated for reelection in 1970 after the Republican-controlled New York legislature gerrymandered his district, Lowenstein remained active in politics. In 1971 he formed Citizens for Alternatives Now, which tried to coordinate a "dump Nixon" campaign. In May 1971 Lowenstein was elected chairman of Americans for Democratic Action and immediately launched a nationwide drive to register 18- to 21-year-olds and to mobilize them in support of peace candidates in 1972. Lowenstein traveled to hundreds of college campuses, urging students to reject violence as a political tactic and to work within the system to make it responsive to the people's will.

Lowenstein's outspoken opposition to the war and to the Nixon administration's policies won him a place on the White House "enemies list" as a top-priority target. A 1972 report issued by Senator SAM ERVIN (D-N.C.) revealed that Lowenstein also was a target of the army's secret surveillance program on domestic political activity. In response to these revelations, Lowenstein urged an official inquiry, citing many "puzzling incidents" in his life during these years.

In 1972 Lowenstein unsuccessfully challenged incumbent representative JOHN ROONEY for the Democratic nomination to Congress from Brooklyn. He ran for a House seat from Nassau County in 1974 and 1976 but lost both times to Republican John Wydler.

He remained active in politics and practiced law in New York City through the late 1970s. On March 14, 1980, Lowenstein was assassinated by a former staff member.

—JD

M

MacGregor, Clark

(1922–2003) *member of the House of Representatives; chairman, Committee to Re-Elect the President*

Born on July 12, 1922, and raised in Minneapolis, MacGregor graduated from Dartmouth in 1946 and received a law degree from the University of Minnesota in 1948. He practiced law until 1960, when he was elected U.S. representative from Minnesota's third district.

In Congress MacGregor emerged as a conservative, opposing President Johnson's reform legislation, amending the anticrime bill of 1967 to put the highest funding priority on thwarting domestic rioting and organized crime, and revising the 1968 gun-control bill to exclude curbs on the sale of rifle and shotgun ammunition. In 1968 MacGregor was one of 10 "surrogate candidates" who spoke on behalf of RICHARD NIXON's presidential candidacy.

During his last term in the House, Mac-Gregor was a leader of the drive to oust Supreme Court justice ABE FORTAS after *Life* magazine revealed that Fortas had accepted (and returned 11 months later) a $20,000 payment from financier Louis E. Wolfson, who was subsequently convicted of selling unregistered securities. One day after MacGregor urged a House probe of the matter, Fortas resigned.

MacGregor captured the Minnesota Republican nomination for senator in 1970 but lost the election to HUBERT H. HUMPHREY, who received 59 percent of the vote. During the Senate race MacGregor pledged support for President Nixon's policies, and Nixon campaigned for MacGregor, calling the candidate "a voice of the future."

Following his election defeat, MacGregor became Nixon's chief congressional liaison. He served on a five-member council appointed to study a wide range of recommendations by black members of the House, including stronger enforcement of civil rights legislation and more emphasis on Africa in foreign policy. After some initial fanfare, however, the council failed to produce concrete results, further alienating the Black Congressional Caucus from the administration. In December 1971 MacGregor coauthored "Richard Nixon's Third Year," a paper describing the president's accomplishments that claimed 1971 "was a year of large conceptions, daring innovation, and substantial progress."

On July 1, 1972, MacGregor became chairman of the Committee to Re-Elect the President (CREEP) in the wake of JOHN MITCHELL's resignation from the post two weeks after the arrest of five burglars at the Democratic National Committee headquarters in the Watergate complex in Washington, D.C. Before accepting the job—MacGregor said in a July 28, 1973, court deposition—he met with Nixon and was assured that CREEP had no involvement in Watergate. At the meeting MacGregor was informed that "no person in a position of authority had any foreknowledge of or involvement in the Watergate." During the campaign MacGregor worked closely with H. R. HALDEMAN. The White House played down the connection, choosing to present the president as a statesman above partisan politics.

MacGregor led the reelection effort in a traditional partisan fashion. He warned of overconfidence when Nixon built an early lead in the polls; praised AFL-CIO neutrality; castigated the American Newspaper Guild's endorsement of Democratic candidate GEORGE MCGOVERN; announced Nixon's refusal to debate McGovern; and labeled the Democratic candidate an advocate of "giveaway" welfare programs, "massive and reckless" defense budget cuts, and a "begging" foreign policy.

MacGregor was not able to avoid entanglement in the Watergate issue. In September the Democrats raised the amount of a previous lawsuit against the Republicans for "blatant political espionage" from $1 million (filed three days after the Watergate break-in) to $3.2 million. MacGregor responded with a countersuit that claimed Democratic national chairman LAWRENCE F. O'BRIEN was using the court "as a forum in which to make public accusations against innocent persons" and asked $2.5 million in damages. Both suits were later dismissed.

In October MacGregor defended the administration against charges that linked CREEP officials to a secret fund used for dirty tricks and political espionage. Earlier MacGregor had denied the existence of the fund and claimed the *Washington Post* was "maliciously linking the White House to Watergate." But on October 26 he vacillated, admitting the existence of a "special fund" used for campaign planning and "in one instance" for gathering information on possible disruptions of Republican rallies in New Hampshire.

In his 1973 court deposition MacGregor said that throughout the campaign he was "misled, deceived, and lied to" by his own staff in CREEP and by top White House aides regarding Watergate. This admission was in direct contradiction of a statement made by the president at a May 22, 1973, press conference in which Nixon said MacGregor was told to "conduct a thorough investigation" of CREEP's relation with the break-in. MacGregor said he did not conduct an investigation and was never told to do so by the president.

The day after Nixon's overwhelming election victory, MacGregor resigned as CREEP chairman and became chief Washington lobbyist for United Aircraft Corp. He testified before the Senate Watergate committee on November 1, 1973, and repeated his court deposition. He died of respiratory failure in 2003.

—BO

Maddox, Lester G(arfield)
(1915–2003) *governor of Georgia*

Born on September 30, 1915, the son of a poor Georgia steelworker, Maddox quit school in the 11th grade to help out at home. He held a variety of jobs until he opened the Pickrick restaurant in 1947. As the restaurant prospered, Maddox turned his attention to politics. He ran unsuccessfully for mayor of Atlanta in 1957 and 1961 and for lieutenant governor in 1962. Throughout these campaigns Maddox maintained an extreme right-wing platform characterized by an emphasis on states' rights and racial segregation. In 1964 Maddox received national attention by defying the provision of the newly adopted Civil Rights Act that outlawed racial segregation in public accommodations. Maddox and his supporters, armed with guns and ax handles, had threatened blacks attempting to integrate the Pickrick. In this first test of the Civil Rights Act, Maddox was ordered by a federal court to integrate the Pickrick. However, he preferred to close the restaurant rather than comply with the court order. The national attention surrounding the affair served to advance Maddox's political career, and he ran for governor of Georgia in 1966. He was selected governor by the Georgia legislature in 1967 after an election in which none of the candidates received an absolute majority.

As governor, Maddox surprised many by the moderation of his racial policies. Certain programs were initiated in Georgia to improve the lot of poor blacks and prisoners. Schools were not closed to prevent desegregation. Maddox's explanations for this change once in office were varied. One observer stated simply, "Maddox didn't practice what he preached," while others pointed to Maddox's lack of administrative experience and argued that he had given subordinates a free hand in initiating social programs.

In 1968 Maddox entered the race for the Democratic presidential nomination. He made his announcement on seeking the nomination less than two weeks before the start of the Democratic National Convention. Maddox ran on the basis of his old right-wing states' rights platform combined with newer themes of complete U.S. military victory in Vietnam and domestic law and order. Maddox's candidacy was not considered seriously at the convention in August 1968, and he withdrew his name from consideration before the balloting began.

Maddox sustained a second political defeat at the convention when a challenge Georgia delegation headed by civil rights activist Julian Bond was seated along with the mostly white, conservative, "official" delegation, which had been handpicked by Maddox in his capacity as Georgia Democratic Party chairman. The convention attempted a compromise, whereby Georgia's votes would be divided between the two delegations. However, this proved unacceptable to Maddox and the majority of his delegation, who resigned. After leaving the convention Maddox characterized the Democrats as the party of "looting, burning, killing, and draft card burning." In the 1968 presidential election Maddox supported the independent candidacy of GEORGE WALLACE.

Maddox continued to be a popular and colorful political figure in Georgia. In 1970 he even offered to ride on top of a train carrying deadly nerve gas through Georgia to prove its safety. Maddox was legally barred from a second consecutive term by a provision in the state constitution. After he attempted to have this provision overturned in court and failed, Maddox ran for lieutenant governor in the 1970 election and won. His running partner for governor was JIMMY CARTER.

During the 1972 presidential election Maddox continued to support the presidential aspirations of George Wallace. After the Democrats nominated GEORGE MCGOVERN, Maddox declared that he hoped RICHARD NIXON would "devastate" McGovern in the coming election. He reasoned that a disastrous political defeat would increase the possibilities for a right-wing turn in sentiment within the Democratic Party.

Maddox was highly critical of the performance of the Nixon administration. In a letter to President Nixon, he sharply denounced the Paris peace talks. He wrote that Nixon's "secret offer of billions of United States dollars to Communist Vietnam . . . is an act giving aid and comfort to the enemy of the first order . . . a pro-Communist act . . . an anti-American act . . . shameful and disgraceful and betrays every American military man who has fought, bled, or died in battle throughout Southeast Asia and the rest of the world."

In 1974 Maddox attempted to gain the Democratic nomination for governor of Georgia once again. The primary battle between Maddox and George Busbee, a state representative, was extremely sharp. The primary was seen as a political struggle between the segregationist policies of Maddox and the racial moderation of the "New South" represented by Busbee and his supporters (which included Maddox's old political enemy Julian Bond). Maddox received the greatest number of votes cast for the dozen candidates in the primary but was defeated by Busbee in the subsequent runoff election. Tearfully admitting defeat, Maddox claimed, "People are quicker to turn out to vote against somebody than they are to vote for somebody."

Maddox entered the 1976 presidential election as the candidate of the right-wing American Independent Party. He asserted that GERALD FORD was a wishy-washy conservative and was dominated by NELSON ROCKEFELLER. He attacked Jimmy Carter as a "leftist-socialist." Maddox's campaign had no appreciable effect on the outcome of the election.

During the mid-1970s Maddox attempted to put together a nightclub act starring himself and his black former dishwasher from the Pickrick. The act, titled the "Governor and his Dishwasher," featured music and jokes. It was not a commercial success. In 1978 Maddox was in debt for over $125,000 and, having recovered from a heart attack, sold his political memorabilia at a public action. He died in 2003 of complications resulting from a fall.

—MIB

Magnuson, Warren G(rant)
(1905–1989) *member of the Senate*

Orphaned at an early age, Magnuson was adopted by a Swedish family and raised in North Dakota. As a young adult he moved to Seattle, where he received his law degree from the University of Washington in 1929. Mag-

nuson was elected to the state legislature in 1932 and to the U.S. House in 1936. In 1944 he won a seat in the Senate.

As a Democrat in the Senate Magnuson consistently supported liberal social welfare legislation. He was an outspoken advocate of increased government spending, both for defense and for domestic programs. He also worked hard to channel federal funds to his home state, which was heavily dependent on shipping, aircraft, fisheries, and timber for its prosperity.

In 1962 Magnuson was reelected with only 52 percent of the vote. The narrowness of his victory led him to take an increasingly active role in sponsoring legislation of national significance. Magnuson played a key role in the passage of the controversial public accommodations section of the Civil Rights Act of 1964. During the Johnson administration he became one of the prime sponsors of consumer protection legislation.

Magnuson continued his advocacy of consumer protection legislation in the NIXON years. In 1970 he drew upon the recommendations of the National Commission on Product Safety and introduced a bill to create an independent consumer product safety agency. No action was taken, but Magnuson reintroduced a similar bill in February 1971. The proposed legislation gave the independent agency broad authority to test products and to set safety standards, allowed it to ban products that constituted an unreasonable hazard, and authorized it to initiate court action against offending producers.

The bill was strongly opposed by industry and by the Nixon administration, which prepared an alternative bill two months later. The administration proposal retained product safety authority within the Department of Health, Education, and Welfare (HEW), gave industry a role in the standard-setting process, and limited the disclosure of product information.

Magnuson's Commerce Committee held intensive hearings on both bills in July 1971, and the following March it reported a revised version. The new bill retained the most important features of Magnuson's original legislation, including the independence of the agency, its right to set mandatory standards and ban products, and the authority to seek court orders against hazardous products. Magnuson was especially adamant about the agency's independence. He argued that HEW was already overburdened with functions and would inadequately perform its consumer protection functions. Magnuson's views prevailed, and in October 1972 Congress approved the creation of an independent Consumer Product Safety Agency with broad regulatory powers.

Magnuson sponsored several other pieces of consumer legislation with varying degrees of success. In 1969 he introduced a bill to ban cigarette advertising on radio and television and strengthen the health warning on cigarette packages. Despite pressure from the tobacco industry, Congress approved it in March 1970, and the bill became effective the following year. In 1970 he sponsored legislation that established federal standards for warranties on consumer products and strengthened the consumer protection powers of the Federal Trade Commission. Although the Senate approved the bill in 1971 and again in 1973, opposition from the Nixon administration kept the House from taking action on it. In December 1974 both houses of Congress finally approved the legislation, and President FORD signed it into law.

Magnuson had less success in his efforts to win passage of a no-fault auto insurance bill. In February 1971 he and Senator PHILIP HART (D-Mich.) introduced legislation to require all motorists to carry insurance providing compensation for bodily injury regardless of who caused an accident. The bill also required each state to enact no-fault laws that met the minimum federal standard set by the bill. The Nixon administration opposed Magnuson's bill, however, and argued instead that no-fault should remain a concern of the states. The Commerce Committee held hearings in 1971 and reported the bill favorably the following year. However, it died in committee in the Senate. The Senate finally approved the bill in May 1974, but heavy lobbying by the American Bar Association killed it in the House. A renewed effort by Magnuson to pass a no-fault law in 1976 also failed.

Magnuson took other legislative initiatives during the Nixon years. In 1971 and 1972 he won extensions of federal unemployment compensation benefits for states with high jobless rates. He sponsored the 1971 Emergency Health Personnel Act, which authorized the Public Health Service to assign medical personnel to areas with critical shortages of health workers. In 1970 Magnuson introduced the constitutional amendment extending the vote to 18-year-olds. He was a strong advocate of increased government funding of cancer research and attacked Nixon's war against cancer as "more myth than reality." Magnuson was highly critical of Nixon's impoundment of funds appropriated by Congress and of President Ford's frequent vetoes of appropriation bills for social welfare programs.

Magnuson was defeated for reelection in 1980 and resumed his law practice. He died at his Seattle home in 1989.

—JD

Magruder, Jeb Stuart

(1934–   ) *special assistant to the president; deputy director of the Committee to Re-Elect the President*

Jeb Stuart Magruder was born on November 5, 1934, in New York City. Magruder served in the army from 1954 to 1956 and graduated from Williams College in 1958. He received an M.B.A. from the University of Chicago in 1963. During the early 1960s he held various jobs in sales, advertising, and merchandising. Magruder became active in Republican politics and in 1968 was in charge of the RICHARD NIXON campaign in Southern California. Nixon intimates ROBERT FINCH and H. R. HALDEMAN liked Magruder and offered him a job as special assistant to the president after the Nixon victory in 1968.

Working under Haldeman, Magruder was involved in multiple political activities centered around public relations and manipulation of the news media. For instance, Magruder thought of the scheme to use antitrust policy to intimidate and coerce large media conglomerates like the *Washington Post* into giving the Nixon administration more favorable news coverage. Magruder was most active in establishing the White House letter-writing campaigns around single issues (e.g., the HARROLD CARSWELL Supreme Court nomination, the Cambodian invasion) and in the formation of dummy "citizens' committees." These committees were supposed to create the impression that Richard Nixon's domestic and foreign policies had broader support than they did.

In May 1971 Haldeman released Magruder from his White House position and told him that as deputy director of the Committee to Re-Elect the President (CREEP), he should begin organizing the personnel on the committee. Magruder ran CREEP until March 1972, when Attorney General JOHN N. MITCHELL officially resigned to become CREEP director. The committee was staffed primarily by former Haldeman White House assistants (35 in all made the move), and Magruder kept in touch with Haldeman on all issues.

Magruder's official job at CREEP was to direct campaign advertising, research, and security operations. In practice he transferred the White House letter-writing campaigns, citizens' committees, and intelligence operations to CREEP.

In August 1971 Magruder and his assistant Kenneth Rietz planned the first in a series of "intelligence operations" to infiltrate the campaigns of the Democratic front-runners, Senators EDMUND MUSKIE of Maine, HENRY JACKSON of Washington, and HUBERT HUMPHREY of Minnesota. The operation was intended not only to gather information but also to sabotage the candidates' respective campaigns. These activities came under the immediate supervision of G. GORDON LIDDY, who was hired by CREEP in December 1971 as general counsel. Liddy also was responsible for initiating his own projects. In early 1972 Magruder ordered HUGH SLOAN to give Liddy $250,000 from CREEP to finance the "Gemstone Plan," which was designed to get information from the Democratic National Committee.

Following the Watergate break-in on June 17, 1972, Magruder played a major role in attempts to get the burglars released and cover up administration involvement in the plot. The cover-up of the burglary and other CREEP activities began immediately. As Magruder later testified, "I do not think there was ever any discussion that there would not be a cover-up." Magruder, Mitchell, and JOHN DEAN worked on strategies to keep the FBI investigation contained to the five burglars, H. HOWARD HUNT, and Liddy. They were afraid that if the FBI investigators probed too deeply, they would uncover the misdeeds of the Nixon administration from 1969 onward and that the adverse publicity would lead to Richard Nixon's defeat in the fall. Magruder also tried to pressure Hugh Sloan into telling the FBI that the sum he gave for the Liddy "Gemstone Plan" was dramatically smaller than it had been. Sloan, however, refused to commit perjury.

In appearances before a grand jury in August, Magruder invented inflated dollar amounts for the expenses of the Liddy operation and claimed that Liddy was a maverick who had broken away from the control of the higher echelon in CREEP. During September 1972, in his last appearance before the grand jury, Magruder was asked about the entries in his and John Mitchell's daily logs for meetings at which the surveillance plan had been discussed. He testified that the first one was canceled, and at the second one, they discussed the new campaign contributions disclosure law. When on September 15, 1972, the Watergate grand jury returned indictments against the five burglars, Hunt, and Liddy, it looked as though the efforts to contain the investigation had been successful.

However, on March 23, 1973, as the Watergate burglars were about to be sentenced, JAMES MCCORD broke his silence and in a letter to Judge JOHN SIRICA claimed that pressure had been applied to the defendants to maintain their silence, that they all committed perjury, and that they had been paid for their silence. The last phase of the cover-up involved the search for scapegoats among the president's men. In early April it appeared to insiders at the White House that Mitchell, Magruder, and Dean were being "set up" by Ehrlichman and Haldeman to assume full responsibility for the break-in and the cover-up.

On April 14, 1973, Magruder followed John Dean to the prosecutor's office with his story to try to work out a bargain for leniency from the courts. A year later, in March 1974, Magruder and six other top presidential aides, including Haldeman and Ehrlichman, were indicted by the Watergate grand jury. On June 4, 1974, after pleading guilty to charges of perjury and conspiring to help others commit perjury, Magruder was sentenced by Judge Sirica to from 10 months to four years in the federal prison at Allenwood, Pennsylvania. On January 8, 1975, Magruder was released after serving seven months of his sentence.

After his release from prison, Magruder earned a master's in divinity from the Prince-

ton Theological Seminary. From 1984 to 1990 he was a Presbyterian minister in Marble Cliff, Ohio; from 1990 to 1998 he served in Lexington, Kentucky. In 1998 he retired from the ministry and now resides in Dallas, Texas.

—SJT

Malek, Frederic

(1936–) *deputy undersecretary of health, education, and welfare; special assistant to the president; deputy director of the Office of Management and Budget*

Born in Berwyn, Illinois, Malek graduated from the U.S. Military Academy in 1959, following which he served as an airborne ranger officer with the special forces (Green Berets) in Vietnam. He also received his M.B.A. from Harvard University in 1964. From 1975 to 1988 Malek worked for Marriott Hotels, becoming its president in 1982. Malek entered the NIXON administration as deputy under secretary of health, education, and welfare. In 1970 he became a special assistant to Nixon, with responsibility for recruiting for positions in the executive office. In 1972 he served as deputy campaign manager for the Committee to Re-Elect the President. He then served as deputy director of the Office of Management and Budget under both Presidents Nixon and Ford.

In 1988 Malek served as the director of the Republican National Convention in New Orleans. Immediately following the convention Malek was named Frank Fahrenkopf's deputy at the Republican National Committee. However, he was forced to resign after it was revealed that while in the Nixon White House, upon the request of the president, he had made a list of the number of Jews who were then working at the Bureau of Labor Statistics. In July 1990 Malek directed the Economic Summit of Industrialized Nations (the G-7 Meeting), for which service he earned the rank of ambassador. From 1989 to 1991 he served as president and vice chairman of Northwest Airlines. In 1992 Malek once again returned to national politics as a campaign manager for the unsuccessful reelection campaign of GEORGE H. W. BUSH.

Following his service to the Bush administration, Malek founded and became chairman of Thayer Capital Partners, a merchant bank in Washington, D.C., where he serves as its president and CEO. He also was a former partner in the Texas Rangers major league baseball team with George W. Bush and successfully spearheaded an effort to get major league baseball back in the Washington, D.C., area.

—JRG

Mandel, Marvin
(1920–   ) *governor of Maryland*

Marvin Mandel came from an Orthodox Jewish background. His father was a clothing cutter in Baltimore. Mandel received his law degree from the University of Maryland in 1942. He was elected a justice of the peace in 1948. His political career began to take off in 1951 after he was appointed to fill a vacancy on the Democratic Party's state central committee. He was elected to the Maryland house of delegates representing the politically important fifth district in 1952. He kept this office for the next 16 years.

Mandel became speaker of the house of delegates in 1963. He replaced Gordon Boone, who had been convicted and jailed in a statewide political scandal involving savings and loan institutions. As Speaker, Mandel became a major figure in Maryland power politics.

In January 1969 Mandel won the special legislative election to fill the remaining two years of SPIRO AGNEW's term as governor. A special election by the legislature was necessary because at that time the Maryland

constitution did not provide for the post of lieutenant governor.

As governor, Mandel's major accomplishment was his attempt to revamp the state's judicial system. Uniform qualifications for judges were imposed, and the practice of electing circuit and appellate judges was ended. Instead, circuit and appellate judges had to seek reconfirmation from the state's senate every 15 years. Mandel also successfully pressed for a state constitutional amendment that provided for the office of lieutenant governor.

In 1973 the governor's personal problems became a potential political liability. Mandel's estranged wife, Barbara, had refused to move out of the governor's mansion even after he had expressed his intention to get a divorce and remarry another woman. Barbara Mandel staged a five-month "sit-in" in the governor's mansion and vacated only after she had concluded that their "marriage had not returned to normal." The Mandels were divorced in 1974, and the governor then remarried.

In the beginning of 1973 a federal grand jury began investigating corruption involving Maryland's politicians. A high point in the investigation was the indictment and conviction of Vice President Agnew for tax evasion. Late in 1973 the grand jury began to investigate Mandel's dealings, particularly his connections to the Tidewater Insurance Co., which was owned in part by close political supporters of Mandel. In an attempt to sidestep criticism, Mandel appointed a study group to inquire into the practice of awarding state contracts by competitive bidding. Mandel also promised to return $40,000 that had been contributed to his upcoming campaign for reelection by consultants who did business with the state.

In November 1975 Mandel and five longstanding political supporters were indicted by a federal grand jury on charges of mail fraud, bribery, and "a pattern of racketeering activity." Mandel was also charged with falsifying his federal income tax return. The charges against Mandel concerned his relationship with the Tidewater Insurance Co. and racetrack interests owned by three of the codefendants. The indictment charged that Mandel had used his powers as governor to veto a bill that would have given Maryland's Marlboro racetrack profitable additional racing days. Mandel and the other five codefendants allegedly proceeded to obtain a concealed interest in the track at greatly reduced prices. According to the indictment, the governor then persuaded the legislature to override his veto, which resulted in prospective windfall profits for the six secret partners. Mandel was said to have received a 5 percent interest in a real estate concern for the services he rendered his partners in this deal.

The charges of mail fraud stemmed from the mailing out of transcripts of Mandel's news conferences in which he lied to newsmen. Mandel responded to his indictment by saying that it could be a positive opportunity because he could now "prove my innocence in a court of law." He also charged that his indictment had been a politically inspired vendetta motivated by "jealousy."

In December 1976 the court declared a mistrial after it was discovered that one of the jurors had been offered $10,000 to hold out against a conviction. After a new trial Mandel and his defendants were convicted on some 18 counts each of mail fraud and racketeering in August 1977. Leaving the courtroom after his conviction, Mandel was jeered by a crowd of spectators who shouted, "Lock him up" and "See you in jail, Marv." In October 1977 Mandel was sentenced to four years in prison, though he escaped paying a fine because he told the court that he was broke.

Mandel refused to resign and was suspended from office. He was replaced by Lieutenant Governor Blair Lee. In January 1979 the conviction was overturned on appeal on technical grounds. The case was returned to federal district court for retrial. Mandel was found guilty and served 19 months in prison before President RONALD REAGAN issued him a pardon. In 1987 an appeals court overturned his conviction. He is presently a lawyer in Baltimore.

—MLB

Mankiewicz, Frank F(abian)
(1924–   ) *political figure*

Frank F. Mankiewicz was born on May 16, 1924, in New York City. A graduate of the University of California at Los Angeles (UCLA) in 1947, Mankiewicz received an M.S. from Columbia the following year. In 1950 he ran an unsuccessful campaign for the California state legislature as a Democrat. After a brief stint as a journalist, he entered the University of California's Law School at Berkeley and was admitted to the bar in 1955. He spent the next six years in private practice.

In 1962 Mankiewicz relocated to Peru, where he served as director of the Peace Corps. Two years later he was promoted to the post of Peace Corps regional director of Latin America. From his Washington office he implemented recruitment drives and supervised the agency's social and educational programs for Latin America.

In 1965 Mankiewicz joined Senator Robert Kennedy's (D-N.Y.) staff as a press assistant. Because of his commitment to Kennedy's goals and his ability to deal with the press, he was appointed Kennedy's press secretary in 1968 and was responsible for coordinating the senator's campaign for the Democratic presidential primary.

After recovering from Kennedy's tragic death later that year, Mankiewicz directed his support to Senator GEORGE MCGOVERN (D-S.D.), whom he considered closest to Kennedy in his liberal perspective. With RICHARD NIXON's victory Mankiewicz returned to his earlier, brief occupation as a journalist and cowrote a liberal syndicated column. In 1969 a Ford Foundation grant subsidized his study of Peace Corps programs in Latin America and the Caribbean.

In 1971 McGovern recruited Mankiewicz to serve as press secretary for his attempt at the Democratic presidential nomination. An astute political observer and strategist extraordinaire, Mankiewicz plunged into the race with cold-blooded realism. The combination of McGovern's lack of recognition beyond the confines of his home state and his vocal opposition to the Vietnam War undermined all possibilities of unified party support. Despite negligible resources and a slim chance for victory, Mankiewicz proceeded to map out logistics for McGovern's state primary entries. A barrage of intensive public exposure was followed by a retreat to analyze repercussions and restructure the campaign.

Mankiewicz formulated a progressive image-building strategy to challenge the media contention that McGovern was a mild-mannered one-issue candidate. In the interests of electability McGovern limited his statements on Vietnam and addressed himself to fundamental economic issues. As a result of campaign staff advice, he became more circumspect in his association with antiwar organizations so that his "radical" image would not foreshadow possible success in the primaries. Elevated to the position of political adviser, Mankiewicz guided his candidate through the requisite gatherings of the party machine in each primary state. McGovern's relatively successful showing laid the foundation for his nomination at the Democratic National Convention in 1972.

Despite Mankiewicz's attempts to enhance McGovern's credibility as a presidential contender, the choice of Senator THOMAS EAGLETON (D-Mo.) as a running mate proved irreversibly damaging to the campaign. Although Mankie-wicz had been assured by Eagleton that his personal background was beyond reproach, the senator's history of psychiatric treatment, including shock therapy, soon surfaced. After a short period of indecision, Eagleton was replaced with SARGENT SHRIVER, but McGovern's already foundering popularity plummeted. Financial and organizational problems and the inescapable "radical" tag together with the Eagleton affair proved to be McGovern's undoing, and his defeat was a harsh one.

After Nixon's victory Mankiewicz turned to television writing and producing. He is now vice chairman of Hill and Knowlton, a public affairs firm.

—DGE

Mansfield, Mike (Michael) (Joseph)
(1903–2001) *member of the Senate; Senate majority leader*

Mike Mansfield was born on March 16, 1903, in New York City. Following the death of his mother, Mansfield's Irish relatives sent him from New York City to live with family in Montana. From 1918 to 1922 Mansfield served in all three branches of the armed service. He then returned home to work for the next eight years as a miner and mining engineer. Mansfield quit mining to obtain both B.A. and M.A. degrees from Montana State University in 1933 and 1934, respectively, where he remained to teach Latin American and Asian history. A Democrat in a traditional Republican state, Mansfield lost his first bid for a political office in his party's congressional primary of 1940, but he won a House seat two years later. In acknowledgment of his specialization in Asian affairs, Mansfield was assigned to the House Foreign Affairs Committee.

Following his election to the Senate in 1952, Mansfield established a liberal record. In an unprecedented move, Senate majority leader Lyndon Johnson selected Mansfield, who had low seniority, to be his assistant, the party whip. It was believed Johnson chose Mansfield because he was a moderate, trustworthy senator who would not threaten the Texan's strong hold on the Senate. In the last years of the Eisenhower administration, Mansfield voted liberal on most issues and supported the nation's foreign policy.

When Johnson became vice president in 1961, the Senate Democrats elected Mansfield their majority leader. During the Kennedy administration Mansfield worked with the White House in its battle for passage of liberal legislation. Unlike Johnson, who had exercised flamboyant leadership over the Senate, Mansfield quietly, with the assistance of his whip, Senator HUBERT H. HUMPHREY (D-Minn.), directed the policies of the majority party. When Johnson took over the presidency, Mansfield watched his power gravitate to the White House.

Mansfield's legislative leadership contrasted sharply with that of Johnson. Demonstrating an inordinate amount of respect for the Senate, Mansfield refused to bully, badger, arm-twist, or make deals to obtain the legislation his party desired. Nevertheless, he held great power as majority leader through his chairmanship of the Democratic Policy and Conference committees, which formulated party policies, scheduled legislation, and voted on and assigned committee chairmanships and positions. Mansfield could, if he desired, control the flow of legislation on the Senate floor. The senator approached this responsibility cautiously. He delegated to his whip, Senator ROBERT BYRD (D-W.Va.), the distasteful task of pressuring for needed votes. This enabled Mansfield to enjoy the prestige of being the aloof, distinguished, statesman legislator who finessed rather than browbeat the Senate into action. Few bills during these years as majority leader bore his name. Mansfield preferred

having other senators introduce legislation. In contrast to senators who thrived on press coverage, Mansfield shied away from publicity. Yet when issues angered him enough, Mansfield joined the political debate.

Mansfield was a particularly strong opponent of the Vietnam War. Although he initially backed the Johnson administration's Indochina policy, Mansfield grew disillusioned with the war effort following a fact-finding trip to Vietnam in 1966. He privately tried to persuade Johnson that military victory would be impossible. When it appeared that the president preferred to settle the war on the battlefield rather than at the conference table, Mansfield publicly criticized the war.

During RICHARD NIXON's first term Mansfield emerged as one of the leading Democratic critics of the administration's Vietnam policy. He particularly deplored how the executive had usurped all the war-making functions from Congress. In 1970 Mansfield enthusiastically supported the Cooper-Church and McGovern-Hatfield amendments. The following year he introduced his own end-the-war amendment. Mansfield's measure declared that it was the policy of the United States to end military operations in Indochina at the earliest possible date and to "provide for the prompt and orderly withdrawal of all United States military forces not later than nine months after the date of [enactment of the bill] subject to the release of all American prisoners of war." The measure also requested the president to negotiate a cease-fire with North Vietnam and establish a final date for the withdrawal of American military forces. It passed the Senate but failed in the House.

Following Nixon's historic visit to China in February 1972, Mansfield, with minority leader HUGH SCOTT (R-Pa.), traveled in April to Beijing. The Chinese Communists' economic and social progress impressed the former Asian scholar, who had visited China for President Roosevelt during World War II. Mansfield downgraded the fear expressed by many Americans that China was acting as an aggressive world revolutionary power. Finding the regime conservative and pragmatic enough to be more concerned with its own internal development, Mansfield informed the American people that the Communist leadership paid only lip-service support to developing countries revolutions. The Mansfield-Scott mission to China accomplished no major breakthroughs in the disputes that had divided Beijing and Washington for close to 25 years; instead, Mansfield and his Chinese hosts engaged in exploratory talks to improve the two nations' economic, political, and cultural contacts.

In addition to Mansfield's opposition to the administration's Vietnam policy, he was particularly incensed about the continued presence of 600,000 U.S. troops in Western Europe. His repeated efforts to introduce legislation to scale down the size of the U.S. forces in the North Atlantic Treaty Organization were rebuffed by the Senate. Supporters of the continued large American military presence in Europe argued that the Mansfield proposal threatened Western security. Mansfield responded that the Europeans should pay for their own defense.

Mike Mansfield had a polite, business-like relationship with both Presidents Nixon and FORD. He breakfasted with them every month to discuss upcoming legislation. But he frequently opposed the administration, particularly on domestic policy. Speaking for the Senate as majority leader, he deplored the Republicans' conservative policies, which he blamed for causing high unemployment and inflation. He quietly lobbied for the Senate to override the Nixon-Ford vetoes of social legislation. During the Watergate scandals Mansfield scorned the administration for its refusal to be honest with the American people, but his criticism was mild in comparison with the partisan attacks launched by fellow Democrats.

Mansfield decided to retire from the Senate following the 1976 election. Those who were impressed with his style of leadership praised him for restoring democracy to the Senate, in contrast to Johnson's dictatorial leadership. On the other hand, Mansfield's critics found him to be a weak leader whose desire to conciliate and patronize left the Senate an unruly body with no direction. Mansfield answered his critics by pointing out that the leadership techniques they called for were not consistent with his basically shy personality.

Mansfield's retirement from public life was short-lived. In 1977 President JIMMY CARTER appointed him ambassador to Japan, a position in which he served until 1988. President RONALD REAGAN awarded him the Presidential Medal of Freedom in 1989. From his retirement until his death in 2001, Mansfield served as senior adviser to Goldman, Sachs, & Co. in Washington, D.C.

—JB

Mardian, Robert C(harles)
(1923–   ) *assistant attorney general*

Born on October 23, 1923, Robert Mardian, the son of a California businessman, attended the University of California from 1941 to 1943. After graduating from the University of Southern California Law School in 1949, he practiced law in California. In 1964 Robert Mardian managed BARRY GOLDWATER's presidential campaign in the western states. Four years later he did the same for RICHARD NIXON. When Nixon was elected, Mardian went to Washington as general counsel under ROBERT FINCH at the Department of Health, Education, and Welfare (HEW). At HEW Mardian carried out the Nixon administration's "southern strategy," formulated by JOHN MITCHELL. The plan called for the administration to stall on public school desegregation in the South to win conservative, segregationist southerners into the Republican Party.

Because of his hard-line anticommunism, Robert Mardian in 1970 was made assistant attorney general in charge of the Internal Security Division. He used the Justice Department's machinery to intimidate and harass a broad spectrum of antiwar protesters, civil rights advocates, and radicals. The 1973 Senate Watergate hearings revealed that on at least two occasions Mardian misused his powers at the request of the White House. First he gave President Nixon confidential FBI information on DANIEL ELLSBERG that was then passed on to JOHN EHRLICHMAN's "Plumbers." He also gave Ehrlichman confidential files on Senator THOMAS EAGLETON (D-Mo.) that revealed that Eagleton had been hospitalized for "exhaustion." Ehrlichman leaked the information to sympathetic newspaper people who published the reports that led to Eagleton's removal as Senator GEORGE MCGOVERN's (D-S.D.) running mate in the 1972 election.

Mardian was involved in the Watergate cover-up from its inception. On June 17, 1972, when the seven Watergate burglars were arrested, John Mitchell told him to have G. GORDON LIDDY, the chief architect of the Watergate burglary and general counsel to the Committee to Re-Elect the President (CREEP), talk to Attorney General RICHARD KLEINDIENST about releasing the burglars, a ploy that Kleindienst rejected. Mardian and FREDERICK LARUE were put in charge of CREEP's "cleaning operation." They supervised the destruction of "potentially embarrassing" documents, including the financial records of important campaign donors received before and after the new Campaign Contributions Disclosure Law went into effect.

Mardian and LaRue also destroyed Liddy's "Gemstone" file, which included memos describing wiretapped conversations of Democratic Party officials and their staffs. In addition, the two men prepared witnesses for their FBI interviews by telling them not to volunteer information. Mardian arranged for his former associates at the FBI to question CREEP officials and staff at the CREEP office instead of at FBI headquarters or in the privacy of their own homes.

During Mardian's 1973 trial for his activities in the Watergate cover-up, he denied participating in any discussion in which he encouraged JEB MAGRUDER to perjure himself. He also argued that he was counsel to CREEP and served in a privileged position vis-à-vis the CREEP staff members. In 1974 he was found guilty of one count of conspiracy and was sentenced to five years in prison and a $5,000 fine. However, in 1975 he won an appeal of his conviction when an appellate court found that Judge JOHN SIRICA should have severed Mardian's case from the other Nixon officials on trial, since the evidence against him was not as strong as that against his codefendants. Mardian was subsequently reinstated to the bar in California and Arizona and returned to private practice.

—SJT

Marshall, Thurgood
(1908–1993) *associate justice, U.S. Supreme Court*

Thurgood Marshall was born on July 2, 1908, in Baltimore, Maryland. Marshall graduated first in his class from Howard University Law School in 1933 and then practiced for several years in Baltimore. He began working for the NAACP in 1936 and served as director-counsel of the NAACP Legal Defense and Educational Fund from 1940 to 1961. In that post Marshall spearheaded a legal assault on racial segregation and discrimination that transformed the law of race relations. His most significant victory came in the 1954 school desegregation decision *Brown v. Board of Education*, but Marshall also successfully challenged discrimination in voting, housing, higher education, public accommodations, and recreation. The nation's foremost civil rights attorney, Marshall was named a judge on the U.S. Second Circuit Court of Appeals in September 1961. He was appointed solicitor general in July 1965, the first black to hold that position. Nominated for the Supreme Court in June 1967, Marshall became the first black on the high bench when he was sworn in that October.

From the start Marshall was a liberal and activist jurist who voted most often with Chief Justice Earl Warren and Justice WILLIAM BRENNAN. He played a subordinate role in his first years on the bench, writing few majority opinions and rarely dissenting. As the Court became more conservative in the 1970s, however, Marshall became increasingly outspoken. The number of his dissents rose sharply, and he was identified as part of the left wing of the Burger Court.

In racial discrimination cases Marshall almost always voted to expand the civil rights of blacks. He supported school desegregation orders and dissented sharply in July 1974 when the Court upset an interdistrict busing plan to remedy school segregation in Detroit. Marshall also objected to a June 1971 decision sanctioning the closing of public swimming pools in Jackson, Mississippi, to avoid desegregation and to a ruling a year later allowing private clubs with state liquor licenses to exclude blacks. Although he generally voted in favor of blacks in employment discrimination cases, Marshall wrote the majority opinion in a February 1975 case holding that an employer could fire employees who bypassed their union's effort to resolve a dispute over racial discrimination and picketed on their own.

In other equal protection cases Marshall urged the Court to adopt a variable standard of review that would take into account the

nature of the classification and of the interests involved in each case. Even under the accepted approach to equal protection claims, however, the justice took a strong stand against all forms of discrimination. He favored making sex a suspect classification that would be subject to strict judicial scrutiny and voted in almost every instance to overturn differences in treatment between men and women. Marshall also opposed government distinctions between legitimate and illegitimate children and between citizens and aliens. However, he did rule in a November 1973 majority opinion that the 1964 Civil Rights Act had not outlawed employment discrimination against aliens. He opposed discrimination against the poor and voted in March 1973 to invalidate public school financing systems based on local property taxes.

Justice Marshall supported expansions of the right to vote. His opinion in a June 1970 case held that residents of a federal enclave in Maryland could vote in state and local elections. In a March 1972 majority opinion Marshall overturned state residency requirements for voting of three months or more. He opposed laws restricting voting on bond issues to property owners and favored a federal law lowering the voting age to 18. Marshall generally supported a strict one-man, one-vote standard of apportionment and dissented in cases that relaxed that standard at the state level.

Marshall spoke for a six-man majority in June 1969 to hold the Fifth Amendment's provision against double jeopardy applicable to the states. In other criminal cases the justice generally favored strong protection of the guarantees afforded by the Bill of Rights. He usually opposed searches without warrants and believed a warrant necessary for electronic eavesdropping. Marshall insisted that a waiver of rights was legitimate only if a defendant was fully informed and uncoerced.

As solicitor general he had argued against the *Miranda* ruling, requiring the police to inform suspects of their rights. But as a justice, Marshall opposed most attempts to cut back that decision. He dissented from rulings authorizing nonunanimous jury verdicts and juries of less than 12 members in state and federal courts and voted in several cases to expand the right to counsel. Marshall took a broad view of the Fifth Amendment's privilege against self-incrimination, and he voted in June 1972 and July 1976 to hold the death penalty totally unconstitutional as a violation of the Eighth Amendment's ban on cruel and unusual punishment.

Marshall took a liberal stance in most First Amendment cases. In a May 1968 opinion for the Court, he held peaceful labor picketing within a suburban shopping center protected by the amendment. He dissented vigorously when the Court narrowed this ruling in June 1972 and then overturned it in March 1976. Marshall voted against prior restraints on the press. However, he did favor narrowing the protection against libel suits enjoyed by the press when the case involved a private citizen rather than a public figure. In an April 1969 decision his opinion for the Court held that the private possession of obscene materials within one's own home could not be made a crime. He also joined in a dissenting opinion in several June 1973 cases urging the Court to ban all government suppression of allegedly obscene material for consenting adults.

In March 1971, however, Marshall spoke for an eight-man majority to rule that Congress could deny conscientious objector status to draft registrants who opposed only the Vietnam War, not all wars, without violating the First Amendment's guarantee of freedom of religion. In August 1973, while the Court was in recess, Marshall upheld a Second Circuit Court order allowing U.S. bombing of Cam-

bodia to continue while the constitutionality of the action was being litigated. When Justice WILLIAM O. DOUGLAS intervened in the case several days later to order a halt in the bombing, Marshall immediately contacted the other members of the Court and issued an order with their support overriding Douglas's action.

Following the NIXON-FORD years Marshall continued to be marginalized on what was largely a conservative Court and authored largely minority opinions. Marshall retired from the Court on October 1, 1991, due to ill health. President GEORGE H. W. BUSH nominated Clarence Thomas as his successor. Marshall died in January 1993.

—CAB

Martin, Graham A(nderson)
(1912–1990) *ambassador to South Vietnam*

Born on September 22, 1912, Graham Martin, the son of a North Carolina minister, joined the Foreign Service in 1947 after a 15-year career in journalism and public administration. President Kennedy appointed Martin ambassador to Thailand in July 1963. Convinced that a lack of adequate U.S. aid had led to a full-scale war in Vietnam, Martin was instrumental in securing and increasing U.S. military and civilian assistance to Thailand in 1964–65. In January 1967 he admitted that the United States had leased large air bases in Thailand for bombing raids against Communist supply lines in Vietnam. Martin returned to Washington in July 1967 to become special assistant to the secretary of state for refugee and migration affairs. He served in that post until named ambassador to Italy by President Nixon in 1969.

As ambassador to Italy Martin allegedly insisted on direct control of covert funds allocated by the CIA for the manipulation of Italian politics. According to the *New York Times* Martin contributed thousands of dollars to the faltering Christian Democratic Party in the 1972 parliamentary election campaign, thereby preventing a victory by the Italian Communists. Although he intended to retire following his tour of duty in Rome, Martin was persuaded by President NIXON in June 1973 to replace ELLSWORTH BUNKER as ambassador to South Vietnam.

Martin's appointment to the embassy in Saigon on March 30, 1973, came six months after the signing of the Paris cease-fire agreement. The political section of the agreement had established a framework to enable the governments of South Vietnam, North Vietnam, and the Provisional Revolutionary Government of South Vietnam (PRG) to work toward reconciliation and eventual reunification of the country. Martin's instructions as ambassador, however, were to reiterate unswerving U.S. support of President Thieu, rally a reluctant Congress to the backing of an unpopular Saigon government, and restore Thieu's wavering faith in the United States. This task became increasingly difficult following the congressional halt to all bombing of Cambodia and the prohibition of further military aid to Vietnam after August 15, 1973.

Martin brooked no criticism of the South Vietnamese government. He distrusted the press and had several notable battles with U.S. correspondents stationed in Saigon as well as a highly publicized flare-up with Senator EDWARD M. KENNEDY (D-Mass.) in March 1974. Martin had suggested that "it would be the height of folly" to give an "honest and detailed answer" to Kennedy's inquiry as to whether an increase in aid would amount to a new commitment to Thieu. The controversy caused a stir at the State Department when Congress killed in May 1974 an administration plan for $474 million in supplementary aid to South Vietnam.

As the situation grew worse for the Saigon regime, it was Martin's hope that by surrendering territory of negligible military value in the northern area of South Vietnam, a political accommodation with the PRG could be reached to keep the Thieu government intact. President Thieu thought that such territorial concessions, if accepted by Hanoi, would be construed as "Communist victories" and would generate sympathy in the United States and support for his position in Congress. But the North Vietnamese would not cooperate. The PRG walked out of the negotiations at Joint Military Command in Saigon, North Vietnam broke off bilateral negotiations with the United States in Paris, and in June 1973 hostilities between North and South Vietnam resumed.

Martin persisted in his belief that a political solution was possible, although he had been advised for weeks by his military analysts of the rapidly deteriorating situation and the Communist preparations for an attack on Saigon. On April 18, 1975, Martin said in an interview, "There has been no advice from Washington for Thieu to step down." At the same time, however, Martin was actively discouraging a military coup against Thieu, assuring former vice president Nguyen Cao Ky that Thieu would soon step down. On April 21 Martin, with the help of French ambassador Jean-Marie Merillon, persuaded Thieu to resign. Martin held back, however, from recommending complete evacuation of Americans and their Vietnamese employees out of fear that such a move would panic the population and precipitate the Communist victory. The result was a chaotic final evacuation that left thousands of Vietnamese who had worked for the Americans stranded in Saigon, while thousands of others perished in hopeless attempts to seek refuge.

In 1976 the FORD White House nominated Martin for the post of ambassador-at-large, but the proposal languished in committee until after the presidential election, when it was withdrawn. Martin died in 1990.

—JAN

Martin, William McChesney
(1906–1998) *chairman, Board of Governors of the Federal Reserve System*

Born on December 17, 1906, William McChesney Martin was the son of a banker who had helped to found the Federal Reserve Bank of St. Louis. After graduating from Yale in 1928, he began the rapid rise in the U.S. financial community that won him acclaim as a "Boy Wonder." After a year as a clerk at the Federal Reserve Bank of St. Louis, Martin took over the statistics department of a St. Louis brokerage firm and in 1931 assumed the firm's seat on the New York Stock Exchange. In 1938, at age 31, Martin became president of the exchange. Martin served in the army during World War II.

In 1946 President Truman appointed him to head the Export-Import Bank. In 1949 he became assistant secretary of the treasury for international finance and played a mediating role in the 1951 accord between the Treasury and the Federal Reserve Bank. In the same year Truman appointed Martin chairman of the Board of Governors of the Federal Reserve Bank.

Known through his 19-year tenure as an advocate of tight money, Martin repeatedly became the center of controversy. During the Eisenhower years Martin was attacked by liberal Democrats who blamed his conservative money management for the recessions and economic sluggishness of these years. Martin, in turn, insisted that the only alternative to such control was increasing inflation and several times proposed tax increases to further restrain demand. In the 1960 presidential campaign John F. Kennedy similarly attacked Martin as part of his overall criticism of the economic stagnation of the Eisenhower years. Once in office, however, Kennedy and his successor, Lyndon Johnson, recognized the importance of Martin's domestic and international prestige for maintaining the soundness of the dollar.

After the mid-1960s, when inflation began to accelerate in conjunction with the Vietnam War, Martin increasingly played a "Cassandra" role with regard to the persistent problems of high government spending, balance-of-payments deficits, and interest rates. Martin's June 1965 speech in which he underlined "disquieting similarities between our present prosperity and the fabulous 20s" depressed the stock market for weeks. In December 1965 he cast the decisive vote in the Fed's move to raise the discount rate to a postwar high at 4 1/2 percent, provoking "easy money" forces led by Representative WRIGHT PATMAN (D-Tex.) to call for his resignation.

While Martin's term as Federal Reserve Board chairman expired one year after RICHARD NIXON assumed office, the year was a propitious one. The new Republican administration was determined to take serious action against inflation, which had reached 4.2 percent in 1968. Hence Martin oversaw the first stages of the 1969–70 credit crunch that culminated in the bankruptcy of the Penn Central and the near-collapse of the commercial paper market.

Martin was positively disposed to the Nixon administration's attempt to combat inflation, although he felt that the situation had deteriorated beyond the point where rising interest and discount rates alone would suffice. Martin had consistently cited expansionary economic programs, massive federal deficits, and chronic balance-of-payments deficits as the real sources of the problem. Nonetheless, during his last year in office he lent support both in his public statements and in policy to anti-inflation measures. He used his February 1969 appearance before the Joint Economic Committee to lay out the Fed plans to fight inflation.

The first major step in this plan, enacted in April 1969, was a 0.5 percent hike in the discount rate to a then-record high of 6 percent.

In the same month the Fed imposed a similar 0.5 percent increase in member bank reserve requirements. In May 1969, during the congressional debate over the extension of the Johnson administration surtax, Martin stated that the Fed would "try anything" to control inflation if the surtax were abolished. In June Martin warned of a financial collapse if inflation were not brought under control. In the event of further serious deterioration of the economy, Martin called for voluntary credit controls, forced savings, and a higher surtax. In the late summer and early fall of 1969, Martin oversaw new moves by the Fed to impose reserve requirements on U.S. foreign branch banks, which had provided an important avenue for circumventing tight credit in the U.S. capital markets. Finally, in December 1969 the Fed also extended reserve requirements to commercial paper issued by bank affiliates.

Martin left office in January 1970, before the general tightening of credit reached its apex in the May–June 1970 corporate liquidity crisis that forced the Nixon administration and Martin's successor, ARTHUR BURNS, into a reversal of monetary policy. After stepping down as Federal Reserve Board chairman, Martin in 1971 was appointed to head a committee established to reorganize the New York Stock Exchange. He also served on the board of directors of several corporations. In addition, he was president of the Tennis Hall of Fame. Martin died in 1998.

—LG

Mathews, (Forrest) David

(1935–   ) *secretary of health, education, and welfare*

The son of a teacher and school superintendent, David Mathews was born on December 6, 1935, and raised in Clarke County, Alabama. He graduated from the University of Alabama in 1958 with a B.A. in history and the following year earned an M.A. In 1965 he received a doctorate in education from Columbia University. Mathews then returned to the University of Alabama, and after rising quickly through the administrative ranks, he was appointed president of the university in 1969.

Mathews instituted innovative programs to involve students in local affairs, including the College of Community Health Services, designed to improve rural health care, and the Law Center, a research group formulated to investigate public policy matters. He also was responsible for progressive curriculum changes, an adult education program, and an "experimental university" of independent study and work-study programs. President GERALD FORD nominated Mathews to be secretary of health, education, and welfare (HEW) in June 1975.

A major task facing Mathews was to curtail the steady rise in HEW's health care budget, much of which was attributed to fraud and mismanagement, particularly in the Medicaid program. In September the new secretary announced a review of hospital procedures in 11 states and the District of Columbia to determine possible violations of federal rules designed to ensure that the government paid only for the care needed by Medicaid patients. Reports submitted by the Joint Commission on Accreditation of Hospitals revealed that two out of three hospitals in those areas did not meet federal standards for reimbursement under Medicaid. Because of an agreement with the commission to keep the reports confidential, Mathews withheld this information from a House subcommittee looking into the matter until the panel subpoenaed the reports in November. Mathews then turned the material over to the House.

At the end of 1975 Mathews reported the formation of a new criminal investigation unit to identify Medicaid fraud and abuse, which was resulting in the loss of an estimated

$750 million a year. Criticism of the program mounted in January 1976, when a report by a House government operations subcommittee charged that HEW's fraud detection resources were "ridiculously inadequate." Two months later Mathews outlined a new campaign that would combine an expanded force of HEW investigators with state officials focusing on criminal violations by nursing homes, clinical laboratories, pharmacists, and doctors receiving Medicaid funds.

But the dimensions of the problem grew even more serious with the release of another report in August by the Senate Subcommittee on Long-Term Care, chaired by Senator FRANK MOSS (D-Utah). The report, based on a four-month investigation, concluded that "rampant" fraud and abuse together with "abysmal" administration were costing the government from one-quarter to one-half of the $15 billion a year spent on Medicaid. During the investigation Moss and six Senate aides posing as patients visited numerous "Medicaid mills," clinics in low-income areas providing various services, where doctors had authorized unwarranted tests, written needless prescriptions, and made referrals to specialists solely to inflate charges paid for by the program. The Moss report recommended either a complete federal takeover of Medicaid or a cutback in funding.

Mathews accused Moss of "grandstanding" and claimed HEW was well ahead of the senator in identifying and resolving the problems. Nevertheless, on October 15 President Ford signed a bill creating an inspector general's office in HEW to investigate abuses and mismanagement in the department's health care programs. The bill gave the inspector general the authority to issue subpoenas, use nondepartmental auditors, and send reports to Congress without prior clearance from the department.

In the early spring 1976 Mathews began President Ford's plan to vaccinate the entire population against a serious new virus called swine flu. When manufacturers of the vaccine were unable to obtain liability insurance, Mathews attempted unsuccessfully to mediate the dispute. Congress intervened to settle the dispute in August by passing legislation that made the government responsible for all suits resulting from the vaccination drive. In mid-December, after almost 40 million people had been immunized, the program was halted because of reports that several people had contracted a rare form of paralysis, known as Guillain-Barré syndrome, within three weeks of receiving the vaccine.

Mathews instituted new procedures at HEW to give interested parties the opportunity to express their views on issues before important regulations were written, rather than after they had been published, as in the past. HEW employees who wrote new regulations were required to take special English courses aimed at making bureaucratic language more understandable. From the time a proposed regulation first appeared in the *Federal Register*, the public was given 90 to 135 days to comment before the final version of the rule was printed.

Mathews returned to his former post as president of the University of Alabama in January 1977, following the inauguration of JIMMY CARTER into the White House. He served in that position until 1981, when he became the president of the Kettering Foundation, a post he continues to hold.

—JR

Mathias, Charles McC(urdy)
(1922–   ) *member of the Senate*

Bon on July 24, 1922, Mathias, the son of an attorney, served in the navy during World War II. He received a bachelors degree from Haverford College in 1944 and a law degree from the University of Maryland in 1949. Mathias served in various local legal posts until 1958, when he won election to the Maryland house of delegates. Two years later he was elected as a Republican to the U.S. House of Representatives from the sixth congressional district, which included wealthy Washington suburbs as well as Maryland's poor western counties.

As a member of the House, Mathias exhibited great concern for the political interests and social welfare of the residents of the District of Columbia and was known as a firm supporter of civil rights. Mathias won election to the Senate in 1968 on an antiwar platform.

Mathias was not close to the NIXON administration. At the 1968 Republican National Convention he was part of a liberal attempt to prevent the nomination of SPIRO AGNEW and to choose instead JOHN LINDSAY for vice president. After the first few months of his administration, Nixon allegedly ranked Mathias with fellow Republican senators MARK HATFIELD of Oregon, CHARLES GOODELL of New York, and CHARLES PERCY of Illinois as men who attacked him personally and opposed an inordinate amount of his policies. Although Mathias had voted against the Carswell nomination to the Supreme Court and for busing and gun control legislation, his record also showed him voting for the WILLIAM REHNQUIST Supreme Court nomination, against the Consumer Protection Agency (he later changed his position and voted for it), for the SST, and against cuts in the oil depletion allowance. Later he was to vote for the Equal Rights Amendment and against judicial review of the environmental aspects of the Alaska oil pipeline. Despite his disagreement with many of the president's policies and his open criticism of the "southern strategy," Mathias campaigned for Nixon's reelection in 1972.

Conflict was greatest between the administration and Mathias over Vietnam and national defense policies. The senator voted against the antiballistic missile and for numerous other cuts in defense spending. In the same year, he cosponsored with Senators HUBERT HUMPHREY (D-Minn.), JACOB JAVITS (R-N.Y.), and Adlai Stevenson (D-Ill.) a resolution prodding the Nixon administration to negotiate with NATO allies and the Soviet Union on mutual troop reductions in Europe. This was rejected 73 to 24. Mathias supported both the Cooper-Church and McGovern-Hatfield amendments to set withdrawal dates of U.S. troops in Southeast Asia. During the debate over the McGovern-Hatfield Amendment he called for the repeal of the Gulf of Tonkin Resolution, which Lyndon Johnson had used as his authority for escalating the war.

In the Senate Mathias pressed forward with several proposals to reform the traditional power base of Congress. In early 1971 he and Oklahoma Democratic senator FRED HARRIS led an unsuccessful move to scrap the seniority system. They sought to amend Senate Rule 24 to require that committee chairmen and the ranking minority members be nominated individually by majority vote of the party caucuses and elected individually by a majority vote of the full Senate. The proposed changes were tabled by the Senate.

In 1973 Mathias sponsored a legislative package to strengthen campaign finance laws, provide matching federal campaign funding, and include the creation of a Federal Elections Commission. Many of his suggestions became law the following year.

Senator Mathias was cochairman, with Democratic senator FRANK CHURCH of Idaho, of the Special Senate Committee on the Termination of National Emergency, which was prompted by the existence of legislation giving the president wide emergency powers that had been on the books since the early days of Franklin Roosevelt's administration. A National Emergencies Act, approved by the Senate in 1974, was the result of the committee's work. Many of the standby powers granted the president were revoked, and a process of periodic congressional review following declaration of emergency was created.

Mathias was reelected to a second term in 1974 by 57 percent over liberal Baltimore councilwoman Barbara Mikulski. Angered at the prospect of having only two conservative Republican candidates, GERALD FORD and RONALD REAGAN, to choose from in 1976, Mathias made several public motions to run for president but withdrew out of fear that his candidacy would simply rebound to the benefit of the more conservative Reagan. He retired from the Senate in 1987 and currently practices law in Washington, D.C.

—GWB

McCall, Tom L(awson)
(1913–1983) *governor of Oregon*

Tom McCall was born on March 11, 1913, in Egypt, Massachusetts. McCall graduated from the University of Oregon in 1936 and worked for the Latah County Wildlife Association. From 1949 to 1952 he was executive assistant to Oregon governor Douglas McKay. McCall lost an initial bid for a seat in the U.S. House of Representatives in 1954. He won election in 1964 as secretary of state, Oregon's second-ranking elective office. In the 1966 gubernatorial contest he defeated his Democratic opponent, state treasurer Robert Straub.

McCall won election as governor on an environmental platform. The new governor attempted to make good his campaign promises by first appointing himself interim chairman of the state's environmental commission to deal with the serious sewage and industrial pollution of the Willamette River. After the 1967 commission hearings he implemented strict measures to control water pollution for every river in the state. The Willamette by 1969 was clean enough for swimming, fishing, boating, and

salmon spawning. McCall obtained increased funds for aid to education by adjusting income taxes rather than raising regressive state sales taxes and property taxes. Viewing the state's antiabortion laws as harmful, he signed a bill in June 1969 making Oregon one of the first states to legalize abortions. That year he also succeeded in pushing through the legislature a reform bill that gave the governor unprecedented control over all state agencies.

Again stressing environmental protection as his main platform, McCall was reelected governor in 1970. During his second term he continued his campaign to preserve Oregon's natural resources. He pushed through bills preventing developers from building on the public beaches along Oregon's Pacific Ocean coastline to control the large influx of tourists, new residents, and the type of new industries entering the state. By 1971 McCall had guided through the legislature over 100 environmental protection bills, including one of the nation's first comprehensive land use plans to prohibit nonreturnable cans and bottles.

The same year McCall also formed the Office of Energy, Research, and Planning to examine problems leading to power shortages and their possible remedies. In response to an energy crisis in the state in 1973, McCall declared a state of emergency and rapidly implemented measures that enlisted the public's cooperation in the conservation of fuel. The following year McCall put into effect the "Oregon Plan," which limited the sale of gasoline to drivers with either odd- or even-numbered license plates on alternate days. In 1973 he signed a bill making Oregon the first state to reduce criminal penalties for possession of less than an ounce of marijuana, making possession a violation rather than a felony. In addition, McCall helped to promote a methadone program to aid the state's heroin addicts.

Although a Republican, McCall was frequently at odds with the administration. He criticized SPIRO AGNEW's tough stand on antiwar protesters and the press in 1971 and feuded openly with conservative RONALD REAGAN on federal funding policies. He was an early critic of Watergate. McCall declared in November 1973 that "we're not going to be housemen for the White House and try to whitewash one of the sorriest pages in American political history." In June 1974 McCall called for President NIXON's immediate resignation.

Restricted by law to two terms, McCall retired in 1975. He died in 1983 after a long battle with prostate cancer.

—LW

McCarthy, Eugene J(oseph)
(1916–2005) *member of the Senate*

Eugene J. McCarthy was born on March 29, 1916, in Watkins, Minnesota. McCarthy entered politics in 1948 as a supporter of Senator HUBERT H. HUMPHREY's (D-Minn.) fight against the Communist-led wing of Minnesota's Democratic-Farmer-Labor Party (DFL). The following year he was elected over a Republican incumbent to the first of his five terms in the House, where he organized a caucus of liberal Democrats—later institutionalized as the Democratic Study Group—that agitated for more progressive legislation than the programs espoused by either Republicans or the Democratic leadership.

After his election to the Senate in 1958, however, McCarthy broke somewhat from his strongly liberal voting record in the House. Although he advocated medical care for the aged and other social reforms enacted by the Kennedy administration, he voted against progressive tax policies considered by the Senate Finance Committee. Prior to 1967 McCarthy's most sustained legislative efforts promoted the reform of federal and state unemployment compensation systems and sought to increase wages for migrant farm workers. He also criticized U.S. intelligence agencies' influence in decisions affecting foreign policy and opposed the sale of U.S. arms to technologically undeveloped nations.

Beginning mildly in 1966, then more vocally in 1967, McCarthy became the Senate's foremost opponent of the Johnson administration's Vietnam War policy. As a candidate for the Democratic presidential nomination, he based his unorthodox campaign almost solely on his opposition to the "morally indefensible" war and President Johnson's "dangerous" domination over Congress in the making of foreign policy. Supported by an unusual army of idealistic young volunteers, he surprised party regulars with strong showings against Johnson in the New Hampshire primary (a chief reason for Johnson's subsequent withdrawal from the race) and a series of close battles with Senator Robert F. Kennedy (D-N.Y.) in the spring primaries. McCarthy failed to garner Kennedy's supporters after the Massachusetts senator's assassination, and he lost the nomination to Humphrey by a vote of 1,041 to 601 in the August convention.

McCarthy's political energy dissipated after the presidential campaign. He answered only 61 percent of the roll call votes in 1969, the third-lowest rating in the Senate. He resigned from the Foreign Relations Committee that year and virtually disappeared from the *Congressional Record*. In 1970 he reemerged to voice opposition to RICHARD NIXON's "Vietnamization" policy. "Even if the South Vietnamese Army could be made into an effective military force," he said, "Asians would still be killing Asians with American arms. . . . The United States would still have moral responsibility for the war." He proposed an alternative plan for a negotiated settlement followed by a withdrawal of American military power, both contingent on Nixon's altering his policy to support a "coalition government to control the process of transition." The administration stood firm in its insistence on free elections in South Vietnam. The only major issue on which McCarthy supported Nixon was the nomination of Minnesota judge HARRY A. BLACKMUN to be an associate justice of the Supreme Court.

McCarthy continued to fight, unsuccessfully, for extended unemployment compensation programs, joining other Senate liberals in opposition to Nixon's Family Assistance Plan in October 1970. He resigned from the Senate in 1971 and ran mediocre campaigns as an independent candidate for the presidency in 1972 and 1976. McCarthy's influence on American politics outlasted his own enthusiasm, as evidenced in the continued vivacious involvement of youth in electoral politics and the long-lived anger against U.S. military involvement in Southeast Asia. In 1982 McCarthy failed in an attempt to reclaim his Senate seat. He died on December 10, 2005, at the Georgetown Retirement Residence in Washington, D.C., of complications from Parkinson's disease.

—AM

McClellan, John L(ittle)

(1896–1977) *member of the Senate; chairman, Government Operations Committee; chairman, Appropriations Committee*

John L. McClellan was born on February 25, 1896, in Sheridan, Arkansas. McClellan never attended college but studied law in his father's law firm for five years and gained admission to the bar in 1913 at age 17. He was the city attorney for Malvern, Arkansas, from 1920 to 1926 and a prosecuting attorney from 1927 to 1930. In 1934 he was elected as a Democrat to the U.S. House of Representatives, where he supported most New Deal programs. Eight years later he was elected to the Senate. He did not face another serious election challenge until 1972, when he was forced into a run-off pri-

mary election by Representative David Pryor (D-Ark.). Despite his age McClellan won the primary and was reelected.

During his Senate career McClellan compiled a basically conservative record, although he supported some social welfare legislation. He gained national prominence during the 1950s and 1960s as a stern, efficient, fair investigator. Over the course of two decades he headed probes of corruption in labor unions, favoritism in the awarding of defense contracts, influence peddling in Congress, and the causes of urban riots.

McClellan continued basically conservative voting patterns during the NIXON-FORD years. In 1972 he cast the first cloture vote of his senatorial career in an unsuccessful effort to stop a filibuster by northern senators opposing an antibusing bill. He usually opposed federal spending for the Model Cities program, mass transit funds, aid for the handicapped, and manpower training. He supported, however, continuing federal farm price subsidies for tobacco in 1972 and opposed limiting crop subsidy payments to $20,000 per grower in 1970. McClellan favored a strong defense posture, continuation of the draft, development of controversial weapons systems like the B-1 bomber, and foreign military aid.

McClellan changed his position on the Vietnam War during the Nixon-Ford years. Although a supporter of the Johnson administration's policies, McClellan voted to bar U.S. troops from Laos and Thailand in 1969. And while he opposed the 1970 Cooper-Church Amendment to limit the president's authority to conduct military operations in Cambodia, he supported the 1971 Mansfield Amendment, which, as adopted by the Senate, called for the withdrawal of U.S. troops from Vietnam within nine months after the release of U.S. prisoners. The administration strongly opposed the move. In 1973, after the Vietnam peace treaty had been signed, McClellan's Appropriations

Committee voted unanimously to bar the use of funds for military operations by U.S. forces in Laos and Cambodia.

In August 1972, upon the death of Senator ALLEN J. ELLENDER (D-La.), McClellan gave up his Government Operations Committee chairmanship to become chairman of the Senate Appropriations Committee and of its Defense Subcommittee. Almost immediately McClellan's new authority was successfully challenged by Senator RUSSELL B. LONG's (D-La.) Finance Committee on the issue of control over the funding of the federal revenue sharing program. The Nixon administration had first proposed the program in 1969. Long's committee had molded the revenue sharing bill specifically to keep the Appropriations Committee from acquiring control of the legislation and eventually the financing of the program. McClellan was rebuffed on the Senate floor by a 49-34 vote when he attempted to amend the bill so his committee would acquire control of it. Twenty-one of the 34 votes for the amendment were cast by members of his own committee.

McClellan's Appropriations Committee and Defense Subcommittee usually cut administration defense budget requests. In 1974 he announced his committee would cut $3.5 billion from the $87.1 billion fiscal 1975 budget request but added that spending cuts would be proposed "only where we are convinced they can be made without unduly diminishing or weakening our defense posture." Despite his support of cuts in defense budget requests, he favored defense spending increases in certain areas. In 1976 he called the $104 billion defense budget lean, noting that the trend of disproportionate cuts could not be continued without seriously impairing national defense. McClellan suffered only occasional floor defeats on major appropriations issues. In 1975 he unsuccessfully opposed the vote to dismantle the controversial Safeguard antiballistic missile system and the vote to bar the use of defense funds to finance activities that could have involved the United States in Angola's civil war.

McClellan also headed the Appropriations Committee's Intelligence Operations Subcommittee. In 1973 that subcommittee was one of several congressional panels investigating the CIA's connections with the Watergate affair. Its probe revealed that several of Nixon's top advisers had discussed the Watergate affair with top CIA officials and told agency members to inform FBI director L. PATRICK GRAY that covert CIA operations would be jeopardized by the FBI Watergate investigation into the source of the money found on the Watergate burglars.

McClellan was the Senate's prime proponent of tough laws to limit protest activities. In 1969 he led a permanent investigation's subcommittee probe into campus disorders and proposed legislation to make it a federal crime to disrupt the operations of federally aided colleges and universities. That year Congress enacted a law that restricted the use of some higher-education funds by students who had participated in campus disorders. When students at Kent State University were killed in 1970, McClellan said on a network news program that "they should have mowed them all down."

As chairman of the Judiciary Committee's Criminal Laws and Procedures Subcommittee, McClellan worked closely with the administration to shape federal anticrime legislative programs during the Nixon-Ford years. In 1969 he introduced the legislation that later became the Organized Crime Control Act of 1970. The law narrowed the immunity granted to witnesses compelled to testify so that they would no longer be granted complete immunity from prosecution. It also broadened the grounds on which perjury convictions could be obtained. The measure generated opposition from many legal groups. The New York City Bar Association warned that it contained "the seeds of official repression."

In 1972 McClellan sponsored the Victims of Crime Act that was eventually incorporated into a broader measure enacted by Congress in 1973 as the Omnibus Crime Control and Safe Streets Act Amendments of 1973. This law provided federal funds to compensate injured law enforcement officers and their families and innocent victims of certain crimes. McClellan had previously opposed such measures because of the inference that society was somehow responsible for crime and should start paying the bill.

McClellan undertook his most sweeping anticrime effort in 1971 when his subcommittee began work on a measure to codify all federal criminal laws. The codification effort had begun in March 1967 when Congress created a commission to study federal criminal laws. McClellan served on the commission, which was headed by former California governor Edmond G. Brown. The Brown Commission submitted its report and a draft code to President Nixon on January 8, 1971. Its proposals included several revisions of federal criminal laws, including the abolishment of the death penalty, a ban on handguns, and reduction of the penalties for marijuana possession.

McClellan's subcommittee held lengthy hearings on the report in 1971 and prepared a much revised version of the proposed code, which was introduced in 1973 as SB 1. After the Nixon administration submitted its own bill, the subcommittee held many hearings in 1973 and 1974 to reconcile the differences between the two versions. The bills drew heavy opposition from legal groups, civil libertarians, and the press who charged the measures contained repressive features that could endanger political and personal liberties. Among other things the committee bill substantially revised the crime classification and sentencing penal-

ties for certain crimes, and it reclassified many crimes as more serious offenses. But the committee also narrowed the definition of treason contained in the commission's draft and the definition of certain national security offenses. A new version was again introduced as SB 1 in 1975, and successor versions were introduced in 1977. Legal groups and civil libertarians continued to oppose them, and by the late 1970s none of the bills had passed. McClellan died of a heart attack in Little Rock, Arkansas, on November 27, 1977.

—AE

McCloskey, Paul N(orton)

(1927–   ) *member of the House of Representatives*

Born on September 29, 1927, "Pete" McCloskey, the son of an attorney, graduated from Stanford University in 1950. After service in the U.S. Marine Corps during the Korean conflict, he earned his law degree from Stanford University Law School in 1953 and then became a deputy district attorney for Alameda County. He went into private practice in 1956 and founded a new law partnership that specialized in conservation cases in 1965. From 1964 to 1967 he taught legal ethics at the Santa Clara and the Stanford University Law Schools.

McCloskey was a progressive Republican and described himself as a fiscal conservative. He refused to support Senator BARRY GOLDWATER for president in 1964 and backed Democrat Pierre Salinger against his conservative Republican opponent, George Murphy, for U.S. senator that year. McCloskey also helped found the California Republican League to oppose extreme rightist factions in the Republican Party.

McCloskey was one of four Republicans who entered the primary election in 1967 to fill the House seat vacated by the death of Representative J. Arthur Younger (R-Calif.). He ran on an antiwar platform calling for immediate efforts to negotiate with the Hanoi government or a two-year deescalation of the war if negotiations failed. McCloskey won the primary and went on to win the general election. He represented an upper- and middle-class suburban district.

In the House McCloskey maintained his independence, voting with the administration and the Republican Party less than 50 percent of the time. As a fiscal conservative, however, he generally supported NIXON-FORD vetoes of federal spending legislation for social welfare measures. A vigorous anticommunist, McCloskey supported a strong defense policy. In 1971 he opposed an all-volunteer army, saying the nation was safer "when its army is made up of reluctant citizen-soldiers than by men who take pride in being professional killers." He fought the cutoff of military aid to Turkey in 1974 and to Chile and South Korea in 1976. At the same time he was skeptical of the cost of defense programs and opposed the administration on funding for the Safeguard antiballistic missile system and the B-1 bomber.

McCloskey always supported environmental programs, believing that conservation was the nation's most vital domestic issue. In 1969 he wrote a minority Government Operations Committee report in which he urged the complete banning of environmental testing of chemical and biological warfare agents after a gas testing accident at the Dugway Proving Grounds killed 6,000 sheep. He was named honorary cochairman of the Environmental Teach-in Group that organized nationwide activities for Earth Day in 1970. He voted to override Nixon's 1972 veto of the Federal Water Pollution Control Act amendments, which authorized $18 billion for grants to states to construct waste treatment plants and set national water quality standards and to override Ford's 1975 veto of a federal strip mining regulation bill. He opposed delaying

the implementation of auto emission standards in 1976.

McCloskey was one of the most outspoken congressional opponents of the Nixon Vietnam policy. Beginning in March 1969 he wrote Nixon the first in a series of five strongly worded letters urging the president to admit the error of U.S. policy and to begin troop withdrawals. He was one of only eight members of Congress who publicly supported the October 15, 1969, Vietnam Moratorium demonstrations that were held in many cities across the country. After the May 1970 invasion of Cambodia, he led the fight for House passage of the Cooper-Church Amendment, curtailing the president's authority to conduct combat operations in that country.

On February 10, 1971, McCloskey called for a national dialogue to discuss the impeachment of President Nixon as a means of inducing him to change his Vietnam policy. He made the proposal after the South Vietnamese Army had launched an American-supported invasion into Laos that had ended in a rout. McCloskey defended his proposal, saying "a reasonable argument can be made that the president's recent decision to employ American airpower in the neutral countries of Laos and Cambodia exceeded his constitutional powers." McCloskey received little support for his proposal, however.

McCloskey formally announced his candidacy for the Republican presidential nomination on July 19, 1971, stating he would enter primaries in New Hampshire, California, and other primary states to lead a slate of delegates to the 1972 Republican Convention who would be pledged to end the Vietnam War. McCloskey recognized that he had little chance of being nominated even if he won in the primaries but insisted that true victory would be an early end to the war rather than his own election. His supporters hoped that McCloskey's candidacy would also help moderate Republicans win grassroots party offices.

McCloskey's presidential campaign also was motivated by what he described as the administration's duplicity in dealing with Congress and the American people. He said, "I am just tired of being lied to by members of the executive branch and having information concealed." In his book *In Truth and Untruth: Political Deceit in America* (1972), he charged that the Nixon administration encouraged "concealment, deception, and news management on a massive scale." Reviewers described the book as loosely written campaign rhetoric and McCloskey's campaign platform rather than a serious examination of the issues he raised.

McCloskey also attacked the administration's position on environmental matters. He pointed out that "we had to fight them tooth and nail to get the water pollution funding money and had to fight over [Nixon's] objections to even get the Environmental Policy Act. This administration has been dragged into the environment issue."

McCloskey campaigned actively for the presidential nomination until the March 7 New Hampshire primary. He received slightly less than 20 percent of the vote, the target he had set for himself. With little money and time running out for filing to be eligible for reelection to Congress, he formally ended his campaign on March 10. But he left his name on the ballot in other primary states "as a symbolic protest."

McCloskey served in the House until 1982, when he was an unsuccessful candidate for the U.S. Senate. He now resides in Woodside, California.

—AE

McCord, James
(1924–) *Watergate figure*

James McCord was born on January 26, 1924, in Waurika, Oklahoma. Unknown to the public prior to 1972, McCord had been deeply involved in U.S. aerial surveillance of the Soviet Union as an officer for the Central Intelligence Agency (CIA).

He officially retired from his duties with the CIA in 1970, and little is known of his activities prior to June 1972. Like many former employees of the agency, McCord obtained employment as a private security officer and in early 1972 placed his services at the disposal of the Republican National Committee and of the Committee to Re-Elect the President (CREEP)

McCord was subsequently one of five men—all with previous ties to the CIA—who was arrested during the June 17 break-in at Democratic Party headquarters in Washington, D.C.'s, Watergate complex. Subsequent investigation revealed that from May 5 through June 17, McCord had conducted surveillance operations on Democratic Party activities in the Watergate. In September 1972 McCord and six other men, including two former White House aides, were indicted for conspiracy to break into the Democratic Party offices in the Watergate.

In January 1973 the U.S. district court presided over by Judge JOHN J. SIRICA found McCord guilty as charged, despite McCord's argument that he had participated in the Watergate break-in without "criminal intent." Just before his sentencing in March 1973, however, McCord sent a letter to Judge Sirica implying that "others" had been involved in Watergate. On March 28, in a secret session before the Senate select committee, McCord implicated White House counsel JOHN DEAN III, presidential aides H. R. HALDEMAN and CHARLES COLSON, and former attorney general JOHN MITCHELL.

Throughout this period McCord was the target of a pressure campaign directed, in his own words, "from the highest levels of the White House" to silence him with threats, offers of leniency, clemency, help with bail, and outright cash.

He recounted these pressure tactics in further Senate select committee testimony on May 18.

It was at McCord's May 22 appearance that he paraphrased a letter he had allegedly written to a former White House aide concerning the desirability of implicating the CIA in Watergate. This testimony later became the object of much speculation that McCord himself was a CIA agent attempting to cover up the agency's role: "If [CIA director Richard] Helms goes," wrote McCord, "and the Watergate operation is laid at the CIA's feet . . . every tree in the forest will fall. It will be a scorched desert. The whole matter is on the precipice right now. Pass the message that if they want it to blow, they are on exactly the right course."

In November 1973 McCord received a one-to-five-year sentence for his role in the break-in. By March 1974 McCord was in open revolt against the White House and its cover-up of Watergate, charging in a letter to various news services that President Nixon had "deliberately concealed and suppressed" evidence of improper government conduct. In June 1974, during hearings to have McCord's case dismissed, his attorney said "there is such a stench attached to this case that it has to be thrown out." In July 1974 the minority report of the Senate Watergate committee on possible CIA involvement in the affair cited McCord's role and described the actions of another CIA agent who had helped McCord's wife destroy private papers immediately after McCord's arrest. Finally, in December 1974 McCord filed a $10 million "legal malpractice" suit against his own attorneys.

In March 1975, his legal options exhausted, McCord entered the minimum-security federal penitentiary in Allenwood, Pennsylvania, to begin serving his sentence. In July 1975 Judge Sirica reduced the sentences of all Watergate burglars, and McCord's time was consequently shortened to four months. On the same day Sirica also dismissed McCord's lawsuit to have the pardon of former president Nixon ruled illegal.

McCord served out his sentence in Allenwood and was released in the late summer of 1975. After his prison term McCord became a booster for the University of Michigan athletic department and was charged with giving players money from an illegal gambling ring.

—LG

McCormack, Ellen
(1926–) *presidential candidate*

Ellen McCormack grew up in New York City and moved with her husband to Merrick, Long Island, New York, in the mid-1950s. The mother of four children and a full-time housewife, McCormack was not active in public affairs until 1970, when New York state adopted a liberal abortion reform law. A practicing Catholic, McCormack helped organize a local antiabortion group on Long Island. In 1974 she worked in the New York senatorial campaign of Barbara Keating, the Conservative Party nominee who took a strong stand against legalized abortions.

Abortion, meanwhile, had become a major public issue. During the 1970s women's liberation groups across the country made the legalization of abortion one of their major goals, and several state legislatures enacted liberal abortion statutes. In January 1973 the Supreme Court struck down statutes banning abortion in 44 states, making it legal for women to obtain abortions, under most conditions, throughout the country. Thereafter the activities of antiabortion forces increased, and by 1975 the Pro-Life Action Committee, of which McCormack was a member, had chapters in 27 states.

At a November 16, 1975, press conference in Boston called by the Pro-Life Action Committee, McCormack declared her candidacy for the 1976 Democratic presidential nomination. Conceding that she was "basically a one-issue candidate," she announced her intention to enter as many primaries as possible but to restrict her campaigning to one appearance per state. The lack of serious campaigning raised suspicions that her candidacy was simply a ruse to gain publicity for antiabortion forces. The suspicion grew stronger when Jay Bowman, the head of Georgia's Right-to-Life Committee, told the press: "She's not a serious candidate. . . . But she can get equal time for the prolife message—and she can get the federal government to pay for the ads."

Controversy over McCormack's candidacy erupted in February 1976 when she applied for matching funds from the Federal Election Commission. Her request was immediately challenged in court by the National Abortion Rights Action League, a feminist group, which charged that "funds have been deceptively solicited for the 'right-to-life' movement and not for a presidential candidacy." The FEC ruled in McCormack's favor, however, and she eventually received over $240,000 in federal matching funds for her campaign, thus becoming the first woman to receive federal funds for a presidential race.

McCormack fared poorly in the primaries. Although she received 9 percent of the vote in Vermont and 8 percent in South Dakota, in no other state did she receive more than 5 percent of the ballots. At the Democratic Convention in July, her name was placed in nomination, but she received only 22 delegate votes. In 1980 she again ran for president, winning 32,327 votes from three states.

—JD

McCormack, John W(illiam)
(1891–1980) *member of the House of Representatives; Speaker of the House*

John McCormack, one of 12 children, was born on December 21, 1891, into a poor Irish-American family in Boston. When McCormack was in the eighth grade, his father died, and he left school to help support the family. He found work as an office boy for a law firm at $4 a week. He took the opportunity to read law books and learn the profession, passing the bar examination in 1913 at age 21—without the benefit of even a formal high school education.

McCormack proved to be a skillful trial lawyer, but he soon pursued a career in politics as a Democrat. He served two terms in the Massachusetts assembly followed by two terms in the state senate. In 1926 he ran for the Boston congressional seat held by Democrat James A. Gallivan and lost, only to win the seat in a special election in 1928 following Gallivan's death. McCormack was a faithful advocate of the New Deal. In 1936 he backed Sam Rayburn's bid for majority leader. When Rayburn became Speaker of the House in 1940, he chose McCormack as the new majority leader.

From Rayburn McCormack learned the various skills of negotiation and compromise that he used with great effect during his congressional career. During the 1940s and 1950s he promoted such liberal legislation as the Marshall Plan, school construction aid, and civil rights bills. In 1962 McCormack, at age 70, became Rayburn's successor as Speaker of the House. His handling of the position evoked much criticism. Many members of Congress felt that he was too compromising and that he lacked the determination of his predecessor. His staunch anticommunism led him to support the war in Vietnam, a position that became increasingly unpopular among liberals, as was his friendship with the conservative southern Democrats.

In January 1969 McCormack faced a serious challenge to his authority as House Speaker. Utah representative MORRIS UDALL offered himself for the position—an audacious move since no Speaker had ever been unseated while his own party was in power. Udall expressed "genuine respect and affection" for McCormack but claimed that there was "an overriding need for new directions and new leadership" in the House. But Udall failed to expand his base of support beyond the young, liberal members of the House, and after a secret balloting of the House Democratic Caucus, McCormack handily defeated his challenger.

In 1970 McCormack faced another challenge to his authority. Liberal California representative Jerome R. Waldie, saying that the Speaker "was not responsive to the problems of the seventies," placed a resolution of no confidence in McCormack before the House Democratic Caucus. But even McCormack's critics felt that the resolution was poorly timed, so it was turned aside without coming to a vote. McCormack said the decision constituted a major victory. Nonetheless, as a concession to disgruntled liberals, the caucus appointed a commission to study the seniority system and agreed to meet more frequently.

In October 1969 a major scandal involving Speaker McCormack erupted on Capitol Hill. Columnist JACK ANDERSON and *Life* magazine revealed that Dr. Martin Sweig, a trusted administrative assistant to McCormack, and Nathan Voloshen, a Sweig associate, had used the Speaker's office as a base for influence peddling in Washington. Sweig and Voloshen had taken payments in exchange for interceding in various criminal cases and arranging government contracts. Sweig had apparently used McCormack's phone, occasionally even impersonating the Speaker's voice.

McCormack bitterly denied any involvement in or knowledge of the scheme and said that the *Life* magazine article, which implicated him in at least one influence-peddling incident, constituted "unwarranted vilification." At a news conference he stated that he would seek reelection the following year both as a representative and as House Speaker, adding that "whether I'm here anymore depends on the people of my district. . . . They know that my life—personal and private—is an open book." In

January 1970 Sweig and Voloshen were indicted by a federal grand jury in New York on charges of conspiracy. McCormack was not named, but he did submit a deposition.

In May 1970 McCormack announced that he would retire at the conclusion of his current term, saying his decision, partly due to the declining health of his wife, had been made during the 1968 Democratic Convention. That same month Nathan Voloshen pleaded guilty. Martin Sweig was found guilty the following month after a trial in which McCormack testified that Sweig was a "devoted aide" and again denied knowledge that his office had been misused.

During his last months in Congress, McCormack continued to work for liberal programs. The House passed a bill lowering the voting age to 18 in June 1970 following a personal campaign by McCormack. In August McCormack spoke out in favor of the Equal Rights Amendment. "This resolution does not undertake to change nature," he said, "but certainly changes conditions." He remained a vocal critic of the NIXON administration, accusing it of "playing on people's fears" and "a callous disregard for the social needs of our less fortunate and disenfranchised and, despite a promise to bring our people together, a pattern of demagoguery that is dividing our nation's rich against poor, white against black, young against old."

As the congressional elections in November drew nearer, McCormack's denunciation of the Nixon administration became more fervent. Following criticism by Nixon of Democratic federal spending policies, McCormack said that the president should "devote his attention to the real problems and quit playing his partisan political games."

McCormack left Congress after 43 years as a representative and the second-longest tenure as Speaker in the history of the House. He died in 1980.

—MDQ

McCracken, Paul W(inston)

(1915–   ) *chairman, Council of Economic Advisers*

Born on December 29, 1915, the son of an Iowa farmer, McCracken studied economics at Harvard, receiving his Ph.D. in 1948. He then left his position at the Federal Reserve Bank of Minneapolis for a teaching job at the University of Michigan School of Business Administration. He became a full professor in 1950. From 1956 to 1959 he served on the President's Council of Economic Advisers (CEA). He then returned to Michigan but was frequently consulted by the Kennedy and Johnson administrations and by private concerns.

In December 1968 President NIXON named McCracken chairman of the CEA. His colleagues were to be HERBERT STEIN and Hendrik S. Houthakker. In his approach to running the national economy, McCracken represented a centrist position between those advocates of "fine tuning" who had run the CEA under the Democrats and the laissez-faire economists of the Chicago School. However, he never rejected Keynesian theory, as did MILTON FRIEDMAN and other members of the Chicago group. In interviews he expressed his admiration for the economic performance of the Johnson administration, but he believed that unwise monetary policy, aggravated by the Vietnam War, had overheated the economy. It was the CEA's responsibility to curb inflation, already identified as the nation's primary domestic problem, but without increasing unemployment. McCracken called his policy "gradualism." It was intended to achieve the goals for which the CEA was originally created by President Harry Truman—full employment with low or no inflation.

In March 1969 McCracken announced the administration's program. He rejected the Johnson administration's policy of pressuring or "jawboning" groups to hold down wages and prices. Both the administration, through its con-

trol over the budget, and the Federal Reserve Board, through its manipulation of credit and the money supply, would apply the brakes to inflation. Thus, the chairman hoped the "psychology of inflation," which had led business and labor to assume its inevitability, could be broken. Yet he believed that because of "inflation-mindedness" there would be a longer lag than one would normally expect between the introduction of new measures and a decline in inflation.

One Johnson measure McCracken favored retaining was the income tax surcharge, which could ensure a budget surplus. The chairman hoped that less inflation would keep demand in line with productivity and lead to fewer imports, more exports, and a resulting improvement in the balance of trade. The price of the inflation fight, as he admitted to the Joint Economic Committee of Congress in February, was a slower economic growth rate. He predicted a growth rate well under the 5 percent achieved in 1968 but did not believe that unemployment would go above 4 percent (it was 3.3 percent at the time).

As McCracken predicted, curbing inflation was not easy. In July 1969 the president ordered a $3.5 billion cut in federal expenditures to offset spending increases due to "uncontrollable" budget items and congressional action. Although by October McCracken claimed he could discern "some early evidence," such as the slowdown in the rise of the consumer price index, that the administration's "fiscal and monetary policies of restraint" were beginning to cool the economy, critics felt that more action was required. Arthur Okun, former CEA chairman, recommended a revival of wage-price guideposts. Members of Congress, business leaders, and representatives of foreign governments concurred, but the chairman argued that such guideposts were of "unproven effectiveness," were often unfair, and might divert attention from the more basic monetary and fiscal causes of inflation.

The president repeated McCracken's reasoning in his annual economic report in January 1970. He foresaw less inflation and less real growth in 1970 than in the previous year but said that if Congress did not help to curb inflation, the Federal Reserve might feel compelled to follow a money and credit policy of "overly long and overly severe restraint." McCracken had already indicated that he favored a more liberal monetary policy than the Fed had been willing to allow, and the differences in policy outlook became clearer under the Fed's new chief, ARTHUR BURNS.

McCracken had not tried to hide his conviction that 1970 would be a difficult year for the nation's businesses and working people, even suggesting that the real output increase "might well be below" the historic annual average of 3 to 3.5 percent. By May progress against inflation had brought such small returns while unemployment had risen that the administration's critics now included Secretary of Housing and Urban Development GEORGE ROMNEY, who demanded wage-price action. A few days later Representative HENRY REUSS (D-Wis.) introduced a bill requiring the CEA to set wage-price guidelines. As before, McCracken rejected the need for such measures.

When the chairman appeared before the Joint Economic Committee in July, there was at least general agreement that the economic decline had "bottomed out." However, there was now disagreement as to how to revive the economy. McCracken wanted more liquidity and thus monetary expansion. Burns and Treasury secretary DAVID M. KENNEDY opposed all stimulative measures. Liberal economists such as Paul Samuelson and Gardner Ackley favored vigorous fiscal measures. It appeared that McCracken was destined to lose. Congress would probably adopt the Samuelson-Ackley prescription and, in retaliation, Burns would keep the lid on the money supply. Burns had already eased restrictions in March, aiming for

a 2 percent growth in the money supply, but McCracken thought the action inadequate.

Although official August 1970 figures showed a rise in second-quarter GNP and the lowest inflation rate (a projected 4.3 percent annual rate) since the third quarter of 1968, in the same month the government issued its first "inflation alert." The alert, McCracken's creation, was viewed by some as an administration attempt to give the appearance of doing something about wages and prices without, in fact, doing anything. Other observers saw it as Nixon and McCracken's first cautious exercise in jawboning. McCracken insisted that the alert was only intended to be informative. Much of it was an analysis of inflationary developments since the Eisenhower administration. He hoped it would "lift the level of visibility and understanding and awareness of these complex developments in the price-cost area" and thus help form public policy. The alert cited developments in specific industries and implied criticism of, among others, the tire and cigarette industries, which had increased prices faster than costs. Yet, if the report represented an abandonment of gradualism and of a laissez-faire attitude on wages and prices, it nonetheless reiterated the chairman's view that monetary and fiscal policy cause inflation. In addition, the report hypothesized that the longer inflation lasts, the harder it is to end. The alert, it was argued, was another measure to combat the "inflation-mindedness" that had overtaken American business and labor. There were two more inflation alerts, in December 1970 and April 1971. Both brought the administration close to "jawboning" and both, in the opinion of union leaders, unjustly assigned too large a share of the responsibility for inflation to labor.

Continuing inflation and unemployment near 6 percent helped the Democrats to do extremely well in the November congressional elections, and the 1972 elections looked equally bad for Nixon and the GOP if the economy were not revitalized. McCracken, who had never been liked by White House advisers because of his unwillingness to disguise unpleasant economic realities, was replaced as the administration's "economic spokesman." The new Treasury secretary, JOHN CONNALLY, assumed that public role, although in fact he worked in close agreement with McCracken.

Nixon, whose first deviation from a strict anti-inflationary policy was the release of $1.5 billion in frozen construction funds in March 1970, announced an "expansionary," but "not inflationary," budget in January 1971. His "full employment" budget called for the government to spend when the economy was sluggish what it would collect if business were brisk and unemployment low. The budget would show a deficit, due not only to inflation and high unemployment, but also to a liberalized depreciation allowance for business. Some Democrats applauded the "Republican conversion to Keynesian economy," but others thought the program inadequate to meet the administration's optimistic predictions. McCracken himself did not share the administration's enthusiastic GNP forecast. In a February report the CEA refused to choose between private predictions of a 7 to 7.5 percent rise in the 1971 GNP and the White House figure of 9 percent. Another move in the further abandonment of gradualism was McCracken's resort to jawboning in January, when he convinced steel industry leaders to moderate price increases.

In a June 1971 interview McCracken admitted that the administration was dissatisfied with its economic "game plan" in view of the persistence of high unemployment and would soon decide whether to change its policies. The following month he announced to the Joint Economic Committee that with inflation at 4 percent and unemployment at 6 percent, the administration was abandoning its GNP target of $1.065 trillion. In order not to aggravate inflation, the government could not take further steps to stimulate the economy. On August 15 Nixon took the last step in rejecting his original program by announcing a 90-day wage and price freeze and the creation of a Cost of Living Council to oversee the freeze. Connally was named council chairman and McCracken vice chairman. The new economic program also included tax cuts and credits, a surtax on imports, and the end of the dollar's convertibility into gold (effectively, the first devaluation of the dollar). Democrats almost unanimously attacked the program as a bonanza for the rich, but it greatly improved the president's standing in the popularity polls.

On November 24 McCracken submitted his resignation, effective January 1, 1972. He conceded that his policy of gradualism had failed against inflationary and psychological pressures that the CEA had underestimated. Some Washington analysts believed that McCracken was the victim of White House "political hatchet men," who wanted the chairman to bend the truth about the economy. Nonetheless, McCracken was credited with getting the president to implement the new program, since he had felt that the administration had been without a coherent policy since it began to hedge on its anti-inflation commitment.

Under the FORD administration McCracken served as a senior consultant to the Treasury Department. He also served as a member of President RONALD REAGAN's Economic Policy Advisory Board. He is now the Edmund Ezra Day Distinguished University Professor Emeritus of Business Administration at the University of Michigan.

—JCH

McGovern, George S(tanley)

(1922–) *member of the Senate; Democratic presidential nominee*

Born on July 19, 1922, the son of a Methodist minister, George McGovern attended Dakota

Wesleyan University and served in the army air corps during World War II. He received his doctorate at Northwestern University in 1953 while also teaching at Dakota Wesleyan from 1949 to 1953. He resigned his professorship to become executive secretary of the Democratic Party in South Dakota and built it into a viable statewide organization. McGovern was elected to the House of Representatives in 1956 and in his two terms established a reputation as a liberal. In 1960 he unsuccessfully challenged Republican incumbent KARL MUNDT for a Senate seat.

In January 1961 President John F. Kennedy appointed McGovern director of the newly created Food for Peace program. McGovern worked to develop the program as a humanitarian instrument of U.S. foreign policy. He resigned in July 1962 to run for the Senate once again and won a narrow victory, becoming South Dakota's first Democratic senator in 26 years.

McGovern was a strong supporter of the liberal social welfare and civil rights legislation of the Kennedy and Johnson administrations. He also quickly became a critic of cold war foreign policy and its "obsession with communism" and urged that defense spending be cut in favor of humanitarian programs abroad and at home. As U.S. military involvement in South Vietnam escalated rapidly in the mid-1960s, McGovern emerged as one of its most vocal Senate critics. Although in the fall of 1967 he turned down a request from ALLARD K. LOWENSTEIN that he head a "dump Johnson" movement, McGovern conducted a brief campaign for the Democratic nomination after the assassination of presidential candidate Robert F. Kennedy. At the Democratic National Convention in August, McGovern placed a distant third in the balloting. In November he was reelected to a second term in the Senate.

McGovern immediately became an outspoken critic of NIXON administration policies. He opposed deployment of the Safeguard

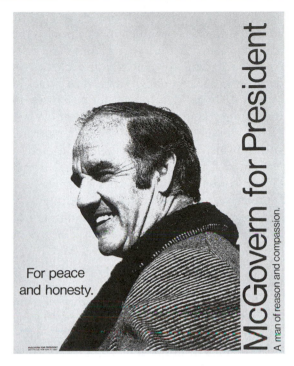

For peace and honesty.

McGovern for President
A man of reason and compassion.

Presidential campaign poster for George McGovern, 1972 *(Library of Congress)*

antiballistic missile (ABM) and was one of only nine senators in November 1969 who voted against a military appropriations bill that included funding for the ABM. McGovern also voted against confirmation of Nixon's Supreme Court nominees CLEMENT HAYNSWORTH and G. HARROLD CARSWELL and in March 1971 voted to cut funding for the controversial supersonic transport plane (SST). McGovern repeatedly called for a reduction in defense spending. In February 1970, after the president promised to veto an education appropriations bill while asking for funds for ABM deployment, McGovern accused him of having a "twisted sense of priorities." He also criticized Nixon's family assistance plan as inadequate and instead endorsed in July 1971 the $6,500 guaranteed annual income plan of the National Welfare Rights Organization.

McGovern received the most public attention for his continuing opposition to the Vietnam War. While other Democratic critics were willing to give Nixon a chance to develop his own policy, McGovern attacked him as early as March 1969 for persisting in the "tragic course" set by Johnson. When Nixon announced in June 1969 his first troop withdrawals, McGovern labeled the action "tokenism." In July McGovern revealed that he had conferred with North Vietnamese and Vietcong representatives in Paris during May and that they had specified a commitment to "unconditional" withdrawal of all U.S. troops as essential for a peace agreement. McGovern called for a unilateral 30-day cease-fire by the United States.

In October he spoke before the Vietnam Moratorium rally in Boston and the following month addressed a massive antiwar demonstration in Washington, D.C. During Senate Foreign Relations Committee hearings in February 1970 on the war, McGovern called Vietnamization a "political hoax" designed to "tranquilize the conscience of the American people while our government wages a cruel and needless war by proxy."

After the invasion of Cambodia by U.S. troops in April 1970, McGovern joined in legislative efforts to mandate an end to the war. In June he voted for the Cooper-Church Amendment to cut off funds for U.S. operations in Cambodia. In July he cosponsored legislation to end the draft and to establish an all-volunteer army. With Senator MARK HATFIELD (R-Ore.) he introduced an "end the war" amendment to a military appropriations bill that would have legislated the withdrawal of all U.S. combat troops from Southeast Asia by the end of 1971. After heated debate the Senate rejected the amendment on September 1 by a vote of 55 to 39. Although the vote was interpreted by many as an administration victory, McGovern thought otherwise. "It is remark-

able," he said, "that for the first time in history more than one-third of the U.S. Senate has voted to cut off funds for a war while we are still in battle." In January 1971 he and Senator Hatfield reintroduced the "end the war" legislation, but in June the Senate again rejected it. McGovern participated in the Senate filibuster to block extension of the Selective Service Act and voted against the bill in September.

McGovern emerged during the Nixon administration as the congressional leader of a fight against hunger in the United States. In December 1968 the Senate created a Select Committee on Nutrition and Human Needs and chose McGovern as its head. The committee conducted extensive hearings throughout the country in 1969. After touring migrant farm worker camps in Florida during March, McGovern declared: "We have seen dirt and living conditions these past two days that one might expect to see in Asia, not America. Most of the cattle and hogs in America are better fed and sheltered than the families we have visited." When HERBERT G. KLEIN, the director of communications for the White House, accused McGovern of making hunger "a political cause," the senator replied that "hunger knows no politics."

In response to the committee's revelations, Nixon announced in May 1969 an expanded drive against hunger and malnutrition. McGovern criticized the president's proposals as "probably less than a third of what is needed." In August his committee reported that an addition $4 billion a year was needed to close "the hunger gap." The following month McGovern scored a major victory when the Senate overruled an Agriculture Committee recommendation of $750 million for food stamps and instead approved a McGovern substitute calling for $1.25 billion and free food stamps to the poorest families.

The House failed to act on the measure until December 1970. Although the final bill provided larger funding, $1.75 billion, it included a "must work" provision for able-bodied recipients. McGovern threatened a filibuster but dropped the threat rather than risk having Congress adjourn without passing any legislation. During 1970 McGovern also led a successful fight for legislation to expand the federal government's school launch program for needy children.

In February 1969 McGovern was chosen by party leaders to head a special commission on party structure and delegate selection. After extensive hearings the commission issued a report in April 1970 declaring that popular control of the party was "necessary for its survival." Among the recommendations accepted by the Democratic national committee were proposals that delegates to the National Convention be chosen during the year of the convention: that the selection process be opened to give wider representation to blacks, women, and the young: and that votes he reapportioned to give fairer representation to the more populous states.

In January 1971 McGovern resigned as head of the party's reform commission and became the first declared contender for the 1972 presidential nomination. In a speech in South Dakota on January 18, he said his campaign "will be rooted not in the manipulation of our fears and divisions but in a national dialogue based on mutual respect and common hope." He pledged to withdraw all U.S. troops from Vietnam and to shift resources from the war to the rebuilding of America.

Political analysts gave McGovern little chance of securing the nomination. He lacked the voter recognition of other Democrats like Senators EDMUND MUSKIE and HUBERT HUMPHREY, was perceived as too radical by many, and seemed to be a single-issue candidate. Nevertheless, McGovern's early declaration gave him time to build a strong campaign organization, and he concentrated his efforts

on winning the allegiance of young people willing to volunteer their time to his antiwar candidacy.

By January 1972 the list of declared candidates had grown considerably, with Senators Muskie, Humphrey, HENRY JACKSON, EUGENE MCCARTHY, and VANCE HARTKE, Alabama governor GEORGE WALLACE, New York mayor JOHN LINDSAY, and Representative SHIRLEY CHISHOLM of New York in the race. Muskie was widely perceived as the front-runner and had the endorsement of important party leaders and labor chiefs, but he fared badly in the primaries. Although he won the New Hampshire primary, Muskie trailed far behind in Florida, Wisconsin, and Pennsylvania. McGovern, meanwhile, polled a respectable second in New Hampshire and won a decisive victory in Wisconsin. Muskie's withdrawal on April 27 and the attempted assassination of George Wallace on May 15 left McGovern and Humphrey the only serious contenders.

After McGovern won primaries in Oregon and Rhode Island on May 23, attention shifted to California, where the two men were to clash on June 6. In a series of preprimary television debates Humphrey lashed into McGovern with unexpected harshness. He charged that McGovern's plan to slash the defense budget by almost one-third would make America a "second-class power" and that tax and welfare proposals revealed McGovern was out to "revolutionize the country by massive redistribution of wealth." Nonetheless, McGovern scored a clear victory in the winner-take-all contest and followed it two weeks later with a big victory in New York that made him an almost certain victor in the quest for the nomination.

The convention reflected the bitter fighting of the primaries. There were rancorous disputes in the credentials committee over the seating of delegates, especially from California and Illinois. McGovern forces won clear-cut victories at the opening of the convention, especially in the denial of representation to Mayor RICHARD DALEY of Chicago. On July 12 McGovern won the nomination on the first ballot; the next day he announced that Missouri senator THOMAS EAGLETON was his choice of running mate.

McGovern's campaign was beset with difficulties from the outset. He was never able to shake off his public image as a "radical," and he failed to win the support of the Democratic Party's traditional sources of strength. AFL-CIO president GEORGE MEANY was hostile to McGovern, and for the first time in its history, the federation's executive council refused to endorse a Democratic candidate for president and remained neutral. Many of the Democratic urban machines were angered by the changes in convention rules, which weakened their influence in the party and which they attributed to McGovern as head of the reform commission, and they remained lukewarm in their support of the candidate.

Further difficulties arose when, on July 25, Eagleton announced that he had hospitalized himself three times for psychiatric treatment of nervous exhaustion and fatigue and had received electroshock therapy. Although McGovern initially announced his unwavering support for his running mate, press reaction showed disapproval of Eagleton's retention, and on July 31 McGovern announced that Eagleton would withdraw from the race. On August 8 the Democratic National Committee chose SARGENT SHRIVER to replace him.

McGovern's campaign never gathered momentum. Throughout the fall attention focused more on his proposals than on President Nixon's record. His tax and welfare plans were attacked as unworkable and too radical, and he was accused of endangering national security with his proposed cuts in the defense budget. Nixon did little campaigning and allowed Vice President SPIRO T. AGNEW and other administration officials to shoulder

most campaign duties. Moreover, McGovern's major issue, the war, was taken from him when Secretary of State HENRY KISSINGER announced on October 26 that "peace is at hand" in Indochina and that a final agreement on a truce and political settlement was almost worked out. Opinion polls on the eve of the election gave Nixon a commanding lead, and the final results were a crushing defeat for McGovern. Nixon captured 61 percent of the popular vote and 521 electoral votes. McGovern carried only Massachusetts and the District of Columbia.

Investigations into the Watergate scandal by the Senate Watergate committee and the Justice Department during 1973 revealed that McGovern and other contenders for the Democratic nomination were the victims of a concerted campaign of "dirty tricks" drawn up by White House officials and the Committee to Re-Elect the President. The aim, according to evidence presented to a grand jury during the spring, was to use political sabotage and espionage to hurt Muskie and Humphrey and to ensure the nomination of McGovern, who was widely assumed to be the weakest of Nixon's potential opponents. Further investigation revealed that former attorney general JOHN MITCHELL drew up plans to bug the McGovern headquarters and that White House chief of staff H. R. HALDEMAN coordinated the political sabotage activities. In August 1973 an Oliver Quayle opinion poll found that in a replay of the 1972 elections the voters would choose McGovern.

Reelected to a third term in 1974, McGovern remained active in the area of nutrition and hunger. In 1975 he led the fight for passage of a $2.7 billion school lunch and child nutrition program that Congress enacted in October over a presidential veto. He also was floor manager of a bill to obstruct a FORD administration attempt to weaken the food stamp program. On November 26, 1974, Ford proposed higher payments for food stamps, and in January the Agriculture Department announced that the amount of monthly income a family was expected to pay for the stamps would be raised to approximately 30 percent. McGovern introduced legislation to freeze costs at the previous level of about 24 percent, and in February Congress approved the legislation by such a wide margin that a veto would have been fruitless.

McGovern took a leading role in urging the normalization of relations with Cuba. After visiting the island in May 1975 at the invitation of Fidel Castro, McGovern called for an immediate end to the U.S. trade embargo. In August McGovern praised the Ford administration's decision to allow foreign subsidiaries of U.S. firms to trade with the Castro regime. McGovern visited Cuba a second time in April 1977.

Initially a supporter of Arizona representative MORRIS UDALL's candidacy for the 1976 presidential nomination, McGovern switched to JIMMY CARTER in June 1976. However, after the election he attacked the "Republican economics" of the Carter administration in May 1977 and the following year was vocal in his criticism of Carter's proposed cuts in domestic social welfare programs to expand the defense budget. In 1980 McGovern was defeated for reelection by James Abdnor. In 1984 he ran again for the Democratic nomination for the presidency but was again unsuccessful. From 1998 to 2001 McGovern served as U.S. ambassador to the United Nations Food and Agriculture agencies.

—JD

McIntyre, Thomas J(ames)
(1915–1992) *member of the Senate*

Thomas J. McIntyre was born on February 20, 1915, in Laconia, New Hampshire. McIntyre, a small-town New Hampshire lawyer active in Democratic politics, won a special November 1962 election to fill the seat of the late Republican senator Styles Bridges. He thereby became the first New Hampshire Democrat elected to the Senate since 1932. During his freshman year McIntyre generally supported the Kennedy administration's foreign and domestic policies. McIntyre later supported key Johnson administration legislation, including the civil rights, antipoverty, Medicare, and school aid bills. He initially backed the president's Vietnam policy.

McIntyre reversed his position on the Vietnam War in 1968. That year he advocated legislation establishing a specific date for troop withdrawal, declaring that the United States should "get out of Vietnam with all due speed." In 1970 he was part of a Nixon-sponsored congressional fact-finding tour of the Vietnam and Cambodian War zones. He wrote the lone dissenting report arguing that while the U.S. invasion of Cambodia may have been a short-term military success, it would not hasten an end to the war.

As chairman of the Research and Development Subcommittee of the Armed Services Committee, McIntyre took a great critical interest in the development of new weapons systems. In 1969 he offered a compromise to an administration proposal to build an anti-ballistic missile (ABM) system. The bill would have allowed development of on-site radar and electronic equipment but no actual missile deployment. The compromise failed. Just before the floor vote in 1970 McIntyre was persuaded to support the ABM by the administration argument that the weapon would be a valuable "bargaining chip" in arms limitation talks with the Soviet Union.

During Nixon's second term McIntyre fought proponents of more sophisticated nuclear weapons systems. His bill to slow the development of the Trident nuclear submarine was defeated in 1973. The next year the Senate rejected McIntyre's bill to defer the $77 million program for a more powerful and accurate intercontinental ballistic missile (ICBM) capable of destroying Soviet missiles in their underground silos. McIntyre feared that these maneuvering reentry vehicles (MaRVs) would "drastically and dangerously alter our national strategic policy" and would undermine the SALT talks. In 1975, however, the Senate passed HUBERT H. HUMPHREY's (D-Minn.) similar amendment halting the testing of MaRVs unless the president certified to Congress that the USSR was testing the same type of weapon.

In 1971 McIntyre introduced his National Healthcare Act, and hearings were held on it in that and subsequent years, but no action was ever taken. His plan called for a nationwide system of health insurance supported by employer-employee contributions, with poor and middle-class people receiving government subsidies according to need.

During the JIMMY CARTER administration McIntyre remained a foe of increased weapons development. He won his 1978 primary campaign but suffered a stunning defeat in November when he lost by only 5,000 votes to conservative Republican Gordon Humphrey. He died in 1992.

—FLM

McNamara, Robert S(trange)
(1916–) *president, World Bank*

Robert S. McNamara was born on June 9, 1916, in San Francisco, California. McNamara majored in mathematics, economics, and philosophy, winning Phi Beta Kappa awards in his sophomore year at the University of California, from which he received a B.A. degree in 1937. He graduated with honors from the Harvard Business School in 1939. After serving in the army air force during World War II, McNa-

mara was employed by the Ford Motor Co. He became general manager, then vice president, as he helped revive the faltering company with emphasis on strict cost-accounting methods and approval of highly profitable projects. In November 1960 McNamara was named company president, but he spent little more than a month in the job. President Kennedy had offered him the position of secretary of defense, and McNamara accepted. He retained this post under the Johnson administration until February 1968, when he resigned to accept an appointment as president of the World Bank.

McNamara, the first president of the World Bank to come from a nonbanking background, instituted new policies with enthusiasm and authority. In a report to the UN Economic and Social Council on December 5, 1968, McNamara laid out his general plan for future World Bank activities. Although the bank would continue its policy of financing large projects such as "power installations and road and rail networks," it would emphasize greater concern to "reach and affect the individual." There would be an effort to quadruple agriculture lending over a five-year period and to triple lending for educational development. In the address McNamara announced a policy revision that would allow the bank and its affiliate the International Development Association to finance state-owned development banks "when we believe that they can be businesslike and self-supporting institutions." McNamara urged President-elect RICHARD NIXON to provide money for easy-term international loans to poor countries.

In July 1969 McNamara completed his first review of the bank's activities. He concluded that it should, over a five-year period, double both its lending to poor countries and its borrowing efforts in the financial markets of rich countries to raise the necessary funds. In its first fiscal year under McNamara, the bank completed about three-fourths of its five-year target. Its total lending during that fiscal year (ending June 30) was $1.78 billion, a record figure and an increase of 87 percent over the year before. In that fiscal year McNamara had obtained funds from some entirely new sources, such as Kuwait. The result was a record total of $1.22 billion raised in the world's capital markets, a 60 percent increase over the previous year.

In an address to the annual meeting of the World Bank on September 21, 1970, McNamara criticized the United States as the "single exception" to the general acceptance by industrial nations of a new aid target of seven-tenths of 1 percent of the gross national product—double the then-current flow. He felt it "inconceivable" that the American public would accept for long a situation in which they—numbering 6 percent of the world's population, but consuming nearly 40 percent of the world's resources—would contribute under "their fair share" to efforts at development in the poor and emerging nations. He pointed out that the United States ranked 11th in terms of percentage of national product among the aid-giving countries.

In October 1972 McNamara instituted a restructuring of the World Bank's regional and technical departments. He felt that regionalization of operations would provide closer integration of the bank's area and project activities and "establish even more firmly that the development of individual countries is the basis on which the Bank's program is built."

In the same month McNamara told the Economic and Social Council of the United Nation that the direction of economic development efforts must attack directly the personal poverty of the bottom 40 percent of populations in the developing countries rather than concentrating on their overall economic growth. He acknowledged that a reorientation of social and economic policy was basically a political problem and that it was up to the developing nations themselves to institute changes that would allow development efforts to reach their poorest citizens. "There is a natural tendency," he stated, "for growth to be concentrated in the modern sectors of the economy, with little current benefit to the lowest income groups." McNamara proposed a five-step program to reach the bottom 40 percent, an aspect of which required financing of rural and urban projects that were low-skill, labor-intensive, but economically useful.

From the time he took office, McNamara stressed, far more than his predecessors, the gravity of the world population problem, which he said was "seriously crippling" economic development efforts. In an effort to help alleviate this growing problem, McNamara instituted family-planning activities and established a Population Projects Department in 1971.

The executive directors unanimously reelected McNamara in 1972 for a second five-year term as World Bank president. He was again reelected to this post for five years in April 1977. He left that organization in 1981. In 1995 he published a memoir, *In Retrospect*.

—MLB

Means, Russell C(harles)
(1940–   ) *Native American activist*

Of mixed white-Native American parentage, Means grew up in poverty in California. He attended California public schools and spent his summers with his grandparents, who were Sioux Indians, on the Pine Ridge reservation in South Dakota, where they lived. Trained as an accountant, Means spent two years as an alcoholic on skid row in Los Angeles. The rising militance of many Native Americans in the late 1960s provided a motive for his rehabilitation. He joined the American Indian Movement (AIM), a radical organization founded in

1968 by Dennis Banks and Clyde Bellecourt, and became director of the American Indian Center in Cleveland, Ohio.

In November 1972 Means participated in the week-long occupation of the offices of the Bureau of Indian Affairs (BIA) in Washington, D.C. The occupation occurred after several hundred Native Americans marched cross-country to dramatize their grievances against the government's policies regarding Native Americans. Before leaving the BIA offices, the occupiers seized files filled with "incriminating" documents.

Means was one of the leaders of the 71-day armed occupation in 1973 of Wounded Knee, a village in the South Dakota Pine Ridge reservation. Means and Dennis Banks, another AIM leader, demanded a Senate investigation of Native American treaties and the ouster of Richard Wilson, the elected tribal chief of the Oglala Sioux. On March 12 Means announced that the occupiers had "seceded" from the United States and would treat U.S. officials as foreign agents. With the aid of their lawyer, William Kunstler, Means and Banks negotiated a cease-fire and went to Washington for talks with government officials. The cease-fire broke down, however, and two Native Americans were killed on April 27.

After the occupation ended in May, Means and Banks were indicted on charges of conspiracy, assault, and theft. The trial began in St. Paul, Minnesota, in February 1974 and ended abruptly in September when Judge Fred J. Nichol dismissed all charges. Nichol accused the prosecutor of deceiving the court, suppressing documents, and lying about evidence and said that the FBI had "stooped to a new low" in its tactics. It was later revealed that Douglas Durham, who coordinated the Wounded Knee legal defense committee and who attended many legal strategy meetings, was a paid informant for the FBI.

In March 1975 Means was indicted for a murder that occurred during a barroom brawl in Scenic, South Dakota. His attorney, William Kunstler, subpoenaed FBI director CLARENCE KELLEY as a defense witness to prove FBI harassment of Means and other AIM leaders. Kunstler argued that the government had created a climate of fear that caused Native Americans to arm themselves in self-defense. On August 6, 1976, a jury acquitted Means of the murder charge.

In 1984 Means ran unsuccessfully for the vice presidency of the United States on a ticket headed by Larry Flynt. In 1987 he unsuccessfully sought the nomination of the Libertarian Party. In 2001 he unsuccessfully ran for governor of New Mexico. That same year he unsuccessfully ran for president of the Oglala Sioux.

—JD

Meany, George
(1894–1980) *president, AFL-CIO*

Born on August 16, 1894, the son of an Irish Catholic plumber and union official, George Meany entered his father's trade at age 16. In 1922 he began his union career as business agent of the Plumbers Union local 463, which included the Bronx and Manhattan. From there Meany moved into the hierarchy of the American Federation of Labor (AFL), winning the posts of president of the New York state federation of labor in 1934 and secretary-treasurer of the national federation in 1940. Twelve years later he succeeded William Green as AFL president.

One of Meany's first important acts as head of the AFL was to negotiate a merger in 1955 with its longtime rival the Congress of Industrial Organizations (CIO). Subsequently, he established virtually complete control over AFL-CIO decision making on both domestic and foreign policy issues. Meany closely identified the federation with both the national Democratic Party and the bipartisan anti-communist foreign policy of the cold war era. The Great Society programs of the Johnson administration, in particular, won his enthusiastic support, and he strongly endorsed U.S. military intervention in Vietnam. Following President Johnson's decision not to run for president in 1968, Meany mobilized AFL-CIO resources on behalf of Vice President HUBERT H. HUMPHREY's presidential candidacy.

Since the late 1950s Meany had been engaged in a feud with WALTER REUTHER, head of the United Auto Workers (UAW) and of the AFL-CIO Industrial Union Department. Reuther continually criticized Meany's hard-line foreign policy posture and complained that the federation lacked the dynamism and imagination needed to stimulate union growth. In early 1968 the UAW began to withhold its dues to the federation, and as a result Meany suspended the 1.6-million-member union on May 16. Along with the independent International Brotherhood of Teamsters, the auto workers then formed the Alliance for Labor Action (ALA), which Meany's executive council promptly denounced as a "dual labor organization, rival to the AFL-CIO."

The split in AFL-CIO ranks was widened at the federation's convention in October 1969, when the delegates voted to expel the Chemical Workers Union for having affiliated with the ALA. In April Meany's staff issued a report on the dispute with the UAW that condemned Reuther for having waged a "two-year campaign of public vilification" and for having refused to resolve the conflict within the "forums of the trade union movement." Meany insisted that the federation would continue to organize the unorganized and to fight for social justice and civil rights.

Despite a long-standing personal and political antipathy to RICHARD NIXON, Meany's relations with the Nixon White House were marked by an ambivalence that puzzled many observers. As he took office in 1969 it seemed possible that the president might win the labor leader's confidence as a result of his aggressive Vietnam policy and his tough stand against the antiwar movement. However, after the economy began to slide into a recession late in the year, Meany criticized the administration's failure to act forcefully to stem the slowdown. Alarmed by the simultaneous rise of unemployment and consumer prices, Meany proposed a variety of countermeasures, including credit rationing by the Federal Reserve and mandatory investment of tax-exempt funds in government-backed mortgages.

When Nixon inaugurated his new economic policy with the announcement on August 15, 1971, of a 90-day wage-price freeze, Meany denounced the president's program as "patently discriminatory" against workers. While union contracts were "highly visible" and thus easy to control, he argued, the administration had failed to establish effective machinery for regulating prices and had exempted entirely corporate profits and stockholders' dividends. Meany warned that labor would not cooperate with the freeze, and he urged unions to cancel their contracts with employers if negotiated benefits were withheld.

As consideration of the postfreeze "Phase Two" period began, Meany called on the administration to create an independent, tripartite control board. Nixon accepted the proposal, and after receiving assurances that the panel would have real authority, Meany agreed to serve on it as one of five labor members. When Phase Two began in mid-November, however, Meany and the other union representatives on the pay board immediately found themselves at odds with the business and public members over the question of implementing existing contracts. On November 18, at the AFL-CIO convention in Bal Harbour, Florida, Meany bitterly attacked the pay board's decision not to grant retroactive payment of wage increases cancelled during the freeze and charged that the administration was trying to destroy collective bargaining. Making a last-minute appearance at the convention on the following day, the president received a pointedly cool reception. After his speech, in which he vowed to pursue his program even if labor refused to cooperate, Nixon's attempt to greet the delegates was cut short when Meany abruptly called the meeting to order. Later, White House aides publicly criticized Meany's "discourteous" treatment of the chief executive. Treasury Secretary JOHN B. CONNALLY called the labor leader boorish and arrogant.

In March 1972 the pay board majority voted to reduce a wage settlement won by the International Longshoremen's and Warehousemen's Union (ILWU) after a lengthy strike on the West Coast docks. Meany and three of the other labor members promptly resigned from the panel (Teamsters president FRANK FITZSIMMONS refused to join the four). In its statement announcing the withdrawal the AFL-CIO indicated its dissatisfaction not only with the ILWU decision but also with the whole trend of administration pay and price policy.

The 1972 presidential campaign brought a measure of reconciliation between Meany and the Nixon administration. At the beginning of the year the AFL-CIO Committee on Political Education (COPE) stated that labor's chief political goal would be the defeat of Nixon's reelection bid. COPE strongly opposed Senator GEORGE MCGOVERN's (D-S.D.) antiwar candidacy, however. Months before the Democratic National Convention, Meany let it be known that Senator HENRY JACKSON (D-Wash.), a firm supporter of the war in Southeast Asia and a leading critic of U.S.-Soviet détente, was his personal preference. The federation provided a speechwriter for Jackson during the primary campaign, and at the convention he was nominated by Steelworkers president I. W. ABEL, a close ally of Meany's. After McGovern won the nomination, Meany

announced on July 19 that the AFL-CIO executive council had voted to withhold endorsement from the Democratic candidate for the first time in its history, adding that personally he would not vote for either Nixon or McGovern.

Some of the federation's major affiliates, as well as some state labor councils, later defied Meany by endorsing McGovern. But the federation's "neutrality" was an expression of the fact that the Republicans had won more labor support, whether open or tacit, in 1972 than at any time since the beginning of the New Deal. Throughout the campaign Meany criticized McGovern's position on the Vietnam War as a policy of "surrender," and in a postelection interview the South Dakota senator called Meany one of the "wreckers" of the Democratic Party.

In November PETER J. BRENNAN, a building trades official, was nominated as secretary of labor after first receiving clearance from Meany. On December 16 Meany rejoined the president's economic administration as a member of the Productivity Commission, and in January of the following year he became a member of the Cost of Living Council. Nixon's decision to drop most mandatory wage-price controls during Phase Three was reported by the *New York Times* to have been influenced by Meany's talks with Secretary of the Treasury GEORGE SHULTZ.

Meany's rapproachement with the administration proved short-lived, however. By April 1973 he was once again scoring the White House on a variety of issues, ranging from unemployment compensation to trade policy. In September Meany assailed the president's veto of an AFL-CIO–backed minimum wage bill as "a callous, cruel blow" to the nation's working poor. The bill would have extended coverage to public employees and to domestics. A long-standing tradition was broken in October when the federation did not invite the president to address its national convention.

After Nixon's resignation Meany continued to blast away at the Republican administration for its failure to spur the economy. As the recession deepened in 1974, he called on Congress to lower interest rates, impose mandatory allocation of credit to priority needs, initiate large-scale public service projects, curb the export of scarce commodities, and take action to spur housing construction. At the same time the federation opposed reintroducing wage-price controls unless they were applied equitably to prices, dividends, and profits as well as wages. Meany bitterly denounced President FORD's repeated vetoes of job-creating projects voted by Congress.

Early in 1976 Meany indicated that he preferred to see either HUBERT HUMPHREY or Jackson as the Democratic presidential nominee. He took little direct part in the political campaigns of that year, however. After the election of JIMMY CARTER, Meany's relations with the White House were distinctly strained. He stepped down from the presidency of the union in 1979 and died the following year.

—TLH

Mills, Wilbur D(aigh)

(1909–1992) *member of the House of Representatives; chairman, Ways and Means Committee*

Wilbur D. Mills was born on May 24, 1909, in Kensett, Arkansas. Mills won election as a Democrat to the House of Representatives in 1938, after having served as a county and probate judge. A protégé of Speaker of the House Sam Rayburn (D-Tex.), he gained appointment under Rayburn's sponsorship to the Ways and Means Committee in 1943, an uncommonly swift ascension to the prestigious tax-writing committee. Through exhaustive study and attention to the details of government finance and trade legislation, Mills by the 1950s became the House's foremost tax expert. He assumed chairmanship of the Ways and Means Committee in 1957. That post and his expertise on tax legislation made Mills, according to some observers, "the most powerful man in Congress" during the 1960s. Mills played a prominent role in the passage of the Trade Expansion Act of 1962, which led to major tariff reductions between the United States and its trading partners. His opposition to Medicare stalled that measure for years until 1965, when Mills decided to support the proposal.

Mills continued to be a major power in the House during the early NIXON administration, although his domination was challenged by both liberals who resented his conservative fiscal policies and his control of the Ways and Means Committee and conservatives who opposed his support of spending for social welfare. A moderate, he urged budget cuts to prevent continued inflation but supported the extension of unemployment insurance and raises in Social Security payments to aid those affected by the economic problems of the period. He refused to support bills establishing a general debt limit and instead proposed setting specific ceilings on individual bills. Mills supported President Nixon's Family Assistance Plan, which would have given the poor a guaranteed income. Despite strong reservations, he believed it better than the existing Aid to Families with Dependent Children program, which he maintained promoted the breakup of families. He pushed for passage of the measure through the House in 1970, but the bill eventually died in the Senate. Mills also backed Nixon's practice of impounding funds allocated by Congress for federal programs, breaking with the Democratic leadership's position on this issue. He argued that the president had the constitutional authority to limit congressional spending for particular programs and urged the House to have faith in Nixon on this measure.

Mills played a prominent role in the passage of the bill extending the Johnson administration's income tax surcharge and in the formation of the Tax Reform Act of 1969. Shortly after his inauguration, Nixon formally asked Congress for a year's extension of the 10 percent surcharge, due to expire in June 1969, in an effort to fight inflation. Mills questioned the surcharge's effectiveness and suggested instead cutting the federal budget and implementing a tight money policy. Nevertheless, he supported the measure, although ill health limited his role in committee deliberations on it. Liberals attempted to tie passage of the surtax to overall tax reform and threatened to block the bill until reform was discussed. But it won close passage in Ways and Means after provisions were added granting low-income individuals tax relief, postponing certain reductions in excise taxes, and repealing a 7 percent tax credit for business investment.

On the House floor Mills campaigned hard for the surcharge bill, noting that a vote against the proposal was a vote for inflation. To convince liberals that the administration would eventually propose broad tax reform, Nixon submitted reform proposals in April, and Mills promised to institute tax restructuring in all sectors. As was his usual practice, Mills got the surtax bill reported under a closed rule that permitted no changes in the measure after it went to the floor, thus forcing liberals to take a clear stand on the bill. The House passed it by five votes in May. The Senate approved it in July, and it was signed into law in August 1969.

Throughout 1969 Mills held extensive hearings on tax reform and played a major role in molding the Tax Reform Act of 1969. In April President Nixon introduced his own tax proposals, including repeal of the 7 percent business investment tax credit, exemption of the poor from federal income tax, and a limit on tax preferences that would set a 50 percent ceiling on most income an individual could shield from taxation. Mills objected to a large number of the president's proposals, and the bill that finally won passage was written almost entirely by Congress. He opposed the limit on tax preferences because it merely restricted access to existing loopholes rather than actually closed them, but he supported the repeal of the 7 percent business investment tax credit. As passed, the Tax Reform Act provided for an increase in the personal income tax exemption by stages from $600 to $750; repealed the 7 percent excise tax for several manufacturing categories; lowered tax rates for single persons; provided a minimum standard deduction designed to remove over 5 million taxpayers from the tax rolls; placed a ceiling on the amount of individual capital gains eligible for low tax rates; and raised capital gains taxes for corporations. It also tightened several loopholes. Despite Nixon's threats of a veto, he signed the bill in late December.

Mills was a vigorous opponent of the president's revenue-sharing proposals, aimed at giving federal funds to state and local governments for uses that they determined. He maintained that the governments that benefited from the monies should also be responsible for raising funds. However, in 1972 he reversed his stand and announced he favored sharing that gave most benefits to urban areas and tied receipt of funds to the intent of local government taxing efforts. The final bill, passed in October, dropped Mills's emphasis on cities but tied funds to relative income and the extent of government taxing efforts.

Mills's power eroded in 1974 because of challenges by House reformers and his personal indiscretions. That year the House voted to force Mills to subdivide his committee into four subcommittees with separate chairmen. In December the Democratic Caucus in the House took away from Ways and Means the power to assign all committee members and gave it to the Democratic Steering Committee, which consisted of House leaders and other influential party members. The caucus also voted to enlarge the Ways and Means Committee from 12 to 35 members—a move that allowed younger and more liberal representation.

Mills's decline in Congress owed much to his own behavior. Before 1974 Mills was one of the hardest-working representatives in the House. He appeared to change considerably in the early 1970s. Reports circulated in 1974 that he was becoming a heavy drinker, and he was frequently seen in Washington, D.C., nightspots. Some people attributed his changed behavior to a difficult operation for a ruptured spinal disk in 1973. Still others explained it as a result of his ill-advised effort in 1971–72 to secure the Democratic nomination for the presidency.

In October 1974 Mills's car containing five passengers was stopped by Washington police. One of the passengers, Annabella Battistella, 38, leaped from the car and either fell or jumped into the Tidal Basin, an estuary of the Potomac River. The media revealed that Battistella was a striptease dancer in a Washington nightclub who performed under the name of Fanne Fox. Mills's career was severely damaged by the incident. Two months later he appeared for a few seconds on a Boston stage with the stripper, now billed as the "Tidal Basin Bombshell." Newspapers had a field day with the story, and Mills's career was in effect ended. He checked himself into the Naval Medical Center in Bethesda, Maryland. House Speaker Carl Albert made it clear that the Steering Committee would not permit him to retain his chairmanship. Mills soon relinquished the post to Al Ullman (D-Ore.).

Mills served one more term as a member of the House before retiring from Congress in 1977. He later admitted his downfall was due to alcoholism. He died at his Arkansas home in 1992.

—HML

Mink, Patsy (Takemoto)
(1927–2002) *member of the House of Representatives*

Born on December 6, 1927, Patsy Takemoto graduated from the University of Honolulu in 1948 and received a law degree from the University of Chicago three years later. Mink served the Hawaii house of representatives as house attorney in 1955 and in the following year became president of the Hawaii Young Democrats. She entered the state house of representatives in 1956 and was voted into the Hawaiian senate in 1958 and 1962. In 1964 Mink won a seat in the U.S. House.

While in Congress Mink established a liberal record on both domestic and foreign affairs. She concentrated her attention on women's rights and education, with particular emphasis on the disabled and minorities. During the last years of the Johnson administration Mink campaigned for federal funding of private and public nonprofit daycare centers. Her campaign culminated in the child development bill of 1971, which passed Congress but was vetoed by President NIXON.

Mink maintained her liberal record in Congress during the Nixon and FORD administrations. In 1972 the liberal Americans for Democratic Action gave her a 100 rating. Mink voted for conservation legislation, busing, family assistance programs, federal aid for abortions, and subsidies for mass transit while opposing much of the "law and order" legislation of the period. She continued as a champion of equality for women and urged the appointment of women to high policy making positions in the Democratic Party. She opposed the nomination of conservative G. HARROLD CARSWELL to the Supreme Court, maintaining that his confirmation would be "an affront to the women of America" because of his record on women's issues. In foreign and defense affairs Mink opposed development of various weapons systems and backed foreign aid. An opponent of the Vietnam War after 1967, she supported the end-the-war resolutions of the period.

As a result of her liberal record and strong support of civil rights and equality for women, Mink was enticed by a group of Oregon Democrats to enter the 1972 presidential primary in that state. In announcing her candidacy, she said, "Without a woman contending for the presidency, the concept of absolute equality will continue to be placed on the back burner as warmed-over lip service." In May she garnered only 2 percent of the vote.

Mink was a vigorous critic of President Nixon during the Watergate controversy. In 1973 she introduced a resolution that called for the impeachment of Nixon, charging his administration with having created "a relentless decadence which had sapped the people's confidence in justice." "Stunned" by President Ford's pardon of Nixon in September 1974, Mink maintained, "I believe that not only was this action unprecedented but perhaps goes beyond the constitutional provisions with respect to executive authority."

In 1976 Mink waged an unsuccessful campaign for the Senate. She served as assistant secretary of state for oceans and international environment and scientific affairs in 1977 and 1978. In 1983 she was elected to the Honolulu city council, where she served until 1990, when she was reelected to the U.S. Congress. She died in September 2002 of viral pneumonia; her name was already on the ballot for reelection to the House, and on November 5, 2002, she was posthumously reelected to her seat in Congress.

—SBB

Mitchell, John N(ewton)
(1913–1988) attorney general

Born on September 15, 1913, John Mitchell grew up on Long Island, New York. Although a Protestant, he attended college and law school at Fordham University, receiving his law degree in 1938. At the firm of Caldwell and Raymond he became an expert in the field of municipal bonds; he was made a partner in 1942. During World War II Mitchell commanded PT boat squadrons in the Pacific. After the war Mitchell returned to his firm, now Caldwell, Trimble, and Mitchell. As the firm prospered, Mitchell became a nationally recognized authority on public finance, a skilled intermediary between politicians seeking to finance projects and the financial community underwriting and selling the bonds. He pioneered in the use of devices such as the semiautonomous agency through which a state could borrow and build while evading its constitutional debt limitation. Mitchell played a key role in the financing of many of New York governor NELSON ROCKEFELLER's grand construction projects.

In 1967 Mitchell's firm merged with that of former vice president RICHARD NIXON to form Nixon, Mudge, Rose, Guthrie, Alexander, & Mitchell. Nixon and Mitchell became close associates, frequently lunching and playing golf together. During Nixon's 1968 presidential campaign Mitchell played a role of growing dominance. Beginning as an adviser to his law partner, Mitchell then organized states for Nixon with a view toward the Republican Convention; he was named campaign manager in May. Many gave Mitchell credit for the smooth professionalism of the Nixon organization, in contrast with the candidate's previous electoral ventures. Nixon admired Mitchell's unflappable demeanor and decisive manner and trusted his pragmatic judgment. Mitchell was a staunch proponent of the so-called southern strategy, which sought to build for the Republicans a coalition of southern and western states by a conservative appeal heavy with "law and order" rhetoric.

During the campaign Mitchell had vociferously denied that he would accept a cabinet post in a Nixon administration. Even after being named attorney general by President-elect Nixon, Mitchell continued to protest that he had not wanted the job and would stay only two years. "This is the last thing in the world I wanted to do," he said. "I've got all the things I ever wanted. I'm a fat and prosperous Wall Street lawyer, which is just what I always wanted to be."

In his acceptance speech before the Republican Convention in August, Nixon had promised: "If we are going to restore order and respect for law in this country, there's one place we're going to begin. We're going to have a new attorney general of the United States." During the campaign Nixon excoriated the liberal, reformist attorney general RAMSEY CLARK for allegedly being "soft on crime." His selection of the conservative Mitchell as attorney general was seen as a signal that the administration intended to pursue a conspicuous hard line against crime, radicalism, and civil disobedience.

Soon after taking office Mitchell stated that he differed from Clark in that he believed the Department of Justice was "an institution for law enforcement, not social improvement." In mid-1969 the administration submitted its anti-crime package, which contained many elements also favored by former administrations, such as federal court reform, an enlarged budget for legal aid, and more job counseling for offenders on parole or probation. The most salient new feature was preventive detention, which would have allowed a federal judge in the District of Columbia to jail a defendant for up to 60 days before trial if the individual was charged with a serious offense and there was a "substantial probability" that he would be a danger to the community if released. Mitchell argued that the high crime rate among defendants out on bail made such legislation imperative. Civil libertarians strenuously opposed preventive detention as unconstitutional, arguing also that speedier trials, not pretrial detention, were the answer.

Other controversial parts of the bill would allow a federal judge to impose a life sentence on anyone convicted of three felonies and permit a police officer with a search warrant to enter a person's premises unannounced. The latter "no-knock" provision also aroused heated opposition. At the same time the Justice Department proposed a narcotics control bill to Congress somewhat more punitive than the existing laws.

Another departure from the Clark tenure was in the area of wiretapping. While his predecessor had refused to use the device except in national security cases, Mitchell pledged to exercise the full wiretapping authority contained in the 1968 omnibus anticrime act. He loosened the restrictions under which the FBI and federal law enforcement officials could tap wires and targeted domestic radicals as well as organized crime.

Mitchell adopted a stern public stance against campus disturbances and civil disobedience. "When you get nihilists on campus," he said, "the thing to do is to get them into court." Against the advice of several career Justice Department lawyers, he approved the prosecution of the Chicago Seven, the radical activists whom the government accused of inciting the Chicago riots outside the Democratic National Convention in 1968. Mitchell also approved the conspiracy indictments against DANIEL ELLSBERG and the Harrisburg Seven and unsuccessfully sought to enjoin newspaper publication of the *Pentagon Papers*.

Mitchell often contended that antiwar demonstrations were inspired by communists. In the aftermath of the mass Mayday antiwar protest in Washington, D.C., in May 1971, he charged that communists and communist sympathizers "have been part of the leadership and makeup of every mass demonstration." Mitchell also compared the May Day protesters to Hitler's Brown Shirts and lauded the mass arrest tactics of the D.C. police, who locked up 13,400 demonstrators. "I hope that Washington's decisive opposition to mob force will set an example for other communities," he said. All the arrests were subsequently ruled unconstitutional.

The Nixon administration's southern strategy was most apparent in the area of civil rights. In mid-1969 Mitchell announced that the administration would not support an outright extension of the Voting Rights Act of 1965 but would propose its own modified version. The two most important revisions would have eliminated the 1965 law's requirement that states could not amend voting procedures without the attorney general's approval and expanded the act's coverage beyond the seven southern states to the entire country. Opponents of the administration's bill argued that it represented a gutting of the 1965 law by encouraging the southern states to institute delaying actions through the courts and by diluting enforcement efforts in the South through the extension of Justice Department jurisdiction to the entire nation. The bill's provisions, said Representative William McCulloch (R-Ohio), "sweep broadly into those areas where the need is least and retreat from those areas where the need is greatest." In response to a group of black civil rights workers protesting the revision of the original act, Mitchell said, "You will be better advised to watch what we do instead of what we say." The House passed the administration's version, but the Senate did not. The final measure enacted in 1970 extended the major features of the 1965 act for five years.

In addition to his duties as attorney general, Mitchell exerted influence over a broad range of administration policies through his position as President Nixon's foremost adviser. Mitchell worked closely with the National Security Council and the national intelligence apparatus. He sat on the Urban Affairs Council. Besides seeing the president once a day, Mitchell said in 1969: "We usually talk on the phone several more times. In the evening he frequently calls me at home." Mitchell oversaw the appointment process after Nixon's election and recommended the conservative WARREN BURGER to Nixon as chief justice. It was also on Mitchell's recommendation that Nixon nominated CLEMENT HAYNSWORTH and G. HARROLD CARSWELL to the Supreme Court. Senate rejection of these nominations was embarrassing to Mitchell, but he remained, in *Newsweek*'s words, "Mr. Nixon's political right arm—his chief domestic strategist, arm-twister and lightning rod, counselor and confidant on problems reaching across the full range of government."

In February 1972 Mitchell resigned as attorney general to head Nixon's campaign for reelection. Mitchell's tenure as head of the Committee to Re-Elect the President (CREEP) was relatively quiet until June 17, when agents of CREEP were arrested for breaking into the Watergate headquarters of the Democratic National Committee. Mitchell said on June 18 that none of those involved in the raid was "operating either on our behalf or with our consent." On July 1 Mitchell resigned as Nixon's campaign manager. He said that his wife, MARTHA MITCHELL, had given him an ultimatum to give up either politics or her. "The happiness and welfare of my wife and daughter" must come first, Mitchell said.

Over the next two and a half years, Mitchell steadfastly reiterated—before FBI agents, grand jurors, reporters, Senate committees, and a District of Columbia jury—that he had had no prior knowledge of or involvement in the Watergate break-in and took no part in the subsequent cover-up. Testifying before the Senate Watergate committee on July 10–12, 1973, Mitchell emphatically repeated his denials and disputed the testimony of former aides JEB STUART MAGRUDER and JOHN DEAN, who had testified that Mitchell approved the break-in as part of an ambitious intelligence program to undermine the political opposition. Dean also testified that Mitchell had participated in arranging payment of hush money to the Watergate defendants.

Mitchell told the committee that he had withheld information from Nixon to forestall an inquiry that might have exposed other "White House horror stories." These included the break-in at the office of DANIEL ELLSBERG's psychiatrist, the proposed firebombing of the Brookings Institution, and the falsification of cables relating to the 1963 assassination of South Vietnamese president Ngo Dinh Diem.

In May 1973 Mitchell and former secretary of commerce MAURICE STANS were indicted by a federal grand jury in New York for perjury and conspiracy to obstruct justice. The indictment charged that they had conspired to obstruct a Securities and Exchange Commission investigation into the mutual funds dealings of financier ROBERT VESCO in return for a secret $200,000 contribution by Vesco to the 1972 Nixon campaign. Both men pleaded not guilty. In April 1974 a federal jury acquitted the pair of all charges.

On March 1, 1974, Mitchell, with former Nixon aides H.R. HALDEMAN, JOHN EHRLICHMAN, CHARLES COLSON, GORDON STRACHAN, ROBERT MARDIAN, and Kenneth Parkinson, was indicted for his role in the Watergate cover-up. Mitchell was charged with conspiracy to obstruct justice, commit perjury, and defraud the United States by manipulating the Central Intelligence Agency, the FBI, and the Justice Department. Mitchell pleaded not guilty to all charges.

The trial took place during October-December 1974. The bulk of the case against Mitchell was contained in the White House tapes and in the detailed testimony of John Dean. Taking the stand in his own defense, Mitchell, adamantly denying any involvement in the criminal conspiracy, was subjected to a blistering cross-examination by prosecutor James Neal. On January 1, 1975, the jury found Mitchell guilty of conspiracy, obstruc-

tion of justice, and perjury. On February 21 Judge JOHN SIRICA sentenced him to a prison term of two and a half to eight years. In July Mitchell was disbarred in New York.

Over the next few years higher courts affirmed the convictions of Mitchell, Haldeman, and Ehrlichman. In June 1977 Mitchell began serving his sentence at a minimum-security prison in Montgomery, Alabama. He was the first U.S. attorney general ever to serve a prison sentence. He was released on parole on January 19, 1979, after serving 19 months. Until his death in 1988 he resided in Georgetown and sometimes served as a consultant.

—TO

Mitchell, Martha (Beall)
(1918–1976)

Martha Elizabeth Beall was born on September 2, 1918, in Pine Bluff, Arkansas. Her father was a cotton broker and her mother a teacher of elocution. Beall graduated from the University of Miami and moved to Mobile, Alabama, where she taught school for a year.

During World War II she married Clyde W. Jennings, a businessman with whom she had one son before their marriage ended in divorce. In 1954 she met JOHN MITCHELL, a New York attorney at the time, and three years later they were married. She gave birth in 1962 to their only child together, a daughter, "Marty."

In January 1967 the Wall Street law firms of John Mitchell and RICHARD NIXON merged to form Nixon, Mudge, Rose, Guthrie, Alexander, & Mitchell. During the following year the Mitchells and the Nixons became friendly, and Mitchell later accepted Nixon's offer to run his 1968 presidential campaign (after the first two campaign managers had resigned). In December 1968 the newly elected President Nixon appointed Mitchell attorney general.

The Mitchells moved to Washington, D.C., and Martha Mitchell, an outspoken, willful southern conservative, soon made it known that the traditional reserve and decorum expected of cabinet wives was not her style. She had strong, often vituperative opinions about many of the politically charged issues of the day, and she was not afraid to express them publicly. Among her favorite targets in 1969 and 1970 were antiwar protesters, whom she described as "very liberal communists," and academics, whom she blamed in one interview for "all the troubles in this country." Even though her public statements were often politically embarrassing, during Nixon's first term John Mitchell and the president seemed more amused than threatened by her. Nixon once said he thought she was "spunky."

The tables began to turn, however, after Nixon's reelection in 1972. As before, John Mitchell served as his campaign manager, but this time their success was soon marred by the Watergate scandal. In early 1973 evidence that John Mitchell was involved in the scandal began to surface. By March Martha Mitchell was coming to his defense. In a phone call to the *New York Times* on March 31, she said somebody was trying to make her husband "the goat" for Watergate and she "was not going to let that happen." She phoned a United Press reporter to say that the Nixon administration had turned "completely against my husband." In April she called the Associated Press to controvert the White House denial of a meeting between Nixon and her husband three days earlier.

On May 5 Martha Mitchell publicly demanded Nixon's resignation as the only way to "give credibility to the Republican Party and credibility to the United States." This time, however, John Mitchell disavowed his wife's comments. He told reporters it was "ridiculous" for anybody to take seriously her suggestion that Nixon resign, and he chided United Press

for printing his wife's statements. But she was not to be silenced.

At a news conference on May 28 Martha Mitchell said she was convinced that her husband had been protecting the president. She also said the White House must bear "all the blame" for Watergate, and that if Nixon did not resign, he would be impeached. Two months later, angered by JOHN EHRLICHMAN's testimony before the Senate Watergate committee, she demanded to be heard by the committee and accused Ehrlichman of being "arrogant, insolent, and insipid." After being informed in September that her testimony was not wanted, she even accused the committee members of protecting Nixon.

Throughout this period the strain on the Mitchells' marriage had grown more severe. In a United Press interview published November 3, 1973, Martha Mitchell not only predicted that Nixon would have to quit and would "be out by April," but confirmed reports that her marriage "was over." In the final settlement John Mitchell retained custody of their daughter, and Martha Mitchell was awarded $1,000 a week alimony. Although her public statements became less frequent and less vociferous after the divorce, she never dropped the contention that her husband had been "framed."

In October 1975 it was discovered she had a rare, terminal form of bone cancer. During her final months she sued John Mitchell for failure to keep up alimony payments. Then days before her death at age 57, she was awarded $36,000 in back alimony. Martha Mitchell died in New York City on May 31, 1976.

—CP

Mondale, Walter F(rederick)
(1928–   ) *member of the Senate*

Born on January 5, 1928, the son of a liberal church minister who was an admirer of Franklin Roosevelt, Walter Mondale graduated from the University of Minnesota in 1951 and served in the army during the Korean War. While in college he worked in HUBERT HUMPHREY's 1948 Senate campaign. He developed a close relationship with Humphrey, which continued throughout his career. Following graduation from the University of Minnesota law school in 1956, Mondale joined the law firm of Governor Orville Freeman, a Humphrey friend. Mondale ran Freeman's reelection campaign of 1958 and then served as special assistant to the state's attorney general. In 1960 Freeman appointed Mondale to complete the unexpired term of the resigning attorney general. In 1960 and 1962 Mondale won this office in his own right. When Hubert Humphrey became vice president in 1965, Mondale was appointed to complete his friend's term. In both 1966 and 1972 he won easy reelection victories.

Mondale compiled one of the most liberal records in the Senate. He supported President Johnson's Great Society legislation, voting for civil rights laws, the War on Poverty programs, and Medicare. Although he originally voted for the appropriations for Vietnam, Mondale soon questioned the war for moral reasons because it diverted funds from social programs. Although he disagreed with Humphrey on the war policies, he helped manage his mentor's losing bid for the presidency in 1968.

During the NIXON-FORD years Mondale emerged as one of the most powerful liberals in the Senate. He earned the highest ratings from the liberal Americans for Democratic Action. The farm lobby organizations also praised him for his work to help their constituency. The Mondale record included support for the continuation and expansion of anti-poverty programs in spite of Nixon and Ford vetoes. He voted for steeper corporate taxes, especially for the oil companies, supported a national no-fault insurance program, and opposed the federal loan to bail out the Lock-

heed Corp. During the 1973–74 recession Mondale lobbied for public works programs and cosponsored with Senator EDWARD KENNEDY (D-Mass.) a tax cut for the middle and working classes. Mondale also supported consumer and environmental legislation. In civil rights he voted against attempts to restrict the federal courts' power to force busing.

Mondale was a leading opponent of the Nixon and Ford defense and foreign policies. He voted for the Cooper-Church and McGovern-Hatfield amendments, both designed to limit the president's freedom to carry on the Vietnam War. Mondale opposed major defense spending programs such as the building of the B-1 bomber, the Trident submarine, and the antiballistic missile system.

Although Mondale was considered a leading liberal activist, he often tended to compromise rather than fight for his goals. In tax and fiscal legislation, for example, Mondale frequently yielded to Senator RUSSELL B. LONG (D-La.), the conservative chairman of the Senate Finance Committee. This refusal to fight to the bitter end for his programs played an important role in ending Mondale's abortive try for the 1976 Democratic presidential nomination. In late 1974 Mondale launched an exploratory campaign for the nomination. Throughout most of 1975 he toured the nation speaking at countless meetings and rallies, but he soon discovered that his public recognition level was still low. At a November 1975 news conference Mondale withdrew his name from contention. He said, "I do not have the overwhelming desire to be president, which is essential for the kind of campaign that is required. I admire those with the determination to do what is required to seek the presidency, but I have found that I am not among them." In his book *The Accountability of Power* (1976), Mondale reviewed his campaign, stressing how he resented the likelihood of having to be packaged by the media to be a viable candidate. He found this reduced the quality of campaigns and removed from the political process the most important reasons for running, namely the issues.

In July 1976 JIMMY CARTER, the Democratic presidential candidate, selected Mondale as his running mate. The former Georgia governor chose Mondale to win favor with the northern liberals, led by Humphrey, who remained skeptical of Carter. In addition, Carter found Mondale to be personally compatible, and he respected Mondale's grasp of the issues and his understanding of the workings of Congress. In the campaign Mondale blasted Gerald Ford's economic policies, which he believed produced unemployment. He raised the issue of the Nixon pardon and condemned HENRY KISSINGER's diplomacy as secretive, counterproductive, and immoral. In his historic debate with his rival, Senator ROBERT DOLE (R-Kan.), Mondale successfully maneuvered Dole to convey the image of a belligerent, insensitive conservative who ignored the needs of the common man. Pollsters believed Mondale's performance in this debate, as well as his anti-Ford campaign, helped Carter win the close victory.

In 1980 Carter and Mondale were defeated in their bid for reelection by RONALD REAGAN and GEORGE H. W. BUSH. Following the 1980 defeat Mondale immediately began to plan for his own presidential run. In 1984 he was chosen as the nominee of the Democratic Party and distinguished his candidacy by choosing Geraldine Ferraro of New York as his running mate—the first female candidate for the vice presidency from either of the two major parties. Running again against Reagan in a time of prosperity, Mondale's effort was doomed to failure; Mondale won only 13 electoral votes to Reagan's 525. From 1987 to 1993 Mondale practiced law in Minnesota and was a distinguished university fellow at the Hubert H. Humphrey Institute of Public Affairs at the University of Minnesota. In 1993 President Bill Clinton chose Mondale as ambassador to Japan, a post Mondale filled until 1997. In 2002 he ran unsuccessfully for his old Senate seat from Minnesota (Mondale replaced incumbent Paul Wellstone, who had died in a plane crash, on the ballot just 11 days before the election). He continues to practice law in Minneapolis.

—JB and JRG

Montoya, Joseph
(1915–1979) *member of the Senate*

Born on September 24, 1915, the son of a New Mexico county sheriff, Montoya graduated from Georgetown University in 1938. He served in the state legislature and was lieutenant governor before being elected to the U.S. House of Representatives in 1957. He won a seat as a Democrat in the Senate in 1964. In the upper house Montoya supported the Johnson administration's Great Society programs. He was especially concerned with poverty programs because his state had a high percentage of poor Mexican Americans and Native Americans. But because New Mexico's wealthy, conservative landowners, livestock dealers, and mining operators—known as "Little Texans"—were also a major political force, Montoya paid close attention to their needs as well. In foreign affairs Montoya was originally a supporter of the Vietnam War but broke with the administration in 1967.

During the NIXON-FORD years Montoya continued to press for legislation to assist the poor of his state. A strong defender of the Office of Economic Opportunity and manpower training programs, Montoya supported increasing the minimum wage, extending unemployment insurance to migrant workers, and establishing special programs to assist Spanish-speaking Americans and Native Americans. Montoya was the floor manager of the unsuccessful 1972 bill attempting to establish a Native American development commission. Montoya also proposed creating a cabinet-level commission on opportunities for Spanish-speaking people. Concerned with the elderly, Montoya cosponsored a bill that would have provided a 100 percent rebate for prescription drugs covered by Medicare.

Montoya also lobbied for consumer interests. He joined in proposing legislation to ensure truth in advertising, fair packaging, and proper labeling of poisonous substances. Montoya introduced legislation to establish a consumer protection agency that would have been independent from the Department of Health, Education, and Welfare. On the Vietnam issue Montoya voted for the Cooper-Church and McGovern-Hatfield Amendments to end the war.

The administration targeted Montoya as one of the leading Democrats to defeat in 1970. Republican money and personnel assisted his conservative opponent, Anderson Carter, a wealthy cattle rancher and oilman who maintained that Montoya was ignoring the interests of the Little Texans. In the campaign Montoya stressed that he represented all of New Mexico's interests, not only those of the poor. When speaking to the state's conservative farmers, Montoya cited his record of opposing the reduction of a ceiling placed on price supports. He also reminded them that he had opposed the nomination of EARL BUTZ, who, he asserted, was an enemy of the family farm. Montoya narrowly won the election with 52.3 percent of the vote.

Senator Montoya was named to the Watergate panel in January 1973. During the early months of the probe, Montoya's skilled interrogation of JOHN DEAN and JOHN MITCHELL led to the development of evidence that President Nixon had known of the Watergate cover-up. As Nixon became increasingly embroiled in the controversy, Montoya managed a bill requiring the president to pay his own legal expenses. After Nixon's resignation he opposed large government grants to help the former president through the transition. Montoya died in Washington, D.C., in June 1979.

—JB

Moorer, Thomas H(inman)
(1912–2004) *chief of naval operations; chairman, Joint Chiefs of Staff*

Thomas H. Moorer was born on February 9, 1912, in Mt. Willing, Alaska. Moorer graduated from the U.S. Naval Academy in 1933. After two years of service as a gunnery officer, he took flight training and received his wings in July 1936. During World War II he saw action in both the Pacific and Atlantic theaters. After the war Moorer attended the Naval War College in Newport, Rhode Island. He took command in 1962 of the Seventh Fleet. In June 1964 Moorer was made a full admiral and named commander in chief of the Pacific Fleet.

In April 1965 Moorer took charge of the allied naval command of the North Atlantic Treaty Organization (NATO). At the same time he became commander of all U.S. forces in the Atlantic. Later that month, with civil war erupting in the Dominican Republic, he directed the U.S. troops sent to the Caribbean nation to restore calm. U.S. forces under Moorer's supervision remained in the Dominican Republic until September.

Johnson appointed Moorer chief of naval operations in August 1967. In that role he served concomitantly as the navy representative on the Joint Chiefs of Staff. Moorer strongly supported the administration's Vietnam War effort. Testifying that summer before the Senate, he argued that only heavier bombing of North Vietnam would force it to the conference table.

President NIXON reappointed Moorer chief of naval operations in June 1969. To counter the growing presence of the Soviet Navy, Moorer worked for the modernization of aging U.S. naval forces and promoted the steady, yearly acquisition of new ships for the fleet. An advocate of the aircraft carrier as a crucial component of U.S. defense strategy throughout his career, he instituted construction of a new phase of quiet, fast nuclear submarines. Pointing to the ongoing dramatic Soviet military buildup, Moorer warned that American indifference to the Soviet threat could lead to the United States being surpassed as a world power.

In April 1970 Nixon named Moorer to succeed General EARLE G. WHEELER as chairman of the Joint Chiefs of Staff. At the time the Nixon administration was involved in ordering U.S. forces to attack Communist sanctuaries along the South Vietnamese border in Cambodia. Moorer helped direct the operation and participated in briefing Nixon on its progress at the end of May. In February 1971 Moorer backed the decision for the U.S. command in Vietnam to provide tactical support for the incursions by South Vietnamese troops into Laos to cut the Ho Chi Minh Trail.

In keeping with the Nixon administration's policy of winding down the war, by 1972 the American military presence in Vietnam stood at 69,000 servicemen. In April North Vietnamese forces launched a major offensive against South Vietnam. Moorer agreed with Nixon's decision to resume bombing North Vietnam, and he orchestrated the mining of the harbors at Hanoi and Haiphong. He was given the responsibility for the military success of the B-52 bombing of the two cities ordered by Nixon in December 1972.

In his role as chairman of the Joint Chiefs, Moorer was one of the president's top assistants in national security and foreign affairs. In September 1970 Moorer was among the high-level officials meeting informally to advise Nixon on the crisis in Jordan precipitated by the civil war between King Hussein and his army and Palestinian guerrillas. In December of the following year, was broke out between India and Pakistan. After deliberation with his chief advisers, Nixon authorized Moorer to dispatch a task force of eight ships from Vietnam to the Bay of Bengal. While U.S. policy recognized the inevitability of an independent East Pakistan, or Bangladesh, the administration made the move to guarantee the defense of West Pakistan.

Moorer appeared before the House Armed Services Committee in March 1971 to express concern over the accelerated development of Soviet missiles. He reiterated his worry that the United States in five years could find itself "in a position of overall strategic inferiority." A year later Moorer told the same committee that the emergence of China as a nuclear power meant that the United States had to reassess its military strategies regarding nuclear warfare.

Moorer told the Senate Armed Services Committee in June 1972 that he endorsed the first set of Strategic Arms Limitation Talks (SALT) accords so long as the United States continued to press forward with programs designed to protect its national security. He said the Joint Chiefs believed a number of assurances were needed to preserve U.S. security under the arms agreements. He identified them as improvement in U.S. intelligence capabilities, continued modernization programs as allowed by the agreements, and a vigorous research and development program to maintain the U.S. lead in weapons technology.

Nixon reappointed Moorer to another two-year tour of duty as chairman of the Joint Chiefs in July 1972. In September General John D. Lavelle told a Senate Armed Services Committee investigation that he had received permission from Moorer and General CREIGHTON W. ABRAMS, commander of U.S. forces in

Vietnam, for a series of unauthorized air raids against North Vietnam in late 1971 and early 1972. Both officers denied knowing that the raids violated the rules of engagement in effect at the time. The committee later ruled that Lavelle had acted on his own without authority in ordering the raids.

The same committee a year later cleared Moorer of charges that he had engaged in military spying on the White House. The committee found that he was not involved in the unauthorized transfer of secret documents from the National Security Council to the Pentagon by two White House liaison officers in 1971. Moorer acknowledged receipt of the documents but thought that they had been sent to him through proper channels.

When the October 1973 Yom Kippur War broke out in the Mideast, Moorer took part in the decision to airlift U.S. military supplies to Israel. In response to the Soviet intention to intervene in the fighting, Moorer carried out Nixon's order to put all U.S. armed forces on a military alert. After the alert the Soviet Union, in diplomatic correspondence, withdrew its threat of intervention.

Moorer resigned as chairman of the Joint Chiefs in July 1974 and retired from the navy. Nixon named General GEORGE S. BROWN to succeed him. In retirement Moorer continued to speak out about the growth of the Soviet military. He died in 2004.

—SF

Morton, Rogers C(lark) B(allard)
(1914–1979) *member of the House of Representatives; chairman, Republican National Committee; secretary of the interior; secretary of commerce*

Born on September 19, 1914, a descendant of the American Revolutionary leader General George Rogers Clark, Morton grew up in Ken-

tucky, where his wealthy and prominent family had long been active in Republican politics. After graduating from Yale in 1937, Morton joined the family milling and flour processing firm. When the firm merged with the Pillsbury Co. in 1951, Morton became a vice president of Pillsbury and later director of its executive committee, a position he held until 1971.

In the early 1950s Morton moved his family to a large farm in Maryland. He was elected U.S. representative from Maryland's predominantly Democratic first district in 1962. Morton was reelected to the House four times by considerable margins. His voting record reflected the conservatism of his Maryland district and a strict adherence to Republican policies.

Morton served as RICHARD NIXON's floor manager at the 1968 Republican National Convention and made the nominating speech for SPIRO T. AGNEW, Nixon's choice for vice president. Shortly after his inauguration President Nixon chose the voluble Morton to be chairman of the Republican National Committee (RNC). Morton kept his House seat and a spot on the powerful House Ways and Means Committee while serving as party chairman without salary.

On April 14, 1969, Morton vowed to wage a campaign on behalf of President Nixon's proposal for a Safeguard antiballistic missile system (ABM). Morton's support of the ABM drew criticism both from Democrats and from Republicans who viewed his plan as a "loyalty test." When President Nixon tacitly rebuked Morton at a press conference, the new RNC chairman backed down. He nevertheless continued to closely support the president's policies.

After a poor Republican showing in the 1970 elections, Morton resigned the RNC chairmanship. In late November 1970 President Nixon designated him to replace WALTER J. HICKEL as secretary of the interior. Hickel, a former governor of Alaska, had become a concerned environmentalist and an outspoken opponent of Nixon's Vietnam policies. Nixon counted upon Morton, a good "team player," to support administration policies. Despite his stated commitment to the environment, opponents pointed to Morton's past indifference to ecological issues and low rating by the League of Conservation Voters while in Congress. They feared his political background might make him soft on industrial polluters.

Although Morton made efforts to strengthen and consolidate the Interior Department and to deal with important environmental problems, he failed to establish coherent national energy and land use policies. The administration ignored Morton's 1971 recommendation to establish a Department of Natural Resources. New Interior offices of conservation, energy data, and fuel allocation created by Morton were absorbed in 1973 by the Federal Energy Administration.

A major controversy during Morton's tenure at the department centered on the proposed construction of an 800-mile oil pipeline across Alaska. Morton announced in early 1971 that he was "a long way" from approving the trans-Alaskan pipeline. He promised that the decision to build the pipeline would be determined by national energy needs and that possible environmental damage and the rights of native Alaskans would be considered. Environmentalists attempted to block approval of the Alaskan route with a series of environmental suits beginning in 1970.

In the spring of 1972, with the nation facing what he described as a "fuel and power crisis," Morton endorsed an increase in the price of natural gas to spur exploration for new gas supplies. He warned of the possible need for gasoline rationing as the United States depleted its oil reserves. Critics accused the Nixon administration of deliberately developing an oil shortage to gain support for fuel price increases and to lessen opposition to the trans-Alaskan oil pipeline.

When Morton approved the Alaskan pipeline route in May 1972, environmental groups accused him of bowing to oil interests, which reportedly had invested more than $2 billion in the project, and continued to block work on the pipeline through legal maneuvers. A bill authorizing the pipeline's construction with appropriate environmental safeguards was approved by Congress on November 13, 1973. When Morton issued the long-awaited construction permit in January 1974, he commented that the project was the first required to comply with strict environmental and technical conditions.

Morton served as a Nixon spokesman during the 1972 presidential campaign. He charged Democratic presidential candidate Senator GEORGE MCGOVERN of South Dakota with a "lack of concern" for environmental issues and attacked McGovern's peace plan for Southeast Asia. Morton remained secretary of the interior through the beginning of Nixon's second term.

Following Nixon's resignation in August 1974, President GERALD FORD appointed Morton to a four-man committee to help oversee the administration transition. A Ford ally since the early 1960s, Morton served as a top adviser to the new president on a variety of subjects. In late August 1974 Morton delivered Ford's first environmental policy message, stressing that the energy crisis had demonstrated the need for more coal mining, offshore oil exploration, oil shale development, and nuclear power plant construction despite possible environmental damage. Morton was named chairman of the new Energy Resources Council in 1974, a post he retained after his transfer from Interior to secretary of commerce in March 1975. The transfer took place amid speculation that as commerce secretary Morton would be in a better position to solicit business support for Ford's 1976 reelection campaign.

As secretary of commerce Morton resisted the demands of the House Commerce Committee's Subcommittee on Investigations for a list of U.S. firms participating in the Arab boycott of Israel. Subcommittee members accused Morton of shielding private corporations that were violating U.S. policy and voted in November 1975 to cite him for contempt of Congress. On December 8 Morton gave the subcommittee the list of U.S. firms that had reported being asked to participate in the Arab boycott. A proponent of détente, Morton opposed the Trade Act of 1974, which denied "most favored nation" trade status to the Soviets until the easing of emigration restrictions on Jews. Morton advocated a return to President Nixon's 1972 trade agreement with the Soviets, calling for unconditional elimination of discriminatory trade restrictions on Soviet-bloc nations.

When Morton resigned as commerce secretary in January 1976, Ford designated him a cabinet-rank counselor to the president on economic and domestic policy matters. Morton served as Ford's campaign chairman prior to the 1976 Republican National Convention. Following Ford's nomination Morton became chairman of the Ford presidential campaign committee but resigned a few weeks later to form a steering committee to promote party unity. After Ford's defeat in November 1976, Morton retired to his farm near Easton, Maryland, and concentrated on boat-building. He died in 1979.

—DAE

Moynihan, Daniel Patrick

(1927–2003) *assistant to the president for urban affairs; counselor to the president; U.S. permanent representative to the United Nations*

Born on March 16, 1927, and raised in Manhattan under difficult financial conditions, Moynihan served in the army during World War II and received a B.A. from Tufts University in 1948. He earned an M.A. from Tuft's Fletcher School of Law and Diplomacy in 1949. Later he did postgraduate work at the London School of Economics. During the 1950s he was assistant and later acting secretary to New York governor W. Averell Harriman. From 1958 to 1960 he was secretary of the public affairs committee of the New York state Democratic Party.

During the 1960 presidential campaign Moynihan wrote position papers on urban affairs for John F. Kennedy. After Kennedy's election Moynihan was appointed special assistant to the secretary of labor, and in March 1963 he was promoted to assistant secretary of labor for policy planning and research.

Moynihan became nationally known in March 1965 when he, Paul Barton, and Ellen Broderick released a Labor Department study called *The Negro Family: The Case for National Action.* Known as the Moynihan Report, this study suggested that the poverty and social problems experienced within the black community were fundamentally related to a deterioration of the black family. The report angered many civil rights leaders who felt that it came close to asserting that the black way of life in America was inherently debilitating. In June 1966 Moynihan was named director of the Harvard-Massachusetts Institute of Technology Joint Center for Urban Studies.

Because Moynihan was widely associated with the liberal wing of the Democratic Party, his colleagues were surprised when in December 1968 he accepted a position in the upcoming NIXON administration as assistant to the president for urban affairs. He also served as the executive secretary of the cabinet-level Urban Affairs Council. Nixon had thought of appointing Moynihan secretary of labor, but the idea was vetoed by GEORGE MEANY, who felt Moynihan did not have the necessary administrative experience.

Moynihan quickly became a Nixon favorite on the White House staff, able to spend long hours in private with the president, a privilege accorded to only a select few. Moynihan charmed the president with loyalty to the administration and a witty, flamboyant speaking style. Moynihan's wry memorandums became a special pleasure for Nixon to read. During his first year at the White House, Moynihan had an important influence on the president, who adopted many of his proposals.

Most prominent among Nixon's domestic programs was welfare reform, of which Moynihan was the chief architect. Moynihan's ideas on welfare reform had been enumerated in a 1967 background study on social welfare called *The Crisis in Welfare*. Moynihan endorsed a form of income maintenance that included children's allowances—fixed sums of cash paid to families on welfare for each child. Moynihan stressed to Nixon the political importance of keeping continuity with Great Society programs. To disarm the liberal Democrats, Nixon needed to enact domestic reform. Moynihan convinced Nixon that as a conservative the president would be able to pass reform legislation that a liberal "wouldn't dare to propose" and suggested that reform could win him support of elements normally allied to the Democratic Party. He persuaded Nixon that substituting cash payments for bureaucratic services was a conservative idea.

On February 2, 1969, Moynihan defended his plan on television: "I feel the problem of the poor people is they don't have enough money and I would sort of put my faith in any effort that put more resources into the hands of those that don't have them . . . Cold cash—it's a surprisingly good cure for a lot of social ills." Yet he had to admit that the American public was unlikely to accept the concept of family allowance payments. At an August 6, 1969, cabinet meeting at Camp David, the president made it clear that after several months of cabinet debate, he had decided to back the welfare program Moynihan had been pushing. The president announced the new program, called the Family Assistance Program (FAP), during a televised national address on August 9.

FAP left the House Ways and Means Committee in February 1970 in an almost unaltered form and was passed by the House in April. But criticism and pressure from liberals and conservatives mounted, and hope for passage of the bill through the Senate faded. In his *Memoirs* Nixon quotes Moynihan as writing in July 1970 that Republicans in the Senate were not resisting efforts to kill FAP and that "increasingly the Democrats see an opportunity to deny you this epic victory and at the same time blame you for the defeat." The Senate Finance Committee voted down the bill in November 1970. When the House again passed the FAP bill, it returned to the Finance Committee, where it was stalled. By 1971 Nixon no longer believed in "the political timing" of the welfare reform proposal, and in the face of the 1972 campaign election, he decided to drop support for the bill. It subsequently died in the Finance Committee as the 91st Congress ended.

Moynihan's influence declined after 1969, as JOHN EHRLICHMAN took control of the Nixon staff and cut off easy access to the president. The Urban Affairs Council was dissolved, and Moynihan was reappointed to the new position of counselor to the president, with cabinet rank. But Moynihan thereafter became an insignificant factor in policy making.

In March 1970 Moynihan was the object of a barrage of criticism when a memorandum he had sent to the president was leaked to the press. In the memo Moynihan offered a general assessment of the position of blacks at the end of the first year of the administration "and of the decade in which their position [had] been the central domestic political issue." Moynihan wrote that "the time may have come when the issue of race could benefit from a period of benign neglect." He countered adverse criticism by contending that within its context the controversial phrase meant that outspoken administration officials, such as Vice President SPIRO T. AGNEW, should cease providing "opportunities for martyrdom, heroics, histrionics, or whatever" to radicals, "hysterics, paranoids, and boodlers" on both ends of the political spectrum. He said he did not mean, as many critics claimed, to recommend neglect of the racial problems besetting the United States.

At the end of 1970 Moynihan returned to a teaching post at Harvard. In 1973 he again left academia, accepting an appointment as ambassador to India, where he remained until May 1975, when President GERALD FORD named Moynihan chief U.S. representative to the United Nations. Moynihan lost no time in establishing himself as a highly assertive and aggressive figure in the United Nation. On October 3 he denounced Uganda president Idi Amin as a "racist murderer" at an address to an AFL-CIO convention in San Francisco. After the United Nation General Assembly passed a resolution declaring Zionism "a form of racism and racial discrimination," Moynihan praised the countries who had voted against the resolution and denounced the assembly's Social, Humanitarian, and Cultural Committee, which had adopted the resolution, saying, "You have degraded this world organization." Drawing increasingly hostile criticism from developing countries' representatives, Moynihan said in December that the General Assembly was "becoming a theater of the absurd," adopting reports "riddled with untruths." After a highly publicized effort to break up an "anti-American" voting bloc at the United Nation, which led to a conflict with the State Department, Moynihan resigned his post at the United Nation in February 1976 to return to Harvard in order to maintain his tenure.

In 1976 Moynihan was elected to the U.S. Senate from New York State, where he served four terms until his retirement in 2001. Throughout his tenure as senator, Moynihan concentrated on domestic issues, particularly welfare reform during the RONALD REAGAN years, and reform of the Social Security system under GEORGE H. W. BUSH and Clinton. While in the Senate, Moynihan continued to write and publish; among his books were *Family and Nation* (1986), *Came the Revolution* (1988), *On the Law of Nations* (1990), and *Secrecy* (1998). Moynihan was replaced in the Senate by Hillary Rodham Clinton. In the years following his retirement from politics he taught at the Maxwell School of Citizenship and Public Affairs at Syracuse University. He died in March 2003 of complications following an emergency appendectomy.

—MLB

Mundt, Karl E(rnst)
(1900–1974) *member of the Senate*

Born on June 3, 1900, the son of Dakota pioneers, Karl Mundt taught speech and sold real estate before his election to the U.S. House in 1938. A virulent anticommunist, Mundt first achieved nationwide recognition in 1948 as acting chairman of the House Un-American Activities Committee investigation of Alger Hiss and as the cosponsor of legislation requiring the registration of communist groups and their officers. Mundt was elected to the Senate in 1948 as a Republican. He chaired the Army-McCarthy hearings and later voted against the Senate censure of Senator Joseph R. McCarthy (R-Wis.). In the early 1960s Mundt was among the first to call for controls on nuclear weapons. Although he staunchly reflected the conservative views of his home state of South Dakota, Mundt supported the farm subsidy, conservation, and civil rights measures of the

Johnson era. In 1967 he led Senate resistance to the ratification of the U.S.-Soviet treaty establishing new consulates on the grounds that the FBI's counterespionage work would be hampered by the treaty's diplomatic immunity provisions.

While he remained active, Mundt continued to be a firm supporter of the Vietnam War. In 1969 the Senate passed a nonbinding resolution expressing its opposition to the commitment of U.S. troops to foreign lands without congressional approval. Mundt introduced a substitute resolution, making exceptions if the United States faced a direct attack or if American citizens or property were endangered, but critics said the measure contained too many loopholes and defeated it.

In 1969 Mundt suffered a debilitating stroke that left him partially paralyzed and prevented him from appearing in the Senate. Over the next two years he occasionally voted by proxy but refused to resign. Finally in 1972 the Senate, in the first major blow to the Old Guard and the rigid seniority system, voted to relieve Mundt of his posts as ranking Republican on the Government Operations Committee and second-ranking member of the Foreign Relations and Appropriations committees. Mundt died in Washington, D.C., in August 1974.

—FLM

Muskie, Edmund (Sixtus)
(1914–1996) *member of the Senate*

Born on March 28, 1914, the son of a Polish emigrant tailor, Muskie grew up in Rumford, Maine. He earned his B.A. degree at Bates College in 1936 and law degree at Cornell University in 1939. His law career was interrupted by naval service during World War II. After the war Muskie served two terms in the state legislature before becoming Maine's first

Democratic governor in 1954. In 1958 Muskie became the first popularly elected Democratic senator in the state's history. He was reelected in 1964, 1970, and 1976.

During Kennedy's administration Muskie earned a reputation as an expert at formulating workable legislation and mobilizing support for it. Through the Johnson administration Muskie gained recognition for his support of environmental and Great Society programs. He received national prominence as the 1968 Democratic vice presidential candidate.

Muskie continued to concentrate on environmental issues during the 1970s. He was a driving force behind the National Air Quality Act, which called for a pollution-free automobile engine by 1985 and established national air quality standards for 10 major contaminants. He criticized President NIXON's 1973 suspension of air pollution emission standards as an answer to the fuel shortage. The Maine legislator played a major role in the design and congressional passage of water quality acts in 1965 and 1966, and he continued this work after 1968. His Subcommittee on Air and Water Pollution was largely responsible for the 1970 Water Pollution Act, which tightened controls on oil and sewage discharge by vessels and mines and established controls of thermal pollution from atomic power plants. Amendments to the act in 1971 set standards to maintain the natural chemical, physical, and biological integrity of the nation's waters and called for an end to discharging pollutants into navigable waters by 1985. He also introduced the 1971 Ocean Dumping Act, which required permits from the Environmental Protection Agency for the dumping of toxic and nontoxic wastes in the oceans and Great Lakes. Muskie also advocated use of tax incentives to encourage industry to assume their responsibility for pollution control.

Muskie continued to support federal aid to education and increased Social Security benefits.

He pressed for urban reform, pointing out that social disintegration caused by lack of jobs and by poor education, housing, and health care remained the fundamental needs of poverty-stricken Americans. He called for an end to the supersonic transport system (SST), space exploration, and atomic energy research and the utilization of those funds for the social benefit of the American poor. He introduced his own Revenue Sharing Act in 1971 and voted for that passed by Congress in 1972. He remained a champion of the small businessman and was a guiding force behind the 1970 Securities Investor Protection Act.

Following Senator EDWARD M. KENNEDY's (D-Mass.) accident on Chappaquiddick Island in July 1969, Muskie emerged as the front-runner for the Democratic Party's 1972 presidential nomination, a position he maintained through 1971. He announced his candidacy officially on January 4, 1972, attacking the Nixon administration for continued inflation and high unemployment and charging the administration with ignoring the nation's social ills. After winning only two state primaries, but not convincingly, Muskie withdrew from the race in May 1972. Analysts explained that because Muskie was the party's early front-runner, his staff became overconfident and conducted a cautious and vague campaign. Also, while his opponents selected primaries they were most likely to win, Muskie entered all, taxing him physically and financially. It was later learned that Muskie also was the focus of a "dirty tricks" campaign instituted by the White House.

Muskie introduced the 1972 Truth in Government Act, which created an independent board authorized to lift secrecy labels from government documents without damaging national security. Believing that a democracy works best when the people have all the information national security permits, Muskie voted for the 1974 changes in the Freedom of Information Act.

Vice presidential campaign poster for Edmund Muskie, 1968 *(Library of Congress)*

Government taxation and finance policies also concerned the Maine legislator. In February 1973 he introduced a bill to amend the tax code with respect to legislative activity by certain tax-exempt organizations. That March he proposed legislation to reform state property taxes by relieving encumbrances on the poor and elderly. He sponsored the 1973 Tax Reform Act, which altered federal income, estate, and gift tax laws, worked for the 1974 Congressional Budget and Impoundment Act, and subsequently became chairman of the new Senate Budget Committee. In April 1975 he defended the committee's $365 billion budget recommendations before the full Senate. Muskie justified the dollars for social services as indispensable and the defense cuts as necessary and projected a $70 billion deficit as essential to help weather the nation through its recession.

In the mid-1960s Muskie publicly supported the administration's Vietnam policy, although privately he took a more "dovish" position. He opposed the antiwar platform of the 1968 Democratic National Convention. After returning to Congress in 1969, Muskie described the American experience in Southeast Asia as a tragedy. Critical of President Nixon's refusal to quickly end the fighting by 1972, Muskie proposed his own peace plan, which called for setting a firm date for U.S. troop withdrawal in return for all American POWs. In 1973 he served as Senate floor manager of the War Powers Act, which passed over a presidential veto. The act more clearly defined presidential and congressional authority in war-making decisions. A critic of the ever-expanding weapons systems, Muskie opposed President Nixon's ABM-Safeguard system in 1969 and approved U.S.-Soviet arms limitation agreements. He opposed creation of an all-volunteer army and instead suggested corrections in the current system. Muskie urged that uniform codes be established for all draft boards to follow and that all men be selected by lottery at age 19 and given several options to choose from, including the military and other national service groups such as the Peace Corps and VISTA.

In January 1976 the Democratic Party selected Muskie as its spokesman to respond to President FORD's State of the Union address. Muskie described Ford's proposed budget as "penny-wise and pound foolish" and designed to maintain a 7 percent unemployment rate. He also called for national energy, environment, and food policies. Late in 1976 Muskie was considered as the possible vice presidential running mate for JIMMY CARTER but was dropped in favor of Senator WALTER MONDALE (D-Minn.). Maine voters returned Muskie to the Senate for a fourth term in November 1976. In 1980 Muskie resigned from the Senate to become President Jimmy Carter's secretary of state, a position he filled until 1981. In January 1981 he was awarded the Presidential Medal of Freedom. He served as a member of the presidential commission investigating the Iran-contra scandal in 1987. He died of heart failure in March 1996.

—TML

N

Nader, Ralph

(1934–) *consumer activist*

The youngest of four children, Ralph Nader was born on February 27, 1934, into a home where political and social affairs were the stuff of dinnertime conversation. His father ran a restaurant and bakery and was heavily involved in community issues. In 1955 Nader graduated from Princeton. He entered Harvard Law School that fall. Graduating in the spring of 1958, Nader served briefly in the army before returning to Connecticut to set up a law practice. During the ensuing years Nader traveled extensively, writing articles for several national magazines and pleading the case for safer motor vehicles before state legislators and civic groups.

In April 1964 the Labor Department's Office of Planning and Research hired Nader to study the federal role in auto safety. He left in May 1965 to write the book *Unsafe at Any Speed: The Designed-in Dangers of the American Automobile*, published in November. It accused the motor industry of placing fashion over safety, singling out General Motors' (GM) Corvair as a serious example. Nader began to attract national attention, especially after he told a Senate subcommittee in March 1966 that GM had hired private detectives to inves-

tigate him. GM first denied, then admitted the charges, publicly apologizing to Nader. The National Traffic and Motor Vehicle Safety Act became law in September, and Nader was widely acknowledged as its principal booster. That fall he sued GM for $26 million, charging invasion of privacy.

In the summer of 1968 Nader assembled a group of student interns in Washington to aid him in a number of projects, principally a study of the effectiveness of the Federal Trade Commission (FTC). Dubbed "Nader's Raiders" by the press, they formed the nucleus for the Center for Study of Responsive Law, the first of several Nader-affiliated organizations that were created during the NIXON years and that transformed Nader's one-man crusade into a broad consumer advocacy apparatus.

The report on the FTC was released in January 1969. It accused the commission of "incompetence by the most modest standards and a lack of commitment to the regulatory mission . . ." and went on to state that FTC officials were "in collusion with business interests." Chairman Paul Rand Dixon was singled out for criticism, and his resignation was urged. The report created such controversy that President Nixon asked the American Bar Association (ABA) to organize an FTC study of its own.

In May Nader publicly endorsed the insurgent candidacy of JOSEPH "JOCK" YABLONSKI for the presidency of the United Mine Workers, a post then held by W. A. Tony Boyle. Nader was a staunch advocate of more stringent occupational safety standards for miners. Earlier in the year he had accused Boyle of "snuggling up to the coal operators," charging that he "neglected his responsibility" to the union members. In August Nader said that the Interior Department had suppressed a report on the harmful environmental effects of underground mining. He was one of the vocal supporters of the Coal Mine Health and Safety Act, which passed that year.

The FTC controversy flared again in September, after the American Bar Association released its study confirming substantially the "Nader's Raiders" report. Chairman Dixon defended the agency before a Senate hearing chaired by EDWARD KENNEDY and called Nader a publicity seeker. Dixon was eventually succeeded by Miles Kirkpatrick, leader of the ABA study.

The year 1970 marked further conflict between Nader and the auto industry. In January the New York state court of appeals ruled that Nader had valid grounds to sue GM, saying that he could sue for "defamation" and "intentional infliction of emotional distress." The following month Nader announced the beginning of "Campaign GM," an effort designed to encourage GM stockholders to influence the company's stance on pollution and safety standards. The largely unsuccessful effort was run by the recently formed Project on Corporate Responsibility, another Nader-affiliated consumer group.

Nader's Center for Responsive Law attracted some criticism when it attacked Senator EDMUND MUSKIE (D-Me.) in May, saying he had "failed the nation in the field of air pollution control." Many environmentalists considered Muskie one of their strongest allies in the

Senate and felt the accusation was unjustified. Muskie himself stated that he was working that year to strengthen the 1967 Air Control Act.

In June two new Nader organizations were established. The Center for Auto Safety, funded in part by Consumers Union, employed the services of three lawyers to monitor the National Highway Safety Bureau. The Public Interest Research Group (PIRG), described as the "action arm" of Nader's consumer conglomerate, was staffed by young lawyers who worked to counteract the influence of corporate lobbyists—in essence, a public-interest law firm. Early PIRG projects included a suit against the Federal Drug Administration for improved birth control pill warnings, an investigation of large corporations paying inadequate amounts of local property taxes, and the organization of "grassroots" opposition in West Virginia to three Union Carbide plants that were polluting the air. PIRG eventually developed a nationwide network of subsidiaries based on college campuses where they were funded through student activity fees. Other Nader groups conducted probes of the medical profession and of Congress.

Nader's long-standing legal battle with GM was settled out of court in August. GM agreed to pay Nader $425,000, while stressing that the settlement was not an admission of guilt but merely a way of ending the protracted court proceedings. Nader used the money to finance Campaign GM and PIRG projects.

Nader and three consumer groups in January 1972 filed a suit in Washington alleging that federal price supports for milk had been raised the previous year as a result of "political considerations." The suit contended that the increase had been granted in return for "promise and expectations of campaign contributions for the reelection campaign of Richard Nixon," offering as evidence the fact that Secretary of Agriculture CLIFFORD HARDIN had at first opposed the increase but reversed himself shortly after dairy interests donated funds to the Nixon organization. The suit touched off a major scandal that ultimately led to a number of indictments.

In January 1973 Nader and the Union of Concerned Scientists held a news conference in which they requested that the Atomic Energy Commission (AEC) impose a moratorium on the construction of new nuclear power plants "until all safety-related issues are resolved." Nader said he would pursue the issue in Congress, the courts, and among electric company stockholders and charged that the AEC was deliberately concealing what he claimed was the belief held by most of the commission's scientists that safety problems might exist. In May he petitioned a federal court in conjunction with Friends of the Earth, seeking the shutdown of 20 nuclear plants because of safety hazards and charging the AEC with a "gross breach of health and safety obligations." The suit was eventually dismissed.

Nader was an early and outspoken critic of the Nixon administration's role in the growing Watergate scandal. In May 1973 he called for the naming of a special prosecutor to investigate the affair. In August he criticized a speech made by the president in defense against charges that he was involved in the scandal, calling the speech a "cowardly and evasive performance." When Nixon fired Watergate special prosecutor ARCHIBALD COX in October, Nader bitterly attacked the action, saying, "Every citizen in this land must strive to reclaim the rule of law which this tyrant has been destroying month by month, strand by strand."

President FORD also was a target of Nader action. In July 1975 Nader announced his opposition to Ford's plan to decontrol domestic oil prices, asserting that it would cost the average family over $900 a year. In November he attacked Ford's consumer policies as "a transparent and phony attempt to mislead the public into thinking that the administration's consumer activities are anything more than a window-dressing deception."

Nader had far kinder words the following year for Ford's opponent in the general election, former Georgia governor JIMMY CARTER. In August 1976 Nader visited Carter in Plains, Georgia, and lauded the candidate as more "admirable" than any presidential prospect in "decades." But once Carter was in the White House, Nader was frequently critical of what he saw as the ineffectiveness of many Carter appointees.

In 1980 Nader resigned as the head of Public Citizen and entered the political arena. In 1992 Nader organized a "None of the Above" campaign in the New Hampshire primary; he ended up garnering a few thousand votes in his own name. In both 1996 and 2000 Nader was the nominee of the Green Party for the presidency. In 1996 he won less than 1 percent of the total vote, refusing to raise or spend more than $5,000 on his total campaign. In 2000, however, Nader's candidacy was instrumental in deciding the disputed election. Overall, Nader received 2.9 million votes (about 2.7 percent of the total votes cast). However, his vote total in Florida exceeded the difference between Al Gore and George W. Bush. Thus, without his name being on the Florida ballot, Gore would have won the state and the presidency (assuming that the Nader votes would have gone to Gore). In 2004 he ran as an independent, winning the support in some states of several smaller parties.

—MQ and JRG

Nelson, Gaylord A(nton)
(1916–2005) *member of the Senate*

Born on June 4, 1916, a country doctor's son, Gaylord Nelson grew up in a small Wisconsin village. His great-grandfather helped found the

Republican Party in Wisconsin, and his father was a loyal supporter of Robert LaFollette's Progressive Party. After receiving his law degree from the University of Wisconsin in 1942, Nelson served in the army during World War II and ran unsuccessfully as a Republican for the state assembly in 1946. After moving to Madison, where he established a law practice, Nelson switched to the Democratic Party and was elected to the state senate in 1948, serving there for 10 years. In 1958 he became Wisconsin's first Democratic governor since 1932. As a state senator and later as governor, Nelson distinguished himself by his interest in tax reform, conservation, and public education.

Elected to the Senate in 1962, Nelson quickly aligned himself with the bloc of liberal Democrats. He was a strong supporter of Lyndon Johnson's Great Society legislation and, with Senator EDWARD M. KENNEDY, cosponsored the legislation creating the Teacher Corps. An early environmentalist, Nelson tried to have curbs placed against the industrial pollution of the Great Lakes, introduced legislation to ban DDT, and worked for legislation requiring industry to restore strip-mined land. Nelson was one of the earliest Senate opponents of the Vietnam War and consistently voted against supplemental appropriation bills to finance the war.

During the NIXON years Nelson emerged as the most visible Senate proponent of the burgeoning environmental movement. In a major Senate speech in January 1970, he charged that the environmental crisis had become a threat to the constitutional rights to life, liberty, and the pursuit of happiness. Using the example of the antiwar movement's national moratorium day, he suggested observation of an "Earth Day" to highlight environmental issues. The idea took hold, and on April 22 demonstrations were held across the country. The following year Nelson proposed an "Earth Week" and urged environmental groups to concentrate on local

issues of environmental deterioration. During April 1971 Nelson toured the country in support of Earth Week.

Nelson continued his campaign against the use of DDT and other dangerous pesticides. In 1969 he introduced legislation to ban the sale or shipment of DDT in the United States and to establish a National Commission on Pesticides to research their safety and effectiveness. Nelson was instrumental in persuading Secretary of Agriculture CLIFFORD HARDIN to impose in July 1969 a temporary ban on the use of DDT pending a study of its effects on human health. When the ban was lifted, however, environmental groups filed suit in federal court to curb the pesticide's use and in January 1971 received a favorable court ruling. Finally, on June 14, 1972, Environmental Protection Agency administrator WILLIAM D. RUCKELSHAUS announced a ban on almost all uses of DDT.

Nelson, meanwhile, with Senator PHILIP HART (D-Mich.), introduced a number of amendments to a pesticide control bill requested by the Nixon administration in 1971. They succeeded in obtaining a provision compelling manufacturers to register pesticides with the EPA even if there was no proof of substantial health hazards. They failed, however, to delete a provision that granted indemnities to manufacturers whose products were removed from the market, nor did they win approval of compulsory information disclosure by a manufacturer before registration of a pesticide. As signed by President Nixon on October 21, 1972, the Federal Environmental Pesticide Control Act was a compromise between industry and environmental interests.

A chairman of the Monopoly Subcommittee of the Senate Select Committee on Small Business, Nelson held extensive hearings on the health hazards of various drugs and on abuses by the drug industry. During 1970 he conducted a controversial inquiry into the dangers posed by birth control pills. Nelson widely publicized the growing body of medical evidence indicating that the pills had serious side effects, including an increased risk of death from blood-clotting disorders. He questioned whether manufacturers had deliberately underemphasized the pills' dangers. The hearings led the Food and Drug Administration to require manufacturers to include a safety warning in packages.

In 1971 Nelson held hearings on the effectiveness of over-the-counter nonprescription tranquilizers. With consumer advocate RALPH NADER he called for an easing of restrictions on the use of generic drugs as a way of reducing costs to the consumer and charged that the American Medical Association was fighting the move for monetary reasons. In 1975 Nelson released a government study on the dangers of "red dye 2," a coloring commonly used in foods and cosmetics, and urged the FDA to ban the dye.

Nelson led the ongoing fight by Senate liberals to preserve antipoverty programs against Nixon's efforts to dismantle them. In April 1969 Nixon announced the closing of 59 Job Corps centers and proposed that federal poverty programs be turned over to the states. In May a sense of the Senate resolution opposing the closings, which Nelson introduced, was defeated by one vote. As chairman of the Subcommittee on Employment, Manpower, and Poverty of the Labor and Public Welfare Committee, Nelson held hearings on legislation to extend the 1964 Economic Opportunity Act and was floor manager of the bill. Under his leadership a bill was reported extending the Office of Economic Opportunity (OEO) for two years, keeping OEO programs under federal control and earmarking funds for specific programs to avoid administrative scuttling. Nixon vetoed the bill in January 1970, and the House sustained the veto.

In 1971 Nelson sponsored a comprehensive child development provision in the OEO extension bill but again was unable to override

the president's veto. Unwilling to risk another confrontation with the president, Nelson engineered a compromise in 1972. Declaring that "Congress has gone the extra mile to meet the president's concerns," he won a three-year extension of the OEO in return for dropping the effort to create an independent legal services agency for the poor and for including his child development proposals in separate legislation. In September Nixon signed the three-year extension into law.

Controversy over the poverty program continued, however, when Nixon proposed in 1973 the abolishment of the OEO and the transfer of its functions to other agencies. The president's preoccupation with the Watergate affair prevented him from winning approval of the OEO's abolishment, and in 1974 Nelson successfully sponsored legislation creating the Community Services Administration, which gave the poverty programs the status of a permanent independent federal agency.

During the Nixon years Nelson continued his opposition to the Vietnam War. He consistently voted against military appropriations for the war, supported the 1970 Cooper-Church Amendment, and opposed the 1971 draft extension bill. In 1971 he introduced legislation to bar the use of draftees in combat operations without their consent, but the Senate rejected the proposal.

Nelson's outspoken opposition to Nixon's foreign and domestic policies won him a place on the infamous White House "enemies list." Nelson voted against confirmation of GERALD FORD as vice president in 1973 and condemned Ford's pardon of Nixon. In December 1974 Congress approved legislation introduced by Nelson to ensure the government's custody of the Nixon tapes and to make them available to the Watergate special prosecutor. That same month Nelson was one of only seven senators who opposed the confirmation of NELSON ROCKEFELLER as vice president.

In 1974 Nelson won reelection to a third Senate term, with 63 percent of the vote. In 1975 he became chairman of the Senate Select Committee on Small Business. In 1977 the Senate appointed him chairman of a special committee charged with formulating a code of ethics for that body.

In 1980 Nelson was defeated by Robert W. Kasten. He then went to a position at the Wilderness Society. In 1995 President Clinton awarded Nelson the Medal of Freedom. He died on July 3, 2005.

—JD

Nessen, Ron(ald Harold)
(1934–) *White House press secretary*

Raised in an upper-middle-class family in Washington, D.C., Nessen attended West Virginia's Shepard College and graduated from American University in 1956. Nessen worked at several jobs in journalism before joining the National Broadcasting Co. in 1962 as a Washington correspondent. He later reported on the Vietnam War and covered numerous foreign stories in such places as Borneo, Panama, Bolivia, and Nigeria.

In August 1973 Nessen, assigned to Washington, D.C., began covering Vice President SPIRO AGNEW's deepening conflict with federal prosecutors investigating charges that he had accepted bribes during his years as governor of Maryland. For two months Nessen reported on his research into Agnew's background and the investigation being launched by the Justice Department. Eventually Agnew subpoenaed Nessen and eight other reporters to reveal their sources of information into the federal inquiry. But the case never came to court in the wake of Agnew's sudden plea of nolo contendere to tax evasion charges and his subsequent resignation.

NBC decided to keep Nessen assigned to the vice presidency following RICHARD NIXON's selection of House minority leader GERALD FORD as Agnew's replacement. Gradually a friendly working relationship developed between the two men. When Nixon resigned from office in August 1974 and Gerald Ford became the new president, Ron Nessen was named NBC's White House correspondent. Following the resignation of JERALD TERHORST, Nessen became Ford's press secretary.

Intent on improving the bitter relationship with the press corps that marked the Watergate era, Nessen adopted an informal, give-and-take atmosphere at his daily briefings, sometimes beginning with a humorous anecdote. He sat in on numerous presidential policy meetings and often passed on direct quotes from these meetings to the press. He increased access to the president by arranging a greater number of press conferences and interviews with Ford and by permitting follow-up questions.

However, Nessen's relations with the press gradually deteriorated. In November Ford departed on a major tour of Asia, including a stop at Vladivostok to meet with Leonid Brezhnev and discuss strategic arms limitation. Nessen's handling of the press during the trip was widely criticized. Reporters complained that he was unavailable at crucial moments during the summit meeting, that they were unable to obtain advance copies of Ford's speeches, and that their questions frequently went unanswered. These was particular resentment of Nessen's attitude toward the reporters themselves, stemming partly from an offhand comment that the journalists were "dazzled" and "amazed" by the Ford-Brezhnev agreement (which was subsequently aborted). Nessen conceded his errors, but many observers felt that the Vladivostok conference had demonstrated that Nessen would in fact be a "salesman" for the new administration. Nessen himself believed that much of the criticism was due to lingering animosity and suspicion that existed between the press and the government during the Nixon years.

The disputes continued. In the early months of 1975, Nessen's credibility was called into question on a number of occasions. He denied Ford planned on dismissing JOHN SAWHILL from his federal energy post, even after the president had personally requested Sawhill's resignation. While Ford was attempting to develop a compromise on his energy policy, Nessen told reporters that no such compromise was being considered. As Nessen's relationship with his erstwhile colleagues deteriorated, the press room was sometimes the scene of heated exchanges.

Nessen remained on good terms with President Ford throughout his tenure but came into conflict with other members of the administration, such as Secretary of State HENRY KISSINGER. In the spring of 1975, as the military forces of the South Vietnamese government began to collapse, a Kissinger staff member told Nessen that "diplomatic initiatives" were under way. Nessen passed this information on to the press, only to discover that it was not true. It was the first of several clashes between the two over the journalistic versus the diplomatic uses of information. A political feud developed when Kissinger began to accuse Nessen of being the source of anti-Kissinger news leaks. The antagonism became public during a December presidential journey to the Far East, when Nessen labeled some reporters "patsies" for agreeing to change a pool report at Kissinger's request.

In January 1976 the National Press Club issued a study of White House press relations that was strongly critical of Nessen. Although it acknowledged his efforts to increase access to the president, the report went on to cite complaints of Nessen's "arrogance" and called his performance during Ford's China trip "the most inept . . . in modern times." Nessen reacted by saying, "I'm learning as I go along, and I still hope to earn their respect."

Following Ford's departure from the White House, Nessen remained in the public eye via his numerous writings and television appearances. In 1978 his memoirs of the Ford presidency, *It Sure Looks Different from the Inside*, were published. From 1980 to 1984 Nessen was the senior vice president for Marston Rothenberg Public Affairs, Inc., in Washington. From 1984 to the present he has served as a vice president for the Mutual Broadcastng System.

—MDQ

Nixon, Richard M(ilhous)
(1913–1994) *president of the United States*

Born on January 11, 1913, into a Quaker family of modest means, Richard Nixon grew up in Yorba Linda and Whittier, California. To supplement the family income, Nixon worked in his father's grocery store and held other jobs. He excelled as a student in public schools and received his B.A. from Whittier College in 1934. Nixon graduated from Duke University Law School in 1937. After rejecting a position in a New York City law firm and failing to receive an appointment as an FBI agent because of the bureau's limited budget, Nixon returned to Whittier to start his own practice. At the outset of World War II he worked for eight months in the Office of Price Administration (OPA); that experience forever left him distrustful of government bureaucracy. From 1942 to 1945 Nixon served as a noncombat navy officer in the South Pacific. Upon his return he won election to the House of Representatives as a Republican, his family's party. During his term in the House from 1947 to 1950, Nixon established a national reputation as an investigator of communist subversives in the federal government. That image helped to secure him election to the U.S. Senate in 1950.

From 1953 to 1960 Nixon served as vice president under Dwight D. Eisenhower. In that position Nixon assumed many of Eisenhower's obligations as leader of the Republican Party and represented the administration in many overseas trips. Nixon's actual role in shaping policy, however, was limited. He nevertheless endeared himself to party leaders and workers, who pressured Eisenhower into accepting Nixon as a running mate again in 1956. Four years later the GOP Convention nominated Nixon for president. He narrowly lost the election to Senator John F. Kennedy (D-Mass.)

During the 1960s Nixon's political fortunes fell sharply and then reversed to net him the presidency. In 1962 Nixon lost a bitter campaign for the California governorship. Despite his 1962 humiliation he enjoyed much influence as a prominent Republican leader at a time of intraparty divisions. Nixon helped to persuade GOP congressmen to support the 1963 nuclear test ban treaty as well as civil rights legislation in 1964 and 1965. After a lame attempt to win the 1964 Republican presidential nomination, Nixon campaigned diligently for the GOP standard-bearer, Senator BARRY GOLDWATER (R-Ariz.), a staunch conservative. Goldwater lost badly and in the process wrecked the prospects of younger Republican figures, preventing them from assuming vital roles in the national party hierarchy. In the ensuing leadership vacuum of 1965–66, Nixon reaffirmed his hold over party officials. He enjoyed a clear lead in the race for the 1968 Republican presidential nomination.

To ensure victory, however, Nixon had to overcome the candidacy of California governor RONALD REAGAN, who better represented the GOP's conservative wing and enjoyed great popularity among southern Republican delegates. Nixon frustrated Reagan's bid by successfully negotiating an alliance with Senator STROM THURMOND (R-S.C.), the de facto leader of the Republican South. Informally, Nixon promised Thurmond at a March meeting that he would not name a "liberal" Republican

as his vice presidential choice, that he would appoint conservatives to the Supreme Court, that he would deemphasize federal desegregation cases, and that he would increase military spending. Prior to his session with Thurmond, Nixon had been embracing most of these positions. But the Nixon-Thurmond alliance signaled the literal adoption of a southern strategy in which the GOP ignored black America and the urban Northeast in favor of the South and conservative West.

Nixon captured the Republican presidential nomination at the GOP's August convention and went on to win a close contest for the presidency. Upon winning the nomination he named Governor SPIRO T. AGNEW of Maryland, moderately acceptable to all wings of the party, as his running mate. Nixon tried to direct a lofty, statesmanlike campaign along the lines of his 1960 effort and that of Thomas E. Dewey in 1948. Because he was well ahead in the polls, he had every reason to follow this strategy. Soon, however, Nixon had to fight more aggressively against the Democratic nominee, Vice President HUBERT H. HUMPHREY. On election eve Nixon spoke of a U.S. "security gap" in defense weaponry and the need for "law and order" amid "the worst crime wave in American history." He also stressed, without revealing the particulars, a "secret plan" to end the war in Vietnam. In results nearly as close as those eight years earlier, Nixon edged out Humphrey and a third-party nominee, Alabama governor GEORGE C. WALLACE, with 43.4 percent of the total vote to 42.7 percent for Humphrey and 13.5 percent for Wallace. Congress, however, remained in Democratic control. Upon acknowledging his victory, Nixon promised a nation torn by racial strife and antiwar protest that his "great objective" would be "to bring the American people together." He echoed that theme in his January 1969 inaugural address. (See *The Kennedy Years* and *The Johnson Years* volumes.)

Nixon's first priority as president in 1969 was to shift U.S. strategy in Vietnam. The president ruled out speedy withdrawal in favor of a more calculated plan designed to preserve the regime of South Vietnamese president Nguyen Van Thieu, an anticommunist and ally of the United States. More importantly, Nixon and his chief foreign policy adviser, HENRY A. KISSINGER, considered it vital to bolster U.S. relations with other powers, large and small, by demonstrating America's firm stand against the threat of communist aggression. In early 1969 Nixon directed General CREIGHTON W. ABRAMS JR., commander of U.S. forces in South Vietnam, to limit offensive operations by American land forces so as to reduce casualties. Simultaneously the president ordered U.S. air forces to escalate bombings of North Vietnam after a vigorous offensive by the North Vietnamese in February.

Perhaps most significantly, the president and defense secretary MELVIN R. LAIRD formulated a policy of "Vietnamization" of the conflict, first suggested by Nixon during the spring of 1968. From 1969 to 1972 the United States gradually withdrew 555,000 armed personnel on the assumption that the well-trained and well-equipped South Vietnamese Army could take over America's vast military role. But the United States continued massive air strikes. Nixon assured Thieu at a June 1969 meeting on Midway Island that the United States would not abandon South Vietnam altogether.

At the same time, in an effort to cut off communist infiltration and supplies into Vietnam, Nixon widened the war. Beginning in 1969 he launched secret air bombing missions over the border provinces of the neutral nations of Laos and Cambodia, where the North Vietnamese maintained supply centers. In March 1970 the United States encouraged a civilian-military coup that brought about a new, pro-Western regime in Cambodia. This government soon lapsed into a corrupt and unpopular military dictatorship. On April 30, 1970, Nixon announced that U.S. and South Vietnamese troops had crossed into Cambodia to wipe out enemy sanctuaries. The president asserted that the short-term action was really "not an invasion of Cambodia" because the areas entered were under North Vietnamese control.

To quiet domestic criticism of the war, the president enunciated the "Nixon Doctrine," which promised that the United States would restrict its use of military intervention in future international crises. The president also reformed the Selective Service System to abolish discriminatory deferments and in 1973 ended the draft entirely. He assumed that the large reduction in the number of troops and the lower casualty rates in Vietnam combined with these other reforms would satisfy those segments of the American public concerned over escalation of the fighting between 1965 and 1968, "graphically demonstrating," Nixon recalled in his memoirs, "that we were beginning to wind down the war."

Despite the president's altered approach, the mass movement against the Vietnam conflict gathered greater force in 1969 and 1970. During that period colleges were torn apart by student protests of the war, while antiwar moratoriums, mass marches, and meetings were held in major U.S. cities. The greatest turbulence, however, followed Nixon's announcement of the U.S. incursion into Cambodia. Violence between police authorities and students culminated at Kent State University when Ohio National Guardsmen fired on a crowd and killed four unarmed students. The Kent State shootings rocked the nation, as did a similar incident at Jackson State College in Mississippi. Initially Nixon dubbed his young critics "bums." However, early on the morning of May 9 he made an attempt to placate students at the Lincoln Memorial who were preparing to march against the war. The gesture proved fruitless.

Nixon and his aides responded to mass protests by developing a "siege" mentality. Since the beginning of his administration, Nixon's assistants had regarded violent antiwar dissidents as potential revolutionaries. Secret data gathering by the federal government commenced against antiwar groups and eventually against less strident politicians and social groups critical of the administration's Vietnam strategy. Concerned that members of antiwar coalitions and later more moderate critics of the president might succeed in crippling Nixon's presidency and in forcing his ouster, White House aides requested government agencies to keep secret files on such individuals. Furthermore, as in the Johnson years, the Nixon foreign policy leadership worried that domestic protest of diplomatic determinations would hurt America's prestige abroad and that in the eyes of foreign leaders, the United States could not be relied on in crisis situations. Thus, Nixon, Kissinger, and other administration officials felt not only free but also obligated to adopt, out of concern for "national security," illegal or extralegal tactics against their more resolute and radical foes.

As a result of these fears, the White House in 1971 waged a campaign against DANIEL ELLSBERG, who had released *The Pentagon Papers* to the *New York Times*. *The Papers* disclosed official misrepresentation to the public about U.S. involvement in Vietnam and revealed confidential information about the formulation of American strategy there. In an extraordinary (though not unprecedented) move, the government secured a court order restraining the *Times* from continuing publication of *The Pentagon Papers*. Nixon secretly ordered staff members to portray Ellsberg as mentally ill. "Win PR [public relations], not just the court case," top White House aide JOHN D. EHRLICHMAN noted at the time. In September agents contracted by Ehrlichman and other assistants broke into the office of Ellsberg's psychiatrist. Nixon had tried to recruit FBI director J. EDGAR HOOVER to have the bureau handle the operation, but Hoover refused to cooperate in extralegal measures to prevent this and other leaks.

The character and background of Nixon's White House staff had a crippling effect on his presidency. From the start of his tenure, the president followed the pattern of Kennedy and Johnson by relying more on his personal White House advisers than members of his cabinet, which included some experienced and able political leaders. Nixon's trusted staff officers came from apolitical backgrounds. His press secretary, RONALD ZIEGLER, had worked for the California amusement park Disneyland. Nixon's chief of staff, H. R. HALDEMAN, had been in advertising, where "image" was highly prized. These aides had contempt for the professional politicians in the cabinet and Congress and succeeded in alienating many of them; the president's men continually betrayed an ignorance of what public officials could or could not do and the bounds that democracy imposed on such officials.

Initially Nixon assisted in partisan causes. He worked hard for GOP candidates in the 1970 elections in the hope of securing a Republican majority in the Senate. Again there were public and private White House efforts. To increase the campaign treasuries of individual Senate candidates, Nixon staff members "laundered" funds their way. Political donations were raised secretly by Nixon assistants, in violation of the law that required them to register publicly as a campaign committee, and then channeled to selected GOP Senate and House nominees. Publicly Nixon and Agnew freely associated campus dissidents and liberal Democrats with professional criminals. The tactic failed generally; the GOP gained two Senate seats, not a majority, while losing a net of nine House seats and 11 governorships. Nixon emerged from the campaign determined to distance himself from the Republican Party.

During his administration Nixon took important new initiatives in domestic affairs. In 1969 the president recommended the "New Federalism," the decentralization of power from Washington to state and local governments. One important aspect of this plan was "revenue sharing," whereby the federal government directly transferred revenues to states and localities to be dispensed as they wished. The concept had originated in 1958 with Representative Melvin Laird (R-Wis.) and had been supported, in modified form, by President Johnson. Congress followed Nixon's proposal in 1972 by voting to provide state and local governments an unrestricted $30 billion over five years. The president also persuaded the Congress in 1969 to reform the Post Office Department by transforming it into a quasi-private corporation. In his January 1971 State of the Union message, Nixon espoused another current cause by championing the building "environment" issue. With his endorsement Congress passed measures limiting air pollution caused by cars, industries, and utilities and restricting pollution from pesticides and industrial wastes. However, during his second term, as economic problems continued to grow, Nixon often advocated easing pollution regulations that might increase spending by industry and local governments.

Nixon inherited a troubled economy from his predecessor. From 1965 to 1968 Lyndon Johnson had attempted a fiscal policy that allowed for expanded federal domestic programs as well as an increasingly expensive military campaign in Vietnam. As early as 1967 this spending policy began to spark inflation. The Consumer Price Index increased from 2.9 percent in 1967 to 4.2 percent in 1968. Nixon had made inflation a major issue in his presidential campaign and in office acted to slow the high economic growth of the late 1960s. He placed his first budget in balance, a feat last accomplished in 1960. By the new conventional wisdom, a balanced budget signaled relatively smaller government expenditures and less of an increase in gross national product, less inflation, and more unemployment. The president also persuaded Congress to repeal the investment tax credit for business, which, initiated under John F. Kennedy, had spurred new plant expansion. He repeatedly vetoed generous social welfare appropriations and ultimately forced Congress to establish its own budget office. In October 1969 Nixon named ARTHUR BURNS chairman of the Federal Reserve Board; Burns acted to curb the growth of the money supply. Nixon's 1969–71 economic policies slowed down the economy and fostered a recession. As forecast, unemployment rose from 3.5 percent in 1968 to 4.9 percent in 1970 and 5.9 percent in 1971. But to the surprise of economists in and outside the White House, inflation did not abate, but increased. Continued inflation tested Nixon severely. Critics demanded price controls, but the president disapproved of such measures because of his experience at the OPA. Despite his opposition, Congress granted the president in August 1970 the power to freeze and otherwise control wages and profits. Nixon signed the bill but maintained that the measure "simply does not fit the economic conditions which exist today."

As inflation continued and his prospects for reelection worsened in 1971, Nixon altered what he liked to dub his economic "game plan." As an indication of his change in policy, in February 1971 he replaced Secretary of the Treasury DAVID KENNEDY with JOHN B. CONNALLY. Connally insisted, for practical political reasons, that Nixon abandon his orthodox economics. In August 1971 Nixon promulgated his New Economic Policy (NEP). He imposed a 90-day freeze on all prices and wage levels (termed Phase One) and established a Cost of Living Council to approve wage and price increases thereafter (Phase Two). The anti-inflation initiatives effectively reduced inflation and helped to restore the president's popularity to a limited degree. Also in 1972 Burns increased the money supply so as to improve economic conditions by November, a policy some observers felt added to the serious inflationary spiral that occurred in 1973 and 1974.

Nixon also had to deal with the decline of the value of the dollar. America's trade deficit had contributed to domestic inflation and over the long run caused U.S. products to become overpriced abroad. High military expenditures in Western Europe and Vietnam added to the problem. By 1971 the United States had the largest balance-of-payments deficit in its history. Most foreign currencies were stronger or "undervalued" compared to the fixed price to gold of the U.S. dollar. Tied to Nixon's NEP of August 1971, the president set a 10 percent surcharge on imported goods. He also delegated sensitive international economic negotiations to Secretary Connally, who "strong-armed" concessions from trading partners. In return the United States removed the 10 percent imports surcharge and devalued the dollar by 8.6 percent in December 1971, the first devaluation since 1934. In February 1973 the government again devalued the dollar by 10 percent.

Partly to help U.S. balance of payments, Nixon twice attempted to aid aircraft manufacturers. In March 1971 Congress voted not to approve further funding of the supersonic transport (SST), thus giving to the Soviet Union and a joint venture sponsored by France and the United Kingdom the world market for such aircraft. Nixon, who had supported continued funding, termed the vote distressing and disappointing, since the United States had heretofore led in the development of aviation technology. The administration enjoyed greater fortune in July and August when Congress agreed to an administration bill allowing

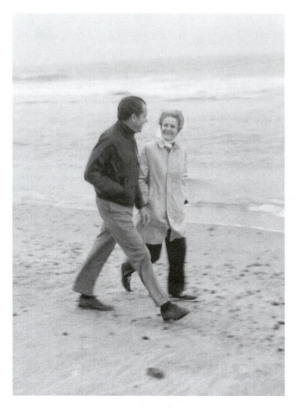

President Nixon and Mrs. Nixon on the beach at San Clemente, January 13, 1971 *(National Archives)*

a $250 million loan to the Lockheed Aircraft Corp., a major exporter of jet planes.

The Nixon administration developed few programs to assist poor and black Americans. During the Johnson presidency the federal government had committed itself to a wide range of programs designed to overcome inequalities suffered by poor people and blacks in the economy and distribution of services. In his 1968 campaign Nixon had tended to ignore black voters. Unlike Johnson, he named no black to his cabinet and few to subcabinet positions. Such subcabinet members as JAMES FARMER, JAMES ALLEN, and Leon E. Panetta fought for more progressive civil rights policies, only to resign in frustration. Similarly, Secretary of

Health, Education, and Welfare (HEW) ROB-ERT FINCH, who had supported these advocates, found himself demoted to White House counselor with an inconsequential role in policy making. Nixon offered little new legislation for minorities and systematically dismantled some "Great Society" programs meant to aid the urban poor. In early 1973, for example, he ordered the abolition of the Office of Economic Opportunity, which had been created under Johnson to aid minorities in the job market. Despite warnings to the contrary, however, Nixon's lack of involvement in civil rights issues did not result in a continuation or revival of the racial rioting that occurred from 1964 to 1968. The race riots of the 1960s all but ceased during his presidency.

Welfare reform stood out as the one exception to Nixon's laissez-faire approach to the problems of blacks and the poor. In August 1969 Nixon offered a major revamping of the welfare system through a guaranteed annual income plan formulated by the president's chief aide on urban policy, DANIEL PATRICK MOYNIHAN. The reform, known as the Family Assistance Plan (FAP), was a departure from traditional Republican philosophy and as such was opposed by such conservative GOP leaders as Governor Reagan and Representative JOHN ASHBROOK (R-Ohio). Black leaders and liberal Democrats looked upon the Nixon-Moynihan plan with skepticism, and Senate liberals combined with conservative Republicans and southern Democrats to scuttle the FAP in late 1970. Fearing Reagan's rivalry for the 1972 presidential nomination, Nixon thereafter all but ignored Moynihan's reform.

The president did monitor more closely the use of busing to end racial segregation in public schools, a controversial legacy of the civil rights revolution of the 1950s and 1960s. Courts increasingly ordered school systems throughout the nation to desegregate their facilities, and Nixon's cabinet officers found themselves having to carry out the court edicts. In 1971, for example, HEW formulated a busing plan for Austin, Texas, that Nixon in turn characterized in August as "the busing of children simply for the busing of children." In June 1972 the president assailed a Detroit court busing order and encouraged legislation to curb the practice. At the same time he did nothing to discourage the violence committed by white extremists and distraught parents during implementation of busing orders. Indeed, in 1972 he commanded the Justice Department to petition the courts on behalf of some school boards opposing lower-court desegregation orders. Despite Nixon's stance, court decisions effectively dictated the desegregation of many school systems during his presidency.

Implicitly related to civil rights was Nixon's preoccupation with the membership of the Supreme Court. Many conservatives in the 1960s had felt that the court under Chief Justice Earl Warren had been too "activist," or liberal, in its decisions regarding school desegregation and the rights of defendants in criminal law proceedings. Nixon shared that concern and pledged to name no liberals and preferably more southerners to the Court. Altogether Nixon chose four justices, including Warren's successor, WARREN E. BURGER in May 1969. That month Nixon and Attorney General JOHN N. MITCHELL forced the resignation of Justice ABE FORTAS after learning of improper actions by Fortas off the bench. To succeed Fortas, a Court liberal, Nixon designated federal judge CLEMENT HAYNSWORTH, a conservative jurist from South Carolina. Although an able judge, Haynsworth, Senate investigators found, had decided one case for a company in which he owned stock. The Senate voted to reject Haynsworth by a 55-45 margin, the first Supreme Court nominee to be disapproved since 1930.

Nixon responded angrily to Haynsworth's rejection in January 1970 by naming federal judge G. HARROLD CARSWELL of Florida. Carswell did not rank highly on anyone's list of potential nominees. He had a mediocre record of court conduct and opinions reversed by higher courts. Indeed, some commentators and senators regarded his designation as a rebuke. Richard Harris of the *New Yorker* wrote that the president "was prepared to insult one branch of the government, the Senate, in order to lower the quality of a second branch, the Judiciary." Again an extended fight over confirmation ensued. Evidence of Carswell's racist past was uncovered. A key supporter, Senator ROMAN HRUSKA (R-Neb.), not only acknowledged Carswell's "mediocrity" as a jurist but also felt that the appointment should be allowed because mediocrity warranted representation on the bench. Nixon's congressional lobbyists added to the damage from Hruska's reasoning by employing clumsy or heavy-handed tactics on GOP senators. In April 1970 the Senate rejected Carswell by a vote of 51 to 45. Nixon bitterly decried the vote as an "act of regional discrimination" against southern judges. He then named a northerner, Judge HARRY BLACKMUN of Minnesota, to the year-long Fortas vacancy; the Senate unanimously confirmed that selection. Two years later Nixon succeeded in appointing a southerner, LEWIS POWELL of Virginia, and then placed WILLIAM REHNQUIST, an Arizona conservative, on the Court.

Nixon's efforts to reshape the Court had mixed results. The Supreme Court veered away from its stands during the Warren era, though the Court's turnabout was by no means complete. The Burger Court upheld some massive school desegregation edicts that employed busing, of which the president publicly disapproved. In January 1973 the Court upheld the right of women to abortions during the first six months of pregnancy, a "liberal" decision, while Nixon was assiduously wooing antiabortion groups. More importantly, the Burger Court did not, as feared, reverse most

of the major decisions handed down during Warren's tenure. Burger proved less persuasive than Warren in mobilizing Court votes and generally preferred to be a legal administrator, calling for Court expansion and procedural reforms rather than advocating new legal initiatives.

Foreign affairs remained Nixon's favorite area and the one in which he demonstrated the greatest imagination. From the time of his 1968 campaign, Nixon had sensed a shift in the global balance of power. China emerged from its "cultural revolution" likely to assume a vital leadership role in the world, yet it was still suspicious of the Soviet Union; sporadic armed border clashes occurred along the Sino-Soviet border in 1969. Although Nixon had long been among those who opposed U.S. diplomatic recognition of China and its admission to the United Nations, the president now felt that Chinese leaders must be approached. As a Republican president with indisputable anti-communist credentials, Nixon could slowly begin to "normalize" U.S.-Chinese relations with little fear of domestic political repercussions. Tentative discussions began soon after Nixon's inauguration. In July 1971 Kissinger secretly flew to Beijing to arrange a presidential visit to China the following year. Announced officially in August, Nixon's trip in February 1972 laid the groundwork for formal relations, which were realized under President JIMMY CARTER in December 1978.

U.S. relations with the Soviet Union improved markedly during Nixon's administration. From the outset Nixon favored the Strategic Arms Limitation Talks (SALT), begun under President Johnson, as a means of containing the arms race. Yet he supported continued increases in new military weapons procurement, notably during the congressional debate over the appropriation for the antiballistic missile system in 1969. The SALT negotiations were designed to culminate not in an overall reduction of U.S. military spending as much as a lessening in the growth rate of military expenditures. The talks ran from 1969 to 1972, when the Soviet leaders agreed to the first of several treaties to limit new armaments. When he went to Moscow in May 1972 to sign the accord, Nixon became the first president to visit the Soviet Union since 1945.

President Nixon fostered a U.S.-Soviet "spirit" of cooperation, or "détente," as cold war tensions between the two great powers lessened. Pushed by Soviet party chairman LEONID BREZHNEV, the USSR aggressively sought America's trade and its high technology and investment for mining Soviet natural resources. In addition, a poor grain harvest forced the USSR to request the right to purchase U.S. grain in 1972. The grain transaction taxed the resources of the Agriculture Department and had the unexpected effect of raising U.S. food prices the following year. That and the question of Soviet domestic repression raised concerns about the gains to accrue from the deal. Senator HENRY M. JACKSON (D-Wash.) delayed approval of SALT-I over the issue of Soviet denial of emigration rights to Russian Jews.

Détente and the new China policy did not, however, resolve the problem of Vietnam. From 1968 to 1972 the United States, North and South Vietnam, and the National Liberal Front (the South Vietnamese Communist faction) continued fruitless negotiations in Paris. As the United States deescalated its military operations, the governments of North and South Vietnam—the one hopeful, the other terrified over what withdrawal portended—hesitated to concede much. Nixon's patience wore thin, especially in light of the upcoming 1972 election and his inability to end the conflict. Continued North Vietnamese offensive operations in early 1972 provoked expanded U.S. air missions over North Vietnam and the mining of Haiphong harbor, the major port

city. Administration sources claimed that the bombing was necessary to protect U.S. troops remaining in the South and was aimed solely at military targets. But there were persistent reports of dikes and hospitals hit by American bombs. The May 1972 offensive prevented a rout of Saigon's forces in the northern tier of South Vietnam, but the North Vietnamese remained uncooperative in the Paris talks, hoping either to wear down Thieu or see Nixon replaced in the November elections.

Nixon appeared to face a tough reelection campaign in 1972. Challenges to Nixon within his own party by Representatives Ashbrook and PAUL N. MCCLOSKEY (R-Calif.) proved inconsequential. But through 1971 he lagged behind Senator EDMUND S. MUSKIE (D-Me.), the leading Democratic contender, in public opinion polls. Indeed, Nixon failed to improve his position greatly even after he announced his new and dramatic policies regarding China and inflation in August 1971. The prospect of political defeat haunted Nixon, who had suffered an inordinate number of voter rebukes. His fears and those of his staff led to complicity in condoning extralegal campaign efforts. The Committee to Re-Elect the President (CREEP) determined to do what it could, legally and illegally, to assist the president. Government officials placed pressure on business executives subject to regulation, including those affected by Nixon's new environmental legislation, to contribute to CREEP. Then CREEP commenced secret political espionage or "dirty tricks" against the Democrats. Muskie was the primary target. CREEP operatives led by DONALD SEGRETTI sought to sabotage his campaign; in the New Hampshire primary, for example, a letter attributing a racial slur about French Canadians to Muskie was sent to the conservative *Manchester Union Leader,* which published the remark along with an anti-Muskie editorial. These and other tactics served to undermine Muskie's lead and encouraged factional

President and Mrs. Richard Nixon visiting the Great Wall of China, 1972 *(Library of Congress)*

rivalries among the Democratic Party's other candidates.

Senator GEORGE S. MCGOVERN (D-S.D.) won the Democratic nomination at the July 1972 National Convention. With impeccably liberal credentials, McGovern had embraced a range of positions on drug use, income redistribution, and other issues that appeared to separate him, like Goldwater in 1964, from the political "mainstream." Furthermore, he secured the nomination without the support of such traditional Democratic blocs as organized labor and the South. Polls taken immediately after the Democratic Convention gave Nixon a 30 percent lead over the South Dakotan.

Ironically, Nixon and his CREEP managers had not anticipated such a vulnerable opponent. They had forecast a close contest along the lines

of Nixon's 1960 and 1968 efforts, and had taken precautions, notably against the expertise of one man, LAWRENCE F. O'BRIEN, chairman of the Democratic National Committee. O'Brien had engineered Humphrey's remarkable showing in 1968 and was commonly considered one of the best political strategists of the postwar period, quite capable of frustrating the president's reelection drive. Shortly before McGovern's nomination, five men hired by CREEP broke into O'Brien's offices in the Democratic headquarters at the Watergate complex in Washington. They set telephone wiretaps and rummaged for intelligence concerning O'Brien's electoral strategy and for any confidential or damaging information on the president. On June 17 these men made a return visit, only to be discovered and arrested by the Washington police.

The White House and Nixon himself denied any knowledge of the Watergate break-in. It was later revealed that Nixon knew that CREEP engaged in surreptitious data-gathering operations and realized that his campaign director, John N. Mitchell, and a White House aide, JEB STUART MAGRUDER, hired the Watergate burglars. However, he chose not to risk public disapproval and reelection; a confession might have evoked old memories of the president as "Tricky Dicky" and clouded his substantive foreign policy initiatives.

Both O'Brien and McGovern attempted to make the Watergate incident a political issue, without avail. At Nixon's direction, Haldeman and Ehrlichman prevailed on Central Intelligence Agency (CIA) deputy director VERNON WALTERS to have the FBI halt its probe of the burglary on the grounds that it might compromise CIA activities. FBI acting director L. Patrick Gray initially agreed to limit the probe but then demanded a written request from Walters, who in turn denied CIA involvement. But Gray joined the successful White House effort to frustrate the Justice Department's initial investigation of the burglary. At about the same time, White House counsel JOHN DEAN, overseeing the "cover-up" for Nixon, requested CIA funds to pay off the captured burglars.

Nixon overwhelmed McGovern in the November balloting. Stressing his duties as chief executive, the president campaigned little and held few press conferences. Surrogate speakers represented Nixon at Republican rallies across the nation and, together with an effective advertising effort, underscored McGovern's contradictory statements and general ineptness as a national candidate. On the eve of the voting Kissinger sealed the victory. Returning from negotiations with the North Vietnamese in Paris, Kissinger proclaimed that "peace is at hand." On November 7 Nixon bested McGovern with 60.8 percent of the vote; he won in 49

states. Other Republican candidates, however, did not fare nearly so well. Democrats actually increased their number of Senate seats. The GOP did win an additional 13 House seats, but Congress remained in Democratic control. Senator ROBERT DOLE (R-Kan.), chairman of the Republican National Committee, termed the results "a personal triumph for Mr. Nixon but not a party triumph."

In the aftermath of victory Nixon moved to solidify his control over the federal government. In November the president asked for the resignations of the top 2,000 executive branch officials; he then arranged for the removal of three of his cabinet members and several federal agency chairmen. His intention was to place cabinet departments directly under the supervision of a few trusted secretaries and White House staff members, while other Nixon loyalists took positions at various levels to monitor activities within each department. Thus, Nixon would effect a plan of "supercabinets" under more direct White House control. Removed from the cabinet were two former GOP governors, GEORGE W. ROMNEY and JOHN A. VOLPE. They were replaced by men known only for their complete loyalty to the president. Rev. THEODORE HESBURGH, president of the University of Notre Dame, was forced out as chairman of the Civil Rights Commission, which had criticized the administration's policies toward blacks. Commerce Secretary PETER PETERSON was dismissed after he was deemed less than sufficiently faithful to Nixon and too closely allied to Senator CHARLES H. PERCY (R-Ill.), a liberal GOP leader.

In the midst of Nixon's personnel shake-up, Kissinger completed a peace agreement with the North Vietnamese. Resolution did not come as swiftly as had been implied in Kissinger's "peace is at hand" statement. Indeed, the North Vietnamese proved unwilling in November and December to make changes in the document demanded by South Vietnam. In response to

North Vietnam's intransigence, in late December the president ordered a "reseeding" of mines in Haiphong Harbor and the most intensive bombing ever of North Vietnam. "The order to renew bombing the week before Christmas," Nixon recalled, "was the most difficult decision I made during the war." It provoked a large outcry from both antiwar spokespersons and others, such as Senator WILLIAM B. SAXBE (R-Ohio), who normally supported the administration. Nevertheless, the "Christmas bombing" forced Hanoi's hand. In early January Kissinger flew to Paris to effect an agreement. On January 15 all bombing and mining operations against the North ceased. North Vietnam provided for the return of U.S. prisoners of war (mainly bomber pilots). On January 23 a cease-fire was announced. Nixon had "won the peace," as he liked to phrase it, and rested on a high crest of popularity. The *Wall Street Journal* reported of an effort to repeal the constitutional limit of two presidential terms so that Nixon could run again in 1976.

In his war against inflation Nixon took issue with the Democratic Congress in late 1972 and early 1973 over government spending. Nixon began "impounding" federal monies, that is, he directed cabinet officers in such departments as HEW not to spend funds allocated by Congress for those departments. Not content to rely on his veto power, the president wished to curb excess expenditures, which he felt contributed much to the inflationary spiral. It appeared to be a practice of doubtful legality and certainly a direct challenge to the authority and independence of the legislative branch.

Just as Nixon's personal popularity rose to new heights, his presidency appeared jeopardized by the incident at the Watergate complex. From June 1972 to March 1973, Nixon and his staff had kept the Watergate conspirators silent by cash payments, coverage of legal fees, and the promise of pardons. For a while these efforts worked. Aside from the *Washing-*

ton Post, most of the news media ignored the possibility that Watergate constituted part of a larger scheme of illegal actions. Federal judge JOHN J. SIRICA, assigned to the Watergate trial, repeatedly asked the defendants if they had acted under authority from CREEP. The men said nothing and pleaded guilty in October; sentencing occurred in January. By that time the *Post* and several other major newspapers stepped up their investigative reportage of the possibility that CREEP or the White House was connected with the burglary. On February 7, 1973, the Senate established a special Judiciary Committee panel, chaired by Senator SAM ERVIN (D-N.C.), to inquire about illegal campaign practices. By the month's end Nixon assumed full charge of all Watergate matters.

Nixon decided he had to make sacrifices in the hope of defusing the Watergate time bomb. On March 22, 1973, Ervin's committee issued its first subpoenas of White House aides and official records. The president refused to honor the requests. Four days later JAMES MCCORD, one of the Watergate burglars, wrote to Judge Sirica asking for a private meeting. Sirica agreed, and McCord told of official culpability. The next day Nixon, Haldeman, and Ehrlichman realized that CREEP would have to acknowledge some guilt and decided to make Mitchell the "fall guy," to blame him for the entire matter. Early the next month John Dean, who had been handling the cover-up, began to talk to federal prosecutors. Now Nixon determined to cast Dean as the "public" culprit and on April 30 forced his resignation. That night, in a televised address, the president tried to defuse the growing scandal by taking responsibility for the Watergate affair but denying personal involvement in the episode or the attempts to cover it up. He asked the nation to let the courts deal with the scandal, urged reform of the political process, and pleaded that he be permitted to continue the tasks for which he was elected.

Public interest in Watergate rose markedly, while faith in the Justice Department and Nixon's handling of the investigation fell. In May Congress compelled Nixon to appoint a new attorney general, ELLIOT L. RICHARDSON, and a Watergate special prosecutor, ARCHIBALD COX, to handle the investigation. Richardson and Nixon both agreed to cooperate with Cox and grant him independence from White House interference, which had severely restricted the Justice Department's inquiry.

Through the late spring and summer of 1973, additional revelations damaged Nixon's reputation further. In June, for example, the General Services Administration reported federal expenditures, many of them extravagant, totaling $1.9 million on Nixon's various estates. Then, too, Dean testified before Ervin's committee; he implicated the president in the cover-up and revealed the existence of the White House "enemies lists." But the greatest surprise came the following month. Alexander Butterfield, a former CIA agent and White House aide, revealed that in 1969 Haldeman had an elaborate taping system installed in the White House to record all the president's conversations. So great had been his and Nixon's concern with the historical record of the Nixon presidency that they had "bugged" themselves. For the next year access to the tapes loomed as the major issue of the Watergate inquiries. Nixon refused to destroy the recordings but also declined, under the rubric of "executive privilege," to turn any over to Sirica, Cox, or congressional panels.

Suddenly another prominent member of the administration fell into disrepute. For some time during 1973, the Justice Department had been assembling evidence indicating that Vice President Agnew had been taking bribes during his term as governor of Maryland and after his election to the vice presidency. The Justice Department's case appeared clear-cut. After a brief fight to salvage his posi-

tion, Agnew pleaded "no contest" to a charge of tax evasion and resigned on October 10. Nixon named Representative GERALD R. FORD JR. (R-Mich.), House minority leader, his new vice president.

Ten days after Agnew's departure from office, on October 20, Nixon tried to resolve the tape controversies by dismissing Special Prosecutor Cox. To Nixon's dismay, Cox had been pursuing many possible White House crimes and activities of questionable legality involving Nixon himself and had been relentless in his quest for access to the White House tapes. When Nixon fired Cox, Attorney General Richardson felt morally obligated to resign in protest; his deputy, WILLIAM RUCKELSHAUS, refused to carry out Nixon's order to remove Cox and in turn was fired even before he could submit his own letter of resignation. Gun-wielding FBI agents moved in to seal Cox's office, and for one terrible moment the special prosecutor's aides thought that the president was executing a coup d'état. The incident became known as the "Saturday night massacre."

Nixon's dismissal of Cox raised a hailstorm of protest. An unprecedented number of telegrams and other messages, overwhelmingly hostile to the president, flooded congressional and White House mail rooms. The House leadership, long loath to act prematurely and fearful of charges of partisan consideration, began organizing impeachment proceedings. Congressional and public opinion thus forced Nixon's hand. He agreed in principle to surrender the tapes, name a new special prosecutor, LEON JAWORSKI, and appoint another independent-minded attorney general, Senator Saxbe.

In the midst of this crisis, foreign policy considerations brought into question the president's basic capacity to govern. In October an alliance of Arab states launched a surprise attack on Israel, an ally of the United States. Since at first the Israeli situation appeared precarious, Nixon ordered a large shipment of arms rushed to the besieged nation. He also placed U.S. armed forces on alert, a grave step apparently related to a threat by the Soviets to intervene militarily in the war. Some observers suspected, however, that the president tried to use the war to distract attention from his serious domestic struggles.

In December the oil-exporting nations of the Middle East instituted a boycott against the United States and other major Western powers allied to Israel. Through the years the United States had become increasingly dependent on the Mideast for its primary oil supply. The boycott created an energy crisis in America; gas stations shut down and thermostats in factories and homes were lowered in warlike sacrifice. In January 1974 Nixon proposed "Project Independence" to Congress, a detailed scheme for lessening America's reliance on imported oil. The quadrupling of oil prices following the boycott, which ended in March 1974, worsened America's trade deficit, fueled inflation, and fostered a worldwide recession in late 1974. Nixon and Kissinger, now secretary of state, increased their involvement in Mideast diplomacy. They wooed Anwar Sadat, president of Egypt, in an attempt to weaken his ties with the Soviet Union and the more militant Arab states and terrorist organizations. As a result, Nixon helped to lay the groundwork for an ease in tensions between Egypt and Israel in the late 1970s.

Watergate proceedings absorbed more and more of the nation's time. In November 1973 a key tape of a conversation transferred to Jaworski revealed an 18-1/2-minute gap, inexplicably and clumsily erased. In early March the Watergate grand jury named the president an "unindicted coconspirator" in the cover-up; the panel elected not to indict Nixon because of doubts that the Supreme Court would allow such an action against a sitting president. By the spring of 1974 the House impeachment inquiry had begun hearings and soon petitioned for 42 White House tapes. By now the president's hopes rested in withholding the tapes themselves. In an attempt to defuse the situation Nixon released edited transcripts of the tapes prepared in April by the White House staff under his direct supervision. The typescripts proved unreliable, and the investigators sued for release of the tapes.

Public opinion clearly worsened for Nixon by mid-1974. News coverage of Watergate overwhelmed that of all other issues. Extensive television network coverage of the Ervin hearings and later the impeachment proceedings revealed for the first time the ethics and personality of Nixon's staff, which had heretofore operated with considerable anonymity. Republicans in Congress by and large remained faithful to the president, though in March Senator JAMES L. BUCKLEY (R-N.Y.) became among the first of a few who publicly asked Nixon to resign. The party suffered for its loyalty; GOP candidates lost in special House elections in 1973 and 1974, a portent of disaster in the November 1974 elections if Nixon remained in office.

Nixon's hopes to retain the presidency all but collapsed in late July 1974 when the Supreme Court unanimously upheld a lower court subpoena directing the president to surrender 64 taped conversations to Jaworski. Events moved swiftly thereafter. The tapes clearly demonstrated that the president had known of and participated in the obstruction of justice in the Justice Department's Watergate investigation and that he had done so largely for personal, political reasons. These revelations provided the basis for the Judiciary Committee's approval of three articles of impeachment in July 1974. For two years the president had lied to the American people; incredibly, he also had totally deceived his own family and GOP leaders whom he had known for years and who had stoutly defended him. It was obvious by early August that the House would impeach the president and that the Senate would vote his removal from office. Republican leaders all but abandoned him. Facing a prolonged and ultimately unsuccessful Senate trial, Nixon resigned from office on August 9, 1974, the first president to do so. He did not admit to criminal wrongdoing, only to rendering "some" bad judgments. In September his successor, Gerald Ford, granted him a blanket pardon.

Following his resignation from the presidency Nixon repaired to his home in San Clemente, California. On September 9, 1974, after a month of furious legal wrangling with the administration, Ford pardoned Nixon for any offenses he "committed, or may have committed," while president. This action unleashed a firestorm of protest that was ultimately more costly for Ford than it was for Nixon. The pardon was at least partially issued because of Nixon's failing health; on October 23, 1974, he underwent surgery for phlebitis, a surgery that, according to several accounts, nearly cost him his life. The intervening years saw Nixon in a protracted legal battle to protect his tapes and papers from the perusal of researchers. After several challenges, one of which was decided by the Supreme Court, on September 15, 1986, the National Archives announced that limited public access to Nixon's papers would begin on December 1, 1986. From that date access to Nixon's papers has been slowly made available to qualified researchers.

Nixon also became a prolific author. He published the second volume of his memoirs, *RN*, in 1978; the event drew a host of criticism when it was learned that a substantial portion of his earnings from the book was going to pay his legal fees. In 1980 he released *Real War;* in 1980, a study of several of the *Leaders* with whom he had worked; in 1987, a generally well-received defense of his policies toward the Vietnam War, *No More Vietnams;* in 1989, a prescient view of the coming end of the

cold war, *1999: Victory without War; Seize the Moment: America's Challenge in a One-Superpower World* (1992); and in 1994, *Beyond Peace.*

In his later years, largely as a result of his writing efforts and the resultant publicity that surrounded each release, Nixon established for himself something of an elder-statesman role. Beginning with RONALD REAGAN, each succeeding president sought his counsel on foreign affairs. Indeed, Nixon's inclusion in the delegation to the 1981 funeral of slain Egyptian president Anwar Sadat—a delegation that included former presidents Ford and Carter—signaled Nixon's reemergence into the community of politics.

Nixon died on April 22, 1994, in New York City following a stroke. His family requested that his not be a state funeral, even though as a former president he was entitled to such a service. He was interred at the Nixon Library and Birthplace in Yorba Linda, California.

—JLB and JRG

Nofziger, (Frank)Lyn C(urran)
(1924–   ) *deputy assistant to the president for congressional liaison*

Franklyn C. Nofziger was born on June 8, 1924, in Bakersfield, California. Nofziger began his journalism career at the *Glendale News-Press* and the *Burbank Daily Review* in 1950. He became managing editor of the *Daily Review* in 1957 but moved on the following year to become a Washington correspondent for the conservative Copley newspaper chain. From 1964 to 1966 he served as the chain's national political writer. He joined RONALD REAGAN's gubernatorial campaign in the middle of January 1966. Following Reagan's inaugural in January 1967, Nofziger was appointed communications director for California, but he emphasized that his work was for the governor, not the state. During his year at the post Nofziger joined other close Reagan aides in promoting the governor's presidential ambitions. In the summer of 1968 Nofziger resigned his position to work for conservative Max Rafferty, the Republican candidate for the U.S. Senate seat in California. Rafferty lost the race to Alan Cranston in November.

In July 1969 Nofziger was appointed by President NIXON to work under presidential assistant BRYCE HARLOW as deputy assistant to the president and chief of congressional liaison. Two years later he became deputy chairman for communications for the Republican National Convention. He also returned to California in 1971 to oversee President Nixon's reelection campaign in that state.

During the Senate Watergate hearings in 1973, it was revealed that Nofziger was involved in an attempt to deter GEORGE WALLACE from entering the presidential race in California; President Nixon feared Wallace would take crucial votes away from his reelection effort. Nofziger gave $10,000 from the Committee to Re-Elect the President (CREEP) to a California advertising executive who had suggested persuading members of Wallace's American Independent Party (AIP) to change their registration. (Insufficient registration would have kept Wallace's name off the ballot.) The attempt failed, however, due in part to a California law allocating a position on the ballot for parties receiving 2 percent of the vote in the prior gubernatorial election; the AIP had achieved this percentage. Nofziger called the effort "legal, moral, and good politics" and said he would "do it again, but it was not very practical."

According to White House counsel JOHN DEAN, Nofziger also was involved in preparing a list of White House "enemies." The list included individuals and institutions from a variety of fields who were considered hostile to the Nixon administration and who were targeted for retaliatory action. After leaving government Nofziger became an independent political consultant. He served for a short time as manager of California lieutenant governor Ed Reinecke's gubernatorial campaign but resigned toward the end of the year, citing differing political approaches. He organized publicity for International Brotherhood of Teamsters president FRANK FITZSIMMONS in June 1974 and worked on a Senate campaign in South Dakota. He left the latter, however, after the Democratic candidate, Senator GEORGE MCGOVERN (D-S.D.), called him "a key member of the Nixon 'dirty tricks' gang."

In 1975 Nofziger rejoined Reagan as a chief organizer of the former governor's unsuccessful campaign for the 1976 Republican presidential nomination. In 1977 Nofziger became executive director of Citizens for the Republic, a conservative group founded to promote Reagan and his views. Nofziger would serve Reagan as an assistant to the president for political affairs. Following the Reagan presidency he founded Nofziger Communications.

—RB

O'Brien, Lawrence F(rancis)

(1917–1990) *chairman, Democratic National Committee; national campaign chairman, McGovern for President Campaign*

Born on July 7, 1917, O'Brien, the son of Irish immigrants, grew up in a political atmosphere spawned by his father's Democratic Party activities in Springfield, Massachusetts. After receiving his law degree from night school at Boston's Northeastern University and serving in the army during World War II, O'Brien worked for Representative Foster Furcola. He became John Kennedy's campaign director in 1952 and served in the same capacity in subsequent campaigns.

O'Brien, considered by some to be one of the best political strategists in the postwar period, was special assistant to the president for congressional relations during Kennedy's presidency. He continued his work under Lyndon Johnson and was the president's campaign director in the 1964 race. He was named postmaster general in 1965, yet he continued his wide-ranging legislative efforts on the president's behalf. As postmaster general, O'Brien oversaw the writing of the report that eventually led to the creation of a quasi-public corporation, taking the Post Office Department out of the cabinet. In 1968 he worked for Robert Kennedy's presidential campaign. After Kennedy's assassination he helped HUBERT HUMPHREY in his presidential campaign. After the election O'Brien joined the Wall Street brokerage house of McDonnell & Co.

In 1970 O'Brien became chairman of the National Democratic Committee, a position he assumed with some reluctance. Upon taking office O'Brien faced the unenviable task of presiding over a party that was $9.3 million in debt with a demoralized staff. The party also was still deeply divided ideologically between the hawks and the doves on Vietnam and reformers and the old guard on domestic issues. O'Brien's role was a difficult one, and he was frequently viewed as a member of the old guard, a front for the power brokers. He attempted to avoid antagonizing any element of the party and forged a strategy to thwart what seemed like a potential emerging Republican majority by becoming a major party spokesman on many issues. He vigorously denounced the RICHARD NIXON economic policies, which he labeled Nixonomics—a blend of inflation and high unemployment that were previously thought to be mutually exclusive. He criticized the Nixon administration's handling of the Vietnam War and its involvement in the ITT scandal.

It was during O'Brien's tenure as party chairman that many of the controversial reforms that later caused such discord at the 1972 Democratic National Convention were formulated. The most significant issue involved the McGovern-Fraser Commission on Party Reform, which sought to establish specific procedural control over the state delegation selection process. The effect of the commission's rulings provided for what seemed to be quotas for youths, minority groups, and women in the delegate selection process and gave the national party an unprecedented amount of control over state party affairs. O'Brien summed up the national party's commitment to the reform agenda when he said in October 1971 that "never before has a political party so totally changed its way of doing business in such a short period of time. . . . And there will be no turning back." Yet he later added that he had wanted reform that "led to party unity, not reform that came at the price of continuing division within the party."

O'Brien stepped down as party chairman after the 1972 Democratic Convention. He was succeeded by Jean Woodward, GEORGE MCGOVERN's choice for the post. However, McGovern was desperate for the services of O'Brien in the fall campaign and pleaded with him to accept the post of national campaign chairman, which O'Brien assumed with some reluctance. He later wrote that they were "the three worst months of my life . . . a nightmare." He became angered and frustrated over the lack of coordination within the campaign organization and the resentment between the McGovern workers who had piloted their candidate through the primaries and those, like O'Brien, who were seen as latecomers.

It was O'Brien's office that the Watergate burglars bugged in the spring of 1972. Discounting many of the widely held theories about the motivation behind the Watergate affair, O'Brien believed the "objective of Watergate was to secure all possible information that would help destroy the Democratic Party and its chairman. It is as simple as that." What par-

ticularly angered him, however, was that during the 1972 presidential campaign when he had tried to raise the break-in as a serious and legitimate political issue, the press and the public still regarded the affair as a joke or a caper "because the hard evidence was still hidden from view."

O'Brien later asserted that he was subjected to harassment long before Watergate through Internal Revenue Service audits and break-ins at his apartment from which documents were stolen. In addition, friends of his were subjected to pressures that he believed were intended to quiet him. He later wrote: "Make no mistake about it, the government can grind you down. The Nixon administration harassment never silenced me, but I would be dishonest if I didn't admit that it hurt me financially, sapped my energies, and often left me deeply depressed." What disturbed O'Brien the most was the great difficulty he had in finding a lawyer to prosecute the Republicans in a civil suit. Even his old friends from the Kennedy and Johnson administrations "felt involvement with me would antagonize the Nixon administration and might jeopardize their law practices." The suit was eventually settled out of court in February 1974 for $775,000.

After he left active politics at the end of 1972, O'Brien spent the next several years writing his autobiography as well as engaging in consulting work on matters of public relations in Washington and New York. In 1975 O'Brien became commissioner of the National Basketball Association, a post he held until 1984. He served as the president of the Basketball Hall of Fame from 1985 to 1987. He died in 1990.

—GWB

Ordaz, Gustavo Díaz
(1911–1979) *president of Mexico*

The period between 1940 and 1960 has been dubbed a "honeymoon" by diplomatic historians because of the tranquillity that characterized relations between Mexico and the United States during those years. Events in Mexico, the United States, and abroad in the 1960s, however, made maintaining such a "special" relationship difficult. Domestic political exigencies, international crises, and the personalities of the leaders involved all contributed to growing tensions between the two countries as the decade came to a close. The Mexican president from 1964 to 1970, Gustavo Díaz Ordaz, was at once complicit in the souring of this relationship and troubled by it.

Gustavo Díaz Ordaz grew up in a once prosperous family made humble by the anti-elitist character of the Mexican Revolution. As an adult, Díaz Ordaz found his career, like his family's fortunes, rested on public perceptions of his relationship to the revolution and its goals. Popular opinion perceived the awkward, painfully self-conscious Díaz Ordaz, like his father, as a man on the wrong side of the revolution. His heavy-handed response to social unrest, his support for increased foreign investment in Mexico, and his relatively cordial relations with the United States provided the ammunition critics needed to suggest he had sold out his country and its revolutionary ideals.

Gustavo Díaz Ordaz owed his entrance into politics and his rapid ascent to the inner circle of the leadership of Mexico's ruling Partido Revolucionario Institucional (PRI) to hard work and good fortune. Díaz Ordaz rose through the ranks of state government before following his political benefactors to Mexico City and various posts within the PRI and the federal government. This rapid ascent through the party and governmental bureaucracy culminated in his being named minister of the interior in 1958 as part of the cabinet of incoming president Adolfo López Mateos. Here Díaz Ordaz occupied the second most powerful position in the government, handled many of the routine details of governance, and sat poised to assume the presidency.

Díaz Ordaz's assumption of that office was guaranteed in 1961 when he skillfully handled one of the most difficult diplomatic situations the López Mateos administration faced while the president was out of the country. Díaz Ordaz crafted a formal Mexican response to the Cuban missile crisis that appealed to the domestic audience by supporting Cuban autonomy and placated the United States by condemning the presence of Soviet weapons on the island. This success proved him worthy of the presidency, and three years later, when it was time for López Mateos to endorse a successor, he chose Díaz Ordaz.

The Cuban missile crisis incident reveals the complexity of Mexican relations with the United States and foreshadows problems Díaz Ordaz would encounter later as president. The early years of his presidency, however, were characterized by cordial relations with the United States and increasing openness to foreign investment. The inherent dichotomies in the Mexican ideology of institutionalized revolution, however, created problems for the president. Anti-Americanism was implicit in the rhetoric of the institutionalized revolution, so any president appearing too close to the United States paid a political price. On the other hand, Mexico could not afford to antagonize the United States. Díaz Ordaz thus had to achieve a delicate balance between domestic rhetoric and international policy in his dealings with Mexican communists, foreign investors, and Cuba.

During the cold war one of the key issues for the United States was anticommunism. While Díaz Ordaz had established his anticommunist credentials on more than one occasion, broad-based support for such measures in Mexico was lacking. Thus, the United States perceived Mexico as soft on communism. The frequent opportunities Díaz Ordaz and his government took to criticize U.S. actions in Vietnam, intervention in the Dominican Republic, and participation in the nuclear arms race exacerbated tensions abroad while quelling discontent at home.

Despite his rhetorical attacks on his North American counterpart, Díaz Ordaz's more private dealings with the United States reveal a relationship that remained strong. The Mexican president loosened controls on foreign investment, peacefully resolved a dispute over the salinity of the Colorado River, and recovered a piece of Mexican territory called the Chamizal made contentious by a change in the course of the Rio Grande. President Díaz Ordaz even addressed the U.S. Congress in 1967.

While public denunciations of U.S. policy and diplomatic successes reveal the complexity of Mexico's relationship with its northern neighbor, the Díaz Ordaz administration's policy on Cuba suggests where the president's priorities were. Mexico maintained formal relations with Cuba and continued to perform all of the ceremonial acts of diplomacy necessary to appease the Mexican left, for whom the Cuban Revolution was kindred to their own. Privately, however, the Mexican government maintained its distance from the island nation, refusing high-level visits, discouraging travel and tourism, and most significantly, allowing U.S. intelligence agencies to monitor Cuban activities from Mexico City and the Mexican embassy in Havana. Thus, President Díaz Ordaz clearly felt it more important to cooperate with the United States than to defend Cuba.

Despite this cooperation, however, Díaz Ordaz's dealings with the United States ended badly when at the close of his presidency a border dispute erupted that overshadowed the goodwill of the previous five years. In 1969 President RICHARD NIXON launched Operation Intercept to crack down on drug trafficking along the U.S.-Mexico border. This initiative essentially closed the border and left the Mexican people and their government with the sense that the new U.S. administration could not be trusted. Ironically for Díaz Ordaz, the pro-U.S. policies that had caused him such political problems at home, in the long run, did little for him abroad.

—JS

P

Packard, David
(1912–1996) *deputy secretary of defense*

David Packard was born on September 7, 1912, in Pueblo, Colorado. Packard received his B.A. from Stanford University in 1934 and his degree in electrical engineering in 1937. He worked for two years at General Electric, and in 1939 he became a cofounder of Hewlett-Packard Co. He served as the company's president from 1947 to 1964 and as chairman of the board from 1964 to 1969. From 1958 to 1969 Packard also was director of the Stanford Research Institute, a prestigious "think tank," and sat on the advisory board of the Hoover Institute of War, Revolution, and Peace. In 1969 President NIXON appointed him deputy secretary of defense.

Because of the obvious potential conflicts of interest for the ranking executive of a large defense contractor, Packard's appointment immediately provoked controversy. He moved to head off Senate opposition by having his $300 million holdings in Hewlett-Packard administered by a charitable trust while he held office. Although Senator ALBERT GORE (D-Tenn.) attacked the arrangement as "only a bookkeeping trust," Packard was confirmed in late January 1969.

Packard served as a spokesman for a number of administration defense proposals.

Throughout 1969 he defended the administration's proposed Safeguard antiballistic missile system before a skeptical Congress. In March 1969 he testified before the Senate Foreign Relations Committee, then holding hearings to build a case against the system. Packard maintained that the Soviet Union was reaching parity with the United States on the total number of missiles and that the system was therefore necessary. Senator Gore countered with the view that the United States was so far ahead in the missile race that its "overkill" capacity was not jeopardized by the Soviet Union's "first strike" capacity. Later that year Packard was forced to admit that the Defense Department was using funds from other programs to begin development of the system despite its promise not to initiate development until Congress approved the plan. Congress approved funds for the project in December.

In 1970 and 1971 Packard led the administration's campaign to save the nearly bankrupt Lockheed Aircraft Corp. In March he told the House Armed Services Committee of the "need to preserve" Lockheed's capabilities while it unraveled its financial difficulties, and in December he disclosed the $1 billion plan to resolve the Pentagon's outstanding disputes with the ailing company. During June 1971 Packard testified before the Senate Banking and Currency Committee in support of the Lockheed bailout bill by which the Nixon administration would guarantee $250 million worth of bank loans to the faltering company.

Packard's support for Treasury Secretary JOHN B. CONNALLY's testimony that Lockheed could not survive without the federal loan guarantee was ambivalent. In his view the financial health of Lockheed was more an economic than a defense matter because of the substantial unemployment and financial losses for the defense and airline industries if Lockheed failed. Under questioning, his support for the bill was diluted by his estimate that Lockheed would need to sell well over 300 aircraft to break even and by his view that the bill potentially set a dangerous precedent for "corporate bailouts" in the future. His testimony exposed a rift within the Nixon administration over the project. Nevertheless, the loan guarantees were passed in July.

Packard also acted as Pentagon spokesman in disputes with civil rights leaders over the Defense Department's alleged failure to follow administration antidiscrimination guidelines. On numerous occasions he also testified before Congress in support of arms sales credit overseas. In May 1970 he was called upon to explain the U.S. invasion of Cambodia. He maintained that the United States would have taken military action against Communist bases in Cambodia earlier except for political considerations dictated by the fact that Prince Sihanouk was in power.

White House press secretary RONALD ZIEGLER announced Packard's resignation from his Pentagon post for "strictly personal reasons" in December 1971. Packard resumed his duties with Hewlett-Packard, where he became chairman of the board in 1972. He also served, beginning in 1973, on DAVID ROCKEFELLER's Trilateral Commission, a group of concerned citizens from the United States, Western Europe, and Japan who met to discuss prob-

lems of the advanced industrialized countries. He died in 1996.

—LG

Passman, Otto E(rnest)

(1900–1988) *member of the House of Representatives; chairman, Foreign Operations Subcommittee of the House Appropriations Committee*

Born on June 27, 1900, Passman, the son of sharecropper parents, left grade school when he was 13 to earn a living. He started a manufacturing company in 1929 and eventually became a well-to-do businessman. He decided to enter politics while serving in the navy during World War II and won his first campaign when he was elected to the House in 1946 as a Democrat.

A staunch conservative and critic of most federal spending, Passman won a seat on the House Appropriations Committee in 1949. A consistent critic of foreign aid programs, he was appointed chairman of the Appropriation Committee's Foreign Operations Subcommittee in 1955. His panel had jurisdiction over all foreign aid appropriations, and he became the most powerful House opponent of the foreign aid program. He sharply cut annual foreign aid requests made by every administration until he was successfully challenged in 1964 by President Johnson and Representative GEORGE H. MAHON (D-Tex.), the newly installed head of the Appropriations Committee. That year Passman was outvoted in his own subcommittee when the fiscal 1965 foreign aid request was cut by only 7.6 percent. His support on the subcommittee eroded further during the following year when the foreign aid request was cut by only 7 percent. These were among the smallest cuts ever made in the foreign aid program.

But Passman was again able to make substantial cuts in foreign aid requests when congressional opposition to the program increased as the cost of the Vietnam War escalated during the late 1960s. Passman cut the fiscal 1969 request by almost 40 percent, which was then the largest reduction ever made in the foreign aid program. Passman described the cut as "about half enough."

During the NIXON-FORD years Passman's subcommittee usually slashed foreign aid requests by more than 25 percent. The cuts, when coupled with the administration's already reduced requests for foreign aid, dropped the annual funding for foreign economic and military assistance programs from the $3 billion level during the 1960s to the $2 billion level during most of the Nixon-Ford years.

Although spending for economic and military assistance was sharply curtailed, total foreign aid appropriations increased significantly after 1973 when American interests focused on the Middle East. During this period most of the increased foreign aid spending financed special programs that benefited four Middle Eastern countries—Israel, Egypt, Jordan, and Syria. Although Passman initially opposed Middle Eastern aid, he eventually sponsored the bill giving $5.8 billion in military and economic assistance to the area.

Passman fully approved the $660 million that the administration requested for Israel and Egypt for fiscal 1975. At the same time, however, he reduced the White House request for foreign economic and military assistance by 41 percent, the largest cut ever made in the program. These cuts reflected congressional concern over the slumping U.S. economy and the mounting federal deficit.

The following year he supported the substantially increased foreign aid appropriations that the House approved for fiscal 1976 and 1977 when it appropriated about $5 billion for all foreign aid programs. Passman argued for the fiscal 1976 increase, noting that most of it was for Middle Eastern programs that sup-

ported the Sinai disengagement agreement between Egypt and Israel.

Although Passman still favored larger foreign aid program cuts than those supported by the Senate, he no longer was the most vocal opponent of the foreign aid program. The strong opposition to the foreign aid requests came from liberal senators on the Senate Foreign Relations Committee who were determined to use their control over foreign aid authorization bills as a lever for changing the administration's foreign policy. Their disputes with the White House over foreign policy issues often stalled the passage of foreign aid appropriations bills during this period when the House and Senate failed to agree on foreign policy positions adopted by the Senate.

Liberal House members tried to unseat Passman as the chairman of the Foreign Operations Subcommittee in 1975 because of his opposition to most social welfare measures sponsored by fellow Democrats. He also was one of two House members publicly opposed to Nixon's impeachment after the White House released the tape transcripts that showed that Nixon had discussed using the CIA to block the FBI's Watergate probe. The liberal challenge failed when the Democratic Caucus confirmed Passman's appointment.

However, Passman's 30-year House career ended the following year when he lost the primary election amid a flurry of corruption charges. In 1978 Passman was indicted on charges of accepting large bribes from South Korean businessman Tong Sun Park in return for using his position to influence federal agencies to increase loans to South Korea and pressure South Korean businessmen into using Park as their agent in dealing with the U.S. government. He was later indicted for income tax evasion. In April 1979 Passman was acquitted of the charges. He retired to his home in Monroe, Louisiana, where he died in 1988.

—AE

Pastore, John O(rlando)

(1907–2000) *member of the Senate*

John O. Pastore was born on March 17, 1907, in Providence, Rhode Island. Pastore, the son of an immigrant tailor, earned his law degree from Northeastern University in 1931 and, after briefly practicing law, launched a career in politics. He won election as lieutenant governor of Rhode Island in 1944 and a year later was elected governor. After serving two terms, Pastore won a seat in the U.S. Senate, becoming the first Italian American ever elected to that body. A liberal on most domestic issues, Pastore supported the Kennedy and Johnson administrations' programs designed to eradicate poverty and discrimination in America. Representing a state that contained two important navy facilities, he also backed President Johnson's defense spending and his conduct of the Vietnam War.

During the early years of the NIXON administration, Pastore continued to support the president's war and defense policies. But in 1970, the same year his Senate seat was challenged by a peace candidate, he voted for the Cooper-Church and Hatfield-McGovern amendments, aimed at ending the Vietnam conflict. That year he also departed from his previous support of defense spending by joining an unsuccessful attempt to place a $66 billion ceiling on Defense Department appropriations for fiscal 1971. Although he sided with Nixon on continued development of the Safeguard antiballistic missile, he voted against purchasing the F-111 fighter-bomber. In 1974 Pastore endorsed the reduction of U.S. troop levels abroad and opposed the resumption of military aid to Turkey. He also took part in the losing effort to block approval of the fiscal 1975 foreign aid bill.

Throughout the Nixon-FORD years Pastore seldom strayed from the liberal record on domestic issues he had compiled throughout his tenure in the Senate. He favored gun control, establishment of a consumer protection agency, federal campaign subsidies, and tax reform. An articulate supporter of civil rights legislation in the 1960s, Pastore in 1969 approved of the administration's Philadelphia Plan to integrate the construction trades through minority hiring quotas. However, he refused to endorse Nixon's Supreme Court nomination of conservative CLEMENT HAYNSWORTH. The Rhode Islander also consistently backed the use of forced busing to achieve school desegregation. He opposed "no-knock" entry legislation and favored the reduction of penalties for marijuana offenses. The major exception to Pastore's liberalism in domestic concerns was his opposition to government abortion aid. A Roman Catholic from a predominantly Catholic state, he voted for a bill in April 1975 that would have barred the use of Medicaid funds for abortions except to save the life of the mother.

As chairman of the Commerce Committee's Subcommittee on Communications, Pastore wielded considerable power in the regulation of TV and other media. He was instrumental in the development of public television and sponsored the 1973 law that lifted TV sports blackouts of professional home games when all tickets were sold out 72 hours in advance. Pastore was a leader in the push for the Federal Election Campaign Act of 1971, the first major reform of campaign financing rules in 50 years. He also helped to write the law's campaign media spending limit in response to election expenditures that had soared in the 1960s with the increased use of television. Under the new law, which took effect in the 1972 presidential and congressional elections, a candidate was allowed to spend 10 cents per voter on media advertising—including TV and radio, newspapers and magazines, and billboards. To allow for inflation, the spending limit was tied to annual increases in the Consumer Price Index, and broadcasters were required to give candidates their lowest possible advertising rates.

Pastore alternated as chairman of the Joint Committee on Atomic Energy. In this role he presided over passage of the Energy Reorganization Act of 1974, which abolished the Atomic Energy Commission (AEC) and established the Energy Research and Development Administration (ERDA) to absorb the AEC's nuclear development and promotional activities and the Nuclear Regulatory Commission to assume AEC regulatory functions. Growing criticism over the conflict between the AEC's promotional efforts and its regulatory duties and a desire to consolidate the government's widely scattered energy programs led to the bill's enactment, which President Gerald Ford had labeled his top priority energy legislation. It was signed into law October 12.

At age 69 Pastore retired from the Senate in 1976 before the end of his term to give his successor, Republican JOHN CHAFEE, seniority. He retired to a North Kingston, Rhode Island, nursing home, where he died of kidney failure in July 2000.

—JR

Patman, (John) (William) Wright
(1893–1976) *member of the House of Representatives; chairman, Banking and Currency Committee*

Born on August 6, 1893, the son of a cotton farmer, Patman worked as a sharecropper to finance his legal studies and obtained his law degree from Cumberland University in Tennessee in 1916. He was elected to the Texas house of representatives in 1920, where he served two terms. In 1924 he was elected district attorney in Texarkana. Four years later he was elected to the U.S. House on an anti–Ku Klux Klan platform.

With the onset of the Depression, Patman became part of the southern Democratic bloc in Congress that supported the liberal social legislation of the New Deal. In 1932 Patman's call for the resignation of Secretary of the Treasury Andrew Mellon had already established his reputation as an enemy of eastern finance capital.

Patman's antibanking crusade was aimed at what he viewed as the excessive interest rates charged by the large eastern banks and promoted by the policies of the Federal Reserve Bank. Patman repeatedly introduced unsuccessful legislation to subject the Fed to government ownership.

Patman became chairman of the House Banking and Currency Committee in 1963. He used this power to conduct extensive investigations into tax-exempt corporations and the interlocking ownership of eastern banks and published the results in highly controversial reports. The "Patman Report," as the Banking Committee's *Commercial Banks and Their Trust Activities* came to be known, appeared in 1968, revealing not only extensive control of nonfinancial corporations by the top 10 U.S. commercial banks, but also massive mutual ownership among the banks themselves.

In early 1969 Patman's committee released a new report severely critical of the power of the one-bank holding companies (OBHCs), which were then exempt from federal regulation. In his introduction to the report Patman asserted that 34 of the largest U.S. commercial banks, with over $100 billion in assets, had established or were planning to establish such companies to avoid Federal Reserve regulations. When President NIXON announced his proposed curbs on OBHCs, Patman attacked them as too weak and filed his own bill.

In mid-1970, due to increasing attention to the U.S. banking system in the wake of the 1969–70 credit crunch, President Nixon established the Commission on Financial Structure and Regulation under Reed O. Hunt to investigate the system. Patman promptly attacked the commission as "little more than a trade association" for the banking industry.

Because of rapidly rising interest rates and tight money sparked by inflation, Patman's lifelong vendettas were accentuated during the Nixon administration. When commercial prime rates reached then-historic highs in mid-1969, reflecting the administration's policies, Patman attacked Secretary of the Treasury DAVID KENNEDY for failing to roll back the rates. Immediately after Kennedy had met with major bank representatives, Patman stated that "the secretary had the 24 largest bankers in the room for 2 1/2 hours, and he could not bring himself to speak up for the American public and ask for a rollback in interest rates."

Patman also played a key role in determining government policy toward the major corporate bankruptcies that emerged in 1970. Just before the Penn Central railroad filed for reorganization under the bankruptcy laws in June 1970, officials of the railroad met with Patman to ask his support for government-guaranteed loans to the Penn Central, which Patman adamantly refused. After the bankruptcy was made public, Patman announced that his committee would investigate the 1950 Defense Production Act to see if aid to the railroad could be provided under its auspices.

In December 1970 Patman's committee issued its report on the Penn Central bankruptcy, which Patman called "one of the saddest, and at times most sordid, pictures of the American business community that has ever been revealed in an official document." In March 1971 the committee issued another report on trading in Penn Central stock prior to bankruptcy, noting that a number of banks had unloaded nearly 2 million shares in the three months prior to June 1970. Patman noted that "it is obvious that many of these sales were undertaken with either the greatest clairvoyance or on the basis of inside information." Later in the summer of 1971, Patman's

committee also held hearings on government aid to the ailing Lockheed Corp., which was eventually granted.

Low-cost housing was another traditional concern of Patman's that occupied his attention during the Nixon years. In January 1971 Patman's committee issued a report charging the Federal Housing Authority with permitting "sheer fraud" and speculation in its federal home ownership program and providing tremendous pork barrels to real estate speculators in slum housing. GEORGE ROMNEY, secretary of the Department of Housing and Urban Development (HUD), initially called the report "inaccurate, misleading, and very incomplete" and said he was shocked that Patman would resort to such tactics. Patman replied that Romney's "emotional blast" showed he was "more interested in attacking the Congress than he was in the real estate speculators and others responsible for the massive abuses in the federal housing program." A week later HUD, conceding widespread abuses uncovered by the report, was forced to suspend the program, which Patman agreed "would do much to restore confidence" in HUD. In January 1973 Romney went much further, freezing all new applications for housing subsidies, public housing, and community development assistance, prompting Patman to announce that his committee "would do everything in its power" to restore these programs on a sound basis.

Patman became increasingly concerned about the deteriorating U.S. economy, warning in July 1971 that a depression was imminent if quick action were not taken, by which Patman meant primarily lower interest rates. He called for a federal agency to regulate interest rates. In early 1973 Patman attacked Nixon's lifting of wage and price controls at the end of Phase Two. Weeks later he called the February 1973 dollar crisis "an international vote of no confidence in the Nixon economic program." He also warned that the United States was taking inadequate measures to deal with the pending energy crisis. When the commercial prime interest rate hit a record 10 percent in August 1973, Patman denounced the "public be damned" attitude of the banks and renewed his efforts to subject the Federal Reserve Bank to audits by the General Accounting Office (GAO). His own committee killed Patman's proposed bill on this question. In May 1974 the House finally approved a bill for GAO audits of the Fed, but all of Patman's proposals had been removed from the legislation. When his last attempt to push through such legislation was killed by the Rules Committee in 1975, Patman announced that "it is no secret that the big business and big banking community, orchestrated by the Federal Reserve, have been working hard to kill or weaken the audit bill."

Patman played a minor role in the early stages of the Watergate scandal. In October 1972, one month before the election, he attempted to convene his committee for hearings on possible violations of banking laws in the Watergate break-in. This move was essentially a pretext to open the affair to congressional scrutiny and to embarrass the president in the midst of the election campaign. Republican members of Patman's committee effectively blocked such hearings despite Patman's renewed efforts to open them a week later. Patman attributed the opposition to the hearings to interference from the highest levels of government and predicted that "the facts will come out."

In January 1975 Patman was deposed as chairman of the Banking and Currency Committee in the "Young Turks" revolt of younger Democratic liberals that also stripped two other long-standing southern Democratic committee chairmen of their posts. Patman was succeeded by Representative HENRY REUSS (D-Wis.) and demoted to chairman of the Subcommittee on Domestic Monetary Policy. In this capacity he supported Reuss's controver-sial bill requiring the Federal Reserve Bank to expand the domestic money supply at a rate of 6 percent per year, but the House turned the bill into a sense-of-Congress resolution. Shortly after announcing that he would not seek reelection in the fall, Patman contracted pneumonia and died on March 7, 1976.

—LG

Pell, Claiborne de Borda
(1918–   ) *member of the Senate*

Born on November 22, 1918, into a socially and politically prominent Newport family, Pell attended the fashionable St. George's School and graduated from Princeton in 1940. He served in the coast guard during World War II and was a special assistant to the State Department in 1945. Commissioned in the Foreign Service in 1946, he worked in various European embassies before returning to Washington in 1950 to work in the State Department. Pell left the department in the early 1950s to return to Rhode Island, where he worked as a partner in an investment banking firm and received political recognition as a top state Democratic fund-raiser. In 1960 he won a seat in the U.S. Senate.

Pell, a liberal, supported most of the Kennedy and Johnson administrations' domestic legislative programs, including all major civil rights legislation of the period. He was instrumental in the passage of legislation in 1964 that established a National Council on the Arts and was a sponsor of legislation designed to provide high-speed intercity rail service for the busy "Northeast corridor." During the Johnson administration he was a firm, if not particularly vocal, opponent of the Vietnam War.

Pell received high ratings from the liberal Americans for Democratic Action (ADA) during the NIXON-FORD years. Pell frequently supported the president's foreign policy but voted against the administration more than 50 percent of the time on domestic policy. Pell supported busing and government abortion aid and opposed the death penalty. He voted against the Supreme Court nominations of G. HARROLD CARSWELL and CLEMENT HAYNSWORTH, both of whom were rejected by the Senate. However, he did vote for the nomination of WILLIAM REHNQUIST to the Supreme Court, differing with many Senate liberals. He advocated national health insurance and aid to mass transit. A supporter of campaign financing reform, Pell cosponsored a bill in March 1974 to provide for public financing of federal election campaigns. Pell was particularly interested in education and in 1971 sponsored a bill to provide federal aid to those attending post–high school vocational and trade schools. The Senate passed the bill without a dissenting vote.

Pell voted for the Cooper-Church Amendment to limit U.S. involvement in Cambodia in 1970. Later that year he criticized U.S. bombing raids of North Vietnam, calling them "counterproductive to an ultimate peace settlement and to our national interests." In June 1972 Pell charged that the U.S. armed forces had used rain-making technology for military purposes in Indochina, causing downpours that killed thousands of people. He then introduced a draft of a treaty barring weather and climate modification activities as weapons of war. President Nixon appointed Pell U.S. representative to the UN General Assembly in 1970. In that post Pell called for the UN to press the North Vietnamese to allow identification of war prisoners and to allow Red Cross access to those held. In the Senate he also voted for the Rhodesian chrome ban and for a reduction in the number of U.S. troops stationed abroad.

With Senator JACOB JAVITS (R-N.Y.), Pell visited Cuba in September 1974 on a personal fact-finding mission during which he met with Premier Fidel Castro on the possible renewal of relations between Washington and Havana. The senators visited Cuba without the official sanction of the State Department, although they had been granted visas. Following the visit Pell recommended that the United States resume normal relations with Cuba and urged the State Department to lift travel restrictions to Cuba. The administration took no action on the suggestions.

Pell was reelected in 1978 with 75 percent of the vote. He was reelected in 1984 and 1990, retiring in January 1997.

—GMS

Pepper, Claude D(enson)
(1900–1989) *member of the House of Representatives*

Born on September 8, 1900, and raised in Alabama, Claude Pepper served in the armed forces during part of World War I before graduating from Alabama State University. After receiving his law degree from Harvard in 1924, he moved to Florida to practice and was elected to the Florida house of representatives in 1929 as a Democrat. Pepper won a U.S. Senate seat in 1936. He served until 1951. In the upper house he compiled a liberal record, voting for New and Fair Deal legislation. He called for a national health insurance plan as early as 1935. An opponent of the cold war, Pepper favored accommodation with the Soviet Union and cuts in the military budget.

In 1950 big business, industry, oil companies, and medical associations united to oust Pepper. George Smathers, running one of the dirtiest campaigns in U.S. history, characterized by slander and red-baiting, defeated him in the primary.

In 1962 Pepper returned to Capitol Hill, easily winning election from Florida's newly created 11th congressional district. During the Johnson years he consistently supported programs for the elderly, who made up a large portion of his constituency. He backed Medicare, increased Social Security benefits, and nutritional programs for senior citizens. A supporter of the Vietnam War in its early years, in 1968 Pepper called for a withdrawal of U.S. troops.

In 1969 Pepper introduced a resolution establishing the Select Committee on Crime with himself as its chairman. While the committee during its three-year existence was responsible for very little legislation and some critics dismissed its work as mere "publicity," Pepper asserted that its hearings, conducted nationwide, had awakened Americans to the magnitude of the drug problem. The committee urged that possession of heroin paraphernalia be a crime, succeeded in reducing the overproduction of amphetamines, and helped sponsor research for a methadone substitute. In 1971 the seven-member panel recommended that Congress pass a preventive detention law to keep drug pushers from jumping bail while awaiting trial and that the United States work for treaties to curb the production of opium around the world.

On foreign policy Pepper's position was more middle-of-the-road during the NIXON-FORD administrations than it had been during his Senate term. While he remained an opponent of the Vietnam War, Pepper voted against large cuts in the military budget. He fought curtailment of the ABM system, the SST, and the F-14 fighter aircraft. Reflecting the feelings of his large Cuban constituency, he opposed recognition of Castro's government.

Pepper was most effective in programs to aid the elderly. He consistently supported increases in Social Security benefits and expansion of Medicare and in 1971 succeeded in amending the Older Americans Act of 1965, setting up low-cost meal programs and nutritional training. Declaring that "mandatory retirement is an extravagant waste of people,"

Pepper guided through the House the 1978 law raising the mandatory retirement age in private industry from 65 to 70 and abolished 70 as the age at which federal employees must retire. In 1989 President GEORGE H. W. BUSH awarded Pepper the Medal of Freedom. Pepper died in office on May 30, 1989.

—FLM

Percy, Charles H(arting)
(1919–   ) *member of the Senate*

Born on September 27, 1919, the son of an office worker, Charles Percy grew up in Chicago. He worked his way through the University of Chicago, where he operated a campus equipment agency that grossed over $150,000 a year. Receiving his B.A. in economics in 1941, Percy joined Bell & Howell, a camera and photographic equipment manufacturer. After serving in the navy during World War II, he returned to Bell & Howell as a corporate secretary and was made president of the firm in 1949. At that time he was the youngest chief executive of a major American corporation.

Under Percy's leadership the corporation grew rapidly during the 1950s and 1960s, becoming the largest camera equipment manufacturer in the country. Concerned about the welfare of his employees, Percy introduced a profit-sharing plan and developed a comprehensive retirement program. He remained president of Bell & Howell until 1963 and chairman of the board of directors until 1966.

Percy's involvement in politics began in earnest during the mid-1950s when he worked as a fund-raiser for the Illinois Republican Party. At his prodding the Republican National Committee created in 1959 a Committee on Program and Progress to formulate party goals and appointed Percy to lead it. In 1960 he was chosen to head the party's Platform Committee at the Republican National Convention.

After an unsuccessful race for the governorship of Illinois in 1964, Percy won a seat in the U.S. Senate in 1966. Entering the Senate in 1967, he quickly distinguished himself as a newcomer who spoke openly on a wide range of issues. His liberalism put him at odds with most of his fellow Republicans. Percy won reelection in 1972 with a margin of over 1 million votes.

A vocal critic of the Vietnam War, Percy consistently supported Senate efforts to end the conflict. In 1970 he voted in favor of the Cooper-Church Amendment to cut off funds for combat operations in Cambodia. He opposed extension of the draft in 1971 and in the following year voted in favor of the Foreign Relations Committee's proposal to cut off funds for combat operations by the end of 1972. Percy repeatedly urged the president to set a timetable for complete withdrawal of U.S. troops and urged a unilateral American cease-fire in Vietnam. In 1973 he cosponsored with Senator JACOB JAVITS (R-N.Y.) the War Powers Act, which limited the president's ability to commit U.S. troops to combat abroad without congressional approval.

A liberal in domestic affairs, Percy took an active legislative role on a wide range of issues. He supported the use of money from the highway trust fund for mass transit, advocated increased federal aid to education, and urged expansion of the food stamp program and stronger efforts to eradicate hunger and malnutrition. As a member of the Senate's Special Committee on Aging, Percy became an advocate of the needs of the elderly, outlining his proposals in *Growing Old in the Country of the Young* (1974). He worked hard to include special provisions for the aged in social welfare legislation and in 1972 helped win passage of a measure that tied Social Security benefits to increases in the cost of living, thus protecting the elderly against inflation. Percy also helped draft the Budget Reform Act of 1974, prohib-

iting the impoundment of funds by the president.

Percy was one of the earliest advocates of consumer protection. In 1972 he cosponsored with Senator Jacob Javits and Senator ABRAHAM RIBICOFF (D-Conn.) a bill to create an independent consumer protection agency. After the bill was killed by a filibuster in 1974, Percy attacked its opponents as the "most powerful and lavishly funded lobbying group" in Washington. Although the bill gained widespread support in Congress in the following years, with both houses passing slightly different versions of the measure in 1975, the inability to override a threatened veto by President FORD kept Senate and House conferees from working out the differences in their respective bills.

During the NIXON years Percy frequently found himself at odds with the president. In addition to his opposition to the president's war policies, he voted against the nominations of CLEMENT HAYNSWORTH and G. HARROLD CARSWELL to the Supreme Court, opposed continued funding of the SST and the Lockheed loan, and sharply attacked Nixon's impoundment of funds appropriated by Congress for domestic programs. His actions won him a place on Nixon's "enemies list" and made him a target of White House attacks.

A vocal critic of Nixon's handling of the Watergate affair, Percy drafted the resolution in 1973 that called for the appointment of a Watergate special prosecutor. In March 1974 Percy predicted that the House would impeach the president; the following month he said that Nixon's resignation would be good for the country, and he urged the Republican Party to reject Watergate in its entirety.

Urging the Republican Party to unite behind Gerald Ford after Nixon's resignation, Percy advised Ford to moderate the strongly conservative tone of his 1976 campaign. A member of the Governmental Affairs Committee that investigated in 1977 the financial dealings of President JIMMY CARTER's budget director, Bert Lance, Percy called for Lance's resignation and urged the appointment of a special prosecutor to investigate the matter further. Percy was defeated for reelection in 1984 by Paul Simon. Residing in Washington, D.C., he is currently president of Charles Percy and Associates, Inc.

—JD

Perot, H(enry) Ross
(1930–) *billionaire businessman and philanthropist*

Born on June 27, 1930, the son of a Texas cotton broker and horse trader, Perot graduated from the U.S. Naval Academy in 1953. After leaving the navy in 1957 he went to Dallas to work as a computer salesman for International Business Machines (IBM), where he remained until 1962. Although offered an executive position, he decided instead to start his own business installing and operating computers for companies by contract. Calling his firm the Electronic Data Systems Corp. (EDS), he rented computers at wholesale rates and then distributed them at retail prices to his clients. His clever management made him and his associates multimillionaires by 1968, when he incorporated his business. From September 1968 to April 1970 the price of his stock rose from $16.50 a share to $150. His investments in his own stock, of which he retained 9 million shares, made him a billionaire.

Determined to make use of his new wealth for humanitarian ends, Perot established a nonprofit philanthropic organization, the Perot Foundation, in April 1969. He donated millions of dollars to the Dallas public school system, including funds to support a ghetto elementary school. He contributed $1 million to the Boy Scouts of America so it could provide increased facilities for blacks and Mexicans in the South. In 1970 he and former astronaut Colonel Frank Borman joined forces to form the American Horizons Foundation, a group that would provide money for public discussion panels on television and sound out public opinion on national issues. A conservative Presbyterian, Perot believed in the strict habits of the small town and untiringly praised the "strong family unit" as the key to solving America's problems.

Perot was intensely involved with helping American prisoners of war (POWs) in Vietnam. His concern was first aroused in 1969 when four women asked him for money with which they could travel to the Paris peace talks to question the North Vietnamese negotiators about the condition of their POW husbands. After granting the women's requests Perot began a nationwide campaign to secure the release of American POWs in Vietnam. The group he established through EDS, called United We Stand, spent over $1 million advertising the plight of the prisoners and urging Americans to stand behind President NIXON's Vietnam policies. It collected tons of mail, clothing, food, and medicine for the POWs, but its cargo planes were denied permission to land by North Vietnam in December 1969.

In January 1970 the Vietnamese rejected his offer of $100 million for the release of American POWs and would not meet with him when he flew to Paris and Vientiane, Laos, in April 1970 to discuss POW release, denouncing his activities as U.S. "propaganda." Nevertheless, Perot's efforts made the U.S. government and the public more aware of the POWs' plight and influenced the Nixon administration to insist on their safety at the Paris peace talks. His activities also forced the North Vietnamese government to improve their treatment and increase the flow of American mail to them.

Perot favored free public discussion and participation among Americans about the war, but urged support of the government as the quickest way of ending the conflict. He claimed to be nonpartisan in politics and to have no political ambitions. The Nixon administration did little of an official nature to encourage his efforts to free the POWs.

Perot's sudden wealth led him into the world of high finance. In 1970 he lent $10 million to the nation's third-largest securities firm, F. I. duPont, Glore Forgan, Inc., and took over the company's ownership to rescue it from debt. After he incorporated the firm in 1971, he was indemnified by the New York Stock Exchange for his efforts. Continuing his stock speculations, Perot organized the duPont Walston, Inc., brokerage firm in July 1973, ostensibly to save the two big brokerage houses from bankruptcy. He invested over $100 million in paying off their previous indebtedness when he effected the 1973 merger, creating the second-largest securities firm in the country, but it went bankrupt in March 1974 and was dissolved. Despite his promises to restore the firm to solvency and efficiency, Perot acquiesced in its dismemberment, realizing he had failed.

W. J. Allegaert, trustee of the bankrupt firm, charged in July 1975 that Perot had merged the two brokerage houses to recoup his earlier losses in duPont, Glore Forgan, Inc. Allegaert filed a $90 million lawsuit against Perot, contending he had deliberately thrust that firm's indebtedness on the stronger Walston firm, thus appeasing the stock exchange, which had threatened to expose duPont's inept management.

In 1974 the Senate Watergate committee disclosed that Representative WILBUR D. MILLS (D-Ark.) had received a secret $100,000 campaign contribution in 1972 from the president of EDS, Milledge A. Hart, and the Dallas regional vice president. Although Perot was not directly involved, his corporation's reputation for honesty was besmirched. In early 1979 Perot again made headlines when he hired a

commando team to incite a riot in Iran. The riot led to the storming of a prison and the freeing of thousands of inmates, including two representatives of EDS.

In the early 1980s Perot became a member of RONALD REAGAN's President's Foreign Intelligence Advisory Board (PFIAB). Perot began a presidential campaign early in 1992 as an unaffiliated candidate who pledged to remain independent and to personally finance his campaign. Reportedly, Perot disliked Vice President GEORGE H. W. BUSH, who was the Republican nominee for president, because he had not done enough as vice president to support efforts to find POWs in Vietnam. He eventually was placed on enough ballots to run for president and poured $37 million of his own money into the race, receiving 19 percent of the vote in the November election. After Bush's loss to Clinton in the 1992 election, Republicans derided Perot for his candidacy.

The following year, 1993, Perot established a watchdog organization called United We Stand to monitor the federal government and the Democratic and Republican parties. In 1995 Perot founded a new political party, the Reform Party, to serve as a springboard for his 1996 presidential election campaign. In 1996, at the Reform Party's national convention, Perot was nominated as the party's candidate for president and won 8 percent of the vote in the November 1996 election. Perot did not run on another platform in 2000 and simply dropped out of the public limelight for the election cycle.

—AES and SAW

Peterson, Peter
(1926–   ) *secretary of commerce*

Peter Peterson was born on June 5, 1926, in Kearney, Nebraska. Peterson had studied at Northwestern University and then at the

University of Chicago, where he obtained his M.B.A. in 1951. He began his business career at Market Facts, Inc., a Chicago research firm, and had become assistant director by the time he moved to the advertising firm of McCann-Erickson in 1953. In 1958 Peterson went to work for the Bell & Howell Co., eventually serving as chairman of the board and chief executive officer from 1968 to 1971.

In 1971 Peterson became an adviser on international economic affairs to President NIXON, working closely with Secretary of the Treasury JOHN CONNALLY. In announcing Peterson's appointment as executive director of the newly created cabinet-level Council on International Economic Policy, a White House spokesman said the council would attempt to provide a "clear top-level focus on international economic issues and to achieve consistency between international and domestic economic policy."

In August 1971 Peterson participated in the special economic meeting at Camp David, Maryland, where Nixon and his top economic advisers devised a large-scale turnabout in administration policy known as the "New Economic Policy" (NEP). At Camp David Peterson generally supported the views of John Connally, whose aggressive plans to stabilize the dollar on international markets signaled a complete departure from the "benign neglect" policies previously advocated by Director of the Office of Management and Budget GEORGE SHULTZ and the Council of Economic Advisors (CEA).

Peterson also was an architect of a new "get tough" policy with developing countries that nationalized U.S. companies. In early January 1972 he announced that the United States would cut off aid to countries that did not swiftly compensate nationalized firms.

In late January 1972 Peterson replaced MAURICE STANS as secretary of commerce. In one of his first statements as secretary, he warned of the intensified competition facing the United States in the world market and called on the United States to undertake a "worldwide economic intelligence effort" to keep abreast of foreign developments. Peterson was committed to free trade. A week before his appointment he appeared with John Connally at a meeting organized by the Conference Board, a New York research organization, to attack the proposed Hartke-Burke bill, which would have curbed certain imports and placed restrictions on the operations of U.S. companies abroad.

Peterson played a key role in laying the foundations for the expansion of U.S.-Soviet trade in the 1970s. During May 1972 he held comprehensive talks with Soviet foreign trade minister Nikolai S. Patolichev, which led to the formation of a U.S.-Soviet trade commission with Peterson as chief U.S. negotiator. Two months later he and Secretary of Agriculture EARL BUTZ signed a three-year $750 million agreement for the sale of domestic wheat, corn, and other grains to the Soviet Union. During July Peterson traveled to the Soviet Union and Poland in an effort to formulate a trade agreement.

On October 18 Peterson signed a three-year trade pact with the Soviet Union. It provided for a settlement of Russia's Lend-Lease debt and included a promise by the U.S. government to ask Congress to grant "most favored nation" status to Soviet goods. The secretary signed a similar pact with Poland in November.

A month later Peterson resigned his post. He remained in the administration to conduct a special study on "how the United States can better coordinate our trading policy with our major trading partners."

Peterson became embroiled in the ITT scandal, which enveloped many members of the Nixon administration. In a July 1972 article Washington columnist JACK ANDERSON alleged that ITT, in October 1971, had submitted a plan to the administration through Peterson to guarantee that the Chilean government of Salvador Allende "would not get through the critical next six months." Peterson admitted receiving the memo but denied receiving an 18-point "action plan" and responding to the overture.

In March 1973 the Securities and Exchange Commission (SEC) published its probe of ITT and named Peterson, with Treasury Secretary Connally, as having been "instrumental" in the delay of three government antitrust suits against ITT. Ten days later Peterson testified before the Senate Foreign Relations Committee on ITT's role in Chile and admitted that he had met with ITT chairman HAROLD GENEEN in December 1971 to discuss ITT's "action plan" against Allende. Peterson, however, asserted that the Nixon administration never seriously considered the ITT proposal.

Upon leaving the government in early 1973, Peterson became chairman of the board at Lehman Brothers, a New York investment bank, a post he held until 1984. In 1985 he cofounded the Blackstone Group and in 1992 was a cofounder of the Concord Coalition. Currently he is chairman of the Council on Foreign Relations.

—LRG

Peterson, Rudolph

(1904–2003) *president, Bank of America; chairman, Presidential Task Force on International Development*

Born on December 6, 1904, Rudolph Peterson came to the United States from Sweden as a youth. After obtaining a bachelor's degree from the University of California in 1925, he began a career in finance with the Commercial Credit Co. In 1936 Peterson became district manager for the Bank of America National

Trust and Savings Association in Fresno, California, and thereafter rose through the Bank of America hierarchy to become its president in 1963. Six years later he was succeeded by A. W. Clausen.

In September 1969 the NIXON administration appointed Peterson chairman of the Presidential Task Force on International Development, established to reassess U.S. foreign aid and international economic development. Peterson had made worldwide headlines in April 1967 when he publicly suggested that the United States place an embargo on shipments of its gold reserve to foreign holders of dollars, thereby signaling an end to the period of dialogue on international liquidity between the United States and its trading partners. The task force, which became known as the Peterson Commission, included future secretary of agriculture EARL BUTZ, Harvard economist Gottfried Haberler, and bankers David Rockefeller and Robert Roosa, as well as other businessmen scholars. The Peterson Commission's report appeared in March 1970 amid a spate of similar development reports, most notably the World Bank's Pearson Report and the Rockefeller Report on Latin America, all aimed at an assessment of the first "development decade" in the developing countries.

Despite secondary differences the Peterson Report and its analogues emphasized the absence of serious economic development in developing countries and called for a vast overhauling of the existing aid programs. Of particular importance, according to the report, was the crisis of U.S. foreign policy in such countries as Cuba and Vietnam and the need for a new strategy to combat insurgency in the developing world.

The overall theme of the Peterson Report was the need for a shift from bilateral to multilateral forms of aid. The report advised that the United States should provide "a supporting rather than a directing role in international development." Poorer countries should establish their own development priorities and receive aid "in relation to the efforts they are making on their own behalf." The report emphasized the need for a reorientation of aid through global lending organizations such as the World Bank and for U.S. aid to be "provided largely within a framework set by the international organization." The task force urged the creation of a U.S.-international development bank and institute, the formation of an overseas private investment corporation to guarantee the security of U.S. foreign investments and loans, and the creation of a U.S. development council. It also suggested that all outright relief and welfare grants to poor nations be consolidated under the control of the State Department.

The Peterson Report posed the need for a shift in control of foreign aid from the legislative to the executive branch to avoid the increasing hostility of Congress toward the foreign aid program that had resulted from frustration over the Vietnam War. It urged a "low profile" U.S. military presence, or "Vietnamization," of the U.S. global defense network in which indigenous troops could bear the brunt of any fighting. A strategy also was outlined in the report for using the aid issue to compete with other major developed countries, particularly the European Economic Community (EEC). By connecting the proposed "multilateralism" with a call for all countries to "untie" their aid from agreements that required a receiving nation to buy only from the donor country, the Peterson Report expressed the hope that much of Europe's nonspecified aid grants to developing countries would ultimately result in purchases of U.S. goods. Finally, warning was issued by the task force against the dangers of social revolution abroad that could be averted by an open international investment environment, a preparation of local populations for military,

police, and counterinsurgency functions, and an emphasis on capital-intensive development and mass population control.

In September 1970 President Nixon submitted a message on foreign aid to Congress that closely paralleled the proposals of the Peterson Report. Many of these proposals were adopted in Congress's shift in foreign aid programs after 1970. In August 1971 Nixon recommended Peterson for the post of director of the UN Development Program, which Peterson assumed in January 1972. He served until 1976. In 1977 he became chairman of the policy committee of S. G. Warburg North American Ltd. and held several bank and corporate directorships. He died in 2003.

—LG

Pike, Otis G(rey)
(1921–   ) *member of the House of Representatives; chairman, Select Committee on Intelligence*

Born on August 31, 1921, in Riverhead, New York, Pike graduated from Princeton's Woodrow Wilson School of Public and International Affairs in 1946 after military service in World War II. He received his law degree from Columbia and practiced law privately in his hometown, where he also held local political office, until elected to the House of Representatives in 1960 as a Democrat.

Pike established himself as a moderate and independent representative during his first decade in Congress. Due to his expertise in military affairs and government operations, Pike was appointed to the House Armed Services Committee, where he supported a strong defense posture while seeking to curtail unnecessary military spending; he particularly opposed cost overruns in Defense Department contracts. He also served briefly on the House Ways and Means Committee.

Pike's moderately liberal views on domestic affairs, coupled with his initial conservatism regarding foreign policy, led him to support about 70 percent of the Kennedy and Johnson administrations' programs. As U.S. involvement in Southeast Asia deepened, however, Pike spoke out increasingly against American defense policy. As early as 1968, when he presided over the Armed Services Committee's investigation of the *Pueblo* incident, Pike criticized the intelligence community for activities whose value "has not been worth the cost."

In July 1975 Pike was named chairman of the new House Select Committee on Intelligence, which was created to succeed the old committee of the same name after disagreements among committee Democrats rendered it inoperative. The committee's mandate, like that of a corresponding Senate special committee, was to probe the performance and practices of the U.S. intelligence establishment. Allegations of illegal covert activities as well as its central role in intelligence gathering made the Central Intelligence Agency (CIA) a major focus of the committee's probe.

Pike's committee received testimony that intelligence reporting relating to several international crises had been tampered with for political reasons. Among the incidents examined were: the Communists' 1968 Tet offensive against South Vietnam, alleged Soviet violations of the 1972 strategic arms limitation agreement, the 1973 Arab-Israeli War, the 1973 coup that ousted Chile's Marxist Allende government, Turkey's 1974 invasion of Cyprus, and the 1974 coup in Portugal.

The investigations of the Pike committee were punctuated by conflicts with the FORD administration over access to classified intelligence information. The central issue involved the extent to which secrecy regarding intelligence operations, with its resulting loss of oversight control, was necessary to preserve national security. Pike's position was that "the foreign affairs of the nation belong to the nation, not just to the executive."

When the administration withheld subpoenaed documents, accusing the committee of releasing sensitive information, Pike threatened contempt of Congress proceedings against Central Intelligence Agency director WILLIAM COLBY. A compromise restored the committee's access to classified information; however, a subsequent dispute over the testimony of midlevel State Department officials again led Pike to seek contempt of Congress citations, this time against Secretary of State HENRY KISSINGER. When Kissinger eventually supplied the required information, Pike recommended that the House not pursue the contempt citations.

In its final report the committee supported increased congressional control over intelligence agencies through oversight of their budgets and proposed covert operations. A permanent intelligence oversight committee was strongly recommended as well as a method for regular declassification of information.

The committee's final report provoked as much controversy as its hearings. Although the panel voted to release its report, the full House agreed to delay publication until the administration certified that it contained no sensitive secrets. Rather than allow the executive branch to "censor the report," Pike favored killing it entirely; however, the question became moot after New York's *Village Voice* published excerpts of the report that had been leaked by CBS news reporter DANIEL SCHORR. The resulting storm over House security procedures obscured the committee's efforts at constructive reform of congressional intelligence oversight.

Pike was reelected in 1976. He declined to seek a 10th term in 1978. From 1979 to 1999 he was a columnist for the Newhouse newspapers. He currently resides in Vero Beach, Florida.

—PG

Powell, Lewis F(ranklin), Jr.

(1907–1998)   *associate justice, U.S. Supreme Court*

Lewis F. Powell Jr. was born on September 19, 1907, in Suffolk, Virginia. Powell received a bachelor's degree in 1929 and a law degree in 1931 from Washington and Lee University. After another year's study at Harvard Law School, he joined an old Richmond, Virginia, firm in 1932, where he became a partner in 1937. A corporate attorney, Powell specialized in securities law, corporate mergers, acquisitions, and reorganizations. He eventually became a director of a number of large companies such as Philip Morris and Ethyl Corp. Powell also engaged in a wide variety of public service work. He headed the Richmond Board of Education from 1952 to 1961 and helped bring peaceful school desegregation to the city at a time when other Virginia schools closed rather than integrate. Powell served on the state board of education, the Virginia constitutional revision commission, and President Lyndon Johnson's National Crime Commission during the 1960s. Long active in the American Bar Association, Powell was president of the organization in 1964 and 1965. He headed the American College of Trial Lawyers from 1969 to 1970 and the American Bar Foundation from 1969 to 1971. Along with WILLIAM H. REHNQUIST, Powell was nominated to the Supreme Court on October 21, 1971. A recognized leader of the legal profession, Powell faced no significant opposition, and the Senate confirmed his appointment on December 6 by an 89-1 vote. He was sworn in on January 7, 1972.

As a justice Powell was frequently compared to JOHN MARSHALL HARLAN. Like Harlan, he showed great regard for the doctrines of federalism and separation of powers. Powell also was skeptical of the Court's ability to achieve social reform and favored a policy of judicial

Justice Lewis F. Powell Jr. *(Library of Congress)*

restraint. He was sensitive to jurisdictional limitations on the Court and adopted Harlan's practice of balancing conflicting interests in deciding cases. Uncomfortable with abstract theories and absolute rules, the justice preferred a flexible approach that allowed him to accommodate the competing values in a suit.

In First Amendment cases, for example, Powell usually weighed free expression against other societal interests. His majority opinion in a June 1972 decision upheld the private property rights of a shopping center owner over the free-speech rights of antiwar protesters and sustained the owner in barring the distribution of political pamphlets on his premises. In April 1974 Powell voided the mail censorship system in California's prisons because it infringed on First Amendment rights more than was necessary to ensure prison security and discipline. Two months later, for a five-man majority, the justice balanced freedom of the press against the right of privacy. He ruled that individuals who were not public figures or officials could recover actual damages for defamatory falsehoods if they proved negligence, not the more limited "actual malice," by the press.

Justice Powell adhered to Harlan's view that state criminal procedures must be "fundamentally fair" but need not meet the standards set for the federal government in the Bill of Rights. He also balanced the claims of defendants and the government in criminal cases but tended to give greater weight to society's interests. In June 1972 Powell voted to guarantee the right to counsel in certain misdemeanor cases and to afford defendants the right to a hearing before their parole could be revoked. However, his majority opinion in a May 1972 case narrowed the scope of the immunity a person must receive before being forced to give up his privilege against self-incrimination. The justice took a restrictive view of the Fifth Amendment in other cases as well. He also favored the government's position in most Fourth Amendment cases. However, he did speak for the Court in June 1972 to hold that the president had no authority to use electronic surveillance in domestic security cases without a warrant. He voted to uphold state death penalty laws in June 1972, arguing that capital punishment was constitutional and that the Court could only rule on the manner of execution used and the appropriateness of the death penalty for a particular crime.

In race discrimination cases Powell urged the Court to abandon the distinction between de facto and de jure school segregation and to establish instead a uniform national desegregation rule. He voted in July 1974 against the use of interdistrict busing to remedy school segregation in Detroit but two years later favored the inclusion of suburbs in a plan to correct intentional segregation in urban public housing. For a five-man majority in April 1977 Powell ruled that suburban zoning regulations,

which effectively barred housing for low-income minorities, were not unconstitutional unless a racially discriminatory motive for the regulations could be proven. In other equal-protection cases Powell employed a balanced approach and frequently voted to overturn government distinctions based on illegitimacy, alienage, and sex. In March 1973, however, the justice wrote for a five-man majority to hold that school financing schemes based on property taxes did not violate the equal protection clause.

Powell supported a trend narrowing the Court's jurisdiction and wrote several significant opinions in this area. His May 1974 opinion for the Court made class action suits more difficult by ruling that plaintiffs in such cases must bear the full cost of notifying all members of the class on whose behalf they were suing. In a June 1975 opinion Powell tightened the requirement that plaintiffs have legal standing to bring a suit before the Court will hear their case. In July 1976 he restricted federal court review of challenges to convictions based on the Fourth Amendment brought by state prisoners.

The justice approached due process claims on a case-by-case basis. He voted with the majority in January 1973 to overturn state laws restricting abortions during the first six months of pregnancy as a denial of due process. However, he dissented in January 1975 when the Court held that due process required public school students to receive a notice and a hearing prior to suspension. Powell was described as a friend of the businessman in Court. He often voted against the government in antitrust cases. In a June 1975 decision Powell ruled that a labor union was subject to antitrust laws if it tried to coerce a general contractor into dealing only with union subcontractors. Powell's most famous opinion came in 1978, where in *Regents of the University of California v. Bakke*, he upheld the principle of affirmative action. Powell retired in 1987 and was replaced on the Court by Anthony Kennedy. He died of pneumonia at his Richmond, Virginia, home in 1998.

—CAB

Price, Raymond K(issam), (Jr.)
(1930–   ) *special assistant to the president; special consultant to the president*

Born on May 6, 1930, Raymond Price grew up in rural Long Island and received his B.A. from Yale University in 1951. After serving as an officer in the navy he began a career in journalism in 1955, working at *Collier's* and *Life* magazines. He joined the *New York Herald Tribune* in 1957 and became editor of the editorial page in 1964. After the demise of that paper in 1966, he was writing a novel when asked by RICHARD NIXON in February 1967 to join a small staff planning a possible Nixon campaign for the presidency.

A month after accepting his offer, Price accompanied Nixon on a three-week round-the-world trip. The tour, the second of four such foreign study trips made in preparation for the presidential race, covered Asia, including Vietnam. During the campaign Price worked as a speechwriter. The nomination assured, Nixon went to Long Island with Price during the Republican National Convention to write his acceptance speech. The address included an "I see" passage, evoking Nixon's vision of America's future that had been suggested by another speechwriter, WILLIAM L. SAFIRE, and ended with a "train whistle" peroration that took the audience back to the candidate's childhood and reaffirmed the American dream.

After Nixon's election Price was charged with the responsibility of drafting his inaugural address. The president-elect asked for recommendations from such aides as newly appointed assistant for national security affairs

HENRY KISSINGER and urban affairs adviser DANIEL PATRICK MOYNIHAN. Nixon worked closely with Price on the speech. In preparing the address Nixon defined the themes of his presidency: a reversal of the flow of power from the federal back to the local level to make government more effective; a desire for peace but a determination to keep America strong; and the need to bring the country together again. The address became most widely remembered for Nixon's appeal to the nation "to lower our voices" at a time of domestic protest and turmoil "so that our words can be heard as well."

Price was named a special assistant to the president in 1969. He served on the White House research and writing staff headed by James Keogh. Other senior writers on the team working on Nixon's speeches, messages, and remarks were Safire and PATRICK J. BUCHANAN JR. When Keogh resigned in December 1970, Nixon named Price to succeed him. Price was among the most eloquent and persuasive of Nixon aides who were moderates on the issues of race relations. Nixon's own position supported desegregation but opposed most busing. Price wrote the white paper on school desegregation that Nixon issued in March 1970. The 8,000-word document examined the legal history and social ramifications of the problem while spelling out the subtle distinctions of Nixon's own policies. It stressed the importance of local leadership in adapting desegregation plans to local circumstances. The following year Price prepared a similar white paper on housing discrimination and in 1972 wrote Nixon's message to Congress proposing new legislation to limit busing.

Price again played an important advisory and speech-writing part in Nixon's reelection campaign. After the election he asked for and was given a new role at the White House. Named a special consultant to the president and given a small staff, Price launched what he called his "house philosopher" project. He planned mainly to pull together the disparate elements of Nixon's philosophy of government into a more readily accessible form. At the same time Price had an informal understanding with the president that he would be available for those speeches with which Nixon particularly wanted his help, beginning with the second inaugural. The speech stressed a central theme of the Nixon presidency, the need to "locate responsibility in more places" and encouraged "individuals at home and nations abroad to do more for themselves, to decide more for themselves."

After the inaugural Price, instead of returning to his project, found himself increasingly devoting his time to Nixon's statements on the growing Watergate scandal. During the remainder of the Nixon presidency Price worked on all the president's major speeches on Watergate and finally on his resignation.

In 1977 Price published *With Nixon*, in which he expressed his feeling that the furor over Watergate was disproportionate to the issues involved. He wondered whether "America's brightest hopes since World War II for a new era of peace abroad and progress at home" had been "sacrificed in a spasm of hysteria on an altar of hypocrisy." Price articulated what he believed to be Nixon's unfulfilled goals: a radical reorganization of the executive branch, a streamlining of the bureaucracy, and implementation of the programs of his New Federalism.

To illustrate what he perceived as the unbalanced press coverage of the Nixon administration, Price devoted a chapter of his book to the night in 1970 that Nixon visited the Lincoln Memorial during the protests over the U.S. military incursion into Cambodia. Price tried to show that the media had covered the events of the evening incompletely and had misquoted Nixon as having called college students "bums." In Price's view the president, troubled by the protesters, had spontaneously gone out to try to communicate with them.

As Watergate unraveled, according to Price, the reporting in the newspapers bordered on a witch hunt. Price did not discount what he described as Nixon's darker side, but he argued that Nixon was both an extraordinary statesman and a "tricky Dick" and that it took the latter to bring the dreams of the former to reality. Price has served as a fellow of the Institute of Politics at Harvard and as editorial coordinator for both the Bipartisan Commission on Central America and the President's Task Force on International Private Enterprise. He is currently president of the Economic Club of New York.

—SF

Proxmire, (Edward) William
(1915–) *member of the Senate*

William Proxmire was born on November 11, 1915, in Lake Forest, Illinois. The son of a surgeon and staunch Republican, Proxmire earned his B.A. from Yale in 1938 and an M.B.A. from Harvard in 1940. He served in the counterintelligence corps of the army during World War II and moved to Wisconsin in 1949, where he entered politics as a Democrat. Elected to the state assembly in 1950, he made three unsuccessful bids for the governorship. In 1957 Proxmire won a special election to fill the Senate seat of the late Joseph McCarthy and in the following year was returned to the Senate for a full term.

In the Senate Proxmire quickly won a reputation as a maverick. In 1958 he challenged the powerful Senate majority leader, Lyndon Johnson, criticizing him for his arbitrary use of authority and demanding more frequent party caucuses. During the 1960s Proxmire supported most of the liberal social welfare legislation of the Kennedy and Johnson administrations. But he attracted attention largely through his persistent attacks on wasteful and extravagant spending by federal agencies, especially the Pentagon. As chairman of the Joint Economic Committee's Subcommittee on Economy in Government, Proxmire was in a position to publicize his concerns, and he frequently commissioned reports by the General Accounting Office to document charges of waste and mismanagement.

Proxmire quickly antagonized the NIXON administration by his determined fight against the controversial supersonic transport plane (SST). In September 1969 Nixon announced his support for continued funding of the plane. Proxmire, who had voted against the initial appropriation for the SST in 1963, immediately declared his opposition to the request. Opposed by the Pentagon, the aerospace industry, and the two powerful senators from Washington, HENRY JACKSON and WARREN MAGNUSON, all of whom supported continued funding, Proxmire marshaled environmental groups to lobby against the SST. He won his first victory in December 1970 when the Senate killed an administration request for $290 million. The following month the Senate reversed itself and approved a three-month extension of funds as part of a Department of Transportation appropriations bill. Proxmire, however, won a pledge from majority leader MIKE MANSFIELD and Senator JOHN STENNIS that there would be a separate SST funding vote. The campaign against the plane received a decisive boost when the president's chief environmental adviser, RUSSELL TRAIN, testified before Proxmire's subcommittee that the SST posed serious health dangers since it could deplete the atmosphere's protective ozone layer. In March 1971 the Senate voted to cut off all SST funds. A final attempt in May to revive the SST was decisively defeated.

Proxmire also targeted the air force's C-5A jet transport plane. In May 1969 he released air force documents showing a $2 billion cost overrun in the production of the plane. In August the Senate rejected Proxmire's proposal to eliminate from the defense budget $533 million earmarked for C-5As, but the air force later cut its purchases of the plane. In 1970 the Defense Department revealed that Lockheed, the nation's largest defense contractor and the maker of the C-5A had appealed for interim financial assistance to cover losses on the plane. When Nixon made a formal request in 1971 for a $250 million federally guaranteed loan to Lockheed to help it avoid bankruptcy, Proxmire scheduled hearings of the Senate Banking Committee and threatened a filibuster against the bill. Nixon successfully outmaneuvered Proxmire by requesting instead a broader federal program to aid financially troubled corporations. Proxmire then agreed not to filibuster if the broader bill were dropped. In July 1971 the Senate approved the Lockheed loan by a one-vote margin.

In 1970 Proxmire published *Report from Wasteland*, a blistering critique of the military-industrial complex. He attacked the common practice of retired military officers accepting executive positions with major defense contractors. Proxmire also accused the Pentagon of deliberately bloating its yearly budget request and of lax budget control procedures that led to billions of dollars wasted yearly. He attacked the lack of competition in the awarding of defense contracts, the de facto subsidization of private industry by the Pentagon, and the lack of mandatory accounting procedures for military procurement.

Initially a supporter of the Vietnam War, Proxmire changed his stand during the Nixon years. He voted for the Cooper-Church Amendment in 1970 and against extending the draft in 1971 and in 1972 unsuccessfully sponsored an amendment to end U.S. bombing in Southeast Asia unconditionally.

Proxmire also opposed the Nixon administration's economic stabilization program. In 1970 Congress passed the Economic Stabilization Act, which provided authority for the president to impose economic controls. Although Nixon initially opposed controls, he reversed himself in August 1971, imposed a 90-day wage-price freeze, and announced a "Phase Two" policy of controls to follow the freeze. In October he asked Congress to expand his authority to control the economy and to extend the Economic Stabilization Act until 1973. Proxmire opposed the request, arguing that Congress should evaluate Phase Two before extending the president's powers. During the Senate debate on the bill Proxmire attacked Phase Two as unworkable and inequitable and charged that it controlled far more of the economy than the parts responsible for inflation. He successfully amended the bill to require the president to report to Congress on action and progress under the stabilization program and to require Senate confirmation of the chairmen of the pay board and price commission. But he failed to defeat the extension of the act through 1973, and in December 1971 Congress complied with the president's request.

Proxmire continued to attack the stabilization program. In 1972 he conducted hearings on the economic outlook and called Phase Two a failure. After Nixon announced the lifting of wage-price controls in January 1973 and replaced them with his "Phase Three" proposal for voluntary constraints, Proxmire criticized Phase Three as "feeble and ineffective" and accused the administration of paralysis in fighting inflation. Proxmire proposed a six-month ceiling on all wages, prices, rents, and profits, but the Senate rejected it. Finally, in 1974 Congress allowed the Economic Stabilization Act to expire.

Becoming chairman of the Senate Banking Committee in 1975, Proxmire played a leading role in winning congressional approval of loans for New York City. Throughout 1975 the nation's largest city was dangerously close to defaulting on its financial obligations. City officials first requested federal aid in May, but President GERALD FORD, Treasury secretary WILLIAM SIMON, and Federal Reserve Board chairman ARTHUR BURNS all opposed it. Proxmire opened hearings on the New York situation in October. Questioning bankers and city officials closely, Proxmire concluded that federal aid was essential to avert a New York City bankruptcy that might jeopardize the nation's economic recovery. In December Congress finally passed legislation allowing the Treasury secretary to make loans of up to $2.3 billion a year through mid-1978.

In 1976 Proxmire won election to a fourth term in the Senate with 73 percent of the vote. In 1978 he presided over New York City's request for an extension of the program of federal loans. Proxmire retired from the Senate in 1989 and resides in Washington, D.C.

—JD

Randolph, Jennings
(1902–1998) *member of the Senate*

Jennings Randolph was born on March 8, 1902, in Salem, West Virginia. Randolph received his B.A. degree in 1924 from Salem College and then pursued a career in journalism and education. From 1933 to 1947 he served in the U.S. House from West Virginia, where he established a record as a supporter of the New Deal. During the next decade he was assistant to the president and director of public relations for Capital Airlines. In 1958 Randolph won election to the Senate to fill a seat vacated by the death of Matthew M. Neely. Two years later Randolph was elected to a full term. During the Kennedy and Johnson years he supported most of the administration's social welfare legislation but devoted himself primarily to measures that dealt with West Virginia's economic problems. As chairman of the Public Works Committee, which was in charge of pork barrel projects, Randolph used his position to promote federal highway programs in his state.

During the NIXON and FORD administrations Randolph continued to focus his attention on the problems of his state and of its largest industry, coal mining. He was a frequent supporter of the United Mine Workers of America and the National Coal Association.

His backing elicited criticism from reformers who charged that he was unwilling to forcefully promote reform of the industry and improve the health and safety of the miners. In 1969 Randolph, in response to the administration's proposed coal mine health and safety bill, submitted a proposal weakening a number of provisions in the Nixon measure.

Randolph called for limited compensation for miners incapacitated by black lung disease. Critics maintained that Randolph's changes wiped "out many of the key reforms needed to cut the death toll in the mines" and failed to deal with the problem of black lung adequately. Randolph admitted that many of the changes were suggested by the National Coal Association but defended the measure, insisting that the owners had a right to be heard. During debate on the administration measure, he warned that hundreds of small mine owners would have to lay off workers and close because of the expense of the program. Nevertheless, the Nixon measure, with the Randolph amendment on black lung disease, passed Congress in December.

In 1971 Randolph, who had initially been unsympathetic to the problem of black lung, began to push harder for federal action in response to wildcat strikes and demonstrations staged in support of relief. In 1972 Congress passed a measure sponsored by Randolph liberalizing eligibility standards for benefits to miners with the disease.

Although Randolph's Public Works Committee had jurisdiction over environmental and conservation legislation, Randolph played only a minor role in this area. Most of that work was handled by Senator EDMUND MUSKIE (D-Me.), chairman of the Subcommittee on Air and Water Pollution. Randolph usually backed Muskie's actions. However, he opposed the Maine senator on the issue of using highway trust funds for mass transit. Despite Randolph's opposition, the measure passed.

During his Senate career Randolph also was interested in measures to aid the handicapped, particularly the blind. In 1972 he sponsored the vocational rehabilitation act, which was designed to aid those with severe handicaps. The measure, which Nixon pocket-vetoed that year, would have authorized $800 million in 1973 and $975 million in 1974 for vocational training of the handicapped.

In September 1975 a report filed with the Securities and Exchange Commission named Randolph as one of several recipients of largely illegal campaign contributions from the Phillips Petroleum Corp. He had received a $1,000 contribution from that corporation in 1972. Phillips also was alleged to have made contributions to Lyndon Johnson's 1964 campaign, Richard Nixon's 1968 campaign, and Gerald Ford's congressional relection campaigns of 1970 and 1972.

Randolph was considered for a time to be in political trouble during his relection campaign in 1978, but after a campaign appearance by President JIMMY CARTER, West Virginians chose to return Randolph to the Senate for another six years. Randolph voted against both Panama Canal treaties. He retired from the Senate in 1985 and died in St Louis, Missouri, in 1998.

—GMS

Ray, Dixy Lee
(1914–1994) *member, Atomic Energy Commission; chair, Atomic Energy Commission; governor of Washington*

Dixy Lee Ray was born on September 3, 1914, in Tacoma, Washington. The second daughter of a commercial printer who anticipated a son, Ray had no first name until age 16, when she adopted Dixy Lee because of her southern heritage and admiration for Robert E. Lee. A Phi Beta Kappa graduate of Mills College in 1937 with a degree in zoology, Ray secured an M.A. the following year and became a science teacher in the California public school system. In 1942 she returned to graduate study and in 1945 was awarded a Ph.D. from Stanford in biological science. The same year she joined the faculty of the University of Washington as an instructor in zoology.

In addition to her university post, in 1945 Ray became a member of Friday Harbor Laboratories, which focused on the impact of various marine organisms on the environment. Her affiliation with the organization extended to 1960. She was then appointed special consultant to the National Science Foundation (NSF) in the area of biological oceanography for two years. An outspoken supporter of environmental preservation, especially when related to the equilibrium of the sea, Ray cautioned her colleagues as early as 1963 about the possible repercussions of pesticides and industrial wastes on marine life. That year she served as special assistant to the director of NSF and assumed the directorship of the Pacific Science Center in Seattle. In 1964, as a visiting professor at Stanford, she joined an international expedition of the Indian Ocean. Ray was appointed to RICHARD NIXON's Task Force on Oceanography in 1969, but she maintained her faculty position as well as functioning in an advisory capacity for several environmental organizations.

In 1972 she was nominated to serve on the Atomic Energy Commission (AEC). With Senate confirmation Ray became the first woman appointee to a full five-year term. "If it hadn"t been for the women's liberation movement I doubt the president would have appointed me," she stated, while denying charges of tokenism.

At the AEC Ray's responsibilities included the supervision of minority hiring and the dissemination of information to the public. At Nixon's request Ray prepared an energy research and development program that would integrate federal and private industry efforts. She structured a plan coordinating the exploitation of nuclear power, coal reserves, and oil shale. The plan also called for further exploration of the potential of solar energy. After AEC chairman JAMES R. SCHLESINGER resigned in 1973, Ray ascended to the post.

As a result of the Arab oil embargo, the AEC was faced with the problem of developing and expanding nuclear power as quickly as possible while, because of public pressure, meeting requisite safety standards. Thus, development would be severely hindered. For Ray the energy crisis had focused on the importance of constructing additional nuclear plants, and she approached the task by separating safety from development and giving each its own staff and budget.

Although many considered this decision a wise move to prevent shortcuts to safety, a number of AEC employees resigned because they regarded the apportionment of funds for safety experiments as a major setback for the development of the costly atomic breeder reactor. Ray defended her move and dismissed charges that nuclear power was inherently perilous. When asked at a news conference if she would allow her two beloved dogs to sleep next to a nuclear reactor, Ray replied, "Yes and you know I sleep next to my dogs."

With the dissolution of the AEC in 1974, Ray was appointed assistant secretary of state for oceans and international environmental and scientific affairs. Although she had been informed she and the division would be the "principal voice and forum" of science-related matters in the State Department, it soon became apparent that she was contacted only for concurrence with department views. In early 1975 Secretary of State HENRY KISSINGER informed the Japan Society that the United States was prepared to enter into a large-scale joint energy research and development program. The offer was made with no prior consultation with Ray. Angered by the move, she handed in her resignation immediately after only six months in the post.

She then began work on her book *Good-bye America* (1976) with a former aide. The central message, according to Ray, is "if we don't change course and get some sense into international and domestic policies we're heading for oblivion."

In 1976 Ray was elected governor of the state of Washington. She ran on the Democratic ticket and won by more than 100,000 votes. She served in that position until 1981. Upon her retirement from politics she became an engineering consultant. She died in 1994.

—DGE

Reagan, Ronald W(ilson)
(1911–2004) *governor of California*

Ronald Reagan's father was an Irish Catholic shoe salesman and his mother an English-Scottish Protestant with a lively interest in the theater. Graduating from Eureka College with a B.A. in 1932, Reagan became a radio sportscaster in Iowa. Five years later he signed a film contract with Warner Brothers. He subsequently appeared in over 50 movies, often playing the all-American "good guy" who fails to "get the girl."

During the 1940s Reagan became active in liberal Democratic politics. However, during

Reagan's five consecutive terms as president of the Screen Actors Guild (1947–52), his political views began to shift to the right. He grew disillusioned with communist influences in the liberal groups he had formerly supported and in 1949 cooperated with the movie industry's effort to purge actors with alleged communist associations. In 1952 Reagan married his second wife, actress Nancy Davis, who strengthened his conservative inclinations and encouraged his political activities. When he became a Republican in 1962, Reagan was already a popular figure among California's extreme right wing. In 1966 he won election as governor, defeating liberal Democrat Pat Brown.

During his first years as governor Reagan and his inexperienced staff struggled to implement their conservative programs. He recruited 250 prominent businessmen to serve on a Businessmen's Task Force, aimed at restructuring the state government. The task force made 1,500 recommendations, and many of its members stayed on as part of Reagan's management team. While a $200 million budget deficit forced Reagan to raise instead of lower taxes, he was able to blame his large budget and tax increases on Brown's administration. Working in cooperation with Democratic assembly Speaker Jesse Unruh, Reagan made the increased levies more palatable by shifting the burden from local property taxes to sales and income taxes and levies on banks and corporations. In addition, he froze state hiring and the purchase of new equipment and cut state mental health and higher education programs. By the time Reagan left office in 1975, he was disbursing $1 billion each year in property tax relief funds to local governments. By 1973 he had a budget surplus that allowed credits of 20 percent to 35 percent on state income taxes and eliminated all such taxes for families earning less than $8,000.

Reagan most prided himself on his successful reform of the state welfare system. In the summer of 1970 he appeared before the U.S. Senate Finance Committee to testify against the Family Assistance Program (FAP), a new federal welfare program favored by President RICHARD NIXON and his adviser DANIEL PATRICK MOYNIHAN. The FAP would have provided a guaranteed federal payment of $1,600 a year for a family of four with no income, provided the head of the family registered for work or training. Viewing the new program as another step toward state socialism, Reagan returned to California determined to design an alternative to FAP.

The governor formed a task force of experts in law, public administration, and business management to review the existing welfare system and in 1971 proposed a series of reforms to cut the welfare rolls, increase benefits to remaining welfare recipients, and require the able-bodied to take public service jobs. Reagan's staff pushed welfare reform through the state legislature by a narrow margin and obtained the necessary Social Security waivers from the federal government only after the program had been in operation for seven months. The California Welfare Reform Program, credited with a 400,000 decrease in state welfare rolls and a $4 billion saving in taxes between 1971 and 1976, proved one of Reagan's most popular measures and served as a model for other states seeking to make similar reforms.

While liberals acknowledged the success of Reagan's welfare reform and were surprised by his support of liberalized abortion, gun-control, and smog-control bills, they remained generally hostile. Critics viewed as naive Reagan's incessant attacks on the evils of big government and dismissed what they regarded as his simplistic solutions to the nation's economic and social problems. Robert Moretti, Democratic Speaker of the California house, described Reagan as "a total negativist," the architect of a program that consisted mostly of saying no to the legislature. The governor's proposals for escalating the Vietnam War and punishing war dissenters further alienated liberals, as did his opposition to farm workers' unions.

After an unsuccessful last-minute bid for the presidential nomination in 1968, Reagan threw his support to Richard Nixon, campaigning vigorously for his party's ticket. Reagan was easily reelected governor in 1970. During the last three years of his term he established task forces to deal with the problems of street crime, taxes, and the restructuring of local government. He tried unsuccessfully to amend California's constitution to limit the percentage of personal income the state could take as revenue in any one year.

Acting on his stated belief that no governor should serve more than two terms, Reagan left office in January 1975, at the end of his second term. One of the most popular Republicans on the national scene, he had proved his effectiveness as a speaker, particularly in the South, during the 1968 presidential primaries. After leaving office Reagan undertook a heavy speaking schedule, expounding on his conservative philosophy several times a week in addition to writing a weekly syndicated column and broadcasting a network radio commentary five times a week.

In March 1976 Reagan declared his presidential candidacy, challenging Republican incumbent GERALD R. FORD. Reagan aimed his major criticism at the Ford administration's policy of détente with the Soviet Union, its heavy defense spending, and the secret diplomacy of Secretary of State HENRY KISSINGER. After losing five primaries to Ford, Reagan scored a decisive victory in North Carolina (52 percent to Ford's 46 percent), marking the first primary victory since 1952 against an incumbent president seeking renomination. As Reagan continued his attacks on U.S. foreign policy with accusations that the United States was retreating from its role as world leader, he chipped away at Ford's base of support, especially in the South and West.

Reagan broke with tradition by announcing his choice for a vice presidential running mate three weeks before the Republican Convention. He picked liberal Pennsylvania senator RICHARD SCHWEIKER. Reagan supporters were dismayed by what they saw as a betrayal of conservative principles, while critics saw the announcement as a blatantly political move, belying Reagan's avowed distaste for professional politics. At the convention in Kansas City in August, Ford supporters successfully resisted Reagan's efforts to force the president to declare his own vice presidential choice before the balloting. Buoyed by this victory, Ford defeated Reagan on the first ballot by 117 votes. Reagan loyalists were able to force Ford, however, to accept a conservative platform, including an amended foreign policy plank.

After his defeat Reagan returned to speech making and writing his newspaper column. Still prominent in the party, Reagan became a leading critic of JIMMY CARTER administration politics.

In 1980 Reagan was elected the 40th president of the United States. He would serve two terms of office, stepping down in 1989. The most popular president since Eisenhower, Reagan's presidency was highlighted by a renewed confidence of ordinary Americans in their government, fueled in part by Reagan's tax cut package of 1981 and his role in bringing about the end of the cold war in Europe. It also was highlighted by a widening fiscal deficit and the problem of the Iran-contra scandal at home. In June 2004 Reagan died at his California home of complications from Alzheimer's disease.

—DAE

Rebozo, (Charles G.) "Bebe"
(1912–1988) *businessman*

Born on November 17, 1912, Rebozo grew up in the Tampa area and by 1964 had become a leading Florida banker and real estate man. He was president of the Key Biscayne Bank and Trust Co. and held the presidencies of several real estate firms. A friend of RICHARD NIXON, Rebozo loaned money to the president in 1969 for the purchase of his San Clemente home and gave the Nixon family personal gifts. Rebozo was a frequent White House guest during the last two years of Nixon's presidency, and the president and his friend often relaxed together on the yacht *Sequoia* during evening cruises down the Potomac River. They talked over strategies in the Oval Office and visited one another in Florida and at ROBERT H. ABPLA-NALP's home in the Bahamas.

During the 1973 Watergate investigation it was revealed that Rebozo played a role in soliciting contributions to a private campaign fund set up by Nixon. One contribution came from billionaire recluse HOWARD HUGHES in the form of $100,000 cash received in July and August 1970. The Hughes contribution was considered by critics a possible payment in return for a favorable Justice Department action on an antitrust suit involving Hughes. Rebozo told the Senate Watergate committee that the money had not been spent for any purpose and had, instead, been returned to Hughes. Rebozo also was alleged to have paid $50,000 out of the fund for personal gifts to Nixon. Money funneled through various trust accounts, the Watergate committee revealed, paid for $46,000 in improvements for Nixon's Key Biscayne home, and another $4,562 paid for a pair of diamond earrings Rebozo had given Mrs. Nixon. The committee noted, however, that Rebozo made these gifts on his own initiative. The fund was again discussed at the Watergate cover-up trial when assistant special prosecutor RICHARD BEN-VENISTE said it was intended to be used to pay $200,000 to $300,000 in legal fees for H. R. HAL-DEMAN and JOHN D. EHRLICHMAN. No charges were brought against Rebozo as a result of his involvement in the fund.

Questions also were raised regarding presidential influence peddling when a possible competitor to Rebozo's Key Biscayne bank was denied a charter in 1973. Representative WRIGHT PATMAN (D-Tex.) sought an investigation of the matter, but after a White House spokesman said there had been no involvement by the president the matter was dropped. Rebozo continued his banking and real estate ventures in Florida until his death in 1998.

—BO

Rehnquist, William H(ubbs)
(1924–2005) *assistant attorney general; associate justice, U.S. Supreme Court*

William H. Rehnquist was born on October 1, 1924, in Milwaukee, Wisconsin. Rehnquist received a B.A. from Stanford University in 1948 and graduated first in his class from Stanford Law School in 1952. He served as a law clerk to Supreme Court justice Robert H. Jackson in 1952 and 1953 and then moved to Phoenix, Arizona, where he practiced privately from 1953 to 1969. Rehnquist also became active in the conservative wing of Arizona's Republican Party and supported Senator BARRY GOLDWATER (R-Ariz.) for the presidency in 1964. On the recommendation of Deputy Attorney General RICHARD G. KLEINDIENST, Rehnquist was appointed assistant attorney general in charge of the office of legal counsel in January 1969.

In that post Rehnquist gave legal advice to the attorney general and the president and the other departments of government. Considered a brilliant attorney, Rehnquist also served as an articulate and well-informed spokesman for the NIXON administration in Congress on a variety of controversial issues. He promoted the unsuccessful nominations of CLEMENT F. HAYNSWORTH and G. HARROLD CARSWELL to the Supreme Court. He defended the president's power to invade Cambodia, the mass arrests

William Rehnquist as associate justice *(Library of Congress)*

of antiwar demonstrators in Washington, and the executive's privilege to withhold information from Congress. Rehnquist supported the administration's criminal law proposals, including authorization of wiretapping and electronic surveillance, preventive detention, and "no-knock" entry. He aroused some controversy in March 1971 when he told a Senate subcommittee that the Justice Department opposed any legislation impairing the government's ability to collect information on citizens. He also said he saw no violation of the First Amendment in the army's surveillance of civilian demonstrators.

On October 21, 1971, President Nixon unexpectedly nominated Rehnquist and LEWIS F. POWELL JR. to the Supreme Court. Opposi-

tion to Rehnquist's appointment soon developed among civil rights, civil liberties, and labor groups who criticized his conservative record on issues of individual and minority rights. Nonetheless, the Senate Judiciary Committee approved Rehnquist's nomination by a 12-4 vote on November 23. After several days of debate the Senate confirmed his appointment 68 to 26. Rehnquist was sworn in as associate justice on January 7, 1972.

The youngest justice at the time of his appointment, Rehnquist soon established himself as the most conservative member of the Court. He advanced a narrow conception of judicial review and insisted that policy making was the function of the political branches of government. He argued that the Court should defer to the judgments of legislatures unless their actions were clearly unconstitutional, and he opposed expansive constitutional interpretations, which he thought allowed the justices to impose their own values on society.

Rehnquist objected, for example, to the Court's extension of the due process clause to a variety of new interests. In cases decided in 1974 and 1975 he voted against granting a right to a notice and a hearing to a federal civil service employee prior to his dismissal, to debtors prior to the seizure of their goods by creditors, and to public school students prior to a disciplinary suspension. He dissented in January 1973 when the Court overturned state laws restricting abortions during the first six months of pregnancy as a violation of the due process right to privacy. In a March 1976 majority opinion Rehnquist stated that police did not deny due process when they identified an individual in a notice to shopkeepers as an "active shoplifter," even though he had never been convicted of theft.

Similarly, Justice Rehnquist took a limited view of the equal protection clause. It was intended, he argued, to protect blacks from racial discrimination by the state and should not be used to overturn other forms of alleged discrimination unless there was no rational basis for the government's action. As a result of this view, Rehnquist voted, often alone, to uphold laws that established different treatment for illegitimate children, aliens, and women. He was the sole dissenter, for example, in May 1973, when the majority invalidated different eligibility requirements for dependency benefits for men and women in the military. He stood alone again in April 1975 when the Court overturned state laws setting a different age of majority for the sexes. Rehnquist spoke for the Court, however, in December 1976 when he ruled that an employer did not violate the 1964 Civil Rights Act, which prohibited sex discrimination in employment, by excluding pregnancy and childbirth from coverage in a disability benefit plan.

The justice also used a rationality test to decide apportionment cases, and he wrote several significant opinions for the Court based on this standard. In February 1973 he upheld a state legislative districting plan that departed from a strict one-person, one-vote rule because the deviations helped the state achieve the goal of providing representation for local communities. For a six-man majority Rehnquist ruled in March 1973 that the one-person, one-vote standard was not required for the election of officials to a special purpose governmental body, such as the board of directors of a state water storage district.

In racial discrimination cases Rehnquist spoke for a unanimous Court in January 1973 to hold that a defendant must be allowed to question potential jurors about possible racial prejudice. However, his majority opinion in a June 1972 case ruled that racial discrimination by a private club did not violate the Constitution, even though the club received a liquor license from the state. In June 1976, for a six-man majority, the justice declared that once school officials had complied with a desegregation order by establishing a racially neutral

pupil assignment system, they could not be required to readjust attendance zones later, when population shifts caused resegregation.

Justice Rehnquist generally voted to sustain governmental actions against individual rights claims, especially in criminal cases. On Fourth Amendment issues, where he was often the Court's spokesman, Rehnquist persistently upheld police searches and seizures against challenge. In a June 1972 decision he ruled that a policeman could stop and frisk a suspect for a weapon on the basis of an informant's tip and then, after arresting him for illegal possession of a handgun, could search the suspect's car without a warrant. His opinion for the Court in a December 1973 case upheld the authority of the police to make a full personal search following a lawful custodial arrest, even for a minor offense such as a traffic violation. In two decisions, in April 1973 and April 1976, Rehnquist stated that a defendant could not claim entrapment into a crime, no matter what the extent of government involvement, if he had shown a predisposition to violate the law. The justice also voted repeatedly to sustain state laws imposing capital punishment.

In First Amendment cases Rehnquist also tended to give greater weight to society's interests than to individual free expression. He joined the majority in several June 1973 cases, for example, to set new guidelines for obscenity laws that allowed greater government control over pornography. The justice generally resolved federal-state conflicts in favor of the states. In a June 1976 majority opinion he overturned a 1968 precedent and held federal minimum wage laws inapplicable to state and local governments. Rehnquist also favored cutbacks in federal court jurisdiction. His opinion for a five-man majority in January 1976 ruled that a federal district judge exceeded his jurisdiction when he ordered Philadelphia officials to establish new procedures for handling complaints of police misconduct.

On September 25, 1986, President RONALD REAGAN nominated Rehnquist to succeed WARREN BURGER as the chief justice of the Supreme Court. Rehnquist was affirmed by a 65-33 Senate vote. In the landmark cases that came before the court during the presidency of GEORGE H. W. BUSH, Rehnquist could be counted on as a conservative voice.

After the Bush administration left office, Rehnquist continued his tenure as chief justice. He acted as the sitting judge in the impeachment of President Bill Clinton and was the lead voice in the decision that gave George W. Bush the election to the presidency in 2000. After being in increasingly frail health in recent years, Rehnquist died on September 3, 2005, after a 33-year career at the Supreme Court.

—AF and CAB

Reuss, Henry S(choellkopf)

(1912–2002) *member of the House of Representatives; chairman, Committee on Banking and Currency*

Henry S. Reuss was born on February 22, 1912, in Milwaukee, Wisconsin. Reuss received his law degree from Harvard in 1936 and shortly thereafter began his public career as counsel to the Office of Price Administration. Reuss served in the army from 1943 to 1945 and after the war was a member of the price control board of the U.S. military government in Germany. In 1949 he served as an administrator for the Marshall Plan in Paris. Returning to legal practice in Wisconsin, Reuss bolted the Republican Party in 1950 to protest McCarthyism and in 1954 was elected to the U.S. House as a Democrat.

Reuss generally aligned himself with liberal Democrats in the House, supporting the social legislation of the Kennedy and Johnson years but emerging as an early opponent of the U.S. war effort in Southeast Asia. Reuss was a member of both the Joint Economic Committee (JEC) and the House Banking and Currency Committee. He also chaired the International Finance Subcommittee, where he sponsored "soft loans" to Latin American countries through the International Development Association. Reuss was an early supporter of environmental legislation and opposed supersonic transport (SST) proposals from 1964 onward.

One of Reuss's primary concerns during the NIXON years was inflation, for which he saw wage-price controls as an essential antidote. When Nixon, immediately after assuming office, announced cuts in the fiscal 1970 budget aimed at achieving a government surplus, Reuss attacked the cuts as "a phony war" on inflation whose sole result would be increased unemployment. In September 1969 Reuss, as a member of the House Government Operations Committee, held hearings on his own bill requiring the administration to adopt voluntary wage-price guidelines. Although the bill cleared committee in May 1970 and drew immediate fire from the administration, it never became law. In July 1970 Reuss stepped up his campaign, calling for "across-the-board freezes on wages, prices, rents, salaries, the whole works" for a three- to four-month period.

Reuss also was deeply involved in liberal tax reform. His principal target was the corporate depreciation tax write-off, which he felt privileged business at the expense of the consumer. In early 1971 Reuss had no less than 10 tax reform bills under consideration. In July of the same year, after the Treasury issued new depreciation guidelines, Reuss filed a joint lawsuit with RALPH NADER, the liberal lobby Common Cause, the United Automobile Workers, the National Rural Electric Cooperative Association, and a real estate developer charging the Treasury with circumventing congressional authority in taxation matters. When the Nixon administration proposed an income tax credit in September 1971, Reuss, who felt that the

1969 tax reform bill had already opened too many loopholes for the wealthy, attacked the proposal and instead called for public works programs to combat unemployment.

Reuss was an important House arbitrator of U.S. policy in the international monetary crises and reform of the early 1970s. When the Nixon administration concluded an agreement with South Africa permitting the sale of South African gold to the International Monetary Fund (IMF), Reuss, in January 1970, attacked the move for "institutionalizing South Africa as a supplier of gold." In June 1971 Reuss introduced a "sense of Congress" resolution to end U.S. gold sales to foreign central banks, and in August 1971, one week before President Nixon officially suspended the gold backing of the dollar, Reuss criticized any increase in the price of gold for giving "windfall profits" to gold-producing nations. Nonetheless, when the Smithsonian Agreement of December 1971 brought about a modest devaluation of the dollar and effected a small increase in the official price of gold, Reuss called the agreement "glorious." In House debate in March 1972 he called for the phasing out of the dollar as a reserve currency. Several months later, when the Smithsonian Agreement was in turn threatened by new chaos in the international money markets, Reuss urged the Joint Economic Committee to permit central banks and the IMF to sell gold on the free market to "help ease the apprehension that currently exists about the viability of the Smithsonian monetary arrangements." When the Smithsonian Agreement collapsed in the spring of 1973, Reuss attacked the Nixon administration for its "much too laggard and lackadaisical attitude" toward the U.S. balance-of-payments deficit. He also welcomed the European currency float of March 1973, expressing his fear that the "United States could be conned into massive intervention" in support of the dollar.

In January 1975 Reuss became chairman of the House Banking and Currency Commit-tee, succeeding Representative WRIGHT PATMAN (D-Tex.). His focus thus turned to questions of domestic banking reform and congressional control of the Federal Reserve. As a member of the JEC, Reuss had already been involved in shaping the One-Bank Holding Company Act of 1970, attacking the banking lobby for pushing the committee "toward wholesale exceptions for a number of bank holding giants." But in 1975, in the wake of the 1974–75 recession, Reuss felt the need for extensive reform was even more urgent. In February 1975 the Banking and Currency Committee rejected a bill introduced by Reuss that would have required the Federal Reserve Bank to force down interest rates and to expand the money supply at a set rate of 6 percent per year. In June 1975 Reuss's ambitious "credit reporting" bill was defeated by the House. The bill would not only have required the top 200 U.S. commercial banks to disclose their lending practices to the Federal Reserve, but also would have required them to channel credit into "national priority areas." Opponents of the bill saw it as a step in the direction of mandatory credit allocation by the government.

In January 1976, after the comptroller of the currency's "problem list" of top commercial banks was leaked to the press showing potential massive illiquidity in the private banking system, Reuss convened the House Banking and Currency Committee for hearings. Federal Reserve chairman ARTHUR BURNS testified to oppose renewed calls for extensive disclosure, but Reuss argued that only such disclosure, together with serious overhaul of the federal regulation of banks, would restore public confidence in the banking system.

Aside from his areas of legislative expertise, Reuss involved himself directly in other liberal issues. In 1969 and 1970 he attacked major corporations involved in pollution and held hearings on population growth. He was a consistent opponent of funds for the SST and fought to reduce allocations for new jets. In 1971 he cosponsored legislation with Senator HUBERT HUMPHREY (D-Minn.) for federal revenue sharing aimed at achieving "modernization" of state and local governments desiring funds. In 1975, after the FORD administration's endorsement of Vice President NELSON ROCKEFELLER's $100 billion "Energy Independence" proposal, Reuss attacked the plan as "grossly inflated, fiscally irresponsible, and susceptible to political manipulation." He also sponsored legislation in late 1975 to provide $4 billion in federal loan guarantees to New York City. Reuss served in the House until 1982, when he retired. He died in 2002.

—LG

Reuther, Walter P.
(1907–1970) *president, United Automobile Workers*

Born on September 1, 1907, Walter Reuther was the son of an immigrant German socialist and union leader. After finishing high school he became a skilled tool and die worker at the Ford Motor Co. plant in Detroit. Fired for his union activity in 1931, Reuther joined the Socialist Party and attended Wayne State University for two years. In 1935 he and his brothers Roy and Victor joined the drive to organize the new United Automobile Workers (UAW). Reuther won his first union post in 1936 as a member of the UAW executive board.

During World War II the Reuther brothers organized their own caucus that fought for control of the UAW against the communist-supported leadership. In 1945 Reuther led the union's General Motors division in an aggressive 113-day strike despite the continued adherence of the Congress of Industrial Organizations (CIO) to the wartime no-strike pledge. He won the support of the UAW's restive membership and, in 1946, the union presidency. Over the next decade, however, Reuther abandoned radicalism and moved toward a

rapprochement with the existing structures of American politics and industrial relations. He served as president of the CIO from 1952 until its merger with the American Federation of Labor (AFL) in 1955 and became a power within the national Democratic Party. At the same time, Reuther sought incremental improvements for UAW members through an innovative collective bargaining program.

Reuther was an enthusiastic supporter of President John F. Kennedy, and he made the UAW an effective lobbying force for the Johnson administration's Great Society and civil rights legislation. Within the UAW, however, as local leaders and rank-and-file members became more concerned with noneconomic grievances involving production standards and working conditions, Reuther encountered serious opposition to his policies and recurrent wildcat strikes following negotiation of each companywide contract.

Since the late 1950s Reuther had been involved in a continuing dispute with AFL-CIO president GEORGE MEANY over the federation's domestic and foreign policies. Reuther complained that the AFL-CIO had become complacent and conservative, and he criticized Meany for refusing to mobilize the federation's resources in an all-out drive to organize the majority of American workers who did not belong to unions. He also took a dim view of AFL-CIO ties to the Central Intelligence Agency and other clandestine government units. In 1967 Reuther and other UAW officials resigned from their AFL-CIO posts, and shortly afterward the union began to withhold its dues to the federation. In May 1968 Meany formally suspended the auto workers.

Upon leaving the AFL-CIO Reuther formed the Alliance for Labor Action (ALA) with the International Brotherhood of Teamsters. The new labor center was later joined by the Chemical Workers Union. In 1969 the

ALA issued a "declaration of purpose," which included a long list of social welfare and trade union goals, with emphasis on coordinated organizing drives among white-collar employees and the working poor. Reuther and Teamster president FRANK FITZSIMMONS also issued a critical statement on the Vietnam War and on the development of the antiballistic missile—positions standing in sharp contrast to those of the AFL-CIO leadership. The federation, for its part, issued a 99-page report on the dispute in April, in which Reuther was denounced for failing to use the "democratic forums" of the AFL-CIO to air his differences. The ALA proved stillborn, however, largely because of the Teamsters' growing friendliness toward the NIXON administration. After several years of relative inactivity, it was formally dissolved by the UAW in 1972.

Approaching the 1970 auto industry negotiations, Reuther drew up a set of demands that centered around wages and retirement benefits. A key feature of the union's bargaining program was the concept of "30 and out," whereby auto workers would start collecting monthly pensions of $500 after 30 years of service, regardless of age. Before negotiations had begun, however, Reuther, his wife, and four others were killed on May 9 when their chartered plane crashed and exploded near Pellston, Michigan. LEONARD WOODCOCK, a former Reuther assistant, was elected to the presidency by the UAW executive board.

—TLH

Rhodes, James A(llen)
(1909–2001) *governor of Ohio*

James A. Rhodes was born in Jackson, Ohio, on September 13, 1909. Rhodes, the only son of a coal miner who was killed in a mine accident, went to work when he was 10 to earn money for his family. He began his political career in 1933 by winning an election for Republican committeeman in Columbus, Ohio. After holding a number of city posts, he was elected state auditor in 1952. He held the post until 1962, when he unseated the incumbent, Governor Michael V. DiSalle, a liberal Democrat who had angered many voters by raising state taxes. He held the governor's office for two terms. While in office Rhodes reduced state expenditures, balanced the state budget, and embarked on an industrial development program that attracted hundreds of companies to the state. He also initiated extensive highway and university construction projects, which he financed by raising $1.4 billion through state bond issues, a program his critics attacked as deficit financing.

Rhodes's political career suffered a setback in the early 1970s. Barred from seeking a third consecutive term as governor, Rhodes ran against ROBERT TAFT JR. in the 1970 Republican senatorial primary. The race became the most bitter intraparty fight in 20 years. Taft ran on an "integrity" platform and indirectly alluded to a critical *Life* magazine article on Rhodes by attacking the governor's "life-style." The April 1969 article criticized Rhodes for commuting the life sentence of a mobster with alleged gangland connections and claimed that Rhodes "had dipped into" campaign funds. Rhodes, on the other hand, ran on a "law and order" platform.

On May 2, 1970, three days before the primary election, Rhodes ordered National Guard troops to the Kent State University campus to quell student demonstrations that had broken out in protest of the U.S. incursion into Cambodia. The next day the Kent State Student Senate charged that Rhodes had ordered the troops to the campus out of political motivations. Rhodes denounced the demonstrators as "the worst type of people we harbor in America." On May 4, the day before the primary, the troops fired their weapons in reaction to sniper shots coming from a nearby building but later admitted they had no evidence of such action. The day after the shooting Rhodes lost the primary by less than 5,000 votes. In November Ohio Republicans suffered a major defeat when their entire slate of candidates for state office was defeated after the disclosure of financial scandals involving members of the Rhodes administration.

The shootings led to lengthy grand jury investigations and bitter legal controversies. Rhodes ordered the state attorney general to convene a grand jury for the purpose of investigating the shootings to determine if those involved were criminally responsible. The grand jury issued a report that found that the guardsmen had acted in self-defense and handed down 25 indictments against demonstrators.

In 1973 a federal grand jury launched a new investigation into the shootings. Although state officials were cleared of criminal responsibility, the parents of the victims and the wounded students filed a $46 million civil damage suit against Rhodes and other state officials in 1975. At the trial Rhodes testified he had not known that the troops carried loaded weapons and described the situation as "almost a state of war." Although the federal jury exonerated Rhodes and 28 other defendants in August 1975, a new trial was ordered after the case was appealed.

When the case was finally settled out of court before the second trial was due to begin in 1979, Rhodes was again governor. He had made an unexpected political comeback by defeating incumbent governor JOHN J. GILLIGAN by 11,000 votes in 1974. Rhodes was surprised by his victory, since he had publicly conceded defeat after the TV networks had declared Gilligan the winner. He was reelected in 1978 to his fourth four-year term—the only person in Ohio history to serve four terms as governor.

The Kent State suit was settled when the state agreed to pay $600,000 in damages and when, as part of the settlement, Rhodes signed a statement saying "in retrospect, the tragedy of May 4, 1970, should not have occurred." He also admitted that the protesting students "may have believed they were right" in continuing the protests in spite of a university ban on rallies. Rhodes would later serve as political adviser to both RONALD REAGAN and GEORGE H. W. BUSH, helping each to carry Ohio's electoral votes. He died in 2001.

—AE

Rhodes, John J(acob)

(1916–2003) *member of the House of Representatives; chairman, Republican Policy Committee; House minority leader*

Rhodes, the youngest son of a retail lumber dealer and Kansas state treasurer, was born on September 18, 1916, in the tiny farming community of Council Grove, Kansas. After graduating from Kansas State University in 1938, he obtained a degree from Harvard Law School. Following service in the army air corps during World War II, he resettled in Mesa, Arizona, opened a law practice, and helped start a firm that later became the Farm and Home Life Insurance Co.

In 1950 Rhodes, a longtime Young Republican activist, and Phoenix city councilman BARRY M. GOLDWATER jointly managed Howard Pyle's successful Republican gubernatorial nomination campaign. Pyle was elected, but Rhodes, running on the ticket for attorney general, lost by a narrow margin. He successfully ran for Congress two years later, becoming the first Republican elected to the House from Arizona. He represented a white, affluent, conservative district comprising parts of Phoenix and its nearby suburbs.

Rhodes consistently supported the NIXON and FORD administrations' legislative programs, voting their positions about 75 percent of the time. He favored a strong defense, endorsed the administrations' Vietnam policy, and backed foreign military aid. Generally Rhodes agreed with the concepts of a balanced federal budget and economy in government. He opposed most major domestic assistance bills, such as mass transit subsidies, aid to education, and federally funded public housing projects. He regularly backed positions taken by the National Association of Businessmen, which gave him its "Watchdog of the Treasury" award for the 1969–70 session of Congress. He supported the policies advocated by the conservative Americans for Constitutional Action more than 70 percent of the time, while he rarely sided with the proposals made by consumer groups or labor organizations.

Rhodes quietly but steadily worked his way up through the Republican leadership in the House. In 1965 he was elected chairman of the Republican Policy Committee, beating an opponent endorsed by newly elected House minority leader Gerald R. Ford (R-Mich.). When Ford became vice president in October 1973, Rhodes immediately announced his candidacy for minority leader. Although he had several rivals for the job, they all dropped out of the race, and Rhodes was elected by acclamation.

The emerging Watergate scandal and the impeachment inquiry dominated the first eight months of Rhodes's leadership. Initially believing in Nixon's innocence, Rhodes tried to defend the president and to disassociate the Republican Party from the scandal. When experts reported in January 1974 that one of the key Watergate tapes might have been deliberately erased, he admitted the report was harmful but cautioned there was "no evidence to connect the president with the erasure." In February he urged the Republican Party to take the offensive, since it had nothing to do with the Watergate abuses. However, by April 1974 he agreed that "the continuing mystery

surrounding Watergate is hurting the image of President Nixon and the Republican Party."

When the White House gave the Judiciary Committee only edited transcripts rather than the actual tapes of presidential conversations subpoenaed by the committee, Rhodes announced that the majority of Republicans believed the White House was in substantial compliance with the subpoena. After the released transcripts had generated a public furor, Rhodes admitted on May 9 that "the contents of the tapes was devastating." He suggested that resignation was now a possible option and said that Nixon's departure would be beneficial to the Republican Party.

Rhodes supported the Judiciary Committee's impeachment inquiry. In January 1974 he headed off Republican efforts to put an April 30 deadline on the committee's impeachment investigation. In June 1974 he opposed conservative Republicans who wanted to turn the case against Nixon into a vote of censure rather than impeachment. Rhodes opposed the action on the grounds that it would be doing the country a great disservice to leave a censured president in office.

Rhodes joined the move toward impeachment after the August 5 release of key transcripts showed Nixon had discussed using the CIA to stop the FBI's Watergate probe. He later endorsed the Nixon pardon, arguing that Nixon had paid a substantial price by resigning and that anything more would be overkill rather than justice. However, he strongly opposed pardons for other Watergate figures, contending they had not suffered the "special consequences that a fallen president must bear."

Rhodes proposed a consensus-type government after the 1974 elections swept an overwhelmingly Democratic majority into Congress. He urged that Democrats cooperate with the administration to prevent a partisan stalemate between the Republican White House and the Democratic Congress. But he warned the Democrats in January 1976 that unless their leadership worked with the administration instead of against it, there would be more presidential vetoes than ever before. Although it was heavily outnumbered in the House, Rhodes successfully held together the Republican minority and gathered enough conservative Democrats to sustain many of President Ford's 61 vetoes.

In 1975 Rhodes unveiled a legislative agenda drafted by the House Republicans. It called for a balanced budget within three years, the automatic extension of unemployment benefits coupled with job training programs during recession periods, catastrophic illness insurance protection, a windfall energy profits tax, and revisions in the food stamp program. The agenda accepted the idea of deficit spending, a position Rhodes had long opposed. Rhodes described the measures as a full-employment budget.

In 1976 Rhodes published *The Futile System*, a highly critical examination of Congress, which he described as "a pitiful, helpless giant, devoid of coordination or purpose." He blamed the Democratic leadership that had controlled Congress for the past 22 years for the existing congressional deficiencies. Rhodes prescribed "a periodic switching of [party] control as a way to keep Congress institutionally fit."

Rhodes continued as minority leader until his retirement in 1981. He died of cancer in 2003.

—AE

Ribicoff, Abraham A(lexander)
(1910–1998) *member of the Senate*

Abraham A. Ribicoff was born in New Britain, Connecticut, on April 9, 1910. The son of an immigrant Jewish factory worker, Ribicoff worked his way through New York University and the University of Chicago Law School. Following graduation in 1933, he returned to Connecticut to open a law practice. In 1938 he won election to the Connecticut general assembly, where he served two terms. He then served five years as a police court judge. In 1948 Ribicoff won a seat in the U.S. House of Representatives, where he remained until 1952, when he lost a close race for the Senate. Two years later he was elected governor of Connecticut. Ribicoff served as secretary of health, education, and welfare during the Kennedy administration and worked unsuccessfully for the passage of Medicare. He resigned to run for Connecticut's Senate seat in 1962. As senator, Ribicoff devoted a great deal of attention to the passage of liberal legislation in areas he was interested in as a member of the administration.

During the NIXON-FORD years Ribicoff was a leader in the campaign for national health insurance. He opposed the ambitious health program supported by Senator EDWARD KENNEDY (D-Mass.) that promised total coverage to all Americans because it was too expensive and would become a bureaucratic nightmare. Rather, he joined Senator RUSSELL LONG (D-La.) in offering an alternative bill that provided insurance only for catastrophic illnesses. Under the plan Medicaid would handle services for the poor and Medicare for the elderly. The remainder of the nation would continue to participate in government-subsidized private or union plans. Testifying on behalf of his bill, Ribicoff stated that the government did not have the administrative capacity to manage a national health care program and suggested that private insurance companies handle the program. Supporters of the Kennedy plan accused Ribicoff of opposing the more ambitious program because his state contained more national insurance companies than any other state in the nation. Congress failed to act on either the Ribicoff or Kennedy bills.

Along with his interest in improving the health delivery system of the nation, Senator

Ribicoff assisted the administration in 1970 in its futile effort to introduce a welfare reform program. The administration proposed a Family Assistance Program (FAP) that promised a guaranteed minimum payment of $1,600 to a family of four. The working poor also were to receive benefits. The proposal encountered stiff opposition in the Senate, where liberals denounced it as too weak and conservatives dismissed the need for the program. In an effort to reach a compromise, Ribicoff introduced an amendment to test the FAP in selected areas and then put it into effect nationally. The Senate Finance Committee voted 9 to 4 to defeat this move endorsed by the administration. The committee then buried the Nixon proposal by a vote of 14 to 1.

As governor of Connecticut, at HEW, and as a senator, Ribicoff was hailed as one of the champions of civil rights in the nation. In 1970 he found himself allied with southern conservatives when he announced his intention to vote for the amendment sponsored by Senator JOHN STENNIS (D-Miss.) that called for a uniform policy on enforcement of school desegregation guidelines regardless of the cause of discrimination. The amendment thus sought to eliminate the distinction between de jure and de facto segregation. Ribicoff called on other northern senators to drop their "monumental hypocrisy" and admit that northern school systems were just as racially segregated as those in the South. But he emphasized that he would not support any antibusing amendment that would "halt federal efforts to enforce school desegregation." Although the Stennis amendment was adopted in the Senate, a House-Senate conference committee reinstated the de jure-de facto distinction.

The following year the Connecticut senator proposed his own two-part plan designed to significantly increase integration in the schools and housing patterns of the nation's suburban communities. The first part of Ribicoff's proposal required all schools within a metropolitan area to have a percentage of minority students at least equal to half the percentage of minority students in the entire metropolitan area. Under his proposal communities would have 12 years to accomplish this integration but would have to show progress annually. If no progress was shown, the schools would face a cutoff of federal funds. The second part of the legislation required suburban communities to maintain federally aided housing facilities for low- and moderate-income families. This section of his plan was to be implemented immediately. In his speech Ribicoff deplored "the seemingly inexorable march toward apartheid in the North as well as the South." Citing U.S. census figures showing northern schools as a whole were more segregated than schools in the South, he said "racial isolation is now just as pervasive in the North as it is in the South."

During the first two years of the JIMMY CARTER presidency, Ribicoff continued to press for national health insurance welfare reform and the creation of a consumer protection agency. Ribicoff, a pro-Zionist Jew, startled the Jewish community when he voted for the 1978 arms sales for Egypt and Syria. Ribicoff announced in 1979 he would not seek reelection the following year. He died in 1998.

—JB

Richardson, Elliot L(ee)
(1920–1999) *undersecretary of state; secretary of health, education, and welfare; secretary of defense; attorney general; ambassador to Great Britain; secretary of commerce*

Elliot L. Richardson was born on July 20, 1920, in Boston, Massachusetts. Descended from early New England settlers and a family of physicians, Richardson attended Harvard College (B.A., magna cum laude, 1941) and Harvard Law School (LL.B., magna cum laude, 1947). He interrupted his studies to serve with distinction as first lieutenant in the army during World War II. He began his legal career with great promise, becoming editor and president of the *Harvard Law Review*, then clerking for the distinguished U.S. court of appeals judge Learned Hand in 1947–48 and for Supreme Court Justice Felix Frankfurter in 1948–49. After three years with the noted Boston law firm Ropes, Gray, Best, Coolidge, and Rugg, he began a career in public service as an aide to Massachusetts senator Leverett Saltonstall in 1953.

In 1957 President Eisenhower appointed Richardson assistant secretary for legislation in the relatively new Department of Health, Education, and Welfare, where he played a major part in drafting the National Defense Education Act and in developing legislation on Social Security, public health, and juvenile delinquency. He returned to Boston in 1959 with an appointment as U.S. attorney for Massachusetts. In this capacity he quickly earned a reputation as a relentless prosecutor. One of his best-known cases involved the prosecution and conviction of Bernard Goldfine for tax evasion after Goldfine's gifts to White House chief of staff Sherman Adams had produced the most scandalous cause célèbre of the Eisenhower administration.

Following the defeat of the Republican national ticket in 1960, Richardson plunged into Massachusetts politics, running for (but losing) the Republican primary contest for state attorney general in 1962. In 1964 he won election as lieutenant governor. For the next two years he took an active role in the administration of Governor JOHN VOLPE, particularly in coordinating social welfare programs. Elected state attorney general in 1966, he pursued such liberal causes as consumer protection and crime prevention measures. He was still serving in this capacity when he was tapped by the new NIXON administration to become undersecretary of state in 1969.

Recommended by President Nixon's close friend WILLIAM ROGERS and endorsed by newly appointed secretary of transportation JOHN VOLPE, Richardson came to the State Department with little experience in foreign affairs. However, Secretary of State Rogers, who knew Richardson from the Eisenhower years, had confidence in his administrative ability and felt that they would be in such personal rapport that Richardson would act as his "alter ego."

During his 17 months at the State Department, Richardson undertook both public and bureaucratic tasks. Traditionally the undersecretary has the responsibility for administering the department, and Richardson assumed these duties, immersing himself in the details and nuances of foreign affairs and introducing administrative and personnel reforms in an attempt to revitalize the Foreign Service. Soon after being sworn in, he represented the United States at the Paris meeting of the Organization for Economic Cooperation and Development, proclaiming an administration policy of increased free trade. Late in 1969 he was actively involved in the preparations for the Strategic Arms Limitation Talks in Helsinki. Richardson proved to be a vigorous supporter of the president's decision to invade Cambodia even though he had serious private reservations about that action. CBS-TV newsman Dan Rather, in *The Palace Guard*, suggested that this support for a controversial policy established Richardson's loyalty in President Nixon's eyes and therefore helped him to receive a promotion to the cabinet as secretary of health, education, and welfare (HEW) in June 1970.

The department Richardson inherited from ROBERT FINCH was badly demoralized, administratively disarrayed, and often ideologically out of tune with the Nixon political orientation. An unwieldy bureaucracy when initially created, HEW had grown during the Johnson Great Society years and then been allowed to drift as that president's attention became consumed with waging the war in Southeast Asia.

When the Nixon administration assumed office, it found HEW difficult to manage and resistant to attempts to cut back the Great Society legacy. During 1969 and 1970 the department was further disrupted when civil rights issues and opposition to the Vietnam War caused mass resignations of liberal departmental officials. Robert Finch, who had found the task of directing HEW frustrating and exhausting, resigned to become a White House adviser.

As a progressive Republican with a reputation and a service record as a strong administrator and a loyal team member, Richardson was suited to both the president's and the department's needs. In addition, he had had experience in HEW during the Eisenhower administration. The combination of these assets led Richardson to declare that he was "returning to an old love," while the president commented that he was "the best qualified man in the country" to head HEW.

With his ability to absorb detail, Richardson soon mastered all of the department's 280 programs. He then began to revitalize the personnel while trying to redirect HEW's efforts. One of Richardson's goals was to decentralize federal control of various social program funds and to streamline HEW's "resource transfer" activities. In this effort Richardson instituted a simpler grant procedure, consolidated programs, and promoted decentralization in keeping with President Nixon's concept of the "New Federalism." Although he personally favored a moderate school busing program to end segregation, he presided over Nixon's more restrained policy of holding federally imposed busing to the minimum required by the law.

Immediately after President Nixon's successful reelection campaign of 1972, he initiated a major personnel shake-up designed to maximize the managerial virtues of thrift, efficiency, and loyalty among his cabinet secretaries and core staff members. As part of this round of bureaucratic musical chairs, Elliot Richardson was moved from HEW to Defense, succeeding MELVIN LAIRD, who retired to private life. Richardson, although trusted and valued for his versatility, was apparently too liberal to achieve the kind of domestic program retrenchment the president envisioned. President Nixon's intentions were clearly indicated by the character of Richardson's successor at HEW, CASPAR WEINBERGER, a fiscal conservative who had already tried paring down the department's budget from his preceding position as budget director.

Richardson's appointment as secretary of defense achieved two other presidential purposes. Assuming command of a departmental conglomerate with a size and budget similar to HEW's, he was expected to trim and tighten the bloated Pentagon bureaucracy. His newest assignment and his replacement by Weinberger at HEW brought two ideologically suited individuals to the president's tasks: "a liberal to make cuts at the conservative Pentagon [and] a conservative [to] swing the ax at the liberal welfare agency." Second, the departure of a strong foreign policy–oriented and defense-experienced Melvin Laird and his replacement by the more generalist and domestic policy–oriented Richardson seemed to crown presidential assistant HENRY KISSINGER as the undisputed paramount foreign policy adviser. The new secretary of defense did not, however, even have time to settle into his new role before being summoned to yet another cabinet position. After only 91 days at the Pentagon, Richardson was drafted attorney general in the first wave of Watergate-related personnel changes.

By May 1973 revelations regarding the original Watergate burglary, its cover-up, and related political subterfuges had forced the resignations of key White House aides JOHN EHRLICHMAN and H. R. HALDEMAN, caused the firing of White House counsel JOHN DEAN, and prompted Attorney General RICHARD KLEINDIENST to resign, claiming that his close friendship with certain Watergate suspects was incompatible with the "impartial enforcement of the law." As a dependably loyal administration member, Richardson was acceptable to the president. As a liberal with a record of success at prosecuting governmental corruption, he also had a good chance of securing Senate confirmation.

Initially reluctant to accept the post of attorney general, Richardson felt it might be more appropriate for the administration to bring in an outsider. Even though he was not close to any of the men implicated in the scandal up to that time, the fact that he had been a key figure throughout the Nixon administration seemed to raise fears that he might "go easy" on administration members involved in the Watergate affair.

At his confirmation hearings (which dragged on for three weeks) Richardson encountered these same misgivings from members of the Senate Judiciary Committee who did not want the administration choosing "one of its own men to hold final responsibility for the Watergate investigations." Indeed, the problem of securing a full and free investigation of the growing scandal led to a disagreement between Richardson and the Senate Judiciary Committee over the independence and authority of a Watergate prosecutor and, for a time, seriously jeopardized his confirmation possibilities. By acquiescing to guidelines that would guarantee the independence of a special prosecutor and announcing the appointment of ARCHIBALD COX to that sensitive position, Richardson allayed the committee's misgivings and secured confirmation for his third cabinet post in as many years.

As the Senate Watergate investigations continued and the special prosecutor's activities gained momentum, Richardson found himself in an increasingly hot crossfire between the White House and Cox. Legally, Richardson as attorney general bore ultimate responsibility for the special prosecutor's actions. Only he could fire Cox, and then only for "extraordinary improprieties."

As early as July 23, 1973, when the special prosecutor issued a subpoena for Watergate-related White House tapes, Richardson realized that the president intended to "get rid" of Cox as soon as possible. During the summer and early autumn of 1973 Richardson and White House chief of staff ALEXANDER HAIG were frequent intermediaries between Nixon and Cox, trying to work out a compromise on the tapes, while the tapes case worked its way through U.S. district and appeals courts. During this same period the Justice Department, under Richardson's direct supervision, developed and pursued a case against Vice President SPIRO AGNEW for tax fraud and bribery. In October, when the evidence against Agnew was firm enough to assure an indictment (and thus precipitate a constitutional crisis), Richardson and the White House negotiated a compromise whereby the vice president resigned from office after pleading no contest to a charge of income tax evasion.

Two days after Agnew's resignation a U.S. appeals court directed the president to surrender the subpoenaed White House tapes to Judge JOHN SIRICA, touching off a new and intense round of behind-the-scenes negotiations through Richardson and Haig. The White House offered edited transcripts of the tapes; Cox refused the arrangement. Richardson proposed that a third party authenticate the transcripts, and the White House proposed that Senator JOHN STENNIS (D-Miss.) be that individual and also insisted that Cox agree not to seek any additional tapes or documents from the White House.

When Cox rejected the plan as an intrusion on his independence, the president directed the attorney general to dismiss him. Richardson, who had pledged at his Senate confirmation hearings to guarantee the independence of the special prosecutor, felt neither justified nor willing to violate that pledge or the public interest as he saw it. Feeling that "the very integrity of the governmental process . . . [he had tried] . . . to help restore" was at stake, he concluded that he "could better serve [his] country by resigning [his] public office rather than by continuing in it."

His deputy, WILLIAM RUCKELSHAUS, also refused to dismiss Cox and was forced to resign. Finally, Solicitor General ROBERT H. BORK, who was next in line as acting attorney general, fired Cox and abolished the office of the special prosecutor. The quartet of resignations and dismissals of October 21, 1973, which became known as the "Saturday night massacre," inflamed public opinion and spurred the commencement of impeachment hearings against President Nixon.

Praised for a principled resignation in protest, Richardson acquired the aura of a folk hero and spent the year following the "Saturday night massacre" fulfilling extensive speaking commitments ranging from television interviews to the Chubb fellowship at Yale and the Godkin lectureship at Harvard. He also directed a project at the Woodrow Wilson International Center for Scholars on the problems of "subnational governments."

Richardson sojourned in academia only long enough to see the demise of the Nixon presidency and the transition to the FORD administration. In December 1974 he was once again summoned to public service when President Ford nominated him to one of the most prestigious diplomatic assignments available—ambassador to Great Britain.

In becoming envoy to the Court of St. James's, Richardson replaced Philadelphia pub-lisher Walter H. Annenberg, who resigned after serving in the post since 1969. At the time of his appointment, Richardson was regarded as a leader of the liberal wing of the Republican Party and was frequently mentioned as a presidential or vice presidential contender. Service in such a distinguished ambassadorship was possibly designed to give him additional foreign experience and thus strengthen his prospects.

After slightly less than a year in London, Richardson expressed disappointment in his diplomatic assignment because, according to the *New York Times*, "he was expected to serve as a 'superambassador' to Western Europe but was getting what he considered only scant attention from Secretary [of State] Kissinger." Wishing to retain Richardson in some capacity and to accommodate Commerce Secretary ROGERS C. B. MORTON's desire to leave the administration, President Ford announced Richardson's return to the cabinet as secretary of commerce. Nominated in November 1975, Richardson easily won Senate confirmation and served in this capacity for the remainder of the Ford presidency. Richardson served the JIMMY CARTER administration as a special representative for the Law of the Sea Conference (1977–80). He died in 1999 of a cerebral hemorrhage.

—MJW

Rivers, L(ucius) Mendel
(1905–1970) *member of the House of Representatives; chairman, Armed Services Committee*

Born on September 30, 1905, in Gumville, South Carolina, Mendel Rivers graduated from the University of South Carolina in 1931. He served as a state representative in South Carolina until 1936, when he became a special attorney for the U.S. Department of Justice. In 1940 he was elected to the House of Representatives. In the House he was a member of the Naval Affairs

Committee, the forerunner of the Armed Services Committee, of which he became chairman in 1965. A strong defender of military spending and the need for the deployment of America's armed forces around the world, Rivers came under increasing attack in the 1960s from critics of the military-industrial complex.

As head of the Armed Services Committee during the first two years of the NIXON administration, Rivers was in a strong position to aid the efforts of the president in a number of areas. He was strongly in favor of both the Sentinel and the Safeguard antiballistic missile systems, nudging Secretary of Defense MELVIN LAIRD to make a "definite statement" sanctioning the programs. He later used his enormous influence in the House to get the Safeguard system passed. He opposed the concept of an all-volunteer army. In April 1969 Rivers objected to a spending ceiling on the C-5A transport because he saw it as part of the effort in Congress to curb military funding.

A vigorous proponent of the war in Vietnam, Rivers lauded Nixon's various actions. In a 1969 speech he told an audience that "we have got to get over our national guilt complex at having kept the world free." Later that year at a Veterans' Day rally in support of the Vietnam War, he said: "there are more of us patriotic Americans than those pro-Hanoicrats. Keep up the fight. SPIRO AGNEW is helping us. You back up Spiro and he will continue to throw it on."

Rivers was thought to have been instrumental in advising Nixon in September 1969 not to hold the murder trial against six Green Berets charged with killing a Vietnamese double agent. He also aggressively opposed the army's prosecution of those implicated in the My Lai incident, contending there was no evidence that U.S. troops were guilty of massacring Vietnamese civilians.

Throughout his career Rivers was easily reelected from his conservative district because he consistently opposed civil rights and social welfare legislation. His popularity was furthered by the large amount of military installations he succeeded in having built in his district as well as the number of defense contractors who opened plants there. It was estimated that defense-related industries accounted for 35 percent of the payroll in the Charleston area.

His reputation in the press and among some of his colleagues was that of an alcoholic and a bully. Allegations of heavy drinking surfaced in the columns of Drew Pearson in the late 1960s, and some critics considered him a security risk for top secret Pentagon information. He made a convenient target for the antiwar movement. Few denied his vast knowledge of military hardware, however, or his assistance in trying to upgrade the pay scale for the military. Rivers underwent open-heart surgery at the University of Alabama Hospital late in 1970 and died three weeks later.

—GWB

Rizzo, Frank L(azzaro)
(1920–1991) *mayor of Philadelphia*

The son of Italian immigrants, Rizzo was born on October 23, 1920, and raised in a poor neighborhood of South Philadelphia. After his mother died in 1938, Rizzo dropped out of high school and joined the navy. In 1943 he entered the Philadelphia police department as a foot patrolman. Working his way up through the ranks, Rizzo was eventually promoted to police commissioner in 1967.

Throughout his career Rizzo tried to live up to the title he proudly gave himself, the "toughest cop in America." His efforts occasionally resulted in charges of police brutality. As police chief he authorized the creation of special teams equipped with shotguns and machine guns to be used for rooftop duty in the event of rioting. As police commissioner he successfully opposed the establishment of a civilian complaint review board. During the late 1960s Rizzo was able to avert racial riots like those plaguing other cities by squelching possible disturbances at the earliest stages and "moving in fast with the most."

Having vowed to "crush black power," Rizzo organized a dawn raid on a Black Panther Party center in Philadelphia on August 29, 1970. Several incidents of racial violence occurred in the following days, resulting in the death of one policeman and the wounding of six others. Rizzo also orchestrated the quelling of the Holmesburg Prison riot in July in which 29 guards and 84 inmates were injured. Rizzo called the prison riot "a complete racial problem." During his tenure Rizzo succeeded in enlarging the department from 6,000 to 7,200, yet despite his efforts crime in Philadelphia increased 19 percent, or three times the national urban average, between 1969 and 1970. Rizzo blamed this increase on the leniency of the courts.

In May 1971 Rizzo won the Democratic mayoral primary with 49 percent of the vote. Shunning campaign debates and refusing to answer questions from the news media, Rizzo campaigned on a "law and order" platform, insisting that he was not a politician but rather a "tough cop." He also promised to lower taxes and reform city government. His style appealed to the white, blue-collar neighborhoods of Philadelphia, and despite the opposition of Governor MILTON SHAPP and of the city's two largest daily newspapers, Rizzo managed to defeat his Republican opponent, Thacher Longstreth, in the mayoral race.

During the early months of his administration, Rizzo undertook an investigation of the use of federal funding. The probe resulted in the prosecution of the head of the Philadelphia Housing Authority's residents advisory board for alleged misappropriation of funds. He gave more disciplinary discretion and power to classroom teachers, appointed blacks to senior city jobs, closed down pornographic movie houses, and investigated the issuing of city contracts. In addition to moving against organized crime, he increased the police department's budget and added to its manpower.

Two Philadelphia newspapers, the *Inquirer* and the *Bulletin*, printed stories on August 3, 1973, alleging that Rizzo deployed a secret, 33-man police squad to spy on city council president George X. Schwartz and Peter J. Camiel, chairman of the Democratic city committee. Learning of this, Camiel revealed that Rizzo and Deputy Mayor Phillip Carrol tried to bribe him on February 27, 1973. According to Camiel, Rizzo and Carroll offered him control over the selection of architects and engineering firms for city contracts in return for his endorsement of Rizzo's candidate for district attorney, incumbent Arlen Specter. Camiel challenged Rizzo and Carrol to submit themselves to a lie detector test administered by an expert hired by the *Philadelphia Daily News.* Rizzo agreed, saying that "If this machine says a man lied, he lied." The test indicated that Rizzo and Carrol lied on six out of 10 questions, while Camiel lied on none. On August 15, 1973, Philadelphia district attorney Arlen Specter announced that a grand jury would investigate charges that Rizzo used a police spy unit for his own purposes and attempted to bribe Camiel.

The Pennsylvania Crime Commission released a 1,404-page report on March 10, 1974, charging that police corruption in Philadelphia was "ongoing, widespread, systematic, and occurring at all levels." The report also accused the Rizzo administration of actively trying to hinder the 18-month investigation by arresting the commission's special agents and failing to act when presented with evidence of corruption. However, after federal district and appellate courts ordered Philadelphia city officials to institute new procedures for handling complaints of police misconduct, the Supreme

Court overturned these rulings in a 5-3 decision. The opinion held there was insufficient proof that city officials were responsible for police misconduct.

Rizzo's popularity began to wane when 211,000 signatures were collected on petitions demanding his recall, but the Pennsylvania supreme court barred a special recall vote from being included on the November 2, 1974, ballot. Nonetheless, Rizzo was able to recapture his office in November 1975 with 57 percent of the vote. In this election the mayor once again campaigned as a "law and order" candidate.

In 1977 Rizzo got the city council to propose a charter change allowing him to run for a third term. This proposed amendment was soundly defeated at the polls. Rizzo would switch to the Republican Party in 1986 and make several unsuccessful runs for mayor of Philadelphia. He also served as a security consultant for Philadelphia Gas Works and had a radio talk show. Rizzo died during the 1991 mayoral campaign.

—AFB

Rockefeller, Nelson A(ldrich)
(1908–1979) *governor of New York; vice president of the United States*

As a grandson of John D. Rockefeller, the Standard Oil magnate, Nelson Rockefeller was born into one of America's wealthiest families. He spent several years working in various family enterprises after graduating from Dartmouth in 1930. Through his directorship of the Creole Petroleum Co., a Latin American-based affiliate of Standard Oil, Rockefeller acquired an interest in Latin American affairs. In 1940 President Franklin D. Roosevelt appointed him to head the office of the Coordinator of Inter-American Affairs.

Over the next 15 years Rockefeller served three presidents in a variety of appointive posts involving both foreign and domestic affairs. From 1944 to 1945 he was assistant secretary of state for Latin American affairs, and in 1950 and 1951 he advised President Harry S. Truman on the Point Four Program. President Eisenhower, whom Rockefeller had endorsed in the 1952 election, appointed him undersecretary of the Department of Health, Education, and Welfare in 1954. Later that year he became a special assistant to Eisenhower on foreign affairs.

Realizing the need for a political base to promote the programs he favored, Rockefeller ran as a liberal Republican for the governorship of New York in 1958 and defeated the incumbent, Democrat W. Averell Harriman. Rockefeller successfully sought reelection in 1962, 1966, and 1970.

As governor of New York, Rockefeller initially won a reputation as an advocate of social welfare legislation and large-scale government spending programs. He transformed an undistinguished state teachers college system into a major statewide liberal arts university. He substantially increased the state's middle-income housing program, won passage of New York's first uniform minimum wage law in 1960, and successfully pressed for civil rights legislation to bar discrimination in housing and public accommodations. In 1965 Rockefeller won expanded powers for the State Commission on Human Rights, launched an ambitious state medicaid plan the following year, and established a Narcotics Addiction Control Commission to provide treatment for addicts regardless of their wishes.

Initially Rockefeller financed these programs on a "pay as you go" basis, increasing taxes to meet rising expenditures. But the enormous growth of the budget made legislators reluctant to approve the ever higher taxes needed, and Rockefeller turned to bond issues to finance such projects as water pollution control and highway construction. When voters began rejecting these, however, Rockefeller and his aides devised a scheme to create quasi-independent agencies to issue so-called moral obligation bonds. Agencies such as the State University Construction Fund and the Urban Development Corporation vastly increased the state's indebtedness through large-scale borrowing from major banks at interest rates higher than those for voter-approved bonds.

Rockefeller was repeatedly frustrated in his ambition to run for the presidency. After Nixon's defeat in 1960, Rockefeller set his sights on the 1964 presidential campaign but lost the Republican nomination to conservative senator BARRY GOLDWATER (R-Ariz.) in a campaign that aroused much bitterness.

Initially declaring himself a "noncandidate" for the 1968 nomination, Rockefeller reversed himself on April 30, 1968, and entered the race. Still campaigning as a liberal, he was unable to catch front-runner RICHARD NIXON. Rockefeller supported Nixon after his nomination, and the two men appeared to have drawn closer ideologically. After the election Nixon chose HENRY KISSINGER, formerly a close aide to Rockefeller, to head the National Security Council.

Rockefeller moved substantially to the right during the latter years of his governorship. He began to speak out against government spending on social welfare programs and to take a tough stand on law-and-order issues.

In January 1969 Rockefeller presented the first of his "austerity" budgets to the state legislature. Although he requested a record $6.4 billion, the increases stemmed from mandated expenditures for existing education and welfare programs, and Rockefeller pointedly did not recommend any new ventures. Instead he warned the legislature that the state faced "a grave fiscal crisis." In his 1971 budget message Rockefeller sounded a graver alarm. Claiming that social welfare programs had "dangerously overloaded the financial capacity of

Vice President Nelson A. Rockefeller *(Ford Library)*

state and local governments," he predicted a "breakdown in local government services" and declared that the state "must tighten its belt and live within its resources."

In April 1971 Rockefeller signed legislation cutting welfare payments by 10 percent, reducing Medicaid allowances, and slashing funds for drug rehabilitation programs. The actions provoked riots in New York City in May as the cutbacks were felt by the city's poor. In June Rockefeller approved a welfare residency law despite the 1969 Supreme Court ruling that such laws were unconstitutional. (The law was voided by the courts in August.) The next month he signed a bill that required welfare recipients to work or lose their benefits. Although Rockefeller's measures received praise from President Nixon, whose own welfare proposals Rockefeller had endorsed, leaders of welfare rights groups and other liberals were extremely critical.

As demonstrations by students, blacks, and other disaffected groups increased in scope and intensity, Rockefeller became an advocate of a tough law-and-order response. Two months later black students at Cornell University occupied the student union building and emerged two days later armed with rifles and shotguns. Calling the situation "intolerable," Rockefeller quickly drafted legislation, which was enacted by the state legislature, outlawing guns on school or college property. He also signed a law that required colleges and universities to adopt regulations for the "maintenance of public order" or face the loss of state financial aid.

Rockefeller came under heavy criticism for his handling of the Attica prison uprising. On September 9, 1971, inmates at the Attica Correctional Facility seized 32 guards and civilian employees as hostages and issued a set of 15 demands, including coverage by the state minimum wage law, an end to censorship of reading materials, and a promise of no reprisals against participants in the rebellion. On September 10 New York state commissioner of corrections Russell G. Oswald agreed to allow a team of observers to participate in the negotiations with the inmates. Among its members were *New York Times* reporter Tom Wicker, Representative Herman Badillo (D-N.Y.), and Clarence Jones, the publisher of the black newspaper the *Amsterdam News*. The observer committee asked Rockefeller to intervene, but he declined.

On September 13 Oswald, with the support of Rockefeller, ordered an air and ground assault of the prison by 1,500 state troopers. Forty-two were killed, including prisoners, guards, and employees. Although early reports accused the inmates of murdering the hostages, autopsies revealed that all of the deaths were caused by gunshot wounds, and subsequent investigation revealed that the convicts were unarmed.

Several commissions were authorized to investigate the uprisings, including one headed by Robert B. McKay, dean of New York University Law School. The McKay Report, issued in September 1972, called the uprising a spontaneous response to legitimate grievances and concluded that Rockefeller should have visited Attica before ordering the assault. The report also was sharply critical of police behavior. A later report, issued in 1975 by special state investigator Bernard S. Meyer, cited "serious errors in judgment" and attacked Rockefeller for making public remarks at the time that were "inappropriate and should not have been made."

Rockefeller continued to make some liberal initiatives during these years. A strong supporter of the burgeoning environmental movement, he won passage in 1970 of a bill that established a state department of the environment, and he drafted legislation to ban the use of the pesticide DDT. In April 1970 Rockefeller signed into law a major abortion reform bill that legalized abortions up to the 24th week of pregnancy. It was considered the most liberal in the nation. In 1972, despite intense pressure from the Roman Catholic Church in New York, Rockefeller vetoed a bill that would have repealed the state's abortion law.

Rockefeller supported most of the initiatives of the Nixon administration. He spoke out in favor of federal revenue sharing and Nixon's Family Assistance Plan and praised Nixon's 1971 imposition of wage and price controls to counter inflation. Rockefeller also supported the administration's policy of "Vietnamization," which called for the gradual withdrawal of U.S. troops from Southeast Asia and the shifting of the military effort to South Vietnamese troops. Rockefeller, however, found himself at odds with Vice President SPIRO AGNEW, especially over the latter's sharp attacks on the liberal antiwar senator from New York CHARLES GOODELL. During Goodell's reelection campaign in 1970, Rockefeller, who endorsed Goodell, sent a message to the White House requesting that Agnew stay out of the campaign, since "outside intervention would be prejudicial to the state Republican ticket."

Rockefeller, meanwhile, retained his interest in foreign affairs. In February 1969 President Nixon announced that he had asked the governor to make a series of visits to Latin America and to formulate policy recommendations to the administration. Rockefeller made the first trip in May 1969, visiting Mexico and several Central American nations. The trip was marred by widespread demonstrations, however, and the Latin American press criticized the tour. Three subsequent visits to South America, in May, June, and July, saw violent demonstrations and battles between police and protesters in almost every country Rockefeller visited. The governments of Peru and Chile withdrew their invitations to avoid violence, and Rockefeller himself canceled the trip to Venezuela. Rockefeller's report, which was released in September 1969, portrayed a sense of crisis in Latin America and pointed to a "climate of growing instability, extremism, and anti-U.S. nationalism." The report recommended major trade concessions, increases in military aid, and the renegotiation of foreign debt.

On December 11, 1973, Rockefeller announced his resignation from the governorship and his intention to devote his time to two national study commissions. The first, a Rockefeller family-funded Commission on Critical Choices for America, was to make a major inquiry into the future role of the federal government in a changing society. The second, a Commission on Water Quality, was a congressionally established panel to study the problem of water pollution.

On August 20, 1974, GERALD FORD, who had just succeeded Richard Nixon as president, nominated Rockefeller for the vice presidency. Under the provisions of the Twenty-fifth Amendment, the nomination required confirmation by both the Senate and the House. Although the selection of Rockefeller was praised by liberals and conservatives of both parties, concern over his wealth and the potential use of it for political purposes led to extensive public hearings on the nomination.

The Senate Rules Committee opened hearings on September 23. Rockefeller promised to cooperate fully, declaring his hope that "the myth or misconception about the extent of the family's control over the economy of this country will be totally brought out and exposed and dissipated." Nonetheless, his disclosures about personal wealth revealed that he, his wife, and his children had assets of almost $230 million, and a spokesman for the family revealed that the entire Rockefeller clan owned securities worth over $1 billion, with large interests in banks and corporations whose assets were far larger.

During October it was revealed that over the years Rockefeller had given or loaned substantial amounts of money to political associates such as Henry Kissinger; William J. Ronan, the chairman of the Port Authority of New York and New Jersey and a Rockefeller appointee; and L. Judson Morhouse, the former chairman of the New York State Republican Party. It was also disclosed that Rockefeller had financed a scurrilous biography of former Supreme Court justice ARTHUR GOLDBERG during Goldberg's 1970 campaign against Rockefeller for the governorship. The Senate Rules Committee held a second set of hearings in November to explore these questions.

Despite misgivings about the propriety of Rockefeller's actions, the committee, on November 22, unanimously recommended his confirmation. Hearings by the House Judiciary Committee reached a similar conclusion. On December 19, after both the House and Senate voted overwhelmingly in favor of confirmation, Rockefeller was sworn in as the nation's 41st vice president.

Almost immediately Rockefeller was given major responsibility by President Ford. On December 22, 1974, the *New York Times* began a series of articles alleging that under President Nixon the CIA had conducted a "massive, illegal domestic intelligence operation" against antiwar activists and other dissenters. In January the *Times* and the *Washington Post* carried further articles that charged the CIA with intercepting the mail of private citizens and labor organizations and with attempting to destroy its domestic intelligence files to stave off investigations. On January 5, 1975, Ford named Rockefeller to head a special commission to investigate the allegations of domestic spying by the CIA.

The Rockefeller Commission began private, closed hearings almost immediately. Extending through the winter and into the spring, the hearings gathered evidence from a wide array of present and former CIA officials. Late in March, when the press reported that the CIA was allegedly involved in plots to assassinate foreign officials, including Fidel Castro of Cuba, Rockefeller extended the investigation. On June 2, before the commission's report was released, Rockefeller told the press that although there were some violations of law, they were not serious. His remarks provoked a sharp response from Senator FRANK CHURCH (D-Idaho), who had conducted a similar investigation for the Senate Foreign Relations Committee. Church said that murder plots were not "a minor matter."

Rockefeller's 299-page report was released on June 10. Although it concluded that the "great majority" of CIA activities were in compliance with the law, the report did concede that the CIA had engaged in actions that were "plainly unlawful and constituted improper invasions upon the rights of Americans." It cited the illegal opening of mail, illegal wiretaps and room buggings, break-ins, and the investigation of confidential tax returns of private citizens. The report also detailed the activities of the Special Operations Group within the CIA, which, beginning in 1967, collected files on over 7,200 protestors, infiltrated domestic political groups, and compiled a computerized index of over 300,000 individuals and organizations involved in political protest.

In February 1975 Ford appointed Rockefeller to head the White House Domestic Council and picked two of Rockefeller's aides for key positions on the council. Under Rockefeller the council shifted its focus from a day-to-day advisory role to one of studying and reviewing long-range domestic policy options. Rockefeller directed the council to study alternative financing for the Social Security system and other approaches to federal-state revenue sharing. He also emphasized the need to free the economy from "stifling" federal regulations and urged the removal of price controls on domestic oil and natural gas.

Almost from the time of his confirmation, there was speculation over whether Rockefeller would remain on Ford's ticket for 1976. Conservative Republicans were strongly opposed to the possibility. Ford, meanwhile, publicly praised Rockefeller as "an exceptionally active and able vice president," and in June he formally endorsed Rockefeller as his desired running mate. To win over party leaders, Rockefeller frequently addressed Republican gatherings throughout the country. During a tour of the South in August 1975, Rockefeller spoke out in favor of states' rights and a balanced budget and against government bureaucracy and welfare "cheats." He also repeatedly urged the party to remain as broad-based in its appeal as possible.

Despite these efforts, conservative opposition to Rockefeller remained strong. On November 3, following a request from Ford, he withdrew from consideration as a possible 1976 vice presidential candidate. The decision was interpreted as a major effort to appease the conservative wing of the party and to stem the threat to Ford's renomination posed by former California governor RONALD REAGAN.

Rockefeller campaigned for Ford during the primaries and won a majority of the New York delegation for the president. After Ford was nominated Rockefeller continued to campaign for his reelection.

Upon the expiration of his term in January 1977, Rockefeller, after a long career as a public official, retired into private life. Two years later, on January 26, 1979, Rockefeller died of a heart attack in New York City.

—JD

Rodino, Peter W(allace)
(1909–2005) *member of the House of Representatives; chairman, Judiciary Committee*

Rodino was born on June 7, 1909, and brought up and educated in the public schools of Newark, New Jersey. He attended the University of Newark and the New Jersey School of Law (now Rutgers), receiving his degree in 1938. From 1930 to 1932 he taught public speaking and citizenship classes at the Young Men's Christian Association. After setting up his law practice in Newark in the late 1930s, Rodino volunteered for military service before America's entry into World War II. After being discharged from the army in 1946, Rodino ran as a Democrat unsuccessfully for the U.S. House against the incumbent, Fred Hartley Jr. The latter retired in 1948, and Rodino was able to win his seat. He represented most of Newark and several surrounding communities.

The representative first served on the Veterans Affairs Committee and then the Judiciary Committee, where he had become the fourth-ranking Democrat by the mid-1960s. A strong supporter of immigration reform, he was influential in the House passage of a 1965 Johnson administration bill that eliminated the old nationality quota system of immigration control. In addition, he was an ardent backer of civil rights legislation, acting as floor manager for the open housing provision of the proposed Civil Rights Act of 1966. In other matters Rodino generally voted for the domestic and foreign policy initiatives of the Johnson administration.

Rodino initially supported the RICHARD NIXON Vietnam policies. However, he broke with the president after the Cambodian invasion of 1970. Soon after he voted for the Cooper-Church Amendment, prohibiting military involvement in Cambodia without specific congressional approval. During the first years of the decade, he voted for other measures to end the war, including an unsuccessful supplemental appropriations bill in June 1973 that provided for the cutoff of all funds for combat activities in Laos and Cambodia. In other foreign policy action Rodino voted against authorizing foreign aid to fund a new squadron of F-4D jet aircraft for Nationalist China in November 1969.

On domestic issues Rodino compiled a generally liberal voting record. He supported consumer protection in various votes as well as the 1969 Nixon administration legislation calling for the government to force the hiring of minority workers on federally financed projects, the so-called Philadelphia Plan. In 1975 Rodino voted for common-site picketing, which would allow workers striking a single subcontractor to picket an entire construction site. That same year he also voted in favor of the federal loan guarantee for financially ailing New York City. He opposed unlimited payments by the government to farmers for not growing crops as well as legislation to continue federal funding for the development of the supersonic transport plane. The representative voted his religious convictions in opposing government aid for abortions and also took what was considered a hard-line position by voting in favor of the controversial "no-knock" provision of the District of Columbia crime bill.

Rodino became chairman of the Judiciary Committee in January 1973 after the defeat of the longtime incumbent, Representative EMMANUEL CELLER. As the Watergate scandal was gaining increasing attention, there were a number of members of Congress who began to call for the impeachment of the president. It was not, however, until October 22, 1973, that the Democratic leaders of the House met to consider these demands. The Speaker, CARL ALBERT, ultimately decided that instead of setting up a separate committee to deal with the matter, all impeachment resolutions would be referred to the Judiciary Committee. The impeachment proceedings were stalled, however, until the committee held hearings on the confirmation of Representative GERALD FORD as vice president. These hearings lasted until November 29.

Shortly before Christmas Rodino named JOHN DOAR, a nominal Republican who had led the Justice Department's Civil Rights Division during the Kennedy and Johnson administrations, as chief counsel of the committee. A staff was somewhat hastily assembled and grew to over 100 lawyers and investigators within a short time.

Many of the more liberal Democratic members of the Judiciary Committee, such as John Conyers of Michigan and Jerome Waldie of California, became irritated by the slow pace of investigation being set by Rodino and Doar. But Rodino refused to be hurried. He was concerned that the proceedings should appear eminently just. As columnist Joseph Kraft wrote: "Mr. Rodino is having his brush with history. He is determined to do everything right. He wants to avoid the slightest hint of partisanship and be fairness itself."

In February 1974, after laying the procedural groundwork for the impeachment investigation, the committee received House authorization to proceed with the formal constitutional process of impeachment. The committee spent much of the spring obtaining transcripts of the tapes of presidential conversations that were believed to be relevant to an understanding of whether Nixon was involved in the Watergate cover-up and whether, in fact, he was guilty of obstructing justice. On April 4, after waiting 38 days for a reply for one group of tapes, the committee decided to give the president five additional days to respond. After a bargaining gambit by presidential lawyer JAMES ST. CLAIR failed, the committee voted 33 to 3 to issue a subpoena to the president on April 11, the first time such action was taken in American history. On April 23, two days before the deadline set by the subpoena, St. Clair asked for and got an extension of five additional days.

The tapes were finally released by the White House, but they contained numerous deletions. In addition, Nixon supplied transcripts that were not accurate renderings of the tape conversations. "The president has not complied with our subpoena," Rodino told the news media. "We did not subpoena a presidential interpretation of what is necessary or relevant to our inquiry." The committee then voted 20 to 18 to reject the transcripts, but the White House responded by saying that it would release no more tapes or transcripts. In the middle of May, after the committee had subpoenaed additional material, the president announced that he would refuse to comply with any "such further subpoenas as may hereafter be issued." In a letter to Rodino the president wrote that "constantly escalating requests" for materials "constitute such a massive invasion into the confidentiality of presidential conversations that the institution of the presidency would be fatally compromised."

By early summer the Judiciary Committee seemed certain to recommend impeachment to the full House, but Rodino was determined to pick up as many Republican votes as possible to avoid the appearance of partisanship. Six weeks of closed hearings had ended on June 21. But before open hearings in front of television cameras began, the *Los Angeles Times* reported that Rodino had said all 21 Democrats would vote for impeachment. Although Rodino denied making the statement, a White House spokesman, Ken Clawson, exploded with indignation. "Now we have our worst fears confirmed out of Rodino's own mouth," Clawson said. "I'm confident that the American people will now once and for all realize that President Nixon is the subject of a witch hunt." Press secretary RON ZIEGLER called the committee a "kangaroo court." But Republican committee member Robert McClory of Illinois came to the chairman's defense when he said that Rodino "has done a good job." All in all, as *New York Times* reporter J. Anthony Lucas wrote in his account, *Nightmare*, "though Rodino miscalculated a few times, he had generally been generous to a fault with the opposition, treating them with great courtesy and deference."

By mid-July the committee released 10 volumes of evidence that in the opinion of its majority and minority counsels warranted impeachment. Televised hearings captured the public's attention in the latter days of July. By this time 29 proposed articles of impeachment had been presented to the committee, and Doar, at Rodino's urging, had at last become an impassioned advocate for impeachment. By the end of the month, the committee voted three articles of impeachment against Nixon—obstruction of justice, abuse of presidential powers, and contempt of Congress. In the case of the first article, Rodino noted that it would be reported to the House that "Richard M. Nixon has prevented, obstructed, and impeded the administration of justice . . . has acted in a manner contrary to his trust as president and subversive of constitutional government, to the great prejudice of the cause of law and justice, and to the manifest injury of the people of the United States . . . [and]

warrants impeachment and trial and removal from office." Nine days before the full House was to start impeachment proceedings, Nixon resigned. Following the presidential pardon of Nixon by GERALD FORD in September, several House members called for the revival of impeachment hearings, but Rodino strongly objected, saying that the principal purpose of impeachment was removal from office and that the procedure should not be used to accomplish any other purpose.

Rodino had gained a fair degree of celebrity status from the exposure he received chairing the Judiciary Committee, and it was not lost on the Democratic Party. He gave a nominating speech for Georgia governor JIMMY CARTER before the national convention in 1976 and was briefly considered to be in the running for the vice presidential nomination. Rodino retired from the House in 1989. He became a professor at Seton Hall University Law School, where he taught until February 2005. He died three months later.

—GWB

Rogers, William P(ierce)
(1913–2001) *secretary of state*

William P. Rogers moved from his small-town, upstate New York beginnings through positions as assistant attorney general to a racket-busting Thomas Dewey of New York in 1938, and as counsel to the Senate Special Committee to Investigate the National Defense Program in 1947, to serve in the Eisenhower Administration as deputy attorney general from 1953 to 1957 and then as attorney general until 1961. As a close friend of the then vice president, RICHARD NIXON, Rogers had been at Nixon's side for three of his "Six Crises"—in the Alger Hiss case he had counselled Nixon to pursue his inquiry, in the 1952 "slush fund" affair he had helped Nixon arrange his "Checkers" speech defense, and after

Eisenhower's 1955 heart attack he had advised Nixon to "act scrupulously like a vice president—not like an acting president." In short, William Rogers was a man Richard Nixon regarded as "a cool man under pressure . . . [with] . . . excellent judgment, a good sense of press relations, and one to whom I could speak with complete freedom."

After acting as a policy adviser during Nixon's 1960 presidential campaign, Rogers decided to drop out of politics for the first time in 15 years and to pursue the practice of law in earnest. An ambitious, self-made, and rather independent individual, Rogers felt he wanted to make it "on his own." He purposely interjected a sense of distance between himself and his old friend Nixon to dispel the notion that he was simply a Nixon crony. During the eight years of the Kennedy-Johnson presidencies he proved himself and prospered as a senior partner in the prestigious New York-Washington-Paris law firm of Royall, Koegel, Rogers, and Wells. He did not even return to play an important role in Richard Nixon's second bid for the presidency in 1968.

Despite the drifting apart that had occurred between Rogers and Nixon during the 1960s, Nixon once again turned to his old friend in 1968, insisting that he accept the ranking cabinet position of secretary of state. In light of Rogers's meager experience in foreign affairs, the appointment was regarded as somewhat surprising and indicative of Nixon's intention "to call the turn" on foreign affairs. Indeed, Rogers's diplomatic experience consisted of having been representative at the independence celebrations of Togo in 1960, a member of the delegation to the United Nations in 1965, and as a 10-week special representative on the Ad Hoc Committee on Southwest Africa in 1967.

His supporters maintained that since he was free of "any commitments or emotional attachments to past policies or procedures," he would be less righteous, doctrinaire, or crusading than his two immediate predecessors, John Foster Dulles and Dean Rusk. In addition, his reputation as one of the most glittering of the "diplomatic yet plain-spoken Hill-crawlers" was viewed as an asset to the administration in soothing the Senate Foreign Relations Committee and thus easing the course of the new administration's Vietnam policy. One lawyer turned diplomat, Nicholas Katzenbach, argued that "technical expertise" was not required in a secretary of state and that "the secretary's job . . . is pulling the government together on foreign problems, dealing with Congress, and . . . dealing with representatives of other governments. All [of which] falls quite naturally in the domain of any successful lawyer. Legal training—questioning, getting at the facts, looking at alternatives—is the greatest possible training." From the president's perspective Rogers's appointment had the advantages of bringing in a comfortable and trusted friend, an individual who would not compete with him for the diplomatic spotlight, and a progressive Republican from the party's eastern, internationalist wing.

Once confirmed, Rogers quickly began to establish good relations with Congress, soliciting the advice of influential senators and representatives and, in turn, being seen as a "force for moderation" within the administration. He also gave more attention than any postwar secretary of state to structural reform. In an effort to modernize and streamline bureaucratic procedures and internal communications, Rogers installed a sophisticated computer system for information storage and retrieval and initiated new personnel, training, and advancement programs designed to develop and keep highly qualified specialists.

By the end of President Nixon's first term, Rogers could claim, probably justifiably, that the department had never been in better shape. Yet management alone was not the solution, since the department's workload was growing.

The secretary pointed out that "apart from the everyday business of diplomacy . . . we've just recently had to become involved in problems that were formerly domestic but have become international. We're dealing now with the environment, communications satellites, air-traffic control, hijacking, and drug suppression."

Early in his tenure Rogers demonstrated that his talents as a negotiator would, at least partially, compensate for his lack of substantive expertise in foreign affairs. In early trips to Europe and the Far East Rogers created a favorable impression with his "ability to gain the quick trust of foreigners by conveying goodwill and personal warmth." However, it was soon apparent that the president looked to Rogers for guidance on the public relations implications of his decisions rather than on policy itself.

Indeed, speculation maintained that HENRY KISSINGER at the National Security Council and MELVIN LAIRD at the Pentagon were more influential in formulating foreign and national security policy than Rogers and the State Department. Certainly Defense Secretary Laird and presidential assistant Kissinger were more conspicuous and were more aggressive bureaucratic politicians than Rogers. Both Laird and Kissinger also had more extensive backgrounds in their fields than Rogers.

By inclination disposed toward keeping a rather low profile, Rogers did not attempt to be a moderating counterweight to Laird. Although rumor and bureaucratic reality pitted Rogers against Kissinger, Rogers seemed content to serve as the top-level confidant while Kissinger acted the part of the stimulator and sifter of policy ideas. While this stance may have resulted in peace among the president's foreign affairs/national security counselors, it also had the effect of lowering public esteem for the State Department and of demoralizing the Foreign Service. One reporter commented that under Rogers the department's personnel seemed "consumed by self-doubt, as if they [were] constantly asking themselves whether what they do really matters."

There is considerable controversy over the extent of Rogers's influence in formulating American foreign policy during his four and a half years as secretary of state. Part of this debate can be attributed to Rogers's contention that he and the president thought "a lot alike." Thus, according to Rogers, he and the president were usually in agreement, so the secretary seldom had to fight for his position. This natural agreement may have given the appearance that Rogers lacked significant policy influence.

Within this like-mindedness, however, it is probable that Rogers exerted a cautious and moderating influence. For instance, in April 1969, when North Korean jets shot down an American EC-121 intelligence plane over the Sea of Japan, Rogers was the voice of caution, speaking against the retaliation urged by the Defense Department and urging a diplomatic resolution, saying that "in international affairs, the weak can be rash, the powerful must be restrained."

Rogers also succeeded in curbing the administration's response to the Peruvian expropriation of American oilfields and installations in the spring of 1969. Instead of provoking a confrontation with Peru (and by extension, with Latin America generally) by a retaliatory cutoff of American foreign aid, Rogers found a loophole in the Hickenlooper Amendment to avoid applying such economic sanctions and implemented a cautious response of diplomatic negotiation.

On policy regarding Vietnam Rogers generally supported the administration's goal of finding a political solution for South Vietnam based on free elections and went along with the military strategy of maintaining a degree of offensive pressure on enemy forces in South Vietnam. Within this context, however, he strenuously objected, without apparent effect, to the 1970 invasion of Cambodia and was a strong proponent for the withdrawal of American forces and for the policy of "Vietnamization."

Although Rogers was clear in expressing the administration's disappointment in the 1971 expulsion of Nationalist China from the United Nations in order to admit Communist China, he also was a potent administration advocate of improving U.S. relations with Beijing. In fact, the secretary of state may have been a "decisive figure" in evolving the dramatic shift in America's China policy that culminated in President Nixon's visit to China in 1972.

In most of the dramatic foreign policy issues of the first Nixon administration, Rogers played a low-keyed, unspectacular role. The one area in which he took a prominent initiative—perhaps the issue he is principally known for—was the Rogers Plan for the Middle East.

Initially proposed to the Soviets in October 1969, Rogers publicly offered his peace proposals to the Middle Eastern belligerents in December. His plan called on Israel to withdraw from Arab territories occupied in the 1967 war in return for Arab assurances of a binding commitment to peace. Although this initial proposal was rejected by both Arabs and Israelis, Rogers persevered in his efforts and during 1970 succeeded in securing Egyptian, Jordanian, and Israeli agreement to a cease-fire and a resumption of negotiations under the auspices of UN ambassador Gunnar Jarring. Eventually Rogers's efforts in the Middle East were eclipsed by his successor's (Henry Kissinger's) "shuttle diplomacy."

Following Nixon's reelection in 1972, rumor began to predict Rogers's imminent departure. Thus, the announcement of his resignation in September 1973 came as no surprise. Apparently everyone concerned was happy with the change—Rogers was eager to

get back to his New York law practice, and the president continued to regard him as a man of "unwavering good spirits, good judgment, and good sense." Kissinger, who had been called the "secretary of state in everything but title," was finally accorded that formal rank.

Rogers returned to the law firm of Rogers and Wells of New York City. In 1986 he headed a presidential task force investigating the *Challenger* shuttle disaster. He died of heart disease in 2001.

—MJW

Rohatyn, Felix G(eorge)
(1928–) *chairman, Municipal Assistance Corporation*

Rohatyn left his native Austria for France in 1933 and immigrated with his family to the United States in 1942, where he was naturalized in 1950. He graduated from Middlebury College in Vermont in 1948 and, through a relative connected with the Paris office of Lazard Frères, took a job with the New York branch of the firm. After service in the U.S. Army in Korea from 1950 to 1952, Rohatyn was assigned to the Paris office of Lazard, where he worked in foreign exchange. He returned to the United States in 1955 and shortly thereafter moved into the area of corporate reorganization, where he later made his reputation. Rohatyn became a partner at Lazard in 1960.

Rohatyn first emerged as a public figure in the years from 1969 to 1971 when he was chairman of the so-called Crisis Committee set up by the New York Stock Exchange. The credit crunch of 1969–70 had put an end to the boom years on Wall Street, and dozens of brokerages were being driven to the wall. Doubt about general stability was further increased when it came to light that over $4 billion in stock certificates had simply been misplaced during large-scale conversion to computerized operations and through slip-shod bookkeeping.

In March 1972 Rohatyn became embroiled in the scandal surrounding the settlement of a government antitrust action against International Telephone and Telegraph (ITT), in which the suit had been dropped in exchange for a pledge from ITT to underwrite a large part of the funds needed to hold the 1972 Republican National Convention in San Diego. In the midst of confirmation hearings for Attorney General-designate RICHARD G. KLEINDIENST, Washington reporter JACK ANDERSON asserted in his column that Kleindienst had negotiated the deal with ITT and quoted Rohatyn, a member of ITT's board of directors, who stated that he had discussed the deal with Kleindienst on several occasions. Kleindienst, for his part, denied any wrongdoing. Two weeks later former attorney general JOHN MITCHELL stated that Rohatyn had indeed attended meetings in the attorney general's office in April 1971 but said that the ITT case had not been discussed. In early April 1972 an associate of consumer advocate RALPH NADER charged that hundreds of thousands of shares of ITT stock had been sold to the public in July 1971 just before the antitrust settlement was announced and prices fell. Because Lazard Frères had handled the sale for ITT and since Rohatyn was associated with both firms, his role in the affair was again subject to some scrutiny.

In June 1975 the New York state legislature created the Municipal Assistance Corp. (MAC), known as "Big Mac," to underwrite further issues of New York City paper and to ensure their marketability, which had been totally undermined by the city's unfolding fiscal crisis. New York governor HUGH CAREY appointed Rohatyn, as a spokesman for the New York banking community, to an advisory panel on the crisis. Rohatyn promptly informed city officials that the banks would

not "roll over," that is, extend, $280 million in short-term notes falling due on June 11 unless the city consented in full to the MAC plan for the redressment of the city's finances.

In September 1975 Rohatyn became chairman of MAC and was effectively the most visible spokesman for the New York City banks throughout the crisis. In July 1975 the dollar price of the initial $1 billion issue of MAC notes fell by 10 percent, indicating that the market had no confidence in the restructured finances of the city. A second $1 billion issue, scheduled for August, had to be canceled. At that point Rohatyn turned to Secretary of the Treasury WILLIAM SIMON and asked for federal guarantees for the next MAC issue. Simon refused. By early August, however, $900 million in MAC paper had been sold to meet the city's short-term cash needs.

A new setback for the marketability of MAC bonds emerged in September when city officials announced that the budget deficit for fiscal 1976 would be $3.3 billion instead of the $641 million previously forecast. Rohatyn called the revelation "shocking" and predicted that default was a "good possibility" with the city's pending $150 million payroll.

Rohatyn also served on the Emergency Financial Control Board (EFCB), a body created by the state legislature to oversee the city's finances at the same time as MAC was established to underwrite new issues. The EFCB, which was characterized by critics as a virtual "bankers' dictatorship," had effective veto power over the city's budget. During the summer of 1975, under Rohatyn's leadership, the EFCB exacted major budget cuts and revisions from New York City, including the end of free tuition at the city's university system, an increase in bus and subway fares from 35 to 50 cents, and layoffs of thousands of New York City employees.

A complex political process surrounded the possible default of New York City throughout the crisis from May 5 to November 1975, when federal guarantees were obtained for the city's security issues. President GERALD FORD and leading government economic spokesmen such as ARTHUR BURNS, William Simon, and ALAN GREENSPAN were initially inclined to let the city default. Rohatyn, on the other hand, was more convinced about the ultimate dangers of default to U.S. and international capital markets. In September 1975 almost all cities in the Northeast region, whatever their local financial situation, were finding it almost impossible to market securities in the shadow of the New York crisis. As Rohatyn put it, "If the market looks this way without a default, think what it will be like with a default."

After the congressional legislation of late 1975, combined with large purchases of MAC bonds by New York City's unions, had temporarily resolved the crisis, Rohatyn continued to serve as chairman of MAC and to work at Lazard Frères. He played an instrumental role in the 1978 congressional legislation, signed by President JIMMY CARTER, that gave further federal assistance to the city.

Rohatyn continued his service as chairman of MAC until 1993. From 1997 to 2000 he served as U.S. ambassador to France.

—LG

Romney, George W(ilcken)
(1907–1995) *governor of Michigan; secretary of housing and urban development*

The son of an American Mormon family living in Mexico, George Romney was born on July 8, 1907, grew up in California and Idaho, and worked his way through Latter-Day Saints University in Utah. After serving two years as a Mormon missionary in England and Scotland, he studied taxation and tariffs at George Washington University. In 1930 Romney joined the Aluminum Corporation of America, returning to Washington in 1932 as a lobbyist for the aluminum industry. As general manager of the Automobile Manufacturers Association from 1942 to 1948, Romney served as chief auto industry spokesman during World War II. Appointed special assistant to the chairman of Nash-Kelvinator in 1948, Romney became president and board chairman of its successor firm, American Motors, six years later.

A Republican, Romney served as governor of Michigan from 1963 to 1969. A member of the liberal wing of the party, Romney was a front-runner for the 1968 presidential nomination. However, a series of political blunders, including a statement that he had been "brainwashed" by U.S. officials during a 1965 Vietnam tour, cut short his campaign.

Following his election in November 1968, RICHARD NIXON appointed Romney secretary of housing and urban development (HUD). During his first months in office, Romney announced a major reorganization of the Model Cities program, giving more direct authority to mayors and local governments in the planning and administration of the federally financed model neighborhoods. A serious shortage of affordable housing, aggravated by a high rate of inflation, led to Romney's announcement in May 1969 of Operation Breakthrough, a plan to build low-cost housing for the poor by mass production methods. In a *New York Times* article in January 1970, Romney described Operation Breakthrough as a blueprint for developing a housing industry capable of producing more than 2 million new units each year. Romney hoped to enlist the cooperation of government, industry, and labor to eliminate such barriers to volume housing construction as the high costs of land and materials, restrictive building codes, zoning ordinances, tax constraints, and labor shortages.

Romney was never entirely comfortable in his cabinet post, where he was restricted to dealing only with housing problems, and broke with the administration on several occasions. In a speech in May 1970 Romney criticized President Nixon's handling of inflation and called for new administration intercession to restrain the wage-price spiral. As his personal contribution to the fight against inflation, Romney announced his intention to return 25 percent of his HUD salary to the U.S. Treasury, suggesting that other business and labor leaders follow suit.

Acting counter to administration housing policy, Romney helped develop plans for the construction of federally subsidized housing outside of inner-city ghettos. President Nixon subsequently declared that his administration would not use the power of the federal government to force integration of suburban communities. Romney denied rumors in November 1970 that he had been asked to resign his HUD post, saying that he remained "deeply involved" in administration policy. A year later Romney gave final approval to the Forest Hills project, a plan to build low-income housing in a white middle-class section of New York City.

After suggesting that all federal housing subsidy programs be abolished and that the Federal Housing Administration be made a private agency, Romney resigned as secretary of HUD on November 27, 1972. In his resignation speech Romney complained that neither President Nixon nor his Democratic opponent in the 1972 election, Senator GEORGE MCGOVERN (D-S.D.), had dealt with the "real issues." Romney stated his intention to form a "coalition of concerned citizens" to enlighten the American public on "life and death" issues. In January 1973 Romney agreed to become chairman and chief executive of the National Center for Voluntary Action, a nonprofit organization he had helped found in 1970 to encourage greater voluntary initiative by individual citizens and groups in solving national problems. In 1991 the center merged with the Points of Light

Foundation, started by President GEORGE H. W. BUSH. Romney died in July 1995 after suffering a heart attack while exercising on his treadmill.

—DAE

Ruckelshaus, William D(oyle)

(1932–   ) *director, Environmental Protection Agency; acting director, FBI; deputy attorney general*

Born on July 24, 1932, in Indianapolis, Indiana, William Ruckelshaus came from a family with strong Republican ties. His father attended every Republican convention between 1920 and 1960 and played a role in writing party platforms. Ruckelshaus graduated from Princeton cum laude in 1957 and received his law degree from Harvard Law School in 1960. He served in the Indiana attorney general's office and helped to write the Indiana Air Pollution Control Act. His work in the state's environmental protection prosecutions gave him the experience he would eventually use as a federal administrator. In 1966 he was elected to the Indiana house of representatives and became the first freshman representative in Indiana to be elected majority leader. He ran unsuccessfully against BIRCH BAYH for the Senate in 1968.

He was brought into the NIXON administration as assistant attorney general and head of the Justice Department's civil division. He directed 200 lawyers dealing with 20,000 cases and was regarded as a good administrator. He became a protégé of Attorney General JOHN MITCHELL. While in the Justice Department he made a point of visiting college campuses to give the administration side on Vietnam—a task he dubbed as the "kamikaze tour."

He was appointed to head the new Environmental Protection Agency (EPA) in 1970. He had to walk carefully between environmental activists who wanted legal action taken against polluters and businessmen who were critical of the high costs of environmental protection. He was able to act with some degree of independence in part because Nixon had hoped to take away attention from a potential Democratic presidential candidate, EDMUND MUSKIE, who had made environmental protection one of his big issues.

Ruckelshaus acted quickly in his first few weeks to prosecute polluters. He moved against Atlanta, Detroit, and Cleveland, threatening to take federal court action if those cities did not stop dumping raw sewage into waterways. Later he filed suit against major industrial polluters such as Republic Steel, Jones & Laughlin, and the Kennebec River Pulp and Paper Co. His strategy was to go after the biggest polluters using a variety of techniques: 180-day notices, enforcement conferences, and civil or criminal suits brought under the revised Refuse Act of 1889. Suits were brought against hundreds of corporations and a few cities. One of his decisions received much criticism from environmental activists, however: the compromise in which he gave auto manufacturers a one-year extension of a 1975 deadline to install antipollution devices on new-model automobiles.

On April 27, 1973, Nixon named Ruckelshaus to replace L. PATRICK GRAY as acting director of the FBI after Gray had become involved in the Watergate cover-up scandal. Ruckelshaus gave up his EPA post to take the FBI job, although he agreed to be acting director temporarily.

Nixon next appointed Ruckelshaus deputy attorney general, and Ruckelshaus was sworn in on September 26, 1973. He served under ELLIOT RICHARDSON and was one of the victims of the "Saturday night massacre," those removals from office that occurred when President Nixon sought to fire ARCHIBALD COX as Watergate prosecutor.

Nixon had ordered Richardson to fire Cox on Saturday, October 20. Richardson refused. He then ordered Ruckelshaus to fire Cox. Ruckelshaus also refused. Although he was never directly informed of his dismissal, Ruckelshaus felt obliged to resign after serving only 24 days in that post. Only when Solicitor General ROBERT BORK was appointed acting attorney general was Cox fired.

After Ruckelshaus left government service, he entered private law practice. In 1976 he supported GERALD FORD for president and was one of the people mentioned as a possible Ford running mate. During the campaign he served as a representative for Ford in negotiations over television arrangements for debates with JIMMY CARTER. In 1983 President RONALD REAGAN appointed Ruckelshaus to serve as interim director of the Superfund project. Ruckelshaus held that position until 1985. He was the chairman and CEO of Browning Ferris Industries of Houston, Texas, until 1999. From 1997 to 1998 he served as the U.S. envoy to the implementing of the Pacific Salmon Treaty. He is currently a strategic director in the Madrona Venture Fund and lives in Seattle, Washington.

—HML

Rumsfeld, Donald

(1932–   ) *director, Office of Economic Opportunity; counselor to the president; director, Cost of Living Council; ambassador to the North Atlantic Treaty Organization; assistant to the president; secretary of defense*

Born on July 9, 1932, the son of a Chicago real estate man, Donald Rumsfeld grew up in the conservative suburbs of Winnetka and Glenview. He won a scholarship to study at Princeton University, became captain of both the football and wrestling teams there, and graduated in 1954 with a major in politics. Contemplating a military career, he joined the navy and spent the next three years as a navy pilot and flight instructor. In 1957 he left the service to test the political waters of Washington.

In 1957 he joined the staff of Ohio representative David Dennison as an administrative assistant. Although Dennison was defeated for reelection in 1958, Rumsfeld had the opportunity to gain much practical experience as his campaign manager that year. Rumsfeld spent the next year as administrative assistant to Representative ROBERT GRIFFIN (R-Mich.), then managed Dennison's unsuccessful attempt to make a comeback in 1960.

Initiated to the legislative waters of Capitol Hill and seasoned in the practice of campaign politics in Illinois, Rumsfeld returned to Chicago to lay the groundwork for his own electoral bid. After two years with the investment banking firm of A. G. Becker & Co., he entered the Republican primary for the 13th congressional district of Illinois. Although classified as an urban district, this North Chicago area was composed mostly of highly mobile, well-educated, young Republicans—an ideal constituency for an ambitious young conservative Republican such as Rumsfeld. Exuding a style suggestive of a Republican Kennedy, Rumsfeld put together a highly personal and enthusiastic campaign organization staffed with numerous young volunteers. He went on to win the primary and handily defeated his Democratic opponent by a tally of 134,442 to 73,998.

In Congress he quickly established his credentials as a conservative. Serving during the heyday of the liberal New Frontier-Great Society presidencies, Rumsfeld consistently voted against the extension of government services, against much progressive legislation, and in favor of holding down government spending and taxation. His voting record for his first year won him a 100 percent rating from the conservative Americans for Constitutional Action and a verdict of only 4 percent from the liberal Americans for Democratic Action. In his six years in the House his conservative stance put him on record against mass transit aid, the antipoverty bill, student loans, federal aid for city and suburban libraries, monies for the arms control and disarmament agency, and creating an executive department of urban affairs. At the same time this conservative record was moderated by strong support for civil rights and a penchant for fighting to reform and modernize the Republican Party. These reform activities included participation in the 1965 transfer of minority leadership from Representative Charles W. Halleck to GERALD FORD as well as an unsuccessful 1968 crusade to reform House rules. Such activities, coupled with the outright "dislike" of senior Illinois representative Les Arends, earned Rumsfeld enough resentment from the Republican old guard in the House to block his advancement. His defeat in seeking the chairmanship of the House Republican Research Committee in early 1969 clearly indicated the ill will he had generated among his colleagues.

Thus, the new NIXON administration's offer of the directorship of the Office of Economic Opportunity (OEO) in the spring of 1969 came as a welcome option to a stalled congressional career. Rumsfeld had tendered valuable campaign service during 1968 as one of 10 surrogate speakers for Mr. Nixon, and the new president needed someone capable and dependable to take on the controversial and the likely to be onerous task of "deescalating the war on poverty." Speculation that Rumsfeld would dismantle the agency was understandable in light of the facts that the administration was hostile to the OEO, that as a congressman Rumsfeld had voted against the creation of the OEO, and that his opinion of the agency was that it "ought to be kept around if for no other reason than that it is important to maintain at least one credible national symbol and program which demonstrates our government's commitment to the poor."

Since he was unwilling, however, to resign a safe seat in Congress simply to preside over the liquidation of the OEO, Rumsfeld was

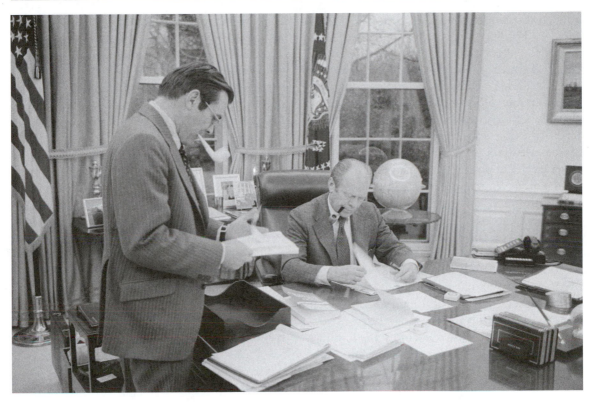

President Gerald Ford meets with Donald Rumsfeld at the White House, 1975. *(Library of Congress)*

simultaneously named a presidential assistant with cabinet rank, made a member of the president's Urban Affairs Council, and paid a salary equal to his congressional rate. In addition, Rumsfeld asserted his mission was not to demolish but to transform the OEO from an "activist" agency to an "initiating agency—an incubator for . . . programs during their initial experimental phases."

During the 19 months of his tenure at the OEO, Rumsfeld tried to reorganize the agency into a more efficient bureaucracy, with emphasis on a lower public profile, on teamwork, and on administrative, mechanical, and bureaucratic matters. Pursuant to these ends, activists in Vista were summarily dropped. Terry Lenzer, the highly committed social activist head of the OEO's Legal Services, was fired,

and similar "advocate types" were weeded out. Rumsfeld was criticized for bowing to political pressure from Nixon's private circle, and the ABA Legal Services Advisory Committee called his dismissal of Lenzer "highly duplicitous." Although under Rumsfeld various OEO programs and activities were farmed out, transferred, or merged to other cabinet departments or agencies, the OEO was not dismantled but streamlined. Rumsfeld viewed his job at the agency as a challenge to make it work in a new way that was more compatible to the Nixon administration.

Pleased with Rumsfeld's performance at the OEO, President Nixon rewarded him with the post of counselor to the president in December 1970, thus taking him off the firing line at the OEO before the actual dismantling occurred. Rumsfeld's successor at the OEO, Howard Phillips, succeeded not only in demolishing the agency but also his own career as a result of the enemies he made in the process.

Rumsfeld's duties and status as counselor were variable and somewhat tenuous, since he shared the title of counselor with former secretary of health, education, and welfare ROBERT FINCH, who was gradually being moved to the outer circles of power. This changed in October 1971 when the president entrusted Rumsfeld with another controversial task—administering Phase II of the Nixon economic program as director of the Cost of Living Council. Rumsfeld approached the task of maintaining wage and price controls as a matter of efficient organization, which was precisely the managerial rather than political image the council required. The effort to remain as neutral as possible while directing the Cost of Living Council also had the result of keeping Rumsfeld away from active involvement in the 1972 presidential campaign.

His position at the council brought Rumsfeld onto the Domestic Council, where he encountered problems with H. R. HALDEMAN and JOHN EHRLICHMAN. In addition, his well-developed sense of timing and instinct for moving on while circumstances were still favorable led Rumsfeld to seek to put distance between himself and both the Cost of Living Council and the White House. His nomination as ambassador to the North Atlantic Treaty Organization (NATO) in December 1972 had the twin advantages of removing him from the Cost of Living Council before prices began to soar and taking him out of the White House before the Watergate scandal began to surface.

In announcing that Rumsfeld had been chosen to replace DAVID KENNEDY at NATO, press secretary RON ZIEGLER stated that the appointment had been prompted by the belief that since Rumsfeld was "considering a return to politics," such a post "would round out" his

background and provide him with a "firm base for challenging ADLAI E. STEVENSON's bid for a second Senate term in 1974." In addition, the president was said to feel that Rumsfeld's "extensive and varied background in American domestic affairs" would be particularly useful "at a time when the United States and Europe are increasingly interdependent economically and socially as well as militarily." Rumsfeld spent the next 18 months acquiring diplomatic and military-related experience and reorganizing his mission to operate more efficiently.

Within hours of Nixon's resignation, President Ford summoned his former House colleague and friend to join a five-man transition group to revise the White House staff and its organization. Rumsfeld, drawing on previous White House experience, quickly assessed the situation, saw the difficulties of trying to shift power from the Nixon appointees, and decided that he did not want to confront those problems by joining the Ford staff. He made his recommendations to the new president and flew back to Brussels. He was at NATO headquarters when Ford made one of the most decisive moves of his presidency—he pardoned Richard Nixon. Once again, Rumsfeld was well out of range of any politically damaging taint.

In the aftermath of the Nixon pardon, Ford began to clean out Nixon staffers. ALEXANDER HAIG was dismissed as chief of staff. In the process NATO gained Haig as a commander and lost Rumsfeld as an ambassador. In September 1974 Rumsfeld was appointed assistant to the president, replacing Haig as chief of staff in function, although he preferred the title of staff coordinator.

Although all nine senior advisers of the Ford staff were theoretically equal, Rumsfeld was a bit more equal than most. While his title of coordinator was less "imperial" than Haig's or Haldeman's, he was as central and influential as they had been. He installed his own team both within the White House and throughout the administration. He held the reins of access and information to the president. His network of allies in the wider administration included Attorney General EDWARD LEVI and Secretary of Transportation WILLIAM COLEMAN. Rumsfeld himself spent more time with the president than any other aide, including HENRY KISSINGER. Rumsfeld used his organizational system to diminish the influence of all potential rivals at the White House. Although the vice president chaired the Domestic Council, Rumsfeld headed off NELSON ROCKEFELLER's hopes for "heavy involvement" in domestic policy making by rigidly controlling the day-to-day operations of the council. He also was instrumental in bringing in HOWARD (BO) CALLAWAY as Ford's campaign manager and in inducing the conservative Callaway to criticize Rockefeller as a "liability" to the national ticket. Rumsfeld took special pains to solicit counterarguments to Kissinger's position papers, to orchestrate rumors of Kissinger's declining influence, and eventually to have him deprived of his White House position as national security assistant.

Rumsfeld, nonetheless, chafed at being staff and wanted to be his own man. President Ford gave him that chance in November 1975 when he appointed him Secretary of defense as part of a startling personnel shake-up that ousted JAMES SCHLESINGER from Defense, WILLIAM COLBY from the Central Intelligence Agency, and Henry Kissinger from his job as presidential assistant for national security affairs. Ford had long been personally uncomfortable with Schlesinger and the growing public controversy between the defense chief and Kissinger over détente policy. In appointing Rumsfeld, Ford got a man more personally agreeable to him as well as an able and diversified administrator. Rumsfeld also was a lifelong proponent of a strong military who had long been suspicious of Kissinger's brand of détente and who wanted "parallel policies of deterrence and détente." Such perspectives put

him in agreement with his predecessor—a similarity the administration took every opportunity to underline.

Despite his NATO experience, Rumsfeld's appointment to the cabinet was criticized as bringing a highly partisan novice to the Pentagon. His supporters argued that since he had the president's confidence and shared Schlesinger's views, he might prove a more effective counterbalance to Kissinger than his predecessor. In addition, the president hoped that Rumsfeld's political savvy would make him more successful in securing legislative approval for defense programs, and, indeed, Rumsfeld's first order of business as secretary was to steer the Defense budget through Congress. Critics argued that Rumsfeld had neither the intellectual capacity nor the strategic breadth to succeed Schlesinger or to compete with Kissinger. Concern also abounded (even at his Senate confirmation hearings) that he would merely use the Defense Department as a stepping-stone to the vice presidential nomination.

Despite such speculation, Rumsfeld was quickly and easily confirmed within two weeks of his nomination. As in all his other executive positions, Rumsfeld proceeded to move in his own team and set about a process of piecemeal immersion in the details and workings of his department in an effort to master the administration of the Pentagon. Given his short tenure in office, the magnitude of the task, and the political environment of the Ford administration, it was no surprise that his secretaryship was not characterized by any substantive changes of policy.

In 1977 Rumsfeld was awarded the Medal of Freedom. From 1977 to 1985 Rumsfeld headed G. D. Searle and Co., a pharmaceuticals company. From 1985 to 1990 he was in business as a consultant. He also served the RONALD REAGAN administration as a special envoy to the Middle East. From 1990 to 1993 he was CEO of General Instrument Corporation. In 1998 he chaired the U.S. Ballistic Missile Threat Commission. Rumsfeld was chosen as secretary of defense by George W. Bush in 2001; this gives Rumsfeld the distinction of being both the youngest secretary of defense (under Ford) and the oldest (under Bush) to have served. Rumsfeld leads the Defense Department in the aftermath of the terrorist attacks on the United States on September 11, 2001, and is instrumental in the conduct of the subsequent war on terrorism in Afghanistan and Iraq.

—MJW and JRG

Rush, (David) Kenneth
(1910–1994) *ambassador to West Germany; deputy secretary of defense; deputy secretary of state; counselor to the president for economic affairs; ambassador to France*

Kenneth Rush was born in Walla Walla, Washington, on January 17, 1910. Rush received his bachelor's degree from the University of Tennessee in 1930 and his law degree from Yale two years later. He practiced law in New York City from 1932 to 1936 and taught law at Duke University in 1936–37, where RICHARD NIXON was one of his students. Rush then joined Union Carbide Corp., eventually becoming president of the company in 1966. In 1969 Nixon made his former law professor ambassador to West Germany. During his short tenure there, Rush continued to assert American resolve to protect West Berlin in the face of Soviet attempts to change its status. Rush served as deputy secretary of defense from February to November 1972 and in February 1973 was confirmed as deputy secretary of state. At that post he became a major spokesman for U.S. policy around the world. He defended increasing trade with Eastern Europe and opposed U.S. unilateral troop withdrawal from the North Atlantic Treaty Organization. Rush was frequently sent on missions to reaffirm U.S. support of Vietnam and to appease Pacific allies disturbed by various defense policy changes.

In May 1974 Rush left the State Department to become counselor to the president for economic affairs, with the role of coordinating domestic and international economic policy. Rush encountered criticism from Congress because he refused invitations to testify formally before the Joint Economic Committee and the Subcommittee on Multinational Corporations, saying that he would meet them only informally. He maintained that formal testimony would inhibit his ability to give President Nixon candid advice. Senator WILLIAM PROXMIRE (D-Wis.) said that Rush's position was "unacceptable and ridiculous" and "based on the same arrogance of power and immaturity of thought that led to Watergate." Rush supported the administration's opposition to congressional efforts to win tax cuts for individuals. "A tax cut for individuals means increased demands without increased productivity." However, he maintained that tax incentives for business would be "noninflationary" if they spurred output.

Rush was named chairman of the eight-member Council on Wage and Price Stability by President FORD in August 1974. The following month he became ambassador to France. He resigned that post at the end of the Ford administration. From 1979 to 1984 Rush served as chairman of the Atlantic Council of the United States. He died in 1994.

—AFB

Russell, Richard B(revard)
(1897–1971) *member of the Senate; president pro tempore of the Senate*

Richard Russell was born on November 2, 1897, in Winder, Georgia. Long one of the Senate's most influential members, Russell was the fourth son in a patrician Georgia family. He served as state assemblyman and governor before his election to the Senate in 1932. Russell generally supported New Deal programs, but as he once said, "I'm a reactionary when times are good. In a depression I'm a liberal." After World War II he was an opponent of civil rights and most social welfare legislation. By the late 1940s Russell had solidly established himself as the leader of the southern bloc. His astute parliamentary skills combined with a dignified and gracious manner made him widely respected in the Senate.

Russell rose to chairman of the Armed Services Committee in 1951 and from that position criticized the Eisenhower and Kennedy administrations for their heavy reliance on a strategy of nuclear deterrence at the expense of conventional weaponry. He headed southern resistance to the Civil Rights acts of 1957 and 1960. Besides his regular House committee positions, Russell was a member of the Democratic Policy Committee and led the conservative majority on the Democratic Steering Committee, which distributed committee assignments. As a key member of what one writer called "an interlocking directorate" of southern power in the Senate, Russell successfully thwarted attempts by liberals in 1965 to reform the Steering Committee.

Russell had opposed Eisenhower's sending arms and technicians to aid the French in Indochina and held strong reservations as Johnson escalated the conflict during the mid-1960s. But believing that America's commitment, once made, must be honored, he helped sponsor the Gulf of Tonkin Resolution in the Senate and supported the president's requests for additional manpower for the war. However, Russell criticized the administration for pursuing a policy that did not promise victory and in 1968 declared that he would not support the sending of additional troops without a drastic escalation of the air war.

In 1969 Russell stepped down as chairman of the Armed Services Committee to head the Appropriations Committee. That year he also became president pro tempore of the Senate, which made him third in line for the presidency. During the NIXON administration Russell supported such liberal measures as aid to mass transit, increased funds for school lunches, and establishment of uniform water quality control. He opposed efforts to ease requirements for invoking cloture and was one of two Democrats to vote against amendments to the tax reform bill of 1969 that increased Social Security benefits and personal tax exemptions and opened or expanded loopholes for certain categories of taxpayers.

Russell continued his battle against forced desegregation. In 1969 he condemned a Justice Department suit to integrate Georgia schools, but he said that court action was preferable to the arbitrary action of the "fanatical bureaucrats" of the Department of Health, Education, and Welfare. Russell opposed forced busing and in 1970 supported efforts to require that racial standards in schools be applied uniformly throughout the country. This proposal would have outlawed the de facto segregation in the North as well as the de jure segregation in the South. Russell believed that the measure would, for the first time, make the North bear the same burden in attempting desegregation as the South bore. Russell applauded President Nixon's Supreme Court nominations of CLEMENT HAYNSWORTH and G. HARROLD CARSWELL, who were opposed by many liberals because of their conservative stands on civil rights.

Russell continued his support of the Vietnam War during his last years in the Senate. He was one of three senators to support the U.S. invasion of Cambodia in 1970 and backed an amendment that provided that limiting U.S. involvement in Cambodia would not preclude the president from taking action necessary to protect U.S. forces in South Vietnam. Russell opposed the administration on the deployment of the Safeguard antiballistic missile system. In 1969 he urged additional development and research on the project rather than immediate deployment.

Once a heavy smoker, Russell had first developed emphysema in 1957. On January 21, 1971, he died of respiratory insufficiency after six weeks of hospitalization.

—FLM

Rustin, Bayard
(1910–1987) *civil rights leader*

Born on March 17, 1910, and raised by his grandparents in West Chester, Pennsylvania, Rustin was influenced by the Quaker pacifism of his grandmother and by his personal experiences with the injustices of segregation. After five years of work for the Young Communist League, Rustin left the organization in 1941 because of its prowar stance during World War II. Rustin served more than two years in jail for his conscientious opposition to the war. An early civil rights activist, he became a close associate of Martin Luther King Jr. and played a leading role in directing the early mass protests of the civil rights movement. He served as an adviser to King throughout the 1950s and 1960s. Rustin was the chief organizer of the 1963 March on Washington, which attracted 250,000 persons to protest discrimination.

In the mid-1960s Rustin, who had previously devoted most of his energies to behind-the-scenes organizing of civil rights protests, began to promote his political views in numerous magazine articles and public speaking engagements. He argued that advances made during the past decade had effectively destroyed the legal basis for discrimination but that in order to effect basic changes in the lives of blacks, the civil rights movement had to shift its focus to fundamental economic problems.

He wrote that poor economic backgrounds had put many blacks at a disadvantage in a job market requiring increasingly sophisticated skills. It was crucial, then, for blacks to promote federal programs for full employment, the abolition of slums, and the reconstruction of the educational system.

Black separatism, he argued, would only isolate blacks politically and foster antiblack sentiments. Instead, he urged black organizations to form a coalition with the AFL-CIO and work through the Democratic Party. In 1964 he formed the A. Philip Randolph Institute to promote political programs for this labor-liberal-black coalition.

In the late 1960s and early 1970s Rustin became increasingly isolated from a black leadership disillusioned with integrationist and coalition politics. In this period his support of the United Federation of Teachers and its president, Albert Shanker, during disputes in New York City over school decentralization and black control was widely denounced within the black community.

Rustin was one of the major critics of the NIXON administration's civil rights policies. In 1970 he joined other blacks in denouncing a memo by DANIEL P. MOYNIHAN, a domestic adviser to President Nixon, that claimed that blacks had made great strides in the past 20 years and called for a period of "benign neglect" on the race issue. The next year Rustin attacked the administration's housing policy. Nixon, in a major policy statement, had differentiated between "racial" and "economic" forms of discrimination, saying the latter was outside the government's domain. Rustin considered the distinction racist in effect and the whole policy "chaotic" and "a disaster."

In a May 1971 article for *Harper's Magazine*, Rustin criticized the president's Philadelphia Plan, ostensibly designed to increase the number of construction jobs available to blacks, as illusionary since it would merely shift black workers from one site to another. Nixon's suspension of the 1931 Davis-Bacon Act, allowing nonunion labor to be hired at less than union rates, was denounced by Rustin as an anti-union device with the effect of pitting black worker against white and placing deflationary pressure on wages. Rustin charged in the same article that near the end of Nixon's first term in office, the administration had "engaged in an assault on the advances of the past decade" with the "intent of building a political majority on the basis of white hostility to blacks."

In the late 1960s and early 1970s, Rustin continued to oppose separatist tendencies. In 1969 he denounced college officials for capitulating to black student demands for "soul courses," contending that black studies would not provide blacks with economically usable skills. In 1972 Rustin became cochairman of the newly merged Socialist Party-Democratic Socialist Federation (later Social Democrats U.S.A.), a group dominated by trade union leaders and others who favored the type of black-labor-union coalition he advocated. The federation had endorsed Democratic presidential nominee GEORGE MCGOVERN, but it criticized both his foreign and domestic policy proposals as "casual" and "vague."

In the mid-1970s Rustin turned his attention to what he considered to be the errors of white liberals. He argued in his *Strategies for Freedom: The Changing Patterns of Black Protest* (1976) that during the past decade the Civil Rights movement had failed to shift from social to economic issues in part because of liberal preoccupation with the Vietnam War, political corruption, the environment, and feminism. In a May 1976 article in the *New York Times Magazine*, he called the "antigrowth" ideas of the environmentalist movement a middle-class elitist tendency that would stunt the economic gains necessary for black equality. Through the 1980s Rustin worked as a delegate for Freedom House, which monitored elections and human

rights violations in developing countries. He died in 1987 of a perforated appendix.

—FM

Ryan, William Fitts
(1922–1972) *member of the House of Representatives*

William Fitts Ryan was born in Albion, New York, on June 28, 1922. After serving under Manhattan district attorney Frank S. Hogan from 1950 to 1957, Ryan helped found an anti-Tammany Democratic Club and became the leading figure in Manhattan reform politics. He was elected by large majorities in his eclectic district throughout his political career and was the only well-supported candidate outside the established party leadership. Ryan vociferously opposed appropriations for the House Un-American Activities Committee during the Kennedy and Johnson administrations. His outspoken support for civil rights and desegregation culminated in 1964 when he led 22 representatives in challenging, unsuccessfully, the all-white Mississippi delegation to Congress.

Under the Johnson administration Ryan began his unrelenting opposition to U.S. involvement in Southeast Asia. In May 1965 Ryan's vote was one of seven against Johnson's supplementary military appropriation, the first request for funds specifically to fight the Vietnam War. Although Ryan supported most of Kennedy's legislation, he disagreed strongly with Johnson on many domestic issues and was critical of the U.S. declaration of neutrality during the 1967 war in the Middle East, favoring a declaration of support for Israel.

Ryan's liberalism became more marked during the NIXON years. While the administration requested annual increases in defense appropriations to fuel the Vietnam War, Ryan proposed amendment after amendment to eliminate or drastically reduce funds for

Vietnam-related operations. Every year his amendments were overwhelmingly defeated. Ryan said the administration's policy was "a product of the outdated cold war mentality, the excessive growth of the military-industrial complex, and, most of all, the war in Vietnam, which is the culmination of disastrously mistaken policies."

Before 1969 most of the issues of defense appropriations were hammered out in committee and behind the closed doors of the Pentagon. But that year nationwide protest against the war and the agitation of a small minority of congressmen, including Ryan, brought Vietnam into unusually open debate in Congress. Ryan said the central issue of the war was who participated in the government of Vietnam; he was one of the first members to identify the conflict as a civil war.

Ryan seldom found himself among the majority of Congress. He and BELLA ABZUG (D-N.Y.) were the sole opponents to the 1972 Atomic Energy Commission's (AEC) appropriations bill, which provided for an AEC license to operate a nuclear reactor in New York City and increased funding for nuclear weapons and reactor development. His amendment to eliminate funds for the nuclear rocket NERVA, designed to transport people and materials into "deep space," was defeated. He said that since the National Aeronautics and Space Administration had proposed no clear mission for the project, it should not receive funds. For similar reasons he repeatedly opposed substantial appropriations for the House Internal Security Commission, which he said was overstaffed, inefficient, and not entirely aboveboard in its dealing with the information it received.

Ryan's liberal politics also found expression in environmental issues. As a member of the Interior and Insular Affairs Committee, he consistently favored the expansion of national park properties and the limitation of their commercial and residential development. In 1970 and 1971 he sought to establish an office of noise abatement and control within the Environmental Protection Agency (EPA) to study noise pollution and its effects. The measure failed but was later incorporated into a more general EPA noise pollution program.

President Nixon's conservative requests for urban renewal angered Ryan, who accused the administration of "misguided" priorities for approving $290 million to finance the construction of the SST while vetoing the House's original requested budget for social services. He was one of three dissenters against an administration bill to strengthen federal laws on the sale and use of explosives; he said the bill was "another dreary episode in the ponderous assault on freedom."

Growth elsewhere in the state of New York necessitated the elimination of Representative Abzug's district for the 1972 election. After painful deliberation she decided to run against Ryan, who was gravely ill at the time. Despite Abzug's popularity, the endorsements went heavily in Ryan's favor, and he won the primary by a 2-to-1 margin. Three months later, however, he died of cancer; another campaign ensued between Ryan's widow, the Liberal Party's choice to replace Ryan, and Abzug, the Democratic committee's candidate. Abzug won with 56 percent of the vote. After Ryan's death Congress broke precedent with the National Parks Service to name the Gateway National Urban Recreation Area after him, honoring Ryan as the principal sponsor of the bill that established the park.

—AM

Safire, William L.
(1929–) *special assistant to the president*

A native New Yorker, William Safire left Syracuse University for financial reasons in 1949 to return to New York to work as a reporter for the *Herald Tribune*. After a stint as a correspondent in Europe and the Middle East for WNBC radio and WNBT-TV in 1951, Safire was inducted into the army the following year, where he was assigned to public relations work. He returned to NBC in 1954. A year later he was named a vice president of Tex McCrary, Inc., a public relations firm.

Safire went to Moscow to represent a home-building firm at the American National Exhibition, which was officially opened by Vice President RICHARD NIXON on July 24, 1959. As the press agent for the company's "typical American house," Safire saw the opportunity to turn Nixon's presence to advantage. By maneuvering the spectators and newsmen trailing after Nixon and Soviet premier Nikita S. Krushchev as they toured the exhibit, he directed the two leaders into the kitchen showroom, prompting the famous "kitchen debate" on the relative merits of capitalism vs. communism. An Associated Press photographer, blocked by the crowds, tossed his camera to Safire, who snapped a widely reproduced picture of the historic encounter.

As he later wrote, Safire decided at that moment to work for Nixon's 1960 presidential campaign. He served as chief of special projects. His photograph of a no-nonsense Nixon besting the Soviet leader was heavily used during the campaign to promote the candidate's tough cold war image. He wrote and edited promotional materials for Republican volunteers and for Nixon administrative assistant ROBERT FINCH.

Safire resigned from the McCrary organization in 1960. He established Safire Public Relations, Inc., in January 1961. His accounts ranged from an ice cream manufacturer to a motor oil firm. Fascinated by politics and the public relations aspects of political campaigns, Safire, in the first half of the decade, worked for such New York Republican candidates as Senator JACOB JAVITS, Governor NELSON ROCKEFELLER, and Mayor JOHN V. LINDSAY.

In his first book, published in 1963, *The Relations Explosion*, Safire presented the emerging public relations concepts. *Plunging into Politics*, written in collaboration with Marshall Loeb in 1964, offered candidates a manual for organizing, staffing, and financing political campaigns. His *The New Language of Politics*, originally published in 1968, contained approximately 1,200 carefully researched entries. Safire described the book in Orwellian terms as a "dictionary of the words and phrases that have misled millions, blackened reputations, held out false hopes, oversimplified ideas to appeal to the lowest common denominator, shouted down inquiry, and replaced searching debate with stereotypes that trigger approval or hatred."

Convinced that Nixon was the best possible Republican candidate for the 1968 presidential race, Safire contacted Nixon at his New York law office in November 1965 and volunteered his services as an unpaid speechwriter. Nixon assigned him to help PATRICK J. BUCHANAN JR. with Nixon's syndicated newspaper column. Safire took part in Nixon's campaign efforts on behalf of Republican candidates in the 1966 elections as Nixon reestablished himself as a force in the party and built up momentum for his 1968 drive.

For the 1968 campaign Safire composed Nixon's "new alignment" speech in which the candidate talked about a "new majority" that was coming into being and affirmed his belief that such disparate groups as traditional Republicans, new liberals, black militants, and progressive southerners "thinking independently, have all reached a new conclusion about the direction of our nation." The speech maintained that the new direction chosen was away from increased federal power and toward more decentralization, local control, and personal freedom. Safire contributed to the form of Nixon's emotive acceptance address at the Republican National Convention. Throughout the presidential campaign he prepared speeches on labor, the economy, youth, and the "American spirit." After the election Nixon, in a victory speech drafted by Safire, outlined among the major objectives of the new administration his determination "to bring the American people together."

In February 1969 Safire moved into a White House office as a special assistant to the president. He became part of a research and writing staff headed by James Keogh that included Buchanan and RAYMOND K. PRICE JR. The team wrote formal speeches, drafted presidential messages to Congress, and prepared material for Nixon's press conferences. Safire's areas of responsibility encompassed the economy and the Vietnam War.

At the same time, Safire was called on to articulate the administration's domestic philosophy as reflected in its programs. Advisers such as DANIEL PATRICK MOYNIHAN, ARTHUR BURNS, and GEORGE P. SHULTZ were in the process of working out initiatives on family assistance, revenue sharing, and desegregation that became known as the "New Federalism." In his "New Federalist Paper #1," written under the pseudonym "Publius," Safire attempted to reconcile traditional Republicanism with Nixonian innovations. The paper advocated a selective decentralization of power, leaving to the federal government the power to set the standards of fairness and to decide what to do and allowing local government to determine how to do it according to their different circumstances. According to Safire, the paper expressed "a need both for national unity and local diversity; a need to establish equality and fairness at the national level and uniqueness and innovation at the local level." The paper provoked vigorous debate within the White House and a rebuttal signed "Cato" by aide Tom Charles Huston.

Safire assisted Vice President SPIRO AGNEW as he campaigned during the 1970 off-year elections. First exposed in 1960 to what he considered the biased reporting of the press in its pro-Kennedy coverage, Safire wrote many of the famous "Agnewisms" used by the vice president to criticize the news media. Agnew identified the national press as "nattering nabobs of negativism" who monopolized the way national news was presented to the country.

During the 1972 campaign Safire abandoned the speechwriter's traditional obscurity to write a series of signed articles for a debate in the *Washington Post* with FRANK MANKIEWICZ, Senator GEORGE S. MCGOVERN's campaign manager. Impressed by Safire's style and political expertise, the *New York Times* offered him a permanent position as a columnist, which Safire accepted. His biweekly column first appeared on the newspaper's op-ed page on April 16, 1973. Almost immediately Safire turned to defending the president's position in the Watergate crisis. When he learned, however, that his telephone had been tapped while he was a White House employee, he responded with "restrained fury." He commended Nixon for putting personal liberty ahead of social security but condemned him for putting national security too far above personal liberty.

Safire's column quickly became controversial. He led the investigation into "Koreagate" and the influence peddling of South Korean Tongsun Park in the U.S. Congress. He won a Pulitzer Prize for a series of columns that led to the resignation of President JIMMY CARTER's budget director, Bert Lance.

In 1975 Safire published *Before the Fall.* He wrote the book in an attempt "to figure out what he [Nixon] was trying to do and how well he succeeded" and as "an effort not to lose sight of all that went right in examining what went wrong." He distinguished between the goals and accomplishments of President Nixon and his administration and Nixon's personal mistakes and failures. Safire summed up Nixon in his "Epilogue" as a president whose greatest achievements were as a peacemaker and whose greatest disappointment was his failure to rally and inspire his countrymen. A winner of the Pulitzer Prize for distinguished commentary in 1978, Safire retired from the writing of his column in January 2005. He serves as chairman of the Dana Foundation.

—SF

St. Clair, James D(raper)

(1920–2001)   *presidential Watergate counsel*

James D. St. Clair was born in Akron, Ohio, on April 14, 1920. After graduating from the University of Illinois in 1941, St. Clair entered Harvard Law School. He interrupted his law studies to serve in the navy during World War II. Following the war he returned to Harvard, graduating in 1947. He joined the prestigious law firm of Hale & Dorr. As chief assistant to Joseph Welch, special counsel for the U.S. Army in the televised Army-McCarthy hearings of 1954, St. Clair was credited with an important behind-the-scenes role in the struggle that helped destroy Senator Joseph McCarthy. St. Clair became known as a meticulous and effective trial lawyer whose clients spanned a broad ideological spectrum. He defended the Boston school committee in its long struggle against mandatory school desegregation. William Sloan Coffin, whom he helped gain acquittal for conspiracy to encourage draft evasion, criticized St. Clair as "all case and no cause."

On the advice of CHARLES COLSON, President NIXON chose St. Clair as his chief Watergate defense counsel in January 1974. St. Clair replaced RED BUZHARDT, who nevertheless remained on the legal staff. In an interview St. Clair said he did not represent Nixon "individually" but rather "the office of the presidency." He defined his role as defending the office of the presidency against any unwarranted incursions. Not only did St. Clair lead President Nixon's legal defense in the courts, but he also personally defended the president before the House Judiciary Committee conducting an inquiry into impeachment.

On February 28 St. Clair presented the president's legal position on the nature of presidential impeachment. According to the report, "a president may only be impeached for indictable crimes" and those crimes must be of "a very serious nature" and committed in one's governmental capacity. It maintained that "the use of a predetermined criminal standard for the impeachment of a president [was] also supported by history, logic, legal precedent, and a sound and sensible public policy which demands stability in our form of government."

St. Clair argued that the impeachment clause, although drafted in the context of English precedents, rejected the British distinction between two types of impeachment—one for "reaching great offenses committed against the government by men of high station," and the other for a politically motivated purpose of maintaining the absolute political supremacy of Parliament. The framers of the Constitution accepted only the former type. St. Clair maintained that the phrase "high crimes and misdemeanors" meant to the framers "such criminal conduct as justified the removal of an officeholder from office." And in light of precedent, there was "no evidence to attribute anything but a criminal meaning" to the phrase. The framers had, according to St. Clair, "emphatically rejected 'maladministration' as a standard for impeachment," and their debates clearly indicated a purely criminal meaning for "other high crimes and misdemeanors."

In the beginning of May St. Clair went to court to quash a subpoena by LEON JAWORSKI, Watergate special prosecutor, for 64 recordings of White House conversations. St. Clair argued that since Jaworski was an employee of the executive branch, the dispute was an "intra-branch" affair in which the courts should play no role. Jaworski protested that such a doctrine would "make a farce of the special prosecutor's charter." Judge JOHN SIRICA upheld Jaworski's argument, refused to quash the subpoena, and ordered Nixon to turn the 64 tapes over to the court. At the end of May the Supreme Court agreed to review the decision.

At the end of May St. Clair tried to quash subpoenas by JOHN EHRLICHMAN and Charles Colson for use in the Ellsberg break-in trial. St. Clair argued that the scope of the subpoenas was too broad and brought a note from Nixon in which the president claimed executive privilege on the documents. U.S. district court judge GERHARD A. GESELL sternly lectured St. Clair that it was not up to the president to decide what documents to produce.

In July St. Clair cross-examined JOHN DEAN before the Judiciary Committee but failed to break Dean as a witness. St. Clair presented President Nixon's rebuttal on impeachment to the committee in a 242-page report. He relied heavily on the lack of a "smoking gun," arguing that the committee had no positive proof of Nixon's participation in the cover-up. To support this point, St. Clair tried to introduce evidence from a conversation that Nixon had refused to supply to the committee. This provoked an outraged reaction from Republicans and Democrats alike, who charged that the president was playing games with the evidence.

Arguments before the Supreme Court on Jaworski's suit for the 64 tapes were heard in July. The Court also heard a countersuit filed by St. Clair contesting the right of the grand jury to charge an incumbent president as "an unindicted co-conspirator" in criminal proceedings. St. Clair argued that such a citation had a prejudicial and damaging effect on the constitutional powers of impeachment vested in the House of Representatives.

St. Clair, in his first appearance before the Supreme Court, contended in the tapes case that the president was not above the law but the only way the law could be applied to him was through impeachment. If the courts could subpoena confidential White House conversations, St. Clair noted, the presidency would be irrevocably weakened. The next day St. Clair said that the president might, for the sake of the "public interest," defy the Supreme Court if it ordered him to give up the tapes.

At the end of July the Supreme Court ruled 8 to 0 that President Nixon must provide the tapes and documents subpoenaed by Jaworski "forthwith." While acknowledging that the generalized claim of executive privilege was "constitutionally based," the justices concluded that in this case it "must yield to the demonstrated, specific need for evidence in a pending criminal trial." The Court left standing the grand jury citation of Nixon as an unindicted coconspirator. The day the decision was announced, St. Clair read a statement to the press that the president would comply with the decision "in all respects."

Judge Sirica ordered St. Clair and Jaworski to work out a timetable for delivery of the tapes. St. clair listened to the tapes to authenticate them and delivered them to Sirica. St. Clair was forced to admit several times to Sirica that there were gaps, and even whole conversations, missing from the tapes he delivered. This was the first time St. Clair had heard the tapes that were so damaging to his client's case. It became clear that Nixon had withheld important evidence from his own counsel.

In the first week of August St. Clair spoke to eight Republicans on the Judiciary Committee who remained Nixon supporters. He told them what was on the tapes and said that it made the president's case hopeless. They then withdrew their support from Nixon.

On August 9 President Nixon resigned. The next day St. Clair said he no longer represented Nixon because Nixon was no longer president. St. Clair remained on the White House payroll for several weeks to deal with the final details of complying with the Supreme Court's decision.

St. Clair returned to private practice in Boston with his old firm of Hale & Dorr. In 1991, at the request of the mayor, he led an investigation of the Boston Police Department. He died in 2001.

—TFS

Sandman, Charles W(illiam), Jr.
(1921–1985) *member of the House of Representatives*

Charles W. Sandman Jr. was born in Philadelphia, Pennsylvania, on October 23, 1921. Sandman graduated from Temple University in 1942, and after service in the army air corps during World War II, he received his law degree from Rutgers in 1948. He practiced law in New Jersey until elected to the state senate in 1956. He served in that body for 10 years, eventually becoming majority leader and president and acting governor from 1962 to 1965, when he ran unsuccessfully for the Republican gubernatorial nomination.

In 1966 Sandman was elected to the U.S. House of Representatives. While a member of the House, Sandman voted a conservative line, receiving an approval rating of from 63 to 96 percent from the Americans for Conservative Action. During the NIXON years he voted for the antiballistic missile system in 1969, the SST in 1971, and against the 1970 Cooper-Church Amendment, an attempt to extricate the United States from military involvement in Southeast Asia.

On domestic issues he opposed busing, establishing a consumer protection agency, lowering the voting age to 18, and funding the Clean Water Act of 1969. He also voted for the controversial state veto provision over the policies of the Office of Economic Opportunity in 1969.

Sandman ran as a fiscal conservative for the New Jersey Republican gubernatorial nomination in 1969 but lost to the more liberal, urban-oriented candidate, WILLIAM CAHILL, by only 13,000 votes. Cahill won the general election.

Later his administration was rocked by the indictment of Secretary of State Paul Sherwin, a close associate of the governor's. With Cahill losing support, Sandman challenged him for the gubernatorial nomination again in 1973. Stressing his opposition to high spending on social welfare and to the proposed state income tax, Sandman beat Cahill. He lost the general election, however, to Judge Brendan T. Byrne, who received a margin of 721,000 votes in what was widely viewed as a repudiation of Sandman's conservatism as well as the waning political appeal of the Nixon administration.

Sandman gained national prominence as a member of the House Judiciary Committee during the 1974 impeachment hearings. There he emerged as one of Nixon's strongest supporters. He openly scorned the televised hearings as a farce. Although in late May Sandman and eight other Republican committee members warned President Nixon that failure to produce the subpoenaed White House tapes might result in his impeachment, by July Sandman had hardened into a belligerent Nixon defender. Eventually he voted against all the articles of impeachment.

Because of his strong identification with Nixon, Sandman lost his reelection bid in 1974, winning only about two-thirds of the votes he had received just two years earlier. Shortly after leaving Congress in 1975, he was hired as township solicitor for Cape May County, New Jersey, at $4,000 a year. He practiced law in a private capacity and died in 1985.

—GWB

Sanford, (James) Terry

(1917–1998) *president, Duke University*

Terry Sanford was born on August 20, 1917, in Laurinburg, North Carolina. The son of a hardware salesman, Sanford attended the University of North Carolina before enter-ing the army during World War II. In 1946 he received a law degree from the University of North Carolina, and during the 1950s he practiced law and became active in state politics. In 1960 Sanford won the election for the North Carolina governorship with the help of urban-based support from blacks, organized labor, and liberal businessmen. His term as governor was characterized by educational reform and increased state expenditures.

During the 1968 presidential campaign Sanford was considered as a possible vice presidential running mate for HUBERT HUMPHREY. His image as a link between the new and old South was seen to have considerable political value. However, Humphrey chose Senator EDMUND MUSKIE (D-Me.), and Sanford had to settle for a minor role in the Democratic campaign. He served as the national chairman of the Citizens for Humphrey-Muskie Committee.

In 1970 Sanford took over the presidency of Duke University. The Durham, North Carolina, campus had for several years been the scene of militant student protest against the Vietnam War. These continued demonstrations culminated in the resignation of Sanford's predecessor, Dr. Douglas Knight. Sanford's policies on student protest were marked by moderation, in contrast to the administration's view that universities should crack down on radicals. In a speech made shortly after his appointment as president of Duke, he stated: "With the self-righteousness of oligarchs the leaders of repression are commanding college presidents to put down the students to shut off the protest and silence dissent. I would suggest that they do not understand young people, do not understand society and have forgotten the lessons of history." Positions such as these led many to believe that Sanford might become the Democratic vice presidential nominee in 1972 as a contrast to conservative vice president SPIRO AGNEW, who had led the call for action against demonstrators.

Sanford entered the race for the Democratic presidential nomination in March 1972. From the beginning he was a "dark horse" candidate who based his election strategy on the expectation that the primary races would prove indecisive and the convention would need a "fresh face" to break out of political deadlock. Sanford ran on a liberal platform advocating speedy U.S. withdrawal from Vietnam. However, on such domestic issues as busing, his stand was less clear. He supported federal legislation that would make desegregated education a national goal but would leave actual desegregation plans in the hands of local government.

Sanford's presidential aspirations were dashed by his defeat in the North Carolina primary in May 1972. He received only 37 percent of the vote in his home state compared to the 50 percent cast for GEORGE WALLACE. The candidacy of SHIRLEY CHISHOLM hurt Sanford's chances from the beginning because it had split the black vote that ordinarily would have gone to Sanford. George Wallace's strong position against busing attracted blue-collar and rural voters and was a major obstacle Sanford could not overcome. In his statement accepting defeat, Sanford said about the busing issue, "To win, I would have to take positions I would be unwilling to take." Sanford continued to work for the Democratic Party during the 1972 election as chairman of the Democratic Charter Commission.

Sanford again made an attempt at gaining his party's presidential nomination in 1976. His chances seemed good in light of the prevailing political current after the NIXON presidency. As one supporter stated: "Terry is clean. Watergate and things like that make a candidate like him more attractive." However, Sanford's hopes were again crushed when, after only three weeks of full-time campaigning, he was hospitalized for chest pains, leading to his withdrawal as a candidate. Sanford stepped down as president of Duke University in 1985. In 1986 Sanford was elected to the U.S. Senate, filling the unexpired position of the deceased John East. He was elected to a full term in 1986 and lost his bid for reelection in 1992. Sanford died in 1998.

—MLB

Sawhill, John C(rittenden)

(1936–2000) *administrator, Federal Energy Administration*

John C. Sawhill was born on June 12, 1936, in Cleveland, Ohio. Sawhill graduated from Princeton in 1958 and began a career in business on Wall Street. In 1960 he returned to academia at New York University, where he received his Ph.D. and became a professor and associate dean. He reentered the business world in 1963 to serve as the director of credit research and then senior vice president for a commercial credit company in Baltimore.

Sawhill entered government service in 1973 when he was named associate director of the Office of Management and Budget for the NIXON administration. In December of that year he was named deputy director of the new Federal Energy Office (FEO) headed by Deputy Secretary of the Treasury WILLIAM E. SIMON. President Nixon had created the office in December by executive order in response to the developing energy crisis sparked by the 1973 Arab oil embargo. At the time Nixon announced that a Federal Energy Administration (FEA) would be established by statute.

The newly enacted FEO turned to devising fuel allocation rules. The guidelines were published January 15 and became effective immediately. Noting that industrial and public service users were favored over those requiring fuel for home heating and private automobiles, Sawhill remarked at the time that the allocation program's aim was "to preserve jobs rather than to have homes at 75 degrees." He prophetically warned, "There will have to be changes in the American lifestyle over the next several years." Sawhill also released details of the administration's contingency plan for gas rationing by coupon in the face of the ongoing Arab oil embargo but insisted that no decision had been made on whether to adopt the plan and voiced hope that rationing could be avoided.

In April Nixon named Simon to succeed GEORGE P. SHULTZ as Treasury secretary. Sawhill was nominated to become head of the recently established FEA. He was confirmed in June. As the nation's new "energy czar," Sawhill found himself at the center of controversy. At the end of the month he accused major oil companies of "foot-dragging and calculated resistance" to the government's regulations requiring them to share their crude oil supplies with independent refiners. At issue, he stated, was the statutory mandate designed "to protect the viability of small and independent sectors of the petroleum industry." Sawhill's criticism of the major oil companies marked the first break in a previously closer, cooperative relationship between the industry and the energy agency. A proponent of the deregulation of natural gas prices, a move unpopular with consumer advocates, Sawhill argued that allowing market conditions to determine prices would stimulate the exploration needed to provide adequate supplies of this energy resource.

Sawhill opposed the strictness of the federal regulations governing the strip mining of coal that were passed by Congress in July. The following month he resumed his confrontation with the oil industry. In a letter to the nation's top 20 oil firms, Sawhill charged the industry with making "efforts to coax the public into buying gasoline that it has indicated it doesn't want or need" while the government was urging stepped-up conservation measures. Sawhill called for an end to "hard-sell tactics" and warned that the agency would take "strong action" to hold down fuel consumption.

The strong action turned out to be administrative proceedings brought by the FEA on August 20 against 14 oil companies accused of inflating prices by roughly $200 million. The next day four of the firms complied with the government's directive to make up overcharges by rolling back prices. Six other firms had previously rolled back prices voluntarily. In a letter on September 13 to Senator HENRY JACKSON (D-Wash.), chairman of the Permanent Investigations Subcommittee, Sawhill said a continuing investigation of about 10 major oil firms revealed that they had profited to the extent of possibly $300 million from the agency's "double recovery" rule, which, until revised in May, allowed refiners to "double-dip" or charge twice for their costs on the volume of crude oil they were required to sell to other refiners under government allocation regulations. To preclude possible conflicts of interest with the oil industry, Sawhill instituted strict standards of conduct for FEA employees, requiring that high- and middle-level officials file financial disclosure reports.

President FORD announced on October 29 the appointment of a "new team that will be in charge of the energy problem." Sawhill was the principal victim of the administrative shake-up. Before leaving office he oversaw the presentation of the FEA's 800-page "Blueprint for Project Independence." Differences in the Nixon and Ford administrations over energy affairs resulted in a lack of continuity on policy matters and diluted the report's impact as a policy-setting document. In November Sawhill told a congressional committee he believed that the oil industry had lobbied for his ouster but added he did not know if its influence had played any part in President Ford's decision to dismiss him.

Sawhill returned to New York University in 1975 to become president of the financially troubled institution. Under his leadership the university executed a series of adroit financial moves that restored its budget's integrity. He stayed at NYU until 1979. From 1981 to 1990 he was a director of McKinsey and Co. In 1990 he became president of the Nature Conservancy. He died in 2000 of complications from diabetes.

—SF

Saxbe, William B(art)

(1916–   ) *member of the Senate, U.S. attorney general*

Born in Mechanicsburg, Ohio, on June 24, 1916, Saxbe took a bachelor's degree in political science from Ohio State University in 1940. During World War II he served for five years in the army air force. While studying law at Ohio State, he was elected to the Ohio house of representatives, where he served four terms and was elected Speaker in the 1953–54 session.

After three years practicing law in Columbus, Saxbe was elected state attorney general in 1957 and was subsequently reelected to four additional two-year terms. His reputation as a "tough, capable crime fighter" who favored capital punishment and long prison sentences for gun-related offenses helped him to become the Republican candidate for the U.S. Senate in 1968. His opponent was liberal Democrat JOHN J. GILLIGAN, who campaigned against the Vietnam War, while Saxbe stressed the law-and-order issues. Saxbe won by 100,000 votes.

Upon taking office in January 1969, he was assigned to the Aeronautical and Space Sciences Committee, the Labor and Public Welfare Committee, and the Special Committee on Aging. In his first year he accumulated one of the lowest scores for individual participation in roll-call votes for the first session of the 91st Congress. He also confounded liberal critics by compiling a moderate 61 percent rating from the Americans for Democratic Action (ADA)

in 1969. However, Saxbe gradually moved to the right politically until in 1972 he was down to a 15 percent ADA rating.

In 1969 Saxbe took a strong stand against the Pentagon's deployment of antiballistic missiles. He asserted that the nation was becoming "militaristic" and a "national security state." In November of the same year he voted to reject the nomination of conservative CLEMENT F. HAYNSWORTH to be an associate justice of the Supreme Court. He denied that there had been any "arm-twisting" from the administration but admitted that "we got tens of hundreds of threatening letters from people in the state [Ohio] who have contributed to his [Nixon's] campaign. It's as strong as anything we've seen." The next year Saxbe was a strong supporter of G. HARROLD CARSWELL's unsuccessful nomination to the Supreme Court despite charges that Carswell was a segregationist. On April 1, 1970, he received a widely publicized letter from President Nixon reaffirming "total support" of Carswell. In the letter Nixon went on to term the charges of segregationist beliefs against the nominee "specious." Saxbe also voted in 1971 to confirm the nomination of WILLIAM H. REHNQUIST to the Supreme Court.

In April 1970 Saxbe joined in an attack against critics of the administration's Vietnam War policies. He declared that while he was "sick and tired" of the war, he was also "sick and tired" of "those who continually played politics with the war." On April 15 Saxbe returned from a trip to Vietnam and told the Senate that the U.S. pullout from that country was proceeding much faster than generally realized. He opposed setting a deadline for complete withdrawals because it might give the enemy an advantage. Saxbe also supported continued funding for the war.

Yet the senator did not fully support the administration's Vietnam policy. In June 1970, following the invasion of Cambodia, he voted for the Cooper-Church Amendment that repealed the Gulf of Tonkin resolution. In February of the next year he cosponsored with Senator WALTER MONDALE (D-Minn.) legislation to bar U.S. participation in or support of any South Vietnamese ground invasion of North Vietnam without explicit approval of Congress. In December 1972 Saxbe delivered a particularly harsh criticism of the bombing of North Vietnam: "I have followed President Nixon through his convolutions and specious arguments, but he appears to have left his senses on this issue. I can't go along with him on this one." On July 20, 1973, the Defense Department admitted that it had knowingly provided the Senate Armed Services Committee, of which Saxbe was a member, with a false report the previous month that did not reveal the secret bombing of Cambodia. Saxbe said he thought that there were stronger grounds for the impeachment of the president because of the secret air war than because of the growing Watergate scandal.

During the early 1970s Saxbe grew increasingly disenchanted with the Senate and the administration, which he considered the "most inept" in history. He was particularly critical of the slow pace of the legislative process. As a result of his frustration Saxbe decided to take as many junkets as possible. Explaining why he took advantage of the often-criticized trips, he stated, "I like to travel."

In October 1973 Saxbe announced that he would retire from the Senate and return to his law practice in Mechanicsburg, Ohio. In so doing he criticized the administration once again. In explaining his decision, he announced: "Nixon had a chance to put businessmen back in the saddle and make the free enterprise system respected again. He blew it. From now on, this town will be full of social planners like Walter Mondale." The next month President Nixon announced he would appoint Saxbe to replace ELLIOT L. RICHARDSON as U.S. attorney general. Richardson resigned after Watergate special prosecutor ARCHIBALD COX and Deputy Attorney General WILLIAM RUCKELSHAUS were fired on October 20 in the so-called Saturday night massacre. The president chose Saxbe because he was not "out to get Nixon" but was not "soft" on him either. In addition, by choosing the maverick, he hoped to avoid a lengthy confirmation battle. Nixon described Saxbe as "eminently qualified" and "an individual who wants this position and who will do everything that he possibly can to serve the nation as the first lawyer in the nation." Saxbe said that he was happy to tackle the job, understanding that the country was in "difficult times" and undergoing a "crisis of leadership." He delayed assuming the office until January 1974 so he would be eligible to collect a Senate pension.

At his swearing-in ceremony Saxbe called himself a "law-and-order man," predicated on his belief in "a society operated in a manner to give each individual the opportunity to express himself without the fear of Big Brother taking over [or] interfering in his personal life." Saxbe also affirmed the independence of the Watergate special prosecutor, LEON JAWORSKI.

Despite his hope of remaining clear of the controversy, Saxbe gradually became embroiled in Watergate. On March 27, 1974, he asked the U.S. court of appeals in Washington to uphold a lower court's refusal to give the Senate Watergate committee access to five White House tape recordings. Committee chairman SAM J. ERVIN said the next day that Saxbe's action was a violation of the "solemn agreement" the attorney general had made before his confirmation that he would leave all matters relating to Watergate to special prosecutor Jaworski. Saxbe denied through a spokesman that he had violated his agreement, since the brief dealt with "institutional issues" rather than the merits of Nixon's refusal to comply with the committee's subpoena.

In a public television interview on June 17, Saxbe said that President Nixon had acted improperly when he relayed secret Watergate grand jury testimony to his former aides who were interested parties in the grand jury proceedings. He implied that Nixon either had a casual attitude toward enforcing the law or lacked knowledge about grand jury proceedings.

Saxbe took office determined to raise Justice Department morale and restore its credibility. In an effort to repair relations with the press, he held frequent conferences, but his blunt, off-the-cuff remarks often caused problems. In February 1974 Saxbe became embroiled in the first of a series of controversies when he stated that police would be guilty of "dereliction of duty" if they knew where the Symbionese Liberation Army (SLA) was holding kidnapped heiress Patricia Hearst and did not "go get her." With regard to the SLA demand that William Randolph Hearst supply $70 worth of food to each of California's needy, Saxbe said, "I certainly wouldn't recommend compliance with such vague and unrealistic demands." Later Saxbe issued a qualifying statement that he did not want "the FBI to pursue any action which would in any way jeopardize the life of the young victim in this case."

During this period Saxbe also caused a flurry of protest when he stated at his weekly press conference that "the Jewish intellectual" of the 1950s tended to be "enamored" of the Communist Party. His comments provoked strongly worded criticism from the Anti-Defamation League (ADL) of B'nai B'rith.

On December 18, 1974, Saxbe became the first cabinet member to resign from the FORD administration. He was nominated the same day to become ambassador to India, replacing DANIEL P. MOYNIHAN. EDWARD H. LEVI was named as the new attorney general by President Ford. Saxbe served at his ambassadorial post until the end of the Ford administration. Following his ambas-

sadorship Saxbe resumed his law practice in Mechanicsburg, Ohio.

—FHM

Scali, John A(lfred)
(1918–1995) *ambassador to the United Nations*

John A. Scali was born on April 27, 1918, in Canton, Ohio. Scali took his B.S. degree in journalism in 1942 at Boston University, where he had been editor in chief of the campus newspaper during his senior year. After graduation he joined the Boston bureau of United Press as a general assignment reporter. Looking for foreign assignments, Scali went to the Associated Press (AP) in 1944. He became a diplomatic and roving correspondent who primarily covered the State Department. In 1961 Scali joined ABC News. During the Cuban missile crisis of 1962 he acted as unofficial liaison between the White House and the Kremlin.

In April 1971 Scali accepted the position of senior White House consultant on foreign affairs information policy. The appointment puzzled many because Scali, a registered Democrat, had been a vocal critic of the NIXON administration's press policies and had denounced "blunderbuss attacks" on the media made by Vice President SPIRO T. AGNEW. Scali explained that his acceptance of the newly created post was due to the fact that it would be "a unique opportunity to see what it's like on the inside after 29 years of watching it from the outside."

Although he agreed with the general goals of Nixon's foreign policy, he opposed the administration's secret diplomacy. Scali hoped to close the "credibility gap" between government and public by allowing maximum disclosure of information to the public. Despite his efforts, the administration continued to suffer from lack of trust by the media and large segments of the population. As a media consultant Scali accompanied Nixon on his official foreign visits, including the historic 1972 trip to China.

In 1973 Scali was appointed ambassador to the United Nations. During his two years at the United Nations Scali had little impact on foreign policy. The United Nations received scant attention from the administration, which was increasingly preoccupied with Watergate. In the General Assembly Scali faced an assertive developing countries bloc that limited the power many of the major Western nations had once had in the world body. In December the United States, joined by other Western nations, denounced the developing countries majority. Scali said that the assembly majority was endangering the future of the United Nations by passing "one-sided, unrealistic resolutions that cannot be implemented" and that disregarded the UN charter. Examples given by Scali were assembly votes to suspend South Africa from the remainder of the 1974 session, to grant to the Palestine Liberation Organization observer status, and to limit Israel's right to speech during a debate on the Palestine issue. "Many Americans are questioning their belief in the United Nations," Scali stated.

In September 1975 Scali returned to ABC News as a Washington-based correspondent, where he worked until his retirement in 1993. Scali died on October 9, 1995.

—MLB

Schlafly, Phyllis S(tewart)
(1924–) *chair, Stop ERA; author; lecturer*

Born on August 15, 1924, the daughter of working-class parents, Phyllis Stewart attended St. Louis Catholic schools and worked in an arms plant at night while earning her B.A. at Washington University in 1944. After receiving an M.A. in political science from Radcliffe in 1945, she worked as a research librarian and in 1949 married Fred Schlafly, a wealthy

St. Louis lawyer. While raising six children, Schlafly ran unsuccessfully for the U.S. House in 1952, was research director of the Cardinal Mindszenty Foundation from 1958 to 1963, and did commentary for the *America Wake Up* radio program from 1962 to 1966.

As author and coauthor of nine books, vice president of the National Federation of Republican Women (NFRW) from 1965 to 1967, and delegate to the Republican National Convention, Schlafly molded a political career around ultraconservative causes. Her first book, *A Choice, Not an Echo*, served as a tract for the 1964 Goldwater campaign. A best seller, the book accused eastern liberal Republicans of successfully conspiring to subvert the majority will of party members for a conservative presidential nominee in all conventions since 1936.

After losing a bitter fight for the presidency of the NFRW in 1967, Schlafly wrote all 500,000 federation members and urged the diversion of a portion of their dues to a war chest to promote conservative candidates and issues. With dues of $5, Schlafly established the Eagle Trust Fund and began the publication from her home in Alton, Illinois, of her newsletter *The Phyllis Schlafly Report*. In 1970 she lost a bid for a House seat from Illinois's 23rd district. The following year she urged President NIXON to hand over leadership of the Republican Party to conservative RONALD REAGAN.

After a 1972 issue of her newsletter condemned the passage of the Equal Rights Amendment (ERA) as subversive of the institution of the family, Schlafly catapulted herself into leadership of the fight against state ratification. By 1973 Schlafly had formed Stop ERA to lobby against the amendment in all state legislatures in which the ERA was up for a vote. Charging that the ERA would destroy the family, force women into combat duty, mandate unisex toilet facilities in all public buildings, promote homosexuality, and dispossess women of their right to be a housewife, Schlafly testified before state legislatures, organized active lobbies in 26 states, appeared on national television and radio, and lectured widely. Affiliates of the American Conservative Union, on whose board of directors Schlafly served, contributed funds for this effort, and the Conservative Caucus helped to raise $50,000 through a direct-mail campaign for the antiratification fight in North Carolina and Florida. Schlafly claimed credit for slowing down the rapid success of the ERA in 1973 and the failure of over 26 attempts at ratification in western and southern state legislatures from 1973 to 1977.

By 1977 Schlafly had become a symbol and spokeswoman for national antifeminist sentiment. Her book *The Power of the Positive Woman* (1977) set forth her belief that a woman's first priority and greatest fulfillment was in the home, that women were the "civilizing force" of history, and that a woman's primary obligation was to "safeguard the values of God, family, and country." In November 1977 Schlafly staged a "profamily" rally at the Houston Astrodome in opposition to the National Women's Conference (NWC). Schlafly claimed that the NWC did not represent her constituency and would prove itself to be "radical, antifeminine, and prolesbian." The ERA was finally defeated in 1982. Schlafly continues her leadership of the Eagle Forum. She served as a member of the Commission on the Bicentennial of the U.S. Constitution from 1985 to 1991.

—JMP

Schlesinger, James R(odney)

(1929–   ) *chairman, Atomic Energy Commission; director, Central Intelligence Agency; secretary of defense*

James R. Schlesinger was born on February 15, 1929, in New York City. Schlesinger graduated summa cum laude from Harvard in 1950. After extended travel abroad he resumed his graduate studies at Harvard, taking his M.A. in economics in 1952 and his Ph.D in 1956. He began teaching at the University of Virginia in 1955 and at the Naval War College two years later. In 1960 Schlesinger's first book, *The Political Economy of National Security*, impressed the staff of the RAND Corp., a defense-oriented "think tank," and consequently Schlesinger worked from 1963 to 1967 at RAND as director of strategic studies. He left RAND in 1967 to serve as assistant director of the Bureau of the Budget. When the new NIXON administration reorganized the bureau into the Office of Management and Budget (OMB), Schlesinger served as acting deputy director during the transition and thereafter as assistant director.

It was at the OMB that Schlesinger first acquired his reputation as a "bureaucracy tamer" and a "budget cutter," trimming $6 billion from the Department of Defense's operating costs and overseeing a study of the U.S. intelligence services with an eye toward cost efficiency. His background at the RAND Corp. qualified him as an expert in nuclear affairs, and this knowledge of nuclear technology made him President Nixon's choice for OMB representative on the Environmental Quality Council. From this position Schlesinger began to play a major role in the Nixon administration's energy policy. With the rise of the environmental movement during Nixon's first term, Schlesinger became increasingly involved with energy and environmental questions. In March 1971 Nixon was prepared to make him secretary of the interior but decided against the move because a number of senators from western states insisted that Schlesinger was out of touch with their constituencies, an early sign of Schlesinger's repeated difficulties in winning congressional support for his policies.

In July 1971 Schlesinger was appointed chairman of the Atomic Energy Commission (AEC), succeeding GLENN T. SEABORG. In a speech soon after his appointment, Schlesinger stated that under his leadership the AEC would become a true advocate of the public interest and not the industry's protector, as it had been in the past. However, he was quickly embroiled in controversy. Legal attempts to prevent a five-megaton nuclear test explosion at Amchitka Island in the Aleutians were defeated by a last-minute Supreme Court decision. Opponents of the test had argued that it could have noxious effects on the environment and pointed to a nearby seismic fault as the source of a possible earthquake. Schlesinger replied to critics by taking his wife and two daughters to observe the test, underlining his complete faith in its safety.

In December 1971 the AEC underwent a major reorganization under Schlesinger's management. The commission established a new office on the environment and safety and announced that it would promote research into nonnuclear sources of energy. Schlesinger defended the reorganization, saying that it marked a shift away from the AEC's old attitude of "technology purely for the sake of technology."

In January 1972 Schlesinger announced the construction of a nuclear breeder reactor for the Tennessee Valley Authority. Foreshadowing the looming energy crisis that would become the focus of public attention in later years, he said, "We are reaching the point that supplies of fossil fuel—coal, gas, and oil—are recognized to be limited" and predicted that nuclear power would be preeminent as a future energy source. In keeping with this outlook, two months later Schlesinger requested an amendment to the National Environmental Policy Act of 1969 that would permit the AEC to issue temporary operating licenses for new nuclear reactors. In December he argued

for allowing private industry to build uranium enrichment facilities. At the same time the AEC published its proposals for nuclear industry regulation, allowing corporate access to secret government technology. Schlesinger argued that private industry's participation was necessary to keep the United States competitive in the export of nuclear reactors.

In December 1972, on what many observers believe was the urging of HENRY KISSINGER, President Nixon appointed Schlesinger to succeed RICHARD HELMS as director of the Central Intelligence Agency (CIA). Schlesinger assumed his duties at the agency in January 1973 and began implementation of budget-trimming proposals developed during his oversight of the earlier OMB study of U.S. intelligence services. Schlesinger's move was generally interpreted as a downgrading of the "cloak and dagger" operations side of the CIA's activities and a bolstering of its research and intelligence-gathering work. Some 1,000 CIA "operations" personnel were scheduled for retirement or dismissal by the end of 1973. A further sign of Schlesinger's growing power over U.S. intelligence services was his appointment as chairman of the Intelligence Resources Advisory Commission, giving him responsibility over the activities of the National Security Agency and the Army Defense Intelligence Agency.

Schlesinger, although never personally linked to Watergate, was obliged to testify, as CIA director, in the spring 1973 Watergate hearings on the role of CIA agents in the burglary of the office of DANIEL ELLSBERG's psychiatrist and in the Watergate burglary itself. Schlesinger said that agency involvement in these activities was "ill-advised" and asserted that he was against CIA involvement in covert domestic operations.

In spring 1973 Nixon once again reshuffled his cabinet in the deepening Watergate crisis. Schlesinger was appointed secretary of defense, succeeding ELLIOT RICHARDSON, who became attorney general. Schlesinger had no difficulty establishing himself as a hard-liner on military and security questions, defending in early speeches the tactical bombing of Cambodia in the Indochina conflict and the 1969–70 secret raids in that country as necessary to "defend U.S. servicemen."

The weakening of the North Atlantic Treaty Organization (NATO) and its alleged lack of preparedness for war with the countries of the Warsaw Pact was a major theme for Schlesinger before and after his move to the Department of Defense. He consistently opposed NATO troop cuts and the withdrawal of U.S. military personnel from Western Europe. These concerns were further aggravated during the October 1973 Mideast crisis when the European allies of the U.S. refused to collaborate openly in the defense of Israel for fear of alienating the Arab countries on which they depended for oil. Schlesinger stated in late October that the actions of these allies would cause the United States to "reflect" on its concepts of military strategy. In June 1974 Schlesinger attended NATO talks in Vienna and then went on to Moscow to participate in talks on strategic arms limitation. In December of that year he warned NATO ministers not to undertake military spending cuts for reasons of economy in the belief that the United States would bail them out militarily. In April 1975, however, as the U.S.-backed regime in Saigon was collapsing, Schlesinger assured America's allies that they would not be abandoned.

One of Schlesinger's attempts to reshape U.S. military strategy in the post-Vietnam world, and one linked to his downfall in November 1975, was his sponsorship of the concept of "limited nuclear warfare." In his view, growing Soviet nuclear capacity had rendered previous U.S. strategy obsolete. He expressed the fear held by many that the Soviets had reached a point where they could withstand a U.S. counterattack and still have the missiles necessary

to devastate the U.S. mainland and stated that "we are seeking to forestall the development of an assymetrical situation which would be beneficial to the Soviet Union." To counter this situation, Schlesinger announced that the United States was "retargeting" Soviet missile bases and placing less emphasis on Soviet population centers.

The "limited nuclear warfare" concept came to the fore in May 1975 when the Pentagon released a paper containing a statement by Schlesinger that the United States was prepared to use such weapons in any general war in Western Europe. He believed a limited nuclear attack on a key Soviet installation could show U.S. determination and force the Soviets to negotiate short of all-out war. Opponents of limited nuclear warfare in Congress argued that such conceptions made nuclear warfare all the more likely. In June 1975 the Stockholm-based Institute of Peace Research charged Schlesinger with promoting the long-term deployment of "mini-nukes" to replace conventional nuclear weapons. In July Schlesinger defended a possible "first strike" with limited nuclear weapons.

Schlesinger's views on such matters won him a reputation as a hard-liner and a general foe of détente with the Soviet Union. After visiting Japan in August 1975 for top-level talks, he described that nation as an "indispensable partner in the Pacific" but "too much of a passive partner." He urged Japan to intensify its rearmament efforts. In early October he toured the NATO capitals of Western Europe, again warning against defense cuts.

On November 3, 1975, in a massive shake-up at the top of the FORD administration, Schlesinger was dismissed from his position as secretary of defense, WILLIAM COLBY was fired from his CIA directorship, and Henry Kissinger, while remaining secretary of state, relinquished his post as head of the National Security Council. Schlesinger's firing in particular was interpreted as a conciliatory gesture to the Soviet Union. The *Washington Post* commented: "Nowhere else in the world is the departure of James Schlesinger likely to be more closely watched—or as warmly received—as in the Kremlin. To the Soviets, Schlesinger was a powerful and persuasive enemy of détente." The Chinese government, in a rare commentary on U.S. domestic politics, attacked Schlesinger's firing as a capitulation to the Soviets.

In the weeks after Schlesinger's firing, President Gerald Ford conceded, after initial denials of administration infighting, that there had been "growing tension" within the government, and Henry Kissinger admitted "differences" with Schlesinger on key questions. On November 23 Schlesinger appeared on *Meet the Press* and attributed his dismissal to, among other things, his opposition to limits on defense spending.

Schlesinger momentarily retired from public life. In the fall of 1976 he was visiting the People's Republic of China on the invitation of Mao Zedong (Mao Tse-tung) at the time of Mao's death. When the JIMMY CARTER administration took office in January 1977, Schlesinger returned to the executive branch as Carter's secretary of energy. Schlesinger helped draft Carter's 1977 energy program, but he drew considerable criticism, particularly in Congress, where many called for his resignation. He was eventually fired by Carter in a major cabinet shake-up in July 1979. Schlesinger then became a senior adviser to Lehman Brothers, Kuhn Loeb (New York). In 2002 President George W. Bush appointed him to the Homeland Security Council.

—LRG

Schorr, Daniel (Louis)

(1916–   ) *news correspondent*

Born on August 31, 1916, a descendant of a Russian-Jewish immigrant family, Schorr worked his way through college. Following graduation from the City College of New York in 1939, he began his career in journalism as an assistant editor for the Jewish Telegraph Agency and then moved over to the *Journal-American*. He took over the New York office of the Netherlands News Agency (ANETA) in 1941 and was drafted two years later. Following his discharge from the army Schorr moved to Amsterdam to work for ANETA until 1948, when he resigned to do freelance work on the Continent.

Schorr's work impressed Edward R. Murrow, who invited him to join the CBS news staff in 1953. Two years later Schorr was appointed CBS's first Moscow correspondent. He remained in the Soviet Union until 1957, when Soviet authorities refused to issue him a return visa following a U.S. vacation. Schorr's broadcasts were denounced by the Russians as being anti-Soviet, and Schorr was accused of being a "provocateur." From 1957 to 1966 Schorr served as a roving diplomatic correspondent, reporting from the United Nations and the major capitals of the world. He transferred to the domestic desk in 1966.

Schorr continued to cover domestic politics during the early NIXON years. His program "Don't Get Sick in America," in April 1970, criticized the Nixon administration's failure to develop a national health care program. Two months later Schorr exposed the existence of "only paper" programs in the U.S. effort to combat hunger abroad. During the debates on the Safeguard antiballistic missile, Schorr uncovered evidence that Dr. James C. Fletcher, a science adviser to the White House, had expressed misgivings to the president about the effectiveness of the system. Schorr informed the evening news viewers that Fletcher personally told him that Nixon also had doubts concerning the program. The following day, at a press conference, President Nixon denied the meeting with Fletcher had ever occurred and called Schorr a liar.

On August 17, 1971, President Nixon promised in an address to the Knights of Columbus a government program to assist Catholic schools. Following a thorough investigation Schorr found no evidence that such a program was being considered. His revelation infuriated the White House. On the morning of August 20 an FBI agent visited Schorr to request an interview because he was being considered for a "position of confidence and trust." Schorr refused to answer questions. He soon learned from relatives, friends, colleagues, and former employees that the FBI had contacted them to investigate his background. Schorr found no evidence that he was being considered for a post and came to believe that the investigation was carried out in retribution for his antiadministration broadcasts. The *Washington Post* broke the FBI-Schorr story on November 10. In response, the White House announced that the investigation was a routine background check for a possible job in the $40,000-a-year range "in the area of the environment." Subsequent Watergate investigations revealed that the White House never intended to offer Schorr a position but that this was one of many ways it used to intimidate its critics.

In August 1972 CBS assigned Schorr to cover the growing Watergate scandal. Of the three national networks, CBS devoted the widest coverage to the story, with Schorr handling most of the reporting. His reports complemented the disclosures made by Woodward and Bernstein of the *Washington Post* and Seymour Hersh of the *New York Times*. After many of Nixon's television appearances to try to exonerate the White House in the Watergate controversy, Schorr would appear and point out the inconsistencies in the president's position. He was considered the leading enemy of the administration on television.

CBS was pressured by a number of its conservative affiliates and Republicans to remove Schorr from the Watergate assignment on the grounds that he lacked objectivity in his reports. For the climax of the Watergate crisis in the summer of 1974, CBS began to divide the coverage assignments among different correspondents. Schorr, for example, did not exclusively report on the impeachment hearings in the House. On the day Nixon resigned CBS instructed its reporters to "go easy" on the president in their analysis of his speech. In his 1977 book *Clearing the Air* Schorr suggested that CBS began to soften the Watergate coverage because of fears of White House retaliation and problems with affiliates.

After Watergate CBS shifted Schorr to cover the growing controversy surrounding the Central Intelligence Agency (CIA). On February 28, 1975, Schorr reported that an internal CIA inquiry had developed evidence of agency involvement in assassination plots against at least three foreign leaders. Schorr said that President FORD was concerned that public disclosure of the plots would embarrass the United States and damage relations with one foreign nation. Schorr then covered the Senate's hearings on illegal action by intelligence agencies.

The House Intelligence Committee headed by Representative OTIS PIKE (D-N.Y.), also conducted an investigation of the FBI and the CIA. Schorr obtained sections of the panel's final report before it was scheduled to be released, but he did not reveal its contents because most of the information had been revealed during the Senate probe. On January 29, 1976, in response to a White House request, the House voted not to open the report to the public. Angered at the action, Schorr secretly gave a copy of the classified report to New York's *Village Voice* for publication. Schorr announced that he had acted on "an inescapable decision of journalist conscience." His action ired the House, which voted on February 19 to conduct an investigation to determine who leaked the material to him. CBS suspended Schorr from reporting until the House completed the investigation, but it did provide him with a lawyer and continued to pay his salary. Testifying before the House Ethics Committee, he refused to divulge his source because of his "professional conscience" as well as the First Amendment rights of freedom of the press. To reveal the source of the report, he contended, would "dry up many future sources for many future reporters." One week later the committee voted to end the probe and recommended that the House not prosecute Schorr for failure to answer its questions. The majority called Schorr's conduct "reprehensible" and urged the House to hire professionals to guard secret materials.

The leaking of the Pike report created additional problems for Schorr within CBS. The network affiliates broadcasting in conservative areas as well as many of Schorr's colleagues were incensed with his conduct and demanded his ouster. On September 28 he resigned, stating; "I would doubt my ability to function effectively if reinstated. . . . My reinstatement would be a source of tension within an organization whose future success I still care about."

Schorr then published his account of covering the Nixon-Ford years titled *Clearing the Air* (1977). In 1980 he was hired as a commentator for the Cable News Network. He left CNN in 1985 and is currently senior news analyst of National Public Radio.

—JB

Schweiker, Richard S(chultz)
(1926–   ) *member of the Senate*

Richard S. Schweiker was born in Norristown, Pennsylvania, on June 26, 1926. The son of a wealthy tile manufacturer, Schweiker, at age 17, enlisted in the navy during World War II.

Following his discharge Schweiker attended Pennsylvania State University, graduating in 1950. After college he joined his family's business and a few years later became involved in local Republican politics in the affluent Main Line suburbs of Philadelphia.

In 1960 Schweiker won a seat in the U.S. House. Cautious and noncommittal as a freshman representative, Schweiker adopted a more liberal stance in his next three terms. Schweiker voted for civil rights legislation, Medicare, Social Security increases, federal rent subsidies, and welfare reform. Schweiker initially supported U.S. involvement in Vietnam but by 1967 began to question the Johnson administration's handling of the conflict. Eventually Schweiker became one of the most determined foes of the war, supporting such end-the-war measures as the Cooper-Church and McGovern-Hatfield amendments in 1970 and 1971, respectively.

Schweiker's election to the Senate in 1968 was considered something of a surprise, as he beat incumbent liberal Democrat Joseph S. Clark, whose defense of gun control legislation had angered many voters. In the Senate Schweiker established a reputation as a maverick who disregarded partisan politics and opposed the NIXON administration on a number of crucial issues. A founding member of the Senate's Wednesday Club of liberal and moderate Republicans, he voted against the administration's Safeguard antiballistic missile system and opposed the president's nominations of CLEMENT HAYNSWORTH and G. HARROLD CARSWELL to the Supreme Court. *Congressional Quarterly* listed Schweiker among the Republican senators who most consistently voted against the Nixon administration's programs. The strained relations between the president and the senator led to Schweiker's inclusion on the White House "enemies list." When confronted with mounting evidence implicating Nixon in the Watergate cover-up,

Schweiker, in May 1974, became the third Republican senator to call for his resignation. Having disassociated himself from the president, Schweiker won reelection in 1974 by defeating Pittsburgh's Democratic mayor Peter F. Flaherty by 247,000 votes.

Overshadowed in some measure by his colleague HUGH SCOTT, the Senate minority leader, Schweiker remained in relative obscurity until his selection in January 1975 to the bipartisan Senate Select Committee on Intelligence Operations. Schweiker drew headlines on July 20, 1975, when he called for a reopening of the investigation of President John F. Kennedy's assassination. But Schweiker's contention of a connection between President Kennedy's death and a CIA plot to murder Cuban premier Fidel Castro was dismissed by other Senate members as a publicity stunt. Subsequently the Senate voted to kill further funding for the committee, leaving Schweiker's allegations unresolved.

Schweiker's voting record was considerably more liberal than the policies endorsed by the FORD administration. Yet Schweiker supported Ford's candidacy and announced in April 1976 that he would vote for the president at the Republican National Convention in Kansas City. But on July 26, 1976, RONALD REAGAN, Ford's rival for the nomination, stunned political observers by nominating Schweiker as his running mate. Schweiker's selection was part of a Reagan plan to force Ford to come out with his vice presidential choice and presumably antagonize some part of his fragile coalition in the process. Arguing that Schweiker could draw off Ford's liberal support in the Northeast, Reagan strategists maintained that a balanced ticket could unite the party and ensure victory. But the plan backfired badly. Schweiker's liberal record enraged Reagan supporters, while at the same time Schweiker could not move a significant number of Pennsylvania delegates to support Reagan.

Schweiker offered to withdraw from the ticket, but Reagan refused. On August 19, 1976, Ford narrowly defeated Reagan on the first ballot, ending a six-month intraparty struggle. In the weeks following the convention Schweiker mended his political fences and endorsed the Ford candidacy.

Despite his liberal voting record Schweiker took a decidedly conservative position on certain issues. He favored abortion only in cases when the mother's life was in danger, disapproved of blanket amnesty for draft evaders, and supported the concept of neighborhood schools and only limited busing to achieve racial integration. In general, however, Schweiker's voting reflected his urban, industrial, Northeast constituency. Americans for Democratic Action gave Schweiker an 89 rating in 1975 (the same as ADA president GEORGE MCGOVERN), while the AFL-CIO's Committee on Political Education awarded Schweiker a 100 rating, the only perfect score in the Senate that year.

In 1977 Schweiker became the second-ranking Republican on the Senate Human Resources Committee. He left the Senate in 1981 and served from 1981 to 1983 as President Ronald Reagan's secretary of health and human services. From 1983 to 1994 he was president of the American Council of Life Insurance. He resides in McLean, Virginia.

—JAN

Scott, Hugh D(oggett)
(1900–1994) *member of the Senate*

Hugh D. Scott was born on November 11, 1900, in Fredericksburg, Virginia. After receiving his law degree from the University of Virginia in 1922, Scott entered private practice in Philadelphia and served as an assistant district attorney there from 1926 to 1941. Elected to the House of Representatives in 1940 and 1942, he served in the navy during World War

II. In 1946 he won reelection to the House and remained a member until 1959. A moderate Republican, Scott was an ardent supporter of Dwight D. Eisenhower in 1952 for the Republican presidential nomination and worked in the general's campaign headquarters.

First elected to the Senate in 1958, Scott successfully challenged the conservative leadership of the Pennsylvania Republican Party in 1962 in his sponsorship of the liberal Republican WILLIAM SCRANTON for the governorship. In 1964 he helped form a "stop Goldwater" movement and after the collapse of NELSON ROCKEFELLER's presidential campaign effort persuaded Scranton to challenge Goldwater at the Republican National Convention. After Goldwater's nomination Scott remained aloof from the presidential race, refusing to campaign for the Arizona senator.

Scott frequently broke with his own party to support liberal legislation. A staunch advocate of civil rights, he was partly responsible for Eisenhower's decision to support such legislation and voted for the civil rights measures of the Johnson administration. Sensitive to the wishes of his liberal constituency in Pennsylvania's large cities, he often supported legislation favored by labor and low-income groups.

In January 1969 Scott was elected party whip by his Republican colleagues in the Senate and in September, after the death of minority leader EVERETT DIRKSEN, was chosen to succeed him. As a party leader and the NIXON administration's chief spokesman in the Senate, Scott was often asked to support measures and adopt strategies that he opposed and that he felt would hurt the Republican Party. Despite frequent statements in support of the administration's legislative program, Scott was at odds with the president on many occasions.

Scott's differences with the administration were especially apparent in the area of civil rights. In June 1969 the White House announced its opposition to an extension of the 1965 Voting Rights Act. Arguing that the law represented "regional legislation," Attorney General JOHN MITCHELL proposed a much weaker substitute. The next day Scott declared that he was willing to lead the fight for a five-year extension of the law. When the House adopted the administration's proposal in December, Scott joined with liberal forces to map a strategy for the Senate debate. With Senator PHILIP HART (D-Mich.) he introduced a compromise measure that extended the act for five years but added a change that would allow certain states an exemption from the ban on literacy tests as a face-saving device for the president. In March 1970 the Senate approved the Scott substitute, and the bill later became law.

Scott also resisted attempts to weaken the federal government's commitment to enforce school desegregation. He opposed the attempt by Senator JOHN STENNIS (D-Miss.) in April 1970 to amend an education appropriation bill to require the desegregation guidelines be uniformly applied in cases of both de jure and de facto segregation. When President Nixon vetoed the education aid bill later that year, Scott voted with the Democratic majority to override the veto. In 1972, as sentiment against court-ordered busing increased, Scott came out publicly against both a constitutional amendment to prohibit busing and any absolute barring of federal funds for busing plans. In February 1972 he and Senator MIKE MANSFIELD (D-Mont.) engineered a Senate compromise that placed a limit on the use of busing but retained it as a tool to achieve integration in some cases.

In other domestic areas Scott's record of support for the White House was mixed. Although he voted against CLEMENT HAYNSWORTH for the Supreme Court, he voted to confirm G. HARROLD CARSWELL. Scott opposed the Nixon administration's uncompromising stand against the Senate's 1969 tax reform bill. When the White House intransigency led to the defeat of a Republican-initiated compromise measure, Scott angrily told the president and his advisers to "listen the next time we try to advise them." He supported Nixon's antiballistic missile proposals and defended the administration's economic measures to control inflation.

For the Republican Party, in Scott's view, to make significant gains in the 1970 elections the administration would have to reduce troop levels in Vietnam by at least 50 percent, substantially lower draft calls, and reduce defense spending. Nevertheless, Scott staunchly defended Nixon's war policies. When New York Republican senator CHARLES GOODELL introduced a bill in September 1969 to cut off all funds for troops in Vietnam by the end of 1970, Scott attacked it as a "cut-and-run and bug-out" resolution. He defended the 1970 invasion of Cambodia and the 1971 invasion of Laos as efforts to end the war and in June 1970 voted against the Cooper-Church Amendment to halt funds for combat operations in Cambodia.

When Senator WILLIAM FULBRIGHT (D-Ark.) initiated hearings in February 1970 into the administration's Vietnamization program, Scott attacked the inquiry and urged the nation to "surmount the hysteria of a limited number of critics." In a sharply partisan speech in April 1971, Scott charged Democratic critics of the war with "irresponsible mud-slinging" and with "giving comfort to the enemy" by "crying the same line of Moscow, Peking, and Hanoi." In June 1971 he urged that Democratic senator MIKE GRAVEL of Alaska be disciplined for reading portions of *The Pentagon Papers* into the Senate record, and in September he voted to extend the draft.

Scott defended Nixon during most of the revelations surrounding the Watergate scandal. In March 1973, after the Senate approved the creation of a special investigating committee, Scott declared that "the White House has nothing to hide." When Nixon announced on

April 30 the resignations of his closest advisers who were implicated in the growing scandal, Scott applauded the speech as proof that Nixon was "determined to see this affair thoroughly cleaned up." In July he predicted that the president would "come out fighting" soon and "reply very, very strongly" to the allegations made at the Senate hearings.

But Scott increasingly found himself on a political limb as White House actions and revelations repeatedly called into question the wisdom of his public support for the president. Scott frequently urged Nixon to make a "full disclosure" of all pertinent information, and he praised Nixon's October 18 decision to hand over partial transcripts to Watergate special prosecutor ARCHIBALD COX. When Cox rejected the compromise and was subsequently fired by Nixon, Scott could only urge the president to hurriedly name a new special prosecutor. A few days later, when the White House made the startling revelation that tapes of two crucial meetings did not exist, Scott lamely defended the announcement by saying "this machine age isn't always perfect."

Late in November 1973 Scott admitted that he had "never been more uncomfortable" than in his current position. "I've had a terribly difficult job," he said, "trying to strike a balance as a party leader and at the same time trying to hold the confidence of people." After the White House gave Scott assurances that evidence existed to clear the president, Scott, in January 1974, reaffirmed his confidence in Nixon's innocence. But he was angered by the refusal of the president to turn over to the House Judiciary Committee the evidence it had requested, and Scott warned Nixon in March that he would definitely be impeached if the White House tapes were not released.

On April 30 Nixon finally released over 1,200 pages of transcripts. A few days later Scott renounced his support of the president. The transcripts revealed, he said, "deplorable, disgusting, shabby, immoral performances" on the part of everyone involved, including President Nixon. After Nixon released further transcripts on August 5 indicating his knowledge of and involvement in the cover-up of the Watergate break-in, Scott met with Nixon and told him that his impeachment and conviction were a virtual certainty, and he urged the president to resign.

Scott's lengthy support of Nixon tarnished his position. On December 4, 1975, he announced that he would not seek reelection the following year. In 1976 his reputation was further hurt by revelations that he had received $45,000 in illegal campaign contributions from the Gulf Oil Corp. Scott admitted receiving the money but denied that he "knowingly" accepted illegal funds, arguing instead that he thought they came from legal, private sources. The Senate Ethics Committee conducted an investigation but decided in September 1976 not to take action against Scott. Scott practiced law in Virginia until his 1994 death.

—JD

Scowcroft, Brent

(1925–   ) *military assistant to the president; deputy assistant to the president for national security affairs; assistant to the president for national security affairs*

A native of Ogden, Utah, Brent Scowcroft graduated from the U.S. Military Academy at West Point in 1947 and earned his fighter pilot wings in 1948, although he never saw combat. Instead he pursued a rather scholarly military career, studying international relations at Columbia University. He received his Ph.D. in 1967. He also studied at Georgetown University's School of Languages and Linguistics, acquiring a fluent knowledge of Russian and Serbo-Croatian. During the middle 1950s he taught Russian history at West Point, and in

the early 1960s he taught political science at the Air Force Academy in Colorado.

Thereafter he held a series of Pentagon assignments. From 1964 to 1967 he was a member of the long-range planning division of the office of the deputy chief of staff for plans and operations. He then worked as staff assistant in the Western Hemisphere region of the office of the assistant secretary of defense for international security affairs during 1968–69. The next year was spent as special assistant to the director of the staff of the Joint Chiefs of Staff. In November 1971 he was brought into the White House as military aide to the president, replacing General J. D. Hughes, who had served RICHARD NIXON since 1969 and who was resigning to become vice commander of the 12th Air Force in Austin, Texas.

Shortly after his appointment to the White House staff, Scowcroft headed the advance party to arrange for President Nixon's trip to Moscow—a delicate mission in view of the concurrent renewal of U.S. bombing of North Vietnam. As a career soldier-administrator with extensive academic background and capable of handling diplomatically tinged scout-and-prepare missions, Scowcroft had much in common with another soldier on the White House staff, General ALEXANDER M. HAIG. Indeed, when Haig left the White House to become army vice chief of staff in January 1973, Scowcroft stepped into his position as deputy to presidential assistant HENRY KISSINGER at the National Security Council (NSC).

As Kissinger's assistant Scowcroft put in a hardworking and low-profile performance. Described as "one of the hardest workers in the White House," "cool under pressure," and "a straightforward and very quiet and very forceful man," he was an able administrator but not a vigorous or dominating one. He was "trained to serve totally and unswervingly the person to whom he was assigned." For more than two years that person was Henry Kissinger, who played a

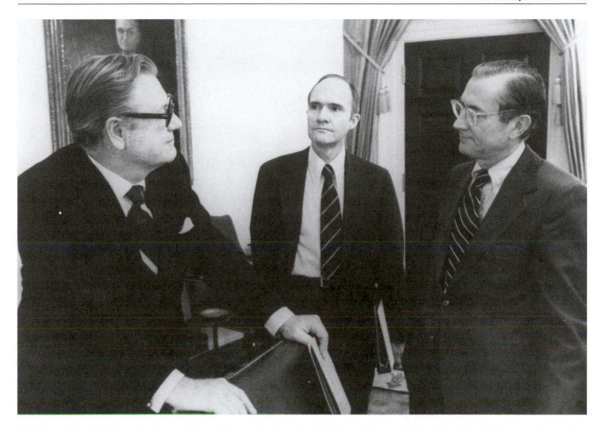

Vice President Nelson A. Rockefeller, Deputy Assistant of National Security Affairs Brent Scowcroft, and CIA director William Colby discuss the situation in Vietnam, 1975. *(Ford Library)*

very prominent position while his deputy stayed quietly, self-effacingly behind the scenes. Kissinger often had a tendency to operate in a highly personalized, secretive manner that cut out even his most trusted assistants. Scowcroft, however, was generally kept well informed, if not by Kissinger, then by his fellow-in-arms Alexander Haig, who had returned to the White House as chief of staff in May 1973.

Not implicated in the Nixon administration scandals, Kissinger and his staff survived intact the transition to the FORD administration. As President Ford sought to "take hold of the foreign policy mechanism" and make it his own, he instituted a major cabinet and White House staff personnel shuffle in November 1975 that replaced Defense Secretary JAMES SCHLESINGER with Ford's White House chief of staff DONALD RUMSFELD. In other shifts GEORGE H. W. BUSH replaced WILLIAM COLBY as the head of the Central Intelligence Agency. ELLIOT RICHARDSON was brought back from the London embassy as secretary of commerce, and Secretary of State Henry Kissinger gave up his dual post as national security affairs assistant. When Kissinger finally left the NSC in 1975, his deputy, Scowcroft, resigned his military commission to accept promotion to Kissinger's former post on the White House staff.

After Ford's 1976 defeat for reelection, from 1982 to 1989 Scowcroft was the vice chairman of Kissinger Associates, Inc., a consulting firm. In 1987 he was once again called to government service, this time as a member of the President's Special Review Board on Iran-Contra (the Tower Commission).

In 1988 president-elect George H. W. Bush offered Scowcroft the position of National Security Advisor. Scowcroft accepted the position and held it for the entirety of the Bush administration. In 1991 President Bush presented Scowcroft with the Medal of Freedom Award. In 1998 he coauthored a volume of memoirs with Bush, *A World Transformed.* Scowcroft is the founder and president of the Scowcroft Group, a consulting firm. He also is the founder and president of the Forum for International Policy.

—MJW and JRG

Scranton, William W(arren)
(1917–   ) *ambassador to the United Nations*

William W. Scranton was born in Madison, Connecticut, on July 19, 1917. A descendant of a wealthy steel and banking family, William Scranton graduated from Yale in 1939 and then received his law degree from Yale Law School in 1946. Following service in the army he returned to his home town of Scranton, Pennsylvania, where he worked for his family. He also became active in local Republican politics. In 1960 he won a seat in the U.S. House. Two years later he won the governorship with 55.4 percent of the vote and immediately emerged as a dark-horse contender for the 1964 Republican presidential nomination. When it appeared certain that Senator BARRY GOLDWATER (R-Ariz.) would get the nomination, moderates and liberals turned to Scranton. Although the Pennsylvania governor initially had refused to run, he belatedly changed his mind and challenged Goldwater, but he was defeated at the convention. In 1966 Scranton completed his term as governor, pledging not

to run "ever for any public office under any circumstances." Although he remained active in Republican politics, he devoted his attention to his family's financial interests and sat on the board of directors of a number of leading corporations.

In December 1968 Scranton visited the Middle East for President-elect RICHARD NIXON. He told reporters at the Jordan River that the United States should follow a "more even-handed" policy toward Israel and its Arab neighbors. This statement infuriated American Jews as well as the Israeli government, and the future administration repudiated it. But Scranton refused to retract his position.

Following the shootings of student protesters at Kent State and Jackson State in the spring of 1970, President Nixon appointed Scranton to chair the President's Commission on Campus Unrest. Eighty-seven witnesses testified at the hearings conducted throughout the summer. The final report advised the president that he "has the platform and prestige to urge all Americans at once, to step back from the battle lines into which they are forming." It urged him to "seek to convince public officials and protesters alike that divisive and insulting rhetoric is dangerous in the current political campaign and throughout the years ahead. The president should insist that no one play irresponsible politics with the issue of 'campus unrest.'" Ending the Vietnam War, promised the report, as well as a renewed commitment to "full social justice at home," would contribute to the reduction of divisiveness on the campuses. When dealing with the controversial question of violence, the report took a balanced position. It blamed student agitators and police for escalating the tensions through overreaction and intimidation of each other. The report recommended the democratization of the governance of the universities, the promulgation of clearly defined rules of permissible conduct and methods of protest, and the termination of defense and intelligence contracts between the federal government and the campuses. The Nixon administration received the controversial report with little comment.

Soon after GERALD FORD became president, he asked Scranton to become the U.S. ambassador to the United Nations. Scranton turned down the offer. When DANIEL PATRICK MOYNIHAN, Ford's second choice, resigned in early March 1976, the president once again asked Scranton. This time he accepted. Because of his 1968 Jordan River statement, the selection of Scranton upset American and Jewish public opinion. Scranton himself added to the problem when he said in a UN debate that he regarded the Israeli settlements in the occupied territories "as an obstacle to the success of the negotiations for a just and final peace between Israel and its neighbors." The Israelis deplored this statement even though Scranton vetoed a UN resolution denouncing their occupation of the West Bank. Scranton was a leading contender to be Ford's running mate in 1976; the position went instead to BOB DOLE. After Ford's defeat Scranton left his UN post. Scranton retired to his home in Dalton, Pennsylvania.

—JB

Seaborg, Glenn T(heodore)
(1912–1999) *chairman, Atomic Energy Commission*

Glenn T. Seaborg was born on April 19, 1912, in Ishpeming, Michigan. Seaborg, a nuclear chemist, discovered the element plutonium in 1940 and worked on the Manhattan Project, which developed the atom bomb during World War II. He served on the Atomic Energy Commission's (AEC) General Advisory Board from 1946 to 1951.

In 1961 Seaborg was appointed head of the AEC by President Kennedy. During his tenure he fought for the maintenance of AEC control over both regulation and development of atomic energy programs despite criticism that the two functions were incompatible. Seaborg supported the nuclear test ban treaty of 1963 and pressed for the confinement of nuclear energy to the five countries already developing their atomic potential. He encouraged the U.S. Plowshare Program designed to formulate peaceful uses of atomic explosives, including excavation and earth-moving. The program, which attracted worldwide attention during the mid-1960s, involved numerous tests at the AEC's nuclear test site in Nevada. In 1970 an AEC report revealed that a 250-square-mile area of its Nevada test site was contaminated with poisonous and radioactive plutonium 239; the area was sealed off from the public. Plowshare was suspended in the early 1970s, primarily due to environmental protest and lack of industry support.

Considerable controversy and publicity surrounded the AEC during Seaborg's remaining years as head of the commission. Its handling of radioactive wastes attracted severe criticism, highlighted by the 1970 release of a 1966 National Academy of Science (NAS) report. The study criticized the poor geographical locations chosen for stockpiling radioactive refuse, the commission's general policy of underground storage, and the varied criteria used to classify the materials at different plants. A subsequent report prepared for Senator FRANK CHURCH (D-Idaho) also found the AEC's disposal techniques careless.

Seaborg became embroiled in a 1971 controversy involving the use of radioactive sand, known as tailings, in construction in Grand Junction, Colorado. Left by companies mining uranium during the 1950s and 1960s, mounds of tailings were carted off for free landfill by both contractors and private citizens. "Elevated" levels of radioactivity were detected in the area by state and federal health officials in 1966. Although some health officials dismissed threats from the low-level radiation, tailings were removed, at state and federal cost, from numerous private homes. In a letter to Governor JOHN LOVE, Seaborg refused to finance a chromosomal study of infants in the town to test for possible abnormalities. Supported by state money, a five-year study was begun on a federal grant at the University of Colorado Medical Center, but the contract was prematurely canceled a year later. The limited tests conducted, however, found significant increases in birth defects and in the death rate due to cancer in the country surrounding Grand Junction.

In 1969 Seaborg gave top priority to the liquid metal fast breeder reactor (LMFBR) development program. LMFBRs were designed to recycle plutonium fuel elements to produce more plutonium. Budget allocations for LMFBRs increased from $85 million (of a nearly $2.3 billion budget) for fiscal year 1970 to $285 million (of an almost $2.6 billion budget) three years later. An accident involving this type of reactor at the Enrico Fermi Atomic Power Plant near Detroit, Michigan, threatened that city in 1966. Two months after it started up in August, emissions of extremely high levels of radiation caused the plant to be shut down. Delicate and tedious testing, conducted over a year and a half, determined the cause of the fuel meltdown and enabled the Power Reactor Development Co. to begin cleanup efforts. The plant resumed operation in July 1970, but financial difficulties caused the AEC to deny the company's application for a license extension in August 1972.

Dr. Seaborg resigned in 1971 to return to teaching chemistry at the University of California at Berkeley. In April 1973 he was appointed director for international relations of the French Société International de Technologie. From 1982 to 1999 he was first director, then chairman, of Lawrence Hall of

Science, University of California at Berkeley. He died in 1999.

—RB

Seale, Bobby
(1937–   ) *black militant*

Born on October 22, 1937, the son of working-class black parents, Seale was raised in Dallas and Oakland, California. After dropping out of high school, he enlisted in the air force but was dishonorably discharged for fighting with a white officer. Returning to Oakland, he finished high school at night and entered Merritt College, where he joined the Afro-American Association. He met Huey Newton, another black student, and together they studied Afro-American and African history and the writings of black militants such as Malcolm X, who especially influenced them. In October 1966 they founded the Black Panther Party. Seale was chairman, and Newton was a minister of defense for the organization.

Although the Panthers received the most publicity for their advocacy of armed self-defense for blacks against police violence, they also had a 10-point platform that emphasized self-help and community control of ghetto institutions such as schools, housing, and businesses. The Black Panthers first came to national attention in May 1967 when Seale led a group of armed Panthers to the California state assembly to protest gun-control legislation aimed at them. The publicity helped increase the Panthers' membership to several thousand, and branches of the group were formed in many cities. Although an all-black organization, the Panthers cooperated with white radical groups, especially in the antiwar movement.

Because of their vocal and militant stand against police brutality, the Panthers were subject to intense government harassment. In

January 1969 Seale announced a campaign to rid the Panthers of FBI and police infiltrators. When the police in several cities raided party offices in June 1969, Seale accused the government of a conspiracy "to destroy the Black Panther Party leadership." In December, after Chicago police had slain fellow members Fred Hampton and Mark Clark, Seale denounced the action as part of a plan to "commit genocide" against the Panthers. It was later revealed that the FBI and local police had indeed infiltrated the Panthers and had encouraged party members to commit acts of violence.

On March 20, 1969, Seale was indicted with seven other leaders of the antiwar movement for violating the antiriot provisions of the 1968 Civil Rights Act in connection with the demonstrations at the Democratic National Convention in Chicago. Their famous "Chicago Eight" conspiracy trial, which began in September 1969, became a cause célèbre for radicals and was the scene of numerous confrontations between the defendants and Judge JULIUS HOFFMAN. When Seale vociferously demanded the right to conduct his own defense (his lawyer, Charles Garry, was sick at the time, and Hoffman refused to grant a delay), the judge ordered him gagged and shackled in court and on November 5 declared a mistrial for Seale. He also sentenced Seale to four years in prison for contempt of court. In 1970 the government dropped the conspiracy charges against him, and in 1972 a court dismissed all of the contempt charges.

Seale, meanwhile, with several other Panther members, was indicted on murder charges in the 1969 torture slaying of Alex Rackley, a former Panther. The trial, scheduled to begin in New Haven, Connecticut, in May 1970, provoked large-scale demonstrations, and the slogan "Free Bobby" became a rallying cry for radicals. The trial of Seale and codefendant Ericka Huggins, which had been postponed until November, was the longest in Connecti-cut history, finally ending on May 25, 1971, when the jury reported that it was hopelessly deadlocked. The judge declared a mistrial and ordered all charges against the defendants dropped. After almost two years in prison Seale was finally released.

With many Panthers killed or jailed over the preceding years, Seale returned to Oakland and helped redirect the Panthers away from armed self-defense and toward community organizing and self-help programs for ghetto residents. In May 1972 Seale announced that he would run for mayor of Oakland the following year. Campaigning on a platform that emphasized community control of police and low-rent housing, he placed second in a field of nine and received over 43,000 votes in the May 1973 runoff.

Soon after the election Seale quietly left the party and retired to private life. In 1978 he published his autobiography, *A Lonely Rage*. In the 1980s he served Youth Employment Strategies.

—JD

Segretti, Donald Henry
(1941–   ) *Watergate figure*

A native Californian, Donald Segretti was born on September 17, 1941, and graduated from the University of Southern California (USC) in 1963. Segretti was a good student and was active in class government at USC, where he attended classes with both DWIGHT CHAPIN and GORDON STRACHAN. He joined the Trojans for Representative Government and became their successful candidate for the student senate. The Trojans were known on the USC campus for their special brand of "dirty tricks," which they called "ratfucking." They stuffed ballot boxes, planted spies in the opposition camp, and distributed false campaign literature about their political opponents. In 1962 with another

USC graduate, RONALD ZIEGLER, Segretti and Chapin were drafted to work on RICHARD NIXON's unsuccessful gubernatorial campaign.

Segretti studied at Cambridge in 1963, returned to California, and entered law school in 1964. He graduated from the University of California at Berkeley in 1966. Segretti worked a year for the Treasury Department before he was drafted into the army to serve as an officer in the judge advocate general's office. A registered Democrat, Segretti was considered a radical for his attempt to integrate private housing in Charlottesville, Virginia. Later Segretti defended soldiers in Long Binh, Vietnam, in their petition for discharge from the army as conscientious objectors. In his last year in the army at Fort Ord, he helped organize the antiwar and antimilitary Concerned Officers Movement.

In spring 1971 Segretti was contacted by his two college friends Chapin and Strachan who, after working under H. R. HALDEMAN in Richard Nixon's successful 1968 presidential campaign, were aides to Haldeman in the White House. Offering the chance for "some fun and travel" plus the opportunity to "work for the president," Chapin and Strachan asked Segretti if he would like to head a "clandestine political activities unit." The purpose of the unit would be to throw the 1972 Democratic primary campaign into disarray and to eliminate the most formidable Nixon rival, EDMUND MUSKIE. In August Segretti met with HERBERT KALMBACH, President Nixon's personal lawyer, and was offered a salary of $16,000 a year plus expenses for his work.

Segretti took his mission seriously and enthusiastically. He hired 28 people in 17 primary states to conduct a campaign of dirty tricks that included forging letters and distributing them under the candidates' letterheads, making dossiers on the candidates' personal lives, seizing confidential files from the candidates, leaking false statements, manufacturing items

for the press, and throwing the candidates' schedules into disarray. He plagued Muskie's campaign with a variety of damaging political literature. His first act was to distribute a leaflet in Florida that read, "If you like Hitler, you'll just love Wallace—vote Muskie." Another flyer from that primary read, "Help Muskie in Busing More Children." It was signed by the "Mothers Backing Muskie." In one of the most vicious attempts to discredit the Democratic front-runners, Segretti arranged for a letter to be sent to various Democrats and the press on stolen Muskie stationery charging both HENRY JACKSON and HUBERT HUMPHREY with sexual misconduct. A falsified Hubert Humphrey press release alleged that SHIRLEY CHISHOLM had been hospitalized in a mental institution.

Segretti kept in contact with Chapin at the White House about his political activities. Altogether Segretti received and disbursed almost $45,000. Segretti's and other "internal security" operations were financed by a slush fund of more than $700,000 in cash collected as illegal campaign gifts and kept in MAURICE STANS's safe at the Committee to Re-Elect the President (CREEP). In 1972 CREEP's deputy director, JEB STUART MAGRUDER, had insisted that the White House Segretti-Chapin operation and the CREEP internal security operation be administered by G. GORDON LIDDY, general counsel for the committee. Although Segretti was contacted on several occasions by E. HOWARD HUNT, chief contact for the Watergate burglars, there is no indication that Segretti, Liddy, or Hunt ever worked on a project together. However, they all met in Miami, Florida, on February 11, 1972. At that meeting Hunt asked Segretti what he was doing, gave him the name of a printer in Miami who would do his leaflets, and promised to get him Muskie's itinerary. Hunt gave Segretti his home phone number and told him to keep in touch.

Donald Segretti's activities were among the first to be uncovered, in October 1972, by the investigation of reporters ROBERT WOOD-WARD and CARL BERNSTEIN of the *Washington Post*. Segretti was traced through Hunt's telephone records. In 1974 Segretti was convicted of political espionage and served four months and 20 days of a six-month sentence. He was released from jail on March 25, 1974, and disappeared from public life.

In 1995 Segretti, who practices law in Orange County, California, entered a race for a judgeship. However, he withdrew his name from the race after one week due to adverse publicity stemming from his role in Watergate.

—SJT

Shapp, Milton J(errold)
(1912–1994) *governor of Pennsylvania*

Born Milton J. Shapiro on June 25, 1912, in Cleveland, Ohio, Shapiro received his B.S. degree in electrical engineering from Case Institute of Technology in 1933. It served little good at the height of the Depression, however; his first job following graduation was driving a truck for 22 cents an hour. He soon found work as a salesman in Philadelphia and changed his name from Shapiro to Shapp when he suspected anti-Semitism was hindering his sales.

Shapp served as an officer in the army's signal corps during World War II. His experience in electronics led him to form Jerrold Electronics in 1948, a small manufacturer and distributor of television-related hardware. Shapp pioneered the practical application of community antenna television (CATV) in the early 1950s and made his multimillion-dollar fortune in CATV franchises.

Shapp was an early supporter of John F. Kennedy and served as a consultant to the administration. He ran in the 1964 Pennsylvania Democratic primary for senator but

dropped out when the party organization endorsed another candidate. In 1966 he ran unsuccessfully for governor. Following his defeat Shapp formed the Pennsylvania Democratic Study Committee, a group of economists and other social scientists that published periodic "Shapp Reports" on various political and economic issues. Despite voter support for Senator EUGENE MCCARTHY in the 1968 Pennsylvania primary, the state delegation's leadership supported Senator HUBERT H. HUMPHREY at the national convention. Shapp vehemently opposed this action and took to the streets to protest with other delegates and citizens the Democratic National Committee's handling of the convention. Presidential primary reform became a major issue for Shapp in later years.

Shapp ran for governor again in 1970. In the general election he presented himself as the enemy of state machine politics. His mass media saturation advertising emphasized his highly successful business activity as a qualification for pulling the state out of the financial bind into which it had been led by machine bosses. To balance the state budget and increase state aid to college education, Shapp suggested a graduated state income tax. His Republican opponent, Lieutenant Governor Raymond J. Broderick, fought the income tax concept as a way of balancing the budget and characterized Shapp's activities at the 1968 Democratic National Convention as being riotous and illegal. Shapp won by a landslide, carrying the Democrats to their first state senate majority since 1962.

At the opening of his administration, Shapp declared himself "the people's advocate." He worked to reform and regulate the state's insurance companies and worked for consumer protection.

Shapp was confronted by several controversial issues in the last years of his first term. In November 1972 he vetoed the first of several strong antiabortion bills, citing its unenforceability. A few months later he proposed sweeping changes in private health care, making hospital budgets and rates subject to state approval, easing health insurance application standards, and providing for public representation on the boards of all health care institutions. Shapp's graduated income tax proposal was quickly adopted by the state legislature but subsequently declared unconstitutional by the conservative Pennsylvania supreme court. The legislature then passed a flat 2.3 percent tax in its place. Shapp established a statewide lottery to lessen the impact of the state income tax on the elderly, whose small, fixed incomes would suffer, and to reduce the property taxes of the elderly poor. Shapp opposed President NIXON's revenue-sharing programs, stating that he considered them part of an attempt to curtail legitimate aid to the poor.

Toward the end of 1973, many of the state's truckers went on strike to protest fuel pricing and allocation practices resulting from the Arab oil embargo; the flow of goods by truck was almost completely stopped. In the strike, marked by violence and bloodshed, Shapp acted as a mediator and helped piece together a pact acceptable to the truckers. Shapp pushed for a no-fault insurance law for the state's automobile drivers, and Pennsylvania's resulting 1974 bill was among the first in the nation.

In 1974 Shapp became the first Pennsylvania governor eligible to run for a second term. He won the Democratic primary handily, defeating an antiabortion candidate, Republican Andrew L. Lewis III, in the November contest with 54 percent of the vote.

Shapp entered the 1975 presidential primary race in September. He eschewed "political rhetoric" and stressed a "businesslike" approach to government, featuring "executive leadership and managerial skill." He entered the Florida and Massachusetts primaries and drew negligible support. In March 1976 he dropped out of the race and in June threw his support to JIMMY CARTER.

Several instances of questionable activity by political allies and administration personnel marred Shapp's last few years as governor. In March 1975 the treasurer of the state Democratic Party, William Casper, was convicted on charges of extortion and conspiracy concerning his activities as a fund-raiser for Governor Shapp's 1974 campaign. Another problem surfaced in 1976 when questions were raised about a 1972 cable TV franchise granted to Shapp from which he later made a $2 million profit. Perjury and conspiracy charges were leveled against the state police commissioner, the deputy commissioner, and the head of the state patrol for incidents involving the alleged falsification of records of patrolmen involved in traffic accidents while intoxicated.

Pennsylvania attorney general Robert P. Kane dismissed Walter M. Phillips, state special prosecutor for Philadelphia, for alleged ineffectiveness in probing municipal corruption; Phillips had been investigating House Speaker Herbert Fineman, a political ally of Governor Shapp, for possible irregularities in the awarding of contracts for the city school system. Shapp's political problems continued into 1977 with the conviction of Fineman on charges of obstructing a federal probe into alleged payoffs by parents seeking to get their children into professional schools. Adjutant General Harry J. Mier was forced to resign from Shapp's cabinet in February 1977; he was alleged to have used military aircraft for personal reasons.

Shapp was not eligible to run for a third term as governor, and Republican Richard Thornburgh took over in 1979. Shapp died in 1994.

—RB

Shriver, R(obert) Sargent, Jr.

(1915–   ) *Democratic vice presidential candidate*

Born on November 9, 1915, into a wealthy and socially prominent Maryland family, Shriver was educated at Yale, where he received an LL.B. in 1941. After serving in the navy during World War II, he worked for Joseph P. Kennedy as assistant manager of the Chicago Merchandise Mart. He married Kennedy's daughter Eunice in 1953, served as a liaison for his brother-in-law Senator John F. Kennedy during the 1960 presidential campaign, and was named the first director of the Peace Corps in 1961. Shriver was named director of the Office of Economic Opportunity (OEO) on February 1, 1964. In February 1968 Shriver left the OEO to accept an appointment as ambassador to France. He continued in that position under President NIXON. He resigned in March 1970 and took up private law practice in Washington and New York.

On August 8, 1972, Shriver was nominated by the Democratic National Committee as the party's candidate for vice president. He replaced Senator THOMAS F. EAGLETON (D-Mo.), who withdrew as the nominee because of the controversy that arose after the disclosure that he had been hospitalized three times in the 1960s for psychiatric treatment. Democratic presidential candidate Senator GEORGE MCGOVERN (D-S.D.) had named Shriver as his choice on August 5, after Senator EDMUND S. MUSKIE (D-Me.) declined an offer to become McGovern's running mate.

Shriver accepted the nomination with "gratitude and joy." In his acceptance speech he stated that he could "already taste the victory." He said he was not embarrassed to be the seventh choice for vice presidential candidate. "Think of the comparison and then you can pity poor Mr. Nixon. His first and only choice was SPIRO AGNEW."

Shriver launched his campaign with an attack on the administration. On August 10 he charged that President Nixon had lost an opportunity for a Vietnam peace settlement when he took office in 1969. Shriver stated: "Nixon had peace handed to him literally in his lap. He blew it." Shriver implied strongly that a 1969 decrease in battlefield activity had signaled North Vietnam's willingness to negotiate a settlement of the war. His statement was quickly rejected by administration officials, but AVERELL HARRIMAN and Cyrus Vance, the two negotiators at the Paris peace talks during the Johnson administration, issued joint statements on August 12 supporting Shriver's assertion.

Ignoring predictions that the Democrats would be routed at the polls in November, Shriver waged an arduous cross-country campaign that focused primarily on maintaining traditional Democratic support for McGovern. In addition to party gatherings, he appeared before labor and college audiences and minority and ethnic groups. His main themes were the state of the economy, unemployment, inflation, and charges against the Nixon administration of special-interest government and of political espionage. He also defended McGovern on the issues of amnesty for Vietnam war resisters and an end to the restrictions on abortion and against the Republican charge of radicalism. The McGovern-Shriver ticket lost by one of the largest electoral and popular margins in U.S. history. Shriver then returned to private life and the practice of international law.

On September 20, 1975, Shriver announced that he was a candidate for the 1976 Democratic presidential nomination. He stated his intention to claim the legacy of his late brother-in-law John F. Kennedy and denied that he was a "stalking horse" for Senator EDWARD M. KENNEDY (D-Mass.), who had said that he would not run in 1976.

The seventh Democrat to declare a candidacy, Shriver was the first to announce that he had qualified for federal matching funds under the 1974 campaign finance law, which required candidates to raise a minimum of $5,000 in sums of $250 or less in 20 states.

In a September 10 speech Shriver advocated putting Americans back to work and "putting the government—as the expression of our common will—on the side of the consumer, the taxpayer, the individual, and the community." He was critical of U.S. foreign policy for having "meddled too much." On January 7, 1976, Shriver issued a 9,000-word economic plan that featured a public service jobs program, tax reductions, tax credits for private employment, and permanent wage-price guidelines.

At the Iowa precinct caucus held on January 19, Shriver garnered only 3.3 percent of the vote. He placed fifth in the New Hampshire primary, third in Mississippi, and third in Illinois. On March 22 he formally withdrew from the race. He asserted that he had achieved remarkable success in light of the handicaps of a late entry into the race, lack of record in elective office or government title, and his reception in some quarters as "nothing more" than a relative by marriage to the Kennedy family. Shriver now resides in Massachusetts. In 1994 he received the Presidential Medal of Freedom.

—FHM

Shultz, George P(ratt)
(1920–   ) *secretary of labor; director, Office of Management and Budget; secretary of the Treasury*

George P. Shultz was born in New York City on December 13, 1920. After receiving a B.A. from Princeton in 1942, Shultz served in the marine corps from 1942 to 1945. He resumed his studies after the war, obtaining his Ph.D. in industrial economics at MIT in 1949. Shultz

taught at MIT from 1946 until 1957, when he was appointed professor of industrial relations at the Graduate School of Business of the University of Chicago. He became dean of the business school in 1962 and remained at that post until 1968, when he left to join President NIXON's cabinet as secretary of labor.

Despite a long academic career, Shultz was no stranger to government. Generally associated with the monetarist "Chicago School" of MILTON FRIEDMAN, Shultz served as an economic adviser to both Republican and Democratic administrations beginning in the mid-1950s. He had been senior staff economist on President Eisenhower's Council of Economic Advisers in 1955–56 and a consultant to the Department of Labor in 1959–60; under Kennedy he served as staff director of a national policy study for the Committee on Economic Development and as a consultant to the President's Advisory Committee on Labor-Management Policy. In the Johnson years he chaired a task force established to review U.S. Employment Service programs. During the same period Shultz produced a steady stream of books, articles, and reports on labor relations.

Shultz's 18-month tenure as secretary of labor coincided with one of the greatest surges of U.S. labor militancy since the immediate postwar period. Directly or indirectly, Shultz involved himself in a six-week East Coast longshoremen's strike, a bitter three-month strike at General Electric, and the March 1970 postal workers' strike, as well as several White House-level bargaining sessions aimed at averting strikes in other industries. Before the postal workers' strike was settled, the National Guard had been sent into New York City to sort the mail, and Shultz had been personally embarrassed by a nationwide rank-and-file rejection of a contract negotiated between union leaders and himself.

This wave of labor militancy jeopardized the entire economic plan of the Nixon administration, which was aimed at deflating the economy and with it the wage push that was held partly responsible for rising prices. As secretary of labor, Shultz was given the assignment of enlisting the trade unions in the fight against inflation. After relatively limited success in this effort, Shultz was appointed in June 1970 to head a study panel on the "blue-collar blues," which attempted to locate the sources of worker discontent.

Under Shultz the Labor Department also became involved in controversies over manpower planning, affirmative action, and union reform. In April 1969 Shultz and other government officials were named in an NAACP lawsuit charging the Nixon administration with failure to enforce equal employment practices. Only three days later Shultz was compelled to publicly defend the administration's $100 million cutback in the funding of the Job Corps, which provided training for unskilled and minority youths.

The Philadelphia Plan, announced by Shultz in July 1969, was a key aspect of the Nixon administration's response to minority criticisms, combining elements of manpower, affirmative action, wage curbs, and union reform in a single stratagem. The plan obliged Philadelphia construction companies with federal contracts to hire a certain quota of minority workers and permitted them to do so at nonunion wage scales. Costly labor settlements in the construction industry and record rates of contract rejections by construction workers were special subjects of concern to Shultz, who called these settlements "disastrous" for the administration's anti-inflation strategy.

Although the U.S. solicitor general ruled that the Philadelphia Plan violated the 1964 Civil Rights Act, a ruling by Attorney General JOHN MITCHELL upheld the constitutionality of the plan in September 1969. In spite of the estrangement of AFL-CIO leaders and "hard-hat" demonstrations across the country, Shultz

in early 1970 warned that if there were not voluntary compliance with the plan, he would extend its provisions to 18 other cities. After a Philadelphia federal court upheld the plan's constitutionality, Shultz in the summer of 1970 announced a similar Washington Plan for the capital. Finally, in February Shultz played a role in the Nixon administration's decision to suspend provisions of the 1934 Davis-Bacon Act, which required union wages to be paid on federal construction projects.

In other important actions promoting direct government involvement in union affairs, Shultz in January 1970 ordered a full-scale Labor Department investigation into the murder of JOSEPH ("JOCK") YABLONSKI, a United Mine Workers (UMW) reform candidate who had been defeated in elections for the union's presidency in December 1969. Two months later Shultz announced a Labor Department suit to void the UMW election results, which ultimately resulted in new, government-supervised elections in 1972 in which UMW president Tony Boyle was unseated by reform candidate Arnold Miller and later indicted for Yablonski's murder.

In June 1970, as part of a larger White House shake-up, President Nixon named Shultz to head the newly created Office of Management and Budget (OMB), which superseded the Bureau of the Budget. In the same move Shultz was appointed presidential adviser. Shultz's appointment to head the OMB marked the beginning of the second phase of Chicago School management of the U.S. economy, in the wake of the Penn Central bankruptcy, the stock market slump, and the corporate liquidity squeeze of May–June 1970, which revealed the dangers inherent in overly rapid deflation and forced the administration and the Federal Reserve Bank into an abrupt about-face in credit policy.

Shultz's move to the OMB did not end his special relationship with labor questions. While appearing more frequently before congressional committees to defend the administration's economic policies, he continued to play a role in opening the construction industry to nonunion labor and preventing costly contract settlements. In July 1971 he called steel industry and union negotiators to the White House on the eve of contract talks in that industry and asked for increases in productivity to justify any wage boosts. In August 1971 Shultz announced a program to limit job promotions for 1.2 million government employees "to get control of wages in the federal government."

In late June 1971 Shultz participated with President Nixon, Federal Reserve Chairman ARTHUR BURNS, and Treasury Secretary JOHN CONNALLY in the so-called Camp David I meeting on national and international economic problems. Although the U.S. economy was showing signs of recovery from the 1969–70 recession, the growing U.S. balance-of-payments deficit was putting heavy pressure on the dollar overseas. In May 1971 the countries of the Common Market jointly floated their currencies, urging the United States to "put its own house in order." Although the administration's economic outlook was in rapid transition and the Chicago School's ideas, which had shown little efficacy, were losing hegemony in policy, Shultz still prevailed over urgings for a more activist intervention—specifically from Secretary Connally—with a "steady as you go" approach. He argued that the immediate crisis was the result of temporary phenomena and would correct itself without precipitous action. While Shultz prevailed in this meeting, it marked the last significant policy move influenced by Chicago School ideas prior to President Nixon's conversion to Keynesianism in August 1971.

Between June and August 1971 it became clear that the administration plan was failing. Unemployment persisted at high levels, inflation did not subside, and, most importantly, the

U.S. balance-of-payments deficit deteriorated still further. Thus, on August 14–15 Shultz and Connally returned to Camp David for a second weekend conference on the economy with President Nixon. On Sunday evening, August 15, Nixon announced on national television a complete policy turnabout toward Keynesian, statist, and interventionist solutions. Nixon's program, which he called the "New Economic Policy" (NEP), included a 90-day wage and price freeze, the end of dollar convertibility into gold, a 10 percent surcharge on imports, a $4.7 billion budget cut, layoffs of federal employees, and tax incentives for investment. As the "Chicago" economist most disposed to go along with this policy turnabout, Shultz stayed on as OMB director, whereas monetarist Hendryk S. Houthakker left the Council of Economic Advisers in mid-July, and CEA chairman PAUL W. MCCRACKEN followed him at the end of the year.

Although Shultz had been a consistent opponent of wage and price controls, seeing them as unnecessary and potentially harmful government interference with the laws of the market, President Nixon appointed him to the Cost of Living Council, established to oversee the control apparatus. As one of the administration's main links to the labor movement, Shultz also was appointed to the National Commission on Productivity, established to revive U.S. industry's lagging competitive position in the world market. In late September he met with Pacific coast shippers and longshoremen's representatives in an effort to settle a three-month dock strike paralyzing West Coast shipping. Shultz also appeared before various congressional committees to report on the progress of the NEP.

In May 1972 Shultz succeeded John Connally as secretary of the Treasury. In this capacity his previous intensive involvement in labor questions gave way to the broader concerns of federal debt management, international monetary reform, and defense of the successive phases of the NEP in Congress. In September 1972 Shultz informed Congress that the expiration of federal debt ceiling legislation would leave the government insolvent before the end of fiscal 1973 if an additional $15.6 billion in debt were not approved. A few days later he stated that President Nixon, if reelected, would increase taxes in his second term. Shultz warned, "If you insist on pushing spending up, it has to come out of the American people sooner or later . . . it will come out first in inflation and then we will have to be facing up to this tax issue."

After Nixon defeated GEORGE MCGOVERN for a second term, Shultz was retained at his Treasury post, and White House press secretary RONALD ZIEGLER said that Shultz "will be the focal point and the overall coordinator of the entire economic policy decision-making process, both domestically and internationally." Shultz also was appointed to head a new cabinet-level Council on Economic Policy. To underline his admission to Nixon's closest circle of advisers, Shultz was given an office in the White House.

For the rest of his tenure at the Treasury, Shultz dealt with the two major problems: administration of economic controls and a renewed dollar crisis that broke out in February 1973. In early January Shultz had met with AFL-CIO president GEORGE MEANY, and immediately thereafter the so-called Phase Two price controls begun in November 1971 were abolished and the apparatus for overseeing them dismantled. Phase Three of the administration's program involved voluntary, or "jawboned," wage and price controls based on informal pressure.

In the first months of 1973, with the lifting of all but essential controls, inflation once again took off at unprecedented rates. Meat prices had been a sensitive issue through 1971–72, and Shultz had earlier abolished all import quotas on meat to assure an adequate supply to the U.S. market. With a dramatic rise in meat prices, President Nixon on March 29 reimposed price controls on meat, and both he and Shultz publicly urged labor to retain the 5.5 percent wage guidelines of Phase Two. Shultz persuaded the commercial banks to forgo a hike in the prime interest rate. In late May he announced a possible excise tax on gasoline to curb demand as a result of sporadic gasoline shortages that anticipated the oil crisis of late 1973 and early 1974.

Shultz's attention to the problems of the domestic economy, however, was increasingly diverted to the international arena. Shultz was a key figure in a complex U.S. strategy to simultaneously prevent a strong European front on international economic questions and to seek economic détente with the Soviet Union. A massive speculative surge against the dollar in February 1973 had compelled Shultz, after consultations with other officials, to announce a 10 percent devaluation of the dollar below the 1971 adjustment. The weakness of the dollar on Western European markets was such that foreign governments were obliged to suspend currency trading for two weeks while international monetary officials convened in Brussels and Paris in early March to resolve the crisis. Representing the United States at the Paris meeting, Shultz, who was seen as a welcome change from the previous "strong-arm" tactics of Connally at such international meetings, rejected European proposals for reform but indicated a cooperative attitude by the United States. The Paris meeting abolished once and for all the fixed-rate exchange system in effect since World War II, and all currencies floated.

From Paris Shultz, who had been appointed head of the East-West Trade Policy Committee on March 6, flew to Moscow for trade discussions with Soviet officials. Before leaving Paris he briefed French finance minister Giscard d'Estaing on Nixon's forthcoming trade policy legislation. In May Shultz presented Nixon's trade bill to the House Ways and Means Committee, promptly drawing the fire of French foreign minister Michel Jobert, who saw the trade policies as an attack on the Common Market and the European Economic Community's (EEC) Common Agricultural Policy. On June 22 Shultz signed a series of trade protocols with the Soviet Union.

Further U.S. inflation once again brought Shultz back to the domestic arena. On June 13, 1973, he admitted that Phase Three voluntary controls had been a failure and announced a new 60-day price freeze. In late August, just before the publication of the latest wholesale price index figures, Shultz warned against "astounding" price increases in the wake of the freeze. August prices for certain agricultural products did in fact show increases of over 100 percent on an annual basis. In early September, echoing public sentiment, Shultz stated that the United States had been "burned" in the massive grain deal with the Soviet Union and linked the deal to runaway American food prices.

In the fall of 1973 Shultz resumed his global travels on behalf of U.S. economic policy. He represented the United States at the Tokyo meeting of the General Agreement on Trade and Tariffs (GATT) on September 12–14. On September 24–28 Shultz represented the United States at the Nairobi meeting of the International Monetary Fund (IMF), where reform of the system and results of the new "floating rates" were assessed. From Nairobi Shultz flew to Moscow for further trade talks and predicted $1.5 billion in Soviet-American trade for 1973. From Moscow Shultz went on to Belgrade for talks with Yugoslav officials.

The Yom Kippur War of October 1973 and the subsequent quadrupling of oil prices placed, according to some observers, an unbearable strain on an already shaky inter-

national monetary system. In November 1973 Shultz met secretly with world monetary officials in Tours, France, for further discussions on monetary reform. In January 1974 Shultz led the U.S. delegation to another IMF meeting, where his call for a rollback of "staggering" oil prices was characterized as "naive" by Arab officials.

Shultz's remaining months at the Treasury—he stepped down in April 1974—were spent in efforts to prepare the U.S. economy for the overall effects of the oil price increase, to avert a recession, and to consolidate the U.S. trade position. At the end of January, after President Nixon ended the so-called Interest Equalization Tax (IET) imposed by Lyndon Johnson to curb U.S. overseas investment, Shultz announced that abolition of the IET had been possible because of renewed dollar strength. In a February 4 report to Congress, Shultz argued that the dramatic increase in 1973 oil company profits had to be viewed against low profits in the preceding years. On February 14, when an international energy conference was held in Washington to discuss the oil emergency, Shultz repeated his call for a reduction in oil prices and urged both developed countries and oil exporters to provide increased aid to non-OPEC developing countries. Earlier Shultz had issued a joint statement with Secretary of State HENRY KISSINGER deploring the House's defeat of a $1.5 billion U.S. contribution to the International Development Agency. He also appeared before Senate committee hearings on the administration's trade bill, opposing the proposed curb on trade with the Soviet Union that tied most favored nation status to Soviet treatment of internal dissidents and Soviet Jews desiring to emigrate.

When Shultz announced his resignation in March 1974 for personal reasons, he was the last original member of President Nixon's cabinet. Although he denied any relationship between his resignation and the Watergate scandal that was slowly enveloping the administration, Shultz was involved in July 1974 House Judiciary Committee hearings on the administration's use of the Internal Revenue Service, a branch of the Treasury Department, for harassment of political opponents.

After leaving his post at the Treasury, Shultz became an executive vice president of the Bechtel Corp. in San Francisco and also taught at Stanford University. From 1982 to 1989 he served as secretary of state in the administration of RONALD REAGAN. In 1989 he was awarded the Medal of Freedom. He is currently the Thomas W. and Susan B. Ford Distinguished Fellow at the Hoover Institution.

—LG

Simon, William E(dward)

(1927–2000) *deputy secretary of the Treasury; secretary of the Treasury*

After receiving his B.A. from Lafayette College in 1952, Simon spent his early career in a series of Wall Street firms, and from 1964 until 1972 he served as director of the municipal and government bond department at Salomon Brothers, an investment bank in which he was a senior partner. Simon's conservative views and extensive knowledge of capital markets were decisive factors in his appointment as deputy secretary of the Treasury, a post he assumed in early 1973.

Simon's first year in government was spent in dealing with the incipient energy crisis. Almost immediately he was named chairman of an interdepartmental Oil Policy Committee, established to confront the first phase of oil and gasoline shortages. His initial public prominence came during a clash with the the Federal Trade Commission (FTC) in September 1973, when he asked the FTC to withdraw its antitrust suit against eight major U.S. oil companies, asserting that the FTC's charges of

company collusion were false. Shortly thereafter Simon warned that U.S. oil imports had reached a record level in 1973, reflecting the country's growing dependency on foreign oil since it ceased to be a net exporter of oil in the mid-1960s.

Simon's role in energy policy entered a new phase in the wake of the October 1973 Yom Kippur War, the subsequent quadrupling of oil prices, and the OPEC organized boycott on oil shipments to the United States. Simon, who became known as the NIXON administration's "energy czar," replaced former Colorado governor JOHN LOVE as top White House energy official in December 1973. In what many saw as a high-level shake-up in which Simon played a role behind the scenes, Love, who had been criticized as ineffectual, resigned, complaining of the Nixon administration's lack of concern about fuel allocation and citing difficulties in even getting to see Nixon or other White House officials about these problems.

Simon's appointment signaled a new awareness of the gravity of the oil crisis, and Simon was made head of the Emergency Energy Action Group, a new cabinet-level committee, as well as director of a new Federal Energy Office. Simon moved quickly to implement tough government controls over the use of gasoline, announcing the administration's desire to reduce private U.S. gasoline consumption by 30 percent in the first three months of 1974. When fuel allocation plans were announced by Simon in mid-December, top priority went to the Defense Department, essential community services, farms, industry, and public transportation. The plans aimed at curtailing private auto use. At the end of the year Simon called for a 10-gallon-per-week limit on private drivers.

In April 1974 Simon became secretary of the Treasury, and his activities turned increasingly to the financial monetary effects, often referred to as "petrodollar recycling," of the sudden sharp increases in Middle Eastern oil revenues. The United States, Japan, and Europe were engaged in heavy competition in the Middle East to solidify political, commercial, and financial relationships with the newly rich Arab states. Thus, in July 1974 Simon toured the Middle East for the U.S. government. His first stop was Egypt, where he negotiated a tax equalization treaty. He also obtained an agreement permitting the operation of four U.S. banks that under the Nasser regime had been expelled in 1957. Terms of U.S. aid to Egypt also were discussed. From Egypt Simon flew to Saudi Arabia and Kuwait, announcing on July 20 a U.S.-Saudi economic agreement. Simon's main concern was to induce the Saudis and Kuwaitis to place their petrodollar surpluses in U.S. bank deposits and in U.S. government securities, particularly Treasury bills, while discouraging them from actual direct investment in U.S. corporations, where they would have direct control over policy. Although a Kuwaiti spokesman asked after Simon's visit why the OPEC countries should help the United States with its problems when it had done nothing for the Arab states, Saudi Arabian oil minister Sheik Ahmed Zaki al-Yamani announced that the bulk of recycled petrodollars would be invested in U.S. capital markets.

Another problem confronting Simon in his first year as secretary of the Treasury was the role of gold in international and domestic transactions. In the spring of 1974 he had reaffirmed the traditional Treasury position of hostility to gold as an international resource. In May 1974 he met with Dutch finance minister Willem Duisenberg to discuss European proposals permitting central banks to sell their gold reserves at the market price instead of the much lower official price. Simon also was in favor of the ownership of gold by private citizens, and when in the summer of 1974 Congress repealed the 40-year ban on private

gold ownership, Simon announced a 2 million-ounce sale for early January 1975. The gold sales were seen as part of an overall U.S. strategy to fully demonetize gold.

Prior to the onset of the 1974–75 recession, Simon was a spokesman for austerity, fiscal constraint, and the maintenance of stable capital markets. Although he had assured adequate flows of petrodollars into U.S. commercial banks and government securities, the accelerating inflation of mid-1974 was threatening to bring the state and municipal bond markets to a standstill. Thus, in August 1974 Simon met with Citibank chairman WALTER WRISTON and Federal Reserve Bank chairman ARTHUR BURNS to arrange for "floating rate bonds," or bonds whose interest rates could be periodically adjusted for inflation throughout the life of the bond. In late August Simon was appointed by President FORD to the Council on Wage and Price Stability, established as part of the administration's short-lived and ill-fated "WIN" program to fight inflation. In late September Simon was appointed to a new 14-member Economic Policy Board and was identified by one commentator as the Ford administration's "principal spokesman on economic policy matters."

Simon continued the general U.S. policy, begun under his predecessor at the Treasury, GEORGE SHULTZ, of pressuring both Europe and the Eastern bloc with U.S. economic weapons and thereby keeping international policy initiative in the hands of the United States. In September 1974 he participated in a secret meeting of the major powers on world financial problems and later in the same month met again with heads of the major capitalist powers to develop a concerted plan to cope with the world energy crisis. Simon's solution was a plan to establish a $25 billion lending facility, or "safety net," to help industrial nations pay their oil deficits, but under conditions set by international bodies with preponderant U.S.

influence. This proposal marked a shift from Simon's earlier position that the private capital markets were capable of financing the oil deficits themselves.

During the same period Simon was a key figure in the Ford administration's use of the "food weapon" for international political leverage. After a meeting of Simon, Secretary of Agriculture EARL BUTZ, and Ford in early October 1974, the U.S. government abruptly canceled contracts for $500 million in grain sales to the Soviet Union. A week later, in Moscow, Simon represented the United States at the second meeting of the U.S.-USSR Economic and Trade Council, where he discussed the grain situation with Soviet leaders. Returning to Washington, Simon announced a limited grain sale to the Soviet Union in exchange for Soviet promises to make no further purchases. Pressure over grain sales, combined with U.S. attempts through the Jackson Amendment to link most favored nation status to Soviet treatment of internal dissidents, pushed the Soviet Union in January 1975 to abrogate the 1972 U.S.-USSR trade agreement.

The 1974–75 recession, which was the most severe contraction of industrial production since 1929–33, greatly enhanced Simon's role as a spokesman for austerity and stabilization on both the international and domestic fronts. In mid-January 1975 the Committee of 10 of the International Monetary Fund (IMF) approved Simon's proposed $25 billion oil "safety net," which effectively made access to oil credits dependent on U.S. approval of domestic austerity measures by governments, such as Italy's, making use of the facility. Simon also had a hand in increasing U.S. contributions to other international agencies, such as the $1.5 billion additional contribution to the Inter-American Development Bank and a $1 billion lending facility established by the World Bank to help poor nations finance their oil deficits. In

each case the United States was acquiring more direct leverage in the domestic economic policies of foreign countries.

Simon also negotiated international monetary policy in preparation for the November 1975 Rambouillet summit of the major Western industrial nations. The major problem confronting the summit was an open rift between the United States and France about the role of gold as an international reserve. The United States, as Simon's repeated statements had made clear, continued to favor the elimination of gold as a reserve asset. Countries like France, on the other hand, with substantial holdings, wanted to sell off their gold at the market price, at the time $150 an ounce, instead of the official rate of $42.22. In the compromise between Simon and French finance minister Jean-Pierre Fourcade, both the IMF and individual central banks agreed to sell off portions of their gold holdings, thus furthering the U.S. policy of demonetizing gold; on the other hand, in keeping with French wishes, they were able to do so at the market and not the official price. Finally, in an additional concession to the French position, it was agreed that a major portion of the IMF's receipts from gold sales would be given to the less-developed countries.

The less-developed countries, or LDCs, constituted a third arena for Simon's international activities. In September 1975 a two-week meeting of the UN Commission on Trade and Development (UNCTAD) witnessed a major confrontation between spokesmen for the LDCs, who demanded a reorganization of the world economy to benefit the poor nations, and the advanced capitalist countries, who resisted such demands. As the major U.S. representative at the UNCTAD meeting along with Secretary of State HENRY KISSINGER, Simon's strategy was to drive a wedge between the developing countries and those Western European nations who were more sympathetic to the developing countries' call for a "new international economic order." Simon was concerned about developing countries' calls for a moratorium or outright cancellation of billions of dollars of LDC debt, which he felt would wreak havoc in Western capital markets. Consequently, with Kissinger Simon floated a plan whereby the United States would agree to large-scale debt relief for the developing countries if Western Europe and Japan, which held over $100 billion from long-standing, U.S. balance-of-payments deficits, would in turn agree to wipe out this "dollar overhang." Simon and Kissinger thereby effectively defused any potential developing countries–European alliance.

Simon became an economic ambassador-at-large for U.S. international policy. He visited Rome in March 1976 and informed the Italian government that further loans to Italy would be dependent on a domestic austerity program, without which any aid would be tantamount to "throwing money down the drain." In May 1976 he met with Chilean government officials for economic talks and a month later consulted with the Spanish minister of finance on possible aid to post-Franco Spain. As the U.S. representative at the June 1976 meeting of the Organization for Economic Cooperation and Development, Simon remarked that "preaching moderate growth is like trying to sell leprosy."

Simon's role in domestic policy was no less oriented toward austerity. With ALAN GREENSPAN, who emerged as the top economist of the Ford administration, Simon increasingly came to feel that the U.S. economy had to turn away from massive government spending to solve its long-term structural problems. Both Simon and Greenspan began to advocate a shift of tax burdens away from corporations to promote capital goods investment, which was the weak element in the recovery of industrial production beginning in March 1975. Simon felt that

federal taxation of both corporate profits and income from dividends and sales of stock was an impediment to capital investment, a "double taxation" of enterprise. He felt that a reduction of federal spending would reduce the need for tax revenues and alleviate the competition between private and public borrowers in the nation's capital markets.

In January 1975 Simon consequently expressed his dismay at the anticipated federal deficit for that year. Several weeks later the House Ways and Means Committee reflected similar concerns in rejecting a $109 billion increase in the federal debt ceiling, which Simon himself had requested to accommodate anticipated government spending. Simon's worries that federal borrowing would crowd out private industry in the capital markets were criticized by economist HERBERT STEIN and former undersecretary of the Treasury PAUL VOLCKER and indeed proved to be exaggerated in the 1975–76 period largely because of stagnant corporate investment.

In the summer of 1975 Simon continued in his public utterances to emphasize the need for price stability, greater discipline in government spending, the dangers of crowding out, and a new theme, tied to stagnant corporate investment, of a "capital gap" confronting U.S. industry. In May 1975 he told the Senate Finance Committee that "we need to get back to price stability in this country, or we'll go down the drain the way Great Britain is going now." Later in the same month he warned that the Social Security system would be bankrupt by 1981 if it continued to run high deficits. He attacked the food stamp program as "a well-known haven for chiselers and rip-off artists." He stated that the main obstacle to solving the energy crisis was the federal government itself and cited "problems created by the Clean Air Act, the moratorium on coal leasing . . . [and] . . . price and supply regulation affecting oil and gas" as examples.

Simon's most controversial role in domestic economic policy, however, was in the New York City fiscal crisis of 1975. Simon, with Greenspan, President Ford, and Federal Reserve Board chairman Burns, opposed federal aid to New York City through most of the crisis, reversing or modifying their position only as it became clear that the national and international repercussions of a default would be impossible to control. In May 1975 Simon rejected an initial New York City plea for aid, stating that "not only is the federal government's legal authority to provide financial assistance limited, but also that such assistance would not be appropriate." Several days later he met with Ford, Vice President NELSON ROCKEFELLER, New York City mayor ABRAHAM BEAME and New York governor HUGH CAREY to discuss the crisis, and he once again rejected pleas for federal guarantees of city bonds. Because of his eight years' experience in the state and municipal bond market at Salomon Brothers, Simon was generally seen as a spokesman for Wall Street hostility to government profligacy and to the social services financed by government borrowing.

Throughout the crisis the major issue was whether the federal government would underwrite New York City's municipal paper, thereby allowing the city to return to the capital markets from which its de facto bankruptcy excluded it. To circumvent this problem the Municipal Assistance Corp. (MAC), or "Big Mac" as it was widely known, and the Emergency Financial Control Board (EFCB) were created to issue further bonds and supervise the city's finances. In spite of this reorganization, Simon rejected the request of EFCB member FELIX ROHATYN, of the Lazard Frères investment bank, for federal underwriting of MAC bonds. Simon used the New York City crisis to underline his capital gap analysis, emphasizing their relationship in congressional testimony on the city fiscal question. On September 16,

just back from the UNCTAD conference on developing countries' debt cancellation, Simon reiterated his view that a New York City default would have no grave consequences and that U.S. capital markets were "capable of handling a default with no more than moderate and relatively short-lived disruption." Simon asserted to the contrary that "there is a serious risk that the capital and credit markets would react adversely" if the federal government acted to prevent default.

Shortly thereafter, however, Simon began to shift his position when numerous New York City bankers warned of impending difficulties in the sale of New York state bonds if the city defaulted on its debts. Simon admitted that default could have a "domino effect" on the capital markets. To meet this danger, he elaborated a three-point plan, calling for an interest moratorium on the city's short-term notes, a temporary increase in the New York state sales tax, and a government study to determine the possibility of transferring local and state welfare burdens to the federal level. At the end of September Simon told Congress that "unprecedented" government borrowing was drawing funds away from housing and business investment, and in early October he once again opposed federal aid to New York City in testimony before the Senate Finance Committee. Only in November, when default had been narrowly averted by last-minute municipal trade union purchases of short-term city paper, did Simon, along with Ford, Greenspan, and Burns, come around to the view—underlined by the personal intervention of West German chancellor Helmut Schmidt—that the effects of a default by New York City on the capital markets could produce an international financial panic.

Simon's high political visibility as a crisis manager led many commentators to see him as a possible running mate for Gerald Ford in the 1976 election, but such speculation proved unfounded. At the end of his term at the Treasury, Simon became president and trustee of the nonprofit John M. Olin Foundation, as well as a consultant to several Wall Street firms. He was treasurer of the U.S. Olympic Committee from 1977 to 1981 and president from 1981 to 1985. From 1985 to 1997 he chaired the U.S. Olympic Foundation. In 1987 he founded WSGP International, Inc. He died on June 3, 2000, of pulmonary fibrosis.

—LG

Sirica, John J(oseph)
(1904–1992) *district court judge*

John J. Sirica was born on March 19, 1904, in Waterbury, Connecticut. The son of a tubercular Italian immigrant, Sirica spent his childhood wandering with his family throughout the South in search of warm climates and business opportunities. As a boy Sirica helped support his family by greasing cars, waiting tables, and selling newspapers. After two unsuccessful attempts at law school, Sirica received his LL.B. from Georgetown University in 1926, where he supported himself as a boxing coach. From 1930 to 1934 Sirica served the Hoover administration as an assistant U.S. attorney in Washington and then went into private practice. In 1949 he joined the prestigious Washington firm of Hogan and Hartson as chief trial attorney. Eight years later, as reward for service in five GOP presidential campaigns, President Eisenhower appointed Sirica to the U.S. District Court for Washington, D.C.

Sirica's work on the district bench earned him a reputation among Washington lawyers as a tough, forthright man of "impeccable integrity," although it was generally conceded that he was not a profound legal scholar. Sirica tried a wide range of cases, many of which were highly complex and controversial. In 1959 he presided over the contempt-of-Congress trial of Teamster vice president Frank W. Brewster, and in 1960 over a 10-month-long, $90 million antitrust action brought against 23 railroads by a Kansas City trucking firm. Because of his firm law-and-order stance and his tendency to give the longest sentences allowed under law, Sirica acquired the nickname "Maximum John." His command of legal niceties and technicalities, however, was sometimes questioned, and he was reversed more frequently than any other judge in the District of Columbia.

By virtue of seniority Sirica became chief judge of the U.S. district court in April 1971. The duties of his new office being largely administrative, he tried few cases and looked forward to his impending retirement on his 70th birthday. His plans changed, however, following the June 1972 arrest of seven undercover operatives of President NIXON's reelection committee at Democratic National Committee headquarters in the Watergate. As the investigation of the incident proceeded, a growing body of evidence suggested that many close associates of Nixon were involved in a wide range of improprieties and illegal actions. Allegations were made that the president himself was personally involved and directly responsible.

Sirica was quick to grasp the full dimensions of the developing Watergate scandal. When the case of the original seven defendants came before his court in January 1973, he did not assign it to any of the 15 judges under his supervision but decided to try it himself. He took that action because as a Republican he would be less vulnerable to charges of political bias, and because unlike other judges who had heavy caseloads, he would have more time to devote to the case.

Impatient at times with the ineffectiveness of the prosecutors and the evasive answers of the defendants, Sirica frequently took over the questioning himself, often refusing to accept the answers he received. When defendant BER-

NARD L. BARKER said that he did not know who had sent him expense money in a plain envelope, Sirica snapped: "Well, I'm sorry, but I don't believe you." When HUGH W. SLOAN JR., the reelection committee's treasurer, testified that he had given $199,000 to defendant G. GORDON LIDDY without knowing what the money was for, yet was not cross-examined, Sirica interrogated Sloan himself with the jury out of the courtroom. On another occasion Sirica dismissed as "ridiculous, frankly," the claim by defendant JAMES MCCORD's attorney that the bugging scheme would help detect plans to incite violence against Republicans in the 1972 campaign: "Whether the jury will believe you is another story." The jury did not, finding both McCord and Liddy guilty of burglary, wiretapping, and attempted bugging.

Going beyond normal procedure, Sirica let the convicted men know that the severity of their sentences would depend heavily on the degree to which they cooperated with their probation officers and investigators still probing the Watergate crime. Sirica's tactics bore fruit on March 20, 1973, several hours before the sentences of the Watergate burglars were due. On that day Sirica received a letter from McCord alleging that there had been "political pressures" on the Watergate defendants to plead guilty, that perjury had been committed, and that "others higher than Liddy" were involved in a massive cover-up. Sirica then deferred sentencing McCord but kept pressure on the other convicted conspirators to talk by meting out provisional sentences of up to 40 years. Promising to review the sentences later, Sirica recommended cooperation with the grand jury and Senator SAM ERVIN's investigating committee, suggesting that such cooperation would be weighed in the final sentencing.

McCord's letter was the final blow for the cover-up. White House counsel JOHN W. DEAN, who had helped coordinate the cover-up, subsequently resigned and testified to

Nixon's prior knowledge of the conspiracy at Senate hearings. JEB S. MAGRUDER, former deputy director of the Committee to Re-Elect the President (CREEP), admitted involvement in the Watergate break-in and cover-up and implicated former attorney general JOHN N. MITCHELL.

Sirica's most dramatic role came later in the year, when he ruled on whether Nixon would be allowed to retain tapes subpoenaed by special prosecutor ARCHIBALD COX pertaining to White House conversations about Watergate. Drawing on Anglo-American jurisprudence, the *Federalist Papers*, and particularly the rulings of Chief Justice John Marshall in the 1807 Burr treason trial, Sirica ordered Nixon on August 29, 1973, to relinquish the secret tapes for a private hearing by himself. In the process Sirica swept aside Nixon's claim that the doctrine of executive privilege placed the president beyond the reaches of the courts and the law. Watergate, in Sirica's view, was a criminal case, one that would not be short-circuited "simply because it is the president of the United States who holds the evidence."

Carving out what he called a "middle ground" between the question of privilege and wholesale delivery of the tapes to the grand jury, Sirica said that he was willing to recognize the validity of a privilege "based on the need to protect presidential privacy," but that it was up to the courts to decide whether such a privilege had been properly claimed. Sirica assigned to himself responsibility for listening to the tapes in camera and deciding what parts should be delivered to the grand jury. Sirica's decision was widely applauded as a "sensible compromise" between the arguments of Cox and presidential counsellor CHARLES A WRIGHT. Although the White House appealed the decision, Sirica's opinion was upheld by the circuit court of appeals, which observed on October 12, 1973, that the president "does not embody the nation's sovereignty" and "is not above the law's commands." However, Sirica was informed by White House counsel J. FRED BUZHARDT, following the president's dismissal of Cox on October 20, 1973, that two of the nine tapes were "nonexistent" and that a conversation of Nixon with aide H. R. HALDEMAN was marred by an 18-minute gap. Sirica then ordered the original tapes submitted to him for safe-keeping. On November 26, 1973, the White House turned over to Sirica the subpoenaed tapes along with a document analyzing the tapes and outlining claims of executive privilege for some of the material.

Convinced that legal procedures were well in motion to get at the Watergate truths, Sirica resentenced the convicted burglars on November 9, 1973, to relatively light terms, mostly to time already served. Sirica played his third major role in the Watergate affair in October 1974, when he chose to preside over the cover-up trial of Mitchell, Haldeman, JOHN EHRLICHMAN, ROBERT MARDIAN, and Kenneth Parkinson. Again, declaring that he would pursue the "truth" rather than adhere to "strict rules of evidence," Sirica played an activist role, although he came under heated criticism for making "gratuitous remarks" regarding the defendants' characters. On January 1, 1975, Haldeman, Ehrlichman, and Mitchell were found guilty, and each was sentenced by Sirica to a prison term of 20 months to five years.

Sirica retired from full-time duty in 1986. He died in 1992.

—JAN

Sisco, Joseph J(ohn)
(1919–2004) *assistant secretary of state for Near Eastern and South Asian affairs; undersecretary of state for political affairs*

Born on October 31, 1919, the son of Italian immigrants, Joseph J. Sisco grew up in Chicago and attended Knox College, graduating with

honors in 1941. After serving in the infantry in the Pacific during World War II, he attended the University of Chicago, receiving a Ph.D. as a specialist in Soviet studies in 1950. Sisco joined the State Department in 1951 and was assigned to the Office of United Nations Affairs. In 1958 he was appointed deputy director of the Office of United Nations Political and Security Affairs. He became assistant secretary for international organization affairs seven years later. Sisco also served on the U.S. delegation to the UN General Assembly from 1952 to 1968. He worked in close harmony with Ambassador ARTHUR J. GOLDBERG during the Six-Day War in June 1967. When Goldberg left government service in 1968, Sisco became the chief U.S. negotiator in the Middle East.

Sisco was promoted in January 1969 to assistant secretary of state for Near Eastern and South Asian affairs. He quickly formulated a position paper that became the basis for the NIXON administration's initial Middle Eastern policy. Sisco's policy had several clear-cut objectives, foremost among these the containment of the USSR's rising influence in the area. Equally important, the Arab states had to be convinced of the administration's impartiality. Israel had to be coaxed into withdrawing from occupied Arab lands, with only "insubstantial" border changes. The United States therefore had to take a direct hand in arranging a "genuine" peace, and the USSR had to be persuaded to join in this effort. During 1969 and 1970 Sisco attempted to implement these ideas.

HENRY KISSINGER and Sisco "disagreed sharply" over the direction of U.S. policy during the 1971 India-Pakistani war. Suspecting that India intended to dismember West Pakistan as well as detach the eastern part, Kissinger wanted the United States "to tilt in favor of Pakistan," according to columnist JACK ANDERSON. Sisco disagreed, arguing that India's ambitions were limited to guaranteeing a free and independent Bangladesh. Sisco predicted a short war, with little chance of intervention by China or Russia, and argued for a policy of cool rhetoric and calm behavior. Although Sisco lost the battle, he reluctantly agreed to present Kissinger's policy to the press.

Following the outbreak of the Yom Kippur War in October 1973, Sisco joined in Kissinger's "step-by-step" diplomacy in the Middle East. Accompanying Kissinger's shuttle between the various Arab capitals and Tel Aviv, Sisco helped work out the disengagement agreement, which called for an Israeli withdrawal from the west bank of the Suez Canal. Although the agreement was criticized by many for demanding harsh concessions from Israel, it did mark the beginning of a new U.S. relationship with the Arab world and a breakthrough in establishing future Arab-Israeli agreements.

Although Sisco had intended to leave public service in early 1974, he agreed to postpone his retirement to become undersecretary of state for political affairs. During his last year in office he attempted to mediate the Greek-Turkish dispute over Cyprus. Eventually a full-scale war was prevented, but not before Congress cut off most U.S. military aid to Turkey.

In February 1976 Sisco retired from the State Department to assume the presidency of American University in Washington, D.C. He served American University until 1980. In 1981 he joined Sisco Associates. He died of complications from diabetes in 2004.

—JAN

Sloan, Hugh, Jr.

(1940–   ) *treasurer, Committee to Re-Elect the President*

Hugh Sloan Jr. was born in Princeton, New Jersey, on November 1, 1940. Sloan, the son of a vice president of the St. Regis Paper Co., graduated from the Hotchkiss School and Princeton University. After service in the army he joined the Republican Congressional Campaign Committee. Sloan rose rapidly in the committee structure, and in 1968 he assumed the post of finance director for the upcoming presidential campaign. After the election he became assistant to the president's appointments secretary, DWIGHT CHAPIN. In early 1971 Sloan joined the Committee to Re-Elect the President (CREEP) and in February 1972 was named its treasurer.

On March 30, 1972, at a meeting attended by JEB STUART MAGRUDER and FREDERICK LARUE, JOHN MITCHELL approved G. GORDON LIDDY's "Gemstone Plan" for political spying. Two days later Magruder told Hugh Sloan that Liddy was authorized to draw up to $250,000 for his political intelligence project. Sloan, unsure of his responsibilities, asked MAURICE STANS, CREEP Finance Committee chairman and Sloan's immediate superior, about the validity of Magruder's request. Stans checked with John Mitchell, who told him that Sloan should make the payment to Liddy. When Sloan questioned Stans about the purpose of the payments, Stans told him, "I do not want to know about it and you do not want to know about it."

In the early days following the foiled break-in at the Democratic National Campaign headquarters in the Watergate, Sloan grew fearful that CREEP was violating the law with its cash disbursements. He reported his fears to JOHN EHRLICHMAN. Nixon's adviser refused to investigate the matter. In June Sloan made his final report to Stans on the cash disbursements of the pre-April contributions. Eventually the money passed through various CREEP officials into the hands of the Watergate burglars as payment for their activities and as "support money" for their silence. On June 23, at HERBERT KALMBACH's

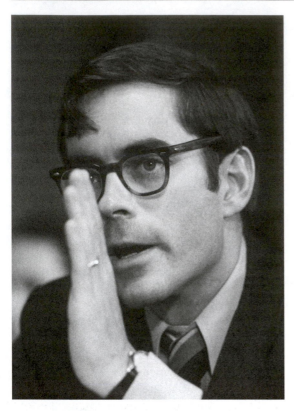

Hugh Sloan Jr. testifies before the Senate Watergate committee, June 6, 1973. *(Bettman/ CORBIS)*

urging, Sloan destroyed the cash book used to prepare his report.

During July various officials connected with CREEP suggested Sloan commit perjury by reporting that he had given only a small amount of money to Liddy instead of the quarter million dollars actually authorized. When Sloan refused to take part in the cover-up, he was forced to resign. On July 20 he met with his lawyers and the prosecutors and told them the whole story of his involvement with CREEP, including the efforts by CREEP officials to silence him.

As the various Watergate trials and hearings progressed from 1973 to 1974, the money Sloan received and disbursed was traced to various sources and destinations. For instance, the $199,000 Sloan gave Liddy came from an original fund that included $30,000 that ROBERT VESCO had given to Maurice Stans, hoping to stave off a Securities and Exchange Commission investigation into his finances. The Liddy money also included $89,000 in illegal campaign contributions that had been "laundered" in Mexico. Sloan disbursed $50,000 to Alexander M. Lahler Jr. of the Maryland Republican Party to inflate the proceeds from a SPIRO AGNEW dinner to make the event look more successful to the voting public and the media than it was. He also provided $10,000 for an anti–GEORGE WALLACE campaign in California that included a $1,200 payment to the American Nazi Party for handing out Wallace leaflets.

Because of his cooperation with the prosecutors and with other investigative bodies and agents, no charges were brought against Hugh Sloan as a result of his activities at CREEP. Sloan, frustrated in his attempts to tell the president that something was wrong and under constant pressure to perjure himself, was the only key official at either CREEP or in the White House who refused to participate in the cover-up. Sloan went on to serve as a trustee of Princeton University. He is a director of the Manulife Financial Corporation.

—SJT

Smith, Gerard C(oad)
(1914–1994) *director, U.S. Arms Control and Disarmament Agency*

Gerard C. Smith was born in New York City on May 4, 1914. Smith received his B.A. from Yale in 1935 and earned his law degree there in 1938. He served with the navy during World War II and after working for various law firms, joined the Atomic Energy Commission in 1950.

During the Kennedy and Johnson administrations he served as counsel to the Washington Center for Foreign Policy Research. In 1969 President NIXON appointed Smith director of the U.S. Arms Control and Disarmament Agency, making him the chief U.S. delegate to all international disarmament conferences, including the Strategic Arms Limitation Talks (SALT) with the Soviet Union.

Smith advocated approaching the talks from a position of strength. During November 1969 he testified before Congress in support of the administration's proposed Safeguard antiballistic missile (ABM) system. He argued that not only would the system be a valuable "bargaining chip" in the talks but also that since the Russians' capability for a surprise attack would be reduced, the ABM would also be "an incentive for a responsible Soviet weapons policy." Before the Senate vote on the ABM in 1970, Smith reportedly convinced several key senators with these arguments, resulting in congressional approval of the system.

When the SALT formally opened in Vienna in April 1970, several main issues separated the two powers. First, the United States sought a comprehensive agreement limiting all forms of offensive and defensive nuclear weaponry, including missile-launching submarines, whereas the Soviets wanted to limit the treaty to defensive arms. The United States demanded on-site inspection, which the Soviet Union refused to consider. Finally, the Soviet Union claimed that the United States sought an unfair advantage by refusing to regard as "strategic," and therefore subject to negotiation, the 500 fighter-bombers based in Western Europe and at sea. The United States replied that the bombers were needed to defend Europe against the Soviets' 700 intermediate-range missiles.

The first breakthrough came in early 1971 when the administration, upon learning that the Soviets would consider limiting their ABM system, dropped its demand for on-site inspections. The major deadlock was broken in May, however, when Nixon announced an agreement to work on limiting the ABM systems. This agreement relieved the delegates temporarily of the need to consider the more difficult questions involving intercontinental ballistic missiles and missiles delivered by bombers and submarines and paved the way for the separate accords that followed.

As Smith brought SALT closer to an agreement, President Nixon flew to Moscow to complete the negotiations and on May 23, 1972, signed the treaties that for the first time put limits on strategic weapons. The first defensive treaty limited each nation to two ABM systems: one centered around its capital, the other to guard part of its offensive missile force. No site could contain more than 100 interceptor missiles, and radar complexes would be limited. Violations would be monitored by surveillance satellites that would not be interfered with. The treaty was of unlimited duration. The second treaty, an interim five-year agreement, forbade any new construction of either land-based or submarine-launched offensive ballistic missiles. It specified the numbers of each type missile to be held by each nation. The treaty left the Soviets with about three times the megatonnage of the United States but allowed the United States about three times as many warheads.

During the summer Smith worked to get congressional support for the agreements. He stated that the treaties were evidence of cooperation between the two nations but warned that strategic forces must be maintained to deter attack. He supported the development of the nuclear submarine Trident and the B-1 bomber as "bargaining chips" in further talks. Congress approved the treaties in August and September.

As SALT I progressed, Smith also had been involved in other areas of arms negotiations with the Russians. In 1971 the two nations concluded the Seabed Arms Control Treaty and the Nuclear Accident Agreement. The first prohibited the installation of nuclear weapons at sea outside a 12-mile limit, and the second established cooperative procedures in the event of a nuclear mishap. Meanwhile, in separate negotiations both nations agreed to ban biological agents in warfare, but the United States would not accede to a Soviet proposal to prohibit chemical agents, saying that their use was primarily tactical, not strategic, and that problems of surveillance made controls impossible to enforce.

In early 1973 Smith resigned his post, having won wide praise as an able negotiator possessing a special rapport with the Russians. He returned to private law practice and headed the Trilateral Commission. He later served as ambassador-at-large for President JIMMY CARTER. From 1981 to 1989 he served as chairman and president of Consultants International Group. He died in 1994.

—FLM

Smith, James E.
(1930–   ) *comptroller of the currency*

James E. Smith was born on September 29, 1930, in Aberdeen, South Dakota. Smith presided over the U.S. government's surveillance of the nation's credit system during the most difficult years experienced by American banks since the Great Depression. Smith had been recruited from the business world by the NIXON administration through its first secretary of the Treasury, DAVID KENNEDY, to serve as deputy undersecretary of the Treasury for legislation. Smith gave up that post to become comptroller of the currency in June 1973.

Smith was immediately pulled into the atmosphere of scandal surrounding the Nixon administration and its ties to various banking groups. In October 1973 he was called before the House Banking and Currency Committee, headed by Representative WRIGHT PATMAN (D-Tex.), to explain his rejection of an application for a national bank charter from a group wishing to compete with a Key Biscayne, Florida, bank headed by CHARLES G. ("BEBE") REBOZO, a personal friend of President Nixon. The lawyers for Rebozo's bank, the sole bank on the island, had argued that there was insufficient loan demand to justify a second bank, although a bank examiner's report had stated that Rebozo's bank was so conservative with loans that it barely qualified as a bank. After Smith's decision the White House issued a statement asserting that "there was no White House involvement whatsoever" in the affair.

In November 1973, after the collapse of the U.S. National Bank of San Diego, headed by Nixon backer C. Arnholt Smith, James Smith was again called before the Patman committee. Although the *Wall Street Journal* had publicized questionable practices by the San Diego bank as early as April 1969, Smith claimed that his office had discovered no problems until much later. Smith told the Patman committee that in spite of "25 separate transactions which might violate" the U.S. Criminal Code, he had tried to prevent the Securities and Exchange Commission (SEC) from bringing a fraud suit against C. Arnholt Smith because he feared a run on the bank. James Smith also denied that he had been pressured in any way by the administration in the affair.

Smith's next embroilment came with the Franklin National bankruptcy of 1974. Smith's position in the affair was particularly delicate because of his ties to former Treasury secretary Kennedy, who was a financial adviser to Italian financier Michele Sindona, the major shareholder in Franklin National's parent company. When Franklin National's pending insolvency became apparent in the first two quarters of 1974, Smith announced that the bank was still solvent. Behind the scenes, however, Smith was involved in a joint investigation of Franklin National conducted by the Federal Reserve Bank, the SEC, and Smith's office of the comptroller of the currency.

The investigation revealed that Franklin National had suffered foreign exchange losses of over $45 million in early 1974. In late May the *Wall Street Journal* revealed that 11 New York banks were involved in a rescue operation for Franklin National, and Smith told the public that the banks had been asked to submit plans for a possible merger. In early October Smith announced the insolvency of Franklin National and the absorption of its assets by the European-American Bank.

In January 1975 Smith announced yet another bank failure, that of Security National Bank of Long Island. While, as in the cases of the U.S. National Bank of San Diego and Franklin National, the failed bank's assets were immediately absorbed by a larger, financially sound bank, Smith had to admit that the 1974–75 recession was undermining the solvency of the nation's financial institutions. He conceded that the comptroller's list of "problem banks" had lengthened considerably in 1974 and included "a few" banks with multibillion-dollar assets. In August 1975 Smith announced the establishment of a national bank surveillance system designed to detect financial problems in advance and to prevent failure. A month later, in the midst of the New York City fiscal crisis, Smith warned that a default by the city would jeopardize 10 to 15 major New York City banks.

Worry over the U.S. financial system increased in January 1976 when the comptroller of the currency's problem-banks list was leaked to the press. The list included both Citibank and Chase Manhattan, the second- and third-largest U.S. commercial banks, respectively. Although Smith "emphatically and unequivocally" defended the solvency of the two banks, he admitted his office was watching them closely. He went on to attack the press for sensationalizing "the well-known fact that loan losses in this nation's largest banks for the years 1974 and 1975 have been above historical norms." He added that the "real news" was that Chase and Citibank had weathered the 1974–75 crisis as well as they had.

Immediately after the disclosure of the list, Senator WILLIAM PROXMIRE (D-Wis.), chairman of the Senate Banking Committee, subpoenaed Smith and reprimanded him for his "failure to do a vigorous job on bank regulation." In his February 6 testimony Smith told the committee that the 1974–75 recession was to blame for the deterioration in bank liquidity. Proxmire rebuked Smith for allowing critical liquidity ratios to deteriorate during his period in office. A week later Smith announced the insolvency of the Hamilton National Bank of Chattanooga, the 195th-largest commercial bank in the United States, but he claimed that his office had foreseen weakness in this case as early as December 1974.

On February 17 Proxmire again criticized Smith for his "laxity" in permitting bank mergers. Mentioning the comptroller's "lush" Washington offices, Proxmire said Smith had earned the title of "King Farouk of the Potomac." In March 1976 Smith rejected a proposal allowing a House subcommittee to conduct a detailed study of the comptroller of the currency's regulation procedures. Smith resigned in July 1976 and returned to his private business career.

—LG

Smith, Margaret Chase
(1898–1995) *member of the Senate*

Margaret Chase was born in Skowhegan, Maine, on December 14, 1898. After graduating from Skowhegan High School and working for the telephone company, the local county newspaper, and as treasurer of the New England Waste Process Co., Margaret Chase married Clyde Smith in May 1930. She was soon absorbed into politics as her husband climbed the ladder to eventually become a liberal Republican representative in the U.S. House following the 1936 election. He died in 1940, and his widow won a special election in September for his seat from the predominantly industrial district. Smith was subsequently to sit on the Naval Affairs Committee, the first woman ever to do so. Her tenure in the House continued until 1948, when she was elected to the Senate. Two years later Smith made a highly publicized speech condemning Senator Joseph R. McCarthy for turning the Senate into a "forum of hate." In 1964 she ran for the Republican nomination for president on a low budget and fared poorly. She was deemed the fifth most popular woman in America in a 1966 Gallup poll, the same year that she was appointed chair of the Senate Republican Conference.

During the NIXON administration Smith oversaw appropriations with Senator JOHN STENNIS while they both served on the Defense Subcommittee of the Armed Services Committee. She ultimately became the ranking Republican member of the full committee. Generally a proponent of Nixon's Vietnam War policies, she voted against both the Cooper-Church Amendment and the more stringent McGovern-Hatfield Amendment, both attempting to fix deadlines for U.S. withdrawal from Indochina. Liberals were particularly angry at her in 1969 when she at first proposed several unsuccessful amendments to block all research and development as well as deployment funds for the Safeguard antiballistic missile system and then voted against the losing compromise effort, the Cooper-Hart measure, which would have allowed only research and development.

Prior to floor action, Smith would frequently withhold announcement of her voting intentions. When the nomination of G. HARROLD CARSWELL to the Supreme Court was before the Senate, she publicly became furious with White House lobbyist BRYCE HARLOW for tipping off a wavering senator about her as yet unsolidified decision. She wound up voting against Carswell. Earlier she also had voted against the Supreme Court nomination of CLEMENT HAYNSWORTH. She was an early advocate of the Equal Rights Amendment, but although the only woman in the Senate from 1967 to 1972, she never considered herself a feminist.

Although she received a 70 percent approval rating by the Americans for Conservative Action on her 1971 voting record, Smith generally defied easy political labeling. She voted against federal aid to big business when such issues as funding for the SST and the loan to the Lockheed Aircraft Corp. came before the Senate. She opposed busing legislation to achieve racial integration of schools and the Philadelphia Plan to integrate the construction trades but voted for the urban-oriented HUGH SCOTT over the conservative ROMAN HRUSKA for the job of Senate minority whip in January 1969.

In a major address before the Senate in June 1970, which was later expanded into a book titled *A Declaration of Conscience*, the Maine senator attempted to give a clearer conception of her concerns. She contrasted her fears of repression engendered by Senator Joseph McCarthy in 1950 with the politically charged climate existing in 1970. "We had a national sickness then from which we recovered," she said. "We have a national sickness now. . . . It is a national feeling of fear and frustration that could result in national suicide. . . ." She warned Americans that "the excessiveness of overreactions on both sides is a clear and present danger to American democracy. That danger is ultimately from the political right, even though it is initially spawned by the anti-democratic arrogance and nihilism from the political left . . . repression is preferable to anarchy and nihilism to most Americans."

In her 1972 reelection bid at age 74, Smith was considered at a disadvantage because of the heart attack suffered by her administrative assistant of 23 years, William C. Lewis, who had been the master strategist of her previous campaigns. She managed to beat a wealthy primary opponent but was upset in the November election by Representative William Hathaway. She retired to her hometown of Skowhegan in January 1973. She served as a visiting professor with the Woodrow Wilson National Fellowship Foundation, and in 1989 she received the presidential Medal of Freedom. She died in 1995 of complications following a stroke.

—GB

Sonnenfeldt, Helmut

(1926–   ) *National Security Council assistant; counselor to the Department of State*

Born on September 13, 1926, the son of German-Jewish physicians who fled Nazi Germany, Helmut Sonnenfeldt was educated in England and at Johns Hopkins University. While serving in the U.S. Army during World War II, Sonnenfeldt was stationed briefly in Germany, where he met a fellow refugee from Hitler, Sergeant HENRY A. KISSINGER. Following the war Sonnenfeldt returned to Johns Hopkins, earning an M.A. in political science in 1951.

Sonnenfeldt joined the State Department in 1952. Assigned to the office of research and analysis, he quickly won recognition as a political analyst. After working briefly on disarmament negotiations, Sonnenfeldt was appointed to the international political activities division in 1961, becoming its director in 1966. In April 1967 Sonnenfeldt was appointed to the office of research analysis for the Soviet bloc, where he headed Soviet and East European research.

Although Sonnenfeldt had developed a reputation as a hard-liner on Soviet affairs, he became the object of intense suspicion by certain State Department security officers, notably Otto F. Otepka, the department's chief security evaluator. Allegations by Otepka and others that Sonnenfeldt had leaked classified information to the press and to foreign diplomats led to surveillance and in late 1960 to sharp interrogation. Sonnenfeldt was eventually cleared, but the taint lingered, and he remained under surveillance for much of his career in the State Department.

When Henry Kissinger was appointed special assistant for national security affairs to President NIXON in January 1969, Sonnenfeldt was the first aide he recruited. Sonnenfeldt ranked among the most experienced experts on Soviet affairs in the government. A close personal friend of Kissinger's, Sonnenfeldt shared similar political views and personality traits with his boss. He staunchly defended Kissinger's policy of détente with the Soviet Union and accompanied Kissinger on his trips to Moscow, where he was on friendly terms with Soviet leader Leonid Brezhnev. Although recognized by his colleagues as a brilliant analyst, Sonnenfeldt developed a reputation as being "difficult to work with" and a harsh and "often irascible" taskmaster. According to one colleague in 1973, "Henry can't live with Hal—nor can he live without him."

In April 1973 the Nixon administration nominated Sonnenfeldt to become undersecretary of the Treasury. Treasury secretary GEORGE P. SHULTZ wanted Sonnenfeldt as his aide to supervise the growing U.S.-Soviet trade and to provide the Treasury Department with political advice and a link to the National Security Council. But Sonnenfeldt's reputation as a "security risk" and persistent charges that he had leaked classified documents held up the appointment for eight months. Eventually Sonnenfeldt's nomination to the Treasury was withdrawn on December 19, 1973. The same day he was confirmed as counselor to the State Department and returned to work for his old boss Kissinger.

In April 1976 Sonnenfeldt became the center of a controversy over the FORD administration's conduct of détente. Republican presidential contender RONALD REAGAN charged in a television address that Sonnenfeldt had proposed that "in effect, captive nations should give up any claims to national sovereignty" and "simply become a part of the Soviet Union." Reagan was upset over press accounts of an off-the-record lecture Sonnenfeldt gave in December 1975 in London to European-based U.S. ambassadors. At the same meeting Kissinger had said that the United States favored maintaining a position of stability with the Soviet Union, "one that would exclude Communists from power in Western Europe but would also acknowledge Moscow's influence in Eastern Europe, Yugoslavia excepted." Sonnenfeldt warned against any Soviet satellite's attempt to break free of Moscow's influence, stressing not only the dubious chances of success but also the possible consequences of international repercussions. Reagan claimed that this amounted to a U.S. underwriting of Soviet dominion in Eastern Europe and that it undercut East European nationalism.

According to the *Washington Post*, however, "the official version of the Sonnenfeldt statement suggested that the United States had not abandoned its efforts to influence events in the Soviet sphere." Referring to the 1,000-word text of the speech, which appeared in London's *Economist*, the *Post* suggested that Sonnenfeldt had actually argued for a more realistic interpretation of the situation in Eastern Europe. Although the USSR was becoming a global superpower, Sonnenfeldt noted, the United States could affect the way in which its power was developed and used by drawing it into a series of dependencies and ties with the West.

Both Kissinger and Sonnenfeldt believed it more important to exclude communists from power in Western Europe than to encourage nationalists in the satellite nations, particularly in light of the limits of the West's military forces during past uprisings. But Reagan's speech put President Ford on the defensive, opening the way to Reagan victories in North Carolina and Texas and forcing a public reappraisal by Ford of détente.

Sonnenfeldt retired from the State Department in 1977. He taught international relations at Johns Hopkins and joined the Rand Corporation in 1978. In the 1980s he was affiliated with the International Institute of Strategic Studies. He is now a guest scholar in foreign policy studies at the Brookings Institution.

—JAN

Spock, Benjamin (McLaine)
(1903–1998) *antiwar activist*

Spock studied medicine at Yale and Columbia, where he obtained an M.D. in 1929, specializing in pediatrics and psychiatry. He practiced in New York and in 1946 wrote *The Common Sense Book of Baby and Child Care*, which by 1969 was the all-time best seller by an American author. From 1947 to 1967 he taught psychiatry and child development alternately at the University of Minnesota and the Mayo Clinic, the University of Pittsburgh, and Case Western Reserve University. During the 1960s Spock, a liberal Democrat, became politically involved as a result of his concern about the dangers of nuclear weapons and later the Vietnam War. In 1963 he became cochairman of the National Committee for a Sane Nuclear Policy (SANE).

During the Johnson administration Spock was a ubiquitous figure at antiwar demonstrations. He resigned his cochairmanship of SANE after the group refused to back the April 1967 antiwar protests. In 1968 Spock was convicted of violations of the Selective Service Act, but his conviction was later overturned on appeal.

After his acquittal Spock continued his crusade for peace. In November he participated in a Washington, D.C., antiwar demonstration of over 250,000 people, sponsored by the New Mobilization Committee, which Spock and others had created on July 4, 1969. Speaking for the group after the invasion of Cambodia in May 1970, Spock told a news conference that "the government is committing titanic violence in Vietnam and Cambodia." He further stated, "We must stand up in opposition to the government's illegal, immoral, and brutal war." He was arrested May 3 during a rally near the White House sponsored by the Fellowship of Reconciliation and other religious groups. Spock was on a list of 65 radical college campus speakers prepared by the House Internal Security Committee in 1970. Nevertheless, he continued undaunted in his antiwar activities, often cooperating with radical groups whose views on personal morality and social and economic reform were far more extreme than his own. Spock was among some 7,000 demonstrators arrested in May 1971 during an antiwar protest in Washington. The People's Coalition for Peace and Justice provided the impetus behind the demonstrations, which were aimed at closing down the capital by means of traffic obstructions. On November 27, 1971, a new left-wing antiwar movement, the People's Party, nominated Spock as its stand-in candidate for president. The party hoped to attract a nationally prestigious political leader as its standard-bearer should the Democrats fail to nominate a progressive, antiwar candidate in 1972. Although he did not support its more extremist views, Spock played a leading, if only titular, role in the party's creation, focusing attention on domestic social and economic injustice as well as the persisting war in Vietnam.

Spock was officially selected the People's Party presidential nominee on July 29, 1972, at its national convention in St. Louis. The party platform stood for immediate withdrawal of all American troops abroad (not only in Vietnam); free medical care for all; tax reforms to eliminate loopholes for the rich; the legalization of marijuana; equal rights for women and homosexuals; legalized abortion on demand; and a guaranteed annual income of $6,500 for a family of four. Spock's name was on the ballot in only 10 states. He received 78,801 votes.

Following his defeat in the election Spock continued to participate in liberal causes. In 1975 he became a member of the Bertrand Russell Tribunal, a 25-member leftist organization that met to condemn violations of human rights in Latin America and Vietnam. He lectured and wrote throughout the 1980s and died in 1998.

—AES

Stans, Maurice H(ubert)

(1908–1998) *secretary of commerce; chairman, Finance Committee to Re-Elect the President*

Born on March 22, 1908, the son of an immigrant Belgian house painter and musician, Stans studied business administration at Northwestern University and worked as a stenographer. In 1928 he joined the small accounting firm of Alexander Grant & Co. as an office boy. In three years he was a partner, and in 1938 he became managing and executive partner. By 1955 he had made Alexander Grant the tenth-largest accounting firm in the country. In 1957 he became deputy director of the Bureau of the Budget and in 1958 bureau chief. A fiscal conservative, Stans achieved a balanced federal budget (in fiscal 1960). He opposed public works programs as an antidote for the recession and was particularly critical of the spending habits of the Democratic Congress.

Stans returned to the business world as an investment banker at the end of the Eisenhower administration but remained close to politics. He wrote a syndicated column during 1961–62 and put his considerable skills as a fund-raiser to use by serving as RICHARD NIXON's finance chairman for the 1962 California gubernatorial campaign. He was chairman of the Nixon Finance Committee and the Republican National Finance Committee in 1968, raising an impressive $34 million for the presidential campaign.

In January 1969 Stans became Nixon's secretary of commerce. Commerce had been an uninfluential post since Herbert Hoover's time, and despite Stans's predictions of a "business-oriented" administration, he could not reverse the trend that had put Commerce's old functions into the hands of the State Department and the Council of Economic Advisers.

The secretary traveled widely in an effort to improve the nation's trade deficit. His November 1971 trip to Moscow was a notable success and an important ingredient in Nixon's pursuit of détente. However, Stans's diplomatic gaffes elsewhere irritated the State Department and damaged his goal of securing trade concessions for American business. In May 1969 his table-pounding demands for voluntary restrictions on Japanese textile exports to the United States only alienated his Tokyo hosts. His effusive praise of the Greek government for its "attitude toward American investment" on a May 1971 visit to Athens went beyond the bounds of protocol and irritated the State Department, which had pointedly refrained from warm endorsements of the regime.

Stans maintained extremely poor relations with American black leaders. His minority small business program aimed to give "minority people a chance to become a capitalist, an employer, to become a success. . . ." Yet the Stans program, like the administration's general approach to social issues, was distrusted by minority spokespersons. Although Nixon and Stans had projected in 1969 that there would be 100 Minority Enterprise Small Business Investment Corporations in operation by June 1970, in fact there were only 39 as of October 1971. The secretary's unpopularity among minorities was underscored at a July 1971 NAACP meeting that greeted him with jeers.

Stans's view that the secretary should be the advocate of business made him one of the most conservative members of the Nixon cabinet. He opposed no-fault auto insurance, product safety standards, and the lifting of oil import quotas. He was able to replace a consumer protection bill backed by Attorney General JOHN MITCHELL with one that made it more difficult for consumers to collect in class-action suits. In July 1971 he urged the nation to "wait a minute" before banning DDT, removing phosphates from detergents, making offshore oil drilling "too difficult," and enforcing air pollution standards without regard for economic considerations.

In January 1972 Stans resigned to become finance chairman of the Committee to Re-Elect the President (CREEP). He worked closely with HERBERT KALMBACH, the president's lawyer, whom he had taught the fine points of political fund-raising in 1968. Because the new Federal Election Campaign Act requiring extensive financial disclosures by candidates was scheduled to go into effect April 7, Stans openly encouraged big contributors who wanted to remain anonymous to act before the deadline. He recommended that big donations be parceled out in $3,000 to $4,000 blocks to "dummy" committees (they were to be abolished by the new law) in Washington and suggested that businessmen donate 1 percent of their profits to the president's campaign treasury. It was later learned that many anonymous contributions were "laundered" in Mexican banks. Stans's forceful, if unorthodox, money-raising techniques brought in over $10 million by April 7.

President-elect Richard Nixon (left) with newly named secretary of commerce, Maurice Stans, December 11, 1968 *(Bettmann/CORBIS)*

The Watergate burglary occurred in June 1972. Stans was almost immediately implicated in the subsequent investigations. In July the Office of Federal Elections, a division of the General Accounting Office (GAO), charged that Stans had failed to keep adequate books on money kept in a safe in CREEP's New York headquarters, part of which was found in the possession of Watergate suspect BERNARD L. BARKER. The GAO believed that a total of $350,000 derived from anonymous contributions made after April 7 was kept unaccounted for so it could be used for "wild card" purposes. Stans told the media that "none of this has anything to do with me," but in August he pointed to G. GORDON LIDDY, campaign finance counsel, as the last man to handle the check

that appeared in Barker's accounts. Stans challenged the GAO report and recommended that in fairness the GAO should investigate the Democrats. In the same manner, when the Democrats in September sought to include him in their civil action suit against the burglars, Stans responded with a personal suit against former Democratic national chairman LAWRENCE O'BRIEN for having "falsely and maliciously" accused him of "a number of criminal acts." Throughout the end of 1972 and all of 1973 reports and charges appeared suggesting that Stans had wrangled large contributions from companies and individuals in exchange for political favors.

Stans was soon involved in a number of lawsuits, the most important of which was a New York grand jury indictment handed down in May 1973. Stans; Mitchell, who had been Nixon's campaign manager; and Harry Sears, a New Jersey politician and associate of financier ROBERT VESCO, were charged with perjury (in their grand jury testimony), conspiracy to defraud the United States, and obstruction of justice. The next month Stans was summoned to appear before the Senate Watergate committee. He sought to avoid testifying on the grounds it would prejudice his upcoming trial (it was later learned that the president wanted to prevent him from giving testimony), but failed. As he had said in public before, he told the committee that he knew nothing about Watergate or any "dirty tricks" operations and was only concerned in collecting "enough money to pay the bills." He noted that CREEP's finance committee was separate from the campaign committee but indicated that he was aware that G. Gordon Liddy handled money for unspecified purposes for which JEB STUART MAGRUDER gave authorization.

Stans and Mitchell were the first cabinet members in 50 years to be formally accused of criminal acts. Sears, who had been indicted with them, was tried separately, since he had agreed to testify against Mitchell and Stans. The prosecution's case asserted that Robert Vesco had made a $200,000 cash contribution to the campaign in exchange for Mitchell's help in stopping a Securities and Exchange Commission (SEC) investigation into the financier's business affairs. Besides Sears, JOHN W. DEAN III, former SEC chairman G. Bradford Cook, and Laurence Richardson, another Vesco associate, testified for the prosecution. It was alleged that when in March 1972 Vesco offered $500,000 to the campaign, Stans said that half that amount would suffice. He supposedly added that it must be delivered before April 7, $200,000 of it in $100 bills. The cash was delivered April 10 and put into Stans's safe to be used for CREEP's espionage activities.

Mitchell then secured a meeting for Vesco with the Securities and Exchange Commission chairman William Casey. The indictment also charged Stans with later seeking SEC general counsel Cook's aid in covering up the Vesco affair, promising to put in a "good word" for Cook (Cook in fact became SEC chairman in February 1974). Cook claimed that it was Stans who persuaded him to perjure himself in grand jury testimony the previous year.

Despite the charges, the evidence was not clear-cut. Stans was helped by the testimony of Edward Nixon, the president's brother and a friend of Vesco's, who stated that when he relayed Vesco's request to make an anonymous contribution to Stans, the finance chairman acted annoyed but informed him that it ought to be in cash. Another point in Stans's favor was the uncontested statement that he rejected a larger offer from Vesco because he could not guarantee privacy to the donor. And since the SEC investigation was not stopped, it was difficult to ascertain whether Stans and Mitchell actually tried to use their considerable influence in Vesco's favor. On April 28, 1974, Stans and Mitchell were acquitted. The most important factor in the defendants' favor, according to the jurors, was the lack of credibility of the prosecution witnesses, especially John Dean and Cook, who had already admitted perjuring himself.

While the trial was in progress the Senate Watergate committee was investigating Stans's role in the handling of payments from the dairy lobby. Corporate representatives testified that Stans and other campaign officials had extorted large contributions from them. Other violations of campaign finance laws were being investigated, including the promise of federal jobs and diplomatic posts to big contributors.

The investigations resulted in another trial. In March 1975 Stans pleaded guilty to five misdemeanor charges of violating election fund-raising laws in Washington federal court. The charges included three counts of failing to properly report on the handling of $150,000 in contributions and two counts of receiving $70,000 in illegal corporate contributions. A prosecution document filed with the court also said that Stans gave $81,000 to FREDERICK C. LARUE, the campaign official who handled "hush money." Stans's conviction for misdemeanors instead of felonies implied that he had broken the law unwittingly. The misdemeanor charge was the result of a plea-bargaining arrangement with the Watergate special prosecutor. In May Stans received his sentence: a $5,000 fine.

In January 1976 the American Institute of Certified Public Accountants trial board found Stans not guilty of bringing discredit to the accounting profession. Stans raised $27 million for the Nixon Library and Birthplace before his death in 1998.

—JCH

Stein, Herbert
(1916–1999) *member and chairman, Council of Economic Advisers*

Herbert Stein was born in Detroit, Michigan, on August 27, 1916. Stein received his bachelor's degree from Williams College in 1935 and immediately entered professional life as an economist. Between 1935 and 1948 he worked for the Federal Deposit Insurance Corp., the National Defense Advisory Commission, the Wages and Price Board, and the Office of War Mobilization and Conversion. In 1945 Stein also began work for the Committee for Economic Development (CED), a private research group sponsored by heads of large business organizations. At the CED Stein rose to the position of director of research, a job he held from 1956. He obtained a Ph.D in economics from the University of Chicago in 1958. Stein was an economic adviser to the presidential

campaign of Republican BARRY GOLDWATER in 1964. In 1966 he went to the Brookings Institution, a Washington "think tank" for analyzing policy issues. He remained at Brookings until President NIXON invited him to join his Council of Economic Advisers (CEA) immediately after the November 1968 election.

Stein, with fellow University of Chicago economist PAUL MCCRACKEN, Nixon's first CEA chairman, felt that the 4 percent inflation rate posted by the U.S. economy in 1968 was far too high and that it could be halted without precipitating a recession. The essential strategy they recommend to the administration was a tightening of credit and a subsequent slowing of growth of the U.S. money supply, aimed at bringing the total money in circulation into harmony with total production. In February 1969 Stein, with CEA colleagues McCracken and Hendrik Houthakker, predicted a "slowdown" in U.S. growth rates but denied that it would be accompanied by a serious rise in unemployment.

Stein also was appointed to head a study of the reconversion problems facing the U.S. economy after the end of hostilities in Vietnam. Stein's earlier experience studying the same problems after World War II and the Korean War made him the obvious choice for the project. When the study appeared in August 1969, its conclusions were not heartening. It argued that the Johnson administration had gravely overestimated the funds that an end to the war would free for social programs.

Throughout 1969 the rapid rise of U.S. interest rates, carried out under Federal Reserve chairman WILLIAM MCCHESNEY MARTIN, brought monetary growth to a virtual halt. From June to December 1969 the U.S. money supply expanded by 0.6 percent, in keeping with the "cold turkey" policies recommended by Stein, McCracken, and other CEA economists. Real production turned downward in November 1969, but in early 1970 inflation was recorded at an annual rate of 6 percent. Stein and other administration economists found themselves confronted with the new phenomenon of "stagflation," or simultaneous inflation and economic contraction, for which neither their monetarist views nor Keynesian theory had any explanation. Many commentators saw these trends as definitive empirical refutation of Stein's theory. But Stein in June 1970 told the Joint Economic Committee (JEC) of Congress that the U.S. economy would have to "go through a period of slack" to cure inflation. While not denying the reality of falling output, rising prices, the 350-point fall in the Dow Jones average since Nixon had taken office, and the corporate liquidity crunch of May–June 1970, Stein deflected criticism from the administration's economic policy and asserted that "we are running below the path . . . we would have chosen," warning against any attempt to "pump up the economy" as Keynesian theory prescribed. In September 1970, when the August Consumer Price Index rise was reported at only 0.2 percent (or a 2.4 percent annual rate), Stein cited this as evidence that the administration strategy was working.

Stein was an important economic spokesman for the administration. In October 1970 he told critics in London who questioned the efficacy of the U.S. government's anti-inflation moves that the Nixon administration was not merely using monetary and fiscal techniques but also manpower programs, direct intervention in collective bargaining (as in the case of construction worker contracts), and a newly established Productivity Committee to improve the performance of the U.S. economy. Stein admitted that reducing U.S. unemployment from its level of 6 percent—compared to 3.2 percent when Nixon took office—by 1972 would require a 6 percent increase in real production and predicted a 3 percent inflation rate for that year.

Another issue that weighted on the Nixon administration in the 1969–71 recession was a wide spectrum of opinion favoring wage-price controls. Stein, a convinced free-market theorist, was strongly opposed to such measures. Late in 1970 he told a meeting of the California Bankers' Association that inflation would slow if wage increases were limited to 8 percent and hinted that wage-price controls might be used in an emergency. The administration, Stein said, was against controls, but "it would be unfortunate to allow ideological purity to stand in the way of our real objectives." Stein asserted that the use of budgetary and monetary measures would be the main tools of the administration's attempts to reach full employment by mid-1972.

By early 1971 it was clear that the Stein-McCracken strategy for the U.S. economy was a failure. The economy had registered virtually zero growth in real terms in 1970, inflation continued, and unemployment hovered at 6 percent. In addition, chronic balance-of-payments deficits were greatly straining the dollar overseas. In the course of an internal discussion of the economy throughout the first half of 1971, these advisers were shunted aside, and President Nixon, with Federal Reserve chairman ARTHUR BURNS, developed a Keynesian strategy—the application of classical deficit spending techniques—to rejuvenate the U.S. economy. In August 1971 Stein participated in the top-level Camp David discussion on the economy, but he played a secondary role because of his association with the policies being discarded. He was assigned to oversee the implementation of the wage and price controls he had previously opposed. In November 1971, however, Stein succeeded Paul McCracken as CEA chairman after the latter's resignation.

Stein had a difficult task. The June–August reversal of administration policy, summarized in President Nixon's assertion that "I am now a Keynesian," was part of a long-term strategy to bring the U.S. economy into "high gear" in time for the 1972 elections. The combined measures succeeded in producing a 5 percent growth rate in 1972 but a runaway inflation in 1973. In March 1972 Stein responded to foreign pressures for an interest hike to protect the U.S. dollar—a move that would have been counter to the entire reflation strategy—by insisting that the August 1971 moves concerning the dollar were sound and that inflation would remain under control. In July 1972 he told a congressional panel that the only way to prevent an "explosion of demand" was "to keep the budget from exploding." In October 1972 he told the JEC that the administration had dropped the traditional 4 percent unemployment target, the usual gauge of "full employment," as "counterproductive." In December, immediately after his reelection, Nixon appointed Stein to his Economic Policy Council.

In February 1973 Stein became embroiled, along with the other leading economic figures in the administration, in the renewed dollar crisis that erupted in that month. At the same time the takeoff of meat prices following the lifting of price controls produced a consumer boycott of meat, which Stein praised as having some downward effect. Stein generally held to his earlier free-market views, rejecting a return to wage-price controls to slow runaway inflation. After the fourfold increase in oil prices in October 1973, he also opposed gas rationing.

Stein came into open conflict with other administration members in early 1974 when Secretary of Labor PETER BRENNAN suggested that U.S. workers should get higher wages to keep up with inflation. Stein retorted that what the country needed was productivity, asserting, "We cannot pay workers for food that was not produced and oil that we didn't get from the Arabs." After the CEA's 1974 report was released to Congress, Stein and Secretary of the Treasury GEORGE SHULTZ defended the report's conclusion that a recession could be averted in the United States in 1974. In doing so, however, Stein conceded that he and Shultz were redefining recession away from textbook definitions, such as a fall in output. In May 1974, when Arthur Burns called for a balanced budget to stop inflation, Stein said that "we don't all talk with the language of an Old Testament prophet," likening Burns to Jeremiah.

In July 1974, three months before the beginning of the worst U.S. recession since the Great Depression, Stein resigned from his post as CEA chairman to return to academic life. He was succeeded by economic consultant ALAN GREENSPAN. Stein began a regular column with the *Wall Street Journal* and resumed his teaching duties at the University of Virginia, where he had taught since 1971. He died in 1999.

—LG

Steinem, Gloria

(1934–) *member, Policy Council, National Women's Political Caucus; founder, Women's Action Alliance; editor, Ms.*

Gloria Steinem was born on March 25, 1934, in Toledo, Ohio. Steinem graduated from Smith College in 1956 and studied for two years in India. In 1960 Steinem moved to New York City to establish a career in journalism. After eight years of writing articles for popular magazines and a stint as a scriptwriter for the TV show *That Was the Week That Was*, Steinem was hired by Clay Felker as a contributing editor to the new magazine *New York*. Through her column "The City Politic," Steinem supported the causes and politics of the American left.

After reporting on a meeting of the Redstockings, a militant feminist group, in November 1968, Steinem concentrated her energies on writing, speaking, and television appearances on behalf of the women's liberation movement.

By 1971 Steinem was nationally recognized as the symbol of the new left feminist leadership. Her picture appeared on the covers of *Newsweek*, *McCall's*, and *Redbook*. Steinem's feminism was based on the belief that women's biological differences "have been used . . . to mark us for an elaborate division of labor . . . [which] is continued for clear reason, conscious or not: the economic and social profit of men as a group."

In July 1971 Steinem, BELLA ABZUG, SHIRLEY CHISHOLM, and BETTY FRIEDAN announced the formation of the National Women's Political Caucus (NWPC) to encourage women to run for public office and lobby for women's issues at the 1972 national party conventions. Although endorsing GEORGE MCGOVERN as "the best of the male candidates" for the Democratic presidential nomination, Steinem later campaigned and ran unsuccessfully as a convention delegate for Chisholm, who had entered the presidential race. As spokeswoman for the NWPC at the Democratic National Convention in Miami, Steinem led unsuccessful floor fights for the inclusion of an abortion plank in the party platform and a challenge of the South Carolina delegation because of underrepresentation of women. She engineered an impressive show of the political strength of women in the nomination vote of Sissy Farenthold for vice president.

In late 1971 Steinem organized and became a member of the board of the Women's Action Alliance, a national information and referral network for women that also gave organizational assistance to women's projects. During this period Steinem gathered support for the publication of a woman's magazine owned and run by women and aimed at the "liberated woman." Financed by Felker's *New York*, all 300,000 copies of the January 1972 preview issue of *Ms.* sold out on newstands. The title, *Ms.*, is a form of address preferred by feminists who consider its use a symbolic refusal to be identified by their relationship to a man.

Under Steinem's editorship, *Ms.*'s circulation had reached 500,000 by 1977.

Despite acrimonious charges from the right in the women's movement that her rhetoric and more militant views threatened to destroy a broad coalition of women and allegations in 1975 that she had been connected with the Central Intelligence Agency, Steinem continued to be active in feminist politics. In 1975 she helped plan the women's agenda for the Democratic National Convention and in 1977 attended the National Conference of Women in Houston, Texas. In 1991 Steinem became the consulting editor for *Ms.* In 1993 she was inducted into the National Women's Hall of Fame.

—JMP

Stennis, John C(ornelius)
(1901–1995) *member of the Senate; chairman, Armed Services Committee*

Born on August 3, 1901, Stennis graduated from Mississippi State College in 1923 and received his law degree from the University of Virginia in 1928. He was elected to the Mississippi house of representatives in 1928. In 1931 he was elected prosecutor for Mississippi's 16th judicial district. He became a circuit judge in 1937 and succeeded Theodore Bilbo in the U.S. Senate in 1947. Stennis was a staunch supporter of segregation and states' rights. He was one of the Senate floor leaders engaged in extended debate and filibuster in opposition to civil rights legislation. He was one of the authors of the "Southern Manifesto," proclaiming resistance to the Supreme Court school desegregation decision of 1954.

In domestic affairs Stennis was a conservative Democrat, opposing most of the New Frontier and Great Society social programs. He did, however, support health programs, including medical research.

Stennis continued his opposition to civil rights legislation during the NIXON-FORD years. In 1970 the Mississippian introduced the Stennis Amendment, requiring uniform national application of school desegregation rules. Stennis made it clear what his objective was: "I want [Northerners] to find out whether or not they want this massive immediate integration." Stennis did not believe that they did and would, consequently, leave the South alone. The proposal, which was attacked by some northern liberals, was enacted in 1972.

Stennis was a staunch supporter of national defense and backed Nixon's antiballistic missile program. In at least one area, however, he disappointed the military. Stennis had insisted that the total number of admirals and generals be kept close to 1,200 rather than the 1,600 the military wanted in the late 1960s. This figure of 1,200 was known among military offices as "the Stennis ceiling." Stennis was a strong supporter of the Central Intelligence Agency (CIA). He was, however, critical of CIA activities in U.S. domestic matters and of its role in the overthrow of the Allende government in Chile.

In foreign policy Stennis expressed strong support of Nixon's Indochina policy. During the late 1960s he had opposed getting the United States involved in the Vietnam War. He voiced the fear that the war might create a precedent for American entry into future conflicts without congressional approval and for the conduct of such conflicts with minimal legislative involvement. However, he believed that once the nation was committed to war, Americans should stand behind the president.

Nevertheless, Stennis worked to curb the president's warmaking power. In 1971 he introduced a resolution that would have curbed the power of the president to commit the nation to war without the consent of Congress. He was a cosponsor, along with Senator JACOB JAVITS (R-N.Y.) of the war powers bill. The measure was a synthesis of previous proposals. It defined emergency conditions under which the president could commit troops without a formal declaration of war and outlined procedures by which Congress could terminate the emergency use if it disapproved. The Vietnam War was exempt from its provisions. The Senate passed the bill in April and the House in August.

Stennis experienced a personal attack that nearly cost him his life. While returning to his home in Washington on January 30, 1973, he was shot in a robbery. He underwent extensive surgery but recovered. The assailants were apprehended.

Stennis almost played a role in the Watergate affair. When in October 1973 Richard Nixon was struggling to keep the White House tapes out of the control of Watergate investigators, he proposed that Stennis listen to them and screen them to make certain that national security secrets would not be divulged. Stennis had agreed to perform this task only if a formal invitation had been tendered to do so by the president and the Senate Watergate committee chairman SAM ERVIN and ranking member HOWARD BAKER. The committee refused. Stennis's relationship with Nixon was close and cordial. He supported Gerald Ford's pardon of Nixon in 1974. Stennis retired from the Senate in 1988 and died at his home in 1995.

—HML

Stevens, John Paul

(1920–   ) *judge, U.S. Seventh Circuit Court of Appeals; associate justice, U.S. Supreme Court*

John Paul Stevens was born on April 20, 1920, in Chicago, Illinois. Stevens received a B.A. from the University of Chicago in 1941 and graduated first in his class from Northwestern University Law School in 1947. He was law clerk to Supreme Court justice Wiley Rutledge in 1947 and 1948. Stevens then entered private practice in Chicago, where he specialized in antitrust and corporate law. He also served in 1950 as counsel to the House Judiciary Subcommittee on Antitrust and Monopoly and as a member of the Attorney General's National Committee to Study Antitrust Laws in 1954 and 1955.

A Republican, Stevens was named a judge on the U.S. Seventh Circuit Court of Appeals in October 1970. During his five years on the appellate bench, he established an excellent reputation for judicial craftsmanship based on opinions that were consistently clear, scholarly, and well written. He was considered a generally moderate jurist with a nonideological approach to cases that made him difficult to categorize. Stevens usually emphasized the facts in each suit and applied the relevant law on a case-by-case basis. Within that framework he tended to favor the prosecution in criminal cases but was responsive to claims of prisoners' rights. He was moderate on discrimination and free-expression issues and overall favored a policy of judicial restraint.

On November 28, 1975, President GERALD FORD nominated Stevens for the Supreme Court seat vacated by the retirement of Justice WILLIAM O. DOUGLAS. Stevens was strongly recommended for the post by Attorney General EDWARD LEVI, who had known him in Chicago, and the nomination was generally well received. Women's rights groups objected to Stevens because he had opposed women's claims in several sex discrimination cases. However, he was confirmed by the Senate on December 17 by a 98-0 vote and sworn in two days later.

Stevens proved to be an independent justice who demonstrated the same case-by-case approach to issues that he had shown on the circuit bench. Nondoctrinaire and individualistic, he was not clearly aligned with either the more liberal or conservative members of the Court. However, Stevens was more liberal in his votes than many observers had anticipated and though hard to categorize, seemed to take a moderate to liberal approach on most issues.

During his first year on the bench, Justice Stevens concurred in an important June 1976 decision holding that a racially discriminatory purpose as well as a discriminatory effect was needed to make a government job test unconstitutional. Later the same month, however, he joined the majority to declare racial discrimination in private nonsectarian schools illegal. Stevens dissented several days later when the Court upheld a Social Security Act provision discriminating against illegitimate children. He also objected to a December 1976 decision ruling that pregnancy and childbirth could be excluded from coverage in a company disability insurance plan without violating a federal law prohibiting sex discrimination in employment.

Justice Stevens spoke for a five-man majority in June 1976 to hold that Civil Service Commission regulations barring resident aliens from federal jobs denied due process of law. However, he also wrote the opinion in a case holding that the dismissal of a state policeman without a hearing did not deprive him of liberty or property without due process. The justice displayed a mixed pattern in First Amendment cases during his first term. His opinion for a five-man majority upheld a Detroit ordinance restricting the location of adult movie theaters. However, Stevens took a strong stand a week later against judicial "gag" orders limiting publication of information about criminal cases.

In July 1976 Stevens voted to overturn laws making death the mandatory penalty for murder. However, he joined in rulings sustaining laws that established death as one possible penalty for murder and set guidelines for the judge or jury in determining the sentence. The justice took a conservative stance in several Fourth Amendment cases in his first months on the Court and was part of a six-man majority that limited state prisoners' right of appeal to federal courts on search and seizure issues. He showed special sensitivity to claims of illegal treatment made by prison inmates. Stevens dissented in June 1976 when the Court ruled that inmates were not entitled to a hearing before being transferred from one prison to another, even when the move was a disciplinary action or conditions in the two prisons differed substantially.

During the next few terms of the Court, Justice Stevens continued to pursue an independent and rather unpredictable course. Quiet and mild-mannered, he was considered a "swing" vote along with Justices POTTER STEWART and BYRON WHITE. Of the three, he was the one most likely to join with the Court's liberals when the justices were divided. He opposed affirmative action in *Regents of California v. Boore* but voted to uphold affirmative action in *Grutter v. Bollinger* (2003).

—CAB

Stewart, Potter

(1915–1985) *associate justice, U.S. Supreme Court*

Potter Stewart was born in Jackson, Michigan, on January 23, 1915. A 1941 graduate of Yale Law School, Stewart joined a prominent Cincinnati firm in 1947. He was appointed to the U.S. sixth circuit court of appeals in April 1954 and to the Supreme Court in October 1958. In his early years on the bench, Stewart was labeled a "swing" justice who cast a pivotal vote in cases dividing the Court's liberal and conservative wings. When a liberal majority emerged on the Warren Court in the early 1960s, Stewart's position was no longer decisive, but he remained a moderate and independent jurist. He took a conservative stance on most loyalty-security, reapportionment, and criminal rights issues but frequently joined the Court's liberals in cases involving civil rights, the right to counsel, obscenity, and eavesdropping.

On the WARREN BURGER Court Stewart, along with BYRON WHITE, once again became a "swing" justice whose vote was crucial in deciding close cases. He occupied a center position between the Court's liberal members and the four more conservative RICHARD NIXON appointees. When those two groups disagreed in a case, Stewart was more likely to vote with the "Nixon bloc," but his progressive views on certain issues still established him as, overall, a moderate and somewhat unpredictable jurist.

Stewart tended toward a policy of judicial restraint, but he defended individual rights against government infringement when he believed there was a clear constitutional mandate for this. He regularly voted to uphold the rights of free speech and assembly. In June 1973 he went beyond his already liberal stance on obscenity to join in a dissent urging the Court to prohibit all attempts to regulate allegedly obscene material for willing adults. Stewart took a broad view of freedom of the press and dissented in June 1972 when the Court held that journalists had no First Amendment right to refuse to identify confidential sources to a grand jury. In an exception to his generally liberal First Amendment views, the justice spoke for the Court in March 1976 to hold that a 1968 ruling that protected the right of union members to picket within a privately owned shopping center was no longer valid.

Stewart usually opposed racial and sexual discrimination. However, he did vote in June 1972 to allow private clubs with state liquor licenses to exclude blacks. He also wrote the opinion in a June 1974 case holding that a California job disability insurance program that excluded pregnancy from coverage did not deny women the equal protection of the laws. In other discrimination cases Stewart's judicial conservatism came to the fore. He believed the Court should normally defer to policy judgments made by legislatures, and so he voted to sustain laws that discriminated against illegitimate children and the poor. In an April 1970 opinion Stewart upheld a state ceiling on the amount of welfare benefits one family could receive and said that the economic, social, and philosophical problems presented by welfare programs were not the business of the federal courts. He also voted to uphold state laws limiting voting on bond issues to property owners or taxpayers. The justice maintained his opposition to a strict one-man, one-vote rule in reapportionment cases and supported February and June 1973 decisions relaxing that standard for state legislative districting.

Justice Stewart insisted that the government adhere to strict procedural standards, and he voted in a series of cases from 1969 on to invalidate state laws that allowed creditors to seize a debtor's wages or goods without notice or hearing. In a potentially far-reaching June 1975 opinion Stewart held that mental patients could not be confined in institutions against their will if they were not dangerous to others and could live outside the institution on their own.

In criminal cases Justice Stewart tended to favor law enforcement authorities. He had opposed the 1966 *Miranda* ruling requiring police to warn suspects of their rights, and in several cases in the 1970s he supported cutbacks on that decision. He took a narrow view of the Fifth Amendment's privilege against self-incrimination and in Fourth Amendment cases backed police "stop and frisk" practices, third-party bugging, and grand jury use of illegally obtained evidence as the basis for questioning witnesses. However, Stewart generally opposed warrantless searches, and in an important June 1969 opinion he limited the scope of the search police could make incident to a lawful arrest. The justice believed that many of the

criminal safeguards in the Bill of Rights took effect only when formal judicial proceedings were instituted. In a June 1972 plurality opinion he restricted the right to counsel at police line-ups to those conducted after a defendant's indictment or arraignment.

Stewart voted in June 1972 to declare the death penalty as then imposed a violation of the Eighth Amendment's ban on cruel and unusual punishment. He announced the judgment of the Court in several capital punishment cases decided in July 1976. In opinions joined by only two other justices, Stewart argued that statutes making the death penalty mandatory for certain crimes were unconstitutional. However, he voted to sustain laws setting death as one possible punishment for murder as long as standards were established to guide the judge or jury in imposing sentence.

President Nixon considered appointing Stewart chief justice in 1969, but Stewart reportedly asked that his name be withdrawn because he believed someone from outside the Court should be given the post. Stewart retired from the Court in 1981 and died four years later on December 7 in Hanover, New Hampshire.

—CAB

Strachan, Gordon C(reighton)
(1943–) *White House aide*

Gordon C. Strachan was born on July 24, 1943, in Berkeley, California. A graduate of the University of Southern California in 1965, Strachan's former classmates included such future associates as DONALD SEGRETTI, RONALD ZIEGLER, and DWIGHT CHAPIN. He received his law degree from the University of California and then joined RICHARD NIXON's old New York law firm, Mudge, Rose, Guthree, and Alexander, to work in the area of estates and trusts. In 1970 Strachan devoted part of his time to "advance work" for the White House in the midterm elections. He left his legal practice shortly afterward and joined the staff of the administration's communications director, HERBERT G. KLEIN. Within a few months Strachan had moved again to become a political aide to Nixon's chief of staff, H. R. HALDEMAN. Referred to by White House staffers as "Haldeman's gofer," Strachan acted as a liaison between Haldeman and the Committee to Re-Elect the President (CREEP). In December he became general counsel to the U.S. Information Agency (USIA.)

In October 1972 the Department of Justice released a report that linked the White House to undercover Republican political sabotage efforts launched against the Democrats. It cited Strachan and Dwight Chapin, Nixon's deputy assistant, as those responsible for hiring Donald Segretti to direct espionage activities in September 1971. Four months later government sources made public information that named Strachan as the initial contact between Segretti and political intelligence operations. Strachan resigned from his position as general counsel to the USIA on April 30, 1973.

Preliminary grand jury evidence revealed May 2, 1973, that such espionage activities, begun in early 1971 and continuing throughout the 1972 election campaign, had been organized by Haldeman, who delegated activities to a variety of aides and minor functionaries. The group's goals entailed the establishment of a sophisticated political intelligence-gathering system and plots to sabotage the presidential campaigns of Senators EDMUND S. MUNSKIE (D-Me.) and HUBERT HUMPHREY (D-Minn.) and ensure the nomination for Senator GEORGE MCGOVERN (D-S.D.), whom the White House considered the weakest candidate.

In July 1973 Strachan testified under a grant of immunity before the Senate Watergate committee. He admitted that after the Watergate break-in he had destroyed documents that might have tied Watergate burglars

to the White House and reported that he had delivered hush money subsequently paid to the burglars by FRED LARUE. Strachan maintained that he did not know what the money was to be used for but became suspicious when LaRue "donned a pair of gloves before touching it." When asked what advice he had to offer youths wishing to enter politics, he replied, "Stay away."

On March 1, 1974, Strachan was one of seven former White House aides indicted by the grand jury for conspiring to cover up Watergate and "other illegal activities." He was charged with one count each of conspiracy, obstruction of justice, and making a false declaration (based on his statement in reference to his knowledge and handling of hush money) before a grand jury. He faced a maximum of 15 years of imprisonment and $20,000 in fines. Because the court had difficulty determining whether Strachan's indictment came as the result of his testimony delivered under the grant of immunity, Strachan's case was separated from the main trial, which took place on January 1, 1975. U.S. District Court Judge JOHN SIRICA dropped all charges against Strachan on May 10, 1975. Strachan moved to Salt Lake City in 1975, where he now practices law.

—SBB

Strauss, Robert S(chwarz)

(1918–) *chairman, Democratic Party National Committee*

Robert S. Strauss was born in Lockhart, Texas, on October 19, 1918. Strauss studied at the University of Texas in Austin, where he obtained his law degree in 1941. Admitted to the Texas bar the same year, he worked as a special agent for the FBI during World War II. In 1945 he became a partner in the Dallas law firm Akin, Gump, Strauss, Hauer, and Feld, where he remained a partner until 1977. Strauss also was involved in the Texas media, becoming president of his own Strauss Broadcasting Company in 1964. Years of work in state Democratic Party politics, where he was generally associated with the right-of-center JOHN CONNALLY faction, won him the job of Democratic national chairman from Texas between 1968 and 1972. In 1969 Strauss also became a member of the party's National Executive Committee. In 1970 he was elected party treasurer, a post he held until 1972, when he stepped aside for an appointee of Senator GEORGE MCGOVERN.

Strauss's ascendancy to the chairmanship of the Democratic National Committee was completed a month after McGovern's crushing defeat in the November 1972 presidential election that led to a wholesale ouster of McGovern supporters from positions of power. On December 3 a meeting of Democratic governors endorsed Strauss for national committee chairman. His support came primarily from the governors of southern and western states. Strauss also had the backing of the AFL-CIO leadership, which had distanced itself from the McGovern campaign and was eager to return prolabor politicians to power within the party.

Strauss was elected to the national chairmanship on December 9 after an acrimonious confrontation with the McGovern forces in which he had to answer accusations that his previous close association with Connally (who had led Democrats for RICHARD NIXON during the 1972 campaign) made him a poor choice. On the TV program *Face the Nation* following his election, Strauss stated that anyone who supported "someone other than the Democratic candidate" for president should not hold high office within the party. "John Connally belongs to the top of the list" of such individuals. He predicted that Connally would soon change his registration to the Republican Party, which Connally did in 1973.

In a gesture of unity Strauss announced that he had no intention of "rolling back the clock" on the party reforms pushed though by McGovern's supporters. He also made overtures to the trade unions by indicating that United Automobile Workers (UAW) president LEONARD WOODCOCK would continue to head a commission studying convention delegate selection and that he would attempt to involve AFL-CIO chairman GEORGE MEANY in the commission as well.

During early 1973 both parties openly wooed Connally. Strauss invited his longtime colleague to "return to this party and bring with him his constituency"—an admitted attempt to compensate for his earlier public criticism of Connally. In March 1973 the Democratic National Committee endorsed 25 new members appointed by Strauss in a further consolidation of control. Strauss's public duties as national chairman consisted primarily of expressing party opinion on the actions of the Republican administration.

In August 1973 President Nixon made a major speech on Watergate that he hoped would clear the air and bring the scandal and its repercussions to an end. Strauss commented that the speech "added nothing, and probably subtracted nothing, from what we knew." After the firing of Watergate special prosecutor ARCHIBALD COX and Deputy Attorney General WILLIAM RUCKELSHAUS, Strauss stated that Nixon had "abandoned the principle of law" and "his oath of office" and expressed doubts about whether Nixon could continue to serve. Strauss advised against openly calling for Nixon's resignation, arguing, "Let us remember what this president was and did when he perceived himself a hero. I ask you what horrors await this nation if he is able to portray himself as a resigned martyr."

Strauss presided over the national comeback of the Democratic Party in the wake of the 1972 elections. He had difficulty, however, coping with the bitter factionary struggles within the party. In August 1974 a Democratic Charter Commission in Kansas City was interrupted by a walkout of liberal and black Democrats who accused Strauss of "stacking" a party committee. Several months later the labor contingent at a Kansas City "mini-convention" expressed anger over what it termed the party's sophisticated discrimination against organized labor in the high councils of the organization.

In June 1976 JIMMY CARTER, who had virtually assured himself of the nomination with victories in the major primaries, asked Strauss to stay on as party chairman through the November election. Strauss stepped down as national chairman in January 1977. Two months later President Carter appointed him a special representative for trade negotiations with the rank of ambassador. In addition to representing the United States at sensitive trade talks, including the 1977–78 negotiations on tariff reductions of the Geneva-based General Agreement on Trade and Tariffs, Strauss served briefly as the Carter administration's "anti-inflation" ombudsman. Strauss served as ambassador to the Soviet Union in 1991 and as ambassador to Russia from 1991 to 1993.

—LRG

Sturgis, Frank A.

(1924–1993) *convicted Watergate burglar*

Frank A. Sturgis was born on December 9, 1924, in Norfolk, Virginia. A onetime commander under Fidel Castro, Frank A. Sturgis was one of five men arrested for breaking into the Democratic National Headquarters at the Watergate in Washington, D.C., on June 17, 1972. The men were equipped with surgical gloves, cameras, electronic equipment, $6,500 in cash, and papers referring to "W. House" and "Howard Hunt." All five had previous Central Intelligence Agency (CIA) connections.

Quickly dismissed by White House press secretary RONALD ZIEGLER as a "third-rate burglary attempt," the incident was cited as "blatant political espionage" by Democratic National chairman LAWRENCE O'BRIEN, who called for an FBI probe of the affair. The Justice Department announced a full-scale inquiry on June 19. Subsequent disclosure tied the five suspects to personnel and funds of the Committee to Re-Elect the President (CREEP).

Sturgis and his associates were indicted by a federal grand jury on September 15, 1972, for conspiracy, burglary, and wiretapping. Two former White House aides—G. GORDON LIDDY and E. HOWARD HUNT—were included in the indictments. In March 1973 the original five pleaded guilty to all counts and were given "provisional" maximum penalties by Judge JOHN J. SIRICA ranging from 35 to 40 years of imprisonment. Although he refused to promise leniency, Sirica recommended that they cooperate fully in the investigation.

In November 1973 Sturgis received a one-to five-year sentence. He was paroled in March 1974. Sturgis was scheduled to begin another prison term at that time due to a conviction for transporting stolen cars into Mexico in 1973. In 1975 his term was set aside because he had cooperated with the authorities.

In April 1975 Sturgis testified before the Rockefeller Commission that he had been party to a 1959 CIA plot to assassinate Fidel Castro and had participated in the agency's 1961 Bay of Pigs invasion. Sturgis and three of the other Watergate burglars brought a $2 million suit on the grounds that they had been tricked into participating in the burglary by being made to believe that they were engaged in national security work that had government approval. In 1977 the case was settled out of court, with each man receiving $50,000 from former president RICHARD NIXON's 1972 campaign fund. Sturgis died on December 4, 1993.

—SBB

Symington, Stuart W(illiam)

(1901–1988) *member of the Senate*

Stuart W. Symington was born in Amherst, Massachusetts, on June 26, 1901. Following his graduation from Yale in 1923, Symington began a successful business career, serving as president of Emerson Electric Manufacturing Co. from 1938 to 1945. During the Truman administration Symington held important posts in several federal agencies and from 1946 to 1950 served as secretary of the air force. A leading proponent of increased defense spending, he advocated the development of a large nuclear-equipped air force.

Symington was elected to the Senate from Missouri as a Democrat in 1952 and argued for greater military preparedness in general and the "big bomber" in particular. In 1960 he campaigned for the Democratic presidential nomination but eventually threw his support behind the unsuccessful candidacy of Lyndon B. Johnson. During the Eisenhower administration he chaired hearings on stockpiling abuses, backed the Defense Department in the "muzzling" probe of 1962, and supported the development of the controversial TFX fighter-bomber.

Early in the Vietnam War Symington, a onetime hawk, became a committed dove. As the only senator to sit on both the Foreign Relations and Armed Services committees, Symington grew convinced that the war was not only unnecessary to U.S. security but also futile, wrong, and harmful to the nation's economy. In October 1967 he urged a unilateral cease-fire aimed at initiating peace negotiations.

A liberal on domestic issues, Symington supported consumer protection, abortion aid, and gun control, positions unpopular in Missouri. During the NIXON years he voted against the Supreme Court nominations of CLEMENT HAYNSWORTH and G. HARROLD CARSWELL, supported legal services for the poor, and championed spending on "human welfare needs" rather than on military projects.

In 1969 Symington headed a subcommittee investigating overseas commitments in an effort to reassess U.S. foreign policy in the wake of the Vietnam War. The subcommittee found that commitments and secret agreements had been made throughout the 1960s to such countries as Ethiopia, Laos, Thailand, South Korea, and Spain and that the United States had 429 major military bases around the world. An agreement permitting U.S. use of bases in Spain in return for grants, loans, and improvements caused particular controversy.

Symington pointed out that many major military commitments of the 1960s and 1970s resulted from executive agreements made without the knowledge or consent of Congress and pressed for a reassertion of congressional authority in foreign policy during the 1970s. For years a supporter of foreign aid, he opposed many aid measures during the Nixon years in his belief that the United States was economically and militarily overcommitted throughout the world. Symington stated, "There has to be a viable economy with a strong dollar. And there has to be faith in the system and confidence of the people in their government. Without the second and third, military strength is not security."

Unlike many other doves, Symington did not completely turn against the "military establishment." Yet he opposed building new military bases, bombers, and an expanded antiballistic missile (ABM) system because he believed alternative systems would be more efficient. His opposition to the ABM hurt him politically. In his 1970 reelection campaign Symington won a narrow 37,000-vote victory over his opponent, state attorney general John C. Danforth, who had received large political contributions from McDonnell Douglas, a builder of missile components.

Symington spoke out against the extension of the Vietnam War into Cambodia and Laos, supporting the Cooper-Church and McGovern-Hatfield amendments. In March 1975 Symington, with Senators HUBERT HUMPHREY, GEORGE MCGOVERN, and Dick Clark (D-Iowa), opposed military aid to the faltering Cambodia government of Lon Nol while supporting additional food and medical help.

Symington also favored measures to ban the importation of Rhodesian chrome ore, withdraw 76,000 U.S. troops stationed abroad, and resume U.S. military aid to Turkey, which was cut off in 1974. In 1973 Symington, as acting chairman of the Armed Services Committee, conducted hearings into the possible involvement of the CIA in the Watergate scandal. According to testimony high administration officials sought to involve the CIA in the Watergate cover-up as well as the burglary of the office of DANIEL ELLSBERG's psychiatrist.

In 1976, after 24 years in the Senate, Symington chose not to seek reelection. He died at his home in Connecticut in 1988.

—JAN

T

Talmadge, Herman E(ugene)
(1913–2002) *member of the Senate*

Herman E. Talmadge was born in McRae, Georgia, on August 9, 1913. After receiving his law degree from the University of Georgia in 1936, Talmadge joined his father's Atlanta law firm. During World War II he served with the navy in several Pacific theater operations. In 1948 he succeeded his father, Eugene Talmadge, as Georgia's governor. In 1950 Talmadge won a seat in the U.S. Senate and quickly gained a reputation as an intelligent and well-informed legislator. During the Kennedy-Johnson years he opposed civil rights and social welfare legislation and supported measures favoring private enterprise.

As chairman of the Agriculture and Forestry Committee, Talmadge was concerned about hunger in America, which he termed a national tragedy. He was the author of the school lunch program passed in 1970 and helped develop the food stamp plan. Beginning in 1969 he sought to improve the food stamp program by eliminating several of its shortcomings, including the high cost of coupons, inadequate food bonuses that deprived stamp program participants of a nutritionally adequate diet, and the inaccessibility of food stamps caused by pay distribution procedures.

Talmadge introduced the 1969 food assistance bill, which authorized $610 billion for the food stamp program and called for a review of changes in the program. He also supported the 1970 bill extending the food stamp program for five years. Talmadge applauded the bill's provision requiring all able-bodied adults to work or register for work in order for their families to be eligible for food stamps. He opposed a guaranteed nutritional income system as financially impractical and unwise.

In 1969 Talmadge introduced the employment opportunity bill, which granted tax credits for certain costs that employers incurred as a result of hiring individuals through work-incentive programs. According to Talmadge the bill had a twofold purpose: (1) to encourage trained workers under existing training programs and (2) to hire individuals through the Social Security Act's work-incentive program. He described the 1970 family assistance bill as the "welfare expansion act" because it allegedly extended welfare benefits to an additional 15 million Americans.

Talmadge's second major concern as chairman of the Agriculture Committee was the plight of rural America. He argued that the redevelopment of small towns was vital to prevent continued migration to big cities. One of his first actions as chairman was to form a subcommittee on rural development chaired by Senator HUBERT HUMPHREY (D-Minn.). Talmadge coauthored the 1972 Rural Development Act, which was designed to encourage rural economic growth and to provide jobs and income required to support better community facilities and improve the general quality of rural life.

With Senator GEORGE AIKEN (R-Vt.) Talmadge introduced the 1972 National Forest and Wild Areas Act, which preserved from development wild areas largely west of the Mississippi River. In 1975 Talmadge supported the Emergency Farm Bill to revise upward target prices of wheat, cotton, and feed grains. He warned that farmers, to reach maximum productivity, must be compensated for increased production costs. He cautioned against continuing America's practice of supplying food to the world and recommended the establishment of a monitoring system to ensure that U.S. agricultural needs were satisfied prior to meeting foreign demand.

Considered an expert on tax legislation, Talmadge worked laboriously for the 1969 tax reform bill. In his struggle for budget control, he supported a proposed 1973 constitutional amendment to prohibit the federal government from spending more than it took in except in a congressionally declared national emergency. He also urged Congress to adopt a legislative program that would cap federal expenditures for each fiscal year, and if expenditures exceeded the ceiling, would require Congress to increase taxes to balance the budget. Continuing his attack on government spending in March 1976, Talmadge introduced a resolution calling for a balanced budget. He charged that continued unrestricted spending brought the nation near bankruptcy.

Talmadge consistently opposed congressional approval of civil rights legislation, believing that such measures went far beyond the Constitution. He declared that forced busing made a mockery of public education. He gained notoriety for his proposed constitutional amendment

Herman E. Talmadge *(Library of Congress)*

to restore state and local control over public education. Talmadge voiced no objections to the conservative civil rights records of President NIXON's Supreme Court nominees and endorsed each of them: CLEMENT F. HAYNSWORTH, G. HARROLD CARSWELL, and WILLIAM H. REHNQUIST.

As a member of the Select Committee on Presidential Campaign Activities (Watergate committee), Talmadge described himself as an "impartial judge and juror." He maintained that the committee's role was to bring to light the facts concerning the Watergate break-in and cover-up. He concurred with the committee's final report, which recommended 35 election campaign reforms, including the establishment of a federal elections commission with supervisory and enforcement powers.

During the early Johnson administration Talmadge supported America's involvement in Vietnam, but during Nixon's administration he became an opponent of the war. He supported the 1970 Cooper-Church Amendment prohibiting further U.S. involvement in Cambodia. He subsequently cosponsored the War Powers Act of 1973, which limited presidential authority to unilaterally order military activities. Talmadge maintained that America's national defense should be second to none. He argued that the United States should deal with the Soviets solely from a position of strength, and therefore in 1969 he supported President Nixon's proposed antiballistic missile system and in 1972 demanded that any strategic arms limitation agreement guarantee U.S. superiority. Talmadge never voted for any foreign aid program, regarding such aid as a global giveaway that the United States did not need and could not afford. Because of this opinion he voted for an end to all foreign aid programs.

In 1979 the Senate Ethics Committee investigated charges that Talmadge had set up a secret bank account into which campaign contributions and expense reimbursements were diverted. He was censured by the Senate that same year. He was defeated for reelection the following year by Mack Mattingly. He retired to his Georgia home, where he died in 2002.

—TML

terHorst, Jerald F(ranklin)
(1922–   ) *White House press secretary*

Born on July 11, 1922, Jerald terHorst was the son of a carpenter who had emigrated from the Netherlands to Grand Rapids, Michigan, shortly before World War I. His journalism-oriented college education at Michigan State was interrupted by service as a captain in the marines during World War II. In 1946 terHorst joined the Grand Rapids *Press* as a city hall reporter and two years later covered GERALD FORD's successful race for a Michigan congressional seat.

In 1952, after a year's active service with the Marine Corps in Korea, terHorst joined the conservative Detroit *News*. For the next 22 years, as Washington correspondent and finally Washington bureau chief, he covered four administrations, national elections, and several presidential trips abroad, earning a reputation as a competent, tireless, and generous reporter.

On August 9, 1974, the day after RICHARD NIXON's resignation announcement, President Ford named terHorst to replace RONALD ZIEGLER as the new White House press secretary. TerHorst and Ford immediately promised a new spirit of openness in the White House, including more frequent presidential press conferences, "pool" reporters, and photographers to cover the day's presidential activities and more complete and accurate information. TerHorst's pledge of better information was supported by his daily meetings with the president and consultations with top members of the administration. This contact stood in marked contrast to the situation of his predecessor, who was generally excluded from policy matters.

His tenure lasted exactly a month. On September 9, 1974, President Ford granted former president Nixon a full pardon for all federal crimes he "committed or may have committed or taken part in" during his term in office. Nixon later issued a statement accepting the pardon. The White House also announced that the Ford administration had concluded an agreement with Nixon (which was later reversed) giving him title to his presidential papers and tape recordings. TerHorst resigned immediately as a matter of "conscience." The next day he told a *New York Times* reporter that he would have felt "a little awkward" defending an absolute pardon for Nixon "but only a conditional pardon for young men who had fled to Canada to escape Vietnam as an act of conscience." Reportedly terHorst's written resignation reached Ford shortly before the president announced the pardon for Nixon.

After his resignation terHorst rejoined the *Detroit News* as a national affairs columnist. In recognition of his "exemplary display of conscience and courage in resigning a highly coveted position which he felt conflicted with his integrity as a journalist," terHorst was awarded the Society of Magazine Writers' first Conscience in Media medal. TerHorst worked for the *News* until 1981, when he became the Washington director of public affairs for the Ford Motor Company.

—FHM

Thompson, Fred D.
(1943–   ) *minority counsel, Senate Watergate committee*

A 1964 graduate of Memphis State University, Thompson earned a law degree from Vanderbilt University in 1967. He then spent two years in private practice before he became an assistant U.S. attorney. An active Republican, Thompson resigned this position in 1972 to direct the successful reelection campaign of Senator HOWARD BAKER (R-Tenn.). He then briefly returned to private practice.

In early 1973 Thompson accepted Baker's offer to serve as minority counsel for the Senate Watergate committee. Although responsible to the Republican members of the committee, Thompson coordinated his efforts along bipartisan lines with majority counsel SAMUEL DASH. In addition to recruiting staff members, Thompson examined voluminous files of Watergate material, including the transcripts from the trial of the seven original Watergate defendants.

During the committee's private and public hearings, Thompson and Dash presented evidence implicating a number of high officials in the Watergate conspiracy and subsequent cover-up. These included Attorney General JOHN MITCHELL, White House counsel JOHN DEAN, and presidential aide H. R. HALDEMAN. As the probe progressed and RICHARD NIXON refused to release White House tapes of conversations about Watergate, Thompson could no longer accept Nixon's innocence. He later stated that "for me the question finally became not, 'are the tapes damaging?' but instead, 'how damaging are they?'"

In the spring of 1974, as a number of grand juries convened to look into various abuses of the Nixon administration, the Watergate committee obtained transcripts of the White House tapes, but, according to Thompson, "even though there was still room for diehards to debate whether Nixon was personally guilty of the obstruction of justice that had taken place, the die was cast." The final transcript, released in August 1974, disclosed that Nixon had ordered the FBI to withdraw from an investigation of Watergate, and with this revelation, the Watergate committee closed its files. Thompson returned to Nashville and began work on a book outlining his role on the Senate Watergate committee titled *At That Point in Time* (1975).

Following this service, in 1980 Thompson became a special assistant to Tennessee governor Lamar Alexander. He then served as a special counsel to the Senate Foreign Relations Committee from 1980 to 1981, and then special counsel to the Senate Intelligence Committee in 1982. From 1985 to 1987 he was a member of the Tennessee Appellate Court Nominating Commission. From 1987 to 1994 he pursued a career as an actor in motion pictures and television. In 1994 he was elected to the U.S. Senate from Tennessee, a seat left vacant by the resignation of Albert Gore Jr. He was reelected in 1996 and served until 2002, when he declined to seek reelection. He continues his career as an actor.

—DGE and JRG

Thurmond, Strom
(1902–2003) *member of the Senate*

The son of a South Carolina politician, Thurmond was a school superintendent, city and county attorney, state senator, and state circuit court judge before World War II. During the war he served in both the European and Pacific theaters. Thurmond became governor of South Carolina in 1946. Two years later he was the presidential candidate of the States' Rights Party, founded in reaction to the strong civil rights plank of the Democratic Party. He carried five states from the Deep South in a losing effort. Thurmond entered the Senate in 1954, becoming the first person ever elected to a major office in a write-in campaign. In 1964 he switched allegiance to the Republican Party and was instrumental in BARRY GOLDWATER's 1964 victories in five southern states.

In 1968 Thurmond supported RICHARD NIXON's presidential candidacy. Reportedly, Nixon's "southern strategy" was based on an agreement with Thurmond. In return for the South Carolinian's support, Nixon pledged to oppose school busing, appoint "strict constructionists" to the Supreme Court, reduce federal spending, and promote a strong military establishment. Thurmond's influence in the White House was apparent; 20 of his friends and aides received administrative jobs. The senator was a frequent supporter of the Nixon administration. He backed the nominations of conservatives CLEMENT HAYNSWORTH and G. HARROLD CARSWELL to the Supreme Court and supported the 1972 Revenue Sharing Act, maintaining that it could reverse the trend toward centralized federal government bureaucracy. As the Watergate crisis unfolded in 1973 and 1974, Thurmond remained loyal to Nixon.

In the early 1970s Thurmond continued to vote against social welfare programs, charging that those people able to work should be given the opportunity. However, he made serious efforts to win housing and welfare funds for his state. In 1972 the senator cosponsored and worked for legislation establishing a 20 percent increase in Social Security benefits. In the same year he voted for the Rural Development Act, which he believed would help alleviate a potential domestic crisis. The bill was designed to ease rural outmigration and improve the quality of rural life. Thurmond also cosponsored the Equal Rights Amendment, stating that it was a "genuine reflection of the needs of many people."

In 1973 Thurmond proposed modification of the Electoral College to make it more representative of the American people's will. His "district plan" provided two electoral votes to the presidential candidate carrying the majority of the popular vote in each state and one electoral vote to the candidate carrying each state district. Thurmond maintained his proposal was constitutional and reflected the "one-man, one-vote" concept. No action was taken on the measure.

School busing was the most controversial issue that concerned Thurmond. He charged that the liberals promoted the very evils they condemned in 1954 when they were against allowing students to attend a particular school because of race. In August 1970 he reportedly persuaded Nixon to call off Justice Department plans to send lawyers south to supervise school openings. Thurmond argued against the 1971 Child Development Act that created child day care centers. He viewed this as a further extension of HEW's bureaucracy and implementation of desegregation guidelines. He also added that rather than parents, government behaviorists would be molding children's character.

An advocate of a strong defense posture, Thurmond was among the first senators to support Nixon's proposed Safeguard-ABM system, passed by Congress in March 1969. He continued to speak for improved weapons systems such as the B-1 bomber, Trident long-range missile, F-14 Tomcat, F-15, and S-3A Viking. In 1972 he was cautious about the SALT agreement, warning against Soviet numerical superiority. He later doubted the wisdom of establishing an all-volunteer army. Thurmond pointed out that Nixon's trip to mainland China had the potential for both triumph and tragedy. He believed this visit to be the beginning of a relationship that could improve U.S. security but might result in tragedy if America's traditional Pacific allies were abandoned.

Thurmond suggested economic foreign policy decisions be made in American interests. Thus, although he condemned the State Department's closing of the American consulate in Rhodesia in 1970, he voted for 1971 legislation lifting the import embargo on Rhodesian chrome ore because of its importance to the U.S. defense program. He advocated ending the export of American industrial technology to the Soviet Union. For the protection of the U.S. textile industry. Thurmond urged President GERALD FORD to impose quotas on textile imports from Japan and other countries. From 1972 to 1976 Thurmond argued against any new Panama Canal treaties that would surrender U.S. sovereignty over the Canal Zone. Should the canal be lost, Thurmond predicted adverse effects upon U.S. commerce and defense.

Because of similar political philosophies, Thurmond supported RONALD REAGAN's political candidacy in 1976. Throughout the 1980s Thurmond distinguished himself as an unwavering supporter of Reagan–GEORGE H. W. BUSH policies. As the ranking Republican on the Judiciary Committee, he was particularly influential in the debates surrounding the Supreme Court appointments of the period. On May 25, 1997, Thurmond broke the longevity record for senators at 42 years, 10 months. When the Republican Party won a Senate majority in 1994, Thurmond became the chairman of the Armed Services Committee. During the 2000 presidential primaries Thurmond was instrumental in delivering his state's delegates to George W. Bush. Beset with rumors about his fading mental capacities, Thurmond decided not to run for reelection in 2002. On December 5, 2002, while still in office, Thurmond turned 100 years old. Upon his retirement Thurmond took a suite at the hospital in Edgewood, South Carolina, where he died on June 26, 2003.

—TML and JRG

Tower, John G(oodwin)
(1925–1991) *member of the Senate*

John G. Tower was born on September 29, 1925, in Houston, Texas. Tower enlisted in the army in 1942 and after his discharge earned a B.A. in 1948 from Southwestern University. From 1948 to 1949 he worked as a radio announcer and became an insurance salesman in Dallas. In 1951 he accepted an assistant professorship of political science at Midwestern University and taught there until 1961.

A conservative, Tower entered Republican politics in the 1950s as a member of his county's executive committee. Elected to the Senate in 1961, Tower emerged to be a leading conservative Republican spokesman. He opposed Kennedy and Johnson social programs and was a vigorous supporter of the Vietnam War.

Tower developed a close relationship with RICHARD NIXON. He campaigned hard for Nixon in 1968 in Texas and became the president's liaison with the growing Texas Republican Party. By the early 1970s he was a leader of the Republicans in the Senate. In 1970 he took over the Republican Senate Campaign Committee, which empowered him to distribute nearly $300,000 to the Republican candidates. Three years later he left this post to head the party's Policy Committee, an important legislative planning group.

Tower enthusiastically backed the Nixon Vietnam War policy and voted against all the attempts to limit U.S. involvement. Extremely critical of the antiwar movement, he characterized GEORGE MCGOVERN in 1972 as "Hanoi's Choice for the President." The following year he lobbied for Congress to sustain Nixon's veto of the JACOB JAVITS War Powers Act, which severely restricted the president's right to commit troops abroad. Tower supported increased defense spending and maintained his conservative stance on domestic issues. He opposed funds allocated to antipoverty programs, spoke out against the establishment of a consumer protection agency, and advocated a constitutional amendment to ban forced busing.

Tower was critical of labor unions. In a December 1971 article in *Nation's Business*, he compared their power to that of the robber barons in the late 19th century. Because Tower believed that curtailing union power would reduce inflation, he introduced legislation to abolish the National Labor Relations Board (NLRB), the government agency charged with monitoring unfair labor practices. Tower accused the board of being "an extension of organized labor." He continued to defend the inclusion of Section 14(b) in the Taft-Hartley Act that permitted states to retain "right to work" laws.

As a leading Republican senator, Tower played a role in persuading Nixon to resign. In early April 1974 he began to publicly express concern over whether the president could govern effectively as long as questions about his role in the Watergate break-in remained unanswered. He joined with the Republican leadership in warning Nixon that impeachment could result if he continued to refuse to furnish all the materials subpoenaed by the Judiciary Committee. During August Tower participated in the Senate Republican Policy Committee decision to send Senator BARRY GOLDWATER (R-Ariz.) to request that Nixon resign.

During 1975 Tower served on the Church committee investigating possible Central Intelligence Agency (CIA) and FBI abuses. He refused to sign the panel's final report, citing evidence of extensive abuses, and opposed publication of the report because of "the diplomatic damage" he felt would result.

In 1978 Tower won another Senate term, narrowly defeating popular Democratic representative Bob Krueger. He was critical of the JIMMY CARTER administration's energy, anti-inflation, disarmament, China, and détente policies.

In 1985 Tower retired from his Senate seat, choosing instead to work as a defense consultant. Two weeks after his retirement President RONALD REAGAN called him back into service as the chief negotiator at the Strategic Arms Reduction Talks in Geneva. The following year Reagan asked Tower to chair the committee charged with investigating the Iran-contra scandal. Known universally as the "Tower committee," the investigation found fault with virtually every member of the president's national security team and did not wholly exonerate the president himself.

In 1988 Tower was one of the first to support the presidential candidacy of GEORGE H. W. BUSH. In 1988 Bush reciprocated by choosing Tower as his secretary of defense-designate. Most observers believed that as a former senator, Tower would be quickly confirmed. However, the nomination stalled amid allegations of Tower's womanizing, drinking, and unacceptably close relationship with key defense contractors. Bush decided not to withdraw the nomination, and it was defeated on the floor of the Senate by a vote of 53 to 47—the first defeat of a cabinet nomination since 1959.

In 1990 Bush appointed Tower chairman of the President's Foreign Intelligence Advisory Board (PFIAB). The next year Tower wrote his memoir, *Consequences: A Personal and Political Memoir*. On April 5, 1991, Tower and his daughter Marian were killed in an airplane crash near New Brunswick, Georgia.

—JB and JRG

Train, Russell E(rrol)

(1920–   ) *chairman, Council on Environmental Quality; administrator, Environmental Protection Agency*

Born on June 4, 1920, the son of an admiral, Train graduated from Princeton University in 1941 and served in the army during World War II. In 1948 he received his law degree from Columbia University and then served as counsel and adviser to various congressional committees and leaders. In 1956 Train joined the Treasury Department as head of its tax legislation staff, and the following year he accepted a judgeship on the Tax Court of the United States. During the 1950s Train became interested in conservation. In 1961 he formed and headed the African Wildlife Leadership Foundation. Train resigned his government post in 1965 to become president of the Conservation Foundation, a nonprofit group interested in research and education on a wide variety of environmental issues. Under Train's leadership the organization broadened its interest to include the problems of hunger, waste disposal, and pesticides.

Shortly after his election RICHARD NIXON asked Train to head a task force on resources and the environment. The group's report, issued in January 1969, criticized the gap between authorized funding and actual money given for antipollution programs and urged the administration to push forward existing environment programs. The panel also recommended the appointment of an adviser on environmental affairs to resolve differences between programs and to serve as leader of a proposed council on the environment.

In January 1969 Nixon announced the appointment of Train as undersecretary of the interior. The choice won the support of conservationists and at the time was seen as a move to placate environmentalists angered by the appointment of WALTER HICKEL as secretary of the interior. Hickel as governor of Alaska had pushed for development rather than preservation of resources.

During his first months in office, Train chaired an intergovernmental task force studying plans for the proposed Alaskan oil pipeline, and by 1970 his group had drawn up strict construction regulations to protect the environment. He also worked to coordinate government programs on the environment and resolve conflicting priorities between existing groups.

As a result of Train's encouragement, Nixon in June 1969 created a cabinet-level Environmental Quality Council composed of the secretaries of agriculture; commerce; health, education, and welfare; housing and urban development; the interior; and transportation. Critics denounced the panel as ineffective, and Congress, under the leadership of Senator HENRY JACKSON (D-Wash.), passed legislation creating an independent environmental council and making protection of natural resources a matter of national policy. Nixon signed the bill in January 1970. At the end of the month he appointed Train chairman of the Council on Environmental Quality. Train's duties included advising the president on environmental problems, developing a means of coordinating government pollution programs, and creating new programs.

The council's first annual report was issued less than three months later. It labeled "the most out-of-hand and irreversible" environmental problem to be the misuse of the nation's available land resources, urged the development of a "strong and consistent federal policy" opposing water pollution, and recommended the monitoring of transportation and energy policies. The report also discussed the problems of noise abatement, endangered species, ocean pollution, and resources, and called for an increase of staff and funds to combat them.

The following year Train recommended a "national contingency plan" for the federal cleanup of oil spills at such times when the responsible party failed to act. It backed long-range planning of land and water resources, timber-cutting regulation, and the banning of commercial trade involving wildlife species in danger of extinction as well as the continuation of tax incentives for organizations engaged in preservation of the environment. Train said that one of his highest priorities was to convince Congress to authorize funds for urban areas that needed mass transit as an alternative to automobiles in order to clean the air.

Train led the U.S. effort in securing an agreement with the Soviet Union to set up a joint environmental improvement program in June 1972 and headed a U.S.-Canadian committee formed to prevent possible oil spills off Canada's western coast resulting from the proposed Alaskan oil pipeline in September. The council's third annual report, appearing in August 1972, stated that while progress was being made in cleaning the air, America's waterways were growing dirtier. The report warned that it would cost nearly three times the original estimates to solve the country's most pressing pollution problems.

In September 1973 Train was confirmed as administrator of the Environmental Protection Agency (EPA), an independent organization created to oversee clean air and water legislation, pesticide control, and radiation-monitoring programs. He frequently clashed with the White House over its attempts to modify or stall enforcement of environmental laws. Shortly after taking the post, Train announced his opposition to a White House suggestion that air quality standards of the Clean Air Act be delayed in light of the anticipated economic consequences of a fuel shortage.

Train eventually backed a compromise between the EPA and the Office of Management and Budget (OMB), which wanted sweeping changes in the law. Under the compromise certain cities were given extensions of the 1977 deadline to meet the act's standards, and power companies were permitted to burn coal in some cases. Auto emission standards also were pushed back. But Train was able to have dropped an OMB proposal that the EPA consider the economic impact and costs of pollution control as well as the health effects in setting air quality standards. Another plan that would have exempted energy-related actions by federal agencies from required environmental impact statements also was dropped. His compromise was denounced by conservationists as an unnecessary weakening of the 1970 law, but it was accepted by Congress.

Near the end of his term Train could report that although the economic slowdown and growing energy crisis had made achievement of environmental goals difficult, progress had been made. Train boasted that carbon monoxide and hydrocarbon auto emissions were down almost 85 percent; dust and soot pollutants were down 14 percent. An $18 million water improvement program had been implemented, and a plan to convert trash into fuel had begun. Under his leadership the EPA had barred the sale of pesticides and the direct industrial discharge of polychlorinated biphenyls (PCBs) into waterways and had set radiation emission limits for nuclear power plants.

Train left government at the end of the FORD administration to return to the Conservation Foundation. In 1978 he was named president and CEO of the World Wildlife Fund; in 1985 he became chairman of its board. In 1991 Train was awarded the Medal of Freedom.

—SBB

U

Udall, Morris K(ing)

(1922–1998) *member of the House of Representatives*

Morris Udall was born on June 15, 1922, and raised in St. Johns, Arizona, a town founded by his grandfather, who was a Mormon missionary. After serving in the army air corps during World War II, he studied law at the University of Arizona and was admitted to the bar in 1949. Entering private practice in Tucson with his older brother Stewart, he also became active in local Democratic politics. In 1950 he was elected chief deputy attorney in Pima County, and in 1953 he won a race for county attorney. In the 1956 presidential campaign Udall chaired Arizona Volunteers for Stevenson and was a delegate to the Democratic National Convention.

In May 1961 Udall won a special election to fill the House seat vacated by his brother Stewart, who had resigned to become secretary of the interior. A supporter of the social welfare legislation of the Kennedy and Johnson administrations, he joined the Democratic Study Group, a liberal faction within the Democratic Party. As a member of the Post Office and Civil Service Committee, Udall wrote the House version of the 1965 federal pay raise bill and in 1967 drafted legislation to set up an independent commission to pass on salary increases for members of Congress. Initially a supporter of the Vietnam War, he broke with the Johnson administration in October 1967 when he declared in a speech given in Tucson that his support of the war had been a "mistake."

As chairman of the Subcommittee on the Environment of the House Interior Committee, Udall emerged as one of the strongest proponents of environmental legislation during the NIXON-FORD era. He supported legislation to fund a program of environmental education and advocated the establishment of a federal commission on population growth and the environment. In 1971 he introduced a resolution to make population stabilization by voluntary means a national goal. In 1974 he successfully sponsored legislation establishing a program of research and development in nonnuclear energy resources. Udall's major concerns, however, were national land use policy and the regulation of strip mining.

In 1964 Congress created the Public Land Law Review Commission and selected Udall as one of the congressional members on the commission. After almost six years of study, it released a report in 1970 that recommended an extensive overhaul of public land legislation and management policies. The report, which urged greater commercial exploitation of federal lands, aroused the ire of environmentalists, and Udall dissented from many of its recommendations.

A national land use policy bill was first introduced in the Senate in 1970 by HENRY JACKSON. It provided grants-in-aid for states to develop and implement statewide land use plans, set federal standards to qualify for the grants, and proposed creation of a federal land and water resources planning council to administer the program. No action was taken by the Senate, but Jackson introduced similar legislation in 1972, and Udall sponsored it in the House. No progress was made in the House until 1974, when Udall's subcommittee held extensive hearings on the bill, and the full Interior Committee reported it favorably. But on June 11 the House killed the legislation on a procedural vote.

In a press conference the next day Udall blamed President Nixon for the defeat, saying that the bill was a victim of "impeachment politics," an attempt by the president to solidify conservative support against his impeachment. Udall was especially bitter because in 1973 Nixon had called land use legislation his "number one environmental priority." In 1975 Udall tried again, but this time the Interior Committee refused to report the bill to the full House. No efforts were made to pass land use legislation in 1976.

Udall also faced stiff opposition in his efforts to have legislation enacted to regulate the strip mining of coal. Although most of the nation's coal reserves were underground, strip mining was considerably cheaper, and coal companies and utilities strongly opposed its regulation. Environmentalists, however, made the regulation of strip mining one of their high-priority items, and Udall acted as their chief proponent in the House. The House passed legislation in 1972, but no action was taken by the Senate.

In 1973 both legislative bodies held extensive hearings on a strip mining bill. Udall's subcommittee held hearings throughout the summer and fall, and in May 1974 the full Interior Committee reported the bill. Its major provisions included establishment of federal standards for the states to follow in setting up mandatory regulatory programs to control the strip mining of coal; the requirement that mining companies restore stripped land to its original contours; and a tax on every ton of coal mined, to be used for the reclamation of previously stripped and abandoned land. Udall, who was floor manager of the bill, described the legislation as an effort to end "a legacy of neglect" of the nation's land. Finally approved by a Senate-House conference on December 3 and passed by Congress on December 13, it was pocket-vetoed by President Ford.

The following month at the opening of the more liberal 94th Congress, Udall reintroduced the legislation. The coal industry mounted a heavy campaign against it, including dispensing $400,000 to finance a demonstration by mine workers in April 1975. Udall accused the industry of "a mischievous and purposeful effort" to "mislead and foster fear among workers." When Congress approved the legislation in May, Ford vetoed it again, and the House failed to override the veto by three votes. In 1976 the House Rules Committee blocked revival of strip mining legislation.

In May 1974 Udall revealed that he was considering a bid for the 1976 presidential nomination. Earlier, in 1969, he had challenged JOHN MCCORMACK's tenure as Speaker of the House, and in 1971 he ran unsuccessfully for House majority leader. Encouraged by Representative HENRY REUSS (D-Wis.) and other House liberals, Udall declared his candidacy in November. Announcing that the "three E's—environment, economy, and energy"—would dominate his campaign, he said that the major challenge facing the nation was "whether we can adapt and change from an era of abundance and cheap natural resources, to an era of scarcity." He advocated federal responsibility for full employment, comprehensive national health insurance, and the federalization of welfare. His platform also included the controversial proposal to break up the huge oil companies through legislation rather than antitrust action through the courts. By July 1975 Udall had raised enough money for his campaign to qualify for federal matching funds under the 1974 campaign finance law. In January 1976 he picked up the endorsement of House Speaker THOMAS O'NEILL.

A large number of candidates ranging across the political spectrum, including Henry Jackson, GEORGE WALLACE, JIMMY CARTER, FRED HARRIS, and BIRCH BAYH, mounted campaigns for the 1976 nomination. Liberal candidates Harris and Bayh dropped out of the race early in the year, however, and Udall urged liberals to unite behind him or else face the prospect of a conservative nominee. Although he failed to win any of the early primaries, Udall placed a strong second in New Hampshire, Massachusetts, New York, and Wisconsin. The race was dominated, however, by dark horse candidate Jimmy Carter, the former governor of Georgia who capitalized on the voters' post-Watergate distrust of Washington politicians.

Carter won seven of the first nine primaries. When Henry Jackson withdrew from active campaigning at the end of April, Udall declared that he and Carter were the only serious candidates left and predicted an "uphill fight" for the nomination. Despite the last-minute challenge of California governor EDMUND "JERRY" BROWN JR., Carter continued to outdistance Udall in delegate strength. Early in June the count stood at 1,117 for Carter and only 327 for Udall. On June 14 Udall met with Carter and announced that he would stop campaigning. Saying that he "will not be a part of any stop-Carter drive," he released his delegates.

Despite the failure of his campaign, Udall's race for the nomination dramatically increased his visibility and gave him added stature in the party. He won inclusion in the platform of a plank committing the party to enact "strip mining legislation designed to protect and restore the environment." Running for reelection to his eighth complete term in the House, Udall won by a substantial majority. Udall retired from the House in 1991. He was awarded the Medal of Freedom in 1996 and died in 1998.

—JD

Ulasewicz, Anthony T. (Tony)
(1918–1997) *Watergate figure*

Anthony Ulasewicz was born in New York City on December 14, 1918. Anthony Ulasewicz was an original member of the team put together by JOHN EHRLICHMAN to investigate persons on the White House "enemies list." Ulasewicz received payment from HERBERT KALMBACH, a leading fund-raiser for the 1968 Republican presidential campaign and later President NIXON's personal lawyer. Ulasewicz had worked earlier for the New York City Police Department's Bureau of Special Services.

Ulasewicz performed a variety of services for Ehrlichman, including illegally wire-tapping columnist Joseph Kraft's telephone in 1969. When Representative Mario Biaggi (D-N.Y.) criticized President Nixon's 1969 call for a war against crime as being "insulting to Italian Americans," he searched Biaggi's past for possible Mafia connections. Ulasewicz reportedly also formulated a plan to search out damaging information on Senator EDWARD KENNEDY concerning the 1969 auto accident at Chappaquiddick that involved the drowning of Mary Jo Kopechne. These and other incidents led the *New York Times* to later describe Ulasewicz as a precursor of the White House "Plumbers."

Ulasewicz first became directly involved in the Watergate cover-up by delivering a message from JOHN DEAN to JAMES MCCORD concerning McCord's course of conduct during the ongoing investigation of the Watergate break-in. On June 28, 1972, Dean approached Kalmbach to secretly raise funds for the defense of the Watergate burglars. At Dean's instruction Ulasewicz was to distribute the money to the defendants. Kalmbach raised money during the summer, and Ulasewicz distributed $220,000, always using secretive methods such as pay telephones, drops, and aliases. In September, when it appeared that the indictments in the Watergate case would include only those directly involved in the break-in, Kalmbach, on the advice of Ulasewicz, declined to raise additional funds for the cover-up effort.

Ulasewicz testified about his activities both during the Senate Watergate committee hearings in July 1973 and the cover-up trial in November 1974. In April 1975 he was indicted for tax evasion regarding the reporting of his income during 1971 and 1972 while he worked for the White House. In December 1976 Ulasewicz was convicted of these charges, and in February 1977 he received the minimum sentence of one year of unsupervised probation. He retired to upstate New York and died in 1997.

—RLN

Usery, W(illie) J(ulian), Jr.
(1923–   ) *secretary of labor*

Born on December 21, 1923, the son of a postal clerk, Usery enrolled in Georgia Military Academy in 1938 but left after three years to work in navy shipyards as a welder. In 1943 he joined the navy and served on a repair ship in the Pacific until 1946. After his discharge he worked as a machinist while attending night school, became active in union politics, and founded a local chapter of the International Association of Machinists (IAM).

Because of his organization skills, Usery was tapped by IAM officials for a union post at Cape Canaveral, later called Cape Kennedy, in 1954. He played a decisive role in most labor negotiations involving the aerospace industry and in 1967 was appointed chairman of the Cape Kennedy Management Relations Council. While stationed in Florida he also became active in the civil rights movement of the 1960s.

In 1968 GEORGE P. SHULTZ, RICHARD NIXON's secretary of labor, offered Usery a position as assistant secretary of labor for labor-management relations. Although he felt that "it's very difficult for a labor leader to come into a Republican administration," he took over the job effective February 1969. His responsibilities included overseeing the federal employee unions, restructuring pension fund regulations, and establishing farm workers' bargaining rights.

In the spring of 1969 Usery served as Nixon's chief mediator for a threatened strike by the Brotherhood of Railroad Signalmen (BRS). Through the use of collective bargaining, he was able to avert a national strike. His decisive role in negotiations with the BRS earned him the reputation of Nixon's "number one labor troubleshooter."

Because of his mediating expertise and interventionist skills, Usery played key roles in the settlement of the 1970 Brotherhood of Railway and Airline Clerks strike and the 1971 United Transportation Union's strike against the railroads. He subsequently intervened in such deadlocked negotiations as the International Brotherhood of Teamsters and Pan American World Airways and also the dispute between black construction workers and the white-controlled building industry in Pittsburgh. In 1971 Usery was instrumental in achieving the first collective bargaining agreement in history between the Council of American Postal Employees and the U.S. Postal Service. With the exception of accusations within the labor movement that he displayed favoritism to AFL-CIO affiliates during union membership drives, Usery was virtually exempt from criticism among national labor leaders and the Department of Labor.

In 1973 the AFL-CIO Executive Council voted unanimously to appoint Usery director of the Department of Organization and Field Services, but he declined because he felt his talents were most needed in the Nixon administration. That same year Usery became the official top labor mediator for the government when he assumed the position of director of the Federal Mediation and Conciliation Service. He continued in his directorship to encourage improved industrywide bargaining procedures and also played a significant role in the formation of joint labor-management committees throughout various industries to avoid possible strikes and deadlocks. He also strengthened his reputation as a negotiator extraordinaire by settling a variety of local labor disputes that threatened to disrupt the clothing and trucking industries. During the Arab oil embargo of 1973, Usery's expendi-

tious handling of a contract dispute prevented a strike by thousands of airline pilots.

Upon the resignation of JOHN T. DUNLOP as secretary of labor in 1975, Usery was considered the likely candidate for the job. Shortly thereafter President FORD nominated Usery, and in February 1976 he assumed the cabinet post. His responsibilities broadened to include the administration of federal antidiscrimination laws, the regulation of government hiring procedures and job training programs, as well as establishment of job safety guidelines. Usery continued in his mediating capacity, and in April 1976 he helped to settle a strike between the Teamsters and the American and General Motors Corps. His tenure with the Labor Department ended at the close of the Ford administration.

Usery left government service in 1977 to start his own business as a labor consultant. In 1990 he mediated a settlement of the United Mine Workers of America's protracted strike at the Pittston, Pennsylvania, mine and chaired a commission concerned with miners' health and pension issues. In 1994–95 Usery participated in the mediation of the major league baseball strike.

—DGE

Vanik, Charles A.

(1913–) *member of the House of Representatives*

Charles A. Vanik was born in Cleveland, Ohio, on April 7, 1913. Vanik received both bachelor's and law degrees from Case-Western Reserve University and served in the navy during World War II. Entering politics at the war's end, Vanik won election to the state senate and a municipal judgeship before unseating a 19-term House incumbent in 1954. Of Czech heritage, Vanik represented the overwhelmingly Democratic 21st district, composed largely of second-generation Eastern European immigrants and blacks.

In January 1965 House leaders transferred Vanik, considered a Johnson administration loyalist, from the Banking and Currency Committee to Ways and Means. The Democratic leadership moved Vanik to the powerful taxation panel because of his strong support for Medicare, long opposed by Ways and Means chairman WILBUR D. MILLS (D-Ark.). It was Vanik's vote that forced Mills to accept a compromise Medicare plan in 1965. While supporting many of the domestic measures of President Johnson, Vanik became highly critical of the administration's Vietnam policy, voting against the 1968 Defense Department authorization that passed the House 213 to 6.

A 1967 Ohio redistricting created a large black majority in Vanik's district. Declaring that the district should now have a black representative, Vanik decided to run in the largely white, suburban 22nd district against 82-year-old incumbent Frances P. Belton (R-Ohio). In a hotly contested election Vanik stressed the need for updating the district's political leadership and defeated the wealthy 14-term representative with 55 percent of the vote.

With his solidly liberal record and excellent constituent services, Vanik easily won reelection in 1970, 1972, and 1974. He maintained two district offices, organizing many district studies and commissions. Vanik's practices of compiling yearly reports on federal aid to his district and on educational aid to his constituents were adopted by federal agencies on a nationwide basis. A strong supporter of environmental protection, Vanik pushed for the cleanup of Lake Erie, advocating improved waste treatment, stricter regulation of industrial waste, and a "no discharge" goal set for 1975. Vanik joined 40 other representatives in offering a package of clean water amendments to the Water Pollution Control Act of 1972. The amendments, which would have made polluters liable to suit and set more stringent waste-dumping standards for the Great Lakes, failed in the House. Vanik also worked actively for consumer protection programs and in 1971 introduced legislation to ensure equal educational and employment opportunities for the handicapped.

In December 1973 Vanik introduced an amendment to President RICHARD NIXON's comprehensive foreign trade bill. The amendment would have placed strict curbs on U.S. trade with the Soviet Union, denying the USSR most favored nation (MFN) status and commercial credit until the Soviets eased emigration restrictions on Soviet Jews. Vanik's amendment passed the House, while the Senate approved a similar amendment introduced by Senators HENRY JACKSON (D- Wash.), ABRAHAM RIBICOFF (D-Conn.), and JACOB JAVITS (R-N.Y.). In the face of strong pressure by the administration, which considered MFN status for the USSR essential to the pursuit of détente, Senator Jackson offered a compromise floor amendment allowing the Soviets an 18-month waiver on the ban of MFN status provided they moved toward free emigration policies. This compromise measure passed in December 1974, but its terms were later rejected by the Soviets.

A longtime advocate of congressional reform, Vanik continued through the Nixon and FORD administrations to oppose the leadership of Ways and Means chairman Wilbur Mills. Often among the dissenting minority on Ways and Means, Vanik supported open committee sessions and fought the "closed rule," frequently invoked by Mills to send Ways and Means bills to the House with a ban on the introduction of floor amendments. At the time of the House Legislative Reorganization Act of 1970, Vanik introduced a measure that would have abolished the seniority system. Terming the system "arbitrary," Vanik proposed the election of new standing committee chairmen every two years. Other congressional reformers opposed Vanik's

amendment, fearing that it had no hope of passage and would weaken other reform efforts. In December 1974 Vanik joined other House Democrats in a successful coalition to strip Wilbur Mills of his Ways and Means chairmanship, a position Mills had held since 1958. On December 19 Ways and Means established its first subcommittees, thus decentralizing the panel's authority. As chairman of the oversight subcommittee, Vanik attacked tax system inequities, citing 11 major firms that paid no income taxes in 1975. Blasting corporate tax loopholes, Vanik charged the Republican administration with aiding the American corporation to become "a freeloader on the American scene." Vanik retired from the House in 1981 and practices law in Washington, D.C.

—DAE

Vesco, Robert L(ee)
(1935–   ) *international financier*

Born on December 4, 1935, the son of an auto worker, Vesco grew up in Detroit. He dropped out of high school at 16 and took a job in an auto repair shop. Eventually he worked his way into the management of several small companies. From 1955 to 1959 he was employed by the Olin Mathieson Corporation, and from 1959 to 1965 he was a financial consultant in New York City. In 1965 he became president of the International Controls Corporation (ICC), a small New Jersey–based firm he used as a vehicle for entering international finance.

In 1970 Vesco used the assets available to him through ICC to gain controlling interest in the foundering Investors Overseas Services Ltd. (IOS), the large mutual fund established by Bernard Cornfeld and one of the more spectacular victims of the 1969–70 international credit crunch. A run on IOS stock, then selling at $10 per share, was the opening phase of a year-long crisis for the "offshore" mutual fund that Cornfeld had built up through the boom of the 1960s. By early September 1970 Vesco had negotiated a bailout package for IOS with conditions effectively giving him control of the conglomerate. Vesco had compelled IOS to deposit $5 million in collateral in a Vesco-controlled bank in the Bahamas, a sum he promptly relent to IOS as the main ingredient of the rescue operation. In effect he used the disarray of the IOS management to take over the conglomerate with its own money. Vesco followed his successful takeover with the ouster of Cornfeld from the organization, ultimately buying for 92 cents a share Cornfeld's 6.6 million shares of IOS stock, or roughly 15 percent of the total stock issued.

The Securities and Exchange Commission (SEC) had intently followed the IOS crisis and Vesco's takeover and in May 1971 won a court battle to subpoena Vesco for an inquiry into the financing of the acquisition of Cornfeld's shares in IOS, which had just been resold to a Canadian subsidiary of Vesco's International Controls. That same month Denver oilman John M. King filed a suit for more than $1 billion against Vesco and IOS, alleging that Vesco had used illegal funds to gain control of various U.S. companies. Dissident IOS officials from Cornfeld's management team fought and lost a proxy battle in July to regain control of IOS from Vesco.

Vesco was arrested in Geneva in November 1971 on charges of misappropriating shares while serving as a director of a former IOS bank subsidiary. The charges stemmed from a complaint by an IOS dissident manager who alleged that his own shares, on deposit in IOS's International Development Bank, had been used by Vesco to defeat the dissident faction in the proxy war for control of the firm. On December 1, however, Vesco and his colleagues were released on bail. Investigations later revealed that the CIA, on orders from the NIXON administration, had intervened to obtain Vesco's release.

In November 1972 a two-year SEC investigation culminated in charges that Vesco, 20 other individuals, and 21 firms they controlled had diverted more than $244 million in assets from four mutual funds holding securities of U.S. companies. The SEC charged Vesco with having controlled IOS through a "shell" corporation created to purchase the Cornfeld shares in 1971. Vesco and his entourage took refuge in Costa Rica, where they could not be extradited. Two days after the SEC civil complaint was announced, the *Wall Street Journal* reported that a company founded by the president of Costa Rica, José Figueres, had received a loan of more than $2 million from Vesco.

In February 1973 Harry L. Sears, a New Jersey Republican who had headed the 1972 Committee to Reelect the President (CREEP) in that state, testified in a pretrial deposition that Vesco had contributed $200,000 to CREEP in hopes of heading off the SEC inquiry into his activities. Sears said that the sum had been delivered in cash to former secretary of commerce MAURICE STANS, who was serving as head of the Republican Finance Committee. The contribution had never been reported to the Government Accounting Office. Sears's account was confirmed by Edward Nixon, the president's brother and a Vesco associate. CREEP announced that it had returned Vesco's contribution because of the pending SEC suit, saying that "under these circumstances, we believe it is in your best interests, as well as ours, that the contribution was returned."

In April 1973 the *Washington Post* alleged that President Nixon and his aide JOHN D. EHRLICHMAN had promised in 1971 to use government channels to help Vesco obtain control of a Lebanese bank. The *Post* reported a December 1971 meeting in the White House involving Gilbert R. J. Straub, a codefendant with Vesco in the SEC suit as well as a friend of Edward and Donald Nixon (the President's brothers), Harry L. Sears, and a man later identified as the courier who delivered Vesco's $200,000 contribution to Stans.

In May 1973 the Justice Department filed charges against the financial committee of CREEP for failure to report the Vesco contribution. A week later Stans and former attorney general JOHN MITCHELL were indicted for their actions while serving on CREEP; the handling of Vesco's contribution was the centerpiece of the government's case against them. At the same time Vesco was indicted on one count of conspiracy and three counts of obstructing justice. In June 1973 the U.S. ambassador to Costa Rica asked the authorities of that country to extradite Vesco. Several days later a New York grand jury indicted Vesco for attempting to defraud the International Controls Corporation. However, in July 1973 the Costa Rican supreme court ruled that Vesco not be extradited.

During October new grand jury indictments were brought against Vesco for his actions in the IOS takeover. A month later he was arrested in the Bahamas in another U.S. attempt to have him extradited, but once again the local court ruled in his favor. In late November a narcotics agent told congressional investigators that Vesco had been involved in a scheme to smuggle 100 pounds of heroin into the United States.

In the spring of 1974 Vesco emerged as the central figure in the Stans-Mitchell trial in New York City in which the government accused both defendants of having attempted to block the SEC investigation of Vesco in exchange for a large cash contribution to the Nixon campaign. In early April 1974 the U.S. prosecutor contended that Vesco's contribution had financed the Watergate break-in. Mitchell and Stans were acquitted, however, and in December 1974 Vesco went on Costa Rican television to defend himself and to portray himself as a victim of "the same political groups that eliminated President Kennedy and then President Nixon and want to eliminate all of Nixon's associates." He further denied having broken any laws in the United States.

In March 1975 charges against Harry L. Sears stemming from his role in CREEP were dropped. Sears's pretrial deposition revealed that Attorney General Mitchell had intervened personally on Vesco's behalf to obtain his release from a Swiss jail in 1971 and that the CIA had informed Swiss intelligence services "that there was unusual interest in higher U.S. government circles . . . in this case, and that we hoped Vesco would be released on his own recognizance." Simultaneously a Senate subcommittee report indicated the possible involvement of Vesco in a scheme to smuggle $200,000 worth of heroin into the United States, and stockholders of International Controls Corporation filed suit against him in Costa Rican courts. During May 1975 New Jersey courts ordered Vesco to pay $5.6 billion to stockholders of IOS Ltd. The following year Vesco was indicted yet again for conspiring to misappropriate $100 million in the assets of mutual funds he controlled.

During the 1970s Vesco made his home in Costa Rica, where he pursued his business and financial interests while resisting the efforts of the United States and local forces hostile to him to achieve his extradition. In 1978 Costa Rica repealed the law that prevented Vesco's extradition. He moved throughout Latin America and by the 1990s had settled in Cuba. On May 31, 1995, Vesco was arrested by Cuban police, along with his wife and Donald Nixon. The following year he was sentenced to 13 years in jail.

—LRG

Volcker, Paul A.

(1927–   ) *undersecretary of the Treasury for monetary affairs*

Paul A. Volcker was born in Cape May, New Jersey, on September 5, 1927. After graduating summa cum laude from Princeton in 1949, Volcker received an M.A. from Harvard in 1951 and did further postgraduate work at the London School of Economics. Upon completion of his studies, he worked as an economist for the Federal Reserve Bank of New York and later for the Chase Manhattan Bank. He served an initial period at the Treasury Department in the 1961–65 period but returned again to Chase as a vice president, remaining there until he was appointed undersecretary of the Treasury for monetary affairs in 1969.

Both publicly and behind the scenes, Volcker played an important role in the international monetary crisis that provided an ever present backdrop to the NIXON administration's economic policies. Volcker was associated with the "hard line," or assertively nationalistic wing of U.S. policy makers on international monetary questions, typified by Secretary of the Treasury JOHN CONNALLY. Like Connally, Volcker often clashed with other U.S. and foreign officials. Central to Volcker's position on such questions was a hostility to any continued significant role for gold in international settlements, which was an important source of friction between the United States and Europe, as well as an advocacy of the extended use of "special drawing rights" (SDRs), or "paper gold" certificates issued by the International Monetary Fund (IMF), which the United States introduced as an international alternative to gold in the late 1960s.

Gold, SDRs, and foreign exchange rates were complexly interrelated issues with which Volcker had to deal repeatedly. In December 1969, as part of the U.S. campaign to ease out gold, Volcker met in Rome with South African officials to negotiate a compromise agreement on South African gold sales to the IMF. In June 1971, as the crisis leading to the August 1971 abrogation of the Bretton Woods Agreement intensified, Volcker, who felt that the existing exchange rate system was adequate, denied any deep structural nature to the U.S. balance-of-payments deficit and blamed the crisis on short-term capital flows. To counter these trends he called for limited mandatory capital controls and "an international open-market operation" in the burgeoning Eurodollar markets. The balance-of-payments crisis persisted, however, and the old exchange rates had to be abandoned.

In August Volcker was sent to Europe to explain the U.S. policy to European governments. Volcker announced that the Europeans "understood and even welcomed" the U.S. unilateral action, but reactions in European capitals did not seem to bear out his optimism. In Brussels, the headquarters of the European Economic Community (EEC), Volcker was seen as representing an "uncompromising" U.S. attitude on Nixon's 10 percent foreign import surcharge. In September, when the IMF Group of 10 met in Paris to discuss the situation, Volcker reaffirmed his opposition to a U.S. gold revaluation and urged the U.S. trading partners to engage in "consultation, not negotiation." Shortly thereafter Volcker disclosed a vastly increased U.S. balance-of-payments deficit, an amount that "shocked" many foreigners.

When the Group of 10 reconvened in November 1971 for new talks and to lay the basis for new fixed rates, Volcker offered America's trading partners an abolition of the 10 percent import surcharge if they consented to revalue their currencies by 11 percent against the dollar, a proposal that elicited little enthusiasm from major exporters to U.S. markets. When the Smithsonian Agreement establishing new fixed rates was finally signed by all countries in Washington in December, most nations agreed to revalue by varying amounts.

After the establishment of new fixed rates, Volcker began to advocate what was known as a "reserve indicator" in international settlements. Under Volcker's proposal, which many observers likened to a 1943 proposal by Keynes that the United States, then a strong creditor nation, had rejected, nations running excessive trade surpluses would be penalized in the same way as deficit nations. Most U.S. trading partners viewed Volcker's plan as a transparent attempt to shift the burden of the United States' chronic deficits onto the surplus producers, and it was never adopted.

Volcker was involved in the public rift, if not actual hostility, between the Treasury and the Federal Reserve Bank on international monetary questions and the administration's so-called benign neglect of the dollar. The Treasury, under Secretary Connally, predominated in U.S. economic policy in this period and was more closely associated with Connally's aggressive international stance, which European and Japanese commentators called "malign neglect," than was the Fed. One dramatic expression of this rift had been the exclusion of Fed chairman ARTHUR BURNS from the "Camp David II" meeting on August 14–15, 1971, when the "New Economic Policy," framed in large part by Connally, had been adopted. In a May 1972 address to the American Bankers' Association in Montreal, Burns referred to the urgent need for overall monetary reform and alluded to a continued limited reserve role for gold. Speaking after Burns, Volcker told the convention that the chairman "was not speaking for the U.S. government" and warned against any "prepackaged reforms."

At the IMF annual meeting in Vienna in September 1972, Volcker attacked what he saw as European efforts to "impose" their solutions on the rest of the world and once again asserted that "gold will have to go the way of silver." Upon his return to the United States, Volcker told the congressional Joint Economic Committee (JEC) that gold "should and must continue to diminish" as a reserve asset and that advocates of an increase in the official gold price—which would be a further devaluation of the dollar—were victims of a "dangerous illusion." Volcker also told the JEC that he opposed Federal Reserve Bank intervention to shore up the dollar, leaving that task to the central banks of other countries.

When the next dollar crisis erupted, in February 1973, the central banks of Europe and Japan did indeed intervene, buying billions of dollars to prevent new revaluations of their currencies. Volcker was sent on a secret tour of the major world capitals to confer with foreign officials, and on February 12, the day of his return to the United States, a further 10 percent devaluation of the dollar was announced. The move proved insufficient. Speculation against the dollar continued, and the market price of gold, in spite of Volcker's repeated statements against gold speculators, soared to $89 an ounce. On March 1 foreign exchange markets closed for two weeks. President Nixon, Volcker, Chairman Burns, and Secretary Connally met to discuss the crisis. Volcker then accompanied an American delegation to Brussels on March 4 for talks with EEC officials. On March 16 in Paris an accord was signed ending the fixed rate system in effect since 1944, and Volcker, in spite of his long-standing opposition to floating rates, announced he was "happy" with the agreement. In June 1973 he appeared before the JEC to reaffirm his satisfaction with the new floating rates system.

Volcker resigned as undersecretary of the Treasury in June 1974. The following year he became president of the Federal Reserve Bank of New York. He served in that position until 1979, when President JIMMY CARTER named him chairman of the Federal Reserve System, a position he held until 1987, when he was succeeded by ALAN GREENSPAN. Since then he has headed a commission that investigated the handling by Swiss banks of Holocaust survivors' accounts and headed an oversight board at Arthur Andersen accountants, the firm responsible for auditing the failed Enron Corp. (2002).

—LG

Volpe, John A(nthony)
(1908–1994) *secretary of transportation; ambassador to Italy*

Volpe, born on December 8, 1908, the eldest son of Italian immigrant parents, rose from a hod carrier to the head of the multimillion-dollar John A. Volpe Construction Co., which he founded in 1933. Volpe's government career began in 1953 when he was appointed public works commissioner for Massachusetts and started the largest highway construction program in the state's history. He served briefly as the interim federal highway administrator when President Eisenhower appointed him to the newly created post in late 1956. In 1960 he was elected governor of Massachusetts, the only Republican to win a statewide race that year. Volpe was the first Italian and Catholic ever elected governor of the state. He was defeated for reelection in 1962, recaptured the office in 1964, and won the state's first four-year gubernatorial term in 1966. He resigned the governorship in 1969 when RICHARD NIXON appointed him the nation's second secretary of transportation. As secretary, Volpe headed the department that was responsible for regulating the automotive, railway, and aviation sectors of the economy. He also supervised the interstate highway construction program, which he helped launch in 1956.

Volpe shaped the Nixon administration's transportation policies and programs and served as the administration's chief Capitol Hill spokesman on many transportation issues during Nixon's first term. These included providing federal loan guarantees for the Penn Central and other bankrupt railroads, reor-

ganizing passenger rail service under Amtrak, and increasing federal safety regulation of the railroads. Volpe also had to cope with the 1970 "sick-out" staged by the nation's air controllers to protest working conditions and the 123-day West Coast dock strike in 1970 that ended after the administration pressured Congress to enact legislation to settle the dispute.

Volpe was a strong supporter of the supersonic transport (SST), which he maintained was needed to preserve the U.S. aviation industry. The program, however, ran into strong congressional opposition led by Senator WILLIAM PROXMIRE (D-Wis.) and Representative HENRY REUSS (D-Wis.). The opponents objected to the plane's excessive development costs, the sonic booms it would create over land, its excessive operating noise on landing and takeoff, and the environmental hazards it might create in the upper atmosphere.

Volpe tried to counter some of the objections to the SST by promising that it would not be flown over land until the plane's 50-mile-wide sonic boom had been reduced to acceptable limits. However, the opponents were able to strengthen their case after they obtained a Department of Transportation report that opposed the plane.

Congress eventually funded the SST in 1969, but the project ran into even stronger congressional opposition during the following year when the administration requested $290 million for fiscal 1971. Congress granted the funds but only for three-fourths of the fiscal year to permit further congressional review. The Nixon administration opened the fight to save the plane in March 1971. Volpe accused the SST opponents of "hysterical sloganeering." He pointed to the long-range benefits of the program, which employed 13,000 people to build the prototypes and which would have employed 50,000 when the plane went into full production. But both Houses voted to end the program in March 1971, after the government had spent about $840 million on the project.

Volpe also was a strong advocate of the administration's mass transit funding proposals that Congress adopted during Nixon's first term. The White House proposed a $10 billion, 12-year program financed by general revenues to upgrade urban transit systems. The program called for an initial $3.1 billion five-year contract authorization. Urban transit proponents, who favored creating an urban transit trust fund similar to the highway trust fund that financed the construction of highways, disapproved of the proposal on the grounds that it failed to ensure full funding for the mass transit program. Instead they favored earmarking the 7 percent excise tax on automobiles to finance an urban transit trust fund. Trust fund spending would have been automatic, as opposed to spending authorizations funded from general revenues that required prior congressional approval before the funds could be spent.

Volpe at first favored the excise tax trust fund concept. But the administration decided against it, and Volpe supported the administration's position. He claimed public transportation was a public responsibility and should be met by all taxpayers out of general revenues. Congress finally resolved the funding controversy without creating a trust fund and enacted the administration's $3.1 billion urban transit aid proposal in 1970.

The urban transit funding controversy broke out again in the next session of Congress. This time the question was whether to divert highway trust funds for mass transit construction. In March 1972 Volpe released a report calling for the diversion of highway trust funds. He proposed a single "urban fund" to be started with a $1 billion authorization from highway trust funds for fiscal 1974. This fund was to be increased to $2.25 billion in later years. The highway construction industry vigorously objected to the proposal to divert highway trust funds from highway construction. Volpe argued that "highway investments alone cannot cope with the pressing and severe problem that is so harmful to the effective functioning of urban areas. Only by proper combination of highway and transit modes can progress be made." Congress failed to pass the measure.

Volpe was a leading supporter of no-fault auto insurance and within the administration lobbied for legislation to create a federal no-fault system. President Nixon, however, opposed the plan, recommending that reform be left to the states, and Volpe eventually presented the president's stand urging that Congress adopt a resolution to encourage states to adopt their own plans.

Volpe was appointed ambassador to Italy in 1973 when Nixon reshuffled his cabinet at the beginning of his second term. He served until 1977, when the JIMMY CARTER administration took office. Volpe retired to his home in Massachusetts, where he died in 1994.

—AE

Wallace, George C(orley)
(1919–1998) *governor of Alabama*

Born on August 25, 1919, the son of a farmer, Wallace received his law degree from the University of Alabama in 1942 and served in the armed forces during World War II. Elected to the state house of representatives in 1947, he served two terms and established a quasi-liberal record. In 1953 he was elected a circuit judge in Alabama and became known as the "fighting judge" because of his open defiance of the U.S. Civil Rights Commission. Having unsuccessfully sought the gubernatorial nomination in 1958, Wallace ran again in 1962, campaigning as a militant segregationist and states' rights advocate. Elected governor, he lived up to his campaign rhetoric. In June 1963, with state troopers, he personally barred the entry of two black students trying to register at the University of Alabama, thereby forcing President Kennedy to federalize the Alabama National Guard. In September he ordered the closing of public schools in several cities to prevent integration. Kennedy again federalized the National Guard to open the schools. In 1965 Wallace used state troops to block Martin Luther King's march from Selma, forcing the federal government to provide the marchers with protection. Prevented by state law from succeeding himself as governor, Wallace ran his wife, Lurleen, who won election in 1966. Wallace was de facto governor during his wife's term.

Capitalizing on the national publicity he received for his segregationist stand, Wallace entered Democratic primaries in Wisconsin, Indiana, and Maryland in 1964. His strong showing impressed political observers and revealed the depth of the white backlash to the civil rights movement. When the Republicans nominated BARRY GOLDWATER, Wallace withdrew from the race. In 1968 he announced a third-party candidacy. Denying that he was a racist, he posed as a defender of the working class and an opponent of the federal government's attempt to "take over and destroy the authority of the states." However, he also spoke out strongly against federal civil rights legislation. Winning a place on the ballot in all 50 states, usually as a candidate of the American Independent Party, Wallace captured 13.6 percent of the vote and carried five states in the South. Political analysts claimed that Wallace's candidacy hurt Republican RICHARD NIXON more than it did HUBERT HUMPHREY.

After the election Wallace supporters took steps to form a national conservative party. In February 1969 Wallace followers met in Dallas and Louisville and in May announced the creation of the American Independent Party. Although it was clearly intended as a vehicle for Wallace, he remained officially aloof from it, wishing to preserve all of his options. He did say, however, that he felt a third party movement was "still necessary," and he continued to address political rallies and speak out on issues.

Wallace quickly became a vocal opponent of the Nixon administration, posing criticism from the right. In a July 1969 television appearance he set out guidelines for the president: "Conclude the war honorably, give some tax reduction to the middle class of our country and cut out unnecessary spending, restore law and order, and get the government out of the control of local institutions such as schools." In November Wallace visited Vietnam and on his return attacked Nixon's policies of troop withdrawal and Vietnamization. Keeping the issue of school desegregation prominent in his speeches, he accused Nixon of breaking his campaign pledge not to bus children to achieve racial balance. In a February 1970 speech in Birmingham, Wallace urged southern governors to disregard federal court orders to integrate schools and told his audience, "We'll see to it that Mr. Nixon is a one-term president." Shrewdly capitalizing on the administration's so-called southern strategy, the effort to win the South over to the Republican Party, Wallace sought to keep pressure on the administration in the area of school desegregation.

Wallace's wife, Lurleen, had died of cancer in 1968 and was succeeded as governor by Albert Brewer. In February 1970 Wallace announced his candidacy against Brewer in the May gubernatorial primary. The outcome of the race was considered decisive for Wallace's political future, and political analysts watched the race closely. Not certain of victory, Wallace turned to explicit racial appeals toward the end of the campaign, charging that Brewer was a favorite of the "bloc vote," a code word

in Alabama politics for blacks. Brewer, on the other hand, subtly appealed to blacks by promising to look to the "future" instead of the past. Although Brewer placed first in the voting, he failed to achieve a majority and was forced into a runoff. Wallace received the support of the Ku Klux Klan and defeated Brewer in the runoff. Immediately after his victory Wallace called on Nixon to deliver his "two-year-old unfulfilled pledges to stop busings and school closings and to reestablish freedom of choice" and pointedly declared that "the Republican Party knows it cannot win without the South in the next election."

With his eye on the 1972 presidential race, Wallace continued to exploit antibusing sentiment. In August 1971 he ordered Alabama school boards to disregard court-ordered integration plans and to keep the schools closed if necessary. The following month, however, schools opened quietly and without incident. Wallace's stand did seem to have an effect. In August Nixon reiterated his opposition to busing and warned federal officials that they risked losing their jobs if they sought to impose busing plans on local school districts. In November the House for the first time overwhelmingly approved an amendment to an education aid bill to prohibit the use of federal money for busing to achieve racial balance.

On January 13, 1972, Wallace formally announced his candidacy for the Democratic presidential nomination. He told a large rally in Tallahassee that he was the only candidate to protest busing and other intrusions of "big government" into their private lives. He also made crime prevention and tax reduction issues in his campaign and claimed to speak for the "little man." Democratic national chairman LAWRENCE F. O'BRIEN immediately disavowed the Wallace candidacy, and AFL-CIO president GEORGE MEANY attacked him as a "bigot" and a "racist" and accused him of being "antilabor right down to the soles of his feet." Wallace's entry into the Democratic race quickly magnified the importance of the busing issue. On February 14 Nixon promised to take steps soon to limit busing, and Senator HENRY JACKSON, another presidential aspirant, proposed a constitutional amendment to prohibit busing. A nonbinding referendum on school busing also was placed on the ballot in the Florida primary.

Wallace made the March 14 primary in Florida a test of his viability as a candidate. Although expected to win, he surprised observers by the size of his victory. Capturing 42 percent of the vote, he had more than double the ballots of second-place finisher Hubert Humphrey. Declaring himself a "serious candidate," Wallace took his campaign North to prove that he had national appeal. In primaries in Wisconsin and Pennsylvania in April, Wallace placed an impressive second, and in Indiana the following month he won over 40 percent of the vote, with strong support in the suburbs and in blue-collar districts. He also easily won primaries in Alabama, Tennessee, and North Carolina. The strength of his campaign led GEORGE MCGOVERN and Hubert Humphrey, the only other serious candidates left, to mount last-minute "stop Wallace" drives in Michigan and Maryland, where primaries were scheduled for May 16.

On May 15 tragedy struck the Wallace campaign. While walking through a crowd of supporters in a shopping center in Laurel, Maryland, he was shot several times and critically wounded. His assailant, a young drifter named Arthur Bremer who had been following Wallace on the campaign trail, was immediately seized by the Secret Service. Wallace was rushed to a hospital, where the bullets were removed, but doctors announced that he would be paralyzed from the waist down. The next day he won easy victories in Michigan and Maryland, but his physical condition considerably diminished the viability of his campaign.

After McGovern won the California primary in June, he was virtually assured the nomination. With McGovern's first-ballot victory and the rejection by the party's Platform Committee of an antibusing plank, Wallace announced that he would remain neutral in the presidential campaign and barred a third-party candidacy for himself.

Wallace's name figured prominently in the Senate Watergate hearings. JOHN DEAN revealed that Wallace was on the president's infamous enemies list, and H. R. HALDEMAN testified that secret campaign funds had been used to aid Wallace's opponents in the 1970 gubernatorial contest. It was also revealed that the Nixon administration had used the Internal Revenue Service to try obtain damaging information on Wallace and members of his family.

Wallace ran for reelection in 1974. The campaign, however, was far different from previous ones. The racial issue remained in the background, and Wallace actively courted black votes, declaring that if reelected he would be governor of both "whites and blacks" and promising "opportunities for all." Although national civil rights leaders opposed him, many local black politicians endorsed Wallace in recognition of his power to disperse federal and state funds and provide political appointments. Wallace easily defeated his opponents without the need for a runoff, receiving 64 percent of the vote, including about one-quarter of the black vote.

Wallace came under increasingly heavy criticism during his new term as governor. Opponents attacked his preoccupation with national politics at the expense of Alabama's daily affairs. Critics charged that Alabama was really run by federal judge Frank M. Johnson who, in the absence of action from Wallace, ordered the desegregation of schools and the state police, the redrawing of the state's political boundaries to ensure fair representation, the cleaning up of the state's decrepit prison system and mental hospitals, and the reassessment of commercial property for tax purposes. Wallace's claim to represent working people also was challenged. Despite his many years as governor, opponents pointed out that Alabama had no minimum wage law, had minimal workmen's and unemployment compensation benefits, had the lowest per-pupil expenditures on education of any state, and was near the bottom in personal income. Its tax system, moreover, was among the most regressive in the country. There also were charges of rampant corruption, with two major kickback convictions, a major theft conviction, and several resignations under fire of top state officials.

Despite the growing disenchantment with his governorship, Wallace, in November 1975, announced his candidacy for the 1976 Democratic presidential nomination. Avoiding for the most part the race issue, he concentrated on crime and high taxes and declared that the main issue in the campaign was whether the middle class could "survive economically." A Gallup poll in December placed him second in popularity among possible candidates, behind Hubert Humphrey, who was not openly campaigning.

Wallace's 1976 race revealed both the limits and the extent of his appeal. By toning down his extremism, he failed to attract the sizable number of disenchanted voters who turned to him in the past to register a protest. On the other hand, his new image did not convince those liberal and middle-of-the-road Democrats who remembered his past record. Wallace's campaign received a serious blow from which it never recovered when he lost the March 14 Florida primary to dark horse candidate JIMMY CARTER. Wallace had predicted a repeat of his 1972 victory, but the ex-Georgia governor won the votes of southerners motivated by regional pride but reluctant to support Wallace. Later in March Carter also defeated Wallace in North Carolina. Wallace

called him a "warmed-over McGovern" and warned Carter supporters that "smiling and grinning a lot" would not bring change. But Carter continued to win primaries and amass delegate strength. In May Wallace announced that he "could support" Carter, and the following month he withdrew from the race and endorsed his opponent.

Although a change in Alabama election law had permitted Wallace to seek a second consecutive term, the law prevented him from running again in 1978. In June 1977 he announced his intention to seek the seat of retiring senator John Sparkman, but the following year he changed his mind. When Alabama's junior senator, JAMES ALLEN, died unexpectedly on June 1, 1978, Wallace said that he was giving "serious consideration" to running in the November special election. However, when November came, Wallace was not in the race. By the end of the 1970s, Wallace had become a born-again Christian and had publicly apologized to the nation's black community for his stand on civil rights while governor. In 1982 he ran for a fourth term as governor, announcing that he had been wrong about "race." He was elected, carrying a majority of the states' black vote. Wallace served as governor until his retirement in 1987. He died in 1998.

—JD

Walters, Vernon A(nthony)
(1917–2002) *deputy director, Central Intelligence Agency*

Born on January 3, 1917, in New York City, Vernon Walters attended Catholic schools in France and Britain. He worked for an insurance firm before entering the army in 1941. He remained in the army after the war and because of his proficiency in languages (French, German, Spanish, Italian, and Portuguese) served as translator for such diplomats as W. Averell Harriman as well as President Dwight D. Eisenhower.

After his election to the White House, President NIXON often turned to Walters as his translator. Beginning in August 1969 Walters functioned as national security adviser HENRY KISSINGER's translator at secret peace talks in Paris with the North Vietnamese. He served as a conduit for subsequent exchanges between the two parties. On the instruction of President Nixon and Kissinger, Walters maintained a strict level of secrecy about the talks. He brought Kissinger in and out of France frequently without the knowledge of the press or the public. The talks were publicized in 1972.

In June 1970 Walters delivered a message from Nixon to the Paris embassy of the People's Republic of China; the message initiated contact between the two countries. Kissinger used Walters as his translator at subsequent secret talks with the Chinese Communists. The contact between Walters and the Chinese ambassador in Paris quickly developed into a link between Washington and Beijing. Eventually Walters arranged the details of the trips by Kissinger and Nixon to China.

Nixon named Walters to be deputy director of the Central Intelligence Agency (CIA) in March 1972, and he was confirmed the following month. He quickly became embroiled in the nascent Watergate scandal. On June 23, six days after the break-in at the Democratic National Committee headquarters in the Watergate office complex, Walters and CIA director RICHARD M. HELMS were summoned to a meeting at the White House with presidential aides H. R. HALDEMAN and JOHN D. EHRLICHMAN. According to Walters, he was asked by the two advisers to inform acting FBI director L. PATRICK GRAY that the bureau's investigation into Republican campaign funds channeled through a Mexican bank might jeopardize CIA activities in that country. Both officials assured Haldeman and Ehrlichman that the CIA was

not involved in the matter, but at their insistence Walters agreed to meet with Gray and relay the message.

Gray initially consented to work only around the periphery of the Watergate case but soon became worried and told Walters he needed a written statement to the effect that CIA interests were at stake before he could call off the FBI's investigation. Walters, at Helms's instruction, then informed Gray that none of the agency's operations were in jeopardy. The FBI investigation continued, and the campaign funds were later linked to the Watergate break-in.

Walters was summoned for three consecutive days at the end of June to meet with presidential counsel JOHN W. DEAN. At these meetings Walters resisted Dean's overtures to involve the CIA in the Watergate cover-up. Walters ultimately testified nearly 20 times under oath about Watergate. He appeared before the House and Senate Armed Services committees, the Senate Watergate committee, and later at the Watergate trials in Washington. His testimony was disputed by Haldeman and Ehrlichman and supported by Helms and internal memos written by Walters at the time. He retired from the CIA and the army in July 1976. He published his memoir, *Silent Missions*, in 1978. Walters was awarded the Medal of Freedom in 1991 and died in 2002.

—SF

Warner, John W(illiam)
(1927–   ) *secretary of the navy*

John W. Warner was born on February 18, 1927, in Washington, D.C. The son of an obstetrician, Warner grew up in Washington, D.C., served in the navy during World War II, and graduated from Washington and Lee University in 1949. After active duty with the marines in Korea, he completed his studies at the University of Virginia Law School. Following graduation he became law clerk to E. Barrett Prettyman, chief judge of the U.S. circuit court of appeals in Washington. In 1955 he joined the Justice Department and worked for four years as an assistant U.S. attorney prosecuting murder and gambling cases. In 1957 he married Catherine Mellon, daughter of multimillionaire Paul Mellon. From 1960 to 1968 Warner was a member of the prestigious Washington law firm of Hogan & Hartson. He also served as an advance man on the campaign staff of RICHARD NIXON. In 1968 he headed the Citizens for Nixon-Agnew.

In February 1969 Nixon named Warner to the post of undersecretary of the navy. In October 1971 Warner led a 10-member U.S. delegation to Moscow to discuss means of avoiding incidents between ships and aircraft of the U.S. and Soviet navies in international waters, especially conflicts involving vessels "shadowing" one another. The talks resulted in a preliminary understanding, although the exact nature of the terms of agreement was not made public.

In May 1972, one month after Warner's appointment as secretary of the navy, U.S. and Soviet officials signed an agreement designed to avoid possible ocean accidents. It was the first military agreement between the two countries since World War II. Recognizing that maneuvers in open waters were subject to regulation by the 1958 Geneva Convention on the high seas, the pact forbade both ships and aircraft from engaging in "simulated attacks" that might "constitute a hazard to navigation."

A conflict arose over the navy's handling of defense contracts under Warner. In July 1972 Warner announced that the navy would pick up out-of-pocket construction costs for five ships under contract to Litton Industries that Litton would otherwise have been forced to pay out of its own funds. However, the following year Warner ruled against rewriting an aircraft contract with Grumman despite claims by company officials that to meet the original terms of the agreement would cost Grumman $100 million.

In response to racial unrest in the navy and the marines, Warner and the chief of naval operations, Admiral ELMO R. ZUMWALT JR., rebuked 100 admirals and generals in November 1972 for failure to act sufficiently against discrimination in their services. Warner stated that racial clashes, such as those aboard the aircraft carriers *Constellation* and *Kitty Hawk* that month, had demonstrated "a lack of communications" but that the navy "was not going to tolerate such things as sit-down strikes" by seamen even when provoked by genuine grievances. Warner said a top-level Human Relations Council would be established to apply "downward pressure" through the ranks. According to a survey in June 1972, blacks constituted 5.8 percent of the navy's enlisted men and 0.7 percent of its officers.

In April 1974 Warner was sworn in as administrator of the American Revolution Bicentennial Administration, which replaced the Bicentennial Commission following Senate hearings into charges that the Nixon administration was using the commission for commercial purposes and political partisanship. In his role as administrator of the new organization, Warner cited as his greatest achievements the Bicentennial Freedom Train; the Fourth of July "Operation Sail," in which tall ships paraded up New York's Hudson River; and the loan of the Magna Carta from Britain. However, he was unable to contain the atmosphere of slick commercialism that marred much of the bicentennial celebration.

Following his divorce from Catherine Mellon, he married actress Elizabeth Taylor in 1977. In 1978 he was elected to a seat in the U.S. Senate from Virginia. In 1979 the governor of Virginia appointed Warner to fill the vacancy of the Senate seat caused by the resignation of William Scott. Warner was reelected in 1984, 1990, 1996, and 2002.

—FHM

Weinberger, Caspar W.

(1917–   ) *chairman, Federal Trade Commission; deputy director, Office of Management and Budget (OMB); director, OMB; secretary of health, education, and welfare*

Weinberger graduated from Harvard magna cum laude and Phi Beta Kappa in 1938 and received an LL.B. there three years later. Following service in the army during World War II, he practiced law in California.

In 1952 he was elected for the first of three terms as a member of the California state legislature. He made a bid for the state attorney generalship in 1958 but lost the Republican primary to a more conservative candidate from Southern California.

Following a two-year hiatus from active politics, Weinberger returned in 1960 as vice chairman of the California Republican Central Committee. Elected its chairman in 1962, he spent the next six years threading a course between conservatives and moderates at both the state and national levels. Thus, he remained neutral in the 1964 primary battle between BARRY GOLDWATER and NELSON ROCKEFELLER and campaigned for RONALD REAGAN in the subsequent election. Reagan reciprocated by appointing him chairman of a California "Little Hoover Commission" and then, in February 1968, director of finance, where Weinberger "set about implementing Reagan's budget-slashing plans" with a fervor. In October 1969 Weinberger was appointed chairman of the Federal Trade Commission (FTC). He delayed active assumption of the directorship until he had seen California through its 1969 budget year.

Weinberger's desire "to direct the agency's attention more toward protection of the nation's consumers" was well attuned to the political needs of the FTC, which was being severely criticized by RALPH NADER's Raiders and the American Bar Association for inefficiency and infighting. In his six short months at the FTC, Weinberger managed to unify the agency behind a tough new program of consumer protection and streamlined the organizational setup from five to two bureaus—the Bureau of Competition (for antitrust matters) and the Bureau of Consumer Protection. He was generally credited with revitalizing the agency.

In June 1970 Weinberger returned to budgetary duties as deputy director of the newly established Office of Management and Budget (OMB), which replaced the former Bureau of the Budget (BOB). His appointment was part of a major personnel shuffle in the NIXON administration that also brought in former labor secretary GEORGE SHULTZ as director of OMB and former BOB director Robert Mayo as White House counselor to the president and added the directorship of the new Domestic Council to JOHN EHRLICHMAN's duties as presidential assistant for domestic affairs. Under the new setup at OMB, director Shultz was to focus on the management and policy-making duties, while Weinberger attended to the preparation of the budget.

Regarded as a "fiscal Puritan," Weinberger concentrated on containing the budget deficit. Although he never managed to balance the federal books, he did keep the 1973 budget within President Nixon's ceiling figure of $250 billion. Indeed, he was so effective a budgetary pruner that he became known as "Cap the Knife."

In May 1972 he moved up to the directorship of OMB. His promotion was taken to be an indicator that the president "was serious about curbing inflation and preventing a tax increase by cutting the federal budget." Although Weinberger prepared a frugal 1974 budget, he did not manage to cut expenditures but merely pared the growth in spending to bare bones, primarily by cutting down or out appropriations for over 100 social welfare programs.

In November 1972 Weinberger moved his campaign to reduce spending into the biggest and perhaps the most open-handed government agency, the Department of Health, Education, and Welfare. His nomination as secretary of health, education, and welfare was part of a more extensive administration reorganization designed to begin implementation of the Ash council's (Advisory Council on Executive Organization) suggestions for restructuring the executive branch. Other concurrent changes moved ELLIOT RICHARDSON from HEW to the Defense Department and brought in ROY L. ASH (the aforementioned commission's chairman) as director of OMB.

Liberal congressional reaction to Weinberger's nomination to head HEW was not favorable initially, since he was expected to "intensify the HEW budget cuts he tried to initiate at OMB." Despite the misgiving of several liberal senators who "questioned Weinberger's sensitivity to social needs," he was confirmed in February 1973.

Further reorganization efforts, described as an attempt to establish a "super cabinet" to oversee and coordinate the functions of the normal cabinet departments, resulted in Weinberger's concurrent appointment as presidential counselor on human resources in January 1973. In this capacity he was responsible for all departmental activities concerning health, education, manpower, development, income security, social services, drug abuse programs, Native American affairs, and consumer protection. The centralization of broad program coordination in a small number of people who were concurrently cabinet secretaries and White House counselors was, perhaps, President Nixon's most overt attempt to bring the executive bureaucracy under the direction of an "administrative presidency."

As secretary, Weinberger proved to be extremely active in pursuing cost-control measures and attempting to decentralize social program control and spending to state and local governments as part of the president's revenue sharing plan. Congress, however, as well as many interested public groups, generally regarded such proposals with suspicion and scorn, thus bringing Weinberger and the president into frequent clashes with the legislature. Congress rejected the administration's proposal for ending narrow categorical funding grants on health and education programs, which would have enabled the states to use federal money with less federal direction. Over administrative objections and occasionally over a presidential veto, the categorical grant system for health services was expanded. After a hard fight Congress eventually did agree to consolidate several elementary, secondary, and vocational educational programs into simple grants to the states, giving the local authorities more discretion over how they would allocate those federal dollars. Indeed, the divergent executive and congressional perspectives on the entire "human resources" topic kept the possibility of major reform and revision at a distance, and most of the administration's achievements in this area were accomplished through tighter administration.

Weinberger, while on the front line of much of this conflict because of his position as secretary of HEW and as human resources counselor to the president, was well regarded personally. On social welfare affairs he was characterized as "not a conservative on human issues . . . [but] a moderate and compassionate man [who] . . . hates waste and ineffective handouts." Many members of Congress admired "his personal grasp of the many programs run by the mammoth department and for his tenacity." Weinberger resigned from HEW in July 1975.

From 1981 to 1987 Weinberger served as secretary of defense for President RONALD

REAGAN. One of the most hawkish of Reagan's advisers, Weinberger advocated and won large increases in Defense Department appropriations. He also advocated strategic modernization of the nation's defenses; most notable within this was his support of the Strategic Defense Initiative ("Star Wars"). After leaving the Reagan administration Weinberger became the publisher and chairman of *Forbes* magazine, where he was a frequent contributor. In 1990 he published his memoir, *Fighting for Peace.* Weinberger was indicted for several counts of lying to the independent counsel investigating the Iran-contra scandals; on his last day in office in 1993, President GEORGE H. W. BUSH pardoned Weinberger for those offenses.

—MJW

Westmoreland, William C(hilds)
(1914–2005) *army chief of staff*

William C. Westmoreland was born on March 26, 1914, in Spartanburg, South Carolina. Westmoreland graduated from West Point in 1936 and was commissioned a second lieutenant in the artillery. During World War II he saw action as a battalion commander in North Africa and Sicily. Following the war Westmoreland took paratrooper and glider training at Fort Benning, Georgia, and he taught at the Army Command and General Staff College at Fort Leavenworth, Kansas. He served as commander of the 187th Airborne Regimental Combat Team in Korea. In 1958 he was named commander of the elite 101st Airborne Division. Two years later President Eisenhower appointed Westmoreland superintendent at West Point.

In 1964 President Johnson named Westmoreland deputy to General Paul D. Harkins, head of the U.S. Military Assistance Command in Vietnam. In June he succeeded Harkins.

During the mid-1960s Westmoreland presided over a gradual escalation of American military involvement in Southeast Asia. To counter the increased infiltration of North Vietnamese troops into South Vietnam, he made repeated requests for additional U.S. troops. By February 1968 there were more than 500,000 American soldiers in South Vietnam. In June 1968 Westmoreland returned to the United States to become chief of staff in a move widely regarded as an indication of President Johnson's refusal to escalate the conflict further.

General CREIGHTON ABRAMS succeeded Westmoreland as U.S. commander in Vietnam. As army chief, Westmoreland in late October was among the Johnson aides who had misgivings about the administration's complete bombing halt of North Vietnam. He doubted that the halt would lead to serious peace talks in Paris.

With the RICHARD NIXON administration came a change in war policy. As formulated broadly in the Nixon Doctrine, the new administration implemented a policy of "winding down" the American presence in Vietnam. The administration emphasized the strengthening of South Vietnamese forces in a program of Vietnamization, a term coined by the new secretary of defense, MELVIN LAIRD, to describe the gradually increasing role of the South Vietnamese in assuming the burden of the fighting. At the same time, Laird prepared a schedule for the withdrawal of U.S. forces. The administration saw the troop withdrawals as part of a larger attempt to break the deadlocked Paris peace talks. Nixon also understood the mood of the country to be such that it would continue to support a policy of U.S. aid for South Vietnam but that increasingly it wanted to see an end to the direct American involvement in the fighting.

Westmoreland was troubled by the decision. He felt that winding down the U.S. role in the fighting risked undoing the accomplishments of four years of American sacrifice in Vietnam. Along with General EARLE WHEELER,

On the occasion of his retirement, General William C. Westmoreland shakes hands with President Richard Nixon as Mrs. Westmoreland looks on, June 26, 1972. *(CORBIS)*

he led an effort to at least modify the president's plan. They were particularly concerned by Nixon's decision to remove combat troops first. The generals would have preferred removal of support troops. Nixon was committed to a policy of withdrawal, though, and the first contingent of 25,000 American combat soldiers left Vietnam in August. American troops continued to withdraw at a constant pace throughout Nixon's first term in office. Westmoreland maintained his misgivings about the troop withdrawals, believing that their timing was more for political than military reasons.

Despite his opposition to the rate and nature of the troop withdrawals, Westmoreland strongly supported the Nixon administration's program of Vietnamization. It was a policy that he had constantly advocated during his tour of duty in South Vietnam and that he believed the Johnson administration had not pursued seriously enough. Westmoreland likewise backed President Nixon's decision in May 1970 to order American combat troops to attack Communist sanctuaries in Cambodia along the South Vietnamese border. The goal, successfully completed, was to buy one year's grace from an enemy attack against South Vietnam to allow Vietnamization needed time. Domestic political reaction against the incursion prompted the administration to limit it to eight weeks. Again in February 1971, in pursuit of the same military results, Westmoreland agreed with the decision for the U.S. command in Vietnam to furnish much of the tactical support for the movement of South Vietnamese troops into Laos to cut the Ho Chi Minh trail.

By the spring of 1972 U.S. forces in Vietnam had been cut back to roughly 70,000 servicemen. At the end of March North Vietnam launched a major offensive across the demilitarized zone (DMZ) into South Vietnam. Westmoreland took an active part in the deliberations among top advisers on how to respond to the invasion. In early April Nixon announced the resumption of full-scale B-52 strikes against North Vietnam.

As army chief, Westmoreland spoke widely at civic functions and campuses to increase public support for the military. He worked to modernize the army and to improve training in light of modern technology and the Vietnam experience. He instituted programs to combat drug abuse, alcoholism, and racial tension and conflict. In anticipation of an end to the draft in 1973, Westmoreland helped to lay the groundwork for a volunteer army. In keeping with America in the 1970s, he oversaw a liberalization of army rules and regulations. Westmoreland also organized the investigation of the 1968 My Lai incident in which Lieutenant WILLIAM L. CALLEY and other army officers were charged with the murder, or the covering up of the murder, of over 100 South Vietnamese civilians. Calley was convicted of the premeditated murder of "at least" 11 civilians in March 1971.

Westmoreland retired from the army in June 1972. President Nixon called him to Washington in October to seek his advice on the secret peace talks between National Security Advisor HENRY KISSINGER and Le Duc Tho, North Vietnam's principal negotiator. Westmoreland urged Nixon to delay action on the new agreement and to hold out for better terms. He argued that it was vital that North Vietnamese troops be required to withdraw from South Vietnam. Accordingly, when the pact, with few

modifications, went into effect in January 1973, Westmoreland claimed that it "had only two virtues: it ended the American involvement and brought the American prisoners of war home." Westmoreland felt that the agreement, because it left North Vietnamese troops in positions in South Vietnam from which they could launch attacks, paved the way for North Vietnam's final April 1975 offensive.

In July 1974 Westmoreland was defeated in a bid for the South Carolina Republican nomination for governor. In retirement he openly denounced the Johnson administration's handling of the war. He strongly criticized its refusal after the Tet offensive to allow him to follow up battlefield successes with attacks on Communist sanctuaries in Cambodia and Laos and across the DMZ into North Vietnam. He argued that this action along with sustained and intensive bombing could have brought the defeat of North Vietnam.

Westmoreland defended the will and determination of South Vietnam to maintain its freedom. He condemned those at home against the war "who went beyond the bounds of reasonable debate and fair dissension." The great majority of Americans, he insisted, had remained firm in their resolve to persevere. Vietnam was lost in the end, Westmoreland asserted, because officials in Washington at first failed to vigorously wage the war and then refused to carry on. He maintained that legislation passed by Congress in the early 1970s designed to limit the president's power to act abroad had hamstrung the FORD administration's final efforts to aid South Vietnam.

In 1982 a CBS documentary, "The Uncounted Enemy: A Vietnam Deception," charged that Westmoreland and others had deliberately undercounted Vietcong strength so as to maintain popular support for the war. Westmoreland sued CBS for libel and settled out of court. He died on July 18, 2005.

—SF

Weyand, Frederick C(arlton)
(1916–) *army chief of staff*

Frederick C. Weyand was born in Arbuckle, California, on September 15, 1916. Weyand graduated from the University of California at Berkeley and received an ROTC commission as a second lieutenant in 1939. He went on active duty in late 1940 and served during World War II in India, Burma, and China. After the war he made the military a career. He was a battalion commander and divisional operations officer in the Korean War. After combat duty Weyand attended the National War College in Washington, D.C. In 1964 he took command of the 25th Infantry Division in Vietnam. He became a field force commander there in 1967. Two years later President NIXON named Weyand military adviser to the U.S. delegation at the Paris peace talks. He returned to Vietnam in 1970 as the deputy commander of the U.S. military command. In 1972 Weyand was appointed commander of the U.S. forces in Vietnam.

When the American military role in Vietnam officially ended on March 29, 1973, Weyand presided over the departure of the last U.S. troops and the deactivation of the U.S. command there. In a farewell speech delivered at formal ceremonies marking the occasion, he declared that "the rights of the people of the Republic of Vietnam to shape their own destiny and to provide their self-defense have been upheld." In a second speech, addressed to the South Vietnamese in their own language, Weyand stated, "Our mission has been accomplished. I depart with a strong feeling of pride in what we have achieved, and in what our achievement represents."

That same year Weyand was named vice chief of staff of the army. President FORD nominated him to succeed General CREIGHTON W. ABRAMS as army chief of staff when Abrams died in office in September 1974. Weyand was confirmed in October. When Weyand took command of the army, the impact of inflation was affecting the military's procurement of new weapons systems, and army weapons stockpiles had been depleted by the massive airlifting of U.S. armaments to Israel during the 1973 Yom Kippur War. Weyand concentrated in particular on increasing U.S. tank strength. In November the Pentagon announced plans to increase the volunteer army's combat divisions from 13 to 16. Continuing the work begun by his predecessor, Weyand attempted to accomplish this by converting support and headquarters troops into combat units.

In early March 1975 North Vietnam launched its final offensive against South Vietnam. Weyand arrived on March 27 in Saigon at President Ford's direction to assess the military situation and recommend whether South Vietnam needed any more U.S. military aid. He conferred on April 2 with President Nguyen Van Thieu on ways of saving South Vietnam from imminent collapse. Weyand reported to Ford on April 4 that the South Vietnamese Army "still has the spirit and the capability to defeat the North Vietnamese." However, in briefing congressional committees on April 8, he said South Vietnam could not survive without additional military aid from the United States. Weyand told reporters later that whether South Vietnam could survive even with the aid was "a very good question." He added that there was no doubt in his mind that South Vietnam would fight.

Over the next several weeks, as North Vietnamese forces approached Saigon, the Ford administration pressed Congress repeatedly for $722 million in emergency military aid and $250 million in humanitarian aid for South Vietnam. Weyand supported the request and warned that South Vietnam could survive only a few months without military assistance. Congress was reluctant to grant further military aid but did authorize a $200 million "contingency fund" that Ford could use to evacuate Americans from South Vietnam and provide humanitarian aid for the South Vietnamese. During the latter days of April the remaining Americans were evacuated from Saigon, and on April 30 South Vietnam fell to the Communists.

During his remaining tour of duty as chief of staff, Weyand continued to work to improve army forces stationed with the North Atlantic Treaty Organization (NATO). He retired in October 1976 and was succeeded by General Bernard W. Rogers. Weyand became an officer with the First Hawaiian Bank.

—SF

Wheeler, Earle G(ilmore)
(1908–1975) *chairman, Joint Chiefs of Staff*

Earle G. Wheeler was born on January 13, 1908, in Washington, D.C. A 1932 graduate of West Point who saw action in World War II as commander of an infantry battalion, Wheeler rose to prominence in the army chiefly as an administrator. A protégé of General Maxwell Taylor, Wheeler was assigned to the office of the Joint Chiefs of Staff as staff director in 1960. In that post he briefed presidential candidate John F. Kennedy on military affairs. Impressed with Wheeler's performance, Kennedy appointed him army chief of staff in October 1962.

As army chief, Wheeler shared General Taylor's philosophy of a balanced military force capable of fighting both conventional and nuclear war. He won the favor of Secretary of Defense ROBERT S. McNAMARA for his implementation of the secretary's program of expansion and modernization of the army and for his articulate public defense of the nuclear test ban treaty in 1963.

President Johnson named Wheeler to succeed Taylor as chairman of the Joint Chiefs of Staff in July 1964. Wheeler stressed the primacy of the country's overall military needs and strategy over the competing demands of the separate armed services. During the Johnson years he increasingly devoted his attention to the war in Vietnam both as a close adviser to the president and as a liaison between the Joint Chiefs and civilian decision makers. Reflecting the policies of the Joint Chiefs, Wheeler advocated an extensive American military presence in Vietnam. As the United States escalated its involvement in the war during the mid-1960s, he consistently supported the military's requests for more troops and weapons.

Wheeler remained chairman of the Joint Chiefs of Staff under President NIXON. As formulated broadly in the Nixon Doctrine, the new administration implemented a policy of "winding down" the American presence in Vietnam. The new secretary of defense, MELVIN LAIRD, charted a schedule for the withdrawal of U.S. forces. The administration saw the troop withdrawals as part of a larger strategy of trying to break the deadlocked Paris peace talks. Wheeler and the army chief of staff, General WILLIAM WESTMORELAND, led a struggle to reverse or at least modify the president's plan. They were especially concerned by his decision to withdraw combat troops first and not backup or support troops. Nixon stuck to his decision, and the first contingent of 25,000 soldiers left Vietnam in August.

As chairman of the Joint Chiefs, Wheeler worked to carry out the Nixon administration's program of Vietnamization. The program sought to improve South Vietnam's armed forces with the goal of having them gradually assume the burden of the fighting. Wheeler visited South Vietnam in July on a fact-finding mission for Nixon. He returned for a second inspection tour in October. In summing up his findings, Wheeler remarked that progress in Vietnamization was being steadily and realistically achieved. At the same time he noted that U.S. forces would have to assist the South Vietnamese for "some time to come." Wheeler forcefully supported Nixon's decision in May 1970 to send American troops into Cambodia to attack Communist sanctuaries along the South Vietnamese border. The military goal, successfully accomplished by the incursion, was to provide the Vietnamization program needed time free from enemy attack.

Throughout America's involvement in Vietnam Wheeler strongly criticized those who protested the war at home. He argued that the single most important factor in prolonging the conflict was Hanoi's perception of America's weakness of purpose. Wheeler steadfastly maintained that the United States could win the war in Vietnam; reflecting the evolution in government policy during the conflict, his definition of victory changed over the years. In 1965 he thought it was possible to guarantee South Vietnam's independence by defeating the Communists on the battlefield. By 1967 he advocated the administration's position that the U.S. goal was to bring Hanoi to the peace table under conditions favorable to the United States. During his service under the Nixon presidency, Wheeler endorsed America's commitment to the process of Vietnamization that would allow South Vietnam to defend itself.

Wheeler retired from the army and from his position as chairman of the Joint Chiefs in July 1970. He was succeeded as chairman by Admiral THOMAS H. MOORER, chief of naval operations. Wheelers became a director of the Monsanto Corp.

In July 1973 the Senate Armed Services Committee called Wheeler to testify about allegations that senior military and civilian officials had falsified reports to conceal secret B-52 strikes against targets in Cambodia in 1969 and 1970. Wheeler told the committee that President Nixon had personally ordered the secret bombing of Cambodia. He denied charges of any falsification of documents. He said a system of dual reports had been instituted using cover targets in South Vietnam for the missions so they could be conducted under stringent security. Later it was revealed that the reason for such secrecy was Prince Sihanouk, the head of the Cambodian government at the time. Sihanouk privately endorsed the U.S. action against the North Vietnamese. But because of his country's neutral status, if the bombing became known publicly he would be forced to protest it publicly. Wheeler died in December 1975.

—SF

White, Byron R(aymond)

(1917–2002) *associate justice, U.S. Supreme Court*

Byron R. White was born in Fort Collins, Colorado, on June 8, 1917. White graduated first in his class from the University of Colorado in 1938. A football all-American, he played professionally for several seasons before receiving a degree from Yale Law School in 1946. White practiced in Denver from 1947 until 1961, when he was named U.S. deputy attorney general. President John F. Kennedy's first Supreme Court nominee, White took his seat on the bench in April 1962.

As a jurist White was not easy to categorize. He refrained from broad statements of philosophy in his opinions and had a pragmatic, nondoctrinaire approach that made it difficult to predict his stance in many cases. Over time, though, his votes showed that he tended to favor government authority over individual rights in First Amendment and criminal cases. White generally supported judicial deference to legislative judgments because he believed it better for the nation to resolve many controversial questions through the political process rather than the courts. The justice also preferred to resolve cases without making dramatic changes in existing law. As a result of such views, White proved to be far more conservative on the Court than had been expected, especially on criminal rights and civil liberties issues. He compiled a more liberal record, however, in civil rights and reapportionment cases.

On the WARREN BURGER Court White occupied a center position and was identified, along with POTTER STEWART, as a "swing" justice whose vote decided cases in which the Court's liberal members were at odds with the more conservative Nixon appointees. When the two groups were sharply divided. White was more likely to vote with the conservatives, especially in criminal cases. He backed police "stop and frisk" practices, upheld warrantless searches he considered reasonable, and urged the Court to limit the application of the exclusionary rule that barred the use of illegally seized evidence at trial. In a March 1969 opinion White ordered the government to let defendants examine the transcripts of illegal electronic eavedropping against them, even in national security cases. In April 1971, however, he upheld "third-party bugging" in which an informer, without a warrant, used an electronic device to transmit his conversation with another person to government agents.

White also joined in decisions cutting back on the 1966 *Miranda* ruling. In three May 1970 cases he upheld plea bargains against charges from defendants that their guilty pleas had been involuntary or improperly induced. In a June 1970 opinion White sustained the use of six-member juries in state courts, and in May 1972 he spoke for the Court to sanction nonunanimous jury verdicts. Justice White joined the Court's liberals in June 1972 to hold the death penalty as then imposed a violation of the Eighth Amendment's ban on cruel and unusual punishment. However, he voted four years later to sustain

capital punishment as the penalty for murder under newer state laws that either made the penalty mandatory or else established guidelines restricting the judge's or jury's discretion in imposing the death sentence.

Justice White opposed the Court's use of an 1866 civil rights law to overturn racial discrimination in housing and in private nonsectarian schools. His majority opinion in a significant June 1976 case held that government action must have a discriminatory purpose as well as a racially disproportionate effect to violate the 14th Amendment. However, White dissented in June 1971 when a majority allowed a city to close its public swimming pools rather than desegregate them and in July 1974 when the Court rejected an interdistrict remedy for school segregation in Detroit. He favored a strict standard of review in sex discrimination cases and voted to overturn most laws discriminating against women and against illegitimate children. White also dissented in March 1973 when the Court held that public school financing systems based on local property taxes did not deny children in poorer districts the equal protection of the laws.

Because he preferred political solutions of controversial issues, White opposed the Court's January 1973 decision invalidating antiabortion laws for the first six months of pregnancy. He also supported virtually all state and federal laws providing aid to parochial schools. In June 1973 he was part of a five-man majority that granted the states greater leeway in regulating allegedly obscene material. To ensure that the political system would be responsive to the popular will, White favored expansion of the electoral process. His opinion in a June 1970 case, for example, opened voting on local bond issues to tenants as well as property owners, and the justice supported a federal law lowering the voting age to 18 in December 1970. Although he had endorsed the one-man, one-vote rule in reapportionment cases, White objected in these years to a very strict application of that standard. For a six-man majority in June 1973 he declared that the states did not have to justify minor deviations from the one-man, one-vote rule in the apportionment of their own legislatures.

In First Amendment cases Justice White most often voted to sustain government power against individual rights claims. He did vote to deny the government's request for an injunction in June 1971 to halt newspaper publication of the *Pentagon Papers*. However, he wrote the opinion in a 5-4 decision a year later holding that journalists had no First Amendment right to refuse to testify before a grand jury about information obtained from confidential sources. In June 1969 White spoke for the Court to sustain the Federal Communications Commission's "fairness doctrine" requiring radio and television stations to air both sides of important issues.

White would later vote to uphold affirmative action plans in *Regents of University of California v. Baake* (1978). He retired from the Court in 1993 and died at his home in 2002.

—CAB

White, Kevin H(agan)
(1929–) *mayor of Boston*

Born on September 25, 1929, White was the son of a politically active family from the West Roxbury section of Boston. He earned a B.A. degree from Williams College in 1952. Three years later he graduated from Boston College Law School and was admitted to the Massachusetts bar.

He was elected Massachusetts secretary of state in 1960, and during his fourth successive term in that post White entered the 1967 race for the Boston mayoralty, facing fellow Democrat LOUISE DAY HICKS in the general election. Hicks, a member of the Boston School Committee, was best known for her vigorous opposition to racial integration in the city's school system. White, with the backing of liberals and blacks, narrowly defeated Hicks.

White's administration quickly demonstrated its commitment to liberal reform. The new mayor appointed blacks to top-level positions, established "mini-city halls" around Boston to serve citizens' needs, set up a 24-hour complaint center, and created the Boston Urban Federation to finance a major low-income housing program. However, his efforts on behalf of Boston's minority groups earned him the epithet "Mayor Black" among the city's working-class white ethnics, and his decision to increase Boston's property tax, already among the highest in the nation, further alienated many Bostonians.

During the NIXON administration White emerged as a leading spokesman for urban America. In March 1970 he joined the mayors of other major cities in announcing a joint lobbying effort on such issues as urban renewal, crime, mass transit, welfare reform, and revenue sharing. The following year, at the San Francisco meeting of the U.S. Conference of Mayors, he and nine other big-city mayors issued a statement condemning President Nixon's budget proposals, including the president's revenue-sharing plan, which they said would result in an overall decrease in urban aid.

After an unsuccessful bid for governor in 1970, White easily defeated former opponent Louise Day Hicks in the November 1971 mayoral election. His victory cut across all economic, ethnic, and racial lines, including the "white ethnic" neighborhoods such as South Boston, a Hicks stronghold.

In January 1972 White publicly endorsed Maine senator EDMUND S. MUSKIE's bid for the Democratic presidential nomination and headed the slate of Muskie delegates running in the Massachusetts primary. After GEORGE MCGOVERN received the nomination in July,

White was briefly considered for the vice presidential spot but was dropped due to the strong protests of John Kenneth Galbraith, head of the Massachusetts delegation.

In March of the same year, the NAACP filed a long-expected suit charging the city of Boston with having established a willful pattern of segregation in the school system. With a court decision imminent, White reversed his previous support of the 1965 Racial Imbalance Law, which cut off state funds to schools with a nonwhite enrollment in excess of 50 percent. He suggested voluntary busing of black students to adjacent white suburban areas as a possible solution, arguing that economic rather than racial integration was the real problem.

On June 21, 1974, district court judge Arthur Garrity Jr. ruled in response to the NAACP suit that Boston had indeed maintained a de facto system of segregated schools and ordered implementation of the Racial Imbalance Law in the fall by whatever means necessary—including large-scale forced busing. When schools reopened in September, whites in South Boston resisted the order with increasingly violent demonstrations. Many white parents kept their children home, and the violence began to spread. Mayor White ordered police escorts for buses carrying black students after they were stoned by white mobs. Despite his stated dissatisfaction with busing, he urged obedience to the law.

At White's request Republican governor Francis Sargent ordered state police to supplement Boston's police force after a refusal by Judge Garrity to send in federal marshals. But on October 15, following a high school melee that resulted in the stabbing of a student, Sargent mobilized the National Guard without consulting White. The mayor, who referred to the guard as an inept militia, accused Sargent of trying to boost his ailing reelection campaign.

In the face of continued federal court intransigence, the antibusing campaign began to subside, with opponents simply acquiescing or transferring their children to private schools. In August a report by the Commission of Human Rights criticized White's coolness to the Garrity decision in the mayor's public statements, saying that it had given support to antibusing sentiment. When schools reopened in the fall of 1975 under an even wider busing program than that of the previous year, there were few reports of violence or protest.

Kevin White was reelected in November following a bitter campaign against Joseph Timilty, a state senator who accused White of corrupt fund-raising practices. Busing was not stressed as a campaign issue, but White's margin of victory was extremely narrow. White held his position as mayor of Boston until 1983, the longest-serving mayor in that city's history.

—MDQ

Wiggins, Charles E.
(1927–2000) *member of the House of Representatives*

Charles E. Wiggins was born in El Monte, California, on December 3, 1927. Wiggins entered the army toward the end of World War II and served again during the Korean War. After Korea he received B.S. and law degrees from the University of Southern California and started a private law practice in El Monte, California, in 1957. Beginning with the 1949 presidency of the El Monte Young Republicans, he held several California Republican Party positions and was active in local and statewide campaigns. In 1960 and 1962 he served on the campaign committee of Representative John Rousselot (R-Calif.) of the John Birch Society. He was chairman of the El Monte Planning Commission from

1954 to 1960, city councilman from 1960 to 1964, and mayor from 1964 to 1966. Wiggins was elected in 1966 to the U.S. House from a wealthy, conservative suburban district.

In Congress Wiggins was a strong supporter of White House legislative policy. He generally sided with the Republicans on party line votes and supported the administration's position about 70 percent of the time during the late 1960s and 1970s. He received ratings of 70 to 80 from the conservative Americans for Constitutional Action. Wiggins backed RICHARD NIXON's Vietnam policy and favored a strong defense posture and foreign military aid. In 1969 he supported the development and deployment of the Safeguard antiballistic missile system. The following year he opposed the Cooper-Church Amendment limiting presidential authority to conduct military operations in Cambodia, and in 1974 he voted against cutting off military aid to Turkey. Two years later he supported development of the B-1 bomber.

Wiggins voted for such anticrime measures as the "no-knock" search warrants proposed by the Nixon administration for its war on drugs. He consistently supported Nixon-Ford vetoes of federal expenditures for the domestic aid programs proposed by the Democrats. But in 1975 he was one of 38 Republicans who voted for the federal loan program for New York City, which the Ford administration finally supported. He seldom supported social welfare or consumer protection programs.

Wiggins served on the House Judiciary Committee, where he became involved in two major battles that brought him to national attention. In 1971 he led the House opposition to the Equal Rights Amendment (ERA), banning sex discrimination. Wiggins convinced the Judiciary Committee to add a clause to the proposed ERA that would have permitted laws that discriminated on the basis of sex in the case of the military draft and in health and safety matters. ERA proponents objected strongly to the Wiggins amendment, contending that it significantly undermined the legislation, especially in the vital occupational health and safety area, where discriminatory laws might continue to bar women from certain occupations. Wiggins lost the ERA fight when the House rejected his amendment by a 265–87 vote and then overwhelmingly adopted the Equal Rights Amendment in 1971.

In 1974 Wiggins became Nixon's chief and most eloquent defender during the House Judiciary Committee's impeachment proceedings. He insisted that the evidence must directly and explicitly link the president to an impeachable offense, a requirement that became known as the "smoking gun" evidence rule. He was one of three members who voted against the first subpoena the committee issued on April 11, 1974, for tapes of presidential conversations and other evidence. Wiggins was one of the 10 committee Republicans who voted against all five impeachment articles, three of which were adopted by the committee.

While he staunchly defended Nixon as long as he felt a case could be made, Wiggins gave up the defense immediately upon discovering the smoking gun he had been demanding. He thus helped precipitate the first presidential resignation in U.S. history. Wiggins found the evidence on August 2, 1974, when White House chief of staff ALEXANDER M. HAIG asked him to inspect the tapes of three critical presidential conversations about Watergate. It was during these conversations, which occurred on June 23, 1973, that Nixon and his chief White House aide, H. R. HALDEMAN, had discussed using the CIA to halt the FBI's Watergate probe. Wiggins, stunned by the contents, told Haig that he could no longer defend Nixon and that he would reveal the contents of the tapes unless the White House made them public.

Following the White House release of the tapes on August 5, Wiggins publicly ended his defense of the president and called for Nixon's resignation or impeachment.

In 1978 Wiggins decided not to seek reelection. Wiggins served as a judge on the U.S. Court of Appeals, Ninth Circuit, from 1984 to 2000. He died while in office in March 2000.

—AE

Wilkins, Roy
(1901–1981) *executive director, NAACP*

Born on August 30, 1901, Roy Wilkins was the grandson of a Mississippi slave and the son of a minister and college graduate who was forced to earn a living doing menial labor. He attended the University of Minnesota from 1919 to 1923, and during his college days he became recognized as an eloquent spokesman against racial injustice. In 1920 he joined the local NAACP chapter, where he served as secretary. Ten years later Wilkins was appointed executive secretary of the national NAACP, serving under Walter White. Throughout the 1930s and 1940s Wilkins established himself as an active arbitrator and speaker on the organization's behalf. His efforts gained him national prominence, and as the NAACP representative he served as a consultant to the War Department in 1941 and to the American delegation to the UN conference in 1945.

With White's death in 1955 Wilkins ascended to the post of executive secretary (the title was changed to executive director in 1965) and assumed leadership of the most influential civil rights group in America. He continued the push for effective legislation, and under his tenure the NAACP's lobbying wing was instrumental in the passage of the Voting Rights Act of 1965 and the Open Housing Act of 1968.

With RICHARD NIXON's succession to the presidency in 1969, the black militant movement, which had become increasingly vocal throughout the 1960s, gained greater momentum. Wilkins's prointegrationist stance and rejection of black power and black nationalism as a return to "segregation and Jim Crow" made him the target of criticism both within the more dissident ranks of the NAACP and from the new generation of black separatists. Undaunted, Wilkins continued to counsel moderation as the most effective means for gaining widespread support for civil rights issues. With the rise of the Black Panther Party and the organization's subsequent clash with police around the country, Wilkins helped form the Commission of Inquiry into Black Panthers and Law Enforcement Officials to explore the reasons for these clashes.

Wilkins led the campaign to extend civil rights laws despite Nixon's informal moratorium on the subject. He successfully opposed Nixon's nomination of civil rights opponent CLEMENT F. HAYNSWORTH to the Supreme Court in 1969 and of conservative G. HARROLD CARSWELL the following year. Frustrated over the Nixon administration's retreat on civil rights, Wilkins mobilized the Washington-based lobbying wing headed by Clarence Mitchell to press for broader legislation and gain extension of the 1965 Voting Rights Act's ban on literacy tests. Although the administration unsuccessfully attempted to modify provisions of the bill, it was signed into law in 1970.

Wilkins also led the fight against Nixon's antibusing stance. Together with the legal wing of the NAACP, he sought to challenge the constitutionality of Nixon's position and won an impressive Supreme Court ruling with the case of *Alexander v. the Holmes County (Mississippi) Board of Education* in 1969. The verdict endorsed the implementation of a desegregation program to take effect immediately.

In 1972 Nixon countered by outlining his desegregation program to Congress, which imposed severe restrictions on busing and delayed school desegregation until the latter part of 1973. The NAACP denounced the Nixon program, but Congress approved the measure. Despite this setback the NAACP made progress in other areas. It succeeded in gaining passage of the Equal Employment Opportunity Act, which broadened the coverage of its predecessor, passed in 1964. The law forbade discrimination by federal, state, and local agencies and allowed the Equal Employment Opportunities Commission to go into court to obtain endorsement of the bill's provisions.

Under Wilkins's leadership the NAACP expanded its fight for equal opportunity on all fronts. The organization established day care centers for low-income working mothers in 1973 and coordinated programs that sponsored housing construction and counseling centers for former prison inmates. Wilkins retired as an NAACP officer in July 1977 at age 76. He died in 1981.

—DGE

Williams, Harrison A(rlington), Jr.

(1919–2001) *member of the Senate; chairman, Special Committee on Aging; chairman, Labor and Public Welfare Committee*

Born on December 10, 1919, Harrison Williams attended Plainfield, New Jersey, public schools and received his B.A. from Oberlin College. He was a seaman and a navy pilot during World War II and then became a steelworker in Ohio for a short while before attending Columbia University Law School, from which he earned his degree in 1948. Elected to the U.S. House of Representatives in 1953 and 1954 but defeated in 1956, Williams revived his political fortunes and was elected in the Democratic landslide

of 1958 to become the first Democratic senator to represent New Jersey since 1936. During the Kennedy-Johnson years he established a reputation as a low-profile urban liberal on domestic policy, favoring the extension of federal government spending for a wide variety of human services. His ratings by lobbying groups up to 1978 showed a consistently prolabor and pro-civil rights record.

An early supporter of President Johnson's Vietnam War policies, Williams gradually shifted his stance so that by the early NIXON years he was speaking out against the extension of the war into Laos and Cambodia and voting for the Cooper-Church Amendment of 1970. Williams supported the War Powers Act of 1973, which limited the president's power to commit troops to combat without congressional approval. He also opposed what he considered to be excessive military spending on such projects as the antiballistic missile system.

Unlike New Jersey's other senator, CLIFFORD CASE, Williams concentrated on domestic rather than foreign affairs. As chairman of the Special Committee on Aging for the first two years of the Nixon administration, Williams was concerned about the impact of inflation on the elderly. He advocated property tax relief for low-income elderly homeowners that was linked to property tax reform and supported the establishment of the national institute on aging.

As a member of the Labor and Public Welfare Committee, the New Jersey senator was coauthor of the Coal Mine Health and Safety Act of 1969, which provided increased protection for coal miners. He became chairman of the committee in 1971 and frequently sought increases in the minimum wage laws as well as more liberalized laws for union organizing.

In the spring of 1972 Williams released a committee report to the public of a yearlong study into private pension plan abuses. He then presented a bill calling for uniform federal standards of fiduciary responsibility, improved disclosure provisions, and the maximum feasible centralization of all federal regulatory functions related to pension plans. With some modifications the Williams bill prevailed and became public law in 1974, known as the Employee Retirement Income Security Act. During the 1975 recession Williams unsuccessfully attempted to get the Senate to authorize 1 million public service jobs at a cost of $7.8 billion.

A strong civil rights advocate, the senator voted for the controversial Philadelphia Plan in December 1969, which mandated that quotas of minority groups be accepted by the construction trades unions. He spearheaded the battle for job equality in 1972 by managing the amendments that gave additional legal enforcement powers to the Equal Employment Opportunities Commission. He was an important proponent of the Occupational Safety and Health Act of 1970, requiring employers to provide working conditions free from recognized hazards likely to cause death or serious physical harm to employees.

As a member of the Banking, Housing, and Urban Affairs Committee, Williams worked for the creation of the Securities Investor Protection Corp. in 1970, which would provide financial protection for customers of brokerage houses, not for the houses themselves, much as the Federal Deposit Insurance Corp., created in 1934, insured bank depositors. One controversial amendment that Williams successfully sponsored in a 1970 banking reform bill prohibiting one-bank holding companies exempted at least 899 companies, including some controlled by the nation's biggest conglomerates. The senator, up for reelection that year, subsequently received a $5,000 contribution from the Bankers Political Action Committee, a lobbying organization. He supported several measures providing for federal financing of urban mass transit as well as the 1975 bill to aid financially beleaguered New York

City. On other issues Williams voted for government abortion aid (in a state with a high proportion of Roman Catholic voters), a consumer protection agency, the licensing of handguns, and against President Nixon's Supreme Court nominees G. HARROLD CARSWELL, CLEMENT HAYNSWORTH, and WILLIAM REHNQUIST.

Williams's 1970 reelection campaign was his most difficult to date. His Republican challenger was a law-and-order Nixon stalwart, Nelson Gross. With Vice President SPIRO AGNEW, Gross attempted to paint Williams as a "radical liberal" who did "nothing to check the violence" then besetting the country. Williams faced a major problem when heavy drinking and "erratic behavior" at the NAACP state conference in October 1968 earned him that organization's censorship. But his public acknowledgment of having conquered alcoholic dependence and $250,000 in labor union support aided him in his 250,000-vote margin of victory (54 percent of the total) over Gross.

When up for reelection in 1976, Williams had a far easier time than in 1970, winning with 62 percent of the vote over David Norcross, commonly considered a sacrificial lamb. That year he also headed the slate of "uncommitted" stop–JIMMY CARTER delegates to the Democratic National Convention who, preferring Senator HUBERT HUMPHREY and California governor EDMUND BROWN JR., took 64 of the 81 delegates. In 1982 Williams resigned his Senate seat after being convicted of bribery charges stemming from the "ABSCAM" investigation. He resided in Bedminster, New Jersey, where he died in 2001.

GB

Williams, John B(ell)
(1918–1983) *governor, of Mississippi*

John Bell Williams attended the University of Mississippi and the Jackson (Miss.) School of

Law, receiving his law degree in 1940. After service in the army air corps during World War II, Williams returned to Mississippi in 1944 as prosecuting attorney for Hinds County. In 1946 he was elected to the U.S. House of Representatives from Mississippi's seventh district and was consistently reelected with little opposition for the next two decades. On Capitol Hill Williams emerged as a strong opponent of civil rights measures and social legislation. In 1967 he won election as governor of Mississippi on a platform emphasizing states' rights and "responsible conservatism."

In his inaugural address Williams called for an end to racial violence in Mississippi and promised to seek funds for federal programs that he had frequently opposed in Congress. During the NIXON administration Williams backed the president's proposals for federal revenue sharing and welfare reform. As governor, Williams remained a strong foe of forced integration. In August 1969 he attended a seminar in Atlanta, Georgia, to defend the South's "freedom of choice" in school desegregation. Delegates from nine southern states accepted Williams's resolution urging President Nixon to "voice support and institute legislation" to bring about "maximum individual freedom" in substitution for bureaucratic directives. An executive committee headed by Williams and Governor LESTER MADDOX of Georgia was established to act as a clearinghouse for proposals to block school desegregation in the South. According to Reg Murphy and Hal Gulliver in *The Southern Strategy*, the Nixon administration was willing to ease up on federally forced desegregation.

On November 6, 1969, however, the U.S. Fifth Circuit Court of Appeals rejected an administration request for "flexible guidelines" and ordered 30 Mississippi school districts to implement effective desegregation plans by December 31, 1969. Williams labeled the ruling "the rawest kind of discrimination" and immediately challenged it. He was rebuffed when the Supreme Court in February 1970 refused to consider his attempts to sue Attorney General JOHN N. MITCHELL and Health, Education, and Welfare (HEW) secretary ROBERT H. FINCH over school desegregation.

Williams backed schemes to avoid school desegregation through the promotion of all-white private "academies." In January 1970 a three-judge federal district court panel in Washington issued an injunction to stop the Internal Revenue Service from granting tax-exempt status to segregated schools in Mississippi. Denouncing the injunction, Williams asked the state legislature to grant tax credits of up to $500 for each taxpayer contributing to the all-white schools. But the state legislature adjourned its 1970 session without approving the plan.

In the aftermath of the May 14, 1970, shootings that left two dead and 12 wounded at predominantly black Jackson State University, Williams defended the Jackson police, stating that they had acted in self-defense. After the Scranton Commission on Campus Unrest reported that the shootings were "unwarranted and unprovoked," Williams blasted the report as "another slanderous diatribe against the state of Mississippi."

Williams was a critic of forced busing as a way to achieve school desegregation. Lambasting the "hypocritical" policy of ending southern de jure segregation while ignoring northern de facto segregation, on September 11, 1971, Williams issued an executive order directing that no state funds be used for busing. However, on October 20 a U.S. district court judge issued a permanent injunction enjoining Mississippi from withdrawing funds meant for busing.

After leaving office in 1972 Williams returned to his law practice in Raymond, Mississippi. He continued to be politically active, however, supporting the presidential campaigns of Nixon in 1972 and GERALD FORD in 1976. He died in Raymond in 1983.

—JAN

Williams, John J(ames)
(1904–1988) *member of the Senate*

John J. Williams was born on May 17, 1904, in Frankford, Delaware. Williams owned a chicken feed business before he entered national politics in 1946. That year he was elected to the U.S. Senate. He ran on a platform that advocated reduction of the government's control over the economy. Representing a state whose politics were strongly influenced by E. I. duPont de Nemours & Co., Williams compiled a conservative voting record as he opposed most social welfare legislation and foreign aid.

Williams's crusades against corruption in government and his efforts to expose official hypocrisy earned him the title of "Conscience of the Senate." His private investigation into the questionable business activities of Senate majority secretary Bobby Baker led to a 16-month investigation of influence peddling and tax fraud by the Senate Rules Committee in 1963. Williams argued that the investigation also should probe into the activities of senators who were involved with Baker, but the Senate refused to go along with his plans.

Williams maintained his conservative record during the NIXON years. He opposed increasing the personal income tax exemption to $800 as part of the tax reform bill of 1969 and was one of six senators who voted against the measure enacted that year. The law cut some taxes by $9.1 billion but increased other taxes by $6.6 billion when it closed various tax loopholes that benefited corporations and wealthy individuals. He was one of the conservatives on Senator RUSSELL B. LONG's (D-La.) Finance Committee who helped to defeat the Nixon administration's welfare reform proposal in 1970. The proposal would have increased the federal government's share of national welfare costs. At the same session he led the unsuccessful 1969 Senate fight to put a $20,000 ceiling on farm subsidy payments. He argued for the proposal by pointing to five farmers who had each received annual subsidies of $1 million.

Williams continued his campaign for high ethical standards in government and kept the spotlight on official hypocrisy. In 1969 he voted against the Supreme Court nomination of Judge CLEMENT F. HYNSWORTH, citing the need to restore public confidence in the Supreme Court. Critics of the Haynsworth nomination charged that the judge had ruled on cases in which he had a financial interest. Haynsworth had been nominated to the seat vacated when Justice ABE FORTAS resigned from the Court amid a controversy involving judicial ethics. Williams introduced legislation in 1969 to revoke the tax-exempt status of foundations that made payments to public officials. He introduced the legislation after it was revealed that Justice Fortas had received payments from a foundation established by financier Louis E. Wolfson and that other justices also had received payments from various foundations.

Williams led the 1969 Senate fight to block pay raises for members of Congress and other top government officials. The pay raise had been proposed by President Johnson in 1968 under the new procedure Congress established in 1967 to help avoid the thorny issue of having House and Senate members vote for their own raises. The Johnson recommendations raised congressional salaries by 41 percent. The increases would cost about $21 million and would go into effect automatically unless Congress vetoed the president's proposal. Williams introduced the resolution to veto the increases on the grounds that Congress should set an example in the fight against inflation. The Senate, however, defeated the resolution.

Williams opposed the Cooper-Church Amendment to end American military involvement in Cambodia, and during debate on the measure he introduced an amendment that also would have prohibited the use of funds to finance U.S. combat troops for Israel. Williams argued that his amendment was consistent with the Senate intent to restrict the use of U.S. combat troops abroad, but the Senate rejected it by a 60–20 vote.

In 1970 Williams sponsored an amendment that stopped the long-standing political practice of giving members of Congress advanced information on the selection of defense contractors. Members used this information for publicity in their home states by releasing it to the media.

Williams ended his 24-year Senate career when he retired at the end of his term in 1971. The Republicans retained his seat when William V. Roth Jr. (R-Del.) easily defeated his Democratic opponent by winning 60 percent of the vote in the 1970 election. Williams died at his Delaware home in 1988.

—AE

Woodcock, Leonard (Freel)

(1911–2001) *president, United Automobile Workers union*

Leonard Woodcock was born in Providence, Rhode Island, on February 15, 1911. Woodcock grew up in England after his father, a manufacturer's representative, was interned in Germany during World War I. He returned to the United States with his family in 1926 and shortly afterward settled in Detroit, where he attended Wayne State University. In 1933 Woodcock became a machine assembler at the Detroit Gear and Machine Co., which manufactured auto parts. There he joined a union, then affiliated with the American Federation of Labor, that later became a local of the United Automobile Workers (UAW). Woodcock served on the UAW's regional staff in Grand Rapids, Michigan, from 1940 to 1944. He returned to the assembly line for two years as a punch press operator at the Continental Motors Corp. before being appointed in 1946 first administrative assistant to WALTER P. REUTHER, who had just been elected UAW president. A year later Woodcock became director of the UAW's regional division for western and upper Michigan.

Elected to an international vice presidency in 1955, Woodcock was put in charge of the UAW's General Motors (GM) and aerospace departments. He gained a reputation as an unusually skillful bargainer, negotiating precedent-setting contracts that included such fringe benefits as dental care programs and bans on discriminatory hiring practices. At the same time, he was regarded with greater friendliness by Detroit's business community than were other members of the top UAW leadership. Like most of the "Reutherites," who had run the union since 1947, Woodcock was an ex-socialist turned left-liberal. Over the years, however, he came to project a somewhat more moderate image than his associates. As the union's chief spokesman on Michigan state politics, for example, Woodcock was the first UAW official to endorse a flat-rate income tax that precluded proportionately higher tax levels for upper-income groups.

During the 1960s Woodcock was increasingly recognized as Walter Reuther's most likely successor. On May 9, 1970, Reuther was killed in a place crash. When the UAW executive board met 12 days later to choose a new president, Victor Reuther, Walter's brother, nominated Douglas Fraser, the head of the Chrysler and skilled trades divisions. A straw poll was taken of the board members giving Woodcock a one-vote majority, whereupon Fraser withdrew his candidacy and made Woodcock's election unanimous.

During Woodcock's presidency the rising tide of discontent among auto workers, which had begun to assume public prominence in the 1960s, became a subject of national debate. Through the early 1970s a flood of books and articles appeared focusing on the problems of boredom, frustration, and alienation associated with the monotony and harsh discipline of assembly line work. Social scientists and managerial personnel were particularly concerned with the effects of the high rates of absenteeism and job turnover on productivity. The UAW's response was ambiguous. In general, the union was willing to back management productivity schemes in return for high wages, on the assumption that this was necessary to meet foreign competition and thus save jobs. As rank-and-file resistance grew, however, the UAW was increasingly forced to take the lead in job actions aimed at blunting the auto makers' rationalizing initiatives.

Shortly after taking office, Woodcock led 400,000 auto workers in an eight-week-long strike against GM in the fall of 1970. Labor writer William Serrin later charged that the walkout was designed as an escape valve for the frustrations of UAW members bitter about what they considered intolerable working conditions. The strike demands, however, which had been drawn up by Reuther before his death, centered around wages and early retirement. The new three-year pacts contained a cost-of-living escalator clause without a ceiling as well as provision for monthly pensions of $500 after 30 years of service if at least 58 years old.

In 1971 the newly organized General Motors Assembly Division (GMAD) began a coordinated campaign to speed up the production of cars. GMAD's show-place, the highly automated Chevrolet Vega factory at Lordstown, Ohio, became the scene of a widely publicized confrontation between plant management, along with its staff of time-study engineers, and the carefully screened, predominantly young, white workforce. In March 1972 Lordstown's UAW local went on strike. In April workers at the GMAD plant in Norwood, Ohio, struck over the same issues and ended up staying out for 174 days. In the fall the UAW national leadership coordinated a series of 17 "ministrikes," each lasting a few days.

The issues of workload and speed-up formed a backdrop to the 1973 contract negotiations. In September, after a nine-day strike, the UAW arrived at an agreement with Chrysler that set the pattern for the entire industry. A key feature of the new contract was the abolition of "compulsory overtime," giving workers the right to refuse overtime work under certain conditions. The union also won recognition of its "30 and out" retirement program, allowing retirement with full benefits after 30 years of service regardless of age. Finally, provision was made for weekly plant inspections by joint union-management health and safety teams.

Woodcock increased the UAW's traditional involvement in Democratic Party politics. During the 1972 presidential primaries the union initially backed Senator EDMUND MUSKIE (D-Me.), but it supported Senator GEORGE MCGOVERN (D-S.D.) at the national convention. During the campaign Woodcock sharply criticized AFL-CIO president GEORGE MEANY for calling McGovern an "apologist from the Communist world."

The UAW had suffered a major embarrassment in 1972 when Alabama governor GEORGE WALLACE won the Michigan primary. Four years later, with busing a volatile issue in Michigan, Woodcock backed JIMMY CARTER in the hope of cutting down Wallace's primary vote. As early as January 1976 UAW locals had campaigned for Carter in the Iowa primary. Woodcock gave his official endorsement in May, thus providing the Carter campaign with what most commentators considered badly needed liberal credentials. Following the Democrats' electoral victory in November, Woodcock was considered for the post of secretary of health, education and welfare in the new administration. He declined the offer, however, on the ground that his position in favor of relaxing some automobile antipollution controls might constitute a "credibility problem."

Under UAW retirement rules Woodcock was ineligible for reelection to the presidency in 1976, after serving his second full two-year term. At the union's national convention in May 1977 he nominated Douglas Fraser as his successor. Earlier, in March, Woodcock had led a commission that visited Vietnam and Laos in search of information on Americans missing in the Indochina War. In May President Carter appointed him head of the U.S. liaison office in Beijing, a position held by Woodcock until 1981. From 1981 until his death in 2001, Woodcock taught at the Center for Chinese Studies at the University of Michigan and was a member of the board of governors of Wayne State University.

—TLH

Woods, Rose Mary

(1917–2005) *private secretary to President Nixon*

Born on December 26, 1917, in Sebring, Ohio, Rose Mary Woods was the daughter of an Irish potter. After graduating from high school in 1935, she worked as a secretary at the Royal China factory. When her fiancé died in 1943, she went to Washington to take a position with the Office of Censorship. She worked for the International Trading Administration from 1945 to 1947, when she joined Christian A. Herter's Committee on Foreign Aid, which was studying the Marshall Plan. RICHARD NIXON was a young congressman on Herter's committee. Ms. Woods was as impressed with Nixon's honesty and frugality as he was impressed with her competence and efficiency. In 1951, after working as a secretary with the Foreign Service Educational Foundation, she began her 23-year career as Richard Nixon's secretary.

Rose Mary Woods entered the Watergate story dramatically in 1973 after the discovery of the 18 1/2-minute gap on the June 20, 1972, tape that had been subpoenaed by Judge JOHN SIRICA. The tape allegedly recorded President Nixon's first discussion of the Watergate break-in with White House chief of staff H. R. HALDEMAN. On November 8, 1973, in routine questioning before Judge Sirica, Woods testified that although the West German Oher 5000 tape recorder was a somewhat complicated machine, she had "caught on" to its use fairly quickly. She rejected the possibility that she could have erased part of the tape.

On November 28 Woods changed her previous testimony and stated that while transcribing the June 20 tape for the court, she had stretched to answer the phone, accidentally pushing the record button while holding her foot on the foot pedal and thereby erasing a section of the tape. She said she reported the mistake to President Nixon, who assured her that the tape was not an essential one. Recording experts and the manufacturers of the Oher 5000 testified that the recorder was specifically designed as a "fail safe" machine, so that Ms. Woods's "accident" was virtually impossible. The experts also testified that someone had tampered with the tape in at least five sections, causing the erasures.

HERBERT KALMBACH, President Nixon's personal lawyer, claimed that Woods, with Donald and Edward Nixon, had received part of a $100,000 campaign contribution from HOWARD HUGHES. Kalmbach testified that he gave $100,000 to Nixon's friend CHARLES G. "BEBE" REBOZO, and Rebozo split the money among the three. Kalmbach's allegations were never substantiated.

Rose Mary Woods was described as a "fiercely loyal" and "totally devoted servant" of Richard Nixon. She was one of the few staff members who broke with the rigid Haldeman discipline to enjoy Washington society. After Nixon's retirement she gave few interviews to the press. Although officially retired, she flew to California to help Nixon with his memoirs. Most often she remained secluded in her Washington apartment. She died in 2005 in a nursing home in Alliance, Ohio.

—SJT

Woodward, Robert U(pshur)
(1943–) *journalist, author*

Born on March 26, 1943, the oldest of six children of an Illinois circuit court judge, Woodward was raised and educated in Wheaton, Illinois. After receiving his B.A. from Yale in 1965, he entered the navy for a four-year tour of duty. Although he had been accepted at Harvard Law School, Woodward applied for a job at the *Washington Post* in September 1970. After failing a two-week tryout, Woodward landed a position with the suburban Montgomery County *Sentinel*. Following a year of covering civic meetings and uncovering scandals in county government, Woodward was rehired by the *Post* in September 1971.

Assigned to the night police beat, Woodward by-lined front-page stories on Medicare abuses, consumer frauds, and health code violations in Washington's most exclusive restaurants. On June 17, 1972, Woodward received a call from *Post* city editor Barry Sussman, who told him that five men carrying expensive electronic gear had been arrested for breaking into the Democratic National Committee headquarters in the Watergate complex. At the arraignment the next day Woodward

heard JAMES MCCORD, one of the burglars, admit that he was a former security consultant for the Central Intelligence Agency (CIA). Following up an Associated Press wire item identifying McCord as a security consultant for the Committee to Re-Elect the President (CREEP), Woodward soon linked the burglars to E. HOWARD HUNT, a White House consultant and a one-time CIA operative.

In July 1972 the *Post*'s editors permanently assigned Woodward and CARL BERNSTEIN to the Watergate story. Using the so-called circle technique of interviewing, Woodward and Bernstein hounded CREEP staffers, FBI and Justice Department employees, and White House aides. Their most valuable source was "Deep Throat," so named because he was always interviewed on "deep background" and could neither be identified nor quoted. Deep Throat, a friend of Woodward's with a "sensitive position in the executive branch," seldom volunteered information but regularly corroborated the reporters' stories before publication.

For the first nine months Woodward and Bernstein pursued the labyrinthine Watergate scandal virtually by themselves. But by April 1973 their list of scoops was staggering: laundered, illegal corporate campaign contributions; the participation of the FBI and the Central Intelligence Agency in the Watergate cover-up; and the harassment of Nixon's "enemies" by the Internal Revenue Service (IRS). Yet when Nixon resigned on August 9, 1974, the reporters "felt no triumph," according to journalist Leonard Downie. "They finally realized with numbing shock that they had helped force the first resignation of a president in American history."

Woodward and Bernstein followed *All the President's Men*, their best-selling re-creation of Watergate, with *The Final Days*, a detailed account of Nixon's last months in office. A few days after Nixon's resignation, Woodward and Bernstein took a year's absence from the *Post*

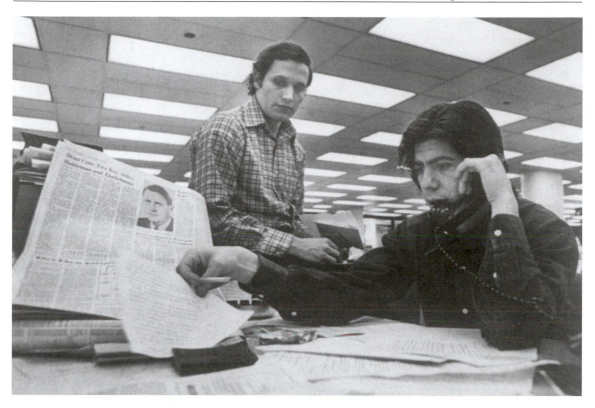

Bob Woodward (left) and Carl Bernstein at their desk at the *Washington Post,* April 29, 1973 *(Bettmann/ CORBIS)*

to begin six months of intensive interviews for the latter book. Despite adverse criticism of its "gossipy" nature, *The Final Days* was acclaimed by journalists and literary critics as a model of reportage and an important contribution to contemporary history.

Woodward returned to work on the *Post*'s national desk in September 1975. As a full-time investigative reporter Woodward looked into Hunt's alleged plot to assassinate columnist JACK ANDERSON, the National Security Administration's wiretaps of antiwar activists, and the IRS's attempts to block an inquiry into Senator JOSEPH MONTOYA's financial affairs. All three stories led to federal investigations.

Woodward continues to be a prolific writer. His post-Watergate works include *The Brethren: Inside the Supreme Court* (1979), *The Command-ers* (1991), *The Agenda* (1994), and *Bush at War* (2002). Most recently he has published *Secret Man* (2005), a look at his relationship with w. MARK FELT of the FBI, who served as Woodward's Watergate background source, Deep Throat. Woodward serves as the assistant managing editor of the *Washington Post.*

—JAN

Wright, Charles A(lan)
(1927–2000) *special White House legal consultant on Watergate*

Charles A. Wright was born in Philadelphia, Pennsylvania, on September 3, 1927. Wright graduated from Wesleyan University in 1947 and obtained his law degree from Yale two years later. He then embarked on a teaching career at the University of Minnesota, moving to the University of Texas in 1955. Wright became a premier authority on court procedure, authoring numerous books on the subject. He represented the state of Texas before the Supreme Court in arguments against the 18-year-old vote and abolition of the death penalty. Wright characterized his political views as "conservative."

In the summer of 1973 Wright was hired as a special legal consultant to President NIXON on constitutional issues involved in the Watergate case. He specialized on issues relating to executive privilege. In his first major assignment at the end of July, Wright drafted a letter rejecting a request by Watergate special prosecutor ARCHIBALD COX for White House tapes relevant to Watergate court proceedings. Wright argued that Cox was part of the executive branch and therefore subject to the instructions of the president. He said the request was an intrusion of the courts into the presidency, in violation of the separation-of-powers doctrine in the Constitution.

Cox filed suit to obtain the tapes, and arguments were heard before U.S. district court judge JOHN SIRICA at the end of August. Wright argued that disclosure of presidential conversations would "impair very markedly" the ability of a president to "perform the constitutional duties vested in him." Sirica ruled against Wright. President Nixon was ordered to make the tapes available to Judge Sirica for a decision on their use by a grand jury. President Nixon, after conferring with Wright and two other staff members, decided to appeal the decision.

On September 11 a U.S. court of appeals heard arguments by Wright and Cox over the tape recordings. Wright reiterated the same arguments as before concerning executive privilege, saying that a president was beyond the jurisdiction of the courts until impeached.

Wright also strongly suggested that Nixon might not obey an adverse judicial decision.

The appeals court, in a surprise move, urged an out-of-court settlement under which Nixon, with Wright and Cox, would examine the tapes to determine what material could go to the grand jury. After three meetings Cox and Wright informed the court that they had failed to come to a compromise settlement. On October 12 the appeals court in a 5–2 decision upheld Judge Sirica's ruling that Nixon must hand over the tape recordings to the U.S. district court.

President Nixon proposed a compromise in which a summary of the tapes verified by Senator JOHN STENNIS (D-Miss.) would be given to Judge Sirica and the Senate Watergate committee. Wright viewed the proposal as a generous offer. Cox refused the offer. Wright called Cox one last time and exchanged letters in an effort to come to an agreement. Cox refused and was fired on October 20 in the so-called Saturday night massacre. Cox later said that Wright had confronted him with a proposal drawn in such a manner that there was no way the special prosecutor could accept it.

In a surprise announcement on October 23, Wright informed Judge Sirica that "the president of the United States would comply in all respects" with the order to turn over the tapes. Two of the tapes Wright agreed to hand over to the court were subsequently discovered to be "nonexistent." Wright was informed of this by a White House secretary the same day it was announced.

Wright returned to his duties at the University of Texas Law School but remained on call for further consultation with Nixon on constitutional issues. He later said he did not resent his dealings with the White House but added that he would have been happier if he had been told of the nonexistent tapes earlier.

In January 1974 Wright returned as a legal consultant to handle executive privilege issues involved in Watergate. Wright played a low-key role in the rest of Watergate, helping to draft briefs for the White House legal defense. After Watergate Wright returned to the University of Texas Law School. He died in Austin in 2000.

—TFS

Wriston, Walter B(igelow)

(1919–2005) *chairman, First National City Corp.; member, National Commission on Productivity, Labor-Management Advisory Committee; member, Advisory Commission on Reform of the International Monetary System*

Walter B. Wriston was born on August 3, 1919, in Middletown, Connecticut. Wriston took a B.A. at Wesleyan University in 1941 and did postgraduate work at the École Française in Middlebury, Vermont. After obtaining an M.A. at the Fletcher School of International Law and Diplomacy in 1942, Wriston entered the army. Discharged as a lieutenant in 1946, Wriston was compelled by a tight job market to accept employment as a junior inspector in the comptroller's office of First National City Bank in New York. He advanced quickly through the ranks, becoming an executive vice president in 1960. In 1961 Wriston helped to develop the "certificate of deposit," or CD, which banks used increasingly in the 1960s and early 1970s to attract corporate funds. Wriston became president of First National City Bank in 1967, and, in the following year, of the reorganized one-bank holding company, First National City Corp. (Citicorp). The constitution of Citicorp under Wriston's auspices permitted a vast expansion of investment in areas closed to commercial banks. Influenced in part by Citicorp's expansion and in spite of Wriston's opposition in personal testimony, Congress in 1970 passed the One-Bank Holdings Company Act in an attempt to circumscribe

such activities. The expansion of Citicorp also was the object of a massive investigation by the RALPH NADER Study Group, published in 1973. A year later, in Citicorp's reply to the Nader study, Wriston bitterly attacked the report as a "reckless misuse of facts."

Wriston's emergence as the head of Citicorp made him a prominent spokesman for the private business sector in the early 1970s. President NIXON appointed him to the National Commission on Productivity in 1970, and in 1971 Wriston was among the business leaders invited to a White House consultation on the implementation of Phase Two controls. When these controls were lifted in January 1973, Wriston was appointed to a Labor-Management Advisory Committee formed under the auspices of the president's Cost of Living Council. In August of the same year Wriston joined other leading bankers and monetary specialists on the administration's Advisory Committee on International Monetary Reform.

Wriston found himself in the midst of controversy in the summer of 1974 when Citibank, in response to accelerating inflation that was driving investors out of the bond market, attempted to issue a 15-year bond with a floating rate set at 1 percent above the average rate on three-month U.S. Treasury bills. The Federal Reserve Bank expressed strong reservations about such an innovation, and Wriston was asked to consult with Fed chairman ARTHUR BURNS on the bond. Citibank eventually consented to a modification of the terms of the bond. After GERALD FORD assumed the presidency, Wriston was appointed to a revamped Labor-Management Advisory Committee.

Wriston played an important role in the controversy over the potential default of New York City in the summer and fall of 1975. Citibank, as one of the largest holders of the city's debt, distinguished itself by a particularly "hard line" in its call for cutbacks in city employment and services to solve the crisis, a hard line Wriston defended in statements to the press. By October 1975, however, as the potentially disastrous effects of a default on U.S. capital markets became more apparent, Wriston came out for some form of federal aid to the city. With Chase Manhattan's David Rockefeller and Morgan Guaranty's Ellmore Patterson, Wriston on October 18 warned the Senate Finance Committee on the dire consequences of default and on October 29 endorsed President Ford's plan for aid to the city.

Wriston's role throughout the crisis was retroactively highlighted a year later when the *New York Times* revealed that the major New York banks had quietly unloaded their own holdings of New York City paper in 1973–74 while continuing to urge small investors to buy them. Wriston and Citibank, however, denied any wrongdoing and any "inside information" on the city's crisis, and Wriston asserted that Citibank had in fact done everything possible to avert default.

After the last-minute bailout of New York Wriston returned to the center of public attention in January 1976 when the *Washington Post* "leaked" a list of "problem banks" that included both Citibank and Chase Manhattan Bank. Wriston, however, attacked the report as "misleading, irresponsible and at variance with the facts."

Wriston remained chairman of Citibank and Citicorp to 1984. In 2004 he received the Medal of Freedom. He died in January 2005 of pancreatic cancer.

—LG

Yablonski, Joseph ("Jock")
(1910–1969) *labor reformer*

Joseph Yablonski was born in Pittsburgh, Pennsylvania, on March 3, 1910. The son of an Eastern European coal miner who was killed on the job in an accident, Yablonski started working in the mines at age 15 to help support his family. He rose in rank in the leadership of the United Mine Workers (UMW), elected as a local president in 1934 and in the late 1930s as a district leader, and from 1942 to 1969 he served on the international executive board of the union. In 1958 Yablonski also was elected president of the Pittsburg area District Five. He served until 1966 when union president Tony Boyle forced him to resign under threat of placing the district in trusteeship.

Although he was originally a loyal supporter of the UMW leadership, Yablonski in the late 1960s became outraged with a number of abuses. He found, for example, Boyle collaborating with management to prevent the implementation of improved safety procedures in the mines and offering of the best possible medical care for black lung disease. Yablonski uncovered evidence of embezzlement of union funds, outrageous expense accounts for the leadership, pension fraud, and examples of nepotism and favoritism in giving out executive positions. He

opposed the clauses in the union's constitution that gave the national near-dictatorial control over the locals. The conventions Yablonski attended appeared to him to be rigged in favor of Boyle. Any attempt by the miners to reform their union, Yablonski learned, was met either with slick parliamentary tricks to muzzle the insurgents or, at the mines, violence and intimidation to silence the workers.

To correct these abuses, Yablonski declared his candidacy for the UMW presidency on May 29, 1969. Boyle immediately fired Yablonski as head of the union's lobbying office in Washington, a position he held concurrent with his other responsibilities. Yablonski's lawyer, Joseph Rauh, sued for his reinstatement, charging the ouster was politically motivated. The court ordered Boyle to return Yablonski to his position. Yablonski encountered difficulty getting the requisite 50 nominations by locals needed to place his name on the presidential ballot.

In a petition to Secretary of Labor GEORGE SHULTZ, Rauh listed 17 examples of illegal actions by Boyle's supporters, including violence and intimidation against the reformers, rigged meetings that denied Yablonski the nominations of locals who did favor him, and the use of patronage and bribes to lure miners away from the insurgents. Rauh also released an FBI report citing the illegal use of union funds in the Boyle campaign. But Shultz was unable to help Yablonski. Under the Landrum-Griffin law, a union election had to take place regardless of charges of irregularities. Only after the voting, upon receiving a petition documenting the charges of corruption, could the election be set aside. Rauh then tried to use the courts to help Yablonski. In one suit Yablonski charged that the *UMW Journal*, paid for by the miners, covered the Boyle campaign but ignored his. The court therefore ordered the union to send at its own expense campaign material for Yablonski.

At a June 23 rally an unidentified miner inflicted a karate chop on the back of Yablonski's neck, leaving him unconscious. Yablonski was rushed to the hospital to recover from this attempt on his life, explained by Boyle supporters as an act by an irrational man. Despite Boyle's attempts to prevent him from getting on the ballot, Yablonski obtained the 50 nominations.

During the election campaign Yablonski's life was threatened on a number of occasions. The federal government refused to act on Rauh's request for setting aside the election because of the dangers his client faced. On December 9 the UMW rank and file reelected Boyle by a vote of 81,000 to Yablonski's 45,000. Yablonski immediately sued for a new election. Rauh cited in the suit 200 examples of irregularities, including ballot stuffing and violence.

On December 30 Yablonski, his wife, and daughter were killed in an amateurish gangland-style execution. Yablonski's two sons, joined by Rauh, and the insurgent miners anxious for a new election accused the UMW leadership of being responsible for the labor reformer's death. The three who assassinated the Yablonski family were immediately arrested, and through confessions two UMW officials were implicated in the case and eventually convicted and imprisoned. It was learned in their trial that the killing of Yablonski was planned during his election campaign but postponed because the conspirators thought the connection between their victim and his campaign would be too obvious.

In the course of the trial of those involved in the case, a mystery person named "Tony" was cited on a number of occasions. Federal investigators identified this individual to be Boyle. Following a long trial with appeals, he was convicted in 1975 as a coconspirator in the killing of Yablonski and received a sentence of three life terms. In 1972, following a series of appeals, the UMW complied with a federal court order and held a new election, in which the reformer Arnold Miller defeated Boyle.

—JB

Yorty, Sam(uel) (William)
(1909–1998) *mayor of Los Angeles*

Samuel Yorty was born on October 1, 1909, in Lincoln, Nebraska. After graduating from high school, Yorty moved to Los Angeles. He attended Southwestern University part time to study law and eventually was admitted to the bar. He also entered politics and was elected in 1936 to the state assembly, where he served two terms. Initially establishing a reputation as a crusading liberal who sponsored a wide range of social and economic welfare legislation, he alienated his liberal supporters by sponsoring the bill that created an un-American activities committee in California. Thereafter he was considered a maverick conservative. For the next 20 years Yorty alternated between political campaigns and his law practice. He won election to the House of Representatives in 1950 and 1952, but lost Senate campaigns in 1940 and 1954 and failed to get the Democratic nomination for the Senate in 1956. In 1960 he antagonized California Democrats by endorsing RICHARD NIXON for president.

Yorty was elected mayor of Los Angeles in 1961 and 1965. He governed during the city's period of rapid population growth and expansion. Although the powers of the Los Angeles mayor were more circumscribed than in most other cities, Yorty managed to lower property taxes and to undertake the renewal of the city's neglected downtown area. He came under serious criticism for his handling of the 1965 Watts riot. The California Advisory Committee to the U.S. Civil Rights Commission charged Yorty with "gross negligence" and "attitudes and actions" that contributed to the ghetto uprising. In 1966 Yorty unsuccessfully challenged Governor Edmund Brown in the gubernatorial primary.

Yorty ran for a third term as mayor in 1969. His main challenger in the technically nonpartisan campaign was Thomas Bradley, a black city council member and former police lieutenant who had the endorsement of state party leaders and national figures such as EDWARD KENNEDY, HUBERT HUMPHREY, and EDMUND MUSKIE. Yorty conducted a vitriolic, racially based campaign. He accused Bradley of running a "racist" campaign by appealing to the "bloc vote" of blacks and "left-wing militants." When the two men faced each other in a runoff, Yorty intensified his campaign rhetoric. "Imagine what would happen here with a Negro mayor," he warned. If Bradley won, Yorty said, the city would become "one big campus" and be taken over by "black militants and left-wing extremists." In the May 27 voting Yorty won by a solid margin.

The following year Yorty entered the Democratic gubernatorial primary. He was defeated by Jesse Unruh, the liberal minority leader of the state assembly, by a more than 2-1 margin. In November 1971 Yorty declared his candidacy for the Democratic presidential nomination. With an initial campaign chest of $250,000 contributed by conservative California businessmen, Yorty was outspokenly conservative. He advocated an aggressive foreign policy, favored raising taxes to increase military spending, and took a tough stand on "law and order" issues. Given little chance of winning, Yorty concentrated his efforts on the New Hampshire primary, where he had the endorsement of WILLIAM LOEB, the ultraconservative publisher of the *Manchester Union-Leader.* Yorty hoped that a good showing in the primary would rally conservatives around his candidacy. When the returns were in, however, he had only 6 percent of the vote. In succeeding primaries Yorty received only a minuscule percentage of the vote, including a showing of 1.5 percent in his home state.

Yorty came under increasing criticism during his third term as mayor. Voters were becoming fed up with growing pollution, traffic congestion, and haphazard development and with a mayor who referred to environmentalists as "kooks" and who spent one out of every four days outside Los Angeles, including six trips to Vietnam. Quipsters remarked that Lost Angeles was the only city with a foreign policy. Yorty also took his law-and-order stance to new extremes, giving virtually complete freedom of action to Los Angeles's tough police chief, Ed Davis. Davis remarked that Yorty was "an automatic champion of safety on the streets and whatever it takes to do that." Under Yorty Los Angeles was continually plagued with charges of police brutality, especially toward blacks, the city's large Chicano population, and antiwar activists.

Yorty ran for a fourth term as mayor in 1973 and again faced Bradley as his main opponent. The two men were forced into a runoff, and Yorty repeated the tactics of the previous campaign. He warned white neighborhoods against the "black bloc vote," and his campaign manager took out full-page newspaper ads accusing Bradley of seeking Black Panther Party support. Bradley won a court order directing Yorty to tone down his more vitriolic campaign literature. In the May 24 runoff Bradley scored a decisive victory over

Yorty, who retired after his term expired. Yorty died in 1998 in Los Angeles.

—JD

Young, Andrew J(ackson), Jr.
(1932–   ) *member of the House of Representatives*

Young, who was born on May 12, 1932, into a middle-class black family, graduated from Howard University in 1951 and the Hartford Theological Seminary in 1955. Ordained as a minister of the United Church of Christ, he served as pastor of churches in Alabama and Georgia. He became involved in the civil rights movement when he helped organize the 1956 Montgomery, Alabama, bus boycott led by Rev. Martin Luther King Jr. He then served on the staff of the National Council of Churches in New York but left when King asked him to become his chief aide in the Southern Christian Leadership Conference (SCLC), which led the civil rights movement during the 1960s. Young was often arrested for participating in the many nonviolent protest demonstrations organized by the SCLC in the South to end discrimination against black people.

In 1969, about a year after King's assassination, Young, who was executive vice president of the SCLC, announced a shift in the organization's strategy. Instead of backing nationwide civil rights protests, the organization would use most of its funds to register black voters to win local elections in the South. The following year Young ran an unsuccessful campaign to unseat Representative Fletcher Thompson Jr. (R-Ga.), a conservative elected from an Atlanta-area district. Young won the seat in 1972 when redistricting had consolidated a district that included most of the city of Atlanta with its black majority and some affluent white suburbs. Young won 53 percent of the vote and became the first black elected to the House from the Deep South since 1898.

During his four years in the House, Young generally opposed the NIXON-FORD legislative programs and regularly voted to override Nixon-Ford vetoes of social welfare legislation. He vigorously supported congressional efforts to legislate an end to the Vietnam War. He compiled a consistently liberal voting record, backing almost every position advocated by the liberal Americans for Democratic Action, the AFL-CIO's Committee on Political Education, and consumer groups.

In 1974 Young opposed the Holt Amendment, which sought to prohibit the Department of Health, Education, and Welfare from withholding funds from school districts to compel them to assign students and teachers to schools and classes on the basis of race, sex, creed, or national origin and to keep records on such factors. Although busing was not mentioned in the amendment, Holt intended it to be an antibusing measure. Young argued that the amendment would increase school busing suits because it closed the door to negotiating settlements of segregation problems. The following year Young vigorously supported extending the Voting Rights Act of 1965, which was due to expire. He pointed out that voter registration of eligible blacks had increased from 29 percent in 1964 to 56 percent in 1972 in the states affected by the law. Young also advocated broadening the law to cover discrimination against language minorities. Congress extended the Voting Rights Act for seven years, included language minorities in its coverage, and permanently banned the use of literacy tests for voter registration eligibility.

Young was among JIMMY CARTER's first supporters for the presidential nomination and actively campaigned for him. The fact that Young, a prominent civil rights leader and Rev. King's former right-hand man, supported the Carter candidacy helped convince many blacks and white liberals that Carter was not a bigot in disguise. Young had an independent power base and was able to give Carter frank and excellent advice during the election campaign. Carter publicly stated that Young was the only man to whom he owed a political debt for his election.

Young was reelected in 1976 but resigned his seat when Carter appointed him U.S. ambassador to the United Nations in 1977. Young served at the United Nations until 1979. In 1981 he was elected mayor of Atlanta; he served two terms in that capacity, until 1990. In 1990 he ran unsuccessfully for governor of Georgia. Young resides in Atlanta, Geogia.

—AE

Young, Milton R(uben)
(1897–1983) *member of the Senate*

A prosperous farmer in North Dakota, Young served in the state legislature from 1933 to 1945, when he was appointed to the U.S. Senate to fill a seat left vacant by the death of Senator John Moses. The following year Young won a special election to complete the term. Representing a farm belt state, Young labored for farm subsidies far exceeding the amount his party was willing to support. In other domestic legislation Young consistently voted conservative well into the 1960s, opposing antipoverty programs and Medicare. Throughout the 1960s Young was at times skeptical of the Vietnam War, but he nevertheless approved the appropriations for it.

During the NIXON-FORD years Young, a senior Republican senator, managed a low profile. He devoted most of his attention to agricultural matters, especially issues concerning his state. Young opposed the nomination of EARL BUTZ as secretary of agriculture because he believed Butz favored lower price supports and showed little interest in helping the small farmer. In 1972 Young was responsible for a 10-cent increase in wheat price supports. He also cosponsored legislation for rural development, crop insurance programs,

and measures to improve market conditions for farm goods. In 1973 Young worked with House Agriculture Committee chairman HERMAN TALMADGE (D-Ga.) to frame legislation continuing farm product supports.

Young's ambivalent attitude toward the Vietnam War continued into the Nixon years. In 1970 he voted against the Cooper-Church Amendment, which would have cut off funds for the Cambodian invasion, and praised the incursion as "a long-overdue decision." Yet Young did support the McGovern-Hatfield Amendment of 1970 and the Mansfield Amendment of 1971, which sought to end the war through congressional intervention. Young consistently supported the administration's defense policies, voting for full appropriations for the antiballistic missile and opposing attempts to cut the defense budget. However, he did support the withdrawal of most U.S. ground troops from Western Europe.

Young consistently voted against welfare, consumer, and environmental legislation. He backed Nixon's nominations of CLEMENT HAYNSWORTH and G. HARROLD CARSWELL to the Supreme Court. He stressed that the conservative Carswell would provide a much-needed "philosophic balance" on the Court. Young countered charges that Carswell was a mediocre judge. He said that Carswell "may be no Abraham Lincoln," but Lincoln, too, was belittled and ridiculed for not being a great intellectual. Young agreed with the administration that the courts had been coddling criminals.

In 1974, at age 76, Young decided to seek reelection despite Republican Senate Campaign Committee advice to retire. In the election he faced the popular former governor William Guy in a spirited campaign in which most issues were avoided. Young narrowly defeated Guy in a contested election in which the December recount gave him a 186-vote majority. Young retired from the Senate in 1980 and died three years later.

Z

Zablocki, Clement J(ohn)
(1912–1983) *member of the House of Representatives*

Clement J. Zablocki was born in Milwaukee, Wisconsin, on November 18, 1912. Zablocki, educated in Milwaukee parochial schools, graduated from Marquette University in 1936 and taught high school before serving in the Wisconsin state senate from 1942 to 1948. That year he was elected representative from Wisconsin's fourth district, comprised of southern Milwaukee and its adjacent suburbs. Reflecting the interests of his working-class Polish-American constituency, Zablocki was an advocate of organized labor, a generous defense budget, and a firm anti-Soviet foreign policy. Both the AFL-CIO Committee on Political Education and the anticommunist, prodefense American Security Council consistently gave Zablocki high ratings.

Despite a reputation of a more conservative approach to social programs than his fellow Wisconsin Democrats, Zablocki voted for the major social welfare legislation of the Johnson administration. As second-ranking member of the House Foreign Affairs Committee, he was of strategic importance as an apologist for the Johnson administration's Vietnam War policy.

During the NIXON administration Zablocki continued to support the Vietnam War effort long after the majority of the House Democrats began to vote for amendments to appropriations bills that prohibited the use of funds for combat activity in Southeast Asia. In May 1973 Zablocki voted against the successful amendment to the Second Supplemental Appropriations bill that cut off funds for bombing in Cambodia. The legislative effort eventually resulted in an administration-congressional compromise to end the bombing by August 15, 1973.

Zablocki was the principal architect and manager of the House legislative effort to define the war-making powers of the president. He introduced the first such House resolution in September 1970. It merely requested that the president consult with Congress "whenever feasible" before committing U.S. troops to combat. This resolution finally passed the House in 1972 but was rejected by Senate conferees as too weak an assertion of the congressional war-making role under the Constitution.

After Zablocki's Subcommittee on National Security reopened hearings on war powers in early 1973 and cooperated with Senate sponsors of a tougher bill, he wrote and reported a much stronger resolution in June. Its major features included a 120-day limit on presidential commitment of U.S. troops without congressional

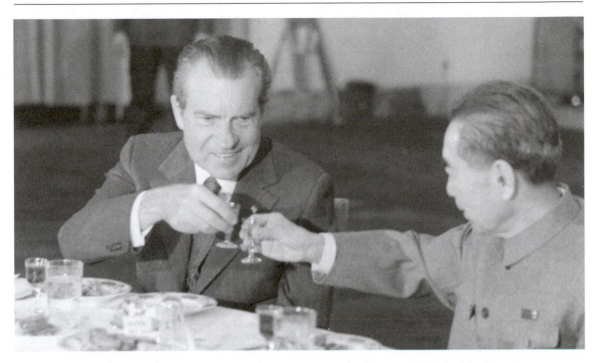

President Nixon with Premier Zhou Enlai (Chou En-lai), February 25, 1972 (National Archives)

authorization and a provision for Congress to direct disengagement before that limit through passage of a concurrent resolution. In conference, major House-Senate differences focused on the granting of "prior authority," that is, allowing the president to commit troops without first obtaining congressional approval. The successful compromise was a general statement of policy that the president had prior authority in emergency situations only. President Nixon vetoed the war powers bill on October 24, but the House overrode it on November 7.

When asked how enough votes were obtained to override the veto (the bill had originally passed three short of the two-thirds necessary to override), Zablocki said, "Some of [them] read the returns of yesterday's elections" and felt that the Watergate scandal, the tapes controversy, and the firing of special prosecutor ACHIBALD COX were decisive in creating the atmosphere necessary for an override.

After chairman of the Foreign Affairs Committee Thomas Morgan (D-Pa.) retired in 1977, Zablocki, by virtue of seniority and his assurances that he would support continued aid to Israel, became chairman of the newly renamed International Relations Committee. Zablocki died in office in 1983.

—JMP

Zhou Enlai

(Chou En-lai) (1898–1976) *premier, People's Republic of China*

Born in Kiangsu Province, Zhou was arrested in 1919 for his participation in student demonstrations. After his release Zhou expatriated to Paris, where he became a member of the Chinese Communist movement in Europe. He returned to China in 1924, where he emerged as a member of both the Chinese Communist

Party and its ally Sun Yat-sen's Kuomintang. After the purge of Kuomintang Communists in 1927, led by Chiang Kai-shek, Zhou went underground. He was elected to the Politburo of the Chinese Communist Party, together with Mao Zedong (Mao Tse-tung) was instrumental in the formation of rural soviets in the Chinese mountains, and helped to plan the Communists' "Long March" of 1934–35. During World War II Chiang was forced to cooperate with the Communists against the Japanese invaders; Zhou served as the link between the Communists and Chiang's Nationalist government.

After the Communist victory in the Chinese civil war in 1949, Zhou emerged as the chief diplomat of the new People's Republic of China (PRC). He negotiated the cease-fire talks in the Korean War and represented his nation at virtually every world conference of import in the 1950s. Clearly the pragmatist to Mao's angry visionary, of Zhou RICHARD NIXON would say: "Without Zhou [the revolution] would have burned out and only the ashes would remain." It was Zhou who negotiated with HENRY KISSINGER what would become Nixon's trip to the PRC in February 1972, ushering in a period of détente between the two nations. More importantly, it was Zhou who negotiated the Shanghai Communiqué with the Nixon administration; released at the end of Nixon's trip, the agreement stated that the PRC was the one true China, and Taiwan was "a part of China."

In 1972 Zhou was diagnosed with liver cancer; he died in January 1976.

—JRG

Ziegler, Ronald L(ewis)
(1939–2003) *White House press secretary*

Ronald L. Ziegler was born on May 12, 1939, in Covington, Kentucky. After receiving a degree in marketing from the University of Southern California in 1961, Ziegler began a brief stint as a salesman for Procter & Gamble. A member of the Young Republicans in his college days and an active volunteer at state Republican headquarters, Ziegler left the firm in October 1961 to serve as press officer for the Republican State Committee.

In 1962 he joined RICHARD NIXON's gubernatorial campaign as assistant to HERBERT G. KLEIN, who served as chief press aide. After Nixon's defeat in late 1962 Ziegler procured an executive post with the prestigious J. Walter Thompson advertising agency, where he became attuned to various facets of television news coverage. During his years at the agency he continued in Republican state politics under the watchful eye of H. R. HALDEMAN, also an adman at the Thompson agency. In 1968 at the urging of Haldeman, who was serving as chief of staff for Nixon's presidential campaign, Ziegler took a leave of absence from advertising to serve again as press chief Klein's assistant.

Following Nixon's victory Ziegler was appointed presidential press secretary. He became the youngest man ever to attain the post. An eager, energetic "PR man," Ziegler's youth, thoroughness, efficiency, and public relations expertise made him popular at the Nixon White House. The news media, however, were less than enthusiastic about the appointment, since Ziegler lacked press credentials, and his knowledge of national and world affairs was limited.

Within months his complacent, humorless, and evasive approach to press briefings came under considerable attack. Ziegler was accused of intentionally passing misinformation and articulating the White House position in a confused "Madison Avenue fuzziness" that required further clarification he was never able to provide. Because of his talent for obfuscation, Ziegler was soon nicknamed "Zigzag," and his statements to the press were labeled

"Ziegles." On one occasion, when asked to elaborate on his expression "the president's least likely decision," he stated, "you should not interpret by my use of 'least likely' that ultimately, or when the final decision is made, that that may not be the decision but what I'm saying is that it is only one of the matters under consideration and the decision has not been made." A number of journalists, while frustrated with Ziegler's obscurantist style, saw the problem more in terms of Nixon's "tight leash" on his press secretary rather than Ziegler's inability to provide background data on administrative policy. Ziegler saw that the press received only what the president intended to reveal. He often admitted ignorance about available detailed information when circuitous statements failed to appease the disgruntled press corps. His ignorance was far from affected, however. He had no input into policy decisions and was seldom given information above and beyond what was to be relayed to the press.

Ziegler experienced no conflict between presidential privacy and the people's right to be kept informed. He also considered it an occupational duty to pass on misinformation to the press. A senatorial press secretary recalled his astonishment when, upon encountering Ziegler one evening, he mentioned that their jobs consisted of "lying to the reporters." After an agitated denial, Ziegler remarked, "Oh, come on, of course you do. We all do."

The full wrath of press interrogations began in June 1972 soon after the Watergate break-in. One judicious reporter had already compared the list of burglars with the list of executive employees at the Committee to Re-Elect the President (CREEP) and pointed out that JAMES MCCORD's name appeared on both. But Ziegler repeatedly refused comment on "a third-rate burglary attempt." As the *Washington Post* published its investigations of the Water-

gate affair and pointed an accusing finger at members of CREEP and the White House staff, Ziegler dismissed the articles as "shabby journalism." Relations between Ziegler and the press had become so strained that members of the White House refused to enter the press room, which they referred to as a "poisoned forum."

As the trial for the Watergate burglars began, a direct path of associations led to Nixon's White House counsel JOHN DEAN. In March 1973 Ziegler informed the press corps that despite this latest development, the president maintained "absolute and total" trust in Dean. Ziegler stated that an investigation would rectify his ambiguous standing in the Watergate affair. When Dean's testimony implicated many in the White House. Ziegler was compelled to issue a revised statement on Watergate developments that, in essence, contradicted the president's previous reluctant statements on the matter. In an attempt to clarify the contradiction, Ziegler labeled his latest remarks the president's "operative" position. Amid a storm of indignation a *New York Times* reporter inquired if that meant "that the other statement is no longer operative, that it is now inoperative." Ziegler replied: "The president refers to the fact that there is new material, therefore this is the operative statement. The others are inoperative."

Whatever smattering of credibility Ziegler retained throughout his tenure had now abruptly vanished. In June 1973 the National Press Club condemned Ziegler by stating, "The White House press secretary has been reduced to a totally programmed spokesman without independent authority. . . . Rather than opening a window into the White House, the press secretary closes doors."

As the result of tension between Watergate special prosecutor ARCHIBALD COX and Nixon, in October 1973 Ziegler announced grimly that Cox and been dismissed. Rather than carry out the president's order to fire Cox, Attorney General ELLIOT RICHARDSON and Deputy Attorney General WILLIAM RUCKELSHAUS resigned. The backlash from the announcements forced Nixon to inform the media a month later, "I am not a crook." As pressure continued to build and cries of impeachment were heard in Congress, Nixon withdrew from the public eye and relied increasingly on Ziegler for solace. Although he encouraged Nixon to fight the impeachment drive, Ziegler had already given up hope. When Nixon resigned, Ziegler accompanied him to his West Coast home.

In 1975 Ziegler attempted to join his former colleagues in an effort to capitalize on Watergate through paid lectures. But Ziegler was less interested in self-vindication than his associates and rather chose to speak in praise of Nixon. Ziegler's lectures were met with hostility, and he soon abandoned the circuit for a job in advertising later that year. From 1987 to 1998 he served as the chief executive of the National Association of Chain Drug Stores. He died of a heart attack in 2003.

—DGE

Zumwalt, E(lmo) R(ussel), Jr.
(1920–2000) *chief of naval operations*

Born on November 29, 1920, in Tulare, California, Zumwalt's parents were both physicians, and at one point he intended to become a military doctor. In 1939 he won an appointment to the U.S. Naval Academy and graduated after three years because of World War II. In June 1942 Zumwalt was commissioned an ensign and assigned to the destroyer USS *Phelps*. After a year on the *Phelps* Zumwalt went to the combat information center of the destroyer USS *Robinson*, where he remained until the end of the war.

After the war Zumwalt served as executive officer on several destroyers. He attended the Naval War College for a year and the National War College in Washington for 10 months. A lecture he delivered there, "The Problems of Succession in the Kremlin," attracted the attention of Paul H. Nitze, the assistant secretary of defense for international affairs. Nitze had Zumwalt assigned to his desk as a staff officer. When Nitze became secretary of the navy in 1963, he made Zumwalt his executive assistant.

In 1965 Zumwalt was promoted to admiral and given command of a cruiser-destroyer flotilla. He went to Vietnam in 1968 as the commander of U.S. naval forces there. While in Vietnam Zumwalt "picked up a whole set of new ideas" about the way the contemporary navy should be run.

Zumwalt was given the chance to apply his reforms after President NIXON nominated him in April 1970 to be chief of naval operations. In July 1970 he succeeded Admiral THOMAS H. MOORER, who became chairman of the Joint Chiefs of Staff. To implement his changes Zumwalt, the youngest chief of naval operations in U.S. history, issued a series of directives known as "Z-Grams." His goal was to bring the navy more into line with the nation's changing lifestyles. He also sought to counter the service's declining enlistment and reenlistment rates. Regulations regarding such matters as conduct, grooming, dress, and shore leave were relaxed, and the navy's promotion procedures were eased. Although the changes met some opposition in the navy hierarchy, Zumwalt contended that his policies were designed "to treat our navy personnel with dignity, discipline, compassion, maturity, and intelligence, but most of all with 20th-century commonsense."

In 1971 Zumwalt was persuaded by senior officers on his staff to rewrite or clarify some of his relaxed rules on personal appearance for sailors. He dismissed, however, the contention of navy traditionalists who feared the new standards would cause a breakdown in discipline. Speaking to the graduating class at Annapolis, he said the navy's problem was not lack of discipline but a need for enlightened leadership. That same year Zumwalt announced a five-year program to recruit more black officers and enlisted men. The aim was to increase the number of black navy personnel to the level of their representation in the U.S. population. In 1973 he disclosed plans to open all navy jobs to women, including assignments for general sea duty. A major reason for the proposed change, he explained, was that the imminence of an all-volunteer armed force had heightened the importance of women as a personnel resource.

After a series of racial incidents between black and white sailors and marines, Zumwalt and Secretary of the Navy JOHN W. WARNER told a meeting of top admirals and Marine Corps generals in November 1972 that race relations were to be given the same priority as professional performance. Later in the month a special House Armed Services subcommittee opened an investigation into the racial disorders aboard the aircraft carriers *Constellation* and *Kitty Hawk*. Appearing before the subcommittee, Zumwalt discounted claims by navy officials and others that a breakdown in discipline had led to the disorders. The *Constellation*'s executive officer, Commander John Schaub, testified that the racial problems could be related to the navy's recruitment of educationally disadvantaged black youths. Speaking later to reporters, he characterized the recruiting of such men as "poorly conceived and totally unfair" because it placed them in competition with other recruits from a "more favorable" background. Zumwalt maintained that the problems stemmed mostly from the failure of commands to fully implement equal opportunity programs. The

servicemen involved in the incidents were eventually disciplined or discharged by the navy.

In February 1973 the navy disclosed that Zumwalt had ordered the discharge of roughly 3,000 enlisted men who were considered a "burden to command." At the same time the navy announced that it was tightening its recruitment standards, with a new emphasis on education and character qualifications.

Faced with budget restraints, Zumwalt supported the development of smaller high-speed craft to offset anticipated reduction in fleet size. In 1971 he initiated guidelines for modernization of the fleet. He was a strong advocate of the navy's controversial new jet fighter, the F-14 Tomcat, and in 1974 he fought successfully for the Trident missile program.

Zumwalt became concerned about the steady growth in Soviet naval power that had begun in the 1960s. In the spring of 1971 he told the House Armed Services Committee that updating the U.S. fleet was necessary to maintain nuclear parity with the Soviet Union and to balance its increasingly active navy. In August 1972 he reported the construction of the first Soviet aircraft carrier. Shortly before his retirement Zumwalt questioned whether the navy would be able to maintain control of the seas in the event of a war with the Soviet Union. Zumwalt left the service in July 1974; he was succeeded as chief of naval operations by Admiral James L. Holloway.

In retirement Zumwalt criticized the conduct of foreign policy under Nixon and Secretary of State HENRY A. KISSINGER, specially the failure to address the issues of détente and the first Strategic Arms Limitation Talks (SALT 1) agreement. In December 1975 he accused Kissinger of witholding information from President GERALD FORD about what Zumwalt described as "gross violations" by the Soviet Union of its 1972 SALT agreement with the United States. Kissinger denied Zumwalt's accusations and the following year refuted the quotes attributed to him in Zumwalt's book *O Watch*. In the book Zumwalt claimed Kissinger had said the United States was in decline and the Soviet Union on the rise. In 1976 Zumwalt ran as the Democratic candidate for the Senate in Virginia and lost to the independent incumbent, Senator HARRY F. BYRD Jr. He became president of American Medical Buildings the following year. He died in 2000.

—SF

APPENDICES

MAPS

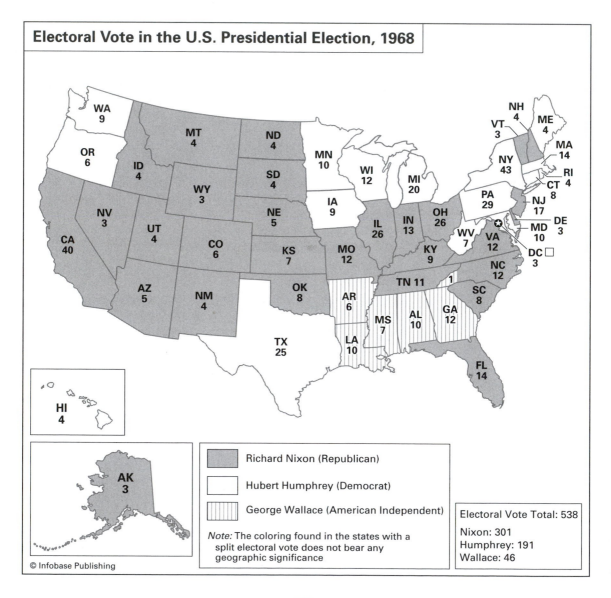

Electoral Vote in the U.S. Presidential Election, 1968

WA 9

OR 6

MT 4

ND 4

MN 10

NH 4

VT 3

ME 4

ID 4

WY 3

SD 4

WI 12

MI 20

NY 43

MA 14

RI 4

CT 4

NV 3

UT 4

NE 5

IA 9

IL 26

IN 13

OH 26

PA 29

NJ 17

DE 3

CA 40

CO 6

KS 7

MO 12

KY 9

WV 7

VA 12

MD 10

DC 3

AZ 5

NM 4

OK 8

AR 6

TN 11

1

NC 12

SC 8

MS 7

AL 10

GA 12

TX 25

LA 10

FL 14

HI 4

AK 3

Richard Nixon (Republican)

Hubert Humphrey (Democrat)

George Wallace (American Independent)

Note: The coloring found in the states with a split electoral vote does not bear any geographic significance

Electoral Vote Total: 538

Nixon: 301
Humphrey: 191
Wallace: 46

© Infobase Publishing

634

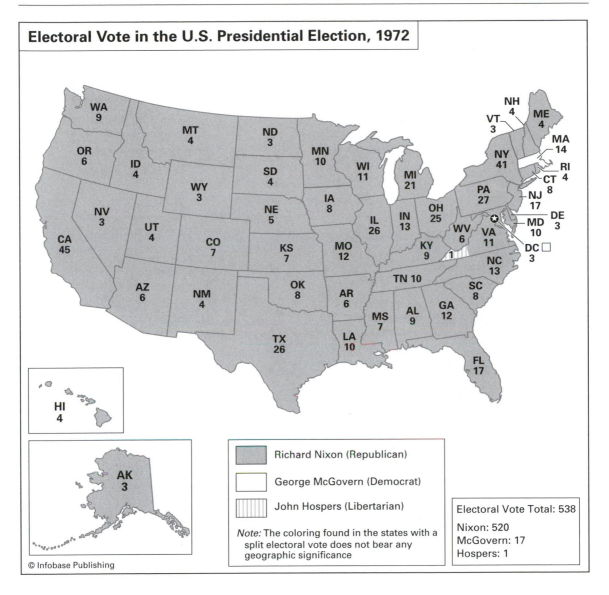

Electoral Vote in the U.S. Presidential Election, 1972

WA 9
OR 6
ID 4
MT 4
ND 3
MN 10
WI 11
MI 21
NH 4
VT 3
ME 4
NY 41
MA 14
RI 4
CT 8
NV 3
UT 4
WY 3
SD 4
NE 5
IA 8
IL 26
IN 13
OH 25
PA 27
NJ 17
DE 3
MD 10
CA 45
CO 7
KS 7
MO 12
KY 9
WV 6
VA 11
DC 3
AZ 6
NM 4
OK 8
AR 6
TN 10
NC 13
SC 8
GA 12
MS 7
AL 9
TX 26
LA 10
FL 17
HI 4
AK 3

Richard Nixon (Republican)

George McGovern (Democrat)

John Hospers (Libertarian)

Note: The coloring found in the states with a split electoral vote does not bear any geographic significance

Electoral Vote Total: 538

Nixon: 520
McGovern: 17
Hospers: 1

© Infobase Publishing

The Vietnam War

PEOPLE'S REPUBLIC
OF CHINA

Legend:

- ☩ U.S. Air Force bases
- ◄—·—· Ho Chi Minh Trail (North Vietnamese supply route)

U.S. and South Vietnamese Offensives

- ◄·········· Invasion of Cambodia, April–June 1970
- ◁═══ Invasion of Laos, February–March 1971

North Vietnamese Offensives

- ◄━━━ Tet offensive, January–February 1968

0 ————— 150 miles
0 ————— 150 km

BURMA

DEMOCRATIC REPUBLIC
OF VIETNAM
(NORTH VIETNAM)

Dien Bien
Phu

Hanoi

Red R.

Haiphong
harbor
mined
1972

Gulf of Tonkin

LAOS

Gulf of Tonkin
incident
Aug. 1964

**Hainan
(CHINA)**

Vientiane

Udon Thani
(Udorn)

Nakhon
Phanom

17th parallel

*Demarcation line
July 1954*

Demilitarized zone
(DMZ)

Quang Tri
Hue

Khe Sahn

Da Nang

*South China
Sea*

THAILAND

☩ Takhli

Nakhon
Ratchasima
(Korat)

Ubon
Ratchathani

My Lai massacre
March 1968

Bangkok

Kontum

Pleiku
Feb. 1965

**REPUBLIC OF
VIETNAM
(SOUTH VIETNAM)**

U Tapao

CAMBODIA

*CENTRAL
HIGHLANDS*

Mekong R.

*Tonle
Sap*

Nha Trang

*Cam Ranh
Bay*

Gulf of Thailand

Phnom Penh

An Loc

Bien Hoa

Kompong Som
(Sihanoukville)

Tan Son
Nhut

☩✪ **Saigon**

*Surrender of
South Vietnam
April 30, 1975*

N

Mekong Delta

© Infobase Publishing

Mekong R.

CHRONOLOGY

1969

January 20—Richard M. Nixon is sworn in as the 37th president of the United States

January 26—Three thousand coal miners meet in Charleston, West Virginia, to demand action against "black lung" disease.

January 30—North Vietnam and the National Liberation Front reject the U.S. proposal to restore neutrality to the Demilitarized Zone.

February 14—A 57-day dock strike, the longest in the history of the Port of New York, ends with a new contract providing a $1.60 hourly package raise and giving longshoremen the right to repack cargo containers when consolidated shipments comprise less than full trailer loads.

February 23–March 2—President Nixon visits five West European nations and consults with their leaders during a tour that he said was intended to create a "new spirit of consultation" and "confidence" between the United States and its European allies.

March 5—Edwin C. Arnett, the first soldier to be court-martialed for deserting from Vietnam to a foreign country, is convicted and sentenced to four years at hard labor.

March 10—James Earl Ray pleads guilty to the assassination of Martin Luther King Jr.

March 14—President Nixon decides to proceed with a revised antiballistic missile (ABM) defense plan.

March 19—A strike against American Airlines by members of the AFL-CIO Transport Workers Union of America, which started February 27, ends with a new contract.

March 26—The Women Strike for Peace pickets Washington in the first large antiwar demonstration since Nixon's inauguration.

March 28—Dwight David Eisenhower dies.

March 29—American combat deaths in Vietnam reach 33,641, exceeding those in the Korean War.

April 2—The nation's longest maritime strike (103 days) ends with a new contract for 8,000 longshoremen in ports from Lake Charles, Louisiana, to Brownsville, Texas. Settlements for Atlantic and other Gulf Coast ports had been reached earlier. The agreements provide a $1.60 an hour package increase and give dockers the right to unpack and repack cargo containers with consolidated shipments of less than full trailer loads.

April 13—A national rail strike is averted by an agreement providing a 22 cents an hour differential for skilled signalmen and a 9 cents adjustment for the semiskilled.

April 15—A U.S. Navy intelligence plane is shot down over North Korea as an intruder in North Korean territorial airspace.

April 23—Sirhan Bishara Sirhan, convicted April 17 of the murder of Robert Kennedy, is sentenced to death.

May 14—President Nixon proposes an eight-point peace plan for Vietnam; it provides for mutual troop withdrawal.

May 15—Supreme Court justice Abe Fortas resigns under criticism after the disclosure that he had accepted (but returned 11 months later) $20,000 from the family foundation of imprisoned financier Louis Wolfson.

June 8—President Nixon announces the withdrawal of 25,000 troops from Vietnam.

June 23—Warren E. Burger is sworn in as chief justice of the United States.

July 18—Senator Edward M. Kennedy's car plunges off a bridge on Chappaquiddick Island; his companion, Mary Jo Kopechne, drowns.

July 22—The Pentagon reveals that the United States has shipped lethal nerve gas to overseas troops.

July 26–August 3—President Nixon tours eight countries in Asia and Europe, emphasizing his belief that peace in Asia depends on Asians themselves. Highlights of the tour are an unannounced visit to South Vietnam and a stop in Romania.

July 30—Neil Armstrong and Air Force Colonel Edwin Eugene (Buzz) Aldrin Jr. become the first men to land and walk on the moon.

August 1—The Justice Department sues Georgia to end segregation in schools.

September 18—President Nixon, addressing the UN General Assembly, urges UN members to aid negotiations for ending the war in Vietnam.

October 1—President Nixon allows draft deferments for graduate students.

October 3—President Nixon blocks a rail strike by imposing a 60-day Railway Labor Act freeze in a dispute between seven railroads and four shopcraft unions.

October 15—Antiwar demonstrations take place throughout the United States in a massive protest coordinated by the Vietnam Moratorium Committee in Washington; among rallies, speeches, and religious services, one of the largest gatherings is a meeting of about 100,000 people in Boston Common.

October 27—Some 147,000 workers go on strike against General Electric Co. at plants across the country in a wage dispute.

November 3—President Nixon announces a U.S.-South Vietnam plan to withdraw U.S. troops from Vietnam.

November 15—In escalating antiwar protests sponsored by the New Mobilization Committee to End the War in Vietnam (the New Mobe), more than 250,000 people participate in Washington in the largest such demonstration ever held; the rally follows a three-day March against Death in which more than 40,000 people took part.

November 17—Preliminary Strategic Arms Limitation Talks (SALT) are opened by U.S. and Soviet negotiators in Helsinki, Finland.

December 1—The first draft lottery since 1942 is held at Selective Service System headquarters.

1970

January 1–2—Vice President Agnew visits Vietnam while on Asian tour.

January 5—Joseph Yablonski, president of the United States Mine Workers of America, is found dead at his home.

January 6—President Nixon announces a major diplomatic agreement with France that will curb heroin traffic.

January 14—The Supreme Court sets the deadline (February 1) for pupil desegregation of public schools.

January 15—Martin Luther King Jr. is honored across the nation on the 41st anniversary of his birthday.

January 19—The second session of the 91st Congress convenes.

January 19—Vice President Agnew concludes a 21-day tour of Pacific and Asian countries.

January 21—Three men are arrested in connection with the Joseph Yablonski murder.

January 22—President Nixon delivers his first State of the Union address.

January 22—The United States rejects Soviet proposals for Middle East peace.

January 30—The International Union of Electrical Workers (IUE) and the United Electrical Workers (UE) end a three-month strike against General Electric Co. by approving a new contract.

January 30—Seven Black Panthers are indicted for attempted murder by a Chicago grand jury.

February 2—The pretrial hearing for 13 Black Panthers in New York City opens.

February 2—President Nixon presents his fiscal 1971 budget to Congress.

February 6—Senator Fred R. Harris resigns as chairman of the Democratic National Committee.

February 6—Walter Cronkite's second interview with Lyndon B. Johnson is broadcast on television.

February 8—Democrats rebut President Nixon's State of the Union address in an hour-long national television program.

February 9—The Democratic Policy Council adopts a resolution urging total withdrawal of U.S. troops from Vietnam.

February 10—The U.S., British, and French embassies in Moscow accept a Soviet proposal for four-power talks on Berlin.

February 10—The Army charges Captain Thomas K. Willingham with unpremeditated murder in connection with the alleged civilian massacre at Songmy (My Lai).

February 10–13—Defense secretary Melvin Laird visits South Vietnam to study Vietnamization and U.S. troop withdrawals.

February 12–17—U.S. and Soviet delegates discuss the peaceful use of nuclear explosions.

February 18—President Nixon submits a foreign policy outline to Congress.

February 18—The "Chicago Seven" are acquitted of conspiring to incite a riot.

March 2—The Lockheed Aircraft Corp. appeals to the Defense Department for interim funding.

March 4—Nixon signs legislation blocking for 37 days a nationwide railroad strike.

March 5—Lawrence F. O'Brien is elected Democratic national chairman.

March 5—The nuclear nonproliferation treaty goes into effect.

March 6—President Nixon appeals to the Soviet Union and Britain to help restore the 1962 Geneva agreements on Laos.

March 6—Pro-Communist Pathet Lao rebels propose a five-point peace plan.

March 9—Gravediggers in the New York metropolitan area end an eight-week strike.

March 10—Thomas A. Foran (chief prosecutor in the "Chicago Seven" conspiracy trial) resigns as U.S. attorney for the northern district of Illinois. (He remains chief prosecutor in the case.)

March 13–16—San Francisco's municipal workers strike successfully for higher wages.

March 13—Bobby G. Seale is extradited from San Francisco to New Haven, Connecticut.

March 14—The *Columbia Eagle*, a U.S. freighter bound for Thailand with air force munitions, is seized by two armed crewmen and diverted to Cambodia. (It may be seen as an antiwar protest by the two crewmen.)

March 16–22—The New Mobilization Committee to End the War in Vietnam (New Mobe) sponsors a national "antidraft week."

March 23—President Nixon orders troops to help move the mail in New York City held up by a postal strike.

March 25—A week-old New York City postal strike ends with the beginning of wage negotiations.

March 26—President Nixon signs a bill increasing G.I. educational monthly allowances.

April 1—The Coal Mine Health and Safety Act of 1969 goes into effect.

April 2—Massachusetts governor Francis W. Sargent signs a bill challenging the legality of the war in Vietnam.

April 4—The largest Washington prowar demonstration since America's involvement in Vietnam is held.

April 7—The drowning case of Mary Jo Kopechne is closed, with no indictments.

April 8—The *Columbia Eagle* is released by Cambodia.

April 11—Willy Brandt concludes a week-long visit to the United States.

April 15—A federal pay raise for postal and civil service employees and military personnel is enacted.

April 16—SALT sessions resume after a recess.

April 17—Assistant Secretary of State Joseph J. Sisco cancels his trip to Jordan after anti-American riots there.

April 17—The *Apollo 13* crew splashes down safely in the Pacific, after experiencing trouble in space (April 13).

April 20—President Nixon announces plans to withdraw more troops from Vietnam.

April 20–May 1—The United States and South Vietnam extend fighting to Cambodia.

April 22—Earth Day is observed across the country.

April 23—President Nixon ends occupational draft deferments and deferments for fathers.

April 30—President Nixon announces the major U.S. troop offensive into Cambodia.

May 4—Four students are killed by National Guardsmen at Kent State University in Ohio.

May 4—The Soviet Union and China assail Nixon's expansion of the war to Cambodia.

May 6—Communist delegates to the Paris peace talks boycott in protest of the U.S. bombing of North Vietnam.

May 6 and May 9—President Nixon confers with student antiwar protesters.

May 8—The "Chicago Seven" are freed, with all charges against them dropped.

May 14—Two students are slain by Mississippi highway patrolmen at Jackson State University.

May 22—Leonard Woodcock is chosen as president of the United Automobile Workers.

June 22—President Nixon signs a bill lowering the voting age for national elections to 18.

June 29—U.S. ground troop withdrawal from Cambodia is completed.

July 1—The nation's most liberal abortion law goes into effect in New York.

July 2–3—The Southeast Asia Treaty Organization (SEATO) holds its annual Ministerial Council meeting.

July 4—Honor America Day demonstrates national unity and faith in American institutions.

July 29—Contracts are signed by the United Farm Workers Organizing Committee and grape growers, increasing farm workers' wages.

July 30—Nixon holds his first nationally televised press conference.

July 31—Israel joins Egypt and Jordan in accepting the U.S. Middle East peace plan.

August 14—The Vienna phase of the SALT sessions ends.

August 20—President Nixon and Mexican president Gustavo Díaz Ordaz meet and propose a treaty concerning U.S.-Mexican border disputes.

August 26—A demonstration is staged for "Women's Strike for Equality" and to celebrate the 50th anniversary of women's right to vote in the United States.

August 30—Vice President Agnew completes a week-long Asian tour.

September 9–12—The Young Americans for Freedom (YAF) hold a 19th anniversary meeting at the University of Hartford in Connecticut.

September 15—Railworkers strike against Southern Pacific Co., Chesapeake & Ohio Railway, and the Baltimore & Ohio Railroad when contract negotiations break down. (A restraining order sends them back to work within a day.)

September 15–20—Golda Meir visits the United States and talks to President Nixon, Secretary of State William P. Rogers, and others.

September 17—The National Liberation Front presents an eight-point peace proposal for Vietnam at the Paris talks.

September 22—President Nixon signs a bill giving the District of Columbia a nonvoting delegate in the House of Representatives.

October 5—President Nixon completes an eight-day trip to Europe.

October 10—North Vietnam denounces Nixon's five-point peace plan (made on October 7).

October 13—Angela Davis is seized and arrested by FBI agents in New York City. (She is charged as an accomplice in a kidnap-escape attempt in California on August 7.)

October 22—President Nixon and Soviet foreign minister Andrei A. Gromyko confer in Washington.

October 23—Nixon addresses the United Nations.

November 12—U.S. policy toward Communist China changes; U.S. delegates to the United Nation argue against Communist China's expulsion from the organization.

November 17—The first anniversary of the SALT sessions is marked.

November 20—The 67-day national strike against General Motors by the United Automobile Workers ends. (An agreement was reached on November 11.)

November 25—President Nixon dismisses Walter J. Hickel as secretary of the interior.

December 8—President Nixon confers with King Hussein of Jordan at the White House.

December 10—A 24-hour nationwide rail strike ends after congressional legislation defers it.

December 10—The Equal Employment Opportunity Commission (EEOC) charges the American Telephone and Telegraph Co. with gross discrimination against women, blacks, and Hispanic Americans.

December 11—President Nixon announces the appointment of Representative George H. W. Bush as the U.S. representative to the United Nation.

December 11—President Nixon confers with Israeli defense minister Moshe Dayan at the White House.

December 21—Angela Davis is extradited from New York to California.

December 21—The Supreme Court rules that the new voting rights of 18-year-olds in federal elections do not extend to state and local elections.

1971

January 2—The 91st Congress adjourns.

January 7—Defense secretary Melvin R. Laird visits Thailand to assess the military situation in Indochina.

January 8–11—Defense secretary Melvin R. Laird visits South Vietnam to assess the military situation in Indochina.

January 12—Rev. Philip F. Berrigan and five others are indicated on charges of conspiring to kidnap Henry Kissinger.

January 14–19—About 85 percent of New York City's police officers go on a wildcat strike.

January 15—Senator Edmund S. Muskie confers with Soviet Premier Aleksei N. Kosygin in Moscow, exchanging views on the Middle East and Indochina.

January 17—The Chicago Teachers' Union accepts a new contract, ending a week-old strike.

January 18—Senator George S. McGovern opens his campaign for the 1972 Democratic presidential nomination in a televised speech.

January 21—The 92nd Congress convenes.

January 22—President Nixon delivers his second State of the Union message.

January 25—The Supreme Court rules that companies cannot deny employment to women with preschool children unless the same criterion applies to men.

January 26—Charles M. Manson and three of his female followers are convicted of first-degree murder in the slaying of actress Sharon Tate and six other persons.

January 29—President Nixon submits his budget for 1972 to Congress.

February 9—*Apollo 14* splashes down after a trip to the moon.

February 11—A treaty prohibiting installation of nuclear weapons on the ocean floor is signed by 63 nations.

February 21—The United States and 20 other UN members sign an international treaty to end illegal drug sales.

February 22—A speech by Eugene J. McCarthy in Boston launches a new effort to mobilize antiwar sentiment on college campuses.

February 23 and February 27—The Columbia Broadcasting System broadcasts "The Selling of the Pentagon."

February 25—President Nixon makes his annual State of the World message.

February 26—The United States and France sign a protocol to crack down on organized narcotics trafficking, formalizing an agreement made in January 1970.

March 2—George H. W. Bush takes over as U.S. ambassador to the United Nations.

March 15—The fourth round of the U.S.-Soviet SALT negotiations begins in Vienna.

March 19—Foreign Minister Abba Eban confers with Secretary of State William P. Rogers and Henry Kissinger.

March 24—The Senate votes against government sponsorship of America's supersonic transport (SST), as did the House on March 18.

March 29—First Lieutenant William L. Calley Jr. is convicted by an army court-martial of the premeditated murder of at least 22 South Vietnamese civilians in the My Lai "massacre" of March 16, 1968. (Calley is sentenced March 31 to life at hard labor, but the sentence is reduced August 20 to 20 years.)

March 29—The jury that convicted Charles M. Manson and his codefendants votes that they be executed in the gas chamber.

April 1—The five-month pilots' strike against Mohawk Airlines ends.

April 3—President Nixon announces that he will personally review the case of Lieutenant William L. Calley Jr. before final sentence is carried out.

April 7—Outtakes of the CBS-TV documentary "The Selling of the Pentagon" are subpoenaed by a House subcommittee.

April 14—President Nixon relaxes a 20-year embargo on trade with Communist China.

April 17—The U.S. table tennis team leaves Communist China after a week-long tour.

April 18—The Newark Teachers' Union and the city's board of education agree to a contract settlement, ending an 11-week strike.

April 18—The White House Conference on Youth is held.

April 24—Marchers mass in Washington and San Francisco and hold peaceful rallies urging Congress to end the war in Indochina immediately.

April 30—Rev. Philip Berrigan and seven others are indicted for plotting to kidnap Henry A. Kissinger and blow up heating tunnels in government buildings.

May 3–5—Antiwar protests organized by the People's Coalition for Peace and Justice are held in Washington.

May 9—Secretary of State William P. Rogers returns after his five-nation tour of the Middle East.

May 21—Secretary of the Army Stanley R. Resor resigns.

May 22—President Nixon joins Lyndon Johnson in dedicating the Lyndon Baines Johnson Library Complex on the University of Texas campus.

May 25—President Nixon signs a bill terminating the project to develop a commercial supersonic transport (SST).

May 26—A new subpoena is issued to replace the one previously issued to CBS to furnish a House subcommittee with outtakes of "The Selling of the Pentagon."

May 28—U.S. and Soviet negotiators conclude the fourth round of SALT in Vienna.

May 30—*Mariner 9*, a U.S. interplanetary space probe bound for Mars, is launched from Cape Kennedy, Florida.

May 31—Vietnam Veterans against the War complete a 20-mile trek to protest the war, tracing in reverse the route of Paul Revere's ride, to "spread the alarm" against the current war.

June 1—The Vietnam Veterans for a Just Peace condemn the protests of the Vietnam Veterans against the War as "irresponsible."

June 3—James R. Hoffa announces from prison that he is not a candidate for reelection as president of the International Brotherhood of Teamsters.

June 12—David Hilliard, the Black Panther chief of staff, is convicted of assault in connection with an April 1968 shootout with police.

June 15—The *New York Times* halts publication of a series of Vietnam War articles drawn from a secret Pentagon study because of a temporary court order. (Publication of the articles began on June 13.)

June 16—The U.S. Conference of Mayors urges President Nixon to withdraw all troops from Vietnam by the end of the year.

June 18 and June 19—The *Washington Post* publishes articles on the involvement of the United States in the Vietnam War based on a classified Pentagon study.

June 21—Communist Chinese premier Zhou Enlai (Chou En-lai) says that withdrawal of U.S. support from Taiwan would facilitate better relations between the United States and Communist China.

June 22 and June 23—The *Boston Globe* and the *Chicago Sun-Times* publish articles based on the classified Pentagon study.

June 30—The Supreme Court rules that articles based on classified Pentagon material may be published by newspapers.

June 30—The 26th Amendment to the Constitution—lowering the minimum voting age to 18 years for all federal, state, and local elections—is ratified by the states.

June 30—Twelve Black Panthers are cleared of charges of murdering a policeman and conspiracy to murder in a gun fight with police at the party's headquarters in Detroit in October 1970.

July 1—David Hilliard is sentenced to a 1- to 10-year prison term for assault in connection with an April 1968 shootout with police.

July 1—President Nixon inaugurates the new volunteer agency Action, which merges the Peace Corps, VISTA, and seven other volunteer service agencies.

July 1—The new semi-independent U.S. Postal Service goes into operation.

July 5–9—The NAACP holds its 62nd annual convention in Minneapolis.

July 7—Seven Black Panthers are indicted in New York on charges of murder and arson in connection with the slaying of a West Coast Panther official.

July 8—Frank E. Fitzsimmons is elected president of the International Brotherhood of Teamsters.

July 8 and July 13—The fifth round of the U.S.-Soviet SALT negotiations are held in Helsinki.

July 9—Representative Paul N. McCloskey announces that he will seek the Republican Party's nomination for president.

July 9—U.S. troops relinquish total responsibility for defense of the area just below the demilitarized zone to South Vietnamese troops.

July 11—President Nixon signs a $5.15 billion education appropriation bill (HR 7016), the largest of its kind in the history of the Office of Education.

July 12—President Nixon signs the Emergency Employment Act (S 31), authorizing $2.25 billion to provide public service jobs in the next two years for the unemployed at state and local levels.

July 16 and 22—The United States, Great Britain, France, and the Soviet Union meet in Berlin to discuss the area's future.

July 18—The National Association of Counties (NACO) opens its annual convention in Milwaukee.

July 22—The Agriculture Department issues new food stamp program regulations.

July 28—Vice President Spiro T. Agnew returns from his 32-day diplomatic tour of 10 nations.

July 31–August 2—Two U.S. astronauts drive an electric car on the moon during scientific exploration and experimentation as part of the *Apollo 15* mission.

August 2—Railroad strikes by the AFL-CIO United Transportation Union end with a contract agreement.

August 2—The United States ends 20 years of opposition to Communist China's presence in the United Nations by announcing future support of China's membership.

August 5—The Selective Service System conducts its third draft lottery since Congress authorized the random selection of men into the armed forces in 1969.

August 6—A New Orleans jury acquits 12 Black Panthers of attempted murder of five New Orleans policemen in a gun fight in September 1970.

August 7—*Apollo 15* splashes down safely in the Pacific. (*Apollo 15* was launched from Cape Kennedy on July 26.)

August 9—President Nixon signs a bill providing a $250 million government-guaranteed loan to Lockheed Aircraft Corp.

August 9—The public service jobs bill is signed by President Nixon to provide 150,000 jobs in state, county, and city governments for the unemployed.

August 9—President Nixon signs a bill appropriating $20,804,622,000 for fiscal 1972 for the Departments of Labor and of Health, Education, and Welfare (HEW).

August 11—New York mayor John V. Lindsay formally switches from the Republican Party to the Democratic Party.

August 13—Attorney General John N. Mitchell drops the federal investigation of the shooting deaths of four students at Kent State University.

August 17—The Export Expansion Finance Act of 1971 is signed by President Nixon.

August 18—A labor agreement between Heublein, Inc., and the AFL-CIO United Farm Workers Organizing Committee ends a nationwide boycott against Heublein products that began August 9.

August 20—Lieutenant William L. Calley Jr.'s sentence of life imprisonment is reduced to 20 years.

August 21—FBI agents and local police foil a Selective Service office raid in Buffalo, New York, arresting five young men and women.

August 21—George Jackson, one of the three black convicts known as the Soledad Brothers charged with killing a Soledad Prison guard, is shot and killed as he attempts to escape from the California State Prison at San Quentin.

August 22—FBI agents and local police foil a Selective Service office raid in Camden, New Jersey, with the arrest of 20 people.

September 13—Nearly 1,500 state troopers, sheriff's deputies, and prison guards put down an uprising by 1,200 inmates at the Attica Correctional Facility in Attica, New York. The insurrection began on September 9 and left dead 31 prisoners and nine guards and civilian employees held as hostages.

September 13—The 63rd National Governors Conference opens in San Juan, Puerto Rico.

September 21—Federal agents seize personal papers and possessions belonging to Dr. Daniel Ellsberg, with the authority of a search warrant.

September 22—The United States formally submits two resolutions to the United Nations bearing on the seating of a Chinese delegation (from Communist China) in the United Nations.

September 24—Senator Fred R. Harris declares himself a candidate for the Democratic nomination for president.

September 24—The fifth round of the U.S.-Soviet SALT negotiations ends in Helsinki.

September 25—Former Supreme Court justice Hugo L. Black dies.

September 26—President Nixon greets Emperor Hirohito of Japan in Anchorage, Alaska, during a stopover on the emperor's flight to Europe.

September 29–October 3—The third annual Black Business and Cultural Exposition, better known as Black Expo, is held in Chicago.

October 4—Secretary of State William P. Rogers address the UN General Assembly, asking for the seating of Communist China on the Security Council and speaking against the expulsion of Nationalist China (Taiwan) from the General Assembly.

October 8—President Nixon becomes the first president to visit all 50 states when he attends the 35th annual Mountain State Forest Festival in Elkins, West Virginia.

October 9—The West Coast dock strike that began July 1 ends in compliance with a court order obtained by the Justice Department under the Taft-Hartley Act.

October 12—Senator Birch Bayh removes himself from the competition for the 1972 Democratic presidential nomination.

October 12–18—Governor Ronald Reagan tours six Asian nations as a special presidential representative, bearing personal letters from President Nixon to the leaders of those countries.

October 16—H. Rap Brown, the fugitive black militant who disappeared 17 months earlier, is shot and captured by police in New York City.

October 16–23—Vice President Spiro Agnew visits Greece for an official conference with Premier George Papadopoulos and a private tour.

October 20–25—Henry Kissinger visits Beijing to arrange the agenda and itinerary for President Nixon's forthcoming trip to Communist China.

October 26—About 300 antiwar demonstrators are arrested for sitting down in the middle of Pennsylvania Avenue during rush hour after a rally at the Washington Monument.

November 6—The most powerful underground nuclear test conducted by the United States is executed on the remote Alaskan island of Amchitka.

November 13—Aubran W. Martin is sentenced to death in the electric chair for his role in the slaying of United Mine Workers official Joseph Yablonski and his wife and daughter.

November 13—The U.S. interplanetary probe *Mariner 9* goes into orbit around Mars as the first man-made object to orbit another planet.

November 16—The first working session of the sixth round of the U.S.-Soviet SALT negotiations is held.

November 19—Senator Henry M. Jackson announces his candidacy for the 1972 Democratic presidential nomination.

November 23–December 2—The White House Conference on Aging is held.

November 29—The East and Gulf Coasts dock strike ends after return-to-work orders are issued by federal courts under provisions of the Taft-Hartley Act.

December 6–8—The first national Conference on Corrections is held in Williamsburg, Virginia, bringing together ex-convicts, judges, lawyers, congressmen, police chiefs, and prison officials.

December 7—The state of Ohio drops for lack of evidence all charges against defendants in the Kent State University riot trials. (Two of the first five defendants were cleared, two pleaded guilty, and charges against one were dismissed.)

December 8–10—The North Atlantic Treaty Organization (NATO) Ministerial Council holds a three-day winter session in Brussels.

December 13–14—President Nixon and French president Georges Pompidou confer on the devaluation of the dollar.

December 17—The first session of the 92nd Congress adjourns.

December 18—President Nixon signs an Alaska native land settlement bill, granting a total of $962.5 million and 40 million acres of land and mineral rights to native Alaskans.

December 18—Rev. Jesse L. Jackson announces the formation of a new black political and economic development organization, PUSH (People United to Save Humanity).

December 20–21—President Nixon meets with British prime minister Edward Heath in Bermuda to discuss world problems.

December 28—President Nixon signs a bill requiring most persons receiving welfare benefits to register for jobs or job training.

December 29—President Nixon signs a bill extending unemployment benefits.

December 30–31—Columnist Jack Anderson publishes reports based on secret material pertaining to formulation of the Nixon administration's policy on the Indian-Pakistani War.

1972

January 4—Senator Edmund S. Muskie announces his candidacy for the 1972 Democratic presidential nomination.

January 6—The Paris peace talks resume after a month's suspension.

January 9—Mrs. Richard M. Nixon returns from an eight-day tour of West Africa during which she met heads of government and visited local institutions representing the president.

January 10—Senator Hubert H. Humphrey announces his candidacy for the 1972 Democratic presidential nomination.

January 11—The Supreme Court rules that a prosecutor only has to show that contested confessions of criminal defendants are voluntary "by a preponderance of the evidence" to have them admitted as evidence.

January 12—U.S. representative James H. Scheuer is questioned by Soviet police on January 12 and is expelled from the USSR January 14, accused of "improper activities" during his visit.

January 12 and 13—Yekaterina A. Furtseva, the Soviet minister of culture, opens an exhibit of Soviet arts and crafts in Washington on January 12. She has tea at the White House with Mrs. Richard Nixon on January 13.

January 13—Senator Edward M. Kennedy announces that he will not be a candidate for the 1972 Democratic presidential nomination.

January 16—Religious leaders from 46 Protestant, Catholic, and Jewish denominations, meeting in Kansas City, Missouri, to discuss Vietnam, ask the administration to withdraw all American troops and refuse aid to the Indochinese governments.

January 18—The 92nd Congress reconvenes to begin its second session.

January 24—President Nixon submits to Congress a $246.3 billion budget for fiscal 1973 with an estimated deficit of $25.5 billion.

January 25—Representative Shirley Chisholm, the only black woman ever to serve in Congress, formally announces that she will seek the Democratic presidential nomination.

January 30—Defense Secretary Melvin R. Laird announces that no men will be called up for military duty until April.

February 2—A new political party, calling itself the Liberty Party, is announced in Denver.

The key planks in the party's platform are its opposition to big government and its dedication to civil and economic freedom.

February 2—The Selective Service System assigns draft lottery numbers to nearly 2 million men born in 1953.

February 4—The sixth round of the U.S.-Soviet Strategic Arms Limitations Talks (SALT) adjourns in Vienna.

February 7—President Nixon signs into law the Federal Election Campaign Act, requiring that candidates report all campaign contributions that are received and spent and limiting campaign spending for media advertising and from the personal funds of the candidate.

February 9—President Nixon delivers his third annual State of the World message to Congress.

February 11—Representative Wilbur D. Mills announces that he is a candidate for the Democratic presidential nomination.

February 11–13—An antiwar rally in Versailles, France, denounces American policy in Indochina and pledges support for the Vietnamese Communists' plans for ending the war.

February 15—Attorney General John N. Mitchell resigns (effective March 1) to head President Nixon's campaign for reelection.

February 18—A seven-month statewide strike by plant craftsmen against the New York Telephone Co. ends.

February 18—Delegates from 34 states attend the opening day of the 20th National Convention of the Communist Party, U.S.A., in New York.

February 18—The California State Supreme Court votes to end the death penalty, thus sparing Sirhan Sirhan and Charles Manson, among others.

February 21—President Nixon arrives in China.

February 21—West Coast longshoremen end a 134-day strike, the nation's longest dock walkout.

February 22 and 23—President Nixon meets with Chinese premier Zhou Enlai (Chou En-lai) for policy discussions.

February 27—President Nixon and Premier Zhou Enlai (Chou En-lai) release a joint communiqué showing the results of their talks.

February 28—President Nixon returns from China.

February 28—The Nationalist Chinese Foreign Ministry (of Taiwan) issues a statement denouncing the Sino-U.S. communiqué.

March—A collection of documents on political surveillance stolen from the FBI's Media, Pennsylvania, office a year before is printed in this month's issue of *Win*, an antiwar magazine.

March 1 and 2—Paul E. Gilly is found guilty of first-degree murder for the 1969 murders of Joseph Yablonski, his wife, and his daughter on March 1. Gilly is sentenced on March 2 to die in the electric chair.

March 2—*Pioneer 10*, a U.S. space probe designed to go past Jupiter, is launched from Cape Kennedy, Florida.

March 8—President Nixon signs an executive order to limit the practice of classifying government documents as secret and to speed the process of declassification.

March 10–12—The first National Black Political Convention is held in Gary, Indiana.

March 11—The Socialist Party and the Democratic Socialist Federation merge at a New York convention, ending a 35-year split.

March 23—The U.S. delegation to the Paris peace talks announces an indefinite suspension of the conference until North Vietnamese and National Liberation Front representatives enter into "serious discussions" on concrete issues determined beforehand.

March 27—Two so-called Soledad Brothers (Fleeta Drumgo and John Cluchette) are found innocent of the 1970 slaying of a guard at Soledad Prison.

March 28—The U.S.-Soviet SALT negotiations begin a seventh round of discussions in Helsinki.

March 31—President Nixon signs executive orders blocking for 60 days two impending railroad strikes by the AFL-CIO United Transportation Union (UTU) and the AFL-CIO Sheet Metal Workers' International Association.

April 3—President Nixon signs into law a bill devaluing the dollar by raising the price of gold from $35 to $50 an ounce.

April 15–20—Hundreds of antiwar demonstrators are arrested in incidents across the country as the escalation of the bombing in Indochina provokes a new wave of protests.

April 20–23—Navy captain John Watts Young and air force lieutenant colonel Charles Moss Duke Jr. spend a record 71 hours, 2 minutes on the moon during the first manned mission to the mountains of the moon, *Apollo 16*.

April 20–24—Henry A. Kissinger, President Nixon's adviser on national security, secretly visits the Soviet Union to confer with Leonid I. Brezhnev, the Soviet Communist Party leader.

April 27—Senator Edmund S. Muskie announces his withdrawal from the presidential primaries.

April 27—The Paris peace talks resume after a one-month break.

May 2—J. Edgar Hoover, the first and only director of the FBI, dies.

May 4—The United States and South Vietnam call an indefinite halt to the Paris peace talks after the 149th session.

May 8—The International Monetary Fund (IMF) formally announces a reduction in the parity of the U.S. dollar to 0.818513 gram of fine gold from 0.888671 gram.

May 11—Interior secretary Rogers C. B. Morton grants a permit for construction of the controversial trans-Alaska oil pipeline.

May 12—North Vietnam's chief negotiator, Le Duc Tho, rejects President Nixon's four-part peace plan.

May 15—Governor George Wallace is shot and seriously wounded in an assassination attempt. The result is paralysis below the waist.

May 15—The Supreme Court rules that the Amish are entitled to exemption from state compulsory education laws.

May 18—Vice President Agnew returns from a six-day visit to Thailand, Japan, and South Vietnam.

May 22—The Supreme Court rules that juries need not return unanimous verdicts to convict defendants in state criminal court cases.

May 26—President Nixon and Soviet general secretary Brezhnev sign agreements limiting offensive and defensive strategic weapons.

June 4—Angela Davis is acquitted on all charges of murder, kidnap, and conspiracy in Santa Clara County Superior Court in San Jose, California.

June 5–7—The National Governors' Conference meets in Houston.

June 9–12—Henry Kissinger makes a private visit to Tokyo but also meets with Japanese government and political leaders to discuss Asian security and Japan's economic differences with the United States.

June 27–28—The Council of Ministers of the Southeast Asia Treaty Organization (SEATO) holds its annual meeting in Canberra, Australia.

July 3–7—The NAACP holds its 63rd annual convention in Detroit.

July 6–17—U.S. and Soviet space planners meet at the U.S. Manned Spacecraft Center in Houston, Texas.

July 7—The United States and the USSR sign an agreement detailing the first areas of study in science and technology in which scientists of both nations will cooperate.

July 8—President Nixon announces the sale of at least $750 million of American wheat, corn, and other grains to the Soviet Union.

July 11—Senators Hubert H. Humphrey and Edmund S. Muskie withdraw from the Democratic presidential nomination race.

July 12—Senator George McGovern wins the Democratic presidential nomination.

July 13—The Paris peace talks resume after a 10-week suspension.

July 14—Jean M. Westwood is selected as the new chairman of the Democratic National Committee.

July 14—Senator Thomas Eagleton is nominated as the Democratic candidate for vice president.

July 16—Thomas Eboli, a reputed East Coast Mafia leader, is shot and killed in New York City.

July 19—Henry Kissinger holds a private meeting with Le Duc Tho, North Vietnamese Politburo member and chief adviser to his country's delegation at the peace talks.

August 1—Senator Thomas F. Eagleton withdraws as the Democratic vice presidential candidate.

August 4—Arthur H. Bremer is found guilty of shooting Governor George C. Wallace and sentenced to 63 years in prison.

August 8—R. Sargent Shriver is nominated by the Democratic National Committee as the party's candidate for vice president.

August 22—President Nixon is renominated as the Republican presidential candidate at the party's 30th National Convention in Miami Beach.

September 1—President Nixon and Japanese premier Kakuei Tanaka hold two days of summit talks in Hawaii.

September 15—A federal grand jury in the District of Columbia indicts seven persons, including two former White House aides, on charges of conspiring to break into the Democratic national headquarters in the capital.

September 21—President Nixon signs into law a bill to improve the benefits program for the widows, widowers, and children of retired U.S. military personnel.

September 26–27—Henry Kissinger holds more private talks with North Vietnamese representatives in Paris.

September 27–31—The fourth annual Black Expo is held in Chicago under the auspices of Operation PUSH.

October 3—President Nixon and Soviet foreign minister Andrei A. Gromyko conclude two days of talks in Washington by signing documents that put into effect the two arms accords reached in Moscow in May.

October 13–December 14—The United Auto Workers undertake a series of 17 "ministrikes" against 10 General Motors Corp. plants.

October 18—The United States and the Soviet Union sign a three-year trade pact.

October 19–20—Henry Kissinger and other U.S. officials hold meetings with South Vietnamese president Nguyen Van Thieu in Saigon.

October 28—President Nixon signs a bill to expand consumer protection.

October 30—President Nixon signs a bill to improve Social Security benefits.

November 7—Richard M. Nixon is reelected president.

November 20 and 21—Henry Kissinger and Le Duc Tho hold more private discussions to work out a final Indochina peace agreement.

December 4—Henry Kissinger and Le Duc Tho resume private Indochina peace talks near Paris after a nine-day recess.

December 4—U.S. and Soviet representatives sign an agreement authorizing each nation to construct a new embassy complex in the other's capital.

December 8—Foreign ministers of the NATO states conclude their regular two-day winter session in Brussels.

December 8—The Pentagon Papers trial in Los Angeles of Daniel Ellsberg and Anthony J. Russo is declared a mistrial.

December 11–14—Navy captain Eugene Andrew Cernan and Dr. Harrison Hagan (Jack) Schmitt explore a mountainous site on the moon during the final Apollo flight, *Apollo 17*.

December 13—Paris peace talks recess with no agreement.

December 15—Arnold R. Miller is elected president of the United Mine Workers' (UMW) union, ousting W. A. Boyle.

December 18—The Supreme Court strikes down a Social Security law that gave a smaller share of a dead father's survivors benefits to illegitimate children than that given to legitimate offspring.

December 21—The U.S.-Soviet SALT negotiators adjourn in Geneva after establishing a four-man consultative commission to ensure adherence to the arms pacts signed in May.

December 26—Harry S. Truman dies.

1973

January 2—Rafael Hernandez Colon is sworn in as Puerto Rico's fourth elected governor.

January 3—The 93rd Congress convenes.

January 8–12—Henry Kissinger and Le Duc Tho hold more secret Indochina peace talks.

January 10—The Watergate trial opens.

January 11—E. Howard Hunt Jr. pleads guilty to all six charges against him relating to Watergate.

January 20—President Nixon is inaugurated for his second term.

January 22—Lyndon B. Johnson dies.

January 26—An agreement is reached between the Chicago school board and the Chicago Teachers' Union, ending a 12-day strike.

January 30—G. Gordon Liddy and James McCord are convicted by a jury in U.S. district court in the District of Columbia of attempting to spy on the Democrats during the 1972 presidential campaign.

February 8—Congress enacts legislation imposing a status quo in the labor stalemate at the Penn Central Railroad, ending a one-day strike.

February 9—The U.S. Circuit Court of Appeals for the District of Columbia orders that a lower court prevent Interior secretary Rogers C. B. Morton from issuing permits for construction of the trans-Alaska oil pipeline.

February 9–11—The first convention of the National Women's Political Caucus (NWPC) is held in Houston.

February 12—The dollar is devalued by 10 percent.

February 15—The United States and Cuba sign a five-year agreement to curb the hijacking of aircraft and ships between the two countries.

February 21—Laos and the Communist Pathet Lao rebels sign a cease-fire agreement aimed at ending the 20-year war in Laos.

February 26—Two of the 15 counts against defendants Daniel Ellsberg and Anthony J. Russo Jr. are dropped.

March 29—H. Rap Brown and three codefendants are convicted in New York of robbery and assault with a deadly weapon.

May 1–2—President Nixon and West Germany chancellor Willy Brandt confer in Washington.

May 2—Former Texas governor John B. Connally, Jr. joins the Republican Party.

May 8—The 70-day confrontation at Wounded Knee, South Dakota, between militant supporters of the American Indian Movement (AIM) and federal agents ends.

May 4—U.S.-Soviet SALT sessions resume in Geneva.

May 9—Henry Kissinger completes four days of intensive talks with Soviet leaders at the estate of Leonid I. Brezhnev.

May 11—Charges against Daniel Ellsberg and Anthony J. Russo Jr. are dismissed in *The Pentagon Papers* trial.

May 14—NATO begins talks on the reduction of military forces in central Europe.

May 14—The Supreme Court rules that female members of the armed services are entitled to the same dependency benefits for their husbands as are servicemen for their dependent wives.

May 22—Henry Kissinger and Le Duc Tho end their talks on implementation of the Vietnam truce agreement.

May 29—President Nixon refuses to give oral or written testimony to the grand jury or the Senate select committee investigating the Watergate case.

June 13—A new accord aimed at strengthening the January 27 cease-fire agreement in South Vietnam is signed in Paris by the United States, North Vietnam, South Vietnam, and the National Liberation Front.

June 20—The Finance Committee to Re-elect the President is found guilty on three misdemeanor counts of concealing a $200,000 cash contribution.

June 22—The three U.S. *Skylab 1* astronauts return from a record 28 days living, working, and performing scientific experiments in space.

June 23—A Soviet consulate general is opened in San Francisco.

June 25—Soviet Communist Party general secretary Leonid Brezhnev ends his visit to the United States.

July 6—A U.S. consulate general is officially opened in Leningrad.

July 9—Secretary of State William P. Rogers and Czechoslovak foreign minister Bohuslav Chnoupek sign a consular convention in Prague to help normalize trade and travel between the two countries.

August 3—Oklahoma officials regain complete control of the state penitentiary at McAlester following an outbreak that left four inmates dead and most of the prison's physical plant in ruins.

August 3—The Justice Department reopens its investigation of the fatal shootings of four students at Kent State University.

August 7—The Senate Select Committee on Presidential Campaign Activities recesses.

August 14—Vice President Agnew makes his personal finance records available to the U.S. attorney's office in Baltimore.

August 29—U.S. District Court judge John J. Sirica orders President Nixon to turn over to him for private examination the tape recordings of presidential conversations involving the Watergate case.

September 22—Henry A. Kissinger is sworn in by U.S. Chief Justice Warren E. Burger as the 56th secretary of state.

September 24—Production resumes at Chrysler Corp. plants with the ratification of a new three-year contract, ending a 10-day strike.

September 25—The crew of *Skylab 2* returns to Earth after 59 1/2 days in space, the longest manned mission so far.

September 25—SALT negotiations resume in Geneva after a summer recess.

September 26—President Nixon signs a vocational rehabilitation bill for the handicapped.

October 5—Oregon becomes the first state to remove criminal penalties for possession of less than one ounce of marijuana.

October 10—Spiro T. Agnew resigns as vice president and pleads no contest to one charge of

income tax evasion. By plea bargaining, he escapes imprisonment on the tax charge and prosecution on charges of bribery and conspiracy.

October 17—President Nixon holds talks with the foreign ministers of Saudi Arabia, Morocco, Kuwait, and Algeria at the White House to end fighting in the Middle East.

December 6—Gerald R. Ford is sworn in as vice president after confirmation by both houses of Congress. President Nixon had chosen him for the post after Vice President Agnew resigned.

December 6—President Nixon signs a bill providing a 10 percent cost-of-living boost to the monthly pension payments for veterans and their dependents.

December 10–11—Henry Kissinger attends the annual NATO winter ministerial meeting in Brussels.

December 11—Nelson A. Rockefeller resigns as governor of New York. He is succeeded by Lieutenant Governor Malcolm Wilson.

December 11—The Supreme Court rules that a person who has been properly arrested for a minor offense might subsequently be searched for evidence relating to a more serious but unrelated crime.

December 19—President Nixon signs a bill ordering the release of approximately $1 billion in impounded funds for education and health programs.

December 22—The 93rd Congress adjourns its first session.

December 28—President Nixon signs a comprehensive manpower training and jobs bill, authorizing needed funding.

December 29—President Nixon signs the Health Maintenance Organization (HMO) Act.

1974

January 4—President Nixon refuses to comply with subpoenas for tapes and documents issued him by the Senate Watergate committee.

January 15—Experts examining the Watergate tape recordings surrendered by President Nixon report that an 18 1/2-minute gap had been caused by at least five separate erasures, rather than a single accidental one, as the White House had contended.

February 4–5—Soviet foreign minister Andrei A. Gromyko confers with President Nixon and Secretary of State Henry Kissinger in Washington.

February 5—Patricia Hearst is kidnapped by the Symbionese Liberation Army (SLA).

February 8—Three astronauts complete a record 84-day space flight as the third and final Skylab crew.

February 12—The trial of militant Native American leaders Russell Means and Dennis Banks in connection with the occupation of Wounded Knee, South Dakota, begins.

February 13—Thirteen major oil-consuming nations endorse a U.S. proposal for international cooperation to fight the world's energy crisis.

February 20—J. Reginald Murphy, editor of the *Atlanta Constitution*, is kidnapped by the American Revolutionary Army.

February 23—J. Reginald Murphy is released by his captors, and an Atlanta couple is arrested in connections with his kidnapping.

February 28—The United States and Egypt resume full-scale diplomatic relations, which were severed in 1967.

March 6–7—The winter meeting of the National Governors' Conference is held in Washington.

March 9–April 16—Hawaii's sugar industry is closed during a strike by field workers.

March 24–28—Henry Kissinger talks with Leonid Brezhnev, Andrei Gromyko, and other Soviet officials in Moscow.

April 3—The White House announces that President Nixon will pay back taxes and interest totaling $465,000 to the Internal Revenue Service.

April 7–29—Hawaii's pineapple industry is closed during a strike by cannery workers.

April 8—President Nixon signs a bill increasing the minimum wage in stages to $2.30 an hour.

April 16—Howard H. Callaway, secretary of the army, halves the 20-year prison sentence being served by Lieutenant William L. Calley Jr.

April 28–May 2—Henry Kissinger confers with officials from the Soviet Union, Algiers, Egypt, and Israel in an effort to promote an Israeli-Syrian troop disengagement.

May 2—Former vice president Spiro T. Agnew is barred from the practice of law by the Maryland Court of Appeals.

May 3–9—Henry Kissinger holds talks with Middle East leaders in continuing efforts to end Israeli-Syrian fighting.

May 21—Jeb Stuart Magruder, former deputy director of the Committee to Re-Elect the President, is sentenced to a prison term of 10 months to four years after being found guilty on charges of plotting the Watergate break-in and cover-up.

May 31—Israeli and Syrian military officials sign a cease-fire agreement in Geneva brought about by Henry Kissinger.

June 1–12—The AFL-CIO Amalgamated Clothing Workers of America strike manufacturers of men's and boys' clothing until a new contract is agreed upon.

June 2–5—The National Governors' Conference is held in Seattle.

June 3—The Supreme Court rules that an employer's retention of night shift pay differentials favoring male employees over female employees violates the Equal Pay Act.

June 7—Former attorney general Richard Kleindienst receives a suspended sentence for his criminal offense in connection with Watergate.

June 8—The United States and Saudi Arabia sign an agreement in Washington for economic and military cooperation.

June 12–18—President Nixon visits Egypt, Saudi Arabia, Syria, Israel, and Jordan.

June 14—President Nixon and President Anwar Sadat sign an accord in Cairo by which the United States will provide Egypt with nuclear technology for peaceful purposes.
June 18–19—NATO meets in Ottawa.

June 26—Government leaders of NATO member nations sign a declaration on Atlantic relations.

June 27–July 3—President Nixon and Soviet Communist Party general secretary Leonid Brezhnev hold summit meetings in Moscow.

June 28—A three-week strike by 4,400 nurses at 43 northern California hospitals ends after ratification of a two-year labor agreement increasing salaries.

June 30—Alberta Williams King, mother of slain civil rights leader Dr. Martin Luther King Jr., is shot and killed.

July 9—Former U.S. chief justice Earl Warren dies.

August 2—John W. Dean III is sentenced to one to four years in prison for his role in the Watergate cover-up.

August 5—President Nixon signs a bill authorizing $22.2 billion for military weapons research and procurement for fiscal 1975.

August 9—At 11:35 a.m., Nixon's letter of resignation is delivered to Secretary of State Henry Kissinger. Nixon leaves Washington for San Clemente.
—12:00 p.m., Ford is sworn in as the thirty-eighth president.

August 12—In his first speech to Congress, Ford announces that inflation is "domestic enemy number one."

August 17—Ford offers Nelson Rockefeller the nomination for the vice presidency under the Twenty-fifth Amendment.

August 18—Speaking to a convention of veterans, Ford announces his intention to create a program that would offer clemency to Vietnam era draft evaders.

August 19–23—The United Mine Workers hold a "memorial week" for men killed or maimed in mines, shutting down the nation's coal mines.

August 22—President Ford signs an $11.1 billion housing and community development bill.

August 28—Ford's first press conference features questions about a possible pardon for Nixon. Ford replies that he is "not ruling it out."

September 4—The United States and the German Democratic Republic (East Germany) establish formal diplomatic relations.

September 6—Nixon signs an agreement with Arthur Sampson, General Services administrator, giving Nixon control of his files (the "Nixon-Sampson agreement").

September 8—In a televised speech, Ford pardons Nixon for all federal crimes he "committed or may have committed or taken part in" while in office.

September 12—Boston city schools open under a new ruling of desegregation. An organized white boycott of the city's schools begins.

September 16—Charges against militant Native American leaders Dennis Banks and Russell Means are dismissed by a federal district court judge.

September 16—President Ford signs a proclamation offering clemency to Vietnam War era draft evaders and military deserters.

September 18—The second round of the Strategic Arms Limitation Talks (SALT II) resumes in Geneva after a six-month recess.

September 23—Senator Edward M. Kennedy announces that he will not be a presidential candidate in 1976.

September 25—The conviction of Lieutenant William L. Calley Jr. is overturned by U.S. district court judge J. Robert Elliott.

September 28—Betty Ford undergoes surgery for breast cancer (radical mastectomy).

October 8—In a speech before a joint session of Congress, Ford calls for a temporary 5 percent tax hike and announces his "Whip Inflation Now" (WIN) program.

October 14—Ford vetoes a congressional ban on aid to Turkey; after being resubmitted and passed again the following day, Ford would once again veto the bill. After compromise the bill would be signed on October 15.

October 17—Ford testifies before the House Judiciary Committee's Subcommittee on Criminal Justice (the "Hungate Committee") regarding the pardon; Ford becomes the first president to testify before Congress since Abraham Lincoln.

October 21—President Ford and President Luis Echeverría Álvarez of Mexico meet at the border.

October 23–November 14—Nixon is hospitalized with phlebitis in his left leg; almost loses his life during the operation.

October 31—A strike by the AFL-CIO International Association of Machinists (IAM), which had grounded flight operations of national airlines since July 15, ends.

November 4—Off-year congressional elections produce large defeats for the Republican Party.

November 5—SALT II sessions recess.

November 5–7—Henry Kissinger visits five Middle East capitals to discuss Arab-Israeli conflict.

November 8—Eight former Ohio National Guardsmen are acquitted of charges stemming from the shooting deaths of four students at Kent State University May 4, 1970.

November 18–22—President Ford becomes the first U.S. chief executive to travel to Japan.

November 18–24—Drivers and terminal workers for Greyhound Lines, Inc., strike, temporarily closing down the nation's largest intercity bus system.

November 19–20—President Ford and Premier Kakuei Tanaka of Japan confer in Japan.

November 21—Senator Walter F. Mondale withdraws from the race for the 1976 Democratic presidential nomination.

November 23—Representative Morris K. Udall announces his candidacy for the 1976 Democratic presidential nomination.

November 23–24—President Ford and Leonid Brezhnev hold talks in Vladivostok to discuss the limitation of nuclear weapons.

December 5—United Mine Workers' president Arnold R. Miller signs a new national coal contract, ending a 24-day strike.

December 13—Attorney General William B. Saxbe resigns.

December 19—Nelson A. Rockefeller is sworn in as the 41st vice president of the United States.

December 19—President Ford signs into law the Presidential Recordings and Materials Preservation Act (PRMPA), giving the federal government custody of the official tapes and papers of former president Nixon. This invalidates the Nixon-Sampson agreement passed earlier by Congress.

December 20—The 93rd Congress adjourns.

December 20—Nixon sues, challenging the constitutionality of the PRMPA.

December 22—The New York Times publishes a story by Seymour Hersh claiming that the CIA "conducted a massive, illegal domestic intelligence operation during the Nixon administration against the antiwar movement and other dissident groups in the United States."

December 22—Construction workers of the United Mine Workers end a five-week strike, which had blocked the return to work of United Mine Workers coal miners since December 6.

1975

January 1—Both the Cambodian Khmer Rouge and the North Vietnamese armies begin what would become their final offensives.

January 3—President Ford signs the Trade Reform Act.

January 4—President Ford signs a bill extending community action programs for the poor.

January 4—Ford announces the creation of the President's Commission on CIA Activities within the United States, chaired by Vice President Rockefeller.

January 11—Former senator Fred R. Harris declares his candidacy for the Democratic nomination for president in 1976.

January 12—Former senator Eugene McCarthy announces that he will campaign as an independent for the presidency backed by the Committee for a Constitutional Presidency.

January 14—The 94th Congress convenes.

January 15—President Ford delivers a State of the Union message to Congress.

January 22—President Ford signs two international agreements banning chemical and biological warfare.

January 27—The Senate announces the formation of a committee to investigate CIA activities within the United States, chaired by Senator Frank Church (D-Idaho).

January 31—SALT II resumes in Geneva after a three-month recess.

February 5—The United Automobile Workers union sponsors a job rally in Washington.

February 6—Senator Henry M. Jackson declares himself a candidate for the 1976 Democratic presidential nomination.

February 7—The Labor Department reports the nation's unemployment rate to be 8.2 percent, the highest since 1941.

February 10–15—Secretary of State Henry Kissinger visits the Middle East to determine the possibility of further negotiations.

February 16–17—Henry Kissinger and Soviet foreign minister Andrei Gromyko meet in Geneva to discuss the Middle East conflict.

February 17—Senator Lloyd M. Bentsen enters the race for the 1976 Democratic presidential nomination.

February 21—John N. Mitchell, H. R. Haldeman, and John D. Ehrlichman are sentenced to two and a half to eight years in prison each for their roles in the Watergate cover-up.

February 24—The United States ends its 10-year arms embargo against India and Pakistan.

March 5—Postmaster General Benjamin Franklin Bailar issues an order prohibiting the Central Intelligence Agency from having access to the mail without authorization.

March 12—The South Vietnamese city of Ban Me Thout, 150 miles northeast of Saigon, falls. Within 10 days both Hue and Danang also have fallen.

March 14—Frederick C. LaRue is sentenced to six months in prison for his role in the Watergate cover-up.

March 17—The Supreme Court rules that the federal government, not the individual states along the Atlantic Coast, has the exclusive right to exploit oil and reserves beneath the continental shelf seabed beyond the three-mile territorial limit.

March 21—In a letter to Yitzhak Rabin, prime minister of Israel, Ford professes his disappointment with Israel's conduct of the recent Sinai peace talks and announces a "reassessment" of U.S. policy toward Israel.

March 22—Henry Kissinger suspends his latest efforts to achieve a second Israeli-Egyptian troop disengagement agreement.

March 29—The withdrawal of all American troops from South Vietnam and release of the last of the U.S. war prisoners held by the Communists are completed.

April 5—John B. Hill and Charley Joe Pernasilice are convicted of criminal charges stemming from an uprising at Attica State Prison while they were inmates there in September 1971.

April 10—Before a joint session of Congress, Ford asks for $722 million in military aid for the South Vietnamese; two Democratic congressmen walk out of the chamber in protest.

April 12—The United States closes its embassy in Phnom Penh, Cambodia, as Khmer Rouge rebel troops take over.

April 14—The American airlift of homeless children to the United States from South Vietnam ends. A total of about 14,000 children had arrived.

April 16—President Ford invokes the Railway Labor Act to avert a nationwide railroad strike by the AFL-CIO Brotherhood of Railway and Airline Clerks.

April 23—Speaking at Tulane University, Ford announces that the Vietnam War is "finished as far as America is concerned."

April 26—About 60,000 participate in a Washington rally, sponsored by the AFL-CIO's Industrial Union Department.

April 28—North Vietnamese troops begin to shell Saigon.

April 29—American personnel are evacuated from the American embassy in Saigon.

April 30—South Vietnamese forces surrender the city of Saigon to the North Vietnamese; the city is renamed Ho Chi Minh City.

May—Unemployment rates reach 9.2 percent, the highest since 1941.

May 11—About 50,000 people gather in the Sheep Meadow in Central Park in New York City to celebrate the end of war in Vietnam and Cambodia.

May 11—Members of the AFL-CIO International Association of Machinists ratify a three-year contract, ending a 13-week strike at McDonnell Douglas Corp.

May 12—The blue-ribbon presidential commission investigating charges of illegal domestic activities by the Central Intelligence Agency (CIA) completes its probe.

May 12—Khmer Rouge forces seize the American merchant ship *Mayaguez* in the Gulf of Siam.

May 14—At 7:09 P.M., U.S. marines storm the island of Koh Tang, off the shore of Cambodia and believed to hold the crew of the *Mayaguez*. Fifteen marines are killed, but the crew is not found. At 9:00 P.M., U.S. air strikes begin to bomb the Cambodian mainland. An hour and a half later, the crew of the *Mayaguez* is released.

May 19–20—Henry Kissinger and Soviet foreign minister Andrei Gromyko hold talks in Vienna.

May 22–23—NATO holds its semiannual talks in Brussels.

May 27—The Supreme Court rules that federal judges do not have the power to block a congressional subpoena issued in connection with an authorized committee investigation.

May 28–29—NATO holds its summit meeting in Brussels, attended by President Ford.

May 28–June 3—President Ford makes his first trip as president to Europe.

May 29—Terry Sanford, president of Duke University, announces his candidacy for the 1976 Democratic presidential nomination.

June 11–12—Israeli prime minister Yitzhak Rabin confers with President Ford and Secretary of State Henry Kissinger in Washington on the possibility of reviving peace negotiations with Egypt.

June 16—The Supreme Court rules that the setting of uniform minimum fee schedules by lawyers is price fixing and a violation of U.S. antitrust laws.

June 28—Dock workers end a strike for a higher guaranteed annual wage that had closed the port of Boston since May 31.

June 29—The National Women's Political Caucus ends a four-day meeting in Boston.

June 30—President Ford signs a bill extending the unemployment compensation program through 1975 for a maximum duration of 65 weeks of aid.

July 1—The U.S. Treasury Department sells 499,500 ounces of gold at auction at $165.05 an ounce.

July 1—Laid-off New York City policemen demonstrate because of the city's financial crisis.

July 1–3—New York City sanitation workers strike because of the city's financial crisis.

July 4—The NAACP ends its 66th annual convention in Washington.

July 8—President Ford officially announces his candidacy for the Republican nomination for president in 1976.

July 11—U.S. judge John J. Sirica reduces the sentences of four Cuban Americans involved in the original Watergate break-in.

July 12—U.S. Army colonel Ernest R. Morgan is released in Beirut after being held hostage for 13 days by a left-wing faction of the Palestine Liberation Army.

July 16—A major purchase of wheat by the Soviet Union from U.S. exporters is announced.

July 17—Spacecraft from the United States and the Soviet Union link in space.

July 18—A nationwide rail strike is averted when a contract agreement is reached between the nation's railroads and the AFL-CIO Brotherhood of Railway Clerks.

July 21—The Postal Service and its employees agree on a new contract, averting a strike.

July 28—A strike by Teamsters that stopped publication of Pittsburgh's two newspapers for a month ends.

July 29—A $2 billion health bill is enacted into law by Congress over a presidential veto.

July 30—Cuban premier Fidel Castro charges the Central Intelligence Agency with at least 24 assassination attempts on himself and other Cuban leaders.

July 30—Leaders of 35 nations meet in Helsinki for the largest summit conference in European history to sign the final document of the Conference on Security and Cooperation in Europe (CSCE). Ford meets twice with Soviet premier Leonid Brezhnev while in Finland.

July 30—The National Urban League ends its annual four-day conference in Atlanta.

July 31—Former Teamsters president James R. Hoffa is reported missing by his family.

August 10—Betty Ford is interviewed by CBS reporter Morley Safer for *60 Minutes*. In the interview, she reveals that she assumed that her children had experimented with marijuana and that she would not be surprised if her daughter, Susan, has had an affair.

August 15—Joanne Little is acquitted of murder in connection with the 1974 killing of a jailer, Clarence Alligood.

August 18—Soviet Communist Party general secretary Leonid Brezhnev meets with a group of 18 U.S. congressmen at Yalta, on the Crimean coast.

August 21—Henry Kissinger arrives in Israel to resume shuttle diplomacy toward attaining Middle East peace.

August 27 and 28—A federal court jury in Cleveland exonerates defendants in connection with the 1970 shooting of students by National Guardsmen at Kent State University.

August 30—The Liberation Party nominates Roger L. MacBride as its candidate for president in the 1976 election.

August 31—The People's Party nominates Margaret Wright as its candidate for president in the 1976 election.

September—The reopening of many schools is held off by a rash of teachers' strikes, affecting at least 961,000 students.

September 1—Frank Aeidler is nominated by the Socialist Party U.S.A. as its candidate for president in the 1976 election.

September 1–5—The International Monetary Fund and the World Bank hold their 30th annual joint meeting in Washington.

September 4—Israel and Egypt sign a U.S.-mediated interim agreement.

September 5—Lynette Alice Fromme is arrested after pointing a pistol at President Ford in Sacramento.

September 9—New York state legislature passes a $2.3 billion aid bill in a last-ditch effort to save New York City from financial collapse.

September 10—The Senate overrides President Ford's veto and passes a $7.9 billion education appropriations bill.

September 16—The New York City teachers' strike ends.

September 18—Patricia Hearst is arrested by agents of the Federal Bureau of Investigation in San Francisco.

September 20—R. Sargent Shriver announces that he is a candidate for the Democratic nomination for president in 1976.

September 20—U.S. astronauts from the Apollo-Soyuz Test Project meet with the Soviet cosmonauts from the flight in Moscow for a two-week tour of the Soviet Union.

September 22—In San Francisco an FBI informant, Sara Jane Moore, fires on President Ford. The gun shot was deflected, and Ford escaped injury.

September 30—Teachers in Boston's public schools end an illegal six-day-old strike after reaching a new contract agreement.

October 2–7—The AFL-CIO holds its convention in San Francisco.

October 7—President Ford signs a $3.96 billion military construction authorization bill for fiscal 1976 and the July–September budget transition period.

October 16—The Federal Reserve Board issues final regulations barring discriminatory credit practices against women.

November 3—Vice President Nelson A. Rockefeller withdraws from consideration as President Ford's running mate in 1976.

November 12—Governor George C. Wallace announces his candidacy for the Democratic presidential nomination in 1976.

November 14—President Ford signs legislation raising the temporary ceiling on the national debt to $595 billion.

November 20—Former California governor Ronald Reagan announces that he will challenge Ford for the Republican nomination for president.

November 26—Lynette Alice Fromme is convicted by a federal jury in Sacramento of attempting to assassinate President Ford.

December 1–5—President Ford visits the People's Republic of China, holding four days of talks with Chinese leaders including Chairman Mao Zedong (Mao Tse-tung) and Deputy Premier Teng Hsiao-ping.

December 8—A veto by the United States blocks a UN Security Council resolution condemning Israel for its air raid on Palestinian refugee camps in Lebanon December 2.

December 9—President Ford signs a bill authorizing the Treasury to loan New York City $2.3 billion annually until 1978.

December 17—Lynette Alice Fromme is sentenced to life imprisonment for attempting to assassinate President Ford.

December 17—The 30th session of the General Assembly of the United Nations ends.

December 19—John Paul Stevens (nominated by Ford) is sworn in as associate justice of the Supreme Court.

December 20—The program to resettle Vietnamese refugees in the United States ends.

December 22—President Ford signs an energy bill providing for an immediate rollback in oil prices and an end to price controls in 40 months.

1976

January 4—Flight attendants at National Airlines sign a new labor agreement and end a 127-day strike.

January 7—In *Nixon v. Administrator* (408 F. Supp. 321, 1976), a district court rules that Nixon's constitutional rights were not violated by the processing of materials by the National Archives.

January 9—Senator Robert C. Byrd announces that he is a candidate for the Democratic presidential nomination in 1976.

January 15—Sara Jane Moore is sentenced to life in prison for having attempted to assassinate President Ford.

January 19—The second session of the 94th Congress convenes.

January 21–23—Henry Kissinger attends meetings with Leonid Brezhnev, Andrei Gromyko, and other Soviet officials in Moscow to discuss SALT.

January 26—The United States vetoes a UN Security Council resolution on the Middle East.

January 30—In *Buckley v. Valeo* the Supreme Court upholds government financing of presidential campaigns and campaign contribution disclosure requirements.

February—Nixon visits China, setting off a storm of press criticism from those who believe he is trying to draw attention away from the New Hampshire primary, where Ford is in a tight race with Ronald Reagan for the Republican nomination.

February 5—President Ford signs a railroad aid bill.

February 8—Public school teachers in Newark ratify a new contract, ending a five-day strike.

February 10—Senator Lloyd Bentsen ends his quest for the Democratic presidential nomination.

February 15—The American Federation of State, County, and Municipal Employees (SCME) withdraws from the AFL-CIO's Public Employee Department.

February 16–24—Henry Kissinger visits Venezuela, Peru, Brazil, Colombia, Costa Rica, and Guatemala to confer with their presidents on trade and other issues.

February 20—SEATO formally disbands.

February 25—The Supreme Court rules that states can outlaw the hiring of illegal aliens when such hiring makes it more difficult for legal residents to obtain jobs.

March 16—The U.S. State Department halts U.S.-Soviet talks because of actions taken by the Soviet Union in Angola.

March 26—Henry Kissinger and Turkish foreign minister Ihsan Sabri Caglayangil sign an accord allowing the reopening of U.S. military installations in Turkey in return for military and economic assistance.

March 30–31—King Hussein of Jordan conducts an official visit to Washington.

April 1—A last-minute settlement averts a New York City subway and bus strike.

April 3—The trucking industry and the Teamsters sign a new contract, ending a three-day strike.

April 12—Patricia Hearst is sentenced to serve 25 years in prison for her conviction on bank robbery charges and 10 years for using a weapon while committing a felony.

April 20—The Supreme Court rules that federal courts can order low-income public housing to be located in white suburbs.

May 20–21—NATO holds its semiannual meeting in Oslo, Norway.

May 24—Supersonic transport (SST) service to Dulles International Airport is inaugurated by the British-French Concorde jetliner.

June 3—The AFL-CIO Amalgamated Clothing and Textile Workers Union is established when the Amalgamated Clothing Workers of America and the Textile Workers Union merge.

June 14—Senator Frank Church withdraws his candidacy for the Democratic presidential nomination.

June 16—Francis E. Meloy Jr., the U.S. ambassador to Lebanon, and Robert O. Waring, his economic counselor, are kidnapped and shot to death in Beirut.

June 16—Frank E. Fitzsimmons is reelected president of the Teamsters union.

June 21—Henry Kissinger addresses the annual ministerial meeting of the Organization for Economic Cooperation and Development (OECD) in Paris.

June 23–24—Henry Kissinger and South African prime minister John Vorster hold talks in West Germany.

June 24—The Supreme Court rules that federal minimum wage laws are not binding on state and local governments.

July 1—Kenneth A. Gibson is elected the first black president of the U.S. Conference of Mayors.

July 1—The Supreme Court rules that states cannot require a woman to obtain her husband's consent before having an abortion.

July 1–4—Celebration of the bicentennial of the signing of the Declaration of Independence.

July 2—The Supreme Court rules that the death penalty does not violate the Constitution's ban on "cruel and unusual" punishment.

July 8—Former president Richard M. Nixon is ordered disbarred in New York State, effective August 9.

July 14—President Ford signs a bill authorizing $32.5 billion in fiscal 1977 for arms procurement and research.

July 14—Jimmy Carter is declared the Democratic presidential nominee. Senator Walter F. Mondale, his choice of a running mate, is approved.

July 17—West German chancellor Helmut Schmidt concludes a three-day visit to Washington, during which he held talks with President Ford.

July 20—The unmanned U.S. spacecraft *Viking 1* lands on Mars, beginning its mission to add to man's knowledge of the planet.

July 20—On orders from Ford, 116 Americans are evacuated from Lebanon.

July 31—An 11-day strike by California cannery workers ends with a new contract.

August 6—Russell C. Means is acquitted of murder in the slaying of Martin Montileaux.

August 9—William and Emily Harris are convicted of kidnapping in the case of Patricia Hearst.

August 14—President Ford signs a bill raising the price of domestic oil.

August 16—A wildcat miners' strike in the East that began July 19 in West Virginia ends.

August 19—Gerald Ford is nominated as the Republican Party's presidential candidate. Senator Robert J. Dole, his choice as a running mate, is approved.

August 28—Members of the United Rubber Workers' union end a 130-day strike against Goodyear Tire and Rubber Co.

August 28 and 31 and September 1—U.S. and North Korean representatives of the Mixed Armistice Commission meet at Panmunjom to discuss easing tension in the Demilitarized Zone.

August 31—William and Emily Harris are sentenced to serve 11 years to life in prison for kidnapping and robbery.

September 3—*Viking 2* lands on Mars.

September 4–6—Henry Kissinger meets with South African prime minister John Vorster in Zurich, Switzerland, for a second round of talks.

September 6—The U.S.-led United Nations Command and North Korea agree to partition the Joint Security Area in the Demilitarized Zone.

September 7 and 8—The AFL-CIO United Rubber Workers sign new contracts with Uniroyal (September 7) and with B. F. Goodrich Co. (September 8), ending a strike that began April 21.

September 14—Henry Kissinger arrives in Tanzania to begin a series of talks with African leaders.

September 20—NATO holds a training exercise to simulate rescue operations against an enemy attack at Namsos, Norway.

September 21—The U.S.-Soviet SALT II sessions resume in Geneva after summer recess.

September 21—SALT II adjourns temporarily.

September 23—In Philadelphia President Ford and Jimmy Carter hold the first of three debates in the presidential campaign on national television.

September 23–October 2—The United Mine Workers of America hold their convention in Cincinnati.

September 24—Rhodesian prime minister Ian Smith accepts a proposal presented by Henry Kissinger for transfer of power to Rhodesia's black majority.

October 4–8—The International Monetary Fund and the World Bank convene in Manila for their 31st annual meeting.

October 6—President Ford and Jimmy Carter have their second nationally televised debate in San Francisco.

October 15—Senators Robert J. Dole and Walter F. Mondale engage in a nationally televised debate, the first campaign debate ever between vice presidential nominees.

October 22—President Ford and Jimmy Carter hold their third and last televised debate in Williamsburg, Virginia.

November 2—Carter defeats Ford for the presidency, winning 49.9 percent of the popular vote to Ford's 47.9 percent, and winning 297 electoral votes to Ford's 241.

November 15—The United States vetoes the admission of Vietnam into the United Nations.

December 6–10—NATO holds year-end meetings in Brussels.

December 13—A strike by the International Brotherhood of Teamsters against United Parcel Service of America, Inc., which began September 16, ends.

PRINCIPAL U.S. GOVERNMENT OFFICIALS OF THE NIXON-FORD YEARS

SUPREME COURT

Earl Warren, Chief Justice 1953–1969
Warren E. Burger, Chief Justice 1969–1986
Hugo L. Black 1937–1971
Harry A. Blackmun 1970–1994
William J. Brennan Jr. 1956–1990
William O. Douglas 1939–1975
Abe Fortas 1965–1969

John Marshall Harlan 1955–1971
Thurgood Marshall 1967–1991
Lewis F. Powell, Jr. 1972–1987
William H. Rehnquist 1972–2005
J. Paul Stevens 1975–?
Potter Stewart 1958–1981
Byron R. White 1962–1993

EXECUTIVE DEPARTMENTS

Department of Agriculture

Secretary
    Clifford M. Hardin 1969–1971
    Earl L. Butz 1971–1976

Undersecretary
    J. Phil Campbell 1969–1975
    John A. Knebel 1975–1976

Assistant Secretary—Rural Development
    Thomas K. Cowden 1969–1972
    William W. Erwin 1973–1975
    William H. Walker 1975–1977

Assistant Secretary—Marketing and Consumer Services
    Richard E. Lyng 1969–1973

    Clayton Yeutter 1973–1974
    Richard Feltner 1974–1977

Assistant Secretary—Department Administration
    Joseph M. Robertson 1969–1971
    Frank B. Elliott 1971–1973
    Joseph R. Wright, Jr. 1973–1976

Assistant Secretary—International Affairs and Commodity Programs*
    Clarence D. Palmby 1969–1972
    Carroll G. Brunthaver Jr. 1972–1974
    Clayton Yeutter 1974–1975
    Richard E. Bell 1975–1977

*The position was originally assistant secretary—international affairs. It was changed in 1969 to the one listed above.

Department of Commerce

Secretary
Maurice H. Stans 1969–1972
Peter G. Peterson 1972–1973
Frederick B. Dent 1973–1975
Rogers C. B. Morton 1975–1977

Undersecretary
Rocco C. Siciliano 1969–1971
James T. Lynn 1971–1973
John K. Tabor 1973–1975
James A. Baker 1975–1976
Edward O. Vetter 1976–1977

Assistant Secretary for Administration
Larry A. Jobe 1969–1973
Joseph E. Kasputys 1976–1977

Assistant Secretary for Domestic and International Business
Kenneth N. Davis, Jr. 1969–1970
Robert McLellan 1970–1972
Andrew E. Gibson 1972
Tilton H. Dobbin 1973–1975
Travis E. Reed 1975–1976
Leonard S. Matthews 1976

Assistant Secretary for Science and Technology
Myron Tribus 1969–1970
James H. Wakelin Jr. 1971–1972
Betsy Ancker-Johnson 1973–1977

Assistant Secretary for Economic Affairs
Harold C. Passer 1969–1972
James L. Pate 1974–1976
Richard G. Darman 1976–1977

Assistant Secretary for Economic Development
Robert A. Podesta 1969–1972
William W. Blunt Jr. 1973–1975
Wilmer D. Mizell 1975–1977

Department of Defense

Secretary
Melvin R. Laird 1969–1973
Elliot Richardson 1973
James R. Schlesinger 1973–1975
Donald H. Rumsfeld 1975–1977

*Deputy Secretary**
David Packard 1969–1971
Kenneth Rush 1972–1973
William P. Clements, Jr. 1973–1977
Robert F. Ellsworth 1975–1977

*The Defense Department received authorization in 1972 to have more than one deputy secretary serving at the same time.

Secretary of the Air Force
Robert C. Seamans Jr. 1969–1973
John L. McLucas 1973–1975
Thomas C. Reed 1976–1977

Secretary of the Army
Stanley R. Resor 1965–1971
Robert F. Froehlke 1971–1973
Howard H. Callaway 1973–1975
Martin R. Hoffmann 1975–1977

Secretary of the Navy
John H. Chafee 1969–1972
John W. Warner 1972–1974
J. William Middendorf 1974–1977

Assistant Secretary (Comptroller)
Robert C. Moot 1968–1973
Terence E. McClary 1973–1976
Fred P. Wacker 1976–?

Assistant Secretary (Installations and Logistics)
Barry J. Shillito 1969–1973
Arthur I. Mendolia 1973–1975
Frank A. Shrontz 1976–1977

Assistant Secretary (International Security Affairs)
G. Warren Nutter 1969–1973
Robert C. Hill 1973–1974
Robert F. Ellsworth 1974–1975
Eugene V. McAuliffe 1976–1977

Assistant Secretary (Manpower)
Roger T. Kelley 1969–1973
William K. Brehm 1973–1976
David P. Taylor 1976–1977

Assistant Secretary (Public Affairs)
Daniel Z. Henkin 1969–1973
Jerry W. Friedheim 1973–1974

Joseph Laitin 1975
M. Allen Woods 1976–1977

*Assistant Secretary (Administration)**
Robert F. Froehlke 1969–1971

*The position was abolished in 1972.

*Assistant Secretary (Intelligence)**
Albert C. Hall 1971–1976

*The position was created in 1971.

*Assistant Secretary (System Analysis)**
Alain C. Enthoven 1965–1969
Gardiner L. Tucker 1970–1973
*The position was abolished in 1973.

Joint Chiefs of Staff

Chairman
General Earle G. Wheeler, U.S. Army
    1964–1970
Admiral Thomas H. Moorer, U.S. Navy
    1970–1974
General George S. Brown, U.S. Air Force
    1974–1978

Chief of Staff, U.S. Army
General William C. Westmoreland 1968–
    1972
General Creighton W. Abrams 1972–1974
General Fred C. Weyand 1974–1976
General Barnard W. Rogers 1976–1979

Chief of Naval Operations
Admiral Thomas H. Moorer 1967–1970
Admiral Elmo R. Zumwalt Jr. 1970–1974
Admiral James L. Holloway III 1974–1978

Chief of Staff, U.S. Air Force
General John P. McConnell 1965–1969
General John D. Ryan 1969–1973
General George S. Brown 1973–1974
General David C. Jones 1974–1978

Commandant of the Marines Corps
General Leonard F. Chapman Jr. 1968–1971
General Robert E. Cushman Jr. 1972–1975
General Louis H. Wilson 1975–1979

Department of Health, Education, and Welfare

Secretary
Robert H. Finch 1969–1970
Elliot L. Richardson 1970–1973
Caspar W. Weinberger 1973–1975
F. David Mathews 1975–1977

Undersecretary
John G. Veneman 1969–1973
Frank C. Carlucci 1973–1975
Marjorie W. Lynch 1975–1977

*Assistant Secretary (Administration and
    Management)**
James Farmer 1969–1971
Rodney H. Brady 1971–1972
Robert A. Marik 1973–1974
John R. Ottina 1974–1976

*The position was originally assistant secretary (administration). It was changed in 1973 to the one listed above.

Assistant Secretary (Education)
James E. Allen Jr. 1969–1970
Sidney P. Marland Jr. 1972–1973
Virginia Y. Trotter 1974–1976

*Assistant Secretary (Health)**
Roger O. Egeberg 1969–1971
Merlin K. DuVal 1971–1972
Charles C. Edwards 1973–1975
Theodore Cooper 1975–1976

*The position was originally assistant secretary (health and scientific affairs). It was changed in 1973 to the one listed above.

Assistant Secretary (Comptroller)
James F. Kelly 1966–1970
James B. Cardwell 1970–1973
John D. Young 1973–1977

Assistant Secretary (Planning and Evaluation)
Lewis H. Butler 1969–1970
Lawrence H. Lynn Jr. 1971–1973
William A. Morrill 1973–1977

*Assistant Secretary (Community and Field Services)**
Patricia Reilly Hitt 1969–1973

*The position was abolished in 1973.

*Assistant Secretary (Human Development)**
Stanley B. Thomas Jr. 1973–1977

*The position was created in 1973.

Assistant Secretary (Legislation)
Creed C. Black 1969–1970
Stephen Kurzman 1971–1976

Department of Housing and Urban Development

Secretary
George Romney 1969–1972
James T. Lynn 1973–1975
Carla A. Hills 1975–1976

Undersecretary
Richard C. Van Dusen 1969–1972
Floyd H. Hyde 1973–1974
James L. Mitchell 1974–1975
John B. Rhinelander 1975–1977

*Assistant Secretary for Housing Production
and Mortgage Credit/Federal Housing
Administration Commissioner**
Eugene A. Gulledge 1969–1973
Sheldon Lubar 1973–1974
David S. Cook 1975–1976

*The position was originally assistant secretary for
mortgage credit and Federal Housing Administration
commissioner. It was changed in 1973 to the one listed
above and abolished in 1976.

*Assistant Secretary for Housing
Management**
Norman Watson 1971–1973
H. R. Crawford 1973–1976

*The position was created in 1971 and abolished in
1976.

*Assistant Secretary for Housing/Federal Housing
Administration Commissioner**
James L. Young 1976

*The position was created in 1976 and it absorbed
the functions of assistant secretary for housing
production and mortgage credit / Federal Housing
Administration commissioner and assistant secretary
for housing management.

*Assistant Secretary for Renewal and Housing
Management**
Lawrence M. Cox 1969–1970

*The position was abolished in 1970.

Assistant Secretary for Administration
Lester P. Condon 1969–1972
Harry T. Morley 1972–1973
W. Boyd Christiansen 1973–1974
Thomas G. Cody 1974–1976

*Assistant Secretary for Fair Housing and Equal
Opportunity*
Samuel J. Simmons 1969–1972
Gloria E. A. Toote 1973–1975
James H. Blair 1975–1977

*Assistant Secretary for Model Cities**
Floyd H. Hyde 1969–1971

*The position was abolished in 1971.

*Assistant Secretary for Community Planning and
Development**
Samuel C. Jackson 1969–1971
Floyd H. Hyde 1971–1973
David O. Meeker Jr. 1973–1976

*The position was originally assistant secretary for
metropolitan planning and development. It was
changed in 1973 to the one listed above.

*Assistant Secretary for Policy Development and
Research**
Harold B. Singer 1969–1972
Michael H. Moskow 1973–1975
Charles J. Orlebeke 1975–1977

*The position was originally assistant secretary for
research and technology. It was changed in 1972 to the
one listed above.

Assistant Secretary for Legislative Affairs
Sol Mosher 1973–1977*

*The position was created in 1973.

*Assistant Secretary for Consumer Affairs and
Regulatory Functions**
Constance Newman 1976–1977

*The position was created in 1976.

Department of the Interior

Secretary
Walter J. Hickel 1969–1970
Rogers C. B. Morton 1971–1975
Stanley K. Hathaway 1975
Thomas S. Kleppe 1975–1977

Undersecretary
Russell E. Train 1969–1970
Fred J. Russell 1970–1971
William T. Pecora 1971–1972
John C. Whitaker 1973–1975
Dale Kent Frizzell 1975–1976

Assistant Secretary—Fish and Wildlife
Leslie L. Glasgow 1969–1971
Nathaniel P. Reid 1971–1977

Assistant Secretary—Energy and Minerals*
Hollis M. Dole 1969–1973
Stephen A. Wakefield 1973–1974
Jack W. Carlson 1974–1976
William L. Fisher 1976–1977

*The position was originally assistant secretary—mineral resources. It was changed in 1973 to the one listed above.

Assistant Secretary—Public Land Management*
Harrison Loesch 1969–1973

*The position was abolished in 1973.

Assistant Secretary—Water and Power Resources*
James R. Smith 1969–1973

*The position was abolished in 1973.

Assistant Secretary—Program Development and Budget*
Laurence Lynn Jr. 1973–1974
Royston Hughes 1974–1976
Ronald Coleman 1976–1977

*The position was created in 1973.

Assistant Secretary—Programs*
John Larson 1971–1973

*The position was created in 1971 and abolished in 1973.

Assistant Secretary—Water Quality*
Carl L. Klein 1969–1970

*The position was abolished in 1970.

Assistant Secretary—Land and Water Resources*
Jack O. Horton 1973–1977

*The position was created in 1973.

Assistant Secretary—Administration
Lawrence H. Dunn 1969–1971
Richard S. Bodman 1971–1973
James T. Clarke 1973–1976
Albert Zapanta 1976–1977

Assistant Secretary—Congressional and Legislative Affairs*
John Kyl 1973–1977

*The position was created in 1973.

Department of Justice

Attorney General
John N. Mitchell 1969–1972
Richard G. Kleindienst 1972–1973
Elliot L. Richardson 1973
William Saxbe 1973–1975
Edward H. Levi 1975–1977

Deputy Attorney General
Richard D. Kleindeinst 1969–1972
Ralph E. Erickson 1972–1973
William D. Ruckleshaus 1973
Laurence H. Silberman 1974–1975
Harold R. Tyler Jr. 1975–1977

Solicitor General
Erwin N. Griswold 1967–1973
Robert H. Bork 1973–1977

Assistant Attorney General/Antitrust Division
Richard W. McLaren 1969–1972
Thomas E. Kauper 1972–1976
Donald Baker 1976–1977

Assistant Attorney General/Civil Division
William D. Ruckleslhaus 1969–1970
L. Patrick Gray III 1970–1972
Harlington Wood Jr. 1972–1973
Carla A. Hills 1974–1975
Rex E. Lee 1975–1977

Assistant Attorney General/Criminal Division
Will R. Wilson 1969–1971
Henry E. Petersen 1972–1974
Richard L. Thornburgh 1975–1977

*Assistant Attorney General/Internal Security
Division**
J. Walter Yeagley 1959–1970
Robert C. Mardian 1970–1972
A. William Olson 1972–1973

*Reorganized in 1973 under assistant attorney general,
criminal division.

Assistant Attorney General/Lands Division
Shiro Kashiwa 1969–1972
D. Kent Frizzell 1972–1973
Wallace H. Johnson Jr. 1973–1975
Peter R. Taft 1975–1977

Assistant Attorney General/Tax Division
Johnnie McK. Walkers 1969–1971
Scott P. Crampton 1971–1976

*Assistant Attorney General/Civil Rights
Division*
Jerris Leonard 1969–1971
David Luke Norman 1971–1973
J. Stanley Pottinger 1973–1977

*Assistant Attorney General/Administrative
Division*
Leo M. Pellerzi 1968–1973
Glen E. Pommerening 1974–1977

*Assistant Attorney General/Office of Legal
Counsel*
William H. Rehnquist 1969–1971
Ralph E. Erickson 1971–1972
Roger E. Cramton 1972–1973
Robert G. Dixon Jr. 1975–1974
Antonin Scalia 1974–1977

*Assistant Attorney General/Office of Legislative
Affairs**
James D. McKevitt 1972–1973
W. Vincent Rakestraw 1974–1975
Michael M. Uhlmann 1975–1977

*The position was created in 1972.

Department of Labor
Secretary
George P. Shultz 1969–1970
James D. Hodgson 1970–1972

Peter J. Brenann 1973–1975
John T. Dunlop 1975–1976
W. J. Usery Jr. 1976–1977

Undersecretary
James D. Hodgson 1969–1970
Laurence H. Silberman 1970–1972
Richard F. Schubert 1973–1975
Robert O. Aders 1975–1976
Michael H. Moskow 1976–1978

Assistant Secretary for Administration
Leo Wertz 1965–1970
Frank Zarb 1970–1973
Fred G. Clark 1973–1977

*Assistant Secretary for Labor-Management
Relations*
W. J. Usery Jr. 1969–1973
Paul J. Fasser Jr. 1973–1976
Bernard E. DeLury 1976–1977

*Assistant Secretary for Occupational Safety and
Health**
John Gunther 1971–1973
Joh H. Stender 1973–1975
Martin Corn 1975–1977

*The position was created in 1971.

*Assistant Secretary for Policy Evaluation and
Research*
Jerome M. Rosow 1969
Richard J. Grunewald 1971–1972
Michael H. Moskow 1972–1974
Abraham Weiss 1974–1977

Assistant Secretary for Employment and Training*
Arnold R. Weber 1969–1970
Malcolm R. Lovell, Jr. 1970–1973
William H. Kolberg 1973–1977

*The position was originally assistant secretary for
manpower administration. It was changed in 1973 to
the one listed above.

Assistant Secretary for Employment Standards*
Arthur A. Fletcher 1969–1972
Richard J. Grunewald 1972–1973
Bernard E. DeLury 1973–1976
John C. Reed 1976–1977

*The position was originally assistant secretary for wage and labor standards. It was changed in 1971 to the one listed above.

Post Office Department*

*Reorganized in 1970 into the U.S. Postal Service, effective 1971.

Postmaster General
Winton M. Blount 1969–1971

Deputy Postmaster General
Elmer T. Klassen 1969–1971

Assistant Postmaster General/Bureau of Operations
Frank J. Nunlist 1969–1971

Assistant Postmaster General/Bureau of Finance and Administration
James W. Hargrove 1969–1971

Assistant Postmaster General/Bureau of Facilities
Henry Lehne 1969–1971

Assistant Postmaster General/Bureau of Personnel
Kenneth A. Housman 1969–1971

Assistant Postmaster General/Research and Engineering
Harold F. Faught 1969–1971

Assistant Postmaster General/Planning and Marketing
Ronald Lee 1969–1971

U.S. Postal Service*

*The service was established as an independent government-owned agency in 1970 by the Postal Reorganization Act of 1970 and was given full authority to operate the U.S. postal system, effective in 1971.

Postmaster General
Elmer T. Klassen 1972–1975
Benjamin F. Bailar 1975–1978

Deputy Postmaster General
Merrill A. Hayden 1971–1972
William F. Bolger 1975–1978

*Senior Assistant Postmaster General/Mail Processing Group**
Harold Faught 1971–1973

*The position was created and abolished in 1973.

*Senior Assistant Postmaster General/Operations Group**
Edward V. Dorsey 1973–1979

*The position was created in 1973.

*Senior Assistant Postmaster General/Employee and Labor Relations Group**
James P. Blaisdell 1972–1973
Darrell F. Brown 1973–1974
James V. P. Conway 1975–1978

*The position was created in 1972.

*Senior Assistant Postmaster General/Support Group**
James W. Hargrove 1971–1972
Benjamin F. Bailar 1972–1973

*The position was created in 1971 and abolished in 1973.

*Senior Assistant Postmaster General/Finance Group**
Ralph W. Nicholson 1973–1974
Richard F. Gould 1975–1977

*The position was created in 1973.

*Senior Assistant Postmaster General/ Administration Group**
Benjamin F. Bailar 1973–1975
J. T. Ellington 1975–1977

*The position was created in 1973.

*Senior Assistant Postmaster General/Manpower and Cost Control**
Carl C. Ulsaker 1974–1978

*The position was created in 1974.

*Senior Assistant Postmaster General/Customer Services Group**
Melvin Baker 1971–1973
Murray Comarow 1972–1973

*The position was created in 1971 and abolished in 1973.

Senior Assistant Postmaster General/Executive Functions Group*
Paul N. Carlin 1972–1973

*The position was created in 1972 and abolished in 1973.

Department of State

Secretary
William P. Rogers 1969–1973
Henry A. Kissinger 1973–1977

Undersecretary
Elliot L. Richardson 1969–1970
John N. Irwin II 1970–1972
Kenneth Rush 1973–1974
Robert S. Ingersoll 1974–1976
Charles W. Robinson 1976–1977

Undersecretary for Economic Affairs
William J. Casey 1973–1974
Charles W. Robinson 1974–1976
William D. Rogers 1976–1977

Deputy Undersecretary for Economic Affairs
Nathaniel Samuels 1969–1972

Undersecretary for Political Affairs
U. Alexis Johnson 1969–1973
William J. Porter 1973–1974
Joseph J. Sisco 1974–1976

Assistant Secretary for Public Affairs
Michael Collins 1970–1971
Carol C. Laise 1973–1975
John E. Reinhardt 1975–1977

Assistant Secretary for Congressional Relations
William B. Macomber Jr. 1967–1969
David M. Abshire 1970–1972
J. Marshall Wright 1973–1974
A. Linwood Holton 1974
Robert J. McCloskey 1975–1976

Assistant Secretary for Inter-American Affairs
Charles A. Meyer 1969–1973
Jack B. Kubisch 1973–1974
William D. Rogers 1974–1976

Assistant Secretary for European Affairs
Martin J. Hillenbrand 1969–1972
Walter J. Stoessel, Jr. 1972–1974
Arthur A. Hartman 1974–1977

Assistant Secretary for Near Eastern and South Asian Affairs
Joseph J. Sisco 1969–1974
Alfred L. Atherton Jr. 1974–1978

Assistant Secretary for East Asian and Pacific Affairs*
Marshall Green 1969–1973
Robert S. Ingersoll 1973–1974
Arthur W. Hummel 1976–1977

*The position was originally assistant secretary of Far Eastern affairs. It was changed in 1966 to the one listed above.

Assistant Secretary for African Affairs
David D. Newsom 1969–1974
Donald Easum 1974–1975
Nathaniel Davis 1975
William E. Schaufele Jr. 1975–1977

Assistant Secretary for Oceans and International, Environmental and Scientific Affairs*
Dixy Lee Ray 1974–1975
Frederick Irving 1976–1977

*The position was created in 1974.

Assistant Secretary for International Organization Affairs
Samuel DePalma 1969–1973
David Popper 1973–1974
William B. Buffum 1974–1975
Samuel W. Lewis 1975–1977

Assistant Secretary for Administration
Francis G. Meyer 1969–1971
Joseph F. Donelan Jr. 1971–1973
John M. Thomas 1973–1979

Assistant Secretary for Educational and Cultural Affairs
John Richardson Jr. 1969–1977

Assistant Secretary for Economic and Business Affairs*
Philip H. Trezise 1969–1972
Willis C. Armstrong 1972–1974
Thomas O. Enders 1974–1975
Joseph A. Greenwald 1976
Julius L. Katz 1976–

*The position was originally assistant secretary for economic affairs. It was changed in 1972 to the one listed above.

Department of Transportation
Secretary
John A. Volpe 1969–1973
Claude Brinegar 1973–1975
William T. Coleman Jr. 1975–1977

Undersecretary
John Robson 1968–1969
James M. Beggs 1969–1973
Egil Krogh 1973
John W. Barnum 1973–1977

Deputy Undersecretary
Charles D. Baker 1969–1970
John P. Olsson 1970–1973
Robert H. Clement 1973–1975
John Snow 1975–1976

Assistant Secretary for Policy Planning and International Affairs
Paul Cherington 1969–1970
Charles D. Baker 1970–1971
John L. Hazard 1972–1973
Robert H. Binder 1974–1977

Assistant Secretary for Public Affairs*
Walter L. Mazan 1969–1970

*The position was abolished in 1970.

Assistant Secretary for Congressional and Intergovernmental Affairs*
Roger Hooker 1973–1974
Robert Monaghan 1975–1977

*The position was created in 1973.

Assistant Secretary for Administration
Alan L. Dean 1967–1969
William S. Heffelfinger 1969–1977

Assistant Secretary for Systems Development and Technology
Secor Browne 1969
Robert Connor 1970–1974
Hamilton Herman 1975–1977

Assistant Secretary for Environment and Urban Systems*
James Braman 1969–1970
Herbert DiSimone 1971–1972
John Hirten 1972–1973

*The position was created in 1969 and abolished in 1973.

Assistant Secretary for Environmental Safety and Consumer Affair*
William J. Smith 1970–1971
Benjamin O. Davis 1971–1975
Judith Connor 1975–1977

*The position was created in 1970 and originally titled assistant secretary for safety. It was changed in 1973 to the one listed above.

Department of the Treasury
Secretary
David M. Kennedy 1969–1971
John B. Connally 1971–1972
George P. Shultz 1972–1974
William E. Simon 1974–1977

Undersecretary
Edwin S. Cohen 1972–1973
Edward C. Schmults 1974–1975
Jerry Thomas 1975–1977

Undersecretary for Monetary Affairs
Paul A. Volcker 1969–1974
Jack F. Bennett 1974–1975
Edwin H. Yeo III 1975–1977

Assistant Secretary for Tax Policy
Edwin S. Cohen 1969–1972
Frederic W. Hickman 1972–1975
Charles M. Walker 1975–1976

Assistant Secretary for Economic Policy
Murray L. Weidenbaum 1969–1971
Edgar R. Fielder 1971–1975
Sidney L. Jones 1975–1977

Assistant Secretary for Enforcement, Operations and Tariff Affairs
Eugene T. Rossides 1969–1973

Edward L. Morgan 1973–1974
David R. MacDonald 1974–1976

Assistant Secretary for International Affairs
John R. Petty 1968–1972
John M. Hennessy 1972–1974
Charles A. Cooper 1974–1975
Gerald L. Parsky 1976–1977

REGULATORY COMMISSIONS AND INDEPENDENT AGENCIES

Atomic Energy Commission*

*Reorganized in 1974 into the Nuclear Regulatory Commission

William A. Anders 1973–1974
Francesco Costagliola 1968–1969
William O. Doub 1971–1974
Wilfrid E. Johnson 1966–1972
William E. Kriegsman 1973–1974
Clarence F. Larson 1969–1974
James T. Ramey 1962–1973
Dixy Lee Ray 1972–1974; chairman, 1973–1974
James R. Schlesinger 1971–1973; chairman, 1971–1973
Glenn T. Seaborg 1961–1971; chairman, 1961–1971
Gerald F. Tape 1963–1969
Theos J. Thompson 1969–1970

Civil Aeronautics Board*

*Abolished in 1985
John G. Adams 1965–1971
Secor D. Browne 1969–1973; chairman, 1969–1973
John H. Crooker Jr. 1968–1969; chairman, 1968–1969
Whitney Gillilland 1959–1975
R. Tenny Johnson 1976–1977
G. Joseph Minetti 1956–1978

Robert Murphy 1961–1973
Richard J. O'Melia 1973–
John Robson 1975–1977; chairman, 1975–1977
Robert Timm 1971–1976; chairman, 1973–1974
Lee R. West 1973–1978

Federal Communications Commission

Robert T. Bartley 1952–1972
Dean Burch 1969–1974; chairman, 1969–1974
Kenneth A. Cox 1963–1970
James R. Fogarty 1976–1983
Benjamin L. Hooks 1972–1977
Thomas J. Houser 1971
Rosel H. Hyde 1946–69; chairman, 1953–1954; 1966–1969
Nicholas Johnson 1966–1973
H. Rex Lee 1968–1973
Robert E. Lee 1953–1981
James H. Quello 1974–1993
Charlotte T. Reid 1971–1976
Glen Robinson 1974–1976
James J. Wadsworth 1965–1969
Abbott M. Washburn 1974–1982
Robert Wells 1969–1971
Margita White 1976–1979
Richard E. Wiley 1972–1977; chairman, 1974–1977

Federal Power Commission

Carl E. Bagge 1965–1970
Albert B. Brooke 1968–1975
John A. Carver 1966–1972
Richard Dunham 1975–1977; chairman, 1975–1977
John Holloman III 1975–1977
Tom Rush Moody Jr. 1971–1975
John N. Nassikas 1969–1975; chairman, 1969–1975
Lawrence J. O'Connor Jr. 1961–1971
Don S. Smith 1973–1979
William Springer 1973–1975
Pinkney Walker 1971–1972
James Watt 1975–1977
Lee C. White 1966–1969; chairman, 1966–1969

Federal Reserve Board

Andrew F. Brimmer 1966–1974
Jeffrey Bucher 1972–1976
Arthur F. Burns 1970–1978; chairman, 1970–1978
Phillip Coldwell 1974–1980
J. Dewey Daane 1963–1974
Stephen Gardner 1976–1978
Robert Holland 1973–1976
Phillip Jackson 1975–1978
David Lilly 1976–1978
Sherman J. Maisel 1965–1972
William McC. Martin Jr. 1951–1970; chairman, 1951–1970
George W. Mitchell 1961–1976
J. Charles Partee 1975–1986
James L. Robertson 1952–1973
John E. Sheehan 1972–1975
William W. Sherill 1967–1971
Henry Wallich 1974–1986

Federal Trade Commission

David Clanton 1976–1981
Calvin J. Collier 1976–1977; chairman, 1976–1977
David S. Dennison 1970–1973

Paul Rand Dixon 1961–?; chairman, 1961–1970
Philip Elman 1961–1970
Lewis A. Engman 1973–1975; chairman, 1973–1975
Mary Elizabeth Hanford 1973–1979
Mary Gardiner Jones 1964–1973
Miles W. Kirkpatrick 1970–1973; chairman, 1970–1973
A. Everette MacIntyre 1961–1973
James M. Nicholson 1967–1969
Stephen Nye 1974–1976
Mayo J. Thompson 1973–1975
Caspar W. Weinberger 1969–1970; chairman, 1969–1970

Nuclear Regulatory Commission*

*The Nuclear Regulatory Commission was established by law on October 11, 1974. It assumed the regulatory functions of the Atomic Energy Commission, which was abolished by the same legislation.

William A. Anders 1974–1976; chairman 1974–1976
Victor Gilinsky 1975–1984
Richard Kennedy 1975–1980
Edward Mason 1975–1978
Marcus Rowden 1975–1977

Securities and Exchange Commission

Hamer H. Budge 1964–1971; chairman, 1969–1971
William J. Casey 1971–1973; chairman, 1971–1973
Manuel F. Cohen 1961–1969; chairman, 1964–1969
G. Bradford Cook 1973; chairman, 1973
John R. Evans 1973–1983
Ray Garrett, Jr. 1973–1975; chairman, 1973–1975
Albert Sydney Herlong Jr., 1969–1973
Roderick Hills 1975–1977; chairman, 1975–1977
Philip Loomis Jr. 1971–1982

James J. Needham 1969–1972
Hugh F. Owens 1964–1973
Irving M. Pollack 1974–1980

Richard B. Smith 1967–1971
A. A. Sommer Jr. 1973–1976
Francis M. Wheat 1964–1969

HOUSE OF REPRESENTATIVES

Alabama
George W. Andrews (D) 1944–1971
Tom Bevill (D) 1967–1996
Walter Flowers (D) 1969–1978
Robert E. Jones Jr. (D) 1947–1976
William Nichols (D) 1967–1988
John H. Buchanan (R) 1965–1980
William L. Dickinson (R) 1965–1992
W. Jack Edwards (R) 1965–1984

Alaska
Nick Begich (D) 1971–1972
Howard W. Pollock (R) 1967–1971
Donald Young (R) 1973–?

Arizona
Morris K. Udall (D) 1961–1992
John B. Conlan (R) 1973–1977
John J. Rhodes (R) 1953–1982
Sam Steiger (R) 1967–1977

Arkansas
William Alexander (D) 1969–1992
Wilbur D. Mills (D) 1939–1977
David Pryor (D) 1966–1973
Ray Thornton (D) 1973–1996
John P. Hammerschmidt (R) 1967–1992

California
Glenn M. Anderson (D) 1969–1992
George E. Brown Jr. (D) 1963–2000
Yvonne Braithwaite Burke (D) 1973–1978
John L. Burton (D) 1974–1982
Phillip Burton (D) 1964–1984
Jeffery Cohelan (D) 1959–1971
James C. Corman (D) 1961–1980
George E. Danielson (D) 1971–1982

Ronald V. Dellums (D) 1971–1996
Don Edwards (D) 1963–1994
Richard T. Hanna (D) 1963–1975
Mark W. Hannaford (D) 1975–1978
Augustus F. Hawkins (D) 1963–1990
Chet Holifield (D) 1943–1975
Harold T. Johnson (D) 1959–1980
John Krebs (D) 1975–1978
Robert L. Leggett (D) 1963–1978
James Lloyd (D) 1975–1980
John J. McFall (D) 1957–1978
George P. Miller (D) 1945–1973
Norman Y. Mineta (D) 1975–1996
John E. Moss (D) 1953–1978
Jerry M. Patterson (D) 1975–1984
Thomas M. Rees (D) 1965–1977
Edward Roybal (D) 1963–1992
Leo J. Ryan (D) 1973–1978
B. F. Sisk (D) 1955–1978
Fortney H. (Pete) Stark (D) 1973–?
John V. Tunney (D) 1965–1971
Lionel Van Deerlin (D) 1963–1980
Jerome R. Waldie (D) 1966–1975
Henry A. Waxman (D) 1975–?
Charles H. Wilson (D) 1963–1980
Alphonzo Bell (R) 1961–1977
Clair W. Burgener (R) 1973–1982
Donald H. Clausen (R) 1963–1982
Delwin Clawson (R) 1963–1978
Barry M. Goldwater Jr. (R) 1969–1982
Charles S. Gubser (R) 1953–1975
Andrew J. Hinshaw (R) 1973–1977
Craig Hosmer (R) 1953–1975
William M. Ketchum (R) 1973–1978
Robert J. Lagomarsino (R) 1974–1992
Glenn P. Lipscomb (R) 1953–1970
William S. Mailliard (R) 1953–1974

R. R. (Bob) Mathias (R) 1967–1975
Paul N. McCloskey Jr. (R) 1967–1992
Carlos J. Moorhead (R) 1973–1996
Jerry L. Pettis (R) 1967–1975
Shirley N. Pettis (R) 1975–1978
Edwin Reinecke (R) 1965–1969
John H. Rousselot (R) 1961–1963; 1970–1982
John G. Schmitz (R) 1970–1973
H. Allen Smith (R) 1957–1973
Burt L. Talcott (R) 1963–1977
Charles M. Teague (R) 1953–1970
James B. Utt (R) 1953–1970
Victor V. Veysey (R) 1971–1975
Charles E. Wiggins (R) 1967–1978
Robert Wilson (R) 1953–1980

Colorado
Wayne N. Aspinall (D) 1949–1973
Frank E. Evans (D) 1965–1978
Byron G. Rogers (D) 1951–1971
Patricia Schroeder (D) 1973–1996
Timothy E. Wirth (D) 1975–1986
William L. Armstrong (R) 1973–1978
Donald G. Brotzman (R) 1963–1965; 1967–1975
James P. (Jim) Johnson (R) 1943–1980
James D. McKevitt (R) 1971–1973

Connecticut
William R. Cotter (D) 1971–1982
Emilio Q. Daddario (D) 1959–1971
Christopher J. Dodd (D) 1975–1980
Robert N. Giaimo (D) 1959–1980
Ella T. Grasso (D) 1971–1975
Anthony Moffett (D) 1975–1982
John S. Monagan (D) 1959–1973
William L. Saint Onge (D) 1963–1970
Stewart B. McKinney (R) 1971–1988
Thomas J. Meskill (R) 1967–1971
Ronald A. Sarasin (R) 1973–1978
Robert H. Steele (R) 1970–1975
Lowell P. Weicker Jr. (R) 1969–1971

Delaware
Pierre S. du Pont IV (R) 1971–1977
William V. Roth Jr. (R) 1967–1970

Florida
Charles E. Bennett (D) 1949–1992
William Chappell Jr. (D) 1969–1988
Dante B. Fascell (D) 1955–1992
Donald Fuqua (D) 1963–1986
Sam M. Gibbons (D) 1963–1996
William D. (Bill) Gunter Jr. (D) 1973–1975
James A. Haley (D) 1953–1977
William Lehman (D) 1973–1992
Claude D. Pepper (D) 1963–1990
Paul G. Rogers (D) 1955–1978
Robert L. F. Sikes (D) 1941–1944;
    1945–1978
Louis Arthur (Skip) Bafalis (R) 1973–1982
J. Herbert Burke (R) 1967–1978
William C. Cramer (R) 1955–1971
Louis Frey Jr. (R) 1969–1978
Richard Kelly (R) 1975–1980
C. W. Bill Young (R) 1971–?

Georgia
Jack Brinkley (D) 1967–1982
John W. Davis (D) 1961–1975
John J. Flynt Jr. (D) 1954–1978
Ronald Bryan "Bo" Ginn (D) 1973–1982
G. Elliott Hagan (D) 1961–1973
Phillip M. Landrum (D) 1953–1976
Elliott H. Levitas (D) 1975–1977
Dawson Mathis (D) 1971–1980
Lawrence McDonald (D) 1975–1984
Maston O'Neal (D) 1965–1971
Robert G. Stephens Jr. (D) 1961–1977
W. S. (Bill) Stuckey Jr. (D) 1967–1977
Andrew Young (D) 1973–1977
Benjamin B. Blackburn (R) 1967–1975
S. Fletcher Thompson (R) 1967–1973

Hawaii
Spark M. Matsunaga (D) 1963–1976
Patsy Takemoto Mink (D) 1965–2002

Idaho
Orval H. Hansen (R) 1969–1974
James A. McClure (R) 1967–1973
Steven D. Symms (R) 1973–1980

Illinois

Frank Annunzio (D) 1965–1992
Cardiss Collins (D) 1973–1996
George Washington Collins (D) 1970–1972
William L. Dawson (D) 1943–1970
John Fary (D) 1975–1982
Kenneth J. Gray (D) 1955–1975
Timothy L. Hall (D) 1975–1977
Ralph H. Metcalfe (D) 1971–1978
Abner J. Mikva (D) 1969–1973
Morgan M. Murphy (D) 1959–1971
Melvin Prince (D) 1945–1988
Roman C. Pucinski (D) 1959–1973
Daniel J. Ronan (D) 1965–1969
Daniel D. Rostenkowski (D) 1959–1994
Martin A. Russo (D) 1975–1992
George E. Shipley (D) 1959–1978
Paul Simon (D) 1975–1984
Sidney R. Yates (D) 1949–1963; 1965–1998
John B. Anderson (R) 1961–1980
Leslie C. Arends (R) 1935–1975
Harold R. Collier (R) 1957–1975
Philip M. Crane (R) 1969–2004
Edward J. Derwinski (R) 1959–1982
John N. Erlenborn (R) 1965–1984
Paul Findley (R) 1961–1982
Robert P. Hanrahan (R) 1973–1975
Henry J. Hyde (R) 1975–?
John C. Klucgynski (R) 1951–1975
Edward R. Madigan (R) 1973–1992
Robert McClory (R) 1963–1982
Robert H. Michel (R) 1957–1994
George M. O'Brien (R) 1973–1986
Tom Railsback (R) 1967–1982
Charlotte T. Reid (R) 1963–1971
Donald Rumsfeld (R) 1963–1969
William L. Springer (R) 1951–1973
Samuel H. Young (R) 1973–1975

Indiana

John Brademas (D) 1959–1980
Floyd J. Fithian (D) 1975–1982
Lee H. Hamilton (D) 1965–1998
Philip H. Hayes (D) 1975–1977
Andrew Jacobs, Jr. (D) 1965–1973

Ray J. Madden (D) 1943–1977
J. Edward Roush (D) 1959–69; 1971–1977
Philip R. Sharp (D) 1975–1994
E. Ross Adair (R) 1951–1971
William G. Bray (R) 1951–1975
David W. Dennis (R) 1969–1975
Elwood H. Hillis (R) 1971–1986
William H. Hudnut, III (R) 1973–1975
Earl F. Landgrebe (R) 1969–1975
John T. Myers (R) 1967–1996
Richard L. Roudebush (R) 1961–1971
Roger H. Zion (R) 1967–1975

Iowa

Berkley Bedall (D) 1975–1986
Michael T. Blouin (D) 1975–1978
John C. Culver (D) 1965–1975
Tom Harkin (D) 1975–1984
Edward Mezvinsky (D) 1973–1977
Neal Smith (D) 1959–1994
Charles E. Grassley (R) 1975–1980
Harold R. Gross (R) 1949–1975
John Kyl (R) 1959–1965; 1967–1973
Wiley Mayne (R) 1967–1975
William J. Sherle (R) 1967–1975
Fred Schwengel (R) 1955–1965; 1967–1973

Kansas

Martha Elizabeth Keys (D) 1975–1978
William R. Roy (D) 1971–1975
Chester L. Mize (R) 1965–1971
Keith G. Sebelius (R) 1969–1980
Garner E. Shriver (R) 1961–1977
Joe Skubitz (R) 1963–1978
Larry Winn Jr. (R) 1967–1984

Kentucky

John Breckinridge (R) 1973–1978
Carroll Hubbard Jr. (D) 1975–1992
Romano L. Mazzoli (D) 1971–1994
William H. Natcher (D) 1953–1994
Carl D. Perkins (D) 1949–1984
Frank A. Stubblefield (D) 1959–1975
John C. Watts (D) 1951–1971
Tim Lee Carter (R) 1965–1980

William O. Cowger (R) 1967–1971
Marion G. Snyder (R) 1963–1965; 1967–?

Louisiana
Corinne C. (Lindy) Boggs (D) 1973–1990
Hale Boggs (D) 1941–1943; 1947–1972
John B. Breaux (D) 1972–1986
Patrick T. Caffery (D) 1969–1973
Edwin W. Edwards (D) 1965–1972
F. Edward Hebert (D) 1941–1977
Gillis W. Long (D) 1973–1986
Speedy O. Long (D) 1965–1973
Otto E. Passman (D) 1947–1976
John R. Rarick (D) 1967–1975
Joe D. Waggonner, Jr. (D) 1961–1978
W. Henson Moore (R) 1975–1986
David C. Treen (R) 1973–1980

Maine
William D. Hathaway (D) 1965–1973
Peter N. Kyros (D) 1967–1975
William S. Cohen (R) 1973–1978
David F. Emery (R) 1975–1982

Maryland
Goodloe E. Byron (D) 1971–1978
George H. Fallon (D) 1945–1971
Samuel N. Friedel (D) 1953–1971
Edward A. Garmatz (D) 1947–1973
Clarence D. Long (D) 1963–1984
Parren J. Mitchell (D) 1971–1986
Paul S. Sarbanes (D) 1971–1976
Gladys Noon Spellman (D) 1975–1980
Robert E. Bauman (R) 1973–1980
J. Glenn Beall Jr. (R) 1969–1971
Lawrence J. Hogan (R) 1969–1975
Marjorie S. Holt (R) 1973–1986
William O. Mills (R) 1971–1973
Rogers C. B. Morton (B) 1963–1971

Massachusetts
Edward P. Boland (D) 1953–1988
James A. Burke (D) 1959–1978
Harold D. Donohue (D) 1947–1975
Robert F. Drinan (D) 1971–1980

Joseph D. Early (D) 1975–1992
Michael J. Harrington (D) 1969–1978
Louise Day Hicks (D) 1971–1973
Torbert H. MacDonald (D) 1955–1976
John W. McCormack (D) 1928–1971
John J. Moakley (D) 1973–2002
Thomas P. O'Neill Jr. (D) 1953–1986
Philip J. Philbin (D) 1943–1971
Gerry E. Studds (D) 1973–1996
Paul E. Tsongas (D) 1975–1978
William H. Bates (R) 1950–1969
Silvio O. Conte (R) 1959–1992
Paul W. Cronin (R) 1973–1975
Margaret M. Heckler (R) 1967–1982
Hastings Keith (R) 1959–1973
F. Bradford Morse (R) 1961–1972

Michigan
James J. Blanchard (D) 1975–1982
William M. Brodhead (D) 1975–1982
Milton Robert Carr (D) 1975–1994
John R. Conyers Jr. (D) 1965–?
Charles C. Diggs Jr. (D) 1955–1980
William D. Ford (D) 1965–1994
Martha W. Griffiths (D) 1955–1975
Lucien N. Nedzi (D) 1961–1980
James G. O'Hara (D) 1959–1976
Richard F. Vander Veen (D) 1974–1977
Robert Traxler (D) 1974–1992
William S. Broomfield (R) 1957–1992
Garry Brown (R) 1967–1978
Elford A. Cederberg (R) 1953–1978
Charles E. Chamberlain (R) 1957–1975
Marvin L. Esch (R) 1967–1977
Gerald R. Ford Jr. (R) 1949–1973
James Harvey (R) 1961–1974
Robert J. Huber (R) 1973–1975
Jack H. McDonald (R) 1967–1973
Donald W. Riegle Jr. (R) 1967–1974
Philip E. Ruppe (R) 1967–1978
Guy Vander Jagt (R) 1966–1992

Minnesota
Robert Bergland (D) 1971–1977
John A. Blatnik (D) 1947–1975

Donald M. Fraser (Dem-Farm Labor) 1963–1978
Joseph E. Karth (D) 1959–1977
Richard Nolan (D) 1975–1980
James L. Oberstar (D) 1975–?
William Frenzel (R) 1971–1998
Tom Hagedorn (R) 1975–1982
Odin Langen (R) 1959–1971
Clark MacGregor (R) 1961–1971
Ancher Nelson (R) 1959–1975
Albert H. Quie (R) 1958–1978
John M. Zwach (R) 1967–1975

Mississippi
Thomas G. Abernathy (D) 1942–1973
David R. Bowen (D) 1973–1982
William M. Colmer (D) 1933–1973
Charles H. Griffen (D) 1968–1973
G. V. (Sonny) Montgomery (D) 1967–1996
Jamie L. Whitten (D) 1941–1994
William Thad Cochran (D) 1973–1978
Chester Trent Lott (R) 1973–1988

Missouri
Richard Walker Bolling (D) 1949–198?
William D. Burlison (D) 1969–1980
William L. Clay (D) 1969–2000
Durward G. Hall (D) 1961–1973
W. R. Hull Jr. (D) 1955–1973
William L. Hungate (D) 1964–1977
Richard H. Ichord (D) 1961–1980
Jerry Litton (D) 1973–1976
William J. Randall (D) 1959–1977
Leonor K. Sullivan (D) 1953–1977
James W. Symington (D) 1969–1977
Gene Taylor (R) 1973–1988

Montana
Max S. Baucus (D) 1975–1978
John Melcher (D) 1969–1977
Arnold Olsen (D) 1961–1971
James F. Battin (R) 1961–1969
Richard G. Shoup (R) 1971–1975

Nebraska
Glenn Cunningham (R) 1957–1971
Robert V. Denney (R) 1967–1971

David T. Martin (R) 1961–1975
John Y. McCollister (R) 1971–1977
Virginia Dodd Smith (R) 1975–1990
Charles Thone (R) 1971–1978

Nevada
Walter S. Baring (D) 1949–1953; 1957–1973
James Santini (D) 1975–1982
David Towell (R) 1973–1975

New Hampshire
Norman E. D'Amours (D) 1975–1984
James C. Cleveland (R) 1963–1980
Louis C. Wyman (R) 1963–1965; 1967–1975

New Jersey
Dominick V. Daniels (D) 1959–1977
James J. Florio (D) 1975–1990
Cornelius E. Gallagher (D) 1959–1973
Henry Helstoski (D) 1965–1977
James J. Howard (D) 1965–1988
Williams J. Hughes (D) 1975–1994
Charles S. Joelson (D) 1961–1969
Gene Andrew Maguire (D) 1975–1980
Helen S. Meyner (D) 1975–1978
Joseph G. Minish (D) 1963–1984
Edward J. Patten (D) 1963–1980
Peter W. Rodino, Jr. (D) 1949–1988
Robert A. Roe (D) 1969–1992
Frank Thompson, Jr. (D) 1955–1980
William T. Cahill (R) 1959–1970
Florence P. Dwyer (R) 1957–1973
Millicent Fenwick (R) 1975–1982
Edwin B. Forsythe (R) 1970–1984
Peter H. B. Frelingheuysen (R) 1953–1975
John E. Hunt (R) 1967–1975
Joseph Maraziti (R) 1973–1975
Matthew J. Rinaldo (R) 1973–1992
Charles W. Sandman Jr. (R) 1967–1975
William B. Widmall (R) 1950–1975

New Mexico
Harold L. Runnels (D) 1971–1980
Ed Foreman (R) 1963–1965 (Texas); 1969–1971
Manuel Lujan (R) 1969–1988

New York

Bella Abzug (D) 1971–1977
Joseph P. Addabo (D) 1961–1986
Jerome Ambro Jr. (D) 1975–1980
Herman Badillo (D) 1971–1978
Mario Biaggi (D) 1969–1988
Jonathan B. Bingham (D) 1965–1982
Frank J. Brasco (D) 1967–1975
Daniel E. Button (D) 1967–1971
Hugh L. Carey (D) 1961–1975
Emanuel Celler (D) 1923–1973
Shirley Chisholm (D) 1969–1982
James J. Delaney (D) 1945–1947;
    1949–1978
John G. Dow (D) 1965–1969; 1971–1973
Thomas J. Downey (D) 1975–1992
Thaddeus J. Dulski (D) 1959–1975
Leonard Farbstein (D) 1957–1971
Jacob H. Gilbert (D) 1960–1971
James M. Hanley (D) 1965–1980
Elizabeth Holtzman (D) 1973–1980
Edward I. Koch (D) 1969–1978
John J. LaFalce (D) 1975–2002
Stanley Lundine (D) 1976–1986
Richard D. McCarthy (D) 1965–1971
Matthew F. McHugh (D) 1975–?
John M. Murphy (D) 1963–1980
Henry J. Nowak (D) 1975–1992
Richard L. Ottinger (D) 1965–1971; 1975–
    1984
Edward W. Pattison (D) 1975–1978
Otis J. Pike (D) 1961–1978
Bertram L. Podell (D) 1968–1975
Adam Clayton Powell (D) 1945–1967; 1969–
    1971
Charles B. Rangel (D) 1971–?
Frederick W. Richmond (D) 1975–1982
John J. Rooney (D) 1944–1974
Benjamin S. Rosenthal (D) 1962–1984
William Fitts Ryan (D) 1961–1972
James H. Scheuer (D) 1965–1973
Stephen J. Solarz (D) 1975–1992
Samuel S. Stratton (D) 1959–1988
Lester L. Wolff (D) 1965–1980
Leo C. Zeferetti (D) 1975–1982

Barber B. Conable Jr. (R) 1965–1984
Hamilton Fish Jr. (R) 1969–1994
Benjamin A. Gilman (R) 1973–2002
James R. Grover Jr. (R) 1963–1975
Seymour Halpern (R) 1959–1973
James F. Hastings (R) 1969–1976
Frank J. Horton (R) 1963–1992
Jack F. Kemp (R) 1971–1988
Carleton J. King (R) 1961–1974
Norman F. Lent (R-C) 1971–1992
Robert C. McEwen (R) 1965–1980
Martin B. McKneally (R) 1969–1971
Donald J. Mitchell (R) 1973–1982
Peter A. Peyser (R) 1971–1976
Alexander Pirnie (R) 1959–1972
Ogden R. Reid (R) 1963–1972; (D) 1972–
    1975
Howard W. Robison (R) 1958–1975
Angelo D. Roncallo (R) 1973–1975
Henry P. Smith III (R) 1965–1975
John H. Terry (R) 1971–1973
William F. Walsh (R-C) 1973–1978
John W. Wydler (R) 1963–1980

North Carolina

Ike F. Andrews (D) 1973–1984
L. H. Fountain (D) 1953–1982
Nick Galifianakis (D) 1967–1973
Willie G. Hefner (D) 1975–1998
David N. Henderson (D) 1961–1977
Walter B. Jones (D) 1966–1992
Alton Lennon (D) 1957–1973
Stephen L. Neal (D) 1975–1994
L. Richardson Preyer (D) 1969–1980
Charles G. Rose, III (D) 1973–1996
Roy A. Taylor (D) 1960–1977
James T. Broyhill (R) 1963–1984
Charles R. Jonas (R) 1953–1973
James Grubbs Martin (R) 1973–1984
Wilmer D. Mizell (R) 1969–1975
Earl B. Ruth (R) 1969–1975

North Dakota

Mark Andrews (R) 1963–1980
Thomas S. Kleppe (R) 1967–1971

Ohio

Thomas Ludlow Ashley (D) 1955–1980
Charles J. Carney (D) 1970–1978
Michael A. Feighan (D) 1943–1971
Wayne L. Hays (D) 1949–1976
Michael J. Kirwan (D) 1937–1970
Thomas A. Luken (D) 1974–1990
Ronald M. Mottl (D) 1975–1982
John F. Seiberling Jr. (D) 1971–1986
Louis Stokes (D) 1969–1998
Charles A. Vanik (D) 1955–1980
John M. Ashbrook (R) 1961–1982
William H. Ayres (R) 1951–1971
Jackson E. Betts (R) 1951–1973
Frank T. Bow (R) 1951–1972
Clarence J. Brown Jr. (R) 1965–1982
Donald D. Clancy (R) 1961–1976
Samuel L. Devine (R) 1959–1980
Willis D. Gradison Jr. (R) 1975–1994
Tennyson Guyer (R) 1973–1982
William H. Harsha (R) 1961–1980
William J. Keating (R) 1971–1974
Thomas N. Kindness (R) 1975–1986
Delbert L. Latta (R) 1959–1988
Donald E. Lukens (R) 1967–1971
William M. McCulloch (R) 1947–1973
Clarence E. Miller (R) 1967–1992
William E. Minshall (R) 1955–1975
Charles A. Mosher (R) 1961–1977
Walter E. Powell (R) 1971–1975
J. William Stanton (R) 1965–1982
Robert Taft Jr. (R) 1963–1965; 1967–1971
Charles W. Whalen Jr. (R) 1967–1978
Chalmers P. Wylie (R) 1967–1992

Oklahoma

Carl Albert (D) 1947–1977
Ed Edmondson (D) 1953–1973
Glenn English (D) 1975–1994
John Jarman (D) 1951–1975; (R) 1975–1977
James R. Jones (D) 1973–1986
Clem Rogers McSpadden (D) 1973–1975
Tom Steed (D) 1949–1980
Theodore M. Risenhoover (D) 1975–?
Page Belcher (R) 1951–1973

Oregon

Les AuCoin (D) 1975–1992
Robert Duncan (D) 1963–1967; 1975–1980
Edith Green (D) 1955–1974
Al Ullman (D) 1957–1980
James Weaver (D) 1975–1986
John R. Dellenback (R) 1967–1975
Wendall Wyatt (R) 1964–1975

Pennsylvania

William A. Barrett (D) 1945–1947; 1949–1976
James A. Byrne (D) 1953–1973
Frank M. Clark (D) 1955–1975
John H. Dent (D) 1958–1978
Robert W. Edgar (D) 1975–1986
Joshua Eilberg (D) 1967–1978
Daniel J. Flood (D) 1945–1947; 1949–1953; 1955–1980
Joseph Gaydon (D) 1968–1990
William J. Green III (D) 1964–1977
William S. Moorhead (D) 1959–1980
Thomas E. Morgan (D) 1945–1977
John P. Murtha (D) 1974–?
Robert N. C. Nix Sr. (D) 1958–1978
Fred B. Rooney (D) 1963–1978
Joseph P. Vigorito (D) 1965–1976
Gus Yatron (D) 1969–1992
Robert J. Corbett (R) 1939–1941; 1945–1971
R. Lawrence Coughlin (R) 1969–1992
James G. Fulton (R) 1945–1971
George A. Goodling (R) 1961–1965; 1967–1975
William F. Goodling (R) 1975–2000
H. John Heinz III (R) 1971–1977
Albert W. Johnson (R) 1963–1977
Joseph M. McDade (R) 1963–1998
Gary A. Myers (R) 1975–1978
John P. Saylor (R) 1949–1973
Herman T. Schneebeli (R) 1960–1977
Richard T. Schulze (R) 1975–1992
John H. Ware III (R) 1970–1975
G. Robert Watkins (R) 1965–1970
J. Irving Whalley (R) 1960–1973
Lawrence G. Williams (R) 1967–1975

Rhode Island

Edward P. Beard (D) 1974–1980
Fernand Joseph Saint Germain (D) 1961–1988
Robert O. Tiernan (D) 1967–1975

South Carolina

Mendel J. Davis (D) 1971–1980
Butler Derrick (D) 1975–1994
William Jennings Bryan Dorn (D) 1947–1949; 1951–1974
Thomas S. Gettys (D) 1964–1975
Kenneth L. Holland (D) 1975–1982
John W. Jenrette Jr. (D) 1975–1980
James R. Mann (D) 1969–1978
John L. McMillan (D) 1939–1973
L. Mendel Rivers (D) 1941–1970
Floyd Spence (R) 1971–2002
Albert Watson (D) 1963–1965; (R) 1965–1971
Edward Young (R) 1973–1975

South Dakota

James Abourezk (D) 1971–1973
F. E. Denholm (D) 1971–1975
James Abdnor (R) 1973–1980
E. Y. Berry (R) 1951–1971
Larry Pressler (R) 1975–1978
Benjamin Reifel (R) 1961–1971

Tennessee

Clifford Allen (D) 1975–1978
William R. Anderson (D) 1965–1973
Ray Blanton (D) 1967–1973
Robert A. Everett (D) 1958–1969
Joe L. Evins (D) 1947–1977
Harold E. Ford (D) 1975–?
Richard Fulton (D) 1963–1975
Ed Jones (D) 1969–1988
Marilyn Lloyd (D) 1975–?
LeMar Baker (R) 1971–1975
Robin L. Beard (R) 1973–1982
William E. (Bill) Brock (R) 1963–1971
John J. Duncan (R) 1965–?

Dan Kuykendall (R) 1967–1975
James H. Quillen (R) 1963–1996

Texas

Jack Brooks (D) 1953–1994
Omar Burleson (D) 1947–1978
Earle Cabell (D) 1965–1973
Robert Casey (D) 1959–1976
Eligio Kika de la Garza (D) 1965–1996
John Dowdy (D) 1952–1973
Robert Eckhardt (D) 1957–1980
O. C. Fisher (D) 1943–1975
Henry B. Gonzaléz (D) 1961–1998
Sam Hall (D) 1976–1986
Jack Hightower (D) 1975–1984
Barbara Jordan (D) 1973–1978
Abraham Kazen Jr. (D) 1967–1984
Robert Kreuger (D) 1975–1978
George H. Mahon (D) 1935–1978
Dale Milford (D) 1973–1978
Wright Patman (D) 1929–1970
J. J. (Jake) Pickle (D) 1963–1994
W. R. Poage (D) 1937–1978
Graham B. Purcell (D) 1962–1973
Herbert Ray Roberts (D) 1962–1980
Olin E. Teague (D) 1946–1978
Charles Wilson (D) 1973–1996
Richard C. White (D) 1965–1982
James C. Wright Jr. (D) 1955–1990
John Young (D) 1957–1978
William Archer Jr. (R) 1971–2000
George H. W. Bush (R) 1967–1971
James M. Collins (R) 1968–1982
Ron Paul (R) 1976–?
Robert D. Price (R) 1967–1975
Alan Steelman (R) 1973–1976

Utah

Allen T. Howe (D) 1975–1976
Douglas W. Owens (D) 1973–1975
Wayne W. Owens (D) 1973–1975
K. Gunn McKay (D) 1971–1980
Lawrence J. Burton (R) 1963–1971
Sherman P. Lloyd (R) 1963–1965; 1967–1973

Vermont
James M. Jeffords (R) 1975–1988
Richard W. Mallary (R) 1972–1975
Robert T. Stafford (R) 1961–1973

Virginia
Watkins M. Abbitt (D) 1948–1973
W. D. (Dan) Daniel (D) 1949–1988
Thomas N. Downing (D) 1959–1977
Joseph L. Fisher (D) 1975–1980
Herbert E. Harris II (D) 1975–1980
John O. Marsh Jr. (D) 1963–1971
David E. Satterfield III (D) 1965–1980
Joel T. Broyhill (R) 1953–1975
M. Caldwell Butler (R) 1972–1982
Robert W. Daniel Jr. (R) 1973–1982
Standord E. Parris (R) 1973–1975
Richard H. Poff (R) 1953–1972
J. Kenneth Robinson (R) 1971–1984
William L. Scott (R) 1967–1973
William C. Wampler (R) 1953–1955; 1967–
    1982
G. William Whitehurst (R) 1969–1986

Washington
Brockman (Brock) Adams (D)
    1965–1977
Don Bonker (D) 1975–1988
Thomas S. Foley (D) 1965–1994
Julia Butler Hansen (D) 1960–1974
Floyd V. Hicks (D) 1965–1977
Mike McCormack (D) 1971–1980
Lloyd Meeds (D) 1965–1978
Catherine May (R) 1959–1971

Thomas M. Pelly (R) 1953–1973
Joel Pritchard (R) 1973–1984

West Virginia
Ken Heckler (D) 1959–1977
James Kee (D) 1965–1973
Robert H. Mollohan (D) 1953–1957; 1969–
    1982
John M. Slack Jr. (D) 1959–1980
Harley O. Staggers (D) 1949–1980

Wisconsin
Leslie Aspin (D) 1971–1994
Alvin Baldus (D) 1975–1980
Robert J. Cornell (D) 1975–1978
Robert Kastenmeier (D) 1959–1990
David R. Obey (D) 1969–?
Henry S. Reuss (D) 1955–1982
Clement J. Zablocki (D) 1949–1982
John W. Byrnes (R) 1945–1973
Glenn R. Davis (R) 1947–1957; 1965–1974
Harold V. Froelich (R) 1973–1975
Robert W. Kasten Jr. (R) 1975–1978
Melvin R. Laird (R) 1953–1969
Alvin E. O'Konski (R) 1943–1973
Henry C. Schadeberg (R) 1961–1965; 1967–
    1971
William A. Steiger (R) 1967–1978
Vernon W. Thomson (R) 1968–1975

Wyoming
Teno Roncalio (D) 1965–1967;
    1971–1978
John Wold (R) 1967–1971

SENATE

Alabama
James B. Allen (D) 1969–1978
John Sparkman (D) 1946–1978

Alaska
Mike Gravel (D) 1969–1980
Ted Stevens (R) 1968–?

Arizona
Paul J. Fannin (R) 1965–1977
Barry Goldwater (R) 1953–1965;
    1969–1986

Arkansas
Dale Bumpers (D) 1975–1998

J. Williams Fulbright (D) 1945–1975
John L. McClellan (D) 1943–1978

California
Alan Cranston (D) 1969–1992
John V. Tunney (D) 1971–1977
George Murphy (R) 1964–1971

Colorado
Gary Hart (D) 1975–1986
Floyd K. Haskell (D) 1973–1978
Gordon Allot (R) 1955–1973
Peter H. Dominick (R) 1963–1975

Connecticut
Thomas J. Dodd (D) 1959–1971
Abraham Ribicoff (D) 1963–1980
Lowell P. Weicker Jr. (R) 1971–1989

Delaware
Joseph R. Biden Jr. (D) 1973–?
J. Caleb Boggs (R) 1961–1973
William V. Roth Jr. (R) 1971–2000
John J. Williams (R) 1947–1970

Florida
Lawton Chiles (D) 1971–1988
Spessard L. Holland (D) 1946–1971
Richard Stone (D) 1975–1980
Edward J. Gurney (R) 1969–1974

Georgia
David H. Gambrell (D) 1971–1973
Sam Nunn (D) 1973–1996
Richard B. Russell (D) 1933–1971
Herman E. Talmadge (D) 1957–1980

Hawaii
Daniel K. Inouye (D) 1963–?
Hiram L. Fong (R) 1959–1977

Idaho
Frank Church (D) 1957–1980
Len B. Jordan (R) 1962–1973
James A. McClure (R) 1973–1990

Illinois
Adlai E. Stevenson III (D) 1970–1980
Everett M. Dirksen (R) 1951–1969
Charles H. Percy (R) 1967–1984
Ralph T. Smith (R) 1969–1970

Indiana
Birch Bayh (D) 1963–1980
Vance Hartke (D) 1959–1977

Iowa
Dick Clark (D) 1973–1978
John C. Culver (D) 1975–?
Harold E. Hughes (D) 1969–1975
Jack Miller (R) 1961–1973

Kansas
Robert J. Dole (R) 1969–1996
James B. Pearson (R) 1962–1978

Kentucky
Wendell H. Ford (D) 1974–1998
Walter Huddleston (D) 1973–1984
Marlow W. Cook (R) 1968–1974
John Sherman Cooper (R) 1946–1949;
    1952–1955; 1956–1973

Louisiana
Allen J. Ellender (D) 1937–1972
Russell B. Long (D) 1948–1986

Maine
William D. Hathaway (D) 1973–1978
Edmund S. Muskie (D) 1959–1980
Margaret Chase Smith (R) 1949–1973

Maryland
Joseph D. Tydings (D) 1965–1971
James Glenn Beall Jr. (R) 1971–1977
Charles McC. Mathias Jr. (R)
    1969–1986

Massachusetts
Edward M. Kennedy (D) 1962–?
Edward W. Brooke (R) 1967–1978

Michigan
Philip A. Hart (D) 1959–1976
Robert P. Griffin (R) 1966–1970

Minnesota
Hubert H. Humphrey (D) 1949–1964;
    1971–1978
Eugene J. McCarthy (D) 1959–1971
Walter F. Mondale (D) 1964–1977

Mississippi
James O. Eastland (D) 1941;
    1943–1978
John Stennis (D) 1947–1988

Missouri
Thomas F. Eagleton (D) 1968–1986
Stuart Symington (D) 1953–1977

Montana
Michael J. Mansfield (D) 1953–1977
Lee Metcalf (D) 1961–1978

Nebraska
Carl T. Curtis (R) 1955–1978
Roman L. Hruska (R) 1954–1977

Nevada
Alan Bible (D) 1954–1974
Howard W. Cannon (D) 1959–1982
Paul Laxalt (R) 1975–1986

New Hampshire
John A. Durkin (D) 1975–1980
Thomas J. McIntyre (D) 1962–1978
Norris Cotton (R) 1954–1974; 1975

New Jersey
Harrison A. Williams Jr. (D) 1959–1982
Clifford P. Case (R) 1955–1978

New Mexico
Clinton P. Anderson (D) 1949–1973
Joseph M. Montoya (D) 1964–1977
Pete V. Domenici (R) 1973–?

New York
James L. Buckley (R) 1971–1977
Charles E. Goodell (R) 1968–1971
Jacob K. Javits (R) 1957–1980

North Carolina
Sam J. Ervin Jr. (D) 1954–1974
B. Everett Jordan (D) 1958–1973
Robert Morgan (D) 1975–1980
Jesse A. Helms (R) 1973–2002

North Dakota
Quentin N. Burdick (D) 1960–1992
Milton R. Young (R) 1945–1980

Ohio
John Glenn (D) 1974–1998
Howard M. Metzenbaum (D)
    1974–1994
Stephen M. Young (D) 1959–1971
William B. Saxbe (R) 1969–1974
Robert Taft Jr. (R) 1971–1977

Oklahoma
Fred R. Harris (D) 1964–1973
Dewey F. Bartlett (R) 1973–1978
Henry Bellmon (R) 1969–1980

Oregon
Mark O. Hatfield (R) 1967–1996
Robert W. Packwood (R) 1969–1996

Pennsylvania
Richard S. Schweiker (R) 1969–1980
Hugh Scott (R) 1959–1977

Rhode Island
John O. Pastore (D) 1950–1976
Claiborne Pell (D) 1961–1996
John Chafee (R) 1976–2000

South Carolina
Ernest F. Hollings (D) 1966–2004
Strom Thurmond (D) 1954–1956; 1956–
    1964; (R) 1964–2002

South Dakota
James Abourezk (D) 1973–1978
George McGovern (D) 1963–1980
Karl E. Mundt (R) 1948–1973

Tennessee
Albert Gore (D) 1953–1971
Howard H. Baker Jr. (R) 1967–1984
William E. Brock III (R) 1971–1977

Texas
Lloyd M. Bentsen Jr. (D) 1971–1994
Ralph Yarborough (D) 1957–1971
John G. Tower (R) 1961–1984

Utah
Frank E. Moss (D) 1959–1977
Wallace F. Bennett (R) 1951–1974
Edwin Jacob (Jake) Garn (R) 1974–1992

Vermont
Patrick J. Leahy (D) 1975–?
George D. Aiken (R) 1941–1975

Winston L. Prouty (R) 1959–1971
Robert T. Stafford (R) 1971–1988

Virginia
Harry F. Byrd Jr. (D) 1965–1971; (I) 1971–1982
William B. Spong Jr. (D) 1966–1973
William Lloyd Scott (R) 1973–1978

Washington
Henry M. Jackson (D) 1953–1982
Warren G. Magnuson (D) 1944–1980

West Virginia
Robert C. Byrd (D) 1959–?
Jennings Randolph (D) 1958–1984

Wisconsin
Gaylord Nelson (D) 1963–1980
William Proxmire (D) 1957–1988

Wyoming
Gale W. McGee (D) 1959–1977
Clifford P. Hansen (R) 1967–1978

GOVERNORS

Alabama
Albert P. Brewer (D) 1968–1971
George C. Wallace (D) 1963–1967; 1971–
    1979; 1983–1987

Alaska
Walter J. Hickel (R) 1966–1969
Keith H. Miller (R) 1969–1971
William A. Egan (D) 1959–1966;
    1971–1974
Jay Hammond (R) 1974–1982

Arizona
John R. (Jack) Williams (R)
    1967–1975
Raoul Castro (D) 1975–1977

Arkansas
Winthrop Rockefeller (R) 1967–1970
Dale Bumpers (D) 1970–1975
David Pryor (D) 1975–1979

California
Ronald Reagan (R) 1967–1975
Edmund G. Brown Jr. (D) 1975–1983

Colorado
John A. Love (R) 1962–1973
John Vanderhoof (R) 1973–1975
Richard D. Lamm (D) 1975–1987

Connecticut
John N. Dempsey (D) 1961–1971

Thomas J. Meskill (R) 1971–1975
Ella T. Grasso (D) 1975–1980

Delaware
Russell W. Peterson (R) 1969–1973
Sherman W. Tribbitt (D) 1973–1977

Florida
Claude R. Kirk Jr. (R) 1967–1971
Reubin Askew (D) 1971–1979

Georgia
Lester G. Maddox (D) 1967–1971
Jimmy Carter (D) 1971–1975
George Busbee (D) 1975–1983

Hawaii
John A. Burns (D) 1962–1975
George R. Ariyoshi (D) 1975–1986

Idaho
Don Samuelson (R) 1967–1971
Cecil D. Andrus (D) 1971–1977

Illinois
Richard B. Ogilvie (R) 1968–1973
Daniel Walker (D) 1973–1977

Indiana
Edgar D. Whitcomb (R) 1969–1973
Otis R. Bowen (R) 1973–1981

Iowa
Robert D. Ray (R) 1969–1983

Kansas
Robert B. Docking (D) 1967–1975
Robert F. Bennett (R) 1975–1979

Kentucky
Wendell H. Ford (D) 1971–1974
Louis B. Nunn (R) 1967–1971
Julian M. Carroll (D) 1975–1979

Louisiana
John J. McKeithen (D) 1967–1972
Edwin W. Edwards (D) 1972–1980, 1984–
1988; 1992–1996

Maine
Kenneth M. Curtis (D) 1967–1975
James Longley (I) 1975–1979

Maryland
Marvin Mandel (D) 1969–1979

Massachusetts
John A. Volpe (R) 1961–1963; 1965–1969
Francis W. Sargent (R) 1969–1975
Michael S. Dukakis (D) 1975–1979; 1983–1991

Michigan
William G. Miliken (R) 1969–1983

Minnesota
Harold LeVander (R) 1967–1971
Wendell R. Anderson (D) 1971–1977

Mississippi
John Bell Williams (D) 1968–1972
William L. Waller (D) 1972–1976
Charles C. Finch (D) 1976–1980

Missouri
Warren E. Hearnes (D) 1965–1973
Christopher S. Bond (R) 1973–1977

Montana
Forrest H. Anderson (D) 1969–1973
Thomas L. Judge (D) 1973–1981

Nebraska
Norbert T. Tiemann (R) 1967–1971
J. James Exon (D) 1971–1979

Nevada
Paul Laxalt (R) 1967–1971
Mike D. N. O'Callaghan (D) 1971–1979

New Hampshire
Walter R. Peterson Jr. (R) 1969–1973
Meldrim Thomson Jr. (R) 1973–1979

New Jersey
Richard J. Hughes (D) 1962–1970
William T. Cahill (R) 1970–1974
Brendan T. Byrne (D) 1974–1982

New Mexico
David F. Cargo (R) 1967–1971
Bruce King (D) 1971–1975
Jerry Apodaca (D) 1975–1979

New York
Nelson A. Rockefeller (R) 1959–1973
Malcolm Wilson (R) 1973–1975
Hugh L. Carey (D) 1975–1983

North Carolina
Robert W. Scott (D) 1969–1972
James E. Holshouser Jr. (R) 1973–1977

North Dakota
William L. Guy (D) 1961–1973
Arthur A. Link (D) 1973–1980

Ohio
James A. Rhodes (R) 1963–1971; 1975–1983
John J. Gilligan (D) 1971–1975

Oklahoma
Dewey F. Bartlett (R) 1967–1971
David Hall (D) 1971–1975
David Boren (D) 1975–1979

Oregon
Tom McCall (R) 1967–1975
Robert Straub (D) 1975–1979

Pennsylvania
Raymond P. Shafer (R) 1967–1971
Milton J. Shapp (D) 1971–1979

Rhode Island
Frank Licht (D) 1969–1973
Philip W. Noel (D) 1973–1977

South Carolina
Robert E. McNair (D) 1965–1971
John C. West (D) 1971–1975
James B. Edwards (R) 1975–1979

South Dakota
Frank Farrar (R) 1969–1970
Richard F. Kneip (D) 1971–1979

Tennessee
Buford Ellington (D) 1959–1963; 1967–1971
Winfield Dunn (R) 1971–1975
Ray Blanton (D) 1975–1979

Texas
Preston Smith (D) 1969–1973
Dolph Briscoe (D) 1973–1979

Utah
Calvin L. Rampton (D) 1965–1977

Vermont
Deanne C. Davis (R) 1969–1973
Thomas P. Salmon (D) 1973–1977

Virginia
Mills E. Godwin Jr. (D) 1966–1970; 1974–1978
Linwood Holton (R) 1970–1974

Washington
Daniel J. Evans (R) 1965–1977

West Virginia
Arch A. Moore Jr. (R) 1969–1977; 1985–1989

Wisconsin
Warren P. Knowles (R) 1964–1971
Patrick J. Lucey (D) 1971–1977

Wyoming
Stanley K. Hathaway (R) 1967–1975
Ed Herschler (D) 1975–1987

SELECTED PRIMARY DOCUMENTS

Nixon Documents

1. First Inaugural Address, January 20, 1969

2. Address to the Nation on Vietnam, May 14, 1969

3. Address to the Nation on the War in Vietnam ("silent majority" speech), November 3, 1969

4. First State of the Union Address, January 22, 1970

5. Statement about Desegregation of Elementary and Secondary Schools, March 24, 1970

6. Address to the Nation on the Situation in Southeast Asia ("pitiful, helpless giant" speech), April 30, 1970

7. Statement on Student Deaths at Kent State University, May 4, 1970

8. Address to the Nation on Economic Policy and Productivity, June 17, 1970

9. State of the Union Address, January 22, 1971

10. Statement to Congress on the Proposed Reorganization of the Executive Branch, March 25, 1971

11. Address to the Nation on the Situation in Southeast Asia, April 7, 1971

12. State of the Union Address, January 20, 1972

13. Speech to the People of the Soviet Union (Broadcast from the Grand Kremlin Palace, Moscow), May 28, 1972

14. Acceptance Speech to Republican National Convention, August 23, 1972

15. Second Inaugural Address, January 20, 1973

16. Address to Nation on Cease-Fire in Vietnam, January 23, 1973

17. Thirtieth Press Conference, January 31, 1973

18. Address to the Nation on Watergate, April 30, 1973

19. Statement on Watergate, May 22, 1973

20. Statement on Watergate, August 15, 1973

21. Introduction of Vice President-Designate Gerald R. Ford, October 12, 1973

22. Statement Regarding Presidential Recordings, October 19, 1973

23. Veto of War Powers Resolution, October 24, 1973

24. Address to the Nation Announcing Answer to the House Judiciary Committee Subpoena for Additional Presidential Tape Recordings, April 29, 1974

25. Resignation of the Presidency, August 8, 1974

Ford Documents

26. Inaugural Address, August 9, 1974

27. Address to Joint Session of Congress, August 12, 1974

28. First Press Conference, August 28, 1974

29. Remarks on Signing Proclamation Pardoning Richard M. Nixon, September 8, 1974

30. First State of the Union Address, January 15, 1975

31. Letter to the Speaker of the House and the President Pro Tempore of the Senate Reporting on United States Actions in the Recovery of the SS *Mayaguez*, May 15, 1975

32. Second State of the Union Address, January 19, 1976

33. Acceptance Speech to Republican National Convention, August 19, 1976

34. Remarks to Press on Election Night, November 3, 1976

35. Third State of the Union Address, January 12, 1977

All documents were taken from Public Papers of the Presidents of the United States: Richard Nixon 1969–1974; Gerald R. Ford, 1974–1977. The Presidency Project. Available online. URL: http://www.presidency.ucsb.edu/ws/.

Nixon Documents

1. First Inaugural Address
January 20, 1969

Senator Dirksen, Mr. Chief Justice, Mr. Vice president, President Johnson, Vice president Humphrey, my fellow Americans—and my fellow citizens of the world community:

I ask you to share with me today the majesty of this moment. In the orderly transfer of power, we celebrate the unity that keeps us free.

Each moment in history is a fleeting time, precious and unique. But some stand out as moments of beginning, in which courses are set that shape decades or centuries.

This can be such a moment.

Forces now are converging that make possible, for the first time, the hope that many of man's deepest aspirations can at last be realized. The spiraling pace of change allows us to contemplate, within our own lifetime, advances that once would have taken centuries.

In throwing wide the horizons of space, we have discovered new horizons on earth.

For the first time, because the people of the world want peace, and the leaders of the world are afraid of war, the times are on the side of peace.

Eight years from now America will celebrate its 200th anniversary as a nation. Within the lifetime of most people now living, mankind will celebrate that great new year which comes only once in a thousand years—the beginning of the third millennium.

What kind of a nation we will be, what kind of a world we will live in, whether we shape the future in the image of our hopes, is ours to determine by our actions and our choices.

The greatest honor history can bestow is the title of peacemaker. This honor now beckons America—the chance to help lead the world at last out of the valley of turmoil and onto that high ground of peace that man has dreamed of since the dawn of civilization.

If we succeed, generations to come will say of us now living that we mastered our moment, that we helped make the world safe for mankind.

This is our summons to greatness.

I believe the American people are ready to answer this call.

The second third of this century has been a time of proud achievement. We have made enormous strides in science and industry and agriculture. We have shared our wealth more broadly than ever. We have learned at last to manage a modern economy to assure its continued growth.

We have given freedom new reach. We have begun to make its promise real for black as well as for white.

We see the hope of tomorrow in the youth of today. I know America's youth. I believe in them. We can be proud that they are better educated, more committed, more passionately driven by conscience than any generation in our history.

No people has ever been so close to the achievement of a just and abundant society, or so possessed of the will to achieve it. And because our strengths are so great, we can afford to appraise our weaknesses with candor and to approach them with hope.

Standing in this same place a third of a century ago, Franklin Delano Roosevelt addressed a nation ravaged by depression and gripped in fear. He could say in surveying the Nation's troubles: "They concern, thank God, only material things." Our crisis today is in reverse.

We find ourselves rich in goods, but ragged in spirit; reaching with magnificent precision for the moon, but falling into raucous discord on earth.

We are caught in war, wanting peace. We are torn by division, wanting unity. We see around us empty fives, wanting fulfillment. We see tasks that need doing, waiting for hands to do them.

To a crisis of the spirit, we need an answer of the spirit. And to find that answer, we need only look within ourselves.

When we listen to "the better angels of our nature," we find that they celebrate the simple things, the basic things—such as goodness, decency, love, kindness.

Greatness comes in simple trappings. The simple things are the ones most needed today if we are to surmount what divides us, and cement what unites us.

To lower our voices would be a simple thing.

In these difficult years, America has suffered from a fever of words; from inflated rhetoric that promises more than it can deliver; from angry rhetoric that fans discontents into hatreds; from bombastic rhetoric that postures instead of persuading.

We cannot learn from one another until we stop shouting at one another—until we speak quietly enough so that our words can be heard as well as our voices.

For its part, government will listen. We will strive to listen in new ways—to the voices of quiet anguish, the voices that speak without words, the voices of the heart—to the injured voices, the anxious voices, the voices that have despaired of being heard.

Those who have been left out, we will try to bring in.

Those left behind, we will help to catch up.

For all of our people, we will set as our goal the decent order that makes progress possible and our lives secure.

As we reach toward our hopes, our task is to build on what has gone before—not turning away from the old, but turning toward the new.

In this past third of a century, government has passed more laws, spent more money, initiated more programs than in all our previous history.

In pursuing our goals of full employment, better housing, excellence in education; in rebuilding our cities and improving our rural areas; in protecting our environment and enhancing the quality of life—in all these and more, we will and must press urgently forward.

We shall plan now for the day when our wealth can be transferred from the destruction of war abroad to the urgent needs of our people at home.

The American dream does not come to those who fall asleep.

But we are approaching the limits of what government alone can do.

Our greatest need now is to reach beyond government, to enlist the legions of the concerned and the committed.

What has to be done, has to be done by government and people together or it will not be done at all. The lesson of past agony is that without the people we can do nothing—with the people we can do everything.

To match the magnitude of our tasks, we need the energies of our people—enlisted not only in grand enterprises, but more importantly in those small, splendid efforts that make headlines in the neighborhood newspaper instead of the national journal.

With these, we can build a great cathedral of the spirit—each of us raising it one stone at a time, as he reaches out to his neighbor, helping, caring, doing.

I do not offer a life of uninspiring ease. I do not call for a life of grim sacrifice. I ask you to join in a high adventure—one as rich as humanity itself, and exciting as the times we live in.

The essence of freedom is that each of us shares in the shaping of his own destiny.

Until he has been part of a cause larger than himself, no man is truly whole.

The way to fulfillment is in the use of our talents. We achieve nobility in the spirit that inspires that use.

As we measure what can be done, we shall promise only what we know we can produce;

but as we chart our goals, we shall be lifted by our dreams.

No man can be fully free while his neighbor is not. To go forward at all is to go forward together.

This means black and white together, as one nation, not two. The laws have caught up with our conscience. What remains is to give life to what is in the law: to insure at last that as all are born equal in dignity before God, all are born equal in dignity before man.

As we learn to go forward together at home, let us also seek to go forward together with all mankind.

Let us take as our goal: Where peace is unknown, make it welcome; where peace is fragile, make it strong; where peace is temporary, make it permanent.

After a period of confrontation, we are entering an era of negotiation.

Let all nations know that during this administration our lines of communication will be open.

We seek an open world—open to ideas, open to the exchange of goods and people—a world in which no people, great or small, will live in angry isolation.

We cannot expect to make everyone our friend, but we can try to make no one our enemy.

Those who would be our adversaries, we invite to a peaceful competition—not in conquering territory or extending dominion, but in enriching the life of man.

As we explore the reaches of space, let us go to the new worlds together—not as new worlds to be conquered, but as a new adventure to be shared.

With those who are willing to join, let us cooperate to reduce the burden of arms, to strengthen the structure of peace, to lift up the poor and the hungry.

But to all those who would be tempted by weakness, let us leave no doubt that we will be as strong as we need to be for as long as we need to be.

Over the past 90 years, since I first came to this Capital as a freshman Congressman, I have visited most of the nations of the world. I have come to know the leaders of the world and the great forces, the hatreds, the fears that divide the world.

I know that peace does not come through wishing for it—that there is no substitute for days and even years of patient and prolonged diplomacy.

I also know the people of the world.

I have seen the hunger of a homeless child, the pain of a man wounded in battle, the grief of a mother who has lost her son. I know these have no ideology, no race.

I know America. I know the heart of America is good.

I speak from my own heart, and the heart of my country, the deep concern we have for those who suffer and those who sorrow.

I have taken an oath today in the presence of God and my countrymen to uphold and defend the Constitution of the United States. To that oath I now add this sacred commitment: I shall consecrate my Office, my energies, and all the wisdom I can summon to the cause of peace among nations.

Let this message be heard by strong and weak alike:

The peace we seek the peace we seek to win—is not victory over any other people, but the peace that comes "with healing in its wings"; with compassion for those who have suffered; with understanding for those who have opposed us; with the opportunity for all the peoples of this earth to choose their own destiny.

Only a few short weeks ago we shared the glory of man's first sight of the world as God sees it, as a single sphere reflecting light in the darkness.

As the Apollo astronauts flew over the moon's gray surface on Christmas Eve, they spoke to us of the beauty of earth—and in that voice so clear across the lunar distance, we heard them invoke God's blessing on its goodness.

In that moment, their view from the moon moved poet Archibald MacLeish to write: "To see the earth as it truly is, small and blue and beautiful in that eternal silence where it floats, is to see ourselves as riders on the earth together, brothers on that bright loveliness in the eternal cold—brothers who know now they are truly brothers."

In that moment of surpassing technological triumph, men turned their thoughts toward home and humanity—seeing in that far perspective that man's destiny on earth is not divisible; telling us that however far we reach into the cosmos, our destiny lies not in the stars but on earth itself, in our own hands, in our own hearts.

We have endured a long night of the American spirit. But as our eyes catch the dimness of the first rays of dawn, let us not curse the remaining dark. Let us gather the light.

Our destiny offers not the cup of despair, but the chalice of opportunity. So let us seize it not in fear, but in gladness—and "riders on the earth together," let us go forward, firm in our faith, steadfast in our purpose, cautious of the dangers, but sustained by our confidence in the will of God and the promise of man.

2. Address to the Nation on Vietnam
May 14, 1969

Good evening, my fellow Americans:

I have asked for this television time tonight to report to you on our most difficult and urgent problem—the war in Vietnam.

Since I took office 4 months ago, nothing has taken so much of my time and energy as the search for a way to bring lasting peace to Vietnam. I know that some believe that I should have ended the war immediately after the inauguration by simply ordering our forces home from Vietnam.

This would have been the easy thing to do. It might have been a popular thing to do. But I would have betrayed my solemn responsibility as President of the United States if I had done so.

I want to end this war. The American people want to end this war. The people of South Vietnam want to end this war. But we want to end it permanently so that the younger brothers of our soldiers in Vietnam will not have to fight in the future in another Vietnam someplace else in the world.

The fact that there is no easy way to end the war does not mean that we have no choice but to let the war drag on with no end in sight.

For 4 years American boys have been fighting and dying in Vietnam. For 12 months our negotiators have been talking with the other side in Paris. And yet the fighting goes on. The destruction continues. Brave men still die.

The time has come for some new initiatives. Repeating the old formulas and the tired rhetoric of the past is not enough. When Americans are risking their lives in war, it is the responsibility of their leaders to take some risks for peace.

I would like to report to you tonight on some of the things we have been doing in the past 4 months to bring true peace, and then I would like to make some concrete proposals to speed that day.

Our first step began before inauguration. This was to launch an intensive review of every aspect of the Nation's Vietnam policy. We accepted nothing on faith, we challenged every assumption and every statistic. We made a systematic, serious examination of all the alternatives open to us. We carefully considered recommendations offered both by critics and supporters of past policies.

From the review, it became clear at once that the new administration faced a set of immediate operational problems:

—The other side was preparing for a new offensive.

—There was a wide gulf of distrust between Washington and Saigon.

—In 8 months of talks in Paris, there had been no negotiations directly concerned with a final settlement.

Therefore, we moved on several fronts at once.

We frustrated the attack which was launched in late February. As a result, the North Vietnamese and the Vietcong failed to achieve their military objectives.

We restored a close working relationship with Saigon. In the resulting atmosphere of mutual confidence, President Thieu and his Government have taken important initiatives in the search for a settlement.

We speeded up the strengthening of the South Vietnamese forces. I am glad to report tonight that, as a result, General Abrams told me on Monday that progress in the training program had been excellent and that, apart from any developments that may occur in the negotiations in Paris, the time is approaching when South Vietnamese forces will be able to take over some of the fighting fronts now being manned by Americans.

In weighing alternate courses, we have had to recognize that the situation as it exists today is far different from what it was 2 years ago or 4 years ago or 10 years ago.

One difference is that we no longer have the choice of not intervening. We have crossed that bridge. There are now more than a half million American troops in Vietnam and 35,000 Americans have lost their lives.

We can have honest debate about whether we should have entered the war in Vietnam. We can have honest debate about how the war has been conducted. But the urgent question today is what to do now that we are there.

Against that background, let me discuss first, what we have rejected, and second, what we are prepared to accept.

We have ruled out attempting to impose a purely military solution on the battlefield.

We have also ruled out either a one-sided withdrawal from Vietnam, or the acceptance in Paris of terms that would amount to a disguised American defeat.

When we assumed the burden of helping defend South Vietnam, millions of South Vietnamese men, women, and children placed their trust in us. To abandon them now would risk a massacre that would shock and dismay everyone in the world who values human life.

Abandoning the South Vietnamese people, however, would jeopardize more than lives in South Vietnam. It would threaten our long-term hopes for peace in the world. A great nation cannot renege on its pledges. A great nation must be worthy of trust.

When it comes to maintaining peace, "prestige" is not an empty word. I am not speaking of false pride or bravado—they should have no place in our policies. I speak rather of the respect that one nation has for another's integrity in defending its principles and meeting its obligations.

If we simply abandoned our effort in Vietnam, the cause of peace might not survive the damage that would be done to other nations' confidence in our reliability.

Another reason for not withdrawing unilaterally stems from debates within the Communist world between those who argue for a policy of confrontation with the United States, and those who argue against it.

If Hanoi were to succeed in taking over South Vietnam by force—even after the power of the United States had been engaged—it would greatly strengthen those leaders who scorn negotiation, who advocate aggression, who minimize the risks of confrontation with the United States. It would bring peace now but it would enormously increase the danger of a bigger war later.

If we are to move successfully from an era of confrontation to an era of negotiation, then we have to demonstrate—at the point at which confrontation is being tested—that confrontation with the United States is costly and unrewarding.

Almost without exception, the leaders of non-Communist Asia have told me that they would consider a one-sided American withdrawal from Vietnam to be a threat to the security of their own nations.

In determining what choices would be acceptable, we have to understand our essential objective in Vietnam: What we want is very little, but very fundamental. We seek the opportunity for the South Vietnamese people to determine their own political future without outside interference.

Let me put it plainly: What the United States wants for South Vietnam is not the important thing. What North Vietnam wants for South Vietnam is not the important thing. What is important is what the people of South Vietnam want for South Vietnam.

The United States has suffered over a million casualties in four wars in this century. Whatever faults we may have as a nation, we have asked nothing for ourselves in return for those sacrifices. We have been generous toward those whom we have fought. We have helped our former foes as well as our friends in the task of reconstruction. We are proud of this record, and we bring the same attitude in our search for a settlement in Vietnam.

In this spirit, let me be explicit about several points:

—We seek no bases in Vietnam.

—We seek no military ties.

—We are willing to agree to neutrality for South Vietnam if that is what the South Vietnamese people freely choose.

—We believe there should be an opportunity for full participation in the political life of South Vietnam by all political elements that are prepared to do so without the use of force or intimidation.

—We are prepared to accept any government in South Vietnam that results from the free choice of the South Vietnamese people themselves.

—We have no intention of imposing any form of government upon the people of South Vietnam, nor will we be a party to such coercion.

—We have no objection to reunification, if that turns out to be what the people of South Vietnam and the people of North Vietnam want; we ask only that the decision reflect the free choice of the people concerned.

At this point, I would like to add a personal word based on many visits to South Vietnam over the past 5 years. This is the most difficult war in America's history, fought against a ruthless enemy. I am proud of our men who have carried the terrible burden of this war with dignity and courage, despite the division and opposition to the war in the United States. History will record that never have America's fighting men fought more bravely for more unselfish goals than our men in Vietnam. It is our responsibility to see that they have not fought in vain.

In pursuing our limited objective, we insist on no rigid diplomatic formula. Peace could be achieved by a formal negotiated settlement. Peace could be achieved by an informal understanding, provided that the understanding is clear, and that there were adequate assurances that it would be observed. Peace on paper is not as important as peace in fact.

And so this brings us to the matter of negotiations.

We must recognize that peace in Vietnam cannot be achieved overnight. A war that has raged for many years will require detailed negotiations and cannot be settled by a single stroke.

What kind of a settlement will permit the South Vietnamese people to determine freely their own political future? Such a settlement will require the withdrawal of all non-South Vietnamese forces, including our own, from South Vietnam, and procedures for political choice that give each significant group in

South Vietnam a real opportunity to participate in the political life of the nation.

To implement these principles, I reaffirm now our willingness to withdraw our forces on a specified timetable. We ask only that North Vietnam withdraw its forces from South Vietnam, Cambodia, and Laos into North Vietnam, also in accordance with a timetable.

We include Cambodia and Laos to ensure that these countries would not be used as bases for a renewed war.

Our offer provides for a simultaneous start on withdrawal by both sides, for agreement on a mutually acceptable timetable, and for the withdrawal to be accomplished quickly.

The North Vietnamese delegates have been saying in Paris that political issues should be discussed along with military issues, and that there must be a political settlement in the South. We do not dispute this, but the military withdrawal involves outside forces, and can, therefore, be properly negotiated by North Vietnam and the United States, with the concurrence of its allies.

The political settlement is an internal matter which ought to be decided among the South Vietnamese themselves, and not imposed by outsiders. However, if our presence at these political negotiations would be helpful, and if the South Vietnamese concerned agreed, we would be willing to participate, along with the representatives of Hanoi, if that also were desired.

Recent statements by President Thieu have gone far toward opening the way to a political settlement. He has publicly declared his Government's willingness to discuss a political solution with the National Liberation Front, and has offered free elections. This was a dramatic step forward, a reasonable offer that could lead to a settlement. The South Vietnamese Government has offered to talk without preconditions. I believe the other side should also be willing to talk without preconditions.

The South Vietnamese Government recognizes, as we do, that a settlement must permit all persons and groups that are prepared to renounce the use of force to participate freely in the political life of South Vietnam. To be effective, such a settlement would require two things: first, a process that would allow the South Vietnamese people to express their choice, and, second, a guarantee that this process would be a fair one.

We do not insist on a particular form of guarantee. The important thing is that the guarantees should have the confidence of the South Vietnamese people, and that they should be broad enough and strong enough to protect the interests of all major South Vietnamese groups.

This, then, is the outline of the settlement that we seek to negotiate in Paris. Its basic terms are very simple: mutual withdrawal of non-South Vietnamese forces from South Vietnam and free choice for the people of South Vietnam. I believe that the long-term interests of peace require that we insist on no less, and that the realities of the situation require that we seek no more.

And now, to make very concrete what I have said, I propose the following specific measures which seem to me consistent with the principles of all parties. These proposals are made on the basis of full consultation with President Thieu.

—As soon as agreement can be reached, all non-South Vietnamese forces would begin withdrawals from South Vietnam.

—Over a period of 12 months, by agreed-upon stages, the major portions of all U.S., allied, and other non-South Vietnamese forces would be withdrawn. At the end of this 12-month period, the remaining U.S., allied, and other non-South Vietnamese forces would move into designated base areas and would not engage in combat operations.

—The remaining U.S. and allied forces would complete their withdrawals as the remaining North Vietnamese forces were withdrawn and returned to North Vietnam.

—An international supervisory body, acceptable to both sides, would be created for the purpose of verifying withdrawals, and for any other purposes agreed upon between the two sides.

—This international body would begin operating in accordance with an agreed timetable and would participate in arranging supervised cease-fires in Vietnam.

—As soon as possible after the international body was functioning, elections would be held under agreed procedures and under the supervision of the international body.

—Arrangements would be made for the release of prisoners of war on both sides at the earliest possible time.

—All parties would agree to observe the Geneva Accords of 1954 regarding South Vietnam and Cambodia, and the Laos Accords of 1962.

I believe this proposal for peace is realistic, and takes account of the legitimate interests of all concerned. It is consistent with President Thieu's six points. It can accommodate the various programs put forth by the other side. We and the Government of South Vietnam are prepared to discuss the details with the other side.

Secretary Rogers is now in Saigon and he will be discussing with President Thieu how, together, we may put forward these proposed measures most usefully in Paris. He will, as well, be consulting with our other Asian allies on these measures while on his Asian trip. However, I would stress that these proposals are not offered on a take-it-or-leave-it basis. We are quite willing to consider other approaches consistent with our principles.

We are willing to talk about anybody's program—Hanoi's 4 points, the NLF's [National Liberation Front's] 10 points—provided it can be made consistent with the very few basic principles I have set forth here tonight.

Despite our disagreement with several of its points, we welcome the fact that the NLF has put forward its first comprehensive program. We are studying that program carefully. However, we cannot ignore the fact that immediately after the

offer, the scale of enemy attacks stepped up and American casualties in Vietnam increased.

Let me make one point clear. If the enemy wants peace with the United States, that is not the way to get it.

I have set forth a peace program tonight which is generous in its terms. I have indicated our willingness to consider other proposals. But no greater mistake could be made than to confuse flexibility with weakness or of being reasonable with lack of resolution. I must also make clear, in all candor, that if the needless suffering continues, this will affect other decisions. Nobody has anything to gain by delay.

Reports from Hanoi indicate that the enemy has given up hope for a military victory in South Vietnam, but is counting on a collapse of American will in the United States. There could be no greater error in judgment.

Let me be quite blunt. Our fighting men are not going to be worn down; our mediators are not going to be talked down; and our allies are not going to be let down.

My fellow Americans, I have seen the ugly face of war in Vietnam. I have seen the wounded in field hospitals—American boys, South Vietnamese boys, North Vietnamese boys. They were different in many ways—the color of their skins, their religions, their races; some were enemies; some were friends.

But the differences were small, compared with how they were alike. They were brave men, and they were so young. Their lives—their dreams for the future—had been shattered by a war over which they had no control.

With all the moral authority of the Office which I hold, I say that America could have no greater and prouder role than to help to end this war in a way which will bring nearer that day in which we can have a world order in which people can live together in peace and friendship.

I do not criticize those who disagree with me on the conduct of our peace negotiations. And I do not ask unlimited patience from a people whose hopes for peace have too often been raised and then cruelly dashed over the past 4 years.

I have tried to present the facts about Vietnam with complete honesty, and I shall continue to do so in my reports to the American people.

Tonight, all I ask is that you consider these facts, and, whatever our differences, that you support a program which can lead to a peace we can live with and a peace we can be proud of. Nothing could have a greater effect in convincing the enemy that he should negotiate in good faith than to see the American people united behind a generous and reasonable peace offer.

In my campaign for the Presidency, I pledged to end this war in a way that would increase our chances to win true and lasting peace in Vietnam, in the Pacific, and in the world. I am determined to keep that pledge. If I fail to do so, I expect the American people to hold me accountable for that failure.

But while I will never raise false expectations, my deepest hope, as I speak to you tonight, is that we shall be able to look back on this day, at that critical turning point when American initiative moved us off dead center, and forward to the time when this war would be brought to an end and when we shall be able to devote the unlimited energies and dedication of the American people to the exciting challenges of peace.

Thank you and good night.

3. Address to the Nation on the War in Vietnam ("silent majority" speech) November 3, 1969

Good evening, my fellow Americans:

Tonight I want to talk to you on a subject of deep concern to all Americans and to many people in all parts of the world—the war in Vietnam.

I believe that one of the reasons for the deep division about Vietnam is that many Americans have lost confidence in what their Government has told them about our policy. The American people cannot and should not be asked to support a policy which involves the overriding issues of war and peace unless they know the truth about that policy.

Tonight, therefore, I would like to answer some of the questions that I know are on the minds of many of you listening to me.

How and why did America get involved in Vietnam in the first place?

How has this administration changed the policy of the previous administration?

What has really happened in the negotiations in Paris and on the battlefront in Vietnam?

What choices do we have if we are to end the war?

What are the prospects for peace?

Now, let me begin by describing the situation I found when I was inaugurated on January 20.

—The war had been going on for 4 years.

—31,000 Americans had been killed in action.

—The training program for the South Vietnamese was behind schedule.

—540,000 Americans were in Vietnam with no plans to reduce the number.

—No progress had been made at the negotiations in Paris and the United States had not put forth a comprehensive peace proposal.

—The war was causing deep division at home and criticism from many of our friends as well as our enemies abroad.

In view of these circumstances there were some who urged that I end the war at once by ordering the immediate withdrawal of all American forces.

From a political standpoint this would have been a popular and easy course to follow. After all, we became involved in the war while my predecessor was in office. I could blame the defeat which would be the result of my action on him and come out as the peacemaker. Some put it to me quite bluntly: This was the only way to avoid allowing Johnson's war to become Nixon's war.

But I had a greater obligation than to think only of the years of my administration and of the next election. I had to think of the effect of my decision on the next generation and on the future of peace and freedom in America and in the world.

Let us all understand that the question before us is not whether some Americans are for peace and some Americans are against peace. The question at issue is not whether Johnson's war becomes Nixon's war.

The great question is: How can we win America's peace?

Well, let us turn now to the fundamental issue. Why and how did the United States become involved in Vietnam in the first place?

Fifteen years ago North Vietnam, with the logistical support of Communist China and the Soviet Union, launched a campaign to impose a Communist government on South Vietnam by instigating and supporting a revolution.

In response to the request of the Government of South Vietnam, President Eisenhower sent economic aid and military equipment to assist the people of South Vietnam in their efforts to prevent a Communist takeover. Seven years ago, President Kennedy sent 16,000 military personnel to Vietnam as combat advisers. Four years ago, President Johnson sent American combat forces to South Vietnam.

Now, many believe that President Johnson's decision to send American combat forces to South Vietnam was wrong. And many others— I among them—have been strongly critical of the way the war has been conducted.

But the question facing us today is: Now that we are in the war, what is the best way to end it?

In January I could only conclude that the precipitate withdrawal of American forces from Vietnam would be a disaster not only for South Vietnam but for the United States and for the cause of peace.

For the South Vietnamese, our precipitate withdrawal would inevitably allow the Communists to repeat the massacres which followed their takeover in the North 15 years before.

—They then murdered more than 50,000 people and hundreds of thousands more died in slave labor camps.

—We saw a prelude of what would happen in South Vietnam when the Communists entered the city of Hue last year. During their brief rule there, there was a bloody reign of terror in which 3,000 civilians were clubbed, shot to death, and buried in mass graves.

—With the sudden collapse of our support, these atrocities of Hue would become the nightmare of the entire nation—and particularly for the million and a half Catholic refugees who fled to South Vietnam when the Communists took over in the North. For the United States, this first defeat in our Nation's history would result in a collapse of confidence in American leadership, not only in Asia but throughout the world.

Three American Presidents have recognized the great stakes involved in Vietnam and understood what had to be done.

In 1963, President Kennedy, with his characteristic eloquence and clarity, said: "we want to see a stable government there, carrying on a struggle to maintain its national independence."

"We believe strongly in that. We are not going to withdraw from that effort. In my opinion, for us to withdraw from that effort would mean a collapse not only of South Viet-Nam, but Southeast Asia. So we are going to stay there."

President Eisenhower and President Johnson expressed the same conclusion during their terms of office.

For the future of peace, precipitate withdrawal would thus be a disaster of immense magnitude.

—A nation cannot remain great if it betrays its allies and lets down its friends.

—Our defeat and humiliation in South Vietnam without question would promote recklessness in the councils of those great powers who have not yet abandoned their goals of world conquest.

—This would spark violence wherever our commitments help maintain the peace—in the Middle East, in Berlin, eventually even in the Western Hemisphere.

Ultimately, this would cost more lives. It would not bring peace; it would bring more war.

For these reasons, I rejected the recommendation that I should end the war by immediately withdrawing all of our forces. I chose instead to change American policy on both the negotiating front and battlefront.

In order to end a war fought on many fronts, I initiated a pursuit for peace on many fronts.

In a television speech on May 14, in a speech before the United Nations, and on a number of other occasions I set forth our peace proposals in great detail.

—We have offered the complete withdrawal of all outside forces within 1 year.

—We have proposed a cease-fire under international supervision.

—We have offered free elections under international supervision with the Communists participating in the organization and conduct of the elections as an organized political force. And the Saigon Government has pledged to accept the result of the elections.

We have not put forth our proposals on a take-it-or-leave-it basis. We have indicated that we are willing to discuss the proposals that have been put forth by the other side. We have declared that anything is negotiable except the fight of the people of South Vietnam to determine their own future. At the Paris peace conference, Ambassador Lodge has demonstrated our flexibility and good faith in 40 public meetings.

Hanoi has refused even to discuss our proposals. They demand our unconditional acceptance of their terms, which are that we withdraw all American forces immediately and unconditionally and that we overthrow the Government of South Vietnam as we leave.

We have not limited our peace initiatives to public forums and public statements. I recognized, in January, that a long and bitter war like this usually cannot be settled in a public forum. That is why in addition to the public statements and negotiations I have explored every possible private avenue that might lead to a settlement.

Tonight I am taking the unprecedented step of disclosing to you some of our other initiatives for peace—initiatives we undertook privately and secretly because we thought we thereby might open a door which publicly would be closed.

I did not wait for my inauguration to begin my quest for peace.

—Soon after my election, through an individual who is directly in contact on a personal basis with the leaders of North Vietnam, I made two private offers for a rapid, comprehensive settlement. Hanoi's replies called in effect for our surrender before negotiations.

—Since the Soviet Union furnishes most of the military equipment for North Vietnam, Secretary of State Rogers, my Assistant for National Security Affairs, Dr. Kissinger, Ambassador Lodge, and I, personally, have met on a number of occasions with representatives of the Soviet Government to enlist their assistance in getting meaningful negotiations started. In addition, we have had extended discussions directed toward that same end with representatives of other governments which have diplomatic relations with North Vietnam. None of these initiatives have to date produced results.

—In mid-July, I became convinced that it was necessary to make a major move to break the deadlock in the Paris talks. I spoke directly in this office, where I am now sitting, with an individual who had known Ho Chi Minh [president of the Democratic Republic of Vietnam] on a personal basis for 25 years. Through him I sent a letter to Ho Chi Minh. I did this outside of the usual diplomatic channels with the hope that with the necessity of making statements for propaganda removed, there might be constructive progress toward bringing the war to an end. Let me read from that letter to you now.

"Dear Mr. President:"

"I realize that it is difficult to communicate meaningfully across the gulf of four years of war. But precisely because of this gulf, I wanted to take this opportunity to reaffirm in all solemnity my desire to work for a just peace. I deeply believe that the war in Vietnam has gone on too long and delay in bringing it to an end can benefit no one—least of all the people of Vietnam. . . ."

"The time has come to move forward at the conference table toward an early resolution of this tragic war. You will find us forthcoming and open-minded in a common effort to bring the blessings of peace to the brave people of Vietnam. Let history record that at this critical juncture, both sides turned their face toward peace rather than toward conflict and war."

I received Ho Chi Minh's reply on August 30, 3 days before his death. It simply reiterated the public position North Vietnam had taken at Paris and flatly rejected my initiative.

The full text of both letters is being released to the press.

—In addition to the public meetings that I have referred to, Ambassador Lodge has met with Vietnam's chief negotiator in Paris in 11 private sessions.

—We have taken other significant initiatives which must remain secret to keep open some channels of communication which may still prove to be productive. But the effect of all the public, private, and secret negotiations which have been undertaken since the bombing halt a year ago and since this administration came into office on January 20, can be summed up in one sentence: No progress whatever has been made except agreement on the shape of the bargaining table. Well now, who is at fault?

It has become clear that the obstacle in negotiating an end to the war is not the President of the United States. It is not the South Vietnamese Government.

The obstacle is the other side's absolute refusal to show the least willingness to join us in seeking a just peace. And it will not do so while it is convinced that all it has to do is to wait for our next concession, and our next concession after that one, until it gets everything it wants.

There can now be no longer any question that progress in negotiation depends only on Hanoi's deciding to negotiate, to negotiate seriously.

I realize that this report on our efforts on the diplomatic front is discouraging to the American people, but the American people are entitled to know the truth—the bad news as well as the good news—where the lives of our young men are involved.

Now let me turn, however, to a more encouraging report on another front.

At the time we launched our search for peace I recognized we might not succeed in bringing an end to the war through negotiation. I, therefore, put into effect another plan to bring peace—a plan which will bring the war to an end regardless of what happens on the negotiating front.

It is in line with a major shift in U.S. foreign policy which I described in my press conference at Guam on July 25. Let me briefly explain what has been described as the Nixon Doctrine—a policy which not only will help end the war in Vietnam, but which is an essential element of our program to prevent future Vietnams.

We Americans are a do-it-yourself people. We are an impatient people. Instead of teaching someone else to do a job, we like to do it ourselves. And this trait has been carried over into our foreign policy.

In Korea and again in Vietnam, the United States furnished most of the money, most of the arms, and most of the men to help the people of those countries defend their freedom against Communist aggression.

Before any American troops were committed to Vietnam, a leader of another Asian country expressed this opinion to me when I was traveling in Asia as a private citizen. He said: "When you are trying to assist another nation defend its freedom, U.S. policy should be to help them fight the war but not to fight the war for them."

Well, in accordance with this wise counsel, I laid down in Guam three principles as guidelines for future American policy toward Asia:

—First, the United States will keep all of its treaty commitments.

—Second, we shall provide a shield if a nuclear power threatens the freedom of a nation allied with us or of a nation whose survival we consider vital to our security.

—Third, in cases involving other types of aggression, we shall furnish military and economic assistance when requested in accordance with our treaty commitments. But we shall look to the nation directly threatened to assume the primary responsibility of providing the manpower for its defense.

After I announced this policy, I found that the leaders of the Philippines, Thailand, Vietnam, South Korea, and other nations which might be threatened by Communist aggression, welcomed this new direction in American foreign policy.

The defense of freedom is everybody's business—not just America's business. And it is particularly the responsibility of the people whose freedom is threatened. In the previous administration, we Americanized the war in Vietnam. In this administration, we are Vietnamizing the search for peace.

The policy of the previous administration not only resulted in our assuming the primary responsibility for fighting the war, but even more significantly did not adequately stress the goal of strengthening the South Vietnamese so that they could defend themselves when we left.

The Vietnamization plan was launched following Secretary Laird's visit to Vietnam in March. Under the plan, I ordered first a substantial increase in the training and equipment of South Vietnamese forces.

In July, on my visit to Vietnam, I changed General Abrams' orders so that they were consistent with the objectives of our new policies. Under the new orders, the primary mission of our troops is to enable the South Vietnamese forces to assume the full responsibility for the security of South Vietnam.

Our air operations have been reduced by over 20 percent.

And now we have begun to see the results of this long overdue change in American policy in Vietnam.

—After 5 years of Americans going into Vietnam, we are finally bringing American men home. By December 15, over 60,000 men will have been withdrawn from South Vietnam including 20 percent of all of our combat forces.

—The South Vietnamese have continued to gain in strength. As a result they have been able to take over combat responsibilities from our American troops.

Two other significant developments have occurred since this administration took office.

—Enemy infiltration, infiltration which is essential if they are to launch a major attack, over the last 3 months is less than 20 percent of what it was over the same period last year.

—Most important—United States casualties have declined during the last 2 months to the lowest point in 3 years.

Let me now turn to our program for the future.

We have adopted a plan which we have worked out in cooperation with the South Vietnamese for the complete withdrawal of all U.S. combat ground forces, and their replacement by South Vietnamese forces on an orderly scheduled timetable. This withdrawal will be made from strength and not from weakness. As South Vietnamese forces become stronger, the rate of American withdrawal can become greater.

I have not and do not intend to announce the timetable for our program. And there are obvious reasons for this decision which I am sure you will understand. As I have indicated on several occasions, the rate of withdrawal will depend on developments on three fronts.

One of these is the progress which can be or might be made in the Paris talks. An announcement of a fixed timetable for our withdrawal would completely remove any incentive for the enemy to negotiate an agreement. They would simply wait until our forces had withdrawn and then move in.

The other two factors on which we will base our withdrawal decisions are the level of enemy activity and the progress of the training programs of the South Vietnamese forces. And I am glad to be able to report tonight progress on both of these fronts has been greater than we anticipated when we started the program in June for withdrawal. As a result, our timetable for withdrawal is more optimistic now than when we made our first estimates in June. Now, this clearly demonstrates why it is not wise to be frozen in on a fixed timetable.

We must retain the flexibility to base each withdrawal decision on the situation as it is at that time rather than on estimates that are no longer valid.

Along with this optimistic estimate, I must—in all candor—leave one note of caution.

If the level of enemy activity significantly increases we might have to adjust our timetable accordingly.

However, I want the record to be completely clear on one point.

At the time of the bombing halt just a year ago, there was some confusion as to whether there was an understanding on the part of the enemy that if we stopped the bombing of North Vietnam they would stop the shelling of cities in South Vietnam. I want to be sure that there is no misunderstanding on the part of the enemy with regard to our withdrawal program.

We have noted the reduced level of infiltration, the reduction of our casualties, and are basing our withdrawal decisions partially on those factors.

If the level of infiltration or our casualties increase while we are trying to scale down the fighting, it will be the result of a conscious decision by the enemy.

Hanoi could make no greater mistake than to assume that an increase in violence will be to its advantage. If I conclude that increased enemy action jeopardizes our remaining forces in Vietnam, I shall not hesitate to take strong and effective measures to deal with that situation.

This is not a threat. This is a statement of policy, which as Commander in Chief of our Armed Forces, I am making in meeting my responsibility for the protection of American fighting men wherever they may be.

My fellow Americans, I am sure you can recognize from what I have said that we really only have two choices open to us if we want to end this war.

—I can order an immediate, precipitate withdrawal of all Americans from Vietnam without regard to the effects of that action.

—Or we can persist in our search for a just peace through a negotiated settlement if possible, or through continued implementation of our plan for Vietnamization if necessary—a plan in which we will withdraw all of our forces from Vietnam on a schedule in accordance with our program, as the South Vietnamese become strong enough to defend their own freedom. I have chosen this second course. It is not the easy way. It is the right way.

It is a plan which will end the war and serve the cause of peace—not just in Vietnam but in the Pacific and in the world.

In speaking of the consequences of a precipitate withdrawal, I mentioned that our allies would lose confidence in America.

Far more dangerous, we would lose confidence in ourselves. Oh, the immediate reaction would be a sense of relief that our men were coming home. But as we saw the consequences of what we had done, inevitable remorse and divisive recrimination would scar our spirit as a people.

We have faced other crises in our history and have become stronger by rejecting the easy way out and taking the right way in meeting our challenges. Our greatness as a nation has been our capacity to do what had to be done when we knew our course was right.

I recognize that some of my fellow citizens disagree with the plan for peace I have chosen. Honest and patriotic Americans have reached different conclusions as to how peace should be achieved.

In San Francisco a few weeks ago, I saw demonstrators. carrying signs reading: "Lose in Vietnam, bring the boys home."

Well, one of the strengths of our free society is that any American has a right to reach that conclusion and to advocate that point of view. But as President of the United States, I would be untrue to my oath of office if I allowed the policy of this Nation to be dictated by the minority who hold that point of view and who try to impose it on the Nation by mounting demonstrations in the street.

For almost 200 years, the policy of this Nation has been made under our Constitution by those leaders in the Congress and the White House elected by all of the people. If a vocal minority, however fervent its cause, prevails over reason and the will of the majority, this Nation has no future as a free society.

And now I would like to address a word, if I may, to the young people of this Nation who are particularly concerned, and I understand why they are concerned, about this war.

I respect your idealism.

I share your concern for peace. I want peace as much as you do. There are powerful personal reasons I want to end this war. This week I will have to sign 83 letters to mothers, fathers, wives, and loved ones of men who have given their lives for America in Vietnam. It is very little satisfaction to me that this is only one-third as many letters as I signed the first week in office. There is nothing I want more than to see the day come when I do not have to write any of those letters.

—I want to end the war to save the lives of those brave young men in Vietnam.

—But I want to end it in a way which will increase the chance that their younger brothers and their sons will not have to fight in some future Vietnam someplace in the world.

—And I want to end the war for another reason. I want to end it so that the energy and dedication of you, our young people, now too often directed into bitter hatred against those responsible for the war, can be turned to the great challenges of peace, a better life for all Americans, a better life for all people on this earth.

I have chosen a plan for peace. I believe it will succeed.

If it does succeed, what the critics say now won't matter. If it does not succeed, anything I say then won't matter.

I know it may not be fashionable to speak of patriotism or national destiny these days. But I feel it is appropriate to do so on this occasion.

Two hundred years ago this Nation was weak and poor. But even then, America was the hope of millions in the world. Today we have become the strongest and richest nation in the world. And the Wheel of destiny has turned so that any hope the world has for the survival of peace and freedom will be determined by whether the American people have the moral stamina and the courage to meet the challenge of free world leadership.

Let historians not record that when America was the most powerful nation in the world we passed on the other side of the road and allowed the last hopes for peace and freedom of millions of people to be suffocated by the forces of totalitarianism.

And so tonight—to you, the great silent majority of my fellow Americans—I ask for your support.

I pledged in my campaign for the Presidency to end the war in a way that we could win the peace. I have initiated a plan of action which will enable me to keep that pledge.

The more support I can have from the American people, the sooner that pledge can be redeemed; for the more divided we are at home, the less likely the enemy is to negotiate at Paris.

Let us be united for peace. Let us also be united against defeat. Because let us understand: North Vietnam cannot defeat or humiliate the United States. Only Americans can do that.

Fifty years ago, in this room and at this very desk, President Woodrow Wilson spoke words which caught the imagination of a war-weary world. He said: "This is the war to end war." His dream for peace after World War I was shattered on the hard realities of great power politics and Woodrow Wilson died a broken man.

Tonight I do not tell you that the war in Vietnam is the war to end wars. But I do say this: I have initiated a plan which will end this war in a way that will bring us closer to that great goal to which Woodrow Wilson and every American President in our history has been dedicated—the goal of a just and lasting peace.

As President I hold the responsibility for choosing the best path to that goal and then leading the Nation along it.

I pledge to you tonight that I shall meet this responsibility with all of the strength and wisdom I can command in accordance with your hopes, mindful of your concerns, sustained by your prayers.

Thank you and goodnight.

4. First State of the Union Address January 22, 1970

Mr. Speaker, Mr. President, my colleagues in the Congress, our distinguished guests and my fellow Americans:

To address a joint session of the Congress in this great Chamber in which I was once privileged to serve is an honor for which I am deeply grateful.

The State of the Union Address is traditionally an occasion for a lengthy and detailed account by the President of what he has accomplished in the past, what he wants the Congress to do in the future, and, in an election year, to lay the basis for the political issues which might be decisive in the fall.

Occasionally there comes a time when profound and far-reaching events command a break with tradition. This is such a time.

I say this not only because 1970 marks the beginning of a new decade in which America will celebrate its 200th birthday. I say it because new knowledge and hard experience argue persuasively that both our programs and our institutions in America need to be reformed.

The moment has arrived to harness the vast energies and abundance of this land to the creation of a new American experience, an experience richer and deeper and more truly a reflection of the goodness and grace of the human spirit.

The seventies will be a time of new beginnings, a time of exploring both on the earth and in the heavens, a time of discovery. But the time has also come for emphasis on developing better ways of managing what we have and of completing what man's genius has begun but left unfinished.

Our land, this land that is ours together, is a great and a good land. It is also an unfinished land, and the challenge of perfecting it is the summons of the seventies.

It is in that spirit that I address myself to those great issues facing our Nation which are above partisanship.

When we speak of America's priorities the first priority must always be peace for America and the world.

The major immediate goal of our foreign policy is to bring an end to the war in Vietnam in a way that our generation will be remembered not so much as the generation that suffered in war, but more for the fact that we had the courage and character to win the kind of a just peace that the next generation was able to keep.

We are making progress toward that goal.

The prospects for peace are far greater today than they were a year ago.

A major part of the credit for this development goes to the Members of this Congress who, despite their differences on the conduct of the war, have overwhelmingly indicated their support of a just peace. By this action, you have completely demolished the enemy's hopes that they can gain in Washington the victory our fighting men have denied them in Vietnam.

No goal could be greater than to make the next generation the first in this century in which America was at peace with every nation in the world.

I shall discuss in detail the new concepts and programs designed to achieve this goal in a separate report on foreign policy, which I shall submit to the Congress at a later date.

Today, let me describe the directions of our new policies.

We have based our policies on an evaluation of the world as it is, not as it was 25 years ago

at the conclusion of World War II. Many of the policies which were necessary and right then are obsolete today.

Then, because of America's overwhelming military and economic strength, because of the weakness of other major free world powers and the inability of scores of newly independent nations to defend, or even govern, themselves, America had to assume the major burden for the defense of freedom in the world.

In two wars, first in Korea and now in Vietnam, we furnished most of the money, most of the arms, most of the men to help other nations defend their freedom.

Today the great industrial nations of Europe, as well as Japan, have regained their economic strength; and the nations of Latin America—and many of the nations who acquired their freedom from colonialism after World War II in Asia and Africa—have a new sense of pride and dignity and a determination to assume the responsibility for their own defense.

That is the basis of the doctrine I announced at Guam. Neither the defense nor the development of other nations can be exclusively or primarily an American undertaking.

The nations of each part of the world should assume the primary responsibility for their own well-being; and they themselves should determine the terms of that well-being.

We shall be faithful to our treaty commitments, but we shall reduce our involvement and our presence in other nations' affairs.

To insist that other nations play a role is not a retreat from responsibility; it is a sharing of responsibility.

The result of this new policy has been not to weaken our alliances, but to give them new life, new strength, a new sense of common purpose.

Relations with our European allies are once again strong and healthy, based on mutual consultation and mutual responsibility.

We have initiated a new approach to Latin America in which we deal with those nations as partners rather than patrons.

The new partnership concept has been welcomed in Asia. We have developed an historic new basis for Japanese-American friendship and cooperation, which is the linchpin for peace in the Pacific.

If we are to have peace in the last third of the century, a major factor will be the development of a new relationship between the United States and the Soviet Union.

I would not underestimate our differences, but we are moving with precision and purpose from an era of confrontation to an era of negotiation.

Our negotiations on strategic arms limitations and in other areas will have far greater chance for success if both sides enter them motivated by mutual self-interest rather than naive sentimentality.

It is with this same spirit that we have resumed discussions with Communist China in our talks at Warsaw.

Our concern in our relations with both these nations is to avoid a catastrophic collision and to build a solid basis for peaceful settlement of our differences.

I would be the last to suggest that the road to peace is not difficult and dangerous, but I believe our new policies have contributed to the prospect that America may have the best chance since World War II to enjoy a generation of uninterrupted peace. And that chance will be enormously increased if we continue to have a relationship between Congress and the Executive in which, despite differences in detail, where the security of America and the peace of mankind are concerned, we act not as Republicans, not as Democrats, but as Americans.

As we move into the decade of the seventies, we have the greatest opportunity for progress at home of any people in world history.

Our gross national product will increase by $500 billion in the next 10 years. This increase alone is greater than the entire growth of the American economy from 1790 to 1950.

The critical question is not whether we will grow, but how we will use that growth.

The decade of the sixties was also a period of great growth economically. But in that same 10-year period we witnessed the greatest growth of crime, the greatest increase in inflation, the greatest social unrest in America in 100 years. Never has a nation seemed to have had more and enjoyed it less.

At heart, the issue is the effectiveness of government.

Ours has become—as it continues to be, and should remain—a society of large expectations. Government helped to generate these expectations. It undertook to meet them. Yet, increasingly, it proved unable to do so.

As a people, we had too many visions—and too little vision.

Now, as we enter the seventies, we should enter also a great age of reform of the institutions of American government.

Our purpose in this period should not be simply better management of the programs of the past. The time has come for a new quest—a quest not for a greater quantity of what we have, but for a new quality of life in America.

A major part of the substance for an unprecedented advance in this Nation's approach to its problems and opportunities is contained in more than two score legislative proposals which I sent to the Congress last year and which still await enactment. I will offer at least a dozen more major programs in the course of this session.

At this point I do not intend to go through a detailed listing of what I have proposed or will propose, but I would like to mention three areas in which urgent priorities demand that we move and move now:

First, we cannot delay longer in accomplishing a total reform of our welfare system. When a system penalizes work, breaks up homes, robs recipients of dignity, there is no alternative to abolishing that system and adopting in its place the program of income support, job training, and work incentives which I recommended to the Congress last year.

Second, the time has come to assess and reform all of our institutions of government at the Federal, State, and local level. It is time for a New Federalism, in which, after 190 years of power flowing from the people and local and State governments to Washington, D.C., it will begin to flow from Washington back to the States and to the people of the United States.

Third, we must adopt reforms which will expand the range of opportunities for all Americans. We can fulfill the American dream only when each person has a fair chance to fulfill his own dreams. This means equal voting rights, equal employment opportunity, and new opportunities for expanded ownership. Because in order to be secure in their human rights, people need access to property rights.

I could give similar examples of the need for reform in our programs for health, education, housing, transportation, as well as other critical areas which directly affect the well-being of millions of Americans.

The people of the United States should wait no longer for these reforms that would so deeply enhance the quality of their life.

When I speak of actions which would be beneficial to the American people, I can think of none more important than for the Congress to join this administration in the battle to stop the rise in the cost of living.

Now, I realize it is tempting to blame someone else for inflation. Some blame business for raising prices. Some blame unions for asking for more wages.

But a review of the stark fiscal facts of the 1960's clearly demonstrates where the primary blame for rising prices must be placed.

In the decade of the sixties the Federal Government spent $57 billion more than it took in in taxes.

In that same decade the American people paid the bill for that deficit in price increases which raised the cost of living for the average family of four by $200 per month in America.

Now millions of Americans are forced to go into debt today because the Federal Government decided to go into debt yesterday. We must balance our Federal budget so that American families will have a better chance to balance their family budgets.

Only with the cooperation of the Congress can we meet this highest priority objective of responsible government. We are on the right track.

We had a balanced budget in 1969. This administration cut more than $7 billion out of spending plans in order to produce a surplus in 1970, and in spite of the fact that Congress reduced revenues by $3 billion, I shall recommend a balanced budget for 1971.

But I can assure you that not only to present, but to stay within, a balanced budget requires some very hard decisions. It means rejecting spending programs which would benefit some of the people when their net effect would result in price increases for all the people.

It is time to quit putting good money into bad programs. Otherwise, we will end up with bad money and bad programs.

I recognize the political popularity of spending programs, and particularly in an election year. But unless we stop the rise in prices, the cost of living for millions of American families will become unbearable and government's ability to plan programs for progress for the future will become impossible.

In referring to budget cuts, there is one area where I have ordered an increase rather than a cut—and that is the requests of those agencies with the responsibilities for law enforcement.

We have heard a great deal of overblown rhetoric during the sixties in which the word "war" has perhaps too often been used—the war on poverty, the war on misery, the war on disease, the war on hunger. But if there is one area where the word "war" is appropriate it is in the fight against crime. We must declare and win the war against the criminal elements which increasingly threaten our cities, our homes, and our lives.

We have a tragic example of this problem in the Nation's Capital, for whose safety the Congress and the Executive have the primary responsibility. I doubt if many Members of this Congress who live more than a few blocks from here would dare leave their cars in the Capitol garage and walk home alone tonight.

Last year this administration sent to the Congress 13 separate pieces of legislation dealing with organized crime, pornography, street crime, narcotics, crime in the District of Columbia.

None of these bills has reached my desk for signature.

I am confident that the Congress will act now to adopt the legislation I placed before you last year. We in the Executive have done everything we can under existing law, but new and stronger weapons are needed in that fight.

While it is true that State and local law enforcement agencies are the cutting edge in the effort to eliminate street crime, burglaries, murder, my proposals to you have embodied my belief that the Federal Government should play a greater role in working in partnership with these agencies.

That is why 1971 Federal spending for local law enforcement will double that budgeted for 1970.

The primary responsibility for crimes that affect individuals is with local and State rather than with Federal Government. But in the field of organized crime, narcotics, pornography, the Federal Government has a special responsibility it should fulfill. And we should make Washington, D.C., where we have the primary responsibility, an example to the Nation and the world of respect for law rather than lawlessness.

I now turn to a subject which, next to our desire for peace, may well become the major concern of the American people in the decade of the seventies.

In the next 10 years we shall increase our wealth by 50 percent. The profound question is: Does this mean we will be 50 percent richer in a real sense, 50 percent better off, 50 percent happier?

Or does it mean that in the year 1980 the President standing in this place will look back on a decade in which 70 percent of our people lived in metropolitan areas choked by traffic, suffocated by smog, poisoned by water, deafened by noise, and terrorized by crime?

These are not the great questions that concern world leaders at summit conferences. But people do not live at the summit. They live in the foothills of everyday experience, and it is time for all of us to concern ourselves with the way real people live in real life.

The great question of the seventies is, shall we surrender to our surroundings, or shall we make our peace with nature and begin to make reparations for the damage we have done to our air, to our land, and to our water?

Restoring nature to its natural state is a cause beyond party and beyond factions. It has become a common cause of all the people of this country. It is a cause of particular concern to young Americans, because they more than we will reap the grim consequences of our failure to act on programs which are needed now if we are to prevent disaster later.

Clean air, clean water, open spaces—these should once again be the birthright of every American. If we act now, they can be.

We still think of air as free. But clean air is not free, and neither is clean water. The price tag on pollution control is high. Through our years of past carelessness we incurred a debt to nature, and now that debt is being called.

The program I shall propose to Congress will be the most comprehensive and costly program in this field in America's history.

It is not a program for just one year. A year's plan in this field is no plan at all. This is a time to look ahead not a year, but 5 years or 10 years—whatever time is required to do the job.

I shall propose to this Congress a $10 billion nationwide clean waters program to put modern municipal waste treatment plants in every place in America where they are needed to make our waters clean again, and do it now. We have the industrial capacity, if we begin now, to build them all within 5 years. This program will get them built within 5 years.

As our cities and suburbs relentlessly expand, those priceless open spaces needed for recreation areas accessible to their people are swallowed up—often forever. Unless we preserve these spaces while they are still available, we will have none to preserve. Therefore, I shall propose new financing methods for purchasing open space and parklands now, before they are lost to us.

The automobile is our worst polluter of the air. Adequate control requires further advances in engine design and fuel composition. We shall intensify our research, set increasingly strict standards, and strengthen enforcement procedures—and we shall do it now.

We can no longer afford to consider air and water common property, free to be abused by anyone without regard to the consequences. Instead, we should begin now to treat them as scarce resources, which we are no more free to contaminate than we are free to throw garbage into our neighbor's yard.

This requires comprehensive new regulations. It also requires that, to the extent possible, the price of goods should be made to include the costs of producing and disposing of them without damage to the environment.

Now, I realize that the argument is often made that there is a fundamental contradiction between economic growth and the quality of life, so that to have one we must forsake the other.

The answer is not to abandon growth, but to redirect it. For example, we should turn toward ending congestion and eliminating smog the same reservoir of inventive genius that created them in the first place.

Continued vigorous economic growth provides us with the means to enrich life itself and to enhance our planet as a place hospitable to man.

Each individual must enlist in this fight if it is to be won.

It has been said that no matter how many national parks and historical monuments we buy and develop, the truly significant environment for each of us is that in which we spend 80 percent of our time—in our homes, in our places of work, the streets over which we travel.

Street litter, rundown parking strips and yards, dilapidated fences, broken windows, smoking automobiles, dingy working places, all should be the object of our fresh view.

We have been too tolerant of our surroundings and too willing to leave it to others to clean up our environment. It is time for those who make massive demands on society to make some minimal demands on themselves. Each of us must resolve that each day he will leave his home, his property, the public places of the city or town a little cleaner, a little better, a little more pleasant for himself and those around him.

With the help of people we can do anything, and without their help, we can do nothing. In this spirit, together, we can reclaim our land for ours and generations to come.

Between now and the year 5000, over 100 million children will be born in the United States. Where they grow up—and how will, more than any one thing, measure the quality of American life in these years ahead. This should be a warning to us.

For the past 30 years our population has also been growing and shifting. The result is exemplified in the vast areas of rural America emptying out of people and of promise—a third of our counties lost population in the sixties.

The violent and decayed central cities of our great metropolitan complexes are the most conspicuous area of failure in American life today. I propose that before these problems become insoluble, the Nation develop a national growth policy.

In the future, government decisions as to where to build highways, locate airports, acquire land, or sell land should be made with a clear objective of aiding a balanced growth for America.

In particular, the Federal Government must be in a position to assist in the building of new cities and the rebuilding of old ones.

At the same time, we will carry our concern with the quality of life in America to the farm as well as the suburb, to the village as well as to the city. What rural America needs most is a new kind of assistance. It needs to be dealt with, not as a separate nation, but as part of an overall growth policy for America. We must create a new rural environment which will not only stem the migration to urban centers, but reverse it. If we seize our growth as a challenge, we can make the 1970's an historic period when by conscious choice we transformed our land into what we want it to become.

America, which has pioneered in the new abundance, and in the new technology, is called upon today to pioneer in meeting the concerns which have followed in their wake—in turning the wonders of science to the service of man.

In the majesty of this great Chamber we hear the echoes of America's history, of debates that rocked the Union and those that repaired it, of the summons to war and the search for peace, of the uniting of the people, the building of a nation.

Those echoes of history remind us of our roots and our strengths.

They remind us also of that special genius of American democracy, which at one critical turning point after another has led us to spot the new road to the future and given us the wisdom and the courage to take it.

As I look down that new road which I have tried to map out today, I see a new America as we celebrate our 200th anniversary 6 years from now.

I see an America in which we have abolished hunger, provided the means for every family in the Nation to obtain a minimum income, made enormous progress in providing better housing, faster transportation, improved health, and superior education.

I see an America in which we have checked inflation, and waged a winning war against crime.

I see an America in which we have made great strides in stopping the pollution of our air, cleaning up our water, opening up our parks, continuing to explore in space.

Most important, I see an America at peace with all the nations of the world.

This is not an impossible dream. These goals are all within our reach.

In times past, our forefathers had the vision but not the means to achieve such goals.

Let it not be recorded that we were the first American generation that had the means but not the vision to make this dream come true.

But let us, above all, recognize a fundamental truth. We can be the best clothed, best fed, best housed people in the world, enjoying clean air, clean water, beautiful parks, but we could still be the unhappiest people in the world without an indefinable spirit—the lift of a driving dream which has made America, from its beginning, the hope of the world.

Two hundred years ago this was a new nation of 3 million people, weak militarily, poor economically. But America meant something to the world then which could not be measured in dollars, something far more important than military might.

Listen to President Thomas Jefferson in 1802: We act not "for ourselves alone, but for the whole human race."

We had a spiritual quality then which caught the imagination of millions of people in the world.

Today, when we are the richest and strongest nation in the world, let it not be recorded that we lack the moral and spiritual idealism which made us the hope of the world at the time of our birth.

The demands of us in 1976 are even greater than in 1776.

It is no longer enough to live and let live. Now we must live and help live.

We need a fresh climate in America, one in which a person can breathe freely and breathe in freedom.

Our recognition of the truth that wealth and happiness are not the same thing requires us to measure success or failure by new criteria.

Even more than the programs I have described today, what this Nation needs is an example from its elected leaders in providing the spiritual and moral leadership which no programs for material progress can satisfy.

Above all, let us inspire young Americans with a sense of excitement, a sense of destiny, a sense of involvement, in meeting the challenges we face in this great period of our history. Only then are they going to have any sense of satisfaction in their lives.

The greatest privilege an individual can have is to serve in a cause bigger than himself. We have such a cause.

How we seize the opportunities I have described today will determine not only our future, but the future of peace and freedom in this world in the last third of the century.

May God give us the wisdom, the strength and, above all, the idealism to be worthy of that challenge, so that America can fulfill its destiny of being the world's best hope for liberty, for opportunity, for progress and peace for all peoples.

5. Statement about Desegregation of Elementary and Secondary Schools March 24, 1970

MY PURPOSE in this statement is to set forth in detail this administration's policies on the subject of desegregation of America's elementary and secondary schools.

Few public issues are so emotionally charged as that of school desegregation, few so wrapped in confusion and clouded with misunderstanding. None is more important to our national unity and progress.

This issue is not partisan. It is not sectional. It is an American issue, of direct and immediate concern to every citizen.

I hope that this statement will reduce the prevailing confusion and will help place public discussion of the issue on a more rational and realistic level in all parts of the Nation. It is time to strip away the hypocrisy, the prejudice, and the ignorance that too long have characterized discussion of this issue.

My specific objectives in this are:

—To reaffirm my personal belief that the 1954 decision of the Supreme Court in Brown v. Board of Education was right in both constitutional and human terms.

—To assess our progress in the 16 years since Brown and to point the way to continuing progress.

—To clarify the present state of the law, as developed by the courts and the Congress, and the administration policies guided by it.

—To discuss some of the difficulties encountered by courts and communities as desegregation has accelerated in recent years, and to suggest approaches that can mitigate such problems as we complete the process of compliance with Brown.

—To place the question of school desegregation in its larger context, as part of America's historic commitment to the achievement of a free and open society.

Anxiety over this issue has been fed by many sources.

On the one hand, some have interpreted various administration statements and actions as a backing away from the principle of Brown—and have therefore feared that the painstaking work of a decade and a half might be undermined. We are not backing away. The constitutional mandate will be enforced.

On the other hand, several recent decisions by lower courts have raised widespread fears that the Nation might face a massive disruption of public education: that wholesale compulsory busing may be ordered and the neighborhood school virtually doomed. A comprehensive review of school desegregation cases indicates that these latter are untypical decisions, and that the prevailing trend of judicial opinion is by no means so extreme.

Certain changes are needed in the Nation's approach to school desegregation. It would be remarkable if 16 years of hard, often tempestuous experience had not taught us something about how better to manage the task with a decent regard for the legitimate interests of all concerned—and especially the children. Drawing on this experience, I am confident the remaining problems can be overcome.

What the Law Requires

In order to determine what ought to be done, it is important first to be as clear as possible about what must be done.

We are dealing fundamentally with inalienable human rights, some of them constitutionally protected. The final arbiter of constitutional questions is the United States Supreme Court.

The President' s Responsibility

There are a number of questions involved in the school controversy on which the Supreme Court has not yet spoken definitely. Where it has spoken, its decrees are the law. Where it has not spoken, where Congress has not acted, and where differing lower courts have left the issue in doubt, my responsibilities as Chief Executive make it necessary that I determine, on the basis of my best judgment, what must be done.

In reaching that determination, I have sought to ascertain the prevailing judicial view

as developed in decisions by the Supreme Court and the various circuit courts of appeals. In this statement I list a number of principles derived from that prevailing judicial view. I accept those principles and shall be guided by them. The departments and agencies of the Government will adhere to them.

A few recent cases in the lower courts have gone beyond those generally accepted principles. Unless affirmed by the Supreme Court, I will not consider them as precedents to guide administration policy elsewhere.

What the Supreme Court Has Said

To determine the present state of the law, we must first remind ourselves of the recent history of Supreme Court rulings in this area.

This begins with the Brown case in 1954, when the Court laid down the principle that deliberate segregation of students by race in the public schools was unconstitutional. In that historic ruling, the Court gave legal sanction to two fundamental truths—that separation by law establishes schools that are inherently unequal, and that a promise of equality before the law cannot be squared with use of the law to establish two classes of people, one black and one white.

The Court requested further argument, however, and propounded the following questions, among others:

"Assuming it is decided that segregation in public schools violates the Fourteenth Amendment"

"a. would a decree necessarily follow providing that, within the limits set by normal geographic school districting, Negro children should forthwith be admitted to schools of their choice, or"

"b. may this Court, in the exercise of its equity powers, permit an effective gradual adjustment to be brought about from existing segregated systems to a system not based on color distinctions?"

In its second Brown decision the following year, the Court addressed itself to these questions of manner and timing of compliance. Its ruling included these principles:

—Local school problems vary: School authorities have the primary responsibility for solving these problems; courts must consider whether these authorities are acting in good faith.

—The courts should be guided by principles of equity, which traditionally are "characterized by a practical flexibility in shaping its remedies and by a facility for adjusting and reconciling public and private needs."

—Compliance must be achieved "with all deliberate speed," including "a prompt and reasonable start" toward achieving full compliance "at the earliest practicable date."

In 1964, the Supreme Court spoke again: "The time for mere 'deliberate speed' has run out, and that phrase can no longer justify denying these . . . children their constitutional rights."

At the same time, Congress also added to the impetus of desegregation by passing the Civil Rights Act of 1964, an act that as a private citizen I endorsed and supported.

Although the Supreme Court in the Brown cases concerned itself primarily, if not exclusively, with pupil assignments, its decree applied also to teacher assignments and school facilities as a whole.

In 1968, the Supreme Court reiterated the principle enunciated in prior decisions, that teacher assignments are an important aspect of the basic task of achieving a public school system wholly freed from racial discrimination. During that same year, in another group of Supreme Court decisions, a significant and new set of principles also emerged:

—That a school board must establish "that its proposed plan promises meaningful and immediate progress toward disestablishing State-imposed segregation," and that the plan

must "have real prospects for dismantling the State-imposed dual system at the earliest 'practicable date.'"

—That one test of whether a school board has met its "affirmative duty to take whatever steps might be necessary to convert to a unitary system in which racial discrimination would be eliminated root and branch" is the extent to which racial separation persists under its plan.

—That the argument that effective desegregation might cause white families to flee the neighborhood cannot be used to sustain devices designed to perpetuate segregation.

—That when geographic zoning is combined with "free transfers," and the effect of the transfer privilege is to perpetuate segregation despite the zoning, the plan is unacceptable.

The most recent decisions by the Supreme Court have now rejected any further delay, adding to the Court's mandate:

—"The obligation of every school district is to terminate dual systems at once and to operate now and hereafter only unitary schools."

—That the obligation of such districts is an affirmative one and not a passive one.

—That freedom of choice plans could no longer be considered as an appropriate substitute for the affirmative obligation imposed by the Court unless they, in fact, discharge that obligation immediately.

The Court has dealt only in very general terms with the question of what constitutes a "unitary" system, referring to it as one "within which no person is to be effectively excluded from any school because of race or color." It has not spoken definitely on whether or not, or the extent to which, "desegregation" may mean "integration."

In an opinion earlier this month, Chief Justice Burger pointed out a number of "basic practical problems" which the Court had not yet resolved, "including whether, as a constitutional matter, any particular racial balance must be achieved in the schools; to what extent school districts and zones may or must be altered as a constitutional matter; to what extent transportation may or must be provided to achieve the ends sought by prior holdings of this Court."

One of these areas of legal uncertainty cited by Chief Justice Burger—school transportation—involves congressional pronouncements.

In the 1964 Civil Rights Act, the Congress stated, ". . . nothing herein shall empower any official or court of the United States to issue any order seeking to achieve a racial balance in any school by requiring the transportation of pupils or students from one school to another or one school district to another in order to achieve such racial balance, or otherwise enlarge the existing power of the court to insure compliance with constitutional standards."

In the 1966 amendments to the Elementary and Secondary Education Act, the Congress further stated, ". . . nothing contained in this Act shall . . . require the assignment or transportation of students or teachers in order to overcome racial imbalance."

I am advised that these provisions cannot constitutionally be applied to de jure segregation. However, not all segregation as it exists today is de jure.

I have consistently expressed my opposition to any compulsory busing of pupils beyond normal geographic school zones for the purpose of achieving racial balance.

What the Lower Courts Have Said

In the absence of definitive Supreme Court rulings, these and other "basic practical problems" have been left for case-by-case determination in the lower courts—and both real and apparent contradictions among some of these lower court rulings have generated considerable public confusion about what the law really requires.

In an often-cited case in 1955 (Briggs v. Elliott), a district court held that "the Constitution . . . does not require integration. . . . It merely forbids the use of governmental power to enforce segregation."

But in 1966 another court took issue with this doctrine, pointing out that it had been used as justifying "techniques for perpetuating school segregation," and declaring that: ". . . the only adequate redress for a previously overt system-wide policy of segregation directed against Negroes as a collective entity is a system-wide policy of integration."

In 1969, the 4th Circuit Court of Appeals declared: "The famous Briggs v. Elliott dictum—adhered to by this court for many years—that the Constitution forbids segregation but does not require integration . . . is now dead."

Cases in two circuit courts have held that the continued existence of some all black schools in a formerly segregated district did not demonstrate unconstitutionality, with one noting that there is "no duty to balance the races in the school system in conformity with some mathematical formula."

Another circuit court decision declared that even though a district's geographic zones were based on objective, nonracial criteria, the fact that they failed to produce any significant degree of integration meant that they were unconstitutional.

Two very recent Federal court decisions continue to illustrate the range of opinion: a plan of a southern school district has been upheld even though three schools would remain all-black, but a northern school system has been ordered by another Federal court to integrate all of its schools completely "by the revising of boundary lines for attendance purposes as well as busing so as to achieve maximum racial integration."

This range of differences demonstrates that lawyers and judges have honest disagreements about what the law requires. There have been some rulings that would divert such huge sums of money to noneducational purposes, and would create such severe dislocations of public school systems, as to impair the primary function of providing a good education. In one, for example—probably the most extreme judicial decree so far—a California State court recently ordered the Los Angeles School Board to establish a virtually uniform racial balance throughout its 711-square-mile district, with its 775,000 children in 561 schools. Local leaders anticipate that this decree would impose an expenditure of $40 million over the next school year to lease 1,600 buses, to acquire site locations to house them, to hire drivers, and to defray operating costs. Subsequent costs would approximate $20 million annually. Some recent rulings by Federal district courts applicable to other school districts appear to be no less severe.

I am dedicated to continued progress toward a truly desegregated public school system. But, considering the always heavy demands for more school operating funds, I believe it is preferable, when we have to make the choice, to use limited financial resources for the improvement of education—for better teaching facilities, better methods, and advanced educational materials—and for the upgrading of the disadvantaged areas in the community rather than buying buses, tires, and gasoline to transport young children miles away from their neighborhood schools.

What Most of the Courts Agree On

Despite the obvious confusion, a careful survey of rulings both by the Supreme Court and by the circuit courts of appeals suggests that the basic judicial approach may be more reasonable than some have feared. Whatever a few lower courts might have held to the contrary, the prevailing trend of judicial opinion appears to be summed up in these principles:

—There is a fundamental distinction between so-called de jure and de facto segregation: de jure segregation arises by law or by the deliberate act of school officials and is unconstitutional; de facto segregation results from residential housing patterns and does not violate the Constitution. (The clearest example of de jure segregation is the dual school system as it existed in the South prior to the decision in Brown—two schools, one Negro and one white, comprised of the same grades and serving the same geographical area. This is the system with which most of the decisions, and the Supreme Court cases up until now, have been concerned.)

—Where school boards have demonstrated a good-faith effort to comply with court rulings, the courts have generally allowed substantial latitude as to method—often making the explicit point that administrative choices should, wherever possible, be made by the local school authorities themselves.

—In devising particular plans, questions of cost, capacity, and convenience for pupils and parents are relevant considerations.

—Whatever the racial composition of student bodies, faculties and staff must be assigned in a way that does not contribute to identifying a given school as "Negro" or "white."

—In school districts that previously operated dual systems, affirmative steps toward integration are a key element in disestablishing the dual system. This positive integration, however, does not necessarily have to result in "racial balance" throughout the system. When there is racial separation in housing, the constitutional requirement has been held satisfied even though some schools remained all-black.

—While the dual school system is the most obvious example, de jure segregation is also found in more subtle forms. Where authorities have deliberately drawn attendance zones or chosen school locations for the express purpose of creating and maintaining racially separate schools, de jure segregation is held to exist. In such a case the school board has a positive duty to remedy it. This is so even though the board ostensibly operates a unitary system.

—In determining whether school authorities are responsible for existing racial separation— and thus whether they are constitutionally required to remedy it—the intent of their action in locating schools, drawing zones, etc., is a crucial factor.

—In the case of genuine de facto segregation (i.e., where housing patterns produce substantially all-Negro or all-white schools, and where this racial separation has not been caused by deliberate official action) school authorities are not constitutionally required to take any positive steps to correct the imbalance.

To summarize: There is a constitutional mandate that dual school systems and other forms of de jure segregation be eliminated totally. But within the framework of that requirement an area of flexibility—a "rule of reason"—exists, in which school boards, acting in good faith, can formulate plans of desegregation which best suit the needs of their own localities.

De facto segregation, which exists in many areas both North and South, is undesirable but is not generally held to violate the Constitution. Thus, residential housing patterns may result in the continued existence of some all-Negro schools even in a system which fully meets constitutional standards. But in any event, local school officials may, if they so choose, take steps beyond the constitutional minimums to diminish racial separation.

School Desegregation Today

The Progress

Though it began slowly, the momentum of school desegregation has become dramatic.

Thousands of school districts throughout the South have met the requirements of law.

In the past year alone, the number of black children attending southern schools held to be in compliance has doubled, from less than 600,000 to nearly 1,900,000—representing 40 percent of the Negro student population.

In most cases, this has been peacefully achieved.

However, serious problems are being encountered both by communities and by courts in part as a consequence of this accelerating pace.

The Problems

In some communities, racially mixed schools have brought the community greater interracial harmony; in others they have heightened racial tension and exacerbated racial frictions. Integration is no longer seen automatically and necessarily as an unmixed blessing for the Negro, Puerto Rican, or Mexican-American child. "Racial balance" has been discovered to be neither a static nor a finite condition; in many cases it has turned out to be only a way station on the road to resegregation. Whites have deserted the public schools, often for grossly inadequate private schools. They have left now resegregated public schools foundering for lack of support. And when they flee the central city in pursuit of all predominantly-white schools in suburbs, it is not only the central schools that become racially isolated, but the central city itself.

These are not theoretical problems, but actual problems. They exist not just in the realm of law, but in the realm of human attitudes and human behavior. They are part of the real world, and we have to take account of them.

The Complexities

Courts are confronted with problems of equity, and administrators with problems of policy. For example: To what extent does desegregation of dual systems require positive steps to achieve integration? How are the rights of individual children and their parents to be guarded in the process of enforcement? What are the educational impacts of the various means of desegregation—and where they appear to conflict, how should the claims of education be balanced against those of integration? To what extent should desegregation plans attempt to anticipate the problem of resegregation?

These questions suggest the complexity of the problems. These problems confront us in the North as well as the South, and in rural communities, suburbs, and central cities.

The troubles in our schools have many sources. They stem in part from deeply rooted racial attitudes; in part from differences in social, economic, and behavioral patterns; in part from weaknesses and inequities in the educational system itself; in part from the fact that by making schools the primary focus of efforts to remedy longstanding social ills, in some cases greater pressure has been brought to bear on the schools than they could withstand.

The Context

Progress toward school desegregation is part of two larger processes, each equally essential:

—The improvement of educational opportunities for all of America's children.

—The lowering of artificial racial barriers in all aspects of American life.

Only if we keep each of these considerations clearly in mind—and only if we recognize their separate natures—can we approach the question of school desegregation realistically.

It may be helpful to step back for a moment, and to consider the problem of school desegregation in its larger context.

The school stands in a unique relationship to the community, to the family, and to the individual student. It is a focal point of community life. It has a powerful impact on the future of all who attend. It is a place not only of learning, but also of living—where a child's

friendships center, where he learns to measure himself against others, to share, to compete, to cooperate—and it is the one institution above all others with which the parent shares his child.

Thus it is natural that whatever affects the schools stirs deep feelings among parents, and in the community at large.

Whatever threatens the schools, parents perceive—rightly—as a threat to their children.

Whatever makes the schools more distant from the family undermines one of the important supports of learning.

Quite understandably, the prospect of any abrupt change in the schools is seen as a threat.

As we look back over these 16 years, we find that many changes that stirred fears when they first were ordered have turned out well. In many southern communities, black and white children now learn together—and both the schools and the communities are better where the essential changes have been accomplished in a peaceful way.

But we also have seen situations in which the changes have not worked well. These have tended to command the headlines, thus increasing the anxieties of those still facing change.

Overburdening the Schools

One of the mistakes of past policy has been to demand too much of our schools: They have been expected not only to educate, but also to accomplish a social transformation. Children in many instances have not been served, but used—in what all too often has proved a tragically futile effort to achieve in the schools the kind of a multiracial society which the adult community has failed to achieve for itself.

If we are to be realists, we must recognize that in a free society there are limits to the amount of Government coercion that can reasonably be used; that in achieving desegregation we must proceed with the least possible disruption of the education of the Nation's children; and that our children are highly sensitive to conflict, and highly vulnerable to lasting psychic injury.

Failing to recognize these factors, past policies have placed on the schools and the children too great a share of the burden of eliminating racial disparities throughout our society. A major part of this task falls to the schools. But they cannot do it all or even most of it by themselves. Other institutions can share the burden of breaking down racial barriers, but only the schools can perform the task of education itself. If our schools fail to educate, then whatever they may achieve in integrating the races will turn out to be only a Pyrrhic victor.

With housing patterns what they are in many places in the Nation, the sheer numbers of pupils and the distances between schools make full and prompt school segregation in every such community impractical—even if there were a sufficient will on the part of the community to it. In Los Angeles, 78 percent of all Negro pupils attend schools that are 95 percent or more black. In Chicago the figure is 85 percent—the same as in Mobile, Alabama. Many smaller cities have the same patterns. Nationwide, 61 percent of all Negro students attend schools which are 95 percent or more black.

Demands that an arbitrary "racial balance" be established as a matter of right misinterpret the law and misstate the priorities.

As a matter of educational policy, some school boards have chosen to arrange their school systems in such a way as to provide a greater measure of racial integration. The important point to bear in mind is that where the existing racial separation has not been caused by official action, this increased integration is and should remain a matter for local determination.

Pupil assignments involve problems which do not arise in the case of the assignment of teachers. If school administrators were truly colorblind and teacher assignments did not reflect the color of the teacher's skin, the law of averages would eventually dictate an approximate racial balance of teachers in each within a system.

Not Just a Matter of Race

Available data on the educational effects of integration are neither definitive nor comprehensive. But such data as we have suggest strongly that, under the appropriate conditions, racial integration in the classroom can be a significant factor in improving the quality of education for the disadvantaged. At the same time, the data lead us into several more of the complexities that surround the desegregation issue.

For one thing, they serve as a reminder that, from an educational standpoint, to approach school questions solely in terms of race is to go astray. The data tell us that in educational terms, the significant factor is not race but rather the educational environment in the home—and indeed, that the single most important educational factor in a school is the kind of home environment its pupils come from. As a general rule, children from families whose home environment encourages learning—whatever their race—are higher achievers; those from homes offering little encouragement are lower achievers.

Which effect the home environment has depends on such things as whether books and magazines are available, whether the family subscribes to a newspaper, the educational level of the parents, and their attitude toward the child's education.

The data strongly suggest, also, that in order for the positive benefits of integration to be achieved, the school must have a majority of children from environments that encourage learning—recognizing, again, that the key factor is not race but the kind of home the child comes from. The greater concentration of pupils whose homes encourage learning—of whatever race—the higher the achievement levels not only of those pupils but also of others in the same school. Students learn from students. The reverse is also true: the greater concentration of pupils from homes that discourage learning, the lower the achievement levels of all.

We should bear very carefully in mind, therefore, the distinction between educational difficulty as a result of race, and educational difficulty as a result of social or economic levels, of family background, of cultural patterns, or simply of bad schools. Providing better education for the disadvantaged requires a more sophisticated approach than mere racial mathematics.

In this same connection, we should recognize that a smug paternalism has characterized the attitudes of many white Americans toward school questions. There has been an implicit assumption that blacks or others of minority races would be improved by association with whites. The notion that an all-black or predominantly-black school is automatically inferior to one which is all—or predominantly—white—even though not a product of a dual system inescapably carries racist overtones. And, of course, we know of hypocrisy: not a few of those in the North most stridently demanding racial integration of public schools in the South at the same time send their children to private schools to avoid the assumed inferiority of mixed public schools.

It is unquestionably true that most black schools—though by no means all—are in fact inferior to most white schools. This is due in part to past neglect or shortchanging of the black schools; and in part to long-term patterns of racial discrimination which caused a greater proportion of Negroes to be left behind educationally, left out culturally, and trapped in low paying jobs. It is not really because they serve black children that most of these schools are inferior, but rather because they serve poor children who often lack the home environment that encourages learning.

Innovative Approaches

Most public discussion of overcoming racial isolation centers on such concepts as compulsory "busing"—taking children out of the schools they would normally attend, and forcing them instead to attend others more distant, often in strange or even hostile neighborhoods. Massive "busing" is seen by some as the only alternative to massive racial isolation.

However, a number of new educational ideas are being developed, designed to provide the educational benefits of integration without depriving the student of his own neighborhood school.

For example, rather than attempting dislocation of whole schools, a portion of a child's educational activities may be shared with children from other schools. Some of his education is in a "home-base" school, but some outside it. This "outside learning" is in settings that are defined neither as black nor white, and sometimes in settings that are not even in traditional school buildings. It may range all the way from intensive work in reading to training in technical skills, and to joint efforts such as drama and athletics.

By bringing the children together on "neutral" territory friction may be dispelled; by limiting it to part-time activities no one would be deprived of his own neighborhood school; and the activities themselves provide the children with better education.

This sort of innovative approach demonstrates that the alternatives are not limited to perpetuating racial isolation on the one hand, and massively disrupting existing school patterns on the other. Without uprooting students, devices of this kind can provide an additional educational experience within an integrated setting. The child gains both ways.

Good Faith and the Courts

Where desegregation proceeds under the mandate of law, the best results require that the plans be carefully adapted to local circumstances.

A sense of compassionate balance is indispensable. The concept of balance is no stranger to our Constitution. Even first amendment freedoms are not absolute and unlimited; rather the scales of that "balance" have been adjusted with minute care, case by case, and the process continues.

In my discussion of the status of school desegregation law, I indicated that the Supreme Court has left a substantial degree of latitude within which specific desegregation plans can be designed. Many lower courts have left a comparable degree of latitude. This does not mean that the courts will tolerate or the administration condone evasions or subterfuges; it does mean that if the essential element of good faith is present, it should ordinarily be possible to achieve legal compliance with a minimum of educational disruption, and through a plan designed to be responsive to the community's own local circumstances.

This matter of good faith is critical.

Thus the farsighted local leaders who have demonstrated good faith by smoothing the path of compliance in their communities have helped lay the basis for judicial attitudes taking more fully into account the practical problems of compliance.

How the Supreme Court finally rules on the major issues it has not yet determined can have a crucial impact on the future of public education in the United States.

Traditionally, the Court has refrained from deciding constitutional questions until it became necessary. This period of legal uncertainty has occasioned vigorous controversy over what the thrust of the law should be.

As a Nation, we should create a climate in which these questions, when they finally are decided by the Court, can be decided in a framework most conducive to reasonable and realistic interpretation.

We should not provoke any court to push a constitutional principle beyond its ultimate limit in order to compel compliance with the court's essential, but more modest, mandate. The best way to avoid this is for the Nation to demonstrate that it does intend to carry out the full spirit of the constitutional mandate.

Policies of This Administration

It will be the purpose of this administration to carry out the law fully and fairly. And where problems exist that are beyond the mandate of legal requirements, it will be our purpose to seek solutions that are both realistic and appropriate.

I have instructed the Attorney General, the Secretary of Health, Education, and Welfare, and other appropriate officials of the Government to be guided by these basic principles and policies:

Principles of Enforcement

—Deliberate racial segregation of pupils by official action is unlawful, wherever it exists. In the words of the Supreme Court, it must be eliminated "root and branch"—and it must be eliminated at once.

—Segregation of teachers must be eliminated. To this end, each school system in this Nation, North and South, East and West, must move immediately, as the Supreme Court has ruled, toward a goal under which "in each school the ratio of White to Negro faculty members is substantially the same as it is throughout the system."

—With respect to school facilities, school administrators throughout the Nation, North and South, East and West, must move immediately, also in conformance with the Court's ruling, to assure that schools within individual school districts do not discriminate with respect to the quality of facilities or the quality of education delivered to the children within the district.

—In devising local compliance plans, primary weight should be given to the considered judgment of local school boards—provided they act in good faith, and within constitutional limits.

—The neighborhood school will be deemed the most appropriate base for such a system.

—Transportation of pupils beyond normal geographic school zones for the purpose of achieving racial balance will not be required.

—Federal advice and assistance will be made available on request, but Federal officials should not go beyond the requirements of law in attempting to impose their own judgment on the local school district.

—School boards will be encouraged to be flexible and creative in formulating plans that are educationally sound and that result in effective desegregation.

—Racial imbalance in a school system may be partly de jure in origin, and partly de facto. In such a case, it is appropriate to insist on remedy for the de jure portion, which is unlawful, without insisting on a remedy for the lawful de facto portion.

—De facto racial separation, resulting genuinely from housing patterns, exists in the South as well as the North; in neither area should this condition by itself be cause for Federal enforcement actions. De jure segregation brought about by deliberate school-board gerrymandering exists in the North as the South; in both areas this must be remedied. In all respects, the law should be applied equally, North and South, East and West.

This is one Nation. We are one people. I feel strongly that as Americans we must be done, now and for all future time, with the divisive notion that these problems are sectional.

Policies for Progress

—In those communities facing desegregation orders, the leaders of the communities will be encouraged to lead—not in defiance, but in smoothing the way of compliance. One clear lesson of experience is that local leadership is a fundamental factor in determining success or failure. Where leadership has been present, where it has been mobilized, where it has been effective, many districts have found that they could, after all, desegregate their schools successfully. Where local leadership has failed, the community has and the schools and the children have borne the brunt of that failure.

—We shall launch a concerted, sustained, and honest effort to assemble and evaluate the lessons of experience: to determine what methods of school desegregation have worked, in what situations, and why—and also what has not worked. The Cabinet-level working group I recently appointed will have as one of its principal functions amassing just this sort of information and helping make it available to the communities in need of assistance.

—We shall attempt to develop a far greater body of reliable data than now exists on the effects of various integration patterns on the learning process. Our effort must always be to preserve the educational benefit for the children.

—We shall explore ways of sharing more broadly the burdens of social transition that have been laid disproportionately on the schools—ways, that is, of shifting to other public institutions a greater share of the task of undoing the effects of racial isolation.

—We shall seek to develop and test a varied set of approaches to the problems associated with de facto segregation, North as well as South.

—We shall intensify our efforts to ensure that the gifted child—the potential leader—is not stifled intellectually merely because he is black or brown or lives in a slum.

—While raising the quality of education in all schools, we shall concentrate especially on racially-impacted schools, and particularly on equalizing those schools that are furthest behind.

Words often ring empty without deeds. In government, words can ring even emptier without dollars.

In order to give substance to these commitments, I shall ask Congress to divert $500 million from my previous budget requests for other domestic programs for fiscal 1971, to be put instead into programs for improving education in racially impacted areas, North and South, and for assisting school districts in meeting special problems incident to court-ordered desegregation. For fiscal 1972, I have ordered that $1 billion be budgeted for the same purposes.

I am not content simply to see this money spent, and then to count the spending as the measure of accomplishment. For much too long, national "commitments" have been measured by the number of Federal dollars spent rather than by more valid measures such as the quality of imagination displayed, the amount of private energy enlisted, or, even more to the point, the results achieved.

If this $1.5 billion accomplishes nothing, then the commitment will mean nothing.

If it enables us to break significant new ground, then the commitment will mean everything.

This I deeply believe: Communities desegregating their schools face special needs—for classrooms, facilities, teachers, teacher-training—and the Nation should help meet those needs.

The Nation also has a vital and special stake in upgrading education where de facto segregation persists—and where extra efforts are needed if the schools are to do their job. These schools, too, need extra money for teachers and facilities.

Beyond this, we need to press forward with innovative new ways of overcoming the effects of racial isolation and of making up for environmental deficiencies among the poor.

I have asked the Vice President's Cabinet committee on school desegregation [Cabinet Committee on Education], together with the Secretary of Health, Education, and Welfare, to consult with experts in and out of government and prepare a set of recommended criteria for the allocation of these funds.

I have specified that these criteria should give special weight to four categories of need:

—The special needs of desegregating (or recently desegregated) districts for additional facilities, personnel, and training required to get the new, unitary system successfully started.

—The special needs of racially impacted schools where de facto segregation persists—and where immediate infusions of money can make a real difference in terms of educational effectiveness.

—The special needs of those districts that have the furthest to go to catch up educationally with the rest of the Nation.

—The financing of innovative techniques for providing educationally sound interracial experiences for children in racially isolated schools.

This money—the $500 million next year, and $1 billion in fiscal 1972—must come from other programs. Inevitably, it represents a further reordering of priorities on the domestic scene. It represents a heightened priority for making school desegregation work, and for helping the victims of racial isolation learn.

Nothing is more vital to the future of our Nation than the education of its children; and at the heart of equal opportunity is equal educational opportunity. These funds will be an investment in both the quality and the equality of that opportunity.

This money is meant to provide help now, where help is needed now.

As we look to the longer-term future, it is vital that we concentrate more effort on understanding the process of learning—and improving the process of teaching. The educational needs we face cannot be met simply with more books, more classrooms, and more teachers—however urgently these are needed now in schools that face shortages. We need more effective methods of teaching, and especially of teaching those children who are hardest to reach and most lacking in a home environment that encourages learning.

In my message on education reform earlier this month, I proposed creation of a National Institute of Education to conduct and to sponsor basic and applied educational research with special emphasis on compensatory education for the disadvantaged, on the Right to Read, on experimental schools, and on the use of television for educational purposes.

I repeat that proposal—and I ask that the Congress consider it a matter of high priority.

A Free and Open Society

The goal of this administration is a free and open society. In saying this, I use the words "free" and "open" quite precisely.

Freedom has two essential elements: the right to choose, and the ability to choose. The right to move out of a mid city slum, for example, means little without the means of doing so. The right to apply for a good job means little without access to the skills that make it attainable. By the same token, those skills are of little use if arbitrary policies exclude the person who has them because of race or other distinction.

Similarly, an "open" society is one of open choices—and one in which the individual has the mobility to take advantage of those choices.

In speaking of "desegregation" or "integration," we often lose sight of what these mean within the context of a free, open, pluralistic society. We cannot be free, and at the same time be required to fit our lives into prescribed places on a racial grid—whether segregated or integrated, and whether by some mathematical formula or by automatic assignment. Neither can we be free, and at the same time be denied because of race—the right to associate with our fellow citizens on a basis of human equality.

An open society does not have to be homogeneous, or even fully integrated. There is room within it for many communities. Especially in a nation like America, it is natural that people with a common heritage retain special ties; it is natural and right that we have Italian or Irish or Negro or Norwegian neighborhoods; it is natural and right that members of those communities feel a sense of group identity and group pride. In terms of an open society, what matters is mobility: the right and the ability of each person to decide for himself where and how he wants to live, whether as part of the ethnic enclave or as part of the larger society—or, as many do, share the life of both.

We are richer for our cultural diversity; mobility is what allows us to enjoy it. Economic, educational, social mobility—all these, too, are essential elements of the open society. When we speak of equal opportunity we mean just that: that each person should have an equal chance at the starting line, and an equal chance to go just as high and as far as his talents and energies will take him.

This administration's programs for helping the poor, for equal opportunity, for expanded opportunity, all have taken a significantly changed direction from those of previous years—and those principles of a free and open society are the keys to the new direction.

Instead of making a man's decisions for him, we aim to give him both the right and and ability to choose for himself—and the mobility to move upward. Instead of creating a permanent welfare class catered to by a permanent welfare bureaucracy, for example, my welfare reform proposal provides job training and a job requirement for all those able to work—and also a regular family assistance payment instead of the demeaning welfare handout.

By pressing hard for the "Philadelphia Plan," we have sought to crack the color bar in the construction unions—and thus to give black and other minority Americans both the right and the ability to choose jobs in the construction trades, among the highest paid in the Nation.

We have inaugurated new minority business enterprise programs—not only to help minority members get started in business themselves, but also, by developing more black and brown entrepreneurs, to demonstrate to young blacks, Mexican-Americans, and others that they, too, can aspire to this same sort of upward economic mobility.

In our education programs, we have stressed the need for far greater diversity in offerings to match the diversity of individual needs—including more and better vocational and technical training, and a greater development of 2-year community colleges.

Such approaches have been based essentially on faith in the individual—knowing that he sometimes needs help, but believing that in the long run he usually knows what is best for himself. Through them also runs a belief that education is the key that opens the door to personal progress.

As we strive to make our schools places of equal educational opportunity, we should keep our eye fixed on this goal: to achieve a set of conditions in which neither the laws nor the institutions supported by law any longer draw an invidious distinction based on race; and going one step further, we must seek to repair the human damage wrought by past segregation. We must give the minority child that equal place at the starting line that his parents were denied—and the pride, the dignity, the self-respect, that are the birthright of a free American.

We can do no less and still be true to our conscience and our Constitution. I believe that most Americans today, whether North or South, accept this as their duty.

The issues involved in desegregating schools, reducing racial isolation, and providing equal educational opportunity are not sim-

ple. Many of the questions are profound, the factors complex, the legitimate considerations in conflict, and the answers elusive. Our continuing search, therefore, must be not for the perfect set of answers, but for the most nearly perfect and the most constructive.

I am aware that there are many sincere Americans who believe deeply in instant solutions and who will say that my approach does not go far enough fast enough. They feel that the only way to bring about social justice is to integrate all schools now, everywhere, no matter what the cost in the disruption of education.

I am aware, too, that there are many equally sincere citizens North and South, black and white—who believe that racial separation is right, and wish the clock of progress would stop or be turned back to 1953. They will be disappointed, too.

But the call for equal educational opportunity today is in the American tradition. From the outset of the Nation, one of the great struggles in America has been to transform the system of education into one that truly provided equal opportunity for all. At first, the focus was on economic discrimination. The system of "fee schools" and "pauper schools" persisted well into the 19th century.

Heated debates preceded the establishment of universal free public education—and even in such States as New York, New Jersey, and Connecticut, the system is barely a century old.

Even today, inequities persist. Children in poor areas often are served by poor schools—and unlike the children of the wealthy, they cannot escape to private schools. But we have been narrowing the gap—providing more and better education in more of the public schools, and making higher education more widely available through free tuition, scholarships, and loans.

In other areas, too, there were long struggles to eliminate discrimination that had nothing to do with race. Property and even religious qualifications for voting persisted well into the 19th century—and not until 1920 were women finally guaranteed the right to vote.

Now the focus is on race—and on the dismantling of all racial bars to equality of opportunity in the schools. As with the lowering of economic barriers, the pull of conscience and the pull of national self-interest both are in the same direction. A system that leaves any segment of its people poorly educated serves the Nation badly; a system that educates all of its people well serves the Nation well.

We have overcome many problems in our 190 years as a Nation. We can overcome this problem. We have managed to extend opportunity in other areas. We can extend it in this area. Just as other rights have been secured, so too can these rights be secured—and once again the Nation will be better for having done so.

I am confident that we can preserve and improve our schools, carry out the mandate of our Constitution, and be true to our national conscience.

6. Address to the Nation on the Situation in Southeast Asia ("pitiful, helpless giant" speech)
April 30, 1970

Good evening, my fellow Americans:

Ten days ago, in my report to the Nation on Vietnam, I announced a decision to withdraw an additional 150,000 Americans from Vietnam over the next year. I said then that I was making that decision despite our concern over increased enemy activity in Laos, in Cambodia, and in South Vietnam.

At that time, I warned that if I concluded that increased enemy activity in any of these areas endangered the lives of Americans remaining in Vietnam, I would not hesitate to take strong and effective measures to deal with that situation.

Despite that warning, North Vietnam has increased its military aggression in all these areas, and particularly in Cambodia.

After full consultation with the National Security Council, Ambassador Bunker, General Abrams, and my other advisers, I have concluded that the actions of the enemy in the last 10 days clearly endanger the lives of Americans who are in Vietnam now and would constitute an unacceptable risk to those who will be there after withdrawal of another 150,000.

To protect our men who are in Vietnam and to guarantee the continued success of our withdrawal and Vietnamization programs, I have concluded that the time has come for action.

Tonight, I shall describe the actions of the enemy, the actions I have ordered to deal with that situation, and the reasons for my decision.

Cambodia, a small country of 7 million people, has been a neutral nation since the Geneva agreement of 1954—an agreement, incidentally, which was signed by the Government of North Vietnam.

American policy since then has been to scrupulously respect the neutrality of the Cambodian people. We have maintained a skeleton diplomatic mission of fewer than 15 in Cambodia's capital, and that only since last August. For the previous 4 years, from 1965 to 1969, we did not have any diplomatic mission whatever in Cambodia. And for the past 5 years, we have provided no military assistance whatever and no economic assistance to Cambodia.

North Vietnam, however, has not respected that neutrality.

For the past 5 years—as indicated on this map that you see here—North Vietnam has occupied military sanctuaries all along the Cambodian frontier with South Vietnam. Some of these extend up to 20 miles into Cambodia. The sanctuaries are in red and, as you note, they are on both sides of the border. They are used for hit and run attacks on American and South Vietnamese forces in South Vietnam.

These Communist occupied territories contain major base camps, training sites, logistics facilities, weapons and ammunition factories, airstrips, and prisoner-of-war compounds.

For 5 years, neither the United States nor South Vietnam has moved against these enemy sanctuaries because we did not wish to violate the territory of a neutral nation. Even after the Vietnamese Communists began to expand these sanctuaries 4 weeks ago, we counseled patience to our South Vietnamese allies and imposed restraints on our own commanders.

In contrast to our policy, the enemy in the past 2 weeks has stepped up his guerrilla actions and he is concentrating his main forces in these sanctuaries that you see on this map where they are building up to launch massive attacks on our forces and those of South Vietnam.

North Vietnam in the last 2 weeks has stripped away all pretense of respecting the sovereignty or the neutrality of Cambodia. Thousands of their soldiers are invading the country from the sanctuaries; they are encircling the capital of Phnom Penh. Coming from these sanctuaries, as you see here, they have moved into Cambodia and are encircling the capital.

Cambodia, as a result of this, has sent out a call to the United States, to a number of other nations, for assistance. Because if this enemy effort succeeds, Cambodia would become a vast enemy staging area and a springboard for attacks on South Vietnam along 600 miles of frontier—a refuge where enemy troops could return from combat without fear of retaliation.

North Vietnamese men and supplies could then be poured into that country, jeopardizing not only the lives of our own men but the people of South Vietnam as well.

Now confronted with this situation, we have three options.

First, we can do nothing. Well, the ultimate result of that course of action is clear. Unless we indulge in wishful thinking, the lives of Americans remaining in Vietnam after our next withdrawal of 150,000 would be gravely threatened.

Let us go to the map again. Here is South Vietnam. Here is North Vietnam. North Vietnam already occupies this part of Laos. If North Vietnam also occupied this whole band in Cambodia, or the entire country, it would mean that South Vietnam was completely outflanked and the forces of Americans in this area, as well as the South Vietnamese, would be in an untenable military position.

Our second choice is to provide massive military assistance to Cambodia itself. Now unfortunately, while we deeply sympathize with the plight of 7 million Cambodians whose country is being invaded, massive amounts of military assistance could not be rapidly and effectively utilized by the small Cambodian Army against the immediate threat. With other nations, we shall do our best to provide the small arms and other equipment which the Cambodian Army of 40,000 needs and can use for its defense. But the aid we will provide will be limited to the purpose of enabling Cambodia to defend its neutrality and not for the purpose of making it an active belligerent on one side or the other.

Our third choice is to go to the heart of the trouble. That means cleaning out major North Vietnamese and Vietcong occupied territories—these sanctuaries which serve as bases for attacks on both Cambodia and American and South Vietnamese forces in South Vietnam. Some of these, incidentally, are as close to Saigon as Baltimore is to Washington. This one, for example [indicating], is called the Parrot's Beak. It is only 33 miles from Saigon.

Now faced with these three options, this is the decision I have made.

In cooperation with the armed forces of South Vietnam, attacks are being launched this week to clean out major enemy sanctuaries on the Cambodian-Vietnam border.

A major responsibility for the ground operations is being assumed by South Vietnamese forces. For example, the attacks in several areas, including the Parrot's Beak that I referred to a moment ago, are exclusively South Vietnamese ground operations under South Vietnamese command with the United States providing air and logistical support.

There is one area, however, immediately above Parrot's Beak, where I have concluded that a combined American and South Vietnamese operation is necessary.

Tonight, American and South Vietnamese units will attack the headquarters for the entire Communist military operation in South Vietnam. This key control center has been occupied by the North Vietnamese and Vietcong for 5 years in blatant violation of Cambodia's neutrality.

This is not an invasion of Cambodia. The areas in which these attacks will be launched are completely occupied and controlled by North Vietnamese forces. Our purpose is not to occupy the areas. Once enemy forces are driven out of these sanctuaries and once their military supplies are destroyed, we will withdraw.

These actions are in no way directed to the security interests of any nation. Any government that chooses to use these actions as a pretext for harming relations with the United States will be doing so on its own responsibility, and on its own initiative, and we will draw the appropriate conclusions.

Now let me give you the reasons for my decision.

A majority of the American people, a majority of you listening to me, are for the withdrawal of our forces from Vietnam. The action I have taken tonight is indispensable for the continuing success of that withdrawal program.

A majority of the American people want to end this war rather than to have it drag on interminably. The action I have taken tonight will serve that purpose.

A majority of the American people want to keep the casualties of our brave men in Vietnam at an absolute minimum. The action I take tonight is essential if we are to accomplish that goal.

We take this action not for the purpose of expanding the war into Cambodia but for the purpose of ending the war in Vietnam and winning the just peace we all desire. We have made—we will continue to make every possible effort to end this war through negotiation at the conference table rather than through more fighting on the battlefield.

Let us look again at the record. We have stopped the bombing of North Vietnam. We have cut air operations by over 20 percent. We have announced withdrawal of over 250,000 of our men. We have offered to withdraw all of our men if they will withdraw theirs. We have offered to negotiate all issues with only one condition—and that is that the future of South Vietnam be determined not by North Vietnam, and not by the United States, but by the people of South Vietnam themselves.

The answer of the enemy has been intransigence at the conference table, belligerence in Hanoi, massive military aggression in Laos and Cambodia, and stepped-up attacks in South Vietnam, designed to increase American casualties.

This attitude has become intolerable. We will not react to this threat to American lives merely by plaintive diplomatic protests. If we did, the credibility of the United States would be destroyed in every area of the world where only the power of the United States deters aggression.

Tonight, I again warn the North Vietnamese that if they continue to escalate the fighting when the United States is withdrawing its forces, I shall meet my responsibility as Commander in Chief of our Armed Forces to take the action I consider necessary to defend the security of our American men.

The action that I have announced tonight puts the leaders of North Vietnam on notice that we will be patient in working for peace; we will be conciliatory at the conference table, but we will not be humiliated. We will not be defeated. We will not allow American men by the thousands to be killed by an enemy from privileged sanctuaries.

The time came long ago to end this war through peaceful negotiations. We stand ready for those negotiations. We have made major efforts, many of which must remain secret. I say tonight: All the offers and approaches made previously remain on the conference table whenever Hanoi is ready to negotiate seriously.

But if the enemy response to our most conciliatory offers for peaceful negotiation continues to be to increase its attacks and humiliate and defeat us, we shall react accordingly.

My fellow Americans, we live in an age of anarchy, both abroad and at home. We see mindless attacks on all the great institutions which have been created by free civilizations in the last 500 years. Even here in the United States, great universities are being systematically destroyed. Small nations all over the world find themselves under attack from within and from without.

If, when the chips are down, the world's most powerful nation, the United States of America, acts like a pitiful, helpless giant, the forces of totalitarianism and anarchy will threaten free nations and free institutions throughout the world.

It is not our power but our will and character that is being tested tonight. The question all Americans must ask and answer tonight is this: Does the richest and strongest nation in the history of the world have the character to meet a direct challenge by a group which rejects every effort to win a just peace, ignores our warning, tramples on solemn agreements, violates the neutrality of an unarmed people, and uses our prisoners as hostages?

If we fail to meet this challenge, all other nations will be on notice that despite its overwhelming power the United States, when a real crisis comes, will be found wanting.

During my campaign for the Presidency, I pledged to bring Americans home from Vietnam. They are coming home.

I promised to end this war. I shall keep that promise.

I promised to win a just peace. I shall keep that promise.

We shall avoid a wider war. But we are also determined to put an end to this war.

In this room, Woodrow Wilson made the great decisions which led to victory in World War I. Franklin Roosevelt made the decisions which led to our victory in World War II. Dwight D. Eisenhower made decisions which ended the war in Korea and avoided war in the Middle East. John F. Kennedy, in his finest hour, made the great decision which removed Soviet nuclear missiles from Cuba and the Western Hemisphere.

I have noted that there has been a great deal of discussion with regard to this decision that I have made and I should point out that I do not contend that it is in the same magnitude as these decisions that I have just mentioned. But between those decisions and this decision there is a difference that is very fundamental. In those decisions, the American people were not assailed by counsels of doubt and defeat from some of the most widely known opinion leaders of the Nation.

I have noted, for example, that a Republican Senator has said that this action I have taken means that my party has lost all chance of winning the November elections. And others are saying today that this move against enemy sanctuaries will make me a one-term President.

No one is more aware than I am of the political consequences of the action I have taken. It is tempting to take the easy political path: to blame this war on previous administrations and to bring all of our men home immediately, regardless of the consequences, even though that would mean defeat for the United States; to desert 18 million South Vietnamese people, who have put their trust in us and to expose them to the same slaughter and savagery which the leaders of North Vietnam inflicted on hundreds of thousands of North Vietnamese who chose freedom when the Communists took over North Vietnam in 1954; to get peace at any price now, even though I know that a peace of humiliation for the United States would lead to a bigger war or surrender later.

I have rejected all political considerations in making this decision.

Whether my party gains in November is nothing compared to the lives of 400,000 brave Americans fighting for our country and for the cause of peace and freedom in Vietnam. Whether I may be a one-term President is insignificant compared to whether by our failure to act in this crisis the United States proves itself to be unworthy to lead the forces of freedom in this critical period in world history. I would rather be a one-term President and do what I believe is right than to be a two-term President at the cost of seeing America become a second-rate power and to see this Nation accept the first defeat in its proud 190-year history.

I realize that in this war there are honest and deep differences in this country about whether we should have become involved, that there are differences as to how the war should have been conducted. But the decision I announce tonight transcends those differences.

For the lives of American men are involved. The opportunity for Americans to come home in the next 12 months is involved. The future of 18 million people in South Vietnam and 7 million people in Cambodia is involved. The possibility of winning a just peace in Vietnam and in the Pacific is at stake.

It is customary to conclude a speech from the White House by asking support for the President of the United States. Tonight, I depart from that precedent. What I ask is far more important. I ask for your support for our brave men fighting tonight halfway around the world—not for territory—not for glory—but so that their younger brothers and their sons and your sons can have a chance to grow up in a world of peace and freedom and justice.

Thank you and good night.

7. Statement on Student Deaths at Kent State University
May 4, 1970

This should remind us all once again that when dissent turns to violence, it invites tragedy. It is my hope that this tragic and unfortunate incident will strengthen the determination of all the Nation's campuses—administrators, faculty, and students alike—to stand firmly for the right which exists in this country of peaceful dissent and just as strongly against the resort to violence as a means of such expression.

8. Address to the Nation on Economic Policy and Productivity
June 17, 1970

Good afternoon, my fellow Americans:

Today I would like to share with you my thoughts on three subjects that reach into the homes and the pocketbooks of every family: your job, your income, and your cost of living.

Specifically, I shall announce actions that will help to move us ahead more quickly towards our goal of full employment, economic growth, and reasonable price stability in peacetime.

Let us begin by recognizing these facts:

The American economy is the strongest in the world. This year, the number of Americans who have jobs is the highest in our history. Even allowing for taxes and inflation, the average real income of Americans is higher this year than ever before, in part because of the increase in Social Security benefits and the reduction of the tax surcharge which will end entirely this month.

Because of that basic economic strength, we can honestly and confidently face up to our current problems:

Unemployment has increased; the price index continues to rise; profits have gone down; the stock market has declined; interest rates are too high.

Today I am presenting a program to deal with these problems.

First we should recognize the causes of our economic difficulties. What we are doing here is to deal with the problems of a nation in transition from a wartime economy to a peacetime economy.

Our economy must consequently make adjustments to two great changes at the same time.

One change is that defense spending is on the way down. For the first time in 20 years, the Federal Government is spending more on human resource programs than on national defense.

This year we are spending $1.7 billion less on defense than we were a year ago; in the next year, we plan to spend $5.2 billion less. This is more than a redirection of resources. This is an historic reordering of our national priorities.

The cuts in defense spending mean a shift of job opportunities away from defense production to the kind of production that meets social needs. This will require adjustment by many employees and businesses.

For example, over 400,000 military and civilian employees have been released in this past year by our Armed Forces. In that time, cutbacks in defense spending have reduced jobs in defense plants by about 300,000. Taken together, that's almost three quarters of a mil-

lion people affected by the reduction in defense spending. Now, while many of these workers have found new jobs, it is not hard to see where much of the current increase in total unemployment has come from.

Despite the difficulties of this transition, progress toward a peacetime economy is a good sign for the labor force and for the business community. Reduction in defense spending gives us more room in the Federal budget to meet human needs at home. It makes it possible to build a much more enduring prosperity in this country.

With its trials and with its hopes, a peacetime economy is clearly on the way. We have already brought home 115,000 from Vietnam. Our success in destroying enemy supply bases in Cambodia has made it possible for us to go forward with the program for withdrawal of 150,000 more men which I announced in my speech of April 20, without jeopardizing the lives of our men who would be brought home after that.

Our scheduled withdrawal of forces from Cambodia by June 30 will be kept. Our scheduled transition from a wartime economy to a peacetime consumer economy will be kept.

While our economy adapts to the reordering of our national priorities and resources, we are undergoing a second great change. We are trying to do something that never has been done before: to avoid a recession while we bring a major inflation to an end.

This administration took office after a long period in which this Nation lived far beyond its means. In the decade of the sixties, Federal deficits totaled $57 billion, and the American consumer was forced to pay the piper in terms of a rising spiral of prices.

Seventeen months ago, when this administration took office, we stood at a crossroads of economic policy. There were actually four roads open to us.

One was the road of runaway inflation: to do nothing about Government spending and rising prices, to let the boom go on booming until the bubble burst. That was the road the Nation was taken on in the sixties, and the people who suffer most along that road are the millions of Americans living on fixed incomes.

The road headed in the opposite direction from that one was a possible choice as well: Let the economy "go through the wringer," as some suggested, and bring on a major recession.

Well, that would stop inflation abruptly, but at a cost in human terms of broken careers and broken lives that this Nation must never again have to pay.

A third choice was the route of wage and price controls. That would lead to rationing, black marketing, total Federal bureaucratic domination, and it would never get at the real causes of inflation.

That left a fourth choice: to cut down the sharp rise in Federal spending and to restrain the economy firmly and steadily. In that way, prices would slow their rise without too great a hardship on the workingman, the business-man, and the investor. That was the road of responsibility, that is the road we chose, and that is the road we are continuing on today.

Because we are concerned with both prices and jobs, we have put the brakes on inflation carefully and steadily.

This did not mean that inflation could end without some slowdown in the economy. But we were willing to make a trade to sacrifice speed in ending inflation in order to keep the economic slowdown moderate.

At the outset of our fight against inflation, we pointed out that it would take time to relieve the heavy spending programs and pres-sures on the economy; after that beginning, it would take more time to see that those reduced pressures result in a slowdown in price rises.

Now many people wonder why we are eas-ing some of the restraints on the economy before we have seen dramatic results in slowing down the rise in the cost of living. Why, they ask, don't we keep on with all of our measures to hold down the economy until price rises stop completely?

Let me put it this way: It is a little like trying to bring a boat into a dock. You turn down the power well before you get to the dock and let the boat coast in. Now if you waited until you reached the dock to turn down the power, you'd soon have to buy a new dock or a new boat.

In the same way, we're heading for the dock of price stability: We have to ease up on the power of our restraint and let our momentum carry us safely into port.

That's why our independent central banking system has seen fit to ease up on the money supply. That is why I relaxed the cutback on federally-assisted construction projects and why I have not asked for a new surtax.

These actions are not a signal that we are giv-ing up our fight against inflation. On the con-trary, they mean that there was already enough power applied to reach the dock and now we'd better make sure that we don't damage the boat.

The Federal Reserve's monetary policy, which permitted no growth in the money supply at all in the second half of 1969, has now been relaxed. In the past 6 months, the money supply has grown at a rate of about 6 percent a year.

The Chairman of the Federal Reserve Board has assured the Nation that there will be enough money and credit to meet future needs, and that the orderly expansion of the economy will not be endangered by a lack of liquidity.

Now I'm not asking anyone to put on rose-colored glasses. We are well aware of the forces working against us.

To make sure the coming upturn in the economy will not be of the kind that brings on a new surge of inflation, we have gained control of the runaway momentum of Federal spending—the spending that triggered the rise in prices in the first place.

In the 3 years before this administration took office, Federal spending rose an average of 15 percent a year—the sharpest rate of increase since the Korean war. In the current fiscal year, we slashed that rate of increase in half, to 7 percent. And in the coming year, we intend to cut that rate of increase in spending by half again.

Now this required some hard decisions—including, as you may recall, the veto of a popular appropriations bill—but it was vital to win the battle to hold down spending so that we could ultimately hold down prices. We are winning that battle but we cannot let up now.

I am convinced that the basic economic road we have taken is the right road, the responsible road, the road that will curb the cost of living and lead us to orderly expansion.

However, we have to face some difficult problems. The momentum of 4 years of inflation was stronger than had been anticipated. The effect on unemployment is greater than we foresaw. The pace of our progress toward price stability and high employment has not been quick enough.

Now this does not mean that we should abandon our strategy. It does mean that we must pay heed to economic developments as we move along and adjust our tactics accordingly.

While relying basically on continued moderation in general fiscal and monetary policies, I think it is necessary, and timely to supplement them with several more specific measures.

Here are the actions I am taking to speed up the fight against inflation:

First, I shall appoint a National Commission on Productivity with representatives from business, labor, the public, and government.

In general, productivity is a measure of how well we use our resources; in particular, it means how much real value is produced by an hour of work. In the past 2 years, productivity has increased far less than usual.

In order to achieve price stability, healthy growth, and a rising standard of living, we must find ways of restoring growth to productivity.

This Commission's task will be to point the way toward this growth in 1970 and in the years ahead. I shall direct the Commission to give first priority to the problems we face now; we must achieve a balance between costs and productivity that will lead to more stable prices.

Productivity in the American economy depends on the effectiveness of management; the investment of capital for research, development, and advanced technology; and most of all on the training and progressive spirit of 86 million working Americans.

To give its efforts the proper base of understanding, the Commission will this summer bring together leaders of business, labor, government, and the general public to meet in a special President's Conference on Productivity.

Second, I have instructed the Council of Economic Advisers to prepare a periodic Inflation Alert. This will spotlight the significant areas of wage and price increases and objectively analyze their impact on the price level. This Inflation Alert will call attention to outstanding cases of price or wage increases and will be made public by the productivity commission.

Third, I am establishing a Regulations and Purchasing Review Board within the Federal Government. All Government actions will be reviewed to determine where Federal purchasing and regulations drive up costs and prices; our import policy will be reviewed to see how supplies can be increased to meet rising demand, without losing jobs here at home.

Now let me specifically spell out what I will do and what I will not do. I intend to help focus the attention of business and labor on the need for increased productivity. This is the way for them to serve their own interest while they serve the public interest. This is the only way to make sure that increases in earnings are not wiped out by the rising cost of living.

This administration, by its spending restraint, has set the example in this past year; we believe we have now earned the credentials to call for similar restraint from business and labor to slow down inflation.

Now is the time for business at every level to take price actions more consistent with a stable cost of living, and now is the time for labor to structure its wage demands to better achieve a new stability of costs.

The fight against inflation is everybody's business. If you act against the national interest, if you contribute to inflation in your price or wage demands, then you are acting against your own best interests and your customers' best interests, and that is neither good business nor good bargaining.

If businessmen and workingmen are willing to raise their sights by lowering their demands, they will help themselves by helping to hold down everybody's cost of living.

I believe there is a new social responsibility growing up in our economic system on the part of unions and corporations. Now is the time for that social concern to take the form of specific action on the wage-price front.

Now, here is what I will not do:

I will not take this Nation down the road of wage and price controls, however politically expedient that may seem.

Controls and rationing may seem like an easy way out but they are really an easy way into more trouble—to the explosion that follows when you try to clamp a lid on a rising head of steam without turning down the fire under the pot.

Wage and price controls only postpone a day of reckoning, and in so doing they rob every American of a very important part of his freedom.

Nor am I starting to use controls in disguise. By that I mean the kind of policy whereby Government makes executive pronouncements to enforce "guidelines" in an attempt to dictate specific prices and wages without authority of law.

Now I realize that there are some people who get satisfaction out of seeing an individual businessman or labor leader called on the carpet and browbeaten by Government officials. But we cannot protect the value of the dollar by passing the buck. That sort of grandstanding distracts attention from the real cause of inflation and it can be a dangerous misuse of the power of Government.

The actions I have outlined today are well within the powers of the President. But there are other actions that the President cannot take alone.

This is not the time for the Congress to play politics with inflation by passing legislation granting the President standby powers to impose wage and price controls. The Congress knows I will not impose controls because they would do more harm than good.

This is the time, however, for Congress and the President to cooperate on a program specifically addressed to help the people who need help most in a period of economic transition from a wartime to a peacetime economy.

Now here is that program:

To provide more help now to those workers who have lost jobs, I urge the Congress to pass the legislation I have proposed to expand and strengthen our unemployment insurance system. This legislation would cover almost 5 million more people who lack this protection now, and the system would be made more responsive to changing economic conditions.

I submitted this legislation to the Congress almost a year ago. It is time for the Congress to act.

To help those in need of job training, I urge the Congress to pass the Manpower Training Act which provides an automatic increase in manpower training funds in times of high unemployment. I submitted this proposal to the Congress 10 months ago. It is time for the Congress to act.

I ask for full appropriation for the Office of Economic Opportunity and I request the Congress to provide at once a supplemental budget of $50 million to provide useful training and support to young people who are out of school in the summer months.

To further protect the small investor, I support the establishment of an insurance corporation with a Federal backstop to guarantee the investor against losses that could be caused by financial difficulties of brokerage houses. While this would not affect the equity risk that is always present in stock market investment, it will assure the investor that the stability of the securities industry itself does not become cause for concern.

To relieve the worries of many of our older citizens living on fixed incomes, I urge the Congress to pass my proposal to tie Social Security benefits to the cost of living. This proposal, passed by the House, awaiting Senate action for the past month, will keep the burden of the fight against inflation from falling on those least able to afford it.

To stimulate an industry bearing the brunt of high interest rates, I urge enactment of the Emergency Home Finance Act of 1970. This would attract as much as $6 billion into the housing market in the coming fiscal year. More than a third of a million families need this legislation for home financing now; and the resulting new construction of more than 200,000 houses will also help provide many new jobs.

This housing bill was passed unanimously by the Senate. It has been awaiting action for 3 months in the House. It is time for the Congress to act.

To help the small businessman who finds it difficult to get necessary credit, I have asked the Congress for greater authority for the Small Business Administration to stimulate banks and others to make loans to small businesses at lower interest rates. I submitted this legislation to the Congress 3 months ago. It is time for the Congress to act.

To strengthen our railroad industry, I am asking for legislation that will enable the Department of Transportation to provide emergency assistance to railroads in financial difficulties. I am also urging the independent Interstate Commerce Commission to give prompt attention to the urgent financial problems of this industry.

And finally, to curb inflationary pressures throughout our economy, I call upon the Congress to join me in holding down Government spending to avoid a large budget deficit. This requires a new restraint on spending programs and the passage of the revenue-producing measures that I have already made.

There is an old and cynical adage that says that in an election year, the smart politician is one who votes for all bills to spend money and votes against all bills to raise taxes.

But in this election year of 1970, that old adage cannot apply. The American people will see through any attempt by anyone to play politics with their cost of living. And whenever a Member of Congress displays the imagination to introduce a bill that calls for more spending, let him display the courage to introduce a bill to raise the taxes to pay for that new program.

Long before the art of economics had a name, it was called "political arithmetic." The American people expect their elected officials to do their political arithmetic honestly.

The actions I have taken today, together with the proposals I have made, are needed now to help us through this time of transition.

I believe this is the right program at the right time and for the right purpose. There is no more important goal than to curb inflation without permitting severe disruption. This is an activist administration, and should new developments call for new action in the future, I shall take the action needed to attain that goal.

Before I close today, I would like to give you a broader view of the significance of what is happening in the American economy.

We have more at stake here than a possible difference of one or two tenths of a percentage point in the price level in 1970. All of us have to make decisions now which will profoundly affect the survival of a free economic system throughout the world.

Industrial countries around the world all face the problems of inflation. By solving our problems here without throwing away our freedom, we shall set an example that will have great impact on the kind of economic systems others may choose.

Our free economic system has produced enormous benefits for the American people. The United States, with 10 percent of the free world's people, produces 40 percent of the free world's output. We did not gain that production power by shackling our free economic system.

The average American has the highest real disposable income in the world, and it is higher today than ever before in our history. We did not reach that height by turning over economic freedom to government.

In the next 5 years, and in real terms, the American consumer will be able to buy almost 20 percent more than he does today. To reach that attainable goal we need no artificial dependence on the production of the weapons of war—on the contrary, we will all share much more fully in a peacetime prosperity.

As I see it, prosperity is not a period of good times between periods of hard times—that's false prosperity, with people riding high but riding for a fall.

Nor is prosperity a time when the well-to-do become better off while everyone else stays the same or falls behind—that's partial prosperity. It only widens the gap between our people.

The true prosperity that I envision offers a new fairness in our national life.

We are working toward a system that will provide "job justice"—open and equal opportunity for every man and woman to build a good career.

We are working toward a system that replaces the old ups and downs with a new steadiness of economic growth within our capacity to produce efficiently.

And we are working toward a system that will deliver a higher standard of living to a people living in peace.

That is the hope offered by a modem free enterprise system—not managed by government and not ignored by government, but helped by a government that creates the climate for steady, healthy growth.

As we move forward into a peacetime economy, I am confident that we will achieve the only kind of prosperity that counts—the prosperity that lasts, the prosperity that can be shared by every American.

Thank you and good afternoon.

9. State of the Union Address January 22, 1971

Mr. Speaker, Mr. President, my colleagues in the Congress, our distinguished guests, my fellow Americans:

As this 92d Congress begins its session, America has lost a great Senator, and all of us who had the privilege to know him have lost a loyal friend. I had the privilege of visiting Senator Russell in the hospital just a few days before he died. He never spoke about himself. He only spoke eloquently about the need for a strong national defense. In tribute to one of the most magnificent Americans of all time, I respectfully ask that all those here will rise in silent prayer for Senator Russell.

[Moment of silence]

Thank you.

Mr. Speaker, before I begin my formal address, I want to use this opportunity to congratulate all of those who were winners in the rather spirited contest for leadership positions in the House and the Senate and, also, to express my condolences to the losers. I know how both of you feel.

And I particularly want to join with all of the Members of the House and the Senate as well in congratulating the new Speaker of the United States Congress.

To those new Members of this House who may have some doubts about the possibilities for advancement in the years ahead, I would remind you that the Speaker and I met just 24 years ago in this Chamber as freshmen Members of the 80th Congress. As you see, we both have come up in the world a bit since then.

Mr. Speaker, this 92d Congress has a chance to be recorded as the greatest Congress in America's history.

In these troubled years just past, America has been going through a long nightmare of war and division, of crime and inflation. Even more deeply, we have gone through a long, dark night of the American spirit. But now that night is ending. Now we must let our spirits soar again. Now we are ready for the lift of a driving dream.

The people of this Nation are eager to get on with the quest for new greatness. They see challenges, and they are prepared to meet those challenges. It is for us here to open the doors that will set free again the real greatness of this Nation—the genius of the American people.

How shall we meet this challenge? How can we truly open the doors, and set free the full genius of our people?

The way in which the 92d Congress answers these questions will determine its place in history. More importantly, it can determine this Nation's place in history as we enter the third century of our independence.

Tonight I shall present to the Congress six great goals. I shall ask not simply for more new programs in the old framework. I shall ask to change the framework of government itself—to reform the entire structure of American government so we can make it again fully responsive to the needs and the wishes of the American people.

If we act boldly—if we seize this moment and achieve these goals—we can close the gap between promise and performance in American government. We can bring together the resources of this Nation and the spirit of the American people.

In discussing these great goals, I shall deal tonight only with matters on the domestic side of the Nation's agenda. I shall make a separate report to the Congress and the Nation next month on developments in foreign policy.

The first of these great goals is already before the Congress.

I urge that the unfinished business of the 91st Congress be made the first priority business of the 92d Congress.

Over the next 2 weeks, I will call upon Congress to take action on more than 35 pieces of proposed legislation on which action was not completed last year.

The most important is welfare reform.

The present welfare system has become a monstrous, consuming outrage—an outrage against the community, against the taxpayer, and particularly against the children it is supposed to help.

We may honestly disagree, as we do, on what to do about it. But we can all agree that we must meet the challenge, not by pouring more money into a bad program, but by abolishing the present welfare system and adopting a new one.

So let us place a floor under the income of every family with children in America-and without those demeaning, soul-stifling affronts to human dignity that so blight the lives of welfare children today. But let us also establish an effective work incentive and an effective work requirement.

Let us provide the means by which more can help themselves. This shall be our goal.

Let us generously help those who are not able to help themselves. But let us stop helping those who are able to help themselves but refuse to do so.

The second great goal is to achieve what Americans have not enjoyed since 1957—full prosperity in peacetime.

The tide of inflation has turned. The rise in the cost of living, which had been gathering dangerous momentum in the late sixties, was reduced last year. Inflation will be further reduced this year.

But as we have moved from runaway inflation toward reasonable price stability and at the same time as we have been moving from a wartime economy to a peacetime economy, we have paid a price in increased unemployment.

We should take no comfort from the fact that the level of unemployment in this transition from a wartime to a peacetime economy is lower than in any peacetime year of the sixties.

This is not good enough for the man who is unemployed in the seventies. We must do better for workers in peacetime and we will do better.

To achieve this, I will submit an expansionary budget this year—one that will help stimulate the economy and thereby open up new job opportunities for millions of Americans.

It will be a full employment budget, a budget designed to be in balance if the economy were operating at its peak potential. By spending as if we were at full employment, we will help to bring about full employment.

I ask the Congress to accept these expansionary policies—to accept the concept of a full employment budget. At the same time, I ask the Congress to cooperate in resisting expenditures that go beyond the limits of the full employment budget. For as we wage a campaign to bring about a widely shared prosperity, we must not reignite the fires of inflation and so undermine that prosperity.

With the stimulus and the discipline of a full employment budget, with the commitment of the independent Federal Reserve System to provide fully for the monetary needs of a growing economy, and with a much greater effort on the part of labor and management to make their wage and price decisions in the light of the national interest and their own self-interest—then for the worker, the farmer, the consumer, for Americans everywhere we shall gain the goal of a new prosperity: more jobs, more income, more profits, without inflation and without war.

This is a great goal, and one that we can achieve together.

The third great goal is to continue the effort so dramatically begun last year: to restore and enhance our natural environment.

Building on the foundation laid in the 37-point program that I submitted to Congress last year, I will propose a strong new set of initiatives to clean up our air and water, to combat noise, and to preserve and restore our surroundings.

I will propose programs to make better use of our land, to encourage a balanced national growth—growth that will revitalize our rural heartland and enhance the quality of life in America.

And not only to meet today's needs but to anticipate those of tomorrow, I will put forward the most extensive program ever proposed by a President of the United States to expand the Nation's parks, recreation areas, open spaces, in a way that truly brings parks to the people where the people are. For only if we leave a legacy of parks will the next generation have parks to enjoy.

As a fourth great goal, I will offer a far-reaching set of proposals for improving America's health care and making it available more fairly to more people.

I will propose:

—A program to insure that no American family will be prevented from obtaining basic medical care by inability to pay.

—I will propose a major increase in and redirection of aid to medical schools, to greatly increase the number of doctors and other health personnel.

—Incentives to improve the delivery of health services, to get more medical care resources into those areas that have not been adequately served, to make greater use of medical assistants, and to slow the alarming rise in the costs of medical care.

—New programs to encourage better preventive medicine, by attacking the causes of disease and injury, and by providing incentives to doctors to keep people well rather than just to treat them when they are sick.

I will also ask for an appropriation of an extra $100 million to launch an intensive campaign to find a cure for cancer, and I will ask later for whatever additional funds can effectively be used. The time has come in America when the same kind of concentrated effort that split the atom and took man to the moon should be turned toward conquering this dread disease. Let us make a total national commitment to achieve this goal.

America has long been the wealthiest nation in the world. Now it is time we became the healthiest nation in the world.

The fifth great goal is to strengthen and to renew our State and local governments.

As we approach our 200th anniversary in 1976, we remember that this Nation launched itself as a loose confederation of separate States, without a workable central government.

At that time, the mark of its leaders' vision was that they quickly saw the need to balance the separate powers of the States with a government of central powers.

And so they gave us a constitution of balanced powers, of unity with diversity-and so clear was their vision that it survives today as the oldest written constitution still in force in the world.

For almost two centuries since—and dramatically in the 1930's—at those great turning points when the question has been between the States and the Federal Government, that question has been resolved in favor of a stronger central Federal Government.

During this time the Nation grew and the Nation prospered. But one thing history tells us is that no great movement goes in the same direction forever. Nations change, they adapt, or they slowly die.

The time has now come in America to reverse the flow of power and resources from the States and communities to Washington, and start power and resources flowing back from Washington to the States and communities and, more important, to the people all across America.

The time has come for a new partnership between the Federal Government and the States and localities—a partnership in which we entrust the States and localities with a larger share of the Nation's responsibilities, and in which we share our Federal revenues with them so that they can meet those responsibilities.

To achieve this goal, I propose to the Congress tonight that we enact a plan of revenue sharing historic in scope and bold in concept.

All across America today, States and cities are confronted with a financial crisis. Some have already been cutting back on essential services—for example, just recently San Diego and Cleveland cut back on trash collections. Most are caught between the prospects of bankruptcy on the one hand and adding to an already crushing tax burden on the other.

As one indication of the rising costs of local government, I discovered the other day that my home town of Whittier, California—which has a population of 67,000—has a larger budget for 1971 than the entire Federal budget was in 1791.

Now the time has come to take a new direction, and once again to introduce a new and more creative balance to our approach to government.

So let us put the money where the needs are. And let us put the power to spend it where the people are.

I propose that the Congress make a $16 billion investment in renewing State and local government. Five billion dollars of this will be in new and unrestricted funds to be used as the States and localities see fit. The other $11 billion will be provided by allocating $1 billion of new funds and converting one-third of the money going to the present narrow-purpose aid programs into Federal revenue sharing funds for six broad purposes for urban development, rural development, education, transportation, job training, and law enforcement but with the States and localites making their own decisions on how it should be spent within each category.

For the next fiscal year, this would increase total Federal aid to the States and localities more than 25 percent over the present level.

The revenue sharing proposals I send to the Congress will include the safeguards against discrimination that accompany all other Federal funds allocated to the States. Neither the President nor the Congress nor the conscience of this Nation can permit money which comes from all the people to be used in a way which discriminates against some of the people.

The Federal Government will still have a large and vital role to play in achieving our national progress. Established functions that are clearly and essentially Federal in nature will still be performed by the Federal Government. New functions that need to be sponsored or performed by the Federal Government—such as those I have urged tonight in welfare and health—will be added to the Federal agenda. Whenever it makes the best sense for us to act as a whole nation, the Federal Government should and will lead the way. But where States or local governments can better do what needs to be done, let us see that they have the resources to do it there.

Under this plan, the Federal Government will provide the States and localities with more money and less interference—and by cutting down the interference the same amount of money will go a lot further.

Let us share our resources.

Let us share them to rescue the States and localities from the brink of financial crisis.

Let us share them to give homeowners and wage earners a chance to escape from ever-higher property taxes and sales taxes.

Let us share our resources for two other reasons as well.

The first of these reasons has to do with government itself, and the second has to do with each of us, with the individual.

Let's face it. Most Americans today are simply fed up with government at all levels. They will not—and they should not—continue to tolerate the gap between promise and performance in government.

The fact is that we have made the Federal Government so strong it grows muscle-bound and the States and localities so weak they approach impotence.

If we put more power in more places, we can make government more creative in more places. That way we multiply the number of people with the ability to make things happen—and we can open the way to a new burst of creative energy throughout America.

The final reason I urge this historic shift is much more personal, for each and for every one of us.

As everything seems to have grown bigger and more complex in America, as the forces that shape our lives seem to have grown more distant and more impersonal, a great feeling of frustration has crept across this land.

Whether it is the workingman who feels neglected, the black man who feels oppressed, or the mother concerned about her children, there has been a growing feeling that "Things are in the saddle, and ride mankind."

Millions of frustrated young Americans today are crying out—asking not what will government do for me, but what can I do, how can I contribute, how can I matter?

And so let us answer them. Let us say to them and let us say to all Americans, "We hear you. We will give you a chance. We are going to give you a new chance to have more to say about the decisions that affect your future—a chance to participate in government—because we are going to provide more centers of power where what you do can make a difference that you can see and feel in your own life and the life of your whole community."

The further away government is from people, the stronger government becomes and the weaker people become. And a nation with a strong government and a weak people is an empty shell.

I reject the patronizing idea that government in Washington, D.C., is inevitably more wise, more honest, and more efficient than government at the local or State level. The honesty and efficiency of government depends on people. Government at all levels has good people and bad people. And the way to get more good people into government is to give them more opportunity to do good things.

The idea that a bureaucratic elite in Washington knows best what is best for people everywhere and that you cannot trust local governments is really a contention that you cannot trust people to govern themselves. This notion is completely foreign to the American experience. Local government is the government closest to the people, it is most responsive to the individual person. It is people's government in a far more intimate way than the Government in Washington can ever be.

People came to America because they wanted to determine their own future rather than to live in a country where others determined their future for them.

What this change means is that once again in America we are placing our trust in people.

I have faith in people. I trust the judgment of people. Let us give the people of America a chance, a bigger voice in deciding for themselves those questions that so greatly affect their lives.

The sixth great goal is a complete reform of the Federal Government itself.

Based on a long and intensive study with the aid of the best advice obtainable, I have concluded that a sweeping reorganization of the executive branch is needed if the Government is to keep up with the times and with the needs of the people.

I propose, therefore, that we reduce the present 12 Cabinet Departments to eight.

I propose that the Departments of State, Treasury, Defense, and Justice remain, but that all the other departments be consolidated into four: Human Resources, Community Development, Natural Resources, and Economic Development.

Let us look at what these would be:

—First, a department dealing with the concerns of people—as individuals, as members of a family—a department focused on human needs.

—Second, a department concerned with the community—rural communities and urban communities—and with all that it takes to make a community function as a community.

—Third, a department concerned with our physical environment, with the preservation and balanced use of those great natural resources on which our Nation depends.

—And fourth, a department concerned with our prosperity—with our jobs, our businesses, and those many activities that keep our economy running smoothly and well.

Under this plan, rather than dividing up our departments by narrow subjects, we would organize them around the great purposes of government. Rather than scattering responsibility by adding new levels of bureaucracy, we would focus and concentrate the responsibility for getting problems solved.

With these four departments, when we have a problem we will know where to go—and the department will have the authority and the resources to do something about it.

Over the years we have added departments and created agencies at the Federal level, each to serve a new constituency, to handle a particular task—and these have grown and multiplied in what has become a hopeless confusion of form and function.

The time has come to match our structure to our purposes—to look with a fresh eye, to organize the Government by conscious, comprehensive design to meet the new needs of a new era.

One hundred years ago, Abraham Lincoln stood on a battlefield and spoke of a "government of the people, by the people, for the people." Too often since then, we have become a nation of the Government, by the Government, for the Government.

By enacting these reforms, we can renew that principle that Lincoln stated so simply and so well.

By giving everyone's voice a chance to be heard, we will have government that truly is of the people.

By creating more centers of meaningful power, more places where decisions that really count can be made, by giving more people a chance to do something, we can have government that truly is by the people.

And by setting up a completely modern, functional system of government at the national level, we in Washington will at last be able to provide government that is truly for the people.

I realize that what I am asking is that not only the executive branch in Washington but that even this Congress will have to change by giving up some of its power.

Change is hard. But without change there can be no progress. And for each of us the question then becomes, not "Will change cause me inconvenience?" but "Will change bring progress for America?"

Giving up power is hard. But I would urge all of you, as leaders of this country, to remember that the truly revered leaders in world history are those who gave power to people, and not those who took it away.

As we consider these reforms we will be acting, not for the next 2 years or for the next 10 years, but for the next 100 years.

So let us approach these six great goals with a sense not only of this moment in history but also of history itself.

Let us act with the willingness to work together and the vision and the boldness and the courage of those great Americans who met in Philadelphia almost 190 years ago to write a constitution.

Let us leave a heritage as they did—not just for our children but for millions yet unborn—of a nation where every American will have a chance not only to live in peace and to enjoy prosperity and opportunity but to participate in a system of government where he knows not only his votes but his ideas count—a system of government which will provide the means for America to reach heights of achievement undreamed of before.

Those men who met at Philadelphia left a great heritage because they had a vision—not only of what the Nation was but of what it could become.

As I think of that vision, I recall that America was founded as the land of the open door—as a haven for the oppressed, a land of opportunity, a place of refuge, of hope.

When the first settlers opened the door of America three and a half centuries ago, they came to escape persecution and to find opportunity—and they left wide the door of welcome for others to follow.

When the Thirteen Colonies declared their independence almost two centuries ago, they opened the door to a new vision of liberty and of human fulfillment—not just for an elite but for all.

To the generations that followed, America's was the open door that beckoned millions from the old world to the new in search of a better life, a freer life, a fuller life, and in which, by their own decisions, they could shape their own destinies.

For the black American, the Indian, the Mexican-American, and for those others in our land who have not had an equal chance, the Nation at last has begun to confront the need to press open the door of full and equal opportunity, and of human dignity.

For all Americans, with these changes I have proposed tonight we can open the door to a new era of opportunity. We can open the door to full and effective participation in the decisions that affect their lives. We can open the door to a new partnership among governments at all levels, between those governments and the people themselves. And by so doing, we can open wide the doors of human fulfillment for millions of people here in America now and in the years to come.

In the next few weeks I will spell out in greater detail the way I propose that we achieve these six great goals. I ask this Congress to be responsive. If it is, then the 92d Congress, your Congress, our Congress, at the end of its term, will be able to look back on a record more splendid than any in our history.

This can be the Congress that helped us end the longest war in the Nation's history, and end it in a way that will give us at last a genuine chance to enjoy what we have not had in this century: a full generation of peace.

This can be the Congress that helped achieve an expanding economy, with full employment and without inflation—and without the deadly stimulus of war.

This can be the Congress that reformed a welfare system that has robbed recipients of their dignity and robbed States and cities of their resources.

This can be the Congress that pressed forward the rescue of our environment, and established for the next generation an enduring legacy of parks for the people.

This can be the Congress that launched a new era in American medicine, in which the quality of medical care was enhanced while the costs were made less burdensome.

But above all, what this Congress can be remembered for is opening the way to a new American revolution—a peaceful revolution in which power was turned back to the people—in which government at all levels was refreshed and renewed and made truly responsive. This can be a revolution as profound, as far-reaching, as exciting as that first revolution almost 200 years ago—and it can mean that just 5 years from now America will enter its third century as a young nation new in spirit, with all the vigor and the freshness with which it began its first century.

My colleagues in the Congress, these are great goals. They can make the sessions of this Congress a great moment for America. So let us pledge together to go forward together—by achieving these goals to give America the foundation today for a new greatness tomorrow and in all the years to come, and in so doing to make this the greatest Congress in the history of this great and good country.

10. Statement to Congress on the Proposed Reorganization of the Executive Branch
March 25, 1971

To the Congress of the United States:

When I suggested in my State of the Union Message that "most Americans today are simply fed up with government at all levels," there was some surprise that such a sweeping indictment of government would come from within the government itself. Yet it is precisely there, within the government itself, that frustration with government is often most deeply experienced.

A President and his associates often feel that frustration as they try to fulfill their promises to the people. Legislators feel that frustration as they work to carry out the hopes of their constituents. And dedicated civil servants feel that frustration as they strive to achieve in action the goals which have been established in law.

Good Men and Bad Mechanisms

The problem with government is not, by and large, the people in government. It is a popular thing, to be sure, for the public to blame elected officials and for elected officials to blame appointed officials when government fails to perform. There are times when such criticism is clearly justified. But after a quarter century of observing government from a variety of vantage points, I have concluded that the people who work in government are more often the victims than the villains when government breaks down. Their spirit has usually been willing. It is the structure that has been weak.

Good people cannot do good things with bad mechanisms. But bad mechanisms can frustrate even the noblest aims. That is why so many public servants—of both political parties, of high rank and low, in both the legislative and executive branches—are often disenchanted with government these days. That is also why so many voters feel that the results of elections make remarkably little difference in their lives.

Just as inadequate organization can frustrate good men and women, so it can dissipate good money. At the Federal level alone we have spent some $1.1 trillion on domestic programs over the last 25 years, but we have not realized a fair return on this investment. The more we spend, the more it seems we need to spend and while our tax bills are getting bigger our problems are getting worse.

No, the major cause of the ineffectiveness of government is not a matter of men or of money. It is principally a matter of machinery. It will do us little good to change personnel or to provide more resources unless we are willing to undertake a critical review of government's overall design.

Most people do not pay much attention to mechanical questions. What happens under the hood of their automobile, for example, is something they leave to the specialists at the garage. What they do care about, however, is how well the automobile performs. Similarly, most people are willing to leave the mechanical questions of government organization to those who have specialized in that subject—and to their elected leaders. But they do care very deeply about how well the government performs.

At this moment in our history, most Americans have concluded that government is not performing well. It promises much, but it does not deliver what it promises. The great danger, in my judgment, is that this momentary disillusionment with government will turn into a more profound and lasting loss of faith.

We must fight that danger. We must restore the confidence of the people in the capacities of their government. In my view, that obligation now requires us to give more profound and more critical attention to the question of government organization than any single group of American leaders has done since the Constitutional Convention adjourned in Philadelphia in September of 1787. As we strive to bring about a new American Revolution, we must recognize that central truth which those who led the original American Revolution so clearly understood: often it is how the government is put together that determines how well the government can do its job.

This is not a partisan matter, for there is no Republican way and no Democratic way to reorganize the government. This is not a matter for dogmatic dispute, for there is no single, ideal blueprint which will immediately bring good order to Federal affairs. Nor is this a matter to be dealt with once and then forgotten. For it is important that our political institutions remain constantly responsive to changing times and changing problems.

Renewed Interest in Comprehensive Reform

The last two years have been a time of renewed interest in the question of how government is organized. The Congress has instituted a number of reforms in its own procedures and is considering others. Judicial reform—at all levels of government—has also become a matter of intense concern. The relationship between various levels of government has attracted increased attention—and so, of course, has the subject of executive reform.

This administration, with the counsel and the cooperation of the Congress, has taken a number of steps to reorganize the executive branch of the Federal Government. We have set up a new Domestic Council and a new Office of Management and Budget in the Executive Office of the President. We have created a new Environmental Protection Agency and a new United States Postal Service. We have worked to rationalize the internal structure of Federal departments and agencies.

All of these and other changes have been important, but none has been comprehensive. And now we face a fundamental choice. We can continue to tinker with the machinery and to make constructive changes here and there—each of them bringing some marginal improvement in the Government's capacities. Or we can step back, take a careful look, and then make a concerted and sustained effort to reorganize the executive branch according to a coherent, comprehensive view of what the Federal Government of this Nation ought to look like in the last third of the twentieth century.

The impulse for comprehensive reorganization has been felt before in recent decades. In fact, the recommendations I am making today stem from a long series of studies which have been made under several administrations over many years. From the report of the President's Committee on Administrative Management (the Brownlow Committee) in 1937, down through the findings of the Commission on Organization of the Executive Branch of the Government (the Hoover Commission) in 1949, the President's Task Force on Government Organization in 1964, and my own Advisory Council on Executive Organization during the last two years, the principles which I am advancing today have been endorsed by a great number of distinguished students of government and management from many backgrounds and from both political parties.

I hope the Congress will now join me in concluding, with these authorities, that we should travel the course of comprehensive reform. For only if we travel that course, and travel it successfully, will we be able to answer affirmatively in our time the fundamental question posed by Alexander Hamilton as the Constitution was being debated in 1788: "whether societies of men are really capable or not of establishing good government from reflection and choice. . . ."

The Fragmentation of Federal Responsibility

As we reflect on organizational problems in the Federal Government today, one seems to stand out above all others: the fact that the capacity to do things—the power to achieve goals and to solve problems—is exceedingly fragmented and broadly scattered throughout the Federal establishment. In addressing almost any of the great challenges of our time, the Federal Government finds itself speaking through a wide variety of offices and bureaus, departments and agencies. Often these units trip over one another as they move to meet a common problem. Sometimes they step on one another's toes. Frequently, they behave like a series of fragmented fiefdoms—unable to focus Federal resources or energies in a way which produces any concentrated impact. Consider these facts:

Nine different Federal departments and twenty independent agencies are now involved in education matters. Seven departments and eight independent agencies are involved in health. In many major cities, there are at least twenty or thirty separate manpower programs, funded by a variety of Federal offices. Three departments help develop our water resources and four agencies in two departments are involved in the management of public lands. Federal recreation areas are administered by six different agencies in three departments of the government. Seven agencies provide assistance for water and sewer systems. Six departments of the government collect similar economic information—often from the same sources—and at least seven departments are concerned with international trade. While we cannot eliminate all of this diffusion, we can do a great deal to bring similar functions under common commands.

It is important that we move boldly to consolidate the major activities of the Government. The programmatic jumble has already reached the point where it is virtually impossible to obtain an accurate count of just how many Federal grant programs exist. Some estimates go as high as 1,500. Despite impressive attempts by individual legislators and by the Office of Economic Opportunity, there is still no agreement on a comprehensive list. Again and again I hear of local officials who are unable to determine how many Federal programs serve their areas or how much Federal

money is coming into their communities. One reason is that the assistance comes from such a wide variety of Federal sources.

The Consequences of Scattered Responsibility

What are the consequences of this scattering of Federal responsibility? There are many.

In the first place, the diffusion of responsibility makes it extremely difficult to launch a coordinated attack on complex problems. It is as if the various units of an attacking army were operating under a variety of highly independent commands. When one part of the answer to a problem lies in one department and other parts lie in other departments, it is often impossible to bring the various parts together in a unified campaign to achieve a common goal.

Even our basic analysis of public needs often suffers from a piecemeal approach. Problems are defined so that they will fit within established jurisdictions and bureaucratic conventions. And the results of government action are typically measured by the degree of activity within each program rather than by the overall impact of related activities on the outside world.

The role of a given department in the policy making process can be fundamentally compromised by the way its mission is defined. The narrower the mission, the more likely it is that the department will see itself as an advocate within the administration for a special point of view. When any department or agency begins to represent a parochial interest, then its advice and support inevitably become less useful to the man who must serve all of the people as their President.

Even when departments make a concerted effort to broaden their perspectives, they often find it impossible to develop a comprehensive strategy for meeting public needs. Not even the best planners can set intelligent spending priorities, for example, unless they have an opportunity to consider the full array of alternative expenditures. But if one part of the problem is studied in one department and another part of the problem is studied elsewhere, who decides which element is more important? If one office considers one set of solutions and a separate agency investigates another set of solutions, who can compare the results? Too often, no official below the very highest levels of the Government has access to enough information to make such comparisons wisely. The result is that the Government often fails to make a rational distribution of its resources among a number of program alternatives.

Divided responsibility can also mean that some problems slip between the cracks and disappear from the Government's view. Everybody's business becomes nobody's business and embarrassing gaps appear which no agency attempts to fill. At other times, various Federal authorities act as rivals, competing with one another for the same piece of "turf."

Sometimes one agency will actually duplicate the work of another; for instance, the same locality may receive two or more grants for the same project. On other occasions, Federal offices will actually find themselves working at cross purposes with one another; one agency will try to preserve a swamp, for example, while another is seeking to drain it. In an effort to minimize such problems, government officials must spend enormous amounts of time and energy negotiating with one another that should be directed toward meeting people's needs. And even when they are able to work out their differences, officials often reach compromise solutions which merely represent the lowest common denominator of their original positions. Bold and original ideas are thus sacrificed in the quest for intergovernmental harmony.

Scattered responsibility also contributes to the over-centralization of public decision making. Because competing offices are often in different chains of command, it is frequently impossible for them to resolve their differences

except by referring them to higher authorities, a process which can mean interminable delays. In an attempt to provide a means for resolving such differences and for providing needed coordination, an entire new layer of bureaucracy has emerged at the interagency level. Last year, the Office of Management and Budget counted some 850 interagency committees. Even so, there are still many occasions when only the White House itself can resolve such interjurisdictional disputes. Too many questions thus surface at the Presidential level that should be resolved at levels of Government closer to the scene of the action.

Inefficient organization at the Federal level also undermines the effectiveness of State and local governments. Mayors and Governors waste countless hours and dollars touching base with a variety of Federal offices—each with its own separate procedures and its own separate policies. Some local officials are so perplexed by the vast array of Federal programs in a given problem area that they miss out on the very ones that would be most helpful to them. Many State and local governments find they must hire expensive specialists to guide them through the jungles of the Federal bureaucracy.

If it is confusing for lower levels of government to deal with this maze of Federal offices, and that challenge can be even more bewildering for individual citizens. Whether it is a doctor seeking aid for a new health center, a businessman trying to get advice about selling in foreign markets, or a welfare recipient going from one office to another in order to take full advantage of Federal services, the people whom the Government is supposed to be serving are often forced to weave their way through a perplexing obstacle course as a condition of receiving help.

The Hobbling of Elected Leadership

Perhaps the most significant consequence of scattered responsibility in the executive branch is the hobbling effect it has on elected leadership—and, therefore, on the basic principles of democratic government. In our political system, when the people identify a problem they elect to public office men and women who promise to solve that problem. If these leaders succeed, they can be reelected; if they fail, they can be replaced. Elections are the people's tool for keeping government responsive to their needs.

This entire system rests on the assumption, however, that elected leaders can make the government respond to the people's mandate. Too often, this assumption is wrong. When lines of responsibility are as tangled and as ambiguous as they are in many policy areas, it is extremely difficult for either the Congress or the President to see that their intentions are carried out.

If the President or the Congress wants to launch a program or change a program or even find out how a program is working, it often becomes necessary to consult with a half dozen or more authorities, each of whom can blame the others when something goes wrong. It is often impossible to delegate to any one official the full responsibility for carrying out a specific mandate, since the machinery for doing that job is divided among various agencies. As a result, there is frequently no single official—even at the Cabinet level—whom the President or the Congress can hold accountable for Government's success or failure in meeting a given need.

No wonder bureaucracy has sometimes been described as "the rule of no one." No wonder the public complains about programs which simply seem to drift. When elected officials cannot hold appointees accountable for the performance of government, then the voters' influence on government's behavior is also weakened.

How Did Things Get This Way?

The American people clearly pay a very high price for the incapacities of governmental structures—one that is measured in disappointment, frustration and wasted tax dollars. But how did things get this way?

What happened, essentially, was that the organization of Government like the grant-in-aid programs which I have discussed in my special messages to the Congress concerning revenue sharing grew up in a haphazard, piecemeal fashion over the years. Whenever Government took on an important new assignment or identified an important new constituency, the chances were pretty good that a new organizational entity would be established to deal with it. Unfortunately, as each new office was set up, little or no attention was given to the question of how it would fit in with the old ones. Thus office was piled upon office in response to developing needs; when new needs arose and still newer units were created, the older structures simply remained in place.

Of the twelve executive departments now in existence, only five can trace their origins to the beginnings of our country. The Departments of State and Treasury were set up in 1789; so was the War Department—the predecessor of the Department of Defense. The positions of Attorney General and Postmaster General were also established in 1789, though it was not until later that the departments they head were set up in their present form. One of these five units, the Post Office Department, will soon become an independent corporation. But, under my proposals, the other four "original" departments would remain intact. It is the seven newer departments of the Government which would be affected by the changes I recommend.

These seven departments were set up to meet the changing needs of a growing nation, needs which have continued to change over the years. The Department of the Interior, for example, was established in 1849 to deal with newly opened western lands and especially with the Indians who inhabited them. The Department of Agriculture was also added in the nineteenth century, at a time when the overwhelming majority of our people were directly affected by the tremendous expansion of agricultural enterprise. In the early years of the twentieth century, in a time of rapid and unsettling industrial growth, the Department of Commerce and Labor was set up. The Labor Department was split off from it in 1913, in response to feelings that labor was suffering from an imbalance of power and needed additional influence. The three newest departments of the Government—Health, Education, and Welfare, Housing and Urban Development, and Transportation—were all created after World War II. Each represented a first step toward bringing together some of the new Federal offices and agencies which had proliferated so rapidly in recent decades.

Organizing around Goals

As we look at the present organization of the Federal Government, we find that many of the existing units deal with methods and subjects rather than with purposes and goals. If we have a question about labor we go to the Labor Department and if we have a business problem we go to the Commerce Department. If we are interested in housing we go to one department and if we are interested in highways we go to another.

The problem is that as our society has become more complex, we often find ourselves using a variety of means to achieve a single set of goals. We are interested, for example, in economic development—which requires new markets, more productive workers, and better transportation systems. But which department do we go to for that? And what if we want to build a new city, with sufficient public facilities, adequate housing, and decent recreation areas—which department do we petition then?

We sometimes seem to have forgotten that government is not in business to deal with sub-jects on a chart but to achieve real objectives for real human beings. These objectives will never be fully achieved unless we change our old ways of thinking. It is not enough merely to reshuffle departments for the sake of reshuffling them. We must rebuild the executive branch according to a new understanding of how government can best be organized to perform effectively.

The key to that new understanding is the concept that the executive branch of the government should be organized around basic goals. Instead of grouping activities by narrow subjects or by limited constituencies, we should organize them around the great purposes of government in modern society. For only when a department is set up to achieve a given set of purposes, can we effectively hold that department accountable for achieving them. Only when the responsibility for realizing basic objectives is clearly focused in a specific governmental unit, can we reasonably hope that those objectives will be realized.

When government is organized by goals, then we can fairly expect that it will pay more attention to results and less attention to procedures. Then the success of government will at last be clearly linked to the things that happen in society rather than the things that happen in government.

Under the proposals which I am submitting, those in the Federal Government who deal with common or closely related problems would work together in the same organizational framework. Each department would be given a mission broad enough so that it could set comprehensive policy directions and resolve internally the policy conflicts which are most likely to arise. The responsibilities of each department would be defined in a way that minimizes parochialism and enables the President and the Congress to hold specific officials responsible for the achievement of specific goals.

These same organizational principles would also be applied to the internal organization of each department. Similar functions would be grouped together within each new entity, making it still easier to delegate authority to lower levels and further enhancing the accountability of subordinate officials. In addition, the proposals I submit today include a number of improvements in the management of Federal programs, so that we can take full advantage of the opportunities afforded us by organizational restructuring.

The administration is today transmitting to the Congress four bills which, if enacted, would replace seven of the present executive departments and several other agencies with four new departments: the Department of Natural Resources, the Department of Community Development, the Department of Human Resources and the Department of Economic Affairs. A special report and summary—which explain my recommendations in greater detail—have also been prepared for each of the proposed new departments.

The Department of Natural Resources

One of the most notable developments in public consciousness in recent years has been a growing concern for protecting the environment and a growing awareness of its highly interdependent nature. The science of ecology—the study of the interrelationships between living organisms and their environments—has experienced a sudden rise in popularity. All of us have become far more sensitive to the way in which each element of our natural habitat affects all other elements.

Unfortunately, this understanding is not yet reflected in the way our Government is organized. Various parts of the interdependent environment are still under the purview of highly independent Federal offices. As a result, Federal land policies, water programs, mineral policies, forestry practices, recreation activities and energy programs cannot be easily coordinated, even though the manner in which each is carried out has a great influence on all the others.

Again and again we encounter intergovernmental conflicts in the environmental area. One department's watershed project, for instance, threatens to slow the flow of water to another department's reclamation project downstream. One agency wants to develop an electric power project on a certain river while other agencies are working to keep the same area wild. Different departments follow different policies for timber production and conservation, for grazing, for fire prevention and for recreational activities on the Federal lands they control, though the lands are often contiguous. We cannot afford to continue in this manner. The challenges in the natural resource field have become too pressing. Some forecasts say that we will double our usage of energy in the next 10 years, of water in the next 18 years, and of metals in the next 22 years. In fact, it is predicted that the United States will use more energy and more critical resources in the remaining years of this century than in all of our history up until now. Government must perform at its very best if it is to help the Nation meet these challenges.

I propose that a new Department of Natural Resources be created that would bring together the many natural resource responsibilities now scattered throughout the Federal Government. This Department would work to conserve, manage and utilize our resources in a way that would protect the quality of the environment and achieve a true harmony between man and nature. The major activities of the new Department would be organized under its five subdivisions: Land and Recreation Resources, Water Resources, Energy and Minerals Resources, Oceanic, Atmospheric and Earth Sciences, and Indian and Territorial Affairs.

The new Department of Natural Resources would absorb the present Department of the Interior. Other major programs which would be joined to it would include: The Forest Service and the soil and water conservation programs from the Department of Agriculture, planning and funding for the civil functions of the Army Corps of Engineers and for the civilian power functions of the Atomic Energy Commission, the interagency Water Resources Council, the oil and gas pipeline safety functions of the Department of Transportation, and the National Oceanic and Atmospheric Administration from the Department of Commerce. Because of their historical association with the Department of the Interior, the programs of the Bureau of Indian Affairs would be administered by the new Department until such time as an acceptable alternative arrangement could be worked out with Indian leaders and other concerned parties.

The Department of Community Development

A restless and highly mobile people, Americans are constantly creating new communities and renewing old ones throughout our land. In an era of rapid change, this process—which once took generations—can now be repeated in just a few years.

At the same time, the process of community development is becoming even more complex, particularly as the problems of urban and rural communities begin to merge. The elements of community life are many and the mark of a cohesive community is the harmonious way in which they interrelate. That is why we hear so much these days about the importance of community planning. And that is why it is essential that Federal aid for community development be designed to meet a wide range of related needs in a highly coordinated manner.

Often this does not happen under the present system. The reason is that the basic community development programs of the Federal Government are presently divided among at least eight separate authorities—including four executive departments and four independent agencies.

A community that seeks development assistance thus finds that it has to search out aid from a variety of Federal agencies. Each agency has its own forms and regulations and timetables—and its own brand of red tape. Each has its own field organizations, often with independent and overlapping boundaries for regions and districts. Sometimes a local community must consult with Federal offices in three or four different States.

The result is that local leaders often find it virtually impossible to relate Federal assistance programs to their own local development strategies. The mayor of one small town has observed that by the time he finishes dealing with eight Federal planning agencies, he has little time to do anything else.

Occasionally, it must be admitted, a community can reap unexpected benefits from this diffusion of Federal responsibility. The story is told of one small city that applied to six different agencies for help in building a sewage treatment plant and received affirmative responses from all six. If all the grants had been completed, the community would have cleared a handsome profit—but at the Federal taxpayer's expense.

To help correct such problems, I propose that the major community development functions of the Federal Government be pulled together into a new Department of Community Development. It would be the overriding purpose of this Department to help build a wholesome and safe community environment for every American. This process would require a comprehensive series of programs which are equal to the demands of growing population and which provide for balanced growth in urban and rural areas. The new Department would operate through three major administrations: a Housing Administration, a Community Transportation Administration and an Urban and Rural Development Administration. A fourth unit, the Federal Insurance

Administration, would be set up administratively by the Secretary.

The new Department of Community Development would absorb the present Department of Housing and Urban Development. Other components would include certain elements of the Economic Development Administration and the Regional Commission programs from the Department of Commerce, the independent Appalachian Regional Commission, various Department of Agriculture programs including water and waste disposal grants and loans, the Rural Electrification Administration, and rural housing programs. The Community Action and Special Impact Programs of the Office of Economic Opportunity would be included, as would the Public Library construction grant program from the Department of Health, Education, and Welfare and certain disaster assistance functions now handled by the Office of Emergency Preparedness and the Small Business Administration. Most Federal highway programs and the Urban Mass Transportation Administration would be transferred from the present Department of Transportation.

I would note that while the Department of Transportation is a relatively new entity, it, too, is now organized around methods and not around purposes. A large part of the Department of Transportation would be moved into the new Department of Economic Affairs—but those functions which particularly support community development would be placed in the Department which is designed to meet that goal.

The Department of Human Resources

The price of obsolete organization is evidenced with special force in those Government programs which are directly designed to serve individuals and families. In part this is because there has been so much new legislation in the human resource field in recent decades; the old machinery is simply overstrained by its new challenges. But whatever the reasons, human resource programs comprise one area in which the Government is singularly ill-equipped to deliver adequate results.

I have already commented on the broad dispersion of Federal health and education activities. Similar examples abound. Income support programs, including those which administer food stamps, welfare payments, retirement benefits and other forms of assistance, are scattered among three departments and a number of other agencies. The Department of Agriculture, the Department of Health, Education, and Welfare, and the Office of Economic Opportunity all handle food and nutrition matters. Child care programs, migrant programs, manpower programs, and consumer programs often suffer from similarly divided attention.

In one city, two vocational training centers were built three blocks apart at about the same time and for the same purpose, with money from two different Federal agencies. And for every case of overattention, there are many more of neglect. Consider the plight of a poor person who must go to one office for welfare assistance, to another for food stamps, to another for financial counseling, to still another for legal aid, to a fifth office for employment assistance, to a sixth place for job training, and to a number of additional offices for various kinds of medical help. The social worker who might guide him through this maze often works in still another location.

Such situations are clearly intolerable, yet the Federal Government—which ought to be working to reform these confused systems—actually is responsible for much of the confusion in the first place.

I believe that we can take a major step toward remedying such problems by establishing a new Department of Human Resources which would unify major Federal efforts to assist the development of individual potential and family well-being. This Department would be subdivided, in turn, into three major administrations: Health, Human Development, and Income Security.

This new Department would incorporate most of the present Department of Health, Education, and Welfare with the following significant additions: a number of food protection, food distribution and nutrition programs from the Department of Agriculture, the College Housing program from the Department of Housing and Urban Development, the independent Railroad Retirement Board, various programs from the Office of Economic Opportunity (including nutrition, health, family planning, alcoholism, and drug rehabilitation efforts), and the Manpower Administration, the Women's Bureau, the Unemployment Insurance Program and a number of other employment service and training activities from the Department of Labor.

The Department of Economic Affairs

One of the first things most students learn about economics is that the material progress of our civilization has resulted in large measure from a growing division of labor. While a single family or a single community once provided most of its own goods and services, it now specializes in providing only a few, depending increasingly on a far-flung, intricate network of other people and other organizations for its full economic well-being.

The only way the Federal Government can deal effectively with such a highly interdependent economy is by treating a wide range of economic considerations in a comprehensive and coordinated manner. And—as our Gross National Product moves beyond the trillion dollar level and as our productive system, which now accounts for approximately 40 percent of the world's wealth, encounters new challenges from other nations—it is becoming even more important that Federal economic policies be carried out as effectively as possible.

But again, the organization of the Government works against the systematic consideration of economic complexities. The step by step evolution of our Federal machinery has created a series of separate entities—each handling a separate part of the economic puzzle. Some of these entities are relatively autonomous units within departments. Others are independent agencies. But perhaps the most dramatic evidence of our fragmented approach to the economy is the existence of four major executive departments which handle highly interdependent economic matters: Commerce, Labor, Agriculture, and Transportation.

This situation can seriously impair governmental efforts to respond effectively to economic challenges. One department, for example, may be concerned with the raw materials a given industry receives from the farms, while a second department is concerned with getting these materials to the factory and getting the product to its market. Meanwhile, a third department is concerned with the workers who harvest the crops, run the transportation systems and manufacture the product, while a fourth department is concerned with the businessmen who own the plant where the product is made and the stores where it is merchandised.

Such a division of responsibility can also create a great deal of overlap. The Agriculture Department, for instance, finds that its interest in agricultural labor is shared by the Labor Department, its regard for agricultural enterprise is shared by the Small Business Administration, and its concern for providing sufficient transportation for farm products is shared by the Department of Transportation. The Commerce, Labor, and Agriculture Departments duplicate one another in collecting economic statistics, yet they use computers and statistical techniques which are often incompatible.

It has sometimes been argued that certain interest groups need a department to act as their special representative within the Government. In my view, such an arrangement serves the best interests of neither the special group nor the general public. Little is gained and much can be lost, for example, by treating our farmers or our workers or other groups as if they are independent participants in our economic life. Their problems cannot be adequately treated in isolation; their well-being is intimately related to the way our entire economy functions.

I would not suggest these reforms if I thought they would in any way result in the neglect of farmers, workers, minorities or any other significant groups within our country. To the contrary, I propose these reforms because I am convinced they will enable us to serve these groups much better. Under my proposals, the new Department of Economic Affairs would be in a much stronger position really to do something about the wide-ranging factors which influence farm income than is the present Department of Agriculture, for example. It could do more to meet the complex needs of workingmen and women than can the present Department of Labor. It would be able to pull together a wider range of resources to help minority businessmen than can the present Department of Commerce.

Federal organization in the economic area has been the target of frequent criticism over the years. During the previous administration alone, two special studies of executive organization recommended that it be substantially altered. I have received a similar recommendation from my Advisory Council on Executive Organization.

I am therefore recommending to the Congress that a new Department of Economic Affairs be established to promote economic growth, to foster economic justice, and to encourage more efficient and more productive relationships among the various elements of our economy and between the United States economy and those of other nations. As this single new Department joined the Treasury Department, the Council of Economic Advisers and the Federal Reserve Board in shaping economic policy, it would speak with a stronger voice and would offer a more effective, more highly integrated viewpoint than four different departments can possibly do at present. The activities of the new Department would be grouped under the following six administrations: Business Development, Farms and Agriculture, Labor Relations and Standards, National Transportation, Social, Economic, and Technical Information and International Economics.

The new Department of Economic Affairs would include many of the offices that are now within the Departments of Commerce, Labor and Agriculture. A large part of the Department of Transportation would also be relocated here, including the United States Coast Guard, the Federal Railroad Administration, the St. Lawrence Seaway Development Corporation, the National Transportation Safety Board, the Transportation Systems Center, the Federal Aviation Administration, the Motor Carrier Safety Bureau and most of the National Highway Traffic Safety Administration. The Small Business Administration, the Science Information Exchange program from the Smithsonian Institution, the National Institute for Occupational Health and Safety from the Department of Health, Education, and Welfare and the Office of Technology Utilization from the National Aeronautics and Space Administration would also be included in the new Department.

Other Organizational Reforms

Regrouping functions among departments can do a great deal to enhance the effectiveness of government. It should be emphasized, however, that regrouping functions within departments is also a critical part of my program for executive reform. Just as like tasks are grouped together within a given department, so similar operations should be rationally assembled within subordinate units. Such a realignment of functions, in and of itself, would make it much easier for appointed officials to manage their agencies and for both the President and the Congress to see that their intentions are carried out.

Toward this same end, I am recommending to the Congress a number of additional steps for bringing greater managerial discipline into Government. In the first place, I am proposing that the Department Secretary and his office be considerably strengthened so that the man whom the President appoints to run a department has both the authority and the tools to run it effectively. The Secretary would be given important managerial discretion that he does not always enjoy today, including the ability to appoint many key department officials, to delegate authority to them and to withdraw or change such delegations of authority, and to marshal and deploy the resources at his command so that he can readily focus the talent available to him at the point of greatest need.

Each of the new Secretaries would be provided with a Deputy Secretary and two Under Secretaries to help him meet his responsibilities. In addition, each major program area within a department would be headed by a high-level administrator who would be responsible for effectively managing a particular group of related activities. These officials would be appointed by the President and their appointments would be subject to Senate confirmation.

It is my philosophy that we should give clear assignments to able leaders—and then be sure that they are equipped to carry them out. As a part of this same effort, we should do all we can to give the best new management tools to those who run the new departments.

There is no better time to introduce needed procedural changes within departments than a time of structural change among departments. We can reap great benefits if we take advantage of this opportunity by implementing the most advanced techniques and equipment for such tasks as planning and evaluation, data collection, systematic budgeting, and personnel administration.

Finally, I would again stress in this message—as I have in my discussions of revenue sharing—the importance of decentralizing government activities as much as possible. As I have already observed, the consolidation of domestic departments would do a great deal to facilitate decentralization, since it would produce fewer interagency disputes that require resolution at higher levels. It is also true, as many management experts have pointed out, that as the reliability and scope of information expand at higher levels of government, officials can delegate authority to lower levels with greater confidence that it will be used well.

In addition to the consolidation of functions, I am also proposing a reform of the field structures of the Federal Government that would also promote decentralization. Each Department, for example, would appoint a series of Regional Directors who would represent the Secretary with respect to all Department activities in the field. Planning, coordination and the resolution of conflicts could thus be more readily achieved without Washington's involvement, since there would be a "Secretarial presence" at the regional level. Further coordination at lower levels of government would be provided by strengthening the ten Regional Councils which include as members the Regional Directors of various departments in a given area of the country.

In the first months of my administration I moved to establish common regional boundaries and regional headquarters for certain domestic departments. I observed at that time that the Federal Government has never given adequate attention to the way in which its departments are organized to carry out their missions in the field. It is now time that we remedied this pattern of neglect. Even the best organized and best managed departments in Washington cannot serve the people adequately if they have to work through inadequate field structures.

Industry and government both have found that even the largest organizations can be run effectively when they are organized according to rational principles and managed according to sound techniques. There is nothing mystical about these principles or these techniques; they can be used to make the Federal Government far more effective in a great many areas.

As we consolidate and rationalize Federal functions, as we streamline and modernize our institutional architecture, as we introduce new managerial techniques and decentralize Government activities, we will give Government the capacity to operate far more efficiently than it does today. It will be able to do more work with fewer mechanisms and fewer dollars. It will be able to use its work force more productively. This could mean significant savings for our taxpayers. I would emphasize, however, that any reductions in the Federal work force attributable to this proposal would come by normal turnover; no civil servant should lose his job as a result of this plan.

It is important that these reforms be seen by our civil servants not as a threat to their security but as an opportunity for greater achievement. We have worked hard to bring able people into Government employment. Executive reorganization can help the Nation make even better use of their talent and their dedication and it can also make it easier for us to attract more men and women of great vision and competence into public service at the Federal level.

Focusing Power Where It Can Be Used Best

These proposals for reorganizing the Federal Government are a natural complement to my proposals for revenue sharing; there is a sense in which these two initiatives represent two sides of the same coin. Both programs can help us decentralize government, so that more decisions can be made at levels closer to the people. More than that, both programs are concerned with restoring the general capacity of government to meet its responsibilities.

On the one hand, through revenue sharing, we would give back to the States and localities those functions which belong at the State and local level. To help them perform those functions more effectively, we would give them more money to spend and more freedom in spending it. At the same time, however, we must also do all we can to help the Federal Government handle as effectively as possible those functions which belong at the Federal level. Executive reorganization can help us achieve this end by bringing together related activities which are now fragmented and scattered.

A healthy Federal system is one in which we neither disperse power for the sake of dispersing it nor concentrate power for the sake of concentrating it. Instead, a sound Federal system requires us to focus power at that place where it can be used to the greatest public advantage. This means that each level of government must be assigned those tasks which it can do best and must be given the means for carrying out those assignments.

The Central Question

Ever since the first settlers stepped upon our shores more than three centuries ago, a central question of the American experience has been: How do we best organize our government to meet the needs of the people? That was the central question as the colonists set up new governments in a new world. It was the central question when they broke from their mother country and made a new nation. It was the central question as they wrote a new Constitution in 1787 and, at each critical turning point since that time, it has remained a dominant issue in our national experience.

In the last forty years, as the Federal Government has grown in scope and complexity, the question of how it should be organized has been asked with even greater intensity and relevance. During this time, we have moved to formulate responsive answers to this question in an increasingly systematic manner. Searching studies of Government management and organization have been made under virtually every national administration since the 1930s and many needed reforms have resulted.

What is now required, however, is a truly comprehensive restructuring of executive organization, one that is commensurate with the growth of the Nation and the expansion of the government. In the last twenty years alone our population has increased by one-third and the Federal budget has quintupled. In the last two decades, the number of Federal civilian employees has risen by almost 30 percent and the domestic programs they administer have multiplied tenfold. Three executive departments and fourteen independent agencies have been tacked on to the Federal organization chart during that brief span.

Yet it still is the same basic organization chart that has set the framework of governmental action for decades. While there have been piecemeal changes, there has been no fundamental overhaul. Any business that grew and changed so much and yet was so patient with old organizational forms would soon go bankrupt. The same truth holds in the public realm. Public officials cannot be patient with outmoded forms when the people have grown so impatient with government.

Thomas Jefferson once put it this way: "I am certainly not an advocate for frequent and untried changes in laws and constitutions," he wrote, "but . . . laws and institutions must go hand in hand with the progress of the human mind. As that becomes more developed, more enlightened, as new discoveries are made, new truths disclosed, and manners and opinions change with the change of circumstances, institutions must advance also, and keep pace with the times." "Institutions must advance." Jefferson and his associates saw that point clearly in the late 18th century, and the fruit of their vision was a new nation. It is now for us—if our vision matches theirs—to renew the Government they created and thus give new life to our common dreams.

RICHARD NIXON
The White House
March 25, 1971

11. Address to the Nation on the Situation in Southeast Asia
April 7, 1971

Good evening, my fellow Americans.

Over the past several weeks you have heard a number of reports on TV, radio, and in your newspapers on the situation in Southeast Asia.

I think the time has come for me as President and as Commander in Chief of our Armed Forces to put these reports in perspective, to lay all the pertinent facts before you and to let you judge for yourselves as to the success or failure of our policy.

I am glad to be able to begin my report tonight by announcing that I have decided to increase the rate of American troop withdrawals for the period from May 1 to December 1. Before going into details, I would like to review briefly what I found when I came into office, the progress we have made to date in reducing American forces, and the reason why I am able to announce a stepped-up withdrawal without jeopardizing our remaining forces in Vietnam and without endangering our ultimate goal of ending American involvement in a way which will increase the chances for a lasting peace in the Pacific and in the world.

When I left Washington in January of 1961, after serving 8 years as Vice President under President Eisenhower, there were no American combat forces in Vietnam. No Americans had died in combat in Vietnam.

When I returned to Washington as President 8 years later, there were 540,000 American troops in Vietnam. Thirty-one thousand had died there. Three hundred Americans were being lost every week and there was no comprehensive plan to end the United States involvement in the war.

I implemented a plan to train and equip the South Vietnamese, to withdraw American forces, and to end American involvement in the war just as soon as the South Vietnamese had developed the capacity to defend their country against Communist aggression. On this chart on my right, you can see how our plan has succeeded. In June of 1969, I announced a withdrawal of 25,000 men; in September, 40,000; December, 50,000; April of 1970, 150,000. By the first of next month, May 1, we will have brought home more than 265,000 Americans—almost half of the troops in Vietnam when I took office.

Now another indication of the progress we have made is in reducing American casualties. Casualties were five times as great in the first 3 months of 1969 as they were in the first 3 months this year, 1971. South Vietnamese casualties have also dropped significantly in the past 2 years. One American dying in combat is one too many. But our goal is no American fighting man dying anyplace in the world. Every decision I have made in the past and every decision I make in the future will have the purpose of achieving that goal.

Let me review now two decisions I have made which have contributed to the achievements of our goals in Vietnam that you have seen on this chart.

The first was the destruction of enemy bases in Cambodia. You will recall that at the time of that decision, many expressed fears that we had widened the war, that our casualties would increase, that our troop withdrawal program would be delayed. Now I don't question the sincerity of those who expressed these fears. But we can see now they were wrong. American troops were out of Cambodia in 60 days, just as I pledged they would be. American casualties did not rise; they were cut in half. American troop withdrawals were not halted or delayed; they continued at an accelerated pace.

Now let me turn to the Laotian operation. As you know, this was undertaken by South Vietnamese ground forces with American air support against North Vietnamese troops which had been using Laotian territory for 6 years to attack American forces and allied forces in South Vietnam. Since the completion of that operation, there has been a great deal of understandable speculation—just as there was after Cambodia—whether or not it was a success or a failure, a victory or a defeat. But, as in Cambodia, what is important is not the instant analysis of the moment, but what happens in the future.

Did the Laotian operation contribute to the goals we sought? I have just completed my assessment of that operation and here are my conclusions:

First, the South Vietnamese demonstrated that without American advisers they could fight effectively against the very best troops North Vietnam could put in the field.

Second, the South Vietnamese suffered heavy casualties, but by every conservative estimate the casualties suffered by the enemy were far heavier.

Third, and most important, the disruption of enemy supply lines, the consumption of ammunition and arms in the battle has been even more damaging to the capability of the North Vietnamese to sustain major offensives in South Vietnam than were the operations in Cambodia 10 months ago.

Consequently, tonight I can report that Vietnamization has succeeded. Because of the increased strength of the South Vietnamese, because of the success of the Cambodian operation, because of the achievements of the South Vietnamese operation in Laos, I am announcing an increase in the rate of American withdrawals. Between May 1 and December 1 of this year, 100,000 more American troops will be brought home from South Vietnam. This will bring the total number of American troops withdrawn from South Vietnam to 365,000. Now that is over two-thirds of the number who were there when I came into office, as you can see from this chart on my left. The Government of South Vietnam fully supports the decision I have just announced.

Now, let's look at the future:

As you can see from the progress we have made to date and by this announcement tonight, the American involvement in Vietnam is coming to an end. The day the South Vietnamese can take over their own defense is in sight. Our goal is a total American withdrawal from Vietnam. We can and we will reach that goal through our program of Vietnamization if necessary.

But we would infinitely prefer to reach it even sooner—through negotiations. I am sure most of you will recall that on October 7 of last year in a national TV broadcast, I proposed an immediate cease-fire throughout Indochina, the immediate release of all prisoners of war in the Indochina area, an all-Indochina peace conference, the complete withdrawal of all outside forces, and a political settlement. Tonight I again call on Hanoi to engage in serious negotiations to speed the end of this war. I especially call on Hanoi to agree to the immediate and unconditional release of all prisoners of war throughout Indochina. It is time for Hanoi to end the barbaric use of our prisoners as negotiating pawns and to join us in a humane act that will free their men as well as ours.

Let me turn now to a proposal which at first glance has a great deal of popular appeal. If our goal is a total withdrawal of all our forces, why don't I announce a date now for ending our involvement? Well, the difficulty in making such an announcement to the American people is that I would also be making that announcement to the enemy. And it would serve the enemy's purpose and not our own.

If the United States should announce that we will quit regardless of what the enemy does, we would have thrown away our principal bargaining counter to win the release of American prisoners of war, we would remove the enemy's strongest incentive to end the war sooner by negotiation, and we will have given enemy commanders the exact information they need to marshal their attacks against our remaining forces at their most vulnerable time.

The issue very simply is this: Shall we leave Vietnam in a way that—by our own actions—consciously turns the country over to the Communists? Or shall we leave in a way that gives the South Vietnamese a reasonable chance to survive as a free people? My plan will end American involvement in a way that would provide that chance. And the other plan would end it precipitately and give victory to the Communists.

In a deeper sense, we have the choice of ending our involvement in this war on a note of despair or on a note of hope. I believe, as Thomas Jefferson did, that Americans will always choose hope over despair. We have it in our power to leave Vietnam in a way that offers a brave people a realistic hope of freedom. We have it in our power to prove to our friends in the world that America's sense of responsibility remains the world's greatest single hope of peace.

And above all, we have it in our power to close a difficult chapter in American history, not meanly but nobly—so that each one of us can come out of this searing experience with a measure of pride in our Nation, confidence in our own character, and hope for the future of the spirit of America.

I know there are those who honestly believe that I should move to end this war without regard to what happens to South Vietnam. This way would abandon our friends. But even more important, we would abandon ourselves. We would plunge from the anguish of war into a nightmare of recrimination. We would lose respect for this Nation, respect for one another, respect for ourselves.

I understand the deep concerns which have been raised in this country, fanned by reports of brutalities in Vietnam. Let me put this into perspective.

I have visited Vietnam many times, and, speaking now from that experience and as Commander in Chief of our Armed Forces, I feel it is my duty to speak up for the two and a half million fine young Americans who have served in Vietnam. The atrocity charges in individual cases should not and cannot be allowed to reflect on their courage and their self-sacrifice. War is a terrible and cruel experience for a nation, and it is particularly terrible and cruel for those who bear the burden of fighting.

But never in history have men fought for less selfish motives—not for conquest, not for glory, but only for the right of a people far away to choose the kind of government they want.

While we hear and read much of isolated acts of cruelty, we do not hear enough of the tens of thousands of individual American soldiers—I have seen them there—building schools, roads, hospitals, clinics, who, through countless acts of generosity and kindness, have tried to help the people of South Vietnam. We

can and we should be very proud of these men. They deserve not our scorn, but they deserve our admiration and our deepest appreciation.

The way to express that appreciation is to end America's participation in this conflict not in failure or in defeat, but in achievement of the great goals for which they fought: a South Vietnam free to determine its own future and an America no longer divided by war but united in peace.

That is why it is so important how we end this war. By our decision we will demonstrate the kind of people we are and the kind of country we will become.

That is why I have chartered the course I have laid out tonight: to end this war—but end it in a way that will strengthen trust for America around the world, not undermine it, in a way that will redeem the sacrifices that have been made, not insult them, in a way that will heal this Nation, not tear it apart.

I can assure you tonight with confidence that American involvement in this war is coming to an end.

But can you believe this? I understand why this question is raised by many very honest and sincere people. Because many times in the past in this long and difficult war, actions have been announced from Washington which were supposed to lead to a reduction of American involvement in Vietnam. And over and over these actions resulted in more Americans going to Vietnam and more casualties in Vietnam.

Tonight I do not ask you to take what I say on faith. Look at the record. Look again at this chart on my left. Every action taken by this Administration, every decision made, has accomplished what I said it would accomplish. They have reduced American involvement. They have drastically reduced our casualties.

In my campaign for the Presidency, I pledged to end American involvement in this war. I am keeping that pledge. And I expect to be held accountable by the American people if I fail.

I am often asked what I would like to accomplish more than anything else while serving as President of the United States. And I always give the same answer: to bring peace—peace abroad, peace at home for America. The reason I am so deeply committed to peace goes far beyond political considerations or my concern about my place in history, or the other reasons that political scientists usually say are the motivations of Presidents.

Every time I talk to a brave wife of an American POW, every time I write a letter to the mother of a boy who has been killed in Vietnam, I become more deeply committed to end this war, and to end it in a way that we can build lasting peace.

I think the hardest thing that a President has to do is to present posthumously the Nation's highest honor, the Medal of Honor, to mothers or fathers or widows of men who have lost their lives, but in the process have saved the lives of others.

We had an award ceremony in the East Room of the White House just a few weeks ago. And at that ceremony I remember one of the recipients, Mrs. Karl Taylor, from Pennsylvania. Her husband was a Marine sergeant, Sergeant Karl Taylor. He charged an enemy machine-gun single-handed and knocked it out. He lost his life. But in the process the lives of several wounded Marines in the range of that machine-gun were saved.

After I presented her the Medal, I shook hands with their two children, Karl, Jr.—he was 8 years old—and Kevin, who was 4. As I was about to move to the next recipient, Kevin suddenly stood at attention and saluted. I found it rather difficult to get my thoughts together for the next presentation.

My fellow Americans, I want to end this war in a way that is worthy of the sacrifice of Karl Taylor, and I think he would want me to end it in a way that would increase the chances that Kevin and Karl, and all those children like them here and around the world, could grow up in a world where none of them would have to die in war; that would increase the chance for America to have what it has not had in this century—a full generation of peace.

We have come a long way in the last 2 years toward that goal. With your continued support, I believe we will achieve that goal. And generations in the future will look back at this difficult, trying time in America's history and they will be proud that we demonstrated that we had the courage and the character of a great people.

Thank you.

12. State of the Union Address January 20, 1972

Mr. Speaker, Mr. President, my colleagues in the Congress, our distinguished guests, my fellow Americans:

Twenty-five years ago I sat here as a freshman Congressman—along with Speaker Albert—and listened for the first time to the President address the State of the Union.

I shall never forget that moment. The Senate, the diplomatic corps, the Supreme Court, the Cabinet entered the Chamber, and then the President of the United States. As all of you are aware, I had some differences with President Truman. He had some with me. But I remember that on that day—the day he addressed that joint session of the newly elected Republican 80th Congress, he spoke not as a partisan, but as President of all the people—calling upon the Congress to put aside partisan considerations in the national interest.

The Greek-Turkish aid program, the Marshall Plan, the great foreign policy initiatives which have been responsible for avoiding a world war for over 25 years were approved by the 80th Congress, by a bipartisan majority of which I was proud to be a part.

Nineteen hundred seventy-two is now before us. It holds precious time in which to accomplish good for the Nation. We must not waste it. I know the political pressures in this session of the Congress will be great. There are more candidates for the Presidency in this Chamber today than there probably have been at any one time in the whole history of the Republic. And there is an honest difference of opinion, not only between the parties, but within each party, on some foreign policy issues and on some domestic policy issues.

However, there are great national problems that are so vital that they transcend partisanship. So let us have our debates. Let us have our honest differences. But let us join in keeping the national interest first. Let us join in making sure that legislation the Nation needs does not become hostage to the political interests of any party or any person.

There is ample precedent, in this election year, for me to present you with a huge list of new proposals, knowing full well that there would not be any possibility of your passing them if you worked night and day. I shall not do that.

I have presented to the leaders of the Congress today a message of 15,000 words discussing in some detail where the Nation stands and setting forth specific legislative items on which I have asked the Congress to act. Much of this is legislation which I proposed in 1969, in 1970, and also in the first session of this 92d Congress and on which I feel it is essential that action be completed this year.

I am not presenting proposals which have attractive labels but no hope of passage. I am presenting only vital programs which are within the capacity of this Congress to enact, within the capacity of the budget to finance, and which I believe should be above partisanship—programs which deal with urgent priorities for the Nation, which should and must be the subject of bipartisan action by this Congress in the interests of the country in 1972.

When I took the oath of office on the steps of this building just 3 years ago today, the Nation was ending one of the most tortured decades in its history.

The 1960's were a time of great progress in many areas. But as we all know, they were also times of great agony—the agonies of war, of inflation, of rapidly rising crime, of deteriorating titles, of hopes raised and disappointed, and of anger and frustration that led finally to violence and to the worst civil disorder in a century.

I recall these troubles not to point any fingers of blame. The Nation was so torn in those final years of the sixties that many in both parties questioned whether America could be governed at all. The Nation has made significant progress in these first years of the seventies:

Our cities are no longer engulfed by civil disorders.

Our colleges and universities have again become places of learning instead of battlegrounds.

A beginning has been made in preserving and protecting our environment.

The rate of increase in crime has been slowed—and here in the District of Columbia, the one city where the Federal Government has direct jurisdiction, serious crime in 1971 was actually reduced by 13 percent from the year before.

Most important, because of the beginnings that have been made, we can say today that this year 1972 can be the year in which America may make the greatest progress in 25 years toward achieving our goal of being at peace with all the nations of the world.

As our involvement in the war in Vietnam comes to an end, we must now go on to build a generation of peace.

To achieve that goal, we must first face realistically the need to maintain our defense.

In the past 3 years, we have reduced the burden of arms. For the first time in 20 years, spending on defense has been brought below spending on human resources.

As we look to the future, we find encouraging progress in our negotiations with the Soviet Union on limitation of strategic arms. And looking further into the future, we hope there can eventually be agreement on the mutual reduction of arms. But until there is such a mutual agreement, we must maintain the strength necessary to deter war.

And that is why, because of rising research and development costs, because of increases in military and civilian pay, because of the need to proceed with new weapons systems, my budget for the coming fiscal year will provide for an increase in defense spending.

Strong military defenses are not the enemy of peace; they are the guardians of peace.

There could be no more misguided set of priorities than one which would tempt others by weakening America, and thereby endanger the peace of the world.

In our foreign policy, we have entered a new era. The world has changed greatly in the 11 years since President John Kennedy said in his Inaugural Address, ". . . we shall pay any price, bear any burden, meet any hardship, support any friend, oppose any foe to assure the survival and the success of liberty."

Our policy has been carefully and deliberately adjusted to meet the new realities of the new world we live in. We make today only those commitments we are able and prepared to meet.

Our commitment to freedom remains strong and unshakable. But others must bear their share of the burden of defending freedom around the world.

And so this, then, is our policy:

—We will maintain a nuclear deterrent adequate to meet any threat to the security of the United States or of our allies.

—We will help other nations develop the capability of defending themselves.

—We will faithfully honor all of our treaty commitments.

—We will act to defend our interests, whenever and wherever they are threatened anyplace in the world.

—But where our interests or our treaty commitments are not involved, our role will be limited.

—We will not intervene militarily.

—But we will use our influence to prevent war.

—If war comes, we will use our influence to stop it.

—Once it is over, we will do our share in helping to bind up the wounds of those who have participated in it.

As you know, I will soon be visiting the People's Republic of China and the Soviet Union. I go there with no illusions. We have great differences with both powers. We shall continue to have great differences. But peace depends on the ability of great powers to live together on the same planet despite their differences.

We would not be true to our obligation to generations yet unborn if we failed to seize this moment to do everything in our power to insure that we will be able to talk about those differences, rather than to fight about them, in the future.

As we look back over this century, let us, in the highest spirit of bipartisanship, recognize that we can be proud of our Nation's record in foreign affairs.

America has given more generously of itself toward maintaining freedom, preserving peace, alleviating human suffering around the globe, than any nation has ever done in the history of man.

We have fought four wars in this century, but our power has never been used to break the peace, only to keep it; never been used to destroy freedom, only to defend it. We now have within our reach the goal of insuring that the next generation can be the first generation in this century to be spared the scourges of war.

Turning to our problems at home, we are making progress toward our goal of a new prosperity without war.

Industrial production, consumer spending, retail sales, personal income all have been rising. Total employment, real income are the highest in history. New home building starts this past year reached the highest level ever. Business and consumer confidence have both been rising. Interest rates are down. The rate of inflation is down. We can look with confidence to 1972 as the year when the back of inflation will be broken.

Now, this a good record, but it is not good enough—not when we still have an unemployment rate of 6 percent.

It is not enough to point out that this was the rate of the early peacetime years of the sixties, or that if the more than 2 million men released from the Armed Forces and defense-related industries were still in their wartime jobs, unemployment would be far lower.

Our goal in this country is full employment in peacetime. We intend to meet that goal, and we can. The Congress has helped to meet that goal by passing our job-creating tax program last month.

The historic monetary agreements, agreements that we have reached with the major European nations, Canada, and Japan, will help meet it by providing new markets for American products, new jobs for American workers.

Our budget will help meet it by being expansionary without being inflationary—a job-producing budget that will help take up the gap as the economy expands to full employment.

Our program to raise farm income will help meet it by helping to revitalize rural America, by giving to America's farmers their fair share of America's increasing productivity.

We also will help meet our goal of full employment in peacetime with a set of major initiatives to stimulate more imaginative use of America's great capacity for technological advance, and to direct it toward improving the quality of life for every American.

In reaching the moon, we demonstrated what miracles American technology is capable of achieving. Now the time has come to move more deliberately toward making full use of that technology here on earth, of harnessing the wonders of science to the service of man.

I shall soon send to the Congress a special message proposing a new program of Federal partnership in technological research and development—with Federal incentives to increase private research, federally supported research on projects designed to improve our everyday lives in ways that will range from improving mass transit to developing new systems of emergency health care that could save thousands of lives annually.

Historically, our superior technology, and high productivity have made it possible for American workers to be the highest paid in the world by far, and yet for our goods still to compete in world markets.

Now we face a new situation. As other nations move rapidly forward in technology, the answer to the new competition is not to build a wall around America, but rather to remain competitive by improving our own technology still further and by increasing productivity in American industry.

Our new monetary and trade agreements will make it possible for American goods to compete fairly in the world's markets—but they still must compete. The new technology program will put to use the skills of many highly trained Americans, skills that might otherwise be wasted. It will also meet the growing technological challenge from abroad, and it will thus help to create new industries, as well as creating more jobs for America's workers in producing for the world's markets.

This second session of the 92d Congress already has before it more than 90 major Administration proposals which still await action.

I have discussed these in the extensive written message that I have presented to the Congress today.

They include, among others, our programs to improve life for the aging; to combat crime and drug abuse; to improve health services and to ensure that no one will be denied needed health care because of inability to pay; to protect workers' pension rights; to promote equal opportunity for members of minorities, and others who have been left behind; to expand consumer protection; to improve the environment; to revitalize rural America; to help the cities; to launch new initiatives in education; to improve transportation; and to put an end to costly labor tie-ups in transportation.

The west coast dock strike is a case in point. This Nation cannot and will not tolerate that kind of irresponsible labor tie-up in the future.

The messages also include basic reforms which are essential if our structure of government is to be adequate in the decades ahead.

They include reform of our wasteful and outmoded welfare system—substitution of a new system that provides work requirements and work incentives for those who can help themselves, income support for those who cannot help themselves, and fairness to the working poor.

They include a $17 billion program of Federal revenue sharing with the States and localities as an investment in their renewal, an investment also of faith in the American people.

They also include a sweeping reorganization of the executive branch of the Federal Government so that it will be more efficient, more responsive, and able to meet the challenges of the decades ahead.

One year ago, standing in this place, I laid before the opening session of this Congress six great goals. One of these was welfare reform. That proposal has been before the Congress now for nearly 2 1/2 years.

My proposals on revenue sharing, government reorganization, health care, and the environment have now been before the Congress for nearly a year. Many of the other major proposals that I have referred to have been here that long or longer.

Now, 1971, we can say, was a year of consideration of these measures. Now let us join in making 1972 a year of action on them, action by the Congress, for the Nation and for the people of America.

Now, in addition, there is one pressing need which I have not previously covered, but which must be placed on the national agenda.

We long have looked in this Nation to the local property tax as the main source of financing for public primary and secondary education.

As a result, soaring school costs, soaring property tax rates now threaten both our communities and our schools. They threaten communities because property taxes, which more than doubled in the 10 years from 1960 to '70, have become one of the most oppressive and discriminatory of all taxes, hitting most cruelly at the elderly and the retired; and they threaten schools, as hard-pressed voters understandably reject new bond issues at the polls.

The problem has been given even greater urgency by four recent court decisions, which have held that the conventional method of financing schools through local property taxes is discriminatory and unconstitutional.

Nearly 2 years ago, I named a special Presidential commission to study the problems of school finance, and I also directed the Federal departments to look into the same problems.

We are developing comprehensive proposals to meet these problems.

This issue involves two complex and inter-related sets of problems: support of the schools and the basic relationships of Federal, State, and local governments in any tax reforms.

Under the leadership of the Secretary of the Treasury, we are carefully reviewing all of the tax aspects, and I have this week enlisted the Advisory Commission on Intergovernmental Relations in addressing the intergovernmental relations aspects.

I have asked this bipartisan Commission to review our proposals for Federal action to cope with the gathering crisis of school finance and property taxes. Later in the year, when both Commissions have completed their studies, I shall make my final recommendations for relieving the burden of property taxes and providing both fair and adequate financing for our children's education.

These recommendations will be revolutionary. But all these recommendations, however, will be rooted in one fundamental principle with which there can be no compromise: Local school boards must have control over local schools.

As we look ahead over the coming decades, vast new growth and change are not only certainties, they will be the dominant reality of this world, and particularly of our life in America.

Surveying the certainty of rapid change, we can be like a fallen rider caught in the stirrups—or we can sit high in the saddle, the masters of change, directing it on a course we choose.

The secret of mastering change in today's world is to reach back to old and proven principles, and to adapt them with imagination and intelligence to the new realities of a new age.

That is what we have done in the proposals that I have laid before the Congress. They are rooted in basic principles that are as enduring as human nature, as robust as the American experience; and they are responsive to new conditions. Thus they represent a spirit of change that is truly renewal.

As we look back at those old principles, we find them as timely as they are timeless.

We believe in independence, and self-reliance, and the creative value of the competitive spirit.

We believe in full and equal opportunity for all Americans and in the protection of individual rights and liberties.

We believe in the family as the keystone of the community, and in the community as the keystone of the Nation.

We believe in compassion toward those in need.

We believe in a system of law, justice, and order as the basis of a genuinely free society.

We believe that a person should get what he works for—and that those who can, should work for what they get.

We believe in the capacity of people to make their own decisions in their own lives, in their own communities—and we believe in their right to make those decisions.

In applying these principles, we have done so with the full understanding that what we seek in the seventies, what our quest is, is not merely for more, but for better for a better quality of life for all Americans.

Thus, for example, we are giving a new measure of attention to cleaning up our air and water, making our surroundings more attractive. We are providing broader support for the arts, helping stimulate a deeper appreciation of what they can contribute to the Nation's activities and to our individual lives.

But nothing really matters more to the quality of our lives than the way we treat one another, than our capacity to live respectfully together as a unified society, with a full, generous regard for the rights of others and also for the feelings of others.

As we recover from the turmoil and violence of recent years, as we learn once again to speak with one another instead of shouting at one another, we are regaining that capacity.

As is customary here, on this occasion, I have been talking about programs. Programs are important. But even more important than programs is what we are as a Nation—what we mean as a Nation, to ourselves and to the world.

In New York Harbor stands one of the most famous statues in the world—the Statue of Liberty, the gift in 1886 of the people of France to the people of the United States. This statue is more than a landmark; it is a symbol—a symbol of what America has meant to the world.

It reminds us that what America has meant is not its wealth, and not its power, but its spirit and purpose—a land that enshrines liberty and opportunity, and that has held out a hand of welcome to millions in search of a better and a fuller and, above all, a freer life.

The world's hopes poured into America, along with its people. And those hopes, those dreams, that have been brought here from every corner of the world, have become a part of the hope that we now hold out to the world.

Four years from now, America will celebrate the 200th anniversary of its founding as a Nation. There are those who say that the old Spirit of '76 is dead—that we no longer have the strength of character, the idealism, the faith in our founding purposes that that spirit represents.

Those who say this do not know America.

We have been undergoing self-doubts and self-criticism. But these are only the other side of our growing sensitivity to the persistence of want in the midst of plenty, of our impatience with the slowness with which age-old ills are being overcome.

If we were indifferent to the shortcomings of our society, or complacent about our institutions, or blind to the lingering inequities—then we would have lost our way.

But the fact that we have those concerns is evidence that our ideals, deep down, are still strong. Indeed, they remind us that what is really best about America is its compassion. They remind us that in the final analysis, America is great not because it is strong, not because it is rich, but because this is a good country.

Let us reject the narrow visions of those who would tell us that we are evil because we are not yet perfect, that we are corrupt because we are not yet pure, that all the sweat and toil and sacrifice that have gone into the building of America were for naught because the building is not yet done.

Let us see that the path we are traveling is wide, with room in it for all of us, and that its direction is toward a better Nation and a more peaceful world.

Never has it mattered more that we go forward together.

Look at this Chamber. The leadership of America is here today—the Supreme Court, the Cabinet, the Senate, the House of Representatives.

Together, we hold the future of the Nation, and the conscience of the Nation in our hands.

Because this year is an election year, it will be a time of great pressure.

If we yield to that pressure and fail to deal seriously with the historic challenges that we face, we will have failed the trust of millions of Americans and shaken the confidence they have a right to place in us, in their Government.

Never has a Congress had a greater opportunity to leave a legacy of a profound and constructive reform for the Nation than this Congress.

If we succeed in these tasks, there will be credit enough for all—not only for doing what is right, but doing it in the right way, by rising above partisan interest to serve the national interest.

And if we fail, more than any one of us, America will be the loser.

That is why my call upon the Congress today is for a high statesmanship, so that in the years to come Americans will look back and say because it withstood the intense pressures of a political year, and achieved such great good for the American people and for the future of this Nation, this was truly a great Congress.

13. Speech to the People of the Soviet Union (Broadcast from the Grand Kremlin Palace, Moscow) May 28, 1972

Dobryy vecher [Good evening]:

I deeply appreciate this opportunity your Government has given me to speak directly with the people of the Soviet Union, to bring you a message of friendship from all the people of the United States and to share with you some of my thoughts about the relations between our two countries and about the way to peace and progress in the world.

This is my fourth visit to the Soviet Union. On these visits I have gained a great respect for the peoples of the Soviet Union, for your strength, your generosity, your determination, for the diversity and richness of your cultural heritage, for your many achievements.

In the 3 years I have been in office, one of my principal aims has been to establish a better relationship between the United States and the Soviet Union. Our two countries have much in common. Most important of all, we have never fought one another in war. On the contrary, the memory of your soldiers and ours embracing at the Elbe, as allies, in 1945, remains strong in millions of hearts in both of our countries. It is my hope that that memory can serve as an inspiration for the renewal of Soviet-American cooperation in the 1970's.

As great powers, we shall sometimes be competitors, but we need never be enemies.

Thirteen years ago, when I visited your country as Vice President, I addressed the people of the Soviet Union on radio and television, as I am addressing you tonight. I said then: "Let us have peaceful competition not only in producing the best factories but in producing better lives for our people."

"Let us cooperate in our exploration of outer space . . . Let our aim be not victory over other peoples but the victory of all mankind over hunger, want, misery, and disease, wherever it exists in the world."

In our meetings this week, we have begun to bring some of those hopes to fruition. Shortly after we arrived here on Monday afternoon, a brief rain fell on Moscow, of a kind that I am told is called a mushroom rain, a warm rain, with sunshine breaking through, that makes the mushrooms grow and is therefore considered a good omen. The month of May is early for mushrooms, but as our talks progressed this week, what did grow was even better: a far-reaching set of agreements that can lead to a better life for both of our peoples, to a better chance for peace in the world.

We have agreed on joint ventures in space. We have agreed on ways of working together to protect the environment, to advance health, to cooperate in science and technology. We have agreed on means of preventing incidents at sea. We have established a commission to expand trade between our two nations.

Most important, we have taken an historic first step in the limitation of nuclear strategic arms. This arms control agreement is not for the purpose of giving either side an advantage over the other. Both of our nations are strong, each respects the strength of the other, each will maintain the strength necessary to defend its independence.

But in an unchecked arms race between two great nations, there would be no winners, only losers. By setting this limitation together, the people of both of our nations, and of all nations, can be winners. If we continue in the spirit of serious purpose that has marked our discussions this week, these agreements can start us on a new road of cooperation for the benefit of our people, for the benefit of all peoples.

There is an old proverb that says, "Make peace with man and quarrel with your sins." The hardships and evils that beset all men and all nations, these and these alone are what we should make war upon.

As we look at the prospects for peace, we see that we have made significant progress at reducing the possible sources of direct conflict between us. But history tells us that great nations have often been dragged into war without intending it, by conflicts between smaller nations. As great powers, we can and should use our influence to prevent this from happening. Our goal should be to discourage aggression in other parts of the world and particularly among those smaller nations that look to us for leadership and example.

With great power goes great responsibility. When a man walks with a giant tread, he must be careful where he sets his feet. There can be true peace only when the weak are as safe as the strong. The wealthier and more powerful our own nations become, the more we have to lose from war and the threat of war, anywhere in the world.

Speaking for the United States, I can say this: We covet no one else's territory, we seek no dominion over any other people, we seek the right to live in peace, not only for ourselves but for all the peoples of this earth. Our power will only be used to keep the peace, never to break it, only to defend freedom, never to destroy it. No nation that does not threaten its neighbors has anything to fear from the United States.

Soviet citizens have often asked me, "Does America truly want peace?"

I believe that our actions answer that question far better than any words could do. If we did not want peace, we would not have reduced the size of our armed forces by a million men,

by almost one-third, during the past 3 years. If we did not want peace, we would not have worked so hard at reaching an agreement on the limitation of nuclear arms, at achieving a settlement of Berlin, at maintaining peace in the Middle East, at establishing better relations with the Soviet Union, with the People's Republic of China, with other nations of the world.

Mrs. Nixon and I feel very fortunate to have had the opportunity to visit the Soviet Union, to get to know the people of the Soviet Union, friendly and hospitable, courageous and strong. Most Americans will never have a chance to visit the Soviet Union, and most Soviet citizens will never have a chance to visit America. Most of you know our country only through what you read in your newspapers and what you hear and see on radio and television and motion pictures. This is only a part of the real America.

I would like to take this opportunity to try to convey to you something of what America is really like, not in terms of its scenic beauties, its great cities, its factories, its farms, or its highways, but in terms of its people.

In many ways, the people of our two countries are very much alike. Like the Soviet Union, ours is a large and diverse nation. Our people, like yours, are hard working. Like you, we Americans have a strong spirit of competition, but we also have a great love of music and poetry, of sports, and of humor. Above all, we, like you, are an open, natural, and friendly people. We love our country. We love our children. And we want for you and for your children the same peace and abundance that we want for ourselves and for our children.

We Americans are idealists. We believe deeply in our system of government. We cherish our personal liberty. We would fight to defend it, if necessary, as we have done before. But we also believe deeply in the right of each nation to choose its own system. Therefore, however much we like our own system for ourselves, we have no desire to impose it on anyone else.

As we conclude this week of talks, there are certain fundamental premises of the American point of view which I believe deserve emphasis. In conducting these talks, it has not been our aim to divide up the world into spheres of influence, to establish a condominium, or in any way to conspire together against the interests of any other nation. Rather we have sought to construct a better framework of understanding between our two nations, to make progress in our bilateral relationships, to find ways of insuring that future frictions between us would never embroil our two nations, and therefore the world, in war.

While ours are both great and powerful nations, the world is no longer dominated by two super powers. The world is a better and safer place because its power and resources are more widely distributed.

Beyond this, since World War II, more than 70 new nations have come into being. We cannot have true peace unless they, and all nations, can feel that they share it. America seeks better relations, not only with the Soviet Union but with all nations. The only sound basis for a peaceful and progressive international order is sovereign equality and mutual respect. We believe in the right of each nation to chart its own course, to choose its own system, to go its own way, without interference from other nations.

As we look to the longer term, peace depends also on continued progress in the developing nations. Together with other advanced industrial countries, the United States and the Soviet Union share a twofold responsibility in this regard: on the one hand, to practice restraint in those activities, such as the supply of arms, that might endanger the peace of developing nations; and second, to assist them

in their orderly economic and social development, without political interference.

Some of you may have heard an old story told in Russia of a traveler who was walking to another village. He knew the way, but not the distance. Finally he came upon a woodsman chopping wood by the side of the road and he asked the woodsman, "How long will it take to reach the village?"

The woodsman replied, "I don't know." The traveler was angry, because he was sure the woodsman was from the village and therefore knew how far it was. And so he started off down the road again. After he had gone a few steps, the woodsman called out, "Stop. It will take you about 15 minutes."

The traveler turned and demanded, "Why didn't you tell me that in the first place?"

The woodsman replied, "Because then I didn't know the length of your stride."

In our talks this week with the leaders of the Soviet Union, both sides have had a chance to measure the length of our strides toward peace and security. I believe that those strides have been substantial and that now we have well begun the long journey which will lead us to a new age in the relations between our two countries. It is important to both of our peoples that we continue those strides.

As our two countries learn to work together, our people will be able to get to know one another better. Greater cooperation can also mean a great deal in our daily lives. As we learn to cooperate in space, in health and the environment, in science and technology, our cooperation can help sick people get well. It can help industries produce more consumer goods. It can help all of us enjoy cleaner air and water. It can increase our knowledge of the world around us.

As we expand our trade, each of our countries can buy more of the other's goods and market more of our own. As we gain experience with arms control, we can bring closer the day when further agreements can lessen the arms burden of our two nations and lessen the threat of war in the world.

Through all the pages of history, through all the centuries, the world's people have struggled to be free from fear, whether fear of the elements or fear of hunger or fear of their own rulers or fear of their neighbors in other countries. And yet, time and again, people have vanquished the source of one fear only to fall prey to another.

Let our goal now be a world free of fear—a world in which nation will no longer prey upon nation, in which human energies will be turned away from production for war and toward more production for peace, away from conquest and toward invention, development, creation; a world in which together we can establish that peace which is more than the absence of war, which enables man to pursue those higher goals that the spirit yearns for.

Yesterday, I laid a wreath at the cemetery which commemorates the brave people who died during the siege of Leningrad in World War II. At the cemetery, I saw the picture of a 12-year-old girl. She was a beautiful child. Her name was Tanya. The pages of her diary tell the terrible story of war. In the simple words of a child, she wrote of the deaths of the members of her family: Zhenya in December. Grannie in January. Leka then next. Then Uncle Vasya. Then Uncle Lyosha. Then Mama. And then the Savichevs. And then finally, these words, the last words in her diary: "All are dead. Only Tanya is left."

As we work toward a more peaceful world, let us think of Tanya and of the other Tanyas and their brothers and sisters everywhere. Let us do all that we can to insure that no other children will have to endure what Tanya did and that your children and ours, all the children of the world can live their full lives together in friendship and in peace.

Spasibo y do svidaniye. [Thank you and good-bye.]

14. Acceptance Speech to Republican National Convention
August 23, 1972

Mr. Chairman, delegates to this convention, my fellow Americans:

Four years ago, standing in this very place, I proudly accepted your nomination for President of the United States.

With your help and with the votes of millions of Americans, we won a great victory in 1968.

Tonight, I again proudly accept your nomination for President of the United States.

Let us pledge ourselves to win an even greater victory this November, in 1972.

I congratulate Chairman Ford. I congratulate Chairman Dole, Anne Armstrong[1] and the hundreds of others who have laid the foundation for that victory by their work at this great convention.

Our platform is a dynamic program for progress for America and for peace in the world.

Speaking in a very personal sense, I express my deep gratitude to this convention for the tribute you have paid to the best campaigner in the Nixon family—my wife, Pat. In honoring her, you have honored millions of women in America who have contributed in the past and will contribute in the future so very much to better government in this country.

Again, as I did last night when I was not at the convention, I express the appreciation of all of the delegates and of all America for letting us see young America at its best at our convention. As I express my appreciation to you, I want to say that you have inspired us with your enthusiasm, with your intelligence, with your dedication at this convention. You have made us realize that this is a year when we can prove the experts' predictions wrong, because we can set as our goal winning a majority of the new voters for our ticket this November.

I pledge to you, all of the new voters in America who are listening on television and listening here in this convention hall, that I will do everything that I can over these next 4 years to make your support be one that you can be proud of, because as I said to you last night, and I feel it very deeply in my heart: Years from now I want you to look back and be able to say that your first vote was one of the best votes you ever cast in your life.

Mr. Chairman, I congratulate the delegates to this convention for renominating as my running mate the man who has just so eloquently and graciously introduced me, Vice President Ted Agnew.

I thought he was the best man for the job 4 years ago.

I think he is the best man for the job today.

And I am not going to change my mind tomorrow.

Finally, as the Vice President has indicated, you have demonstrated to the Nation that we can have an open convention without dividing Americans into quotas.

Let us commit ourselves to rule out every vestige of discrimination in this country of ours. But my fellow Americans, the way to end discrimination against some is not to begin discrimination against others.

Dividing Americans into quotas is totally alien to the American tradition.

Americans don't want to be part of a quota. They want to be part of America. This Nation proudly calls itself the United States of America. Let us reject any philosophy that would make us the divided people of America.

In that spirit, I address you tonight, my fellow Americans, not as a partisan of party, which would divide us, but as a partisan of principles, which can unite us.

Six weeks ago our opponents at their convention rejected many of the great principles of the Democratic Party. To those millions who have been driven out of their home in the Democratic Party, we say come home. We say come home not to another party, but we say come home to the great principles we Americans believe in together.

And I ask you, my fellow Americans, tonight to join us not in a coalition held together only by a desire to gain power. I ask you to join us as members of a new American majority bound together by our common ideals.

I ask everyone listening to me tonight—Democrats, Republicans, independents, to join our new majority—not on the basis of the party label you wear in your lapel, but on the basis of what you believe in your hearts.

In asking for your support I shall not dwell on the record of our Administration which has been praised perhaps too generously by others at this convention.

We have made great progress in these past 4 years.

It can truly be said that we have changed America and that America has changed the world. As a result of what we have done, America today is a better place and the world is a safer place to live in than was the case 4 years ago.

We can be proud of that record, but we shall never be satisfied. A record is not something to stand on; it is something to build on.

Tonight I do not ask you to join our new majority because of what we have done in the past. I ask your support of the Principles I believe should determine America's future.

The choice in this election is not between radical change and no change. The choice in this election is between change that works and change that won't work.

I begin with an article of faith.

It has become fashionable in recent years to point up what is wrong with what is called the American system. The critics contend it is so unfair, so corrupt, so unjust, that we should tear it down and substitute something else in its place.

I totally disagree. I believe in the American system.

I have traveled to 80 countries in the past 25 years, and I have seen Communist systems, I have seen Socialist systems, I have seen systems that are half Socialist and half free.

Every time I come home to America, I realize how fortunate we are to live in this great and good country.

Every time I am reminded that we have more freedom, more opportunity, more prosperity than any people in the world, that we have the highest rate of growth of any industrial nation, that Americans have more jobs at higher wages than in any country in the world; that our rate of inflation is less than that of any industrial nation, that the incomparable productivity of America's farmers has made it possible for us to launch a winning war against hunger in the United States, and that the productivity of our farmers also makes us the best fed people in the world with the lowest percentage of the family budget going to food of any country in the world.

We can be very grateful in this country that the people on welfare in America would be rich in most of the nations of the world today.

Now, my fellow Americans, in pointing up those things, we do not overlook the fact that our system has its problems.

Our Administration, as you know, has provided the biggest tax cut in history, but taxes are still too high.

That is why one of the goals of our next Administration is to reduce the property tax which is such an unfair and heavy burden on the poor, the elderly, the wage earner, the farmer, and those on fixed incomes.

As all of you know, we have cut inflation in half in this Administration, but we have got to cut it further. We must cut it further so that we can continue to expand on the greatest accomplishment of our new economic policy: For the first time in 5 years wage increases in America are not being eaten up by price increases.

As a result of the millions of new jobs created by our new economic policies, unemploy-

ment today in America is less than the peacetime average of the sixties, but we must continue the unparalleled increase in new jobs so that we can achieve the great goal of our new prosperity—a job for every American who wants to work, without war and without inflation. The way to reach this goal is to stay on the new road we have charted to move America forward and not to take a sharp detour to the left, which would lead to a dead end for the hopes of the American people.

This points up one of the clearest choices in this campaign. Our opponents believe in a different philosophy.

Theirs is the politics of paternalism, where master planners in Washington make decisions for people.

Ours is the politics of people—where people make decisions for themselves.

The proposal that they have made to pay $1,000 to every person in America insults the intelligence of the American voters.

Because you know that every politician's promise has a price—the taxpayer pays the bill.

The American people are not going to be taken in by any scheme where Government gives money with one hand and then takes it away with the other.

Their platform promises everything to everybody, but at an increased net in the budget of $144 billion, but listen to what it means to you, the taxpayers of the country. That would mean an increase of 50 percent in what the taxpayers of America pay. I oppose any new spending programs which will increase the tax burden on the already overburdened American taxpayer.

And they have proposed legislation which would add 82 million people to the welfare rolls.

I say that instead of providing incentives for millions of more Americans to go on welfare, we need a program which will provide incentives for people to get off of welfare and to get to work.

We believe that it is wrong for anyone to receive more on welfare than for someone who works. Let us be generous to those who can't work without increasing the tax burden of those who do work.

And while we are talking about welfare, let us quit treating our senior citizens in this country like welfare recipients. They have worked hard all of their lives to build America. And as the builders of America, they have not asked for a handout. What they ask for is what they have earned—and that is retirement in dignity and self-respect. Let's give that to our senior citizens.

Now, when you add up the cost of all of the programs our opponents have proposed, you reach only one conclusion: They would destroy the system which has made America number one in the world economically.

Listen to these facts: Americans today pay one-third of all of their income in taxes. If their programs were adopted, Americans would pay over one-half of what they earn in taxes. This means that if their programs are adopted, American wage earners would be working more for the Government than they would for themselves.

Once we cross this line, we cannot turn back because the incentive which makes the American economic system the most productive in the world would be destroyed.

Theirs is not a new approach. It has been tried before in countries abroad, and I can tell you that those who have tried it have lived to regret it.

We cannot and we will not let them do this to America.

Let us always be true to the principle that has made America the world's most prosperous nation—that here in America a person should get what he works for and work for what he gets.

Let me illustrate the difference in our philosophies. Because of our free economic system, what we have done is to build a great building of economic wealth and money in America. It is by far the tallest building in the world, and we are still adding to it. Now because some of the windows are broken, they say tear it down and start again. We say, replace the windows and keep building. That is the difference.

Let me turn now to a second area where my beliefs are totally different from those of our opponents.

Four years ago crime was rising all over America at an unprecedented rate. Even our Nation's Capital was called the crime capital of the world. I pledged to stop the rise in crime. In order to keep that pledge, I promised in the election campaign that I would appoint judges to the Federal courts, and particularly to the Supreme Court, who would recognize that the first civil right of every American is to be free from domestic violence.

I have kept that promise. I am proud of the appointments I have made to the courts, and particularly proud of those I have made to the Supreme Court of the United States. And I pledge again tonight, as I did 4 years ago, that whenever I have the opportunity to make more appointments to the courts, I shall continue to appoint judges who share my philosophy that we must strengthen the peace forces as against the criminal forces in the United States.

We have launched an all-out offensive against crime, against narcotics, against permissiveness in our country.

I want the peace officers across America to know that they have the total backing of their President in their fight against crime.

My fellow Americans, as we move toward peace abroad, I ask you to support our programs which will keep the peace at home.

Now, I turn to an issue of overriding importance not only to this election, but for generations to come—the progress we have made in building a new structure of peace in the world.

Peace is too important for partisanship. There have been five Presidents in my political lifetime—Franklin D. Roosevelt, Harry Truman, Dwight Eisenhower, John F. Kennedy, and Lyndon Johnson.

They had differences on some issues, but they were united in their belief that where the security of America or the peace of the world is involved we are not Republicans, we are not Democrats. We are Americans, first, last, and always.

These five Presidents were united in their total opposition to isolation for America and in their belief that the interests of the United States and the interests of world peace require that America be strong enough and intelligent enough to assume the responsibilities of leadership in the world.

They were united in the conviction that the United States should have a defense second to none in the world.

They were all men who hated war and were dedicated to peace.

But not one of these five men, and no President in our history, believed that America should ask an enemy for peace on terms that would betray our allies and destroy respect for the United States all over the world.

As your President, I pledge that I shall always uphold that proud bipartisan tradition. Standing in this Convention Hall 4 years ago, I pledged to seek an honorable end to the war in Vietnam. We have made great progress toward that end. We have brought over half a million men home, and more will be coming home. We have ended America's ground combat role. No draftees are being sent to Vietnam. We have reduced our casualties by 98 percent. We have gone the extra mile, in fact we have gone tens of thousands of miles trying to seek a negotiated settlement of the war. We have offered a cease-fire, a total withdrawal of all American forces, an exchange of all prisoners of war, internationally supervised free elections with the Communists participating in the elections and in the supervision.

There are three things, however, that we have not and that we will not offer.

We will never abandon our prisoners of war.

Second, we will not join our enemies in imposing a Communist government on our allies—the 17 million people of South Vietnam.

And we will never stain the honor of the United States of America.

Now I realize that many, particularly in this political year, wonder why we insist on an honorable peace in Vietnam. From a political standpoint they suggest that since I was not in office when over a half million American men were sent there, that I should end the war by agreeing to impose a Communist government on the people of South Vietnam and just blame the whole catastrophe on my predecessors.

This might be good politics, but it would be disastrous to the cause of peace in the world. If, at this time, we betray our allies, it will discourage our friends abroad and it will encourage our enemies to engage in aggression.

In areas like the Mideast, which are danger areas, small nations who rely on the friendship and support of the United States would be in deadly jeopardy.

To our friends and allies in Europe, Asia, the Mideast, and Latin America, I say the United States will continue its great bipartisan tradition—to stand by our friends and never to desert them.

Now in discussing Vietnam, I have noted that in this election year there has been a great deal of talk about providing amnesty for those few hundred Americans who chose to desert their country rather than to serve it in Vietnam. I think it is time that we put the emphasis where it belongs. The real heroes are 2 1/2 million young Americans who chose to serve their country rather than desert it. I say to you tonight, in these times when there is so much of a tendency to run down those who have served America in the past and who serve it today, let us give those who serve in our Armed Forces and those who have served in Vietnam the honor and the respect that they deserve and that they have earned.

Finally, in this connection, let one thing be clearly understood in this election campaign: The American people will not tolerate any attempt by our enemies to interfere in the cherished right of the American voter to make his own decision with regard to what is best for America without outside intervention.

Now it is understandable that Vietnam has been a major concern in foreign policy. But we have not allowed the war in Vietnam to paralyze our capacity to initiate historic new policies to construct a lasting and just peace in the world.

When the history of this period is written, I believe it will be recorded that our most significant contributions to peace resulted from our trips to Peking and to Moscow.

The dialogue that we have begun with the People's Republic of China has reduced the danger of war and has increased the chance for peaceful cooperation between two great peoples.

Within the space of 4 years in our relations with the Soviet Union, we have moved from confrontation to negotiation, and then to cooperation in the interest of peace.

We have taken the first step in limiting the nuclear arms race.

We have laid the foundation for further limitations on nuclear weapons and eventually of reducing the armaments in the nuclear area.

We can thereby not only reduce the enormous cost of arms for both our countries, but we can increase the chances for peace.

More than on any other single issue, I ask you, my fellow Americans, to give us the chance to continue these great initiatives that can contribute so much to the future of peace in the world.

It can truly be said that as a result of our initiatives, the danger of war is less today than it was; the chances for peace are greater.

But a note of warning needs to be sounded. We cannot be complacent. Our opponents have proposed massive cuts in our defense budget which would have the inevitable effect of making the United States the second strongest nation in the world.

For the United States unilaterally to reduce its strength with the naive hope that other nations would do likewise would increase the danger of war in the world.

It would completely remove any incentive of other nations to agree to a mutual limitation or reduction of arms.

The promising initiatives we have undertaken to limit arms would be destroyed.

The security of the United States and all the nations in the world who depend upon our friendship and support would be threatened.

Let's look at the record on defense expenditures. We have cut spending in our Administration. It now takes the lowest percentage of our national product in 20 years. We should not spend more on defense than we need. But we must never spend less than we need.

What we must understand is, spending what we need on defense will cost us money. Spending less than we need could cost us our lives or our freedom.

So tonight, my fellow Americans, I say, let us take risks for peace, but let us never risk the security of the United States of America.

It is for that reason that I pledge that we will continue to seek peace and the mutual reduction of arms. The United States, during this period, however, will always have a defense second to none.

There are those who believe that we can entrust the security of America to the good will of our adversaries.

Those who hold this view do not know the real world. We can negotiate limitation of arms, and we have done so. We can make agreements to reduce the danger of war, and we have done so.

But one unchangeable rule of international diplomacy that I have learned over many, many years is that, in negotiations between great powers, you can only get something if you have something to give in return.

That is why I say tonight: Let us always be sure that when the President of the United States goes to the conference table, he never has to negotiate from weakness.

There is no such thing as a retreat to peace.

My fellow Americans, we stand today on the threshold of one of the most exciting and challenging eras in the history of relations between nations.

We have the opportunity in our time to be the peacemakers of the world, because the world trusts and respects us and because the world knows that we shall only use our power to defend freedom, never to destroy it; to keep the peace, never to break it.

A strong America is not the enemy of peace; it is the guardian of peace.

The initiatives that we have begun can result in reducing the danger of arms, as well as the danger of war which hangs over the world today.

Even more important, it means that the enormous creative energies of the Russian people and the Chinese people and the American people and all the great peoples of the world can be turned away from production of war and turned toward production for peace.

In America it means that we can undertake programs for progress at home that will be just as exciting as the great initiatives we have undertaken in building a new structure of peace abroad.

My fellow Americans, the peace dividend that we hear so much about has too often been described solely in monetary terms—how much money we could take out of the arms budget and apply to our domestic needs. By far the biggest dividend, however, is that achieving our goal of a lasting peace in the world would reflect the deepest hopes and ideals of all of the American people.

Speaking on behalf of the American people, I was proud to be able to say in my television address to the Russian people in May: We covet no one else's territory. We seek no dominion over any other nation. We seek peace not only for ourselves, but for all the people of the world.

This dedication to idealism runs through America's history.

During the tragic War Between the States, Abraham Lincoln was asked whether God was on his side. He replied, "My concern is not whether God is on our side, but whether we are on God's side."

May that always be our prayer for America.

We hold the future of peace in the world and our own future in our hands. Let us reject therefore the policies of those who whine and whimper about our frustrations and call on us to turn inward.

Let us not turn away from greatness.

The chance America now has to lead the way to a lasting peace in the world may never come again.

With faith in God and faith in ourselves and faith in our country, let us have the vision and the courage to seize the moment and meet the challenge before it slips away.

On your television screen last night, you saw the cemetery in Leningrad I visited on my trip to the Soviet Union—where 300,000 people died in the siege of that city during World War II.

At the cemetery I saw the picture of a 12-year-old girl. She was a beautiful child. Her name was Tanya.

I read her diary. It tells the terrible story of war. In the simple words of a child she wrote of the deaths of the members of her family. Zhenya in

December. Grannie in January. Then Leka. Then Uncle Vasya. Then Uncle Lyosha. Then Mama in May. And finally—these were the last words in her diary: "All are dead. Only Tanya is left."

Let us think of Tanya and of the other Tanyas and their brothers and sisters everywhere in Russia, in China, in America, as we proudly meet our responsibilities for leadership in the world in a way worthy of a great people.

I ask you, my fellow Americans, to join our new majority not just in the cause of winning an election, but in achieving a hope that mankind has had since the beginning of civilization. Let us build a peace that our children and all the children of the world can enjoy for generations to come.

15. Second Inaugural Address January 20, 1973

Mr. Vice President, Mr. Speaker, Mr. Chief Justice, Senator Cook, Mrs. Eisenhower, and my fellow citizens of this great and good country we share together:

When we met here 4 years ago, America was bleak in spirit, depressed by the prospect of seemingly endless war abroad and of destructive conflict at home.

As we meet here today, we stand on the threshold of a new era of peace in the world.

The central question before us is: How shall we use that peace?

Let us resolve that this era we are about to enter will not be what other postwar periods have so often been: a time of retreat and isolation that leads to stagnation at home and invites new danger abroad.

Let us resolve that this will be what it can become: a time of great responsibilities greatly borne, in which we renew the spirit and the promise of America as we enter our third century as a nation.

This past year saw far-reaching results from our new policies for peace. By continuing to revitalize our traditional friendships, and by our missions to Peking and to Moscow, we were able to establish the base for a new and more durable pattern of relationships among the nations of the world. Because of America's bold initiatives, 1972 will be long remembered as the year of the greatest progress since the end of World War II toward a lasting peace in the world.

The peace we seek in the world is not the flimsy peace which is merely an interlude between wars, but a peace which can endure for generations to come.

It is important that we understand both the necessity and the limitations of America's role in maintaining that peace.

Unless we in America work to preserve the peace, there will be no peace.

Unless we in America work to preserve freedom, there will be no freedom.

But let us clearly understand the new nature of America's role, as a result of the new policies we have adopted over these past 4 years.

We shall respect our treaty commitments.

We shall support vigorously the principle that no country has the right to impose its will or rule on another by force.

We shall continue, in this era of negotiation, to work for the limitation of nuclear arms and to reduce the danger of confrontation between the great powers.

We shall do our share in defending peace and freedom in the world. But we shall expect others to do their share.

The time has passed when America will make every other nation's conflict our own, or make every other nation's future our responsibility, or presume to tell the people of other nations how to manage their own affairs.

Just as we respect the right of each nation to determine its own future, we also recognize the responsibility of each nation to secure its own future.

Just as America's role is indispensable in preserving the world's peace, so is each nation's role indispensable in preserving its own peace.

Together with the rest of the world, let us resolve to move forward from the beginnings we have made. Let us continue to bring down the walls of hostility which have divided the world for too long, and to build in their place bridges of understanding—so that despite profound differences between systems of government, the people of the world can be friends.

Let us build a structure of peace in the world in which the weak are as safe as the strong, in which each respects the right of the other to live by a different system, in which those who would influence others will do so by the strength of their ideas and not by the force of their arms.

Let us accept that high responsibility not as a burden, but gladly—gladly because the chance to build such a peace is the noblest endeavor in which a nation can engage; gladly also because only if we act greatly in meeting our responsibilities abroad will we remain a great nation, and only if we remain a great nation will we act greatly in meeting our challenges at home.

We have the chance today to do more than ever before in our history to make life better in America—to ensure better education, better health, better housing, better transportation, a cleaner environment—to restore respect for law, to make our communities more livable—and to ensure the God-given right of every American to full and equal opportunity.

Because the range of our needs is so great, because the reach of our opportunities is so great, let us be bold in our determination to meet those needs in new ways.

Just as building a structure of peace abroad has required turning away from old policies that have failed, so building a new era of progress at home requires turning away from old policies that have failed.

Abroad, the shift from old policies to new has not been a retreat from our responsibilities, but a better way to peace.

And at home, the shift from old policies to new will not be a retreat from our responsibilities, but a better way to progress.

Abroad and at home, the key to those new responsibilities lies in the placing and the division of responsibility. We have lived too long with the consequences of attempting to gather all power and responsibility in Washington.

Abroad and at home, the time has come to turn away from the condescending policies of paternalism—of "Washington knows best."

A person can be expected to act responsibly only if he has responsibility. This is human nature. So let us encourage individuals at home and nations abroad to do more for themselves, to decide more for themselves. Let us locate responsibility in more places. And let us measure what we will do for others by what they will do for themselves.

That is why today I offer no promise of a purely governmental solution for every problem. We have lived too long with that false promise. In trusting too much in government, we have asked of it more than it can deliver. This leads only to inflated expectations, to reduced individual effort, and to a disappointment and frustration that erode confidence both in what government can do and in what people can do.

Government must learn to take less from people so that people can do more for themselves.

Let us remember that America was built not by government, but by people; not by welfare, but by work; not by shirking responsibility, but by seeking responsibility.

In our own lives, let each of us ask—not just what will government do for me, but what can I do for myself?

In the challenges we face together, let each of us ask—not just how can government help, but how can I help?

Your National Government has a great and vital role to play. And I pledge to you that where this Government should act, we will act boldly and we will lead boldly. But just as important is the role that each and every one of us must play, as an individual and as a member of his own community.

From this day forward, let each of us make a solemn commitment in his own heart: to bear his responsibility, to do his part, to live his ideals—so that together we can see the dawn of a new age of progress for America, and together, as we celebrate our 200th anniversary as a nation, we can do so proud in the fulfillment of our promise to ourselves and to the world.

As America's longest and most difficult war comes to an end, let us again learn to debate our differences with civility and decency. And let each of us reach out for that one precious quality government cannot provide—a new level of respect for the rights and feelings of one another, a new level of respect for the individual human dignity which is the cherished birthright of every American.

Above all else, the time has come for us to renew our faith in ourselves and in America.

In recent years, that faith has been challenged.

Our children have been taught to be ashamed of their country, ashamed of their parents, ashamed of America's record at home and its role in the world.

At every turn we have been beset by those who find everything wrong with America and little that is right. But I am confident that this will not be the judgment of history on these remarkable times in which we are privileged to live.

America's record in this century has been unparalleled in the world's history for its responsibility, for its generosity, for its creativity, and for its progress.

Let us be proud that our system has produced and provided more freedom and more abundance, more widely shared, than any system in the history of the world.

Let us be proud that in each of the four wars in which we have been engaged in this century, including the one we are now bringing to an end, we have fought not for our selfish advantage, but to help others resist aggression.

And let us be proud that by our bold, new initiatives, by our steadfastness for peace with honor, we have made a breakthrough toward creating in the world what the world has not known before—a structure of peace that can last, not merely for our time, but for generations to come. We are embarking here today on an era that presents challenges as great as those any nation, or any generation, has ever faced.

We shall answer to God, to history, and to our conscience for the way in which we use these years.

As I stand in this place, so hallowed by history, I think of others who have stood here before me. I think of the dreams they had for America and I think of how each recognized that he needed help far beyond himself in order to make those dreams come true.

Today I ask your prayers that in the years ahead I may have God's help in making decisions that are right for America, and I pray for your help so that together we may be worthy of our challenge.

Let us pledge together to make these next 4 years the best 4 years in America's history, so that on its 200th birthday America will be as young and as vital as when it began, and as bright a beacon of hope for all the world.

Let us go forward from here confident in hope, strong in our faith in one another, sustained by our faith in God who created us, and striving always to serve His purpose.

16. Address to Nation on Cease-Fire in Vietnam
January 23, 1973

Good evening:

I have asked for this radio and television time tonight for the purpose of announcing that we today have concluded an agreement to end the war and bring peace with honor in Vietnam and in Southeast Asia.

The following statement is being issued at this moment in Washington and Hanoi:

At 12:30 Paris time today, January 23, 1973, the Agreement on Ending the War and Restoring Peace in Vietnam was initialed by Dr. Henry Kissinger on behalf of the United States, and Special Adviser Le Duc Tho on behalf of the Democratic Republic of Vietnam.

The agreement will be formally signed by the parties participating in the Paris Conference on Vietnam on January 27, 1973, at the International Conference Center in Paris.

The cease-fire will take effect at 2400 Greenwich Mean Time, January 27, 1973. The United States and the Democratic Republic of Vietnam express the hope that this agreement will insure stable peace in Vietnam and contribute to the preservation of lasting peace in Indochina and Southeast Asia.

That concludes the formal statement. Throughout the years of negotiations, we have insisted on peace with honor. In my addresses to the Nation from this room of January 25 and May 8 [1972], I set forth the goals that we considered essential for peace with honor.

In the settlement that has now been agreed to, all the conditions that I laid down then have been met:

A cease-fire, internationally supervised, will begin at 7 p.m., this Saturday, January 27, Washington time.

Within 60 days from this Saturday, all Americans held prisoners of war throughout Indochina will be released. There will be the fullest possible accounting for all of those who are missing in action.

During the same 60-day period, all American forces will be withdrawn from South Vietnam.

The people of South Vietnam have been guaranteed the right to determine their own future, without outside interference.

By joint agreement, the full text of the agreement and the protocol to carry it out will be issued tomorrow.

Throughout these negotiations we have been in the closest consultation with President Thieu and other representatives of the Republic of Vietnam. This settlement meets the goals and has the full support of President Thieu and the Government of the Republic of Vietnam, as well as that of our other allies who are affected.

The United States will continue to recognize the Government of the Republic of Vietnam as the sole legitimate government of South Vietnam.

We shall continue to aid South Vietnam within the terms of the agreement, and we shall support efforts by the people of South Vietnam to settle their problems peacefully among themselves.

We must recognize that ending the war is only the first step toward building the peace. All parties must now see to it that this is a peace that lasts, and also a peace that heals—and a peace that not only ends the war in Southeast Asia but contributes to the prospects of peace in the whole world.

This will mean that the terms of the agreement must be scrupulously adhered to. We shall do everything the agreement requires of us, and we shall expect the other parties to do everything it requires of them. We shall also expect other interested nations to help insure that the agreement is carried out and peace is maintained.

As this long and very difficult war ends, I would like to address a few special words to each of those who have been parties in the conflict.

First, to the people and Government of South Vietnam: By your courage, by your sacrifice, you have won the precious right to determine your own future, and you have developed the strength to defend that right.

We look forward to working with you in the future—friends in peace as we have been allies in war.

To the leaders of North Vietnam: As we have ended the war through negotiations, let us now build a peace of reconciliation. For our part, we are prepared to make a major effort to help achieve that goal. But just as reciprocity was needed to end the war, so too will it be needed to build and strengthen the peace.

To the other major powers that have been involved even indirectly: Now is the time for mutual restraint so that the peace we have achieved can last.

And finally, to all of you who are listening, the American people: Your steadfastness in supporting our insistence on peace with honor has made peace with honor possible. I know that you would not have wanted that peace jeopardized. With our secret negotiations at the sensitive stage they were in during this recent period, for me to have discussed publicly our efforts to secure peace would not only have violated our understanding with North Vietnam, it would have seriously harmed and possibly destroyed the chances for peace. Therefore, I know that you now can understand why, during these past several weeks, I have not made any public statements about those efforts.

The important thing was not to talk about peace, but to get peace—and to get the right kind of peace. This we have done.

Now that we have achieved an honorable agreement, let us be proud that America did not settle for a peace that would have betrayed our allies, that would have abandoned our prisoners of war, or that would have ended the war for us but would have continued the war for the 50 million people of Indochina. Let us be proud of the 2 1/2 million young Americans who served in Vietnam, who served with honor and distinction in one of the most selfless enterprises in the history of nations. And let us be proud of those who sacrificed, who gave their lives so that the people of South Vietnam might live in freedom and so that the world might live in peace.

In particular, I would like to say a word to some of the bravest people I have ever met—the wives, the children, the families of our prisoners of war and the missing in action. When others called on us to settle on any terms, you had the courage to stand for the right kind of peace so that those who died and those who suffered would not have died and suffered in vain, and so that where this generation knew war, the next generation would know peace. Nothing means more to me at this moment than the fact that your long vigil is coming to an end.

Just yesterday, a great American, who once occupied this office, died. In his life, President Johnson endured the vilification of those who sought to portray him as a man of war. But there was nothing he cared about more deeply than achieving a lasting peace in the world.

I remember the last time I talked with him. It was just the day after New Year's. He spoke then of his concern with bringing peace, with making it the right kind of peace, and I was grateful that he once again expressed his support for my efforts to gain such a peace. No one would have welcomed this peace more than he.

And I know he would join me in asking—for those who died and for those who live—let us consecrate this moment by resolving together to make the peace we have achieved a peace that will last. Thank you and good evening.

17. Thirtieth Press Conference January 31, 1973

THE PRESIDENT. In view of the announcement that has already been made this morning, I know that you will have questions on that and other matters, so we will go right to the questions.

Questions
Meeting with President Thieu

[1.] I think Miss Thomas [Helen Thomas, United Press International] has the first question.

Q. Can you tell us whether you are going to meet with President Thieu sometime this spring and also give us a better feeling on Dr. Kissinger's trip, the purpose and so forth?

THE PRESIDENT. At some time this spring I do plan to meet with President Thieu. I have discussed the matter with him in correspondence and I also discussed it yesterday in my meeting with the Foreign Minister. It will be at a time mutually convenient.

The UPI story, incidentally, was on the mark except for the location. The location we have agreed on will be the Western White House this spring.

Dr. Kissinger's Trip to Hanoi

As far as Dr. Kissinger's trip is concerned, this is a matter that we feel is very important in terms of developing the postwar relationship with North Vietnam. When we look at this very intricate agreement, which Dr. Kissinger so brilliantly briefed for the members of the press, and if you have read it, you will see why I use the word "intricate," we can see that, insofar as its terms are concerned, if the agreement is kept, there is no question about the fact that we will have peace in not only Vietnam but in Indochina for a very long period of time. But the question is whether both parties—in fact, all parties involved—have a will to peace, if they have incentives to peace, if they have desire to peace.

Now, on this particular point, it is necessary, of course, for us to talk to the South Vietnamese, as we are. It is also vitally important that we have a direct communication with the

North Vietnamese. And Dr. Kissinger will be going to Hanoi to meet with the top leaders of the Government of the DRV. There he will discuss the postwar relationship. He will, of course, discuss the current status of compliance with the peace agreements which we have made, and he will also discuss, in terms of postwar relationships, the matter of the reconstruction program for all of Indochina.

As the leaders probably reported after my meeting with them the day after I announced the cease-fire agreement, I raised with the leaders the point that the United States would consider for both North Vietnam and South Vietnam and the other countries in the area a reconstruction program.

I, of course, recognized in raising this with the leaders that there would have to be Congressional consultation and Congressional support. In terms of this particular matter at this time, Dr. Kissinger will be having an initial conversation with the North Vietnamese with regard to this whole reconstruction program.

I should also say that I have noted that many Congressmen and Senators and many of the American people are not keen on helping any of the countries in that area, just as they are not keen on foreign aid generally. But as far as I am concerned, whether it is with the North or the South or the other countries in the area, I look upon this as a potential investment in peace. To the extent that the North Vietnamese, for example, participate with us and with other interested countries in reconstruction of North Vietnam, they will have a tendency to turn inward to the works of peace rather than turning outward to the works of war.

This, at least, is our motive, and we will know more about it after Dr. Kissinger completes his talks with them, which we think will be quite extensive and very frank since he has already, obviously, paved the way for it.

Welcoming of Prisoners of War

[2.] Q. Mr. President, Dr. Kissinger is going to Vietnam and is due there in Hanoi on February 10. Is this related in any way with the first prisoners of war to come out of Hanoi?

THE PRESIDENT. Not at all.

Q. I mean, is the date a coincidence?

THE PRESIDENT. The date is a pure coincidence, and Dr. Kissinger will not be meeting with the prisoners of war. Incidentally, speaking of the POW question, I have noted some speculation in the press, and it isn't—I should say—it's speculation that is justified, because I understand there was a Defense Department report to this effect, that I was going to go out to Travis Air Force Base to meet the first POW's when they came in.

I do not intend to do so. I have the greatest admiration for the prisoners of war, for their stamina and their courage and the rest, and also for their wives and their parents and their children who have been so strong during this long period of their vigil.

This is a time that we should not grandstand it; we should not exploit it. We should remember that it is not like astronauts coming back from the Moon after what is, of course, a very, shall we say, spectacular and dangerous journey, but these are men who have been away sometimes for years. They have a right to have privacy, they have a right to be home with their families just as quickly as they possibly can. And I am going to respect that right, of course, to the extent that any of them or their families desiring to visit the White House can be sure that they will be very high on the list.

Domestic Divisions and Amnesty

[3.] Q. Mr. President, do you have anything specifically in mind to help heal the wounds in this country, the divisions over the war, and specifically, anything down the road much farther in terms of amnesty?

THE PRESIDENT. Well, it takes two to heal wounds, and I must say that when I see that the most vigorous criticism or, shall we say, the least pleasure out of the peace agreement comes from those that were the most outspoken advocates of peace at any price, it makes one realize whether some want the wounds healed. We do.

We think we have taken a big step toward ending a long and difficult war which was not begun while we were here, and I am not casting any aspersions on those Presidents who were in office who can no longer be here to speak for themselves, for the causes of the war. I am simply saying this: that as far as this Administration is concerned, we have done the very best that we can against very great obstacles, and we finally have achieved a peace with honor.

I know it gags some of you to write that phrase, but it is true, and most Americans realize it is true, because it would be peace with dishonor had we—what some bare used, the vernacular—"bugged out" and allowed what the North Vietnamese wanted: the imposition of a Communist government or a coalition Communist government on the South Vietnamese. That goal they have failed to achieve. Consequently, we can speak of peace with honor and with some pride that it has been achieved.

Now, I suppose, Mr. Sheldon [Courtney R. Sheldon, *Christian Science Monitor*], that your question with regard to amnesty may deal with the problems of healing the wounds. Certainly I have sympathy for any individual who has made a mistake. We have all made mistakes. But also, it is a rule of life, we all have to pay for our mistakes.

One of the most moving wires I received, of the many thousands that have come in to the White House since the peace announcement, was from a man who was in prison in Michigan, I believe it is, and he spoke about a group of his fellow inmates. They are in a work camp, so I suppose they are being rehabilitated to come out.

He wrote very emotionally about what we had done and he felt it was an achievement they were very proud of. I feel sorry for that man; on the other hand, it is not my right, and I should not exercise such a right, because he so wrote to me, to say "Now you are forgiven for what you did."

Now, as far as amnesty is concerned, I have stated my views, and those views remain exactly the same. The war is over. Many Americans paid a very high price to serve their country, some with their lives, some as prisoners of war for as long as 6 to 7 years, and of course, 2 1/2 million, 2 to 3 years out of their lives, serving in a country far away in a war that they realize had very little support among the so-called better people, in the media and the intellectual circles and the rest, which had very little support, certainly, among some elements of the Congress—particularly the United States Senate—but which fortunately did have support among a majority of the American people, who some way, despite the fact that they were hammered night after night and day after day with the fact that this was an immoral war, that America should not be there, that they should not serve their country, that morally what they should do was desert their country.

Certainly as we look at all of that, there might be a tendency to say now, to those few hundreds who went to Canada or Sweden or someplace else and chose to desert their country, that because they had a higher morality, we should now give them amnesty.

Now, amnesty means forgiveness. We cannot provide forgiveness for them. Those who served paid their price. Those who deserted must pay their price, and the price is not a junket in the Peace Corps, or something like that, as some have suggested. The price is a criminal penalty for disobeying the laws of the United States. If they want to return to the United States they must pay the penalty. If they don't want to return, they are certainly welcome to stay in any country that welcomes them.

Postwar Reconstruction in Indochina

[4.] Mr. Theis [J. William Theis, Hearst Newspapers and Hearst Headline Service].

Q. Do you have any floor or ceiling dollar figure in mind for the rehabilitation of North Vietnam or the rest of Indochina?

THE PRESIDENT. Mr. Theis, that is a matter that the Members of the Congress raised with me, as you might imagine, and they raised it not only with regard to North Vietnam but with regard to South Vietnam and Cambodia and Laos in this period as we move into the cease-fire and, we hope, peacetime reconstruction.

I cannot give you that figure now, because it is a matter that has to be negotiated, and it must be all part of one pattern. The figure, of course, will come out. The figures will come out, but they must first be discussed with the bipartisan leadership because, with all of this talk about the powers of the Presidency, let me say I am keenly aware of the fact that even though I might believe that a program of reconstruction for North Vietnam, as well as South Vietnam, is an investment in peace, the Congress has to believe it. The Congress has to support it. And this is going to be one of the more difficult assignments I have had as President, but I think we can make it if the Congress sees what the stakes are.

Interest Rates on Agricultural Loans

[5.] Q. Mr. President, sir, Senator Hollings says on a recent trip to Southeast Asia, he discovered that we are letting some countries, including Japan, have 2 percent money, yet we have denied our own farmers in rural cooperatives 2 percent money. We are telling them they have to have their loans at 5 percent. Would you comment on this and how this might relate to your upcoming program of aid to Southeast Asia?

THE PRESIDENT. Well, as far as the program of aid is concerned and the percentage of interest that is paid, we will, of course, have in mind the interest of the American people. We want to be fair, of course, to those who have been our allies and in the great tradition of America when it fights wars, to those who have been our enemies, like Germany and Japan who, with America's help, now have become our two greatest competitors in the free world.

Now, when you get down to whether the percentage will be 2 percent or 5 percent or 3 percent, that is a matter to be negotiated, but we will be fair and we will see that our farmers also are treated fairly.

Let me say, if I could, with regard to REA [Rural Electrification Administration]—and Miss McClendon [Sarah McClendon, Sarah McClendon News Service], because you are somewhat of an expert on this—I have always supported REA because I used to represent the old 12th District. When I lived there and represented it, it was primarily agricultural, orange groves; now it is primarily people, subdivided. But as one who came from that area, I naturally had a great interest in this matter of REA and the rest, and supported it.

But what I have found is that when I first voted for REA, 80 percent of the loans went for the purpose of rural development and getting electricity to farms. Now 80 percent of this 2 percent money goes for country clubs and dilettantes, for example, and others who can afford living in the country. I am not for 2 percent money for people who can afford 5 percent or 7.

Relations with Europe

[6.] Q. Mr. President, you and people in your Administration have been quoted as calling 1973 the year of Europe. Could you tell us exactly what that means to you, and specifically, will you be making a trip to Europe in the next month or so?

THE PRESIDENT. I will not be making any trips to Europe certainly in the first half of this year. Whether I can make any trips later on remains to be seen. As a matter of fact, so that all of you can plan not to take shots, I plan no trips whatever in the first half of this year outside the United States. The meeting with President Thieu, if it does work out, at a time mutually convenient, will take place sometime in the spring.

Now, the fact that I don't take a trip to Europe does not mean that this will not be a period when there will be great attention paid to Europe, because it just happens as we complete the long and difficult war in Vietnam, we now must turn to the problems of Europe. We have been to the People's Republic of China. We have been to the Soviet Union. We have been paying attention to the problems of Europe, but now those problems will be put on the front burner.

There is the problem of trade, for example. There is the problem of the European Security Conference which we must discuss.

There is the problem of mutual balanced force reduction. All of this will require consultation with our European allies. And in that connection, that is one of the reasons that the Heath visit is so enormously important. I am spending more time with Mr. Heath than I have with some other visitors. I mean by that not that time proves everything, but not only will we have the usual dinners and luncheons and so forth, but I am spending a full day with him at Camp David because I want to get his thoughts about what the position of the United States and our European friends should be with regard to the European Security Conference, with regard to the MBFR [mutual and balanced force reductions], and of course, what the position of the United States should be and the new, broader European Community should be in this period when we can either become competitors in a constructive way or where we can engage in economic confrontation that could lead to bitterness and which would hurt us both.

We want to avoid that, even though it has been predicted by some in this country who really fear the new Europe. I do not fear it if we talk to them and consult at this time.

Governor Connally and the 1976 Election

[7.] Mr. Deakin [James Deakin, *St. Louis Post-Dispatch*]

Q. You are quoted as telling a recent visitor that you believe that Governor Connally will be the Republican nominee of 1976. Is that correct?

THE PRESIDENT. Well, I had thought we had just completed an election.

Q. Just a little foresight there.

THE PRESIDENT. Having just completed one, let me give some advice, if I can, to all of those who may be thinking of becoming candidates in 1976.

I have a considerable amount of experience in getting nominations and winning elections and also losing them. So, consequently, I would suggest that as far as the Presidential candidate is concerned, he is out of his mind if he allows any activity in his behalf or participates in any activity in his behalf, running for the nomination before the elections of 1974 are concluded.

If I were advising people who are interested in becoming and running for President, for the nomination in either party, I would say the best way to get the nomination now is not to be out seeking it. The best way to get it is to work as hard as you can for the success of the candidates of your party, be they for the House or the Senate or Governor, and do it in a selfless way until after 1974 and immediately after 1974 take off and run as fast as you can. And I have always done that and with mixed results. [Laughter]

But as far as Governor Connally is concerned, you all know my very high respect for him. I have stated my belief that he could handle any job that I can think of in this country or in the world for that matter, but I would be out of my mind if I were to be endorsing anybody for the Presidency at the present time when there are a number of people who have indicated—or whose friends have indicated that they might have an interest in the position and that is just fine.

If Governor Connally—and, of course, many have suggested that the Vice President would be interested—I assume that several Governors might be interested. In fact, one of these days, perhaps right after the '74 elections, I will give you my list, and it will be quite a long one because I am not going to make my choice until after they have been through a few primaries.

Shooting of Senator Stennis

[8.] Q. Can you give us your reaction to the shooting of Senator Stennis?

THE PRESIDENT. Well, I called Mrs. Stennis last night, as I am sure many others of his friends did, and it is just one of those senseless things that happens, apparently. When she told me that all they got was his billfold, she said it didn't have much in it, and his Phi Beta Kappa key and also his watch, apparently. So, it's one of those things that happens in our cities today—fortunately not happening as much as it did previously.

The point that I would make with regard to Senator Stennis—and this is what I told her is that I just hope that the doctors did the most superb job they have ever done. I hope that his spirit would see him through this physically and in every other way, because of all the Senators in the United States Senate, Democrat or Republican, in terms of our being able to achieve the honorable peace we have achieved, John Stennis was the most indispensable.

Gun Control

[9.] Q. Mr. President, I would like to ask you, along those lines, you said it was such a senseless thing. The White House, this Administration, has not spoken out very strongly against gun controls, particularly handguns. I would like to know perhaps if maybe you are going to have second thoughts about that now?

THE PRESIDENT. Well, as you know, the problem with that is not so much the White House speaking out on handguns and Saturday night specials, which I think this may have been. I haven't seen the latest reports, but the doctor last night told me it was a .22 caliber cheap gun kind of a thing, and Mrs.

Stennis said it sounded like firecrackers. Obviously if they had had a .45, he would be dead.

We have, and I have, as you know, advocated legislation to deal with what we call the Saturday night specials, which can be acquired by anybody, including juveniles, and apparently there are some suggestions that juveniles were those involved in this case. I am not charging that, incidentally. I am saying what I read in the papers, most of which, as you know, is true.

So, under the circumstances, I feel that Senator Hruska, who introduced the bill before and then it came a cropper in the Senate Judiciary Committee, will now work with the Judiciary Committee in attempting to find the formula which will get the support necessary to deal with this specific problem, without, at the same time, running afoul of the rights of those who believe that they need guns for hunting and all that sort of thing.

Let me say, personally, I have never hunted in my life. I have no interest in guns and so forth. I am not interested in the National Rifle Association or anything from a personal standpoint. But I do know that, in terms of the United States Congress, what we need is a precise definition which will keep the guns out of the hands of the criminals and not one that will impinge on the rights of others to have them for their own purposes in a legitimate way.

Incidentally, the legislation that we originally suggested or that we discussed with Senator Hruska, I thought precisely dealt with the problem, but it did not get through the Senate. My guess is that Senator Stennis—everything perhaps has a down side and an up side; I guess everything really does—but the very fact that Senator Stennis was the victim of one of these things—we thought this was the case when Governor Wallace was—but in this instance, it was apparently one of these small handguns that most people, most reasonable people, except for the all-out opponents of any kind of legislation in this field, most reasonable people believe it should be controlled. Perhaps we can get some action. I hope the Senate does act.

I have asked the Attorney General—had asked incidentally before this happened—as one of his projects for this year to give us a legislative formula, not one that would simply speak to the country, and not get through, but one that can get through the Congress. That is the problem.

Executive Privilege

[10.] Mr. Mollenhoff [Clark R. Mollenhoff, *Des Moines Register and Tribune*].

Q. Did you approve of the use of executive privilege by Air Force Secretary Searoans in refusing to disclose the White House role in the firing of air cost analyst Fitzgerald?

It came up yesterday in the Civil Service hearings. He used executive privilege. You had stated earlier that you would approve all of these uses of executive privilege, as I understood it, and I wondered whether your view still prevails in this area, or whether others are now entitled to use executive privilege on their own in this type of case?

THE PRESIDENT. Mr. Mollenhoff, your first assumption is correct. In my dealings with the Congress—I say mine, let me put it in a broader sense—in the dealings of the Executive with the Congress, I do not want to abuse the executive privilege proposition where the matter does not involve a direct conference with or discussion within the Administration, particularly where the President is involved. And where it is an extraneous matter as far as the White House is concerned, as was the

case when we waived executive privilege for Mr. Flanigan last year, as you will recall, we are not going to assert it.

In this case, as I understand it—and I did not approve this directly, but it was approved at my direction by those who have the responsibility within the White House in this case it was a proper area in which the executive privilege should have been used.

On the other hand, I can assure you that all of these cases will be handled on a case-by-case basis, and we are not going to be in a position where an individual, when he gets under heat from a Congressional committee, can say, "Look, I am going to assert executive privilege."

He will call down here, and Mr. Dean, the White House Counsel, will then advise him as to whether or not we approve it.

Q. I want to follow one question on this.

THE PRESIDENT. Sure.

Q. This seems to be an expansion of what executive privilege was in the past, and you were quite critical of executive privilege in 1948 when you were in the Congress—

THE PRESIDENT. I certainly was.

Q. You seem to have expanded it from conversation with the President himself to conversation with anyone in the executive branch of the Government and I wonder, can you cite any law or decision of the courts that supports that view?

THE PRESIDENT. Well, Mr. Mollenhoff, I don't want to leave the impression that I am expanding it beyond that. I perhaps have not been as precise as I should have been. And I think yours is a very legitimate question because you have been one who has not had a double standard on this. You have always felt that executive privilege, whether I was complaining about its use when I was an investigator or whether I am now defending its use when others are doing the investigating—I understand that position.

Let me suggest that I would like to have a precise statement prepared which I will personally approve so that you will know exactly what it is. I discussed this with the leaders and we have talked, for example— the Republicans, like Senator Javits and Senator Percy, are very interested in it, not just the Democrats, and I understand that. But I would rather, at this point, not like to have just my off-the-top-of-my-head press conference statement delineate what executive privilege will be.

I will simply say the general attitude I have is to be as liberal as possible in terms of making people available to testify before the Congress, and we are not going to use executive privilege as a shield for conversations that might be just embarrassing to us, but that really don't deserve executive privilege.

A. Ernest Fitzgerald

[11.] Q. The specific situation with regard to Fitzgerald, I would like to explore that. That dealt with a conversation Seamans had with someone in the White House relative to the firing of Fitzgerald and justification or explanations. I wonder if you feel that that is covered, and did you have this explained to you in detail before you made the decision?

THE PRESIDENT. Let me explain. I was totally aware that Mr. Fitzgerald would be fired or discharged or asked to resign. I approved it and Mr. Seamans must have been talking to someone who had discussed the matter with me.

No, this was not a case of some person down the line deciding he should go. It was a decision that was submitted to me. I made it and I stick by it.

Impoundment of Funds

[12.] Q. Mr. President, how do you respond to criticism that your impoundment of funds abrogates power or authority that the Constitution gave to Congress?

THE PRESIDENT. The same way that Jefferson did, and Jackson did, and Truman did.

When I came in on this, Mr. Mollenhoff—he is one of the few old-timers around here who will remember it—you remember when Senator Symington, who has now turned the other way on this, but you remember when we were talking about the 70 group air force. You remember that on that case I voted as a Congressman to override President Truman's veto. I think it was 70 wing or 70 group air force, where we insisted on a 70 group air force and he said the budget would only provide for 48.

Despite the fact that the Congress spoke, not just as the leaders spoke to me the other day but by veto, overwhelming in both Houses, President Truman impounded the money. He did not spend it. And he had a right to. The constitutional right for the President of the United States to impound funds—and that is not to spend money, when the spending of money would mean either increasing prices or increasing taxes for all the people—that right is absolutely clear.

The problem we have here is basically that the Congress wants responsibility, they want to share responsibility. Believe me, it would be pleasant to have more sharing of responsibility by the Congress. But if you are going to have responsibility, you have to be responsible, and this Congress—and some of the more thoughtful Members of Congress and that includes most of the leadership, in the very good give-and-take we had the other day—this Congress has not been responsible on money.

We simply had this. There is a clear choice. We either cut spending or raise taxes and I made a little check before the leaders meeting. I checked on the campaigns of everybody who had run for office across this country, Democrat and Republican. I didn't find one Member of Congress, liberal or conservative, who had campaigned on the platform of raising taxes in order that we could spend more.

Now the point is, the Congress has to decide, does it want to raise taxes in order to spend more or does it want to cut, as the President is trying to cut? The difficulty, of course—and I have been a Member of Congress—is that the Congress represents special interests.

The Interior Committee wants to have more parks and the Agriculture Committee wants cheap REA loans and the HEW Committee or the Education and Labor Committee wants more for education and the rest, and each of these wants we all sympathize with. But there is only one place in this Government where somebody has got to speak not for the special interests which the Congress represents but for the general interest.

The general interest of this country, the general interest, whether it be rich or poor or old, is don't break the family budget by raising the taxes or raising prices, and I am going to stand for that general interest. Therefore, I will not spend money if the Congress overspends, and I will not be for programs that will raise the taxes and put a bigger burden on the already overburdened American taxpayer.

American Prisoners in China

[13.] Q. Mr. President, there are two American fliers still being held prisoner in China, and they are sort of in limbo—well, three Americans but two fliers. I wonder if you could give us their status, and do you expect them to be returned with the other prisoners?

THE PRESIDENT. This matter we discussed when we were in the People's Republic of China, and we have every reason to believe that these fliers will be released on the initiative of the People's Republic of China as the POW situation is worked out in Vietnam.

I won't go beyond that because this is a matter that should be left to the People's Republic of China, but we have, we believe, every assurance that will happen.

Q. Downey, also?

THE PRESIDENT. Downey is a different case, as you know. Downey involves a CIA agent. His sentence of 30 years has been, I think, commuted to 5 years, and we have also discussed that with Premier Chou En-lai. I would have to be quite candid: We have no assurance that any change of action, other than the commutation of the sentence, will take place, but we have, of course, informed the People's Republic through our private channels that we feel that would be a very salutary action on his part.

But that is a matter where they must act on their own initiative, and it is not one where any public pressures or bellicose statements from here will be helpful in getting his release.

REPORTER. Thank you, Mr. President.

18. Address to the Nation on Watergate April 30, 1973

Good evening:

I want to talk to you tonight from my heart on a subject of deep concern to every American.

In recent months, members of my Administration and officials of the Committee for the

Re-Election of the President—including some of my closest friends and most trusted aides—have been charged with involvement in what has come to be known as the Watergate affair. These include charges of illegal activity during and preceding the 1972 Presidential election and charges that responsible officials participated in efforts to cover up that illegal activity.

The inevitable result of these charges has been to raise serious questions about the integrity of the White House itself. Tonight I wish to address those questions.

Last June 17, while I was in Florida trying to get a few days rest after my visit to Moscow, I first learned from news reports of the Watergate break-in. I was appalled at this senseless, illegal action, and I was shocked to learn that employees of the Re-Election Committee were apparently among those guilty. I immediately ordered an investigation by appropriate Government authorities. On September 15, as you will recall, indictments were brought against seven defendants in the case.

As the investigations went forward, I repeatedly asked those conducting the investigation whether there was any reason to believe that members of my Administration were in any way involved. I received repeated assurances that there were not. Because of these continuing reassurances, because I believed the reports I was getting, because I had faith in the persons from whom I was getting them, I discounted the stories in the press that appeared to implicate members of my Administration or other officials of the campaign committee.

Until March of this year, I remained convinced that the denials were true and that the charges of involvement by members of the White House Staff were false. The comments I made during this period, and the comments made by my Press Secretary in my behalf, were based on the information provided to us at the time we made those comments. However, new information then came to me which persuaded me that there was a real possibility that some of these charges were true, and suggesting further that there had been an effort to conceal the facts both from the public, from you, and from me.

As a result, on March 21, I personally assumed the responsibility for coordinating intensive new inquiries into the matter, and I personally ordered those conducting the investigations to get all the facts and to report them directly to me, right here in this office.

I again ordered that all persons in the Government or at the Re-Election Committee should cooperate fully with the FBI, the prosecutors, and the grand jury. I also ordered that anyone who refused to cooperate in telling the truth would be asked to resign from Government service. And, with ground rules adopted that would preserve the basic constitutional separation of powers between the Congress and the Presidency, I directed that members of the White House Staff should appear and testify voluntarily under oath before the Senate committee which was investigating Watergate.

I was determined that we should get to the bottom of the matter, and that the truth should be fully brought out—no matter who was involved.

At the same time, I was determined not to take precipitate action and to avoid, if at all possible, any action that would appear to reflect on innocent people. I wanted to be fair. But I knew that in the final analysis, the integrity of this office—public faith in the integrity of this office—would have to take priority over all personal considerations.

Today, in one of the most difficult decisions of my Presidency, I accepted the resignations of two of my closest associates in the White House—Bob Haldeman, John Ehrlichman—two of the finest public servants it has been my privilege to know.

I want to stress that in accepting these resignations, I mean to leave no implication whatever of personal wrongdoing on their part, and I leave no implication tonight of implication on the part of others who have been charged in this matter. But in matters as sensitive as guarding the integrity of our democratic process, it is essential not only that rigorous legal and ethical standards be observed but also that the public, you, have total confidence that they are both being observed and enforced by those in authority and particularly by the President of the United States. They agreed with me that this move was necessary in order to restore that confidence.

Because Attorney General Kleindienst—though a distinguished public servant, my personal friend for 20 years, with no personal involvement whatever in this matter—has been a close personal and professional associate of some of those who are involved in this case, he and I both felt that it was also necessary to name a new Attorney General.

The Counsel to the President, John Dean, has also resigned.

As the new Attorney General, I have today named Elliot Richardson, a man of unimpeachable integrity and rigorously high principle. I have directed him to do everything necessary to ensure that the Department of Justice has the confidence and the trust of every law-abiding person in this country.

I have given him absolute authority to make all decisions bearing upon the prosecution of the Watergate case and related matters. I have instructed him that if he should consider it appropriate, he has the authority to name a special supervising prosecutor for matters arising out of the case.

Whatever may appear to have been the case before, whatever improper activities may yet be discovered in connection with this whole sordid affair, I want the American people, I want you to know beyond the shadow of a doubt that during my term as President, justice will be pursued fairly, fully, and impartially, no matter who is involved. This office is a sacred trust and I am determined to be worthy of that trust.

Looking back at the history of this case, two questions arise:

How could it have happened?

Who is to blame?

Political commentators have correctly observed that during my 27 years in politics I have always previously insisted on running my own campaigns for office.

But 1972 presented a very different situation. In both domestic and foreign policy, 1972 was a year of crucially important decisions, of intense negotiations, of vital new directions, particularly in working toward the goal which has been my overriding concern throughout my political career—the goal of bringing peace to America, peace to the world.

That is why I decided, as the 1972 campaign approached, that the Presidency should come first and politics second. To the maximum extent possible, therefore, I sought to delegate campaign operations, to remove the day-to-day campaign decisions from the President's office and from the White House. I also, as you recall, severely limited the number of my own campaign appearances.

Who, then, is to blame for what happened in this case?

For specific criminal actions by specific individuals, those who committed those actions must, of course, bear the liability and pay the penalty.

For the fact that alleged improper actions took place within the White House or within my campaign organization, the easiest course would be for me to blame those to whom I delegated the responsibility to run the campaign. But that would be a cowardly thing to do.

I will not place the blame on subordinates—on people whose zeal exceeded their judgment and who may have done wrong in a cause they deeply believed to be right.

In any organization, the man at the top must bear the responsibility. That responsibility, therefore, belongs here, in this office. I accept it. And I pledge to you tonight, from this office, that I will do everything in my power to ensure that the guilty are brought to justice and that such abuses are purged from our political processes in the years to come, long after I have left this office.

Some people, quite properly appalled at the abuses that occurred, will say that Watergate demonstrates the bankruptcy of the American political system. I believe precisely the opposite is true. Watergate represented a series of illegal acts and bad judgments by a number of individuals. It was the system that has brought the facts to light and that will bring those guilty to justice—a system that in this case has included a determined grand jury, honest prosecutors, a courageous judge, John Sirica, and a vigorous free press.

It is essential now that we place our faith in that system—and especially in the judicial system. It is essential that we let the judicial process go forward, respecting those safeguards that are established to protect the innocent as well as to convict the guilty. It is essential that in reacting to the excesses of others, we not fall into excesses ourselves.

It is also essential that we not be so distracted by events such as this that we neglect the vital work before us, before this Nation, before America, at a time of critical importance to America and the world.

Since March, when I first learned that the Watergate affair might in fact be far more serious than I had been led to believe, it has claimed far too much of my time and my attention.

Whatever may now transpire in the case, whatever the actions of the grand jury, whatever the outcome of any eventual trials, I must now turn my full attention—and I shall do so—once again to the larger duties of this office. I owe it to this great office that I hold, and I owe it to you—to my country.

I know that as Attorney General, Elliot Richardson will be both fair and he will be fearless in pursuing this case wherever it leads. I am confident that with him in charge, justice will be done.

There is vital work to be done toward our goal of a lasting structure of peace in the world—work that cannot wait, work that I must do.

Tomorrow, for example, Chancellor Brandt of West Germany will visit the White House for talks that are a vital element of "The Year of Europe," as 1973 has been called. We are already preparing for the next Soviet-American summit meeting later this year.

This is also a year in which we are seeking to negotiate a mutual and balanced reduction of armed forces in Europe, which will reduce our defense budget and allow us to have funds for other purposes at home so desperately needed. It is the year when the United States and Soviet negotiators will seek to work out the second and even more important round of our talks on limiting nuclear arms and of reducing the danger of a nuclear war that would destroy civilization as we know it. It is a year in which we confront the difficult tasks of maintaining peace in Southeast Asia and in the potentially explosive Middle East.

There is also vital work to be done right here in America: to ensure prosperity, and that means a good job for everyone who wants to work; to control inflation, that I know worries every housewife, everyone who tries to balance a family budget in America; to set in motion new and better ways of ensuring progress toward a better life for all Americans.

When I think of this office—of what it means—I think of all the things that I want to accomplish for this Nation, of all the things I want to accomplish for you.

On Christmas Eve, during my terrible personal ordeal of the renewed bombing of North

Vietnam, which after 12 years of war finally helped to bring America peace with honor, I sat down just before midnight. I wrote out some of my goals for my second term as President. Let me read them to you.

"To make it possible for our children, and for our children's children, to live in a world of peace.

"To make this country be more than ever a land of opportunity—of equal opportunity, full opportunity for every American.

"To provide jobs for all who can work, and generous help for those who cannot work.

"To establish a climate of decency and civility, in which each person respects the feelings and the dignity and the Godgiven rights of his neighbor.

"To make this a land in which each person can dare to dream, can live his dreams—not in fear, but in hope—proud of his community, proud of his country, proud of what America has meant to himself and to the world."

These are great goals. I believe we can, we must work for them. We can achieve them. But we cannot achieve these goals unless we dedicate ourselves to another goal.

We must maintain the integrity of the White House, and that integrity must be real, not transparent. There can be no whitewash at the White House.

We must reform our political process—ridding it not only of the violations of the law but also of the ugly mob violence and other inexcusable campaign tactics that have been too often practiced and too readily accepted in the past, including those that may have been a response by one side to the excesses or expected excesses of the other side. Two wrongs do not make a right.

I have been in public life for more than a quarter of a century. Like any other calling, politics has good people and bad people. And let me tell you, the great majority in politics in the Congress, in the Federal Government,

in the State government—are good people. I know that it can be very easy, under the intensive pressures of a campaign, for even well-intentioned people to fall into shady tactics—to rationalize this on the grounds that what is at stake is of such importance to the Nation that the end justifies the means. And both of our great parties have been guilty of such tactics in the past.

In recent years, however, the campaign excesses that have occurred on all sides have provided a sobering demonstration of how far this false doctrine can take us. The lesson is clear: America, in its political campaigns, must not again fall into the trap of letting the end, however great that end is, justify the means.

I urge the leaders of both political parties, I urge citizens, all of you, everywhere, to join in working toward a new set of standards, new rules and procedures to ensure that future elections will be as nearly free of such abuses as they possibly can be made. This is my goal. I ask you to join in making it America's goal.

When I was inaugurated for a second time this past January 20, I gave each member of my Cabinet and each member of my senior White House Staff a special 4-year calendar, with each day marked to show the number of days remaining to the Administration. In the inscription on each calendar, I wrote these words: "The Presidential term which begins today consists of 1,461 days—no more, no less. Each can be a day of strengthening and renewal for America; each can add depth and dimension to the American experience. If we strive together, if we make the most of the challenge and the opportunity that these days offer us, they can stand out as great days for America, and great moments in the history of the world."

I looked at my own calendar this morning up at Camp David as I was working on this speech. It showed exactly 1,361 days remaining in my term. I want these to be the best days in America's history, because I love America. I deeply believe that America is the hope of the world. And I know that in the quality and wisdom of the leadership America gives lies the only hope for millions of people all over the world that they can live their lives in peace and freedom. We must be worthy of that hope, in every sense of the word. Tonight, I ask for your prayers to help me in everything that I do throughout the days of my Presidency to be worthy of their hopes and of yours.

God bless America and God bless each and every one of you.

19. Statement on Watergate
May 22, 1973

Recent news accounts growing out of testimony in the Watergate investigations have given grossly misleading impressions of many of the facts, as they relate both to my own role and to certain unrelated activities involving national security.

Already, on the basis of second- and third-hand hearsay testimony by persons either convicted or themselves under investigation in the case, I have found myself accused of involvement in activities I never heard of until I read about them in news accounts.

These impressions could also lead to a serious misunderstanding of those national security activities which, though totally unrelated to Watergate, have become entangled in the case. They could lead to further compromise of sensitive national security information.

I will not abandon my responsibilities. I will continue to do the job I was elected to do.

In the accompanying statement, I have set forth the facts as I know them as they relate to my own role.

With regard to the specific allegations that have been made, I can and do state categorically:

1. I had no prior knowledge of the Watergate operation.

2. I took no part in, nor was I aware of, any subsequent efforts that may have been made to cover up Watergate.

3. At no time did I authorize any offer of executive clemency for the Watergate defendants, nor did I know of any such offer.

4. I did not know, until the time of my own investigation, of any effort to provide the Watergate defendants with funds.

5. At no time did I attempt, or did I authorize others to attempt, to implicate the CIA in the Watergate matter.

6. It was not until the time of my own investigation that I learned of the break-in at the office of Mr. Ellsberg's psychiatrist, and I specifically authorized the furnishing of this information to Judge Byrne.

7. I neither authorized nor encouraged subordinates to engage in illegal or improper campaign tactics.

In the accompanying statement, I have sought to provide the background that may place recent allegations in perspective. I have specifically stated that executive privilege will not be invoked as to any testimony concerning possible criminal conduct or discussions of possible criminal conduct, in the matters under investigation. I want the public to learn the truth about Watergate and those guilty of any illegal actions brought to justice.

Allegations surrounding the Watergate affair have so escalated that I feel a further statement from the President is required at this time.

A climate of sensationalism has developed in which even second- or third-hand hearsay charges are headlined as fact and repeated as fact.

Important national security operations which themselves had no connection with Watergate have become entangled in the case.

As a result, some national security information has already been made public through court orders, through the subpoenaing of documents, and through testimony witnesses have given in judicial and Congressional proceedings. Other sensitive documents are now threatened with disclosure. Continued silence about those operations would compromise rather than protect them and would also serve to perpetuate a grossly distorted view—which recent partial disclosures have given—of the nature and purpose of those operations.

The purpose of this statement is threefold:

—First, to set forth the facts about my own relationship to the Watergate matter;

—Second, to place in some perspective some of the more sensational—and inaccurate— of the charges that have filled the headlines in recent days, and also some of the matters that are currently being discussed in Senate testimony and elsewhere;

—Third, to draw the distinction between national security operations and the Watergate case. To put the other matters in perspective, it will be necessary to describe the national security operations first.

In citing these national security matters, it is not my intention to place a national security "cover" on Watergate, but rather to separate them out from Watergate—and at the same time to explain the context in which certain actions took place that were later misconstrued or misused.

Long before the Watergate break-in, three important national security operations took place which have subsequently become entangled in the Watergate case.

—The first operation, begun in 1969, was a program of wiretaps. All were legal, under the authorities then existing. They were undertaken to find and stop serious national security leaks.

—The second operation was a reassessment, which I ordered in 1970, of the adequacy of internal security measures. This resulted in a plan and a directive to strengthen our intelligence operations. They were protested by Mr. Hoover, and as a result of his protest, they were not put into effect.

—The third operation was the establishment, in 1971, of a Special Investigations Unit in the White House. Its primary mission was to plug leaks of vital security information. I also directed this group to prepare an accurate history of certain crucial national security matters which occurred under prior administrations, on which the Government's records were incomplete.

Here is the background of these three security operations initiated in my Administration.

1969 Wiretaps

By mid-1969, my Administration had begun a number of highly sensitive foreign policy initiatives. They were aimed at ending the war in Vietnam, achieving a settlement in the Middle East, limiting nuclear arms, and establishing new relationships among the great powers. These involved highly secret diplomacy. They were closely interrelated. Leaks of secret information about any one could endanger all.

Exactly that happened. News accounts appeared in 1969, which were obviously based on leaks—some of them extensive and detailed—by people having access to the most highly classified security materials.

There was no way to carry forward these diplomatic initiatives unless further leaks could be prevented. This required finding the source of the leaks.

In order to do this, a special program of wiretaps was instituted in mid-1969 and terminated in February 1971. Fewer than 20 taps, of varying duration, were involved. They produced important leads that made it possible to tighten the security of highly sensitive materials. I authorized this entire program. Each individual tap was undertaken in accordance with procedures legal at the time and in accord with long-standing precedent.

The persons who were subject to these wiretaps were determined through coordination among the Director of the FBI, my Assistant for National Security Affairs, and the Attorney General. Those wiretapped were selected on the basis of access to the information leaked, material in security files, and evidence that developed as the inquiry proceeded.

Information thus obtained was made available to senior officials responsible for national security matters in order to curtail further leaks.

The 1970 Intelligence Plan

In the spring and summer of 1970, another security problem reached critical proportions. In March a wave of bombings and explosions struck college campuses and cities. There were 400 bomb threats in one 24-hour period in New York City. Rioting and violence on college campuses reached a new peak after the Cambodian operation and the tragedies at Kent State and Jackson State. The 1969–70 school year brought nearly 1,800 campus demonstrations and nearly 250 cases of arson on campus. Many colleges closed. Gun battles between guerrilla style groups and police were taking place. Some of the disruptive activities were receiving foreign support.

Complicating the task of maintaining security was the fact that, in 1966, certain types of undercover FBI operations that had been conducted for many years had been suspended. This also had substantially impaired our ability to collect foreign intelligence information. At the same time, the relationships between the FBI and other intelligence agencies had been deteriorating. By May 1970, FBI Direc-

tor Hoover shut off his agency's liaison with the CIA altogether.

On June 5, 1970, I met with the Director of the FBI (Mr. Hoover), the Director of the Central Intelligence Agency (Mr. Richard Helms), the Director of the Defense Intelligence Agency (Gen. Donald V. Bennett), and the Director of the National Security Agency (Adm. Noel Gayler). We discussed the urgent need for better intelligence operations. I appointed Director Hoover as chairman of an interagency committee to prepare recommendations.

On June 25, the committee submitted a report which included specific options for expanded intelligence operations, and on July 23 the agencies were notified by memorandum of the options approved. After reconsideration, however, prompted by the opposition of Director Hoover, the agencies were notified 5 days later, on July 28, that the approval had been rescinded. The options initially approved had included resumption of certain intelligence operations which had been suspended in 1966. These in turn had include authorization for surreptitious entry—breaking and entering, in effect—on specified categories of targets in specified situations related to national security.

Because the approval was withdrawn before it had been implemented, the net result was that the plan for expanded intelligence activities never went into effect.

The documents spelling out this 1970 plan are extremely sensitive. They include—and are based upon—assessments of certain foreign intelligence capabilities and procedures, which of course must remain secret. It was this unused plan and related documents that John Dean removed from the White House and placed in a safe deposit box, giving the keys to Judge Sirica. The same plan, still unused, is being headlined today.

Coordination among our intelligence agencies continued to fall short of our national security needs. In July 1970, having earlier discontinued the FBI's liaison with the CIA, Director Hoover ended the FBI's normal liaison with all other agencies except the White House. To help remedy this, an Intelligence Evaluation Committee was created in December 1970. Its members included representatives of the White House, CIA, FBI, NSA, the Departments of Justice, Treasury, and Defense, and the Secret Service.

The Intelligence Evaluation Committee and its staff were instructed to improve coordination among the intelligence community and to prepare evaluations and estimates of domestic intelligence. I understand that its activities are now under investigation. I did not authorize nor do I have any knowledge of any illegal activity by this Committee. If it went beyond its charter and did engage in any illegal activities, it was totally without my knowledge or authority.

The Special Investigations Unit

On Sunday, June 13, 1971, the New York Times published the first installment of what came to be known as "The Pentagon Papers." Not until a few hours before publication did any responsible Government official know that they had been stolen. Most officials did not know they existed. No senior official of the Government had read them or knew with certainty what they contained.

All the Government knew, at first, was that the papers comprised 47 volumes and some 7,000 pages, which had been taken from the most sensitive files of the Departments of State and Defense and the CIA, covering military and diplomatic moves in a war that was still going on.

Moreover, a majority of the documents published with the first three installments in the Times had not been included in the 47-volume study—raising serious questions about what and how much else might have been taken.

There was every reason to believe this was a security leak of unprecedented proportions.

It created a situation in which the ability of the Government to carry on foreign relations even in the best of circumstances could have been severely compromised. Other governments no longer knew whether they could deal with the United States in confidence. Against the background of the delicate negotiations the United States was then involved in on a number of fronts—with regard to Vietnam, China, the Middle East, nuclear arms limitations, U.S.-Soviet relations, and others—in which the utmost degree of confidentiality was vital, it posed a threat so grave as to require extraordinary actions.

Therefore during the week following the Pentagon Papers publication, I approved the creation of a Special Investigations Unit within the White House—which later came to be known as the "plumbers." This was a small group at the White House whose principal purpose was to stop security leaks and to investigate other sensitive security matters. I looked to John Ehrlichman for the supervision of this group.

Egil Krogh, Mr. Ehrlichman's assistant, was put in charge. David Young was added to this unit, as were E. Howard Hunt and G. Gordon Liddy.

The unit operated under extremely tight security rules. Its existence and functions were known only to a very few persons at the White House. These included Messrs. Haldeman, Ehrlichman, and Dean.

At about the time the unit was created, Daniel Ellsberg was identified as the person who had given the Pentagon Papers to the New York Times. I told Mr. Krogh that as a matter of first priority, the unit should find out all it could about Mr. Ellsberg's associates and his motives. Because of the extreme gravity of the situation, and not then knowing what additional national secrets Mr. Ellsberg might disclose, I did impress upon Mr. Krogh the vital importance to the national security of his assignment. I did not authorize and had no knowledge of any illegal means to be used to achieve this goal.

However, because of the emphasis I put on the crucial importance of protecting the national security, I can understand how highly motivated individuals could have felt justified in engaging in specific activities that I would have disapproved had they been brought to my attention.

Consequently, as President, I must and do assume responsibility for such actions despite the fact that I at no time approved or had knowledge of them.

I also assigned the unit a number of other investigatory matters, dealing in part with compiling an accurate record of events related to the Vietnam war, on which the Government's records were inadequate (many previous records having been removed with the change of administrations) and which bore directly on the negotiations then in progress. Additional assignments included tracing down other national security leaks, including one that seriously compromised the U.S. negotiating position in the SALT talks.

The work of the unit tapered off around the end of 1971. The nature of its work was such that it involved matters that, from a national security standpoint, were highly sensitive then and remain so today.

These intelligence activities had no connection with the break-in of the Democratic headquarters, or the aftermath.

I considered it my responsibility to see that the Watergate investigation did not impinge adversely upon the national security area. For example, on April 18, 1973, when I learned that Mr. Hunt, a former member of the Special Investigations Unit at the White House, was to be questioned by the U.S. Attorney, I directed Assistant Attorney General Petersen to pursue every issue involving Watergate but to confine his investigation to Watergate and related mat-

ters and to stay out of national security matters. Subsequently, on April 25, 1973, Attorney General Kleindienst informed me that because the Government had clear evidence that Mr. Hunt was involved in the break-in of the office of the psychiatrist who had treated Mr. Ellsberg, he, the Attorney General, believed that despite the fact that no evidence had been obtained from Hunt's acts, a report should nevertheless be made to the court trying the Ellsberg case. I concurred, and directed that the information be transmitted to Judge Byrne immediately.

Watergate

The burglary and bugging of the Democratic National Committee headquarters came as a complete surprise to me. I had no inkling that any such illegal activities had been planned by persons associated with my campaign; if I had known, I would not have permitted it. My immediate reaction was that those guilty should be brought to justice, and, with the five burglars themselves already in custody, I assumed that they would be.

Within a few days, however, I was advised that there was a possibility of CIA involvement in some way.

It did seem to me possible that, because of the involvement of former CIA personnel, and because of some of their apparent associations, the investigation could lead to the uncovering of covert CIA operations totally unrelated to the Watergate break-in.

In addition, by this time, the name of Mr. Hunt had surfaced in connection with Watergate, and I was alerted to the fact that he had previously been a member of the Special Investigations Unit in the White House. Therefore, I was also concerned that the Watergate investigation might well lead to an inquiry into the activities of the Special Investigations Unit itself.

In this area, I felt it was important to avoid disclosure of the details of the national security matters with which the group was concerned. I knew that once the existence of the group became known, it would lead inexorably to a discussion of these matters, some of which remain, even today, highly sensitive.

I wanted justice done with regard to Watergate; but in the scale of national priorities with which I had to deal—and not at that time having any idea of the extent of political abuse which Watergate reflected—I also had to be deeply concerned with ensuring that neither the covert operations of the CIA nor the operations of the Special Investigations Unit should be compromised. Therefore, I instructed Mr. Haldeman and Mr. Ehrlichman to ensure that the investigation of the break-in not expose either an unrelated covert operation of the CIA or the activities of the White House investigations unit—and to see that this was personally coordinated between General Waiters, the Deputy Director of the CIA, and Mr. Gray of the FBI. It was certainly not my intent, nor my wish, that the investigation of the Watergate break-in or of related acts be impeded in any way.

On July 6, 1972, I telephoned the Acting Director of the FBI, L. Patrick Gray, to congratulate him on his successful handling of the hijacking of a Pacific Southwest Airlines plane the previous day. During the conversation Mr. Gray discussed with me the progress of the Watergate investigation, and I asked him whether he had talked with General Walters. Mr. Gray said that he had, and that General Walters had assured him that the CIA was not involved. In the discussion, Mr. Gray suggested that the matter of Watergate might lead higher. I told him to press ahead with his investigation.

It now seems that later, through whatever complex of individual motives and possible misunderstandings, there were apparently wide-ranging efforts to limit the investigation or to conceal the possible involvement of members of the Administration and the campaign committee.

I was not aware of any such efforts at the time. Neither, until after I began my own investigation, was I aware of any fund-raising for defendants convicted of the break-in at Democratic headquarters, much less authorize any such fund-raising. Nor did I authorize any offer of executive clemency for any of the defendants.

In the weeks and months that followed Watergate, I asked for, and received, repeated assurances that Mr. Dean's own investigation (which included reviewing files and sitting in on FBI interviews with White House personnel) had cleared everyone then employed by the White House of involvement. In summary, then:

1. I had no prior knowledge of the Watergate bugging operation, or of any illegal surveillance activities for political purposes.

2. Long prior to the 1972 campaign, I did set in motion certain internal security measures, including legal wiretaps, which I felt were necessary from a national security standpoint and, in the climate then prevailing, also necessary from a domestic security standpoint.

3. People who had been involved in the national security operations later, without my knowledge or approval, undertook illegal activities in the political campaign of 1972.

4. Elements of the early post-Watergate reports led me to suspect, incorrectly, that the CIA had been in some way involved. They also led me to surmise, correctly, that since persons originally recruited for covert national security activities had participated in Watergate, an unrestricted investigation of Watergate might lead to and expose those covert national security operations.

5. I sought to prevent the exposure of these covert national security activities, while encouraging those conducting the investigation to pursue their inquiry into the Watergate itself. I so

instructed my staff, the Attorney General, and the Acting Director of the FBI.

6. I also specifically instructed Mr. Haldeman and Mr. Ehrlichman to ensure that the FBI would not carry its investigation into areas that might compromise these covert national security activities, or those of the CIA.

7. At no time did I authorize or know about any offer of executive clemency for the Watergate defendants. Neither did I know until the time of my own investigation of any efforts to provide them with funds.

Conclusion

With hindsight, it is apparent that I should have given more heed to the warning signals I received along the way about a Watergate cover-up and less to the reassurances.

With hindsight, several other things also become clear:

—With respect to campaign practices, and also with respect to campaign finances, it should now be obvious that no campaign in history has ever been subjected to the kind of intensive and searching inquiry that has been focused on the campaign waged in my behalf in 1972.

It is clear that unethical, as well as illegal, activities took place in the course of that campaign.

None of these took place with my specific approval or knowledge. To the extent that I may in any way have contributed to the climate in which they took place, I did not intend to; to the extent that I failed to prevent them, I should have been more vigilant.

It was to help ensure against any repetition of this in the future that last week I proposed the establishment of a top level, bipartisan, independent commission to recommend a comprehensive reform of campaign laws and practices. Given the priority I believe it deserves, such reform should be possible before the next Congressional elections in 1974.

—It now appears that there were persons who may have gone beyond my directives, and sought to expand on my efforts to protect the national security operations in order to cover up any involvement they or certain others might have had in Watergate. The extent to which this is true, and who may have participated and to what degree, are questions that it would not be proper to address here. The proper forum for settling these matters is in the courts.

—To the extent that I have been able to determine what probably happened in the tangled course of this affair, on the basis of my own recollections and of the conflicting accounts and evidence that I have seen, it would appear that one factor at work was that at critical points various people, each with his own perspective and his own responsibilities, saw the same situation with different eyes and heard the same words with different ears.

What might have seemed insignificant to one seemed significant to another; what one saw in terms of public responsibility, another saw in terms of political opportunity; and mixed through it all, I am sure, was a concern on the part of many that the Watergate scandal should not be allowed to get in the way of what the Administration sought to achieve.

The truth about Watergate should be brought out—in an orderly way, recognizing that the safeguards of judicial procedure are designed to find the truth, not to hide the truth.

With his selection of Archibald Cox—who served both President Kennedy and President Johnson as Solicitor General—as the special supervisory prosecutor for matters related to the case, Attorney General-designate Richardson has demonstrated his own determination to see the truth brought out. In this effort he has my full support.

Considering the number of persons involved in this case whose testimony might be subject to a claim of executive privilege, I recognize that a clear definition of that claim has become central to the effort to arrive at the truth.

Accordingly, executive privilege will not be invoked as to any testimony concerning possible criminal conduct or discussions of possible criminal conduct, in the matters presently under investigation, including the Watergate affair and the alleged coverup.

I want to emphasize that this statement is limited to my own recollections of what I said and did relating to security and to the Watergate. I have specifically avoided any attempt to explain what other parties may have said and done. My own information on those other matters is fragmentary, and to some extent contradictory. Additional information may be forthcoming of which I am unaware. It is also my understanding that the information which has been conveyed to me has also become available to those prosecuting these matters. Under such circumstances, it would be prejudicial and unfair of me to render my opinions on the activities of others; those judgments must be left to the judicial process, our best hope for achieving the just result that we all seek.

As more information is developed, I have no doubt that more questions will be raised. To the extent that I am able, I shall also seek to set forth the facts as known to me with respect to those questions.

20. Introduction of Vice President-Designate Gerald R. Ford
October 12, 1973

Members of the Cabinet, Members of the Congress, members of the diplomatic corps, all of our distinguished guests here in the East Room, and my fellow Americans:

I have invited you here tonight so that I could share with all of you, not only in this room but the millions listening on television and radio, my announcement of the man whose name I shall submit to the Congress tomorrow for confirmation as Vice President of the United States.

I shall ask the Congress tonight, and also when I submit the name tomorrow, to act as expeditiously as possible on this nomination because of the great challenges we face at home and abroad today.

We live at a time in which we face great dangers, but also a time of very great opportunities. We can be thankful tonight that for the first time in five years the United States is at peace with every nation in the world. We can also be thankful that we are in the midst of a rising expansion of our economy in which more Americans have better jobs at higher wages than at any time in the history of our country.

But also on the other side, we have to recognize the fact that the peace that we have worked so hard to build, not only for ourselves but for all the world, is now threatened because of a new outbreak of war in the Mideast.

And also we must recognize the fact that the prosperity that we seek is plagued by an inflation which is a burden on the family budget of millions of Americans.

This is a time, therefore, that we need strong and effective leadership, because the hope of the world for peace lies with the leadership that we have here in the United States of America. And our ability to build a new prosperity in this country, a prosperity without war and without inflation, lies in the need for strong leadership in the United States of America.

Never in our history has the world more needed a strong America, a united America, with both the power and the will to act in the spirit that made this a great country and that has kept it a free country.

That is why at this particular time it is vital that we turn away from the obsessions of the past and turn to the great challenges of the future. This is a time for a new beginning for America, a new beginning in which we all dedicate ourselves to the tasks of meeting the challenges we face, seizing the opportunities for greatness, and meeting the dangers wherever they are, at home or abroad.

I am confident tonight as I stand here before leaders of both parties, I am confident we shall meet those dangers and also seize those opportunities. I am confident that we shall do so, but we can and will do so only if we have the support of millions of our fellow Americans all across this land. We can and will do so only if we have bipartisan support in the Congress of the United States in matters in which no partisanship should ever enter. We can and will do so only if we have strong effective leadership in the executive branch of this Government.

These were the considerations that I had in mind as I considered what man or other individual to select as the nominee for Vice President of the United States. Let me tell you what the criteria were that I had in mind. First, and above all, the individual who serves as Vice President must be qualified to be President. Second, the individual who serves as Vice President of the United States must be one who shares the views of the President on the critical issues of foreign policy and national defense, which are so important if we are to play our great role, our destined role to keep peace in the world. Third, at this particular time when we have the Executive in the hands of one party and the Congress controlled by another party, it is vital that the Vice President of the United States be an individual who can work with members of both parties in the Congress in getting approval for those programs of the Administration which we consider are vital for the national interest.

It was these criteria that I had in mind when I pondered this decision last night and early this morning in the quiet beauty of Camp David. And the man I have selected meets those three criteria.

First, he is a man who has served for 25 years in the House of Representatives with great distinction. [Applause]

Ladies and gentlemen, please don't be premature. There are several here who have served 25 years in the House of Representatives.

In addition to that service in the House, I should point out that in that period of time he has earned the respect of both Democrats and Republicans. He is a man also who has been unwavering in his support of the policies that brought peace with honor for America in Vietnam and in support of a policy for the strong national defense for this country, which is so essential if we are to have peace in the world. And above all, he is a man who, if the responsibilities of the great office that I hold, should fall upon him, as has been the case with eight Vice Presidents in our history, we could all say, the leadership of America is in good hands.

Our distinguished guests and my fellow Americans, I proudly present to you the man whose name I will submit to the Congress of the United States for confirmation as the Vice President of the United States, Congressman Gerald Ford of Michigan.

Ladies and gentlemen, Congressman Ford knows the rules, that since he now has to be confirmed by both Houses, his remarks will be very brief.

VICE PRESIDENT-DESIGNATE FORD. Mr. President, I am deeply honored, and I am extremely grateful, and I am terribly humble, but I pledge to you, Mr. President, and I pledge to my colleagues in the Congress, and I pledge to the American people, that to the best of my ability, if confirmed by my colleagues in the

Congress, that I will do my utmost, to the best of my ability, to serve this country well and to perform those duties that will be my new assignment, as effectively and as efficiently and with as much accomplishment as possible.

Mr. President, with pride I have supported our country's policies, both at home and abroad, aimed at seeking peace worldwide and a better well-being for all of our citizens throughout our great land, and I will continue to work with you and with the Congress in the further implementation of those policies in the months and years ahead.

It seems to me that we want, in America, a united America. I hope I have some assets that might be helpful in working with the Congress in doing what I can throughout our country to make America a united America. I pledge to you my full efforts, and I pledge the same to my colleagues and to the American people. Thank you very much.

THE PRESIDENT. I know that all of you will want to meet Congressman Ford and Mrs. Ford. We will be in the Blue Room if you would like to come by and say hello and congratulate them. Also there will be refreshments, I understand, in the State Dining Room in case some of you did not have supper.

Thank you and good evening.

22. Statement Regarding Presidential Recordings
October 19, 1973

For a number of months, there has been a strain imposed on the American people by the aftermath of Watergate, and the inquiries into and court suits arising out of that incident. Increasing apprehension over the possibility of a constitutional confrontation in the tapes cases has become especially damaging.

Our Government, like our Nation, must remain strong and effective. What matters most, in this critical hour, is our ability to act— and to act in a way that enables us to control events, not to be paralyzed and overwhelmed by them. At home, the Watergate issue has taken on overtones of a partisan political contest. Concurrently, there are those in the international community who may be tempted by our Watergate-related difficulties at home to misread America's unity and resolve in meeting the challenges we confront abroad.

I have concluded that it is necessary to take decisive actions that will avoid any possibility of a constitutional crisis and that will lay the groundwork upon which we can assure unity of purpose at home and end the temptation abroad to test our resolve.

It is with this awareness that I have considered the decision of the Court of Appeals for the District of Columbia. I am confident that the dissenting opinions, which are in accord with what until now has always been regarded as the law, would be sustained upon review by the Supreme Court. I have concluded, however, that it is not in the national interest to leave this matter unresolved for the period that might be required for a review by the highest court.

Throughout this week, the Attorney General, Elliot Richardson, at my instance, has been holding discussions with Special Prosecutor Archibald Cox, looking to the possibility of a compromise that would avoid the necessity of Supreme Court review. With the greatest reluctance, I have concluded that in this one instance, I must permit a breach in the confidentiality that is so necessary to the conduct of the Presidency. Accordingly, the Attorney General made what he regarded as a reasonable proposal for compromise and one that goes beyond what any President in history has offered. It was a proposal that would comply with the spirit of the decision of the court of appeals. It would have allowed justice to proceed undiverted, while maintaining the principle of an independent executive branch. It would have given the Special Prosecutor the information he claims he needs for use in the grand jury. It would also have resolved any lingering thought that the President himself might have been involved in a Watergate coverup.

The proposal was that, as quickly as the materials could be prepared, there would be submitted to Judge Sirica, through a statement prepared by me personally from the subpoenaed tapes, a full disclosure of everything contained in those tapes that has any bearing on Watergate. The authenticity of this summary would be assured by giving unlimited access to the tapes to a very distinguished man, highly respected by all elements in American life for his integrity, his fairness, and his patriotism, so that that man could satisfy himself that the statement prepared by me did indeed include fairly and accurately anything on the tapes that might be regarded as related to Watergate. In return, so that the constitutional tensions of Watergate would not be continued, it would be understood that there would be no further attempt by the Special Prosecutor to subpoena still more tapes or other Presidential papers of a similar nature.

I am pleased to be able to say that Chairman Sam Ervin and Vice Chairman Howard Baker of the Senate Select Committee have agreed to this procedure and that at their request, and mine, Senator John Stennis has consented to listen to every requested tape and verify that the statement I am preparing is full and accurate. Some may ask why, if I am willing to let Senator Stennis hear the tapes for this purpose, I am not willing merely to submit them to the court for inspection in private. I do so out of no lack of respect for Judge Sirica, in whose discretion and integrity I have the utmost confidence, but because to allow the tapes to be heard by one judge would create a precedent that would be available to 400 district judges. Further, it would create a precedent that Presidents are required to submit to judicial demands that purport to override

Presidential determinations on requirements for confidentiality.

To my regret, the Special Prosecutor rejected this proposal. Nevertheless, it is my judgment that in the present circumstances and existing international environment, it is in the overriding national interest that a constitutional confrontation on this issue be avoided. I have, therefore, instructed White House Counsel not to seek Supreme Court review from the decision of the court of appeals. At the same time, I will voluntarily make available to Judge Sirica—and also to the Senate Select Committee—a statement of the Watergate-related portions of the tapes, prepared and authenticated in the fashion I have described.

I want to repeat that I have taken this step with the greatest reluctance, only to bring the issue of Watergate tapes to an end and to assure our full attention to more pressing business affecting the very security of the Nation. Accordingly, though I have not wished to intrude upon the independence of the Special Prosecutor, I have felt it necessary to direct him, as an employee of the executive branch, to make no further attempts by judicial process to obtain tapes, notes, or memoranda of Presidential conversations. I believe that with the statement that will be provided to the court, any legitimate need of the Special Prosecutor is fully satisfied and that he can proceed to obtain indictments against those who may have committed any crimes. And I believe that by these actions I have taken today, America will be spared the anguish of further indecision and litigation about tapes.

Our constitutional history reflects not only the language and inferences of that great document, but also the choices of clash and accommodation made by responsible leaders at critical moments. Under the Constitution, it is the duty of the President to see that the laws of the Nation are faithfully executed. My actions today are in accordance with that duty, and in that spirit of accommodation.

23. Veto of War Powers Resolution
October 24, 1973

To the House of Representatives:

I hereby return without my approval House Joint Resolution 542—the War Powers Resolution. While I am in accord with the desire of the Congress to assert its proper role in the conduct of our foreign affairs, the restrictions which this resolution would impose upon the authority of the President are both unconstitutional and dangerous to the best interests of our Nation.

The proper roles of the Congress and the Executive in the conduct of foreign affairs have been debated since the founding of our country. Only recently, however, has there been a serious challenge to the wisdom of the Founding Fathers in choosing not to draw a precise and detailed line of demarcation between the foreign policy powers of the two branches.

The Founding Fathers understood the impossibility of foreseeing every contingency that might arise in this complex area. They acknowledged the need for flexibility in responding to changing circumstances. They recognized that foreign policy decisions must be made through close cooperation between the two branches and not through rigidly codified procedures.

These principles remain as valid today as they were when our Constitution was written. Yet House Joint Resolution 542 would violate those principles by defining the President's powers in ways which would strictly limit his constitutional authority.

Clearly Unconstitutional

House Joint Resolution 542 would attempt to take away, by a mere legislative act, authorities which the President has properly exercised under the Constitution for almost 200 years. One of its provisions would automatically cut off certain authorities after sixty days unless the Congress extended them. Another would allow the Congress to eliminate certain authorities merely by the passage of a concurrent resolution—an action which does not normally have the force of law, since it denies the President his constitutional role in approving legislation.

I believe that both these provisions are unconstitutional. The only way in which the constitutional powers of a branch of the Government can be altered is by amending the Constitution—and any attempt to make such alterations by legislation alone is clearly without force.

Undermining Our Foreign Policy

While I firmly believe that a veto of House Joint Resolution 542 is warranted solely on constitutional grounds, I am also deeply disturbed by the practical consequences of this resolution. For it would seriously undermine this Nation's ability to act decisively and convincingly in times of international crisis. As a result, the confidence of our allies in our ability to assist them could be diminished and the respect of our adversaries for our deterrent posture could decline. A permanent and substantial element of unpredictability would be injected into the world's assessment of American behavior, further increasing the likelihood of miscalculation and war.

If this resolution had been in operation, America's effective response to a variety of challenges in recent years would have been vastly complicated or even made impossible. We may well have been unable to respond in the way we did during the Berlin crisis of 1961, the Cuban missile crisis of 1962, the Congo rescue operation in 1964, and the Jordanian crisis of 1970—to mention just a few examples. In addition, our recent actions to bring about a peaceful settlement of the hostilities in the Middle East would have been seriously impaired if this resolution had been in force.

While all the specific consequences of House Joint Resolution 542 cannot yet be predicted, it is clear that it would undercut the ability of the United States to act as an effective influence for peace. For example, the provision automatically cutting off certain authorities after 60 days unless they are extended by the Congress could work to prolong or intensify a crisis. Until the Congress suspended the deadline, there would be at least a chance of United States withdrawal and an adversary would be tempted therefore to postpone serious negotiations until the 60 days were up. Only after the Congress acted would there be a strong incentive for an adversary to negotiate. In addition, the very existence of a deadline could lead to an escalation of hostilities in order to achieve certain objectives before the 60 days expired.

The measure would jeopardize our role as a force for peace in other ways as well.

It would, for example, strike from the President's hand a wide range of important peace-keeping tools by eliminating his ability to exercise quiet diplomacy backed by subtle shifts in our military deployments. It would also cast into doubt authorities which Presidents have used to undertake certain humanitarian relief missions in conflict areas, to protect fishing boats from seizure, to deal with ship or aircraft hijackings, and to respond to threats of attack. Not the least of the adverse consequences of this resolution would be the prohibition contained in section 8 against fulfilling our obligations under the NATO treaty as ratified by the Senate. Finally, since the bill is somewhat vague as to when the 60 day rule would apply, it could lead to extreme confusion and dangerous disagreements concerning the prerogatives of the two branches, seriously damaging our ability to respond to international crises.

Failure to Require Positive Congressional Action

I am particularly disturbed by the fact that certain of the President's constitutional powers as Commander in Chief of the Armed Forces would terminate automatically under this resolution 60 days after they were invoked. No overt Congressional action would be required to cut off these powers—they would disappear automatically unless the Congress extended them. In effect, the Congress is here attempting to increase its policy-making role through a provision which requires it to take absolutely no action at all.

In my view, the proper way for the Congress to make known its will on such foreign policy questions is through a positive action, with full debate on the merits of the issue and with each member taking the responsibility of casting a yes or no vote after considering those merits. The authorization and appropriations process represents one of the ways in which such influence can be exercised. I do not, however, believe that the Congress can responsibly contribute its considered, collective judgment on such grave questions without full debate and without a yes or no vote. Yet this is precisely what the joint resolution would allow. It would give every future Congress the ability to handcuff every future President merely by doing nothing and sitting still. In my view, one cannot become a responsible partner unless one is prepared to take responsible action.

Strengthening Cooperation between the Congress and the Executive Branch

The responsible and effective exercise of the war powers requires the fullest cooperation between the Congress and the Executive and the prudent fulfillment by each branch of its constitutional responsibilities. House Joint Resolution 542 includes certain constructive measures which would foster this process by enhancing the flow of information from the executive branch to the Congress. Section 3, for example, calls for consultations with the Congress before and during the involvement of the United States forces in hostilities abroad. This provision is consistent with the desire of this Administration for regularized consultations with the Congress in an even wider range of circumstances.

I believe that full and cooperative participation in foreign policy matters by both the executive and the legislative branches could be enhanced by a careful and dispassionate study of their constitutional roles. Helpful proposals for such a study have already been made in the Congress. I would welcome the establishment of a non-partisan commission on the constitutional roles of the Congress and the President in the conduct of foreign affairs. This commission could make a thorough review of the principal constitutional issues in Executive-Congressional relations, including the war powers, the international agreement powers, and the question of Executive privilege, and then submit its recommendations to the President and the Congress. The members of such a commission could be drawn from both parties—and could represent many perspectives including those of the Congress, the executive branch, the legal profession, and the academic community.

This Administration is dedicated to strengthening cooperation between the Congress and the President in the conduct of foreign affairs and to preserving the constitutional prerogatives of both branches of our Government. I know that the Congress shares that goal. A commission on the constitutional roles of the Congress and the President would provide a useful opportunity for both branches to work together toward that common objective.

RICHARD NIXON

24. Address to the Nation Announcing Answer to the House Judiciary Committee Subpoena for Additional Presidential Tape Recordings
April 29, 1974

Good evening:

I have asked for this time tonight in order to announce my answer to the House Judiciary Committee's subpoena for additional Watergate tapes, and to tell you something about the actions I shall be taking tomorrow—about

what I hope they will mean to you and about the very difficult choices that were presented to me.

These actions will at last, once and for all, show that what I knew and what I did with regard to the Watergate break-in and coverup were just as I have described them to you from the very beginning.

I have spent many hours during the past few weeks thinking about what I would say to the American people if I were to reach the decision I shall announce tonight. And so, my words have not been lightly chosen; I can assure you they are deeply felt.

It was almost three years ago, in June 1972 that five men broke into the Democratic National Committee headquarters in Washington. It turned out that they were connected with my reelection committee, and the Watergate break-in became a major issue in the campaign.

The full resources of the FBI and the Justice Department were used to investigate the incident thoroughly. I instructed my staff and campaign aides to cooperate fully with the investigation. The FBI conducted nearly 1,500 interviews. For 9 months—until March 1973—I was assured by those charged with conducting and monitoring the investigations that no one in the White House was involved.

Nevertheless, for more than a year, there have been allegations and insinuations that I knew about the planning of the Watergate break-in and that I was involved in an extensive plot to cover it up. The House Judiciary Committee is now investigating these charges.

On March 6, I ordered all materials that I had previously furnished to the Special Prosecutor turned over to the committee. These included tape recordings of 19 Presidential conversations and more than 700 documents from private White House files.

On April 11, the Judiciary Committee issued a subpoena for 42 additional tapes of conversations which it contended were necessary for its investigation. I agreed to respond to that subpoena by tomorrow.

In these folders that you see over here on my left are more than 1,200 pages of transcripts of private conversations I participated in between September 15, 1972, and April 27 of 1973 with my principal aides and associates with regard to Watergate. They include all the relevant portions of all of the subpoenaed conversations that were recorded, that is, all portions that relate to the question of what I knew about Watergate or the coverup and what I did about it.

They also include transcripts of other conversations which were not subpoenaed, but which have a significant bearing on the question of Presidential actions with regard to Watergate. These will be delivered to the committee tomorrow.

In these transcripts, portions not relevant to my knowledge or actions with regard to Watergate are not included, but everything that is relevant is included—the rough as well as the smooth—the strategy sessions, the exploration of alternatives, the weighing of human and political costs.

As far as what the President personally knew and did with regard to Watergate and the coverup is concerned, these materials—together with those already made available—will tell it all.

I shall invite Chairman Rodino and the committee's ranking minority member, Congressman Hutchinson of Michigan, to come to the White House and listen to the actual, full tapes of these conversations, so that they can determine for themselves beyond question that the transcripts are accurate and that everything on the tapes relevant to my knowledge and my actions on Watergate is included. If there should be any disagreement over whether omitted material is relevant, I shall meet with them personally in an effort to settle the matter. I believe this arrangement is fair, and I think it is appropriate.

For many days now, I have spent many hours of my own time personally reviewing these materials and personally deciding questions of relevancy. I believe it is appropriate that the committee's review should also be made by its own senior elected officials, and not by staff employees.

The task of Chairman Rodino and Congressman Hutchinson will be made simpler than was mine by the fact that the work of preparing the transcripts has been completed. All they will need to do is to satisfy themselves of their authenticity and their completeness.

Ever since the existence of the White House taping system was first made known last summer, I have tried vigorously to guard the privacy of the tapes. I have been well aware that my effort to protect the confidentiality of Presidential conversations has heightened the sense of mystery about Watergate and, in fact, has caused increased suspicions of the President. Many people assume that the tapes must incriminate the President, or that otherwise, he would not insist on their privacy.

But the problem I confronted was this: Unless a President can protect the privacy of the advice he gets, he cannot get the advice he needs.

This principle is recognized in the constitutional doctrine of executive privilege, which has been defended and maintained by every President since Washington and which has been recognized by the courts, whenever tested, as inherent in the Presidency. I consider it to be my constitutional responsibility to defend this principle.

Three factors have now combined to persuade me that a major unprecedented exception to that principle is now necessary:

First, in the present circumstances, the House of Representatives must be able to reach an informed judgment about the President's role in Watergate.

Second, I am making a major exception to the principle of confidentiality because I believe such action is now necessary in order to restore the principle itself, by clearing the air of the central question that has brought such pressures upon it—and also to provide the evidence which will allow this matter to be brought to a prompt conclusion.

Third, in the context of the current impeachment climate, I believe all the American people, as well as their representatives in Congress, are entitled to have not only the facts but also the evidence that demonstrates those facts.

I want there to be no question remaining about the fact that the President has nothing to hide in this matter.

The impeachment of a President is a remedy of last resort; it is the most solemn act of our entire constitutional process. Now, regardless of whether or not it succeeded, the action of the House, in voting a formal accusation requiring trial by the Senate, would put the Nation through a wrenching ordeal it has endured only once in its lifetime, a century ago, and never since America has become a world power with global responsibilities.

The impact of such an ordeal would be felt throughout the world, and it would have its effect on the lives of all Americans for many years to come.

Because this is an issue that profoundly affects all the American people, in addition to turning over these transcripts to the House Judiciary Committee, I have directed that they should all be made public—all of these that you see here.

To complete the record, I shall also release to the public transcripts of all those portions of the tapes already turned over to the Special Prosecutor and to the committee that relate to Presidential actions or knowledge of the Watergate affair.

During the past year, the wildest accusations have been given banner headlines and ready credence as well. Rumor, gossip innuendo, accounts from unnamed sources of what a pro-spective witness might testify to, have filled the morning newspapers and then are repeated on the evening newscasts day after day.

Time and again, a familiar pattern repeated itself. A charge would be reported the first day as what it was—just an allegation. But it would then be referred back to the next day and thereafter as if it were true.

The distinction between fact and speculation grew blurred. Eventually, all seeped into the public consciousness as a vague general impression of massive wrongdoing, implicating everybody, gaining credibility by its endless repetition.

The basic question at issue today is whether the President personally acted improperly in the Watergate matter. Month after month of rumor, insinuation, and charges by just one Watergate witness—John Dean—suggested that the President did act improperly.

This sparked the demands for an impeachment inquiry. This is the question that must be answered. And this is the question that will be answered by these transcripts that I have ordered published tomorrow.

These transcripts cover hour upon hour of discussions that I held with Mr. Haldeman, John Ehrlichman, John Dean, John Mitchell, former Attorney General Kleindienst, Assistant Attorney General Petersen, and others with regard to Watergate.

They were discussions in which I was probing to find out what had happened, who was responsible, what were the various degrees of responsibilities, what were the legal capabilities, what were the political ramifications, and what actions were necessary and appropriate on the part of the President.

I realize that these transcripts will provide grist for many sensational stories in the press. Parts will seem to be contradictory with one another, and parts will be in conflict with some of the testimony given in the Senate Watergate committee hearings.

I have been reluctant to release these tapes, not just because they will embarrass me and those with whom I have talked—which they will—and not just because they will become the subject of speculation and even ridicule—which they will—and not just because certain parts of them will be seized upon by political and journalistic opponents—which they will.

I have been reluctant because, in these and in all the other conversations in this office, people have spoken their minds freely, never dreaming that specific sentences or even parts of sentences would be picked out as the subjects of national attention and controversy.

I have been reluctant because the principle of confidentiality is absolutely essential to the conduct of the Presidency. In reading the raw transcripts of these conversations, I believe it will be more readily apparent why that principle is essential and must be maintained in the future. These conversations are unusual in their subject matter, but the same kind of uninhibited discussion—and it is that—the same brutal candor is necessary in discussing how to bring warring factions to the peace table or how to move necessary legislation through the Congress.

Names are named in these transcripts. Therefore, it is important to remember that much that appears in them is no more than hearsay or speculation, exchanged as I was trying to find out what really had happened, while my principal aides were reporting to me on rumors and reports that they had heard, while we discussed the various, often conflicting stories that different persons were telling.

As the transcripts will demonstrate, my concerns during this period covered a wide range. The first and obvious one was to find out just exactly what had happened and who was involved.

A second concern was for the people who had been, or might become, involved in Watergate. Some were close advisers, valued friends, others whom I had trusted. And I was also concerned about the human impact on others, especially some of the young people and their families who had come to Washington to work in my Administration, whose lives might be suddenly ruined by something they had done in an excess of loyalty or in the mistaken belief that it would serve the interests of the President.

And then, I was quite frankly concerned about the political implications. This represented potentially a devastating blow to the Administration and to its programs, one which I knew would be exploited for all it was worth by hostile elements in the Congress as well as in the media. I wanted to do what was right, but I wanted to do it in a way that would cause the least unnecessary damage in a highly charged political atmosphere to the Administration.

And fourth, as a lawyer, I felt very strongly that I had to conduct myself in a way that would not prejudice the rights of potential defendants.

And fifth, I was striving to sort out a complex tangle, not only of facts but also questions of legal and moral responsibility. I wanted, above all, to be fair. I wanted to draw distinctions, where those were appropriate, between persons who were active and willing participants on the one hand, and on the other, those who might have gotten inadvertently caught up in the web and be technically indictable but morally innocent.

Despite the confusions and contradictions, what does come through clearly is this:

John Dean charged in sworn Senate testimony that I was "fully aware of the coverup" at the time of our first meeting on September 15, 1972. These transcripts show clearly that I first learned of it when Mr. Dean himself told me about it in this office on March 21—some 6 months later.

Incidentally, these transcripts—covering hours upon hours of conversations—should place in somewhat better perspective the controversy over the 18 1/2 minute gap in the tape of a conversation I had with Mr. Haldeman back in June of 1972.

Now, how it was caused is still a mystery to me and, I think, to many of the experts as well. But I am absolutely certain, however, of one thing: that it was not caused intentionally by my secretary, Rose Mary Woods, or any of my White House assistants. And certainly, if the theory were true that during those 18 1/2 minutes, Mr. Haldeman and I cooked up some sort of a Watergate coverup scheme, as so many have been quick to surmise, it hardly seems likely that in all of our subsequent conversations—many of them are here—which neither of us ever expected would see the light of day, there is nothing remotely indicating such a scheme; indeed, quite the contrary.

From the beginning, I have said that in many places on the tapes there were ambiguities—a statement and comments that different people with different perspectives might interpret in drastically different ways—but although the words may be ambiguous, though the discussions may have explored many alternatives, the record of my actions is totally clear now, and I still believe it was totally correct then.

A prime example is one of the most controversial discussions, that with Mr. Dean on March 21—the one in which he first told me of the coverup, with Mr. Haldeman joining us midway through the conversation.

His revelations to me on March 21 were a sharp surprise, even though the report he gave to me was far from complete, especially since he did not reveal at that time the extent of his own criminal involvement.

I was particularly concerned by his report that one of the Watergate defendants, Howard Hunt, was threatening blackmail unless he and his lawyer were immediately given $121,000 for legal fees and family support, and that he was attempting to blackmail the White House, not by threatening exposure on the Watergate matter, but by threatening to reveal activities that would expose extremely sensitive, highly secret national security matters that he had worked on before Watergate.

I probed, questioned, tried to learn all Mr. Dean knew about who was involved, what was involved. I asked more than 150 questions of Mr. Dean in the course of that conversation.

He said to me, and I quote from the transcripts directly: "I can just tell from our conversation that these are things that you have no knowledge of."

It was only considerably later that I learned how much there was that he did not tell me then—for example, that he himself had authorized promises of clemency, that he had personally handled money for the Watergate defendants, and that he had suborned perjury of a witness.

I knew that I needed more facts. I knew that I needed the judgments of more people. I knew the facts about the Watergate coverup would have to be made public, but I had to find out more about what they were before I could decide how they could best be made public.

I returned several times to the immediate problem posed by Mr. Hunt's blackmail threat, which to me was not a Watergate problem, but one which I regarded, rightly or wrongly, as a potential national security problem of very serious proportions. I considered long and hard whether it might in fact be better to let the payment go forward, at least temporarily, in the hope that this national security matter would not be exposed in the course of uncovering the Watergate coverup.

I believed then, and I believe today, that I had a responsibility as President to consider every option, including this one, where production of sensitive national security matters was at issue—protection of such matters. In the course of considering it and of "just thinking out loud," as I put it at one point, I several times suggested that meeting Hunt's demands might be necessary.

But then I also traced through where that would lead. The money could be raised. But money demands would lead inescapably to clemency demands, and clemency could not be granted. I said, and I quote directly from the tape: "It is wrong, that's for sure." I pointed out, and I quote again from the tape: "But in the end we are going to be bled to death. And in the end it is all going to come out anyway. Then you get the worst of both worlds. We are going to lose, and people are going to—"

And Mr. Haldeman interrupts me and says: "And look like dopes!"

And I responded, "And in effect look like a coverup. So that we cannot do."

Now, I recognize that this tape of March 21 is one which different meanings could be read in by different people. But by the end of the meeting, as the tape shows, my decision was to convene a new grand jury and to send everyone before the grand jury with instructions to testify.

Whatever the potential for misinterpretation there may be as a result of the different options that were discussed at different times during the meeting, my conclusion at the end of the meeting was clear. And my actions and reactions as demonstrated on the tapes that follow that date show clearly that I did not intend the further payment to Hunt or anyone else be made. These are some of the actions that I took in the weeks that followed in my effort to find the truth, to carry out my responsibilities to enforce the law:

As a tape of our meeting on March 22, the next day, indicates, I directed Mr. Dean to go to Camp David with instructions to put together a written report. I learned 5 days later, on March 26, that he was unable to complete it. And so on March 27, I assigned John Ehrlichman to try to find out what had happened, who was at fault, and in what ways and to what degree.

One of the transcripts I am making public is a call that Mr. Ehrlichman made to the Attorney General on March 28, in which he asked the Attorney General to report to me, the President, directly, any information he might find indicating possible involvement of John Mitchell or by anyone in the White House. I had Mr. Haldeman separately pursue other, independent lines of inquiry.

Throughout, I was trying to reach determinations on matters of both substance and procedure on what the facts were and what was the best way to move the case forward. I concluded that I wanted everyone to go before the grand jury and testify freely and fully. This decision, as you will recall, was publicly announced on March 30, 1973. I waived executive privilege in order to permit everybody to testify. I specifically waived executive privilege with regard to conversations with the President, and I waived the attorney-client privilege with John Dean in order to permit him to testify fully and, I hope, truthfully.

Finally, on April 14—3 weeks after I learned of the coverup from Mr. Dean—Mr. Ehrlichman reported to me on the results of his investigation. As he acknowledged, much of what he had gathered was hearsay, but he had gathered enough to make it clear that the next step was to make his findings completely available to the Attorney General, which I instructed him to do.

And the next day, Sunday, April 15, Attorney General Kleindienst asked to see me, and he reported new information which had come to his attention on this matter. And although he was in no way whatever involved in Watergate, because of his close personal ties, not only to John Mitchell but to other potential people who might be involved, he quite properly removed himself from the case.

We agreed that Assistant Attorney General Henry Petersen, the head of the Criminal Division, a Democrat and career prosecutor, should be placed in complete charge of the investigation.

Later that day, I met with Mr. Petersen. I continued to meet with him, to talk with him, to consult with him, to offer him the full cooperation of the White House—as you will see from these transcripts—even to the point of retaining John Dean on the White House Staff for an extra few weeks after he admitted his criminal involvement, because Mr. Petersen thought that would make it easier for the prosecutor to get his cooperation in breaking the case if it should become necessary to grant Mr. Dean's demand for immunity.

On April 15, when I heard that one of the obstacles to breaking the case was Gordon Liddy's refusal to talk, I telephoned Mr. Petersen and directed that he should make clear not only to Mr. Liddy but to everyone that—and now I quote directly from the tape of that telephone call—"As far as the President is concerned, everybody in this case is to talk and to tell the truth." I told him if necessary I would personally meet with Mr. Liddy's lawyer to assure him that I wanted Liddy to talk and to tell the truth.

From the time Mr. Petersen took charge, the case was solidly within the criminal justice system, pursued personally by the Nation's top professional prosecutor with the active, personal assistance of the President of the United States.

I made clear there was to be no coverup.

Let me quote just a few lines from the transcripts—you can read them to verify them—so that you can hear for yourself the orders I was giving in this period.

Speaking to Haldeman and Ehrlichman, I said: ". . . It is ridiculous to talk about clemency. They all knew that."

Speaking to Ehrlichman, I said: "We all have to do the right thing. . . . We just cannot have this kind of a business. . . ."

Speaking to Haldeman and Ehrlichman, I said: "The boil had to be pricked. . . . We have to prick the boil and take the heat. Now that's what we are doing here."

Speaking to Henry Petersen, I said: "I want you to be sure to understand that you know we are going to get to the bottom of this thing."

Speaking to John Dean, I said: "Tell the truth. That is the thing I have told everybody around here."

And then speaking to Haldeman: "And you tell Magruder, 'now Jeb, this evidence is coming in, you ought to go to the grand jury. Purge yourself if you're perjured and tell this whole story.'"

I am confident that the American people will see these transcripts for what they are, fragmentary records from a time more than a year ago that now seems very distant, the records of a President and of a man suddenly being confronted and having to cope with information which, if true, would have the most far-reaching consequences, not only for his personal reputation but, more important, for his hopes, his plans, his goals for the people who had elected him as their leader.

If read with an open and a fair mind and read together with the record of the actions I took, these transcripts will show that what I have stated from the beginning to be the truth has been the truth: that I personally had no knowledge of the break-in before it occurred, that I had no knowledge of the coverup until I was informed of it by John Dean on March 21, that I never offered clemency for the defendants, and that after March 21, my actions were directed toward finding the facts and seeing that justice was done, fairly and according to the law.

The facts are there. The conversations are there. The record of actions is there.

To anyone who reads his way through this mass of materials I have provided, it will be totally, abundantly clear that as far as the President's role with regard to Watergate is concerned, the entire story is there.

As you will see, now that you also will have this mass of evidence I have provided, I have tried to cooperate with the House Judiciary Committee. And I repeat tonight the offer that I have made previously: to answer written interrogatories under oath and, if there are then issues still unresolved, to meet personally with the chairman of the committee and with Congressman Hutchinson to answer their questions under oath.

As the committee conducts its inquiry, I also consider it only essential and fair that my counsel, Mr. St. Clair, should be present to cross-examine witnesses and introduce evidence in an effort to establish the truth.

I am confident that for the overwhelming majority of those who study the evidence that I shall release tomorrow—those who are willing to look at it fully, fairly, and objectively—the evidence will be persuasive and, I hope, conclusive.

We live in a time of very great challenge and great opportunity for America.

We live at a time when peace may become possible in the Middle East for the first time in a generation.

We are at last in the process of fulfilling the hope of mankind for a limitation on nuclear arms—a process that will continue when I meet with the Soviet leaders in Moscow in a few weeks.

We are well on the way toward building a peace that can last, not just for this but for other generations as well.

And here at home, there is vital work to be done in moving to control inflation, to develop our energy resources, to strengthen our economy so that Americans can enjoy what they have not had since 1956: full prosperity without war and without inflation.

Every day absorbed by Watergate is a day lost from the work that must be done by your President and by your Congress work that must be done in dealing with the great problems that affect your prosperity, affect your security, that could affect your lives.

The materials I make public tomorrow will provide all the additional evidence needed to get Watergate behind us and to get it behind us now.

Never before in the history of the Presidency have records that are so private been made so public.

In giving you these records—blemishes and all—I am placing my trust in the basic fairness of the American people.

I know in my own heart that through the long, painful, and difficult process revealed in these transcripts, I was trying in that period to discover what was right and to do what was right.

I hope and I trust that when you have seen the evidence in its entirety, you will see the truth of that statement.

As for myself, I intend to go forward, to the best of my ability, with the work that you elected me to do. I shall do so in a spirit perhaps best summed up a century ago by another President when he was being subjected to unmerciful attack. Abraham Lincoln said:

"I do the very best I know how—the very best I can; and I mean to keep doing so until the end. If the end brings me out all right, what is said against me won't amount to anything. If the end brings me out wrong, ten angels swearing I was right would make no difference."

Thank you and good evening

25. Resignation of the Presidency August 8, 1974

Good evening:

This is the 37th time I have spoken to you from this office, where so many decisions have been made that shaped the history of this Nation. Each time I have done so to discuss with you some matter that I believe affected the national interest.

In all the decisions I have made in my public life, I have always tried to do what was best for the Nation. Throughout the long and difficult period of Watergate, I have felt it was my duty to persevere, to make every possible effort to complete the term of office to which you elected me.

In the past few days, however, it has become evident to me that I no longer have a strong enough political base in the Congress to justify continuing that effort. As long as there was such a base, I felt strongly that it was necessary to see the constitutional process through to its conclusion, that to do otherwise would be unfaithful to the spirit of that deliberately difficult process and a dangerously destabilizing precedent for the future.

But with the disappearance of that base, I now believe that the constitutional purpose has been served, and there is no longer a need for the process to be prolonged.

I would have preferred to carry through to the finish, whatever the personal agony it would have involved, and my family unanimously urged me to do so. But the interests of the Nation must always come before any personal considerations.

From the discussions I have had with Congressional and other leaders, I have concluded that because of the Watergate matter, I might not have the support of the Congress that I would consider necessary to back the very difficult decisions and carry out the duties of this office in the way the interests of the Nation will require.

I have never been a quitter. To leave office before my term is completed is abhorrent to every instinct in my body. But as President, I must put the interests of America first. America needs a full-time President and a full-time Congress, particularly at this time with problems we face at home and abroad.

To continue to fight through the months ahead for my personal vindication would almost totally absorb the time and attention of both the President and the Congress in a period when our entire focus should be on the great issues of peace abroad and prosperity without inflation at home.

Therefore, I shall resign the Presidency effective at noon tomorrow. Vice President Ford will be sworn in as President at that hour in this office.

As I recall the high hopes for America with which we began this second term, I feel a great sadness that I will not be here in this office working on your behalf to achieve those hopes in the next 2 1/2 years. But in turning over direction of the Government to Vice President Ford, I know, as I told the Nation when I nominated him for that office 10 months ago, that the leadership of America will be in good hands.

In passing this office to the Vice President, I also do so with the profound sense of the weight of responsibility that will fall on his shoulders tomorrow and, therefore, of the understanding, the patience, the cooperation he will need from all Americans.

As he assumes that responsibility, he will deserve the help and the support of all of us. As we look to the future, the first essential is to begin healing the wounds of this Nation, to put the bitterness and divisions of the recent past behind us and to rediscover those shared ideals that lie at the heart of our strength and unity as a great and as a free people.

By taking this action, I hope that I will have hastened the start of that process of healing which is so desperately needed in America.

I regret deeply any injuries that may have been done in the course of the events that led to this decision. I would say only that if some of my judgments were wrong—and some were wrong—they were made in what I believed at the time to be the best interest of the Nation.

To those who have stood with me during these past difficult months—to my family, my friends, to many others who joined in supporting my cause because they believed it was right—I will be eternally grateful for your support.

And to those who have not felt able to give me your support, let me say I leave with no bitterness toward those who have opposed me, because all of us, in the final analysis, have been concerned with the good of the country, however our judgments might differ.

So, let us all now join together in affirming that common commitment and in helping our new President succeed for the benefit of all Americans.

I shall leave this office with regret at not completing my term, but with gratitude for the privilege of serving as your President for the past 5 1/2 years. These years have been a momentous time in the history of our Nation and the world. They have been a time of achievement in which we can all be proud, achievements that represent the shared efforts of the Administration, the Congress, and the people.

But the challenges ahead are equally great, and they, too, will require the support and the efforts of the Congress and the people working in cooperation with the new Administration.

We have ended America's longest war, but in the work of securing a lasting peace in the world, the goals ahead are even more far-reaching and more difficult. We must complete a structure of peace so that it will be said of this generation, our generation of Americans, by the people of all nations, not only that we ended one war but that we prevented future wars.

We have unlocked the doors that for a quarter of a century stood between the United States and the People's Republic of China.

We must now ensure that the one quarter of the world's people who live in the People's Republic of China will be and remain not our enemies, but our friends.

In the Middle East, 100 million people in the Arab countries, many of whom have considered us their enemy for nearly 20 years, now look on us as their friends. We must continue to build on that friendship so that peace can settle at last over the Middle East and so that the cradle of civilization will not become its grave.

Together with the Soviet Union, we have made the crucial breakthroughs that have begun the process of limiting nuclear arms. But we must set as our goal not just limiting but reducing and, finally, destroying these terrible weapons so that they cannot destroy civilization and so that the threat of nuclear war will no longer hang over the world and the people.

We have opened the new relation with the Soviet Union. We must continue to develop and expand that new relationship so that the two strongest nations of the world will live together in cooperation, rather than confrontation.

Around the world in Asia, in Africa, in Latin America, in the Middle East—there are millions of people who live in terrible poverty, even starvation. We must keep as our goal turning away from production for war and expanding production for peace so that people everywhere on this Earth can at last look forward in their children's time, if not in our own time, to having the necessities for a decent life.

Here in America, we are fortunate that most of our people have not only the blessings of liberty but also the means to live full and good and, by the world's standards, even abundant lives. We must press on, however, toward a goal, not only of more and better jobs but of full opportunity for every American and of what we are striving so hard right now to achieve, prosperity without inflation.

For more than a quarter of a century in public life, I have shared in the turbulent history of this era. I have fought for what I believed in. I have tried, to the best of my ability, to discharge those duties and meet those responsibilities that were entrusted to me.

Sometimes I have succeeded and sometimes I have failed, but always I have taken heart from what Theodore Roosevelt once said about the man in the arena, "whose face is marred by dust and sweat and blood, who strives valiantly, who errs and comes short again and again because there is not effort without error and shortcoming, but who does actually strive to do the deed, who knows the great enthusiasms, the great devotions, who spends himself in a worthy cause, who at the best knows in the end the triumphs of high achievements and who at the worst, if he fails, at least fails while daring greatly."

I pledge to you tonight that as long as I have a breath of life in my body, I shall continue in that spirit. I shall continue to work for the great causes to which I have been dedicated throughout my years as a Congressman, a Senator, Vice President, and President, the cause of peace, not just for America but among all nations—prosperity, justice, and opportunity for all of our people.

There is one cause above all to which I have been devoted and to which I shall always be devoted for as long as I live.

When I first took the oath of office as President 5 1/2 years ago, I made this sacred commitment: to "consecrate my office, my energies, and all the wisdom I can summon to the cause of peace among nations."

I have done my very best in all the days since to be true to that pledge. As a result of these efforts, I am confident that the world is a safer place today, not only for the people of America but for the people of all nations, and that all of our children have a better chance than before of living in peace rather than dying in war.

This, more than anything, is what I hoped to achieve when I sought the Presidency. This, more than anything, is what I hope will be my legacy to you, to our country, as I leave the Presidency.

To have served in this office is to have felt a very personal sense of kinship with each and every American. In leaving it, I do so with this prayer: May God's grace be with you in all the days ahead.

Ford Documents

26. Inaugural Address
August 9, 1974

Mr. Chief Justice, my dear friends, my fellow Americans:

The oath that I have taken is the same oath that was taken by George Washington and by every President under the Constitution. But I assume the Presidency under extraordinary circumstances never before experienced by Americans. This is an hour of history that troubles our minds and hurts our hearts.

Therefore, I feel it is my first duty to make an unprecedented compact with my countrymen. Not an inaugural address, not a fireside chat, not a campaign speech—just a little straight talk among friends. And I intend it to be the first of many.

I am acutely aware that you have not elected me as your President by your ballots, and so I ask you to confirm me as your President with your prayers. And I hope that such prayers will also be the first of many.

If you have not chosen me by secret ballot, neither have I gained office by any secret promises. I have not campaigned either for the Presidency or the Vice Presidency. I have not subscribed to any partisan platform. I am indebted to no man, and only to one woman—my dear wife—as I begin this very difficult job.

I have not sought this enormous responsibility, but I will not shirk it. Those who nominated and confirmed me as Vice President were my friends and are my friends. They were of both parties, elected by all the people and acting under the Constitution in their name. It is only fitting then that I should pledge to them and to you that I will be the President of all the people.

Thomas Jefferson said the people are the only sure reliance for the preservation of our liberty. And down the years, Abraham Lincoln renewed this American article of faith asking, "Is there any better way or equal hope in the world?"

I intend, on Monday next, to request of the Speaker of the House of Representatives and the President pro tempore of the Senate the privilege of appearing before the Congress to share with my former colleagues and with you, the American people, my views on the priority business of the Nation and to solicit your views and their views. And may I say to the Speaker and the others, if I could meet with you right after these remarks, I would appreciate it.

Even though this is late in an election year, there is no way we can go forward except together and no way anybody can win except by serving the people's urgent needs. We cannot stand still or slip backwards. We must go forward now together.

To the peoples and the governments of all friendly nations, and I hope that could encompass the whole world, I pledge an uninterrupted and sincere search for peace. America will remain strong and united, but its strength will remain dedicated to the safety and sanity of the entire family of man, as well as to our own precious freedom.

I believe that truth is the glue that holds government together, not only our Government but civilization itself. That bond, though strained, is unbroken at home and abroad.

In all my public and private acts as your President, I expect to follow my instincts of openness and candor with full confidence that honesty is always the best policy in the end.

My fellow Americans, our long national nightmare is over.

Our Constitution works; our great Republic is a government of laws and not of men. Here the people rule. But there is a higher Power, by whatever name we honor Him, who ordains not only righteousness but love, not only justice but mercy.

As we bind up the internal wounds of Watergate, more painful and more poisonous than those of foreign wars, let us restore the golden rule to our political process, and let brotherly love purge our hearts of suspicion and of hate.

In the beginning, I asked you to pray for me. Before closing, I ask again your prayers, for Richard Nixon and for his family. May our former President, who brought peace to millions, find it for himself. May God bless and comfort his wonderful wife and daughters, whose love and loyalty will forever be a shining legacy to all who bear the lonely burdens of the White House.

I can only guess at those burdens, although I have witnessed at close hand the tragedies that befell three Presidents and the lesser trials of others.

With all the strength and all the good sense I have gained from life, with all the confidence my family, my friends, and my dedicated staff impart to me, and with the good will of countless Americans I have encountered in recent visits to 40 States, I now solemnly reaffirm my promise I made to you last December 6: to uphold the Constitution, to do what is right as God gives me to see the right, and to do the very best I can for America.

God helping me, I will not let you down.

Thank you.

27. Address to Joint Session of Congress August 12, 1974

Mr. Speaker, Mr. President, distinguished guests, and my very dear friends:

My fellow Americans, we have a lot of work to do. My former colleagues, you and I have a lot of work to do. Let's get on with it.

Needless to say, I am deeply grateful for the wonderfully warm welcome. I can never express my gratitude adequately.

I am not here to make an inaugural address. The Nation needs action, not words. Nor will this be a formal report of the state of the Union. God willing, I will have at least three more chances to do that.

It is good to be back in the People's House. But this cannot be a real homecoming. Under the Constitution, I now belong to the executive branch. The Supreme Court has even ruled that I am the executive branch—head, heart, and hand.

With due respect to the learned Justices—and I greatly respect the judiciary—part of my heart will always be here on Capitol Hill. I know well the coequal role of the Congress in our constitutional process. I love the House of Representatives. I revere the traditions of the Senate despite my too-short internship in that great body. As President, within the limits of basic principles, my motto toward the Congress is communication, conciliation, compromise, and cooperation.

This Congress, unless it has changed, I am confident, will be my working partner as well as my most constructive critic. I am not asking for conformity. I am dedicated to the two-party system, and you know which party I belong to.

I do not want a honeymoon with you. I want a good marriage.

I want progress, and I want problem solving which requires my best efforts and also your best efforts.

I have no need to learn how Congress speaks for the people. As President, I intend to listen.

But I also intend to listen to the people themselves—all the people—as I promised last Friday. I want to be sure that we are all tuned in to the real voice of America.

My Administration starts off by seeking unity in diversity. My office door has always been open, and that is how it is going to be at the White House. Yes, Congressmen will be welcomed—if you don't overdo it. [Laughter]

The first seven words of the Constitution and the most important are these: "We the People of the United States . . ." We the people ordained and established the Constitution and reserved to themselves all powers not granted to Federal and State government. I respect and will always be conscious of that fundamental rule of freedom.

Only 8 months ago, when I last stood here, I told you I was a Ford, not a Lincoln. Tonight I say I am still a Ford, but I am not a Model T.

I do have some old-fashioned ideas, however. I believe in the very basic decency and fairness of America. I believe in the integrity and patriotism of the Congress. And while I am aware of the House rule that no one ever speaks to the galleries, I believe in the first amendment and the absolute necessity of a free press.

But I also believe that over two centuries since the First Continental Congress was convened, the direction of our Nation's movement has been forward. I am here to confess that in my first campaign for President—of my senior class in South High School in Grand Rapids, Michigan—I headed the Progressive Party ticket, and lost. Maybe that is why I became a Republican. [Laughter]

Now I ask you to join with me in getting this country revved up and moving.

My instinctive judgment is that the state of the Union is excellent. But the state of our economy is not so good. Everywhere I have been as Vice President, some 118,000 miles in 40 States and some 55 press conferences, the unanimous concern of Americans is inflation.

For once all the polls seem to agree. They also suggest that the people blame Government far more than either management or labor for the high cost of everything they have to buy.

You who come from 50 States, three territories, and the District of Columbia, know this better than I do. That is why you have created, since I left, your new Budget Reform Committee. I welcome it, and I will work with its members to bring the Federal budget into balance in fiscal year 1976.

The fact is that for the past 25 years that I had the honor of serving in this body, the Federal budget has been balanced in only six.

Mr. Speaker, I am a little late getting around to it, but confession is good for the soul. I have sometimes voted to spend more taxpayer's money for worthy Federal projects in Grand Rapids, Michigan, while I vigorously opposed wasteful spending boondoggles in Oklahoma. [Laughter]

Be that as it may, Mr. Speaker, you and I have always stood together against unwarranted cuts in national defense. This is no time to change that nonpartisan policy.

Just as escalating Federal spending has been a prime cause of higher prices over many years, it may take some time to stop inflation. But we must begin right now.

For a start, before your Labor Day recess, Congress should reactivate the Cost of Living Council through passage of a clean bill, without reimposing controls, that will let us monitor wages and prices to expose abuses.

Whether we like it or not, the American wage earner and the American housewife are a lot better economists than most economists care to admit. They know that a government big enough to give you everything you want is a government big enough to take from you everything you have.

If we want to restore confidence in ourselves as working politicians, the first thing we all have to do is to learn to say no.

The first specific request by the Ford Administration is not to Congress but to the voters in the upcoming November elections. It is this, very simple: Support your candidates, Congressmen and Senators, Democrats or Republicans, conservatives or liberals, who consistently vote for tough decisions to cut the cost of government, restrain Federal spending, and bring inflation under control.

I applaud the initiatives Congress has already taken. The only fault I find with the Joint Economic Committee's study on inflation, authorized last week, is that we need its expert findings in six weeks instead of six months.

A month ago, the distinguished majority leader of the United States Senate asked the White House to convene an economic conference of Members of Congress, the President's economic consultants, and some of the best economic brains from labor, industry, and agriculture.

Later, this was perfected by resolution [S. Res. 363] to assemble a domestic summit meeting to devise a bipartisan action for stability and growth in the American economy. Neither I nor my staff have much time right now for letter writing. So, I will respond. I accept the suggestion, and I will personally preside.

Furthermore, I propose that this summit meeting be held at an early date, in full view of the American public. They are as anxious as we are to get the right answers.

My first priority is to work with you to bring inflation under control. Inflation is domestic enemy number one. To restore economic confidence, the Government in Washington must provide some leadership. It does no good to blame the public for spending too much when the Government is spending too much.

I began to put my Administration's own economic house in order starting last Friday. I instructed my Cabinet officers and Counsellors and my White House Staff to make fiscal restraint their first order of business, and to save every taxpayer's dollar the safety and genuine welfare of our great Nation will permit. Some economic activities will be affected more by monetary and fiscal restraint than other activities. Good government clearly requires that we tend to the economic problems facing our country in a spirit of equity to all of our citizens in all segments of our society.

Tonight, obviously, is no time to threaten you with vetoes. But I do have the last recourse, and I am a veteran of many a veto fight right here in this great chamber. Can't we do a better job by reasonable compromise? I hope we can.

Minutes after I took the Presidential oath, the joint leadership of Congress told me at the White House they would go more than halfway to meet me. This was confirmed in your unanimous concurrent resolution of cooperation, for which I am deeply grateful. If, for my part, I go more than halfway to meet the Congress, maybe we can find a much larger area of national agreement.

I bring no legislative shopping list here this evening. I will deal with specifics in future messages and talks with you, but here are a few examples of how seriously I feel about what we must do together.

Last week, the Congress passed the elementary and secondary education bill, and I found it on my desk. Any reservations I might have about some of its provisions—and I do have—fade in comparison to the urgent needs of America for quality education. I will sign it in a few days.

I must be frank. In implementing its provisions, I will oppose excessive funding during this inflationary crisis.

As Vice President, I studied various proposals for better health care financing. I saw them coming closer together and urged my friends in the Congress and in the Administration to sit down and sweat out a sound compromise. The comprehensive health insurance plan goes a long ways toward providing early relief to people who are sick.

Why don't we write—and I ask this with the greatest spirit of cooperation—why don't we write a good health bill on the statute books in 1974, before this Congress adjourns?

The economy of our country is critically dependent on how we interact with the economies of other countries. It is little comfort that our inflation is only a part of a worldwide problem or that American families need less of their paychecks for groceries than most of our foreign friends.

As one of the building blocks of peace, we have taken the lead in working toward a more open and a more equitable world economic system. A new round of international trade negotiations started last September among 105 nations in Tokyo. The others are waiting for the United States Congress to grant the necessary authority to the executive branch to proceed.

With modifications, the trade reform bill passed by the House last year would do a good job. I understand good progress has been made in the Senate Committee on Finance. But I am optimistic, as always, that the Senate will pass an acceptable bill quickly as a key part of our joint prosperity campaign.

I am determined to expedite other international economic plans. We will be working together with other nations to find better ways to prevent shortages of food and fuel. We must not let last winter's energy crisis happen again. I will push Project Independence for our own good and the good of others. In that, too, I will need your help.

Successful foreign policy is an extension of the hopes of the whole American people for a world of peace and orderly reform and orderly freedom. So, I would say a few words to our distinguished guests from the governments of other nations where, as at home, it is my determination to deal openly with allies and adversaries.

Over the past 52 years in Congress and as Vice President, I have fully supported the outstanding foreign policy of President Nixon. This policy I intend to continue.

Throughout my public service, starting with wartime naval duty under the command of President Franklin D. Roosevelt, I have upheld all our Presidents when they spoke for my country to the world. I believe the Constitution commands this. I know that in this crucial area of international policy I can count on your firm support.

Now, let there be no doubt or any misunderstanding anywhere, and I emphasize anywhere: There are no opportunities to exploit, should anyone so desire. There will be no change of course, no relaxation of vigilance, no abandonment of the helm of our ship of state as the watch changes.

We stand by our commitments and we will live up to our responsibilities in our formal alliances, in our friendships, and in our improving relations with potential adversaries.

On this, Americans are united and strong. Under my term of leadership, I hope we will become more united. I am certain America will remain strong.

A strong defense is the surest way to peace. Strength makes detente attainable. Weakness invites war, as my generation—my generation—knows from four very bitter experiences.

Just as America's will for peace is second to none, so will America's strength be second to none.

We cannot rely on the forbearance of others to protect this Nation. The power and diversity of the Armed Forces, active Guard and Reserve, the resolve of our fellow citizens, the flexibility in our command to navigate international waters that remain troubled are all essential to our security.

I shall continue to insist on civilian control of our superb military establishment. The Constitution plainly requires the President to be Commander in Chief, and I will be.

Our job will not be easy. In promising continuity, I cannot promise simplicity. The problems and challenges of the world remain complex and difficult. But we have set out on a path of reason, of fairness, and we will continue on it. As guideposts on that path, I offer the following:

—To our allies of a generation in the Atlantic community and Japan, I pledge continuity in the loyal collaboration on our many mutual endeavors.

—To our friends and allies in this hemisphere, I pledge continuity in the deepening dialog to define renewed relationships of equality and justice.

—To our allies and friends in Asia, I pledge a continuity in our support for their security, independence, and economic development. In Indochina, we are determined to see the observance of the Paris agreement on Vietnam and the cease-fire and negotiated settlement in Laos. We hope to see an early compromise settlement in Cambodia.

—To the Soviet Union, I pledge continuity in our commitment to the course of the past 3 years. To our two peoples, and to all mankind, we owe a continued effort to live and, where possible, to work together in peace, for in a thermonuclear age there can be no alternative to a positive and peaceful relationship between our nations.

—To the People's Republic of China, whose legendary hospitality I enjoyed, I pledge continuity in our commitment to the principles of the Shanghai communique. The new relationship built on those principles has demonstrated that it serves serious and objective mutual interests and has become an enduring feature of the world scene.

—To the nations in the Middle East, I pledge continuity in our vigorous efforts to advance the progress which has brought hopes of peace to that region after 25 years as a hotbed of war. We shall carry out our promise to promote continuing negotiations among all parties for a complete, just, and lasting settlement.

—To all nations, I pledge continuity in seeking a common global goal: a stable international structure of trade and finance which reflects the interdependence of all peoples.

—To the entire international community—to the United Nations, to the world's nonaligned nations, and to all others—I pledge continuity in our dedication to the humane goals which throughout our history have been so much of America's contribution to mankind.

So long as the peoples of the world have confidence in our purposes and faith in our word, the age-old vision of peace on Earth will grow brighter.

I pledge myself unreservedly to that goal. I say to you in words that cannot be improved upon: "Let us never negotiate out of fear, but let us never fear to negotiate."

As Vice President, at the request of the President, I addressed myself to the individual rights of Americans in the area of privacy. There will be no illegal tappings [tapings], eavesdropping, buggings, or break-ins by my Administration. There will be hot pursuit of tough laws to prevent illegal invasion of privacy in both government and private activities.

On the higher plane of public morality, there is no need for me to preach tonight. We have thousands of far better preachers and millions of sacred scriptures to guide us on the path of personal right-living and exemplary official conduct. If we can make effective and earlier use of moral and ethical wisdom of the centuries in today's complex society, we will prevent more crime and more corruption than all the policemen and prosecutors governments can ever deter. If I might say so, this is a job that must begin at home, not in Washington.

I once told you that I am not a saint, and I hope never to see the day that I cannot admit having made a mistake. So I will close with another confession.

Frequently, along the tortuous road of recent months from this chamber to the President's House, I protested that I was my own man. Now I realize that I was wrong.

I am your man, for it was your carefully weighed confirmation that changed my occupation.

The truth is I am the people's man, for you acted in their name, and I accepted and began my new and solemn trust with a promise to serve all the people and do the best that I can for America.

When I say all the people, I mean exactly that.

To the limits of my strength and ability, I will be the President of black, brown, red, and white Americans, of old and young, of women's liberationists and male chauvinists [laughter]—and all the rest of us in-between, of the poor and the rich, of native sons and new refugees, of those who work at lathes or at desks or in mines or in the fields, of Christians, Jews, Moslems, Buddhists, and atheists, if there really are any atheists after what we have all been through.

Fellow Americans, one final word: I want to be a good President. I need your help. We all need God's sure guidance. With it, nothing can stop the United States of America.

Thank you very much.

28. First Press Conference
August 28, 1974

THE PRESIDENT. Good afternoon.

At the outset, I have a very important and a very serious announcement. There was a little confusion about the date of this press conference. My wife Betty had scheduled her first press conference for the same day. And obviously, I had scheduled my first press conference for this occasion. So, Betty's was postponed.

We worked this out between us in a calm and orderly way. She will postpone her press conference until next week, and until then, I will be making my own breakfast, my own lunch, and my own dinner. [Laughter]

Helen [Helen Thomas, United Press International].

Questions

Immunity or Pardon for Former President Nixon

[1.] Q. Mr. President, aside from the Special Prosecutor's role, do you agree with the bar association that the law applies equally to all men, or do you agree with Governor Rockefeller that former President Nixon should have immunity from prosecution? And specifically, would you use your pardon authority, if necessary?

THE PRESIDENT. Well, let me say at the outset that I made a statement in this room a few moments after the swearing in. And on that occasion I said the following: that I had hoped that our former President, who brought peace to millions, would find it for himself.

Now, the expression made by Governor Rockefeller, I think, coincides with the general view and the point of view of the American people. I subscribe to that point of view, but let me add, in the last 10 days or 2 weeks I have asked for prayers for guidance on this very important point.

In this situation, I am the final authority. There have been no charges made, there has been no action by the courts, there has been no action by any jury. And until any legal process has been undertaken, I think it is unwise and untimely for me to make any commitment.

Action by the Special Prosecutor

[6.] Q. Do you feel the Special Prosecutor can in good conscience pursue cases against former top Nixon aides as long as there is the possibility that the former President may not also be pursued in the courts?

THE PRESIDENT. I think the Special Prosecutor, Mr. Jaworski, has an obligation to take whatever action he sees fit in confor-

mity with his oath of office, and that should include any and all individuals.

Prevention of Further "Watergates"

[7.] Q. What do you plan to do as President to see to it that we have no further Watergates?

THE PRESIDENT. Well, I indicated that, one, we would have an open Administration. I will be as candid and as forthright as I possibly can. I will expect any individuals in my Administration to be exactly the same. There will be no tightly controlled operation of the White House Staff. I have a policy of seeking advice from a number of top members of my staff. There will be no one person, nor any limited number of individuals, who make decisions. I will make the decisions and take the blame for them or whatever benefit might be the case.

I said in one of my speeches after the swearing in, there would be no illegal wiretaps, there would be none of the other things that to a degree helped to precipitate the Watergate crisis.

Possibility of Pardon for the Former President

[24.] Q. Mr. President, you have emphasized here your option of granting a pardon to the former President.

THE PRESIDENT. I intend to.

Q. You intend to have that option. If an indictment is brought, would you grant a pardon before any trial took place?

THE PRESIDENT. I said at the outset that until the matter reaches me, I am not going to make any comment during the process of whatever charges are made.

29. Remarks on Signing Proclamation Pardoning Richard M. Nixon
September 8, 1974

Ladies and gentlemen:

I have come to a decision which I felt I should tell you and all of my fellow American citizens, as soon as I was certain in my own mind and in my own conscience that it is the right thing to do.

I have learned already in this office that the difficult decisions always come to this desk. I must admit that many of them do not look at all the same as the hypothetical questions that I have answered freely and perhaps too fast on previous occasions.

My customary policy is to try and get all the facts and to consider the opinions of my countrymen and to take counsel with my most valued friends. But these seldom agree, and in the end, the decision is mine. To procrastinate, to agonize, and to wait for a more favorable turn of events that may never come or more compelling external pressures that may as well be wrong as right, is itself a decision of sorts and a weak and potentially dangerous course for a President to follow.

I have promised to uphold the Constitution, to do what is right as God gives me to see the right, and to do the very best that I can for America.

I have asked your help and your prayers, not only when I became President but many times since. The Constitution is the supreme law of our land and it governs our actions as citizens. Only the laws of God, which govern our consciences, are superior to it.

As we are a nation under God, so I am sworn to uphold our laws with the help of God. And I have sought such guidance and searched my own conscience with special diligence to determine the right thing for me to do with respect to my predecessor in this place, Richard Nixon, and his loyal wife and family.

Theirs is an American tragedy in which we all have played a part. It could go on and on and on, or someone must write the end to it. I have concluded that only I can do that, and if I can, I must.

There are no historic or legal precedents to which I can turn in this matter, none that precisely fit the circumstances of a private citizen who has resigned the Presidency of the United States. But it is common knowledge that serious allegations and accusations hang like a sword over our former President's head, threatening his health as he tries to reshape his life, a great part of which was spent in the service of this country and by the mandate of its people.

After years of bitter controversy and divisive national debate, I have been advised, and I am compelled to conclude that many months and perhaps more years will have to pass before Richard Nixon could obtain a fair trial by jury in any jurisdiction of the United States under governing decisions of the Supreme Court.

I deeply believe in equal justice for all Americans, whatever their station or former station. The law, whether human or divine, is no respecter of persons; but the law is a respecter of reality.

The facts, as I see them, are that a former President of the United States, instead of enjoying equal treatment with any other citizen accused of violating the law, would be cruelly and excessively penalized either in preserving the presumption of his innocence or in obtaining a speedy determination of his guilt in order to repay a legal debt to society.

During this long period of delay and potential litigation, ugly passions would again be aroused. And our people would again be polarized in their opinions. And the credibility of our free institutions of government would again be challenged at home and abroad.

In the end, the courts might well hold that Richard Nixon had been denied due process, and the verdict of history would even more be inconclusive with respect to those charges arising out of the period of his Presidency, of which I am presently aware.

But it is not the ultimate fate of Richard Nixon that most concerns me, though surely it deeply troubles every decent and every compassionate person. My concern is the immediate future of this great country.

In this, I dare not depend upon my personal sympathy as a long-time friend of the former President, nor my professional judgment as a lawyer, and I do not.

As President, my primary concern must always be the greatest good of all the people of the United States whose servant I am. As a man, my first consideration is to be true to my own convictions and my own conscience.

My conscience tells me clearly and certainly that I cannot prolong the bad dreams that continue to reopen a chapter that is closed. My conscience tells me that only I, as President, have the constitutional power to firmly shut and seal this book. My conscience tells me it is my duty, not merely to proclaim domestic tranquillity but to use every means that I have to insure it.

I do believe that the buck stops here, that I cannot rely upon public opinion polls to tell me what is right.

I do believe that right makes might and that if I am wrong, 10 angels swearing I was right would make no difference.

I do believe, with all my heart and mind and spirit, that I, not as President but as a humble servant of God, will receive justice without mercy if I fail to show mercy.

Finally, I feel that Richard Nixon and his loved ones have suffered enough and will continue to suffer, no matter what I do, no matter what we, as a great and good nation, can do together to make his goal of peace come true.

[At this point, the President began reading from the proclamation granting the pardon.]

"Now, therefore, I, Gerald R. Ford, President of the United States, pursuant to the par-

don power conferred upon me by Article II, Section 2, of the Constitution, have granted and by these presents do grant a full, free, and absolute pardon unto Richard Nixon for all offenses against the United States which he, Richard Nixon, has committed or may have committed or taken part in during the period from July [January] 20, 1969 through August 9, 1974."

[The President signed the proclamation and then resumed reading.]

"In witness whereof, I have hereunto set my hand this eighth day of September, in the year of our Lord nineteen hundred and seventy-four, and of the Independence of the United States of America the one hundred and ninety-ninth."

30. First State of the Union Address January 15, 1975

Mr. Speaker, Mr. Vice President, Members of the 94th Congress, and distinguished guests:

Twenty-six years ago, a freshman Congressman, a young fellow with lots of idealism who was out to change the world, stood before Sam Rayburn in the well of the House and solemnly swore to the same oath that all of you took yesterday—an unforgettable experience, and I congratulate you all.

Two days later, that same freshman stood at the back of this great Chamber—over there someplace—as President Truman, all charged up by his single-handed election victory, reported as the Constitution requires on the state of the Union.

When the bipartisan applause stopped, President Truman said, "I am happy to report to this 81st Congress that the state of the Union is good. Our Nation is better able than ever before to meet the needs of the American people, and to give them their fair chance in the pursuit of happiness. [It] is foremost among the nations of the world in the search for peace."

Today, that freshman Member from Michigan stands where Mr. Truman stood, and I must say to you that the state of the Union is not good: Millions of Americans are out of work.

Recession and inflation are eroding the money of millions more.

Prices are too high, and sales are too slow.

This year's Federal deficit will be about $30 billion; next year's probably $45 billion.

The national debt will rise to over $500 billion.

Our plant capacity and productivity are not increasing fast enough.

We depend on others for essential energy.

Some people question their Government's ability to make hard decisions and stick with them; they expect Washington politics as usual.

Yet, what President Truman said on January 5, 1949, is even more true in 1975. We are better able to meet our people's needs. All Americans do have a fairer chance to pursue happiness. Not only are we still the foremost nation in the pursuit of peace but today's prospects of attaining it are infinitely brighter.

There were 59 million Americans employed at the start of 1949; now there are more than 85 million Americans who have jobs. In comparable dollars, the average income of the American family has doubled during the past 26 years.

Now, I want to speak very bluntly. I've got bad news, and I don't expect much, if any, applause. The American people want action, and it will take both the Congress and the President to give them what they want. Progress and solutions can be achieved, and they will be achieved.

My message today is not intended to address all of the complex needs of America. I will send separate messages making specific recommendations for domestic legislation, such as the extension of general revenue sharing and the Voting Rights Act.

The moment has come to move in a new direction. We can do this by fashioning a new partnership between the Congress on the one hand, the White House on the other, and the people we both represent.

Let us mobilize the most powerful and most creative industrial nation that ever existed on this Earth to put all our people to work. The emphasis on our economic efforts must now shift from inflation to jobs.

To bolster business and industry and to create new jobs, I propose a 1-year tax reduction of $16 billion. Three-quarters would go to individuals and one-quarter to promote business investment.

This cash rebate to individuals amounts to 12 percent of 1974 tax payments—a total cut of $12 billion, with a maximum of $1,000 per return.

I call on the Congress to act by April 1. If you do—and I hope you will—the Treasury can send the first check for half of the rebate in May and the second by September.

The other one-fourth of the cut, about $4 billion, will go to business, including farms, to promote expansion and to create more jobs. The 1-year reduction for businesses would be in the form of a liberalized investment tax credit increasing the rate to 12 percent for all businesses.

This tax cut does not include the more fundamental reforms needed in our tax system. But it points us in the right direction—allowing taxpayers rather than the Government to spend their pay.

Cutting taxes now is essential if we are to turn the economy around. A tax cut offers the best hope of creating more jobs. Unfortunately, it will increase the size of the budget deficit. Therefore, it is more important than ever that we take steps to control the growth of Federal expenditures.

Part of our trouble is that we have been self-indulgent. For decades, we have been voting ever-increasing levels of Government benefits, and now the bill has come due. We have been adding so many new programs that the size and the growth of the Federal budget has taken on a life of its own.

One characteristic of these programs is that their cost increases automatically every year because the number of people eligible for most of the benefits increases every year. When these programs are enacted, there is no dollar amount set. No one knows what they will cost. All we know is that whatever they cost last year, they will cost more next year.

It is a question of simple arithmetic. Unless we check the excessive growth of Federal expenditures or impose on ourselves matching increases in taxes, we will continue to run huge inflationary deficits in the Federal budget.

If we project the current built-in momentum of Federal spending through the next 15 years, State, Federal, and local government expenditures could easily comprise half of our gross national product. This compares with less than a third in 1975.

I have just concluded the process of preparing the budget submissions for fiscal year 1976. In that budget, I will propose legislation to restrain the growth of a number of existing programs. I have also concluded that no new spending programs can be initiated this year, except for energy. Further, I will not hesitate to veto any new spending programs adopted by the Congress.

As an additional step toward putting the Federal Government's house in order, I recommend a 5-percent limit on Federal pay increases in 1975. In all Government programs tied to the Consumer Price Index—including Social Security, civil service and military retirement pay, and food stamps—I also propose a 1-year maximum increase of 5 percent.

None of these recommended ceiling limitations, over which Congress has final authority, are easy to propose, because in most cases they involve anticipated payments to many, many deserving people. Nonetheless, it must be done. I must emphasize that I am not asking to eliminate, to reduce, to freeze these payments. I am merely recommending that we slow down the rate at which these payments increase and these programs grow.

Only a reduction in the growth of spending can keep Federal borrowing down and reduce the damage to the private sector from high interest rates. Only a reduction in spending can make it possible for the Federal Reserve System to avoid an inflationary growth in the money supply and thus restore balance to our economy. A major reduction in the growth of Federal spending can help dispel the uncertainty that so many feel about our economy and put us on the way to curing our economic ills.

If we don't act to slow down the rate of increase in Federal spending, the United States Treasury will be legally obligated to spend more than $360 billion in fiscal year 1976, even if no new programs are enacted. These are not matters of conjecture or prediction, but again, a matter of simple arithmetic. The size of these numbers and their implications for our everyday life and the health of our economic system are shocking.

I submitted to the last Congress a list of budget deferrals and rescissions. There will be more cuts recommended in the budget that I will submit. Even so, the level of outlays for fiscal year 1976 is still much, much too high. Not only is it too high for this year but the decisions we make now will inevitably have a major and growing impact on expenditure levels in future years. I think this is a very fundamental issue that we, the Congress and I, must jointly solve.

Economic disruptions we and others are experiencing stem in part from the fact that the world price of petroleum has quadrupled in the last year. But in all honesty, we cannot put all of the blame on the oil-exporting nations. We, the United States, are not blameless. Our growing dependence upon foreign sources has been adding to our vulnerability for years and years, and we did nothing to prepare ourselves for such an event as the embargo of 1973.

During the 1960's, this country had a surplus capacity of crude oil which we were able to make available to our trading partners whenever there was a disruption of supply. This surplus capacity enabled us to influence both supplies and prices of crude oil throughout the world. Our excess capacity neutralized any effort at establishing an effective cartel, and thus the rest of the world was assured of adequate supplies of oil at reasonable prices.

By 1970, our surplus capacity had vanished, and as a consequence, the latent power of the oil cartel could emerge in full force. Europe and Japan, both heavily dependent on imported oil, now struggle to keep their economies in balance. Even the United States, our country, which is far more self-sufficient than most other industrial countries, has been put under serious pressure.

I am proposing a program which will begin to restore our country's surplus capacity in total energy. In this way, we will be able to assure ourselves reliable and adequate energy and help foster a new world energy stability for other major consuming nations.

But this Nation and, in fact, the world must face the prospect of energy difficulties between now and 1985. This program will impose burdens on all of us with the aim of reducing our consumption of energy and increasing our production. Great attention has been paid to the considerations of fairness, and I can assure you that the burdens will not fall more harshly on those less able to bear them.

I am recommending a plan to make us invulnerable to cutoffs of foreign oil. It will require sacrifices, but it—and this is most important—it will work.

I have set the following national energy goals to assure that our future is as secure and as productive as our past:

First, we must reduce oil imports by 1 million barrels per day by the end of this year and by 2 million barrels per day by the end of 1977.

Second, we must end vulnerability to economic disruption by foreign suppliers by 1985.

Third, we must develop our energy technology and resources so that the United States has the ability to supply a significant share of the energy needs of the free world by the end of this century.

To attain these objectives, we need immediate action to cut imports. Unfortunately, in the short term there are only a limited number of actions which can increase domestic supply. I will press for all of them.

I urge quick action on the necessary legislation to allow commercial production at the Elk Hills, California, Naval Petroleum Reserve. In order that we make greater use of domestic coal resources, I am submitting amendments to the Energy Supply and Environmental Coordination Act which will greatly increase the number of powerplants that can be promptly converted to coal.

Obviously, voluntary conservation continues to be essential, but tougher programs are needed—and needed now. Therefore, I am using Presidential powers to raise the fee on all imported crude oil and petroleum products. The crude oil fee level will be increased $1 per barrel on February 1, by $2 per barrel on March 1, and by $3 per barrel on April 1. I will take actions to reduce undue hardships on any geographical region. The foregoing are interim administrative actions. They will be rescinded when the broader but necessary legislation is enacted.

To that end, I am requesting the Congress to act within 90 days on a more comprehensive energy tax program. It includes: excise taxes and import fees totaling $2 per barrel on product imports and on all crude oil; deregulation of new natural gas and enactment of a natural gas excise tax.

I plan to take Presidential initiative to decontrol the price of domestic crude oil on April 1. I urge the Congress to enact a windfall profits tax by that date to ensure that oil producers do not profit unduly.

The sooner Congress acts, the more effective the oil conservation program will be and the quicker the Federal revenues can be returned to our people.

I am prepared to use Presidential authority to limit imports, as necessary, to guarantee success.

I want you to know that before deciding on my energy conservation program, I considered rationing and higher gasoline taxes as alternatives. In my judgment, neither would achieve the desired results and both would produce unacceptable inequities.

A massive program must be initiated to increase energy supply, to cut demand, and provide new standby emergency programs to achieve the independence we want by 1985. The largest part of increased oil production must come from new frontier areas on the Outer Continental Shelf and from the Naval Petroleum Reserve No. 4 in Alaska. It is the intent of this Administration to move ahead with exploration, leasing, and production on those frontier areas of the Outer Continental Shelf where the environmental risks are acceptable.

Use of our most abundant domestic resource—coal—is severely limited. We must strike a reasonable compromise on environmental concerns with coal. I am submitting Clean Air [Act] amendments which will allow greater coal use without sacrificing clean air goals.

I vetoed the strip mining legislation passed by the last Congress. With appropriate changes, I will sign a revised version when it comes to the White House.

I am proposing a number of actions to energize our nuclear power program. I will submit legislation to expedite nuclear leasing [licensing] and the rapid selection of sites.

In recent months, utilities have cancelled or postponed over 60 percent of planned nuclear expansion and 30 percent of planned additions to non-nuclear capacity. Financing problems for that industry are worsening. I am therefore recommending that the 1-year investment tax credit of 12 percent be extended an additional 2 years to specifically speed the construction of power plants that do not use natural gas or oil. I am also submitting proposals for selective reform of State utility commission regulations.

To provide the critical stability for our domestic energy production in the face of world price uncertainty, I will request legislation to authorize and require tariffs, import quotas, or price floors to protect our energy prices at levels which will achieve energy independence.

Increasing energy supplies is not enough. We must take additional steps to cut long-term consumption. I therefore propose to the Congress: legislation to make thermal efficiency standards mandatory for all new buildings in the United States; a new tax credit of up to $150 for those homeowners who install insulation equipment; the establishment of an energy conservation program to help low-income families purchase insulation supplies; legislation to modify and defer automotive pollution standards for 5 years, which will enable us to improve automobile gas mileage by 40 percent by 1980.

These proposals and actions, cumulatively, can reduce our dependence on foreign energy supplies from 3 to 5 million barrels per day by 1985. To make the United States invulnerable to foreign disruption, I propose standby emergency legislation and a strategic storage program of 1 billion barrels of oil for domestic needs and 300 million barrels for national defense purposes.

I will ask for the funds needed for energy research and development activities. I have established a goal of 1 million barrels of synthetic fuels and shale oil production per day by 1985 together with an incentive program to achieve it.

I have a very deep belief in America's capabilities. Within the next 10 years, my program envisions: 200 major nuclear power plants; 250 major new coal mines; 150 major coal-fired power plants; 30 major new [oil] refineries; 20 major new synthetic fuel plants; the drilling of many thousands of new oil wells; the insulation of 18 million homes; and the manufacturing and the sale of millions of new automobiles, trucks, and buses that use much less fuel.

I happen to believe that we can do it. In another crisis—the one in 1942 President Franklin D. Roosevelt said this country would build 60,000 [50,000] military aircraft. By 1943, production in that program had reached 125,000 aircraft annually. They did it then. We can do it now.

If the Congress and the American people will work with me to attain these targets, they will be achieved and will be surpassed. From adversity, let us seize opportunity. Revenues of some $30 billion from higher energy taxes designed to encourage conservation must be refunded to the American people in a manner which corrects distortions in our tax system wrought by inflation.

People have been pushed into higher tax brackets by inflation, with consequent reduction in their actual spending power. Business taxes are similarly distorted because inflation exaggerates reported profits, resulting in excessive taxes.

Accordingly, I propose that future individual income taxes be reduced by $16.5 billion. This will be done by raising the low-income allowance and reducing tax rates. This continuing tax cut will primarily benefit lower- and middle-income taxpayers.

For example, a typical family of four with a gross income of $5,600 now pays $185 in Federal income taxes. Under this tax cut plan, they would pay nothing. A family of four with a gross income of $12,500 now pays $1,260 in Federal taxes. My proposal reduces that total by $300. Families grossing $20,000 would receive a reduction of $210.

Those with the very lowest incomes, who can least afford higher costs, must also be compensated. I propose a payment of $80 to every person 18 years of age and older in that very limited category.

State and local governments will receive $2 billion in additional revenue sharing to offset their increased energy costs.

To offset inflationary distortions and to generate more economic activity, the corporate tax rate will be reduced from 48 percent to 42 percent.

Now let me turn, if I might, to the international dimension of the present crisis. At no time in our peacetime history has the state of the Nation depended more heavily on the state of the world. And seldom, if ever, has the state of the world depended more heavily on the state of our Nation.

The economic distress is global. We will not solve it at home unless we help to remedy the profound economic dislocation abroad. World trade and monetary structure provides markets, energy, food, and vital raw materials—for all nations. This international system is now in jeopardy.

This Nation can be proud of significant achievements in recent years in solving problems and crises. The Berlin agreement, the SALT agreements, our new relationship with China, the unprecedented efforts in the Middle East are immensely encouraging. But the world is not free from crisis. In a world of 150 nations, where nuclear technology is proliferating and regional conflicts continue, international security cannot be taken for granted.

So, let there be no mistake about it: International cooperation is a vital factor of our lives today. This is not a moment for the American people to turn inward. More than ever before, our own well-being depends on America's determination and America's leadership in the whole wide world.

We are a great Nation—spiritually, politically, militarily, diplomatically, and economically. America's commitment to international security has sustained the safety of allies and friends in many areas—in the Middle East, in Europe, and in Asia. Our turning away would unleash new instabilities, new dangers around the globe, which, in turn, would threaten our own security.

At the end of World War II, we turned a similar challenge into an historic opportunity and, I might add, an historic achievement. An old order was in disarray; political and economic institutions were shattered. In that period, this Nation and its partners built new institutions, new mechanisms of mutual support and cooperation. Today, as then, we face an historic opportunity. If we act imaginatively and boldly, as we acted then, this period will in retrospect be seen as one of the great creative moments of our Nation's history. The whole world is watching to see how we respond.

A resurgent American economy would do more to restore the confidence of the world in its own future than anything else we can do. The program that this Congress passes can demonstrate to the world that we have started to put our own house in order. If we can show that this Nation is able and willing to help other nations meet the common challenge, it can demonstrate that the United States will fulfill its responsibilities as a leader among nations.

Quite frankly, at stake is the future of industrialized democracies, which have perceived their destiny in common and sustained it in common for 30 years.

The developing nations are also at a turning point. The poorest nations see their hopes of feeding their hungry and developing their societies shattered by the economic crisis. The long-term economic future for the producers of raw materials also depends on cooperative solutions.

Our relations with the Communist countries are a basic factor of the world environment. We must seek to build a long-term basis for coexistence. We will stand by our principles. We will stand by our interests. We will act firmly when challenged. The kind of a world we want depends on a broad policy of creating mutual incentives for restraint and for cooperation.

As we move forward to meet our global challenges and opportunities, we must have the tools to do the job.

Our military forces are strong and ready. This military strength deters aggression against our allies, stabilizes our relations with former adversaries, and protects our homeland. Fully adequate conventional and strategic forces cost many, many billions, but these dollars are sound insurance for our safety and for a more peaceful world.

Military strength alone is not sufficient. Effective diplomacy is also essential in preventing conflict, in building world understanding. The Vladivostok negotiations with the Soviet Union represent a major step in moderating strategic arms competition. My recent discussions with the leaders of the Atlantic community, Japan, and South Korea have contributed to meeting the common challenge.

But we have serious problems before us that require cooperation between the President and the Congress. By the Constitution and tradition, the execution of foreign policy is the responsibility of the President.

In recent years, under the stress of the Vietnam war, legislative restrictions on the President's ability to execute foreign policy and military decisions have proliferated. As a Member of the Congress, I opposed some and I approved others. As President, I welcome the advice and cooperation of the House and the Senate.

But if our foreign policy is to be successful, we cannot rigidly restrict in legislation the ability of the President to act. The conduct of negotiations is ill-suited to such limitations. Legislative restrictions, intended for the best motives and purposes, can have the opposite result, as we have seen most recently in our trade relations with the Soviet Union.

For my part, I pledge this Administration will act in the closest consultation with the Congress as we face delicate situations and troubled times throughout the globe.

When I became President only 5 months ago, I promised the last Congress a policy of communication, conciliation, compromise, and cooperation. I renew that pledge to the new Members of this Congress.

Let me sum it up. America needs a new direction, which I have sought to chart here today—a change of course which will: put the unemployed back to work; increase real income and production; restrain the growth of Federal Government spending; achieve energy independence; and advance the cause of world understanding.

We have the ability. We have the know-how. In partnership with the American people, we will achieve these objectives.

As our 200th anniversary approaches, we owe it to ourselves and to posterity to rebuild our political and economic strength. Let us make America once again and for centuries more to come what it has so long been—a stronghold and a beacon-light of liberty for the whole world.

Thank you

31. Letter to the Speaker of the House and the President Pro Tempore of the Senate Reporting on United States Actions in the Recovery of the SS *Mayaguez*
May 15, 1975

On 12 May 1975, I was advised that the S.S. Mayaguez, a merchant vessel of United States registry en route from Hong Kong to Thailand with a U.S. citizen crew, was fired upon, stopped, boarded, and seized by Cambodian naval patrol boats of the Armed Forces of Cambodia in international waters in the vicinity of Poulo Wai Island. The seized vessel was then forced to proceed to Koh Tang Island where it was required to anchor. This hostile act was in clear violation of international law.

In view of this illegal and dangerous act, I ordered, as you have been previously advised, United States military forces to conduct the necessary reconnaissance and to be ready to respond if diplomatic efforts to secure the return of the vessel and its personnel were not successful. Two United States reconnaissance aircraft in the course of locating the Mayaguez sustained minimal damage from small firearms. Appropriate demands for the return of the Mayaguez and its crew were made, both publicly and privately, without success.

In accordance with my desire that the Congress be informed on this matter and taking note of Section 4(a)(1) of the War Powers Resolution, I wish to report to you that at about 6:20 a.m., 13 May, pursuant to my instructions to prevent the movement of the Mayaguez into a mainland port, U.S. aircraft fired warning shots across the bow of the ship and gave visual signals to small craft approaching the ship. Subsequently, in order to stabilize the situation and in an attempt to preclude removal of the American crew of the Mayaguez to the mainland, where their rescue would be more difficult, I directed the United States Armed Forces to isolate the island and interdict any movement between the ship or the island and the mainland, and to prevent movement of the ship itself, while still taking all possible care to prevent loss of life or injury to the U.S. captives. During the evening of 13 May, a Cambodian patrol boat attempting to leave the island disregarded aircraft warnings and was sunk. Thereafter, two other Cambodian patrol craft were destroyed and four others were damaged and immobilized. One boat, suspected of having some U.S. captives aboard, succeeded in reaching Kompong Som after efforts to turn it around without injury to the passengers failed.

Our continued objective in this operation was the rescue of the captured American crew along with the retaking of the ship Mayaguez. For that purpose, I ordered late this afternoon [May 14] an assault by United States Marines on the island of Koh Tang to search out and rescue such Americans as might still be held there, and I ordered retaking of the Mayaguez by other marines boarding from the destroyer escort Holt. In addition to continued fighter and gunship coverage of the Koh Tang area, these Marine activities were supported by tactical aircraft from the Coral Sea, striking the military airfield at Ream and other military targets in the area of Kompong Som in order to prevent reinforcement or support from the mainland of the Cambodian forces detaining the American vessel and crew.

At approximately 9:00 p.m. EDT on 14 May, the Mayaguez was retaken by United States forces. At approximately 11:30 p.m., the entire crew of the Mayaguez was taken aboard the Wilson. U.S. forces have begun the process of disengagement and withdrawal.

This operation was ordered and conducted pursuant to the President's constitutional executive power and his authority as Commander-in-Chief of the United States Armed Forces.

Sincerely,

GERALD R. FORD

32. Second State of the Union Address January 19, 1976

Mr. Speaker, Mr. Vice President, Members of the 94th Congress, and distinguished guests:

As we begin our Bicentennial, America is still one of the youngest nations in recorded history. Long before our forefathers came to these shores, men and women had been strug-

gling on this planet to forge a better life for themselves and their families.

In man's long, upward march from savagery and slavery—throughout the nearly 2,000 years of the Christian calendar, the nearly 6,000 years of Jewish reckoning—there have been many deep, terrifying valleys, but also many bright and towering peaks.

One peak stands highest in the ranges of human history. One example shines forth of a people uniting to produce abundance and to share the good life fairly and with freedom. One union holds out the promise of justice and opportunity for every citizen: That union is the United States of America.

We have not remade paradise on Earth. We know perfection will not be found here. But think for a minute how far we have come in 200 years.

We came from many roots, and we have many branches. Yet all Americans across the eight generations that separate us from the stirring deeds of 1776, those who know no other homeland and those who just found refuge among our shores, say in unison:

I am proud of America, and I am proud to be an American. Life will be a little better here for my children than for me. I believe this not because I am told to believe it, but because life has been better for me than it was for my father and my mother. I know it will be better for my children because my hands, my brains, my voice, and my vote can help make it happen.

It has happened here in America. It has happened to you and to me. Government exists to create and preserve conditions in which people can translate their ideas into practical reality. In the best of times, much is lost in translation. But we try. Sometimes we have tried and failed. Always we have had the best of intentions.

But in the recent past, we sometimes forgot the sound principles that guided us through most of our history. We wanted to accomplish great things and solve age-old problems. And we became overconfident of our abilities. We tried to be a policeman abroad and the indulgent parent here at home.

We thought we could transform the country through massive national programs, but often the programs did not work. Too often they only made things worse. In our rush to accomplish great deeds quickly, we trampled on sound principles of restraint and endangered the rights of individuals. We unbalanced our economic system by the huge and unprecedented growth of Federal expenditures and borrowing. And we were not totally honest with ourselves about how much these programs would cost and how we would pay for them. Finally, we shifted our emphasis from defense to domestic problems while our adversaries continued a massive buildup of arms.

The time has now come for a fundamentally different approach for a new realism that is true to the great principles upon which this Nation was founded.

We must introduce a new balance to our economy—a balance that favors not only sound, active government but also a much more vigorous, healthy economy that can create new jobs and hold down prices.

We must introduce a new balance in the relationship between the individual and the government—a balance that favors greater individual freedom and self-reliance.

We must strike a new balance in our system of federalism—a balance that favors greater responsibility and freedom for the leaders of our State and local governments.

We must introduce a new balance between the spending on domestic programs and spending on defense—a balance that ensures we will fully meet our obligation to the needy while also protecting our security in a world that is still hostile to freedom.

And in all that we do, we must be more honest with the American people, promising them no more than we can deliver and delivering all that we promise.

The genius of America has been its incredible ability to improve the lives of its citizens through a unique combination of governmental and free citizen activity.

History and experience tells us that moral progress cannot come in comfortable and in complacent times, but out of trial and out of confusion. Tom Paine aroused the troubled Americans of 1776 to stand up to the times that try men's souls because the harder the conflict, the more glorious the triumph.

Just a year ago I reported that the state of the Union was not good. Tonight, I report that the state of our Union is better—in many ways a lot better—but still not good enough.

To paraphrase Tom Paine, 1975 was not a year for summer soldiers and sunshine patriots. It was a year of fears and alarms and of dire forecasts—most of which never happened and won't happen.

As you recall, the year 1975 opened with rancor and with bitterness. Political misdeeds of the past had neither been forgotten nor forgiven. The longest, most divisive war in our history was winding toward an unhappy conclusion. Many feared that the end of that foreign war of men and machines meant the beginning of a domestic war of recrimination and reprisal. Friends and adversaries abroad were asking whether America had lost its nerve. Finally, our economy was ravaged by inflation—inflation that was plunging us into the worse recession in four decades. At the same time, Americans became increasingly alienated from big institutions. They were steadily losing confidence, not just in big government but in big business, big labor, and big education, among others. Ours was a troubled land.

And so, 1975 was a year of hard decisions, difficult compromises, and a new realism that taught us something important about America. It brought back a needed measure of common sense, steadfastness, and self-discipline.

Americans did not panic or demand instant but useless cures. In all sectors, people met their difficult problems with the restraint and with responsibility worthy of their great heritage.

Add up the separate pieces of progress in 1975, subtract the setbacks, and the sum total shows that we are not only headed in a new direction, a direction which I proposed 12 months ago, but it turned out to be the right direction.

It is the right direction because it follows the truly revolutionary American concept of 1776, which holds that in a free society the making of public policy and successful problemsolving involves much more than government. It involves a full partnership among all branches and all levels of government, private institutions, and individual citizens.

Common sense tells me to stick to that steady course.

Take the state of our economy. Last January, most things were rapidly getting worse. This January, most things are slowly but surely getting better.

The worst recession since World War II turned around in April. The best cost-of-living news of the past year is that double-digit inflation of 12 percent or higher was cut almost in half. The worst—unemployment remains far too high.

Today, nearly 1,700,000 more Americans are working than at the bottom of the recession. At year's end, people were again being hired much faster than they were being laid off.

Yet, let's be honest. Many Americans have not yet felt these changes in their daily lives. They still see prices going up far too fast, and they still know the fear of unemployment.

We are also a growing nation. We need more and more jobs every year. Today's economy has produced over 85 million jobs for Americans, but we need a lot more jobs, especially for the young.

My first objective is to have sound economic growth without inflation.

We all know from recent experience what runaway inflation does to ruin every other worthy purpose. We are slowing it. We must stop it cold.

For many Americans, the way to a healthy, noninflationary economy has become increasingly apparent. The Government must stop spending so much and stop borrowing so much of our money. More money must remain in private hands where it will do the most good. To hold down the cost of living, we must hold down the cost of government.

In the past decade, the Federal budget has been growing at an average rate of over 10 percent a year. The budget I am submitting Wednesday cuts this rate of growth in half. I have kept my promise to submit a budget for the next fiscal year of $395 billion. In fact, it is $394.2 billion.

By holding down the growth of Federal spending, we can afford additional tax cuts and return to the people who pay taxes more decisionmaking power over their own lives.

Last month I signed legislation to extend the 1975 tax reductions for the first 6 months of this year. I now propose that effective July 1, 1976, we give our taxpayers a tax cut of approximately $10 billion more than Congress agreed to in December.

My broader tax reduction would mean that for a family of four making $15,000 a year, there will be $227 more in take-home pay annually. Hardworking Americans caught in the middle can really use that kind of extra cash.

My recommendations for a firm restraint on the growth of Federal spending and for greater tax reduction are simple and straightforward. For every dollar saved in cutting the growth in the Federal budget, we can have an added dollar of Federal tax reduction.

We can achieve a balanced budget by 1979 if we have the courage and the wisdom to continue to reduce the growth of Federal spending.

One test of a healthy economy is a job for every American who wants to work.

Government—our kind of government—cannot create that many jobs. But the Federal Government can create conditions and incentives for private business and industry to make more and more jobs.

Five out of six jobs in this country are in private business and in industry. Common sense tells us this is the place to look for more jobs and to find them faster. I mean real, rewarding, permanent jobs.

To achieve this we must offer the American people greater incentives to invest in the future. My tax proposals are a major step in that direction. To supplement these proposals, I ask that Congress enact changes in Federal tax laws that will speed up plant expansion and the purchase of new equipment. My recommendations will concentrate this job-creation tax incentive in areas where the unemployment rate now runs over 7 percent. Legislation to get this started must be approved at the earliest possible date.

Within the strict budget total that I will recommend for the coming year, I will ask for additional housing assistance for 500,000 families. These programs will expand housing opportunities, spur construction, and help to house moderate- and low-income families.

We had a disappointing year in the housing industry in 1975. But with lower interest rates and available mortgage money, we can have a healthy recovery in 1976.

A necessary condition of a healthy economy is freedom from the petty tyranny of massive government regulation. We are wasting literally millions of working hours costing billions of taxpayers' and consumers' dollars because of bureaucratic red tape. The American farmer, who now feeds 215 million Americans, but also millions worldwide, has shown how touch more he can produce without the shackles of government control.

Now, we badly need reforms in other key areas in our economy: the airlines, trucking, railroads, and financial institutions. I have submitted concrete plans in each of these areas, not to help this or that industry, but to foster competition and to bring prices down for the consumer.

This administration, in addition, will strictly enforce the Federal antitrust laws for the very same purposes.

Taking a longer look at America's future, there can be neither sustained growth nor more jobs unless we continue to have an assured supply of energy to run our economy. Domestic production of oil and gas is still declining. Our dependence on foreign oil at high prices is still too great, draining jobs and dollars away from our own economy at the rate of $125 per year for every American.

Last month, I signed a compromise national energy bill which enacts a part of my comprehensive energy independence program. This legislation was late, not the complete answer to energy independence, but still a start in the right direction.

I again urge the Congress to move ahead immediately on the remainder of my energy proposals to make America invulnerable to the foreign oil cartel.

My proposals, as all of you know, would reduce domestic natural gas shortages; allow production from Federal petroleum reserves; stimulate effective conservation, including revitalization of our railroads and the expansion of our urban transportation systems; develop more and cleaner energy from our vast coal resources; expedite clean and safe nuclear power production; create a new national energy independence authority to stimulate vital energy investment; and accelerate development of technology to capture energy from the Sun and the Earth for this and future generations.

Also, I ask, for the sake of future generations, that we preserve the family farm and family-owned small business. Both strengthen America and give stability to our economy. I will propose estate tax changes so that family businesses and family farms can be handed down from generation to generation without having to be sold to pay taxes.

I propose tax changes to encourage people to invest in America's future, and their own, through a plan that gives moderate-income families income tax benefits if they make long-term investments in common stock in American companies.

The Federal Government must and will respond to clear-cut national needs—for this and future generations.

Hospital and medical services in America are among the best in the world, but the cost of a serious and extended illness can quickly wipe out a family's lifetime savings. Increasing health costs are of deep concern to all and a powerful force pushing up the cost of living. The burden of catastrophic illness can be borne by very few in our society. We must eliminate this fear from every family.

I propose catastrophic health insurance for everybody covered by Medicare. To finance this added protection, fees for short-term care will go up somewhat, but nobody after reaching age 65 will have to pay more than $500 a year for covered hospital or nursing home care, nor more than $250 for 1 year's doctor bills.

We cannot realistically afford federally dictated national health insurance providing full coverage for all 215 million Americans. The experience of other countries raises questions about the quality as well as the cost of such plans. But I do envision the day when we may use the private health insurance system to offer more middle-income families high quality health services at prices they can afford and shield them also from their catastrophic illnesses.

Using resources now available, I propose improving the Medicare and other Federal health programs to help those who really need protection—older people and the poor. To help States and local governments give better health care to the poor, I propose that we combine 16

existing Federal programs, including Medicaid, into a single $10 billion Federal grant.

Funds would be divided among States under a new formula which provides a larger share of Federal money to those States that have a larger share of low-income families.

I will take further steps to improve the quality of medical and hospital care for those who have served in our Armed Forces.

Now let me speak about Social Security. Our Federal social security system for people who have worked and contributed to it for all their lives is a vital part of our economic system. Its value is no longer debatable. In my budget for fiscal year 1977, I am recommending that the full cost-of-living increases in the Social Security benefits be paid during the coming year.

But I am concerned about the integrity of our Social Security Trust Fund that enables people—those retired and those still working who will retire—to count on this source of retirement income. Younger workers watch their deductions rise and wonder if they will be adequately protected in the future. We must meet this challenge head on. Simple arithmetic warns all of us that the Social Security Trust Fund is headed for trouble. Unless we act soon to make sure the fund takes in as much as it pays out, there will be no security for old or for young.

I must, therefore, recommend a three-tenths of 1 percent increase in both employer and employee Social Security taxes effective January 1, 1977. This will cost each covered employee less than 1 extra dollar a week and will ensure the integrity of the trust fund.

As we rebuild our economy, we have a continuing responsibility to provide a temporary cushion to the unemployed. At my request, the Congress enacted two extensions and two expansions in unemployment insurance which helped those who were jobless during 1975. These programs will continue in 1976.

In my fiscal year 1977 budget, I am also requesting funds to continue proven job training and employment opportunity programs for millions of other Americans.

Compassion and a sense of community—two of America's greatest strengths throughout our history—tell us we must take care of our neighbors who cannot take care of themselves. The host of Federal programs in this field reflect our generosity as a people.

But everyone realizes that when it comes to welfare, government at all levels is not doing the job well. Too many of our welfare programs are inequitable and invite abuse. Too many of our welfare programs have problems from beginning to end. Worse, we are wasting badly needed resources without reaching many of the truly needy.

Complex welfare programs cannot be reformed overnight. Surely we cannot simply dump welfare into the laps of the 50 States, their local taxpayers, or their private charities, and just walk away from it. Nor is it the right time for massive and sweeping changes while we are still recovering from the recession.

Nevertheless, there are still plenty of improvements that we can make. I will ask Congress for Presidential authority to tighten up the rules for eligibility and benefits.

Last year I twice sought long overdue reform of the scandal-riddled food stamp program. This year I say again: Let's give food stamps to those most in need. Let's not give any to those who don't need them.

Protecting the life and property of the citizen at home is the responsibility of all public officials, but is primarily the job of local and State law enforcement authorities.

Americans have always found the very thought of a Federal police force repugnant, and so do I. But there are proper ways in which we can help to insure domestic tranquility as the Constitution charges us.

My recommendations on how to control violent crime were submitted to the Congress last June with strong emphasis on protecting the innocent victims of crime. To keep a convicted

criminal from committing more crimes, we must put him in prison so he cannot harm more law-abiding citizens. To be effective, this punishment must be swift and it must be certain.

Too often, criminals are not sent to prison after conviction but are allowed to return to the streets. Some judges are reluctant to send convicted criminals to prison because of inadequate facilities. To alleviate this problem at the Federal level, my new budget proposes the construction of four new Federal facilities.

To speed Federal justice, I propose an increase this year in the United States attorneys prosecuting Federal crimes and the reinforcement of the number of United States marshals. Additional Federal judges are needed, as recommended by me and the Judicial Conference.

Another major threat to every American's person and property is the criminal carrying a handgun. The way to cut down on the criminal use of guns is not to take guns away from the law-abiding citizen, but to impose mandatory sentences for crimes in which a gun is used, make it harder to obtain cheap guns for criminal purposes, and concentrate gun control enforcement in high-crime areas.

My budget recommends 500 additional Federal agents in the 11 largest metropolitan high-crime areas to help local authorities stop criminals from selling and using handguns.

The sale of hard drugs is tragically on the increase again. I have directed all agencies of the Federal Government to step up law enforcement efforts against those who deal in drugs. In 1975, I am glad to report, Federal agents seized substantially more heroin coming into our country than in 1974.

As President, I have talked personally with the leaders of Mexico, Colombia, and Turkey to urge greater efforts by their Governments to control effectively the production and shipment of hard drugs.

I recommended months ago that the Congress enact mandatory fixed sentences for persons convicted of Federal crimes involving the sale of hard drugs. Hard drugs, we all know, degrade the spirit as they destroy the body of their users.

It is unrealistic and misleading to hold out the hope that the Federal Government can move into every neighborhood and clean up crime. Under the Constitution, the greatest responsibility for curbing crime lies with State and local authorities. They are the frontline fighters in the war against crime.

There are definite ways in which the Federal Government can help them. I will propose in the new budget that Congress authorize almost $7 billion over the next 5 years to assist State and local governments to protect the safety and property of all their citizens.

As President, I pledge the strict enforcement of Federal laws and—by example, support, and leadership—to help State and local authorities enforce their laws. Together, we must protect the victims of crime and ensure domestic tranquility.

Last year I strongly recommended a 5-year extension of the existing revenue sharing legislation, which thus far has provided $230 billion to help State and local units of government solve problems at home. This program has been effective with decisionmaking transferred from the Federal Government to locally elected officials. Congress must act this year, or State and local units of government will have to drop programs or raise local taxes.

Including my health care program reforms, I propose to consolidate some 59 separate Federal programs and provide flexible Federal dollar grants to help States, cities, and local agencies in such important areas as education, child nutrition, and social services. This flexible system will do the job better and do it closer to home.

The protection of the lives and property of Americans from foreign enemies is one of my primary responsibilities as President.

In a world of instant communications and intercontinental ballistic missiles, in a world

economy that is global and interdependent, our relations with other nations become more, not less, important to the lives of Americans.

America has had a unique role in the world since the day of our independence 200 years ago. And ever since the end of World War II, we have borne—successfully—a heavy responsibility for ensuring a stable world order and hope for human progress.

Today, the state of our foreign policy is sound and strong. We are at peace, and I will do all in my power to keep it that way.

Our military forces are capable and ready. Our military power is without equal, and I intend to keep it that way.

Our principal alliances with the industrial democracies of the Atlantic community and Japan have never been more solid.

A further agreement to limit the strategic arms race may be achieved.

We have an improving relationship with China, the world's most populous nation. The key elements for peace among the nations of the Middle East now exist. Our traditional friendships in Latin America, Africa, and Asia continue.

We have taken the role of leadership in launching a serious and hopeful dialog between the industrial world and the developing world.

We have helped to achieve significant reform of the international monetary system.

We should be proud of what America, what our country, has accomplished in these areas, and I believe the American people are.

The American people have heard too much about how terrible our mistakes, how evil our deeds, and how misguided our purposes. The American people know better.

The truth is we are the world's greatest democracy. We remain the symbol of man's aspiration for liberty and well-being. We are the embodiment of hope for progress.

I say it is time we quit downgrading ourselves as a nation. Of course, it is our responsibility to learn the right lesson from past mistakes. It is our duty to see that they never happen again. But our greater duty is to look to the future. The world's troubles will not go away.

The American people want strong and effective international and defense policies. In our constitutional system, these policies should reflect consultation and accommodation between the President and the Congress. But in the final analysis, as the framers of our Constitution knew from hard experience, the foreign relations of the United States can be conducted effectively only if there is strong central direction that allows flexibility of action. That responsibility clearly rests with the President.

I pledge to the American people policies which seek a secure, just, and peaceful world. I pledge to the Congress to work with you to that end.

We must not face a future in which we can no longer help our friends, such as Angola, even in limited and carefully controlled ways. We must not lose all capacity to respond short of military intervention.

Some hasty actions of the Congress during the past year—most recently in respect to Angola—were, in my view, very shortsighted. Unfortunately, they are still very much on the minds of our allies and our adversaries.

A strong defense posture gives weight to our values and our views in international negotiations. It assures the vigor of our alliances. And it sustains our efforts to promote settlements of international conflicts. Only from a position of strength can we negotiate a balanced agreement to limit the growth of nuclear arms. Only a balanced agreement will serve our interests and minimize the threat of nuclear confrontation.

The defense budget I will submit to the Congress for fiscal year 1977 will show an essential increase over the current year. It provides for real growth in purchasing power over this year's defense budget, which includes the cost of the all-volunteer force.

We are continuing to make economies to enhance the efficiency of our military forces. But the budget I will submit represents the necessity of American strength for the real world in which we live.

As conflict and rivalry persist in the world, our United States intelligence capabilities must be the best in the world.

The crippling of our foreign intelligence services increases the danger of American involvement in direct armed conflict. Our adversaries are encouraged to attempt new adventures while our own ability to monitor events and to influence events short of military action is undermined. Without effective intelligence capability, the United States stands blindfolded and hobbled.

In the near future, I will take actions to reform and strengthen our intelligence community. I ask for your positive cooperation. It is time to go beyond sensationalism and ensure an effective, responsible, and responsive intelligence capability.

Tonight I have spoken about our problems at home and abroad. I have recommended policies that will meet the challenge of our third century. I have no doubt that our Union will endure, better, stronger, and with more individual freedom. We can see forward only dimly—1 year, 5 years, a generation perhaps. Like our forefathers, we know that if we meet the challenges of our own time with a common sense of purpose and conviction, if we remain true to our Constitution and to our ideals, then we can know that the future will be better than the past.

I see America today crossing a threshold, not just because it is our Bicentennial but because we have been tested in adversity. We have taken a new look at what we want to be and what we want our Nation to become.

I see America resurgent, certain once again that life will be better for our children than it is for us, seeking strength that cannot be counted in megatons and riches that cannot be eroded by inflation.

I see these United States of America moving forward as before toward a more perfect Union where the government serves and the people rule.

We will not make this happen simply by making speeches, good or bad, yours or mine, but by hard work and hard decisions made with courage and with common sense.

I have heard many inspiring Presidential speeches, but the words I remember best were spoken by Dwight D. Eisenhower. "America is not good because it is great," the President said. "America is great because it is good."

President Eisenhower was raised in a poor but religious home in the heart of America. His simple words echoed President Lincoln's eloquent testament that "right makes might." And Lincoln in turn evoked the silent image of George Washington kneeling in prayer at Valley Forge.

So, all these magic memories which link eight generations of Americans are summed up in the inscription just above me. How many times have we seen it? "In God We Trust."

Let us engrave it now in each of our hearts as we begin our Bicentennial.

33. Acceptance Speech to Republican National Convention
August 19, 1976

Mr. Chairman, delegates and alternates to this Republican Convention:

I am honored by your nomination, and I accept it with pride, with gratitude, and with a total will to win a great victory for the American people. We will wage a winning campaign in every region of this country, from the snowy banks of Minnesota to the sandy plains of Georgia. We concede not a single State. We concede not a single vote.

This evening I am proud to stand before this great convention as the first incumbent President since Dwight D. Eisenhower who can tell the American people America is at peace.

Tonight I can tell you straightaway this Nation is sound, this Nation is secure, this Nation is on the march to full economic recovery and a better quality of life for all Americans.

And I will tell you one more thing: This year the issues are on our side. I am ready, I am eager to go before the American people and debate the real issues face to face with Jimmy Carter. The American people have a right to know firsthand exactly where both of us stand.

I am deeply grateful to those who stood with me in winning the nomination of the party whose cause I have served all of my adult life. I respect the convictions of those who want a change in Washington. I want a change, too. After 22 long years of majority misrule, let's change the United States Congress.

My gratitude tonight reaches far beyond this arena to countless friends whose confidence, hard work, and unselfish support have brought me to this moment. It would be unfair to single out anyone, but may I make an exception for my wonderful family—Mike, Jack, Steve, and Susan and especially my dear wife, Betty.

We Republicans have had some tough competition. We not only preach the virtues of competition, we practice them. But tonight we come together not on a battlefield to conclude a cease-fire, but to join forces on a training field that has conditioned us all for the rugged contest ahead. Let me say this from the bottom of my heart: After the scrimmages of the past few months, it really feels good to have Ron Reagan on the same side of the line.

To strengthen our championship lineup, the convention has wisely chosen one of the ablest Americans as our next Vice President, Senator Bob Dole of Kansas. With his help, with your help, with the help of millions of Americans who cherish peace, who want freedom preserved, prosperity shared, and pride in

America, we will win this election. I speak not of a Republican victory, but a victory for the American people.

You at home listening tonight, you are the people who pay the taxes and obey the laws. You are the people who make our system work. You are the people who make America what it is. It is from your ranks that I come and on your side that I stand.

Something wonderful happened to this country of ours the past 2 years. We all came to realize it on the Fourth of July. Together, out of years of turmoil and tragedy, wars and riots, assassinations and wrongdoing in high places, Americans recaptured the spirit of 1776. We saw again the pioneer vision of our revolutionary founders and our immigrant ancestors. Their vision was of free men and free women enjoying limited government and unlimited opportunity. The mandate I want in 1976 is to make this vision a reality, but it will take the voices and the votes of many more Americans who are not Republicans to make that mandate binding and my mission possible.

I have been called an unelected President, an accidental President. We may even hear that again from the other party, despite the fact that I was welcomed and endorsed by an overwhelming majority of their elected representatives in the Congress who certified my fitness to our highest office. Having become Vice President and President without expecting or seeking either, I have a special feeling toward these high offices. To me, the Presidency and the Vice-Presidency were not prizes to be won, but a duty to be done.

So, tonight it is not the power and the glamour of the Presidency that leads me to ask for another 4 years; it is something every hard-working American will understand—the challenge of a job well begun, but far from finished.

Two years ago, on August 9, 1974, I placed my hand on the Bible, which Betty held, and took the same constitutional oath that was administered to George Washington. I had faith in our people, in our institutions, and in myself. "My fellow Americans," I said, "our long national nightmare is over."

It was an hour in our history that troubled our minds and tore at our hearts. Anger and hatred had risen to dangerous levels, dividing friends and families. The polarization of our political order had aroused unworthy passions of reprisal and revenge. Our governmental system was closer to stalemate than at any time since Abraham Lincoln took the same oath of office. Our economy was in the throes of runaway inflation, taking us headlong into the worst recession since Franklin D. Roosevelt took the same oath.

On that dark day I told my fellow countrymen, "I am acutely aware that you have not elected me as your President by your ballots, so I ask you to confirm me as your President with your prayers."

On a marble fireplace in the White House is carved a prayer which John Adams wrote. It concludes, "May none but honest and wise men ever rule under this roof." Since I have resided in that historic house, I have tried to live by that prayer. I faced many tough problems. I probably made some mistakes, but on balance, America and Americans have made an incredible comeback since August 1974. Nobody can honestly say otherwise. And the plain truth is that the great progress we have made at home and abroad was in spite of the majority who run the Congress of the United States.

For 2 years I have stood for all the people against a vote-hungry, free-spending congressional majority on Capitol Hill. Fifty-five times I vetoed extravagant and unwise legislation; 45 times I made those vetoes stick. Those vetoes have saved American taxpayers billions and billions of dollars. I am against the big tax spender and for the little taxpayer.

I called for a permanent tax cut, coupled with spending reductions, to stimulate the economy and relieve hard-pressed, middle-income taxpayers. Your personal exemption must be raised from $750 to $1,000. The other party's platform talks about tax reform, but there is one big problem—their own Congress won't act.

I called for reasonable constitutional restrictions on court-ordered busing of schoolchildren, but the other party's platform concedes that busing should be a last resort. But there is the same problem—their own Congress won't act.

I called for a major overhaul of criminal laws to crack down on crime and illegal drugs. The other party's platform deplores America's $90 billion cost of crime. There is the problem again—their own Congress won't act.

The other party's platform talks about a strong defense. Now, here is the other side of the problem—their own Congress did act. They slashed $50 billion from our national defense needs in the last 10 years.

My friends, Washington is not the problem; their Congress is the problem. You know, the President of the United States is not a magician who can wave a wand or sign a paper that will instantly end a war, cure a recession, or make bureaucracy disappear. A President has immense powers under the Constitution, but all of them ultimately come from the American people and their mandate to him. That is why, tonight, I turn to the American people and ask not only for your prayers but also for your strength and your support, for your voice, and for your vote.

I come before you with a 2-year record of performance without your mandate. I offer you a 4-year pledge of greater performance with your mandate. As Governor Al Smith used to say, "Let's look at the record."

Two years ago inflation was 12 percent. Sales were off. Plants were shut down. Thousands were being laid off every week. Fear of the future was throttling down our economy and threatening millions of families.

Let's look at the record since August 1974. Inflation has been cut in half. Payrolls are up. Profits are up. Production is up. Purchases are up. Since the recession was turned around, almost 4 million of our fellow Americans have found new jobs or got their old jobs back. This year more men and women have jobs than ever before in the history of the United States. Confidence has returned, and we are in the full surge of sound recovery to steady prosperity.

Two years ago America was mired in withdrawal from Southeast Asia. A decade of Congresses had shortchanged our global defenses and threatened our strategic posture. Mounting tension between Israel and the Arab nations made another war seem inevitable. The whole world watched and wondered where America was going. Did we in our domestic turmoil have the will, the stamina, and the unity to stand up for freedom?

Look at the record since August, 2 years ago. Today America is at peace and seeks peace for all nations. Not a single American is at war anywhere on the face of this Earth tonight.

Our ties with Western Europe and Japan, economic as well as military, were never stronger. Our relations with Eastern Europe, the Soviet Union, and mainland China are firm, vigilant, and forward looking. Policies I have initiated offer sound progress for the peoples of the Pacific, Africa, and Latin America. Israel and Egypt, both trusting the United States, have taken an historic step that promises an eventual just settlement for the whole Middle East.

The world now respects America's policy of peace through strength. The United States is again the confident leader of the free world. Nobody questions our dedication to peace, but nobody doubts our willingness to use our strength when our vital interests are at stake, and we will. I called for an up-to-date, powerful Army, Navy, Air Force, and Marines that will keep America secure for decades. A strong military posture is always the best insurance for peace.

But America's strength has never rested on arms alone. It is rooted in our mutual commitment of our citizens and leaders in the highest standards of ethics and morality and in the spiritual renewal which our Nation is undergoing right now.

Two years ago people's confidence in their highest officials, to whom they had over-whelmingly entrusted power, had twice been shattered. Losing faith in the word of their elected leaders, Americans lost some of their own faith in themselves.

Again, let's look at the record since August 1974. From the start my administration has been open, candid, forthright. While my entire public and private life was under searching examination for the Vice-Presidency, I reaffirmed my lifelong conviction that truth is the glue that holds government together—not only government but civilization itself. I have demanded honesty, decency, and personal integrity from everybody in the executive branch of the Government. The House and Senate have the same duty.

The American people will not accept a double standard in the United States Congress. Those who make our laws today must not debase the reputation of our great legislative bodies that have given us such giants as Daniel Webster, Henry Clay, Sam Rayburn, and Robert A. Taft. Whether in the Nation's Capital, the State capital, or city hall, private morality and public trust must go together.

From August of 1974 to August of 1976, the record shows steady progress upward toward prosperity, peace, and public trust. My record is one of progress, not platitudes. My record is one of specifics, not smiles. My record is one of performance, not promises. It is a record I am proud to run on. It is a record the American people—Democrats, Independents, and Republicans alike—will support on November 2.

For the next 4 years I pledge to you that I will hold to the steady course we have begun.

But I have no intention of standing on the record alone.

We will continue winning the fight against inflation. We will go on reducing the dead weight and impudence of bureaucracy. We will submit a balanced budget by 1978.

We will improve the quality of life at work, at play, and in our homes and in our neighborhoods. We will not abandon our cities. We will encourage urban programs which assure safety in the streets, create healthy environments, and restore neighborhood pride. We will return control of our children's education to parents and local school authorities.

We will make sure that the party of Lincoln remains the party of equal rights.

We will create a tax structure that is fair for all our citizens, one that preserves the continuity of the family home, the family farm, and the family business.

We will ensure the integrity of the Social Security system and improve Medicare so that our older citizens can enjoy the health and the happiness that they have earned. There is no reason they should have to go broke just to get well.

We will make sure that this rich Nation does not neglect citizens who are less fortunate, but provides for their needs with compassion and with dignity.

We will reduce the growth and the cost of government and allow individual breadwinners and businesses to keep more of the money that they earn.

We will create a climate in which our economy will provide a meaningful job for everyone who wants to work and a decent standard of life for all Americans. We will ensure that all of our young people have a better chance in life than we had, an education they can use, and a career they can be proud of.

We will carry out a farm policy that assures a fair market price for the farmer, encourages full production, leads to record exports, and eases the hunger within the human family. We will never use the bounty of America's farmers as a pawn in international diplomacy. There will be no embargoes.

We will continue our strong leadership to bring peace, justice, and economic progress where there is turmoil, especially in the Middle East. We will build a safer and saner world through patient negotiations and dependable arms agreements which reduce the danger of conflict and horror of thermonuclear war. While I am President, we will not return to a collision course that could reduce civilization to ashes.

We will build an America where people feel rich in spirit as well as in worldly goods. We will build an America where people feel proud about themselves and about their country.

We will build on performance, not promises; experience, not expediency; real progress instead of mysterious plans to be revealed in some dim and distant future. The American people are wise, wiser than our opponents think. They know who pays for every campaign promise. They are not afraid of the truth. We will tell them the truth.

From start to finish, our campaign will be credible; it will be responsible. We will come out fighting, and we will win. Yes, we have all seen the polls and the pundits who say our party is dead. I have heard that before. So did Harry Truman. I will tell you what I think. The only polls that count are the polls the American people go to on November 2. And right now, I predict that the American people are going to say that night, "Jerry, you have done a good job, keep right on doing it."

As I try in my imagination to look into the homes where families are watching the end of this great convention, I can't tell which faces are Republicans, which are Democrats, and which are Independents. I cannot see their color or their creed. I see only Americans.

I see Americans who love their husbands, their wives, and their children. I see Americans who love their country for what it has been and what it must become. I see Americans who work hard, but who are willing to sacrifice all they have worked for to keep their children and their country free. I see Americans who in their own quiet way pray for peace among nations and peace among themselves. We do love our neighbors, and we do forgive those who have trespassed against us.

I see a new generation that knows what is right and knows itself, a generation determined to preserve its ideals, its environment, our Nation, and the world.

My fellow Americans, I like what I see. I have no fear for the future of this great country. And as we go forward together, I promise you once more what I promised before: to uphold the Constitution, to do what is right as God gives me to see the right, and to do the very best that I can for America.

God helping me, I won't let you down.

Thank you very much.

34. Remarks to Press on Election Night November 3, 1976

It is perfectly obvious that my voice isn't up to par, and I shouldn't be making very many comments, and I won't. But I did want Betty, Mike, Jack, Steve, Susan, and Gayle to come down with me and to listen while Betty read a statement that I have sent to Governor Carter. I guess Ron [Nessen] has told you that I called him.

But I do want to express on a personal basis my appreciation and that of my family for the friendship that all of us have had. And after Betty reads the statement that was sent to Governor Carter by me, I think all of us—Betty, the children, and myself—would like to just come down and shake hands and express our appreciation personally.

Let me call on the real spokesman for the family. Betty.

Mrs. FORD. The President asked me to tell you that he telephoned President-elect Carter a short time ago and congratulated him on his victory.

The President also wants to thank all those thousands of people who worked so hard on his behalf and the millions who supported him with their votes. It has been the greatest honor of my husband's life to have served his fellow Americans during 2 of the most difficult years in our history.

The President urges all Americans to join him in giving your united support to President-elect Carter as he prepares to assume his new responsibilities.

I would like to read you the telegram the President sent to President-elect Carter this morning.

[At this point, Mrs. Ford read the telegram, the text of which follows:]

Dear Jimmy:

It is apparent now that you have won our long and intense struggle for the Presidency. I congratulate you on your victory.

As one who has been honored to serve the people of this great land, both in Congress and as President, I believe that we must now put the divisions of the campaign behind us and unite the country once again in the common pursuit of peace and prosperity.

Although there will continue to be disagreements over the best means to use in pursuing our goals, I want to assure you that you will have my complete and wholehearted support as you take the oath of office this January.

I also pledge to you that I, and all members of my Administration, will do all that we can

to insure that you begin your term as smoothly and as effectively as possible.

May God bless you and your family as you undertake your new responsibilities.

Signed, "Jerry Ford."

Thank you very much.

35. Third State of the Union Address January 12, 1977

Mr. Speaker, Mr. Vice President, Members of the 95th Congress, and distinguished guests:

In accordance with the Constitution, I come before you once again to report on the state of the Union.

This report will be my last—maybe—[laughter]—but for the Union it is only the first of such reports in our third century of independence, the close of which none of us will ever see. We can be confident, however, that 100 years from now a freely elected President will come before a freely elected Congress chosen to renew our great Republic's pledge to the Government of the people, by the people, and for the people.

For my part I pray the third century we are beginning will bring to all Americans, our children and their children's children, a greater measure of individual equality, opportunity, and justice, a greater abundance of spiritual and material blessings, and a higher quality of life, liberty, and the pursuit of happiness.

The state of the Union is a measurement of the many elements of which it is composed—a political union of diverse States, an economic union of varying interests, an intellectual union of common convictions, and a moral union of immutable ideals.

Taken in sum, I can report that the state of the Union is good. There is room for improvement, as always, but today we have a more perfect Union than when my stewardship began.

As a people we discovered that our Bicentennial was much more than a celebration of the past; it became a joyous reaffirmation of all that it means to be Americans, a confirmation before all the world of the vitality and durability of our free institutions. I am proud to have been privileged to preside over the affairs of our Federal Government during these eventful years when we proved, as I said in my first words upon assuming office, that "our Constitution works; our great Republic is a Government of laws and not of men. Here the people rule."

The people have spoken; they have chosen a new President and a new Congress to work their will. I congratulate you—particularly the new Members—as sincerely as I did President-elect Carter. In a few days it will be his duty to outline for you his priorities and legislative recommendations. Tonight I will not infringe on that responsibility, but rather wish him the very best in all that is good for our country.

During the period of my own service in this Capitol and in the White House, I can recall many orderly transitions of governmental responsibility—of problems as well as of position, of burdens as well as of power. The genius of the American system is that we do this so naturally and so normally. There are no soldiers marching in the street except in the Inaugural Parade; no public demonstrations except for some of the dancers at the Inaugural Ball; the opposition party doesn't go underground, but goes on functioning vigorously in the Congress and in the country; and our vigilant press goes right on probing and publishing our faults and our follies, confirming the wisdom of the framers of the first amendment.

Because of the transfer of authority in our form of government affects the state of the Union and of the world, I am happy to report to you that the current transition is proceeding very well. I was determined that it should; I wanted the new President to get off on an easier start than I had.

When I became President on August 9, 1974, our Nation was deeply divided and tormented. In rapid succession the Vice President and the President had resigned in disgrace. We were still struggling with the after-effects of a long, unpopular, and bloody war in Southeast Asia. The economy was unstable and racing toward the worst recession in 40 years. People were losing jobs. The cost of living was soaring. The Congress and the Chief Executive were at loggerheads. The integrity of our constitutional process and other institutions was being questioned. For more than 15 years domestic spending had soared as Federal programs multiplied, and the expense escalated annually. During the same period our national security needs were steadily shortchanged. In the grave situation which prevailed in August 1974, our will to maintain our international leadership was in doubt.

I asked for your prayers and went to work.

In January 1975 I reported to the Congress that the state of the Union was not good. I proposed urgent action to improve the economy and to achieve energy independence in 10 years. I reassured America's allies and sought to reduce the danger of confrontation with potential adversaries. I pledged a new direction for America. 1975 was a year of difficult decisions, but Americans responded with realism, common sense, and self-discipline.

By January 1976 we were headed in a new direction, which I hold to be the right direction for a free society. It was guided by the belief that successful problem-solving requires more than Federal action alone, that it involves a full partnership among all branches and all levels of government and public policies which nurture and promote the creative energies of private enterprises, institutions, and individual citizens.

A year ago I reported that the state of the Union was better—in many ways a lot better—but still not good enough. Common sense told me to stick to the steady course we were on, to continue to restrain the inflationary growth of government, to reduce taxes as well as spending, to return local decisions to local officials, to provide for long-range sufficiency in energy and national security needs. I resisted the immense pressures of an election year to open the floodgates of Federal money and the temptation to promise more than I could deliver. I told it as it was to the American people and demonstrated to the world that in our spirited political competition, as in this chamber, Americans can disagree without being disagreeable.

Now, after 30 [29] months as your President, I can say that while we still have a way to go, I am proud of the long way we have come together.

I am proud of the part I have had in rebuilding confidence in the Presidency, confidence in our free system, and confidence in our future. Once again, Americans believe in themselves, in their leaders, and in the promise that tomorrow holds for their children.

I am proud that today America is at peace. None of our sons are fighting and dying in battle anywhere in the world. And the chance for peace among all nations is improved by our determination to honor our vital commitments in defense of peace and freedom.

I am proud that the United States has strong defenses, strong alliances, and a sound and courageous foreign policy.

Our alliances with major partners, the great industrial democracies of Western Europe, Japan, and Canada, have never been more solid. Consultations on mutual security, defense, and East-West relations have grown closer. Collaboration has branched out into new fields such as energy, economic policy, and relations with the Third World. We have used many avenues for cooperation, including summit meetings held among major allied countries. The friendship of the democracies is deeper, warmer, and more effective than at any time in 30 years.

We are maintaining stability in the strategic nuclear balance and pushing back the specter of nuclear war. A decisive step forward was taken in the Vladivostok Accord which I negotiated with General Secretary Brezhnev—joint recognition that an equal ceiling should be placed on the number of strategic weapons on each side. With resolve and wisdom on the part of both nations, a good agreement is well within reach this year.

The framework for peace in the Middle East has been built. Hopes for future progress in the Middle East were stirred by the historic agreements we reached and the trust and confidence that we formed. Thanks to American leadership, the prospects for peace in the Middle East are brighter than they have been in three decades. The Arab states and Israel continue to look to us to lead them from confrontation and war to a new era of accommodation and peace. We have no alternative but to persevere, and I am sure we will. The opportunities for a final settlement are great, and the price of failure is a return to the bloodshed and hatred that for too long have brought tragedy to all of the peoples of this area and repeatedly edged the world to the brink of war.

Our relationship with the People's Republic of China is proving its importance and its durability. We are finding more and more common ground between our two countries on basic questions of international affairs.

In my two trips to Asia as President, we have reaffirmed America's continuing vital interest in the peace and security of Asia and the Pacific Basin, established a new partnership with Japan, confirmed our dedication to the security of Korea, and reinforced our ties with the free nations of Southeast Asia.

An historic dialog has begun between industrial nations and developing nations. Most proposals on the table are the initiatives of the United States, including those on food, energy, technology, trade, investment, and commodities. We are well launched on this process of shaping positive and reliable economic relations between rich nations and poor nations over the long term.

We have made progress in trade negotiations and avoided protectionism during recession. We strengthened the international monetary system. During the past 2 years the free world's most important economic powers have already brought about important changes that serve both developed and developing economies. The momentum already achieved must be nurtured and strengthened, for the prosperity of the rich and poor depends upon it.

In Latin America, our relations have taken on a new maturity and a sense of common enterprise.

In Africa the quest for peace, racial justice, and economic progress is at a crucial point. The United States, in close cooperation with the United Kingdom, is actively engaged in this historic process. Will change come about by warfare and chaos and foreign intervention? Or will it come about by negotiated and fair solutions, ensuring majority rule, minority rights, and economic advance? America is committed to the side of peace and justice and to the principle that Africa should shape its own future, free of outside intervention.

American leadership has helped to stimulate new international efforts to stem the proliferation of nuclear weapons and to shape a comprehensive treaty governing the use of oceans.

I am gratified by these accomplishments. They constitute a record of broad success for America and for the peace and prosperity of all mankind. This administration leaves to its successor a world in better condition than we found. We leave, as well, a solid foundation for progress on a range of issues that are vital to the well-being of America.

What has been achieved in the field of foreign affairs and what can be accomplished by the new administration demonstrate the genius of Americans working together for the common good. It is this, our remarkable ability to work together, that has made us a unique

nation. It is Congress, the President, and the people striving for a better world.

I know all patriotic Americans want this Nation's foreign policy to succeed. I urge members of my party in this Congress to give the new President loyal support in this area. I express the hope that this new Congress will reexamine its constitutional role in international affairs.

The exclusive right to declare war, the duty to advise and consent on the part of the Senate, the power of the purse on the part of the House are ample authority for the legislative branch and should be jealously guarded. But because we may have been too careless of these powers in the past does not justify congressional intrusion into, or obstruction of, the proper exercise of Presidential responsibilities now or in the future. There can be only one Commander in Chief. In these times crises cannot be managed and wars cannot be waged by committee, nor can peace be pursued solely by parliamentary debate. To the ears of the world, the President speaks for the Nation. While he is, of course, ultimately accountable to the Congress, the courts, and the people, he and his emissaries must not be handicapped in advance in their relations with foreign governments as has sometimes happened in the past.

At home I am encouraged by the Nation's recovery from the recession and our steady return to sound economic growth. It is now continuing after the recent period of uncertainty, which is part of the price we pay for free elections.

Our most pressing need today and the future is more jobs—productive, permanent jobs created by a thriving economy. We must revise our tax system both to ease the burden of heavy taxation and to encourage the investment necessary for the creation of productive jobs for all Americans who want to work.

Earlier this month I proposed a permanent income tax reduction of $10 billion below current levels, including raising the personal exemption from $750 to $1,000. I also recommended a series of measures to stimulate investment, such as accelerated depreciation for new plants and equipment in areas of high unemployment, a reduction in the corporate tax rate from 48 to 46 percent, and eliminating the present double taxation of dividends. I strongly urge the Congress to pass these measures to help create the productive, permanent jobs in the private economy that are so essential for our future.

All the basic trends are good; we are not on the brink of another recession or economic disaster. If we follow prudent policies that encourage productive investment and discourage destructive inflation, we will come out on top, and I am sure we will.

We have successfully cut inflation by more than half. When I took office, the Consumer Price Index was rising at 12.2 percent a year. During 1976 the rate of inflation was 5 percent.

We have created more jobs—over 4 million more jobs today than in the spring of 1975. Throughout this Nation today we have over 88 million people in useful, productive jobs—more than at any other time in our Nation's history. But there are still too many Americans unemployed. This is the greatest regret that I have as I leave office.

We brought about with the Congress, after much delay, the renewal of the general revenue sharing. We expanded community development and Federal manpower programs. We began a significant urban mass transit program. Federal programs today provide more funds for our States and local governments than ever before—$70 billion for the current fiscal year. Through these programs and others that provide aid directly to individuals, we have kept faith with our tradition of compassionate help for those who need it. As we begin our third century we can be proud of the progress that we have made in meeting human needs for all of our citizens.

We have cut the growth of crime by nearly 90 percent. Two years ago crime was increasing at the rate of 18 percent annually. In the first three quarters of 1976, that growth rate had been cut to 2 percent. But crime, and the fear of crime, remains one of the most serious problems facing our citizens.

We have had some successes, and there have been some disappointments. Bluntly, I must remind you that we have not made satisfactory progress toward achieving energy independence. Energy is absolutely vital to the defense of our country, to the strength of our economy, and to the quality of our lives.

Two years ago I proposed to the Congress the first comprehensive national energy program— a specific and coordinated set of measures that would end our vulnerability to embargo, blockade, or arbitrary price increases and would mobilize U.S. technology and resources to supply a significant share of the free world's energy after 1985. Of the major energy proposals I submitted 2 years ago, only half, belatedly, became law. In 1973 we were dependent upon foreign oil imports for 36 percent of our needs. Today, we are 40-percent dependent, and we'll pay out $34 billion for foreign oil this year. Such vulnerability at present or in the future is intolerable and must be ended.

The answer to where we stand on our national energy effort today reminds me of the old argument about whether the tank is half full or half empty. The pessimist will say we have half failed to achieve our 10-year energy goals; the optimist will say that we have half succeeded. I am always an optimist, but we must make up for lost time.

We have laid a solid foundation for completing the enormous task which confronts us. I have signed into law five major energy bills which contain significant measures for conservation, resource development, stockpiling, and standby authorities. We have moved forward to develop the naval petroleum reserves; to build a 500-million barrel strategic petroleum stockpile; to phase out unnecessary Government allocation and price controls; to develop a lasting relationship with other oil consuming nations; to improve the efficiency of energy use through conservation in automobiles, buildings, and industry; and to expand research on new technology and renewable resources such as wind power, geothermal and solar energy. All these actions, significant as they are for the long term, are only the beginning.

I recently submitted to the Congress my proposals to reorganize the Federal energy structure and the hard choices which remain if we are serious about reducing our dependence upon foreign energy. These include programs to reverse our declining production of natural gas and increase incentives for domestic crude oil production. I proposed to minimize environmental uncertainties affecting coal development, expand nuclear power generation, and create an energy independence authority to provide government financial assistance for vital energy programs where private capital is not available.

We must explore every reasonable prospect for meeting our energy needs when our current domestic reserves of oil and natural gas begin to dwindle in the next decade. I urgently ask Congress and the new administration to move quickly on these issues. This Nation has the resources and the capability to achieve our energy goals if its Government has the will to proceed, and I think we do.

I have been disappointed by inability to complete many of the meaningful organizational reforms which I contemplated for the Federal Government, although a start has been made. For example, the Federal judicial system has long served as a modal for other courts. But today it is threatened by a shortage of qualified Federal judges and an explosion of litigation claiming Federal jurisdiction. I commend to the new administration and the Congress the recent report and recommendations of the Department of Justice, undertaken at my request, on "the needs of the Federal Courts." I especially endorse its proposals for a new commission on the judicial appointment process.

While the judicial branch of our Government may require reinforcement, the budgets and payrolls of the other branches remain staggering. I cannot help but observe that while the White House staff and the Executive Office of the President have been reduced and the total number of civilians in the executive branch contained during the 1970's, the legislative branch has increased substantially although the membership of the Congress remains at 535. Congress now costs the taxpayers more than a million dollars per Member; the whole legislative budget has passed the billion dollar mark.

I set out to reduce the growth in the size and spending of the Federal Government, but no President can accomplish this alone. The Congress sidetracked most of my requests for authority to consolidate overlapping programs and agencies, to return more decisionmaking and responsibility to State and local governments through block grants instead of rigid categorical programs, and to eliminate unnecessary red tape and outrageously complex regulations.

We have made some progress in cutting back the expansion of government and its intrusion into individual lives, but believe me, there is much more to be done—and you and I know it. It can only be done by tough and temporarily painful surgery by a Congress as prepared as the President to face up to this very real political problem. Again, I wish my successor, working with a substantial majority of his own party, the best of success in reforming the costly and cumbersome machinery of the Federal Government.

The task of self-government is never finished. The problems are great; the opportunities are greater.

America's first goal is and always will be peace with honor. America must remain first in keeping peace in the world. We can remain first in peace only if we are never second in defense.

In presenting the state of the Union to the Congress and to the American people, I have a special obligation as Commander in Chief to report on our national defense. Our survival as a free and independent people requires, above all, strong military forces that are well equipped and highly trained to perform their assigned mission.

I am particularly gratified to report that over the past 25 years, we have been able to reverse the dangerous decline of the previous decade in real resources this country was devoting to national defense. This was an immediate problem I faced in 1974. The evidence was unmistakable that the Soviet Union had been steadily increasing the resources it applied to building its military strength. During this same period the United States real defense spending declined. In my three budgets we not only arrested that dangerous decline, but we have established the positive trend which is essential to our ability to contribute to peace and stability in the world.

The Vietnam war, both materially and psychologically, affected our overall defense posture. The dangerous anti-military sentiment discouraged defense spending and unfairly disparaged the men and women who serve in our Armed Forces.

The challenge that now confronts this country is whether we have the national will and determination to continue this essential defense effort over the long term, as it must be continued. We can no longer afford to oscillate from year to year in so vital a matter; indeed, we have a duty to look beyond the immediate question of budgets and to examine the nature of the problem we will face over the next generation.

I am the first recent President able to address long-term, basic issues without the burden of Vietnam. The war in Indochina consumed enormous resources at the very time that the overwhelming strategic superiority we once enjoyed was disappearing. In past years, as a result of decisions by the United States,

our strategic forces leveled off, yet the Soviet Union continued a steady, constant buildup of its own forces, committing a high percentage of its national economic effort to defense.

The United States can never tolerate a shift in strategic balance against us or even a situation where the American people or our allies believe the balance is shifting against us. The United States would risk the most serious political consequences if the world came to believe that our adversaries have a decisive margin of superiority.

To maintain a strategic balance we must look ahead to the 1980's and beyond. The sophistication of modern weapons requires that we make decisions now if we are to ensure our security 10 years from now. Therefore, I have consistently advocated and strongly urged that we pursue three critical strategic programs: the Trident missile launching submarine; the B-1 bomber, with its superior capability to penetrate modern air defenses; and a more advanced intercontinental ballistic missile that will be better able to survive nuclear attack and deliver a devastating retaliatory strike.

In an era where the strategic nuclear forces are in rough equilibrium, the risks of conflict below the nuclear threshold may grow more perilous. A major, long-term objective, therefore, is to maintain capabilities to deal with, and thereby deter, conventional challenges and crises, particularly in Europe.

We cannot rely solely on strategic forces to guarantee our security or to deter all types of aggression. We must have superior naval and marine forces to maintain freedom of the seas, strong multipurpose tactical air forces, and mobile, modern ground forces. Accordingly, I have directed a long-term effort to improve our worldwide capabilities to deal with regional crises.

I have submitted a 5-year naval building program indispensable to the Nation's maritime strategy. Because the security of Europe and the integrity of NATO remain the cornerstone of American defense policy, I have initiated a special, long-term program to ensure the capacity of the Alliance to deter or defeat aggression in Europe.

As I leave office I can report that our national defense is effectively deterring conflict today. Our Armed Forces are capable of carrying out the variety of missions assigned to them. Programs are underway which will assure we can deter war in the years ahead. But I also must warn that it will require a sustained effort over a period of years to maintain these capabilities. We must have the wisdom, the stamina, and the courage to prepare today for the perils of tomorrow, and I believe we will.

As I look to the future—and I assure you I intend to go on doing that for a good many years—I can say with confidence that the state of the Union is good, but we must go on making it better and better.

This gathering symbolizes the constitutional foundation which makes continued progress possible, synchronizing the skills of three independent branches of Government, reserving fundamental sovereignty to the people of this great land. It is only as the temporary representatives and servants of the people that we meet here, we bring no hereditary status or gift of infallibility, and none follows us from this place.

Like President Washington, like the more fortunate of his successors, I look forward to the status of private citizen with gladness and gratitude. To me, being a citizen of the United States of America is the greatest honor and privilege in this world.

From the opportunities which fate and my fellow citizens have given me, as a Member of the House, as Vice President and President of the Senate, and as President of all the people, I have come to understand and place the highest value on the checks and balances which our founders imposed on government through the separation of powers among co-equal legislative, executive, and judicial branches. This often results in difficulty and delay, as I well know, but it also places supreme authority under God, beyond any one person, any one branch, any majority great or small, or any one party. The Constitution is the bedrock of all our freedoms. Guard and cherish it, keep honor and order in your own house, and the Republic will endure.

It is not easy to end these remarks. In this Chamber, along with some of you, I have experienced many, many of the highlights of my life. It was here that I stood 28 years ago with my freshman colleagues, as Speaker Sam Rayburn administered the oath. I see some of you now—Charlie Bennett, Dick Bolling, Carl Perkins, Pete Rodino, Harley Staggers, Tom Steed, Sid Yates, Clem Zablocki—and I remember those who have gone to their rest. It was here we waged many, many a lively battle— won some, lost some, but always remaining friends. It was here, surrounded by such friends, that the distinguished Chief Justice swore me in as Vice President on December 6, 1973. It was here I returned 8 months later as your President to ask not for a honeymoon, but for a good marriage.

I will always treasure those memories and your many, many kindnesses. I thank you for them all.

My fellow Americans, I once asked you for your prayers, and now I give you mine: May God guide this wonderful country, its people, and those they have chosen to lead them. May our third century be illuminated by liberty and blessed with brotherhood, so that we and all who come after us may be the humble servants of thy peace. Amen.

Good night. God bless you.

SELECTED BIBLIOGRAPHY

NIXON AND THE NIXON ADMINISTRATION: 1969–1974

a. General Studies

Berman, William C. *America's Right Turn: From Nixon to Bush.* Baltimore: Johns Hopkins University Press, 1994.

Drury, Allen. *Courage and Hesitation: Notes and Photographs of the Nixon Administration.* Garden City, N.Y.: Doubleday, 1971.

Evans, Rowland, and Robert Novak. *Nixon in the White House: The Frustration of Power.* New York: Random House, 1971.

Genovese, Michael A. *The Nixon Presidency: Power and Politics in Turbulent Times.* New York: Greenwood Press, 1990.

Greene, John Robert. *The Limits of Power: The Nixon and Ford Administrations.* Bloomington: Indiana University Press, 1992.

Hoff, Joan. *Nixon Reconsidered.* New York: Basic Books, 1994.

Reichley, James. *Conservatives in an Age of Change: The Nixon and Ford Administrations.* Washington, D.C.: Brookings Institution, 1981.

Schell, Johnathan. *The Time of Illusion: An Historical and Reflective Account of the Nixon Era.* New York: Vintage Books, 1976.

Small, Mevin. *The Presidency of Richard Nixon.* Lawrence: University Press of Kansas, 1999.

b. Historiographical Studies and Bibliographies

Bremer, Howard F., ed. *Richard M. Nixon: Chronology, Documents, Bibliographical Aids.* Dobbs Ferry, N.Y.: Oceana Publications, 1975.

c. Published Papers

Oudes, Bruce, ed. *From the President: Richard Nixon's Secret Files.* New York: Harper & Row, 1988.

d. Nixon Biographies, Part I: The Sycophants

Aitken, Jonathan. *Nixon: A Life.* Washington, D.C.: Regnery Publishing, 1994.

Costello, William. *The Facts about Nixon.* New York: Viking Press, 1960.

de Toledano, Ralph. *Nixon.* New York: Duell, Sloan, & Pearce, 1960.

———. *One Man Alone: Richard Nixon.* New York: Funk & Wagnalls, 1969.

Kornitzer, Bela. *The Real Nixon: An Intimate Biography.* New York: Rand McNally, 1960.

Mazo, Earl. *Richard Nixon: A Political and Personal Portrait.* New York: Harper Brothers, 1959.

e. Nixon Biographies, Part II: Assailants, Critics, and Psychobiographers

Abrahamsen, David. *Nixon vs. Nixon.* New York: New American Library, 1976.

Allen, Gary. *Richard Nixon: The Man behind the Mask.* Boston: Western Islands, 1971.

Brodie, Fawn. *Richard Nixon: The Shaping of His Character.* Cambridge, Mass.: Harvard University Press, 1981.

Mankiewicz, Frank. *Perfectly Clear: Nixon from Whittier to Watergate*. New York: Popular Library, 1973.

Mazlish, Bruce. *In Search of Nixon: A Psychohistorical Inquiry*. Baltimore: Penguin Books, 1972.

Voorhis, Jerry. *The Strange Case of Richard Milhous Nixon*. New York: Paul S. Eriksson, 1972.

Wicker, Tom. *One of Us: Richard Nixon and the American Dream*. New York: Random House, 1991.

Wills, Garry. *Nixon Agonistes: The Crisis of the Self-Made Man*. Boston: Houghton Mifflin, 1968.

Witcover, Jules. *The Resurrection of Richard Nixon*. New York: Putnam, 1970.

Woodstone, Arthur. *Inside Nixon's Head*. New York: Popular Library, 1976.

f. Nixon Biographies, Part III: The Equalizers

Alsop, Stewart. *Nixon and Rockefeller: A Double Portrait*. Garden City, N.Y.: Doubleday, 1960.

Ambrose, Stephen E. *Nixon: The Education of a Politician, 1913–1962*. New York: Simon & Schuster, 1987.

———. *Nixon: The Triumph of a Politician, 1962–1972*. New York: Simon & Schuster, 1989.

———. *Nixon: Ruin and Recovery, 1973–1990*. New York: Simon & Schuster, 1991.

Morris, Roger. *Richard Milhous Nixon: The Rise of an American Politician*. New York: Henry Holt, 1989.

g. Books by Nixon

———. *Six Crises*. Garden City, N.Y.: Doubleday, 1962.

———. *Nixon on the Issues*. Nixon-Agnew Campaign Committee, 1969.

———. *Nixon Speaks Out: Major Statements by Richard Nixon in the Presidential Campaign of 1968*. Nixon-Agnew Campaign Committee, 1969.

———. *Setting the Course: The Major Policy Statements of President Richard Nixon*. New York: Funk & Wagnalls, 1970.

———. *A New Road for America: Major Policy Statements, March 1970 to October 1971*. Garden City, N.Y.: Doubleday, 1972.

———. *Memoirs of Richard Nixon*. New York: Grosset & Dunlap, 1978.

———. *The Real War*. New York: Warner Books, 1980.

———. *Leaders*. New York: Touchstone, 1982.

———. *Real Peace*. New York: Simon & Schuster, 1983.

———. *No More Vietnams*. New York: Arbor House, 1985.

———. *1999: Victory without War*. New York: Pocket Books, 1988.

———. *In the Arena: A Memoir of Victory, Defeat, and Renewal*. New York: Simon & Schuster, 1990.

h. Memoirs of Administration Alumni

Atkins, Ollie. *The White House Years: Triumph and Tragedy*. Chicago: Playboy Press, 1977.

Buchanan, Patrick J. *The New Majority: President Nixon at Mid-Passage*. Philadelphia: Girard Bank, 1973.

———. *Right from the Beginning*. Washington, D.C.: Regnery Publishing, 1998.

Ehrlichman, John. *Witness to Power: The Nixon Years*. New York: Simon & Schuster, 1981.

Garment, Leonard. *Crazy Rhythm*. New York: Times Books, 1996.

Hickel, Walter. *Who Owns America?* Englewood Cliffs, N.J.: Prentice Hall, 1971.

Keogh, James. *President Nixon and the Press*. New York: Funk & Wagnalls, 1972.

Kissinger, Henry. *White House Years*. Boston: Little, Brown, 1979.

———. *Years of Upheaval*. Boston: Little, Brown, 1982.

Klein, Herbert G. *Making It Perfectly Clear*. Garden City, N.Y.: Doubleday, 1980.

Malek, Frederick V. *Washington's Hidden Tragedy: The Failure to Make Government Work*. New York: Free Press, 1978.

Mollenhoff, Clark R. *Gameplan for Disaster: An Ombudsman's Report on the Nixon Years*. New York: W. W. Norton, 1976.

Price, Ray. *With Nixon*. New York: Viking Press, 1977.

Safire, William. *Before the Fall*. Garden City, N.Y.: Doubleday, 1975.

Simon, William E. *A Time for Truth*. New York: Berkeley Books, 1978.

Stans, Maurice H. *The Terrors of Justice*. New York: Everest House, 1978.

Thompson, Kenneth W., ed. *The Nixon Presidency*. Lanham, Md.: University Press of America, 1987.

i. "Watergate Memoirs"

Colson, Charles W. *Born Again*. Lincolns, Va.: Chosen Books, 1976.

Cox, Archibald. *The Court and the Constitution*. Boston: Houghton Mifflin, 1987.

Dash, Samuel. *Chief Counsel: Inside the Ervin Committee—The Untold Story of Watergate*. New York: Random House, 1976.

Dean, John. *Blind Ambition: The White House Years*. New York: Simon & Schuster, 1976.

———. *Lost Honor*. Los Angeles: Stratford Press, 1982.

Doyle, James. *Not above the Law: The Battles of Watergate Prosecutors Cox and Jaworski*. New York: William Morrow, 1977.

Ervin, Sam J. *The Whole Truth: The Watergate Conspiracy*. New York: Random House, 1980.

Haldeman, H. R. *The Ends of Power*. New York: Times Books, 1978.

Jaworski, Leon. *The Right and the Power*. New York: Reader's Digest Press, 1976.

Liddy, G. Gordon. *Will*. New York: Dell Publishing, 1980.

Magruder, Jeb Stuart. *An American Life: One Man's Road to Watergate*. New York: Atheneum, 1974.

Sirica, John J. *To Set the Record Straight*. New York: W. W. Norton, 1979.

j. Domestic Policies

Arno Press/New York Times. *Earth Day: The Beginning*. New York: Arno Press and New York Times, 1970.

Burke, Vincent and Vee. *Nixon's Good Deed: Welfare Reform*. New York: Columbia University Press, 1974.

Moynihan, Daniel P. *The Politics of a Guaranteed Income: The Nixon Administration and the Family Assistance Plan*. New York: Random House, 1973.

Nathan, Richard. *The Plot That Failed: Nixon and the Administrative Presidency*. New York: John Wiley & Sons, 1975.

Rathesberger, James, ed. *Nixon and the Environment: The Politics of Devastation*. New York: Taurus Communications, 1972.

Unger, Irwin. *The Best of Intentions: The Triumph and Failure of the Great Society under Kennedy, Johnson, and Nixon*. New York: Brandywine Press, 1996.

Whitaker, John C. *Striking a Balance: Environmental and Natural Resources Policy in the Nixon-Ford Years*. Washington, D.C.: American Enterprise Institute for Public Policy Research, 1976.

Congress

An essential source for examining Congress on a year-to-year basis is the annual *Congressional Quarterly Almanac* (Washington, D.C.: Congressional Quarterly Service, 1945–   ). It describes major bills and traces their evolution in both chambers. Important committee investigations are examined, and roll call votes, studies of voting patterns, and committee membership lists are included.

For those not familiar with the work of Congress, Dennis W. Brezina and Allen Overmeyer, *Congress in Action* (New York: Free Press, 1974) is recommended. This is a case study of the 1970 Environmental Education Act from its inception to implementation. A thought-provoking study is Gary Orfield's *Congressional Power: Congress and Social Change* (New York: Harcourt Brace Jovanovich, 1975). He critically examines three theses: that Congress is fundamentally conservative; that the only solution to problems comes from the presidency; and that Congress opposes institutional reform. This final point is the subject of Robert H. Davidson and Walter J. Oleszek, *Congress against Itself* (Bloomington: Indiana University Press, 1977). The authors were staff members working on the limited restructuring of the House in 1974. The staffs of congressmen, committees, and even the General Accounting Office are reviewed favorably in *Congressional Staffs: The Invisible Force in America* (New York: The Free Press, 1977) by Harrison W. Fox and Susan W. Hammond.

Relationships between the president and Congress were often less than amicable. The White House tactics and strategies to gain influence with Congress are the subject of Abraham Holtzman, *Legislative Liaison: Executive Leadership in Congress* (Chicago: Indiana University Press, 1976). In a wide range of essays, including such topics as the budget, executive appointments, and the black caucus, Harvey C. Mansfield, ed., *Congress against the President* (New York: Academy of Political Science, 1975) analyzes the philosophical and practical differences between the executive and the legislative.

Other Works

Abzug, Bella S. *Bella! Ms. Abzug Goes to Washington.* New York: Saturday Review Press, 1972.

Asbell, Bernard. *The Senate Nobody Knows.* Garden City, N.Y.: Doubleday, 1978.

Bailey, Stephen K. *Congress in the Seventies.* New York: St. Martin's Press, 1970.

Beard, Edmund, and Stephen Horn. *Congressional Ethics: The View from the House.* Washington, D.C.: Brookings Institution, 1975.

Blanchard, Robert O., comp. *Congress and the News Media.* New York: Hastings House, 1974.

Buckley, James L. *If Men Were Angels: A View from the Senate.* New York: Putnam, 1975.

Clark, Peter K. "The Effect of Inflation on Federal Expenditures." U.S. Congressional Budget Office (June 18, 1976).

Clausen, Aage R. *How Congressmen Decide: A Policy Focus.* New York: St. Martin's Press, 1973.

Congressional Quarterly, Inc. *Guide to Congress.* Washington, D.C.: Congressional Quarterly, 1976.

———. *Inside Congress.* Washington, D.C.: Congressional Quarterly, 1976.

———. *Powers of Congress.* Washington, D.C.: Congressional Quarterly, 1976.

Frye, Alton. *A Responsible Congress: The Politics of National Security.* New York: McGraw-Hill, 1975.

Green, Mark J., et al. *Who Runs Congress?* New York: Bantam Books, 1972.

Griffith, Ernest S., and Francis R. Valeo. *Congress: Its Contemporary Role.* New York: New York University Press, 1975.

Harris, Joseph P. *Congress and the Legislative Process.* New York: McGraw-Hill, 1972.

Jones, Charles O. *The Minority Party in Congress.* Boston: Little, Brown, 1970.

Jordan, Barbara. *Barbara Jordan: A Self-Portrait.* Garden City, N.Y.: Doubleday, 1979.

MacCann, Richard Dyer. "Televising Congress." *American Scholar* (Summer 1976).

Mann, Kenneth Eugene. "John Roy Lynch: U.S. Congressman from Mississippi." *Negro Historical Bulletin* (April/May 1974).

Matsunaga, Spark, and Yung Chen. *Rulemakers of the House.* Urbana: University of Illinois Press, 1976.

Matthews, Donald R. and James A. Stimson. *Yeas and Nays: Normal Decision-Making in the U.S. House of Representatives.* New York: John Wiley & Sons, 1975.

Mayhew, David R. *Congress: The Electoral Connection.* New Haven, Conn.: Yale University Press, 1974.

McGovern, George S. *Grassroots.* New York: Random House, 1977.

Ogul, Morris S. *Congress Oversees the Bureaucracy: Studies in Legislative Supervision.* Pittsburgh, Pa.: University of Pittsburgh Press, 1976.

Ornstein, Norman J. *Congress in Change: Evolution and Reform.* New York: Praeger, 1975.

Polsby, Nelson W. *Congress and the Presidency.* Englewood Cliffs, N.J.: Prentice Hall, 1971.

Ralph Nader Congress Project, *The Commerce Committees*, David E. Price, director. New York: Grossman Publishers, 1975.

———. *The Environment Committees*. New York: Grossman Publishers, 1975.

———. *The Judiciary Committees*, Peter H. Schuck, director. New York: Grossman Publishers, 1975.

———. *The Money Committees*, Lester M. Salamon, director. New York: Grossman Publishers. 1975.

———. *The Revenue Committees*, Richard Spohn and Charles McCollum, directors. New York: Grossman Publishers, 1975.

———. *Ruling Congress: A Study of How the House and Senate Rules Govern the Legislative Process*, Ted Siff and Alan Weil, directors. New York: Grossman Publishers, 1975.

Rapoport, Daniel. *Inside the House: An Irreverent Guided Tour through the House of Representatives, from the Days of Adam Clayton Powell to Those of Peter Rodino*. Chicago: Follett, 1975.

Rhodes, John J. *The Futile System: How to Unchain Congress and Make the System Work Again*. McLean, Va.: EPM Publications, 1976.

Riegle, Donald. *O Congress*. Garden City, N.Y.: Doubleday, 1972.

Rieselbach, Leroy N. *Congressional Politics*. New York: McGraw-Hill, 1973.

———. *Congressional Reform in the Seventies*. Morristown, N.J.: General Learning Press, 1977.

Ripley, Randall B. *Congress: Process and Policy*. New York: W. W. Norton, 1975.

Schneider, Jerrold E. *Ideological Coalitions in Congress*. Westport, Conn.: Greenwood Press, 1979.

Shapiro, David L. "Mr. Justice Rehnquist: A Preliminary View." *Harvard Law Journal* (December 1976).

Shepsle, Kenneth A. *The Giant Jigsaw Puzzle: Democratic Committee Assignments in the Modern House*. Chicago: University of Chicago Press, 1978.

Uslaner, Eric M. *Congressional Committee Assignments: Alternative Models for Behavior*. Beverly Hills, Calif.: Sage Publications, 1974.

Vatz, Richard E. "The Defeats of Judges Haynsworth and Carswell: Rejection of Supreme Court Nominees." *Quarterly Journal of Speech* (December 1974).

Vogler, David J. *The Politics of Congress*. Boston: Allyn & Bacon, 1974.

State and Local Government

Of paramount concern to state and local government from 1969 to 1976 were the problems associated with urban decay. The scope of these problems is covered by Alan K. Campbell and Roy W. Bahl, eds., in *State and Local Government: The Political Economy of Reform* (New York: Free Press, 1976). The diverse demands of urban dwellers and the cities' inability to raise adequate revenue to meet those demands are the subject of two important works: William G. Coleman, *Cities, Suburbs, and States: Governing and Financing Urban America* (New York: Free Press, 1975), and Douglas Yates, *The Ungovernable City: The Problem of Urban Politics and Policy Making* (Cambridge, Mass.: MIT Press, 1977).

Federal efforts to aid in the solution of urban problems are examined by Bernard Friedman and Marshall Kaplan in *The Politics of Neglect: Urban Aid from Model Cities to Revenue Sharing* (Cambridge, Mass.: MIT Press, 1975). This study analyzes the efforts of Presidents Lyndon Johnson and Richard Nixon to aid the cities and finds that urban America saw little improvement under either administration. Gary D. Brewer's *Politicians, Bureaucrats, and the Consultant: A Critique of Urban Problem Solving* (New York: Basic Books, 1973) focuses on federal aid programs to San Francisco and Pittsburgh. Brewer concludes that the magnitude of urban problems was not fully appreciated by bureaucratic researchers and planners, thus reform efforts fell short of success. In contrast, Paul Terrell's *The Social Impact of Revenue Sharing* (New York: Praeger Publishers, 1976) is more optimistic. This study of seven Pacific Coast areas points out that President Nixon's revenue-sharing program had positive local effects, due largely to increased citizen participation in government.

New York City's fiscal crisis evoked several pessimistic essays, including two in the 1976 journal *Society*: George Sternlieb and James W. Hughes, "New York: Future without a Future?" and Wolfgang Quante, "Flight of the Corporate Headquarters." Both articles comment on New York's bleak economic future because of its eroding tax base and labor market.

Other Works

Allswang, John M. *Bosses, Machines and Urban Voters*. New York: Kennikat Press, 1977.

Bartley, Numan V., and Hugh D. Graham. *Southern Politics and the Second Reconstruction*. Baltimore: Johns Hopkins University Press, 1975.

Beramn, David R. *State and Local Politics*. Boston: Holbrook Press, 1975.

Berg, Larry, et al. *Corruption in the American Political System*. Morristown, N.J.: General Learning Press, 1976.

Bingham, Richard D. *Public Housing and Urban Renewal: An Analysis of Federal-Local Relations*. New York, Praeger, 1975.

Bollens, John C., and Grant B. Geyer. *Yorty: Politics of a Constant Candidate*. Pacific Palisades, Calif.: Palisades Publishers, 1973.

Boyarsky, Bill. *Backroom Politics*. Los Angeles: J. P. Tarcher, 1974.

Buel, Ronald A. *Dead End: The Automobile in Mass Transportation*. Englewood Cliffs, N.J.: Prentice Hall, 1972.

Bulton, James W. *Black Violence: Political Impact of the 1960s Riots*. Princeton, N.J.: Princeton University Press, 1978.

Callow, Alexander B., ed. *The City Boss in America: An Interpretive Reader*. New York: Oxford University Press, 1976.

Cash, Kevin. *Who the Hell Is William Loeb?* Manchester, N.H.: Amoskeag Press, 1975.

Connery, Robert H., and Gerald Benjamin, eds. *Governing New York State: The Rockefeller Years*. New York: Academy of Political Science, 1974.

Conot, Robert. *American Odyssey*. New York: Bantam, 1974.

Davidson, Chandler. *Biracial Politics: Conflict and Coalition in the Metropolitan South*. Baton Rouge: Louisiana State University Press, 1972.

Davies, Richard O. *The Age of Asphalt: The Automobile, the Freeway, and the Condition of Metropolitan America*. Philadelphia: Lippincott, 1975.

Downes, Bryan T. *Politics, Change and the Urban Crisis*. North Scituate, Duxbury, Mass.: 1976.

Dye, Thomas R. *Politics in States and Communities*. Englewood Cliffs, N.J.: Prentice Hall, 1977.

Edsall, Thomas B. "Racetracks, Banks, and Liquor Stores." *Washington Monthly* (October 1974).

Eisinger, Peter K. *The Patterns of Interracial Politics: Conflict and Cooperation in the City*. New York: Academic, 1976.

Ershkowitz, Miriam, and Joseph Zikmund, II. *Black Politics in Philadelphia*. New York: Basic Books, 1973.

Gardiner, John A. *The Politics of Corruption; Organized Crime in an American City*. New York: Russell Sage Foundation, 1970.

Gellhorn, Walter. "The Ombudsman's Relevance to American Municipal Affairs," *American Bar Association* (February 1968).

Gray, Francine du Plessix. *Hawaii: The Sugar-Coated Fortress*. New York: Random House, 1972.

Harbert, Anita S. *Federal Grants-in-Aid: Maximizing Benefits to the States*. New York: Praeger, 1976.

Havard, William C., ed. *Politics of the Contemporary South*. Baton Rouge: Louisiana State University Press, 1972.

Hawley, Willis D. *Blacks and Metropolitan Governance: The Stakes of Reform*. Berkeley: Institute of Governmental Studies, University of California, 1972.

Howard, Perry H. *Political Tendencies in Louisiana*. Baton Rouge: Louisiana State University Press, 1972.

Hutcheson, John D., Jr., and Jann Shevin. *Citizens Groups in Local Politics; A Bibliographic Review*. Santa Barbara, Calif.: CLIO Books,1976.

Jones, Charles O., and Robert D. Thomas, eds. *Public Policy Making in a Federal System*. Beverly Hills, Calif.: Sage Publications, 1976.

Juster, F. Thomas, ed. *The Economic and Political Impact of General Revenue Sharing*. Ann Arbor: Survey Research Center, Institute for Social Research, University of Michigan: 1977.

Klein, Woody. *Lindsay's Promise: The Dream That Failed*. New York: Macmillan, 1970.

Kutz, Myer. *Rockefeller Power*. New York: Simon & Schuster, 1974.

Lamb, Curt. *Political Power in Poor Neighborhoods*. Cambridge, Mass.: Schenkman, 1975.

Levin, Melvin R., et al. *New Approaches to State Land Use Policies*. Lexington, Mass.: Lexington Books, 1974.

Liebert, Roland, J. *Disintegration and Political Action: The Changing Functions of City Government in America*. New York: Academic Press, 1976.

Lufkin, Dan W. *Many Sovereign States: A Case for Strengthening State Government*. New York: McKay, 1975.

Mirenghoff, William. *The Comprehensive Employment and Training Act: Impact on People, Places, Programs*. Washington, D.C.: National Academy of Sciences, 1976.

Nathan, Richard P., et al. *Revenue Sharing: The Second Round*. Washington, D.C.: Brookings Institution, 1977.

Parker, Thomas F. *Violence in the U.S.* New York: Facts On File, 1974.

Petshek, Kirk R. *The Challenge of Urban Reform; Policies and Program in Philadelphia*. Philadelphia: Temple University Press, 1973.

Phelan, James, and Robert Pozen. *The Company State: Ralph Nader's Study Group Report on DuPont in Delaware*. New York: Grossman Publishers, 1973.

Peirce, Neal R. *The Megastates of America*. New York: Norton, 1972.

———. *The Border South States*. New York: Norton, 1975.

———. *The Deep South States*. New York: Norton, 1974.

———. *The Great Plains States*. New York: Norton, 1973.

———. *The Mountain States*. New York: Norton, 1972.

Putnam, Jackson, K. *Old-Age Politics in California: From Richardson to Reagan*. Stanford, Calif.: Stanford University Press, 1970.

Ravitch, Diane. *The Great School Wars, New York City, 1805–1973: A History of the Public Schools as Battlefield of Social Change*. New York: Basic Books, 1974.

Revesz, Etta. *Hate Don't Make No Noise: Anatomy of a New Ghetto*. New York: Viking Press: 1978.

Rosenthal, Alan, and John Blydenburgh, eds. *Politics in New Jersey*. New Brunswick, N.J.: Eagleton Institute of Politics, Rutgers University, 1975.

Royko, Mike. *Boss: Richard J. Daley of Chicago*. New York: Dutton, 1971.

Sacks, Seymour. *City Schools/Suburban Schools: A History of Fiscal Conflict*. Syracuse, N.Y.: Syracuse University Press, 1972.

Shank, Alan. *Political Power and the Urban Crisis*. Boston: Holbrook Press, 1976.

Steiner, Henry M. *Conflict in Urban Transportation: The People against the Planners*. Lexington, Mass.: Lexington Books, 1978.

Sternlieb, George. "New York; Future without a Future?" *Society* (May/June 1976).

Widick, B. J., Jr. *Detroit: City of Race and Class Violence*. Chicago: Quadrangle Books, 1972.

Wilkstrom, Gunnar. *Municipal Government Response to Urban Riots*. San Francisco: R and E Research Associates, 1972.

Winter-Berger, Robert N. *The Washington Payoff*. New York: L. Stuart, 1972.

The Supreme Court

General studies of the Burger Court include Robert G. McCloskey, The *Modern Supreme Court* (Cambridge, Mass.: Harvard University Press, 1972) and Archibald Cox, *The Role of the Supreme Court in American Government* (New York: Oxford University Press; 1976), which concentrates on recent Court trends in the area of liberty and equality. Since 1949 the *Harvard Law Review* has presented in every fall issue a discussion analysis of the work of the preceding Court term. *The Supreme Court Review* (Chicago: University of Chicago Press, 1960–), ed. Philip B. Kurland, is an excellent annual publication containing articles on recent Court decisions and trends. Law reviews are often the best source of material on constitutional history, current legal issues, and Supreme Court cases. *The Index to Legal Periodicals* allows easy location of articles on a particular topic. Stephen M. Millet, *A Selected Bibliography of American Constitutional History* (Santa Barbara, Calif.: CLIO Books, 1975) is a useful starting point for locating sources on constitutional law and history. Richard Y. Funston, *Constitutional Counterrevolution?* (New York: Halsted Press, 1977) examines continuities and discontinuities between the Warren and Burger Courts. James F. Simon, *In His Own Image: The Supreme Court in Richard Nixon's America* (New York: McKay, 1973) is a balanced assessment of the Burger Court through the 1971–72 term. Philip B. Kurland analyzes the first three terms of the Burger Court in detail in articles in *The Supreme Court Review* for 1970, 1971, and 1972. Articles giving an overview and assessment of the Burger Court's work include William F. Swindler, "The Court, the Constitution, and Chief Justice Burger," *Vanderbilt Law Review* 27 Vanderbilt University School of Law (April 1974), pp. 443–474; "The Burger Court: New Directions in Judicial Policy-Making," *Emory Law Journal*, 23 (Summer, Emory University School of Law, 1974), pp. 643–779; "The Burger Court and the Constitution," *Columbia Journal of Law and Social Problems*, 11 (Fall 1974), pp. 35–71; and Henry J. Abraham, "Some Observations on the Burger Court's Record on Civil Rights and Liberties," *Notre Dame Lawyer*, 52 Notre Dame Law School, (October 1976), pp. 77–86 and A. E. Dick Howard, "From Warren to Burger: Activism and Restraint," *Wilson Quarterly* (Spring 1977), pp. 109–120. Raoul Berger, *Government by Judiciary* (Cambridge, Mass.: Harvard University Press, 1977) looks at the Court's recent use of the 14th Amendment in various fields and discusses both Warren and Burger Court rulings.

Other Works

Abraham, Henry, J. *Freedom and the Court: Civil Rights and Liberties in the United States*, 3d ed. New York: Oxford University Press, 1977.

Bell, Derrick A., Jr. *Race, Racism and American Law*. Boston: Little, Brown, 1973.

Bosmajian, Haig A., ed. *Obscenity and Freedom of Expression*. New York: Burt Franklin & Co., 1975.

———. *The Principles and Practice of Freedom of Speech*. Boston: Houghton Mifflin, 1971.

Casper, Jonathan D. *American Criminal Justice: The Defendant's Perspective*. Englewood Cliffs: Prentice Hall, 1972.

Clark, Leroy D. *The Grand Jury: The Use and Abuse of Political Power*. New York: Quadrangle, 1975.

Dorsen, Norman, et al. *Political and Civil Rights in the United States*, 4th ed. Boston: Little, Brown, 1976.

Elliott, Ward E. Y. *The Rise of Guardian Democracy: The Supreme Court's Role in Voting Rights Disputes, 1845–1969*. Cambridge, Mass.: Harvard University Press, 1974.

Fellman, David. *The Defendant's Rights Today.* Madison: University of Wisconsin Press, 1976.

Galloway, John, ed. *The Supreme Court and the Rights of the Accused.* New York: Facts On File, 1973.

Kurland, Philip B., ed. *Free Speech and Association: The Supreme Court and the First Amendment.* Chicago: University of Chicago Press, 1975.

Lawhorne, Clifton O. *Defamation and Public Officials: The Evolving Law of Libel.* Carbondale: Southern Illinois University Press, 1971.

Lewis, Felice F. *Literature, Obscenity and Law.* Carbondale: Southern Illinois University Press, 1976.

Levy, Leonard W. *Against the Law: The Nixon Court and Criminal Justice.* New York: Harper and Row, 1974.

Liston, Robert A. *The Right to Know: Censorship in America.* New York: Franklin Watts, Inc., 1973.

Meltsner, Michael. *Cruel and Unusual: The Supreme Court and Capital Punishment.* New York: Random House, 1973.

Milner, Neil. *The Court and Local Law Enforcement: The Impact of Miranda.* Beverly Hills: Sage Publications, 1971.

Morgan, Richard E. *The Supreme Court and Religion.* New York: Free Press, 1972.

Paul, Arnold M., ed. *Black Americans and the Supreme Court Since Emancipation.* New York: Holt, Rinehart & Winston, 1972.

Paulsen, Monrad G., and Charles H. Whitebread. *Juvenile Law and Procedure.* Reno: National Council of Juvenile Court Judges, 1974.

Pember, Don R. *Privacy and the Press: The Law, the Mass Media and the First Amendment.* Seattle: University of Washington Press, 1972.

Pennock, J. Roland, and John W. Chapman, eds. *Due Process.* New York: New York University Press, 1977.

Pfeffer, Leo. *Church, State and Freedom*, rev. ed. Boston: Beacon Press, 1967.

————. *God, Caesar and the Constitution: The Court as Referee of Church-State Confrontations.* Boston: Beacon Press, 1975.

Pious, Richard M., ed. *Civil Rights and Liberties in the 1970s.* New York: Random House, 1973.

Regan, Richard J. *Private Conscience and Public Law: The American Experience.* New York: Fordham University Press, 1972.

Schauer, Frederick F. *The Law of Obscenity.* Washington, D.C.: Bureau of National Affairs, 1976.

Schmidt, Benno C., Jr. *Freedom of the Press vs. Public Access.* New York: Praeger, 1976.

Smith, Elwyn A. *Religious Liberty in the United States.* Philadelphia: Fortress Press, 1972.

Sorauf, Francis J. *The Wall of Separation: The Constitutional Politics of Church and State.* Princeton, N.J.: Princeton University Press, 1976.

Stephens, Otis. *The Supreme Court and Confessions of Guilt.* Knoxville: University of Tennessee Press, 1973.

Sunderland, Lane V. *Obscenity: The Court, the Congress and the President's Commission.* Washington, D.C.: American Enterprise Institute for Public Policy Research, 1974.

Twentieth Century Fund, Task Force on the Government and the Press. *Press Freedom under Pressure.* New York: 1972.

Ungar, Sanford J. *The Papers and the Papers: An Account of the Legal and the Political Battle over the Pentagon Papers.* New York: Dutton, 1972.

Wasby, Stephen L., ed. *Civil Liberties: Policy and Policy Making.* Lexington, Mass.: Lexington Books, 1976.

Foreign Affairs

In the forefront of the Nixon and Ford administrations were several global issues. Tad Szule's *The Illusion of Peace: Foreign Policy in The Nixon Years* (New York: Penguin, 1978) provides an excellent overview of the Richard Nixon-Henry Kissinger stewardship of U.S. foreign policy. A more critical analysis of the period can be found in George F. Kennan's *The Cloud of Danger* (Boston: Little, Brown, 1977). Kennan charged that the United States had overcommitted itself and recommended a paring down, so as to more easily cope with important issues. In contrast, Henry Brandon in *The Retreat of American Power* (Garden City, N.Y.: Doubleday, 1973) praises the Nixon-Kissinger team for overseeing the rapid withdrawal of the United States from world domination. Secretary of State Henry Kissinger has been the subject of many writers. Marvin and Bernard Kalb, *Kissinger* (Boston: Little, Brown, 1974) presents a favorable account of Kissinger's diplomatic efforts through 1973. A sympathetic intellectual evaluation of Kissinger's foreign policy philosophy can be found in John G. Stoessinger, *Henry Kissinger: The Anguish of Power* (New York: Norton, 1976). In his *Diplomacy for a Crowded World* (Boston: Little, Brown, 1976), George Ball criticizes Kissinger's unilateral diplomacy, asserting that it was successful for gaining domestic political support but not in establishing lasting structures of world peace and American security.

An abundant amount of foreign policy literature focused on Asia. An excellent starting point is Peter Poole's *The United States and Indochina: From FDR to Nixon* (Hinsdale, Ill.: Dryden Press, 1973). Former Central Intelligence Agency official Robert G. Sutter describes the Chinese efforts to improve U.S. relations in his *China Watch: Toward Sino-American Reconciliation* (Baltimore: Johns Hopkins University Press, 1978). Sutter concludes that "realists" in both Peking and Washington finally won out in 1972, when both nations recognized the need to balance power. Of growing concern during the Nixon-Ford years were problems in the Middle East. Robert W. Stookey's *America and the Arab States: An Uneasy Encounter* (New York: John Wiley & Sons, 1975) stresses that U.S. economic health and security are linked directly to the volatile Arab states. The Arab-Israeli issue is placed

into the larger context of Middle East policy by Bernard Reich in *Quest for Peace: United States-Israeli Relations and the Arab-Israeli Conflict* (New Brunswick, N.J.: Transaction Books, 1977).

General Works

Andrews, Craig Neal. *Foreign Policy and the New American Military.* Beverly Hills: Sage Publications, 1974.

Aron, Raymond. *The Imperial Republic: The United States and the World, 1945–1973.* Englewood Cliffs, N.J.: Weidenfeld & Nicolson, 1974.

Azyliowicz, Bard E. O'Neill, ed. *The Energy Crisis and U.S. Foreign Policy.* New York: Praeger, 1975.

Barber, Stephen. *America in Retreat.* New York: Barnes & Noble, 1970.

Blaufarb, Douglas S. *The Counterinsurgency Era: U.S. Doctrine and Performance, 1950 to the Present.* New York: Free Press, 1977.

Buckley, William Frank. *Inveighing We Will Go.* New York: Putnam, 1972.

Buncher, Judith F., ed. *Human Rights and American Diplomacy, 1975–1977.* New York: Facts On File, 1977.

Combs, Jerald A., comp. *Nationalist, Realist and Radical: Three Views of American Diplomacy.* New York: Harper & Row, 1972.

Coolidge, Archibald Cary. *The United States as a World Power.* New York: Macmillan, 1971.

Coufoudaki, Van. "U.S. Foreign Policy and the Cyprus Question: An Interpretation," *Millenium* 5, no. 3 (Winter, 1976–77: 245–268).

Edwards, David V. *Creating a New World Politics: From Conflict to Cooperation.* New York: McKay, 1973.

Falk, Richard A. *What's Wrong with Henry Kissinger's Foreign Policy.* Princeton, N.J.: Center of International Studies, Princeton University, 1974.

Falk, Stanley L., ed. *The World in Ferment: Problem Areas for the United States.* Washington, D.C.: Industrial College of the Armed Forces, 1970.

Falkowski, Lawrence S. *Presidents, Secretaries of State and Crises in U.S. Foreign Relations: A Model and Predictive Analysis.* Boulder, Colo.: Westview Press, 1978.

Gilpin, Robert. *U.S. Power and the Multinational Corporation: The Political Economy of Foreign Direct Investment.* New York: Basic Books, 1975.

Graubard, Stephen. *Kissinger.* New York: WW Norton and Co., 1973.

Gujiral, M. L. *U.S. Global Involvement: A Study of American Expansionism.* New Delhi: Arnold Heinemann Publishers, 1975.

Halloran, Richard. *Conflict and Compromise: The Dynamics of American Foreign Policy.* New York: John Day, 1973.

Hickman, Martin B., comp. *Problems of American Foreign Policy.* Beverly Hills: Sage Publications, 1975.

Hoxie, Ralph Gordon. *Command Decision and the Presidency: A Study in National Security Policy and Organization.* New York: Reader's Digest Press, 1977.

Jones, Alan M., ed. *U.S. Foreign Policy in a Changing World: The Nixon Administrations, 1969–1973.* New York: McKay, 1973.

Kaplan, Morton A. *Dissent and the State in Peace and War; An Essay on the Grounds of Public Morality.* New York: Dunellen Co., 1970.

Kintner, William Roscoe, and Richard B. Foster, eds. *National Strategy in a Decade of Change: An Emerging U.S. Policy.* Lexington, Mass.: Lexington Books, 1973.

Krasner, Stephen D. *Defending the National Interest: Raw Materials, Investments and U.S. Foreign Policy.* Princeton, N.J.: Princeton University Press, 1978.

Landau, David. *Kissinger: The Uses of Power.* Boston: Houghton Mifflin, 1972.

Lehman, John F. *The Executive, Congress and Foreign Policy: Studies of the Nixon Administration.* New York: Praeger, 1974.

Lesh, Donald R., ed. *A Nation Observed: Perspectives on America's World Role.* Washington, D.C.: Potomac Associates, 1974.

Nixon, Richard. *United States Foreign Policy for the 1970s. A Report by President Richard Nixon to the Congress, February 25, 1971.* New York: Harper & Row, 1971.

Osgood, Robert E. *Retreat from Empire? The First Nixon Administration.* Baltimore: Johns Hopkins University Press, 1973.

Owen, Henry, and Charles L. Shultze, eds. *Setting National Priorities.* Washington: The Brookings Institution, 1976.

Parenti, Michael. *The Anti-Communist Impulse.* New York: Random House, 1970.

Paul, Roland A. *American Military Commitments Abroad.* New Brunswick, N.J.: Rutgers University Press, 1973.

Perusse, Roland I., ed. *Contemporary Issues in Inter-American Relations.* San Juan: North-South Press, 1972.

Pusey, Merlo John. *The U.S.A. Astride The Globe.* Boston: Houghton Mifflin, 1971.

Roberts, Chalmers M. "Foreign Policy under a Paralyzed Presidency," *Foreign Affairs* (July 1974).

Rostow, Eugene V. *Peace in the Balance: The Future of American Foreign Policy.* New York: Simon & Schuster, 1972.

Scheer, Robert. *America after Nixon; The Age of the Multinationals.* New York: McGraw-Hill, 1974.

Schlafly, Phyllis, and Chester Ward. *Kissinger on the Couch.* New York: Arlington House, 1974.

Schneider, William. "Public Opinion: The Beginning of Ideology," *Foreign Policy* (Winter 1974–75).

Schurmann, Herbert Franz. *The Role of Ideas in American Foreign Policy; A Conference Report.* Hanover, N.H.: University Press of New England, 1971.

Sorensen, Theodore C. "Watergate and American Foreign Policy," *World Today* (December 1974).

Stegenga, James A., ed. *Toward A Wiser Colossus; Reviewing and Recasting United States Foreign Policy.* Lafayette, Ind.: Purdue University Studies, 1972.

Stern, Laurence, *The Wrong Horse: The Politics of Intervention and the Failure of American Diplomacy*. New York: Times Books, 1977.

The Middle East

Alroy, Gil C. *The Kissinger Experience: American Policy in the Middle East*. New York: Horizon Press, 1975.

Arakie, Margaret. *The Broken Sword of Justice: America, Israel and the Palestine Tragedy*. London: Quartet Books, 1973.

Churba, Joseph. *The Politics of Defeat: America's Decline in the Middle East*. New York: Cyrco Press, 1977.

Drinan, Robert F. *Honor the Promise: America's Commitment to Israel*. Garden City, N.Y.: Doubleday, 1977.

Golan, Matti. *The Secret Conversations of Henry Kissinger: Step-By-Step Diplomacy in the Middle East*. New York: Quadrangle/New York Times Book Co., 1976.

Harris, George S. *Troubled Alliance: Turkish-American Problems in Historical Perspective, 1945–1971*. Washington: American Enterprise Institute for Public Policy Research, 1972.

Klebanoff, Shoshana. *Middle East Oil and U.S. Foreign Policy, With Special Reference to the U.S. Energy Crisis*. New York: Praeger, 1974.

Mangold, Peter. *Superpower Intervention in the Middle East*. New York: St. Martin's Press, 1978.

Nakhleh, Emile A. *Arab-American Relations in the Persian Gulf*. Washington, D.C.: American Enterprise Institute for Public Policy, 1975.

Pranger, Robert J. *American Policy for Peace in the Middle East, 1969–1971: Problems of Principle, Maneuver and Time*. Washington, D.C.: American Enterprise Institute for Public Policy Research, 1971.

Quandt, William B. *Decade of Decisions: American Policy toward the Arab-Israeli Conflict, 1967–1976*. Berkeley: University of California Press, 1977.

Rostow, Eugene V., ed. *The Middle East: Critical Choices for the United States*. Boulder, Colo.: Westview Press, for the National Committee for American Foreign Policy, 1976.

Safran, Nadav. *Israel, The Embattled Ally*. Cambridge, Mass.: Belknap Press, 1978.

Sheehan, Edward. *The Arabs, Israelis and Kissinger: A Secret History of American Diplomacy in the Middle East*. New York: Reader's Digest Press, 1976.

"Step by Step in the Middle East," *Journal of Palestine Studies* (Spring/Summer 1976) Issue 19–20.

Tucker, Robert W. "Israel and the United States: From Dependence to Nuclear Weapons?" *Commentary* (May 1975) vol. 60.

Ullman, Richard H. "After Rabat: Middle East Risks and American Roles," *Foreign Affairs* (December 1975).

Asia

Barnett, A. Doak. *China and the Major Powers in East Asia*. Washington, D.C.: Brookings Institution, 1977.

———. *A New U.S. Policy toward China*. Washington, D.C.: Brookings Institution, 1971.

Brodine, Virginia, comp. *Open Secret: The Kissinger-Nixon Doctrine in Asia*. New York: Harper & Row, 1972.

Bueler, William M. *U.S. China Policy and the Problem of Taiwan*. Boulder: Colorado Associated University Press, 1971.

Chay, John, ed. *The Problems and Prospects of American-East Asian Relations*. Boulder, Colo.: Westview Press, 1977.

Clough, Ralph N. *East Asia and U.S. Security*. Washington, D.C.: Brookings Institution, 1975.

———. *Island China*. Cambridge, Mass.: Harvard University Press, 1978.

Cohen, Jerome Alan, et al. *Taiwan and American Policy; The Dilemma in U.S.-China Relations*, New York: Praeger, 1971.

Destler, I. M. *Managing an Alliance: The Politics of U.S.-Japanese Relations*. Washington, D.C.: Brookings Institution, 1976.

Fairbanks, John K. *The United States and China.* Cambridge, Mass.: Harvard University Press, 1971.

Fifield, Russell Hunt. *Americans in Southeast Asia: The Roots of Commitment.* New York: Crowell, 1973.

Gelb, Leslie H., and Richard K. Betts. *The Irony of Vietnam: The System Worked.* Washington, D.C.: Brookings Institution, 1979.

Goldstein, Martin E. *American Policy Toward Laos.* Rutherford, N.J.: Fairleigh Dickinson University Press, 1973.

Haendel, Dan. *The Process of Priority Formulation: U.S. Foreign Policy in the Indo-Pakistani War of 1971.* Boulder, Colo.: Westview Press, 1977.

Harrison, Selig S. *The Widening Gulf: Asian Nationalism and American Policy.* New York: Free Press, 1978.

Hinton, Harold C. *Three and a Half Powers: The New Balance In Asia.* Bloomington: Indiana University Press, 1975.

Hohenberg, John. *New Era in the Pacific: An Adventure in Public Diplomacy.* New York: Simon & Schuster, 1972.

Hon, Eugene. *Nixon's Trip—The Road to China's Russian War.* San Francisco: Henson Co., 1972.

Johnson, Stuart E. *The Military Equation in Northeast Asia.* Washington, D.C.: Brookings Institution, 1979.

Kalb, Marvin L. *Roots of Involvement: The U.S. in Asia, 1784–1971* New York: Norton, 1971.

Kintner, William Roscoe. *The Impact of President's Nixon's Visit to Peking on International Politics.* Philadelphia: Foreign Policy Research Institute, 1972

Kirk, Donald. *Wider War: The Struggle for Cambodia, Thailand and Laos.* New York: Praeger, 1972.

Kubek, Anthony. *The Red China Papers: What Americans Deserve to Know about U.S.-China Relations.* New Rochelle, N.Y.: Arlington House, 1975.

Kunhi Krishnan, T. V. *The Unfriendly Friends, India and America.* Thompson, Conn.: 1974.

MacFarquhar, Roderick, comp. *Sino-American Relations 1949–1971.* New York: Praeger, 1972.

May, Ernest R., and James C. Thompson, Jr. *American-East Asian Relations: A Survey.* Cambridge, Mass.: Harvard University Press, 1972.

Meyers, William, and M. Vincent Hayes, eds. *China Policy; New Priorities and Alternatives.* New York: Gordon and Breach, 1972.

Moorsteen, Richard Harris, and Morton Abramovitz. *Remaking China Policy: U.S.-China Relations and Governmental Decision-making.* Cambridge, Mass.: Harvard University Press, 1971.

Ravenal, Earl, ed. *Peace with China? U.S. Decisions for Asia.* New York: Liveright, 1971.

Rosovsky, Henry, ed. *Discord in the Pacific: Challenges to the Japanese-American Alliance.* Washington, D.C.: Columbia Books, 1972.

Scalapino, Robert A. *American-Japanese Relations in a Changing Era.* New York: Library Press, 1972.

———. *Asia and the Road Ahead: Issues for the Major Powers.* Berkeley: University of California Press, 1975.

Selden, Mark. *Remaking Asia; Essays on the American Uses of Power.* New York: Pantheon Books, 1973.

Shawcross, William. *Sideshow: Kissinger, Nixon and the Destruction of Cambodia.* New York: Simon and Schuster, 1979.

Sih, Paul K. ed. *Asia and Contemporary World Problems: A Symposium.* New York: St. John's University Press, 1972.

Sihanouk Varman, Norodom. *My War with the CIA: The Memoirs of Prince Norodom Sihanouk.* New York: Pantheon Books, 1973.

Simon, Sheldon W. *Asian Neutralism and U.S. Policy.* Washington: American Enterprise Institute for Public Policy Research, 1975.

Sullivan, Marianna P. *France's Vietnam Policy: A Study in French-American Relations.* Westport, Conn.: Greenwood Press, 1978.

Van der Linden, Frank. *Nixon's Quest for Peace.* Washington: R. B. Luce, 1972.

Yung-hwan, Jo, ed. *Foreign Policy in Asia: An Appraisal.* Santa Barbara: ABC-CLIO, 1978.

The Western Hemisphere

Black, Jan Knippers. *United States Penetration of Brazil.* Philadelphia: University of Pennsylvania Press, 1977.

Fox, Annette B., et al. *Canada and the United States: Transnational and Transgovernmental Relations.* New York: Columbia University Press, 1976.

Kaufman, Edy. *The Superpowers and Their Spheres of Influence: The United States and the Soviet Union in Eastern Europe and Latin America.* New York: St. Martin's Press, 1977.

MacEoin, Gary. *No Peaceful Way: Chile's Struggle for Dignity.* New York: Sheed & Ward, 1974.

Martin, John Bartlow. *U.S. Policy in the Caribbean.* Boulder, Colo.: Westview Press, 1978.

Petras, James F. *The United States and Chile: Imperialism and the Overthrow of the Allende Government.* New York: Monthly Review Press, 1975.

Uribe Arce, Armando. *The Black Book of American Intervention in Chile.* Boston: Beacon Press, 1975.

Europe and the Soviet Union

Barnet, Richard J. *The Giants: Russia and America.* New York: Simon & Schuster, 1977.

Beam, Jacob. *Multiple Exposure: An American Ambassador's Unique Perspective on East-West Issues.* New York: Norton, 1978.

Bell, Coral. *The Diplomacy of Detente: The Kissinger Era.* New York: St. Martin's Press, 1977.

Calleo, David P. *The Atlantic Fantasy: The U.S., Nato and Europe.* Baltimore: Johns Hopkins University Press, 1970.

Catlin, George Edward Gordon, Sir, *Kissinger's Atlantic Charter.* Gerrards Cross, Britain: C. Smythe, 1974.

Donovan, John, ed. *U.S. and Soviet Policy in the Middle East.* New York: Facts On File, 1972.

Griffith, William E. *Peking, Moscow and Beyond: The Sino-Soviet-American Triangle.* Washington, D.C.: Center for Strategic and International Studies, Georgetown University, 1973.

Kaiser, Karl. *Europe and the United States: The Future of the Relationship.* Washington, D.C.: Columbia Books, 1973.

Mally, Gerhard. *Interdependence: The European-American Connection in the Global Context.* Lexington, Mass.: Lexington Books, 1976.

Mazlish, Bruce. *Kissinger: The European Mind in American Policy.* New York: Basic Books, 1976.

Newhouse, John. *DeGaulle and the Anglo-Saxons.* New York: Viking Press, 1970.

Pfaltzgraff, Robert L., Jr. "The United States and Europe; Partners in a Multipolar World?" *Orbis* (Spring 1973).

Pittman, John. "Détente-Main Stake in the Struggle," *World Marxist Review* (October 1974).

Sakharov, Andrei Dimitrievich. *My Country and the World.* New York: Knopf, 1975.

Sheldon, Della W. ed. *Dimensions of Détente.* New York: Praeger Publishers, 1978.

Sobel, Lester A. ed. *Kissinger and Détente.* New York: Facts On File, 1975.

Stessinger, John George. *Nation in Darkness—China, Russia and America.* New York: 1975.

Strauss, David. *Menace in the West: The Rise of French Anti-Americanism in Modern Times.* Westport, Conn.: Greenwood Press, 1978.

Africa

Arkhurst, Frederick S., ed. *U.S. Policy toward Africa.* New York: Praeger Publishers, 1975.

Packenham, Robert A. *Liberal America and the Third World: Political Development Ideas in Foreign Aid and Social Science.* Princeton, N.J.: Princeton University Press, 1973.

U.S. National Security Council, Interdepartmental Group for Africa, *The Kissinger Study of Southern Africa: National Security Study Memorandum 39 (Secret)*. Westport, Conn.: Greenwood Press, 1976.

Defense

The problem of resolving defense needs with détente was the major focus of policy formulation in the Nixon/Ford years. Détente meant an easing of tensions between Moscow and Washington, but critics were fearful that the United States was giving away too much and that the Soviets would gain an advantage. A monograph, directed to the general public, that discusses the issue in global terms is Drew Middleton's *Retreat from Victory* (New York: Hawthorn Books, 1973). A pessimistic theme is pursued by Rudolph J. Rummel in *Peace Endangered: The Reality of Détente* (Beverly Hills, Sage Publications, 1976). The questions of adjusting defense options to foreign policy is assessed by Morton H. Halperin, *Defense Strategies for the Seventies* (Boston: Little, Brown, 1971).

Alarmed by the magnitude of global weapons expenditure, Henry Kissinger calls for clearly defined doctrines and a new international order to deal with the problem in the second edition of his *Nuclear Weapons and Foreign Policy* (New York: Norton, 1969). Adding credence to Kissinger's claim is *World Military Expenditures and Arms Control Transfers 1967–1976* (Washington, GPO, 1978), issued by the United States Arms Control and Disarmament Agency. The volume is an invaluable source of statistical data, revealing the amount of money spent by each nation on its military establishment. An excellent analysis of American and Soviet capabilities is Edward Luttwack's *The U.S.-U.S.S.R. Nuclear Weapons Balance* (Beverly Hills, Calif.: Sage Publications, 1974). Despite rhetoric to the contrary, the Senate had little influence on the Strategic Arms Limitation Talks (SALT), according to Alan Platt, *The U.S. Senate and Strategic Arms Policy 1969–1977* (Boulder, Colo.: Westview Press, 1978).

The frustration of Vietnam contributed, in part, to the end of the draft and the creation of an all-voluntary army. Two excellent studies of the topic are: Jerald C. Bachman et al., *The All-Volunteer Force: A Study of Ideology in the Military* (Ann Arbor: University of Michigan Press, 1977); and Harry A. Marmion, *A Case against a Volunteer Army* (New York, Quadrangle Books, 1971).

Other Works

Andrews, Craig N. *Foreign Policy and the New American Military*. Beverly Hills, Calif.: Sage Publications, 1974.

Beard, Edmund. *Developing the ICBM: A Study in Bureaucratic Politics*. New York: Columbia University Press, 1976.

Betts, Richard K. *Soldiers, Statesmen and Cold War Crises*. Cambridge, Mass.: Harvard University Press, 1977.

Bezboruah, Monorajan. *U.S. Strategy in the Indian Ocean: The International Response*. New York: Praeger, 1977.

Binkin, Martin. *Support Costs in the Defense Budget: The Submerged One-Third*. Washington, D.C.: Brookings Institution, 1972.

Blechman, Barry M., et al. *The Soviet Military Buildup and U.S. Defense Spending*. Washington, D.C.: Brookings Institution, 1977.

Bletz, Donald F. *The Role of the Military Professional in U.S. Foreign Policy*. New York: Praeger, 1972.

Bottome, Edgar M. *The Missile Gap*. Rutherford, N.J.: Farleigh Dickinson University Press, 1971.

Boyle, Richard. *The Flower of the Dragon: The Breakdown of the U.S. Army in Vietnam*. San Francisco: Ramparts Press, 1972.

Chase, John D. "U.S. Merchant Marine—For Commerce and Defense," *U.S. Naval Institute Proceedings* (May 1976) pp. 133–134.

Clemens, Walter C. *The Superpowers and Arms Control: From Cold War to Interdependence*. Lexington, Mass.: Lexington Books, 1973.

Clough, Ralph N., et al. *The United States, China and Arms Control*. Washington, D.C.: Brookings Institution, 1975.

Coffey, Joseph I. *Strategic Power and National Security*. Pittsburgh, Pa.: University of Pittsburgh Press, 1971.

Congressional Quarterly Staff. *U.S. Defense Policy: A Study of Conflict and the Policy Process*. Boston: Congressional Quarterly, 1977.

Corson, Williams R. *Consequences of Failure*. New York: Norton, 1974.

Cox, Arthur M. *The Dynamics of Détente: How to End the Arms Race*. New York: WW Norton, 1976.

Dvorin, Eugene P., ed. *The Senate's War Powers: Debate on Cambodia from the Congressional Record*. Chicago: Markham Pub. Co., 1971.

Endicott, John E., and Roy W. Stafford. *American Defense Policy*. Baltimore: Johns Hopkins University Press, 1977.

Farley, Philip. *Arms across the Sea*. Washington, D.C.: Brookings Institution, 1978.

Fitzgerald, Frances. *Fire in the Lake: The Vietnamese and the Americans in Vietnam*. Boston: Little, Brown, 1972.

Fox, T. Ronald. *Arming America: How the U.S. Buys Weapons*. Cambridge, Mass.: Harvard University Press, 1974.

Gerhardt, James M. *The Draft and Public Policy*. Columbus: Ohio State University Press, 1971.

Goode, Stephen. *The National Defense System*. New York: Watts, 1972.

Goodpaster, Andrew J. *For the Common Defense*. Lexington, Mass.: Lexington Books, 1977.

Greenbacker, John E. "Where Do We Go from Here?" *U.S. Naval Institute Proceedings* (June, 1976).

Greenwood, John, et al. *American Defense Policy Since 1945: A Preliminary Bibliography*. Lawrence: University Press of Kansas, 1973.

Habib, Philip C. "Department of State Urges Congressional Approval of Agreement with Turkey in Defense Cooperation," *Department of State Bulletin* (October 1976).

Holst, T. T., and W. Schneider, eds. *Why ABM? Policy Issues in the Missile Defense Controversy*. Elmsford, N.Y.: Pergamon Press, 1965.

Johnson, David T., and Barry R. Schneider. *Current Issues in U.S. Defense Policy*. New York: Praeger, 1976.

Kaplan, Morton A., ed. *Isolation or Interdependence? Today's Choices for Tomorrow's World*. New York: Free Press, 1975.

Keelye, John B. *The All-Volunteer Force and American Society*. Charlottesville: University Press of Virginia, 1978.

Lambeth, Benjamin. *Selective Nuclear Options in American and Soviet Strategic Policy*. Santa Monica, Calif.: Rand, 1976.

Lansdeal, Edward G. *In the Midst of Wars: An American's Mission to Southeast Asia*. New York: Harper & Row, 1972.

Lens, Sidney. *The Day before Doomsday*. Garden City, N.Y.: Doubleday. 1977.

Liska, George. *Quest for Equilibrium: America and the Balance of Power on Land and Sea*. Baltimore: Johns Hopkins University Press, 1977.

Littauer, Raphael, and Norman Uphoff, eds. *The Air War in Indochina*. Boston: Beacon Press, 1972.

Long, Franklin A., et al. *Arms, Defense Policy and Arms Control*. New York: W. W. Norton, 1976.

Luttwak, Edward N. "The Defense Budget and Israel" *Commentary* (February, 1975).

Marmion, Harry A. *A Case against a Volunteer Army*. New York: Quadrangle Books, 1971.

Martin, Lawrence, ed. *The Management of Defense*. New York: 1976.

Myrdal, Alva. *The Game of Disarmament: How the United States and Russia Run the Arms Race*. New York: Pantheon, 1977.

Nathan, James A., and James K. Oliver. "Public Opinion and U.S. Security Policy," *Armed Forces and Society* (January 1975).

Owen, David. *The Politics of Defense*. New York: Taplinger, 1972.

Palmer, Bruce, Jr., and Tarr Curtis. "A Careful Look at Defense Manpower," *Military Review* (September 1976).

Philips, David Morris. "Foreign Investment in the United States: The Defense Industry," *Boston University Law Review* (November 1976).

Quanbeck, Alton H., and Barry M. Blechman. *Strategic Forces: Issues for the Mid-Seventies.* Washington, D.C.: Brookings Institution, 1973.

Reeves, Thomas, and Karl Hess. *The End of the Draft.* New York: Random House, 1970.

Russett, Bruce M. *What Price Vigilance: The Burden of National Defense.* New Haven, Conn.: Yale University Press, 1970.

Schlesinger, James R. "A Testing Time for America," *Fortune* (Spring 1976 75–77, 147–153).

Smith, Clyde A. "Constraints of Naval Geography on Soviet Naval Power," *Naval War College Review* (February 1974).

"U.S. Defense Policy and the B-1 Bomber Controversy: Pros and Cons," *Congressional Digest* (December 1976).

Useem, Michael. *Conscription, Protest and Social Conflict.* New York: Wiley & Sons, 1973.

Weidenbaum, Murray L. *The Economics of Peacetime Defense.* New York: Praeger, 1974.

Business, Labor, and Economic Policy

An excessive rate of inflation played havoc with the U.S. economy through the mid-1970s. The Nixon and Ford administrations chose to deal with the problem in traditional conservative fashion, except for Nixon's efforts at controls in the early 1970s. Critics spoke of "Nixonomics": recession and inflation. In his *Nixonomics: How the Dismal Science of Free Enterprise Became the Bleak Art of Controls* (New York: Praeger Publishers, 1972), Leonard S. Silk explores Nixon's basic economic conservatism, analyzing the factors, including the desire for reelection, that resulted in the president's intervention in the economy. The economic problems of the 1970s are traced to the Vietnam War by Robert W.

Stevens in *Vain Hopes, Grim Realities: The Economic Consequences of the Vietnam War* (New York: New Viewpoints, 1976). Stevens argued that both Presidents Johnson and Nixon made errors in economic planning because of the war. The Vietnam War ruined chances for a full-employment cycle and a successful campaign against poverty and left a devalued dollar and a large future expenditure commitment. Whatever the cause of inflation, it remained the central problem from which all others—unemployment, recession, and a confused international monetary situation—arose, according to conservative economist Ezra Solomon. *The Anxious Economy* (San Francisco: W. H. Freeman, 1975). On the other hand, Keynesian economist Walter Heller, *The Economy: Old Myths and New Realities* (New York: Norton, 1976) concludes that contemporary economic problems were the result of traditional Republican Party policy aggravated by OPEC decisions to increase crude oil prices.

Other Works

Abel, I. W. *Labor's Role in Building a Better Society.* Austin: Bureau of Business Research, University Press of Texas at Austin, 1972.

Albin, Peter S. *Progress Without Poverty: Socially Responsible Economic Growth.* New York: Basic Books, 1978.

Bach, George L. *Making Monetary and Fiscal Policy.* Washington, D.C.: Brookings Institution, 1971.

Backman, Jules. *Business Problems of the Seventies.* New York: New York University Press, 1973.

Bauer, Raymond A., et al. *American Business and Public Policy: The Politics of Foreign Trade.* Chicago: Aldine, Atherton, 1972.

Bergsten, C. Fred. *Toward a New International Economic Order: Selected Papers of C. Fred Bergsten, 1971–1974.* Lexington, Mass.: Lexington Books, 1975.

Berman, Peter I. *Inflation and the Money Supply in the United States, 1956–1977.* Lexington, Mass.: Lexington Books, 1978.

Boulding, Kenneth, et al. *From Abundance to Scarcity: Implication for the American Tradition.* Columbus: Ohio State University Press, 1978.

Brandis, Royall, comp. *Current Economic Problems: A Book of Readings.* Homewood, Ill.: R. D. Irwin, 1972.

Brenner, Philip, comp. *Exploring Contradictions; Political Economy in the Corporate State.* New York: D. McKay, 1974.

Brookstone, Jeffrey M. *The Multinational Businessman and Foreign Policy: Entrepreneural Politics in East-West Trade and Investment.* New York: Praeger, 1976.

Cagan, Phillip, and Robert E. Tipsey. *The Financial Effects of Inflation.* Cambridge, Mass.: Ballinger Pub. Co., 1978.

Carson, Robert B. *Government in the American Economy: Conventional and Radical Studies on the Growth of State Economic Power.* Lexington, Mass.: Heath, 1973.

Congressional Quarterly Staff. *The U.S. Economy: Challenges in the '70's.* Washington: Congressional Quarterly, 1972.

Dahlberg, Arthur Olaus. *How to Save Free Enterprise.* Old Greenwich, Conn.: Devin-Adair Co., 1974.

Diebold, William. *The United States and the Industrial World: American Foreign Economic Policy in the 1970's.* New York: Praeger, 1972.

Eckstein, Otto. *Parameters and Policies in the U.S. Economy.* New York: American Elsevier Pub. Co., 1975.

Eyestone, Robert. *Political Economy: Politics and Policy Analysis.* Chicago: Markham Pub. Co., 1972.

Fatemi, Nasrollah S., ed. *Problems of Balance of Payment and Trade.* Rutherford, N.J.: Farleigh Dickinson University Press, 1974.

Fellner, William J., et al. *Correcting Taxes for Inflation.* Washington: American Enterprise Institute for Public Policy Research, 1975.

Friedman, Milton. *There's No Such Thing as a Free Lunch.* La Salle, Ill.: Open Court, 1975.

Galbraith, John Kenneth. *Economics and the Public Purpose.* Boston: Houghton Mifflin Co., 1973.

———. *The New Industrial State.* Boston: Houghton Mifflin Co., 1978.

Goldman, Marshall I. *Détente and Dollars: Doing Business with the Soviets.* New York: Basic Books, 1975.

Graham, Otis L. *Toward a Planned Society: From Roosevelt to Nixon.* New York: Oxford University Press, 1976.

Harrington, Michael. *The Twilight of Capitalism.* New York: Simon and Schuster, 1976.

Harris, Fred R. *The New Populism.* New York: Saturday Review Press, 1973.

Jensen, Ralph. *Let Me Say This about That: A Primer on Nixonomics.* New York: Holt, Rinehart and Winston, 1972.

Keyserling, Leon H. *Full Employment without Inflation.* Washington, D.C.: Conference on Economic Progress, 1975.

Lanzillotti, Robert F., et al. *Phase II in Review: The Price Commission Experience.* Washington, D.C.: Brookings Institution, 1975.

La Velle, Michael. *Red, White and Blue-Collar Views: A Steelworker Speaks His Mind about America.* New York: Saturday Review Press, 1975.

Leasure, J. William. *Prices, Profit and Production: How Much Is Enough?* Albuquerque: University of New Mexico Press, 1974.

Leng, Shao-chuan, ed. *Post-Mao China and U.S.-China Trade.* Charlottesville: University Press of Virginia, 1977.

Levison, Andrew. *The Working Class Majority.* New York: Coward, McCann & Geoghegan, 1974.

Levitan, Sari, and Robert Taggart. *The Promise of Greatness.* Cambridge, Mass.: Harvard University Press, 1976.

Levy, Harold. "Civil Rights in Employment and the Multinational Corporations," *Cornell International Law Journal* (December 1976) vol. 10.

Mayer, Joseph. "Inflation Fancies versus Facts," *Social Science* (December 1973).

Meany, George. "Common Sense in Labor Law," *Labor Law Journal* (October 1976).

Miller, Roger LeRoy, and Raburn M. Williams, *The New Economics of Richard Nixon: Freezes, Floats and Fiscal Policy*. New York: Harper's Magazine Press, 1972.

Morrison, Rodney J. *Expectations and Inflation: Nixon, Politics and Economics*. Lexington, Mass.: Lexington Books, 1973.

Moynihan, Daniel P., et al. *Business and Society in Change*. New York: American Telephone and Telegraph Co., 1975.

National Urban Coalition. *Counterbudget: A Blueprint for Changing National Priorities 1971–1976*. New York: National Urban Coalition, 1971.

Nixon, Richard Milhous. *Setting The Course, The First Years*. New York: Funk & Wagnalls, 1970.

Nothstein, Gary Z., and Jeffrey P. Ayers. "The Multinational Corporation and the Extraterritorial Application of the Labor Management Relations Act," *Cornell International Law Journal* (December 1976) vol 10, no. 1.

Parker, James E. "Inflation's Impact on Corporate Tax Rates," *Taxes* (September 1976) pp. 580–586.

Pohlman, Jerry E. *Inflation under Control?* Reston, Va.: Reston Pub. Co., 1976.

Popkin, Joel, ed. *Analysis of Inflation: 1965–1974*. Cambridge, Mass.: Ballinger Pub. Co., 1977.

Reynolds, Floyd G., comp. *Current Issues of Economic Policy*. Homewood, Ill.: R.D. Irwin, 1973.

Rostow, Walt W. *Getting from Here to There*. New York: McGraw-Hill, 1978.

Scheer, Robert. *America after Nixon; The Age of the Multinationals*. New York: McGraw-Hill, 1974.

Schultze, Charles L. "Inflation and Unemployment: The Dilemma of the Humphrey-Hawkins Jobs Bill," *Wage-Price Law and Economic Review* (January 1976).

Sichel, Werner, ed. *Economic Advice and Executive Policy: Recommendations from Past Members of the Council of Economic Advisers*. New York: Praeger, 1977.

Simon, William E. *A Time for Truth*. New York: Berkley Pub. Co., 1978.

Smith, Allen W. *Understanding Inflation and Unemployment*. Chicago: Nelson-Hall, 1976.

Sommers, Albert T. *Answers to Inflation and Recession: Economic Policies for a Modern Society*. New York: Conference Board, 1975.

———. *The Widening Cycle: An Examination of U.S. Experience with Stabilization Policy in the Last Decade*. New York: Conference Board, 1975.

Twight, Charlotte. *America's Emerging Fascist Economy*. New Rochelle, N.Y.: Arlington House Publishers, 1975.

Weidenbaum, Murray L. *The Economics of Peacetime Defense*. New York: Praeger, 1974.

———. *Government-Mandated Price Increases: A Neglected Aspect of Inflation*. Washington, D.C.: American Enterprise Institute for Public Policy Research, 1975.

Woodruff, William. *America's Impact on the World: A STudy of the Role of the United States in the World Economy, 1750–1970*. New York: Wiley, 1975.

Young, John Parke. *An American Alternative: Steps toward a More Workable and Equitable Economy*. Los Angeles: Crescent Publications, 1976.

Social Dissent, Civil Rights, and the Women's Movement

Student protest marked the late 1960s and early 1970s. The protests ranged from antiwar discontent to demands for continued civil rights progress and attacks upon the corporate state. Excellent surveys of the protest movement include Irwin Unger, *The Movement: A History of the American New Left 1959–1972* (New York: Addison-Wesley, 1974) and James L. Wood, *Political Consciousness and Student Activism* (Beverly Hills: Sage, 1974). Charles A. Reich's *The Greening of America* (New York: Crown Publishing Group, 1970) describes the student revolution as an effort to overcome the dominance of the corporate state and make the nation more livable. A valuable study of the draft defectors from their initial resistance to their life in Canada is Roger N. Williams, *The New Exiles; American War Resisters in Canada* (New York: Liveright Publishing Corp., 1971).

In the areas of civil rights and federal aid to the poor, the Nixon and Ford administrations did not receive high marks. Lawrence N. Bailis in *Bread or Justice* (Lexington, 1974) traces the development of welfare rights groups since the 1960s. A more recent study is Francis Piven and Richard A. Cloward, *Poor People's Movement: Why They Succeed: How They Fail* (New York: Knopf, 1977). Peter H. Ross et al., *The Roots of Urban Discontent* (New York: John Wiley & Sons, 1974) provides an analysis of the reasons why ghetto dwellers continued to mistrust politicians and municipal institutions.

Black inequality was still an area of discontent in 1976. An attack upon Nixon's first years in the White House is Leon E. Panetta and Peter Gall, *Bring Us Together: The Nixon Team and the Civil Rights Retreat* (Philadelphia: J. B. Lippincott, 1971). Less militant but pessimistic is Charles S. Bullock and Harrell R. Rodgers, *Racial Equality in America* (Pacific Palisades: Scott Foresman & Co., 1975). Bayard Rustin's *Strategies for Freedom: The Changing Patterns of Black Protest* (New York: Columbia University Press, 1976) noted that much had been done regarding social inequities and recommended that future efforts be directed toward economic gains.

Women's rights emerged as a formidable movement during the time period. A comprehensive survey emphasizing the recent period is Barbara S. Deckard's *The Women's Movement: Political, Socio-Economic, and Psychological Issues* (New York: Addison-Wesley, 1975). The range of women's views on their quest for equality can be found in Leslie Tanner, ed., *Voices from Women's Liberation* (New York: Signet, 1971). The difficulties of overcoming the social and psychological impact of the past is the central theme of Gayle G. Yates's *What Women Want: The Ideas of the Movement* (Cambridge, Mass.: Harvard Univ. Press, 1975).

Social Dissent

Adams, Elsie B., and Mary L. Briscoe. *Up against the Wall, Mother.* Beverly Hills: Glencoe Press, 1971.

Adams, Michael Vannoy, "From Texas to Sussex: An Odyssey of Campus Protest," *Encounter* (January 1975) pp. 83–89.

Altbach, Philip G. *Student Politics in America: A Historical Analysis.* New York: McGraw-Hill, 1973.

Arendt, Hannah. *Crises of the Republic; Lying in Politics, Civil Disobedience, on Violence, Thoughts on Politics, and Revolution.* New York: Harcourt Brace Jovanovich, 1972.

Bacciocco, Edward J. *The New Left in America: Reform to Revolution, 1956 to 1970.* Stanford, Calif.: Hoover Institution Press, 1974.

Bannan, John F., and Rosemary S. *Law, Morality and Vietnam: The Peace Militants and the Courts.* Bloomington: Indiana University Press, 1974.

Berrigan, Daniel. *The Dark Night of Resistance.* Garden City, N.Y.: Doubleday, 1971.

Bingham, Jonathan B., and Alfred M. *Violence and Democracy.* New York: World Pub. Co., 1970.

Bowers, John W., and Donovan J. Ochs. *The Rhetoric of Agitation and Control.* Reading, Mass.: Addison-Wesley Pub. Co., 1971.

Cantor, Milton. *The Divided Left: American Radicalism, 1900–1975.* New York: Hill and Wang, 1978.

Chomsky, Noam. *For Reasons of State.* New York: Pantheon Books, 1973.

Christy, Jim. *The New Refugees: American Voices in Canada.* Toronto: Peter Martin Associates, 1972.

Cohane, John P. *White Papers of an Outraged Conservative.* Indianapolis: Bobbs-Merrill, 1972.

Cutler, Richard L. *The Liberal Middle Class: Maker of Radicals.* New Rochelle, N.Y.: Arlington House, 1973.

Decter, Midge. *Liberal Parents, Radical Children.* New York: Coward, McCann & Geoghegan, 1975.

Dellinger, David T. *More Power Than We Know: The People's Movement toward Democracy* Garden City, N.Y.: Anchor Press, 1975.

Dolbeare, Kenneth M., and Patricia Dolbeare. *American Ideologies: The Competing Political Beliefs of the 1970's.* Chicago: Markham Pub. Co., 1971.

Emerick, Kenneth Fred. *War Resisters Canada.* Knox: Pennsylvania Free Press, 1972.

Erskine, Hazel. "Civil Liberties and the American Public," *Journal of Social Issues* (Spring 1975) vol. 31, no. 2, pp. 12–29.

Evans, Mark. *Will the Real Young America Please Stand Up? The Until Now Silent, Youthful Majority's Call for a Return to the Traditional Principles That Made This Country Great.* Harrisburg, Pa.: Stackpole Books, 1973.

Flacks, Richard. *Youth and Social Change.* Chicago: Markham Pub. Co., 1971.

Gerzon, Mark. *The Whole World Is Watching: A Young Man Looks at Youth's Dissent.* New York: Popular Library, 1969.

Gore, Albert. *The Eye of the Storm; A People's Politics of the Seventies.* New York: Herder and Herder, 1970.

Graubard, Mark A. *Campustown in the Throes of the Counterculture (1968–1972).* Minneapolis, Minn.: Campus Scope Press, 1974.

Hatfield, Mark O., et al. *Amnesty? The Unsettled Question of Vietnam.* Croton-on-Hudson, N.Y.: Sun River Press, 1973.

Heath, G. Louis, ed. *Mutiny Does Not Happen Lightly: The Literature of the American Resistance.* Metuchen, N.J.: Scarecrow Press, 1976.

———. *Vandals in the Bomb Factory: The History and Literature of the Students for a Democratic Society.* Metuchen, N.J.: Scarecrow Press, 1976.

Hendel, Samuel, comp. *The Politics of Confrontation.* New York: Appleton-Century-Crofts, 1971.

Horowitz, Irving Louis. *The Struggle Is the Message: The Organization and Ideology of the Anti-War Movement.* Berkeley, Calif.: Glendessary Press, 1970.

Jacquency, Mona G. *Radicalism on Campus: 1969–1971; Backlash in Law Enforcement and in the Universities.* New York: Philosophical Library, 1972.

Kasinsky, Renee G. *Refugees from Militarism: Draft-Age Americans in Canada.* New Brunswick, N.J.: Transaction Books, 1976.

Keniston, Kenneth. *Youth and Dissent; The Rise of the New Opposition.* New York: Harcourt Brace Jovanovich, 1971.

Killmer, Richard L., et al. *They Can't Go Home Again: The Story of America's Political Refugees.* Philadelphia: United Church Press, 1971.

Kruger, Marlis, and Frieda Silvert. *Dissent Denied: The Technocratic Response to Protest.* New York: Elsevier, 1975.

Lipset, Seymour Martin. *Rebellion in the University.* Boston: Little, Brown, 1971.

Murphy, Jeeire G., comp. *Civil Disobedience and Violence.* Belmont, Calif.: Wadsworth Pub. Co., 1971.

Ramparts Magazine Editors. *Divided We Stand.* San Francisco: Canfield Press, 1970.

Reitman, Alan. *The Pulse of Freedom; American Liberties: 1920–1970s.* New York: WW Norton, 1975.

Rice, Donald F., comp. *The Agitator: A Collection of Diverse Opinions from America's Not-So-Popular Press.* Chicago: American Library Association, 1972.

Rinzler, Alan, ed. *Manifesto Addressed to the President of the United States from the Youth of America.* New York: Macmillan, 1970.

Sale, Kirkpatrick. *SDS.* New York: Random House, 1973.

Salisbury, Harrison E., comp. *The Indignant Years: Art and Articles from the Op-Ed Page of the New York Times.* New York: Crown/ Arno Press, 1973.

Samberg, Paul, ed. *Fire! Reports from the Underground Press.* New York: E.P. Dutton, 1970.

Stiehm, Judith. *Nonviolent Power: Active and Passive Resistance in America.* Lexington, Mass.: Lexington Books, 1972.

Taylor, Clyde, comp. *Vietnam and Black America: An Anthology of Protest and Resistance.* Garden City, N.Y.: Anchor Press, 1973.

Useem, Michael. *Protest Movements in America.* Indianapolis, Ind.: Bobbs-Merrill, 1975.

Civil Rights

Bardolph, Richard. *The Civil Rights Record: Black Americans and the Law, 1849–1970.* New York: Crowell, 1970.

Bender, Paul. "The Reluctant Court," *Civil Liberties Review* (June/July 1975).

Bickel, Alexander M. *The Supreme Court and the Idea of Progress.* New York: Harper & Row, 1970.

Billington, Monroe Lee. *The Political South in the Twentieth Century.* New York: Scribner, 1975.

Black, Earl. *Southern Governors and Civil Rights.* Cambridge, Mass.: Harvard University Press, 1976.

Bond, Julian. *A Time to Speak, A Time to Act.* New York: Simon and Schuster, 1972.

Brooks, Thomas R. *Walls Come Tumbling Down: A History of the Civil Rights Movement, 1940–1970.* Englewood Cliffs, N.J.: Prentice Hall, 1974.

Button, James W. *Black Violence: Political Impact of the 1960s Riots.* Princeton, N.J.: Princeton University Press, 1978.

Commission on Civil Rights, "Twenty Years after Brown: Equal Opportunity in Housing," Washington: The Commission, 1975.

Davis, Angela Yvonne. *Angela Davis: An Autobiography.* New York: Random House, 1974.

Draper, Theodore. *The Rediscovery of Black Nationalism.* New York: Viking Press, 1970.

Fogelson, Robert M. *Violence as Protest: A Study of Riots and Ghettos.* Garden City, N.Y.: Doubleday, 1971.

Forman, James. *The Making of Black Revolutionaries.* New York: Macmillan, 1972.

Franklin, John Hope. *Racial Equality in America.* Chicago: University of Chicago Press, 1976.

Gregory, Dick. *Up from Nigger.* New York: Stein and Day, 1976.

Jackson, George. *Blood in My Eye.* New York: Random House, 1972.

Jackson, Larry R., and William A. Johnson. *Protest by the Poor: The Welfare Rights Movement in New York City.* Lexington, Mass.: Lexington Books, 1974.

Killian, Lewis M. *The Impossible Revolution, Phase II: Black Power and the American Dream.* New York: Random House, 1975.

Kotz, Nick, and Mary Lynn Kotz. *A Passion for Equality: George A. Wiley and the Movement.* New York: WW Norton, 1977.

Kousser, J. Morgan. *The Shaping of Southern Politics.* New Haven, Conn.: Yale University Press, 1974.

Newton, Huey P. *Revolutionary Suicide.* New York: Harcourt Brace Jovanovich, 1973.

Parris, Guichard, and Lester Brooks. *Blacks in the City: A History of the National Urban League.* Boston: Little, Brown, 1971.

Roberts, Sylvia. "Equality of Opportunity in Higher Education: Impact of Contract Compliance and the Equal Rights Amendment," *Liberal Education* (Spring 1973).

Rustin, Bayard. *Down the Line.* Chicago: Quadrangle Books, 1971.

Seale, Bobby. *A Lonely Rage: The Autobiography of Bobby Seale.* New York: Bantam Books, 1978.

Wolk, Allan. *The Presidency and Black Civil Rights: Eisenhower to Nixon.* Rutherford, N.J.: Farleigh Dickinson University Press, 1971.

The Women's Movement

Altbach, Edith H., comp. *From Feminism to Liberation.* Cambridge, Mass.: Schenkman Pub. Co., 1971.

Amundsen, Kirsten. *The Silenced Majority: Women and American Democracy.* Englewood Cliffs, N.J.: Prentice Hall, 1971.

Andreas, Carol. *Sex and Caste in America.* Englewood Cliffs, N.J.: Prentice Hall, 1971.

Babcox, Deborah, and Madeline Belkin. *Liberation Now!* New York: Dell Pub. Co., 1971.

Blahna, Loretta J. *The Rhetoric of the Equal Rights Amendments.* Lawrence: University of Kansas Press, 1973.

Brady, David W., and Kent L. Tedin. "Ladies in Pink: Religion and Political Ideology in the Anti-ERA Movement," *Social Science Quarterly* (March 1976)

Brown, Barbara A., et al. *Women's Rights and the Law: The Impact of ERA on State Laws.* New York: Praeger, 1977.

Chesler, Phyllis, and Emily Jane Goodman. *Women, Money and Power.* New York: Morrow, 1976.

Decter, Midge. *The Liberated Woman and Other Americans.* New York: Coward, McCann & Geoghegan, 1971.

Flexner, Eleanor. *Century of Struggle: The Women's Rights Movement in the United States.* Cambridge, Mass.: Belknap Press of Harvard University Press, 1975.

Foss, Sonja Kay. *A Fantasy Theme Analysis of the Rhetoric of the Debate on the Equal Rights Amendment, 1970–1976: Toward a Theory of Rhetoric Movements.* Evanston, Ill.: Northwestern University Press, 1976.

Freeman, Jo. *The Politics of Women's Liberation: A Case Study of an Emerging Social Movement and Its Relation to the Policy Process.* New York: 1975, McKay.

Giele, Janet Z. *Women and the Future: Changing Sex Roles in Modern America.* New York: Free Press, 1978.

Ginsburg, Ruth Bader. "The Need for the Equal Rights Amendment," *American Bar Association Journal* (September 1973).

Sedwick, Cathy, and Reba Williams. "Black Women and the Equal Rights Amendment," *Black Scholar* (July/August 1976) vol. 7, no. 10, pp. 24–29.

U.S. Senate, Subcommittee on Constitutional Amendments. *Women and the "Equal Rights" Amendment.* New York: R.R. Bowker Co., 1972.

Wohl, Lisa Cronin. "White Gloves and Combat Boots. The Fight for ERA," *Civil Liberties Review* (April 1974).

Watergate

The break-in at the Democratic National Committee's headquarters in the Watergate office complex resulted in a large-scale investigation of crimes linked to the White House, which became collectively known as the Watergate affair. Sensing possible impeachment and removal from office, President Richard Nixon resigned in August 1974. The incident has produced an abundance of literature, usually of a sensational nature. In *All the President's Men* (New York: William Morrow & Co., 1974), *Washington Post* reporters Carl Bernstein and Robert Woodward tell how they uncovered the story behind the Watergate break-in. The book holds a distinguished place in any Watergate history. Many participants in illegal and extralegal White House activities have published their memoirs, including John W. Dean, *Blind Ambition: The White House Years* (New York: Simon & Schuster, 1977): H. R. Haldeman, *The Ends of Power* (New York: Crown, 1978); and Jeb Stuart Magruder, *An American Life* (Paterson: Atheneum, 1974). These personal accounts narrate similar stories. Special Watergate Prosecutor Leon Jaworski's *The Right and the Power: The Prosecution of Watergate* (New York: Reader's Digest, 1977) weaves trial briefs and other documents into a narrative about how the prosecutor successfully pursued evidence of the Watergate cover-up. The efforts of the special prosecutor's office to obtain White House materials used in the trials of presidential assistants are told by Richard Ben-Veniste and George Frampton in their *Stonewall* (New York: Simon & Schuster, 1977). A personal story about the workings of the Senate Select Committee on Presidential Campaign Activities is Samuel Dash's *Chief Counsel: Inside the Ervin Committee—The Untold*

Story of Watergate (New York: Random House, 1976). Following the Watergate affair many proposals to limit executive power were made. These proposals are challenged by Theodore C. Sorenson in *Watchman in the Night: Presidential Accountability after Watergate* (Cambridge, Mass.: MIT Press, 1975).

Other Works

Anderson, John B. *Vision and Betrayal in America.* Waco, Tex.: Word Books, 1975.

Ball, Howard. *No Pledge of Privacy: The Watergate Tapes Litigation.* Port Washington, N.Y.: Kennikat Press, 1977.

Bromwell, Dana G. *The Tragedy of King Richard: Shakespearean Watergate.* Salina, Kan.: Survey Publishers, 1974.

Boyd, Marjorie. "The Watergate Story: Why Congress Didn't Investigate until after the Election," *Washington Monthly* (February 1973).

Candee, Dan. "The Moral Psychology of Watergate," *Journal of Social Issues* (Spring 1975) vol. 31, no. 2, 183–192.

Caraley, Demetrios. "Separation of Powers and Executive Privilege: The Watergate Briefs," *Political Science Quarterly* (December 1973) vol 120, no. 3.

Cohen, Alden. *The Women of Watergate.* New York: Stein and Day, 1975.

Cohen, Jacob. "Conspiracy Fever," *Commentary* (April 1975).

Colson, Charles W. *Born Again.* Tappan, N.J.: Chosen Books, Inc., 1976.

Conrad, Paul. *The King and Us: Editorial Cartoons.* Los Angeles: Clymer Publications, 1974.

Congressional Quarterly Staff. *Watergate: Chronology of a Crisis.* Washington, D.C.: Congressional Quarterly, Inc., 1975.

Cox, Archibald. "Watergate and the Constitution of the United States," *University of Toronto Law Journal* (Spring 1976).

Dean, Maureen. *"Mo": A Woman's View of Watergate.* New York: Bantam Books, 1975.

Drew, Elizabeth. *Washington Journal: The Events of 1973–1974.* New York: Random House, 1975.

Evans, Les, and Allen Myers. *Watergate and the Myth of American Democracy.* New York: Pathfinder Press, 1974.

Friedman, Leon, comp. *United States v. Nixon: The President before the Supreme Court.* New York: Chelsea House Publishers, 1974.

Halpern, Paul J., ed. *Why Watergate?* Pacific Palisades: Palisades Pub., 1975.

Harrell, Jackson. "Failure of Apology in American Politics: Nixon on Watergate," *Speech Monographs* (Winter 1975).

Hendel, Samuel. "Separation of Powers Revisited in Light or 'Watergate'" *Western Political Quarterly* (December 1974).

Higgins, George V. *The Friends of Richard Nixon.* Boston: Little, Brown, 1975.

Hunt, Howard. *Undercover: Memoirs of an American Secret Agent.* New York: Putnam, 1974.

Hurst, James Willard. "Watergate: Some Basic Issues," *Center Magazine* (January 1974) pp. 11–25.

Knappman, Edward W., ed. *Watergate and the White House,* 3 vols. New York: Facts On File, 1973–1974.

Kurland, Philip B. *Watergate and the Constitution.* Chicago: University of Chicago Press, 1978.

Lasky, Victor. *It Didn't Start with Watergate.* New York: Dial Press, 1977.

Lukas, J. Anthony. *Nightmare: The Under Side of the Nixon Years, 1969–1974.* New York: Viking Press, 1976.

Lurie, Leonard. *The Impeachment of Richard Nixon.* New York: Berkley Pub. Corp., 1973.

McGeever, Patrick J. "Guilty, Yes; Impeachment, No," *Political Science Quarterly* (June 1974) pp. 289–299.

Magruder, Jeb S. *An American Life: One Man's Road to Watergate.* New York: Atheneum, 1974.

Mankiewicz, Frank. *U.S. v. Richard M. Nixon: The Final Crisis.* New York: Ballantine, 1975.

Myers, Robert J. *The Tragedies of King Richard, the Second; The Life and Times of Richard II (1367–1400), King of England (1377–1399), Compared to Those of Richard of America in His Second Administration.* Washington: Acropolis Books, 1973.

Moseley, Clifton L. *John Smith Views Watergate.* Memphis: Capsule Volume Series, 1974.

Mosher, Frederick C. *Watergate: Implications for Responsible Government.* New York: Basic Books, 1974.

New York Times Staff. *The End of a Presidency.* New York: Holt, Rinehart and Winston, 1974.

New York Times Staff. *The Watergate Hearings: Break-in and Cover-up; Proceedings of the Senate Select Committee on Presidential Campaign Activities.* New York: Bantam Books, 1973.

Nixon, Richard M. *Submission of Recorded Presidential Conversations to the Committee on the Judiciary of the House of Representatives.* Washington, D.C.: U.S. News & World Report, 1974.

Osborne, John. *The Fifth Year of the Nixon Watch.* New York: Liveright, 1974.

Pynn, Ronald, comp. *Watergate and the American Political Process.* New York: Praeger, 1975.

Ripon Society, and Clifford W. Brown, Jr. *Jaws of Victory: The Game-Plan Politics of 1972, the Crisis of the Republican Party, and the Future of the Constitution.* Boston: Little, Brown, 1974.

Robinson, Michael J. "The Impact of the Televised Watergate Hearings," *Journal of Communications* (Spring 1974) pp. 17–30.

Rosenberg, Kenyon C., and Judith K. *Watergate: An Annotated Bibliography* Littleton, Colo.: Libraries, unlimited, 1975.

Royster, Vermont. "The Public Morality: Afterthoughts on Watergate," *American Scholar* (Spring 1974).

Saffell, David C., comp. *Watergate: Its Effects on the American Political System.* Cambridge, Mass.: Winthrop Publishers, 1974.

Shannon, William. *They Could Not Trust the King: Nixon, Watergate and the American People.* New York: Macmillian Publishing Co., 1974.

Sobel, Lester A., comp. *Money and Politics: Contributions, Campaign Abuses and the Law.* New York: Facts On File, 1974.

Stein, Howard F. "The Silent Complicity at Watergate," *American Scholar* (Winter 1973).

"Table Talk: A British View of Watergate," *Center Magazine* (June 1974).

Thompson, Fred D. *At That Point in Time: The Inside Story of the Senate Watergate Committee.* New York: Quadrangle/New York Times Book Co., 1975.

U.S. Department of Justice. *Watergate Special Prosecution Force, Final Report.* Washington, D.C.: 1977.

U.S. House of Representatives. *Independent Special Prosecutor.* Washington, D.C.: 1973.

———. Committee on the Judiciary. *Comparison of White House and Judiciary Transcripts of Eight Recorded Presidential Conversations.* Washington, D.C.: 1974.

———. *Impeachment Inquiry.* Washington, D.C.: 1975.

———. *Testimony of Witnesses.* Washington, D.C.: 1974.

———. *Transcripts of Eight Recorded Presidential Conversations.* Washington: 1974.

———, Special Subcommittee on Intelligence. *Inquiry into the Alleged Involvement of Central Intelligence Agency in the Watergate and Ellsberg Matters.* Washington, D.C.: 1975.

———. Subcommittee on Criminal Justice. *Authority to Issue Final Report by Special Prosecutor.* Washington: 1975.

———. *Pardon of Richard Nixon and Related Matters.* Washington: 1975.

U.S. Senate. *The Final Report of the Select Committee on Presidential Campaign Activities, United States Senate.* Washington: 1974.

———. Select Committee on Presidential Campaign Activities. *Presidential Campaign Activities of 1972.* Washington: 1973.

———. *Presidential Campaign Activities of 1972.* Washington: 1974.

Van, Sickle, Clifford Kenneth. *The Oral Communication of Senator Sam J. Ervin, Jr. in the Watergate Hearings: A Study in Consistency.* Michigan State University, 1976.

Van Hoffman, Nicholas, and Gary Trudeau. *The Fireside Watergate.* New York: Sheed and Ward, 1973.

Washington Post Staff. *The Fall of a President.* New York: Dell Publishing Co., 1974.

"Watergate: Its Implications for Responsible Government," *Administration and Society* (August 1974).

Watergate: The View from the Left. New York: Pathfinder Press, 1973.

Weissman, Stephen R., comp. *Big Brother and the Holding Company. The World behind Watergate.* Palo Alto, Calif.: Ramparts Press, 1974.

White, Theodore H. *Breach of Faith: The Fall of Richard Nixon.* New York: Atheneum, 1975.

Wise, Helen D. *What Do We Tell the Children? Watergate and the Future of Our Country.* New York: G. Braziller, 1974.

FORD AND THE FORD ADMINISTRATION: 1974–1976

a. General Studies

Berman, William C. *America's Right Turn: From Nixon to Bush.* Baltimore: Johns Hopkins University Press, 1994.

Firestone, Bernard J., and Alexej Ugrinsky. *Gerald R. Ford and the Politics of Post-Watergate America, 2 vols.* (Volume 2 contains John Robert Greene, "A Nice Person Who Worked at the Job: The Dilemma of the Ford Image") Westport, Conn.: Greenwood Press, 1993.

Greene, John Robert. *The Limits of Power: The Nixon and Ford Administrations.* Bloomington: Indiana University Press, 1992.

———. *The Presidency of Gerald R. Ford.* Lawrence: University Press of Kansas, 1995.

Hartmann, Robert. *Palace Politics: An Insider's Account of the Ford Years.* New York: McGraw-Hill, 1980.

Hersey, John. *The President.* New York: Knopf, 1975.

Johnson, Richard. "Rediscovering Gerald Ford." *Denver Post Magazine* (January 17, 1993), pp. 12–18.

Kennerly, David Hume. *Shooter.* New York: Newsweek Books, 1979.

Nessen, Ron. *It Sure Looks Different from the Inside.* New York: Playboy Press, 1978.

Porter, Roger B. "Gerald R. Ford: The Healing Presidency." In Fred I. Greenstein, ed., *Leadership in the Modern Presidency.* Cambridge, Mass.: Harvard University Press, 1978.

———. "Ford's Presidency: Brief but Well Run." *New York Times* (May 15, 1988).

Reichley, A. James. *Conservatives in an Age of Change: The Nixon and Ford Administrations.* Washington, D.C.: Brookings Institution, 1981.

Shabecoff, Philip. "Appraising Presidential Power: The Ford Presidency." In Thomas E. Cronin and Rexford G. Tugwell, eds., *The Presidency Appraised,* 2nd ed. Westport, Conn.: Praeger, 1977.

Sidey, Hugh, and Fred Ward. *Portrait of a President.* New York: Harper & Row, 1975.

Thompson, Kenneth W., ed. *The Ford Presidency: Twenty-two Intimate Perspectives of*

Gerald R. Ford. Lanham, Md.: University Press of America, 1988.

b. Historiographical Studies and Bibliographies

Greene, John Robert. *Gerald R. Ford: A Bibliography*. Westport, Conn.: Greenwood Press, 1994.

Lankevich, George J., ed. *Gerald R. Ford: Chronology, Documents, Bibliographical Aids*. Dobbs Ferry, N.Y.: Oceana Publications, 1977.

c. By Gerald R. Ford

Ford, Gerald R. "Why the President Died: The Warren Commission Report—A Participant's View." *California Magazine* (Autumn 1964), 14–15ff.

———. "Impeachment: A Mace for the Federal Judiciary." *Notre Dame Lawyer* 46 (Summer 1974): 669–677.

———. *A Time to Heal: The Autobiography of Gerald R. Ford*. New York: Harper & Row, 1979.

———. "The White House and Congress: Congressional Restraints on Presidential Authority." *Houston Law Review* 21 (May 1984): 447–456.

———. "Attorney General Edward H. Levi." *University of Chicago Law Review* 52 (Spring 1985): 284–289.

———. *Humor and the Presidency*. New York: Arbor House, 1987.

———, and John R. Stiles. *Portrait of the Assassin*. New York: Simon & Schuster, 1965.

d. Biographies of Gerald R. Ford

Aaron, Jan. *Gerald Ford: President of Destiny*. New York: Fleet, 1975.

Cannon, James. *Time and Chance: Gerald Ford's Appointment with Destiny*. New York: Harper-Collins, 1994.

LeRoy, Dave. *Gerald Ford: The Untold Story*. Arlington, Va.: R.W. Beatty, 1974.

Mollenhoff, Clark R. *The Man Who Pardoned Nixon*. New York: St. Martin's Press, 1976.

Reeves, Richard. *A Ford, Not a Lincoln*. New York: Harcourt Brace Jovanovich, 1975.

Schapsmeier, Edward L., and Frederick H. Schapsmeier. *Gerald R. Ford's Date with Destiny: A Political Biography*. New York: Peter Lang Publishing, 1989.

Vestal, Bud. *Jerry Ford, Up Close: An Investigative Biography*. New York: Coward, McCann, & Geohegan, 1974.

e. Cabinet and White House Staff

Casserly, John J. *The Ford White House: The Diary of a Speechwriter*. Boulder: University Press of Colorado, 1977.

Chapel, Gage William. "Speechwriting in the Ford Administration: An Interview with Speech Writer Robert Orben." *Exetasis* (June 15, 1976): 16–17.

Coyne, John R., Jr. *Fall in and Cheer: A Thoughtful, Often Irreverent View of American Politics*. Garden City, N.Y.: Doubleday, 1979.

Feigenbaum, Edward D. "Staffing, Organization, and Decision-Making in the Ford and Carter White Houses." *Presidential Studies Quarterly* 10 (Summer 1980): 364–377.

Haig, Alexander M., Jr. *Inner Circles: How America Changed the World*. New York: Warner Books, 1992.

Hoxie, R. Gordon. "Staffing the Ford and Carter Presidencies." In Bradley D. Nash, ed., *Organizing and Staffing the Presidency*. Washington, D.C.: Center for the Study of the Presidency, 1980.

Kernell, Samuel, and Samuel L. Popkin. *Chief of Staff: Twenty-five Years of Managing the Presidency*. Berkeley: University of California Press, 1986.

Liebetreu, Sharon. "On Robert Hartmann: Ford's Alter Ego." *Michigan Speech Association Journal*, 18 (1983): 26–34.

Medved, Michael. *The Shadow Presidents: The Secret History of the Chief Executives and Their Top Aides*. New York: Times Books, 1979.

Patterson, Bradley. *The Ring of Power*. New York: Basic Books, 1988.

Shearer, Lloyd. "Don Rumsfeld: He's President Ford's Number One Man." *Parade* (February 2, 1975): 4–5ff.

Sidey, Hugh. "Ford's Forgotten Legacy." *Time* (March 25, 1991): 20.

Storing, Herbert J., ed. *The Ford White House.* Lanham, Md.: University Press of America, 1986.

Warshaw, Shirley Anne. "Cabinet Government in the Modern Presidency." In James P. Pfiffner and R. Gordon Hoxie, *The Presidency in Transition.* Washington, D.C.: Center for the Study of the Presidency, 1989.

Wayne, Stephen J. "Running the White House: The Ford Experience." *Presidential Studies Quarterly* (Spring–Summer 1977): 95–101.

———. *The Legislative Presidency.* New York: Harper & Row, 1978.

f. The Pardon of Richard Nixon

Anson, Robert Sam. *Exile: The Unquiet Oblivion of Richard M. Nixon.* New York: Simon & Schuster, 1984.

Ben-Veniste, Richard, and George Frampton, Jr. *Stonewall: The Real Story of the Watergate Prosecution.* New York: Simon & Schuster, 1977.

Cowlishaw, Patrick R. "The Conditional Presidential Pardon." *Stanford Law Review* (November 1975): 149–177.

Doyle, James. *Not above the Law: The Battles of Watergate Prosecutors Cox and Jaworski.* New York: William Morrow, 1977.

Haig, Alexander M., Jr. *Inner Circles: How America Changed the World.* New York: Warner Books, 1992.

Hersh, Seymour. "The Pardon: Nixon, Ford, Haig, and the Transfer of Power." *Atlantic* (August 1983): 55–78.

Humbert, W. H. *The Pardoning Power of the President.* Washington, D.C.: American Council on Public Affairs, 1941.

Jaworski, Leon. *The Right and the Power.* New York: Harper & Row, 1977.

Kutler, Stanley I. *The Wars of Watergate: The Last Crisis of Richard Nixon.* New York: W. W. Norton, 1990.

McClory, Robert. "A Rebuttal: Was the Fix in between Ford and Nixon?" *National Review* (October 14 1983): 1,264–1,272.

Nixon, Richard M. *In the Arena: A Memoir of Victory, Defeat, and Renewal.* New York: Simon & Schuster, 1990.

Rozell, Mark J. "President Ford's Pardon of Richard M. Nixon: Constitutional and Political Considerations." *Presidential Studies Quarterly* (Winter 1994): 121–138.

Williston, Samuel. "Does a Pardon Blot Out Guilt?" *Harvard Law Review* 28 (May 1915): 647–663.

g. Clemency Program for Vietnam Era Draft Evaders—President's Clemency Board (PCB)

Baskir, Lawrence M., and William A. Strauss. "The Wounded Generation." *American Heritage* (April/May 1978): 23–29.

———. *Chance and Circumstance: The Draft, the War, and the Vietnam Generation.* New York: Random House, 1978.

Bell, Bruce D., and Beverly W. Bell. "Desertion and Antiwar Protest: Findings from the Ford Clemency Program." *Armed Forces and Society* 3 (Spring 1977): 433–443.

MacPherson, Myra. *Long Time Passing: Vietnam and the Haunted Generation.* Garden City, N.Y.: Doubleday, 1984.

Presidential Clemency Board: Report to the President. Washington, D.C.: U.S. Government Printing Office, 1975.

U.S. Department of Defense, Office of the Deputy Chief of Staff for Personnel, Department of the Army. *After Action Report. Implementation of President's Clemency Program,* 2 vols. (October 1975).

h. Economic Policy

Ellison, Julian, and Robert S. Browne. "Impact of the 1975 Tax Cut on Income and Employment in the Black Community." *Review of Black Political Economy* 17 (Fall 1988): 5–9.

Hargrove, Irwin C., and Samuel A. Morley, eds. *The President and the Council of Economic Advisors: Interviews with CEA Chairmen.* Boulder, Colo.: Westview Press, 1984.

Ippolito, David S. *Uncertain Legacies: Federal Budget Policy from Roosevelt through Reagan.* Charlottesville: University Press of Virginia, 1990.

Kettl, Donald F. *Leadership at the Fed.* New Haven, Conn.: Yale University Press, 1986.

Mustell, Deborah, and David Lee. "An Economic Overview of Recent Administrations." *Illinois Business Review* 41 (December 1984): 1–3.

Porter, Roger B. *Presidential Decision-Making: The Economic Policy Board.* Cambridge: Cambridge University Press, 1980.

Simon, William E. *A Time for Truth.* New York: Berkley Publishing, 1978.

Sloan, John W. "Economic Policymaking in the Johnson and Ford Administrations." *Presidential Studies Quarterly* (Winter 1990): 111–125.

Sobel, Lester A., ed. *Ford and the Economy.* New York: Facts On File, 1976.

i. New York City Fiscal Crisis

Auletta, Ken. "Who's to Blame for the Fix We're In." *New York* (October 27, 1975): 29–41.

Bailey, Robert W. *The Crisis Regime: The New York City Financial Crisis.* Albany: State University of New York Press, 1984.

Loverd, Richard A. "Presidential Decision-Making during the 1975 New York Financial Crisis: A Conceptual Analysis." *Presidential Studies Quarterly* 21 (Spring 1991): 251–267.

Shalala, Donna, and Carol Bellamy. "A State Saves a City: The New York Case." *Duke Law Journal* (1976): 1,119–1,132.

Shefter, Martin. *Political Crisis/Fiscal Crisis: The Collapse and Revival of New York City.* New York: Basic Books, 1985.

j. Energy Policy

Davis, David Howard. "Energy Policy in the Ford Administration." In David A. Caputo, ed., *The Politics of Policy-Making in America: Five Case Studies.* San Francisco: W. H. Freeman, 1977.

k. Environmental Policy

Whitaker, John C. *Striking a Balance: Environmental and Natural Resource Policy in the Nixon-Ford Years.* Washington, D.C.: American Enterprise Institute for Public Policy Research, 1976.

l. Swine Flu Scare

Begley, Sharon L. "The Failure of the Swine Flu Program." *Yale Journal of Biology and Medicine* 50 (1977): 645–656.

Bernstein, Barton. "The Swine Flu Vaccination Campaign of 1976: Politics, Science, and the Public." *Congress and the Presidency* 10 (Spring 1983): 95–103.

Fielding, Jonathan E., M.D. "Swine Flu Immunization Program Revisited." *American Journal of Law and Medicine* 4 (1978): 35–43.

Neustadt, Richard E., and Harvey Fineberg. *The Epidemic That Never Was: Policy-Making and the Swine Flu Affair.* New York: Vintage Books, 1982.

Silverstein, Arthur. *Pure Politics and Impure Science: The Swine Flu Affair.* Baltimore: Johns Hopkins University Press, 1981.

Wecht, Cyril J., M.D. "The Swine Flu Vaccination Program: Scientific Venture or Political Folly?" *American Journal of Law and Medicine* 3 (1977–1978): 425–445.

m. Supreme Court/Judicial Issues/Nomination of John Paul Stevens

Felkenes, George T. "Domestic Tranquility: President Ford's Policy Positions on Criminal Justice Issues." *Presidential Studies Quarterly* 13, no. 3 (Summer 1993): 519–532.

Ford, Gerald R. "Attorney General Edward H. Levi." *University of Chicago Law Review* 52 (Spring 1985): 284–289.

Kramer, Victor H. "The Case of Justice Stevens: How to Select, Nominate, and Confirm a Justice to the U.S. Supreme Court." *Constitutional Commentary* 7 (Summer 1990): 325–340.

O'Brien, David M. "The Politics of Professionalism: President Gerald R. Ford's Appointment of Justice John Paul Stevens." *Presidential Studies Quarterly* 21 (Winter 1991): 103–126.

Woodward, Bob, and Scott Armstrong. *The Brethren: Inside the Supreme Court.* New York: Simon & Schuster, 1979.

n. Africa/Angolan Civil War

Klinghoffer, Arthur Jay. *The Angolan War: A Study of Soviet Policy in the Third World.* Boulder, Colo.: Westview Press, 1980.

Noer, Thomas J. "International Credibility and Political Survival: The Ford Administration's Intervention in Angola." *Presidential Studies Quarterly* (Fall 1993): 771–786.

Prados, John. *Presidents' Secret Wars: CIA and Pentagon Covert Operations since World War II.* New York: William Morrow, 1986.

Smith, Wayne S. "A Trap in Angola." *Foreign Policy* (Spring 1986): 61–74.

Weissman, Stephen R. "CIA Covert Action in Zaire and Angola: Patterns and Consequences." *Political Science Quarterly* 94 (1979): 263–286.

o. Defense Policies

Kinnard, Douglas. "James R. Schlesinger as Secretary of Defense." *Naval War College Review* 32 (1979): 22–34.

Laird, Melvin R. "A Strong Start in a Difficult Decade: Defense Policy in the Nixon-Ford Years." *International Security* (Fall 1985): 5–26.

p. Rescue of the *Mayaguez*

DesBrisbay, Captain Thomas D. "Fourteen Hours on Koh Tang." USAF Southeast Asia Monograph Series 3. Washington, D.C.: U.S. Government Printing Office, 1975.

Guilmartin, John F. *A Very Short War: The* Mayaguez *and the Battle of Koh Tang.* Col-

lege Station: Texas A&M University Press, 1995.

Hahn, Dan F. "Corrupt Rhetoric: President Ford and the *Mayaguez* Affair." In Theodore Windt, ed., *Essays in Presidential Rhetoric.* Dubuque, Iowa: Kendall-Hunt, 1983.

Head, Richard G., F. W. Short, and R. C. McFarlane. *Crisis Resolution: Presidential Decision-Making in the* Mayaguez *and Korean Confrontations.* Boulder, Colo.: Westview Press, 1978.

Lamb, Christopher Jon. "Belief Systems and Decision-Making in the *Mayaguez* Crisis." *Presidential Studies Quarterly* 99 (Winter 1984–1985): 681–702.

———. *Belief Systems and Decision-Making in the* Mayaguez *Crisis.* Gainesville: University of Florida Press, 1988.

Nathan, James. "The *Mayaguez*, Presidential War, and Congressional Senescence." *Intellect* (February 1976): 360–362.

"The Recapture of the S.S. *Mayaguez*: Failure of the Consultation Clause of the War Powers Resolution." *New York University Journal of International Law and Politics* 8 (1976): 457–478.

Rowan, Roy. *The Four Days of* Mayaguez. New York: W. W. Norton, 1975.

q. Middle East

Fisk, Robert. *Pity the Nation: The Abduction of Lebanon.* New York: Atheneum, 1990.

Golden, Peter. "Max Fisher, Diplomat." *Detroit Free Press Magazine* (May 3 1992): 6–7ff.

Lenczowski, George. *American Presidents and the Middle East.* Durham, N.C.: Duke University Press, 1990.

Quandt, William B. *Decade of Decisions: American Policy toward the Arab-Israeli Conflict, 1967–1976.* Berkeley: University of California Press, 1977.

Teslik, Kennan Lee. *Congress, the Executive Branch, and Special Interests: The American Response to the Arab Boycott of Israel.* Westport, Conn.: Greenwood Press, 1982.

r. Soviet Union/SALT II

Edmonds, Robin. *Soviet Foreign Policy: The Brezhnev Years.* New York: Oxford University Press, 1983.

Gaddis, John Lewis. "The Rise, Fall, and Failure of Détente." *Foreign Affairs* (Winter 1983): 354–373.

Maresca, John J. *To Helsinki: The Conference on Security and Cooperation in Europe, 1973–1975.* Durham, N.C.: Duke University Press, 1985.

Mastny, Vojtech, ed. *Helsinki, Human Rights, and European Security: Analysis and Documentation.* Durham, N.C.: Duke University Press, 1986.

Nelson, Keith L. *The Making of Détente: Soviet-American Relations in the Shadow of Vietnam.* Baltimore: Johns Hopkins University Press, 1995.

Newhouse, John. *War and Peace in the Nuclear Age.* New York: Knopf, 1989.

Porter, Roger B. *The U.S.-U.S.S.R. Grain Agreement.* Cambridge: Cambridge University Press, 1984.

Ribuffo, Leo. "Is Poland a Soviet Satellite? Gerald Ford, the Sonnenfeldt Doctrine, and the Election of 1976." *Diplomatic History* 14 (Summer 1990): 385–403.

Stern, Paula. *Water's Edge: Domestic Politics and the Making of American Foreign Policy.* Westport, Conn.: Greenwood Press, 1979.

Teriff, Terry. *The Nixon Administration and the Making of U.S. Nuclear Strategy.* Ithaca, N.Y.: Cornell University Press, 1995.

Zimmerman, Warren. "Making Moscow Pay the Price for Rights Abuses." *New York Times* (August 1, 1986): A27.

s. Investigations of the Intelligence Community

Ashby, LeRoy, and Rod Gramer. *Fighting the Odds: The Life of Senator Frank Church.* Pullman: Washington State University Press, 1994.

Bamford, James. *The Puzzle Palace: A Report on NSA, America's Most Secret Agency.* Boston: Houghton Mifflin, 1982.

Belin, David W. *Final Disclosure: The Full Truth about the Assassination of President Kennedy.* New York: Scribner, 1988.

Colby, William. *Honorable Men: My Life in the CIA.* New York: Simon & Schuster, 1978.

Johnson, Loch. *A Season of Inquiry: The Senate Intelligence Investigation.* Lexington: University Press of Kentucky, 1985.

Olmsted, Kathryn S. *Challenging the Secret Government: The Post-Watergate Investigations of the CIA and the FBI.* Chapel Hill: University of North Carolina Press, 1996.

Prados, John. *President's Secret Wars: CIA and Pentagon Covert Operations since World War II.* New York: William Morrow, 1986.

Ranelagh, John. *The Agency: The Rise and Decline of the CIA.* London: Weidenfeld & Nicolson, 1986.

Report to the President by the Commission on CIA Activities within the United States. Washington, D.C.: U.S. Government Printing Office, 1975.

Richelson, Jeffrey T. *The U.S. Intelligence Community.* Cambridge, Mass.: Ballinger, 1985.

Smist, Frank J., Jr. *Congress Oversees the United States Intelligence Community, 1947–1989.* Knoxville: University of Tennessee Press, 1990.

Wise, David. "Colby of CIA—CIA of Colby." *New York Times Magazine* (July 1, 1973): 9ff.

Woodward, Bob. *Veil: The Secret Wars of the CIA: 1981–1987.* New York: Lyons Press, 1987.

———, and Walter Pincus. "At the CIA, Bush Jollied Up the Troops but Avoided the Issues." *Washington Post National Weekly Edition* (September 5–11, 1988): 14–15.

t. The Presidential Election of 1976

Alexander, Herbert E. *Financing the 1976 Election.* Washington, D.C.: CQ Press, 1979.

Anderson, Patrick. *Electing Jimmy Carter: The Campaign of 1976.* Baton Rouge: Louisiana State University Press, 1994.

Bitzer, Lloyd F., and Theodore Rueter. *Carter vs. Ford: The Counterfeit Debates of 1976*. Madison: University of Wisconsin Press, 1980.

Chagall, David. *The New Kingmakers*. New York: Harcourt Brace Jovanovich, 1981.

Devlin, L. Patrick. "President Ford's Ad Man Reviews the 1976 Media Campaign [interview with Doug Bailey]." *Indiana Speech Journal* 13 (April 1978): 14–28.

Dobriansky, Lev E. "The Unforgettable Ford Gaffe." *Ukrainian Quarterly* 3 (1977): 366–377.

Drew, Elizabeth. *American Journal: The Events of 1976*. New York: Random House, 1976.

Gold, Vic. *PR as in President*. Garden City, N.Y.: Doubleday, 1977.

Kondrake, Morton. *The Citizen's Guide to the 1976 Presidential Candidates: Ford*. Washington, D.C.: Capitol Hill News Service, 1976.

Kraus, Sidney, ed. *The Great Debates: Carter vs. Ford, 1976*. Bloomington: Indiana University Press, 1979.

Lamis, Alexander P. *The Two-Party South*. New York: Oxford University Press, 1984.

MacDougall, Malcolm. *We Almost Made It*. New York: Crown, 1977.

Moore, Jonathan, and Janet Fraser, eds. *Campaign for President: The Managers Look at '76*. Cambridge, Mass.: Ballinger, 1977.

Speakes, Larry. *Speaking Out: The Reagan Presidency from inside the White House*. New York: Scribner, 1988.

U.S. Congress, House Committee on House Administration. *The Presidential Campaign, 1976*, 2 vols. Washington, D.C.: U.S. Government Printing Office, 1978–1979.

Witcover, Jules. *Marathon: The Pursuit of the Presidency, 1972–1976*. New York: Viking Press, 1977.

u. The First Lady

Greene, John Robert. *Betty Ford: Candor and Courage in the White House*. Lawrence: University Press of Kansas, 2005.

INDEX

Boldface page numbers indicate primary discussions. *Italic* page numbers indicate illustrations. Page numbers followed by *c* indicate an item in the chronology.